PETERSON'S®

SAT® PREP GUIDE:
THE ULTIMATE GUIDE TO MASTERING THE SAT® EXAM 2019

PETERSON'S®

About Peterson's®

Peterson's has been your trusted educational publisher for over 50 years. It's a milestone we're quite proud of, as we continue to offer the most accurate, dependable, high-quality educational content in the field, providing you with everything you need to succeed. No matter where you are on your academic or professional path, you can rely on Peterson's for its books, online information, expert test-prep tools, the most up-to-date education exploration data, and the highest quality career success resources—everything you need to achieve your education goals. For our complete line of products, visit **www.petersons.com.**

For more information, contact Peterson's, 8740 Lucent Blvd., Suite 400, Highlands Ranch, CO 80129; 800-338-3282 Ext. 54229; or visit us online at **www.petersons.com**.

SAT® is a trademark registered and/or owned by the College Board, which was not involved in the production of, and does not endorse, this product.

SAT Subject Tests™ is a trademark registered and/or owned by the College Board, which was not involved in the production of, and does not endorse, this product.

©Copyright 2019 Peterson's.

ALL RIGHTS RESERVED. No part of this work covered by the copyright herein may be reproduced or used in any form or by any means—graphic, electronic, or mechanical, including photocopying, recording, taping, Web distribution, or information storage and retrieval systems—without the prior written permission of the publisher.

For permission to use material from this publication, complete the Permission Request Form at **www.petersonspublishing.com/spa/permissions.aspx.**

ISBN: 978-0-7689-4249-1

Printed in the United States of America

10 9 8 7 6 5 4 3 2 1   21 20 19

Third Edition

Peterson's Updates and Corrections

Check out our website at **www.petersonspublishing.com/publishingupdates** to see if there is any new information regarding the test and any revisions or corrections to the content of this book. We've made sure the information in this book is accurate and up-to-date; however, the test format or content may have changed since the time of publication.

Access 3 Additional Online Practice Tests PLUS Peterson's® Online Course for the SAT® Exam

For access to Peterson's 3 online practice tests, visit **www.petersons.com/testprep/sat.** Interested in improving your skills with *Peterson's Online Course for the SAT® Exam*? A special discount is available to customers, like you, who have purchased *Peterson's SAT® Prep Guide*. For more information, go to **www.petersons.com/testprep/sat** and enter the code: **SAT2019.**

TABLE OF CONTENTS

Introduction to *Peterson's SAT® Prep Guide* vii
The Peterson's Suite of SAT® Exam Products xi

PART I: BASICS FACTS ABOUT THE SAT® EXAM

1 ALL ABOUT THE SAT® EXAM
How the SAT® Exam is Used for College Admissions . 4
When to Take the SAT® Exam (and SAT Subject Tests™).... 4
How Your Scores Are Reported 5
How Often to Take the SAT® Exam 5
Registering for the SAT® Exam 5
Get to Know the Current SAT® Exam Format 7
Get to Know the SAT® Exam Question Types 8
Reading Test 8
Writing and Language Test 14
Math Test 18
Grid-Ins 20
SAT® Exam Essay (Optional) 24
The SAT® Exam Answer Sheet 24
How the SAT® Exam Is Scored 25
Strategies for SAT® Exam Success 26
Make an SAT® Exam Study Plan 27
Measuring Your Progress 28
Simulate Test-Taking Conditions 29
The Night Before and Day of the Exam 31
Top 10 Strategies to Raise Your Score 32
Summing It Up 33

PART II: THE DIAGNOSTIC TEST

2 THE DIAGNOSTIC TEST
Introduction to the Diagnostic Test 37
Answer Sheets 39
Section 1: Reading Test 45
Section 2: Writing and Language Test 57
Section 3: Math Test—No Calculator 69
Section 4: Math Test—Calculator 79
Section 5: Essay 95
Answer Keys and Explanations 99
Computing Your Scores 122

PART III: READING STRATEGIES FOR THE SAT® EXAM

3 READING TEST STRATEGIES
A Closer Look at the Reading Test 131
Basic Steps for Answering Reading Questions 132
Tips for Taking the Reading Test 138
Strategies for Answering Specific Question Types ... 140
Exercise: Reading Test 141
Summing It Up 153

PART IV: WRITING STRATEGIES FOR THE SAT® EXAM

4 WRITING AND LANGUAGE TEST STRATEGIES
A Closer Look at the Writing and Language Test 157
The Three Most Common Multiple-Choice
Editing Questions 158
Expression of Ideas Questions: Words In Context..... 159
Expression of Ideas Questions: Adding or
Deleting Text 160
Expression of Ideas Questions:
Reordering Sentences 161
Expression of Ideas Questions: Combining
Sentences and Using Transitional Words and
Phrases Correctly 162
Graphic Organizer Questions 162
Exercise: Writing and Language Test 164
Summing It Up 173

5 STANDARD ENGLISH CONVENTIONS
Sentence Formation 176
Verb Tense, Mood, and Voice 183
Conventions of Usage 188
Agreement 192
Frequently Confused Words 196
Conventions of Punctuation 229
Summing It Up 244

PART V: ESSAY WRITING STRATEGIES FOR THE SAT® EXAM

6 THE SAT® ESSAY
A Closer Look at the Essay Question 248
Pacing Your Writing 248
Prewriting 248
Writing the Introduction 250
Developing Your Ideas 252
Writing the Conclusion 254
The Scoring Rubric for the SAT® Essay 256
Exercise: Practicing Your Essay Skills 257
Additional Essay Writing Practice 263
Summing It Up 266

PART VI: MATH STRATEGIES FOR THE SAT® EXAM

7 MULTIPLE-CHOICE MATH
Why Multiple-Choice Math Is Easier 271
Question Format 272
Solving Multiple-Choice Math Questions 273
Know When to Use Your Calculator 274
Learn the Most Important Multiple-Choice
Math Tips 275
Exercises: Multiple-Choice Math 288
Summing It Up 301

8 GRID-IN STRATEGIES

Why Grid-Ins Are Easier Than You Think 303
How to Record Your Answers 304
Guessing on Grid-Ins Can't Hurt You 308
Exercises: Grid-Ins 309
Summing It Up 324

9 NUMBERS AND OPERATIONS

Operations with Fractions 326
Tests for Divisibility 326
Exercise: Operations with Fractions 329
Word Problems Involving Fractions 333
Exercise: Word Problems Involving Fractions 335
Complex Numbers 341
Exercise: Complex Numbers 344
Direct and Inverse Variation 349
Exercise: Direct and Inverse Variation 351
Finding Percentages 356
Exercise: Finding Percentages 362
Percentage Word Problems 366
Exercise: Percentage Word Problems 370
Summing It Up 374

10 BASIC ALGEBRA

Signed Numbers 375
Exercise: Signed Numbers 376
Linear Equations 380
Exercise: Linear Equations 383
Simultaneous Equations 387
Exercise: Simultaneous Equations 394
Exponents 399
Exercise: Exponents 401
Quadratic Equations 405
Exercise: Quadratic Equations 408
Literal Equations 412
Exercise: Literal Equations 413
Roots and Radicals 418
Exercise: Roots and Radicals 421
Monomials and Polynomials 424
Exercise: Monomials and Polynomials 427
Problem Solving in Algebra 430
Exercise: Problem Solving in Algebra 435
Inequalities 440
Exercise: Inequalities 444
Summing It Up 448

11 GEOMETRY

Geometric Notation 449
Angle Measurement 451
Intersecting Lines 453
Area 455
Circles 456
Volume 459
Triangles 461
Parallel Lines 467
Coordinate Geometry 468
Exercise: Geometry 476
Summing It Up 487

12 FUNCTIONS AND INTERMEDIATE ALGEBRA

Functions 489
Exercise: Functions 495
Integer and Rational Exponents 499
Exercise: Integer and Rational Exponents 502
Solving Complex Equations 507
Exercise: Solving Complex Equations 511
Linear, Quadratic, and Exponential Functions 515
Exercise: Linear, Quadratic, and
Exponential Functions 524
Summing It Up 528

13 DATA ANALYSIS, STATISTICS, AND PROBABILITY

Calculating Measures of Center and Spread 529
Weighted Average 532
Exercise: Calculating Measures of
Center and Spread 533
Probability 539
Exercise: Probability 543
Data Interpretation 550
Exercise: Data Interpretation 556
Statistics 564
Exercise: Statistics 572
Summing It Up 580

PART VII: PRACTICE TESTS FOR THE SAT® EXAM

14 SAT® EXAM PRACTICE TESTS

Introduction to the Practice Tests 583
Practice Test 1—Answer Sheets 585
Practice Test 1 591
Practice Test 1—Answer Keys and Explanations 641
Computing Your Scores 664
Practice Test 2—Answer Sheets 671
Practice Test 2 677
Practice Test 2—Answer Keys and Explanations 729
Computing Your Scores 754
Practice Test 3—Answer Sheets 761
Practice Test 3 767
Practice Test 3—Answer Keys and Explanations 821
Computing Your Scores 847
Practice Test 4—Answer Sheets 855
Practice Test 4 861
Practice Test 4—Answer Keys and Explanations 917
Computing Your Scores 942
Practice Test 5—Answer Sheets 949
Practice Test 5 955
Practice Test 5—Answer Keys and Explanations 1007
Computing Your Scores 1033

PART VIII: APPENDICES

Parents' Guide to College Admission Testing 1043
Math Formulas for Memorization 1065

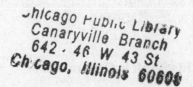
INTRODUCTION TO *PETERSON'S SAT® PREP GUIDE*

Whether you have three long months or just four short weeks to prepare for the exam, *Peterson's® SAT® Prep Guide* can help you develop a study plan that caters to your individual needs and personal timetable. These step-by-step plans are easy to follow and remarkably effective. No matter which plan you select, begin by taking a diagnostic practice test.

The Diagnostic Practice Test and Process

The diagnostic practice test does more than give you testing experience. Easy-to-use diagnostic tables help you track your performance, identify your strengths, and pinpoint areas for improvement. At the end of the diagnostic testing process, you will know which question formats are giving you the most difficulty. You will also know which topics to review in depth and which ones you can spend less time on, whether they are algebra or geometry, literary analysis, or reading charts and graphs. By understanding your testing profile, you can immediately address your weak areas by working through the relevant review chapters, learning the important test-taking tips, and completing the additional practice exercises.

Five Full-length Practice Tests in This Book

When you have completed your formal review, take the practice tests to sharpen your skills further. Even if you understand the SAT® perfectly, you still need to practice applying the methods you have learned in *Peterson's® SAT® Prep Guide*. Take the practice tests under simulated test conditions. Find a quiet place where you won't be interrupted, set a timer for the required time for each section, and work through each test as though it were test day. Doing so will help you to get used to the time limits and to learn to pace yourself. If you don't have time to take full-length practice tests, *Peterson's® SAT® Prep Guide* explains how to use timing drills to take shorter sections of the exams to combat your weaknesses, work on your pacing, and increase your level of confidence.

Comprehensive Answer Explanations

At the end of each practice session, read all the answers and explanations, even for the questions that you answered correctly. There are comprehensive explanations for every one of the book's 2,100+ questions! By reading the answer explanations, you can learn from your mistakes.

You'll also find that *Peterson's® SAT® Prep Guide* discusses all of the "big picture issues" other books ignore. For example, it addresses questions such as the following:

- How is the SAT® exam really used for college admission?

- When should you take the test?

- How many times should you plan to take the SAT® exam?

- Do all SAT® exam scores "count" in college admissions?

By addressing these questions, *Peterson's® SAT® Prep Guide* debunks prevailing myths and helps you put the SAT® exam into its proper perspective. It also serves as your "college guidance counselor," giving you the expert advice you need to apply to college. And when you think about it, that's our number-one goal here. Our objective is to help you dramatically raise your scores so that you can maximize the likelihood of getting into the college of your choice.

How This Book Is Organized

Peterson's SAT® Prep Guide is divided into eight parts to facilitate your study.

- **Part I** explains everything you need to know about the SAT® exam and provides an overview with examples of the different question types you'll find on the actual test.

- **Part II** offers a diagnostic test to help you identify your areas of strength and those areas where you need to spend more time in your review sessions.

- **Part III** explores the Reading Test section and offers expert strategies for answering each type of question.

- **Part IV** goes into detail about the different types of questions you'll see on the Writing and Language Test section of the SAT® exam. You'll also find a helpful review of Standard English Conventions.

- **Part V** describes the optional Essay part of the SAT® exam and provides strategies for developing a well-supported and coherent response to the essay prompt in this section.

- **Part VI** offers a thorough review of all math topics you'll see on the Math Test–No Calculator and Math Test–Calculator sections. You'll find helpful information on multiple-choice and grid-in math strategies, plus helpful reviews of numbers and operations, basic algebra, geometry, functions and intermediate algebra, and data analysis, statistics, and probability.

- **Part VII** includes five more tests that provide you with practice for the SAT® exam so you can simulate taking the test under timed conditions. Each of the practice tests has detailed answer explanations plus instructions on how to determine your scores for the Evidence-Based Reading and Writing section and the two Math sections. You'll also be able to calculate your subscores in the categories of Expression of Ideas, Standard English Conventions, Words in Context, Command of Evidence, Heart of Algebra, Problem Solving and Data Analysis, and Passport to Advanced Math as well as the cross-test scores for the Analysis in History/Social Studies and Analysis in Science questions.

- **Part VIII** contains the Appendices. Appendix A is the **Parents' Guide to College Admission Testing**, offering great information to assist parents in creating a plan to help their teens prepare for college-admissions tests. It discusses the various roles parents play, how to approach teens on this subject matter, and how to work with the guidance counselor. It also provides great tips on how to help teens improve their time management—essential when preparing for standardized tests like the SAT® exam. Appendix B is an exhaustive list of essential math formulas to memorize for test day.

Special Study Features

You will find four kinds of special study features scattered throughout the book. In addition to providing insight into how to best use this guide for test-prep success, each study feature highlights specific types of information:

 Tips point out valuable information you need to know when taking the SAT® exam. Tips provide quick and simple hints for selecting the correct answers for the most common SAT® question types.

Alerts identify potential pitfalls in the testing format or question types that can cause common mistakes in selecting answers.

NOTES: **Notes** address information about the test structure itself.

 Cautions provide warnings, such as common grammatical errors or possible errors in computation or formulas that can result in choosing incorrect answers.

How to Use This Book

It's understandable that all of the information you'll be reading about the SAT® exam might seem a little overwhelming. But even if you are feeling confused by everything the exam requires, take some comfort in the knowledge that you are holding a great resource to help you do well on test day. This book's job is not to make you a genius; its job is to make sure you are prepared to take the SAT® exam. If you become a genius in the process, consider that a bonus.

The following four steps will help you get the most out of using this guide:

Step 1: First Things First—Get to Know the Exam

You will get the most out of *Peterson's SAT® Prep Guide* by using this book as it is organized. You may want to skip Chapter 1: All About the SAT® because you're anxious to get right to the lessons, since that's where the real preparation begins, but Chapter 1 is very useful for giving you a picture of the exam's content as a whole.

 ALERT: If you skip Chapter 1, you'll miss out on vital information about the SAT® exam: when and how many times you should take it; how to register; how the exam is scored and how scores are reported; the test format and question types, including a first look at kinds of questions on the Reading Test, the Writing and Language Test, and the Math Tests (Calculator and No Calculator); strategies for test-taking success, and much more!

Step 2: The Diagnostic Test Is Your Friend—Don't Skip It!

Once you've learned the essential information about the SAT® exam in general, you will need to take the first step toward getting your scores where you want them to be by taking the diagnostic test. The diagnostic test is a full-length practice test that you take before you start studying or reviewing any subject material.

Understandably, taking a long diagnostic test may not seem the ideal way to get started on your test-preparation path. However, the point of a diagnostic test is to give you an idea of what your strengths and weaknesses are before you dive into your SAT® exam preparation. By taking the diagnostic test and analyzing your answers, you may discover that you retained more information from your English classes than you realized. You might also learn that you aren't quite the math expert you thought you were. Or maybe you will find that most of your math skills are really strong, but you need some help when it comes to quadratic equations. Getting a clear idea of your strengths and weaknesses will help you know which chapters of this book really demand your focus. The diagnostic test will help you get that clear idea.

Step 3: Build Your Skills—Practice, Practice, Practice!

After evaluating your diagnostic test results, you should know the skills on which you need to focus. By diligently studying the information presented, you will become familiar with not only the question types that will appear on the SAT®, but also the language of the exam to help you be prepared for how the test will be worded.

Familiarizing yourself with the way certain questions are worded on the SAT® may help you figure out the kind of question you are answering, which may help you select the best answer.

Throughout each review chapter (Chapters 3–13), you will find numerous practice questions, which will help familiarize you with the language and presentation of the SAT® exam. The exercises and quizzes in these review chapters are a great way to practice, and the thorough answer explanations will help you understand why an answer is right—or more importantly, why an answer is wrong. This can hopefully keep you from making a similar mistake again when you take the real test.

Step 4: See What You Have Learned—Test Yourself Again

Near the end of the book, in Part VII, you will have the opportunity to take five complete practice tests for the SAT® exam. With each practice test, you should see an improvement in your score since taking the diagnostic test.

You should take these tests under the same circumstances you will encounter on test day. That means completing each test section in the same time that will be allotted for the actual test:

- Reading Test: 65 minutes
- Writing and Language Test: 35 minutes
- Math Test—No Calculator: 25 minutes
- Math Test—Calculator: 55 minutes
- Essay: 50 minutes

Print or Online? You Decide!

To accommodate your preferred test-taking style, Peterson's now gives you the option to take the diagnostic and practice tests in this book either on paper or online. Our paper-based tests are also available in an online format so that you can choose how you want to take them—on paper to simulate the actual SAT® test-taking experience, or online for a more interactive experience with automated timing, and instant feedback and scoring results. Take all the tests on paper, all online, or a combination of the two. The choice is yours.

For more information, go to **www.petersons.com/testprep/sat**.

If you begin using this book to prepare for the SAT® well in advance of test day, you might want to hold off taking the last practice test until a few days before taking the actual SAT® to refamiliarize yourself with the test's format and content.

THE PETERSON'S SUITE OF SAT® EXAM PRODUCTS

In addition to *Peterson's SAT® Prep Guide,* Peterson's has an array of cutting-edge SAT® exam preparation resources designed to give you the best test preparation possible. Our online course and interactive practice tests can be used alone or combined with other Peterson's SAT®-focused products to help you succeed and get the test scores you want. Take a few minutes to discover what's available in Peterson's suite of SAT® products or visit our website at **www.petersons.com/testprep/sat.**

Peterson's SAT® Prep Guide

Peterson's SAT® Prep Guide features content and strategies that will help you master the SAT® exam. It contains a full-length diagnostic test and access to eight full-length practice tests—five within the book and three online. The expert subject review and skill-specific exercises in *Peterson's SAT® Prep Guide* can help familiarize you with the unique content, structure, and format of the test. Test-taking tips and advice guide you smoothly from your first day of test preparation to test day.

In addition, taking online practice tests is ideal because you get immediate feedback and automated scoring. *Peterson's SAT® Prep Guide* gives you access to three full-length online practice tests, with detailed feedback to help you understand the concepts presented. The content in these three practice tests was created by the test-prep experts at Peterson's to help you boost your test-prep confidence so you can score well on test day. You can access these three practice tests at **www.petersons.com/testprep/sat.**

REMEMBER: You have the option to take Peterson's SAT® Prep Guide practice tests either in the book or online. For more information, go to **www.petersons.com/testprep/sat**.

Peterson's Practice Tests for the SAT® Exam

Looking for even more online test practice? You can find it with *Peterson's Practice Tests for the SAT® Exam.* This test-prep tool provides three full-length tests with immediate feedback and explanations for each question. Your purchase allows you 90-day access to these tests, which feature the Essay Self-Score option—you can compare your essay to samples provided to give you an idea of how your essay will be evaluated based on official scoring guidelines. Equipped with on-the-spot feedback and sample essays for comparison, you can be confident that you're getting the guidance you need to improve your score in all sections of the SAT® exam.

Peterson's Online Course for the SAT® Exam

Peterson's Online Course for the SAT® Exam is a comprehensive test prep course that is customized for you. In addition to practice tests, the online course allows access to supplemental content, including additional subject-specific strategies and lessons, tips, and college search options tailored to your projected test scores and interests.

Here's how the course works:

1. An initial diagnostic pretest determines your strengths and weaknesses.
2. Based on your diagnostic test results, interactive lessons teach you the subject areas you need to learn.
3. Quizzes after each lesson gauge how well you have learned the materials just taught.
4. Full-length practice tests allow you to apply all the skills you've learned and monitor your progress.

Peterson's Online Course for the SAT® Exam gives you the opportunity to solidify your understanding and build your confidence about any concept you may encounter on the SAT®—no matter how close it is to test day!

Interested in going the extra mile and using additional online practice tests or the online course? Take advantage of customer-friendly discounts available only to customers who purchase *Peterson's SAT® Prep Guide.* For more information and to obtain your special discount on Peterson's online courses, go to **www.petersons.com/testprep/sat** and enter the code: **SAT2019.**

Give Us Your Feedback

- Peterson's publishes a full line of books—test prep, career preparation, education exploration, and financial aid. Peterson's publications can be found at high school guidance offices, college libraries and career centers, and your local bookstore and library. Peterson's books are also available for purchase online at **www.petersonsbooks.com.**

- We welcome any comments or suggestions you may have about this publication. Your feedback will help us make education dreams possible for you—and others like you.

Now that you know why *Peterson's SAT® Prep Guide* is an essential resource to prepare you to take a very important test, it's time to make the most of this powerful preparation tool. Turn the page and find out everything you need to know about the SAT®!

PART I: BASIC FACTS ABOUT THE SAT® EXAM

Chapter 1: All About the SAT® Exam

CHAPTER 1:
ALL ABOUT THE SAT® EXAM

OVERVIEW

- How the SAT® Exam Is Used for College Admissions
- When to Take the SAT® Exam (and SAT Subject Tests™)
- How Your Scores Are Reported
- How Often to Take the SAT® Exam
- Registering for the SAT® Exam
- Get to Know the Current SAT® Exam Format
- Get to Know the SAT® Exam Question Types
- Reading Test
- Writing and Language Test
- Math Test
- Grid-Ins
- SAT® Exam Essay (Optional)
- The SAT® Exam Answer Sheet
- How the SAT® Exam Is Scored
- Strategies for SAT® Exam Success
- Make an SAT® Exam Study Plan
- Measuring Your Progress
- Simulate Test-taking Conditions
- The Night Before and Day of the Exam
- Top 10 Strategies to Raise Your Score
- Summing It Up

Chapter 1

All About
the SAT®
Exam

HOW THE SAT® EXAM IS USED FOR COLLEGE ADMISSIONS

The explicitly stated purpose of the SAT® exam is to predict how students will perform academically as first-year college students. But the more practical purpose of the test is to help college admissions officers make acceptance decisions. When you think about it, admissions officers have a difficult job, particularly when they are asked to compare the academic records of students from different high schools in different parts of the country taking different classes. It's not easy to figure out how one student's grade point average (GPA) in New Mexico correlates with that of another student in Florida. Even though admissions officers can do a good deal of detective work to evaluate candidates fairly, they benefit a great deal from the SAT®. The SAT® provides a single, standardized means of comparison. After all, virtually every student takes the SAT®, and the SAT® is the same for everyone. It doesn't matter whether you hail from Maine, Maryland, or Montana.

So the SAT® is an important test. But it is not the be-all, end-all. Keep it in perspective! It is only one of several important pieces of the college admissions puzzle. Other factors that weigh heavily into the admissions process include GPA, difficulty of course load, level of extracurricular involvement, and the strength of the college application itself.

WHEN TO TAKE THE SAT® EXAM (AND SAT SUBJECT TESTS™)

When you decide which schools you're going to apply to, find out if they require the SAT® exam. Most do! Your next step is to determine when they need your SAT® scores. Write that date down. That's the one you really don't want to miss.

You do have some leeway in choosing your test date. The SAT® is typically offered on one Saturday morning in October, November, December, March, May, June, and August. Check the exact dates to see which ones meet your deadlines. Tests are offered on select Sundays, usually the Sunday after each Saturday test date, for students who cannot take the test on Saturday due to religious observance. Students who wish to take the SAT® exam on a Sunday must provide a letter printed on stationery from their house of worship explaining the religious reason for the request. An official religious leader must sign the letter.

What if you don't know which schools you want to apply to? Don't panic! Even if you take the exam in December of your senior year, you'll probably have plenty of time to send your scores to most schools.

When you plan to take the SAT®, there is something even more important than the application deadlines of particular schools. You need to select a test date that works best with your schedule. Ideally, you should allow yourself at least two to three months to use this book to prepare. Many students like to take the test in March of their junior year. That way, they take the SAT® several months before final exams, the prom, and end-of-the-year distractions. Taking the test in March also gives students early feedback as to how they are scoring. If they are dissatisfied with their scores, there is ample opportunity to take the test again in the spring or following fall. But your schedule might not easily accommodate a March testing. Maybe you're involved in a winter sport or school play that will take too much time away from studying. Maybe you have a family reunion planned over spring break in March. Or maybe you simply prefer to prepare during a different time of year. If that's the case, just pick another date.

If the schools you've decided on also require SAT Subject Tests™, here's one good piece of advice: Try to take SAT Subject Tests™ immediately after you finish the subject(s) in school. For most of you, this means taking the SAT Subject Tests™ in June. By taking the exam then, you'll save an awful lot of review work. Remember this, too: you have to register for the SAT Subject Tests™ separately, and you can't take the Subject Tests on the same day as the SAT®. So check the dates, think ahead, and plan it out. It's worth it in the end.

Are you starting to prepare a little later than you had planned? Don't get upset; it happens. Using the accelerated plan, you should be able to cover most of the material within a month. You probably won't have much time to practice, but you'll get the most important facts about the test and be able to take a few sample exams.

HOW YOUR SCORES ARE REPORTED

After you have taken the SAT® exam, College Board scores your test and creates a score report. We will discuss in detail how the SAT® is scored later in this chapter. You and your high school receive score reports from each SAT® and SAT Subject Test™ that you decide to take.

At the time of registration, you can pick four colleges or universities to receive your score report. College Board will send your scores to these four schools for free. Within nine days of taking the test, you can change your school selection. If you want to send more than four reports or change your mind more than nine days after your test date, you will have to pay to do so.

If you decide to take the SAT®, or any SAT Subject Test™, more than once, you have the option to decide which scores to send to the schools you've picked—scores from one, several, or all test dates.

Some colleges do not allow you to designate the test date or dates for your score reports; you cannot designate individual test sections. In other words, if you take the SAT® exam in October, December, and March, you cannot pick the Evidence-Based Reading and Writing section score from October, Math score from December, and Essay score from March and ask to have those results sent to the schools of your choice. You can only choose whether to send your complete results from one, two, or all three test dates. However, some colleges do allow students to send in their best score for each subject, regardless of whether they are from the same test date, so be sure to check on the individual policy of each college to which you are applying.

If you choose not to take advantage of this option, all of your scores will be sent to the schools you've selected. However, no score reports will ever be sent without your specific consent. You and your counselor will receive e-mail reminders, asking which scores you want to send. You can also choose your schools and send your scores online using the College Board's Score Choice™ tool. Learn more about Score Choice™ at the website **https://collegereadiness.collegeboard.org/sat/scores/sending-scores/score-choice**.

HOW OFTEN TO TAKE THE SAT® EXAM

Different colleges evaluate the exam in different ways. Some take your highest Math, Evidence-Based Reading and Writing, and Essay scores, even if they were earned on different test days. So if you nailed the Math section in March, the Evidence-Based Reading and Writing section in October, and the Essay section in December, the colleges will combine those scores to maximize your overall score. However, many other colleges won't do that. Some pay most attention to your highest combined score from a single day. Many others will average all of your scores or lend equal weight to all of them.

So what does this mean? It means that you should take the SAT® exam only when you are truly prepared. There is nothing wrong with taking the SAT® two or three times, as long as you are confident that your scores will improve substantially each time. Let's say that you scored an 1100 on your first SAT®. If you would have been thrilled to have hit 1120, it's probably not worth taking the test again. Most colleges look at SAT® scores in ranges and will not hold 20 points against you. They understand that scoring an 1100 means that you were only one or two questions away from 1120. But if you scored an 1100 and expected to score closer to 1200 or 1300 based on practice testing, then you should probably retake the exam. In other words, it is of little value to take the SAT® multiple times if you expect to earn roughly the same score. But it is worthwhile if you expect to score significantly higher on a second or third try. For more advice about this, see your high school guidance counselor.

REGISTERING FOR THE SAT® EXAM

You should register for the SAT® exam at least six weeks before your testing date. That way you will avoid late registration fees and increase your chances of taking the exam at your first-choice testing center. You can register through the mail by completing the SAT® registration form found inside *The SAT®* and *SAT Subject Tests™ Student Registration Booklet*, which can be found in your guidance counselor's office or online (printable PDF) at **https://collegereadiness.collegeboard.org/pdf/sat-registration-booklet-students.pdf**. Registering online is probably the quickest and easiest method, and you will receive immediate registration confirmation. You will need to pay by credit card, and you will need to upload a photo with your registration. The photo you provide will become part of your Admission Ticket on test day. For more information, visit **https://sat.collegeboard.org/register**.

Photo ID

The photo you provide (either uploaded with your online registration or mailed in with the printed registration) becomes part of your Admission Ticket on test day.

Photos must be properly focused with a full-face view. The photo must be clearly identifiable as you, and it must match your appearance on test day. **IMPORTANT:** If you are not easily recognizable in your photo, you will not be admitted to the test center.

Choose a photo that:

- Shows only you—no other people in the shot
- Shows a head-and-shoulders view, with the entire face, both eyes, and hair clearly visible
- Is properly focused and has no dark spots or shadows
- Shows a head covering only if it is worn for religious purposes

Visit **https://collegereadiness.collegeboard.org/sat/register/policies-requirements/photo** for more information about the required photo ID.

In addition, you are responsible for bringing an acceptable form of identification.

Some acceptable examples include:

- State-issued driver's license
- State-issued nondriver ID
- School identification card
- Passport (required in India, Ghana, Nepal, Nigeria, and Pakistan)
- Government-issued ID
- School ID Form* prepared by your school
- Talent Search Identification Program ID/Authorization to Test Form (grades 7 and 8 only); photo not required

* Your school can prepare an ID form for you. This form must include a recognizable photo, and the school seal must overlap the photo. Sign the ID form in the presence of your counselor or principal. You will be asked to sign the ID form again at the test center. This form must be dated and is good only for one year.

 ALERT: You must provide a photo when you sign up for the SAT®. The photo will be part of your Admission Ticket, and it will be checked against your photo ID on test day.

REGISTRATION FEES

At the time of this book's printing, the fee for the SAT® (no essay) is $47.50. If you are planning to take the SAT® with the Essay section, you will need to pay $64.50. To determine if you are eligible for a fee waiver, visit **https://collegereadiness.collegeboard.org/sat/register/fees/fee-waivers**. (Students who qualify for a fee waiver may also be eligible to apply to college, send their scores, and apply for finanical aid (through CSS Profile) to as many colleges as they choose, at no cost.)

GET TO KNOW THE CURRENT SAT® EXAM FORMAT

The SAT® consists of sections on math, evidence-based reading and writing, and an optional essay. The sections are timed to range from 25 to 65 minutes. The whole test takes 3 hours, plus 50 minutes for the optional essay. Don't worry. There are breaks. The following chart gives you an idea of what to expect. The test sections appear in the following order: Reading Test, Writing and Language Test, Math Test—No Calculator, Math Test—Calculator, and the Essay.

Format of the SAT® Test

Evidence-Based Reading and Writing	**Score 200–800**
Reading questions based on: • Passages in US and world literature, history/social studies, and science • Paired passages • Lower and higher text complexities • Words in context, command of evidence, and analysis Writing and Language questions based on: • Passages in careers, history/social studies, humanities, and science • Argument, informative/explanatory, and nonfiction narrative passages • Words in context, grammar, expression of ideas, and analysis	Time—Total: 100 Minutes • Reading Test (65 minutes) • Writing and Language Test (35 minutes) Question Types • Multiple-choice with 4 answer choices
Math	**Score 200–800**
Real-world problems solved using: • Algebra • Problem solving and data analysis • Advanced math • Lines, triangles, and circles using theorems • Trigonometric functions	Time—Total: 80 Minutes • Math Test—No Calculator (25 minutes) • Math Test—Calculator (55 minutes) Question Types • Multiple-choice with 4 answer choices • Student-produced responses (grid-ins)
Optional Essay	
What's involved: • Read an argument-type passage written for a general audience • Analyze the passage in terms of how the writer uses evidence, reasoning, and stylistic elements to build an argument to persuade his or her audience	Time—Total: 50 minutes Question Type • One prompt that emphasizes analyzing the argument presented in the passage Score: 3–12 (Reading: 1–4 scale, Analysis: 1–4 scale, Writing: 1–4 scale)

7

Chapter 1

All About the SAT® Exam

GET TO KNOW THE SAT® EXAM QUESTION TYPES

The question types in the SAT® exam don't cover a wide variety of topics. They are very limited—no science, no world languages, no social studies. You'll find only questions testing reading comprehension, writing skills, and math skills—skills that you've been working on since kindergarten.

Most of the questions are multiple-choice. That's good, because it means the correct answer is right there on the page for you. You just have to find it—easier said than done sometimes, but true. Only the math grid-ins and the essay require student-produced answers. For the grid-ins, you'll need to do the calculations and then fill in circles on the answer sheet to show your answers. (More about the answer sheets later in this chapter.) The following pages provide you with a closer look at the question types and question formats that you will find in each section of the SAT®.

 On the SAT®, all questions count the same. You won't get more points for answering a really difficult question than you will get for answering a very simple one. Remember that when you're moving through the test. The more time you spend wrestling with the answer to one "stumper," the less time you have to whip through several easier questions.

READING TEST

The Reading Test assesses your knowledge of words in context, command of evidence in the passages, and your analysis of the passage, including graphics. All the questions are multiple-choice. The questions on the Reading Test are all passage-based. All passages are from previously published sources and cover topics in US and world literature, history/social studies, and science.

WORDS IN CONTEXT

Just as the name implies, words-in-context questions assess your ability to determine the meaning of words or phrases in the context of an extended passage. If you do not recognize the meaning of the word, its meaning may be determined by context. Your job is to read the passage and the question, and then analyze the answer choices to figure out which one makes the most sense based on the words around it. That means you must look for clues in the passage.

Here is an excerpt from a passage on the opah fish, followed by three sample words-in-context questions. Read the passage excerpt and try to answer each question on your own before you read the answer explanations on the next page.

Nicholas Wegner of NOAA Fisheries' Southwest Fisheries Science Center in La Jolla, California, is lead author of a new paper on the opah, or moonfish. He and his coauthor, biologist Owyn Snodgrass, discovered that the opah has the unusual ability to keep its body warm, even in the cold depths of the ocean. An excerpt on their findings follows.

Courtesy: NOAA Fisheries

Warm Blood Makes Opah an Agile Predator

New research by NOAA Fisheries has revealed the opah, or moonfish, as the first fully warm-blooded fish that circulates heated blood throughout its body much like mammals and

Line
birds, giving it a competitive advantage in the cold ocean

5 depths.

The silvery fish, roughly the size of a large automobile tire, is known from oceans around the world and dwells hundreds of feet beneath the surface in chilly, dimly lit waters. . . .

10 Fish that typically inhabit such cold depths tend to be slow and sluggish, conserving energy by ambushing prey instead of chasing it. But the opah's constant flapping of its fins heats its body, speeding its metabolism, movement and reaction times, scientists report today in the journal

15 *Science*. . . .

"Before this discovery, I was under the impression this was a slow-moving fish, like most other fish in cold environments," Wegner said. "But because it can warm its body, it turns out to be a very active predator that chases

20 down agile prey like squid and can migrate long distances."

Questions:

1. As used in the first paragraph, "competitive advantage" refers to

   A. a way to seek out a mate.

   B. an ability to outperform rivals.

   C. an aptitude for keeping itself moving.

   D. a capacity to conceal itself from predators.

2. As it is used in paragraph 3, "ambushing" most nearly means

   A. pursuing for long distances.

   B. moving slowly at first.

   C. hiding and then attacking.

   D. weakening and then killing.

3. As it is used in paragraph 4, "agile" most nearly means

   A. nimble.

   B. inactive.

   C. strong.

   D. clever.

Explanations:

1. Clues to the meaning of the phrase don't appear until the fourth paragraph: "I was under the impression . . . like most other fish in cold environments" and "But . . . it turns out to be a very active predator." Here, you're told that the opah is *unlike* other fish in that it can swim faster and farther and catch more prey. Choices A, C, and D are specific traits that might help the fish in its environment. But choice B is the only one that makes sense in the context of the passage. **The correct answer is B.**

2. The biggest clue to the meaning of *ambushing* is "instead of chasing it." Because you know that the fish don't chase their prey, you can exclude choice A. Choices B and D don't make sense in the context of the sentence because neither is a method for capturing prey, as chasing is. Choice C, however, makes sense when you consider the context clue. **The correct answer is C.**

3. The clue "very active predator" is your clue that *agile* must mean that the squid provides a challenge for the opah. This eliminates choice B. Choice D can also be eliminated because the context emphasizes physical, not mental, abilities. Likewise, you can eliminate choice C because the level of activity, not strength, is the focus. Choice A fits the context, as it suggests that the squid is able to move quickly and easily. **The correct answer is A.**

 In SAT® reading questions, the answers will always be directly stated or implied in the passage.

COMMAND OF EVIDENCE

The Evidence-Based Reading and Writing sections of the SAT® require you to interpret information or ideas in a passage and then use evidence to support your conclusion. This element of the Reading Test, which makes up 20 percent of the questions, works like this: You answer a multiple-choice question in which you analyze a portion of the passage or pair of passages. You then answer a second question requiring you to cite the best evidence in the text for the answer.

The passages include literary texts from US and world literature, as well as nonfiction texts in science and history/social studies. In some cases, related passages are paired and require you to make connections between the texts.

The following is an example of how these "command of evidence" questions work. The passage is a continuation of the NOAA article cited previously, "Warm Blood Makes Opah an Agile Predator."

Gills Show Unusual Design

Courtesy: NOAA Fisheries

Wegner realized the opah was unusual when a coauthor of the study, biologist Owyn Snodgrass, collected a sample of its gill tissue. Wegner recognized an unusual design:

Line Blood vessels that carry warm blood into the fish's gills wind
5 around those carrying cold blood back to the body core after absorbing oxygen from water.

The design is known in engineering as "counter-current heat exchange." In opah it means that warm blood leaving the body core helps heat up cold blood returning from the
10 respiratory surface of the gills, where it absorbs oxygen. Resembling a car radiator, it's a natural adaptation that conserves heat. The unique location of the heat exchange within the gills allows nearly the fish's entire body to maintain an elevated temperature, known as endothermy,
15 even in the chilly depths.

"There has never been anything like this seen in a fish's gills before," Wegner said. "This is a cool innovation by these animals that gives them a competitive edge. The concept of counter-current heat exchange was invented in fish long
20 before we thought of it."

The researchers collected temperature data from opah caught during surveys off the West Coast, finding that their body temperatures were regularly warmer than the surrounding water. They also attached temperature monitors
25 to opah as they tracked the fish on dives to several hundred feet and found that their body temperatures remained steady even as the water temperature dropped sharply. The 20 fish had an average muscle temperature about 5 degrees C above the surrounding water while swimming about 150
30 to 1,000 feet below the surface, the researchers found. . . .

A few other fish . . . warm certain parts of their bodies . . . boosting their swimming performance. But internal organs, including their hearts, cool off quickly and begin to slow down when they dive into cold depths, forcing them to
35 return to shallower depths to warm up.

Questions:

1. The author discusses the adaptations of some fish in the last paragraph mainly to show that

    A. opah swim faster because they are able to keep themselves warm.

    B. some fish maintain a body temperature warmer than the sea water.

    C. biologists have found evidence that some fish are warm-blooded.

    D. opah have a distinctive design that keeps them warm at greater depths.

2. Which choice provides the best evidence for the answer to the previous question?

    A. Lines 12–15 ("The unique . . . chilly depths.")

    B. Lines 18–20 ("The concept . . . of it.")

    C. Lines 21–24 ("The researchers . . . surrounding water.")

    D. Lines 27–30 ("The 20 fish . . . researchers found.")

Explanations:

1. In the first question, the author's intention is to contrast the warming ability of other fish with the warming ability of the opah. Though the passage does note that some fish maintain a body temperature warmer than seawater for a short period, this is not the reason the author includes details about other fish. Thus, choice B is not correct. Choices A and C are incorrect because neither idea is noted in the text. **The correct answer is D.**

2. The second question asks you to determine which of four segments of the passage provides the best evidence to support your answer to the first question. Choices B, C, and D do not provide textual support for the contrast the author makes in the last paragraph. **The correct answer is A.**

ANALYSIS AND GRAPHICS

Two passages in the SAT® Reading Test include a graphic. Your job is to analyze the passage and interpret the information in the graphic as it relates to the passage. Questions based on the graphic are multiple-choice. Here is a sample reading passage with an accompanying graphic, in this case a map, and a question that requires your analysis.

From "About John Snow," by Professor Paul Fine, London School of Hygiene & Tropical Medicine and The John Snow Society.

John Snow (1813–1858)

John Snow is an iconic figure in epidemiology and public health, best known for his work on cholera, for a famous map, and for organizing the removal of a pump handle in Soho.

Line
5 Less well-known are his important contributions to anesthesia and to epidemiological methods, and his engagement in public debates of the time. The breadth and depth of Snow's activities provide a model for population researchers concerned not only with sound method but also with bringing their results to public benefit.

10 Indeed, though epidemiology is often described as the study of health-related aspects of populations, its methods are applicable to studies of virtually anything in populations, and disciplines which now acknowledge the methods and terminology of epidemiology range from education to crime
15 science and economics.

Snow was born in York on 15 March 1813, one of eight children in a family of modest means. He apprenticed with a surgeon-apothecary in Newcastle from 1827 to 1833, and there witnessed the first epidemic of cholera in the UK. He
20 then moved to London, qualified as physician in 1843 and

set up general practice in Soho. Early in his career he became interested in the physiology of respiration in recognition of the major problem of asphyxia of the newborn.

These interests led him to be invited to witness one of the
25 first applications of ether anesthesia in the UK in December 1846. He immediately recognized the importance of ambient temperature and within one month published tables of the vapor pressure of ether. This initiated an important line of research on instruments for administering anesthetics
30 and led to his becoming the most prominent authority on anesthesia in the UK. He administered chloroform to Queen Victoria at the birth of Prince Leopold in 1853.

The second great cholera epidemic arrived in London in 1848, and many attributed its cause to an atmospheric
35 "effluence" or "miasma." Snow's firsthand experience of the disease in 1832, combined with studies of respiration, led him to question miasma theories and to publish the first edition of *On the Mode of Communication of Cholera* in 1849, in which he proposed that cholera was attributable to a
40 self-replicating agent which was excreted in the cholera

evacuations and inadvertently ingested, often, but not necessarily, through the medium of water.

When cholera returned in 1853, Snow recognized an ideal opportunity to test his hypothesis by comparing cholera mortality rates in populations of south London supplied by water drawn from sewage-contaminated versus uncontaminated regions of the Thames. He personally carried out a cohort study to make this comparison, recognizing the need to confirm the water source of each case and to assure comparability of the populations concerned. On 30 August 1854 while involved in these studies, a dramatic cholera epidemic began near his home in Soho, leading to more than 550 deaths within two weeks. Analysis of the addresses of the cholera deaths and interviews of residents of the area led him to suspect that water from a pump on Broad Street was responsible—and he prevailed upon the local council to remove the handle of the pump on 8 September 1854.

Though the epidemic was already in decline by that date, the rapidity of his action, the logic of the analysis, and the pragmatism of the response has made this a classic event in the history of public health, well known to students and practitioners the world over. The combination of these studies provided overwhelming evidence for an infectious agent, known now as *Vibrio cholerae*.

Snow described this work in the second edition of *On the Mode of Communication of Cholera*. He then expanded his public health interests by becoming involved in debates over legislation concerning nuisance industries in London, while maintaining his research and practice in anesthesia until his death in 1858.

The 200th anniversary of Snow's birth provides an occasion to celebrate his achievements, to consider their original context, to discuss their place in contemporary epidemiology, and consider their likely future, not only as the armamentarium of public health, but as a framework of method for science and society.

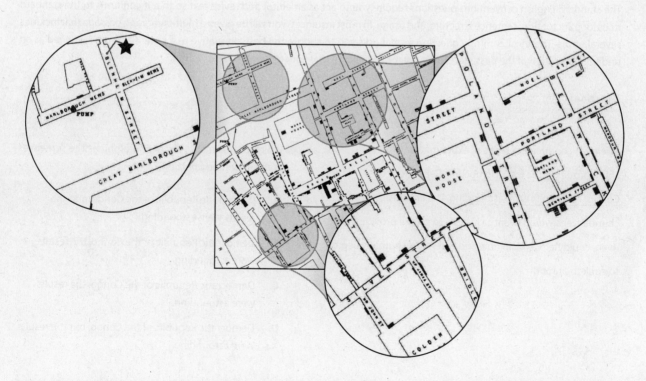

Question:

On John Snow's map, deaths from the 1854 cholera epidemic are represented by stacks of black lines. Based on the image and the passage, what can we assume about Blenheim Street (shown magnified in the upper-left side of the map)?

A. No one lived there.

B. Broad Street did not supply their water.

C. Its residents were as affected as the rest of the neighborhood.

D. Relatives came to stay there to avoid the cholera outbreak.

Explanation:

The passage explains that Snow determined that the pump on Broad Street supplied contaminated water to nearby residents. You can infer that people living on streets containing stacks of bars used the Broad Street pump. Based on the map, then, people on Blenheim Street likely did not use the Broad Street pump. **The correct answer is B.**

WRITING AND LANGUAGE TEST

The SAT® Exam Writing and Language Test consists of multiple-choice questions based on passages. The multiple-choice questions test how well you understand and use standard English conventions, as well as recognize words in context and command of evidence in the passages. Analysis of the passages and graphics is also included.

STANDARD ENGLISH CONVENTIONS AND WORDS IN CONTEXT

The standard English conventions questions require you to act as an editor and revise text so that it conforms to the standard rules for punctuation, sentence structure, and usage. In most instances, you will be given a multiparagraph passage that includes several errors. The most common question format asks you to choose the best alternative to a potential error, identified as an underlined portion of the passage. Here is a sample question that concerns sentence structure:

Question:

Scientists conducted a series of experiments with chimpanzees in the **1** Democratic Republic of the Congo. The results were astounding. The conclusion, that chimpanzees would eventually learn to cook if provided an oven, could help explain how and when early humans began to cook their food.

1 Which choice most effectively combines the sentences at the underlined portion?

A. Democratic Republic of the Congo, and the results were astounding.

B. Democratic Republic of the Congo, the results were astounding.

C. Democratic Republic of the Congo: the results were astounding.

D. Democratic Republic of the Congo, but the results were astounding.

Explanation:

Choice B creates a comma splice, which is a form of a run-on sentence, so that's not correct. Likewise, the colon in choice C is not correct, as the clause it introduces does not really explain the first part of the sentence. Introducing *but* in choice D changes the meaning of the sentences by setting up a contrasting scenario. Only choice A maintains the two sentences' meanings and combines them without confusion. **The correct answer is A.**

The words-in-context questions on the test measure your ability to choose appropriate words based on the context of the passage. These questions are multiple-choice and include the option to keep the word that is used.

Question:

There is a debate about whether early humans had the mental capacity to cook. Though it may not seem sophisticated, cooking requires planning, an ability to interrupt gratification, and the complex use of tools.

2

A. NO CHANGE

B. apprehend

C. delay

D. restrain

Explanation:

Here, you must choose the word that makes the most sense in the context. The words *interrupt*, *apprehend*, and *restrain* don't convey what is meant here—to hold off. Only *delay* (choice C) conveys that sense. **The correct answer is C.**

COMMAND OF EVIDENCE

To answer the command of evidence questions in the Writing and Language Test, you need to carefully read the passage in question. Here is an example of this type of question. The excerpt comes from the passage "About John Snow."

Question:

The second great cholera epidemic arrived in London in 1848, and many attributed its cause to an atmospheric "effluence" or "miasma." Snow's firsthand experience of the disease in 1832, combined with studies of respiration, led him to question miasma theories and to publish the first edition of *On the Mode of Communication of Cholera* in 1849, in which he proposed that cholera was attributable to a self-replicating agent which was excreted in the cholera evacuations and inadvertently ingested, often, but not necessarily, through the medium of water. **3**

3 Which choice best summarizes the main idea of the paragraph?

A. In 1848, many people were incorrect to blame atmospheric miasma for the spread of cholera.

B. John Snow's study, *On the Mode of Communication of Cholera*, was read by scholars worldwide.

C. John Snow was curious, and he never took anything at face value.

D. Snow's questioning of the miasma theory and theories on water contamination changed the conversation about disease circulation.

Explanation:

The question asks you to determine which sentence best summarizes the main idea of the paragraph. Choices A, B, and C all contain ideas that are important in the paragraph. But choice D contains the crux of the paragraph: that Snow questioned the prevailing wisdom and then proposed his own theory about how cholera was transmitted. **The correct answer is D.**

EXPRESSION OF IDEAS

Some questions require you to analyze the passage's topic development, organization, and language use and make improvements for maximum impact. You may be asked to improve the wording or structure of the passage or strengthen the writer's point. Here is an excerpt from a passage about Harriet Tubman and a sample question to help illustrate this concept.

Question:

At the beginning of the Civil War, Harriet Tubman worked for the Union Army as a cook and nurse. Later in the war she shifted to a more decisive position as a spy and scout. Tubman was the first woman to lead an expedition of armed fighters, and her leadership during a raid at Combahee Ferry resulted in the liberation of 700 enslaved people. **4** Tubman was born in Dorchester County, Maryland, around 1822.

4 The writer is considering deleting the underlined sentence from the paragraph. Should the writer delete this sentence?

A. Yes, because the sentence has nothing to do with the main topic of the passage.

B. Yes, because the sentence veers from the topic of Tubman's role in the war.

C. No, because the sentence provides valuable historical information about Tubman.

D. No, because the sentence provides a strong conclusion to the paragraph.

Explanation:

Here you are being asked if the sentence in question is relevant to the paragraph. In this case, basic information about where and when Tubman was born has little to do with a paragraph about her role in the Civil War. **The correct answer is B.**

ANALYSIS AND GRAPHICS

One or two of the passages in the Writing and Language Test include graphics. You will be asked to determine how the passage needs to be revised based on the information in the graphic. Here is an excerpt from another paragraph in "About John Snow" and a sample question to help illustrate this concept.

Question:

Snow's mapping of the outbreak showed few surprising results. Little Pulteney Street is a case in point. The street is blocks from Broad Street and closer to two other water pumps. Among residents of the street, there [5] were no cases of cholera reported during the outbreak.

[5] Which choice completes the sentence using accurate data based on the map?

A.   NO CHANGE

B.   was one new case of cholera

C.   were fewer than ten new cases of cholera

D.   were more than twenty new cases of cholera

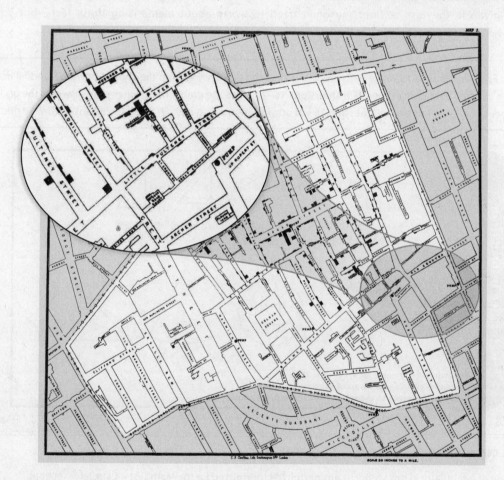

Explanation:

Here, you are being asked to interpret the information in the passage based on the map. If you look closely at the area in question, Little Pulteney Street, you'll see that there are about six bars, and we can infer that each bar represents a case of cholera. **The correct answer is C.**

MATH TEST

The questions in the Math sections (Math Test—No Calculator and Math Test—Calculator) address concepts, skills, and practices that are most useful for students after they graduate from high school. There are two question formats for math questions: multiple-choice and grid-ins (student-produced responses).

 A four-function, battery-powered, scientific or graphing calculator is allowed for the Math Test—Calculator section of the SAT®. You may not use the following: handheld mini-computers, laptop computers, pocket organizers, calculators that print or "talk," or calculators with letters on the keyboard.

MULTIPLE-CHOICE MATH

Multiple-choice math questions on the SAT® exam look like all the other standard multiple-choice math questions you've ever seen. A problem is given in algebra, problem solving, data analysis, advanced math, or additional topics, and four choices are presented from which you must choose the correct answer. The major concepts that you might need in order to solve math problems are given in the test section. You don't need to worry about memorizing these facts, but you do need to know when to use each one. The directions are similar to the following:

DIRECTIONS: For **Questions 1–15,** solve each problem, select the best answer from the choices provided, and fill in the corresponding circle on your answer sheet. For **Questions 16–20**, solve the problem and enter your answer in the grid on the answer sheet. The directions **before Question 16** will provide information on how to enter your answers in the grid.

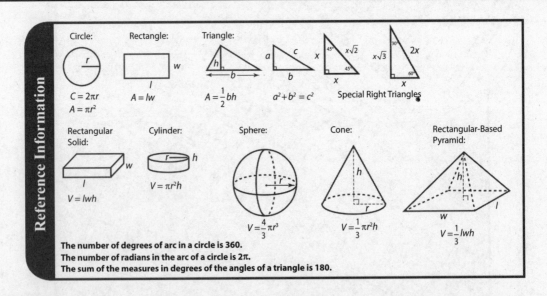

ADDITIONAL INFORMATION:

1. The use of a calculator in this section is **not permitted** (**permitted** for the Math Test—Calculator section).
2. All variables and expressions used represent real numbers unless otherwise indicated.
3. Figures provided in this test are drawn to scale unless otherwise indicated.
4. All figures lie in a plane unless otherwise indicated.
5. Unless otherwise specified, the domain of a given function f is the set of all real numbers x for which $f(x)$ is a real number.

Here are some sample multiple-choice math questions. Try them yourself before looking at the solutions that are given.

Example:

Michele is at the airport renting a car that costs $39.95 per day plus tax. A tax of 7% is applied to the rental rate, and an additional one-time untaxed fee of $5.00 is charged by the airport where she picks up the car. Which of the following represents Michele's total charge $c(x)$, in dollars, for renting a car for x days?

A. $c(x) = (39.95 + 0.07x) + 5$

B. $c(x) = 1.07(39.95)x + 5$

C. $c(x) = 1.07(39.95x + 5)$

D. $c(x) = 1.07(39.95 + 5)x$

Solution:

The total cost, $c(x)$, can be found by multiplying any daily charges by the number of days, x, and then adding any one-time charges. The daily charges include the $39.95 daily rate and the 7% tax. This can be computed by:

$$\$39.95 + 0.07(\$39.95) = 1(\$39.95) + 0.07(\$39.95) = 1.07(\$39.95)$$

Multiply the daily charge by x and add the one-time charge of $5 to obtain the function rule:

$$c(x) = 1.07(39.95)x + 5$$

The correct answer is B.

Example:

The graph of $y = (3x + 9)(x - 5)$ is a parabola in the xy-plane. In which of the following equivalent equations do the x- and y-coordinates of the vertex of the parabola appear as constants or coefficients?

A. $y = 3x^2 - 6x - 45$

B. $y = 3x(x - 2) - 45$

C. $y = 3(x - 1)^2 + (-48)$

D. $y = (x + 3)(3x - 15)$

Solution:

The equation $y = (3x + 9)(x - 5)$ can be written in vertex form $y = a(x - h)^2 + k$, where the vertex of the parabola is (h, k). To put the equation in vertex form, first multiply the factors, then complete the square. **The correct answer is C.**

Example:

The same final exam is given to two separate groups of students taking the same class. The students who took the exam on the first floor had a mean score of 84. The students who took the exam on the second floor had a mean score of 78. Which of the following represents the mean score x of both groups of students?

A. $x = 81$

B. $x < 81$

C. $x > 81$

D. $78 < x < 84$

Solution:

Many students will select choice A as the answer because 81 is the mean of 78 and 84, but there is no information about the size of the two groups that are being averaged. If the groups were equal in size, choice A would be correct. If there were more students on the second floor, then choice B would be the correct answer. Similarly, if there were more students on the first floor, then choice C would be correct. Since we don't know which floor has more students taking the exam or if the number of students is equal, we can only say that choice D is true. **The correct answer is D.**

GRID-INS

Unlike multiple-choice math, the grid-in section of the SAT® does not give you the answers. You have to compute the answer and then fill in your answer in the circles on your answer sheet. You may use the Reference Information table that appeared earlier in this chapter for these problems also.

On the SAT® exam, each set of grid-in questions starts with directions that look approximately like this:

> **DIRECTIONS:** For these questions, solve the problem and enter your answer in the grid, as described below, on the answer sheet.

1. Although not required, it is suggested that you write your answer in the boxes at the top of the columns to help you fill in the circles accurately. You will receive credit only if the circles are filled in correctly.

2. Mark no more than one circle in any column.

3. No question has a negative answer.

4. Some problems may have more than one correct answer. In such cases, enter only one answer.

5. Mixed numbers such as $3\frac{1}{2}$ must be entered as 3.5 or $\frac{7}{2}$.

   If $3\frac{1}{2}$ is entered into the grid as , it will be interpreted as $\frac{31}{2}$, not $3\frac{1}{2}$.

6. **Decimal answers:** If you obtain a decimal answer with more digits than the grid can accommodate, it may be either rounded or truncated, but it must fill the entire grid.

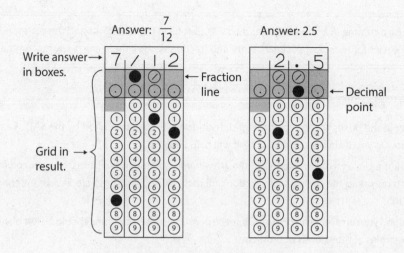

Answer: $\frac{7}{12}$

Answer: 2.5

Write answer → in boxes.

← Fraction line

← Decimal point

Grid in → result.

Answer: 201
Either position is correct.

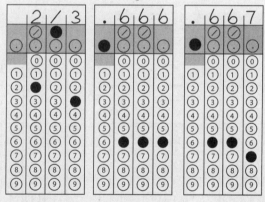

Acceptable ways to grid $\frac{2}{3}$ are:

Once you understand the following six rules, you can concentrate on just solving the math problems in this section.

1. Write your answer in the boxes at the top of the grid.

2. Mark the corresponding circles, one per column.

3. Start in any column.

4. Work with decimals or fractions.

5. Express mixed numbers as decimals or improper fractions.

6. If more than one answer is possible, enter any one.

Now let's look at these rules in more detail:

1. Write your answer in the boxes at the top of the grid. Technically, this isn't required by the SAT®. Realistically, it gives you something to follow as you fill in the circles. Do it—it will help you.

2. Make sure to mark the circles that correspond to the answer you entered in the boxes, one per column. The machine that scores the test can only read the circles, so if you don't fill them in, you won't get credit. Just entering your answer in the boxes is not enough!

3. You can start entering your answer in any column, if space permits. Unused columns should be left blank; don't put in zeroes. Here are some examples of these kinds of problems:

Examples:

Use the grids provided to try the following grid-in quesions.

1. The circumference of a circle is 20π. If the area of a sector of the circle with a central angle of

   $\frac{3\pi}{2}$ is $a\pi$, what is the value of a?

2. There are 70 students in a school who participate in the music program. If 35% of the students participate in the music program, how many students are in the school?

3. What is one possible solution to the equation $\frac{1}{x}+\frac{3}{x-1}=-4$?

1.

2.

3.

Solutions:

1. $C = 2\pi r = 20\pi$

   $r = 10$

   $A = \dfrac{3}{4}\pi r^2 = \dfrac{3}{4}\pi(10)^2 = 75\pi = a\pi$

   $a = 75$

2. $\dfrac{35}{100} = \dfrac{70}{x}$

   $35x = 7{,}000$

   $x = 200$

3. $\dfrac{1}{x} + \dfrac{3}{x-1} = -4$

   $x - 1 + 3x = -4x(x-1)$

   $4x - 1 = -4x^2 + 4x$

   $0 = -4x^2 + 1$

   $0 = (-2x+1)(2x+1)$

   $x = \pm 0.5$

Only 0.5 or $\dfrac{1}{2}$ (1/2) can be entered in the grid because, as the directions stated, no answer requires a minus sign.

You will learn more about grid-ins in Chapter 8: "Grid-In Strategies."

SAT® EXAM ESSAY (OPTIONAL)

For the essay, you will be given a previously published passage that examines ideas in the sciences and arts, as well as in civic, cultural, and political life. The passages are written for a broad-based audience, and prior knowledge of the topic is not expected. Your task in writing the essay is to read and comprehend the text sufficiently to write a thoughtful analysis of the passage.

Though the passage contents may vary from test to test, the prompt will not change. You will be asked to explain how the author of the passage builds an argument to persuade an audience. The prompt will likely look something like this:

> As you read the following passage, consider how the author uses the following:
>
> - Evidence, such as facts, statistics, or examples, to support claims.
> - Reasoning to develop ideas and to connect claims and evidence.
> - Stylistic or persuasive elements, such as word choice or appeals to emotion, to add power to the ideas expressed.

Your response will be evaluated based on your comprehension of the text, as well as on the quality of your analysis and writing. This means that you must show thoughtful understanding of the source text and appropriate use of textual evidence to support your arguments. You will also be expected to organize your ideas in a coherent way and to express them clearly, using the conventions of Standard Written English. The essay does not elicit your opinion or ask you to use your imagination to write creatively. Instead, your response should depend entirely on the source text to support your analysis. You can learn more about the optional Essay in Chapter 6: "The SAT® Exam Essay."

THE SAT® EXAM ANSWER SHEET

On the day of the test when you are given your test booklet, you'll also be given a separate answer sheet. For each multiple-choice question, you'll see a corresponding set of answer circles. The circles are labeled A, B, C, and D. Remember the following about the answer sheet:

- Answer sheets are read by machines—and machines can't think. That means it's up to you to make sure you're in the right place on the answer sheet every time you record an answer. The machine won't know that you really meant to answer Question 25 when you marked the space for Question 26.

- If you skip a question, list the number on your scratch paper. Don't mark the answer sheet in any way as a reminder. Any stray marks may affect how the machine scores your answer sheet.

- Always check to see that the answer space you have filled in corresponds to the question you are answering.

- Be sure to fill in the answer circles completely so that there can be no mistake about which answers you chose.

These seem like simple things, but you'd be surprised how many students fail to do them, especially keeping track of answer lines if they skip a question.

 TIP Make sure you're in the right place! Always check to see that the answer space you fill in corresponds to the question you are answering.

As you just read in the "Grid-Ins" section of this chapter, grid-in responses are only for questions you will see in the math sections. You'll still be filling in circles, but they will look a little different from the multiple-choice circles. Again, here's a sample of the special grid you will use.

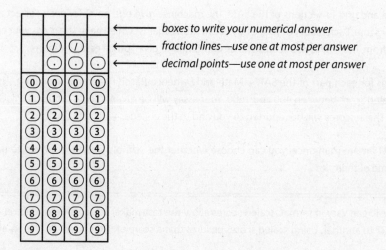

boxes to write your numerical answer
fraction lines—use one at most per answer
decimal points—use one at most per answer

At the top of the grid, you'll write in the numerical answer. The slashes that appear in the second row are used for answers with fractions. If you need one of these fraction lines in your answer, darken one of the circles. The circles with the dots are for answers with decimal points—use these circles just as you do the fraction line circles. In the lower part of the grid, fill in the numbered circles that correspond to the numbers in your answer.

Here are some examples. Note that for grid-in responses, answers can begin on the left or the right.

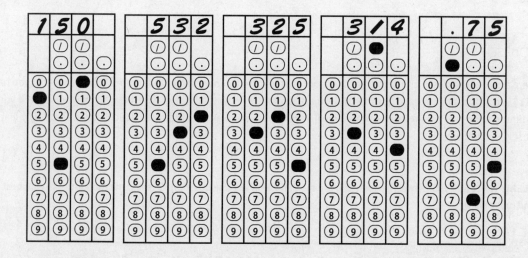

HOW THE SAT® EXAM IS SCORED

OK, you've filled in all your answer circles and perhaps written an essay. The 3 hours (and 50 minutes if you are taking the optional essay portion) are up (not a minute too soon), and you've turned in your answer sheet and your essay sheet. What next? Off your answers go to the machines at College Board and to the high school and college teachers who have been trained to read and score the essays. The machines can scan the bubble sheets in seconds and calculate a score for most of your test. If you are taking the optional essay portion, two readers will score it based on three criteria: reading, analysis, and writing. Their scores will be combined and reported separately from the main portion of the SAT®.

In scoring the multiple-choice and grid-in sections of the SAT®, the machines give one point for each correct answer. Incorrect answers have no effect on your score. Each reader of your essay uses a rubric against which he or she reads your essay. Each reader then gives your essay a score from 1 to 4. The two scores will be combined to give you an essay subscore.

The result of these calculations for each part of the SAT®—Math and Evidence-Based Reading and Writing—is your raw score. This is then converted to a scaled score between 400 and 1600. Your essay will be given a score ranging between 6 and 24, and it will be reported separately. These scores will be reported to you and to the colleges you have chosen.

Remember, if you take the SAT® more than once, you can choose whether the schools you are applying to receive the scores from each test date or just some of them.

NOTE: Because the SAT® can vary in format, scaled scores allow the test-maker to account for differences from one version of the SAT® to another. Using scaled scores ensures that a score of 500 on one SAT® is equivalent to 500 on another.

STRATEGIES FOR SAT® EXAM SUCCESS

What makes some people better test-takers than others? The secret isn't just knowing the subject; it's knowing specific test-taking strategies that can add up to extra points. This means psyching out the test, knowing how the test-makers think and what they're looking for, and using this knowledge to your advantage. Smart test-takers know how to use pacing and guessing to add points to their score.

PACE YOURSELF

Suppose there are 20 questions in one of the math sections that need to be answered in 25 minutes. That means that you have 1 minute and 15 seconds to answer each question. But smart test-takers know that's not the best way to use their time. If you use less than a minute to answer the easier questions, you'll have extra time to answer the more difficult ones. That's why learning to pace yourself is so important.

ALERT: Don't spin your wheels by spending too much time on any one question. Give it some thought, take your best shot, and move along.

Question Sets in Math Usually Go from Easiest to Most Difficult—You Should Too

A question set is one set of similar questions within the larger Math and Reading and Writing sections. In the Math sections, SAT® questions follow the pattern of easiest to hardest. Work your way through the easier questions as quickly as you can. That way you'll have more time for the more difficult ones.

But two words of caution: First, what may be easy to the test-writer may not be to you. Don't panic if Question 3 seems hard. Try to work through it, but don't spend too much time on it if it's a topic such as factoring that has just never been easy for you to understand. Second, work quickly but carefully. Don't work so fast that you make a silly mistake and lose a point that you should have gained.

You Can Set Your Own Speed Limit

All right, how will you know what your speed limit is? Use the practice tests to check your timing, and see how it affects your answers. If you've answered most of the questions in the time limit but have a lot of incorrect answers, you'd better slow down. On the other hand, if you are very accurate in your answers but aren't answering every question in a section, you can probably pick up the pace a bit.

It's Smart to Keep Moving

It's hard to let go, but sometimes you have to. Don't spend too much time on any one question before you've tried all the questions in a section. There may be questions later on in the test that you can answer easily, and you don't want to lose points just because you didn't get to them.

The Easy Choice Isn't Always Best

Are you at the end of a math section? Remember, that's where you'll usually find the hardest questions, which means that the answers are more complex. Look carefully at the choices and really think about what the question is asking.

You Don't Have to Read the Directions

What? Yes, you read it correctly the first time—you don't have to read the directions. By the time you actually sit down to take the SAT®, you've studied this book, taken all the practice tests you could find, and read enough SAT® directions to fill a library. So when the exam clock starts ticking, don't waste time rereading directions you already know. Instead, go directly to Question 1.

You're Going to Need a Watch

If you're going to pace yourself, you need to keep track of the time—and what if there is no clock in your room or if the only clock is out of your line of vision? That's why it's a good idea to bring a watch to the test. A word of warning: Don't use a watch alarm or your watch will end up on the proctor's desk.

MAKE AN SAT® EXAM STUDY PLAN

As with almost any form of learning, preparing for the SAT® is an investment of time. The more you have, the better your chances of boosting your score significantly. Next, we'll walk you through two different study plans, each tailored to a specific amount of preparation time. Choose the plan that fits your circumstances and adapt it to your needs.

Regardless of how much time you have before the actual exam, your first step should be to take the Diagnostic Test in Part II of this book. After you score it, compute your category percentages to assess your relative strengths and weaknesses. Hang on to the scoring sheet so you know where to get started.

THE COMPLETE PLAN

If you have three or more months to prepare, you should congratulate yourself! This will give you sufficient time to familiarize yourself with the test, learn critical strategies, review grammar and math fundamentals, practice writing, and take full-length tests.

You'll get the most out of your SAT® preparation if you follow these steps:

- Reread this chapter to ensure that you understand the format, structure, and scoring of the SAT®.
- Take the Diagnostic Test and identify your areas that need improvement.
- Read each and every strategy and review chapter.
- Work through all the examples, exercises, and practice exams.
- Read all the answer explanations.
- Focus on the chapters where your scores show you need to improve.

THE ACCELERATED PLAN

If you have one month or less to prepare for the SAT®, or if you cannot devote a lot of time to studying for any other reason, follow the accelerated plan. You'll get the most out of this plan if you take these steps:

- Reread this chapter to ensure that you understand the format, structure, and scoring of the SAT®.
- Take the Diagnostic Test and identify your areas that need improvement.
- Focus on the chapters that cover material that is most problematic for you and work through all the examples and exercises in these chapters.
- Work through as many practice exams as you can.
- Read all the answer explanations.

NOTE: You may be wondering how you can possibly wade through all this information in time for the test. Don't be discouraged! We wrote this book knowing that some of you would be on very condensed schedules. The information in this section will help you construct a study plan that works for you—one that will help you boost your score no matter how limited your time may be. Remember, though, that practice and targeted study are essential elements of that score boosting, so invest as much time as possible in your SAT® preparation.

MEASURING YOUR PROGRESS

It does seem as if you're on a treadmill sometimes, doesn't it? Question after question after question—are you really getting anywhere? Is all of this studying really working?

The way to find out is to monitor your progress throughout the preparation period, whether it's three months or four weeks. By taking a diagnostic examination at the beginning, you'll establish your skill baseline, and you'll be able to craft the study plan that's right for you. Then, you can either start to read the entire book (if you are using the complete plan) or go directly to the chapters that address your weaknesses (if you are using the accelerated plan). At the end of each chapter, complete the exercises and compare your percentages to your original diagnostic percentages. How have you improved? Where do you still need work? Even if you haven't reached your ultimate performance goal, are you at least applying new test-taking methods?

Here's an important point: You don't have to go through the book in order. You might want to start with the topic that you find most difficult, such as functions or grammar, or the question type that you're most unsure about, such as grid-ins. Then move to the next most difficult and so on down the line, saving the easiest topics or question types until the end. If you use the accelerated plan, you should definitely take this approach.

SIMULATE TEST-TAKING CONDITIONS

The five full-length practice exams in Chapter 14 can help you prepare for the experience of taking a timed, standardized test. Taking these tests will improve your familiarity with the SAT®, reduce your number of careless errors, and increase your overall level of confidence. To make sure that you get the most out of this practice, you should do everything in your power to simulate actual test-taking conditions.

FIND A BLOCK OF TIME

Because the SAT® is administered in one long block of time, the best way to simulate test-taking conditions is to take an entire practice exam in one sitting. This means that you should set aside 3½–4 hours of consecutive time.

If you find it difficult to find approximately 4 quiet hours at home, maybe take the test in the library. If you decide to take a test at home, take precautions. Let your friends know you are taking a practice test, put your phone in another room, and convince siblings to stay out of your room. Easier said than done, right? Although infrequent interruptions won't completely invalidate your testing experience, you should try to avoid them.

WORK AT A DESK AND WEAR A WATCH

Don't take a practice test while you are lounging on your bed. After all, the SAT® proctors won't let you take the test lying down! Clear off sufficient space on a desk or table to work comfortably. Wear a watch to properly administer the sections under timed conditions. Or use a timer. The time for each section is marked on the section, so check the beginning of each section and set your timer or your watch for that amount of time.

You are not allowed to explore other sections on the test while you are supposed to be working on a particular one. So when you take your practice tests, don't look ahead or back. Take the full time to complete each section.

 **CAUTION** If you're worried that you won't be able to resist the temptation to check the answer keys during the practice tests, cover them up before you take a test. Don't allow yourself to become dependent upon a sneak look now and then. You won't have answer keys available on test day, and the main purpose of the practice tests is to prepare you for the real experience.

PRACTICE ON A WEEKEND MORNING

Since the SAT® is typically administered at 8:30 a.m. on Saturday (or Sunday for religious observers), why not take the practice test at the exact same time on a weekend morning? You should be most energetic in the morning anyway. If you are not a morning person, now is a good time to become one since that's when you'll have to take the actual SAT®! When you take the practice test, allow yourself two breaks. Give yourself a 5-minute break after Section 2: Writing and Language Test to run to the bathroom, eat a snack, and re-sharpen your pencils. You can take another 5-minute break after Section 4: Math Test—Calculator.

Remember that your goal is to take these practice tests in as true an environment as possible so that you're prepared to take the real SAT®. You will be accustomed to sitting for a long period of time, but you will get two breaks. This knowledge will make you considerably less anxious on test day.

The following table puts all of the SAT® section times in a one-stop format, so you can refer to it often when planning your SAT® study time.

Section	Number of Questions	Time Allowed
Reading	52	65 minutes
Writing and Language	44	35 minutes
Math Test—No Calculator	20	25 minutes
Math Test—Calculator	38	55 minutes
Essay	--	50 minutes

ONE THIRD OF THE WAY THROUGH YOUR STUDY

When you are approximately one third of the way through your plan of study—this can be after ten days or a month—it's time to take one of the practice tests. When you have finished scoring and reading the answer explanations, compare your scores with your original diagnostic scores. Hopefully, you're doing better. But if you're not, don't panic. At this point in test preparation, it's not unusual to score about the same as you did at the beginning.

What's more important than *what* you scored is *how* you took the practice test. Did you really use the test-taking strategies to which you've been introduced? If you didn't, go back to the strategy chapters and either reread them, if you are doing the complete plan, or at least reread the summaries, if you are on the accelerated plan. Then continue your review. Read more review chapters and complete the exercises.

30

Chapter 1

All About
the SAT®
Exam

TWO THIRDS OF THE WAY THROUGH YOUR STUDY

After you have worked through most of the review chapters (under the complete plan) or all of the material relating to your areas of weakness (under the accelerated plan), it's time to take another practice test. By now, you should be seeing some real improvement in your scores. If you are still having trouble with certain topics, review the problematic material again.

THE HOME STRETCH

For the most part, the last phase of study should involve *less learning* and *more practice*. Take more practice tests! By now, you probably understand how to take the exam. What you need is more practice taking the test under simulated test-day conditions to work on your pacing and test-taking strategies.

When you take additional practice exams, be sure to do so in a near-test environment. Keep analyzing your scores to ensure that all of this practice is working. Determine which areas need additional work. If you skipped over any of the review chapters in this book, go back and use the exercises to improve your skills.

THE FINAL WEEK

One last word of advice: no matter which study plan you select, you should probably take one full-length, timed practice test the week before you take the actual SAT®. This will get you ready for the big day. But don't take the practice test the day before the real exam. That's a time when you should be relaxing, not cramming.

THE NIGHT BEFORE AND DAY OF THE EXAM

If you follow the guidelines in this book, you will be extremely well prepared. You will know the format inside and out, you will know how to approach every type of question, you will have worked hard to strengthen your weak areas, and you will have taken multiple practice tests under simulated testing conditions. The last 24 hours before the SAT® exam is not the time to cram—it's actually the time to relax. Remember that the SAT® is primarily a test of how you think, not what you know. So last-minute cramming can be more confusing than illuminating.

In the morning, take a shower to wake up and then eat a sensible breakfast. If you are a person who usually eats breakfast, you should probably eat your customary meal. If you don't usually eat breakfast, don't gorge yourself on test day because it will be a shock to your system. Eat something light (like a granola bar and a piece of fruit), and pack a snack.

Test Day Checklist

On the night before the big day, find a diversion to keep yourself from obsessing about the SAT®. Maybe stay home and watch some of your favorite television shows. Or go out to an early movie. Do whatever is best for you. Just make sure you get plenty of sleep.

You should also lay out the following items before you go to bed:

 Test ticket

 Acceptable photo ID

 Sharp pencils with erasers

 Permissible calculator

 Snack and bottle of water

 A sweater or sweatshirt in case of cooler test center conditions (optional)

> **NOTE:** Make sure you allow enough time to arrive at the test site at least 15 minutes before the 8 a.m. arrival time. You don't want to raise your level of anxiety by having to rush to get there.

TOP 10 STRATEGIES TO RAISE YOUR SCORE

When it comes to taking the SAT®, some test-taking skills will do you more good than others. There are concepts you can learn and techniques you can follow that will help you do your best. Here are our picks for the top 10 strategies to raise your score:

1. Create a study plan and follow it. The right SAT® study plan will help you get the most out of this book in whatever time you have.

2. Don't get stuck on any one question. Since you have a specific amount of time to answer questions, you can't afford to spend too much time on any one problem.

3. Learn the directions in advance. If you already know the directions, you won't have to waste your time reading them. You'll be able to jump right in and start answering questions as soon as the testing clock starts.

4. If you choose to take the essay portion of the test, it's important to develop your ideas and express them clearly, using examples to back them up. Your essay doesn't have to be grammatically perfect, but it does have to be focused and organized, and it should explain how the author develops his or her argument.

5. For the Writing and Language Test multiple-choice questions, think about the simplest, clearest way to express an idea. If an answer choice sounds awkward or overly complicated, chances are good that it's wrong.

6. For relevant words in context, be sure to read the sentences around the word carefully. The SAT® is no longer testing obscure words but instead is focusing on defining words in the context of a passage.

7. For Reading Test questions, first skim the passage to see what it's about. Look for the main ideas, and then tackle the questions that direct you straight to the answer by referring you to a specific line in the passage. Then work on the detailed questions that require a closer reading of the passage.

8. For the Math multiple-choice questions, it can help if you know how to approach the problems. If you're stuck, try substituting numbers for variables. You can also try plugging in numbers from the answer choices. Start with one of the middle numbers. That way, if it doesn't work, you can strategically choose one that's higher or lower, since the answer choices are normally presented in ascending order.

9. For the Math grid-in questions, you determine the answer and enter it into a grid. Be sure to make your best guess, even if you're not sure.

10. Finally, relax the night before the test. Don't cram. Studying at the last minute will only stress you out. Go to a movie or hang out with a friend—anything to get your mind off the test!

SUMMING IT UP

- Learning the question types is the best way to prepare for the SAT® exam. Knowing the test format and question types will relieve test anxiety because you'll know exactly what to expect on test day.

  1. **Reading:** The answer to every question will be either directly stated or implied in the passage.

  2. **Writing and Language:** These question sets test your ability to spot and correct grammatical errors, usage problems, and wordiness. You will also be expected to answer questions to improve the development and organization of a particular paragraph or the passage as a whole.

  3. **Multiple-Choice Math:** A set of reference formulas is given at the beginning of each math section, so you don't have to worry about forgetting an important formula.

  4. **Grid-ins:** You have to calculate the answer and then fill in circles on the grids provided on the answer sheet. Only the circles count, so fill in each one correctly.

  5. **Essay (Optional):** You will have 50 minutes to write your essay, which tests reading, analysis, and writing skills. You will be asked to produce a written analysis of a provided source text. You will need to explain how the author has effectively built an argument to persuade his or her audience. The readers are trained to evaluate the essays as first drafts, not polished final products.

- When you take a full practice examination, try to simulate test-taking conditions:

  - You'll need to set aside approximately 4 quiet hours.

  - Work at a desk and wear a watch.

  - Cover the answers before you start the test.

  - Whenever possible, take the full practice tests on weekend mornings.

- You may use a calculator on the SAT®, but only in one math section. For some questions, you will need to decide if the calculator will help you or slow you down.

- Every SAT® exam question is worth 1 point, whether it is an easy question or a difficult one. So nail the easier questions—and quickly accumulate points.

- Fill in the answer circles cleanly and completely, or you won't get credit for your answers.

- Random guessing will have little effect on your score, but educated guessing can boost your score.

- Pace yourself and move through the test relatively quickly.

- Relax the evening before the SAT®, but also be sure you're prepared.

  - Assemble the supplies you will need for the test.

  - Pick out what you'll wear and remember to layer your clothes.

  - Be sure your calculator has fresh batteries.

- On the morning of the exam, eat breakfast, pack your snack, and leave for the test site in plenty of time to get there at least 15 minutes before the start time.

33

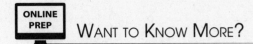

Access more practice questions, valuable lessons, helpful tips, interactive games and flashcards, and expert strategies from *Peterson's Online Course for the SAT® Exam:*

To purchase and access the course, go to **https://www.petersons.com/testprep/sat/**.

34

Chapter 1

All About
the SAT®
Exam

PART II: THE DIAGNOSTIC TEST

Chapter 2: The Diagnostic Test

CHAPTER 2:
THE DIAGNOSTIC TEST

OVERVIEW

- Introduction to the Diagnostic Test
- Answer Sheets
- Section 1: Reading Test
- Section 2: Writing and Language Test
- Section 3: Math Test—No Calculator
- Section 4: Math Test—Calculator
- Section 5: Essay
- Answer Keys and Explanations
- Computing Your Scores

INTRODUCTION TO THE DIAGNOSTIC TEST

Before you begin preparing for the SAT® exam, it's important to know your strengths and the areas where you need improvement. If you find the questions for the Reading Test easy, for example, it would be a mistake to spend hours practicing them. Taking the Diagnostic Test in this chapter and then working out your scores will help you determine how you should apportion your study time.

PREPARING TO TAKE THE DIAGNOSTIC TEST

If possible, take the Diagnostic Test in one sitting. Give yourself at least 4 hours to complete it. The actual test is 3 hours and 45 minutes, and you'll be allowed to take three short breaks—you may even want to have some healthy snacks nearby for a quick break you'll want to take. Simulating the test this way will give you an idea of how long the sections are and how it feels to take the entire test. You will also get a sense of how long you can spend on each question in each section, so you can begin to work out a pacing schedule for yourself.

First, assemble all the things you will need to take the test, including the following items:

- No. 2 pencils, at least three
- A calculator with fresh batteries
- A timer
- The answer sheets and the lined paper for the essay—provided on the following pages

Set a timer for the time specified for each section, which is noted at the top of the first page of each test section. Stick to that time, so you are simulating the real test. At this point, it's as important to know how many questions you can answer in the time allotted as it is to answer questions correctly. Good luck!

Section 1: Reading Test

1. Ⓐ Ⓑ Ⓒ Ⓓ   12. Ⓐ Ⓑ Ⓒ Ⓓ   23. Ⓐ Ⓑ Ⓒ Ⓓ   33. Ⓐ Ⓑ Ⓒ Ⓓ   43. Ⓐ Ⓑ Ⓒ Ⓓ
2. Ⓐ Ⓑ Ⓒ Ⓓ   13. Ⓐ Ⓑ Ⓒ Ⓓ   24. Ⓐ Ⓑ Ⓒ Ⓓ   34. Ⓐ Ⓑ Ⓒ Ⓓ   44. Ⓐ Ⓑ Ⓒ Ⓓ
3. Ⓐ Ⓑ Ⓒ Ⓓ   14. Ⓐ Ⓑ Ⓒ Ⓓ   25. Ⓐ Ⓑ Ⓒ Ⓓ   35. Ⓐ Ⓑ Ⓒ Ⓓ   45. Ⓐ Ⓑ Ⓒ Ⓓ
4. Ⓐ Ⓑ Ⓒ Ⓓ   15. Ⓐ Ⓑ Ⓒ Ⓓ   26. Ⓐ Ⓑ Ⓒ Ⓓ   36. Ⓐ Ⓑ Ⓒ Ⓓ   46. Ⓐ Ⓑ Ⓒ Ⓓ
5. Ⓐ Ⓑ Ⓒ Ⓓ   16. Ⓐ Ⓑ Ⓒ Ⓓ   27. Ⓐ Ⓑ Ⓒ Ⓓ   37. Ⓐ Ⓑ Ⓒ Ⓓ   47. Ⓐ Ⓑ Ⓒ Ⓓ
6. Ⓐ Ⓑ Ⓒ Ⓓ   17. Ⓐ Ⓑ Ⓒ Ⓓ   28. Ⓐ Ⓑ Ⓒ Ⓓ   38. Ⓐ Ⓑ Ⓒ Ⓓ   48. Ⓐ Ⓑ Ⓒ Ⓓ
7. Ⓐ Ⓑ Ⓒ Ⓓ   18. Ⓐ Ⓑ Ⓒ Ⓓ   29. Ⓐ Ⓑ Ⓒ Ⓓ   39. Ⓐ Ⓑ Ⓒ Ⓓ   49. Ⓐ Ⓑ Ⓒ Ⓓ
8. Ⓐ Ⓑ Ⓒ Ⓓ   19. Ⓐ Ⓑ Ⓒ Ⓓ   30. Ⓐ Ⓑ Ⓒ Ⓓ   40. Ⓐ Ⓑ Ⓒ Ⓓ   50. Ⓐ Ⓑ Ⓒ Ⓓ
9. Ⓐ Ⓑ Ⓒ Ⓓ   20. Ⓐ Ⓑ Ⓒ Ⓓ   31. Ⓐ Ⓑ Ⓒ Ⓓ   41. Ⓐ Ⓑ Ⓒ Ⓓ   51. Ⓐ Ⓑ Ⓒ Ⓓ
10. Ⓐ Ⓑ Ⓒ Ⓓ   21. Ⓐ Ⓑ Ⓒ Ⓓ   32. Ⓐ Ⓑ Ⓒ Ⓓ   42. Ⓐ Ⓑ Ⓒ Ⓓ   52. Ⓐ Ⓑ Ⓒ Ⓓ
11. Ⓐ Ⓑ Ⓒ Ⓓ   22. Ⓐ Ⓑ Ⓒ Ⓓ

Section 2: Writing and Language Test

1. Ⓐ Ⓑ Ⓒ Ⓓ   10. Ⓐ Ⓑ Ⓒ Ⓓ   19. Ⓐ Ⓑ Ⓒ Ⓓ   28. Ⓐ Ⓑ Ⓒ Ⓓ   37. Ⓐ Ⓑ Ⓒ Ⓓ
2. Ⓐ Ⓑ Ⓒ Ⓓ   11. Ⓐ Ⓑ Ⓒ Ⓓ   20. Ⓐ Ⓑ Ⓒ Ⓓ   29. Ⓐ Ⓑ Ⓒ Ⓓ   38. Ⓐ Ⓑ Ⓒ Ⓓ
3. Ⓐ Ⓑ Ⓒ Ⓓ   12. Ⓐ Ⓑ Ⓒ Ⓓ   21. Ⓐ Ⓑ Ⓒ Ⓓ   30. Ⓐ Ⓑ Ⓒ Ⓓ   39. Ⓐ Ⓑ Ⓒ Ⓓ
4. Ⓐ Ⓑ Ⓒ Ⓓ   13. Ⓐ Ⓑ Ⓒ Ⓓ   22. Ⓐ Ⓑ Ⓒ Ⓓ   31. Ⓐ Ⓑ Ⓒ Ⓓ   40. Ⓐ Ⓑ Ⓒ Ⓓ
5. Ⓐ Ⓑ Ⓒ Ⓓ   14. Ⓐ Ⓑ Ⓒ Ⓓ   23. Ⓐ Ⓑ Ⓒ Ⓓ   32. Ⓐ Ⓑ Ⓒ Ⓓ   41. Ⓐ Ⓑ Ⓒ Ⓓ
6. Ⓐ Ⓑ Ⓒ Ⓓ   15. Ⓐ Ⓑ Ⓒ Ⓓ   24. Ⓐ Ⓑ Ⓒ Ⓓ   33. Ⓐ Ⓑ Ⓒ Ⓓ   42. Ⓐ Ⓑ Ⓒ Ⓓ
7. Ⓐ Ⓑ Ⓒ Ⓓ   16. Ⓐ Ⓑ Ⓒ Ⓓ   25. Ⓐ Ⓑ Ⓒ Ⓓ   34. Ⓐ Ⓑ Ⓒ Ⓓ   43. Ⓐ Ⓑ Ⓒ Ⓓ
8. Ⓐ Ⓑ Ⓒ Ⓓ   17. Ⓐ Ⓑ Ⓒ Ⓓ   26. Ⓐ Ⓑ Ⓒ Ⓓ   35. Ⓐ Ⓑ Ⓒ Ⓓ   44. Ⓐ Ⓑ Ⓒ Ⓓ
9. Ⓐ Ⓑ Ⓒ Ⓓ   18. Ⓐ Ⓑ Ⓒ Ⓓ   27. Ⓐ Ⓑ Ⓒ Ⓓ   36. Ⓐ Ⓑ Ⓒ Ⓓ

Section 3: Math Test—No Calculator

1. Ⓐ Ⓑ Ⓒ Ⓓ   4. Ⓐ Ⓑ Ⓒ Ⓓ   7. Ⓐ Ⓑ Ⓒ Ⓓ   10. Ⓐ Ⓑ Ⓒ Ⓓ   13. Ⓐ Ⓑ Ⓒ Ⓓ
2. Ⓐ Ⓑ Ⓒ Ⓓ   5. Ⓐ Ⓑ Ⓒ Ⓓ   8. Ⓐ Ⓑ Ⓒ Ⓓ   11. Ⓐ Ⓑ Ⓒ Ⓓ   14. Ⓐ Ⓑ Ⓒ Ⓓ
3. Ⓐ Ⓑ Ⓒ Ⓓ   6. Ⓐ Ⓑ Ⓒ Ⓓ   9. Ⓐ Ⓑ Ⓒ Ⓓ   12. Ⓐ Ⓑ Ⓒ Ⓓ   15. Ⓐ Ⓑ Ⓒ Ⓓ

Diagnostic Test—ANSWERS

Peterson's SAT® Prep Guide 2019

Section 3: Math Test—No Calculator

16.   17.   18.   19.   20.

Section 4: Math Test—Calculator

1. Ⓐ Ⓑ Ⓒ Ⓓ   7. Ⓐ Ⓑ Ⓒ Ⓓ   13. Ⓐ Ⓑ Ⓒ Ⓓ   19. Ⓐ Ⓑ Ⓒ Ⓓ   25. Ⓐ Ⓑ Ⓒ Ⓓ
2. Ⓐ Ⓑ Ⓒ Ⓓ   8. Ⓐ Ⓑ Ⓒ Ⓓ   14. Ⓐ Ⓑ Ⓒ Ⓓ   20. Ⓐ Ⓑ Ⓒ Ⓓ   26. Ⓐ Ⓑ Ⓒ Ⓓ
3. Ⓐ Ⓑ Ⓒ Ⓓ   9. Ⓐ Ⓑ Ⓒ Ⓓ   15. Ⓐ Ⓑ Ⓒ Ⓓ   21. Ⓐ Ⓑ Ⓒ Ⓓ   27. Ⓐ Ⓑ Ⓒ Ⓓ
4. Ⓐ Ⓑ Ⓒ Ⓓ   10. Ⓐ Ⓑ Ⓒ Ⓓ   16. Ⓐ Ⓑ Ⓒ Ⓓ   22. Ⓐ Ⓑ Ⓒ Ⓓ   28. Ⓐ Ⓑ Ⓒ Ⓓ
5. Ⓐ Ⓑ Ⓒ Ⓓ   11. Ⓐ Ⓑ Ⓒ Ⓓ   17. Ⓐ Ⓑ Ⓒ Ⓓ   23. Ⓐ Ⓑ Ⓒ Ⓓ   29. Ⓐ Ⓑ Ⓒ Ⓓ
6. Ⓐ Ⓑ Ⓒ Ⓓ   12. Ⓐ Ⓑ Ⓒ Ⓓ   18. Ⓐ Ⓑ Ⓒ Ⓓ   24. Ⓐ Ⓑ Ⓒ Ⓓ   30. Ⓐ Ⓑ Ⓒ Ⓓ

31.   32.   33.   34.   35.

36.   37.   38.

Section 5: Essay

SECTION 1: READING TEST

65 Minutes—52 Questions

TURN TO SECTION 1 OF YOUR ANSWER SHEET TO ANSWER THE QUESTIONS IN THIS SECTION.

> **DIRECTIONS:** Each passage (or pair of passages) in this section is followed by a number of multiple-choice questions. After reading each passage, select the best answer to each question based on what is stated or implied in the passage or passages and in any supplementary material, such as a table, graph, chart, or photograph.

Questions 1–10 are based on the following passage.

John James Audubon (1785–1851) is known primarily for his bird studies, but as this passage from Ornithological Biography *shows, he wrote about the behavior of other animals as well.*

Black Bear

The Black Bear (*Ursus americanus*), however clumsy in appearance, is active, vigilant, and persevering; possesses great strength, courage, and address; and
Line undergoes with little injury the greatest fatigues and
5 hardships in avoiding the pursuit of the hunter. Like the Deer, it changes its haunts with the seasons, and for the same reason, namely, the desire of obtaining suitable food, or of retiring to the more inaccessible parts, where it can pass the time in security, unobserved by man,
10 the most dangerous of its enemies. During the spring months, it searches for food in the low rich alluvial lands that border the rivers, or by the margins of such inland lakes as, on account of their small size, are called by us ponds. There it procures abundance of succulent roots,
15 and of the tender juicy stems of plants, on which it chiefly feeds at that season. During the summer heat, it enters the gloomy swamps, passes much of its time wallowing in the mud, like a hog, and contents itself with crayfish, roots, and nettles, now and then, when hard pressed
20 by hunger, seizing on a young pig, or perhaps a sow, or even a calf. As soon as the different kinds of berries which grow on the mountain begin to ripen, the Bears betake themselves to the high grounds, followed by their cubs. In such retired parts of the country where there are no
25 hilly grounds, it pays visits to the maize fields, which it ravages for a while. After this, the various species of nuts, acorns, grapes, and other forest fruits, that form what in the western country is called mast, attract its attention. The Bear is then seen rambling singly through
30 the woods to gather this harvest, not forgetting to rob every Bee tree it meets with, Bears being, as you well know, expert at this operation. You also know that they are good climbers, and may have been told, or at least may now be told, that the Black Bear now and then
35 houses itself in the hollow trunks of the larger trees for weeks together, when it is said to suck its paws. You are probably not aware of a habit in which it indulges, and which, being curious, must be interesting to you. At one season, the Black Bear may be seen examining
40 the lower part of the trunk of a tree for several minutes with much attention, at the same time looking around, and snuffing the air, to assure itself that no enemy is near. It then raises itself on its hind legs, approaches the trunk, embraces it with its forelegs, and scratches
45 the bark with its teeth and claws for several minutes in continuance. Its jaws clash against each other, until a mass of foam runs down both sides of the mouth. After this it continues its rambles. In various portions of our country, many of our woodsmen and hunters
50 who have seen the Bear performing the singular operation just described, imagine that it does so for the purpose of leaving behind an indication of its size and power. They measure the height at which the scratches are made, and in this manner, can, in fact, form an
55 estimate of the magnitude of the individual. My own opinion, however, is different. It seems to me that the Bear scratches on the trees, not for the purpose of showing its size or its strength, but merely for that of sharpening its teeth and claws, to enable it better to
60 encounter a rival of its own species during the amatory season. The Wild Boar of Europe clashes its tusks and scrapes the earth with its feet, and the Deer rubs its antlers against the lower part of the stems of young trees or bushes, for the same purpose.

CONTINUE

Diagnostic Test — READING

1 As used in line 3, "address" refers to

A. habitat.

B. anxiety.

C. skill.

D. direction.

2 What is the most likely reason that Audubon wrote about the black bear?

A. He wanted to provide more information about another animal to his readers.

B. He was fascinated by mammals.

C. He wanted to prove he had interests other than birds.

D. He wanted to show the commonalities in behavioral patterns of bears and birds.

3 Which choice provides the best evidence for the answer to the previous question?

A. Lines 5–8 ("Like the Deer, . . . obtaining suitable food . . .")

B. Lines 29–32 ("The Bear is then seen . . . this operation.")

C. Lines 36–38 ("You are probably . . . interesting to you.")

D. Lines 55–59 ("My own opinion . . . teeth and claws")

4 Huntsmen and woodsmen claim that the bear scratches tree bark with its teeth and claws to

A. sharpen its teeth.

B. mark the tree for winter hibernation.

C. ward off potential predators by showing its size.

D. mark the tree so that other animals can't harvest its nuts and acorns.

5 What is the main rhetorical effect of the author's description of how black bears behave in swamps, lines 16–21?

A. To show that the bear is an exceptional predator

B. To explain why humans might want to hunt bears

C. To impress the reader with how varied a bear's diet is

D. To create an image of a bear placidly foraging for food

6 Which choice provides the best evidence for the answer to the previous question?

A. Lines 16–17 ("During . . . swamps")

B. Lines 17–18 ("passes . . . mud")

C. Lines 19–20 ("now and . . . hunger")

D. Lines 20–21 ("seizing on . . . calf.")

7 According to Audubon, how are the claws of the black bear like the tusks of the wild boar?

A. Both are parts of the body that warn other animals that they are predators.

B. Both animals use these parts of their bodies to forage for crayfish and roots.

C. Both animals use these body parts to defend themselves from human predators.

D. Both are parts of the body that the animal sharpens to better compete for a mate.

8 The fact that Audubon calls man the bear's "most dangerous" enemy (line 10) indicates that he

A. is a hunter himself.

B. has some sympathy for hunted bears.

C. does not believe that bears are dangerous.

D. thinks bears are more dangerous than people.

9 Which choice provides the best evidence for the answer to the previous question?

A. Lines 5–6 ("Like the Deer . . . seasons")

B. Lines 6–8 ("for the same . . . food")

C. Line 8 ("retiring . . . parts")

D. Lines 9–10 ("man, . . . enemies.")

10 The author indicates that he believes that the reader

A. knows absolutely nothing about bears.

B. already has some knowledge of bears.

C. needs help overcoming a fear of bears.

D. believes bears can climb trees as well as apes.

Thomas Jefferson wrote in 1787 to his nephew, Peter Carr, a student at the College of William and Mary.

Paris, August 10, 1787

Dear Peter, I have received your two letters of
December 30 and April 18 and am very happy to find by
Line them, as well as by letters from Mr. Wythe,* that you have
5 been so fortunate as to attract his notice and good will: I
am sure you will find this to have been one of the more
fortunate events of your life, as I have ever been sensible
it was of mine. I enclose you a sketch of the sciences to
which I would wish you to apply in such order as Mr. Wythe
10 shall advise: I mention also the books in them worth your
reading, which submit to his correction. Many of these
are among your father's books, which you should have
brought to you. As I do not recollect those of them not in
his library, you must write to me for them, making out a
15 catalogue of such as you think you shall have occasion for
in 18 months from the date of your letter, and consulting
Mr. Wythe on the subject. To this sketch I will add a few
particular observations.

1. Italian. I fear the learning of this language will
20 confound your French and Spanish. Being all of them
degenerated dialects of the Latin, they are apt to mix in
conversation. I have never seen a person speaking the
three languages who did not mix them. It is a delightful
language, but late events having rendered the Spanish
25 more useful, lay it aside to prosecute that.

2. Spanish. Bestow great attention on this, and
endeavor to acquire an accurate knowledge of it. Our
future connections with Spain and Spanish America will
render that language a valuable acquisition. The ancient
30 history of a great part of America too is written in that
language. I send you a dictionary.

3. Moral philosophy. I think it lost time to attend
lectures in this branch. He who made us would have been
a pitiful bungler if he had made the rules of our moral
35 conduct a matter of science. For one man of science, there
are thousands who are not. What would have become of
them? Man was destined for society. His morality therefore
was to be formed to this object. He was endowed with a
sense of right and wrong merely relative to this. This sense
40 is as much a part of his nature as the sense of hearing,
seeing, feeling; it is the true foundation of morality. . . . The
moral sense, or conscience, is as much a part of man as
his leg or arm. It is given to all human beings in a stronger
or weaker degree, as force of members is given them
45 in a greater or less degree. . . . State a moral case to a

ploughman and a professor. The former will decide it
as well, and often better than the latter, because he has
not been led astray by artificial rules.

*George Wythe, a well-respected scholar, the first American
law professor, and one of the signatories of the Declaration of
Independence, became an important teacher and mentor to
Thomas Jefferson.

11 What is the best description of Mr. Wythe and his relationship to the Jefferson family?

A.   Teacher

B.   Cousin

C.   Family friend

D.   Public servant

12 What is the purpose of Jefferson's letter to his nephew?

A.   To advise him about his education

B.   To advise him about leading a moral life

C.   To make sure he will learn a second language

D.   To keep in touch with his family while abroad

13 What does Jefferson suggest his reader do about studying
the Italian language?

A.   Ignore it to pursue Spanish instead

B.   Ignore it to study French instead

C.   Use it as a building block to studying Spanish

D.   Use it in conversation with Spanish people

14 Which choice provides the best evidence for the answer
to the previous question?

A.   Lines 19–20 ("I fear . . . Spanish.")

B.   Lines 20–22 ("Being all . . . conversation.")

C.   Lines 22–23 ("I have . . . mix them.")

D.   Lines 23–25 ("It is a . . . prosecute that.")

CONTINUE

15 In lines 42–43, Jefferson compares conscience to a physical limb of the body to show

   A. that it is natural and present in all human beings.

   B. how easily we take it for granted.

   C. that without it, humans are powerless.

   D. how mental and physical states are integrated.

16 Based on the passage, what country does Jefferson think will most closely align with the newly independent colonies in the future?

   A. England

   B. France

   C. Italy

   D. Spain

17 By "lost time" (line 32), Jefferson means

   A. wasted time.

   B. the past.

   C. missing time.

   D. youth.

18 Jefferson tells his nephew to lay Italian aside because it is

   A. a degenerated dialect.

   B. not necessary since he already knows French.

   C. not useful to be multilingual.

   D. too easy to get it mixed up with Spanish.

19 Which of the following best summarizes Jefferson's overall view of morality?

   A. Morality is a science that can be taught by professors and scholars.

   B. Moral philosophy is self-taught.

   C. A sense of morality is part of human nature.

   D. Humans are moral beings who need rules to guide their behavior.

Three Generations of the Jefferson Family

Peter Jefferson (b: 1708; d: 1757) - [spouse] Jane Randolph (b: 1721; d: 1776)

[children: 10]

Thomas (1743 - 1826) - [spouse] Martha Wales (1748 - 1782)   Martha (1746 - 1811) - [spouse] Dabney Carr (1743 - 1773)

[children: 6]   [children: 6]

(others died before reaching adulthood)

Martha (b: 1772; d: 1836)   Mary (b: 1778; d: 1782)   Peter (b: 1770; d: 1815)

20 Based on information in the family tree, Peter may have relied on advice from his uncle Thomas because Peter

   A. considered Thomas to be a better parental figure than his father was.

   B. did not receive reliable advice from his own mother.

   C. did not have a father, and his mother was busy with her 5 other children.

   D. wanted the best education so he could help take care of his 5 siblings.

21 Which of the following best describes the tone of Jefferson's letter to his nephew?

   A. Invested and warm

   B. Anxious and worried

   C. Objective and matter-of-fact

   D. Distant and preoccupied

This excerpt is from the article "New Link in the Food Chain? Marine Plastic Pollution and Seafood Safety," by Nate Seltenrich. It has been reproduced from the journal Environmental Health Perspectives.

World plastics production has experienced almost constant growth for more than half a century, rising from approximately 1.9 tons in 1950 to approximately 330 million tons in 2013. The World Bank estimates that 1.4 billion tons of trash are generated globally each year, 10% of it plastic. The International Maritime Organization has banned the dumping of plastic waste (and most other garbage) at sea. However, an unknown portion of the plastic produced each year escapes into the environment—instead of being landfilled, incinerated, or recycled—and at least some of it eventually makes its way to sea.

Plastics that reach the ocean will gradually break down into ever-smaller pieces due to sunlight exposure, oxidation, and the physical action of waves, currents, and grazing by fish and birds. So-called microplastics—variably defined in the scientific literature and popular press as smaller than 1 or 5 mm in diameter—are understood to be the most abundant type of plastic in the ocean. The 5 Gyres' authors* found microplastics almost everywhere they sampled, from near-shore environments to the open ocean, in varying concentrations, and they estimated that particles 4.75 mm or smaller—about the size of a lentil—made up roughly 90% of the total plastic pieces they collected.

But the degradation of larger pieces of plastic is not the only way microplastics end up in the ocean. Nurdles—the plastic pellets used as a feedstock for producing plastic goods—can spill from ships or land-based sources, and "microbeads" used as scrubbing agents in personal care products such as skin cleansers, toothpastes, and shampoos, can escape water-treatment facilities and pass into water-sheds with treated water. (In June 2014, Illinois became the first US state to ban the manufacture and sale of products containing microbeads, which have been documented in the Great Lakes and Chicago's North Shore Channel.)

Marine organisms throughout the food chain commonly consume plastics of various sizes. The tiniest microplastics are small enough to be mistaken for food by zooplankton, allowing them to enter the food chain at very low trophic levels. Some larger predators are thought to confuse nurdles (which typically measure less than 5 mm in diameter) with fish eggs or other food sources.

Once plastics have been consumed, laboratory tests show that chemical additives and adsorbed pollutants and metals on their surface can desorb (leach out) and transfer into the guts and tissues of marine organisms. . . .

Research has shown that harmful and persistent substances can both bioaccumulate (or increase in concentration as exposures persist) and biomagnify (or increase in concentration at higher trophic levels) within organisms as they assume some of the chemical burden of their prey or environment. Yet again, no research has yet demonstrated the bioaccumulation of sorbed pollutants in the environment.

Three key questions remain to be determined. To what extent do plastics transfer pollutants and additives to organisms upon ingestion? What contribution are plastics making to the contaminant burden in organisms above and beyond their exposures through water, sediments, and food? And, finally, what proportion of humans' exposure to plastic ingredients and environmental pollutants occurs through seafood? Researchers are moving carefully in the direction of answers to these questions. . . .

New laws . . . could require handling plastics more responsibly at the end of their useful life through recycling, proper disposal, and extended producer responsibility.

Rolf Halden, director of the Center for Environmental Security at the Biodesign Institute at Arizona State University, advocates for another solution: manufacturing more sustainable plastics from the start. "We need to design the next generation of plastics to make them more biodegradable so that they don't have a long half-life, they don't accumulate in the oceans, and they don't have the opportunity to collect chemicals long-term," he says. "There's just no way we can shield people from all exposures that could occur. Let's design safer chemicals and make the whole problem moot."

The 5 Gyres Institute addresses plastic pollution in the ocean.

22 According to the passage, plastic is

A. wasted more than any other material.

B. responsible for a massive amount of waste.

C. not being produced as much as it once was.

D. the single most dangerous material to the planet.

CONTINUE

23 Which choice provides the best evidence for the answer to the previous question?

    A. Lines 1–2 ("World . . . century")

    B. Lines 4–6 ("The World . . . it plastic.")

    C. Lines 6–8 ("The International . . . at sea.")

    D. Lines 8–10 ("However . . . environment")

24 Which best describes the overall tone of the article?

    A. Neutral and scientific

    B. Emotional and persuasive

    C. Personal and human

    D. Subjective and opinionated

25 What solution does Rolf Halden support to decrease the effects of pollution from plastics on humans?

    A. Passing laws to mandate more rigorous recycling

    B. Developing plastics that are biodegradable

    C. Making plastics that are safe to ingest

    D. Banning the production of new plastic products

26 This article was most likely written to

    A. offer a theory about why the environment is in danger.

    B. inform the public of the problems of plastic in the ocean.

    C. start a movement to halt all plastic production.

    D. inspire readers to clean up the oceans personally.

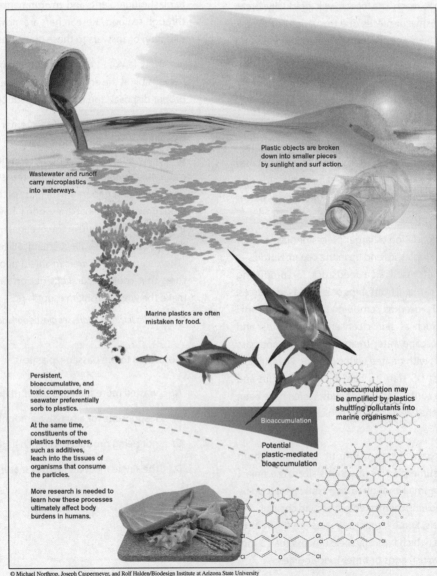

Wastewater and runoff carry microplastics into waterways.

Plastic objects are broken down into smaller pieces by sunlight and surf action.

Marine plastics are often mistaken for food.

Persistent, bioaccumulative, and toxic compounds in seawater preferentially sorb to plastics.

At the same time, constituents of the plastics themselves, such as additives, leach into the tissues of organisms that consume the particles.

More research is needed to learn how these processes ultimately affect body burdens in humans.

Bioaccumulation

Bioaccumulation may be amplified by plastics shuttling pollutants into marine organisms.

Potential plastic-mediated bioaccumulation

© Michael Northrop, Joseph Caspermeyer, and Rolf Halden/Biodesign Institute at Arizona State University

27 Which choice provides the best evidence for the answer to the previous question?

A. Lines 45–48 ("Once plastics . . . organisms.")

B. Lines 49–51 ("Research . . . biomagnify")

C. Lines 54–56 ("Yet again . . . environment.")

D. Line 57 ("Three key . . . determined.")

28 Based on the passage, which of the following statements is true?

A. The percentage of plastic being recycled has increased by over 300 percent in the past 60 years.

B. Microplastics are the most common type of plastic found in the ocean.

C. Plastic breaks down into smaller pieces in the ocean, making it less dangerous to marine organisms.

D. Harmful nurdles leak into the environment from shampoo.

29 Why did Illinois ban the sale of certain personal care products?

A. Residues from the products were ending up in the ocean.

B. The containers couldn't be recycled.

C. The products were determined to be carcinogenic.

D. The products contained microbeads that were getting into the water system.

30 Which of the following words would be most helpful in figuring out the meaning of the word "adsorbed" (line 46)?

A. Absolve

B. Adhere

C. Absorb

D. Sorbet

31 One of the questions the author raises in lines 57–65 deals with

A. how much plastic waste from the oceans people might be ingesting.

B. how sea creatures happen to ingest plastic waste in the oceans.

C. what kinds of plastic waste can be found in the oceans.

D. why people are so careless about dumping plastic waste into the oceans.

32 Which choice provides the best evidence for the answer to the previous question?

A. Lines 57–59 ("To what . . . ingestion?")

B. Lines 59–62 ("What contribution . . . food?")

C. Lines 62–64 ("And, finally . . . seafood?")

D. Line 64–65 ("Researchers . . . questions.")

CONTINUE

Angel Decora was born Hinookmahiwikilinaka on the Winnebago Reservation in Nebraska in 1871. She worked as a book illustrator, particularly on books by and about Native Americans, and lectured and wrote about Indian art. The story from which this excerpt is taken, "The Sick Child," may be autobiographical.

It was about sunset when I, a little child, was sent with a handful of powdered tobacco leaves and red feathers to make an offering to the spirit who had caused
Line the sickness of my little sister. It had been a long, hard
5 winter, and the snow lay deep on the prairie as far as the eye could reach. The medicine-woman's directions had been that the offering must be laid upon the naked earth, and that to find it I must face toward the setting sun.

10 I was taught the prayer: "Spirit grandfather, I offer this to thee. I pray thee restore my little sister to health." Full of reverence and a strong faith that I could appease the anger of the spirit, I started out to plead for the life of our little one.

15 But now where was a spot of earth to be found in all that white monotony? They had talked of death at the house. I hoped that my little sister would live, but I was afraid of nature.

I reached a little spring. I looked down to its pebbly
20 bottom, wondering whether I should leave my offering there, or keep on in search of a spot of earth. If I put my offering in the water, would it reach the bottom and touch the earth, or would it float away, as it had always done when I made my offering to the water spirit?

25 Once more I started on in my search of the bare ground.

The surface was crusted in some places, and walking was easy; in other places I would wade through a foot or more of snow. Often I paused, thinking to clear
30 the snow away in some place and there lay my offering. But no, my faith must be in nature, and I must trust to it to lay bare the earth.

It was a hard struggle for so small a child.

I went on and on; the reeds were waving their tas-
35 selled ends in the wind. I stopped and looked at them. A reed, whirling in the wind, had formed a space round its stem, making a loose socket. I stood looking into the opening. The reed must be rooted in the ground, and the hole must follow the stem to the earth. If I poured
40 my offerings into the hole, surely they must reach the

ground; so I said the prayer I had been taught, and dropped my tobacco and red feathers into the opening that nature itself had created.

No sooner was the sacrifice accomplished than a
45 feeling of doubt and fear thrilled me. What if my offering should never reach the earth? Would my little sister die?

Not till I turned homeward did I realize how cold I was. When at last I reached the house they took me in and warmed me, but did not question me, and I said
50 nothing. Everyone was sad, for the little one had grown worse.

The next day the medicine woman said my little sister was beyond hope; she could not live. Then bitter remorse was mine, for I thought I had been unfaithful,
55 and therefore my little sister was to be called to the spirit-land. I was a silent child, and did not utter my feelings; my remorse was intense.

My parents would not listen to what the medi-cine-woman had said, but clung to hope. As soon as
60 she had gone, they sent for a medicine-man who lived many miles away.

He arrived about dark. He was a large man, with a sad, gentle face. His presence had always filled me with awe, and that night it was especially so, for he
65 was coming as a holy man. He entered the room where the baby lay, and took a seat, hardly noticing any one. There was silence saving only for the tinkling of the little tin ornaments on his medicine-bag. He began to speak: "A soul has departed from this house, gone to the
70 spirit-land. As I came I saw luminous vapor above the house. It ascended, it grew less, it was gone on its way to the spirit-land. It was the spirit of the little child who is sick; she still breathes, but her spirit is beyond our reach . . .

33 The narrator wants to place her offering correctly because she

A. will have to explain her choice to everyone else.

B. wants to be trusted with similar tasks in the future.

C. thinks doing so will save her little sister's life.

D. is afraid of being punished if she does it incorrectly.

34 The medicine man describes the appearance of the spirit of the narrator's sister as

A. luminous vapor.

B. a tin ornament.

C. a baby.

D. beyond our reach.

35 Why didn't the girl's parents send for the medicine man in the first place?

A. He was busy helping another family at the time.

B. He had to come from a long distance.

C. They thought the medicine woman would be able to help their daughter.

D. They preferred a woman to cure their female child.

36 What evidence from the text shows the girl's dilemma in following the medicine woman's directions?

A. Lines 7–8 ("the offering . . . naked earth")

B. Lines 21–23 ("If I put . . . away")

C. Lines 27–29 ("The surface . . . of snow. ")

D. Lines 34–35 ("I went on . . . the wind.")

37 Which title best expresses an important theme of the passage?

A. "The Medicine-Man"

B. "Acts of Faith"

C. "Native American Culture"

D. "Walking on Snow"

38 Which choice provides the best evidence for the answer to the previous question?

A. Lines 1–4 ("It was . . . little sister.")

B. Lines 12–13 ("Full of . . . spirit")

C. Lines 44–45 ("No sooner . . . thrilled me.")

D. Lines 59–61 ("As soon . . . away.")

39 Based on the passage, which choice best describes the narrator's relationship with her parents?

A. The parents seem to treat the narrator as if she were an adult.

B. The narrator wishes her parents would give her more responsibility.

C. The parents love their youngest child, but not the narrator.

D. The narrator receives warmth and validation from her parents.

40 What is the central idea in the passage?

A. A Native American recalls her experience of trying to save and losing her baby sister.

B. A Native American child is called upon to make an offering to the spirits.

C. A Native American family struggles with illness in the depths of winter on the Plains.

D. A Native American family uses their religious beliefs to try to save their daughter.

41 When the girl says, "bitter remorse was mine" (lines 53–54), she feels

A. that she is responsible for her sister's illness.

B. badly because she didn't listen to the medicine woman.

C. angry about being given so much responsibility.

D. guilty because she feels as though she has failed her sister.

42 Which of the following best describes the meaning of "thrilled" in line 45?

A. Inspired

B. Refreshed

C. Frightened

D. Stimulated

CONTINUE

Passage 1: Fanny Wright was a reformer, author, and orator, which were unusual occupations for a woman in the early nineteenth century.

Passage 2: Young Robert Emmet was condemned to death for treason after organizing a rebellion against the English in Ireland. He, too, had achieved fame as an orator, with speeches decrying tyranny.

PASSAGE 1

Fanny Wright to a Fourth-of-July Audience at New Harmony, Indiana (1828)

In continental Europe, of late years, the words *patriotism* and *patriot* have been used in a more enlarged sense than it is usual here to attribute to them, or than
Line is attached to them in Great Britain. Since the political
5 struggles of France, Italy, Spain, and Greece, the word *patriotism* has been employed, throughout continental Europe, to express a love of the public good; a preference for the interests of the many to those of the few; a desire for the emancipation of the human race from the thrall of
10 despotism, religious and civil: in short, *patriotism* there is used rather to express the interest felt in the human race in general than that felt for any country, or inhabitants of a country, in particular. And *patriot*, in like manner, is employed to signify a lover of human liberty and human
15 improvement rather than a mere lover of the country in which he lives, or the tribe to which he belongs. Used in this sense, patriotism is a virtue, and a patriot is a virtuous man. With such an interpretation, a patriot is a useful member of society capable of enlarging all minds
20 and bettering all hearts with which he comes in contact; a useful member of the human family, capable of establishing fundamental principles and of merging his own interests, those of his associates, and those of his nation in the interests of the human race. Laurels and statues
25 are vain things, and mischievous as they are childish; but could we imagine them of use, on such a patriot alone could they be with any reason bestowed. . . .

PASSAGE 2

Robert Emmet to the Court That Condemned Him to Death (1803)

I am charged with being an emissary of France. An emissary of France! and for what end? It is alleged that
30 I wish to sell the independence of my country; and for what end? . . .

No; I am no emissary. . . . Sell my country's independence to France! and for what? Was it a change of masters? No, but for ambition. Oh, my country! Was it personal
35 ambition that could influence me? Had it been the soul of my actions, could I not, by my education and fortune, by the rank and consideration of my family, have placed myself amongst the proudest of your oppressors? My country was my idol! To it I sacrificed every selfish, every
40 endearing sentiment; and for it I now offer up myself, O God! No, my lords; I acted as an Irishman, determined on delivering my country from the yoke of a foreign and unrelenting tyranny, and the more galling yoke of a domestic faction, which is its joint partner. . . . It was
45 the wish of my heart to extricate my country from this double riveted despotism—I wished to place her independence beyond the reach of any power on earth. I wished to exalt her to that proud station in the world. Connection with France was, indeed, intended, but only
50 as far as mutual interest would sanction or require.

Were the French to assume any authority inconsistent with the purest independence, it would be the signal for their destruction . . .

I wished to prove to France and to the world that
55 Irishmen deserved to be assisted . . . I wished to procure for my country the guarantee which Washington procured for America—to procure an aid, . . . which would perceive the good, and polish the rough points of our character . . . These were my objects; not to receive new
60 taskmasters, hilt to expel old tyrants. And it was for these ends I sought aid from France . . .

Let no man dare, when I am dead, to charge me with dishonor; let no man attaint my memory by believing that I could have engaged in any cause but that of my
65 country's liberty and independence . . . The proclamation of the provisional government speaks for our views; no inference can be tortured from it to countenance barbarity or debasement at home, or subjection, humiliation, or treachery from abroad. I would not have
70 submitted to a foreign oppressor, for the same reason that I would resist the foreign and domestic oppressor. In the dignity of freedom, I would have fought upon the threshold of my country, and its enemy should enter only by passing over my lifeless corpse. And am I, who lived
75 but for my country, and who have subjected myself to the dangers of the jealous and watchful oppressor, and the bondage of the grave, only to give my countrymen their rights, and my country its independence . . . —no, God forbid!

43 Which of the following statements from Emmet's speech shows that he thinks he is a martyr?

    A. Lines 36–38 ("could I not . . . your oppressors?")

    B. Lines 46–47 ("I wished to . . . on earth.")

    C. Lines 54–55 ("I wished to . . . to be assisted")

    D. Lines 62–63 ("Let no man . . . with dishonor;")

44 Which of the following of Emmet's statements shows that he thinks he is a patriot?

    A. Line 32 ("No; . . . emissary.")

    B. Lines 34–35 ("Was it . . . influence me?")

    C. Lines 54–55 ("I wished . . . assisted")

    D. Lines 65–66 ("The proclamation . . . for our views;")

Timeline	
1707	Acts of Union between Scotland and England create the Kingdom of Great Britain
1776–1783	American colonies declare and win independence
1789	French storm the Bastille (prison), fight to end French monarchy
1798	Society of United Irishmen rebel unsuccessfully against British rule
1800	British Parliament passes The Act of Union, abolishing the Irish parliament
1801	United Kingdom of Great Britain and Ireland created
1803	United States purchases Louisiana Territory from France
	Robert Emmet leads a rebellion in Dublin against the union
1803–1815	Napoleonic Wars in Europe (France vs. European powers)
1808–1833	Spanish wars of independence
1823	France invades Spain to help restore monarchy
1828	Andrew Jackson elected president of United States

45 Based on the timeline, the historical events of which year most likely influenced the American concept of patriotism?

    A. 1707

    B. 1776

    C. 1803

    D. 1828

46 Based on information shown in the timeline, why might France have turned down Emmet's request for help?

    A. France was in the midst of trying to restore the monarchy in Spain.

    B. France was engaged in the drawn-out Napoleonic Wars.

    C. France had fought its own revolution and didn't want to get involved in that of another country.

    D. France was trying to keep the United States from taking Louisiana.

47 Emmet would not fit Wright's definition of a patriot because he

    A. saw no dishonor in his actions.

    B. wanted to free his people.

    C. idolized his own country above all others.

    D. declared the court's sentence to be unjust.

48 Which one of the following statements is true?

    A. Although years apart, both Wright and Emmet were advocating to rethink their country's ideas about patriotism.

    B. Emmet was focused on freedom and independence for his own country, while Wright was focused on freedom and independence for all humankind.

    C. Emmet loved his country more than Wright loved her country.

    D. Wright didn't understand tyranny because she lived in a democracy, while Emmet fought against tyranny.

CONTINUE

49 How does the tone of Wright's speech compare with that of Emmet's speech?

A. Both express anger, although in response to different causes.

B. Wright's expresses a calm plea while Emmet expresses desperation and anger.

C. Emmet speaks calmly, and Wright speaks passionately.

D. Both use a tone that prevents their specific positions from being convincing.

50 Which of the following statements is most analogous to Emmet's statement: "In the dignity of freedom, I would have fought upon the threshold of my country, and its enemy should enter only by passing over my lifeless corpse." (lines 72–74)

A. Never yield to force; never yield to the apparently overwhelming might of the enemy.

B. With the enemy at their back, with our bayonets at their breasts, in the day of their distress, perhaps the Americans would have submitted . . .

C. Give me liberty or give me death.

D. It is sweet and fitting to die for one's country.

51 Which of the following fits Wright's definition of a patriot?

A. A person willing to die for his country

B. A person who fights for improving the lives of others

C. A person who enlists in the armed forces of his country

D. A person who loves his country

52 When the British government claims that Emmet is an "emissary" (line 29) of France, they are accusing him of being

A. an ambassador.

B. a spy.

C. a minister.

D. a mercenary.

STOP

If you finish before time is called, you may check your work on this section only.
Do not turn to any other section.

SECTION 2: WRITING AND LANGUAGE TEST

35 MINUTES—44 QUESTIONS

TURN TO SECTION 2 OF YOUR ANSWER SHEET TO ANSWER THE QUESTIONS IN THIS SECTION.

DIRECTIONS: Each passage below is accompanied by a number of multiple-choice questions. For some questions, you will need to consider how the passage might be revised to improve the expression of ideas. Other questions will ask you to consider how the passage might be edited to correct errors in sentence structure, usage, or punctuation. A passage may be accompanied by one or more graphics—such as a chart, table, or graph—that you will need to refer to in order to best answer the question(s).

Some questions will direct you to an underlined portion of a passage—it could be one word, a portion of a sentence, or the full sentence itself. Other questions will direct you to a particular paragraph or to certain sentences within a paragraph, or you'll be asked to think about the passage as a whole. Each question number refers to the corresponding number in the passage.

After reading each passage, select the answer to each question that most effectively improves the quality of writing in the passage or that makes the passage follow the conventions of Standard Written English. Many questions include a "NO CHANGE" option. Select that option if you think the best choice is to leave that specific portion of the passage as it is.

Questions 1–11 are based on the following passage.

While most American cities must adapt to constant growth, Detroit is undergoing change as a result of depopulation.

A city of 139 square miles, with a long history of growth and middle-class success, Detroit now faces an unusual, though not entirely novel, situation for US cities: depopulation. **1** Economic transformations caused by recessions, the loss of manufacturing, and other factors have wreaked havoc on the once prosperous city, driving away its middle class and **2** it left behind vast tracts of urban blight.

1 Which choice provides the most logical introduction to the sentence?

- **A.** NO CHANGE
- **B.** Civic growth caused by the depression
- **C.** The improvement in living conditions
- **D.** The decrease in pollution

2

- **A.** NO CHANGE
- **B.** having left behind vast tracts of urban blight.
- **C.** to leave behind vast tracts of urban blight.
- **D.** leaving behind vast tracts of urban blight.

CONTINUE

The statistics (3) are staggering—since 1950, some 60 percent of the population has gone elsewhere, leaving the city with (4) 20,000 new residents. When the people left, thousands of businesses went with them.

City planners have been responding to the challenge of depopulation. Over several years, they have studied their urban spaces and used varying and innovative techniques to (5) confuse the input of some 30,000 of their residents. Planners have come up with what (6) she calls Detroit Future City, a vision that takes the long view and is projected to take some fifty years to implement. Within this plan are different strands of redevelopment, development, and—most dramatically—un-development. (7) Similarly, the strategic plan includes a concept not often seen in US city planning: downsizing, or what some prefer to call "right sizing."

3

A. NO CHANGE
B. are staggering since: 1950 some
C. are staggering since 1950 some
D. are staggering since; 1950 some

4 Which choice provides information that best supports the claim made by this sentence?

A. NO CHANGE
B. 100,000 vacant residences or lots
C. 50,000 more middle-class residents
D. 30,000 homeless people

5

A. NO CHANGE
B. belittle
C. solicit
D. return

6

A. NO CHANGE
B. they call
C. he calls
D. we call

7

A. NO CHANGE
B. In fact,
C. Nevertheless,
D. Besides,

[1] One of the boldest suggestions of the plan is a basic conversion of about one third of all Detroit's urban space. [2] Making the city more compact, the planners **8** <u>reasoned</u>, would save money on services and allow them to devote more resources to a smaller total area. [3] Walking paths, parks, ponds for rainwater collection and retention (the city's sewage system is overburdened), sports fields, meadows, forested areas, campgrounds, and other green space initiatives would then gradually transform the shutdown area.

9 [4] The plan contained some creative and bold suggestions. [5] Controversially, the plan suggests shutting down services in certain areas to drive current residents out of them and into neighborhoods being targeted for strengthening. [6] The plan also calls for remaining neighborhoods to be **10** <u>transformed but—not by the</u> traditional models of economic growth. [7] For example, the city, if organized carefully with viable public transportation options, hopes to create jobs right where people live. In part, the plan is predicated on the idea that within their own various redevelopment areas, or "natural economic zones," people can both live and work in fields that every city **11** <u>has, namely, healthcare, education, government, transportation, and local businesses</u> that meet core needs, such as grocery stores and eating places. The plan is also predicated on the idea that the well-planned urban space generates its own economic success, as well as on the idea that such areas will eventually draw some outside business and industry. Debt-ridden Detroit is definitely going to need the latter. A recent NPR report on Detroit posited that commercial real estate taxes can make up a substantial 70 percent of the revenue for a city.

8

A. NO CHANGE
B. insisted
C. noted
D. commented

9 To improve the flow of this paragraph, sentence 4 should be placed

A. where it is now.
B. before sentence 1.
C. after sentence 5.
D. after sentence 6.

10

A. NO CHANGE
B. transformed—but not by the
C. transformed but not—by the
D. transformed, but not by—the

11

A. NO CHANGE
B. has; namely, healthcare and education; government and transportation, local businesses
C. has; namely, healthcare; education; government; transportation; and local businesses
D. has; namely, healthcare, education, government, transportation; and local businesses

Questions 12–22 are based on the following passage.

In a public square on the Indonesian island of Java, dusk falls. Families gather; it is a festival day. Children dart around while, on the edges of the square, vendors **12** hawk snacks and toys. A large screen, lit from behind, stands prominently in the square. A twenty-piece percussion orchestra, or *gamelan*, prepares to play.

13 The scene is traditional Java, hundreds of years ago. The performance is *wayang kulit*, or shadow puppetry, one of the world's oldest storytelling **14** traditions its origins stretch back to the ancient spiritual practices of Indonesia's original inhabitants, who believed that the spirits of the ancestors governed the living world. Ceremonial puppet plays addressed the spirits, asking them to help the living.

Over two thousand years ago, islands such as Java, Bali, and Sumatra saw their first **15** Indian migrants, a nation to which Indonesia was linked through trade relations. In the centuries that followed, Indian culture influenced every aspect of Indonesian life.

The puppet plays reflected these cultural changes. **16** They began to depict narratives from Hindu religious texts, including the *Mahabharata*, the *Ramayana*, and the *Serat Menak*. Traditional Indonesian stories were blended into Hindu epics or lost altogether. Later, when Islam began to spread throughout Indonesia, puppet plays again transformed.

12

A. NO CHANGE
B. stock
C. advertise
D. trade

13 At this point, the author is considering deleting the underlined sentence. Should the writer do this?

A. Yes, because it inserts an irrelevant opinion.
B. Yes, because it distracts from the main ideas of the paragraph.
C. No, because it provides a transition from the previous paragraph to this one.
D. No, because it explains what *wayang kulit* is.

14

A. NO CHANGE
B. traditions and its origins stretch
C. traditions, its origins stretch
D. traditions. Its origins stretch

15

A. NO CHANGE
B. migrants from India, a nation to which Indonesia
C. Indian migrants, to which a nation Indonesia
D. Indian migrants, a nation of people to which Indonesia

16 At this point, the writer is considering adding the following sentence:

A master of shadow puppetry is called a *dalang*.

The Islamic religion **17** prohibited the display of gods in human form, so Indonesians adapted their art by making flat, leather puppets that cast shadows on a screen. The puppets **18** themselves remain unseen during the performances; only their shadows were visible. *Wayang kulit* was born.

Java is particularly well-known for its continuation of the shadow puppet tradition. **19** Performances are epic events, lasting all night long from sunset to sunrise with no break at all. They take place in public spaces and are performed on holidays and at family celebrations. At the center is a large screen, backlit by a gas or electrical light. Behind this screen sits the *dalang*, or shadow master, traditionally a man. He manipulates the puppets—sometimes more than a hundred of them in one show—with rods, voicing and singing all of the roles. **20** Simultaneously he directs the *gamelan* the large percussive orchestra which consists of percussive instruments some of which are mallets.

17

- **A.** NO CHANGE
- **B.** discouraged
- **C.** hindered
- **D.** restricted

18

- **A.** NO CHANGE
- **B.** themselves will remain unseen during the performances
- **C.** themselves remained unseen during the performances
- **D.** themselves had been remaining unseen during the performances

19

- **A.** NO CHANGE
- **B.** Performances are epic events, lasting from sunset to sunrise with no break.
- **C.** Performances are epic events, lasting all night long from sunset to sunrise without taking a break.
- **D.** Performances are epic events, lasting all night.

20

- **A.** NO CHANGE
- **B.** Simultaneously he directs, the *gamelan* the large, percussive orchestra which consists of percussive, instruments some of which are mallets.
- **C.** Simultaneously, he directs the *gamelan*—the large percussive orchestra, which consists of percussive instruments, some of which are mallets.
- **D.** Simultaneously, he directs, the *gamelan*, the large, percussive orchestra, which consists, of percussive instruments, some of which, are mallets.

CONTINUE

Each puppet is carefully crafted, a flat figure that is perforated to project a detailed shadow. Artists begin creating a puppet by tracing the outline of a paper model on leather. The leather figure is painstakingly smoothed and treated before being passed onto another craftsperson, who paints it. Then, the puppet's moving parts—the arms and hands—are added, along with the sticks used **21** to manipulate their parts. These puppets follow an established set of conventions: evil characters have grotesque faces, while noble ones have more refined features. They are highly stylized caricatures, rather **22** then realistic figures.

21
A. NO CHANGE
B. to manipulate his parts
C. to manipulate its parts
D. to manipulate her parts

22
A. NO CHANGE
B. that
C. than
D. this

Questions 23–33 are based on the following passage and supplementary material.

Water issues are hardly unknown to the American Southwest, but they have recently taken on a new urgency.

23 The arid climate and limited water resources of the American Southwest **24** has always influenced the peoples of the region. The Anasazi, ancient people of some of the most inhospitable areas of the Southwest, made a series of accommodations to **25** they're hot, arid environment by means of adaptive agricultural practices, cliff-side residences, and elaborate catchment systems.

23 Which of the following sentences would make the most effective introductory sentence to this passage?

A. Consider a vacation to the American Southwest!
B. What do you know about the majestic American Southwest?
C. The Anasazi are the original people who inhabited the American Southwest.
D. There's a serious problem occurring in the American Southwest.

24
A. NO CHANGE
B. had always influence
C. have always influenced
D. is always influenced

25
A. NO CHANGE
B. their hot, arid environment
C. there hot, arid environment
D. its hot, arid environment

Today, the American Southwest, simplistically defined in this document as encompassing all of Utah, Nevada, New Mexico, Arizona, and California, is the country's fastest-growing **26** region. It is home to more than 50 million people who are the source of ever-increasing water demands. Yet, the region is dependent for its water on just two river systems, the Colorado and the Rio Grande, of which the former is unequivocally the primary.

The Colorado supplies water to some 38 million users and irrigates some 300 million acres of farmland, much of it in **27** California! However, the mighty Colorado's flow was apportioned almost one hundred years ago to include not just the southwestern United States but also Mexico. It was also apportioned according to a volume that simply does not exist in current years; for example, in the years 2001–2006, river water that had been **28** projected to flow versus river water that did flow came up a staggering 34 percent short.

In 2014, the US Department of the Interior warned that the Colorado River basin area "is in the midst of a fourteen-year drought nearly unrivaled in 1,250 years." **29** It further noted that the river's two major reservoirs, Lake Powell and Lake Mead—the once-massive backup systems for years in which drought occurs—were, alarmingly, more than 50 percent depleted. **30** Equally dire, and possibly, more alarming, predictions came out of a recent study, cited in the Proceedings of the National Academy of Science of the United States, that suggested a 50 percent chance of Lakes Powell and Mead reaching a level so low that they become inoperable by the 2020s. **31** For all intensive purposes, the Southwest's water supply is drying up.

26 Which choice most effectively combines the sentences at the underlined portion?

- **A.** region, but it is home
- **B.** region; home
- **C.** region it is home
- **D.** region, home

27

- **A.** NO CHANGE
- **B.** California. However,
- **C.** California? However,
- **D.** California, however,

28

- **A.** NO CHANGE
- **B.** hoped
- **C.** desired
- **D.** thought

29 At this point, the writer is considering deleting this sentence. Should the writer do this?

- **A.** Yes, because it repeats information that has already been presented in the passage.
- **B.** Yes, because it blurs the paragraph's focus by introducing a new idea.
- **C.** No, because it illustrates the severity of drought conditions with a specific example.
- **D.** No, because it introduces the argument that the Southwest's water supply is drying up.

30

- **A.** NO CHANGE
- **B.** Equally dire, and possibly more alarming,
- **C.** Equally dire and possibly more alarming
- **D.** Equally dire and, possibly more alarming,

31

- **A.** NO CHANGE
- **B.** For all intentional purposes,
- **C.** For all intents and purposes,
- **D.** For all intended purposes,

CONTINUE

32 Compounding the problems of drought, increasing population, and an overly optimistic historical assessment of water resources are problems related to climate change. For example, between 2000 and 2014, the 33 highest air temperatures in much of the Southwest rose as much as 2 degrees, increasing the negative effects of evapotranspiration, the evaporation of water from the soil. Finally, climate change and drought are leading to the greater prevalence and intensity of fires, including so-called "super fires," a result, in part, of the beetle infestations and dying trees that are weakened by the lack of water.

32

A. NO CHANGE

B. Escalating

C. Inflating

D. Exaggerating

33 Which choice makes appropriate and effective use of the data in the accompanying map?

A. NO CHANGE

B. lowest air temperatures

C. hottest water temperature

D. average air temperatures

Average Temperatures in the Southwestern United States 2000–2014 Versus Long-Term Average

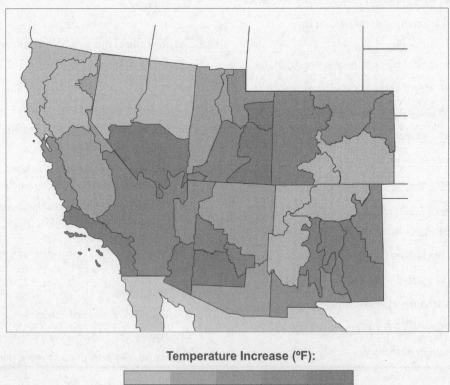

Temperature Increase (°F):

1   1.2   1.4   1.6   1.8   2

This map shows how the average air temperature from 2000 to 2014 has differed from the long-term average (1895–2014). To provide more detailed information, each state has been divided into climate divisions, which are zones that share similar climate features.

Women in Film: Troubling Inequalities

34 In a society in which television and movies have been well documented as **35** <u>roles</u> of social change, current data about women in the movies are far from reassuring.

36 <u>Women simply can't expect to play the leading roles men play or even, in general, to be on-screen for as many minutes as men are in any given film, while there seems to be no end of extraordinary acting talent among women in Hollywood.</u> As for other categories of filmmaking, at least by Oscar standards, women seem barely to exist at all.

34 Which choice most effectively establishes the main topic of the paragraph?

A. There are many actresses in Hollywood with extraordinary talent, but they cannot seem to get the same roles as men.

B. Though women land far fewer leading roles than men, in other categories of filmmaking, they do a little better.

C. Women are not adequately represented in Hollywood, either by the roles they play or by the amount of time they appear on-screen.

D. The movie industry needs to pay female actresses more than their male counterparts, in an effort to attract new and extraordinary talent.

35

A. NO CHANGE
B. agents
C. necessities
D. relationships

36

A. NO CHANGE

B. Women simply can't expect to play the leading roles men play or even, in general, while there seems to be no end of extraordinary acting talent among women in Hollywood, to be on-screen for as many minutes as men are in any given film.

C. Women simply can't expect to play the leading roles men play or to be on-screen for as many minutes as men, and there seems to be no end of extraordinary acting talent among women in Hollywood in general.

D. While there seems to be no end of extraordinary acting talent among women in Hollywood, women simply can't expect to play the leading roles men play or even, in general, to be on-screen for as many minutes as men are in any given film.

CONTINUE

Indeed, **37** women were the protagonists in only 15 percent of the top grossing films of 2013, according to a study conducted at San Diego State University. Other study findings included the fact that when women are on-screen, **38** their marriage status is more identifiable than men. Also, males over age 40 are much more commonly represented on-screen than women in the same age group.

Other inequities have been revealed by Cinemetrics, which strives to gather objective data on movies, and by other organizations. **39** For example, in 2013, lead actresses in full-length films spent 57 minutes on-screen, while lead actors spent 85 minutes on-screen. Compounding the inequity is the tendency of the camera to stay on a female actress longer in a single shot, or stare at **40** them passively, while the camera moves more actively when it shows a male character. In other aspects of films, women **41** are treated even more outrageously. Since the Oscars began in 1928, only 16 percent of all nominees have been women. In fact, there were no women nominees at all in seven categories of achievement for the 2014 Oscars. More significantly, Oscar trends do not seem to be improving over time.

37

A. NO CHANGE

B. women were the protagonist

C. a woman was the protagonists

D. the protagonists were a woman

38

A. NO CHANGE

B. their marriage status is more identifiable than of a man.

C. their marriage status is more identifiable than that of men.

D. their marriage status is more identifiable than men's marriage.

39 Which choice most effectively maintains support for claims or points in the text?

A. NO CHANGE

B. For example, women direct more documentaries than narrative films.

C. For example, the highest paid actress in 2013 made $33 million dollars.

D. For example, women buy about half of movie tickets purchased in the United States.

40

A. NO CHANGE

B. him

C. her

D. us

41

A. NO CHANGE

B. are taken advantage of.

C. are cheated.

D. fare even worse.

Some women, however, have managed to shine despite these inequities. Actress Meryl Streep has been nominated for 19 Oscars as of 2015, easily surpassing both male and female competitors for the record of most Academy Award nominations. She is **42** confused for her strong, authoritative roles; she portrayed a powerful—if terrifying—boss in *The Devil Wears Prada* (2006) and a formidable leader in *The Giver* (2014). Streep has received **43** accolades for such parts, as 15 of her 19 Academy Award nominations were in the category of Best Actress in a Leading Role. Even Streep, however, is subject to the inequities of the film industry: in *The Devil Wears Prada* her **44** characters love life was brought to the forefront and depicted as a sacrifice that she, as a woman in power, had to continually make for the good of her career.

42

A. NO CHANGE
B. famous
C. forgotten
D. lambasted

43

A. NO CHANGE
B. privileges
C. recognition
D. attention

44

A. NO CHANGE
B. character love life
C. character's love life
D. character loves life

STOP

If you finish before time is called, you may check your work on this section only.
Do not turn to any other section.

SECTION 3: MATH TEST—NO CALCULATOR 🔲

25 Minutes—20 Questions

TURN TO SECTION 3 OF YOUR ANSWER SHEET TO ANSWER THE QUESTIONS IN THIS SECTION.

DIRECTIONS: For **Questions 1–15,** solve each problem, select the best answer from the choices provided, and fill in the corresponding circle on your answer sheet. For **Questions 16–20,** solve the problem and enter your answer in the grid on the answer sheet. The directions **before Question 16** will provide information on how to enter your answers in the grid.

ADDITIONAL INFORMATION:

1. The use of a calculator in this section is **not permitted**.
2. All variables and expressions used represent real numbers unless otherwise indicated.
3. Figures provided in this test are drawn to scale unless otherwise indicated.
4. All figures lie in a plane unless otherwise indicated.
5. Unless otherwise specified, the domain of a given function f is the set of all real numbers x for which $f(x)$ is a real number.

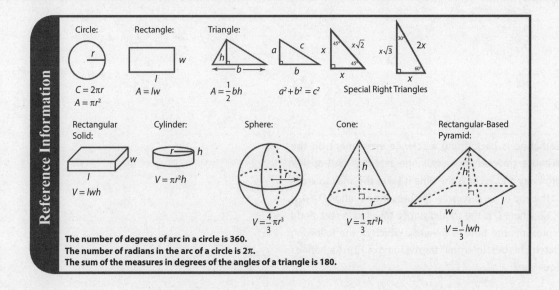

CONTINUE

1

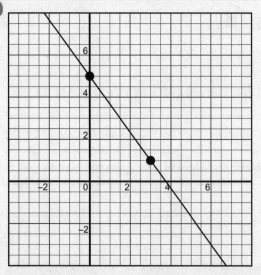

If the line drawn above is translated 3 units to the left and 6 units down, what is the slope of the new line?

A. $-\dfrac{1}{9}$

B. $-\dfrac{4}{3}$

C. $-\dfrac{7}{10}$

D. -2

2 Catherine is performing a science experiment on the distance traveled by a snail. She sets the snail on her driveway and records the time it takes the snail to crawl to the end of her driveway. She uses the equation $D = 0.4t + 12$, where D is the total distance traveled in feet, and t represents the time in minutes. Which of the following statements best interprets the meaning of 12 in Catherine's equation?

A. It would take the snail 12 minutes to reach the end of the driveway.

B. The snail began 12 feet from the beginning of the driveway.

C. The snail traveled a total distance of 12 feet.

D. The snail traveled at a rate of 12 feet per minute.

3 If $-2x + 5 = 2 - (5 - 2x)$, what is the value of x?

A. -2

B. 2

C. 3

D. 5

4 When the expression $\dfrac{10i}{1-2i}$ is simplified to the form $a + bi$, what is the coefficient b?

A. -5

B. $-\dfrac{10}{3}$

C. 2

D. 5

5 Write $5\sqrt{-16}$ as a complex number, using $i = \sqrt{-1}$.

A. $5 + 4i$

B. $-20i$

C. $20i$

D. $80i$

6 A grain silo has a maximum capacity of 45,000 cubic feet. It currently contains 32,500 cubic feet of grain. Each week, farmers add 1,000 bushels of grain. If one cubic foot is approximately 0.8 bushel, which of the following inequalities can be used to model the number of weeks, w, until the silo reaches its maximum capacity?

A. $32,500 + 1,250w \le 45,000$

B. $32,500 + 800w \le 45,000$

C. $32,500 + 1,250w \ge 45,000$

D. $32,500 + 800w \ge 45,000$

CONTINUE

7 The graph of $y = (3x - 4)(x + 3)$ is a parabola in the xy-plane.

In which of the following equivalent equations do the x- and y-coordinates of the vertex show as constants or coefficients?

SHOW YOUR WORK HERE

A. $y = 3x^2 + 5x - 12$

B. $y = 3\left(x - \dfrac{4}{3}\right)(x - (-3))$

C. $y = 3\left(x^2 + \dfrac{5}{3}x - 4\right)$

D. $y = 3\left(x - \left(-\dfrac{5}{6}\right)\right)^2 - \dfrac{169}{12}$

8 What is the difference when $-x - y$ is subtracted from $-x^2 + 2y$?

A. $-x^2 - x - 3y$

B. $x^2 + 3y$

C. $-x^2 + x + 3y$

D. $-x^2 + x - 3y$

9 A semitruck has a fuel tank that holds 125 gallons of diesel fuel. When driven at 55 miles per hour, the truck can travel 6 miles on 1 gallon of fuel. If Jorge fills the tank in his truck and drives at 55 miles per hour, which of the following functions of d shows the number of gallons of diesel fuel that remains after driving h hours?

A. $d(h) = 125 - \dfrac{6}{55h}$

B. $d(h) = 125 - \dfrac{55h}{6}$

C. $d(h) = \dfrac{125 - 6h}{55}$

D. $d(h) = \dfrac{125 - 55h}{6}$

10

$$A = \frac{M}{M-N}$$

Solve for M.

A. $M = \dfrac{AN}{A-1}$

B. $M = \dfrac{AN}{1-A}$

C. $M = \dfrac{N}{A-1}$

D. $M = \dfrac{N}{1-A}$

11 Donna bought a sofa with 0% interest for the first 36 months. She makes a small down payment, and then she makes equal monthly payments until she pays off the sofa. The equation $y = 90x + 75$ models the number of payments, x, that she makes to pay for a sofa that costs y dollars. What does the 90 represent in this equation?

A. The total paid after x months.

B. The pay-off amounts for the loan.

C. Donna's monthly payment.

D. Donna's down payment.

12 What is the sum of all values of n that satisfy $2n^2 - 11n + 15 = 0$?

A. −11

B. −5.5

C. 5.5

D. 15

CONTINUE

13 The Matthews family is driving to the beach, which is 480 miles away. The function that represents the distance (in miles) it takes them to get to the beach is $f(t) = 480 - 60t$, where t represents time (in hours). In this equation, t is the independent variable, and $f(t)$ is the dependent variable. At which point does the graph of the function $f(t) = 480 - 60t$ cross the x-axis?

A. (0, 480)

B. (6, 0)

C. (0, 8)

D. (8, 0)

14 The population of a small town is growing. The town currently has 500 people. Based on the growth of the population in past years, it is estimated that the population will be 650 after 1 year. Similarly, it is estimated that after 2 years, the population will be 845, and after 3 years, the population will be 1,099. Which of the following is an expression which represents the town's population growth?

A. 500×1.3^x

B. $150x + 500$

C. $500 \times (1.3)^{x-1}$

D. $650 \times (1.3)^{x-1t}$

15 The expression $\dfrac{4x+1}{x+2}$ is equivalent to which of the following?

A. $\dfrac{4+1}{2}$

B. $4 + \dfrac{1}{2}$

C. $4 + \dfrac{1}{x+2}$

D. $4 - \dfrac{7}{x+2}$

SHOW YOUR WORK HERE

DIRECTIONS: For **Questions 16–20,** solve the problem and enter your answer in the grid, as described below, on the answer sheet.

1. Although not required, it is suggested that you write your answer in the boxes at the top of the columns to help you fill in the circles accurately. You will receive credit only if the circles are filled in correctly.

2. Mark no more than one circle in any column.

3. No question has a negative answer.

4. Some problems may have more than one correct answer. In such cases, enter only one answer.

5. **Mixed numbers** such as $3\frac{1}{2}$ must be entered as 3.5 or $\frac{7}{2}$.

    If $3\frac{1}{2}$ is entered into the grid as $\begin{array}{|c|c|c|c|}\hline 3 & 1 & / & 2 \\\hline\end{array}$, it will be interpreted as $\frac{31}{2}$, not $3\frac{1}{2}$.

6. **Decimal answers:** If you obtain a decimal answer with more digits than the grid can accommodate, it may be either rounded or truncated, but it must fill the entire grid.

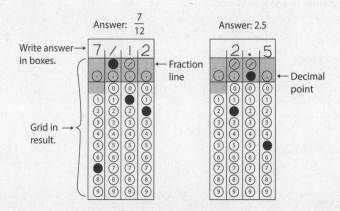

Answer: $\frac{7}{12}$ Answer: 2.5

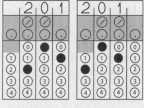

Answer: 201
Either position is correct.

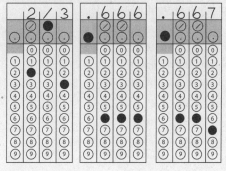

Acceptable ways to grid $\frac{2}{3}$ are:

CONTINUE

16

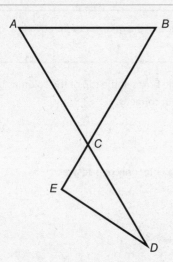

In the figure above, $AC = BC$. If $m\angle B = 50°$, what is the measure of $\angle ECD$? (Do not enter the degree symbol.)

17

$$5x - 4y = 13$$
$$x + 2y = 4$$

If (x, y) is a solution of the system of equations above, what is the value of the ratio $\dfrac{x}{y}$?

18

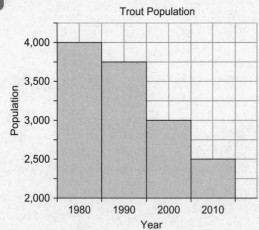

The bar graph above shows the population of trout in a lake, from 1980 to 2010.

By what percentage did the population decline from 1980 to 2000? Round to the nearest percentage point if necessary, and enter your answer as a two-digit number. (Do not grid the percent sign.)

19 If $f(x) = 5x + 12$, what is the value of $f(p + 3) - f(p)$?

SHOW YOUR WORK HERE

20 What is the sum of the solutions of the equation

$$\frac{9}{x-2} + \frac{16}{x+3} = 5\,?$$

STOP

If you finish before time is called, you may check your work on this section only.

Do not turn to any other section.

SECTION 4: MATH TEST—CALCULATOR ▣

55 Minutes—38 Questions

TURN TO SECTION 4 OF YOUR ANSWER SHEET TO ANSWER THE QUESTIONS IN THIS SECTION.

DIRECTIONS: For **Questions 1–30,** solve each problem, select the best answer from the choices provided, and fill in the corresponding circle on your answer sheet. For **Questions 31–38**, solve the problem and enter your answer in the grid on the answer sheet. The directions **before Question 31** will provide information on how to enter your answers in the grid.

ADDITIONAL INFORMATION:

1. The use of a calculator in this section **is permitted**.
2. All variables and expressions used represent real numbers unless otherwise indicated.
3. Figures provided in this test are drawn to scale unless otherwise indicated.
4. All figures lie in a plane unless otherwise indicated.
5. Unless otherwise specified, the domain of a given function *f* is the set of all real numbers *x* for which *f(x)* is a real number.

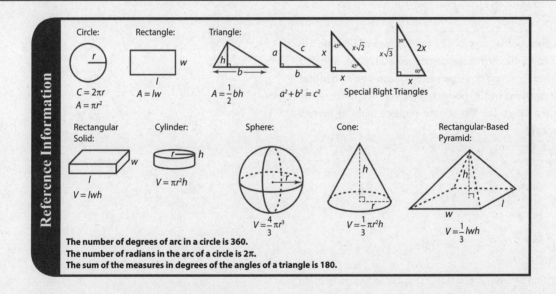

The number of degrees of arc in a circle is 360.
The number of radians in the arc of a circle is 2π.
The sum of the measures in degrees of the angles of a triangle is 180.

CONTINUE

SHOW YOUR WORK HERE

1 The usual price for 10 audio singles sold by an online vendor is $12.50. During a sale, this price is reduced by 15%. What is the savings if one were to purchase 40 audio singles during such a sale?

    A. $1.88

    B. $2.50

    C. $7.50

    D. $10.00

2 If it costs $1.30 a square foot to lay linoleum, what will be the cost of laying 20 square yards of linoleum? (3 ft. = 1 yd.)

    A. $26

    B. $78

    C. $156

    D. $234

3 Bill averaged a score of 182 for 6 games of bowling. His scores for the first three games were 212, 181, and 160. Of the remaining three games, two scores were identical, and the third was 20 points higher than one of these two games. What was the second highest score of these 6 games?

    A. 173

    B. 181

    C. 183

    D. 193

4 A gallon of water is equal to 231 cubic inches. How many gallons of water are needed to fill a fish tank that measures 11" high, 14" long, and 9" wide?

    A. 6

    B. 9

    C. 12

    D. 14

5 The recommended daily protein intake for an adult weighing 50 kg (approximately 110 pounds) is 40 grams. One cup of milk contains 8 grams of protein, and one egg contains 6 grams of protein. Which of the following inequalities represents the possible number of cups of milk, *m*, and eggs, *n*, an adult weighing 50 kg could consume in a day to meet or exceed the recommended daily protein intake from these alone?

A. $8m + 6n \geq 40$

B. $8m + 6n > 40$

C. $\dfrac{8}{m} + \dfrac{6}{n} \geq 40$

D. $\dfrac{8}{m} + \dfrac{6}{n} > 40$

6 Amy is renting a moving van for $19.99 per day, plus an additional $0.15 per mile. A tax of 7.5% is applied to both the daily rate and the mileage rate. Which of the following represents the total charge, *y*, that Amy will pay to rent the van for one day and drive it *x* miles?

A. $y = 19.99 + 0.075x + 0.15$

B. $y = 1.075(19.99) + 0.15x$

C. $y = 1.075(19.99 + 0.15x)$

D. $y = 1.075(19.99 + 0.15)x$

7 If nails are bought at 35 cents per dozen and sold at 3 for 10 cents, the total profit on $5\dfrac{1}{2}$ dozen is

A. 25 cents.

B. $27\dfrac{1}{2}$ cents.

C. $31\dfrac{1}{2}$ cents.

D. 35 cents.

8 A cubic foot of concrete weighs approximately 150 pounds. How many pounds will a similar block of concrete weigh if the edges are twice as long?

A. 300 pounds

B. 450 pounds

C. 800 pounds

D. 1,200 pounds

SHOW YOUR WORK HERE

CONTINUE

9. Which of the following expressions is equivalent to $-2(1-x)^2 + 2(1-x^2)$?

A. $-2x$

B. $-4x^2 + 4x$

C. $-4x^2 - 4x - 4$

D. 0

10. An organization is giving away T-shirts for its 5-kilometer road race. The cost to produce the T-shirts is defined by the equation $C(x) = 7x + 60$, where x is the number of T-shirts produced. The organization gives away the T-shirts for free to people who sign up for the race more than one month in advance and pay the $20 sign-up fee. What is the fewest number of people who must sign up in order for the organization to profit if the only cost is manufacturing the T-shirts and the only income is the sign-up fee?

A. 3

B. 5

C. 13

D. 20

11. A small college, which has a population of 2,180 students, recently held a fundraiser in which each male student raised $20, and each female student raised $25. Together, they raised a total of $50,000. If x represents the number of male students in the college and y represents the number of female students in the college, which system of equations can be used to represent the scenario?

A. $x + y = 50,000$
$20x + 25y = 2,180$

B. $x + y = 2,180$
$20x + 25y = 50,000$

C. $x + y = 2,180$
$25x + 20y = 50,000$

D. $x + y = 50,000$
$25x + 20y = 50,000$

12 Which of the following is an expression equivalent to $\sqrt[3]{9x^3y^5z^6}$?

A. $3y^2z^3$

B. $3xy^2z^3$

C. $9^{\frac{1}{3}}xy^2z^3$

D. $9^{\frac{1}{3}}xy^{\frac{5}{3}}z^2$

13

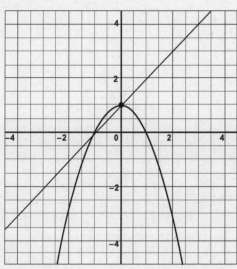

$y = x + 1$

$y = -x^2 + 1$

A system of equations and their graphs are shown above. Which of the following are solutions to the system?

   I.   (0, 1)

   II. (1, 0)

   III. (−1, 0)

   IV. (0, −1)

A. I only

B. II only

C. I and III only

D. II and IV only

14 If $\dfrac{x}{3} - \dfrac{y}{4} = 5$, what is the value of $8x - 6y$?

A. −120

B. −60

C. 60

D. 120

CONTINUE

15 At a restaurant, the rates for meals are $7.50 for a lunch and $12 for a dinner. One weekend, the restaurant sold a total of 241 meals for $2,523. Which of the following systems of equations can be used to determine the number of lunches, x, and the number of dinners, y, that the restaurant sold?

SHOW YOUR WORK HERE

A. $7.5x + 12y = 241$
$\quad\quad x + y = 2,523$

B. $12x + 7.5y = 241$
$\quad\quad x + y = 2,523$

C. $7.5x + 12y = 2,523$
$\quad\quad x + y = 241$

D. $12x + 7.5y = 2,523$
$\quad\quad x + y = 241$

16

United States Population

The graph shows the relationship between the population of the United States (in millions) and the year the population was recorded. Which of the following statements is true about the data shown on the graph?

A. There is a weak correlation between the variables.

B. There is a strong correlation between the variables.

C. There is no clear correlation between the variables.

D. There is an exponential correlation between the variables.

17

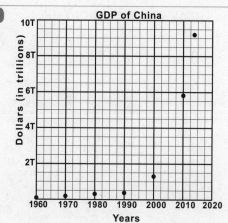

The graph shows data representing the gross domestic product (GDP), in trillions of dollars, of China from 1970 through 2013. Which of the following function types would best represent the data?

A. Linear

B. Logarithmic

C. Cubic

D. Exponential

18 A college graduate goes to work for x dollars per week. After several months, the company gives all the employees a 10% pay cut. A few months later, the company gives all the employees a 10% raise. Which expression is equal to the college graduate's weekly salary resulting from these changes?

A. $0.90x$

B. $0.99x$

C. x

D. $1.01x$

19 Which of the following systems of inequalities has a solution set that intersects the first quadrant of the xy-plane?

A. $\begin{cases} y \le -2x+4 \\ y > -2x+2 \end{cases}$

B. $\begin{cases} x \le -2 \\ y \ge 5 \end{cases}$

C. $\begin{cases} y \ge x \\ y < -3-x \end{cases}$

D. $\begin{cases} y > 5+3x \\ y \le -3+3x \end{cases}$

CONTINUE

20 If $\dfrac{(1-2i)^2}{2}$ is rewritten as $a + bi$, then what is the value of b? (Note: $i = \sqrt{-1}$)

A. -2

B. $\dfrac{-3}{2}$

C. $\dfrac{1}{2}$

D. 2

21 What is the original price of an item if it costs $12.60 after a 10% discount is applied to the selling price?

A. $11.34

B. $12.48

C. $13.86

D. $14

22 A recipe for a homemade weed killer calls for $1\dfrac{1}{3}$ gallons of white vinegar and 2 cups of table salt. Miguel made a large batch of the weed killer and used 7 cups of table salt. If he followed the recipe correctly, how many gallons of white vinegar did he use?

A. 4

B. $4\dfrac{2}{3}$

C. $5\dfrac{1}{3}$

D. 6

23 Given $(1.26 + 4.52i) + (-0.89 + xi) = 0.37 + 7.4i$, what is the value of x? (Note: $i = \sqrt{-1}$)

A. -1.64

B. 1.64

C. 2.88

D. 11.92

24 If $(x-4)$ and $(x+2)$ are factors of $f(x)$, which of the following graphs could represent the function $f(x)$?

SHOW YOUR WORK HERE

A.

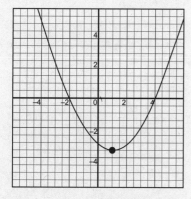

B.

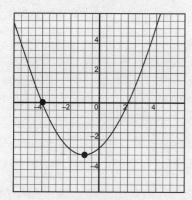

C.

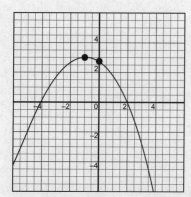

D.

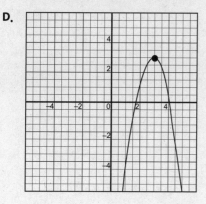

25

	None	1 to 3	4 or more
Group A	8	23	19
Group B	14	21	5
Total	22	44	24

The table above shows data from demographic researchers studying the number of living siblings people have. If a person is chosen at random from Group A, what is the probability that the person has no living siblings?

A. $\dfrac{4}{25}$

B. $\dfrac{4}{11}$

C. $\dfrac{7}{11}$

D. $\dfrac{22}{25}$

26 During the *Apollo* 14 mission, astronaut Alan Shepard hit a golf ball on the moon. The height of the ball in meters is modeled by the function $f(t) = -0.81t^2 + 55t + 0.02$, where t is the time in seconds after the ball was hit. What does 0.02 stand for in this equation?

A. Acceleration of the ball due to gravity

B. Vertical velocity of the ball

C. Horizontal velocity of the ball

D. Height of the ball before it is hit

SHOW YOUR WORK HERE

27 If k is a positive constant other than 1, which of the following could be the graph of $kx + y = c$?

A.

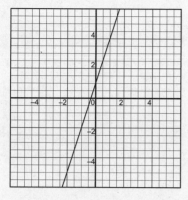

B.

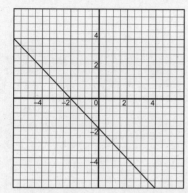

C.

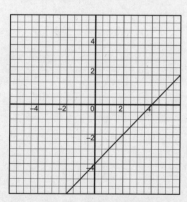

D.

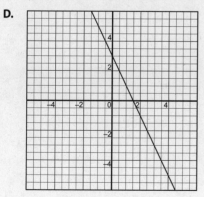

28 The Cyber Corporation buys a new machine for $80,000. If the machine loses 15% of its value each year, what is its value after 4 years?

A. $41,760.50

B. $42,750.50

C. $48,000.00

D. $49,130.00

29 The table below shows the total number of medals won by the United States in the Winter Olympics for the years 1994 to 2014.

Number of Medals	Year
12	1994
13	1998
31	2002
25	2006
37	2010
28	2014

How many medals would the United States have had to win in the 2018 Olympics in order for the average number of medals for the years 1994 to 2018 to be one more than the average number of medals won during the years 1994 to 2014?

A. 29

B. 31

C. 32

D. 36

30 If the expression $\dfrac{6x}{2x+4}$ is written in the form $3+\dfrac{A}{x+2}$, what is the value of A?

A. −12

B. −6

C. 6

D. 12

DIRECTIONS: For **Questions 31–38,** solve the problem and enter your answer in the grid, as described below, on the answer sheet.

1. Although not required, it is suggested that you write your answer in the boxes at the top of the columns to help you fill in the circles accurately. You will receive credit only if the circles are filled in correctly.

2. Mark no more than one circle in any column.

3. No question has a negative answer.

4. Some problems may have more than one correct answer. In such cases, enter only one answer.

5. **Mixed numbers** such as $3\frac{1}{2}$ must be entered as 3.5 or $\frac{7}{2}$.

   If $3\frac{1}{2}$ is entered into the grid as $\overline{3\ |\ 1\ /\ 2}$, it will be interpreted as $\frac{31}{2}$, not $3\frac{1}{2}$.

6. **Decimal answers:** If you obtain a decimal answer with more digits than the grid can accommodate, it may be either rounded or truncated, but it must fill the entire grid.

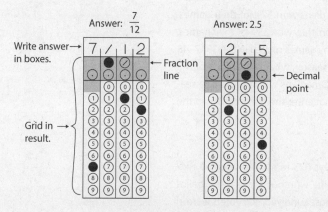

Answer: $\frac{7}{12}$

Answer: 2.5

Write answer in boxes.

Fraction line

Decimal point

Grid in result.

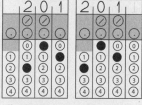

Answer: 201
Either position is correct.

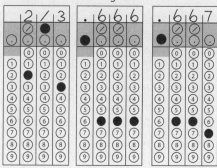

Acceptable ways to grid $\frac{2}{3}$ are:

31 If $(ax - 1)(2x + b) = 4x^2 + 4x - 3$, what is the value of $a + b$?

32 Derek has $50 to spend on organic produce at the local farmer's market. A pint of berries costs $4, a 1-pound bag of peaches costs $3.75, and a head of lettuce costs $1.50. If he buys at least two of each item, what is the maximum number of pints of berries he could purchase?

33 In a 3-hour examination of 350 questions, there are 50 mathematical problems. If twice as much time should be allowed for each mathematical problem as for each of the other questions, how many minutes should be spent on the mathematical problems?

34 In the 1924–25 season of the National Hockey League (NHL), the Montreal Canadiens won 57% of their games. During the 1947–48 season, they won 33% of their games. If there were twice as many games played in the 1947–48 season as in the1924–25 season, what percentage of the games did the Montreal Canadiens win in these two seasons of the league? (Do not enter the percent sign in the grid.)

35 A polling company surveys 625 randomly selected registered voters to determine whether a proposed ballot measure might pass. Of those surveyed, 400 voters were in favor of the ballot measure. The polling company reports that the poll results have a conservative margin of error of 4%. If 9,000 people actually vote, what is the minimum number of people likely to vote for the ballot measure?

36 The average weight of a medium-sized bottlenose dolphin is 400 pounds. If a particular medium-sized bottlenose dolphin weighs 110% of the average, how many pounds does the dolphin weigh?

37

$$3x + y = -4$$
$$x + y = 13$$

If (x, y) is a solution for the system of equations above, what is the value of y?

38

$$-3x + 2y = -1$$
$$6x - by = 8$$

What is the value for b that will make the system above have no solution?

STOP

If you finish before time is called, you may check your work on this section only.
Do not turn to any other section.

SECTION 5: ESSAY

50 Minutes—1 Essay

Directions: The essay gives you an opportunity to show how effectively you can read and comprehend a passage and write an essay analyzing the passage. In your essay, you should demonstrate that you have read the passage carefully, present a clear and logical analysis, and use language precisely.

Your essay will need to be written on the lines provided in your answer booklet. You will have enough space if you write on every line and keep your handwriting to an average size. Try to print or write clearly so that your writing will be legible to the readers scoring your essay.

As you read the passage below, consider how Peter Krapp uses the following:

- Evidence, such as facts, statistics, or examples, to support claims
- Reasoning to develop ideas and to connect claims and evidence
- Stylistic or persuasive elements, such as word choice or appeals to emotion, to add power to the ideas expressed

Adapted from "Penn State Hack Exposes Theft Risk of Student Personal Data" by Peter Krapp, originally published in The Conversation *on May 20, 2015. Peter Krapp is a professor of film & media studies at University of California, Irvine. (This passage was edited for length.)*

1   Pennsylvania State University's College of Engineering took its computer network offline on May 15 after disclosing two cyberattacks. The perpetrators were able to access information on 18,000 students, who are being contacted this week with the news that their personal identifying information is in hackers' hands.

2   Three days later, the computer network is back online, with new protections for its users. One of the two attacks is ascribed by a forensic cybersecurity corporation retained by Penn State to computers apparently based in China.

3   As a researcher who has published on hacking and hacktivism and serves on the board of the UC Irvine data science initiative, I believe two aspects of this news story deserve particular attention.

Compromising student data

4   Penn State announced last week that the FBI alerted it on November 21, 2014, about an attack with custom malware that started as early as September 2012.

5   Why did it take so long for Penn State to disclose the breach, despite the fact that the experience of large-scale hacks in 2013 and 2014 (against Target, Home Depot, and others) clearly demonstrated an urgent need for quick and full disclosure—both to help the victims and to preserve a modicum of trust?

6   Penn State stated only that any disclosure would have tipped off the perpetrators before their access to the College of Engineering computers could be cut off. Meanwhile, student data may have been compromised for at least six months, maybe longer.

7   Another conspicuous problem with public discussion of events like this is, in fact, the lack of distinction often made in the media between actual appropriation of data (as at Penn State) and mere temporary disabling or defacement of websites (as happened to Rutgers University last month). That is like being unable to make a difference between a grand theft auto and keying a car.

8   The question is, what can universities do to limit the risk to their students?

CONTINUE

9   The exposure of student data in higher education is not limited to Social Security numbers or email passwords. Information collected and retained by educational institutions includes full name, address, phone number, credit and debit card information, workplace information, date of birth, personal interests and of course academic performance and grade information.

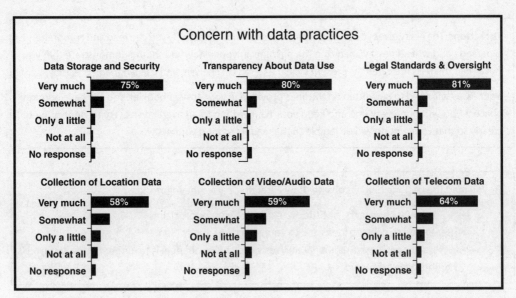

A survey conducted by the Obama administration collected responses from 24,092 individuals on how much they trusted various institutions to keep their data safe. There was a high level of concern around transparency and legal standards.

. . .

10 President Obama only recently called for laws covering data hacking and student privacy. "We're saying that data collected on students in the classroom should only be used for educational purposes," he stated in his speech to the Federal Trade Commission (FTC) earlier this year.

Data privacy concerns

11 If students' right to privacy needs to be protected from the specter of foreign intelligence agencies poking around the Penn State Engineering School, then by the same logic it should be protected also against data-mining by for-profit actors right here in the US.

12 Until May 2014, Google, for instance, routinely mined its apps for education services for advertising and monetizing purposes. When *Education Week* reported that Google was mining student emails, it quickly led not only to lawsuits but also to landmark legislation. The California Senate Bill 1177 was enacted to prevent educational services from selling student information or mining it for advertising purposes.

13 Yet, almost a year later, students in California remain just as concerned about their data privacy as before—since the new state law was watered down to apply only to K–12 and not to higher education. And when it was disclosed earlier this spring that education publisher Pearson secretly monitored social media to discern references to their content, the legislative response was one that, according to the Electronic Privacy Information Center (EPIC) in Washington, DC, "fails to uphold President Obama's promise that the data collected in an educational context can be used only for educational purposes."

14 Students in higher education nationwide are still in a position where they cannot opt out of the computer services of their learning institutions, and so they have no expectation of privacy.

15 Despite President Obama's promises for safeguarding the privacy of consumers and families, and despite the fact that a number of technology companies concerned with growing consumer distrust recently signed a pledge to safeguard student privacy, neither Google nor Apple signed on.

16   The President's Council of Advisors on Science and Technology (PCAST) was tasked to examine current and likely future capabilities of key technologies, both those associated with the collection, analysis, and use of big data and those that can help to preserve privacy, resulting in a direct recommendation to strengthen US research in privacy-related technologies.

17   And overwhelmingly, respondents to a White House survey recently expressed severe reservations about the collection, storage, and security and use of private information.

18   Maybe it is time for higher education to heed those signals.

> Write an essay in which you explain how Peter Krapp builds an argument to persuade his audience that the use of college students' personal information for anything other than educational purposes is a serious violation of privacy and a major breach of computer security. In your essay, analyze how Peter Krapp uses one or more of the features listed above (or features of your own choice) to strengthen the logic and persuasiveness of his argument. Be sure that your analysis focuses on the most relevant features of the passage. Your essay should not explain whether you agree with the writer's claims, but rather explain how he builds an argument to persuade his audience.

STOP

If you finish before time is called, you may check your work on this section only.
Do not turn to any other section.

1. C	12. A	23. B	33. C	43. D
2. A	13. A	24. A	34. A	44. D
3. C	14. D	25. B	35. C	45. B
4. C	15. A	26. B	36. B	46. B
5. D	16. D	27. B	37. B	47. C
6. B	17. A	28. B	38. B	48. B
7. D	18. D	29. D	39. A	49. B
8. B	19. C	30. B	40. A	50. C
9. D	20. C	31. A	41. D	51. B
10. B	21. A	32. C	42. C	52. B
11. A	22. B			

READING TEST RAW SCORE ☐
(Number of correct answers)

1. **The correct answer is C.** *Address* appears in the author's description of the black bear, including qualities that the bear possesses. So the context here tells us that *address* is not being used to mean direction (choice D), because one can possess a great *sense of direction* but not direction. *Habitat* (choice A) can also be eliminated because the correct answer choice should refer to a trait of the black bear, and one's habitat is not a personal trait. Anxiety is a personal trait, but it contradicts the author's description of the black bear as possessing great courage, so choice B can be eliminated. Therefore, the correct answer is choice C, since *skill* is a positive personality trait that would be listed among traits such as strength and courage.

2. **The correct answer is A.** Choice A is correct because Audubon clearly wanted to inform readers about black bears even though he was mainly known as a studier of birds. Had this not been his goal, he would not have written this particular passage, nor would he address the reader directly with phrases such as, "You are probably not aware . . . " Choice B can be eliminated because its conclusion is too general; Audubon seems as though he was likely fascinated by the black bear, but there is no strong evidence that this man, who mostly studied birds, was fascinated by *all* mammals. Choice C

is incorrect because it assumes the reader is more interested in what Audubon knows than the topic he is actually discussing, shifting the focus from bears and placing it onto the author himself. Choice D is incorrect because Audubon never compared the black bear to any species of bird in the passage.

3. **The correct answer is C.** In lines 36–38, Audubon addresses the reader in a direct way in order to engage the reader's interest in bears. In lines 29–32, he also addresses the reader directly, but doesn't attempt to provide "more information." Instead, he reinforces information assumed to be already known by the reader, making choice B incorrect. Although he mentions other mammals in the passage, such as in lines 5–8 (choice A), there is not enough evidence to conclude that he was fascinated by mammals in general. Although it's interesting that Audubon inserts his own opinion so directly in lines 55–59 (choice D), these lines do not provide any evidence for the answer to the previous question.

4. **The correct answer is C.** The author explicitly states that "many of our woodsmen and hunters who have seen the Bear performing the singular

operation just described, imagine that it does so for the purpose of leaving behind an indication of its size and power," which supports choice C. Choice A represents Audubon's claim, which begins with the phrase "It seems to me," not that of the huntsmen and woodsmen. There's no indication that the tree will be used for hibernation (choice B), nor that such behavior is a way of obtaining food (choice D).

5. **The correct answer is D.** The author explains how bears forage for food by using descriptive phrases that create a placid, or peaceful, image. The author mentions that bears may eat livestock, but that is not the main focus, so choices A and B are incorrect. While the lines in choice C do show that the bear eats a wide range of foods, the author's use of descriptive phrases is evidence that he is creating an image as opposed to making a scientific list of what the bear eats.

6. **The correct answer is B.** The previous question indicated that the author was trying to create a placid, or peaceful, effect with his description of how bears behave in swamps in lines 17–18, and the words "passes much of its time" and "wallowing" help achieve that effect. The wording in lines 16–17 creates a sense of discomfort by using phrases such as "During the summer heat" and "gloomy," so choice A is not the best answer. Focusing on the bear's hunger, as choice C does, or how it seizes prey, as choice D does, does not contribute to the placid atmosphere the author is trying to achieve.

7. **The correct answer is D.** Audubon explains that the bear sharpens its claws and the wild boar sharpens its tusks for the same purpose: to prepare themselves for competition during the mating season, choice D—not for defense from human predators (choice C), which are only mentioned very briefly in the passage. A predator would not be very effective if it went out of its way to warn potential prey that it was a predator, so choice A does not make much sense. The author only mentions that the black bear forages for crayfish and roots and does not indicate what the wild boar eats, so choice B is incorrect.

8. **The correct answer is B.** The fact that Audubon calls man the bear's "most dangerous" enemy shows that he has some sympathy for hunted bears, making choice B the correct answer. Nothing indicates that Audubon hunts, so choice A is incorrect. He never denies that bears are dangerous nor does he state that bears are more dangerous than people, so choices C and D are also incorrect.

9. **The correct answer is D.** By referring to man as "the most dangerous of its enemies," Audubon creates an image of man as almost villainous in his treatment of hunted bears, which indicates that he has sympathy for the creatures. Choice A refers to the bear's migratory habits in a neutral way, indicating nothing about the author's feelings for the bear. Neither does choice B, which merely refers to a basic instinct of the bear. Choice C only indicates how the bear protects itself from its most dangerous enemies; it does not comment on those enemies in a way that expresses the author's sympathy for bears.

10. **The correct answer is B.** The author addresses the reader directly with such phrases as "as you well know" and "you also know that" when stating information about bears. This shows that he believes the reader already has some knowledge about bears and contradicts the assumption in choice A. While it is entirely possible that some readers may have a fear of bears, there is no evidence that the author believes this in the passage, so choice C is not the best answer. Although the author assumes that the reader knows that bears are "good climbers," he never compares their climbing abilities to that of apes, so choice D is incorrect.

11. **The correct answer is A.** The first paragraph of the letter indicates that Wythe and Jefferson have an established relationship and Jefferson believes Wythe had a positive influence on Jefferson's education, thus we can infer that Wythe was a teacher. The letter does not imply any familial relationship or that Wythe and Jefferson are friends (choices B and C); rather, it shows a more formal connection. There is no indication of how Wythe is employed (choice D). While he could be a public servant of some kind, that conclusion could not be drawn from the information provided.

12. **The correct answer is A.** Jefferson's overall concern is that his nephew should receive a solid education, choice A. This letter has a greater purpose than merely staying in touch (choice D). His advice about studying languages (choice C) is part of the overall advice about education, and morality is also a part of his course of study (choice B).

13. **The correct answer is A.** Jefferson indicates that learning Italian might actually make it harder to learn Spanish, which he views as the more useful language. This contradicts the conclusion in choice C. Jefferson only briefly mentions French to indicate that it is a similar language to Italian and Spanish and never indicates he believes that it is more important to learn French than Spanish or Italian, so choice B is incorrect.

Although he mentions that Spanish and Italian are similar, Jefferson never suggests that they are so similar that it makes sense to speak Italian to Spanish people, which eliminates choice D.

14. **The correct answer is D.** The word *prosecute* in this context is used to mean "pursue," so in lines 23–25, Jefferson is suggesting that Peter lay Italian aside to learn Spanish instead. Choices A and B introduce the problem of learning Italian and Spanish at the same time, but neither choice suggests how Peter should deal with this problem. Choice C is incorrect because it merely indicates Jefferson's own observations about people who speak Italian, French, and Spanish.

15. **The correct answer is A.** Jefferson compares conscience to a physical limb of the body to show that it is natural and present in all human beings (choice A). Choices B, C, and D may be true, but Jefferson only covers the first point: that morality is as natural as an arm or leg and is given to all "in a stronger or weaker degree" (lines 43–44).

16. **The correct answer is D.** In advising Peter about language studies, Jefferson tells him to learn Spanish (lines 26–29). He predicts that it will be valuable in the future because of "connections with Spain and Spanish America." He dismisses Italian (choice C) as unworthy of Peter's attention and doesn't discuss America's future with France (choice B) or England (choice A).

17. **The correct answer is A.** By "lost time," Jefferson means "wasted time." In his third point, Jefferson tells Peter that he shouldn't bother to study moral philosophy because it is something everyone knows intuitively, stating that morality "is as much a part of his nature as the sense of hearing, seeing, feeling." "Lost time" could refer to the past (choice B) or mean "missing time" (choice C), but Jefferson is not discussing the past or a gap in time in this context. He says nothing about youth either, so choice D does not make much sense.

18. **The correct answer is D.** Jefferson claims that he has never seen anyone who spoke French, Spanish, and Italian who didn't get them confused. All three languages are derived from Latin (choice A), as Jefferson notes ("all of them degenerated dialects of the Latin"), but that is not the reason he gives to avoid the study of Italian. Jefferson does think it is necessary to learn a language other than French (choice B) because he recommends learning Spanish. Jefferson states that it is useful to be multilingual, as he advocates the study of Spanish; he only suggests that one should be careful when choosing which languages to study, so choice C is incorrect.

19. **The correct answer is C.** Jefferson says morality is innate, therefore it doesn't need to be taught. In fact, he argues, teaching it can have the negative effect of leading "astray" (lines 47–48).

20. **The correct answer is C.** The family tree shows that Peter's father died when Peter was only 3 years old, and that his mother had 5 other children to care for, so choice C is the best conclusion to reach. The fact that Peter's father was already dead when Thomas wrote this letter eliminates choice A, since a comparison cannot be fairly made between someone currently living and someone who is dead. Choice B is too speculative and is not as logical a conclusion as choice C. Choice D assumes that Peter was responsible for caring for his 5 siblings, and there is no evidence of this in the family tree or the passage.

21. **The correct answer is A.** The letter shows Jefferson to be very involved in ensuring that his nephew gets the best education since it refers to a number of important study topics and how Peter should approach them. Expressing that he felt "very happy" to receive letters from Peter also helps create a warm tone. Although Jefferson clearly cares for his nephew, he does not seem particularly worried about the boy since there is no anxious language in this letter, so choice B can be eliminated. The letter's warmth also eliminates choices C and D since an "objective and matter-of-fact" tone would be contrary to warmth, as would a "distant and preoccupied" tone.

22. **The correct answer is B.** In the first paragraph, the author provides a number of statistics that support choice B. However, the author never compares plastic waste to the impact of other forms of waste, so choice A cannot be concluded based on information in this particular passage. The author writes that "World plastics production has experienced almost constant growth for more than half a century," which contradicts choice C. While the entire passage discusses the impact of plastic waste on the planet, the author never compares that to the impact of other forms of waste, so choice D is not the best answer.

23. **The correct answer is B.** Lines 4–6 provide specific statistics about how plastic accounts for 10 percent of the 1.4 billion tons of trash the world generates each year. By any standards, that is a massive amount of waste. Choice A indicates that plastic production continues to grow, but without specific numbers, there

is no way to use this information to conclude that plastic is responsible for a massive amount of waste. That the International Maritime Organization has had to ban dumping of plastic waste indicates it is a big enough problem to warrant such action, but choice C is simply not as specific as choice B is, so it is not the best answer choice. Choice D also refers to a problem but fails to supply specific numbers.

24. **The correct answer is A.** The overall tone is neutral, choice A. The author provides facts and data using scientific terminology and explanations. Nowhere does he attempt to persuade the reader to a particular view (choice B), inject a personal story (choice C), or offer his own opinion (choice D), although he does offer differing viewpoints on possible solutions.

25. **The correct answer is B.** In lines 72–74, Halden's quote ("We need to design the next generation of plastics to make them more biodegradable…") shows that he believes science can find a way to make plastics biodegradable, which he says will eliminate the problem. The author states that new laws may help minimize the problem ("New laws … could require handling plastics more responsibly at the end of their useful life through recycling, proper disposal, and extended producer responsibility"), not Halden, so choice A is incorrect. The author describes how some sea creatures have ingested plastic, but Halden never advocates for the invention of edible plastic in this passage, so choice C is incorrect. Banning all new plastic production is an extreme and unrealistic solution that Halden never suggests, so choice D is incorrect.

26. **The correct answer is B.** The article includes scientific data and explanations of the effects of plastics in the ocean and waterways, offering information to the public. The specific data in this passage contradict the idea that the author is merely theorizing that the environment could be in danger, and this conclusion is too general in any event, so choice A is not the best answer. Choices C and D are too extreme and unrealistic; it is unlikely a movement will halt all plastic production, which is not even something the author advocates, and cleaning up the oceans is too huge a job for readers to take on personally. Choice B remains the most logical and realistic answer.

27. **The correct answer is B.** Lines 49–51: "Research has shown that harmful and persistent substances can both bioaccumulate … and biomagnify …" indicate that plastic pollution in the ocean is a problem by specifying that they are "harmful." Choice A merely states what happens when animals eat plastics without suggesting

that this is or is not a problem, so choice A is not the best answer. Choice C describes how certain problems associated with plastic pollution are still unknown, so it fails to support the previous question's conclusion that plastic pollution is a problem. Choice D merely sets up questions to follow without providing evidence that plastic pollution in the ocean is a problem.

28. **The correct answer is B.** In lines 16–19, the author explains that microplastics are "the most abundant type of plastic in the ocean." Although it is likely that recycling has increased in the past 60 years, the passage doesn't mention it, making choice A incorrect. Although it's true that plastic breaks down into smaller pieces in the ocean, it is stated in the passage that microplastics are more dangerous to marine organisms, who mistake them for food, rather than less dangerous, making choice C incorrect. As explained in lines 27–29, nurdles are plastic pellets used in plastic production, making choice D incorrect. In lines 30–33, the passage mentions that scrubbing agents in shampoo that leak into the environment are called microbeads, not nurdles.

29. **The correct answer is D.** The author explains that a law was passed in Illinois to prevent infiltration of these tiny microbeads into the water system (lines 33–37). The microbeads were ending up in the Great Lakes and Chicago's waterways. None of the other options are offered as a reason for the law.

30. **The correct answer is B.** Knowing the meaning of *absorb* (choice C) does not assist in understanding the meaning of *adsorbed*. The words share the same suffix, but it's the prefix that makes the word less familiar. *absolve* (choice A) has the same prefix as *absorb* but does not help in figuring out the meaning of *adsorb*. The *sorb-* in *sorbet* (a frozen dessert) has nothing to do with the word *adsorbed*, so choice D is incorrect. *Adhere* (choice B) is to hold fast or stick to something else; so *adsorb* must mean when one substance sticks to another.

31. **The correct answer is A.** The author indicates that there are ways humans may be ingesting plastic waste in lines 57–65. The author had already discussed how sea creatures ingest such waste in the previous paragraphs, so choice B is not the best answer. Choice C had already been discussed earlier, too. Choice D is incorrect because the author never theorizes about why people dump plastic waste into the oceans in this passage.

32. **The correct answer is C.** Lines 62–64 ("And, finally, what proportion of humans' exposure to plastic

ingredients and environmental pollutants occurs through seafood?") deal with how much plastic waste from the oceans people might be ingesting by eating seafood. Choice A has to do with the transference of plastic pollutants, not the amount of such pollutants people are ingesting. Choice B deals with the effects of plastic pollutants. Choice D is a general statement about the efforts to answer the questions the author raises.

33. **The correct answer is C.** As she places the offering, the narrator wonders whether her sister will die, so it is logical to conclude that she wants to place her offering correctly to prevent that from happening. No one at home asks her about the offering once she returns, so choices A and D can be eliminated. By worrying about her sister's potential death, the narrator indicates that she has more important things on her mind than whether she'll be trusted to make offerings again in the future, so choice B is not the best answer.

34. **The correct answer is A.** In line 70, the medicine man describes seeing a "luminous vapor above the house," and clarifies that "It was the spirit of the little child who is sick" in line 72. Choice B describes objects that were in his medicine bag, not the appearance of the sister's spirit. The sister was a baby, but the medicine man never describes her as a baby, so choice C is not the best answer. In line 73, the medicine man says the "spirit is beyond our reach," but this describes the spirit's location, not its appearance.

35. **The correct answer is C.** The family didn't send for the medicine man until the medicine woman had given up hope, which makes choice C the most logical answer. What the medicine man had been doing before arriving at the family's house is never indicated, so there is no evidence for choice A. Although we are told that the medicine man had to travel quite a distance, choice B, this is not offered as a reason why he was not contacted in the first place. Although the family did have a medicine woman attempt to cure their child before calling the medicine man, the narrator never implies that the healers' genders were of any significance.

36. **The correct answer is B.** Lines 21–23 show the girl having trouble analyzing how nature will affect the delivery of her offering and unsure if she is making the right decision. Choice A describes the instructions given by the medicine woman; it doesn't explain why they were difficult to follow. Choice C describes the variance in the terrain where she was searching for the right spot, but it does not describe any particular problem. Choice D describes the narrator's surroundings without

indicating that they were causing her any particular problem.

37. **The correct answer is B.** The narrator has faith that her offering will save her sister, and the medicine man has faith that the girl's spirit still exists. Choice B emphasizes the theme of faith in this passage. Choice A is not the best answer because it places the medicine man at the center of the story when it is mainly about the narrator's faith that her actions will save her sister. Choice C implies that the passage is mostly concerned with Native American culture when the rituals in the story are not as important as how the characters feel about them. Choice D describes one passing incident in the passage that says nothing about the story's overall theme.

38. **The correct answer is B.** Choice B most effectively indicates the strength of the narrator's faith by describing how she believes her offering will save her sister. Choice A merely describes the offering without indicating the narrator's faith that it has any power to save her sister. Choice C describes a moment in the story in which the narrator's faith is shaken, so it contradicts the conclusion in the previous question. Choice D mistakes the correct answer to the previous question.

39. **The correct answer is A.** The parents seem oblivious to the natural emotions of a child. Though they give the narrator responsibility and take care of her physical needs (lines 48–49), they don't seem to offer comfort or consolation. The narrator is probably given more responsibility than she wants, which makes choice B incorrect. The parents naturally focus on the child likely to die, but there is no indication they prefer the younger child, so choice C is incorrect. The narrator seems very alone and her parents display little warmth or affection, making choice D incorrect.

40. **The correct answer is A.** Choice A covers the central idea of the passage best by including its most important details: the sister's death and the narrator's efforts to save her. Choice B narrowly focuses on the girl following the instructions of the medicine woman without indicating why she was following those instructions. Choices C and D do not capture the concept of the narrative and the point of view because they both shift focus from the narrator to the entire family.

41. **The correct answer is D.** The narrator feels remorseful because she feels as if she had failed, since her sister dies despite her efforts to save the baby. The narrator may feel responsible for her sister's death, but there is

no evidence that she has any reason to feel as though she *caused* her sister's illness, so choice A is not the best answer. The narrator follows the instructions of the medicine woman meticulously, so choice B is not the best conclusion. The narrator may have felt burdened by the amount of responsibility she took on, but her remorse is more directly related to her sister's death, so choice C is not the best answer.

42. **The correct answer is C.** The modern meaning of *thrilled* is usually "excited," but in line 45, the author is talking about fear and doubt. Choices A, B, and D all have positive connotations that fail to capture the feelings of heightened fear the narrator was experiencing when she began thinking that her offering had failed to save her sister's life.

43. **The correct answer is D.** In choice D, Emmet acknowledges his death sentence and declares that he is dying for a cause. Choice C explains why he asked France for assistance, and choice B explains that he was fighting for his country's independence and freedom from tyranny. In choice A, he defends his actions by saying that he could have stood by and done nothing, given his family's privileged position, but chose instead to defend liberty.

44. **The correct answer is D.** Choice D shows Emmet's pride in his country by saying that his government speaks for him. In choice A, he merely states that he is not working for France, but this alone does not prove that he feels pride in his own country. In choice B, he theorizes about the different influences that could have caused him to betray his country. Choice C makes a statement about how he feels the people in his country deserve assistance from France, but that alone does not make a strong case for the author's patriotism.

45. **The correct answer is B.** According to the timeline, "American colonies declare" independence in 1776, and the fact that the country needed to define itself outside of the rule of another country probably caused America's view of patriotism to focus more on the country itself, rather than a greater concern for all people. Choice A refers to events that did not concern America. Choices C and D do refer to events that concerned America, but neither had as significant an impact on the country and its views as declaring independence in 1776 did.

46. **The correct answer is B.** Noting the date of Emmet's speech in his defense of his actions prior to his execution, choice A is not possible. The Louisiana Purchase by the United States (choice D), would have given

France more resources to help. However, the Napoleonic Wars were draining the French treasury (choice B), leaving the country overburdened and uninterested in becoming involved elsewhere. The French Revolution had started in 1789, triggering the rise of Napoleon, but this was not directly related to its refusal to aid Emmet.

47. **The correct answer is C.** Emmet loved his country and declared his patriotism toward Ireland as his reason for his actions (choice C). Wright's view was more inclusive, defining it as freeing all people, whatever the country. Emmet's primary focus was on his own people (choice B), not all of humankind. He defended his actions (choice A), but this action is unrelated to Wright's concept of a patriot, as is a court that renders an unjust sentence (choice D).

48. **The correct answer is B.** Although both Emmet and Wright wanted freedom from tyranny, Emmet's focus was on Ireland, and Wright had a broader objective of freedom and independence for all humankind, choice B. Choice A is incorrect because only Wright states that her country's concept of patriotism needs to be rethought. Wright was focused on advancing an expansive concept of patriotism that included other countries, which does not mean that she did not love her country, so choice C is not the best answer. Choice D is incorrect because Wright indicates that she does understand tyranny by advocating for its opposite: freedom and concern for all people.

49. **The correct answer is B.** Wright's speech reads as a sincere yet calm plea for understanding and concern for all people, while Emmet's feels more motivated by his desperation to save himself and his anger regarding the charges of treason against him, which is clear through his regular use of exclamations throughout his speech. Wright does not express anger, so choice A is incorrect. It is Emmet who is passionate and angry and Wright who is calm, not the other way around, so choice C is incorrect. Someone can speak calmly yet sincerely, as Wright does, or desperately and angrily, as Emmet does, and still be convincing, so choice D is not the best answer.

50. **The correct answer is C.** All the options refer to patriotism, but choice A is mostly about perseverance and the importance of freedom. Choice B speculates on how Americans might react if attacked and suggests submission as one possibility. Choice C sets up the either-or scenario in which there can only be one of two outcomes: liberty or death. Emmet's statement is analogous because there are only two choices: if the enemy wishes to come

into his homeland (symbolized by the word "threshold"), he will defend it to the death. Choice D expresses too much pleasure in the act of fighting for and dying for one's country, while Emmet's statements show that he is motivated more by his belief in the righteousness of freedom than more romantic ideas about dying for one's country.

51. **The correct answer is B.** Wright says Americans' idea of a patriot is someone who loves his/her country, choice D, but that idea is too narrow. She explains that Europeans see patriotism as a more expansive concept that extends to freedom for all humans. This idea, she explains, includes working toward the best interests of all human lives, wherever they are, so that they are free from despotism. This statement suggests that she herself holds these ideas (choice B) and wants others to consider them. Physically fighting for one's country, choices A and C, is an example of vanity.

52. **The correct answer is B.** Emmet speaks of being accused of secretly selling his country out to France, which would be the actions of a spy. In this context, an emissary is a spy (choice B). The government wouldn't accuse someone of being an ambassador, an official position as a representative (choice A). Similarly, a minister is an official head of a government department, which eliminates choice C. Choice D is incorrect because a mercenary is a paid soldier, and there is nothing that suggests the government thinks Emmet is a "hired gun."

Answer Keys and Explanations

SECTION 2: WRITING AND LANGUAGE TEST

1. A	10. B	19. B	28. A	37. A
2. D	11. A	20. C	29. C	38. C
3. A	12. A	21. C	30. B	39. A
4. B	13. C	22. C	31. C	40. C
5. C	14. D	23. D	32. A	41. D
6. B	15. B	24. C	33. D	42. B
7. B	16. D	25. B	34. C	43. A
8. A	17. A	26. D	35. B	44. C
9. B	18. C	27. B	36. D	

WRITING AND LANGUAGE TEST RAW SCORE
(Number of correct answers)

1. **The correct answer is A.** Choice A correctly sets up the sentence's focus on the various causes of depopulation and their negative impact. Choices B, C, and D are incorrect because they present potentially positive developments.

2. **The correct answer is D.** Choice D follows the same parallel construction as the preceding phrase, "driving away its middle class." Choices A, B, and C are incorrect because they do not demonstrate parallel construction.

3. **The correct answer is A.** Choice A is correct because the dash is being used to indicate the following explanation of what is staggering. Choice C is incorrect because it creates a run-on sentence. Choices B and D are incorrect because they move the punctuation to the wrong part of the sentence.

4. **The correct answer is B.** Choice B correctly maintains the sentence's focus on the effects of depopulation. Choices A and C are incorrect because they suggest a growth in residency, which contradicts the main argument of the passage. Choice D is incorrect because homelessness is unrelated to the main focus of the passage, which is Detroit's depopulation.

5. **The correct answer is C.** *Solicit* (choice C) correctly establishes the implied intent of the city planners within the context of the passage—to *solicit*, or ask for, the input of city residents while studying their urban spaces. Choices A, B, and D do not make sense within the context of the passage, as all of these terms imply the opposite of the city planners' intent.

6. **The correct answer is B.** The plural pronoun *they* is required here to agree with the plural noun *planners*, so *they call* (choice B) is the correct answer. Choices A and C are incorrect because they incorrectly use singular pronouns. Choice D is incorrect because "we call" is first-person plural, not third-person plural, which is what is required here.

7. **The correct answer is B.** Choice B is correct because "in fact" properly suggests an elaboration of the previous sentence. Choice A is incorrect because it suggests the second sentence is an equal and additional example, rather than an elaboration of the first. Choice C is incorrect because it implies the author is drawing a conclusion despite a contradiction. Choice D is also incorrect because it implies that the second sentence is a second example supporting a contrast scenario, which is not the case.

8. **The correct answer is A.** In choice A, the sentence explains the planners' logic. Choice B implies that there was resistance to their thinking or that their thinking was absolute, which is incorrect. Choices C and D do not denote the careful calculation that the rest of the sentence implies.

9. **The correct answer is B.** This sentence would best serve as a transition between the previous and current paragraphs. The previous paragraph refers to the city planners' strategic plan, and the current paragraph begins with an example of one of the plan's boldest suggestions. A sentence that mentions that the plan contained bold suggestions (choice B) would work well here. The other choices would place this notion *after* providing examples of the plan's bold suggestions, rendering it ineffective and unnecessary.

10. **The correct answer is B.** Choice B correctly places the dash so that it separates the two clauses. Choices A, C, and D are incorrect because they place the dash in the wrong place.

11. **The correct answer is A.** Choice A is correct because items in a series should be separated by commas. Choice B is incorrect because it is unnecessarily wordy and misuses semicolons. Choice C is incorrect because it misuses semicolons. Choice D is also incorrect because it incorrectly mixes a semicolon with commas.

12. **The correct answer is A.** Choice A is correct because *hawk* means "to call out and sell," which is what vendors at festivals do. Choice B is incorrect because, while the vendors may stock merchandise, the author's intent here is to describe *how* they sell that merchandise. Similarly, choices C and D are incorrect because the vendors are selling—not advertising or trading—goods.

13. **The correct answer is C.** Choice C correctly suggests that this sentence provides a transition between the scene depicted in the first paragraph and the ancient and modern tradition of puppetry, and the writer should not delete it. Choice A is incorrect because this sentence is not an opinion. Choice B is incorrect because this sentence does not distract from but rather helps in contextualizing the main ideas of the paragraph. Choice D is incorrect because it is the following sentence that explains what *wayang kulit* is.

14. **The correct answer is D.** Choice D correctly uses end punctuation to correct this run-on sentence. Choices A, B, and C are incorrect because they do not employ the correct punctuation to denote two independent clauses.

15. **The correct answer is B.** Choice B is correct because the phrase, "a nation to which Indonesia was linked through trade relations" should refer to the country of India, not "migrants." Choices A and D are incorrect because the modifier is misplaced. Choice C is incorrect because it is awkward and doesn't make sense.

16. **The correct answer is D.** Choice D is correct because this sentence is tangential to the paragraph's focus on the cultural influences of Hindu culture on the Indonesian way of life. Choice A is incorrect because this information is not relevant. Choice B is incorrect because this paragraph is not focused on the actual practice of shadow puppetry. Choice C is incorrect because this information has not been presented before this sentence.

17. **The correct answer is A.** Choice A reflects the paragraph's emphasis that depicting gods in human form was not allowed under any circumstance. Choices B, C, and D are incorrect because these words do not suggest complete proscription the way choice A does.

18. **The correct answer is C.** Choice C is correct because it places the verb in the past tense. Choice A is incorrect because the present tense is an inappropriate shift from the past tense that the rest of the paragraph uses. Choices B and D are incorrect because the sentence requires the simple past tense.

19. **The correct answer is B.** Choice B conveys both the duration of the events and the lack of interruptions without being redundant or wordy. Choice A is incorrect because "all night long" is redundant. Choice C is incorrect because it is redundant and wordy; while it is constructed better by omitting "at all," "all night long from sunset to sunrise" is still redundant. Choice D is incorrect because just noting that the performance lasted all night isn't as informative as noting that, from dusk to dawn, the performance had no interruptions.

20. **The correct answer is C.** As written, the sentence is a run-on and needs some added punctuation to reduce confusion. Choice C fixes the run-on by adding the appropriate commas and an em-dash. Choices B and D add commas in inappropriate places, creating additional confusion.

21. **The correct answer is C.** Choice C is correct because the pronoun *its* should refer back to the antecedent "the puppet." Choice A is incorrect because *their* is plural and *puppet* is not. Choices B and D are incorrect because "the puppet" is neither male nor female.

22. **The correct answer is C.** Choice C is correct because comparisons require *than*, not *then*. Choice A is incorrect because *then* is an adverb that refers to time. Choices B and D are incorrect because they don't make sense in the sentence.

Answer Keys and Explanations

23. **The correct answer is D.** The intent of this passage is to bring attention to the serious water issues occurring in the American Southwest, so choice D would be the most effective introductory sentence. The passage is not an enticement to vacation in the American Southwest, so choice A is incorrect. It is also not focused on pointing out the majestic aspects of the American Southwest, so choice B is incorrect. The Anasazi people are a supporting detail about the American Southwest in the context of this passage, so choice C is also incorrect.

24. **The correct answer is C.** Choice C is correct because the sentence subject that includes "arid climate and limited water resources," is a compound subject, which means the verb must also be plural. Choice A is incorrect because "has" is singular. Choice B is incorrect because it is the past perfect instead of the present perfect tense. Choice D is incorrect because it is present tense and changes the meaning of the sentence.

25. **The correct answer is B.** Choice B is correct because the sentence requires a possessive pronoun in order to refer back to the Anasazi people. Choice A is incorrect because *they're* is a contraction, not a possessive. Choice C is incorrect because *there* is an adverb, not a possessive. Choice D is incorrect because *its* is singular possessive, while the antecedent, *people*, is plural.

26. **The correct answer is D.** Choice D combines the sentences in a way that helps emphasize the connection between the two. Choice A is incorrect because *but* implies that the two ideas are contradictory. Choice B is incorrect because it misuses a semicolon to connect an independent clause and what is now a dependent clause. Choice C is incorrect because it creates a run-on sentence.

27. **The correct answer is B.** Choice B is correct because the sentence is a statement, and thus it should end in a period. Choice A is incorrect because the sentence does not warrant the excitement or surprise that an exclamation point conveys. Choice C is incorrect because the sentence is not a question. Choice D is incorrect because it creates a run-on sentence.

28. **The correct answer is A.** Choice A is correct because the context of the sentence suggests that a scientific forecast or prediction about water flow has been made. Choices B and C are incorrect because they reflect subjective impulses and do not maintain the neutral and scientific tone of the passage. Choice D is incorrect because it is vague and fails to suggest a basis in research.

29. **The correct answer is C.** This sentence adds new and relevant information by providing an example that shows the reader how severe the drought really is. Choice A is incorrect because this information has not been presented previously in the passage. Choice B is incorrect because this sentence does not blur the paragraph's focus; rather, it is relevant to the paragraph's main argument. Choice D is incorrect because this sentence does not introduce this argument; rather, it supports the argument.

30. **The correct answer is B.** Choice B is correct because the dependent clause "and possibly more alarming" must be set off by commas. Choice A is incorrect because it contains one too many commas. Choice C is incorrect because it contains no commas. Choice D is incorrect because the comma should be before *and*.

31. **The correct answer is C.** Although it may sound otherwise, the conventional expression is "for all intents and purposes." Choices A, B, and D are incorrect.

32. **The correct answer is A.** Choice A is correct because the author's intent is to suggest that there are other factors that make the problems of drought worse and more complicated. Choices B, C, and D are incorrect because each word emphasizes an increase in severity rather than an increase in the number of factors contributing to problems in the area.

33. **The correct answer is D.** The accompanying map measures average air temperatures, so choice D is correct. The map does not measure the highest or lowest air temperatures, so choices A and B are incorrect. It also doesn't measure water temperature, so choice C is incorrect.

34. **The correct answer is C.** Choice C is correct because this first paragraph establishes that women do not get as many leading roles as men nor do they spend as much time on-screen. Choice A is incorrect because it does not stress the number of roles nor the amount of on-screen time. Choice B is incorrect because it does not cite the amount of on-screen time, alluding to it only vaguely. Choice D is incorrect because the main idea of the passage is not a plea to pay female actresses more than their male counterparts to attract new talent.

35. **The correct answer is B.** Choice B is correct because only *agents* expresses the idea that television and movies play an active role in causing social change. Choices A, C, and D are incorrect because they don't suggest a causal relationship to social change.

36. **The correct answer is D.** Choice D is correct because the subordinate clause that begins with *while* is tied to the central premise of the sentence and needs to be at the beginning. Choice A is incorrect because at the end of the sentence, the relationship of the clause to the central idea is lost. Choices B and C are incorrect because they obscure the relationship of the clause to the central idea of the sentence.

37. **The correct answer is A.** Choice A is correct because the noun *women* should agree in number with *protagonists*. Choice B is incorrect because *protagonist* should be plural. Choice C is incorrect because *protagonist* should be singular if it is to agree with the subject. Choice D is incorrect because "a woman" is not plural.

38. **The correct answer is C.** Choice C clarifies that the comparison is between women's marital status and the marital status of men. Choice A is incorrect because it makes an illogical comparison between women's marital status and men in general. Choice B is incorrect because it uses the singular *man*, meaning that only one man's marriage status is being compared. Choice D is incorrect because it compares women's marital status to the grammatically incorrect phrase "men's marriage."

39. **The correct answer is A.** Choice A supports the paragraph's claim that women are underrepresented in the film industry. Choices B, C, and D are incorrect because they don't support the paragraph's main focus that women are underrepresented in the film industry.

40. **The correct answer is C.** Choice C is correct because the pronoun should refer to the female actress using *her*. Choice A is incorrect because it is plural. Choice B is incorrect because it is masculine. Choice D is incorrect because it is plural and first person.

41. **The correct answer is D.** Choice D maintains the objective and neutral tone of the passage while noting unfavorable comparisons. Choices A, B, and C are incorrect because the tone of each choice is emotionally charged, which is inconsistent with the objective tone of the passage.

42. **The correct answer is B.** Given the context of the sentence and paragraph, *famous* is the most appropriate word choice. Streep is offered as an example of a woman who has achieved great acclaim as an actress, despite gender inequalities in the film industry. The previous sentence mentions her many award nominations, so referring to her fame here makes the most sense. The other answer choices either don't make sense given the context, or we are not given enough information to determine if they are appropriate choices, so they are incorrect.

43. **The correct answer is A.** Choice A is correct because *accolades* connotes the achievements, honor, and respect that the passage goes on to describe. Choice B is incorrect because the awards were not privileges. Choices C and D are incorrect because they do not connote the honor and respect that *accolades* does.

44. **The correct answer is C.** The word *characters* should be the possessive *character's*, so choice C is correct. Choice A is incorrect because *characters* is plural instead of possessive. Choice B is incorrect because *character* is not possessive. Choice D is incorrect because it does not convey the appropriate meaning.

Section 3: Math Test—No Calculator

1. B	**5.** C	**9.** B	**13.** D	**17.** 6
2. B	**6.** A	**10.** A	**14.** A	**18.** 25
3. B	**7.** D	**11.** C	**15.** D	**19.** 15
4. C	**8.** C	**12.** C	**16.** 80	**20.** 4

MATH TEST—NO CALCULATOR RAW SCORE

(Number of correct answers)

1. **The correct answer is B.** The slope of a line can be determined by finding the difference in the y-coordinates divided by the difference in the x-coordinates for any two points on the line. Using the points indicated, the slope is $\frac{5-1}{0-3}=-\frac{4}{3}$. Translating the line moves all the points on the line the same distance in the same direction, and the image will be a parallel line. Therefore, the slope of the line is $-\frac{4}{3}$.

2. **The correct answer is B.** The constant 12 represents the starting distance on the driveway. In other words, before the snail even moved, it was already 12 feet from the beginning of the driveway. Therefore, Catherine must have placed the snail 12 feet from the start of her driveway before she began recording the time it took for the snail to get to the end of her driveway.

3. **The correct answer is B.** Solve for x:

   $$-2x+5=2-(5-2x)$$
   $$-2x+5=2-5+2x$$
   $$-2x+5=-3+2x \qquad \text{Add } 2x \text{ to both sides.}$$
   $$5=-3+4x \qquad \text{Add } +3 \text{ to both sides.}$$
   $$8=4x \qquad \text{Divide by 4.}$$
   $$2=x$$

4. **The correct answer is C.** Multiply both the numerator and the denominator by the complex conjugate of the denominator, which is equivalent to multiplying by 1. The resulting rational expression has a real denominator and can be simplified to $-4 + 2i$.

   $$\frac{10i}{1-2i}\left(\frac{1+2i}{1+2i}\right)=\frac{\left(10i+20i^2\right)}{1-4i^2}$$
   $$=\frac{10i-20}{1+4}$$
   $$=2i-4$$

5. **The correct answer is C.**

   $$5\sqrt{-16}$$
   $$=5\left(\sqrt{16}\cdot\sqrt{-1}\right)$$
   $$=5(4i)$$
   $$=20i$$

6. **The correct answer is A.** The amount of grain added each week is 1,000 bushels. Divide 1,000 bushels by 0.8 bushels per cubic foot to obtain 1,250 cubic feet per week. So the total amount of grain in the silo is 32,500 (what is already there) plus 1,250w (the amount added each week times the number of weeks), which must be less than or equal to the volume of the silo, 45,000 cubic feet.

7. **The correct answer is D.** The vertex of a parabola is found when the equation is written in the form $y = a(x - h)^2 + k$. You don't need to perform any calculations, because only choice D is written in this form.

8. **The correct answer is C.**

   $$-x^2+2y-(-x-y)=-x^2+2y+x+y$$
   $$=-x^2+x+3y$$

9. **The correct answer is B.** Since Jorge's truck is traveling at an average speed of 55 miles per hour and the truck gets 6 miles per gallon, the number of gallons of diesel used each hour can be found by the equation $\frac{55 \text{ miles}}{1 \text{ hour}} \times \frac{1 \text{ gallon}}{6 \text{ miles}} = \frac{55}{6}$. The truck uses $\frac{55}{6}$ gallons of diesel per hour, so it uses $\frac{55}{6}h$ gallons of diesel in h hours. The truck's fuel tank has 125 gallons of diesel at the beginning of the trip. Therefore, the function that models the number of gallons of diesel remaining in the tank h hours after the trip begins is $d(h) = 125 - \frac{55h}{6}$.

10. **The correct answer is A.**

$$A = \frac{M}{M-N}$$
$$A(M-N) = M$$
$$AM - AN = M$$
$$AM - M = AN$$
$$M(A-1) = AN$$
$$M = \frac{AN}{A-1}$$

11. **The correct answer is C.** The total cost of the sofa, y, is equal to the number of monthly payments multiplied by the amount of each payment, plus the down payment. The number of monthly payments is x, and x is multiplied by 90 in the given equation. So 90 represents the monthly payment. 75 represents the down payment.

12. **The correct answer is C.** The sum of the values that satisfy the equation is the sum of the solution $2.5 + 3 = 5.5$.

$$2n^2 - 11n + 15 = 0$$
$$(2n - 5)(n - 3) = 0$$
$$2n - 5 = 0, n - 3 = 0$$
$$n = 2.5, n = 3$$

13. **The correct answer is D.** The graph will cross the x-axis at the point where the function (that is, the y-coordinate) has a value of 0. As a result, the following equation needs to be solved:

$$480 - 60t = 0$$
$$-60t = -480$$
$$t = 8$$

Since t represents the independent variable, the point is (8, 0).

14. **The correct answer is A.** The initial population of the town is 500. The rate of change between consecutive x values (1 year, 2 years, 3 years) is not constant. As a result, the expression cannot be linear, and choice B is eliminated. Determine the ratio of each year's population to the previous year's population to the previous year's population. Comparing the population after one year to the initial population, we have:

$$\frac{650}{500} = 1.3$$

If the population is growing exponentially, then we can calculate the population after x years by multiplying the initial population by 1.3 raised to the x power. Choice A represents that calculation. (You can eliminate choice C by substituting $x = 1$ year, and choice D doesn't make sense because it introduces the undefined quantity t.)

15. **The correct answer is D.** For questions of this type, you often can identify the correct answer by substituting values for the variable. Zero (or any value that simplifies the necessary arithmetic) is a good choice. When you substitute 0 for x, $\frac{4x+1}{x+2}$ simplifies to $\frac{1}{2}$. Because any equivalent expression must have the same value as the original expression for all x, look for the expression that equals $\frac{1}{2}$ when $x = 0$. Among the answers, only choice D is such an expression. You can also arrive at this answer using algebra, but it takes longer.

16. **The correct answer is 80.** If $AC = BC$, then $m\angle A = m\angle B = 50°$.

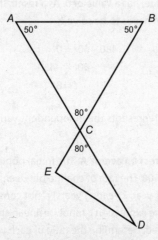

In $\triangle ABC$, $m\angle ACB = 180° - (m\angle A + m\angle B)$. So $m\angle ACB = 80°$. Further, $m\angle ACB = m\angle ECD$ because they are opposite angles. Therefore, $m\angle ECD = 80°$.

17. **The correct answer is 6.** First, solve for x by multiplying the second equation by 2 so that the coefficient of y will be 4, the additive inverse (the opposite) of the y coefficient in the first equation. Add the two equations to eliminate y.

$$
\begin{array}{r}
5x - 4y = 13 \\
x + 2y = 4 \\
\hline
5x - 4y = 13 \\
2x + 4y = 8 \\
\hline
7x = 21 \\
x = 3
\end{array}
$$

Then, substitute $x = 3$ into the second equation to get the value of y:

$$3 + 2y = 4$$
$$2y = 1$$
$$y = \frac{1}{2}$$

Finally, substitute $x = 3$ and $y = \frac{1}{2}$ into $\frac{x}{y}$ to get the value of the ratio:

$$\frac{x}{y} = \frac{3}{\frac{1}{2}} = 6$$

18. **The correct answer is 25.** According to the graph, the trout population was 4,000 in the year 1980 and 3,000 in the year 2000. The decrease in number of fish is 1,000, whereas the initial trout population for the year 1980 was 4,000. So the percent decrease equals the ratio of the change in population to the original population. This relationship can be represented as $\frac{1,000}{4,000}$.

This ratio simplifies as $\frac{1}{4}$, or 25%.

19. **The correct answer is 15.** To begin, $f(p + 3) = 5(p + 3) + 12 = 5p + 15 + 12 = 5p + 27$. Similarly, $f(p) = 5p + 12$. Thus,

$$
\begin{aligned}
f(p+3) - f(p) &= 5p + 27 - (5p + 12) \\
&= 5p + 27 - 5p - 12 \\
&= 15
\end{aligned}
$$

20. **The correct answer is 4.** Solve for x:

$$\frac{9}{x-2} + \frac{16}{x+3} = 5$$
$$\left(\frac{9}{x-2} + \frac{16}{x+3}\right)(x-2)(x+3) = 5(x-2)(x+3)$$
$$9x + 27 + 16x - 32 = 5x^2 + 5x - 30$$
$$0 = 5x^2 - 20x - 25$$
$$0 = 5(x+1)(x-5)$$
$$x = -1 \text{ or } x = 5$$

To get the sum of the solutions, simply add -1 and 5: $-1 + 5 = 4$.

1. C	**9.** B	**17.** D	**25.** A	**33.** 45
2. D	**10.** B	**18.** B	**26.** D	**34.** 41
3. D	**11.** B	**19.** A	**27.** D	**35.** 5400
4. A	**12.** D	**20.** A	**28.** A	**36.** 440
5. A	**13.** C	**21.** D	**29.** B	**37.** 21.5
6. C	**14.** D	**22.** B	**30.** B	**38.** 4
7. B	**15.** C	**23.** C	**31.** 5	
8. D	**16.** B	**24.** A	**32.** 9	

MATH TEST—CALCULATOR RAW SCORE
(Number of correct answers)

1. **The correct answer is C.** 15% of $12.50 is (0.15)($12.50) = $1.875. So the discount for every 10 audio singles purchased is $1.875. Multiply this by 4 to get the savings when purchasing 40 audio singles: 4($1.875) = $7.50.

2. **The correct answer is D.** When measuring length, 1 yard = 3 feet. When measuring area, 1 square yard = 9 square feet. So 20 square yards = 180 square feet. At $1.30 per square foot, it will cost 180 × $1.30 = $234.

3. **The correct answer is D.** Let x represent the score of one of the two games in which he scored identically. Then, the score of the third game is $x + 20$. Since the average of all six games is 182, solve the following equation for x:

$$\frac{212+181+160+x+x+(x+20)}{6}=182$$

$$\frac{573+3x}{6}=182$$

$$573+3x=1,092$$

$$3x=519$$

$$x=173$$

So his six scores were 160, 173, 173, 181, 193, and 212. Therefore, the second highest score is 193.

4. **The correct answer is A.** The volume of the fish tank is 11(14)(9) = 1,386 cubic inches. The amount needed to fill the tank is 1,386 ÷ 231 = 6 gallons.

5. **The correct answer is A.** The amount of protein in m cups of milk is $8m$ grams, and the amount of protein in n eggs is $6n$ grams. The problem asks for the amount to meet *or* exceed the recommended daily intake, which sets up a greater-than-or-equal-to scenario.

6. **The correct answer is C.** The total charge that Amy will pay is the daily rate, the mileage rate, and the 7.5% tax on both. If Amy drove x miles, then the total charge is $(19.99 + 0.15x) + 0.075(19.99 + 0.15x)$, which can be rewritten as $1.075(19.99 + 0.15x)$.

7. **The correct answer is B.** $5\frac{1}{2}$ dozen nails are bought for $5\frac{1}{2}$ dozen × 35 cents per dozen = 192.5 cents. There are 66 nails in $5\frac{1}{2}$ dozen and 66 ÷ 3 = 22 sets sold at 10 cents per set, so 22 sets × 10 cents per set = 220 cents. The profit is 220 – 192.5 = $27\frac{1}{2}$ cents.

8. **The correct answer is D.** The weights are proportional to the volumes, and the volumes vary as the cubes of their linear dimensions. If the edges are doubled, the volume becomes $2^3 = 8$ times as large (see the figure). Therefore, the weight is 8 × 150 = 1,200 pounds.

1 ft.

9. **The correct answer is B.**

$$-2(1-x)^2 + 2(1-x^2) = -2(1-2x+x^2) + 2(1-x^2)$$
$$= -2 + 4x - 2x^2 + 2 - 2x^2$$
$$= -4x^2 + 4x$$

10. **The correct answer is B.** One method of finding the correct answer is to create an inequality. The income from the sign-up fees for x people is $20x$. For the organization to profit, $20x$ must be greater than the cost of x T-shirts. Therefore, $20x > 7x + 60$ can be used to model the situation. Solving this inequality yields $x > 4.6$. Since there can't be 4.6 people, round the answer up to 5.

11. **The correct answer is B.** The total number of students, $x + y$, is equal to 2,180, so the answer must be choice B or choice C. The male students raised $20 each, and the female students raised $25 each. Since x represents the number of male students, then the amount the male students raised is represented by $20x$, and the amount the female students raised is represented by $25y$. The total amount raised is $50,000, so the sum is $20x + 25y = 50,000$. That leaves choice B as the only correct answer.

12. **The correct answer is D.** The cube root of an expression is equal to that expression raised to the $\frac{1}{3}$ power, so

$$\sqrt[3]{9x^3y^5z^6} = \left(9x^3y^5z^6\right)^{\frac{1}{3}}$$
$$= 9^{\frac{1}{3}}xy^{\frac{5}{3}}z^2$$

13. **The correct answer is C.** The two intersections of the graphs of the equations are at the points (0, 1) and (−1, 0). Substituting 0 for x and 1 for y makes both equations true. Also, substituting −1 for x and 0 for y makes both equations true.

14. **The correct answer is D.** Find the solution to this problem by using the structure of the given equation. Multiplying both sides of the equation $\frac{x}{3} - \frac{y}{4} = 5$ by 24 will clear fractions from the equation and yield $8x - 6y = 120$.

15. **The correct answer is C.** If x is the number of lunches sold and y is the number of dinners sold, then $x + y$ represents the number of meals sold during the weekend. The equation $7.5x + 12y$ represents the total amount collected in the weekend. Therefore, the correct system of equations is $x + y = 241$ and $7.5x + 12y = 2,523$.

16. **The correct answer is B.** The scatterplot shows a strong correlation between the variables. As the years increase, the population also increases.

17. **The correct answer is D.** The points on the graph display a pattern of exponential growth, as a rapidly upward-turning curve could be used to connect them; therefore, an exponential curve would best represent the data.

18. **The correct answer is B.** The graduate starts at x dollars per week. After the pay cut, the graduate receives 90% of the original salary. The 10% raise adds 9% to the salary (10% of 90%), so the new salary is $0.99x$.

19. **The correct answer is A.** The solution set is as follows. Note that it extends into all quadrants except the third.

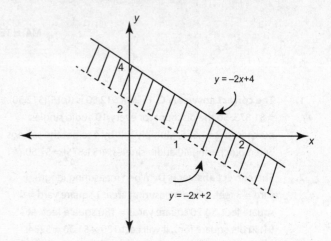

20. **The correct answer is A.**

$$\frac{(1-2i)^2}{2}$$
$$= \frac{1 - 2i - 2i + 4i^2}{2}$$
$$= \frac{1 - 4i + 4i^2}{2}$$
$$= \frac{1 - 4i + 4(-1)}{2}$$
$$= \frac{1 - 4i - 4}{2}$$
$$= \frac{-3 - 4i}{2}$$
$$= -\frac{3}{2} - 2i$$
$$= -\frac{3}{2} + (-2)i$$

Hence, $b = -2$.

21. **The correct answer is D.** If the discount is 10%, then $12.60 is 90% of $14.

22. **The correct answer is B.** To solve for the number of gallons of white vinegar, set up a proportion.

$$\frac{1\frac{1}{3}}{2}=\frac{x}{7}$$

$$2x=\frac{28}{3}$$

$$x=4\frac{4}{6}=4\frac{2}{3}$$

23. **The correct answer is C.** When adding complex numbers, we add the real parts of each number and the imaginary parts separately.

$$(1.26 + 4.52i) + (-0.89 + xi)$$
$$= (1.26 + (-0.89)) + (4.52 + x)i$$

We are given that this sum equals 0.37 + 7.4i. So we know that (4.52 + x), or the coefficient of i, equals 7.4. (We can disregard the real number part of the sum.) We can write: 4.52 + x = 7.4.

Solving for x gives: $x = 7.4 - 4.52$
$$x = 2.88$$

24. **The correct answer is A.** Because the function f has (x – 4) and (x + 2) as factors, the function should have zeros when x – 4 = 0 and x + 2 = 0. The only graph that shows a curve that has x-intercepts at –2 and 4 is choice A.

25. **The correct answer is A.** There are a total of 8 + 23 + 19 = 50 people in Group A, and 8 of them have no living siblings. So the probability is $\frac{8}{50}=\frac{4}{25}$.

26. **The correct answer is D.** When t = 0, the height of the ball is 0.02 m, so 0.02 represents the height of the ball before it is hit.

27. **The correct answer is D.** If k is a positive constant other than 1, then the equation kx + y = c can be rewritten as y = –kx + c. If k is positive, then –k is negative, and it must be something other than –1. The only graph with a negative slope other than –1 is answer choice D.

28. **The correct answer is A.** If the machine loses 15% of its value each year, then each year its value is 85% of what it was the year before. Therefore, the value of the machine can be modeled by $V(x) = 80{,}000 \times (0.85)^x$, where x = the number of years since the machine was purchased. After 4 years, its value is $80,000 × (0.85)^4 = $41,760.50.

29. **The correct answer is B.** To find the current average, add all of the medals and divide by 6:

$$\frac{12+13+31+25+37+28}{6}=\frac{146}{6}$$
$$=24.3$$
$$\approx 24$$

The new average has to be one more than that, or 25.3. However, it will be spread over seven Winter Olympics:

$$\frac{12+13+31+25+37+28+x}{7}=\frac{146+x}{7}=25.3$$
$$146+x=177.1$$
$$x=31.1$$

30. **The correct answer is B.** Simplify the ratio $\frac{6x}{2x+4}$ by factoring out the greatest common factor (2). The result is $\frac{3x}{x+2}$. Set $\frac{3x}{x+2}=3+\frac{A}{x+2}$ and solve.

$$3x=3(x+2)+A$$
$$3x=3x+6+A$$
$$A=-6$$

31. **The correct answer is 5.** Expand the left side and then equate corresponding coefficients:

$$(ax-1) \cdot (2x+b)=4x^2+4x-3$$
$$2ax^2-2x+abx-b=4x^2+4x-3$$
$$2ax^2+(ab-2)x-b=4x^2+4x-3$$

So 2a = 4, ab – 2 = 4, and –b = –3. So a = 2 and b = 3. Therefore, a + b = 5.

32. **The correct answer is 9.** Since he must buy at least two of each item, first determine the cost of buying exactly 2 of each:

$$2(\$4.00 + \$3.75 + \$1.50) = \$18.50$$

Now, subtract that from $50: $50 – $18.50 = $31.50.

Divide this difference by the cost of a pint of berries ($4.00) to get 7.875.

So Derek would be able to buy at most 7 more pints of berries. This, together with the 2 pints we accounted for at the start of the solution, gives a maximum of 9 pints of berries that he could purchase.

33. **The correct answer is 45.** Letting m be the time per regular question, $2m$ is the time per math problem. The total time for all the regular questions is $300m$, and the total time for all the math problems is $50(2m)$. Since the exam is 3 hours, or 180 minutes, $300m + 100m = 180$ minutes, $400m = 180$, and $m = \dfrac{180}{400} = \dfrac{9}{20}$. The time to do a math problem is $2\left(\dfrac{9}{20}\right) = \dfrac{9}{10}$. All 50 math problems can be done in $50\left(\dfrac{9}{10}\right) = 45$ minutes.

34. **The correct answer is 41.** The number of games that the Montreal Canadiens played is not provided, but it is given that the ratio of the number of games played in the 1947–48 season to that in the 1924–25 season is 2:1. Problems like this can be solved by plugging in real numbers. Let's say that there were 100 games in the 1924–25 season, so they won 57 of those games. In the 1947–48 season, there were twice as many games, or 200 games, so they won 33% of 200 games, or 66 games. Altogether they won 123 out of 300 games, and this fraction can be simplified to 41 out of 100, or 41%.

35. **The correct answer is 5400.** Of the number of voters polled, 400 of 625, or 64%, were in favor of the measure. If the margin of error is 4%, the likely population proportion will be between 60% and 68%: 60% of 9,000 total voters is $(0.6)(9,000) = 5,400$.

36. **The correct answer is 440.** If the dolphin weighs 110% of the average, it weighs 10% more than the average weight of 400 pounds, or $0.10 \times 400 = 40$ pounds. The dolphin weighs $400 + 40 = 440$ pounds.

37. **The correct answer is 21.5.** First, combine the equations by subtracting $(x + y = 13)$ from $(3x + y = -4)$:

$$
\begin{array}{r}
3x + y = -4 \\
-(x + y = 13) \\
\hline
2x = -17 \\
x = -8.5
\end{array}
$$

Then solve for x and substitute into one of the equations to solve for y:

$$-8.5 + y = 13$$
$$y = 21.5$$

38. **The correct answer is 4.** In general, a system of equations that has no solution takes this form, where a, b, m, and n are constants:

$$ax + by = m$$
$$ax + by = n$$

To rewrite the given system in this form, we must multiply $-3x + 2y = -1$ by some factor so that the coefficient of x will be 6, making it equal to the coefficient in the second equation. That factor is -2. When we multiply the first equation by -2, the given system becomes this equivalent system:

$$6x - 4y = 2$$
$$6x - by = 8$$

Now the coefficients are equal, and the y coefficients would be equal if $b = 4$. So if $b = 4$, then the system has no solution.

SECTION 5: ESSAY

ANALYSIS OF PASSAGE

The following is an analysis of the passage by Peter Krapp, noting how the writer used evidence, reasoning, and stylistic or persuasive elements to support his claims, connect the claims and evidence, and add power to the ideas he expressed. Check to see if you evaluated the passage in a similar way.

1   Pennsylvania State University's College of Engineering took its computer network offline on May 15 after disclosing two cyberattacks. The perpetrators were able to access information on 18,000 students, who are being contacted this week with the news that their personal identifying information is in hackers' hands.

   Three days later, the computer network is back online, with new protections for its users.

2   One of the two attacks is ascribed by a forensic cybersecurity corporation retained by Penn State to computers apparently based in China.

3   As a researcher who has published on hacking and hacktivism and serves on the board of the UC Irvine data science initiative, I believe two aspects of this news story deserve particular attention.

Compromising student data

4   Penn State announced last week that the FBI alerted it on November 21, 2014, about an attack with custom malware that started as early as September 2012.

5   Why did it take so long for Penn State to disclose the breach, despite the fact that the experience of large-scale hacks in 2013 and 2014 (against Target, Home Depot, and others) clearly demonstrated an urgent need for quick and full disclosure—both to help the victims and to preserve a modicum of trust?

6   Penn State stated only that any disclosure would have tipped off the perpetrators before their access to the College of Engineering computers could be cut off.

7   Meanwhile, student data may have been compromised for at least six months, maybe longer.

1   The writer cites a specific example of a computer security breach and uses facts and statistics to show the seriousness of the problem.

2   By mentioning that the computer hackers appear to be located in China, the writer underscores the global risks of the security breach.

3   The writer establishes his credentials to write about and offer an argument on this topic.

4   The writer uses facts and dates to lay the groundwork for the point he is about to make.

5   The writer poses a rhetorical question to address one aspect of this story that he earlier said deserves "particular attention." His first point is that Penn State took too long to disclose the security breach. He cites two past breaches to support his argument about the need for quick disclosure and uses evocative words ("help the victims and to preserve a modicum of trust") to emphasize how important early disclosure is.

6   The writer states Penn State's justification for delaying disclosure. He uses the word <u>only</u> to imply that Penn State should have been more forthcoming, thus strengthening his own position. At the same time, he presents himself as reasonable because he offers Penn State's argument before going on with his own.

7   The writer shows why, in his opinion, Penn State's position is weak.

8   Another conspicuous problem with public discussion of events like this is, in fact, the lack of distinction often made in the media between actual appropriation of data (as at Penn State) and mere temporary disabling or defacement of websites (as happened to Rutgers University last month). That is like being unable to make a difference between a grand theft auto and keying a car.

The question is, what can universities do to limit the risk to their students?

9   The exposure of student data in higher education is not limited to Social Security numbers or email passwords. Information collected and retained by educational institutions includes full name, address, phone number, credit and debit card information, workplace information, date of birth, personal interests and of course academic performance and grade information.

10 A survey conducted by the Obama administration collected responses from 24,092 individuals on how much they trusted various institutions to keep their data safe. There was a high level of concern around transparency and legal standards. (https://www.whitehouse.gov/issues/technology/big-data-review)

. . .

11 President Obama only recently called for laws covering data hacking and student privacy. "We're saying that data collected on students in the classroom should only be used for educational purposes," he stated in his speech to the Federal Trade Commission (FTC) earlier this year.

Data privacy concerns

12 If students' right to privacy needs to be protected from the specter of foreign intelligence agencies poking around the Penn State Engineering School, then by the same logic it should be protected also against data-mining by for-profit actors right here in the US.

13 Until May 2014, Google, for instance, routinely mined its apps for education services for advertising and monetizing purposes. When *Education Week* reported that Google was mining student emails, it quickly led not only to lawsuits but also to landmark legislation.

14 The California Senate Bill 1177 was enacted to prevent educational services from selling student information or mining it for advertising purposes.

15 Yet, almost a year later, students in California remain just as concerned about their data privacy as before—since the new state law was watered down to apply only to K–12 and not to higher education.

8   *The writer now addresses the second point that he feels "deserve[s] particular attention" — The media do not treat breaches like the one at Penn State seriously, often viewing them more like nuisance problems. He supports his view that the media should be able to make a distinction between serious and non-serious security breaches by juxtaposing a significant crime (grand theft auto) with a minor infraction (keying a car).*

9   *The writer shows how dangerous these kinds of security breaches are, using specific examples of the kinds of information that can fall into hackers' hands.*

10 *The writer strengthens his viewpoint by providing statistical evidence in the form of a survey that reveals how concerned people are about the safety of their personal data.*

11 *The writer supports his argument by quoting an authority no less than the president of the United States. (He also makes the point that he believes the president's concern is overdue, by saying this statement was made "only recently.")*

12 *The writer underscores the depth of the problem by pointing out that there are many entities that might access students' computer data: not only foreign intelligence agencies (as was the case with the Penn State breach), but US companies that mine computer data for profit. The writer argues that just as foreign breaches have been recognized as serious, so should domestic for-profit breaches.*

13 *The writer offers a specific example of a US company mining personal data for profit to strengthen his case.*

14 *The writer underscores the validity of his argument by citing legislation enacted to address the problem.*

15 *The writer points out that the final form of the legislation to protect students' data does not extend to college students.*

16 And when it was disclosed earlier this spring that education publisher Pearson secretly monitored social media to discern references to their content, the legislative response was one that, according to the Electronic Privacy Information Center (EPIC) in Washington, DC, "fails to uphold President Obama's promise that the data collected in an educational context can be used only for educational purposes."

16 The writer reinforces his argument that not enough is being done to protect college students' personal data by citing another example of a US company data-mining for profit. He also quotes an authoritative source to support this claim.

17 Students in higher education nationwide are still in a position where they cannot opt out of the computer services of their learning institutions, and so they have no expectation of privacy.

17 The writer points out a reality that makes and keeps college students vulnerable: "they cannot opt out of the computer services of their learning institutions."

18 Despite President Obama's promises for safeguarding the privacy of consumers and families, and despite the fact that a number of technology companies concerned with growing consumer distrust recently signed a pledge to safeguard student privacy, neither Google nor Apple signed on.

18 The writer underscores college students' vulnerability by pointing out that two major companies (Google and Apple) have refused to sign a pledge to safeguard student privacy.

19 The President's Council of Advisors on Science and Technology (PCAST) was tasked to examine current and likely future capabilities of key technologies, both those associated with the collection, analysis, and use of big data and those that can help to preserve privacy, resulting in a direct recommendation to strengthen US research in privacy-related technologies.

19 The writer points out that an advisory board to the US president has recommended strengthening research on the problem.

20 And overwhelmingly, respondents to a White House survey recently expressed severe reservations about the collection, storage, and security and use of private information.

20 The writer cites a White House survey that reflected "severe reservations about the collection, storage, and security and use of private information." The survey shows that despite the measures that have been put in place, the public still feels its data is at risk.

21 Maybe it is time for higher education to heed those signals.

21 The writer concludes his argument by saying it's time for colleges (where people are particularly vulnerable) to pay attention to—and act on—the information they have, in order to remedy the situation.

Sample Essays

The following are examples of a high-scoring and low-scoring essay, based on the passage by Peter Krapp.

High-Scoring Essay

Peter Krapp builds a well-constructed argument designed to persuade readers that computer hacking is a danger that steals our most valuable possession—personal information—from our most vulnerable people—students. The article focuses on personal information about college students stolen from college computer networks. The writer builds his argument brick by brick. He starts by giving an example of student data stolen from a college by hackers in China, relating his topic to an event that really happened. The writer quickly establishes himself as an expert in the topic so readers can trust his information. Krapp asks and answers questions about the theft of data, goes into more depth about the type of information stolen from college networks, and then briefly touches on the laws, or the lack of laws, to protect students. He points out that data is stolen from students by not only foreign hackers, but also by American companies. The writer finishes with a call for colleges to protect student data, clearly stating his purpose.

The theft of 18,000 students' data from Pennsylvania State University's College of Engineering is a strong example to start the article. Naming the college and identifying the large number of students tells the reader immediately that a single incident affected many people. The location of the hackers shows that protecting the physical location of the data is useless, and it adds a bit of foreign intrigue.

The second paragraph is a single sentence, but accomplishes two important things. It gives the reader his credentials, proving that he is qualified to speak as an authority on the topic. It also provides structure for the next section by telling the reader that the writer will focus on two aspects of the news story.

Krapp reveals the first aspect to be discussed right away—Penn State knew that data was being stolen for six months before doing anything about it. To emphasize just how astonishing Penn State's behavior is, Krapp asks the same question that any reader might ask: Why? He asks the question in words that urge a fast response such as "urgent need" and "help the victims." He demonstrates that Penn State's response is weak by describing the response as "stated only."

The next paragraph starts with "Another conspicuous problem." This phrase presents the second aspect he wants to discuss, which is the media's lack of understanding about the difference between the major problem of stealing data and the minor problem of disabling a website for a short period of time. He helps readers to understand the difference by comparing stealing a car to causing only minor damage to the car.

Krapp follows the reader's natural thought process by asking the next question: If it's a problem, how do we fix it? He presents information in two ways, listing the type of information at risk and displaying bar charts that show the results of a presidential survey on the public's perception of data security.

The section title, "Data privacy concerns," informs readers that Krapp is addressing another concern, the theft of student data by US companies that want to mine data for profit. He gives two examples that are recognized and used by college students: Google and Pearson. He points out that students are particularly vulnerable to theft by the corporations that provide the apps and class materials that students must use for school. The school dictates which apps are to be used, so students "cannot opt out." He touches again on the law, but reveals that it doesn't protect college students. This information reinforces his arguments that college students are vulnerable to data theft. Presenting the facts this way says that college students are not only vulnerable, they are betrayed by the universities, US companies, and laws that should protect them.

The argument Krapp has built leads to a solid conclusion that Krapp states in a single, final sentence that is brief but summarizes the conclusion readers should draw. The brevity of the statement ensures that readers will get the point of the article and remember it in the future. The information that Krapp presents in examples, lists, survey results and bar charts provides a solid foundation for the conclusion that becomes obvious to any reader. Protect student data.

Low-Scoring Essay

Peter Krapp tries to persuade us that students should be allowed to opt out of giving their data to colleges and companies. This would protect them from having their full name, address, phone number, credit and debit card information, workplace information, date of birth, personal interests and of course academic performance and grade information stolen by people like Chinese hackers and companies like Google and Pearson.

Peter Krapp persuades us by giving lots of examples of data being stolen, like Pennsylvania State University's College of Engineering, Target, Home Depot, Google, and Pearson. One of the examples includes a chart that shows how much 24,092 individuals trusted various institutions to keep their data safe. Most of them didn't think their data was safe.

All of this information, charts, and examples that Peter Krapp included in his essay is very convincing. I think we should pass some laws like Peter Krapp suggested. The laws would keep American companies from stealing our data and punish hackers from other countries who steal our data.

All college students should try to opt out of giving away all of their private information because we know the colleges won't protect it. The colleges actually tell students to use apps that they know companies steal data from. This makes college students more vulnerable than anyone else to losing their data.

If companies are going to use the data they take from students, they should pay the students for the data. Then, students might not mind so much if companies take their data because the students would make money from it and college is very expensive.

When I go to college, I will opt out of giving my data to colleges and companies. My information is important to me and I don't want it stolen from me.

COMPUTING YOUR SCORES

Now that you've completed this diagnostic test, it's time to compute your scores. Simply follow the instructions on the following pages, and use the conversion tables provided to calculate your scores. The formulas provided will give you as close an approximation as possible of how you might score on the actual SAT® exam.

TO DETERMINE YOUR PRACTICE TEST SCORES

1. After you go through each of the test sections (Reading, Writing and Language, Math—No Calculator, and Math—Calculator) and determine which questions you answered correctly, be sure to enter the number of correct answers in the box below the answer key for each of the sections.

2. Your total score on the practice test is the sum of your Evidence-Based Reading and Writing Section score and your Math Section score. To get your total score, convert the raw score—the number of questions you answered correctly in a particular section—into the "scaled score" for that section, and then calculate the total score. It sounds a little confusing, but we'll take you through the steps.

TO CALCULATE YOUR EVIDENCE-BASED READING AND WRITING SECTION SCORE

Your Evidence-Based Reading and Writing Section score is on a scale of 200–800. First determine your Reading Test score, and then determine your score on the Writing and Language Test.

1. Count the number of correct answers you got on the **Section 1: Reading Test.** Remember that there is no penalty for wrong answers. **The number of correct answers is your raw score.**

2. Go to **Raw Score Conversion Table 1: Section and Test Scores** on page 125. Look in the "Raw Score" column for your raw score, and match it to the number in the "Reading Test Score" column.

3. Do the same with **Section 2: Writing and Language Test** to determine that score.

4. Add your Reading Test score to your Writing and Language Test score.

5. Multiply that number by 10. This is your Evidence-Based Reading and Writing Section score.

TO CALCULATE YOUR MATH SECTION SCORE

Your Math score is also on a scale of 200–800.

1. Count the number of correct answers you got on the **Section 3: Math Test—No Calculator** and the **Section 4: Math Test—Calculator**. Again, there is no penalty for wrong answers. **The number of correct answers is your raw score.**

2. Add the number of correct answers on the Section 3: Math Test—No Calculator and the Section 4: Math Test—Calculator.

3. Use the **Raw Score Conversion Table 1: Section and Test Scores** on page 125 and convert your raw score into your Math Section score.

TO OBTAIN YOUR TOTAL SCORE

Add your score on the Evidence-Based Reading and Writing Section to the Math Section score. This is your total score on this SAT® Practice Test, on a scale of 400–1600.

SUBSCORES PROVIDE ADDITIONAL INFORMATION

Subscores offer you greater details about your strengths in certain areas within literacy and math. The subscores are reported on a scale of 1–15 and include Heart of Algebra, Problem Solving and Data Analysis, Passport to Advanced Math, Expression of Ideas, Standard English Conventions, Words in Context, and Command of Evidence.

Heart of Algebra

The **Heart of Algebra subscore** is based on questions from the **Math Test** that focus on linear equations and inequalities.

- Add up your total correct answers from these questions:
    ◦ Math Test—No Calculator: Questions 1–3, 6, 9, 11, 17, 18
    ◦ Math Test—Calculator: Questions 5, 6, 10, 11, 14, 15, 19, 27, 29, 37, 38
- Your Raw Score = the total number of correct answers from all of these questions
- Use the **Raw Score Conversion Table 2: Subscores** on page 126 to determine your **Heart of Algebra** subscore.

Problem Solving and Data Analysis

The **Problem Solving and Data Analysis subscore** is based on questions from the **Math Test** that focus on quantitative reasoning, the interpretation and synthesis of data, and solving problems in rich and varied contexts.

- Add up your total correct answers from these questions:
    ◦ Math Test—No Calculator: None
    ◦ Math Test—Calculator: Questions 1–3, 7, 8, 16–18, 21, 22, 25, 28, 32–36
- Your Raw Score = the total number of correct answers from all of these questions
- Use the **Raw Score Conversion Table 2: Subscores** on page 126 to determine your **Problem Solving and Data Analysis** subscore.

Passport to Advanced Math

The **Passport to Advanced Math subscore** is based on questions from the **Math Test** that focus on topics central to your ability to progress to more advanced math, such as understanding the structure of expressions, reasoning with more complex equations, and interpreting and building functions.

- Add up your total correct answers from these questions:
    ◦ Math Test—No Calculator: Questions 7, 8, 10, 12–15, 19, 20
    ◦ Math Test—Calculator: Questions 9, 12, 13, 24, 26, 30, 31
- Your Raw Score = the total number of correct answers from all of these questions
- Use the **Raw Score Conversion Table 2: Subscores** on page 126 to determine your **Passport to Advanced Math** subscore.

Expression of Ideas

The **Expression of Ideas subscore** is based on questions from the **Writing and Language Test** that focus on topic development, organization, and rhetorically effective use of language.

- Add up your total correct answers from these questions in Section 2: Writing and Language Test:
    ◦ Questions 1, 4, 5, 7–9, 12, 13, 16, 17, 19, 20, 23, 26, 28, 29, 32–35, 39, 41–43
- Your Raw Score = the total number of correct answers from all of these questions
- Use the **Raw Score Conversion Table 2: Subscores** on page 126 to determine your **Expression of Ideas** subscore.

Standard English Conventions

The **Standard English Conventions subscore** is based on questions from the **Writing and Language Test** that focus on sentence structure, usage, and punctuation.

- Add up your total correct answers from these questions in Section 2: Writing and Language Test:
    ◦ Questions 2, 3, 6, 10, 11, 14, 15, 18, 21, 22, 24, 25, 27, 30, 31, 36–38, 40, 44
- Your Raw Score = the total number of correct answers from all of these questions
- Use the **Raw Score Conversion Table 2: Subscores** on page 126 to determine your **Standard English Conventions** subscore.

Words in Context

The **Words in Context subscore** is based on questions from the **Reading Test** and the **Writing and Language Test** that address word/phrase meaning in context and rhetorical word choice.

- Add up your total correct answers from these questions in Sections 1 and 2:
  - Reading Test: Questions 1, 5, 12, 16, 27, 30, 41, 42, 51, 52
  - Writing and Language Test: Questions 5, 8, 12, 17, 28, 32, 35, 43
- Your Raw Score = the total number of correct answers from all of these questions
- Use the **Raw Score Conversion Table 2: Subscores** on page 126 to determine your **Words in Context** subscore.

Command of Evidence

The **Command of Evidence subscore** is based on questions from the **Reading Test** and the **Writing and Language** Test that ask you to interpret and use evidence found in a wide range of passages and informational graphics, such as graphs, tables, and charts.

- Add up your total correct answers from these questions in Sections 1 and 2:
  - Reading Test: Questions 6, 9, 14, 19, 28, 32, 36, 38, 43, 44
  - Writing and Language Test: Questions 1, 4, 13, 16, 29, 33, 34, 42
- Your Raw Score = the total number of correct answers from all of these questions
- Use the **Raw Score Conversion Table 2: Subscores** on page 126 to determine your **Command of Evidence** subscore.

CROSS-TEST SCORES

The SAT® exam also reports two cross-test scores: Analysis in History/Social Studies and Analysis in Science. These scores are based on questions in the Reading Test, Writing and Language Test, and both Math Tests that ask you to think analytically about texts and questions in these subject areas. Cross-test scores are reported on a scale of 10–40.

Analysis in History/Social Studies

- Add up your total correct answers from these questions:
  - Reading Test: Questions 11–21, 43–52
  - Writing and Language Test: Questions 12, 13, 16, 17, 19, 20
  - Math Test—No Calculator: Question 14
  - Math Test—Calculator: Questions 11, 16, 17, 25, 29, 34, 35
- Your Raw Score = the total number of correct answers from all of these questions
- Use the **Raw Score Conversion Table 3: Cross-Test Scores** on page 127 to determine your **Analysis in History/Social Studies** cross-test score.

Analysis in Science

- Add up your total correct answers from these sections:
- Reading Test: Questions 1–10, 22–32
- Writing and Language Test: Questions 23, 26, 28, 29, 32, 33
  - Math Test—No Calculator: Questions 2, 13
  - Math Test—Calculator: Questions 4, 5, 8, 22, 26, 36
- Your Raw Score = the total number of correct answers from all of these questions
- Use the **Raw Score Conversion Table 3: Cross-Test Scores** on page 127 to determine your **Analysis in Science** cross-test score.

Raw Score Conversion Table 1: Section and Test Scores

Raw Score	Math Section Score	Reading Test Score	Writing and Language Test Score	Raw Score	Math Section Score	Reading Test Score	Writing and Language Test Score	Raw Score	Math Section Score	Reading Test Score	Writing and Language Test Score
0	200	10	10	20	450	22	23	40	610	33	36
1	200	10	10	21	460	23	23	41	620	33	37
2	210	10	10	22	470	23	24	42	630	34	38
3	230	11	10	23	480	24	25	43	640	35	39
4	240	12	11	24	480	24	25	44	650	35	40
5	260	13	12	25	490	25	26	45	660	36	
6	280	14	13	26	500	25	26	46	670	37	
7	290	15	13	27	510	26	27	47	670	37	
8	310	15	14	28	520	26	28	48	680	38	
9	320	16	15	29	520	27	28	49	690	38	
10	330	17	16	30	530	28	29	50	700	39	
11	340	17	16	31	540	28	30	51	710	40	
12	360	18	17	32	550	29	30	52	730	40	
13	370	19	18	33	560	29	31	53	740		
14	380	19	19	34	560	30	32	54	750		
15	390	20	19	35	570	30	32	55	760		
16	410	20	20	36	580	31	33	56	780		
17	420	21	21	37	590	31	34	57	790		
18	430	21	21	38	600	32	34	58	800		
19	440	22	22	39	600	32	35				

Conversion Equation 1 Section and Test Scores

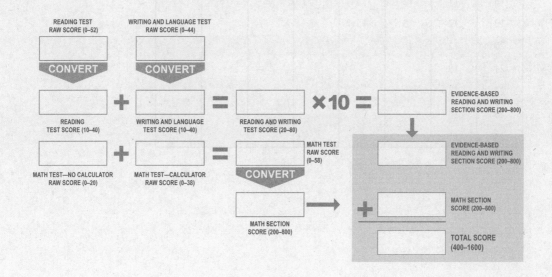

RAW SCORE CONVERSION TABLE 2: SUBSCORES

Raw Score (# of correct answers)	Expression of Ideas	Standard English Conventions	Heart of Algebra	Problem Solving and Data Analysis	Passport to Advanced Math	Words in Context	Command of Evidence
0	1	1	1	1	1	1	1
1	1	1	1	1	3	1	1
2	1	1	2	2	5	2	2
3	2	2	3	3	6	3	3
4	3	2	4	4	7	4	4
5	4	3	5	5	8	5	5
6	5	4	6	6	9	6	6
7	6	5	6	7	10	6	7
8	6	6	7	8	11	7	8
9	7	6	8	8	11	8	8
10	7	7	8	9	12	8	9
11	8	7	9	10	12	9	10
12	8	8	9	10	13	9	10
13	9	8	9	11	13	10	11
14	9	9	10	12	14	11	12
15	10	10	10	13	14	12	13
16	10	10	11	14	15	13	14
17	11	11	12	15		14	15
18	11	12	13			15	15
19	12	13	15				
20	12	15					
21	13						
22	14						
23	14						
24	15						

CONVERSION EQUATION 2 SUBSCORES

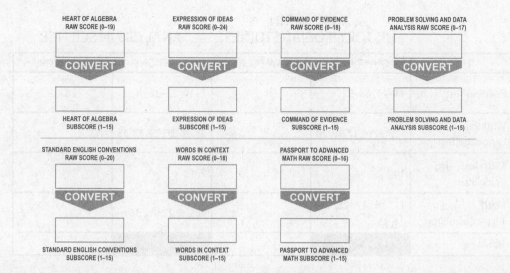

HEART OF ALGEBRA RAW SCORE (0–19)	EXPRESSION OF IDEAS RAW SCORE (0–24)	COMMAND OF EVIDENCE RAW SCORE (0–18)	PROBLEM SOLVING AND DATA ANALYSIS RAW SCORE (0–17)
CONVERT	CONVERT	CONVERT	CONVERT
HEART OF ALGEBRA SUBSCORE (1–15)	EXPRESSION OF IDEAS SUBSCORE (1–15)	COMMAND OF EVIDENCE SUBSCORE (1–15)	PROBLEM SOLVING AND DATA ANALYSIS SUBSCORE (1–15)

STANDARD ENGLISH CONVENTIONS RAW SCORE (0–20)	WORDS IN CONTEXT RAW SCORE (0–18)	PASSPORT TO ADVANCED MATH RAW SCORE (0–16)
CONVERT	CONVERT	CONVERT
STANDARD ENGLISH CONVENTIONS SUBSCORE (1–15)	WORDS IN CONTEXT SUBSCORE (1–15)	PASSPORT TO ADVANCED MATH SUBSCORE (1–15)

RAW SCORE CONVERSION TABLE 3: CROSS-TEST SCORES

Raw Score (# of correct answers)	Analysis in History/Social Studies Cross-Test Score	Analysis in Science Cross-Test Score
0	10	10
1	10	11
2	11	12
3	12	13
4	14	14
5	15	15
6	16	16
7	17	17
8	18	18
9	20	19
10	21	20
11	22	20
12	23	21
13	24	22
14	25	23
15	26	24
16	27	24
17	28	25

Raw Score (# of correct answers)	Analysis in History/Social Studies Cross-Test Score	Analysis in Science Cross-Test Score
18	28	26
19	29	27
20	30	27
21	30	28
22	31	29
23	32	30
24	32	30
25	33	31
26	34	32
27	35	33
28	35	33
29	36	34
30	37	35
31	38	36
32	38	37
33	39	38
34	40	39
35	40	40

CONVERSION EQUATION 3: CROSS-TEST SCORES

TEST	ANALYSIS IN HISTORY/SOCIAL STUDIES QUESTIONS	RAW SCORE	ANALYSIS IN SCIENCE QUESTIONS	RAW SCORE
Reading Test	11–21, 43–52		1–10, 22–32	
Writing and Language Test	12, 13, 16, 17, 19, 20		25, 26, 28, 29, 32, 33	
Math Test—No Calculator	14		2, 13	
Math Test—Calculator	11, 16, 17, 25, 29, 34, 35		4, 5, 8, 22, 26, 36	
TOTAL				

ANALYSIS IN HISTORY/
SOCIAL STUDIES
RAW SCORE (0–35)

CONVERT

ANALYSIS IN HISTORY/
SOCIAL STUDIES
CROSS-TEST SCORE (10–40)

ANALYSIS IN SCIENCE
RAW SCORE (0–35)

CONVERT

ANALYSIS IN SCIENCE
CROSS-TEST SCORE (10–40)

PART III: READING STRATEGIES FOR THE SAT® EXAM

Chapter 3: Reading Test Strategies

CHAPTER 3:
READING TEST STRATEGIES

OVERVIEW

- A Closer Look at the Reading Test
- Basic Steps for Answering Reading Questions
- Tips for Taking the Reading Test
- Strategies for Answering Specific Question Types
- Exercise: Reading Test
- Summing It Up

A CLOSER LOOK AT THE READING TEST

The SAT® Reading Test is focused on demonstrating comprehension and reasoning skills through responses to a variety of reading passages. The passages are chosen to reflect the complexity and reading levels appropriate to college and career readiness. The questions will require you to analyze the text and use textual evidence to assess meaning and to support ideas. The emphasis is on using the text to support your answers and on understanding the overall concepts and how they are developed through the course of the passage.

Passage topics are drawn from US and world literature, historical and social science documents, and scientific writing. There will be four single passages and one paired passage, and a total of 52 questions. The single passage lengths are between 500–750 words; the paired passage divides the 500–750-word length between the two passages.

The reading comprehension questions are designed to assess how well you read and understand information. The questions don't test the specifics you have learned in your course work. They are based solely on explicit and implicit information contained in the passage. At least one passage will be accompanied by an informational graphic from which one or more questions will be drawn. These questions require you to analyze the data presented in such formats as tables, graphs, and charts.

> **NOTE:** Reading questions are not arranged in order of difficulty. The questions for each passage will generally begin with broader questions about the overall ideas in the text and will then focus on specific portions of the passage.

131

Chapter 3

Reading Test
Strategies

QUESTION FORMAT

On the SAT® exam, each reading passage and question set starts with a direction line that looks like this:

> **Questions 1–10 are based on the following passage.**

OR

> **Questions 1–10 are based on the following passage[s] and supplementary material.**

OR

> **Questions 1–10 are based on the following two passages.**

The direction line is followed by a brief introduction to the text. The introduction describes the origin of the passage. Sometimes, the introduction will include additional background information.

The questions for each passage are in standard multiple-choice format with four answer choices each. Most often, these questions ask you to do one of the following:

- Determine central themes and ideas as presented in the passage.
- Determine the author's purpose or point of view of the text.
- Cite textual evidence to support inferences, conclusions, or arguments.
- Cite evidence to illustrate or support interpretations of meaning, mood, or tone of the passage.
- Analyze words and phrases in the context of the passage.
- Analyze information in an accompanying table, graph, chart, etc.

Chapter 3

Reading Test Strategies

BASIC STEPS FOR ANSWERING READING QUESTIONS

To answer the reading questions, follow these five steps:

1. Read the introduction.
2. Read the questions.
3. Read the passage with the questions in mind.
4. Answer the questions.
5. For any question you're not sure of, eliminate obviously wrong answers and take your best guess. Answer all the questions.

Let's look at the five steps in more detail.

1. You don't want to blow past the introductory paragraph because it can be very helpful to you. It might provide some important background information about the passage, or it might set the stage so you know what you're reading about.

2. Read the questions so you know what to look for in the passage. For example, if there's a question about the theme, consider that as you read. If there's a question that references a particular word or phrase, or perhaps a quotation in the text, look for it as you read the passage.

3. Now read the passage as quickly as you can without getting lost. Don't fret over details; focus on the larger ideas and try to follow the sequence, argument, or plot.

4. Answer the questions that are easiest for you. Then tackle the others in order, referring to the text to find and confirm answers as time permits.

5. Eliminate answer choices that you know are incorrect and guess at the remaining choices. Remember, there is no penalty for incorrect answers, so be sure not to leave any answer circles blank.

Now that you're familiar with how to approach reading passages and questions, let's try a few. Note that in the SAT® Exam and all of the practice tests in this book, the reading passages will appear in two columns. For instructional purposes, we have placed the passages full page in this chapter.

NOTE: Never skip the introduction, as it is likely to contain some important information about both the passage and the types of questions that accompany it. The introduction will identify the type of passage being presented, the source or author of the passage, the era in which the passage was written, or the event that the passage describes. All of this information will help you focus your reading and find the correct answers to the questions.

SAMPLE READING PASSAGE 1

Questions 1–4 are based on the following passage.

José Martí was a Cuban teacher, organizer, writer, and poet. The lyrics to the popular folk song "Guantanamera" were adapted from one of Martí's poems. Although Cuban by birth, he is considered one of the most influential writers in all of Latin America. He died in the battle for Cuba's independence from Spain, a cause to which he had devoted much of his life.

The following excerpt comes from an article by Martí that was published in El Partido Liberal *(Mexico City), March 5, 1892.*

Our America

The prideful villager thinks his hometown contains the whole world, and as long as he can stay on as mayor or humiliate the rival who stole his sweetheart or watch his nest egg accumulating in its strongbox he believes the universe to be in good order, unaware of the giants in seven-league boots who can crush him underfoot or the battling comets
Line in the heavens that go through the air devouring the sleeping worlds. … It is the hour of reckoning and of marching in
5 unison, and we must move in lines as compact as the veins of silver that lie at the roots of the Andes. …

Our youth go out into the world wearing Yankee- or French-colored glasses and aspire to rule by guesswork a country they do not know. … To know is to solve. To know the country and govern it in accordance with that knowledge is the only way of freeing it from tyranny. The European university must yield to the American university. The history of America from the Incas to the present must be taught in its smallest detail, even if the Greek Archons go untaught. Our
10 own Greece is preferable to the Greece that is not ours; we need it more. Statesmen who arise from the nation must replace statesmen who are alien to it. …

What a vision we were: the chest of an athlete, the hands of a dandy, and the forehead of a child. We were a whole fancy dress ball, in English trousers, a Parisian waistcoat, a North American overcoat, and a Spanish bullfighter's hat. The Indian circled about us, mute, and went to the mountaintop to christen his children. The black, pursued from afar,
15 alone and unknown, sang his heart's music in the night, between waves and wild beasts. The campesinos, the men of the land, the creators, rose up in blind indignation against the disdainful city, their own creation. We wore epaulets and judge's robes, in countries that came into the world wearing rope sandals and Indian headbands. The wise thing would have been to pair, with charitable hearts and the audacity of our founders, the Indian headband and the judicial robe, to undam the Indian, make a place for the able black, and tailor liberty to the bodies of those who rose up and
20 triumphed in its name. … No Yankee or European book could furnish the key to the Hispanoamerican enigma. So the people tried hatred instead, and our countries amounted to less and less each year. Weary of useless hatred … we are beginning, almost unknowingly, to try love. The nations arise and salute one another. "What are we like?" they ask, and

begin telling each other what they are like. … The young men of America are rolling up their sleeves and plunging their hands into the dough, and making it rise with the leavening of their sweat. They understand that there is too much
25 imitation, and that salvation lies in creating. Create is this generation's password. Make wine from plantains; it may be sour, but it is our wine! …

Anyone who promotes and disseminates opposition or hatred among races is committing a sin against humanity. … To think is to serve. We must not, out of a villager's antipathy, impute some lethal congenital wickedness to the continent's light-skinned nation simply because it does not speak our language or share our view of what home life should be or
30 resemble us in its political failings, which are different from ours, or because it does not think highly of quick-tempered, swarthy men or look with charity, from its still uncertain eminence, upon those less favored by history who, in heroic stages, are climbing the road that republics travel. But neither should we seek to conceal the obvious facts of the problem, which can, for the peace of the centuries, be resolved by timely study and the urgent, wordless union of the continental soul. For the unanimous hymn is already ringing forth, and the present generation is bearing industrious America along
35 the road sanctioned by our sublime forefathers. From the Rio Bravo to the Straits of Magellan, the Great Cemi,* seated on a condor's back, has scattered the seeds of the new America across the romantic nations of the continent and the suffering islands of the sea!

*Cemi is a deity or ancestral spirit of the Taíno people—one of the indigenous groups of the Caribbean.

1. What is the most likely reason Martí wrote this article?

    A. To appeal to fellow Latin Americans to be more like the Europeans

    B. To gain support from fellow Latin Americans to join in a fight against European invaders

    C. To rally support for himself as a leader of a revolution to free his country from tyranny

    D. To encourage fellow Latin Americans to educate themselves about their own mixed heritage

Review the introduction and note that Martí was a teacher, writer, and organizer and that he spent a good part of his life fighting for Cuban independence. You can infer from that information that he would try to persuade people to educate themselves. Martí talks about how little his fellow countrymen know of their own heritage and says that they cannot expect to govern themselves unless they understand their own heritage (lines 6–8). Choice D pinpoints one rationale Martí gives for education. Overall, the excerpt does not address revolution, nor does Martí present himself as revolutionary. He appeals to pride in one's heritage. These ideas are connected, because Martí believes that his fellow Latin Americans can free themselves through education (lines 7–8: "To know the country and govern it in accordance with that knowledge is the only way of freeing it from tyranny."). **The correct answer is D.**

2. As used in line 12, "vision" refers to

    A. how others perceive the peoples of Latin America.

    B. a picture of a unified culture.

    C. Martí's ideals about freedom.

    D. the opportunity to create a new beginning.

When a question refers to a specific part of the text, quickly reread the line(s) and the surrounding text. In paragraph 3, Martí offers a detailed, mocking description of the disparate parts blended to compose the peoples of Latin America. The picture he paints is of a person comprising various elements of other cultures—none his or her own. This, he says, is how Europeans saw the people of Latin America. The vision is the image others have of them and how it is misunderstood and even hated by others. **The correct answer is A.**

3. Which statement represents Martí's attitude toward education?

    A. Universal education is of the utmost importance.

    B. Everyone should learn about Latin American history.

    C. Education is necessary for new leadership.

    D. Education should include the study of Greek democracy as a model for freedom.

This question is asking for an overview, so you need to think about the points Martí makes and his overall message. You can eliminate choices A and B because they are general statements that anyone could make—they are not ideas that are represented in the passage (though they are related). Choice D is an incorrect interpretation of the text. Choice C is the best answer because Martí says that education is important for new leaders, and these leaders must be well-versed in the history of Latin America. People who are educated about their own country and heritage will rise as leaders and take over for "statesmen who are alien to it" (line 11). **The correct answer is C.**

4. Which of the following best describes of the overall tone of the article?

    A. Passionate and resolute

    B. Angry and bitter

    C. Scolding and arrogant

    D. Inflammatory and rebellious

This type of question also requires you to think about the point of view and presentation, which determine the tone. Martí tries to persuade his readers, advising them to wake up to threats from those who don't understand them or hate them (lines 20–21: "No Yankee or European book could furnish the key to the Hispanoamerican enigma. So the people tried hatred instead, and our countries amounted to less and less each year."). His passion comes through in the use of flowery and emotional language: "the hour of reckoning and of marching in unison" (lines 4–5); similes: "move in lines as compact as the veins of silver" (line 5); and metaphors: "sang his heart's music in the night, between waves and wild beasts" (line 15). He expresses a resolve, not anger or bitterness: "Make wine from plantains; it may be sour, but it is our wine!" (lines 25–26). Although Martí admonishes his fellow countrymen for being naïve and for ignoring dangers (line 3): they are "unaware of the giants in seven-league boots who can crush him underfoot"), he does not take the position of preacher. Rather, he speaks as one of the people (lines 4–5: "It is the hour of reckoning and of marching in unison, and we must move in lines as compact as the veins of silver that lie at the roots of the Andes."). Martí does not use inflammatory language; nor does he call for rebellion (choice D). Rather, he tries to persuade his fellow Latin Americans to unite in spite of their differences and to defend their lands from foreigners who do not understand them. **The correct answer is A.**

SAMPLE READING PASSAGE 2

Questions 1–4 are based on the following two passages.

The following passages discuss theories of how culture and language spread across Europe and Central Asia to form modern European and Asian peoples. Two teams of scientists—one based at the University of Copenhagen and one at the University of Adelaide—presented studies about the DNA of ancient Europeans, based on 170 skeletons found in countries from Spain to Russia.

Passage 1 is excerpted from "When modern Eurasia was born," originally published by the University of Copenhagen on June 10, 2015, by the Center for GeoGenetics and the Natural History Museum of Denmark.

When modern Eurasia was born

With this new investigation, the researchers confirm that the changes came about as a result of migrations. The researchers think that this is interesting also because later developments in the Bronze Age are a continuation of this new social perception. Things add up because the migrations can also explain the origin of the northern European language *Line* families. Both language and genetics have been with us all the way up to the present. Kristian Kristiansen [professor of
5 archaeology at the University of Gothenburg, Sweden] even thinks that it was crucial that events happened during these few centuries, as crucial as the colonization of the Americas.

One of the main findings from the study is how these migrations resulted in huge changes to the European gene-pool, in particular conferring a large degree of admixture on the present populations. Genetically speaking, ancient Europeans from the time post these migrations are much more similar to modern Europeans than those prior to the Bronze Age.

Mobile warrior people

10 The re-writing of the genetic map began in the early Bronze Age, about 5,000 years ago. From the steppes in the Caucasus, the Yamnaya Culture migrated principally westward into North and Central Europe, and to a lesser degree, into western Siberia. Yamnaya was characterized by a new system of family and property. In northern Europe the Yamnaya mixed with the Stone Age people who inhabited this region and along the way established the Corded Ware Culture, which genetically speaking resembles present-day Europeans living north of the Alps today.

15 Later, about 4,000 years ago, the Sintashta Culture evolved in the Caucasus. This culture's sophisticated new weapons and chariots were rapidly expanding across Europe. The area east of the Urals and far into Central Asia was colonized around 3,800 years ago by the Andronovo Culture. The researchers' investigation shows that this culture had a European DNA background.

During the last part of the Bronze Age, and at the beginning of the Iron Age, East Asian peoples arrived in Central Asia.
20 Here it is not genetic admixture we see, but rather a replacement of genes. The European genes in the area disappear.

A new scale

These new results derive from DNA analyses of skeletons excavated across large areas of Europe and Central Asia, thus enabling these crucial glimpses into the dynamics of the Bronze Age. In addition to the population movement insights, the data also held other surprises. For example, contrary to the research team's expectations, the data revealed that lactose tolerance rose to high frequency in Europeans, in comparison to prior belief that it evolved earlier in time (5,000–7,000 years ago).

Passage 2 is excerpted from "European invasion: DNA reveals the origins of modern Europeans," published in March 2015, by Alan Cooper, a director at the Australian Centre for Ancient DNA at the University of Adelaide, and Wolfgang Haak, a senior research fellow at the University of Adelaide.

European invasion: DNA reveals the origins of modern Europeans

25 What we have found is that, in addition to the original European hunter-gatherers and a heavy dose of Near Eastern farmers, we can now add a third major population: steppe pastoralists. These nomads appear to have "invaded" central Europe in a previously unknown wave during the early Bronze Age (about 4,500 years ago).

This event saw the introduction of two very significant new technologies to western Europe: domestic horses and the wheel. It also reveals the mysterious source for the Indo-European languages.

30   The genetic results have answered a number of contentious and long-standing questions in European history. The first big issue was whether the first farmers in Europe were hunter-gatherers who had learnt farming techniques from neighbours in southeast Europe, or did they instead come from the Near East, where farming was invented.

The genetic results are clear: farming was introduced widely across Europe in one or two rapid waves around 8,000 years ago by populations from the Near East—effectively the very first skilled migrants.

35   At first the original hunter-gatherer populations appear to have retreated to the fringes of Europe: to Britain, Scandinavia and Finland. But the genetics show that within a few thousand years they had returned, and significant amounts of hunter-gatherer genomic DNA was mixed in with the farmers 7,000 to 5,000 years ago across many parts of Europe.

Wheeling across Europe

But there was still a major outstanding mystery. Apart from these two groups, the genomic signals clearly showed that a third—previously unsuspected—large contribution had been made sometime before the Iron Age, around 2,000
40   years ago. But by whom?

We have finally been able to identify the mystery culprit, using a clever new system invented by our colleagues at Harvard University.

Instead of sequencing the entire genome from a very small number of well-preserved skeletons, we analysed 400,000 small genetic markers right across the genome. This made it possible to rapidly survey large numbers of skeletons from
45   all across Europe and Eurasia.

This process revealed the solution to the mystery. Our survey showed that skeletons of the Yamnaya culture from the Russian/Ukrainian grasslands north of the Black Sea, buried in large mounds known as kurgans, turned out to be the genetic source we were missing.

1.   How do the passages illustrate the contributions of DNA evidence to scientific inquiry?

   A.   Both provide examples of how DNA evidence enabled scientists to fill in gaps in their knowledge about human migrations.

   B.   Both describe how DNA analysis is used in scientific investigations.

   C.   The passages imply that DNA evidence can solve evolutionary questions.

   D.   The passages show how scientists solved the mysteries of DNA evidence.

Both passages illustrate how DNA has been used to answer questions about human migration patterns—questions that had been unresolved before the ability to use DNA as evidence for such studies (choice A). Neither passage gives details about the actual scientific methodology as both are focused on the results. Choices C and D are not correct interpretations of the passages. **The correct answer is A.**

2.   Which lines from the text support the idea that migration of human populations can be tracked through DNA testing?

   A.   Line 1: ("With this … migrations.")

   B.   Lines 8–9: ("Genetically … the Bronze Age.")

   C.   Lines 26–27: ("These nomads … 4,500 years ago.")

   D.   Lines 28–29: ("This event … Indo-European languages.")

This type of question requires that you find specific text to support an answer to a question. Although the concept given—that DNA testing was used to track population migrations—can be found in both passages, you only need to review the specific lines given in the answer choices to find the correct answer. Review only the options to find the one that that best supports the concept.

Choices C and D are not directly related to DNA evidence. Choice A confirms the idea of migration, but the text does not refer to DNA as the process that tracked the migration. Choice B refers to the genetic evidence, another term for DNA, which shows a similarity between ancient and modern Europeans. This evidence illustrates that scientists have been tracking the migration patterns. **The correct answer is B.**

3. What is the best description of the two passages?

    A. They show conflicting claims about the migrations.

    B. They describe different scientific methodologies.

    C. They provide supplementary information.

    D. They are written from a different perspective.

When reading paired passages, compare the passages as you read. This question asks you to compare the information. On your first reading, you probably noticed that they do not contradict one another (choice A); nor do they show different points of view (choice D). Both passages describe scientific studies and what scientists were able to learn from them, and both describe using DNA as the methodology, so you can eliminate choice B. But the second passage adds to the information in the first, making them supplements (choice C) to one another. **The correct answer is C.**

4. Based on information in the two passages, which of the following statements could be made about scientific inquiry?

    A. DNA evidence showed why many Europeans are lactose intolerant.

    B. Research can provide historical information.

    C. Evidence showed that the steppe pastoralists introduced horses and the wheel to Western Europe.

    D. Scientific investigation can provide evidence about human history not obtainable through other means.

Like the preceding question, this one asks you to compare the two passages, except this question looks at a topic not directly discussed in the passages but one that is implicit within it—the nature of scientific inquiry. So while choices A and C are true, neither one answers the question. Choice B is also true, but it doesn't address the nature of scientific investigations; it is simply a general statement that could apply to many texts. Choice D, however, states a fact about scientific inquiry that can be gleaned from the text: Both passages describe how scientists were able to use DNA data to answer questions they were unable to address before the use of DNA testing was available. **The correct answer is D.**

> **NOTE:** The paired passages have the same types of questions as the single passages. Some of the questions, however, may ask you to synthesize the information presented in the two passages by noting commonalities or comparing them in some way.

TIPS FOR TAKING THE READING TEST

You will be allotted 65 minutes to answer the 52 questions in the Reading section. That's a lot of questions in a short period of time. However, you can use some specific strategies and techniques to move through this portion of the SAT® exam efficiently. Check out these strategies for answering the reading questions quickly and accurately.

ANSWER ALL OF THE QUESTIONS BEFORE YOU START THE NEXT PASSAGE

There won't be time to go back to reread the passages and recheck your answers, so answer every question that you can about the passage. If you don't know an answer, skip the question and return to it when you have answered the other questions in the passage. Check your time, and if you think you can answer one of the skipped questions with a quick reread of part of the passage, go ahead. If not, or if you find it is taking too long, just give it your best guess and then move on. Remember, wrong answers are not held against you, so don't leave anything blank. Make sure you have answered every question for each passage before you move on to the next one.

Remember That the Questions Get More Specific

The question order often holds a key to understanding a passage. The SAT® Reading Test organizes the questions from broader questions about themes, purpose, point of view, and main ideas to more specific questions about explicit and implicit meaning, specific language, and structure of the text. Review the questions and take note of the information they ask for before reading the passage. As you read, underline or make notes to highlight text that may answer a question. Remember, answers will be in the text—either stated or implied.

Paired Passages

For the paired passages, look for the characteristics in each passage that tie them together. Skim the questions so you know what to look for and underline parts of the text that you may want to refer to. Try to form an overview of the two passages. Ask yourself why they are paired: what do they have in common; how are they different. In answering the questions for this type of passage, follow the same strategy: first answer all the questions you are fairly sure about. Then fill in the others based on best guesses, and, if time allows, review the evidence in the text to support your guess and answer the question accordingly. Make sure you have answered all the questions, and then go to the next passage.

Don't Panic When You Read an Unfamiliar Passage

The passages can be unfamiliar. In their attempt to be fair, the test-makers purposely choose a variety of passages. This helps make sure that each test-taker can demonstrate his or her reading and analysis skills. Remember, you're not being tested on your knowledge of the topic but on how well you do the following:

- Understand the author's assumptions, point of view, and theme
- Determine how the author supports the main ideas in the text
- Determine how the author uses specific language to create mood or tone
- Analyze the logical structure of the text
- Analyze overall meaning as well as specific words and phrases in context of the passage

Remember That Everything You Need to Know Is Right There in Front of You

The introductory paragraph and the passage have all the information you'll need to answer the questions. Even if the passage is about the price of beans in Bulgaria or the genetic makeup of a wombat, don't worry. It's all right there on the page.

Start with the Passages That Interest You

A point is a point. It doesn't matter if the point comes from answering correctly a question about a piece of fiction or a scientific experiment. If the style and subject matter appeal to you, you will probably go through a passage more quickly and answer the questions more easily. So before you start, quickly check the topics by skimming the titles and introductions. Start with the topics that are most familiar or most interesting. Then work your way down to the ones that you think will be hardest. Make a notation so you know which passages you have completed, and double check that your answers on the answer sheet correspond to the correct question numbers.

Highlight Important Information as You Read the Passages

It pays to be an active reader, and making quick notes is a part of this process. Let the questions guide your notations. Based on the questions, actively use your pencil to look for and bracket the text evidence that addresses questions about the big ideas, themes, and purpose as you read. Use other markings to indicate places in the text that may provide evidence for other questions, for example, a specific word or phrase referred to in a question. The questions will be related to the most important information in the passage. If you've highlighted those pieces of information, you'll be able to find them more easily to help answer the questions.

Don't Get Bogged Down in the Details

Remember, you don't have to understand every bit of information. You just have to find the information you need to answer the questions. Don't waste your time trying to analyze technical details or information not related to a question.

Don't Confuse a "True" Answer with a "Correct" Answer

The fact that an answer choice is true doesn't mean it's right. What does that mean? It means that a certain answer choice may be perfectly true—in fact, all of the answer choices may be true. But the *right* answer must be the correct answer to the question that's being asked. Only one of the answer choices will be correct and, therefore, the right choice. Read carefully—and don't be fooled!

STRATEGIES FOR ANSWERING SPECIFIC QUESTION TYPES

As you learned earlier, each reading question asks you to do one of the following:

- Determine central themes and ideas as presented in the passage.
- Determine the author's purpose or point of view of the text.
- Cite textual evidence to support inferences, conclusions, or arguments.
- Cite evidence to illustrate or support interpretation of meaning, mood, or tone of the passage.
- Analyze words and phrases in the context of the passage.
- Analyze quantitative information in an accompanying graphic, such as a table, graph, or chart.

The following tips present strategies for dealing with specific types of SAT® exam reading questions. You should use these strategies in combination with the basic steps for approaching the reading test. These strategies don't take the place of the basic steps but are extra tools to help you with certain types of questions. These tools work with both single and paired passages on any topic.

1. A broad question about the passage requires you to think about the passage as a whole. Keep this in mind as you read the passage, noting any references to an overview in the introduction and/or conclusion of the passage.

2. Before you begin, note the subject of the passage and the voice/perspective. These items can often be found in the introduction. Ask yourself if the author is providing information about a specific topic, making an argument for or against something, or telling a story. Whether fiction or nonfiction, ask yourself who is telling the story and why.

3. Look for evidence of inferences in the text and evaluate how they support the author's ideas.

4. As you read, notice the overall tone and mood of the passage and find textual evidence—specific words or phrases—that contribute to these elements.

5. If a question asks about a specific word, read the surrounding text to verify the context in which the word is used.

6. Examine the graphic illustration specifically in response to the question associated with it. If it asks to apply the illustration to the text, read that portion of the text in conjunction with the graphic illustration.

To help you see how these tips work, read the passage in the exercise on the next page. Then read each tip and try to use it to help you answer each question before you read the answer explanation. Note, again, that on the real exam and in the practice tests in this book, reading passages will appear in two columns. For instructional purposes, the following passages appear full page.

140

Chapter 3

Reading Test Strategies

EXERCISE: READING TEST

30 Minutes—23 Questions

> **DIRECTIONS:** Each passage or pair of passages below is followed by a number of questions. After reading each passage or pair, choose the best answer to each question based on what is stated or implied in the passage or passages and in any accompanying graphics (such as a table or graph).

Questions 1–6 are based on the following passage.

*The passage below discusses how Alaska Native cultural practices and heritage are being preserved in the twenty-first century. (For the full article, please visit **www.nps.gov**.)*

Alaska Native cultural practices continue to be a central force in virtually all villages throughout Alaska. In order to maintain cultural knowledge and ensure its survival, Alaska Native people need to learn the best methods of recording and archiving music, dance, and oral history. Along with the expansion of Europeans and Americans into Alaska were
Line accompanying hardships for the indigenous people: epidemic diseases, strong Christian missionary activities, and western
5 educational policies such as English language-only rules. These resulted in decimated populations throughout the entire territory of Alaska, a decline in indigenous languages, and, in many cases, the abolishment of traditional religion and associated music and dance repertoires.

Native people are deeply spiritual people; historically, they had a rich ceremonial life that was profoundly expressed through music and dance—core means by which people communicate their identities and beliefs. With the introduction
10 of Christianity, traditional cultures, including aspects such as music and dance, were not viewed favorably by the missionaries. Sadly, most of the missionaries did not tolerate masked dancing and other forms of religious expressions. Dance, language, and ceremonial practices either had to be practiced in secret, or were lost.

In the 1960s, during the Native Solidarity Movement, as Alaska Native people became more politically active, their re-identification with their cultures, languages, music, and dance became a banner of their newfound political and social
15 strength. One of the major outcomes of that movement has been a renaissance in traditional music and dance practices, resulting in multiple dance festivals and younger people becoming actively involved in their village dance groups. …

The Fifth Annual Kingikmiut Dance Festival featured a large Russian dance group, as well as the Tikigaq Traditional Dancers of Point Hope and dance groups from Brevig Mission and other villages on the Seward Peninsula. Kingikmiut, or Wales, was once known as the dance capital of the Seward Peninsula. Captain Henry Trollope visited Wales in 1853–54
20 and wrote "… the place is sort of a capital in these parts and has four dancing houses, which is a very expressive manner of estimating the extent and population for a place." (Ray 1975) Because of its strategic location, Kingikmiut flourished. Before the 1900 and 1917 epidemics, it consisted of two related villages and consolidated into one village once the populations had been decimated by disease. After these terrible epidemics, western educators' English-only policies forced music, dance, and other expressions of traditional Native culture to go underground.

25 Repression of Native culture by western educators and missionaries was common all over Alaska and is a major reason why many Alaska Native languages are threatened today. In the first part of the twentieth century, traditional dance and music became associated with the old ways and were looked down upon. After the 1960s, a strong revitalization movement arose. Today there is a renaissance in traditional music and dance practices. In Wales and other Seward Peninsula communities, the younger people, who make up a large percentage of the population, have a great thirst for
30 learning to sing and dance their traditional songs.

1. Which of the following best reflects the main idea of the passage?

   A. There has been a recent surge in interest in Native cultures everywhere.

   B. Native Alaskans have always tried to preserve their history and culture.

   C. Western expansion into Alaska resulted in loss of native cultures.

   D. Native Alaskan traditions were revived in the 1960s.

2. What can you infer about the fact that a large collection of traditional dance masks once used by Alaska's Yup'ik people is now exhibited at the National Museum of Natural History at the Smithsonian Institution?

   A. The dance ceremonies in which the museum's masks were once used were likely religious ceremonies.

   B. The masks are more important as works of art than as items in traditional dances.

   C. The masks in the museum's exhibit were used in traditional Alaskan native dances during the 1960s revival.

   D. The museum intends the exhibition of masks to send a strong pro-tolerance message to Christian missionaries..

3. What was the relationship between Europeans and the health of Alaska's native people?

   A. Europeans brought newer and more effective medicines to Alaska's native people.

   B. Europeans actively sought to wipe out Alaska's native people with new diseases.

   C. Europeans received many medical tips from the Alaska's unusually healthy native people.

   D. Europeans caused Alaska's native people to fall fatally ill.

4. What evidence does the passage provide to suggest that Captain Henry Trollope helped introduce Kingikmuit to the rest of the world?

   A. Lines 19–20: ("Captain Henry…and wrote…")

   B. Lines 20–21: ("…the place is…for a place.")

   C. Lines 21–23: ("Because of its…by disease.")

   D. Lines 23–24: ("After these terrible…go underground.")

5. What conclusion can you infer from the passage?

   A. Traditional Alaskan culture thrived without obstacles after the 1960s.

   B. The Native Solidarity Movement's efforts were not completely effective.

   C. Music and dance are never involved in Christian ceremonies.

   D. Older Alaskan natives have no interest in Alaska's traditional culture.

6. As used in line 28, "renaissance" most nearly means

   A. repression.

   B. reconsideration.

   C. rebirth.

   D. reservation.

142

Chapter 3

Reading Test
Strategies

The following is an excerpt from "The Purloined Letter," a short story by Edgar Allan Poe. Poe is best known for writing poems and stories in the horror and mystery genre. However, he is also considered the inventor of detective fiction. The Mystery Writers of America call their awards for excellence in the genre "Edgars," in honor of Poe.

The Purloined Letter

… "Well, then; I have received personal information, from a very high quarter, that a certain document of the last importance, has been purloined from the royal apartments. The individual who purloined it is known; this beyond a doubt; he was seen to take it. It is known, also, that it still remains in his possession."

Line "How is this known?" asked Dupin.

5 "It is clearly inferred," replied the Prefect, "from the nature of the document, and from the non-appearance of certain results which would at once arise from its passing out of the robber's possession; that is to say, from his employing it as he must design in the end to employ it."

"Be a little more explicit," I said.

"Well, I may venture so far as to say that the paper gives its holder a certain power in a certain quarter where such

10 power is immensely valuable." The Prefect was fond of the cant of diplomacy.

"Still I do not quite understand," said Dupin.

"No? Well; the disclosure of the document to a third person, who shall be nameless, would bring in question the honor of a personage of most exalted station; and this fact gives the holder of the document an ascendancy over the illustrious personage whose honor and peace are so jeopardized."

15 "But this ascendancy," I interposed, "would depend upon the robber's knowledge of the loser's knowledge of the robber. Who would dare—"

"The thief," said G., "is the Minister D—, who dares all things, those unbecoming as well as those becoming a man. The method of the theft was not less ingenious than bold. The document in question—a letter, to be frank—had been received by the personage robbed while alone in the royal boudoir. During its perusal she was suddenly interrupted

20 by the entrance of the other exalted personage from whom especially it was her wish to conceal it. After a hurried and vain endeavor to thrust it in a drawer, she was forced to place it, open as it was, upon a table. The address, however, was uppermost, and, the contents thus unexposed, the letter escaped notice. At this juncture enters the Minister D—. His lynx eye immediately perceives the paper, recognises the handwriting of the address, observes the confusion of the personage addressed, and fathoms her secret. After some business transactions, hurried through in his ordinary manner, he produces

25 a letter somewhat similar to the one in question, opens it, pretends to read it, and then places it in close juxtaposition to the other. Again he converses, for some fifteen minutes, upon the public affairs. At length, in taking leave, he takes also from the table the letter to which he had no claim. Its rightful owner saw, but, of course, dared not call attention to the act, in the presence of the third personage who stood at her elbow. The minister decamped; leaving his own letter—one of no importance—upon the table." …

30 "You looked among D—'s papers, of course, and into the books of the library?"

"Certainly; we opened every package and parcel; we not only opened every book, but we turned over every leaf in each volume, not contenting ourselves with a mere shake, according to the fashion of some of our police officers. We also measured the thickness of every book-cover, with the most accurate ad measurement, and applied to each the most jealous scrutiny of the microscope. Had any of the bindings been recently meddled with, it would have been utterly

35 impossible that the fact should have escaped observation. Some five or six volumes, just from the hands of the binder, we carefully probed, longitudinally, with the needles."

"You explored the floors beneath the carpets?"

"Beyond doubt. We removed every carpet, and examined the boards with the microscope."

"And the paper on the walls?"

40 "Yes."

"You looked into the cellars?"

"We did."

"Then," I said, "you have been making a miscalculation, and the letter is not upon the premises, as you suppose."

"I fear you are right there," said the Prefect. "And now, Dupin, what would you advise me to do?"

45 "To make a thorough re-search of the premises."

"That is absolutely needless," replied G—. "I am not more sure that I breathe than I am that the letter is not at the Hotel."

7. Which of the following best describes the Prefect G?

    A. He delights in being obscure and frustrating his colleagues.

    B. He tends to talk a great deal about things about which he knows nothing.

    C. He is concerned with protecting other people's privacy and honor.

    D. He possesses investigative skills that are greater than those of anyone else.

8. According to Prefect G, where did the royal lady hide the letter?

    A. In plain sight

    B. Behind the wallpaper

    C. Beneath the floorboards

    D. At a hotel

9. What is the most likely reason that Prefect G measured each book cover in the library?

    A. To obey Dupin's command to measure each book cover

    B. To prove that the letter was not actually stolen

    C. To show his fellow investigators that he was very thorough

    D. To detect whether the letter was hidden in one of them

10. As used in line 13, "ascendency" most nearly means

    A. rise.

    B. advantage.

    C. joy.

    D. weakness.

11. Which of the following is a line that could be in the letter?

    A. It would be such an honor to have you in attendance at this surprise gala.

    B. You know how much I would like to be in your employ again.

    C. I'm so sorry that this is late notice, but can I meet with you and the prince next week?

    D. I beg of you to meet me on Monday when the prince is in Monaco.

144

Chapter 3

Reading Test
Strategies

12. Why didn't the royal lady stop Minister D from taking the letter?

    A. She did not see that Minister D was stealing the letter.

    B. She did not want the other person in the room to read the letter.

    C. She had written the letter for Minister D to read.

    D. She knew that the letter was not very important.

> **Questions 13–17 are based on the following passage and supplementary material.**

This passage is the introduction to a report from the Office of the Chief Technologist at the US space agency NASA, entitled "Emerging Space: The Evolving Landscape of the 21st Century American Spaceflight" (www.nasa.gov/sites/default/files/files/Emerging_Space_Report.pdf).

America stands today at the opening of a second Space Age. Innovative NASA programs and American entrepreneurs together are transforming the space industry. These initiatives—both at NASA and in the private sector—are expanding the nation's opportunities for exploration and for the economic development of the solar system.

Line
5   Today's space economy extends some 36,000 kilometers (22,369 miles) from the surface of the Earth and includes an array of evidence-based technologies—satellite communications, global positioning satellites, and imaging satellites—on which our economy depends. These technologies are now an integral part of our economy, and they would not exist if not for the over 50 years of research, development, and investment in the enabling technologies by NASA and other government agencies that seeded these efforts and allowed them to bloom. As we expand our activities in the solar system over the next decades, NASA programs and investments will provide the seed and soil that encourage economic
10 development increasingly farther from Earth. The first signs of this are already visible.

The next era of space exploration will see governments pushing technological development and the American private sector using these technologies as they expand their economic activities to new worlds. NASA's next objectives for exploration—visits to asteroids and Mars— are more complex than any previous space mission attempted. They will happen in the context of relatively smaller NASA budgets and an expanding commercial space economy. Teaming with
15 private-sector partners to develop keystone markets like low Earth orbit (LEO) transportation and technological capabilities like asteroid mining will help NASA achieve its mission goals, help the space economy evolve to embrace new ambitions, and provide large economic returns to the taxpayer through the stimulation and growth of new businesses and 21st-century American jobs.

Motivated by an intrinsic desire to explore space, successful American entrepreneurs have pledged and spent
20 hundreds of millions of dollars to develop technologies aimed at fundamentally improving space access. Since 2003, commercial human spaceflight has received $2.5 billion in private investment.[1] At the same time, a new generation of space enthusiasts are engaging directly though small-scale projects. Through cubesats, suborbital and orbital adventures, and citizen science opportunities, the United States is transitioning from a spacefaring nation to a nation of spacefarers.

In addition to executing its scientific and human spaceflight programs, NASA also has a legislated responsibility to
25 "encourage, to the maximum extent possible, the fullest commercial use of space." As part of fulfilling this responsibility, this report examines how NASA has collaborated with American private-sector individuals and companies investing in space exploration, collectively known as "emerging space." Today, more than fifty years after the creation of NASA, our goal is no longer just to reach a destination. Our goal is to develop the capabilities that will allow the American people to explore and expand our economic sphere into the solar system. Although when NASA was founded only a government
30 program could undertake a voyage from the Earth to the Moon, this may not be true in the future. By taking full advantage of the combined talents of government and the American private sector, our next journeys beyond Earth will come sooner and we will catalyze new industries and economic growth in the process.

---

1. 2013 Commercial Spaceflight Industry Indicators, Commercial Spaceflight Federation

NASA provides a number of resources for people willing to contribute as citizen scientists. All are available online, meaning all you need is access to the Internet. Software tools are also provided. More than 1.2 million people from 80 countries have participated in NASA's citizen science projects. This table captures just a few of the projects.

Project	Citizen Scientist Role	Number of Participants
Be a Martian	Tag rover images and map craters from satellite pictures	1,230,000
HiTranslate	Help translate NASA's HiRISE project captions into different languages	1,021 new in 2012
International Space Apps Challenge	Develop mobile applications, software, hardware, data visualization, and platforms to address current challenges relevant to space exploration and social need	2,083 from 17 countries in 2012
Lunar Impacts	Independent observers can monitor the rates and sizes of large meteoroids striking the far side of the moon	26 impact candidates
Rock Around the World	Help Mars scientists better understand the red planet by sending rocks to NASA for analysis	12,461 rocks received
Stardust at Home	Search for the first samples of solid matter from outside the solar system	30,649 from 2006 to 2012
Target Asteroids!	Observe asteroids, to help scientists refine orbits and determine the composition of near-Earth objects (NEOs) in support of the OSIRIS-Rex mission	104 registered users from 23 countries

13. As used in line 1, "Space Age" most nearly means

A. an era of space exploration and exploitation.

B. the year that space was first explored.

C. the time it takes to travel to outer space.

D. an advanced age in one's life.

14. What was NASA's first goal?

A. To expand the US economy

B. To visit asteroids and Mars

C. To provide commercial travel

D. To reach the moon

15. Which of the following is the best summary of the passage?

   A. NASA is ushering in a new chapter in the Space Age that will allow the commercialization of space.

   B. In the next decades, ordinary people will be able to travel in space.

   C. NASA is the US agency that is charged with developing space programs.

   D. The Second Space Age will expand the economy and increase complex technologies in space exploration.

Questions 16 and 17 refer to the table.

16. What is the most likely reason that the "Be a Martian" project has so many more participants than the other projects?

   A. More people are interested in exploring Mars than in other aspects of the program.

   B. Other projects require more sophisticated/complex technology skills.

   C. It is the only project that is designed for young people.

   D. The other projects all require more time as a volunteer.

17. What skills are needed to participate in the NASA projects as a citizen-scientist?

   A. The ability to identify different kinds of rocks

   B. The ability to use a telescope

   C. The ability to use software technology and the Internet

   D. The ability to locate and recognize the planets and other celestial bodies

---

Questions 18–23 are based on the following two passages.

The following passages are excerpted from narratives written by two explorers. Passage 1 is by Sir Earnest Shackleton from an account he wrote entitled: South! The Story of Shackleton's Last Expedition (1914–1917). Passage 2 is part of an account by Hiram Bingham III, from "The Discovery of Machu Picchu," first published in Harper's Monthly magazine in 1913.

PASSAGE 1

Some intangible feeling of uneasiness made me leave my tent about 11 p.m. that night and glance around the quiet camp. The stars between the snow-flurries showed that the floe had swung round and was end on to the swell, a position exposing it to sudden strains. I started to walk across the floe in order to warn the watchman to look carefully

Line for cracks, and as I was passing the men's tent the floe lifted on the crest of a swell and cracked right under my feet. The
5 men were in one of the dome-shaped tents, and it began to stretch apart as the ice opened. A muffled sound, suggestive of suffocation, came from beneath the stretching tent. I rushed forward, helped some emerging men from under the canvas, and called out, "Are you all right?"

"There are two in the water," somebody answered. The crack had widened to about four feet, and as I threw myself down at the edge, I saw a whitish object floating in the water. It was a sleeping-bag with a man inside. I was able to
10 grasp it, and with a heave lifted man and bag on to the floe. A few seconds later the ice-edges came together again with tremendous force. Fortunately, there had been but one man in the water, or the incident might have been a tragedy. The rescued bag contained Holness, who was wet down to the waist but otherwise unscathed. The crack was now opening again. The *James Caird* and my tent were on one side of the opening and the remaining two boats and the rest of the camp on the other side. With two or three men to help me I struck my tent; then all hands manned the painter and rushed
15 the *James Caird* across the opening crack. We held to the rope while, one by one, the men left on our side of the floe

jumped the channel or scrambled over by means of the boat. Finally I was left alone. The night had swallowed all the others and the rapid movement of the ice forced me to let go the painter. For a moment I felt that my piece of rocking floe was the loneliest place in the world. Peering into the darkness; I could just see the dark figures on the other floe.

PASSAGE 2

Nor was I in a great hurry to move. The water was cool, the wooden bench, covered with a woolen poncho, seemed
20 most comfortable, and the view was marvelous. On both sides tremendous precipices fell away to the white rapids of the Urubamba River below. In front was the solitary peak of Huay-na Picchu, seemingly inaccessible on all sides. Behind us were rocky heights and impassable cliffs. Down the face of one precipice the Indians had made a perilous path, which was their only means of egress in the wet season, when the bridge over which we had come would be washed away. Of the other precipice we had already had a taste. We were not surprised to hear the Indians say they only went away from
25 home about once a month.

Leaving the huts, we climbed still farther up the ridge. Around a slight promontory the character of the stone-faced andenes began to improve, and suddenly we found ourselves in the midst of a jungle-covered maze of small and large walls, the ruins of buildings made of blocks of white granite, most carefully cut and beautifully fitted together without cement. Surprise followed surprise until there came the realization that we were in the midst of as wonderful ruins as any
30 ever found in Peru. It seemed almost incredible that this city, only five days' journey from Cuzco, should have remained so long undescribed and comparatively unknown. Yet so far as I have been able to discover, there is no reference in the Spanish chronicles to Machu Picchu. It is possible that not even the conquistadors ever saw this wonderful place. From some rude scrawls on the stones of a temple we learned that it was visited in 1902 by one Lizarraga, a local muleteer. It must have been known long before that, because, as we said above, Wiener [an Austrian-French explorer], who was
35 in Ollantaytambo in the 70's, speaks of having heard of ruins at a place named "Matcho Picchu," which he did not find.

18. How do the two passages differ in their tone?

   A. Passage 1 has a tone of surprise, and Passage 2 has a tone of fear.

   B. Passage 1 has a threatening tone, and Passage 2 has an adventurous tone.

   C. Passage 1 exhibits a tone of danger, and Passage 2, a tone of awe.

   D. Passage 1 features a gloomy tone, and Passage 2, a festive tone.

19. What does the passage reveal about Hiram Bingham III?

   A. He tends to be overwhelmed by his experiences.

   B. He is a naturally mistrustful person.

   C. He has a cold and calculating attitude.

   D. He embraces and enjoys life.

20. Which of the following best describes a purpose common to both passages?

   A. To tell the world about the dangers of undeveloped places

   B. To tell the world about new and undiscovered places

   C. To persuade others to visit undeveloped places

   D. To persuade people to help develop the locales described

21. What is meant by "The night had swallowed all the others" (lines 16–17)?

   A. An animal swallowed some of the men.

   B. Some of the men had fallen asleep.

   C. Some of the men were impossible to see in the dark.

   D. Some of the men had returned home.

22. What idea in the text leads to the conclusion that Shackleton shared a special connection with his men?

   A. Shackleton was concerned with rescuing them from the water.

   B. Shackleton told the watchman to look for cracks in the floe.

   C. Shackleton sensed they were in trouble before he knew it.

   D. Shackleton asked them if they were all right.

23. Based on the two passages, what can be inferred about the nature of expeditions?

   A. They are often dangerous and can't be undertaken alone.

   B. They usually add to the knowledge about a place.

   C. They are good travel destinations for people who enjoy going to little-known places.

   D. They represent undiscovered parts of the world.

149

Chapter 3

Reading Test Strategies

1. C	6. C	11. D	16. B	20. B
2. A	7. C	12. B	17. C	21. C
3. D	8. A	13. A	18. C	22. C
4. B	9. D	14. D	19. D	23. B
5. B	10. B	15. D		

1. **The correct answer is C.** The first paragraph in the passage provides a summary. It explicitly states the reasons that the Native Alaskan culture was almost wiped out and what needs to be done to ensure that it is not lost forever. The rest of the passage supports the concepts introduced here.

2. **The correct answer is A.** The second paragraph of the passage indicates that Alaska's native people used masks in religious ceremonies, so choice A is a reasonable conclusion to draw. Choice B, however, makes a judgment regarding importance that the passage does not support. Since the passage provides no evidence that masks were once again used when politically active people revived traditional dances in the 1960s, there is no way to reach the conclusion in choice C. There can be a number of intentions behind the decision to create a particular exhibit, and no evidence in the passage supports the conclusion in choice D.

3. **The correct answer is D.** According to the first paragraph of the passage, Europeans brought epidemic diseases with them to Alaska, and this resulted in "decimated populations," which supports the conclusion in choice D. While it is conceivable that a new culture could bring both disease and medicine with it, there is no evidence in the passage that supports the conclusion in choice A. Choice B implies that the fact that Europeans brought epidemic diseases to Alaska was intentional, but there is no evidence in the passage that supports this conclusion. There is no evidence that supports the conclusion in choice C either.

4. **The correct answer is B.** The fact that Captain Henry Trollope's observations regarding the Kingikmuit people are quoted in lines 20–21 indicates that they were significant and likely helped introduce Kingikmuit culture to the rest of the world. Lines 19–20 (choice A) merely introduce Captain Henry Trollope without indicating anything about how he might have helped introduce Kingikmuit to the rest of the world. Choices C and D have nothing to do with Captain Henry Trollope.

5. **The correct answer is B.** While the Native Solidarity Movement helped spark a revival of traditional Alaskan culture in the 1960s, the final paragraph of the passage indicates that threats to Alaskan culture still exist today, so choice B is the best answer and choice A cannot be correct. While Christian missionaries clearly disapproved of music and dancing in Native Alaskan ceremonies, they may have had a different attitude regarding dance and music in Christian ceremonies, so there is no clear evidence to support the inference in choice C. While the final paragraph of the passage does specify the enthusiasm of younger Alaskan natives for traditional Alaskan culture, this does not really support the rather extreme conclusion in choice D.

6. **The correct answer is C.** The word *renaissance* is used in connection with the revitalization of traditional Alaskan music and dance, so choice C makes the most sense.

   Choice A is incorrect because it would convey the opposite of the author's intention. While choice B might make sense in this context, it does not fit the context as strongly as choice C does. Choice D simply does not make sense in this context.

7. **The correct answer is C.** Prefect G's refusal to name suspects, his tendency toward "diplomacy" and his refusal to dishonor the accused illustrate his concern to protect the privacy and honor of others. While he does speak in an obscure manner that frustrates his colleagues, Prefect G is not speaking in such a way because he enjoys it, so choice A is not the best answer. Prefect G does seem to know what he is saying; he just says it unclearly, so choice B is not the best answer either. While Prefect G does know certain things, Dupin could be right when he points out that Prefect G made a "miscalculation," so choice D may not be true.

8. **The correct answer is A.** Prefect G explains that the royal lady was forced to leave the letter open "upon a table" (line 21), which supports choice A. While Dupin asks if Prefect G looked behind the wallpaper (choice B), beneath the floorboards (choice C), and at the hotel (choice D), Prefect G says that he checked in all of these places and he could not find the letter in any of them.

9. **The correct answer is D.** According to line 33 of the passage, Prefect G measured the cover of each book in the library, and he did so while searching for the letter. This suggests that he thought the letter could have been hidden in one of the book covers. Dupin does not command Prefect G to measure each book cover, so choice A is incorrect. Measuring the book covers would not provide proof that the letter was not stolen, so choice B is incorrect. Prefect G was very thorough, but choice C does not accurately indicate his motivation for measuring each book cover.

10. **The correct answer is B.** In line 13, Prefect G uses *ascendency* to suggest the advantage the possessor of the letter would have over the person who is the subject of the letter. *Rise* (choice A) can be a synonym of *ascendency*, but it does not match how the word is used in this particular context. *Joy* (choice C) is not usually used as a synonym for *ascendency*, and *weakness* (choice D) has the opposite meaning of *ascendency*.

11. **The correct answer is D.** We know that the royal lady is being blackmailed. Therefore, the contents must reveal something she is hiding from the man in the room with her, most likely her husband. Choice D is the only one that contains information that is to be kept from the prince.

12. **The correct answer is B.** Her fear of a third person in the room knowing the contents of the letter prevented the royal lady from stopping Minister D's theft. Prefect G states that the royal lady saw Minister D take the letter (lines 27–28), so choice A is incorrect. The royal lady did not write the letter, so choice C is incorrect, and if the letter were not important, as choice D suggests, there would be no reason to investigate its theft.

13. **The correct answer is A.** "Space Age" is an idiom meaning "an era of space exploration and exploitation." Since one cannot do something first more than once, choice B does not make sense. Choice C is not an accurate definition of the idiom "Space Age," and choice D has nothing to do with the context of the idiom's use in the passage.

14. **The correct answer is D.** According to lines 27–28, NASA's first goal was "to reach a destination," and line 30 indicates that the destination was the moon. Choice A describes a goal of NASA today, not its very first goal. Choice B describes a goal of NASA beyond its first one, and choice C misinterprets the idea of reaching a destination.

15. **The correct answer is D.** This statement represents the best summary because it states the main idea by providing the two most important aspects of the commercialization of space exploration.

16. **The correct answer is B.** The table shows that the "Be a Martian" project involves tagging on the Internet, and the table caption explains that participants are provided with any needed software. According to the descriptions of the other projects, they all require some additional skill, for example, translating text or doing more complex searches.

17. **The correct answer is C.** Reading the descriptions, the skill required in all of the projects is how to use the Internet to conduct searches. Even for projects that involve language translation, a participant would have to access the Internet to get the text that needs to be translated.

18. **The correct answer is C.** The first line of Passage 1 sets the tone of danger (feeling of uneasiness) that continues after the crack in the ice. Although the men aren't killed, the path to the boat was nevertheless full of danger. Passage 2 begins with Bingham's observations that show his appreciation of the beauty of the place. He marvels at the Indians who make their way down the steep precipice on a regular basis (lines 22–23). As Bingham makes his way through the jungle and sees Machu Picchu for the first time, detailed descriptions show awe and surprise at the "wonderful ruins" (line 29).

19. **The correct answer is D.** In the second passage, Bingham speaks of how much he enjoys the sensations and sights during his exploration, which supports choice D and eliminates choice C. While he seems to be in a somewhat heightened state of enjoyment, choice A is much too extreme a conclusion. There is no evidence in the passage that Bingham is mistrustful (choice B).

20. **The correct answer is B.** Both passages record the experiences of men who are drawn to exploring places that most people don't ever see. Both use detailed descriptions of the physical terrain of remote places that are void of other people. There is no call inviting others to join them—just descriptions that inform.

21. The correct answer is C. Choice C is an accurate interpretation of line 16. Evidence in the passage does not support the interpretations in choices A, B, or D.

22. The correct answer is C. Passage 1 opens with a line indicating that Shackleton had an "intangible feeling" that something was wrong, and his feeling was proven correct when it turned out some of his men were in trouble. One can be concerned with someone without sharing a special connection with that person, so choices A, B, and D are not the best answers.

23. The correct answer is B. Both passages describe places about which little was known at the time. Both men undertook the trip and wrote detailed accounts of their experiences so that others could learn about them and perhaps follow their footsteps to gain even more knowledge.

SUMMING IT UP

- In the Reading Test section, there are four single passages, one paired passage, and a total of 52 questions. You will have 65 minutes to complete this section.

- You do not need information beyond what is provided by the passage to answer any question.

- Complete familiar and interesting passages first.

- Read the introduction; it often provides background that will help form an overview of the passage.

- Read the questions and their answer choices.

- Read the passage as quickly as possible, marking the text to note information that may be relevant to the questions. Let the questions drive your focus and the notations you make.

- Don't get bogged down in details. Most questions will not be focused on details unless they are used to support a major idea or theme.

- Go back into the passage to find answers as needed.

- Reading Test questions are presented in order from those related to the central ideas and overall themes to those involving structural and language-related concepts. Approach each passage by first looking for the big ideas and then the more structural concepts.

- For any question you're not sure of, eliminate obviously wrong answers and take your best guess. Wrong answers are not counted against you, so answer every question.

- Answer every question for a passage before starting the next passage.

Access more practice questions, helpful lessons, valuable tips, and expert strategies for the following reading topics in *Peterson's Online Course for the SAT® Exam*:

- Advanced Reading Strategies

- Advanced Question Types

- Analyzing Arguments

- Analyzing Structure

- Common Question Types

- Hard Prose Passages

- Hard Science Passages

- Other Reading Questions

- Pacing in Evidence-Based Reading

- Paired Passages

- Passage Technique

- Point of View

- Quantitative Information

- Reading Actively

- Understanding Difficult Text

- Wrong Answer Types

To purchase and access the course, go to **www.petersons.com/testprep/sat.**

PART IV: WRITING STRATEGIES FOR THE SAT® EXAM

Chapter 4: Writing and Language Test Strategies

Chapter 5: Standard English Conventions

CHAPTER 4: WRITING AND LANGUAGE TEST STRATEGIES

OVERVIEW

- A Closer Look at the Writing and Language Test
- The Three Most Common Multiple-Choice Editing Questions
- Expression of Ideas Questions: Words in Context
- Expression of Ideas Questions: Adding or Deleting Text
- Expression of Ideas Questions: Reordering Sentences
- Expression of Ideas Questions: Combining Sentences and Using Transitional Words and Phrases Correctly
- Graphic Organizer Questions
- Exercise: Writing and Language Test
- Summing It Up

A CLOSER LOOK AT THE WRITING AND LANGUAGE TEST

The Writing and Language Test gives you opportunities to demonstrate your college and career readiness by revising and editing four passages. Each passage is 400–450 words long. There are 11 multiple-choice questions about each one—a total of 44 questions in all. You have 35 minutes to complete this section; that is about 48 seconds per question. If that doesn't sound like enough time to you, be assured that you will be able to answer many of the questions in *fewer* than 48 seconds. You can save up your extra seconds for the harder questions you'll encounter.

One passage of the four will be career-related; for example, this chapter includes a passage on technical writing careers. Another passage will be humanities-related; it might be about visual art, music, theater arts, or literature. For example, this chapter includes a short critical essay on a nineteenth-century novel by British author Jane Austen. The other two passages will be about history/social studies and science. Some of the passages will be accompanied by graphic organizers such as tables, charts, or graphs.

The writing modes used in the passages will include argument, informative/explanatory text, and nonfiction narrative. For example, this chapter's sample passage on technical writing is an informative/explanatory text. The essay on Jane Austen that appears later in this chapter includes both argument and nonfiction narrative.

Answering the multiple-choice questions on each passage will place you in an editor's role. You will be revising and editing the work of an unspecified writer. You will be asked to improve each passage's development, organization, and use of language. Your tasks will include making sure that each passage conforms to standard rules of English grammar, usage, and punctuation. When a passage is accompanied by one or more graphic organizers, you may need to correct the passage's inaccurate interpretation of data.

These editing and revising goals may sound overwhelming, but don't worry. Every answer is right there on your test page. All you have to do is to select one out of four possible solutions (A, B, C, or D) to choose the best use of language.

THE THREE MOST COMMON MULTIPLE-CHOICE EDITING QUESTIONS

The Writing and Language Test contains three primary categories of multiple-choice questions:

1. EXPRESSION OF IDEAS QUESTIONS

More than half of the questions fall into this category. This group includes questions about the following:

- Words in context
- Adding, deleting, or changing text
- Transitional language that smoothly and clearly takes the reader from one idea to another
- Relevant (or irrelevant) details
- Combining sentences to make text more concise and to flow more smoothly
- Eliminating awkward language and wordiness
- Reordering sentences so that paragraphs make better sense
- Consistency of style and tone
- Cohesion and precision of language

You will learn how to approach Expression of Ideas questions later in this chapter.

158

Chapter 4

Writing and
Language
Test
Strategies

2. STANDARD ENGLISH CONVENTIONS QUESTIONS

About 45 percent of the questions fall into this category of grammar, usage, and punctuation rules. It includes questions that require you to demonstrate your knowledge of the following:

- Consistent (or inconsistent) verb tenses
- Punctuation
- Sentence structure
- Correct (or incorrect) word usage

The Exercise section of this chapter provides practice with answering some questions from this category. In Chapter 5, you will learn more about grammar, usage, and punctuation questions.

3. GRAPHIC ORGANIZER QUESTIONS

This is the smallest percentage of the three primary categories. There may be only a few questions that deal with graphic organizers on the Writing and Language Test. This type of question asks you to make revising and editing decisions about passages in light of information and ideas conveyed through graphic organizers such as tables, charts, and graphs. However, you will not need to do any mathematical computation in order to answer the questions in this category. Later in this chapter, you will learn how to approach Graphic Organizer questions.

EXPRESSION OF IDEAS QUESTIONS: WORDS IN CONTEXT

Words-in-Context questions are perhaps the easiest type of question on the Writing and Language Test. Most of the questions on the test, including words in context, do not have a question right before the answer choices. Instead, you should choose the response that corrects the sentence or paragraph and makes the writing stronger. Review the example below.

Jane Austen and Fanny Price

In real life, one is sometimes left out because of actual purposeful **1** problems on the parts of those doing the leaving out, but sometimes one is simply left out—and culpability **2** was beside the point. **3** The second case is much less satisfying to the left-out person, but it is also much more usual. **4** Novels such as "Cinderella" are satisfying because, in them, it is clearly the nastiness of the villains and villainesses that causes the heroes and heroines to be excluded from pleasurable activities.

A. NO CHANGE

B. Fairy tales

C. Stories

D. Articles

First, quickly read the paragraph to get a general sense of its meaning—you don't need to understand every word. Right now you are answering Question 4 only, so don't worry about any errors you might spot in the rest of the paragraph—you will deal with those later in the "Exercise" portion of this chapter.

Question **4** asks you to decide which word best fits the context. Your four choices are:

A. NO CHANGE (Novels); B. Fairy tales; C. Stories; and D. Articles.

Use the context clue *Cinderella* to make the best choice. Right away you can eliminate choice D: "Cinderella" is *not* an article—most articles are nonfiction. Choice C is a possibility: "Cinderella" *is* a story—set this choice aside for a moment. Is "Cinderella" a novel? No—novels are long, and the story of Cinderella is fairly short. Eliminate choice A. Is Cinderella a fairytale? Yes, it is: it has magical elements, and it is a traditional tale that has been passed down for many generations. Is *Fairy tales* a better answer than *Stories*? Yes, it is, because this description is more precise. Fairy tales are a specific type of story. **The correct answer is B.**

Let's try a words-in-context question that goes with a different passage.

A Technical Writing Career

Technical **11** communicators, better known as "technical writers," plan, write, and edit instruction manuals, print and online articles, and other documents that transform **12** intense technical information into simpler language that end users can understand.

A. NO CHANGE

B. engineers

C. manuals

D. workers

Quickly read the one-sentence paragraph to figure out what it is mainly about. Again, focus on the question you're answering (Question 11).

Here are some clue words and phrases that will help you figure out which word belongs after the numeral **11**: *writers; write, and edit;* and *simpler language that . . . users can understand.* To which answer choice do these clues direct you? You can eliminate *manuals* (choice C): a manual is a thing (a set of instructions), not a person. Might *engineers* (choice B) and *workers* (choice D) be writers who write and edit text?

Maybe, but the word *communicators* is the best choice because it is most precise—a writer's main job is to communicate with others by writing understandable sentences, paragraphs, and so on.

Since the word *communicators* already appears in the paragraph after the **11**, **the correct answer is A,** NO CHANGE.

 If you are somewhat stuck, but not totally, make an educated guess. If you can eliminate at least one answer choice that you know is wrong (eliminating two is even better), you won't be guessing at random. Remember that you will not be penalized for wrong answers, so educated guessing is a fine strategy to use.

EXPRESSION OF IDEAS QUESTIONS: ADDING OR DELETING TEXT

Here is a question that asks you whether it is a good or bad idea to delete a certain sentence.

160

Chapter 4

Writing and
Language
Test
Strategies

When I was in elementary school, I was a shy little girl. . . . The stories I made up always had the same plot: I was carried off by a prince (David) on a flying horse to his castle where I became his wife and got to live in the lap of luxury. **5** <u>From there I would go into elaborate detail about the décor of the castle, how many horses we owned, what colors they were, and so on.</u> It was a silly, childish fantasy, but it comforted me.

5 The writer is considering deleting the underlined sentence. Should the writer do this?

A. Yes, because it adds unnecessary technical details.

B. Yes, because it makes the grown-up writer seem silly and childish.

C. No, because it adds funny details and helps to show that the narrator was a child at the time.

D. No, because, without this sentence, the last sentence in the paragraph would not make sense.

This question truly casts you in an editor's role. You're asked whether the paragraph would be better or worse if this sentence were deleted. Not only that, you're asked *why* your choice is the correct one.

You can eliminate choice B. The underlined sentence doesn't make the grown-up writer seem "silly and childish"—it makes her *subject* (her younger self) seem so. The writer explicitly states this in the last sentence of the paragraph—she is having fun making fun of her younger self.

Also eliminate choice A: This sentence *does* contain details, but they are not technical. How about choice D? Would the paragraph's last sentence fail to make sense if the underlined sentence were deleted? Read the first two sentences and the last one *without* the middle (underlined) one. The last sentence still makes sense, so you can eliminate choice D.

You are left with choice C. Even if you disagree that the underlined sentence is funny, it definitely "helps to show that the narrator was a child at the time." **The correct answer is C.**

EXPRESSION OF IDEAS QUESTIONS: REORDERING SENTENCES

Next, let's try a question that asks you to reorder sentences in a paragraph.

[1] A few years ago, US government experts predicted that employment of technical writers would grow 1.5 percent from 2012 to 2022, a gain of about 7,400 jobs per year. [2] (This is faster than the average for all occupations on which the US Department of Labor gathers statistics.) [3] This causes a greater need for professionals with the talent and skills to write instructional manuals that users can easily understand and follow. **16** [4] The high-tech and electronics industries continue to change and grow.

16 For the sake of cohesion, sentence 4 should be placed

   A. where it is now.

   B. before sentence 1.

   C. after sentence 1.

   D. after sentence 2.

In this type of question, each sentence in a paragraph is numbered with a numeral in brackets. Your job is to decide whether a specific sentence should stay where it is; move to a different spot in the paragraph; and if it *should* move, where it should go.

The best way to answer this question would be to read the paragraph out loud to yourself. During the SAT® exam, you won't be able to do that, but try it now if possible. You will probably notice that sentence 4 sounds odd at the end of the paragraph—it seems "tacked on" somehow. So it needs to be moved, but where?

Try each option one at a time. You will discover that this sentence belongs right after sentence 2—before sentence 3. Sentence 3 says that "This causes a greater need . . . [for good technical writers]." *What* causes this need? The cause is the fact that "the high-tech and electronics industries continue to change and grow." If sentences 3 and 4 were to swap places, the paragraph would be "most logical"—it would make better sense than it does now, for sure. **The correct answer is D.**

If a particular question seems overwhelming, circle it in your test booklet and go on to the next question. When you're done with all of the easier ones, come back to any questions you circled.

161

Chapter 4

Writing and Language Test Strategies

EXPRESSION OF IDEAS QUESTIONS: COMBINING SENTENCES AND USING TRANSITIONAL WORDS AND PHRASES CORRECTLY

Here is a question that asks you to complete two tasks at once: combine two shorter sentences into one longer one and choose the transitional word or phrase that makes the best sense in the new, longer sentence.

Most novel readers do not like it when story events seem artificially "rigged" by the author in order to teach a moralistic lesson. In this novel, Jane Austen rigs **7** events. Whenever Fanny is left out, we can be sure that one or some of the other characters are engaged in something sinful. This is an unrealistic (fairytale) element in what is otherwise a highly developed, realistic novel.

7 Which choice most effectively combines the two sentences at the underlined portion?

A.   events, but whenever Fanny is left out,

B.   events so that whenever Fanny is left out,

C.   events, because, whenever Fanny is left out,

D.   events, and the cause is that whenever Fanny is left out,

Again, the best way to solve this editing problem is to imagine reading the paragraph out loud. If you try one answer choice at a time, you will soon find the one that makes the best sense. The writer is saying that Jane Austen heavy-handedly rigs events in her novel in order that such and such happens. The transitional words and phrases in the other answer choices (A: *but*; C: *because*; D: *and the cause is that*) do not relay that same idea; only *so that* communicates this thought clearly. **The correct answer is B.**

GRAPHIC ORGANIZER QUESTIONS

Every Writing and Language Test contains one or more passages with graphic organizers such as tables, charts, and graphs. One or more of the questions following such a passage deals with its organizers. This type of question asks you to compare information given in the passage to similar information or data that the graphic organizer presents. If the two sets of information are inconsistent, you will need to make editing changes to the passage.

Here is an example:

A TECHNICAL WRITING CAREER	
Quick Facts: Technical Writers	
2017 Median Pay	$70,930 per year $34.10 per hour
Entry-level Education	Bachelor's degree
Work Experience in a Related Occupation	Less than 5 years
On-the-job Training	Short-term on-the-job training
Number of Jobs, 2016	52,400
Job Outlook, 2016–26	11% (faster than average)
Employment Change, 2016–26	5,700

[Source: **www.bls.gov/ooh/Media-and-Communication/Technical-writers.htm**]

Technical communicators, better known as "technical writers," plan, write, and edit instruction manuals, print and online articles, and other documents. Requirements for this well-paid profession include **17** a bachelor's degree and five to ten years of on-the-job training in a technical field.

17 Which choice most accurately and effectively represents the information in the chart?

A. NO CHANGE

B. a bachelor's degree and less than ten years of on-the-job work experience in a related occupation

C. a master's degree, less than five years of work experience in a related occupation, and a short period of on-the-job training

D. a bachelor's degree, less than five years of work experience in a related occupation, and a short period of on-the-job training

To find the correct answer choice, you will need to pay close attention to details in the chart. In this case, carefully read the three rows beginning with "Entry-level Education" and ending with "On-the-job Training." Choice A is incorrect because the chart does not specify "five to ten years of on-the-job training in a technical field." Choice B is incorrect because the chart does not specify "less than ten years of on-the-job work experience in a related occupation." Choice C is incorrect because the chart lists a bachelor's degree, not a master's, as a prerequisite for an entry-level technical writing job. The only answer choice that perfectly matches the chart is choice D. **The correct answer is D.**

EXERCISE: WRITING AND LANGUAGE TEST

18 MINUTES—22 QUESTIONS

DIRECTIONS: Each of the following passages is accompanied by a set of questions. For some questions, you will consider how the passage might be revised to improve the expression of ideas. For other questions, you will consider how the passage might be edited to correct errors in sentence structure, usage, or punctuation. A passage or a question may be accompanied by one or more graphics (such as a table, chart, graph, or photograph) that you will consider as you make revising and editing decisions.

Some questions will direct you to an underlined portion of a passage. Other questions will direct you to a location in a passage or ask you to think about the passage as a whole.

After reading each passage, choose the answer to each question that most effectively improves the quality of writing in the passage or that makes the passage conform to the conventions of Standard Written English. Many questions include a "NO CHANGE" option. Choose that option if you think the best choice is to leave the relevant portion of the passage as it is.

164

Chapter 4

Writing and
Language
Test
Strategies

Questions 1–11 are based on the following passage.

Jane Austen and Fanny Price

. . . In real life, one is sometimes left out because of actual purposeful **1** problems on the parts of those doing the leaving out, but sometimes one is simply left out—and culpability **2** was beside the point. **3** The second case is much less satisfying to the left-out person, but it is also much more usual. Fairy tales such as "Cinderella" are satisfying because, in them, it is clearly the nastiness of the villains and villainesses that causes the heroes and heroines to be excluded from pleasurable activities.

1

A. NO CHANGE
B. wrongdoing
C. issues
D. charity

2

A. NO CHANGE
B. had been
C. is
D. would have been

3 The writer is considering deleting the underlined sentence. Should the writer do this?

A. Yes, because it does not provide a good transition between the first and third sentences in the paragraph.

B. Yes, because it fails to support the main argument of the passage: that *Mansfield Park* presents a fairytale conception of being left out.

C. No, because it identifies important distinctions among three different "cases."

D. No, because it provides a good transition between the first and third sentences in the paragraph.

---

[1] When I was in elementary school, I was a shy little girl not unlike Fanny Price of Jane Austen's [4] *Mansfield Park*. [2] Sometimes when I was feeling left out, I would sit on a bench at the very edge of the playground and put spit on my cheeks to simulate tears, in case David Gould, [5] a boy I knew, should pass by and take pity on me. [6] [3] I also had a fairytale conception of being left out (as Fanny and Jane Austen have in this novel). [4] He never did, but it didn't really [7] matter. My imagination would take over from that point. [5] The stories I made up always had the same [8] plot I was carried off by a prince David on a flying horse to his castle, where I became his wife and got to live in the lap of luxury. [6] (From there I would go into elaborate detail about the décor of the castle, how many horses we owned, what colors they were, and so on.)

4. The writer is considering adding the phrase "magnificent work of art" here. Should the writer do this?

A. Yes, because it identifies the genre of *Mansfield Park*.

B. Yes, because it sums up the writer's true opinion of the book.

C. No, because it is an unnecessary and possibly confusing addition.

D. No, because it contradicts the writer's previous, more critical statement.

5. Which choice provides the most relevant detail?

A. NO CHANGE

B. the shortest boy in my classroom

C. the handsomest boy in the school

D. my sister's best friend's boyfriend

6. To make this paragraph most logical, sentence 3 should be placed

A. where it is now.

B. after sentence 1.

C. after sentence 4.

D. after sentence 6.

7. Which choice most effectively combines the two sentences at the underlined portion?

A. matter, because my imagination

B. matter; for example, my imagination

C. matter; in other words, my imagination

D. matter—consequently, my imagination

8.

A. NO CHANGE

B. plot I was carried off by a prince (David) on

C. plot; I was carried off by a prince (David) on

D. plot: I was carried off by a prince (David) on

In the course of *Mansfield Park*, Fanny goes through one big suffer-and-be- **9** victorious cycle (her ultimate marriage to Edmund after many, many years of being left out) and many little suffer-and-be-comforted cycles:

> "Edmund . . . going quietly to another table . . . brought a glass of Madeira to Fanny [who had a headache as a result of being deprived of proper exercise by the thoughtless disregard of others], and obliged her to drink the greater part. She wished to be able to decline it, but the tears which a variety of feelings created, made it easier to swallow than to speak." [*Mansfield Park*, page 513; from *The Complete Novels of Jane Austen*, Modern Library edition]

The little gush of passionate, passive gratefulness that Fanny feels when Edmund "obliges" her to drink the Madeira feels to me similar to the sweet rush of vindicated personal pathos that I felt at the moment in my David Gould fantasy when he would suddenly appear and sweep me up and away from my wrongfully left-out state into one of well-deserved bliss. This way of thinking is childish, self-pitying, and self-deluded; **10** accordingly, Jane Austen (who is usually far more astute) lets Fanny get away with it.

The author rigs things so that whenever Fanny is left out, we can be sure that one or some of the other characters are engaged in something sinful; this is an unrealistic **11** (fairy tale) element in what is otherwise a highly developed, realistic novel.

9

A. NO CHANGE
B. vindicated
C. validated
D. vaulted

10

A. NO CHANGE
B. yet,
C. predictably,
D. on the other hand,

11 Which choice provides the most relevant list of details?

A. NO CHANGE
B. fairy tale element in
C. fairy tale (element) in
D. [fairy tale] element in

166

Chapter 4

Writing and
Language
Test
Strategies

A Technical Writing Career

Technical communicators, better known as "technical writers," plan, write, and edit instruction manuals, print and online articles, and other documents that [12] maintain complex technical information into simpler language that end users can understand.

A typical technical writer

- determines end users' needs.

- [13] studies and examines product samples and gets into discussions about them with designers and developers.

- outlines, writes, and edits documents that support a variety of technical products.

- gathers and/or creates graphics that illustrate instructions and other technical documents.

- writes scripts for online instructional videos.

- decides which medium [14] (how-to manuals, "frequently asked questions" pages, online videos) will most effectively convey the information.

- gathers feedback on products' usability from customers, designers, and manufacturers.

- revises documents to fit product changes.

- works with customer service specialists to improve the end-user experience through product design changes.

12

A. NO CHANGE

B. function

C. transform

D. construct

13

A. NO CHANGE

B. studies product samples and discusses them with designers and developers.

C. studies and scrutinizes product samples and discusses them with designers and developers.

D. studies product samples and gets into discussions about them with designers and developers.

---

14 Which choice provides the most relevant list of details?

A. NO CHANGE

B. (books, magazines, newspapers, television news shows)

C. (drawing, painting, sculpture, computer-generated graphics)

D. (keyboards, monitors, hard drives, software, cloud computing)

167

Chapter 4

Writing and
Language
Test
Strategies

Technical writers must be able to fully comprehend complex information. Their work colleagues may include computer hardware engineers, scientists, computer support specialists, and software developers.

15 How else can they be expected to communicate with people from such an array of professional backgrounds?

15 Which change most effectively ends this paragraph and is also consistent with information provided in the chart?

A. NO CHANGE

B. Prior knowledge about such colleagues' fields enables technical writers to understand and translate "tech speak" into clear, useful instructions for users.

C. It takes years of graduate study to enable a technical writer to understand various work colleagues' fields—a master's degree or Ph.D. in technical writing is advisable.

D. DELETE the underlined sentence and do not replace it.

168

Chapter 4

Writing and
Language
Test
Strategies

Quick Facts: Technical Writers	
2017 Median Pay	$70,930 per year $34.10 per hour
Entry-Level Education	Bachelor's degree
Work Experience in a Related Occupation	Less than 5 years
On-the-job Training	Short-term on-the-job training
Number of Jobs, 2016	52,400
Job Outlook, 2016–26	11% (Faster than average)
Employment Change, 2016–26	5,700

[Source: **www.bls.gov/ooh/Media-and-Communication/Technical-writers.htm**]

16 [1] Why is the technical writing field growing so quickly? [2] A few years ago, US government experts predicted that employment of technical writers would grow **17** 1.1 percent from 2016 to 2026, a gain of about 5,700 jobs per year. [3] (This is faster than the average for all occupations on which the U.S. Department of Labor gathers statistics.) [4] As the high-tech and electronics industries continue to **18** stall, they reflect a greater need for professionals with the talent and skills to write instructional manuals that users can easily understand and follow.

16 For the sake of cohesion, sentence 1 should be placed

    A. where it is now.

    B. after sentence 2.

    C. after sentence 3.

    D. after sentence 4.

17 Which choice most accurately and effectively represents the information in the chart (on the previous page)?

    A. NO CHANGE

    B. 10 percent from 2016 to 2026, a gain of about 5,000 jobs per year.

    C. 11 percent from 2016 to 2026, a gain of about 5,700 jobs per year.

    D. 11 percent from 2016 to 2026, a gain of about 5,700 jobs total.

18

    A. NO CHANGE

    B. evolve

    C. shift

    D. compress

169

Job opportunities **19** abound. This is especially true for applicants with both technical skills and writing skills. Increasingly, consumers rely on technologically sophisticated products in the home as well as in the workplace. In addition—for many people—ordinary daily life requires us to **20** misconstrue complex medical and scientific information. **21** All of these factors are combining, joining, and uniting to create many new opportunities for technical writers. As older workers retire, their jobs will become **22** vacant. Yet, competition among freelance technical writers will remain lively.

19 Which choice most effectively combines the two sentences at the underlined portion?

  A. abound, especially for applicants with

  B. abound, especially is this the case for applicants with

  C. abound; especially positively impacted are applicants with

  D. abound—and especially for those lucky applicants who have acquired

20

  A. NO CHANGE

  B. comprehend complex medical and scientific information

  C. comprehend simplistic medical and scientific information

  D. comprehend complex medical scientific information

21

  A. NO CHANGE

  B. All of these factors are combining to create

  C. All of these factors are combining and uniting to create

  D. All of these factors are combining and joining to create

22

  A. NO CHANGE

  B. occupied

  C. unaltered

  D. profitable

170

Chapter 4

Writing and
Language
Test
Strategies

ANSWER KEYS AND EXPLANATIONS

PASSAGE 1

1. B	**4.** C	**6.** B	**8.** D	**10.** B
2. C	**5.** C	**7.** A	**9.** A	**11.** A
3. D				

1. **The correct answer is B.** In this sentence, the writer is indicating an act to deliberately do wrong to another person, so the best word choice is *wrongdoing*. While wrongdoing is a problem of sorts, the word *problems* is not specific enough, so it is not the best answer choice. *Issues* (choice C) is similarly lacking in specificity. *Charity* (choice D) has almost the opposite meaning of *wrongdoing*.

2. **The correct answer is C.** Except for this verb, *was*, the writer uses the present tense throughout the paragraph. Therefore, to be consistent, the correct answer is choice C.

3. **The correct answer is D.** The writer should not delete the sentence because it provides a good transition between the first and third sentences in the paragraph.

4. **The correct answer is C.** The writer should not add this phrase here because it is unnecessary and may confuse readers into thinking *Mansfield Park* is a work of visual art, such as a painting.

5. **The correct answer is C.** It makes sense that a girl would cast the handsomest boy in the school in the role of a prince who saves her from her unhappy state. Choices A, B, and D are incorrect because, while they are possible choices, they are not as relevant as choice C.

6. **The correct answer is B.** Sentence 3 makes the best sense when it follows sentence 1.

7. **The correct answer is A.** The linking word *because* makes sense in context: the writer is explaining *why* it did not matter that David Gould never noticed or pitied her when she was a shy little girl.

8. **The correct answer is D.** As originally written, the sentence lacks the necessary punctuation, and choice D corrects this issue by separating an idea (the stories the writer always made up had the same plot) from its explanation with a colon and placing the non-essential information (the prince's name) within parentheses. Choice B uses parentheses correctly but fails to include the colon. Choice C uses a semicolon instead of a colon.

9. **The correct answer is A.** The parenthetical information in this sentence describes a situation in which someone suffers (Fanny is left out) before achieving success (she gets married), and *victorious* means "achieving success." *Vindicated* (choice B) means "being cleared of blame," and does not make much sense in this context. To be validated (choice C) is to be proven truthful or correct, so *validated* is not a strong answer either. *Vaulted* (choice D) means "domed" and makes no sense in this context."

10. **The correct answer is B.** The transitional word *yet* makes sense in context: the writer is explaining that, even though Jane Austen is usually astute about her characters, in this case, the author "lets Fanny get away with" childishness, self-pity, and self-delusion.

11. **The correct answer is A.** As originally written, the parentheses enclose an alternate and inessential term for unrealistic, and inessential information should be enclosed in parentheses. Therefore, choice B is incorrect. Choice C encloses the wrong term in parentheses. Choice D uses brackets instead of parentheses.

Chapter 4

Writing and Language Test Strategies

12. C	15. B	17. D	19. A	21. B
13. B	16. C	18. B	20. B	22. A
14. A				

12. **The correct answer is C.** The sentence describes a situation in which text is changed from something complex to something easily understandable, and *transform* means "change." *Maintain* means the opposite of *transform*, so the sentence as originally written (choice A) does not make sense. One cannot "function" something such as text, so choice B does not make sense in this context. *Construct* means "create," but the sentence is describing something that has already been created, so choice D is not the best answer

13. **The correct answer is B.** Only choice B offers clear and concise wording without redundancy. Choice A is incorrect because "studies and examines" is redundant and "gets into discussions about" is less concise than simply "discusses." Choice C eliminates the original redundancy, but then it creates a new one: *scrutinizes* and *studies* mean the same thing. Choice D is incorrect because it fails to correct the original sentence's wordiness.

14. **The correct answer is A.** No change is needed because the writer is using the word *medium* to refer to a genre or method of effectively conveying technical information.

15. **The correct answer is B.** This sentence clarifies information presented earlier in the paragraph.

16. **The correct answer is C.** Sentence 1 makes the most sense when it follows sentence 3.

17. **The correct answer is D.** The last two lines of the chart say that the projected job outlook for technical writers during the ten years from 2016 to 2026 is 11 percent growth and that, during those ten years, the technical writing field will gain 5,700 jobs total. Choices A, B, and C are incorrect because the statistics they give do not match those shown in the chart.

18. **The correct answer is B.** The sentence describes how industries change and grow, and this is what *evolve* means. *Stall* (choice A) means the opposite of *evolve*. *Shift* is not as specific a word as *evolve*, so choice C is not the very best answer choice. *Compress* (choice D) means "squeeze" and does not make sense in this context.

19. **The correct answer is A.** This is the simplest, clearest way to combine the two sentences. Choices B, C, and D are incorrect because each is either awkward or too wordy or does not match the rest of the passage's style and tone.

20. **The correct answer is B.** The sentence describes how ordinary life requires people to understand complex medical and scientific information, and *comprehend* means "understand." *Misconstrue* means "confuse," which is the opposite of *understand*, so choice A is incorrect. Choice C introduces a new error by changing *complex* to its opposite: *simplistic*. Choice D turns the sentence into a run-on by eliminating the conjunction *and*.

21. **The correct answer is B.** As originally written, the sentence is redundant since *combining*, *joining*, and *uniting* all share the same meaning. Choice B corrects this error by using only one of these terms. Choices C and D make the mistake of eliminating only one of the redundant terms.

22. **The correct answer is A.** When one retires from a job, that job is no longer filled by a worker, and *vacant* means "not filled." *Occupied* means "filled," so choice B has the opposite meaning of the correct answer. Leaving a position alters that position, so choice C does not make sense. *Profitable* means "money-making," so choice D does not really fit the context of this sentence.

172

Chapter 4

Writing and
Language
Test
Strategies

SUMMING IT UP

- In the Writing and Language Test section of the SAT® exam, there are four passages and 44 multiple-choice questions (11 questions about each passage). You will have 35 minutes to complete this section.

- The multiple-choice questions in this section put you in an editor's role. Each question consists of an "editing problem" with four possible solutions.

- Some passages are accompanied by informational graphics, such as graphs, charts, tables, and photographs. You'll need to refer to these supplementary graphics to answer a question or two, but no math will be required in this section.

- There are three main categories of multiple-choice questions:

  1. Expression of Ideas questions, including questions on words in context; adding, deleting, or changing text; transitional language; relevant details; combining sentences; eliminating awkward language and wordiness; reordering sentences so that paragraphs make better sense; consistency of style and tone; cohesion and precision of language

  2. Standard English Conventions questions covering grammar, usage, and punctuation

  3. Graphic Organizer questions asking you to compare information that is in the passage to similar information or data that are presented in a chart, graph, table, or photograph

- In addition to your Writing and Language Test score, the following subscores and cross-test scores will be provided:

  - Command of Evidence: Questions asking you to interpret and use evidence in the passages and informational graphics, such as graphs, tables, and charts
  - Expression of Ideas: Questions that focus on topic development, organization, and rhetorically effective use of language
  - Words in Context: Questions that address the meaning of a particular word or phrase in context
  - Standard English Conventions: Questions that focus on sentence structure, usage, and punctuation
  - Analysis in History/Social Studies: Questions based on history/social studies–related passages
  - Analysis in Science: Questions based on science-related passages

Writing and
Language
Test
Strategies

WANT TO KNOW MORE?

Access additional practice questions, valuable lessons, helpful tips, and expert strategies for the following Writing and Language Test topics in *Peterson's Online Course for the SAT® Exam*:

- Frequently Confused Words

- Grammar Question Types

- Organization Questions

- Pacing in Writing

- Parallelism

- Pronouns

- Punctuation

- Style Questions

- Verb Tenses

To purchase and access the course, go to **www.petersons.com/testprep/sat**.

CHAPTER 5:
STANDARD ENGLISH CONVENTIONS

OVERVIEW

- Sentence Formation
- Verb Tense, Mood, and Voice
- Conventions of Usage
- Agreement
- Frequently Confused Words
- Conventions of Punctuation
- Summing It Up

This chapter reviews Standard English language conventions. While we're not attempting to teach you all the rules of punctuation and grammar, we do want you to review those rules that may be tested or that you may need to call on for your own writing.

Each of the three main domains covered in this chapter—sentence structure, conventions of usage, and conventions of punctuation—is broken down into smaller sections. These instructional sections are followed by exercises with answers and explanations. Be sure to read all the answer explanations, even for the questions you answered correctly. Review is an important part of your SAT® exam preparation.

175

Chapter 5

Standard
English
Conventions

SENTENCE FORMATION

SENTENCE BOUNDARIES

Fragments

Basic Rule

Every sentence must have a complete subject and verb and express a full idea. A group of words that is missing one of these elements is called a sentence fragment or an incomplete sentence.

There are three ways to correct incomplete sentences:

1. Add the fragment to the sentence that precedes it.

    Incorrect: Zoologists and wildlife biologists study animals and other wildlife. How they interact with their ecosystems.

    Correct: Zoologists and wildlife biologists study animals and other wildlife and how they interact with their ecosystems.

    Explanation: The fragment is added to the sentence that precedes it by adding the word *and*.

2. Add the fragment to the sentence that follows it.

    Incorrect: By studying animal behaviors. Wildlife biologists seek to understand how animals interact with their ecosystems.

    Correct: By studying animal behaviors, wildlife biologists seek to understand how animals interact with their ecosystems.

    Explanation: The fragment is added to the sentence that follows it by inserting a comma.

3. Add a subject and verb to the fragment.

    Incorrect: Considerable time studying animals in their natural habitats.

    Correct: Wildlife biologists may spend considerable time studying animals in their natural habitats.

    Explanation: A subject (*wildlife biologists*) and verb (*may spend*) are added to the fragment.

Run-ons

A run-on sentence occurs when a writer fails to use either end-stop punctuation to divide complete thoughts or suitable conjunctions to join two ideas.

The following rules will help you avoid and fix run-on sentences:

1. Though the result can be short, choppy sentences, the most common way to correct a run-on sentence is to simply divide the sentence using end-stop punctuation.

    Incorrect: Zoologists need a bachelor's degree for entry-level positions a master's degree or Ph.D. is often needed for advancement.

Correct: Zoologists need a bachelor's degree for entry-level positions. A master's degree or Ph.D. is often needed for advancement.

2. A more advanced technique is to create a compound sentence by joining independent clauses using a coordinating conjunction (e.g., *and, but,* or *so*).

   Incorrect: Zoologists need a bachelor's degree for entry-level positions a master's degree is often needed for advancement.

   Correct: Zoologists need a bachelor's degree for entry-level position, but a master's degree is often needed for advancement. (Remember that a comma is required when you use a coordinating conjunction to join two independent clauses.

3. Another option is to create a complex sentence by adding a subordinating conjunction (e.g., *because, although,* or *while*), making one of the independent clauses a dependent clause.

   Incorrect: Zoologists need only a bachelor's degree for entry-level positions a master's degree is often needed for advancement.

   Correct: Zoologists need only a bachelor's degree for entry-level positions although a master's degree is often needed for advancement. (In general, commas are not required when the dependent clause follows the independent clause.)

   Also Correct: Although a master's degree is often needed for advancement, zoologists need only a bachelor's degree for entry-level positions. (Commas are required when the dependent clause precedes the independent clause.)

4. Use a semicolon when ideas are very closely related in meaning and full end-stop punctuation seems too strong.

   Incorrect: Zoologists and wildlife biologists study how animals and other wildlife interact with their ecosystems these scientists work in offices, laboratories, or outdoors.

   Correct: Zoologists and wildlife biologists study how animals and other wildlife interact with their ecosystems; these scientists work in offices, laboratories, or outdoors.

Skill Builder: Fragments and Run-ons

> **DIRECTIONS:** Revise the following sentences to correct fragments and eliminate run-ons.

1. Zoologists and wildlife biologists perform a variety of scientific tests and experiments for example, they take blood samples from animals to assess their levels of nutrition, check animals for disease and parasites, and tag animals in order to track them.

2. In order to track potential threats to wildlife. Wildlife biologists often use computer programs.

3. Zoologists and wildlife biologists work to expand our knowledge of wildlife species. Work closely with public officials to develop wildlife management and conservation plans.

4. Herpetologists study reptiles, such as snakes. And amphibians, such as frogs.

5. Some wildlife biologists develop conservation plans and make recommendations on conservation and management issues. To policymakers and the general public.

6. Ecologists study ecosystems. And the relationships between organisms and the surrounding environments.

7. Evolutionary biologists study the origins of species. The changes in their inherited characteristics over generations.

8. Zoologists and wildlife biologists conduct experimental studies they also collect biological data for analysis.

Answers

In some cases, there are many possible correct answers. Here are some examples:

1. Zoologists and wildlife biologists perform a variety of scientific tests and experiments. For example, they take blood samples from animals to assess their levels of nutrition, check animals for disease and parasites, and tag animals in order to track them.

2. In order to track potential threats to wildlife, wildlife biologists often use computer programs.

3. Zoologists and wildlife biologists work to expand our knowledge of wildlife species and work closely with public officials to develop wildlife management and conservation plans.

4. Herpetologists study reptiles and amphibians, such as snakes and frogs.

5. Some wildlife biologists develop conservation plans and make recommendations on conservation and management issues to policymakers and the general public.

6. Ecologists study ecosystems and the relationships between organisms and the surrounding environments.

7. Evolutionary biologists study the origins of species and the changes in their inherited characteristics over generations.

8. Zoologists and wildlife biologists conduct experimental studies and collect biological data for analysis.

COORDINATION AND SUBORDINATION

Basic Rule

Coordinating and subordinating conjunctions are used to join together clauses and form compound and complex sentences.

Some common coordinating and subordinating conjunctions follow.

Coordinating conjunctions	Subordinating conjunctions
and, but, for, nor, or, so, yet	*after, although, as, as if, because, before, even if, even though, if, if only, rather than, since, that, though, unless, until, when, where, whereas, wherever, whether, which, while*

Basic Rule of Coordinating Conjunctions

Coordinating conjunctions are used to join independent clauses to make compound sentences. In these sentences, each piece of information carries the same weight.

Independent clauses: There was a Treaty of Paris signed in 1763. There was also one signed in 1783.

Joined together: There were Treaties of Paris signed in 1763 and 1783.

When two clauses are joined, if the second remains an independent clause, a comma must be used before the coordinating conjunction.

Independent clauses: There was a Treaty of Paris signed in 1763. There was also one signed in 1783.

Joined together: There was a Treaty of Paris signed in 1763, but there was another Treaty of Paris signed in 1783.

Basic Rule of Subordinating Conjunctions

Subordinating conjunctions are used to join independent and dependent clauses to make complex sentences. In these sentences, the dependent clause establishes a place, a time, a reason, a condition, a concession, or a comparison for the independent clause.

Independent clauses: A tax on imported goods from another country is called a tariff. A tax on imported goods from another country to protect a home industry is called a protective tariff.

Joined together: A tax on imported goods from another country is called a tariff, while a tax on imported goods from another country to protect a home industry is called a protective tariff.

Here, the subordinate clause is at the end. You can also place a subordinate clause at the beginning of a sentence, as long as you use a comma.

Independent clauses: A tax on imported goods from another country is called a tariff. A tax on imported goods from another country to protect a home industry is called a protective tariff.

Joined together: While a tax on imported goods from another country is called a tariff, a tax on imported goods from another country to protect a home industry is called a protective tariff.

Skill Builder: Subordination and Coordination

DIRECTIONS: Join the following sentences using subordinating or coordinating conjunctions.

1. A democracy is a form of government that is run for the people. It is also run by the people.

2. A primary source is an original record of an event. A secondary source is something that was written later.

3. The Industrial Revolution ushered in a time of unparalleled human progress. People often forget the damage that this progress did, and continues to do, to the environment.

4. Elizabeth Cady Stanton became famous as an advocate of women's rights. During the Civil War, she was also an ardent abolitionist.

Answers

In some cases, there are many possible correct answers. Here are some examples:

1. A democracy is a form of government that is run for the people, and it is also run by the people.

2. Whereas a primary source is an original record of an event, a secondary source is something that was written later.

3. While the Industrial Revolution ushered in a time of unparalleled human progress, people often forget the damage that this progress did, and continues to do, to the environment.

4. Elizabeth Cady Stanton became famous as an advocate of women's rights, and, during the Civil War, she was also an ardent abolitionist.

Parallel Structure

Parallel structure is the repetition of a grammatical form within a sentence. Parallel structure is a hallmark of effective writing and is often used to emphasize ideas and present compared items in an equal light. Coordinating conjunctions are often used in parallel constructions.

> **Non-parallel structure:** As a child, George Washington Carver enjoyed reading, learned about plants, and he made art.

> **Parallel structure:** As a child, George Washington Carver enjoyed reading, learning about plants, and making art.

Modifier Placement

A modifier is a word, phrase, or clause that adds detail to a sentence. In order to avoid confusion, modifiers should be placed as close as possible to the things they modify.

Examples of different modifiers are underlined in the sentences below.

<u>Within the field of marine biology</u>, employment is <u>highly</u> competitive. (The phrase "within the field of marine biology" modifies the subject of the sentence, which is *employment*. The word *highly* modifies our understanding of the competitive nature of finding employment.)

The <u>abundant</u> supply of <u>marine</u> scientists far exceeds the demands, and the number of federal and state government jobs is <u>limited</u>. (*Abundant* modifies *supply*. *Marine* modifies *scientists*. *Limited* modifies our understanding of *jobs*.)

When the subject of a modifier is unclear or is not included in the sentence, it is considered a dangling modifier.

> **Incorrect:** Not realizing that the job title of marine biologist rarely exists, *marine biology* is a term recognized by most people. (What is the first phrase modifying?)

> **Possible revision:** Not realizing that the job title of marine biologist rarely exists, most people recognize the term *marine biology*.

Misplaced modifiers occur when a modifier is poorly placed and it doesn't express the writer's intent accurately.

> **Incorrect:** The term *marine biologist* is used to almost describe all of the disciplines and jobs that deal with the study of marine life, not just those that deal with the physical properties of the sea.

> **Possible revision:** The term *marine biologist* is used to describe almost all of the disciplines and jobs that deal with the study of marine life, not just those that deal with the physical properties of the sea.

Skill Builder: Modifier Placement

> **DIRECTIONS:** Revise the following sentences to eliminate problems with modifier placement.

1. Critical for getting a competitive edge in the job market, fishery science requires a strong background in advanced mathematics and computer skills.

2. A fishery scientist studies population dynamics of fish and marine mammals after taking course work in the animal and aquatic sciences.

3. Another increasingly important field within marine biology, more universities are starting to offer programs in fisheries or wildlife management.

4. As well as their interactions, biological oceanographers study both the biological and physical aspects of the sea.

5. A student may take course work weighted heavily in physics, mathematics, and computer modeling in the field of physical oceanography.

Answers

In some cases, there are many possible correct answers. Here are some examples:

1. A strong background in advanced mathematics and computer skills is critical for getting a competitive edge in the fishery science job market.

2. After taking course work in the animal and aquatic sciences, a fishery scientist studies fish and marine mammal population dynamics.

3. More universities are starting to offer programs in fisheries or wildlife management, another increasingly important field within marine biology.

4. Biological oceanographers study both the biological and physical aspects of the sea, as well as their interactions.

5. A student in the field of physical oceanography may take course work weighted heavily in physics, mathematics, and computer modeling.

VERB TENSE, MOOD, AND VOICE

Basic Rule

Use the same verb tense whenever possible within a sentence or paragraph. Do not shift from one tense to another unless there is a valid reason.

> **Incorrect:** The Magna Carta *was* signed in 1215 by King John of England and *has been* the first document of its kind to limit the power of the British monarchy.

> **Correct:** The Magna Carta *was* signed in 1215 by King John of England and *was* the first document of its kind to limit the power of the British monarchy.

WHEN TO USE THE PERFECT TENSES

Basic Rule

Use *present perfect* for an action begun in the past and extended to the present.

> **Example:** Scientists at NASA *have seen* an alarming increase in the accumulation of greenhouse gases.

> **Explanation:** In this case, *scientists at NASA saw* would be incorrect. What they *have seen* (present perfect) began in the past and extends to the present.

Basic Rule

Use *past perfect* for an action begun and completed in the past before some other past action.

> **Example:** Despite their preparations, Lewis and Clark *had never encountered* the kinds of challenges that awaited them before their expedition.

> **Explanation:** In this case, *never encountered* would be incorrect. The action *had never encountered* (past perfect) is used because it is referring to events prior to their expedition.

Basic Rule

Use *future perfect* for an action begun at any time and completed in the future.

> **Example:** When the American astronauts arrive, the Russian cosmonauts *will have been* on the International Space Station for six months.

> **Explanation:** In this case, although both actions occur in the future, the Russian cosmonauts *will have been* on the space station before the American astronauts *arrive*. When there are two future actions, the action completed first is expressed in the future perfect tense.

Tenses: Common Verbs

Refer to the following chart to familiarize yourself with some common verbs and their tenses.

Infinitive	Present	Past	Future	Present Perfect	Past Perfect	Future Perfect
to ask	ask	asked	will ask	have asked	had asked	will have asked
to be	am	was	will be	have been	had been	will have been
to become	become	became	will become	have become	had become	will have become
to begin	begin	began	will begin	have begun	had begun	will have begun
to come	come	came	will come	have come	had come	will have come
to do	do	did	will do	have done	had done	will have done
to eat	eat	ate	will eat	have eaten	had eaten	will have eaten
to feel	feel	felt	will feel	have felt	had felt	will have felt
to find	find	found	will find	have found	had found	will have found
to get	get	got	will get	have gotten	had gotten	will have gotten
to give	give	gave	will give	have given	had given	will have given
to go	go	went	will go	have gone	had gone	will have gone
to grow	grow	grew	will grow	have grown	had grown	will have grown
to have	have	had	will have	have had	had had	will have had
to hear	hear	heard	will hear	have heard	had heard	will have heard
to hide	hide	hid	will hide	have hidden	had hidden	will have hidden
to keep	keep	kept	will keep	have kept	had kept	will have kept
to know	know	knew	will know	have known	had known	will have known
to leave	leave	left	will leave	have left	had left	will have left
to like	like	liked	will like	have liked	had liked	will have liked

Infinitive	Present	Past	Future	Present Perfect	Past Perfect	Future Perfect
to look	look	looked	will look	have looked	had looked	will have looked
to make	make	made	will make	have made	had made	will have made
to meet	meet	met	will meet	have met	had met	will have met
to put	put	put	will put	have put	had put	will have put
to say	say	said	will say	have said	had said	will have said
to see	see	saw	will see	have seen	had seen	will have seen
to sleep	sleep	slept	will sleep	have slept	had slept	will have slept
to speak	speak	spoke	will speak	have spoken	had spoken	will have spoken
to study	study	studied	will study	have studied	had studied	will have studied
to take	take	took	will take	have taken	had taken	will have taken
to think	think	thought	will think	have thought	had thought	will have thought
to walk	walk	walked	will walk	have walked	had walked	will have walked
to want	want	wanted	will want	have wanted	had wanted	will have wanted
to work	work	worked	will work	have worked	had worked	will have worked
to write	write	wrote	will write	have written	had written	will have written

*Note: For consistency, all verbs are conjugated in the first person singular.

Skill Builder: Verb Tense

DIRECTIONS: Circle the word with the correct verb tense for each sentence.

1. (was, has been) Founded in Jamestown, Virginia, the House of Burgesses ___ the first representative body founded in the new world.

2. (have been, were) There ___ many great American explorers, but some scholars argue that none is as historically significant as Lewis and Clark.

3. (had never been, never was) Before 1804, Meriwether Lewis ___ on an expedition of any significance, let alone led one.

4. (will have added, has added) By the time this article is published, the United States ___ 250,000 new jobs.

5. (was, has been) Civil Disobedience, or the refusal to obey a government law or laws, ___ one of Martin Luther King, Jr.'s key tactics during the Civil Rights Movement.

Answers

1. **The correct answer is *was*.** The past tense is used because the action occurred in the past.

2. **The correct answer is *have been*.** The present perfect tense is used because the sentence refers to action that began in the past and extended to the present.

3. **The correct answer is *had never been*.** The past perfect tense is used because the sentence contains a past tense action that occurred before another action.

4. **The correct answer is *will have added*.** The future perfect tense is used because the sentence refers to action begun at any time and completed in the future.

5. **The correct answer is *was*.** The past tense is used because the action occurred in the past.

Mood

Basic Rule

Mood, as it relates to verb forms, refers to the kind of message the writer intends to communicate.

The *indicative mood* is the most common mood and is used to state facts or opinions.

> **Example:** Zora Neale Hurston's novel *Their Eyes Were Watching God* was forgotten for many years but is now considered a literary classic.

The *imperative mood* is used when a writer wants to give a directive or make a request. Though not stated, the subject of an imperative sentence is *you*.

> **Example:** Stop pretending that it doesn't matter.

> **Example:** George Washington peered across the Potomac as the frigid wind lashed his face. "Hurry!" he exclaimed. (*Peered* is in the indicative. *Hurry* is in the imperative.)

186

Chapter 5

Standard
English
Conventions

www.petersons.com

The *subjunctive mood* expresses a condition contrary to fact, a wish, a supposition, or an indirect command. Although it is going out of use in English, the subjunctive can still be seen in the following forms:

- To express a wish not likely to be fulfilled or impossible to be realized

  Example: I wish it *were* possible for us to approve his transfer at this time. (It is *not* possible.)

- In a subordinate clause after a verb that expresses a command, a request, or a suggestion

  Example: It was recommended by the White House *that* the Office of Homeland Security *be* responsible for preparing the statements.

- To express a condition known or supposed to be contrary to fact

  Example: If Ann were chosen to be our company's president, women would earn more than their male counterparts.

- After *as if* or *as though*. In formal writing and speech, *as if* and *as though* are followed by the subjunctive, since they introduce as supposition something not factual. In informal writing and speaking, the indicative is sometimes used.

  Example: Before defecting to the British Army, Benedict Arnold talked as if he were a true American patriot. (He was not.)

Avoid shifts in mood. Once you have decided on the mood that properly expresses your message, use that mood throughout the sentence or the paragraph. A shift in mood is confusing to the listener or reader; it indicates that the speaker or writer himself has changed his way of looking at the conditions.

Incorrect: It is requested by the White House that a report of Congressional proceedings *be* prepared and copies *should be* distributed to all citizens. (*Be* is subjunctive; *should be,* indicative.)

Correct: It is requested by the White House that a report of the Congressional proceedings *be* prepared and that copies *be* distributed to all citizens.

Voice

Basic Rule

Voice tells us whether the subject of a sentence is the actor or is acted upon. In formal writing, active voice is preferred because it is more immediate and places the reader closer to the action.

Active voice example: According to legend, George Washington chopped down the whole cherry tree.

Passive voice example: According to legend, the cherry tree was chopped down by George Washington.

Skill Builder: Mood and Voice

> **DIRECTIONS:** In the following sentences, choose the correct mood or voice.

1. (was, were) The team of Russian engineers ___ unable to prevent the nuclear reactor in Chernobyl from melting down.

2. (was, were) If climate change ___ not such a threat to life on this planet, the scientific community would not be making such a big deal about carbon emissions.

3. (is, were) If inflation ___ to continue to rise, the effects on the economy would be disastrous.

4. (be, should be) The president asked that the Speaker of the House ___ present when the special announcement was made.

5. (passive or active voice) The stony coral polyps were placed in a cup made of calcium carbonate.

6. (passive or active voice) For over 40 years, Henry Clay played a central role on the national political stage.

Answers and Explanations

1. **The correct answer is *was*.** This sentence uses the indicative mood and requires the simple past tense.

2. **The correct answer is *were*.** The subjunctive is correct because the sentence is making a supposition.

3. **The correct answer is *were*.** The subjunctive is correct because the sentence is making a supposition.

4. **The correct answer is *be*.** The subjunctive is correct because the subordinate clause after the verb is making a request.

5. **The correct answer is *passive voice*.** This sentence is passive because the subject of the sentence is acted upon.

6. **The correct answer is *active voice*.** This sentence is active because the subject of the sentence is the actor.

CONVENTIONS OF USAGE

PRONOUNS

Pronouns substitute for nouns.

Examples: George Washington was born on February 22, 1732, in Pope's Creek, Virginia; *he* was the first American president.

Did you know that Besty Ross and George Washington both went to the same church? *It* was called Christ Church, and *it* was located in Philadelphia.

The following pronoun chart may prove helpful:

Number	Person	Subjective Case	Objective Case	Possessive Case
Singular	1st person	I	me	mine
	2nd person	you	you	yours
	3rd person	he, she, it, who	him, her, it, whom	his, hers, whose
Plural	1st person	we	us	ours
	2nd person	you	you	yours
	3rd person	they, who	them, whom	theirs, whose

Basic Rule

A pronoun uses the *subjective* case when it is the subject of the sentence or when it renames the subject as a subject complement.

Incorrect: That night, George Washington, Robert Morris, and *him* asked Betsy Ross to sew the first flag.

Correct: That night, George Washington, Robert Morris, and *he* asked Betsy Ross to sew the first flag. (*He* is part of the subject of the sentence.)

Incorrect: George Ross is *him*.

Correct: George Ross is *he*. (*He* renames the subject.)

Basic Rule

If a pronoun is the object of a verb or preposition, it is placed in the *objective* case.

Incorrect: After the plot was discovered, they accused Benedict Arnold and *he* of treason.

Correct: After the plot was discovered, they accused Benedict Arnold and *him* of treason. (*Him* is the object of the verb *accused*.)

Incorrect: Despite the fact that we turned in our marine biology paper late, "A" grades were given to Franklin and *I*.

Correct: Despite the fact that we turned in our marine biology paper late, "A" grades were given to Franklin and *me*. (*Me* is the object of the verb *given*.)

Pronoun Clarity

Avoid ambiguity and confusion by placing a pronoun as close as possible to its *antecedent* (the word it refers to) and by making sure that the antecedent is clear.

> **Incorrect:** At the height of his career, Frank Lloyd Wright told an architectural scholar that *he* thought *his* work was improving. (Is Wright talking about his own work or the work of the scholar?)

> **Correct:** At the height of his career, Frank Lloyd Wright told an architectural scholar that he thought *his own* work was improving.

> **Incorrect:** Frank Lloyd Wright and his wife Olgivanna founded a school for aspiring artists in Spring Green, Wisconsin, where they could "learn by doing." (Does *they* refer to the Wrights or the artists?)

> **Correct:** Frank Lloyd Wright and his wife Olgivanna founded a school in Spring Green, Wisconsin, where aspiring artists could "learn by doing."

Possessive Determiners

When a pronoun expresses ownership, it is placed in the possessive case.

 Possessive determiners (*its, your, their*), contractions (*it's, you're, they're*), and adverbs (*there*) are often confused. Remember that personal pronouns that express ownership never require an apostrophe.

> **Incorrect:** Frank Lloyd Wright believed that *an architectural structure* should be in harmony with *it's* environment.

> **Correct:** Frank Lloyd Wright believed that an architectural structure should be in harmony with *its* environment.

Skill Builder: Pronouns

> **DIRECTIONS:** In the space provided, identify and explain the pronoun error contained in each statement.

1. The Battle of Yorktown was an important turning point in the American Revolution and the British defeat signaled the end of it.

2. The American Bill of Rights was based on the English Bill of Rights; it protected the rights of the citizens.

3. While the Articles of Confederation is less famous than other historical documents like the Declaration of Independence and the Constitution, it's historical significance cannot be overstated.

4. Federalists and Anti-Federalists felt differently about the division of power between national and state governments. They preferred more power be given to the states.

5. Thomas Paine was an American patriot who's pamphlets *Common Sense* and *The Crisis* helped stir the American independence movement.

Answers and Explanations

1. It is unclear whether the *it* at the end of the sentence refers to the American Revolution or the Battle of Yorktown.

2. It is unclear whether the *it* that follows the semicolon refers to the American or English Bill or Rights or both.

3. *It's* is a contraction; the correct word should be the possessive pronoun *its*.

4. It is unclear whether *they* refers to the Federalists or the Anti-Federalists.

5. *Who's* is a contraction; the correct word should be the possessive pronoun *whose*.

AGREEMENT

Pronoun-Antecedent Agreement

A pronoun agrees with its antecedent in both person and number.

>**Example:** The archaeologists examined the fossilized bone with great care to make sure they didn't damage *it*.

>**Explanation:** The pronoun *they* refers to archaeologists, its antecedent. The pronoun *it* refers to *bone*, its antecedent.

 Remember to use a singular pronoun when you refer to indefinite pronouns such as *everyone, everybody, each, every, anyone, anybody, nobody, none, no one, one, either,* and *neither*.

Examples:

Although Union High School's male lacrosse players operate as a team, each knows it's his (*not their*) responsibility to arrive on time and in uniform.

Despite the fact that many of the women came from wealthy families, everyone who attended the Seneca Falls conference on women's rights risked her (not *their*) life and reputation.

When the programmers were questioned, neither could be certain if it was *his* or *her* (not *their*) mistake that caused the computer network to crash.

Subject-Verb Agreement

Basic Rule

A verb agrees in number with its subject. A singular subject takes a singular verb. A plural subject takes a plural verb.

>**Examples:** <u>Coral reefs</u> <u>are</u> an important part of the marine ecosystem.
>

>My <u>teacher</u> <u>believes</u> that <u>coral reefs</u> <u>are</u> an important part of the marine ecosystem.
>

For the following sentence, choose the correct verb: (is, am, are)

>Booker T. Washington, Frederick Douglass, and W.E.B. DuBois _____ all important historical figures.

>**Explanation:** Remember that the verb must agree with the subject. Since the subject is plural—subjects joined by *and* are plural—a plural verb is needed. The correct response therefore should be:

>Booker T. Washington, Frederick Douglass, and W.E.B. DuBois are all important historical figures.

Sometimes the subject comes after the verb, but the rule still applies.

Choose the correct verb: (is, are)

While the lecture has lasted two hours already, there _____ still three more speakers.

Explanation: The correct choice is *are* since the subject *speakers* is plural and requires a plural verb.

 There is one major exception to this rule. When the sentence is introduced by the word "there" and the verb is followed by a compound (double) subject, the first part of the subject dictates whether the verb should be singular or plural.

Example: There *is one American astronaut* in the shuttle and four Russian astronauts in the space station.

When compound subjects are joined by *either-or* or *neither-nor,* the verb agrees with the subject closest to the verb.

Examples:

Neither the violinist nor *the other musicians have had* much experience performing for an audience.

Neither you nor *I am* willing to make the sacrifices required of a professional musician.

Explanation:

In the first example, *musicians* (plural) is closest to the verb; in the second example, *I* (singular) is closest to the verb.

Sometimes a word or a group of words may come between the subject and the verb. The verb still must agree with the simple subject, and the *simple subject is never part of a prepositional phrase.*

Example:

Stephen King, the author of hundreds of best-selling novels, novellas, and short stories, *is* also a guitarist and singer in a band.

The simple subject is *Stephen King*, a singular noun. The verb must be *is.*

Choose the correct verb: (was, were)

The causes of the deterioration of coral reefs _____ not known until recently.

Explanation:

The simple subject is *causes;* "of the deterioration of coral reefs" is a prepositional phrase. Since the subject is plural, the plural verb *were* is required. So, the correct answer is *were.*

 The third person singular of most verbs ends in "s." First person: I, we speak; second person: you speak; third person: he, she, it speaks. Examples: He runs. She jogs. It jumps. The man sees. Mary laughs. The child walks.

COLLECTIVE NOUNS

Collective nouns present special problems. A collective noun names a group of people or things. Although usually singular in form, it is treated as either singular or plural according to the sense of the sentence:

- A *collective* is treated as singular when members of the group act, or are considered, as a unit:

  Example: The citizens' *assembly is drafting* a petition that would seek to protect local aquifers from chemical run-off and hazardous waste.

- A *collective* is treated as plural when the members act, or are considered, as multiple individuals:

  Example: After one of the longest and most fabled droughts in baseball history, the *Boston Red Sox have* finally overcome the "Curse of the Bambino" to win another World Series.

Common collective nouns include:

assembly, association, audience, board, cabinet, class, commission, committee, company, corporation, council, counsel, couple, crowd, department, family, firm, group, jury, majority, minority, number, pair, press, public, staff, United States

The following short words—though seldom listed as collective nouns—are governed by the same rules. They are singular or plural according to the intended meaning of the sentence.

all, any, more, most, some, who, which

Skill Builder: Agreement

> **DIRECTIONS:** Follow the principles of agreement and choose the correct word.

1. (is, are) The president and vice president of the United States of America ___ expected to attend tomorrow's historic ceremony honoring Rosa Parks.

2. (have, has) Either the chair of the department or one of the professors ___ the necessary paperwork.

3. (was, were) In the time of the first settlers, there ___ no antibiotics to prevent outbreaks of disease.

4. (its, their) Because of ___ biodiversity, coral reefs are often called "the rainforests of the sea."

5. (her, their) After a brief introduction, each of the doctors presented ___ findings at the medical conference.

6. (is, are) Many young people are surprised to find out that the music of Verdi's operas ___ as vibrant and fun as anything on the radio.

7. (his, their) As the conductor took the podium, the musicians finished tuning ___ instruments.

8. (know, knows) Neither Sherlock Holmes nor the detectives of Scotland Yard ___ who the perpetrator is.

9. (is, are) According to preliminary market reports, either Xiaomi or Huawei ___ the biggest smartphone provider in China.

10. (is, are) However, neither the Republicans nor the Democrats ___ satisfied with the language of the new nuclear weapons treaty.

Answers and Explanations

1. **The correct answer is *are*.** The plural subject *president and vice president* requires the plural *are*.

2. **The correct answer is *has*.** The verb must agree with the subject closest to it, in this case the singular *one*.

3. **The correct answer is *were*.** The plural subject *antibiotics* requires the plural *were*.

4. **The correct answer is *their*.** The plural subject *coral reefs* requires the plural *their*.

5. **The correct answer is *her*.** The singular subject *each* requires the singular *her*.

6. **The correct answer is *is*.** The singular subject *music* requires the singular *is*.

7. **The correct answer is *their*.** The plural antecedent *musicians* requires the plural *their*.

8. **The correct answer is *know*.** In a *neither-nor* construction, the verb is governed by the closest subject, *detectives*.

9. **The correct answer is *is*.** The singular determiner *either* requires the singular verb *is*.

10. **The correct answer is *are*.** In a *neither-nor* construction, the verb is governed by the closest subject, *Democrats*.

Skill Builder: Agreement

> **DIRECTIONS:** Revise the underlined words to eliminate agreement errors. If the underlined word is grammatically correct, write C above it. If a change is necessary, indicate the change and give a grammatical reason for it. Do not make unnecessary changes.

Joseph, one of my best friends, <u>are</u> considering becoming a medical doctor. He and I <u>believe</u> that medicine, compared to

　　　　　　　　　　　　　　　　　1　　　　　　　　　　　　　　　　　　　　　　　**2**

other professions, <u>are</u> an exciting and fulfilling field. In order to help him decide, he asked each of his friends to give his or her

　　　　　　　　　　3

opinion about why medicine would or would not be a fulfilling career choice. After that, he also asked his parents for their

opinions. It seems that his friends and his mother <u>is</u> in agreement, but his father <u>do</u> not agree.

　　　　　　　　　　　　　　　　　　　　　　　　　　　4　　　　　　　　　　　　　　**5**

Jacob's father feels strongly that the medical profession, unlike other professions, <u>requires</u> an excessive amount of study and is

　　　　　　　　　　　　　　　　　　　　　　　　　　　　　　　　　　　　　　6

too emotionally taxing. On the other hand, his friends and his mother <u>agree</u> that while the schooling is rigorous, the practice

　　　　　　　　　　　　　　　　　　　　　　　　　　　　　7

itself would be very rewarding.

Jacob <u>is</u> still deciding what he wants to be, but he and I <u>has</u> learned that there <u>is</u> always many possible answers to a question.

　　　8　　　　　　　　　　　　　　　　　　　　　　**9**　　　　　　　　　**10**

Answers and Explanations

1. **The correct answer is *is*.** The subject, *Joseph*, is singular.

2. **The correct answer is C.** The subject, *He and I*, is plural.

3. **The correct answer is *is*.** The subject, *medicine*, is singular.

4. **The correct answer is *are*.** The subject, *his friends and his mother*, is plural.

5. **The correct answer is *does*.** The subject, *father*, is singular.

6. **The correct answer is C.** The subject, *medical profession*, is singular.

7. **The correct answer is C.** The subject, *friends and mother*, is plural.

8. **The correct answer is C.** The subject, *Jacob*, is singular.

9. **The correct answer is *have*.** The subject, *he and I*, is plural.

10. **The correct answer is *are*.** The subject, *answers*, is plural.

FREQUENTLY CONFUSED WORDS

The following pages review groups of words that are similar in sound and/or meaning and are generally found to be confusing to students and adults alike. Misunderstanding what they mean or how they are used results in various usage problems. The word groups have been broken down into manageable sections to help you learn them more easily. Do not try to master all the information at once. Study one section at a time.

At the end of each section there is a practice exercise. See how well you do on the exercise by checking your answers against the answers and explanations given. If you do well, go on to the next section. If you find that you have made a number of errors, review the section. It is important that you master each section before moving on to the next one.

FREQUENTLY CONFUSED WORDS: GROUP 1

a is used before words that start with a consonant sound

an is used before words that start with a vowel sound

> Please give the baby *a* toy.
>
> He is *an* only child. We put up *a* united front. (*United* begins with a consonant sound—*y*.)
>
> We spent *an* hour together. (*Hour* begins with a vowel sound, since the *h* is silent.)

and is used to join words or ideas

> We enjoy shopping *and* sightseeing.
>
> She is a very serious student, *and* her grades are the best in the class.

accept means to receive or to agree to something

except means to exclude or excluding

> I'll *accept* the gift from you.
>
> Everyone *except* my uncle went home.
>
> My uncle was *excepted* from the group of losers.

advice means counsel (noun), opinion

advise means *to* offer advice (verb)

> Let me give you some free *advice*.
>
> I'd *advise* you to see your doctor.

affect means to influence (verb)

effect means to cause or bring about (verb) or a result (noun)

> The pollution can *affect* your health.
>
> The landmark decision will *effect* a change in the law.
>
> The *effect* of the storm could not be measured.

all ready means everybody or everything ready

already means previously

> They were *all ready* to write when the test began.
>
> They had *already* written the letter.

all together means everybody or everything together

altogether means *completely*

> The boys and girls stood *all together* in line.
>
> His action was *altogether* strange for a person of his type.

desert (DEZZ-ert) means an arid area

desert (di-ZERT) means to abandon, or a reward or punishment (usually plural)

dessert (di-ZERT) means the final course of a meal

> I have seen several movies set in the Sahara *desert*.
>
> The soldier was warned not to *desert* his company.
>
> We're certain that execution is a just *desert* for his crime.
>
> He received his just *deserts*.
>
> We had strawberry shortcake for *dessert*.

in is used to indicate inclusion, location, or motion within limits

into is used for motion toward one place from another

> The spoons are *in* the drawer.
>
> We were walking *in* the room.
>
> I put the spoons *into* the drawer.
>
> She walked *into* the room.

it's is the contraction of *it is* or *it has*

its is a possessive pronoun meaning belonging to it

> *It's* a very difficult assignment.
>
> We tried to analyze *its* meaning.

lay means to put

lie means to recline

> *To lay:*
>
> | (present) | I lay |
> |---|---|
> | (past) | I laid the gift on the table. |
> | (present perfect) | I have laid |
>
> *To lie:*
>
> | (present) | I lie |
> |---|---|
> | (past) | I lay on my blanket at the beach. |
> | (present perfect) | I have lain |

lets is third person singular present of *let*

let's is a contraction for *let us*

> He *lets* me park my car in his garage.
>
> *Let's* go home early today.

loose means not fastened or restrained, or not tight-fitting

lose means to mislay, to be unable to keep, to be defeated

> The dog got *loose* from the leash.
>
> Try not to *lose* your umbrella.

passed is the past tense of to pass

past means just preceding or an earlier time

> The week *passed* very quickly.
>
> The *past* week was a very exciting one.

principal means chief or main (adjective), or a leader, or a sum of money (noun)

principle means a fundamental truth or belief

> His *principal* support comes from the real estate industry.
>
> The *principal* of the school called a meeting of the faculty.
>
> He earned 10 percent interest on the *principal* he invested last year.
>
> As a matter *of principle,* he refused to register for the draft.

quiet means silent, still

quit means to give up, to discontinue

quite means very or exactly, to the greatest extent

> My brother is very shy and *quiet*.
>
> I *quit* the team last week.
>
> His analysis is *quite* correct.

raise means to lift, to erect

raze means to tear down

rise means to get up, to move from a lower to a higher position, to increase in value

> The neighbors helped him *raise* a new barn.
>
> The demolition crew *razed* the old building.
>
> The price of silver will *rise* again this month.

set means to place something down (mainly)

sit means to seat oneself (mainly)

> *To set:*
>
> (present)   He sets
>
> (past)   He set the lamp on the table.
>
> (present perfect)   He has set
>
> *To sit:*
>
> (present)   He sits
>
> (past)   He sat on the chair.
>
> (present perfect)   He has sat

stationary means standing still

stationery means writing material

> In ancient times, people thought that the earth was *stationary*.
>
> We bought our school supplies at the *stationery* store.

suppose means to assume or guess

supposed is the past tense and also past participle of *suppose*

supposed also means ought to or should (when followed by *to*)

> I *suppose* you will be home early.
>
> I *supposed* you would be home early.
>
> I had *supposed* you would be there.
>
> I am *supposed to* be in school tomorrow.

than is used to express comparison

then is used to express time or a result or consequence

> Jim ate more *than* we could put on the large plate.
>
> I knocked on the door, and *then* I entered.
>
> If you go, *then* I will go, too.

their means belonging to them

there means in that place

they're is the contraction for they are

> We took *their* books home with us.
>
> Your books are over *there* on the desk.
>
> *They're* coming over for dinner.

though means although or as if

thought is the past tense of to think, or an idea (noun)

through means in one side and out another, by way of, finished

> *Though* he is my friend, I can't recommend him for this job.
>
> I *thought* you were serious!
>
> We enjoyed running *through* the snow.

to means in the direction of (preposition); it is also used before a verb to indicate the infinitive

too means very, also

two is the numeral 2

> We shall go *to* school.
>
> It is *too* hot today.
>
> We shall go, *too*.
>
> I ate *two* sandwiches for lunch.

use means to employ, put into service

used is the past tense and the past participle of *use*

> I want to *use* your chair.
>
> I *used* your chair.

used, meaning in the habit of or accustomed to, is followed by *to*

used is an adjective meaning not new

> I am *used to* your comments.
>
> I bought a *used* car.

weather refers to *atmospheric conditions*

whether introduces a choice; it should not be preceded by *of* or *as to*

> I don't like the *weather* in San Francisco.
>
> He inquired *whether* we were going to the dance.

were is a past tense of *be*

we're is a contraction of *we are*

where refers to place or location

> They *were* there yesterday.
>
> *We're* in charge of the decorations.
>
> *Where* are we meeting your brother?

who's is the contraction for *who is* (or *who has*)

whose means of whom, implying ownership

> *Who's* the next batter?
>
> *Whose* notebook is on the desk?

your is a possessive, showing ownership

you're is a contraction for *you are*

> Please give him *your* notebook.
>
> *You're* very sweet.

Skill Builder: Usage

> **DIRECTIONS:** Circle the correct word to complete the sentence while adhering to formal American English conventions.

1. The patriot Samuel Adams was one of the (principal, principle) organizers of the Boston Tea Party.

2. Merchants in Boston refused to (accept, except) the taxes imposed upon them by the Tea Act of 1773.

3. Though the significance of the Tea Act of 1773 cannot be overrestimated, (weather, whether) or not the Tea Act of 1773 led to the American Revolution is hard to say.

4. In late November of 1773, the ship the Dartmouth sailed (in, into) Boston Harbor.

5. Governor Hutchinson was determined to collect the taxes and (adviced, advised) the tea consignees not to back down.

6. More (than, then) 40 tons of tea were thrown into the water during the Boston Tea Party.

7. Tea smuggling was (all ready, already) a significant problem, especially in New York and Philadelphia.

8. The overall (affect, effect) of the Boston Tea Party was to bolster the revolutionary fervor that was sweeping New England.

9. The British Crown reacted swiftly and harshly in order to dispel the idea that they were (loosing, losing) control of the colonies.

10. (All together, Altogether) 342 chests of tea, weighing over 92,000 pounds, were dumped into the water.

Answers

1. principal
2. accept
3. whether
4. into
5. advised
6. than
7. already
8. effect
9. losing
10. altogether

Frequently Confused Words: Group 2

abbreviate means to shorten by omitting

abridge means to shorten by condensing

> New York is *abbreviated* to NY.
>
> In order to save time in the reading, the report was *abridged*.

ad is used informally, but in formal usage *advertisement* is correct; similarly: *exam* (examination), *auto* (automobile), *phone* (telephone), *gym* (gymnasium)

advantage means a superior position

benefit means a favor conferred or earned (as a profit)

> He had an *advantage* in experience over his opponent.
>
> The rules were changed for his *benefit*.

aggravate means to make worse

annoy means to bother or to irritate

> Your nasty comments *aggravated* a bad situation.
>
> Your nasty comments *annoyed* him. (Not: Your nasty comments aggravated him.)

ain't is an unacceptable contraction for *am not, are not,* or *is not,* although *ain't* is sometimes heard in very informal speech

alibi is an explanation on the basis of being in another place

excuse is an explanation on any basis

> The accused man's *alibi* was that he was in another town when the robbery occurred.
>
> Whenever he is late, he makes up a new *excuse*.

all ways means in every possible way

always means at all times

> He was in *all ways* acceptable to the voters.
>
> He was *always* ready to help.

almost means nearly, not quite

most refers to the greatest amount or number or to the largest part, a majority

> We are *almost* finished writing the book.
>
> *Most* of the credit should be given to his uncle.

alongside of means side by side with

alongside means parallel to the side

He stood *alongside of* her at the corner.

Park the car *alongside* the curb.

allot means to give or apportion

I will *allot* 3 hours for painting the table.

alot is a misspelling of a lot

He earned *a lot* of money. (Better: He earned *a great deal* of money.)

alright is now often employed in common usage to mean *all right* (In formal usage, *all right* is still preferred by most authorities.)

all right means satisfactory, very well, uninjured, or without doubt

I'm *alright,* thank you.

It was his responsibility, *all right.*

alternate, as a noun, means a substitute or second choice

alternate, as a verb, means to perform by turns

alternative means a choice between two things, only one of which may be accepted

She served as an *alternate* delegate to the convention.

The cook *alternated* green beans and cauliflower on the menu.

Is there an *alternative* to the proposition? (In less formal usage, *alternative* is not always limited to a choice between *two.)*

alumna means a female graduate (plural: *alumnae*; *ae* rhymes with key)

alumnus means a male graduate (plural: *alumni*; *ni* rhymes with high)

She is an *alumna* of Mrs. Brown's School for Young Women.

He is an *alumnus* of City College.

among is used to discuss more than two items

between is used to discuss *two* items only

The work was divided *among* the four brothers.

She divided the pie *between* Joe and Marie.

amount is used to refer to a quantity not individually countable

number is used to refer to items that can be counted individually

A tremendous *amount* of work had piled up on my desk.

We ate a great *number* of cookies at the party.

annual means yearly

biannual means twice a year (also semiannual)

biennial means once in two years or every two years

Skill Builder: Usage

DIRECTIONS: Circle the correct word to complete the sentence while adhering to formal American English conventions.

1. The (abbreviated, abridged) jobs report omitted jobs in the arts in order to make the report more manageable.

2. Detectives often ask suspects if they have an (alibi, excuse) for where they were on the night of a given crime.

3. Animal trainers must (allot, a lot) a significant amount of their work time to building a relationship with their animals.

4. The famous dog trainer Felix Ho is an (alumna, alumnus) of La Trobe University in Melbourne, Australia.

5. Animal care and service workers often divide their time (among, between) training, feeding, grooming, and exercising their animals.

6. Learning how to be an effective animal trainer requires a tremendous (amount, number) of work.

7. Animals form very real bonds with their trainers; likewise, trainers are often (anxious, eager) to see their animals when they have been away.

8. While horse trainers rarely have formal schooling in their field, they can't get their training just (anywhere, anywheres).

9. Becoming a good animal trainer requires experience that can be (awfully, very) difficult to attain.

10. Many animal trainers feel (bad, badly) when they have to leave their animals for long periods of time.

11. (Because, Being that) zookeepers and marine mammal trainers require formal education, they tend to make more money than other animal care professionals.

Answers

1. abbreviated

2. alibi

3. allot

4. alumnus

5. among

6. amount

7. eager

8. anywhere

9. very

10. bad

11. Because

207

Chapter 5

Standard
English
Conventions

Frequently Confused Words: Group 3

beside means at the side of

besides means in addition to

> In our tennis game, he played *beside* me at the net.
>
> We entertained Jim, Sue, and Louise, *besides* the members of the chorus.

better means recovering

well means completely recovered

better is used with the verb *had* to show desirability

> He is *better* now than he was a week ago.
>
> In a few more weeks, he will be *well.*
>
> He *had better* (not *he better)* follow instructions or pay the penalty.

between you and I is the incorrect form, since the object of the preposition *between* should be the objective case *me*, not the subjective case *I*

> *Between you and me,* he has not been very helpful this week.

both means two considered together

each means one of two or more

> *Both* of the applicants qualified for the position.
>
> *Each* applicant was given a good reference.

bring means to carry toward the speaker

take means to carry away from the speaker

> *Bring* the coat to me.
>
> *Take* money for carfare when you leave.

bunch is used informally to describe a group of people, but in formal usage *group* is preferred

> When he returned to his office, he learned that a *group* of students was waiting for him.

burst is used in present and past tenses to mean to explode (or to break)

bust and *busted* are incorrect forms of burst

> I do hope the balloon will not *burst.*
>
> He cried when the balloon *burst.* (not *busted)*

but that is sometimes heard in informal usage, but in formal usage *that* is correct

> He never doubted *that* she would visit him.

can means able

may implies permission or possibility

> *I can* eat both desserts.
>
> *May I* eat both desserts?
>
> It *may* snow tonight.

cannot seem is sometimes used informally, but in formal usage *seems unable* is correct

> My elderly uncle *seems unable* to remember his own phone number.

complected should not be used for complexioned

> At the beach, the fair-*complexioned* boy stayed under an umbrella.

consistently means in harmony

constantly means regularly, steadily

> If you give me advice, you should act *consistently* with that advice.
>
> I *constantly* warned him about leaving the door unlocked.

continual means happening again and again at short intervals

continuous means without interruption

> The teacher gave the class *continual* warnings.
>
> Noah experienced *continuous* rain for forty days.

could of is an incorrect form of *could have,* which can be contracted to *could've* in speech or informal writing

> I wish that I *could've gone.* (Better: I wish that I *could have gone.*)

couple refers to two; *several* or *a few* refers to more than two

> Alex and Frieda are the most graceful *couple* on the dance floor.
>
> A *few* of my cousins—Mary, Margie, Alice, and Barbara—will be at the reunion tonight.

data is the Latin plural of *datum,* meaning information (*data* is preferred with plural verbs and pronouns, but is now acceptable in the singular)

> These *data* were very significant to the study. (Or: This *data* was very significant to the study.)

did is the past tense of *do*

done is the past participle of *do*

> I *did* whatever was required to complete the job.
>
> I have *done* what you requested.

different than is often used informally, but in formal usage *different from* is correct

>Jack is *different from* his brother.

disinterested means impartial

uninterested means not interested

>The judge must be a *disinterested* party in a trial.
>I'm an *uninterested* bystander, so I find the proceedings boring.

doesn't is a contraction of *does not* (third person singular)

don't is a contraction of *do not* and is not a substitute for *doesn't*

>She *doesn't* go to school.
>They *don't* go to school.

doubt whether is often heard in informal usage, but *doubt that* is the correct form

>I *doubt that* I will be home this evening.

due to is sometimes used informally at the beginning of a sentence, but in formal usage *because of, on account of,* or some similar expression is preferred

>*Because of* (not *due to*) the rain, the game was postponed. (But: The postponement was *due to* the rain.)

each other refers to two persons

one another refers to more than two persons

>Jane and Jessica have known *each other* for many years.
>Several of the girls have known *one another* for many years.

either … or is used to refer to choices

neither … nor is the negative form

>*Either* Lou *or* Jim will drive you home.
>*Neither* Alice *nor* Carol will be home tonight.

else than is sometimes heard in informal usage, but in formal usage *other than* is correct

>Shakespeare was rarely regarded by students as anything *other than* the writer of plays.

enthuse or *enthused* should be avoided; use *enthusiastic*

>We were *enthusiastic* when given the chance to travel abroad.

equally as good is an incorrect form; *equally good* or *just as good* is correct

>This bicycle is *just as good* as that one.

etc. is the abbreviation for the Latin term *et cetera,* meaning and so forth, and other things. In general, it is better to be specific and not use *etc.*

I think that oranges, peaches, cherries, *etc.,* are healthful. (*Etc.* is not preceded by *and*)

everyone, written as one word, is a pronoun

every one, written as two words, is used to refer to each individual

Everyone present voted for the proposal.

Every one of the voters accepted the proposal.

every bit is incorrect usage for *just as*

You are *just as* (not *every bit as*) clever as she is.

ever so often means frequently or repeatedly

every so often means occasionally or now and again

He sees his brother *ever so often,* practically every day.

Since tickets are so expensive, we only attend the theater *every so often.*

expect is sometimes used incorrectly to mean assume or presume

I *assume* (not *expect*) that he won the race.

211

Chapter 5

Standard
English
Conventions

Skill Builder: Usage

> **DIRECTIONS:** Circle the correct word to complete the sentence while adhering to formal American English conventions.

1. (Beside, Besides) needing a bachelor's degree in marine biology, animal science, biology, or a related field, marine mammal trainers often need to have SCUBA certification.

2. Between you and (me, I), training lions does not sound like fun!

3. After a rigorous application process, (both, each) of the trainers were hired.

4. A dog trainer might begin with a simple task, such as training a dog to (bring, take) a rubber ball back to him.

5. Young students often ask zookeepers, "(Can, May) I help you feed the animals?"

6. While job opportunities in kennels, grooming shops, and pet stores are increasing, many advanced animal care professionals, such as zookeepers and marine mammal trainers, (cannot seem, seem unable) to find work.

7. In jobs surveys, the percentage of nonfarm animal caretakers (consistently, constantly) outnumbers the number of actual animal trainers.

8. Here are a (couple, few) examples of what an animal care specialist might do: give food and water to animals; clean equipment and the living spaces of animals; monitor animals and record details of their diet, physical condition, and behavior; and examine animals for signs of illness or injury.

9. Even though they sound the same, the job of a pet groomer is very (different from, different than) the job of a horse groom.

10. (Because of, Due to) employment growth and high job turnover, job opportunities in the animal care and services field will continue to grow.

11. The starting salary for animal care and service workers is (equally as good, just as good) as the starting salary for nonfarm animal caretakers.

212

Chapter 5

Standard English Conventions

Answers

1. Besides

2. me

3. both

4. bring

5. May

6. seem unable

7. constantly

8. few

9. different from

10. Because of

11. just as good

FREQUENTLY CONFUSED WORDS: GROUP 4

fewer is used to refer to items that can be counted

less is used to refer to something viewed as a mass, not as a series of individual items

> I made *fewer* repairs on the new car than on the old one.
>
> After the scandal, the company enjoyed *less* prestige than it had the previous year.

finalized is used to mean concluded or completed, usually in informal usage; in formal usage, *completed* is preferred

> Labor and management *completed* arrangements for a settlement.

flaunt means to make a display of

flout means to show contempt, scorn

> He *flaunted* his new wealth in an ostentatious manner.
>
> She *flouted* the policeman's authority.

former means the first of two

latter means the second of two

> The *former* half of the story was in prose.
>
> The *latter* half of the story was in poetry.

good is an adjective; *good* is often used informally as an adverb, but the correct word is *well*

> She is a *good* singer.
>
> She sings *well*.

graduated is followed by the preposition *from* when it indicates completion of a course of study

graduated also means divided into categories or marked intervals

> He *graduated from* high school last year. (Or: He *was graduated from* high school last year.)
>
> A *graduated* test tube is one that has markings on it to indicate divisions.

guess is sometimes used informally to mean *think* or *suppose,* but it is incorrect in formal use

> I *think* (not *guess*) I'll go home now.

habit means an individual tendency to repeat a thing

custom means group habit

> He had a *habit* of breaking glasses before each recital.
>
> The *custom* of the country was to betroth girls at an early age.

had ought is an incorrect form for *ought* or *should*

hadn't ought is an incorrect form for *should not* or *ought not*

> The men *ought* (not *had ought*) to go to the game now.
>
> He *ought not* (not *hadn't ought*) to have spoken.
>
> He *should not* (not *hadn't ought*) have spoken.

hanged is used in reference to a person

hung is used in reference to a thing

> The prisoner was *hanged* in the town square.
>
> The drapes were *hung* unevenly.

have got is incorrect usage; *got* should be omitted

> I *have* an umbrella.

healthful is used to express whatever *gives* health

healthy is used to express whatever *has* health

> He follows a *healthful* diet.
>
> He is a *healthy* person.

hisself is a misspelling of *himself*

> Let him do it *himself.*

humans is used informally to refer to human beings, but in formal usage *human beings* is correct

> He says that love is a basic need of all *human beings.* (But used as an adjective: He says that love is a basic *human* need.)

if introduces a condition

whether introduces a choice

> I shall go to Greece *if* I win the prize.
>
> He asked me *whether* I intended to go to Greece.

if it was implies that something might have been true in the past

if it were implies doubt or indicates something that is contrary to fact

> If your book *was* there last night, it is there now.
>
> *If it were* summer now, we would all go swimming.

imply means to suggest or hint at (the speaker *implies*)

infer means *to deduce* or *conclude* (the listener *infers*)

> Are you *implying* that I have disobeyed orders?
>
> From your carefree tone, what else are we *to infer?*

in back of means behind

in the back of (or *at the back of*) means in the rear of

>   The shovel is *in back of* (behind) the barn.

>   John is sitting *in the back of* the theater.

in regards to is an incorrect form for *in regard to*

>   He called me *in regard to* your letter.

instance where is sometimes used informally, but the correct term is *instance in which*

>   Can you tell me of one *instance in which* such a terrible thing occurred?

irregardless in an incorrect form for *regardless*

>   I'll be your friend *regardless* of what people say, even if the people are accurate.

is when and *is where* are sometimes used informally, but in formal usage *occurs when* and *is a place where* are correct

>   The best scene *occurs when* the audience least expects it.

>   My favorite vacation spot *is a place where* there are no telephones.

kind of and *sort of* are informal expressions that should be rephrased in formal writing—for instance, *somewhat* or *rather* are preferable

>   I am *rather* sorry he retired.

>   He was *somewhat* late for the meeting.

kid is used informally to mean child (noun) or to make fun of (verb) but is incorrect in formal usage

>   My cousin is a very sweet *child*.

>   They always laugh when you *make fun of me*.

learn means to acquire knowledge

teach means to give knowledge

>   We can *learn* many things just by observing carefully.

>   He is one actor who likes to *teach* his craft to others.

least means the *smallest in degree* or *lowest rank*

less means the smaller or lower of two

>   This is the *least* desirable of all the apartments we have seen.

>   This apartment is *less* spacious than the one we saw yesterday.

leave means to go away from (a verb is NOT used with *leave*)

let means to permit (a verb IS used with *let*)

> *Leave* this house at once.
>
> *Let* me remain in peace in my own house.

lend is a verb meaning to give to

loan is a noun denoting what is given

borrow means to take from

> The bank was willing to *lend* him $500.
>
> He was granted a *loan* of $500.
>
> I'd like to *borrow* your electric drill for an hour.

liable means responsible according to the law

likely suggests probable behavior

> If he falls down the stairs, we may be *liable* for damages.
>
> A cat, if annoyed, is *likely* to scratch.

libel is a written and published statement injurious to a person's character

slander is a spoken statement of the same sort

> The unsubstantiated negative comments about me in your book constitute *libel*.
>
> When you say these vicious things about me, you are committing *slander*.

like is a preposition used to introduce a phrase

as if is used to introduce a clause (a subject and a verb)

as is a conjunction used to introduce a clause

like if is an incorrect form for *like, as,* or *as if*

> It seems *like* a sunny day.
>
> It seems *as if* it is going to be a sunny day.
>
> He acted *as* he was expected to act.

many refers to a number

much refers to a quantity or amount

> How *many* inches of rain fell last night?
>
> *Much* rain fell last night.

may of is an incorrect form for *may have*

might of is an incorrect form for *might have*

> **NOTE:** Contractions of these terms are unacceptable in formal usage.
>
> He *may have* been there, but I didn't see him.
>
> I *might have* gone to the party if I hadn't been ill.

Skill Builder: Usage

> **DIRECTIONS:** Circle the correct word to complete the sentence while adhering to formal American English conventions.

1. As of 2012, the median annual wage for nonfarm animal caretakers is (less, fewer) than $20,000.

2. During the interrogation, the lawyer (flaunted, flouted) his authority as he questioned the accused thief.

3. In addition to being patient with animals, animal caretakers must also work (good, well) with people!

4. She is one of 2,200 people to (graduate, graduate from) the National Association of Professional Pet Sitters' certification program.

5. While in captivity, many animals develop nervous (customs, habits), such as pacing and over-grooming.

6. While it is usually not required, animal caretakers in shelters (ought, had ought) to attend training programs through the Humane Society of the United States and the American Humane Association.

7. Keepers in zoos plan diets, monitor eating patterns, and clean enclosures in order to maintain (healthful, healthy) animals.

8. Often, the difference between the needs of animals and (human beings, humans) is not as great as you think.

9. (Irregardless, Regardless) of one's education, the number one trait an animal trainer must have is a love for animals.

10. While it does happen, it is (rather, sort of) rare for a groom to be hired who does not have significant prior experience with horses.

11. Animal trainers take good care of their animals because when animals are neglected, they are more (liable, likely) to become aggressive and dangerous.

Answers

1. less

2. flaunted

3. well

4. graduate from

5. habits

6. ought

7. healthy

8. human beings

9. Regardless

10. rather

11. likely

Frequently Confused Words: Group 5

maybe means perhaps, possibly (adverb)

may be shows possibility (verb)

> *Maybe* he will meet us later.
>
> He *may be* here later.

mighty means powerful or great; it should not be used in formal writing to mean *very*

> He was *very* (not *mighty*) sleepy.

media is the Latin plural of *medium*; it refers to a means of mass communication or artistic expression and is used with a plural verb

> Most *media* that report the news realize their responsibility to the public.
>
> That artist's favorite *medium* is watercolor.

must of is an incorrect form for *must have*

> I *must have* been sleeping when you called. (A contraction of this term is unacceptable in formal usage.)

myself is used as an intensifier if the subject of the verb is *I*

myself instead of *I* or *me* is not correct

> Since I know *myself* better, let me try it my way.
>
> My daughter and *I* (not *myself*) will play.
>
> They gave my son and *me* (not *myself*) some food.

nice is used informally to mean pleasing, good, fine, but a more exact, less overused word is preferred

> This is *sunny* (or *good* or *fine*) weather (not *nice* weather).
>
> He is a *good* (or *kind*) person.

nowheres is incorrect usage for *nowhere*

> The dog was *nowhere* to be found.

off of is sometimes used informally, but *off* is correct in formal usage

> Joe was taken *off* the team.

okay (O.K.) is used informally but is to be avoided in formal writing

> *Informal:* His work is *okay.*
>
> *Formal:* His work is *acceptable* (or *good*).

on account of is an incorrect form of *because*

> We could not meet you *because* we did not receive your message in time.

oral means spoken

verbal means expressed in words, either spoken or written

> Instead of writing a note, she gave him an *oral* message.

> Shorthand must usually be transcribed into *verbal* form.

outdoor is an adjective

outdoors is an adverb

> We spent the summer at an *outdoor* music camp.

> We played string quartets *outdoors*.

owing to is used informally, but in formal usage *because* is preferred

> *Because* of a change of management, his company canceled the takeover attempt.

people comprise a united or collective group of individuals

persons are individuals who are separate and unrelated

> The *people* of our city will vote next week.

> Only ten *persons* remained in the theater after the first act.

per is a Latin term used mainly in business: *per diem* (by the day), *per hour* (by the hour). In formal writing, *according to* or *by the* is preferred

> As *per* your instructions... (Better: *According to* your instructions...)

plan on is used informally, but in formal usage *plan to* is correct

> Do you *plan to go* (not *plan on going*) to the lecture?

plenty means abundance (noun)

plenty is incorrect as an adverb or adjective

> There is *plenty* of room in that compact car.

> That compact car is *very* large (not *plenty* large).

prefer that than is the incorrect form for *prefer that to*

> I *prefer that to* anything else you might suggest.

put in is incorrect for to *spend, make,* or *devote*

> Every good student should *spend* (not *put in*) several hours a day doing homework.

> Be sure *to make* (not *put in*) an appearance at the meeting.

quit is sometimes used informally to mean *stop,* but in formal usage *stop* is preferred

> Please *stop* your complaining.

quite is used to mean *very* in informal usage, but in formal usage *very* is preferred

> Your comment was *very* (not *quite*) intelligent.

quite a few is used to mean *many* in informal usage, but in formal usage *many* is preferred

> My car has *many* (not *quite a few*) dents.

read where is heard in informal usage, but in formal usage *read that* is correct

> I *read that* the troops were being reviewed today.

real is sometimes used informally instead of *really* or *very*, but in formal usage *really* is correct

> He's a *very* (not *real*) good ballplayer.
> He plays *really* (not *real*) well with the band.

reason is because is used informally in speech, but in formal usage *the reason is that* is correct

> The *reason* she calls *is that* (not *because*) she is lonely. (Or: She calls *because* she is lonely.)

refer back/report back: since *re* means back or again, the word *back* is redundant and should be omitted

> Please *refer* to your notes.
> Please *report* to the supervisor.

repeat again is redundant; *again* should be omitted

> Please *repeat* the instructions.

respectfully means with respect and decency

respectively means as relating to each, in the order given

> The students listened *respectfully* to the principal.
> Jane and Lena are the daughters *respectively* of Mrs. Smith and Mrs. Jones.

run is used informally to mean *conduct, manage,* but in formal usage *conduct* or a similar word is preferred

> He wants to *conduct* (not *run*) the operation on a profitable basis.

said is sometimes used in business or law to mean *the* or *this*; in formal usage, *the* or *this* is correct

said is also used incorrectly to mean told someone

> When *the* (not *said*) coat was returned, it was badly torn.
> The professor *told us* (not *said*) to study for the examination.

same as is an incorrect form for *in the same way as* or *just as*

> The owner's son was treated *in the same way as* any other worker.

says is present tense of *say*

said is past tense of *say*

> He *says* what he means.
> He *said* what he meant. (*Goes* or *went* should not be used instead of *says* or *said.*)

Skill Builder: Usage

1. If you are interested in the social and organizational side of businesses, the field of organizational psychology (may be, maybe) the field for you.

2. As the economy continues to grow and more businesses are created, organizational psychology is becoming a (mighty, very) important field.

3. (Because of, On account of) their collaborative work with social workers and healthcare professionals, demand for psychologists is expected to increase in tandem with the healthcare industry overall.

4. (Nowhere, Nowheres) is the demand for psychologists growing more than in the field of organization psychology.

5. Because of the importance of talking with patients, clinical psychologists are expected to have good (oral, verbal) communication skills.

6. Psychologists typically work in offices, so if you prefer working (outdoor, outdoors), this might not be the job for you.

7. Over the next decade, the job market for psychologists will continue to grow in large part (because of, owing to) increased demand for psychological services in schools, hospitals, mental health centers, and social services agencies.

8. Most (people, persons) don't realize that there is a difference between a Ph.D. in psychology (a research degree) and a Psy.D. (a clinical degree).

9. While a master's degree is sufficient for some positions, most aspiring psychologists (plan on getting, plan to get) a Ph.D. or a Psy.D.

10. In addition to formal schooling, most clinical psychologists (put in, spend) hundreds of unpaid hours as interns in their fields of specialization.

11. The reason most aspiring psychologists get Ph.D.'s and Psy.D.'s is (because, that) there are more jobs available for psychologists with terminal degrees.

Answers

1. may be

2. very

3. Because of

4. Nowhere

5. oral

6. outdoors

7. because of

8. people

9. plan to get

10. spend

11. that

Frequently Confused Words: Group 6

saw is the past tense of *see*

seen is the past participle of *see*

> We *saw* a play yesterday.

> I have never *seen* a Broadway show.

seem is used in informal speech and writing in the expressions *I couldn't seem to* and *I don't seem to* but in formal usage:

> We *can't find* the address. (Not: We *can't seem to find* the address.)

seldom ever is used informally, but in formal usage *ever* is redundant and should be omitted, or *if* should be inserted

> I *seldom* swim in January.

> I *seldom if ever* swim in January.

shall is used with *I* and *we* in formal usage; informally, I *will (would)* may be used

will is used with *you, he, she, it, they*

> When an emphatic statement is intended, the rule is reversed

> I *shall* be there today.

> We *shall* pay the rent tomorrow.

> I certainly *will* be there.

> They *shall* not pass.

shape is incorrect when used to mean state or condition

> The refugees were in *serious condition* (not *shape*) when they arrived here.

should of is an incorrect form for *should have,* which can be contracted to *should've* in speech or informal writing

> You *should've* returned that sweater. (Better: You *should have* returned that sweater.)

sink down is sometimes heard in informal usage, but *down* is redundant and should be omitted

> You can *sink* into the mud if you are not careful.

some time means a segment of time

sometime means at an indefinite time in the future

sometimes means occasionally

> I'll need *some time* to make a decision.

> Let's meet *sometime* next week.

> *Sometimes* I have an urge to watch a late movie on television.

stayed means remained

stood means took or remained in an upright position or erect

> He *stayed* in bed for three days.

> The scouts *stood* at attention while the flag was lowered.

still more yet is redundant; *yet* should be omitted

> There is *still more* to be said.

sure is used informally to mean surely or certainly, but in formal usage *surely* or *certainly* is preferred

> She *certainly* (not *sure)* is pretty!

> We will *surely* be in trouble unless we get home soon.

testimony means information given orally

evidence means *i*nformation given orally or in writing; an object that is presented as proof

> He gave *testimony* to the grand jury.

> He presented written *evidence* to the judge.

than any is used informally in a comparison, but in formal usage *than any other* is preferred

> He is smarter *than any other* boy in the class.

the both is used informally, but in formal usage *the* should be omitted

> I intend to treat *both* of you to lunch.

their, in informal usage, often appears in the construction, "Anyone can lose their card," but because *anyone* takes a singular personal pronoun, *his* or *her* is the correct form

theirselves is an incorrect form for *themselves*

> They are able to care for *themselves* while their parents are at work.

them is the objective case of *they*; it is not used instead of *those* (the plural of *that)* before a noun

> Give me *those* (not *them)* books!

try and is sometimes used informally instead of *try to,* but in formal usage *try to* is correct

> My acting teacher is going to *try to* attend the opening of my play.

unbeknownst to is unacceptable for *without the knowledge of*

> The young couple decided to get married *without the knowledge of* (not *unbeknownst to)* their parents.

upwards of is an incorrect form for *more than*

> There are *more than* (not *upwards of)* 60,000 people at the football game.

valuable means of great worth

valued means held in high regard

invaluable means priceless

> This is a *valuable* manuscript.
>
> You are a *valued* friend.
>
> A good name is an *invaluable* possession.

wait on is sometimes used informally, but in formal usage *wait for* is correct

> We *waited for* (not *on*) him for over an hour.

which is sometimes used incorrectly to refer to people; it refers to things

who is used to refer to people

that is used to refer to people or things

> He decided to wear his orange striped tie, *which* had been a gift from his daughter.
>
> I am looking for the girl *who* made the call.
>
> He finally returned the books *that* he had borrowed.

while is unacceptable for *and, but, whereas,* or *though*

> The library is situated on the south side, *whereas* (not *while*) the laboratory is on the north side.
>
> *Though* (not *while*) I disagree with you, I shall not interfere with your right to express your opinion.

who is, who am is used with these constructions:

> It is *I who am* the most experienced.
>
> It is *he who is...*
>
> It is *he or I who am...*
>
> It is *I or he who is...*
>
> It is *he and I who are...*

who, whom To determine whether to use *who* or *whom* (without grammar rules), use *he, him*:

(Who, Whom) do you think should represent our company?

Step 1:	Change the *who—whom* part of the sentence to its natural order:
	Do you think *(who, whom)* should represent our company?
Step 2:	Substitute *he* for *who*, and *him* for *whom*:
	Do you think *(he, him)* should represent our company?
Step 3:	Since *he* would be used in this case, the correct form is:
	Who do you think should represent our company?

whoever, whomever (see *who, whom* above)

> Give the chair to *whoever* wants it (subject of verb *wants*).

> Speak to *whomever* you see (object of preposition *to*).

win is used when you win a game

beat is used when you beat another player; *beat* is incorrect usage for *swindle*

> We *won* the contest.

> We *beat* (not *won*) the other team.

> The hustler *swindled* the gambler out of twenty dollars.

without is incorrect usage for *unless*

> You will not receive the tickets *unless* (not *without*) you pay for them in advance.

worst kind and *worst way* are incorrect usages for terms such as *very badly* or *extremely*

> The school is *greatly in need* of more teachers (not *needs teachers in the worst way*).

would of is an incorrect form for *would have,* which can be contracted to *would've* in informal usage

> He *would've* treated you to the movies. (Better: He *would have* treated you to the movies.)

would have is *not* used instead of *had* in an *if* clause

> If I *had* (not *would have*) gone, I would have helped him.

225

Chapter 5

Standard
English
Conventions

Skill Builder: Usage

DIRECTIONS: Circle the correct word to complete the sentence while adhering to formal American English conventions.

1. In Sir Arthur Conan Doyle's story, "A Scandal in Bohemia," Sherlock Holmes (can't believe, can't seem to believe) that he's been outsmarted by the beautiful and alluring Irene Adler.

2. Forest conservation workers are (seldom, seldom ever) required to have education beyond a basic bachelor's degree.

3. According to his fictional biography, Sherlock Holmes's friend, John H. Watson, returns to England in serious (condition, shape) after being wounded in the Second Anglo-Afghan War.

4. (Some time, Sometime) in the near future, the U.S. Forest Service may be forced to undertake its own fire suppression duties, which will result in higher levels of employment.

5. At the end of all Sherlock Holmes stories, Holmes presents (evidence, testimony) that shows how a crime was committed and whom it was committed by.

6. According to some scholars, Sherlock Holmes is more recognizable (than any, than any other) fictional detective in the world.

7. The complexity of the Tube, Britain's underground railway system, makes it possible for anyone to lose (his or her, their) way.

8. In the event that they get lost, forest service workers need to be able to take care of (theirselves, themselves) in the wild.

9. If formal schooling is unavailable, aspiring forest and conservation services workers should (try and, try to) gain experience working in forestry-related fields.

10. As of 2012, there were (more than, upwards of) 10,000 jobs in the forest and conservation services field.

Answers

1. can't believe

2. seldom

3. condition

4. Some time

5. evidence

6. than any other

7. his or her

8. themselves

9. try to

10. more than

CONVENTIONAL EXPRESSIONS

A conventional expression is a phrase or clause that has become a characteristic way of expressing a certain idea. Ironically, despite these expressions being conventional, they are often misused.

Here is a list of commonly misused conventional expressions and their correct usages.

Incorrect Usage	Correct Usage
It's a doggy-dog world	It's a dog-eat-dog world
For all intensive purposes	For all intents and purposes
I'm *suppose to* go running	…supposed to…
statue of limitations	statute of limitations
I could care less	I couldn't care less
Fall by the waste side	Fall by the wayside
Irregardless	Regardless
Escape goat	Scapegoat
I guess we'll *make due*	…make do…
Peak my interest	Pique my interest
The criminal got away *scott free*	…scot free…
I'm waiting with *baited breath*	…bated breath…
Without further adieu	Without further ado
The boy had *free reign*	…free rein…
Hunger pains	Hunger pangs
I *should of* called	…should have…
Don't *step foot* on this carpet	…set foot…
Nipped in the butt	Nipped in the bud
The waiter was at his *beckon call*	…beck and call…
The lawyer made a *mute point*	…moot point…
Case and point	Case in point
The cops were starting to *hone in*	…home in…
One in the same	One and the same

LOGICAL COMPARISON

Basic Rule

In order for a comparison to make sense, it must be logical and complete.

In an incomplete comparison, what is being compared is unclear.

> **Incomplete:** According to some scholars of US history, the Magna Carta is more important because it was the first document to limit the powers of the King of England.

> **Complete:** According to some scholars of US history, the Magna Carta is more important than the Declaration of Independence because it was the first document to limit the powers of the King of England.

> **Incomplete:** At 864,000 miles across, the sun is more than 100 times the size.

> **Complete:** At 864,000 miles across, the sun is more than 100 times the size of Earth.

For a comparison to be logical, you must be comparing the same things.

> **Illogical:** Despite popular opinion, many scholars believe that the political achievements of Thomas Jefferson were much more significant to American history than George Washington. (Thomas Jefferson's achievements are being compared to the person George Washington.)

> **Logical:** Despite popular opinion, many scholars believe that the political achievements of Thomas Jefferson were much more significant to American history than the achievements of George Washington.

> **Illogical:** The distance from the sun to the planet Neptune is 30 times greater than the sun and Earth. (This distance from the sun to Neptune is being compared to the sun and Earth, not the distance between them.)

> **Logical:** The distance from the sun to the planet Neptune is 30 times greater than the distance from the sun to Earth.

Skill Builder: Logical Comparisons

DIRECTIONS: Revise the following comparisons to make sure they are logical.

1. According to scientists, the brain mass of a dolphin is actually slightly greater than a human.

2. Although they are on the same hemisphere, the average rainfall in South America differs greatly from North America.

3. In the 2015 World Happiness Report, the people of Switzerland ranked happier than America.

4. The tallest mountain in the United States is still 9,000 feet shorter than Nepal.

Answers

1. According to scientists, the brain mass of a dolphin is actually slightly greater than the brain mass of a human.

2. Although they are on the same hemisphere, the average rainfall in South America differs greatly from the average rainfall in North America.

3. In the 2015 World Happiness Report, the people of Switzerland ranked happier than the people of America.

4. The tallest mountain in the United States is still 9,000 feet shorter than the tallest mountain in Nepal.

CONVENTIONS OF PUNCTUATION

END-OF-SENTENCE PUNCTUATION

There are three types of punctuation used to end a sentence: the period, the question mark, and the exclamation mark.

1. A period is used at the end of a sentence that makes a statement.

    Examples:

    Toni Morrison's first novel, *The Bluest Eye,* was published in 1970.

    In 1620, the Pilgrims in Plymouth signed the Mayflower Compact.

2. A question mark is used after a direct question. A period is used after an indirect question.

    Examples:

    Direct Question—Were *The Federalist Papers* written by James Madison, John Jay, or Alexander Hamilton?

    Indirect Question—Profession Mahin wanted to know if you knew who wrote *The Federalist Papers.*

3. An exclamation mark is used after an expression that shows strong emotion or issues a command. It may follow a word, a phrase, or a sentence.

    Examples:

    Koko the gorilla knows more than 1,000 sign-language signs and can communicate with humans. Amazing!

    One of the most famous quotes in American history is Patrick Henry's, "Give me liberty or give me death!"

Chapter 5

Standard
English
Conventions

The Colon

Basic Rule

The colon is used to precede a list of three or more items or a long quotation.

Examples:

Christopher Columbus led three ships to the New World: *La Nina, La Pinta,* and *La Santa Maria.*

In the United States, there are three branches of government: the Executive, the Legislative, and the Judicial.

 Avoid using the colon after a verb. It can interrupt the natural flow of language.

Incorrect: The Louisiana Purchase included territory that would become: Montana, South Dakota, Nebraska, Kansas, Oklahoma, Arkansas, Louisiana, and Missouri.

Correct: The Louisiana Purchase included territory that would become many of today's states: Montana, South Dakota, Nebraska, Kansas, Oklahoma, Arkansas, Louisiana, and Missouri.

The Semicolon

Basic Rule

A semicolon may be used to separate two complete ideas (independent clauses) in a sentence when the two ideas have a close relationship and are *not* connected with a coordinating conjunction.

Example: "Inalienable rights" are basic human rights that many believe cannot and should not be given up or taken away; life, liberty, and the pursuit of happiness are some of those rights.

The semicolon is often used between independent clauses connected by conjunctive adverbs such as *consequently, therefore, also, furthermore, for example, however, nevertheless, still, yet, moreover,* and *otherwise.*

Example: In 1867, critics thought William H. Seward foolish for buying the largely unexplored territory of Alaska for the astronomical price of $7 million; however, history has proven that it was an inspired purchase.

 Do not use the semicolon between an independent clause and a phrase or subordinate clause.

Incorrect: While eating ice cream for dessert; Clarence and Undine discussed their next business venture.

Correct: While eating ice cream for dessert, Clarence and Undine discussed their next business venture.

230

Chapter 5

Standard
English
Conventions

www.petersons.com

Skill Builder: Punctuation

> **DIRECTIONS:** Decide whether the colons and semicolons are correctly placed in the following sentences or whether another mark of punctuation would be better. Write the correct punctuation in the space provided.

1. He is an excellent student and a fine person; as a result, he has many friends.

2. Because he is such an industrious student; he has many friends.

3. We tried our best to purchase the books; but we were unsuccessful.

4. The students were required to pass the following exit tests: English, science, math, and social studies.

5. The rebuilt vacuum cleaner was in excellent condition; saving us a good deal of expense since we didn't have to purchase a new one.

6. Marie has a very soft voice; however, it is clear and distinct.

7. Don't open the door; the floor is still wet.

8. Don't open the door; because the floor is still wet.

9. To the campers from the city, every noise in the night sounded like a bear: a huge, ferocious, meat-eating bear.

10. We worked for three days painting the house; nevertheless, we still needed more time to complete the job.

11. The telephone rang several times, as a result; his sleep was interrupted.

12. Peter was chosen recently to be vice president of the business; and will take over his duties in a few days.

231

Chapter 5

Standard
English
Conventions

Answers

1. Correct.

2. Substitute a comma for the semicolon.

3. Substitute a comma for the semicolon.

4. Correct.

5. Substitute a comma for the semicolon.

6. Correct.

7. Correct.

8. Delete the semicolon.

9. Substitute a comma for the colon.

10. Correct.

11. The telephone rang several times; as a result, his sleep was interrupted. (Note the two punctuation changes. The semicolon is placed in front of the conjunctive adverb and the comma after it.)

12. Delete the semicolon; no punctuation is necessary in its place.

The Em-Dash

Basic Rule

Em-dashes are used to set off parenthetical material that you want to emphasize.

> **Example:** Benjamin Franklin's many intellectual pursuits—from printmaking to politics—exemplify his eclectic personality.

Em-dashes can also be used when you are renaming a nearby noun. Typically, you would use a comma to set this clause off, but since it includes commas already, you use an em-dash.

> **Example:** Benjamin Franklin—a printer, writer, inventor, and statesman—was the son of a soap maker.

An em-dash also indicates a list, a restatement, an amplification, or a dramatic shift in tone or thought.

> **Example:** Eager to write for his brother's newspaper, young Benjamin began submitting letters to the editor under the pseudonym, Silence Dogood—they were a hit!

Skill Builder: Punctuation

> **DIRECTIONS:** Revise the following sentences to eliminate end-of-sentence and within-sentence punctuation errors.

1. Architects design houses, office buildings, and other structures!

2. On any given day, architects might perform the following tasks; prepare structural specifications; meet with clients to determine objectives and structural requirements; direct workers to prepare drawings and documents.

3. Architects are responsible for designing the places where we live: work: play: learn: shop: and eat?

4. Architects—design both indoor and outdoor—spaces on public and private projects.

5. Architects often provide various predesign services: from environmental impact studies to cost analyses: depending on a project's needs.

6. For actual blueprints, traditional paper-and-pencil drafting has been replaced by computer-aided design and drafting (CADD): however, hand-drawing skills are still important during the conceptual stages of a project.

7. Did you know that BIM stands for business information modeling.

8. Architects often collaborate with workers in related fields; civil engineers, urban planners, interior designers, and landscape architects.

9. In addition to years of schooling, being a good architect requires a mix of artistic talent and mathematical ability: it's not easy!

10. The path to becoming an architect requires a college education: a five-year Bachelor of Architecture degree program is typical.

Answers

1. Architects design houses, office buildings, and other structures.

2. On any given day, architects might perform the following tasks: prepare structural specifications, meet with clients to determine objectives and structural requirements, and direct workers to prepare drawings and documents.

3. Architects are responsible for designing the places where we live, work, play, learn, shop, and eat.

4. Architects design both indoor and outdoor spaces on public and private projects.

5. Architects often provide various predesign services—from environmental impact studies to cost analyses—depending on a project's needs.

6. For actual blueprints, traditional paper-and-pencil drafting has been replaced by computer-aided design and drafting (CADD); however, hand-drawing skills are still important during the conceptual stages of a project.

7. Did you know that BIM stands for business information modeling?

8. Architects often collaborate with workers in related fields: civil engineers, urban planners, interior designers, and landscape architects.

9. In addition to years of schooling, being a good architect requires a mix of artistic talent and mathematical ability—it's not easy!

10. The path to becoming an architect requires a college education; a five-year Bachelor of Architecture degree program is typical.

233

Chapter 5

Standard
English
Conventions

The Apostrophe

The apostrophe is usually either misused or omitted because of the writer's failure to proofread his paper or because he is not certain about its use. The apostrophe is used in the following situations:

- To indicate the possessive case *of nouns*: If the noun does not end in *s*—whether singular or plural—add an *'s*; if the noun ends in *s* simply add the *'*. Some writers like to add *'s* to all nouns, even those that already end in *s*.

    Examples:

    The impact of Allen Ginsberg's poem "Howl" on the cultural landscape of the United States cannot be overstated.

    A car's headlights are typically wired in parallel so that if one burns out the other will keep functioning.

    The women's club sponsored many charity events.

    Charles Mingus' (or Mingus's) skill as a jazz musician is widely recognized.

 Do not use apostrophes with possessive pronouns such pronouns as *yours*, *hers*, *ours*, *theirs*, and *whose*, which indicate possession already.

- To indicate a *contraction*—the omission of one or more letters: Place the apostrophe exactly where the missing letters occur.

    Examples:

    can't = cannot

    it's = it is

    we're = we are

- To indicate *plurals* of letters, abbreviations, and numbers: Usually, the apostrophe is used to form the plurals of lowercase letters (*a*'s, *b*'s, *c*'s, and so on) and numbers (3's, 6's). With capital letters, abbreviations without periods (PhD, RN), and even with numbers when no confusion results, you have a choice. In either case, the writer should be consistent in his or her style.

    Examples:

    Tiffani signed her texts with *x*'s and *o*'s.

    The class learned their multiplication tables for 2's and 4's.

    BUT:

    Jocelyn recited her ABCs for her parents.

    The room was filled with those who had earned their PhDs.

Skill Builder: Apostrophe Use

> **DIRECTIONS:** Revise the following sentences to correct any apostrophe errors.

1. Poet William <u>Wordsworths</u> most famous work is *The Prelude*, which was published in 1850.

2. <u>Its</u> how Wordsworth uses the language of the "common man" that strikes most <u>readers</u>.

3. While most of his <u>poems</u> are considered classics, *The Prelude* stands as one of the crowning <u>achievements</u> of British Romanticism.

4. <u>Wordsworths</u> poem *The Prelude* was published by his wife Mary three <u>months</u> after his death.

5. <u>Sonnet 18s</u> theme revolves around the idea of expressing <u>ones</u> self through language.

6. What proportion of <u>humans</u> exposure to plastic ingredients and environmental <u>pollutants</u> occurs through seafood?

7. The use of <u>student's</u> personal information for anything other than educational <u>purposes</u> is a violation of privacy.

Answers

1. Poet William <u>Wordsworth's</u> most famous work is *The Prelude*, which was published in 1850.

2. <u>It's</u> how Wordsworth uses the language of the "common man" that strikes most <u>readers</u>.

3. While most of his <u>poems</u> are considered classics, *The Prelude* stands as one of the crowning <u>achievements</u> of British Romanticism.

4. <u>Wordsworth's</u> poem *The Prelude* was published by his wife Mary three <u>months</u> after his death.

5. <u>Sonnet 18's</u> theme revolves around the idea of expressing <u>one's</u> self through language.

6. Do you know what proportion of <u>humans'</u> exposure to plastic ingredients and environmental <u>pollutants</u> occurs through seafood?

7. The use of <u>students'</u> personal information for anything other than educational <u>purposes</u> is a violation of privacy.

235

Chapter 5

Standard
English
Conventions

Skill Builder: Apostrophe Use

DIRECTIONS: Circle the word with the correct spelling in the following sentences.

1. According to (statistics, statistic's), 55 percent of the nursing workforce holds a (bachelors, bachelor's) degree or higher.

2. Over the past decade, the average age of (nurses, nurse's) has increased by almost two years for (RNs, RN's) and 1.75 years for (LPNs, LPN's).

3. According to the Board of Registered (Nurse's, Nurses') list of (regulations, regulation's), registered (nurses, nurse's) must have a high school diploma, appropriate pre-licensure schooling, and required certification.

4. Despite teaching similar (skills, skill's), one nursing (program, program's) (requirements, requirement's) can be very different from another (programs, program's) (requirements, requirement's).

5. Many future (RNs, RN's) attend the following types of pre-licensure degree (programs, program's): Associate Degree in Nursing (ADN); Bachelor of Science in Nursing (BSN); Entry-Level Master's Program in Nursing (ELM).

6. Based on recent (studies, studies'), an (RNs, RN's) salary is about $50,000 a year.

Answers

1. statistics; bachelor's

2. nurses; RNs; LPNs

3. Nurses'; regulations; nurses

4. skills; program's; requirements; program's; requirements

5. RNs; programs

6. studies; RN's

ITEMS IN A SERIES

Basic Rule

Use a comma between items in a series when three or more items are present. Items can be expressed as words, phrases, or clauses.

> **Example:** The following wildlife biologists study animals based on where they live: limnologists, marine biologists, and terrestrial biologists.

When the items themselves contain commas, use a semicolon to separate them.

> **Example:** Some kinds of biologists study specific species of animals. For example, cetologists study marine mammals, such as whales and dolphins; entomologists study insects, such as beetles and butterflies; and ichthyologists study wild fish, such as sharks and lungfish.

Skill Builder: Items in a Series

> **DIRECTIONS:** Revise the following sentences to make sure the items in a series are punctuated correctly.

1. A typical architectural program includes courses on such topics as architectural history, building design, computer-aided design, and math.

2. Architects must possess certain qualities: analytical skills, in order to understand the content of designs, communication skills, in order to communicate with clients, creativity, in order to develop attractive and functional structures, and organizational skills, in order to keep track of big projects.

3. In order to be hired as an architect, you typically need to: complete a professional degree in architecture: gain relevant experience through a paid internship: and pass the Architect Registration Exam.

4. Because of growing concerns about the environment, today's architects need to understand sustainable design, which emphasizes the efficient use of resources, such as energy and water conservation, waste and pollution reduction, and environmentally friendly specifications and materials.

5. In addition to structural plans architects often provide drawings of the air-conditioning heating and ventilating systems electrical systems communications systems plumbing and possibly site and landscape plans.

Answers

1. *No corrections are needed. The sentence reads fine as follows:* A typical architectural program includes courses on such topics as architectural history, building design, computer-aided design, and math.

2. Architects must possess certain qualities: analytical skills, in order to understand the content of designs; communication skills, in order to communicate with clients; creativity, in order to develop attractive and functional structures; and organizational skills, in order to keep track of big projects.

3. In order to be hired as an architect, you typically need to complete a professional degree in architecture, gain relevant experience through a paid internship, and pass the Architect Registration Exam.

4. Because of growing concerns about the environment, today's architects need to understand sustainable design, which emphasizes the efficient use of such resources as energy and water; waste and pollution reduction; and environmentally friendly specifications and materials.

5. In addition to structural plans, architects often provide drawings of the air-conditioning, heating, and ventilating systems; electrical systems; communications systems; plumbing; and possibly site and landscape plans.

237

Chapter 5

Standard
English
Conventions

Nonrestrictive and Parenthetical Elements

Basic Rule

Nonrestrictive and parenthetical elements provide extra information that is not essential to the meaning or grammatical correctness of a sentence. A nonrestrictive or parenthetical element can be removed from a sentence without making the sentence grammatically incorrect and without interfering with the rest of the sentence's meaning.

Parenthetical elements are identified by commas, parentheses, or em-dashes. While each of these punctuation marks serves a similar purpose, the difference between them is one of emphasis.

Commas indicate a slight interruption.

Example: Toni Morrison, who won the Nobel Prize in Literature in 1993, is a Professor Emeritus at Princeton University.

Parentheses are seen as "quieter" than commas and are reserved for asides that are less important and more tangential than those indicated by commas. They also allow the inclusion of material that doesn't have a specific grammatical connection to the rest of the sentence.

Example: Toni Morrison's novel *Beloved* (1987) explores the themes of love and the supernatural.

Example: While at Princeton, Toni Morrison (the writer) established a special creative workshop for writers and performances called the Princeton Atelier.

If parentheses are used for "quiet" asides, dashes are used when you want to call attention to something. Dashes interrupt the flow of your sentence, thereby calling attention to the information they contain.

Example: Toni Morrison—winner of both the Pulitzer and Nobel Prizes in Literature—is considered one of the greatest writers of her generation.

238

Chapter 5

Standard
English
Conventions

www.petersons.com

Skill Builder: Nonrestrictive and Parenthetical Elements

> **DIRECTIONS**: Select a comma, parentheses, or em-dash to set off the underlined portion of each sentence.

1. Samuel Clemens <u>1835–1910</u> was born in Florida, Missouri, to John and Jane Clemens.

2. Mark Twain <u>whose given name was Samuel Clemens</u> was the sixth of seven children.

3. In 1861, Sam's dreams of becoming a steamboat pilot ended abruptly <u>the Civil War started</u>.

4. Sam's commitment to the Confederate cause was short-lived <u>he quit the army after just two weeks</u>.

5. Twain's "big break" came with the publication of his short story, "Jim Smiley and His Jumping Frog" <u>1865</u>, which was picked up by papers across the country.

6. After the success of his story, "Jim Smiley and His Jumping Frog," Clemens was hired by the Sacramento Union to visit and report on the Sandwich Islands <u>now Hawaii</u>.

7. Clemens' writings for the Sacramento Union were so popular that <u>upon his return</u> he was asked to undertake a lecture tour across the United States.

8. Like all good writers, Mark Twain <u>Samuel Clemens</u> spent his life observing and writing about life as he saw it, with all of its joys and horrors.

Answers

1. Samuel Clemens (1835–1910) was born in Florida, Missouri, to John and Jane Clemens.

2. Mark Twain, whose given name was Samuel Clemens, was the sixth of seven children. *(Em-dashes might also be acceptable here if the writer wished to emphasize the information.)*

3. In 1861, Sam's dreams of becoming a steamboat pilot ended abruptly—the Civil War started.

4. Sam's commitment to the Confederate cause was short-lived—he quit the army after just two weeks.

5. Twain's "big break" came with the publication of his short story, "Jim Smiley and His Jumping Frog" (1865), which was picked up by papers across the country.

6. After the success of his story, "Jim Smiley and His Jumping Frog," Clemens was hired by the Sacramento Union to visit and report on the Sandwich Islands (now Hawaii).

7. Clemens' writings for the Sacramento Union were so popular that, upon his return, he was asked to undertake a lecture tour across the United States.

8. Like all good writers, Mark Twain (Samuel Clemens) spent his life observing and writing about life as he saw it, with all of its joys and horrors.

THE COMMA

Basic Rule

In previous sections, we covered the way that commas are used to separate the following:

- Independent clauses that are connected by a coordinating conjunction

- Items in a series

- Nonrestrictive elements

In addition to these uses, commas have several other purposes:

- To set off introductory clauses and phrases.

    Example: The year after winning her Nobel Prize, Toni Morrison published the novel *Jazz*.

- To set off nouns that are being addressed directly.

    Example: Toni Morrison, the Nobel Prize committee commends you on your achievements and thanks you for your contribution to world literature.

- To separate the different parts of dates, addresses, and geographical names.

    Example: Toni Morrison was born on February 18, 1931, in Lorain, Ohio, to Ramah and George Wofford.

- To introduce a titles and quotations.

    Example: Toni Morrison began her lecture, "The Future of Time: Literature and Diminished Expectations," with the line, "Time, it seems, has no future."

- To separate contrasted elements or to indicate a distinct pause or shift.

    Examples: To her handlers, Koko the gorilla seemed thoughtful, almost human.

    You're one of the senator's close friends, aren't you?

- To separate coordinate adjectives that precede the noun they describe. Coordinate adjectives are of equal importance and related meaning.

    Examples: Toni Morrison is rumored to be a fun, entertaining speaker.

Note how the word *and* can be substituted for the comma. If you cannot substitute *and* without changing the meaning, the adjectives are not coordinate, and no comma is needed.

Example: Toni Morrison is a well-respected American writer.

240

Chapter 5

Standard
English
Conventions

UNNECESSARY PUNCTUATION

Unnecessary punctuation can break a sentence into confusing and illogical fragments.

Here are some common mistakes to look out for.

- Don't use a comma to connect independent clauses. This is called a comma splice.

    Incorrect: Toni Morrison grew up in an integrated neighborhood, she did not become fully aware of racial divisions until she was in her teens.

    Possible revision: Toni Morrison grew up in an integrated neighborhood and did not become fully aware of racial divisions until she was in her teens.

- Don't use a comma between compound elements that are not independent clauses.

    Incorrect: In 1998, Oprah Winfrey, and Danny Glover starred in a film adaptation of Morrison's novel *Beloved*.

    Possible revision: In 1998, Oprah Winfrey and Danny Glover starred in a film adaptation of Morrison's novel *Beloved*.

- Do not use an apostrophe when making a noun plural.

    Incorrect: In 2006, the *New York Times Book Review* named *Beloved* the best American novel published in the last 25 year's.

    Possible revision: In 2006, the *New York Times Book Review* named *Beloved* the best American novel published in the last 25 years.

 While any punctuation mark can be misused, overused commas tend to be a common problem.

241

Chapter 5

Standard English Conventions

Skill Builder: Commas and Unnecessary Punctuation

> **DIRECTIONS**: Revise the following sentences to correct errors, with special attention to unnecessary, misused, and missing punctuation marks. In some cases, there are multiple ways to fix these errors. Consider the answers a partial list of possible revisions.

1. The job of an art director is a creative one he or she is responsible for the visual style and images in magazines newspapers product packaging, and movie and television productions.

2. An art director's job includes creating the overall design of a project; and directing others who develop artwork and layouts.

3. People interested in becoming art director's often work as graphic designer's, illustrator's, copy editor's, or photographer's, or in some other types of art and design occupations.

4. Some art directors work for advertising and public relations firms and others work in print media and entertainment.

5. In order to become an art director you typically need at least a bachelor's degree in an art or design subject, and previous work experience.

6. Art direction is a management position, that oversees the work of other designers and artists.

7. An art director might choose the overall style or tone, desired for a project, and communicate this vision to the artists he or she manages.

8. In the movie industry an art director might collaborate with a director; in order to determine the look and style of a movie.

9. As of 2012: art directors held about 74,800 jobs.

10. Even though the majority of art directors are self-employed they often work under pressure to meet strict deadlines.

242

Chapter 5

Standard
English
Conventions

www.petersons.com

Answers

1. The job of an art director is a creative one; he or she is responsible for the visual style and images in magazines, newspapers, product packaging, and movie and television productions.

2. An art director's job includes creating the overall design of a project and directing others who develop artwork and layouts.

3. People interested in becoming art directors often work as graphic designers, illustrators, copy editors, or photographers or in some other types of art and design occupations.

4. Some art directors work for advertising and public relations firms, and others work in print media and entertainment.

5. In order to become an art director, you typically need at least a bachelor's degree in an art or design subject and previous work experience.

6. Art direction is a management position that oversees the work of other designers and artists.

7. An art director might choose the overall style or tone desired for a project and communicate this vision to the artists he or she manages.

8. In the movie industry, an art director might collaborate with a director in order to determine the look and style of a movie.

9. As of 2012, art directors held about 74,800 jobs.

10. Even though the majority of art directors are self-employed, they often work under pressure to meet strict deadlines.

243

Chapter 5

Standard
English
Conventions

SUMMING IT UP

- The SAT® Writing and Language Test is designed to test your mastery of Standard English conventions. On the test, you will read multiple passages that may cover careers, science, history, or the humanities. The questions will require you to read the passages and select the answers that improve the writing in the passage. The correct answer will be the one that best follows Standard English conventions.

- The Standard English conventions reviewed in this lesson are keys to good writing. When you utilize proper sentence structure, grammar, and punctuation, your writing is stronger, clearer, and more focused. That is why the use of Standard English conventions is important for both college writing and any writing you will do in your future career.

 WANT TO KNOW MORE?

Access more practice questions, lessons, helpful tips, and expert strategies for the following English language conventions topics in *Peterson's Online Course for the SAT® Exam*:

- Ambiguous Pronouns
- Comparisons
- Frequently Confused Words
- Modifiers
- Noun Agreement
- Parallelism
- Pronoun Case
- Pronouns: Number
- Punctuation
- Sentence Improvements
- Subject-Verb Agreement
- Verb Tenses
- What Makes a Sentence?

To purchase and access the course, go to **www.petersons.com/testprep/sat**.

PART V:
ESSAY WRITING STRATEGIES
FOR THE SAT® EXAM

Chapter 6: The SAT® Essay

CHAPTER 6:
THE SAT® ESSAY

OVERVIEW

- A Closer Look at the Essay Question
- Pacing Your Writing
- Prewriting
- Writing the Introduction
- Developing Your Ideas
- Writing the Conclusion
- The Scoring Rubric for the SAT® Essay
- Exercise: Practicing Your Essay Skills
- Additional Essay Writing Practice
- Summing It Up

The Essay section of the SAT® exam is 50 minutes long. In this time, you need to read the essay prompt and plan and write your essay. It doesn't need to be—and isn't supposed to be—a final, polished version. The high school and college English teachers who will score your essay are trained to view the essays as first drafts. They will be assessing your essay and hundreds of others against a rubric that guides them to look at the essays holistically. They are reading for an overall general impression of your reading, writing, and analyzing skills. Later in this chapter, you will analyze a rubric that is similar to the one the scorers will use.

A CLOSER LOOK AT THE ESSAY QUESTION

You will be given one essay prompt and asked to write an analytical essay in response. You won't have a choice of questions to answer. This is good because it saves you time, as you don't have to decide which one to choose. The essay section is made up of a prompt that directs you to read and analyze a high-quality source text. In this text, the author makes an argument or examines a current debate, idea, or trend.

Once you have closely read and analyzed the source text, you can begin your planning. You don't need any specific subject-area knowledge to write your essay. The purpose of the essay is to demonstrate for the scorers that you can then analyze it in writing using your own critical reasoning and evidence drawn from the source text.

PACING YOUR WRITING

You want to use everything you've been taught in English class about the writing process—but sped up to fit within 50 minutes. Pacing yourself is important so that you are able to get your ideas down on paper in a complete, coherent, and unified essay. As you practice writing essays in this chapter and in the practice tests in this book, work out a pacing schedule for yourself. Begin by trying out the following timetable and see how it works for you. If necessary, adjust it as you practice, but be sure to give yourself enough time to finish a complete draft.

- Prewriting: 10 to 15 minutes
- Writing the introduction: 4 to 5 minutes
- Writing the body of the essay: 15 to 20 minutes
- Writing the conclusion: 3 to 4 minutes
- Revising: 3 to 5 minutes
- Proofing: 3 to 5 minutes

NOTE: Remember that the readers do not take off points for specific errors in grammar, usage, and mechanics, but they will take note of a pattern of errors. These can contribute to a lower score. Check the rubric (later in this chapter).

PREWRITING

Before you begin to write your analysis, read the prompt and the source text. Pay attention to the text author's key claims. Underline the author's key claims. Then circle or highlight evidence the author uses to support those claims. Finally, take notes on important stylistic features or persuasive techniques the author uses in the source text.

You want to spend about 10 to 15 minutes on prewriting, as this will give you time to carefully read the prompt and then read and analyze the source text. Your goals in this planning stage are as follows:

- Identify and underline the author's key claims.
- Find and then circle or highlight specific evidence the author uses to support his or her key claims.
- Take notes on ways the author has used logic, reasoning, rhetoric (persuasive language techniques), and evidence to convince readers that his or her key claims are valid.

FAMILIARIZING YOURSELF WITH THE PROMPT AND THE PASSAGE

The Essay prompt will not change much at all, no matter when and where you are taking the SAT®. This is great news because it means you can become very familiar and comfortable with the prompt before you take the test. The source text (passage) that accompanies the prompt *will* be new to you; however, it will share important qualities with other passages you will read and analyze as you prepare to write the SAT® Essay.

All passages:

- Come from high-quality, previously published sources
- Contain arguments written for a broad audience
- Examine ideas, opinions, views, debates, or trends
- Discuss topics in the arts; the sciences; or civic, cultural, or political life
- Are interesting, relevant, and accessible to college-bound students at your grade level
- Tend NOT to consist of simple pro/con debates on issues
- Strive to convey nuanced views on complex subjects
- Use evidence, logical reasoning, and/or stylistic and persuasive elements
- Are similarly complex: all are challenging—but not *too* difficult—for readers at your grade level
- Do NOT require test-takers to possess prior knowledge of specific topics

The prompt that introduces the passage will be identical or very similar to this:

> As you read the passage below, consider how [the author] uses the following:
>
> - Evidence, such as facts or examples, to support claims
>
> - Reasoning to develop ideas and to connect claims and evidence
>
> - Stylistic or persuasive elements, such as word choice or appeals to emotion, to add power to the ideas expressed

After the passage, the prompt will continue as follows:

> Write an essay in which you explain how [the author] builds an argument to persuade [his/her] audience that [the author's claim is true or valid]. In your essay, analyze how [the author] uses one or more of the features listed above [see bullet points above] (or features of your own choice) to strengthen the logic and persuasiveness of [his/her] argument. Be sure that your analysis focuses on the most relevant aspects of the passage. Your essay should not explain whether you agree with [the author's] claims, but rather explain how [he/she] builds an argument to persuade [his/her] audience.

It is vital that you read, reread, and thoroughly understand everything the prompt asks you to do. Pay particular attention to the bullet points that tell you exactly what to look for in the passage. Also note that the prompt gives you the option of mentioning other "features of your own choice." Finally, let's take a close look at the last sentence in the prompt (we have capitalized and underlined the word *not*):

> Your essay should <u>NOT</u> explain whether you agree with [the author's] claims, but rather explain how [he/she] builds an argument to persuade [his/her] audience.

In other words, your task is *not* to present your own arguments—the passage author has already done that. Your task is to analyze the author's argument: "explain how the author builds an argument to persuade [his/her] audience."

The people who develop the SAT® believe that if you complete this essay-writing task, your work will exhibit three types of skills:

1. Close reading skills
2. Analyzing skills
3. Writing skills

ORGANIZING YOUR ESSAY

Decide how many paragraphs you need to write to develop your analysis of the passage. Remember that length is not a valid substitute for strength. Your answer booklet provides a certain number of pages for your essay. You can't write more than the lines provided, but you can write less. It is more important to do a good job of analyzing the passage than it is to fill up all the lines. However, an essay of five sentences won't earn you a high score.

A safe number of paragraphs is five. Use the first paragraph for the introduction and the last one for the conclusion. That gives you three paragraphs to develop your ideas. That doesn't mean that you can't write a fourth or even fifth paragraph in the body of your essay to develop your ideas. It's more important to have a tightly written and well-developed shorter essay than a longer, rambling, repetitious one that you didn't have time to revise or proofread. There is a limit to what you can write in 50 minutes. Use the opportunity that you have for practice in this book to work on your pacing and see how much you can plan and write well in 50 minutes.

WRITING THE INTRODUCTION

Now it's time to write. You've analyzed the prompt and the passage in your prewriting step and identified the author's key claims, use of evidence and reasoning, and stylistic or persuasive language features. Now begin writing your introduction.

In your introduction, it is important to introduce the source text to your reader. State the author's name and the title of the passage. Then give a brief summary of the author's key claim. Two to four sentences should accomplish these tasks.

As you practice writing essays in this book, and as you write the real one on test day, keep the following five ideas in mind:

1. In writing your introduction, keep the key words and phrases of the prompt in mind.
2. Avoid being cute, funny, ironic, satiric, overly emotional, or too dramatic. Set the tone or attitude in your first sentence. You want to be sincere, clear, and straightforward.
3. Don't bother repeating the key claims from the source text word for word. A paraphrase in your own words is far better than just copying the words of the source text.
4. In your first paragraph, in addition to introducing the passage's author, title, topic, and the author's key claim about the topic, make it clear to your readers that you are about to analyze the passage and explain how the author accomplishes his or her persuasive purpose. This can be accomplished in a clear topic sentence.
5. Each sentence should advance your topic and be interesting to your reader.

Skill Builder: Topic Sentence

> **DIRECTIONS:** Which of the following is the best topic sentence?

1. I agree with the author that the use of motorized boats and watercraft should be limited in freshwater streams and lakes.

2. The author believes that the use of motorized boats and other watercraft should be limited in freshwater ecosystems in order to decrease pollution.

3. In this essay, I will examine the author's argument in favor of limiting the use of motorized boats and watercraft in freshwater streams and lakes.

4. The author introduces her argument with startling statistics on the negative effects of motorized watercraft on freshwater ecosystems; she then builds on those statistics with careful reasoning to reach the logical conclusion that we should limit the use of motorized watercraft in freshwater ecosystems.

Answer and Explanation

Of the four sentences presented, choice 4 is the best answer since it states the topic clearly, limits the scope of the essay, and presents the key points of the analysis. Sentence 4 also implies that the essay writer will expand on these key points in the body of the essay.

 ALERT: Remember that you are writing an analysis of the passage author's work. You are NOT writing a persuasive essay on the author's topic.

RECOGNIZING EFFECTIVE INTRODUCTIONS

An *effective* introduction often refers to the subject of the essay, explains the value of the topic, or attracts the attention of the reader by giving a pertinent illustration. Ineffective beginnings often contain unrelated material, ramble, and lack clarity.

Skill Builder: Effective Introductions

> **DIRECTIONS:** Examine the following excerpts from five introductory paragraphs and decide whether each is effective or ineffective. Be able to defend your decision.

1. The pollution of freshwater streams and lakes has become a pretty big problem in the United States. Part of the problem is due to the unrestricted use of motorized boats and other stuff. I mostly agree with the author that something needs to be done about it, but I don't know that you should tell people where they can drive their boats.

2. Freshwater lakes and streams are popular recreational destinations for many Americans. These bodies of water are also the principal ecosystems of many different animals and plants. In her essay, "Bringing Fresh Back to Freshwater Lakes and Streams," activist River Pura makes the claim that the unrestricted use of motorized watercraft is to blame for polluting these ecosystems.

3. River Pura makes a very persuasive argument to persuade her audience that motorized boats should be restricted in freshwater streams and lakes. She persuades her audience with some facts and emotional appeals.

4. The author makes an argument to persuade her audience about what she is thought about. It's pollution.

5. Pollution in freshwater ecosystems has been growing over the past decade. Author River Pura, in her essay titled "Bringing Fresh Back to Freshwater Streams and Lakes," claims that motorized watercraft are the primary source of that pollution. While Pura presents her readers with startling statistical information, her argument is anticlimactic and builds to no logical conclusion.

Answers and Explanations

1. *Ineffective.* This paragraph is focused on the topic of the source text, not on the author's writing. Although the prompt specifically says *not* to present opinions on the topic, the writer states that he or she "mostly agrees" with the passage author. Also, the writer uses vague, informal expressions: "pretty big" and "mostly agree."

2. *Effective.* This paragraph effectively introduces the author, the passage title, and the topic. The paragraph also identifies the author's key claim and begins to analyze the author's work.

3. *Ineffective.* While this paragraph identifies the author's key claim, nonspecific phrases like "some facts" and "emotional appeal" weaken the paragraph. Also, the writer uses three different forms of the word *persuade*, which sounds repetitious.

4. *Ineffective.* The paragraph does not introduce the author, the passage title, or the author's key claim. It does not explain that the writer is going to analyze the passage. The writing is poorly constructed and misuses verb tense.

5. *Effective.* This paragraph clearly introduces the source text, highlights the author's key claim, and explains how the passage author fails to build an effective argument.

DEVELOPING YOUR IDEAS

The heart of your essay is the development, or middle paragraphs. In these paragraphs, you must use explanations, details, and examples from the source text to support the main ideas in your essay. All the sentences in the development paragraphs must explain and support your analysis of the source text and must not digress.

In the limited time you have on the Essay section of the SAT®, you can take only 15 to 20 minutes to write the body of your essay. In this time, you need to support your analysis of the author's work with careful reasoning, and back up your analysis with evidence from the source text. Your writing must be coherent, logical, unified, and organized.

Avoid the following three pitfalls in the development of your essay:

1. Using sentences that are irrelevant and contain extraneous material
2. Using sentences that do not follow a logical sequence of thought but seem to jump from one idea to another
3. Using sentences that do not relate to the topic sentence or do not flow from the preceding sentence

USING TRANSITIONS

The successful writer uses transitional words and phrases to connect thoughts and provide a logical sequence of ideas. Become familiar with the following list of transitions and use them in your practice essays. They will help make your writing smoother:

therefore	for example	nevertheless
first of all	in any case	but
then	consequently	still
moreover	for instance	yet
second	on the other hand	also
indeed	of course	in addition
however	finally	furthermore

Skill Builder: Using Transitions

> **DIRECTIONS:** In the following three samples, the transition is missing. Supply a transitional word or phrase that will allow the second sentence to follow smoothly or logically from the first.

1. Freshwater ecosystems hold only 0.01% of Earth's water supply. Over half of the people on Earth live near freshwater ecosystems.

2. Human activity comprises the primary threat to freshwater ecosystems. Damming lakes, extracting water, and filling shallow wetlands all lead to the destruction of these ecosystems.

3. Constructing dams and levees can lead to a significant loss of habitat for land animals and plant species. The restricted water flow changes natural water temperatures and impacts marine life.

Answers and Explanations

1. The sentences require a transition that indicates contrast, such as *yet, but, however, still, although* and *either . . . or.*

   Although freshwater ecosystems hold only 0.01% of Earth's water supply, over half of the people on Earth live near these ecosystems.

2. These sentences require a transition that indicates an example is to follow.

   Human activity comprises the primary threat to freshwater ecosystems; for example, damming lakes, extracting water, and filling shallow wetlands all lead to the destruction of these ecosystems.

3. These sentences require a transition that indicates additional information is to follow.

   The construction of dams and levees can lead to a significant loss of habitat for land animals and plant species. Furthermore, the restricted water flow changes natural water temperatures and impacts marine life.

WRITING EFFECTIVELY

There are three important elements that will be considered in scoring an SAT® essay:

1. Reading
2. Analysis
3. Writing

Essays are scored according to how well they meet these three basic criteria. To improve an essay you are writing, ask yourself these questions:

Reading

- Does my essay demonstrate a thorough understanding of the source text?
- Does my essay identify the author's key claims?
- Does my essay explain how the author uses evidence to support his or her key claims?
- Does my essay effectively use evidence from the source text?

253

Chapter 6

The SAT®
Essay

Analysis

- Does my essay offer an in-depth evaluation of the author's use of evidence in building and supporting an argument?
- Does my essay offer an in-depth evaluation of the author's use of stylistic or persuasive language features to build and support his or her argument?
- Does my essay use supporting evidence from the passage that is relevant and focused on my task (analyzing the passage)?

Writing

- Does my essay include a precise central claim that is supported with body paragraphs?
- Does my essay include an effective introduction and a strong conclusion?
- Does my essay incorporate a variety of sentence structures? Is each of my sentences clearly written? Does each sentence flow well?
- Is my essay virtually error-free in spelling, grammar, usage, and mechanics?

WRITING THE CONCLUSION

Lewis Carroll, the author of *Alice in Wonderland,* once gave some very good advice for writers. He said, "When you come to the end, stop!"

When you come to the end of your ideas, stop writing the development—and begin writing your conclusion. You can't just end your essay with your last development paragraph. You need to draw your comments together in a strong, clear concluding paragraph.

A good concluding paragraph for your essay should assure your scorers that you have successfully read, understood, and analyzed the source text. You should be able to do this in three to six sentences written in 3 to 4 minutes. The following are three possible ways to end your essay:

1. Through a *restatement* of your most important or most central idea
2. Through a *summary* of the material covered in the essay
3. Through a *clear statement* about the effectiveness of the passage author's work

Keep in mind that a good conclusion is an integral part of your essay. It may be a review or a restatement, or it may leave your readers with an intriguing question to think about (one that is closely related to your essay, of course). In any case, your conclusion must be strong, clear, and effective.

What *Not* to Say in Your Conclusion

Just as there are good techniques, there are also some very ineffective methods that essay writers may be tempted to use in drawing a composition to a close. Try to avoid falling into the following three traps:

1. Apologizing for your inability to more thoroughly analyze the passage in the allotted time
2. Complaining that the source text did not interest you or that you don't think it was fair to be asked to write an analysis of the source text without giving your own opinions on the topic
3. Introducing material that you will not develop, rambling on about nonpertinent matters, using material that is trite or unrelated, or making a sarcastic joke that indicates your disdain for the topic you just spent 50 minutes writing about

Recognizing Effective Conclusions

Remember that an *effective* concluding paragraph may restate or summarize main idea(s) in your essay, draw a logical conclusion, or offer a strong opinion about the effectiveness of the author's work. An *ineffective* final paragraph introduces new material in a scanty fashion, apologizes for the ineffectiveness of your essay, or is illogical or unclear. Use the following skill-builder exercises to test yourself.

Skill Builder: Effective Conclusions

DIRECTIONS: Why are the following sentences ineffective in a concluding paragraph?

1. I wish I had more time to write a better, more in-depth analysis, but I find that in the allotted time this is all that I could do.
2. Although I have not mentioned this before, my family enjoys boating on freshwater lakes. We often pick up litter from the water in the hopes of decreasing pollution.
3. This passage was incredibly difficult to understand, and I felt like the author droned on and on about nothing.

DIRECTIONS: Examine the following five excerpts from concluding paragraphs and decide whether each is effective or ineffective.

4. That's all I have to say about the topic. I know I'm not an expert, but at least this is an actual analysis of the work. I also used a lot of supporting details from the source text. So, I think you should give me at least a 3.
5. While River Pura is a passionate spokesperson for freshwater ecosystems, her argument for limiting the use of motorized watercraft lacks cohesion. Furthermore, a careful examination of the issue shows that motorized watercraft are not the main cause of pollution in freshwater ecosystems. Had Pura taken the time to structure her impassioned pleas around valid statistical evidence, her argument would be stronger.
6. I forgot to mention earlier that the author uses a variety of descriptive words and phrases to appeal to the emotions of readers. She also uses figurative language and makes some illusions to other articles the reader may have read.
7. Protecting the biodiversity of freshwater ecosystems is a topic of importance for all of those who depend upon these ecosystems for survival. River Pura makes a solid case for the restriction of motorized watercraft in freshwater areas. Pura begins her argument with startling facts and statistics designed to capture the reader's attention. She then moves into a well-reasoned discourse that effectively negates any counter-claims opponents might make.
8. In conclusion, the author makes a pretty good case for protecting freshwater ecosystems. However, most people I know aren't going to stop boating because an environmentalist says they should.

Answers and Explanations

1. *Ineffective.* Don't apologize for doing a poor job. (Maybe your essay is better than you think. And if it *is* bad, why would you want to call attention to its weaknesses?) Also, don't blame the fact that you did a poor job on the time limit.
2. *Ineffective.* Don't include asides like this anywhere in your essay—but especially not in your conclusion. You're supposed to be concluding your analysis, not cramming in extra details that are only loosely related to the topic.
3. *Ineffective.* Do not complain about the task in the conclusion. Your essay should maintain a formal tone throughout.
4. *Ineffective.* Do not speak directly to or "butter up" the scorers in your concluding paragraph. Maintain a formal tone.
5. *Effective.* This paragraph sums up the key points of the analysis and states the essay writer's opinion of the passage author's persuasive writing.

6. *Ineffective*. Do not introduce new ideas into a concluding paragraph. If you have more information to add that would improve or add depth to your analysis, consider adding another body paragraph. Also, the essay writer has misused the word *illusion*: he or she should have used *allusion*.

7. *Effective*. This paragraph effectively summarizes the key points of the analysis.

8. *Ineffective*. This paragraph gives only a vague summary of the analysis and offers an opinion that is irrelevant to the essay-writing task.

THE SCORING RUBRIC FOR THE SAT® ESSAY

The SAT® Essay will be scored based on a 4-point rubric. Points will be awarded in three areas: reading, analysis, and writing. Each essay will be scored by two graders who will give a score of 1 to 4 in each of the three areas. Scores in each area will be reported separately from the other two. For example, a test-taker might earn a score of 3/4/3. This means that the test-taker scored 3 out of 4 points in both reading and writing and 4 out of 4 points in analysis.

All the scorers read the essays against the same rubric developed by the College Board, which administers the SAT®. This rubric guides the scorers in considering overall impression, development, organization, diction, sentence structure, grammar, usage, and mechanics. The rubric also directs scorers in evaluating essay writers' comprehension of the source text, use of relevant evidence from the passage, and their analysis of the passage author's argument. The scoring guidelines are similar to the following:

Essay Scoring 4 (Advanced)

- *Reading:* shows a comprehensive understanding of the source text, including the author's key claims, use of details and evidence, and the relationship between the two
- *Analysis:* offers an "insightful" and in-depth evaluation of the author's use of evidence and stylistic or persuasive features in building an argument; uses relevant supporting details that address the task
- *Writing:* includes all of the features of a strong essay, including a precise central claim, body paragraphs, and a strong conclusion; incorporates a variety of sentence structures; is virtually free of all convention errors

Essay Scoring 3 (Proficient)

- *Reading:* shows an appropriate understanding of the source text, including the author's key claims and use of details in developing an argument
- *Analysis:* offers an effective evaluation of the author's use of evidence and stylistic or persuasive features in building an argument; uses appropriate supporting details and evidence that are relevant and focused on the task
- *Writing:* includes all of the features of an effective essay, including a precise central claim, body paragraphs, and a strong conclusion; incorporates a variety of sentence structures and is relatively free of common grammatical errors

Essay Scoring 2 (Partial)

- *Reading:* shows some understanding of the source text, including the author's key claims; uses limited textual evidence; incorporates unimportant details
- *Analysis:* offers a limited evaluation of the author's use of evidence and stylistic or persuasive features in building an argument; supporting details are lacking and/or irrelevant to task
- *Writing:* does not provide a precise central claim, nor an effective introduction, body paragraphs, and conclusion; incorporates little variety of sentence structures and contains numerous errors in grammar and conventions

Essay Scoring 1 (Inadequate)

- *Reading:* demonstrates little or no understanding of the source text or the author's use of key claims
- *Analysis:* offers no clear evaluation of the author's use of evidence and stylistic or persuasive features in building an argument; supporting details and evidence are nonexistent or irrelevant to task
- *Writing:* lacks any form of cohesion or structure; incorporates little variety in sentence structure and includes significant errors in convention that make it difficult to read

Read the rubric several times. As you practice writing essays for the SAT®, keep this rubric in mind. As you write each essay, try to focus on one or two qualities of good writing that the rubric measures. After you have finished writing your essay, come back to the rubric and see how your essay measures up.

Use the following table to help you. Give yourself anywhere from 1 to 4 points for each quality of good writing.

PRACTICE TEST SCORING TABLE

Reading:	_____
Analysis:	_____
Writing:	_____
Final Score:	_____ / _____ / _____

EXERCISE: PRACTICING YOUR ESSAY SKILLS

Use the following prompt to practice writing an effective essay. Carefully read the prompt and write a response. Make use of the effective writing techniques discussed in this chapter. Use the scoring rubric to evaluate your work. Then read and evaluate the three sample responses.

As you read the passage below, consider how the writer uses the following:

- Evidence, such as facts or examples, to support claims

- Reasoning to develop ideas and to connect claims and evidence

- Stylistic or persuasive elements, such as word choice, emotional appeal, intellectual appeal, or ethical appeal, to add power to the ideas expressed

---

Henry Clay (1777–1852) served several terms in Congress and was Secretary of State in 1825. In the following speech, given in 1818, he argues that the United States should support South America in gaining independence from Spain.

The Emancipation of South America

1 Spain has undoubtedly given us abundant and just cause for war. But it is not every cause of war that should lead to war. . . . If we are to have war with Spain, I have, however, no hesitation in saying that no mode of bringing it about could be less fortunate than that of seizing, at this time, upon her adjoining province. There was a time, under certain circumstances, when we might have occupied East Florida with safety; had we then taken it, our posture in the negotiation with Spain would have been totally different from what it is.

2 But we have permitted that time, not with my consent, to pass by unimproved. If we were now to seize upon Florida after a great change in those circumstances, and after declaring our intention to acquiesce in the procrastination desired by Spain, in what light should we be viewed by foreign powers—particularly Great Britain? We have already been accused

of inordinate ambition, and of seeking to aggrandize ourselves by an extension, on all sides, of our limits. Should we not, by such an act of violence, give color to the accusation? No, Mr. Chairman; if we are to be involved in a war with Spain, let us have the credit of disinterestedness. Let us put her yet more in the wrong. Let us command the respect which is never withheld from those who act a noble and generous part. I hope to communicate to the committee the conviction which I so strongly feel, that the adoption of the amendment which I intend to propose would not hazard, in the slightest degree, the peace of the country....

3   In contemplating the great struggle in which Spanish America is now engaged, our attention is fixed first by the immensity and character of the country which Spain seeks again to subjugate. Stretching on the Pacific Ocean from about the fortieth degree of north latitude to about the fifty-fifth degree of south latitude, and extending from the mouth of the Rio del Norte (exclusive of East Florida), around the Gulf of Mexico and along the South Atlantic to near Cape Horn, it is nearly five thousand miles in length, and in some places nearly three thousand in breadth....

4   Throughout all the extent of that great portion of the world which I have attempted thus hastily to describe, the spirit of revolt against the dominion of Spain has manifested itself. The Revolution has been attended with various degrees of success in the several parts of Spanish America. In some it has been already crowned, as I shall endeavor to show, with complete success, and in all I am persuaded that independence has struck such deep root, that the power of Spain can never eradicate it. What are the causes of this great movement?

5   Three hundred years ago, upon the ruins of the thrones of Montezuma and the Incas of Peru, Spain erected the most stupendous system of colonial despotism that the world has ever seen—the most vigorous, the most exclusive. The great principle and object of this system have been to render one of the largest portions of the world exclusively subservient, in all its faculties, to the interests of an inconsiderable spot in Europe....

6   Thus upon the ground of strict right, upon the footing of a mere legal question, governed by forensic rules, the Colonies, being absolved by the acts of the parent country from the duty of subjection to it, had an indisputable right to set up for themselves. But I take a broader and a bolder position. I maintain that an oppressed people are authorized, whenever they can, to rise and break their fetters. This was the great principle of the English Revolution. It was the great principle of our own....

7   In the establishment of the independence of Spanish America, the United States have the deepest interest. I have no hesitation in asserting my firm belief that there is no question in the foreign policy of this country, which has ever arisen, or which I can conceive as ever occurring, in the decision of which we have had or can have so much at stake. This interest concerns our politics, our commerce, our navigation....

8   I would invoke the spirits of our departed fathers. Was it for yourselves only that you nobly fought? No, no! It was the chains that were forging for your posterity that made you fly to arms, and, scattering the elements of these chains to the winds, you transmitted to us the rich inheritance of liberty.

Write an essay in which you explain how Henry Clay builds an argument to persuade his audience that the United States should support South America in its efforts to secure freedom from Spain. In your essay, analyze how Clay uses one or more of the features previously listed (or features of your own choice) to strengthen the logic and persuasiveness of his argument. Be sure that your analysis focuses on the most relevant aspects of the passage.

Your essay should not explain whether you agree with Clay's claims, but rather explain how he builds an argument to persuade his audience.

Use the following scoring guide to help you evaluate Sample Essay 1. Then, read our analysis of the essay, as well as suggestions for improvement.

Score Point	Reading	Analysis	Writing
4 (Advanced)	The essay shows a comprehensive understanding of the source text, including the author's key claims, use of details and evidence, and the relationship between the two.	The essay offers an "insightful" and in-depth evaluation of the author's use of evidence and stylistic or persuasive features in building an argument. Supporting details and evidence are relevant and focus on those details that address the task.	The essay includes all of the features of a strong essay, including a precise central claim, body paragraphs, and a strong conclusion. There is a variety of sentence structures used in the essay, and it is virtually free of all convention errors.
3 (Proficient)	The essay shows an appropriate understanding of the source text, including the author's key claims and use of details in developing an argument.	The essay offers an "effective" evaluation of the author's use of evidence and stylistic or persuasive features in building an argument. Supporting details and evidence are appropriate and focus on those details that address the task.	The essay includes all of the features of an effective essay, including a precise central claim, body paragraphs, and a strong conclusion. There is a variety of sentence structures used in the essay, and it is free of significant convention errors.
2 (Partial)	The essay shows some understanding of the source text, including the author's key claims, but uses limited textual evidence and/or unimportant details.	The essay offers limited evaluation of the author's use of evidence and stylistic or persuasive features in building an argument. Supporting details and evidence are lacking and/or are not relevant to the task.	The essay does not provide a precise central claim, nor does it provide an effective introduction, body paragraphs, and conclusion. There is little variety of sentence structure used in the essay, and there are numerous errors in grammar and conventions.
1 (Inadequate)	The essay demonstrates little or no understanding of the source text or the author's use of key claims.	The essay offers no clear evaluation of the author's use of evidence and stylistic or persuasive features in building an argument. Supporting details and evidence are nonexistent or irrelevant to the task.	The essay lacks any form of cohesion or structure. There is little variety of sentence structures, and significant errors in convention make it difficult to read.

Sample Essay 1

In his speech to Congress, Henry Clay emphasizes the importance of supporting South America in their revolt against Spain. Clay begins his argument by talking about the significance of the state of Florida, which isn't actually a state yet. Clay urges Congress not to invade Florida (which apparently has been captured by Spain) because it would make the US look bad. Clay's goal is for Spain to be "in the wrong" and for the US to "command the respect which is never withheld from those who act a noble and generous part."

Clay goes on to remind his listeners that the majority of South America is already involved in a Revolution against Spain. This is a key point of persuasion. Finally, Clay makes the comparison between the Revolution in South America and the Revolution against Great Britain. He even goes so far as to "invoke the spirits of our departed fathers" and uses other images like "fly to arms" and "the rich inheritance of liberty." While Clay's argument is okay, it's long-winded and focuses too much on emotional appeal.

Analysis of Sample Essay 1

This response scored a 2/2/2.

- **Reading—2:** The writer demonstrates some comprehension of the source text. In the first paragraph, the writer conveys the basic central claim—*the importance of supporting South America in their revolt against Spain*. The writer also shows a partial understanding of Clay's position on Florida—*Clay's goal is for Spain to be "in the wrong"*—but does not effectively tie it to the central claim. In the following paragraph, the writer correctly identifies Clay's comparison of the South American Revolution to the US Revolution. However, there is little demonstration of the relationship between the central claim and the supporting details. Overall, the writer shows a partial understanding of the source text.

- **Analysis—2:** The response offers a limited analysis of the source text, showing only partial understanding of the task. The writer mentions the *significance of the state of Florida* but then does not elaborate on this significance or explain how Florida's significance contributes to Clay's argument. In the second paragraph, the writer makes note of *a key point of persuasion*; however, there is no further discussion of why South America's revolution against Spain is a key point of persuasion. Furthermore, the writer does not develop the effect of Clay's comparison of the South American Revolution to the US Revolution. While the writer includes the use of *emotional appeal* in the analysis, there is no explanation of it. Overall, this response is only a partially successful analysis.

- **Writing—2:** This response reflects limited cohesion and some skill in the use of language. There is no precise central claim, nor is there an effective introduction and conclusion. Phrases like *isn't actually a state yet* and *which apparently has been captured by Spain* use an informal, almost flippant tone. Calling the source text *long-winded* is subjective and inappropriate for a formal analysis. Overall, this response represents a partially developed essay.

Suggestions for Improvement

1. The response needs a clearly developed introduction that establishes the topic and presents a precise central claim. While the first paragraph makes a start, a precise central claim should briefly summarize the key points that the writer will make in his or her analysis.

2. Each body paragraph should begin with a topic sentence that summarizes the key point of the paragraph. For instance, the writer could begin the second paragraph with the sentence: *Clay begins his argument with reason rather than rhetoric, logically appealing to those who are hesitant to engage in open warfare.*

3. The use of evidence from the source text should directly support key aspects of the essay writer's analysis. Look at this sentence from paragraph 2 of Sample Essay 1: He even goes so far as to "invoke the spirits of our departed fathers" and uses other images like "fly to arms" and "the rich inheritance of liberty." The quotations here do not support the writer's analysis of the source text. A better use of quotations might be:

   Clay uses emotionally powerful language as a persuasive tool in making the correlation between the US quest for independence from Great Britain and South America's quest for independence from Spain. He wants to inspire the same passionate support for South America's struggle that most of his listeners feel about their own country's revolution, so he *uses emotional phrases like "invoke the spirits of our departed fathers," "fly to arms," and "rich inheritance of liberty."*

4. The response should include a strong conclusion that restates the thesis, recaps the most important parts of the analysis, or leaves the reader with a final thought. The conclusion should provide a sense of closure on the topic.

5. All SAT® essays should maintain a formal and objective tone. The writer should limit the use of contractions and refrain from using derogatory adjectives like *long-winded* to describe the source text.

Sample Essay 2

In Henry Clay's 1818 address to Congress, he is building an argument to persuade his listeners to support South America in their revolution against Spain. He builds his argument in three different ways. Clay demonstrates an understanding of his audience, underscores the action that they need to take, and closes with an emotional appeal for liberty by referencing the Revolutionary War.

Clay begins building his argument by demonstrating an understanding of his audience. He demonstrates an understanding of his audience when he assures them at the outset of his speech that he is not calling for open warfare against Spain. This is significant because many members of Congress still remembered the bloodshed from the Revolutionary War. Clay reassures his audience and seeks to get them on his side by stating "it is not every cause of war that should lead to war." Once Congresses minds are put at ease, Clay can move onto talking about his central claim.

After Clay reassures his listeners, he then attempts to underscore the amount of involvement they would have to take in the conflict. He is seeking to minimize the nature of the conflict in order to win support for it. Clay says that, "The Revolution has been attended with various degrees of success in the several parts of Spanish America. In some it has been already crowned, as I shall endeavor to show, with complete success. . . ."

Finally, Clay seeks to draw a parallel for his listeners between the revolution they had recently won and the revolution being fought in South America. This is his emotional appeal. Clay is telling his listeners, "Remember your fight for independence? Remember how greatly you desired freedom? This is the same thing." By getting his listeners to remember how passionately they desired freedom from Great Britain, he is hoping to sway their emotions in favor of supporting South America against Spain.

Henry Clay uses logic, minimizing, and emotional appeal to build an argument. He shows that he understands his audience and seeks to give them what they need so that they will agree with him.

Analysis of Sample Essay 2

This essay scored a 3/3/3.

- **Reading—3:** This response demonstrates effective understanding of the source text with appropriate use of evidence through the analysis. In the second paragraph, the author discusses Clay's understanding of his audience and what the audience most fears. Although the source text does not refer explicitly to this fear, the writer picks up on it from a careful reading of the passage. In the next paragraph, the writer cites and discusses a claim Clay makes that supporting South America requires a minimal response. Finally, the last body paragraph paraphrases Clay's emotional call to remember the principles that guided the American Revolution. The writer shows an effective understanding of both the central idea and important details.

- **Analysis—3:** The writer shows an effective understanding of the task by identifying three ways Clay builds his argument (*Clay demonstrates an understanding of his audience, underscores the action that they need to take, and closes with an emotional appeal . . .*) and then elaborating on each point in the body paragraphs. Each body paragraph carefully evaluates how pieces of evidence from the source text, the author's use of reasoning, or stylistic or persuasive features are used to develop an argument. For example, in the final body paragraph the writer claims that Clay is *getting his listeners to remember how passionately they desired freedom from Great Britain* and explains that this is *to sway their emotions in*

261

Chapter 6

The SAT®
Essay

favor of supporting South America against Spain. The response could have made stronger use of evidence from the text, offering a direct quote rather than a paraphrase. However, this response shows an effective analysis of the source text using relevant support.

- **Writing—3:** This essay includes most of the features of an effective essay, including a precise central claim and body paragraphs. The introduction and conclusion lack development, although the introduction presents the central claim and the conclusion restates it. There is appropriate variety of sentence structure, and the few errors of convention and grammar do not detract from the overall reading of the response. Overall, this analysis is proficient.

Suggestions for Improvements

1. The author should work to develop a stronger introduction and conclusion. For example, the introduction could explain the significance of the topic, and the conclusion might provide a final thought or statement.

2. Paragraph 3 could further discuss Clay's reasons for minimizing the support needed in South America. While the writer effectively points out Clay's use of minimization, the importance of this technique to Clay's argument is not fully clear.

3. In paragraph 4, the writer paraphrases Clay's emotional appeal. When discussing an author's use of emotional language to persuade listeners to share his point of view or take a certain action, direct quotes from the source text are best.

Sample Essay 3

In 1818, South America was rising in revolt against Spain. Congressman Henry Clay believed that it was in America's best interest to support their neighbors to the south. In his speech to the 1818 Congress, Clay builds an argument tailor-made for his audience, outlining action steps Congress should take while at the same time appealing to their passionate belief in democracy. Through a combination of careful rhetoric, logic, and emotional appeal, Clay hopes to convince Congress to adopt an amendment that would put the US at war with Spain.

Clay begins his argument with careful rhetoric designed specifically for his audience. Clay understands that some may be thinking of the bloodshed of the American Revolution and have no desire to engage in another war. "It is not every cause of war that should lead to war …" Clay maintains. However, Clay goes on to suggest to his audience that, had they acted prior to this moment in time, war might have been avoided. In essence, Clay is telling his audience that he does not condone war; however, Congress has brought about the necessity to engage in war by previous inaction. Clay tells his audience, "There was a time . . . "when . . . our posture in the negotiation with Spain would have been totally different . . . " Yet, Clay maintains, that time has passed. Now is the time for more heavy-handed action.

Clay furthers the appeal of his argument by insisting that the action steps he proposes would not lead the country into another violent conflict. Rather, Clay maintains " . . . " the adoption of the amendment which I intend to propose would not hazard, in the slightest degree, the peace of the country. . . . " He uses logic to reason that, because of the size of South America, and because of the success that some South American people have already had in their fight against Spain, the revolution in some areas is already "a complete success." Therefore, Clay is demonstrating to his audience that supporting his amendment poses no risk to them.

Finally, Clay uses an emotional appeal to ultimately convince Congress to pass the amendment. Clay draws a parallel between the ideals of freedom and democracy that underscored the fight for American independence and the ideals of freedom and democracy that are bolstering the fight in South America. His emotional appeal is summed up in the last paragraph of the speech: "I would invoke the spirits of our departed fathers. Was it for yourselves only that you nobly fought? No, no! It was the chains that were forging for your posterity that made you fly to arms . . . ""

Speaking to Congress of the imminent threat of Spain, Henry Clay seeks to persuade his listeners to pass an amendment that would essentially put the fledgling nation at war with another European nation. With careful rhetoric, logic, and emotional appeals, Clay seeks to convince his listeners that freedom is something for which one should always be willing to fight.

Analysis of Sample Essay 3

This essay scored a 4/4/4.

- **Reading—4:** This response demonstrates thorough understanding of the source text with skillful use of paraphrases and direct quotations. The writer briefly summarizes the main idea of Clay's argument (*Clay believed that it was in America's best interest to support their neighbors to the south*) and presents many details from the text, including Clay's reflection that Congress had an opportunity to negotiate with Spain but missed it, to demonstrate why Clay's argument is significant. There are few long direct quotations from the source text. Instead, the author accurately and precisely paraphrases the key points of the speech.

- **Analysis—4:** The writer demonstrates an insightful understanding of the task by identifying three ways Clay builds his argument (*Through a combination of careful rhetoric, logic, and emotional appeal...*) and then elaborating on each point in the body paragraphs. Each body paragraph carefully evaluates how pieces of evidence from the source text, the author's use of reasoning, or stylistic or persuasive features are used to develop an argument. For example, in the final body paragraph the writer claims that Clay "draws a parallel between the ideals of freedom and democracy that underscored the fight for American independence and the ideals of freedom and democracy that are bolstering the fight in South America." The response demonstrates a thorough understanding of both the source text and its effect on the audience.

- **Writing—4:** This essay is cohesive and shows an effective command of language, including a precise central claim and body paragraphs. The introduction and conclusion are well developed. There is ample variety of sentence structures and no errors of convention and grammar that detract from the overall reading of the response. Overall, this analysis shows advanced writing proficiency.

ADDITIONAL ESSAY WRITING PRACTICE

For more practice, carefully read the following prompt and source text. Then write an analysis of the passage. Score your analytical response using the rubric provided.

> As you read the passage below, consider how the writer uses the following:
>
> - Evidence, such as facts or examples, to support claims
>
> - Reasoning to develop ideas and to connect claims and evidence
>
> - Stylistic or persuasive elements, such as word choice, emotional appeal, intellectual appeal, and ethical appeal, to add power to the ideas expressed

Padre Island National Seashore separates the Gulf of Mexico from the Laguna Madre, one of a few hypersaline lagoons in the world. The park protects 70 miles of coastline, dunes, prairies, and wind tidal flats teeming with life. It is a safe nesting ground for the Kemp's Ridley sea turtle and a haven for 380 bird species. It also has a rich history, including the Spanish shipwrecks of 1554.

The Importance of the 1554 Shipwrecks

1   In April, 1554, three Spanish *naos* (a type of cargo and passenger ship similar to Columbus's *Santa Maria*) went aground on Padre Island following a storm that had blown them across the Gulf of Mexico from the coast of Cuba. At the time this was the greatest disaster to ever befall the Spanish fleet in the New World. Tons of treasure bound for Spain was lost in addition to the lives of approximately three hundred passengers and crew who died from hunger, thirst, and attacks by natives as they attempted to walk back to the port of Vera Cruz.

2   But the story of the 1554 shipwreck does not end there, nor does it end with the conclusion of the salvage operations that took place later that year. As with any important historical event, its effects resonate through the centuries and can still be felt today—if one looks for them.

3   First of all, the wrecks were the first documented occurrence of Europeans on the island and one of the first occurrences of Europeans in what was to become Texas. The salvage operation was the first documented instance of Europeans intentionally coming to the island and staying for an extended period.

4   Second, the three ships that wrecked (the *Santa Maria de Yciar*, the *Espiritu Santo*, and the *San Esteban*) are the oldest shipwrecks ever found in North America (excluding the Caribbean and Latin America).

5   Third, when the remains of the ships were discovered in 1967, a private company called Platoro, Ltd. began excavating them. This set off a long legal battle over ownership of the remains, as Texas had no laws governing antiquities at the time. In the long run, the state won its case and the remains were turned over to the National Park Service, which has transferred curation of the artifacts to the Corpus Christi Museum of Science and History, where they may now be viewed.

6   Historian and Marine Archeologist Dr. Donald Keith, president of the Ships of Discovery at the Corpus Christi Museum of Science and History, notes that:

7   "The 1554 shipwrecks are important for a lot of reasons. The 'mining' of them by Platoro caused the state of Texas to realize that shipwrecks and archaeological sites in general are important, and the property of the people and the state. They are cultural resources that have to be cared for. Some of the earliest experiments in the conservation of artifacts from the sea were done on the objects and hull remains that were recovered from the sites that Platoro and the State worked. . . . The Platoro conflict did lead to the establishment of the Texas Antiquities Committee, which led to the Texas Historical Commission, which led to the discovery and excavation of *La Belle* [the ship of the French explorer La Salle, found on the Texas coast within the past few years] among other accomplishments."

8   This third and last effect on our present society is undoubtedly the most important, because it resulted in new Texas laws to protect archeological resources. These laws follow the federal Antiquities Act in spirit, which gives federal agencies custody of relics found within their jurisdictions so that they may be properly protected and studied. Thus, instead of ending up in private collections where they become curiosities for a fortunate few, the knowledge derived from the artifacts goes to the public in the form of publications and exhibits in museums and on websites.

9   Bits and pieces of the 1554 wrecks and many other historical events still wash up on the island or can be found emerging from the sands. If you discover something, please remember that the right thing to do is leave it where it is and report it to us, so that we may conduct a proper archeological dig and learn more about the rich history of the island and share our findings (and yours) with the world.

> Write an essay in which you explain how the writer builds an argument to persuade his or her audience of the importance of the 1554 shipwrecks. In your essay, analyze how the author uses one or more of the features listed previously (or features of your own choice) to strengthen the logic and persuasiveness of his/her argument. Be sure that your analysis focuses on the most relevant aspects of the passage.
>
> Your essay should not explain whether you agree with the writer's claims, but rather explain how the writer builds an argument to persuade his or her audience.

Score Point	Reading	Analysis	Writing
4 **(Advanced)**	The essay shows a comprehensive understanding of the source text, including the author's key claims, use of details and evidence, and the relationship between the two.	The essay offers an "insightful" and in-depth evaluation of the author's use of evidence and stylistic or persuasive features in building an argument. Supporting details and evidence are relevant and focus on those details that address the task.	The essay includes all of the features of a strong essay, including a precise central claim, body paragraphs, and a strong conclusion. There is a variety of sentence structures used in the essay, and it is virtually free of all convention errors.
3 **(Proficient)**	The essay shows an appropriate understanding of the source text, including the author's key claims and use of details in developing an argument.	The essay offers an "effective" evaluation of the author's use of evidence and stylistic or persuasive features in building an argument. Supporting details and evidence are appropriate and focus on those details that address the task.	The essay includes all of the features of an effective essay, including a precise central claim, body paragraphs, and a strong conclusion. There is a variety of sentence structures used in the essay, and it is free of significant convention errors.
2 **(Partial)**	The essay shows some understanding of the source text, including the author's key claims, but uses limited textual evidence and/or unimportant details.	The essay offers limited evaluation of the author's use of evidence and stylistic or persuasive features in building an argument. Supporting details and evidence are lacking and/or are not relevant to the task.	The essay does not provide a precise central claim, nor does it provide an effective introduction, body paragraphs, and conclusion. There is little variety of sentence structure used in the essay, and there are numerous errors in grammar and conventions.
1 **(Inadequate)**	The essay demonstrates little or no understanding of the source text or the author's use of key claims.	The essay offers no clear evaluation of the author's use of evidence and stylistic or persuasive features in building an argument. Supporting details and evidence are nonexistent or irrelevant to the task.	The essay lacks any form of cohesion or structure. There is little variety of sentence structures, and significant errors in convention make it difficult to read.

SUMMING IT UP

- The Essay section of the SAT® exam is 50 minutes long. You will be given one essay prompt and asked to write an analytical essay in response.

- SAT® essays are scored based on how well they meet the following three criteria:

    1. Reading—Does the essay demonstrate a thorough understanding of the source text, identify the author's key claims and explain how he or she uses evidence to support them, and use evidence from the source text effectively?

    2. Analysis—Does the essay offer in-depth evaluations of the author's use of evidence and stylistic or persuasive language features to build and support his or her argument? Does the essay include relevant supporting evidence from the passage to aid in its analysis?

    3. Writing—Does the essay include an effective introduction, a precise central claim supported by body paragraphs, and a strong conclusion? Does the essay include a variety of clearly written sentences that flow well together? Is the essay mostly error-free in grammar, usage, and mechanics?

- Your essay should not explain whether you agree with the author's claims, but, rather, it should explain how the author builds an argument to persuade his or her audience.

- Practice pacing yourself so that you are able to get your ideas down on paper in a complete, coherent, and unified essay.

- Prewriting should take 10 to 15 minutes. Use this time to do the following:

    ○ Identify and underline the author's key claims.

    ○ Find and then circle or highlight specific evidence the author uses to support his or her key claims.

    ○ Take notes on ways the author has used logic, reasoning, and rhetoric (persuasive language techniques), and evidence to convince readers that his or her key claims are valid.

- Writing the introduction should take 4 to 5 minutes. Keep these five ideas in mind:

    1. Keep the key words and phrases of the prompt in mind.

    2. Be sincere, clear, and straightforward. Avoid being cute, funny, ironic, satiric, overly emotional, or too dramatic.

    3. Paraphrase key claims from the source text.

    4. Write a clear topic sentence that introduces the passage's author, title, topic and the author's key claim about the topic, and makes it clear to your readers that you are about to analyze the passage and explain how the author accomplishes his or her persuasive purpose.

    5. Write sentences that advance the topic and interest the reader.

- Writing the body of the essay should take 15 to 20 minutes. Support your analysis of the author's work with careful reasoning, and back up your analysis with evidence from the source text. Your writing must be coherent, logical, unified, and organized.

- Writing the conclusion should take 3 to 4 minutes. A good concluding paragraph should assure your scorers that you have successfully read, understood, and analyzed the source text. There are three possible ways to end your essay:

    1. Through a *restatement* of your most important or most central idea

    2. Through a *summary* of the material covered in the essay

    3. Through a *clear statement* about the effectiveness of the passage author's work

- Revising (3 to 5 minutes) and proofing (3 to 5 minutes) are important steps in the writing process. Be sure to leave yourself enough time to polish your essay, even though it is considered a first draft by the test graders.

266

Chapter 6

The SAT®
Essay

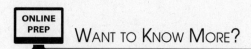

WANT TO KNOW MORE?

Access more practice questions, valuable lessons, helpful tips, and expert strategies for the following essay writing topics in *Peterson's Online Course for the SAT® Exam:*

- Avoiding Common Errors

- Effective Style in Essays

- Essay Scoring

- Essay Writing Method

- Organize and Develop Ideas

- Putting It All Together

To purchase and access the course, go to **www.petersons.com/testprep/sat.**

267

Chapter 6

The SAT®
Essay

PART VI:
MATH STRATEGIES
FOR THE SAT® EXAM

Chapter 7:   Multiple-Choice Math
Chapter 8:   Grid-In Strategies
Chapter 9:   Numbers and Operations
Chapter 10: Basic Algebra
Chapter 11: Geometry
Chapter 12: Functions and Intermediate Algebra
Chapter 13: Data Analysis, Statistics, and Probability

CHAPTER 7: MULTIPLE-CHOICE MATH

OVERVIEW

- Why Multiple-Choice Math Is Easier
- Question Format
- Solving Multiple-Choice Math Questions
- Know When to Use Your Calculator
- Learn the Most Important Multiple-Choice Math Tips
- Exercises: Multiple-Choice Math
- Summing It Up

WHY MULTIPLE-CHOICE MATH IS EASIER

How can one kind of math possibly be easier than another? Multiple-choice math questions on the SAT® exam are easier than those on the math tests you take in class because the answers are right there in front of you. As you know from taking other standardized tests, multiple-choice questions always give you the answer. You just have to figure out which answer is the correct one. So even if you aren't sure and have to guess, you can use estimating to narrow your choices and improve your odds.

The questions in each multiple-choice math section are arranged from easiest to most difficult. The questions don't stick to one content area. They jump around from algebra to geometry to advanced math to data analysis to statistics and back to algebra in no particular pattern.

QUESTION FORMAT

On the SAT® Math test, each set of multiple-choice math questions starts with directions and a reference section that look like this:

DIRECTIONS: For **Questions 1–30,** solve each problem, select the best answer from the choices provided, and fill in the corresponding circle on your answer sheet. For **Questions 31–38,** solve the problem and enter your answer in the grid on the answer sheet. The directions **before Question 31** will provide information on how to enter your answers in the grid.

ADDITIONAL INFORMATION:

- The use of a calculator **is permitted**. (In the Math Test—No Calculator section, this will say: "The use of a calculator is **not permitted**.)

- All variables and expressions used represent real numbers unless otherwise indicated.

- Figures provided in this test are drawn to scale unless otherwise indicated.

- All figures lie in a plane unless otherwise indicated.

- Unless otherwise specified, the domain of a given function f is the set of all real numbers x for which is $f(x)$ is a real number.

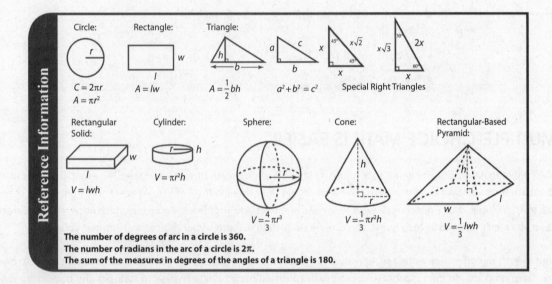

The information in the reference section should all be familiar to you from your schoolwork. Know that it's there in case you need it. But remember: the formulas themselves aren't the answers to any problems. You have to know when to use them and how to apply them.

Some multiple-choice questions ask to solve a given equation or system of equations, while others are presented in the form of word problems. Some include graphs, charts, or tables that you will be asked to interpret. All of the questions have four answer choices. These choices are arranged in order when the answers are numbers, usually from smallest to largest, but occasionally from largest to smallest.

SOLVING MULTIPLE-CHOICE MATH QUESTIONS

These five steps will help you solve multiple-choice math questions:

1. Read the question carefully and determine what's being asked.

2. Decide which math principles apply and use them to solve the problem.

3. Look for your answer among the choices. If it's there, mark it and go on.

4. If the answer you found is not there, recheck the question and your calculations.

5. If you still can't solve the problem, eliminate obviously wrong answers and take your best guess.

Now let's try out these steps on a couple of SAT®-type multiple-choice math questions.

Example:

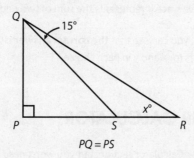

$PQ = PS$

In the figure above, $x =$

A. 15°

B. 30°

C. 60°

D. 75°

Solution:

1. The problem asks you to find the measure of one angle of right triangle PQR.

2. Two math principles apply: (1) the sum of the measures in degrees of the angles of a triangle is 180, and (2) 45-45-90 right triangles have certain special properties. Since $PQ = PS$, $\triangle PQS$ is a 45-45-90 right triangle. Therefore, angle $PQS = 45°$ and angle $PQR = 45 + 15 = 60°$. Therefore, angle $x = 180 - 90 - 60 = 30°$.

3. Look to see if 30° is among the answer choices. You'll see that it's choice B. No further steps are needed.
   The correct answer is B.

Example:

If x and y are negative numbers, which of the following is negative?

A. xy

B. $(xy)^2$

C. $(x - y)^2$

D. $x + y$

Solution:

1. The problem asks you to pick an answer choice that is a negative number.

2. The principles that apply are those governing operations with signed numbers. Since x and y are negative, choice A must be positive. As for choices B and C, as long as x and y are not equal to each other, both expressions must be positive. (If they're equal, the expression equals zero, and any number other than zero squared gives a positive result.) Choice D, however, is negative since it represents the sum of two negative numbers.

3. Looking among the answer choices, you can see that **the correct answer is D.** If you have trouble working with letters, try substituting easy numbers for x and y in each choice.

KNOW WHEN TO USE YOUR CALCULATOR

Calculators are allowed in the SAT® Math Test—Calculator section, but you won't *need* a calculator to solve any SAT® math questions. Calculators can be helpful in solving most of the problems, whether you use the calculator for simplifying expressions or graphing equations. But remember that your calculator is not some sort of magic brain. If you don't understand the questions in the first place, the calculator won't give you a solution.

Most calculators that you would use in class are allowed. It is best to use whichever calculator you are already comfortable using instead of trying to learn how to use a new one.

The most important thing to remember is to set up your work on paper first, and then plug the information into the calculator. For example, if you have a question that deals with an equation, set up the equation on your scratch paper. Then make your number substitutions on the calculator. This way, you always have something to refer to without having to think, "Oh, nuts, how did I set that up?" as the seconds tick by.

When you use your calculator, check the display each time you enter numbers to make sure you entered them correctly. Make sure to hit the Clear key after each finished operation; otherwise, it could get ugly.

LEARN THE MOST IMPORTANT MULTIPLE-CHOICE MATH TIPS

You've probably heard some of these tips before, but some will be new to you. Whatever the case, read them, learn them, and remember them. They will help you.

 ALERT: Don't automatically reach for your calculator. If it can't help you solve the problem, you'll just waste time fiddling with it. Save the calculator for what it does best, especially simplifying numeric expressions.

The Question Number Tells You How Hard the Question Is

Just as in most of the other SAT® sections, the questions go from easy to hard as you work toward the end. The first third of the questions is easy, the middle third is average but harder, and the final third gets more and more difficult. Take a look at these three examples. Don't solve them yet (you'll be doing that in a couple of minutes); just get an idea of how the level of difficulty changes from Question 1 to Question 12 to Question 25.

1. If $\dfrac{a+5}{6} = m$, and $m = 9$, what is the value of a?

   A. 24

   B. 49

   C. 59

   D. 84

12. Line a intersects the x-axis at $(3, 0)$ and the y-axis at $(0, -2)$. Line b passes through the origin and is parallel to line a. Which of the following is an equation of line b?

   A. $y = \dfrac{3}{2}x$

   B. $y = \dfrac{2}{3}x$

   C. $y = -\dfrac{3}{2}x$

   D. $y = -\dfrac{2}{3}x$

275

Chapter 7

Multiple-Choice Math

25. Yasmine owns a coffee shop and orders both coffee and tea from a wholesale supplier. The supplier will send no more than 600 kg in a shipment. Coffee beans come in packages that weigh 18.5 kg, and tea leaves come in packages that weigh 10 kg. Yasmine wants to buy at least twice as many packages of coffee as packages of tea. If c stands for the number of packages of coffee, and t stands for the number of packages of tea, which of the following systems of inequalities best represents Yasmine's order? Both c and t are nonnegative integers.

A. $18.5c + 10t \leq 600$
          $c \geq 2t$

B. $18.5c + 10t \leq 600$
          $2c \geq t$

C. $37c + 10t \leq 600$
          $c \geq 2t$

D. $37c + 10t \leq 600$
          $2c \geq t$

 TIP Look for shortcuts. SAT® math problems test your math reasoning, not your ability to make endless calculations. If you find yourself calculating too much, you've probably missed a shortcut that would have made your work easier.

Can you see the difference? You can probably do Question 1 very quickly. For Question 12, you might have to think for a bit. Question 25 may cause you to wince a little and then get started on some heavy-duty thinking.

EASY QUESTIONS HAVE EASY ANSWERS—DIFFICULT QUESTIONS DON'T

The easy questions are straightforward and don't have any hidden tricks. The obvious answer is almost always the correct answer. So for Question 1, the answer is indeed choice B.

When you hit the difficult stuff, you have to think harder. The information is not straightforward, and the answers aren't obvious. You can bet that your first-choice, easy answer will be wrong. If you don't believe it, let's take another look at Question 25.

Example:

25. Yasmine owns a coffee shop and orders both coffee and tea from a wholesale supplier. The supplier will send no more than 600 kg in a shipment. Coffee beans come in packages that weigh 18.5 kg, and tea leaves come in packages that weigh 10 kg. Yasmine wants to buy at least twice as many packages of coffee as packages of tea. If c stands for the number of packages of coffee, and t stands for the number of packages of tea, which of the following systems of inequalities best represents Yasmine's order? Both c and t are nonnegative integers.

A. $18.5c + 10t \leq 600$
          $c \geq 2t$

B. $18.5c + 10t \leq 600$
          $2c \geq t$

C. $37c + 10t \leq 600$
          $c \geq 2t$

D. $37c + 10t \leq 600$
          $2c \geq t$

Solution:

This question is difficult mostly because it takes a little longer to think through the problem and set up the inequalities laid out in the question stem. Let's tackle this step by step.

We will use the variables c for coffee beans and t for tea. The total weight, in kg, of coffee beans and tea that the wholesale supplier sends can be expressed as the weight of each package multiplied by the number of each type of package, which is $18.5c$ for coffee beans and $10t$ for tea leaves. Since the supplier will not send shipments that weigh more than 600 kg, it follows that $18.5c + 10t \leq 600$ expresses the first part of the problem.

Since Yasmine wants to buy at least twice as many packages of coffee beans as packages of tea leaves, the number of packages of coffee beans should be greater than or equal to two times the number of packages of tea leaves. This can be expressed by $c \geq 2t$.

Thus, **the correct answer is A.**

Why are the other answers wrong? Choice B misrepresents the relationship between the numbers of each package that Yasmine wants to buy. Choice C is incorrect because the first inequality of the system incorrectly doubles the weight per package of coffee beans. The weight of each package of coffee beans is 18.5 kg, not 37 kg. Choice D doubles the weight per package of coffee beans and transposes the relationship between the numbers of packages.

 ALERT: Beware of the obvious. Don't be fooled by what look like obvious answers to difficult questions. The answers to difficult questions require some digging. They never jump out at you.

BE CERTAIN TO ANSWER THE QUESTION BEING ASKED

Suppose that you were asked to solve the following problem:

Example:

If $5x + 11 = 31$, what is the value of $x + 4$?

A. 4

B. 6

C. 8

D. 10

Solution:

The first step is to solve the equation $5x + 11 = 31$.

$$5x + 11 = 31 \quad \text{Subtract 11 from both sides.}$$
$$5x = 20 \quad \text{Divide both sides by 5.}$$
$$x = 4$$

Remember that the problem does not ask for the value of x, it asks for the value of $x + 4$, so the answer is actually 8. Make certain that the answer you select is the answer to the question that is being asked. **The correct answer is C.**

When Guessing at Hard Questions, You Can Toss Out Easy Answers

Now that you know the difficult questions won't have easy or obvious answers, use a guessing strategy. (Use all the help you can get!) When you have less than a clue about a difficult question, scan the answer choices and eliminate the ones that seem easy or obvious, such as any that just restate the information in the question. Then take your best guess.

Questions of Average Difficulty Won't Have Trick Answers

Let's look again at Question 12:

12. Line *a* intersects the *x*-axis at (3, 0) and the *y*-axis at (0, –2). Line *b* passes through the origin and is parallel to line *a*. Which of the following is an equation of line *b*?

    A. $y = \dfrac{3}{2}x$

    B. $y = \dfrac{2}{3}x$

    C. $y = -\dfrac{3}{2}x$

    D. $y = -\dfrac{2}{3}x$

This is a bit more difficult than Question 1, but it's still pretty straightforward. Since we know points on line *a*, we can calculate the slope of this line:

$$\frac{y_2 - y_1}{x_2 - x_1} = \frac{-2 - 0}{0 - 3} = \frac{2}{3}$$

Since line *b* is parallel to line *a*, the two have the same slope, that is, $\dfrac{2}{3}$. The problem tells us that line *b* passes through the origin, which means that it intercepts the *y*-axis at 0. Thus, line *b* can be expressed by the equation $y = \dfrac{2}{3}x$. **The correct answer is B.**

It's Smart to Work Backward

Every standard multiple-choice math problem includes four answer choices. One of them has to be correct; the other three are incorrect. This means that it's always possible to solve a problem by testing each of the answer choices. Just plug each choice into the problem and sooner or later you'll find the one that works! Testing answer choices can often be a much easier and surer way of solving a problem than attempting a lengthy calculation.

When Working Backward, Always Start from the Middle

When working on multiple-choice math questions, remember that all of the numeric answer choices are presented in order—either smallest to largest, or vice versa. As a result, it's always best to begin with a middle option, choice B or choice C. This way, if you start with choice C and it's too large, you'll only have to concentrate on the smaller choices. There, you've just knocked off at least two choices in a heartbeat! Now let's give it a test run!

Example:

If $\frac{8}{9}y = \frac{9}{4}$, what is the value of y?

A. $\frac{32}{81}$

B. $\frac{1}{2}$

C. 2

D. $\frac{81}{32}$

Solution:

Start with choice C, because it will be easier to compute with than choice B: $\frac{8}{9}(2) = \frac{16}{9} < \frac{9}{4}$.
Since choice C is too small, the only possible answer is choice D.

You can check that $\frac{8}{9}\left(\frac{81}{32}\right) = \frac{9}{4}$.

The correct answer is D.

Now try this testing business with a more difficult question:

Example:

In the *xy*-plane, the line determined by the points (8, *c*) and (*c*, 18) passes through the origin. Which of the following could be the value of *c*?

A. 10

B. 11

C. 12

D. 13

Solution:

Start with choice C, because it may be easier to compute with than choice B. The line through (8, 12) and (12, 18)

is $y = \frac{18-12}{12-8}x + b$. This equation simplifies to $y = \frac{3}{2}x$, which is a line through the origin.

Plug (8, 12) or (12, 18) into $y = \frac{3}{2}x$, and both sides will be equal.

$$12 = \frac{3}{2}(8) \text{ or } 18 = \frac{3}{2}(12)$$
$$12 = 12 \qquad 18 = 18$$

The other values of *c* will not result in an equivalent equation. **The correct answer is C.**

It's Easier to Work with Numbers Than with Letters

Because numbers are more meaningful than letters, try plugging them into equations and formulas in place of variables. This technique can make problems much easier to solve. Here are some examples:

Example:

If $x - 4$ is 2 greater than y, then $x + 5$ is how much greater than y?

A. 3

B. 7

C. 9

D. 11

Solution:

Choose any value for x. Let's say you decide to make $x = 4$. Solve for x in the first equation. If $4 - 4 = 0$, and 0 is 2 greater than y, then $y = -2$. In the second equation, if $x = 4$, then $4 + 5 = 9$. Therefore, $x + 5$ is 11 more than y. **The correct answer is D.**

Example:

The cost of renting office space in a building is $2.50 per square foot per month. Which of the following represents the total cost c, in dollars, to rent p square feet of office space each year in the building?

A. $c = 2.50(12p)$

B. $c = 2.50p + 12$

C. $c = \dfrac{2.50p}{12}$

D. $c = \dfrac{12p}{2.50}$

Solution:

Let $p = 100$, then the rent for one month is $250 and the rent for one year is $3,000. The only equation that will provide that answer is $c = 2.50(12p)$. **The correct answer is A.**

If a question asks for an odd integer or an even integer, go ahead and pick any odd or even integer you like.

 Leave a paper trail! If you need to set up an equation, jot it down in your test booklet. That way, if you come back to recheck your work, you'll know what you were originally thinking.

Solving for Variables with Restricted Values

When solving problems involving variables, you must pay careful attention to any restrictions on the possible values of the variables

Consider the following question:

Example:

If $x \geq 2$, which of the following is a solution to the equation $x(x-3)(x+4)(x+2)(3x-5) = 0$?

A. 2

B. 3

C. 4

D. 5

Solution:

This equation has five solutions, but the problem is looking only for a solution that is at least 2. Set each of the factors equal to 0 and solve for x. The only answer that is greater than or equal to 2 is 3. **The correct answer is B.**

Now, consider this slightly different version of the same problem.

Example:

If $x < -2$, which of the following is a solution to the equation $x(x-3)(x+4)(x+2)(3x-5) = 0$?

A. –3

B. –4

C. –5

D. There is more than one solution.

Solution:

The solutions to the equation can be found by setting each of the factors equal to zero. So $x = 0$, $x - 3 = 0$, $x + 4 = 0$, $x + 2 = 0$, and $3x - 5 = 0$.

These lead to the solutions $x = 0, 3, -4, -2$, and $\frac{5}{3}$ respectively.

Of these five solutions only –4 (choice B) is less than –2. **The correct answer is B.**

The test booklet is yours, so feel free to use it for your scratchwork. Also, go ahead and mark up any diagrams with length or angle information; it helps. But don't waste time trying to redraw diagrams; it's just not worth it.

SOLVING EQUATIONS IN THE THREE-STATEMENT FORMAT

You may find a three-statement format in certain questions in the multiple-choice math section. The best way to answer this kind of question is by process of elimination, tackling one statement at a time and marking it as true or false. Here is an example:

Example:

Note: Figure not drawn to scale.

In the figure above, lines k and m intersect at a point, and lines k and n intersect at a different point. If $v + s = p + q$, which of the following statements must be true?

I. $r = w$

II. $t = s$

III. $q = x$

A. I only

B. II only

C. I and II only

D. I, II, and III

Solution:

Because $v + s = p + q$, we know that $p + q = 180$. Because they both make a straight line, lines m and n must be parallel. Since m and n are parallel, then statements I and II, must be true. While statement III might be true, it is only true if line k is perpendicular to lines m and n, and that does not have to be true. **The correct answer is C.**

TIP For multiple-choice math questions, circle what's being asked so that you don't pick a wrong answer by mistake. That way, for example, you won't pick an answer that gives perimeter when the question asks for an area.

SOLVING EQUATIONS INVOLVING SQUARE ROOTS OR ALGEBRAIC FRACTIONS

The procedure for solving equations involving square roots or algebraic fractions occasionally results in what are known as *extraneous solutions*. An extraneous solution is a number that is correctly obtained from the equation-solving process but doesn't actually solve the equation, be sure to check your answer.

Example:

Solve for x: $\sqrt{x+4} + 15 = 10$

A. -29

B. -21

C. 21

D. There are no solutions.

Solution:

First, solve the equation.

$$\sqrt{x+4} + 15 = 10 \quad \text{Subtract 15 from both sides.}$$
$$\sqrt{x+4} = -5 \quad \text{Square both sides.}$$
$$\left(\sqrt{x+4}\right)^2 = (-5)^2$$
$$x + 4 = 25$$
$$x = 21$$

It appears that the solution is choice C. However, if you check the solution $x = 21$ in the original equation, you will see that it doesn't solve it.

$$\sqrt{x+4} + 15 = 10?$$
$$\sqrt{21+4} + 15 = 10?$$
$$\sqrt{25} + 15 = 10?$$
$$5 + 15 \neq 10.$$

The correct answer is D.

Solving Geometry Problems of Measure

When you are asked to find the measure of a side or angle of a figure, using the measure of an angle or a side of another shape can help you find the measure you need.

Example:

In the figure, what is the length of *NP*?

A. 8

B. 9

C. 12

D. 15

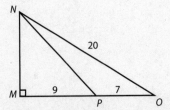

Solution:

This figure is really two right triangles, *NMO* and *NMP*. Since *NM* is a side of both triangles, once you find its length, you can find the length of *NP*. The Pythagorean theorem is what you need:

$$NM^2 + MO^2 = NO^2$$

$$NM^2 + (16)^2 = (20)^2$$

Note that 16 and 20 are multiples of 4 and 5, respectively, so you now know that this is a 3-4-5 right triangle, which means that *NM* = 12.

Since you just found out that triangle *NMP* has sides of 9 and 12, it's also a 3-4-5 right triangle, so *NP* must be 15. **The correct answer is D.**

 Draw a diagram if none is supplied. Drawing a diagram is a great way to organize information. Mark it up with the information you're given, and you'll have a better idea of what you're looking for.

284

Chapter 7

Multiple-Choice Math

Solving Right Triangles Using the Pythagorean Theorem

The Pythagorean theorem is usually needed to solve problems involving a right triangle for which you are given the lengths of some of the sides. The Pythagorean theorem enables you to compute the length of the third side of a right triangle if you know the lengths of the other two sides. It is one of the most useful and common SAT® exam geometry facts. Consider the problem below.

Example:

Line segment $\overline{PQ}$ is tangent to the circle with center O at point T. If T is the midpoint of $\overline{PQ}$, $OQ = 13$, and the radius of the circle is 5, what is the length of $\overline{PQ}$?

A. 10

B. 12

C. 24

D. 26

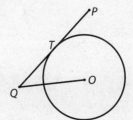

Solution:

This is a tricky question since, at the moment, it doesn't appear to involve any triangles at all. However, you are told that the radius of the circle is 5, and if you draw in radius $\overline{OT}$, you will create triangle OTQ. Use the fact that a tangent line to a circle is perpendicular to the radius at the point of contact to deduce that $\angle OTQ$ is a right angle.

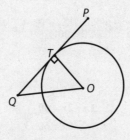

The diagram now depicts right triangle OTQ, and $OT = 5$ and $OQ = 13$. Now, use the Pythagorean theorem to determine that $TQ = 12$, as shown here:

$$OT^2 + TQ^2 = OQ^2$$
$$5^2 + TQ^2 = 13^2$$
$$25 + TQ^2 = 169$$
$$TQ^2 = 144$$
$$TQ = 12$$

Finally, since T is the midpoint of line segment $\overline{PQ}$, the entire length of the line segment is $12 + 12 = 24$.
The correct answer is C.

ELIMINATE ANSWERS THAT CAN'T POSSIBLY BE RIGHT

Knowing whether your calculations should produce a number that's larger or smaller than the quantity you started with can point you toward the right answer. It's also an effective way of eliminating wrong answers. Here's an example:

Example:

Daryl can set up the display for the science fair in 20 minutes. It takes Francisco 30 minutes to set it up. How long will it take the two boys to complete the setup if they work together?

- **A.** 8 minutes
- **B.** 12 minutes
- **C.** 20 minutes
- **D.** 30 minutes

Solution:

Immediately you can see that choices C and D are impossible because the two boys working together will have to complete the job in less time than either one of them working alone.

	Daryl	Francisc
Actual time spent	x	x
Time needed to do entire job alone	20	30

$$\frac{x}{20} + \frac{x}{30} = 1$$

Multiply by 60 to clear fractions:

$$3x + 2x = 60$$
$$5x = 60$$
$$x = 12$$

The correct answer is B.

YOUR EYE IS A GOOD ESTIMATOR

Figures in the standard multiple-choice math section are always drawn to scale unless you see the warning "Note: Figure not drawn to scale." That means you can sometimes solve a problem just by looking at the picture and estimating the answer. Here's how this works:

Example:

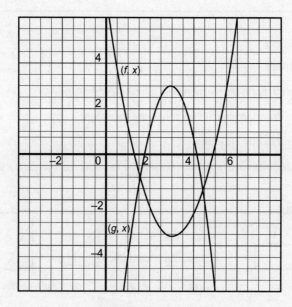

$$f(x) = (x-3)^2 - 3$$
$$g(x) = -2(x-3)^2 + 3$$

Graphs of the functions f and g are shown in the xy-plane above. For which of the following values of x does $f(x) + g(x) = 0$?

A. 1

B. 2

C. 3

D. 4

Solution:

The sum of the function values is 0 when the function values for f and g are opposites. That appears to be true at $x = 3$. **The correct answer is C.**

IF SOME QUESTIONS ALWAYS GIVE YOU TROUBLE, SAVE THEM FOR LAST

You know which little demons haunt your math skills. If you find questions that you know will give you nightmares, save them for last. They will take up a lot of your time, especially if you're panicking, and you can use that time to do more of the easier questions.

Chapter 7

Multiple-
Choice Math

EXERCISES: MULTIPLE-CHOICE MATH

EXERCISE 1

18 MINUTES—15 QUESTIONS

For **Questions 1–15,** solve each problem, choose the best answer from the choices provided, and put a circle around the correct answer. You may use any available space for scratch work.

ADDITIONAL INFORMATION:

- The use of a calculator **is permitted**.

- All variables and expressions used represent real numbers unless otherwise indicated.

- Figures provided in this test are drawn to scale unless otherwise indicated.

- All figures lie in a plane unless otherwise indicated.

- Unless otherwise specified, the domain of a given function *f* is the set of all real numbers *x* for which *f(x)* is a real number.

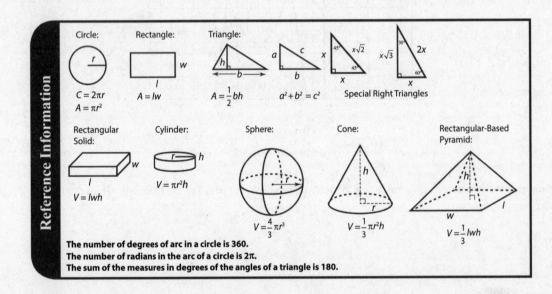

1. A linear function $g(x)$ has x-intercept $(-3, 0)$ and y-intercept $(0, -6)$. Compute $g\left(-\dfrac{1}{2}\right)$.

   A. -7

   B. -6

   C. -5

   D. -2

2. For what values of x, if any, does the graph of $f(x) = 2 - |4 - x|$ cross the x-axis?

   A. 4

   B. 2 and 6

   C. -2

   D. No such values

3. If $H(x) = 3 - 2x^2$, compute $H(x - 1)$.

   A. $-2x^2 + 1$

   B. $-2x^2 - 2x + 4$

   C. $-2x^2 + 4x + 5$

   D. $-2x^2 + 4x + 1$

4. For what value of the constant a, if any, does this system have infinitely many solutions?

   $$3x - \frac{1}{2}y = 4$$
   $$ax = 2 - y$$

   A. -6

   B. 0

   C. 6

   D. No such value

5. Which of these is equivalent to $(2x - 7)^2$?

   A. $4x^2 - 49$

   B. $4x^2 + 49$

   C. $4x^2 - 28x + 49$

   D. $4x^2 - 14x - 49$

6. A chiropractor charges a flat fee of $45 plus $15 per 10 minutes for the duration of a patient's visit. Which equation gives the cost, C, of a visit in terms of the number of hours, h?

- **A.** $C = 45 + 10h$
- **B.** $C = 45 + 60h$
- **C.** $C = 45 + 90h$
- **D.** $C = 90h$

7. To which of the following is this equation equivalent?

$$\frac{R_1 - R_2}{\dfrac{1}{R_2} + \dfrac{1}{R_1}} = R_2$$

- **A.** $\dfrac{R_1 - R_2}{R_1 + R_2} = \dfrac{1}{R_1}$
- **B.** $\dfrac{R_1}{R_2} - \dfrac{R_2}{R_1} = R_2$
- **C.** $\dfrac{R_1^2 - R_2^2}{R_1} = R_2$
- **D.** $\dfrac{(R_1 - R_2)(R_1 + R_2)}{2} = R_2$

8. What is the solution set of the equation $\sqrt{4x^2 + 1} = 3$?

- **A.** $\{-2, 2\}$
- **B.** $\left\{-\sqrt{\dfrac{1}{2}}, \sqrt{\dfrac{1}{2}}\right\}$
- **C.** $\{-\sqrt{5}, \sqrt{5}\}$
- **D.** $\{-\sqrt{2}, \sqrt{2}\}$

9. The endpoints of a diameter of a circle are (−2, −1) and (0, −4). What is the circumference of this circle?

A. $\dfrac{\sqrt{13}}{2}\pi$

B. $\sqrt{13}\,\pi$

C. $\dfrac{13}{2}\pi$

D. 13π

SHOW YOUR WORK HERE

10. Determine the value of $x + y$ given the following:

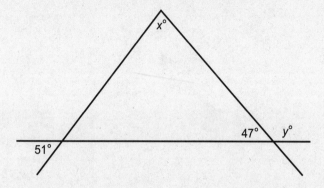

A. 82

B. 133

C. 215

D. 266

11. Find the equation of the line with x-intercept (−4, 0) that is parallel to the line with equation $3x − 4y = 1$.

A. $3x − 4y = −12$

B. $3x − y = −12$

C. $4x + 3y = −16$

D. $3x − 4y = −3$

12. Find the solution set of this nonlinear system:

$$4x + y = 0$$
$$y = 2(x − 1)^2 − 10$$

A. $\{(−4, 16), (4, −16)\}$

B. $\{(−2, 8), (2, −8)\}$

C. $\{(−2, -8), (2, 8)\}$

D. Empty set

291

Chapter 7

Multiple-Choice Math

13. Solve this equation for y, assuming a is a non-zero real number:

$$\frac{ay-1}{a-y} = a$$

A. $y = \dfrac{2a+1}{a+1}$

B. $y = a^2 - 2a + 1$

C. $y = \dfrac{a^2 + 1}{2a}$

D. $y = \dfrac{a^2 + 1}{a+1}$

14. Which of these is equivalent to $(3 - 2i)^2$? (Note: $i = \sqrt{-1}$)

A. 29

B. 8

C. −13

D. −22

15. What is the solution set for the following equation?

$$x(4x - 1) = -\frac{1}{16}$$

A. Empty set

B. $\left\{\dfrac{1}{8}\right\}$

C. $\left\{-\dfrac{1}{8}, \dfrac{1}{8}\right\}$

D. $\left\{-\dfrac{1}{16}, \dfrac{15}{64}\right\}$

EXERCISE 2

12 MINUTES—10 QUESTIONS

For **Questions 1–10**, solve each problem, choose the best answer from the choices provided, and put a circle around the correct answer. You may use any available space for scratch work.

ADDITIONAL INFORMATION:

- The use of a calculator is **permitted**.

- All variables and expressions used represent real numbers unless otherwise indicated.

- Figures provided in this test are drawn to scale unless otherwise indicated.

- All figures lie in a plane unless otherwise indicated.

- Unless otherwise specified, the domain of a given function f is the set of all real numbers x for which $f(x)$ is a real number.

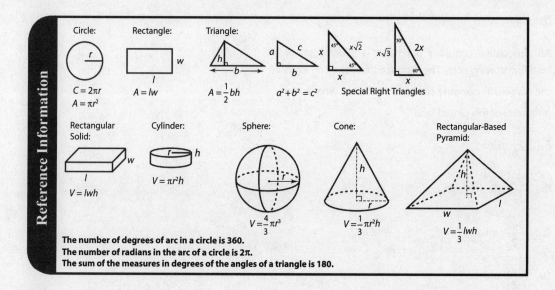

1. Jack is training for a marathon. Currently, he runs a 5K in 29 minutes. His goal is to reduce this time by 15 seconds each week. Which of the following would be his completion time, in minutes, after w weeks?

   A. $29 - 15w$

   B. $29 \times 60 - 15w$

   C. $29 - \dfrac{1}{4}w$

   D. $29 + 15w$

2. If $\dfrac{x}{2y} = -\dfrac{1}{4}$, which of these is equal to $x - 2y$?

   A. $5x$

   B. $3x$

   C. $-\dfrac{5}{2}y$

   D. $-4y$

3. An agricultural company purchased a square plot of land for growing corn. The distance from one corner to the diagonally opposite corner is $1\dfrac{1}{4}$ miles. What is the perimeter of this plot of land?

   A. $3\dfrac{1}{8}$ miles

   B. $\dfrac{25}{32}$ mile

   C. $\dfrac{5\sqrt{2}}{2}$ miles

   D. $\dfrac{5\sqrt{2}}{8}$ miles

4. Two canoes leave a dock, traveling in opposite directions, at noon. One canoe travels at 6 miles per hour, and the other at 4 miles per hour. Which equation can be used to determine the number of hours, x, it takes before the canoes are 36 miles apart?

   A. $\dfrac{x}{4} + \dfrac{x}{6} = 36$

   B. $10x = 36$

   C. $(4x)(6x) = 36$

   D. $2x = 36$

5. Determine the value of a so that the points $(-a, 2)$ and $(3, 4a)$ lie on a line perpendicular to the line with the equation $x = \frac{1}{2}y - 1$.

A. $\dfrac{1}{9}$

B. $\dfrac{1}{7}$

C. 4

D. $-\dfrac{2}{3}$

6. Margaret is practicing her soccer goal shots. She made 23 of the last 36 shots. If she misses every shot thereafter, which of the following equations could be used to determine the number of shots, s, she missed in a row so that her "percentage of goals made" drops to 55%?

A. $\dfrac{23 - s}{36 + s} = 0.55$

B. $\dfrac{23 + s}{36 + s} = 0.55$

C. $\dfrac{23}{36 + s} = 0.55$

D. $\dfrac{23}{36} + s = 0.55$

7. The ratio of "Yes" to "No" votes at a town hall meeting regarding the installation of a new gas pipeline is 2 to 5. If there were 42 "Yes" votes, how many people, all told, voted?

A. 105

B. 126

C. 147

D. 252

8. Assume *RSTU* is a rhombus. What is the value of $x + y + z$?

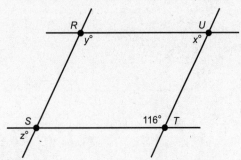

- **A.** 64
- **B.** 128
- **C.** 244
- **D.** 360

9. If $-3 \leq y \leq 1$ and $-4 \leq -x \leq 2$, what is the smallest value $x - y$ can be?

- **A.** -7
- **B.** -5
- **C.** -3
- **D.** -1

10. A basketball player can spin a basketball on her finger at a rate of 100 revolutions per minute. What is the rate in revolutions per second?

- **A.** $\dfrac{3}{5}$ revolutions per second
- **B.** 6,000 revolutions per second
- **C.** $\dfrac{5}{3}$ revolutions per second
- **D.** $\dfrac{1}{6,000}$ revolutions per second

Exercise 1: Answer Key and Explanations

1. C	4. D	7. A	10. C	13. C
2. B	5. C	8. D	11. A	14. A
3. D	6. C	9. B	12. B	15. B

1. **The correct answer is C.** The slope is $m = \dfrac{0-(-6)}{-3-0} = -2$. Using this in $y = mx + b$ with the y-intercept $b = -6$ yields the equation $y = -2x - 6$. This is $g(x)$. So $g\left(-\dfrac{1}{2}\right) = -2\left(-\dfrac{1}{2}\right) - 6 = 1 - 6 = -5$.

2. **The correct answer is B.** Solve the equation $2 - |4 - x| = 0$. This is the same as $|4 - x| = 2$, which breaks down into two equations, namely $4 - x = 2$ and $4 - x = -2$. Solving these for x yields the solutions $x = 2$ and $x = 6$.

3. **The correct answer is D.** Substitute the expression $x - 1$ in for x and simplify:
$$H(x-1) = 3 - 2(x-1)^2$$
$$= 3 - 2\left(x^2 - 2x + 1\right)$$
$$= 3 - 2x^2 + 4x - 2$$
$$= -2x^2 + 4x + 1$$

4. **The correct answer is D.** A system of two linear equations has infinitely many solutions when the equations are multiples of each other. If you multiply the first equation by -2, you get the equation $-6x + y = -8$, so that $-6x = -8 - y$. No matter what value of a is used, the second equation $ax = 2 - y$ can never be equivalent to this.

5. **The correct answer is C.** FOIL as follows:
$$(2x-7)^2 = (2x-7)(2x-7)$$
$$= 4x^2 - 14x - 14x + 49$$
$$= 4x^2 - 28x + 49$$

6. **The correct answer is C.** There are 60 minutes in one hour. This equates to six 10-minute installments, each of which costs $15. So the hourly rate is $90. A visit of h hours costs the flat fee plus the hourly rate times h. That is, $C = 45 + 90h$.

7. **The correct answer is A.** Get a common denominator in the bottom of the left side and simplify, as follows:
$$\frac{R_1 - R_2}{\dfrac{1}{R_2} + \dfrac{1}{R_1}} = R_2$$
$$\frac{R_1 - R_2}{\dfrac{R_1 + R_2}{R_1 R_2}} = R_2$$
$$(R_1 - R_2) \cdot \frac{R_1 R_2}{R_1 + R_2} = R_2$$
$$\frac{R_1 - R_2}{R_1 + R_2} = \frac{\cancel{R_2}}{R_1 \cancel{R_2}}$$
$$\frac{R_1 - R_2}{R_1 + R_2} = \frac{1}{R_1}$$

8. **The correct answer is D.** Square both sides and then solve the resulting quadratic equation, as follows:
$$\sqrt{4x^2 + 1} = 3$$
$$4x^2 + 1 = 9$$
$$4x^2 = 8$$
$$x^2 = 2$$
$$x = \pm\sqrt{2}$$

9. **The correct answer is B.** Calculate the distance between the endpoints. The length of the diameter, d, is $d = \sqrt{(-2-0)^2 + (-1-(-4))^2} = \sqrt{4+9} = \sqrt{13}$. The circumference of a circle is $\pi d = \sqrt{13}\,\pi$.

10. The correct answer is C. The interior angles of a triangle sum to 180. Since vertical angles are congruent, the three angles are x, 47, and 51.

$$x + 47 + 51 = 180$$
$$x = 180 - 98$$
$$x = 82$$

In addition, the angles with measures 47 and y are supplementary.

$$47 + y = 180$$
$$y = 133$$

Thus, the value of $x + y$ is $82 + 133 = 215$.

11. The correct answer is A. First, find the slope of the given line by putting it into slope-intercept form; solving for y yields $3x - 1 = 4y$ and so, $y = \frac{3}{4}x - \frac{1}{4}$. The slope is $\frac{3}{4}$. This is the slope of the desired line as well, since parallel lines have the same slope. Using point-slope formula for a line with the point $(-4, 0)$ yields:

$$y - 0 = \frac{3}{4}(x - (-4))$$
$$y = \frac{3}{4}x + 3$$
$$4y = 3x + 12$$
$$3x - 4y = -12$$

12. The correct answer is B. Solve the first equation for y so $y = -4x$. Substitute this into the second equation and solve for x:

$$-4x = 2(x - 1)^2 - 10$$
$$-4x = 2(x^2 - 2x + 1) - 10$$
$$-4x = 2x^2 - 4x + 2 - 10$$
$$-4x = 2x^2 - 4x - 8$$
$$2x^2 = 8$$
$$x^2 = 4$$
$$x = \pm 2$$

Now substitute these values back into the first equation to get the corresponding y-values. Doing so yields the solutions $(-2, 8)$ and $(2, -8)$.

13. The correct answer is C. Multiply both sides by the denominator of the fraction on the left; then gather the y-terms on one side:

$$\frac{ay - 1}{a - y} = a$$
$$ay - 1 = a(a - y)$$
$$ay - 1 = a^2 - ay$$
$$2ay = a^2 + 1$$
$$y = \frac{a^2 + 1}{2a}$$

14. The correct answer is A. FOIL and simplify:

$$(3 - 2i)^2 = (3 - 2i)(3 - 2i)$$
$$= 9 - 6i - 6i + 4i^2$$
$$= 9 - 12i - 4$$
$$= 5 - 12i$$

15. The correct answer is B. Gather all terms to the left side and factor the resulting quadratic expression:

$$x(4x - 1) = -\frac{1}{16}$$
$$4x^2 - x + \frac{1}{16} = 0$$
$$\left(2x - \frac{1}{4}\right)\left(2x - \frac{1}{4}\right) = 0$$
$$2x - \frac{1}{4} = 0$$
$$2x = \frac{1}{4}$$
$$x = \frac{1}{8}$$

Exercise 2: Answer Key and Explanations

1. C	3. C	5. A	7. C	9. C
2. C	4. B	6. C	8. C	10. C

1. **The correct answer is C.** There are 60 seconds in one minute and 15 seconds equals $\frac{1}{4}$ minute. The number of minutes reduced after w weeks is $\frac{1}{4}w$. Subtracting this from 29 yields the number of minutes equal to Jack's completion time after w weeks.

2. **The correct answer is C.** Cross-multiply to obtain the equivalent equation $4x = -2y$. Hence, $x = -\frac{1}{2}y$. Therefore, $x - 2y = -\frac{1}{2}y - 2y = -\frac{5}{2}y$.

3. **The correct answer is C.** Let x miles be the length of a side of the plot of land purchased. The following is a diagram of the plot of land:

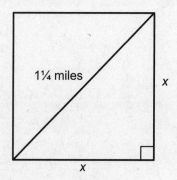

Use the Pythagorean theorem to find x:

$$x^2 + x^2 = \left(\frac{5}{4}\right)^2$$
$$2x^2 = \frac{25}{16}$$
$$x^2 = \frac{25}{32}$$
$$x = \sqrt{\frac{25}{32}}$$
$$x = \frac{5}{4\sqrt{2}} = \frac{5\sqrt{2}}{8}$$

The perimeter is $4\left(\frac{5\sqrt{2}}{8}\right) = \frac{5\sqrt{2}}{2}$ miles.

4. **The correct answer is B.** Since the canoes are traveling in the exact opposite direction, add the distances traveled after a given time to determine how far they are apart at that time. In one hour, the canoes are $6 + 4 = 10$ miles apart. The rate at which they are separating is 10 miles per hour. Let x be the number of hours it takes for the canoes to be 36 miles apart. Using distance equals rate times time yields the equation $10x = 36$.

5. **The correct answer is A.** First, find the slope of the given line by putting it into $y = mx + b$ form:

$$2x = y - 2$$
$$y = 2x + 2$$

The slope of the given line is 2. The slope of the desired line, being perpendicular to this one, is $-\frac{1}{2}$. Use the definition of slope to set up the following equation to determine the value of a:

$$\frac{4a - 2}{3 - (-a)} = -\frac{1}{2}$$
$$\frac{4a - 2}{3 + a} = -\frac{1}{2}$$
$$2(4a - 2) = -(3 + a)$$
$$8a - 4 = -3 - a$$
$$9a = 1$$
$$a = \frac{1}{9}$$

6. **The correct answer is C.** After missing s shots, the number of shots attempted is $36 + s$. Having missed all of these, Margaret has made 23 goals. The fraction made is $\frac{23}{36 + s}$. To find the value of s for which this is 55%, or 0.55, set up this equation:

$$\frac{23}{36 + s} = 0.55$$

7. **The correct answer is C.** Let x be the number of "No" votes. Set up the following proportion and solve for x:

$$\frac{2}{5} = \frac{42}{x}$$
$$2x = 42(5)$$
$$x = 105$$

The number of people who voted, all told, is the sum of "Yes" and "No" votes, namely $105 + 42 = 147$.

8. **The correct answer is C.** Since the sum of the measures of adjacent angles in a rhombus is 180, we see that $x = 64$ and $y = 116$. Since vertical angles are congruent, we have $z = 64$. Thus, $x + y + z = 64 + 116 + 64 = 244$.

9. **The correct answer is C.** Look at the values of $x - y$ for all pairs of choices of extreme values of x and y. Note that $-3 \leq y \leq 1$ and $-2 \leq x \leq 4$: The smallest value of $x - y$ is -3.

x	y	$x - y$
-2	-3	$-2 - (-3) = 1$
-2	1	$-2 - 1 = -3$
4	-3	$4 - (-3) = 7$
4	1	$4 - 1 = 3$

10. **The correct answer is C.** Since one minute equals 60 seconds, we convert the units as follows: In one hour, the train will cover 6(14), or 84, miles.

$$\frac{100 \text{ revolutions}}{1 \text{ minute}} \times \frac{1 \text{ minute}}{60 \text{ seconds}} = \frac{100}{60} = \frac{5}{3} \text{ revolutions per second}$$

300

Chapter 7

Multiple-Choice Math

SUMMING IT UP

- Follow the five-step plan for answering basic multiple-choice math questions:

  1. Read the question carefully and determine what's being asked.

  2. Decide which math principles apply and use them to solve the problem.

  3. Look for your answer among the choices. If it's there, mark it and go on.

  4. If the answer you found is not there, recheck the question and your calculations.

  5. If you still can't solve the problem, eliminate obviously wrong answers and take your best guess.

- In the Math Test—Calculator section, use a calculator where it can help the most: on basic arithmetic calculations, when calculating square roots and percentages, and comparing and converting fractions.

- Always set up your work on paper, then enter the numbers in your calculator; that way, if your calculation becomes confused, you don't have to try to replicate your setup from memory.

- The question number tells you how hard the question will be, though some questions may be easier for you.

- Work backward from the answer choices. When you do, start with choice B or choice C.

- Try to work with numbers instead of letters. This will help you avoid unnecessary algebraic calculations.

- Figures in the math section are always drawn to scale unless you see a warning. If you need to do so, use your eye as an estimator.

WANT TO KNOW MORE?

Access more practice questions, valuable lessons, helpful tips, and expert strategies for the following multiple-choice math topics in *Peterson's Online Course for the SAT® Exam:*

- Calculator Strategy

- Guessing in Math

- Pacing in Math

- Plugging in Numbers

- Problem Solving

- Working Backwards

To purchase and access the course, go to **www.petersons.com/testprep/sat**.

Chapter 7

Multiple-Choice Math

CHAPTER 8:
GRID-IN STRATEGIES

OVERVIEW

- Why Grid-Ins Are Easier Than You Think
- How to Record Your Answers
- Guessing on Grid-Ins Can't Hurt You
- Exercises: Grid-Ins
- Summing It Up

WHY GRID-INS ARE EASIER THAN YOU THINK

Let's take a quick break from multiple-choice questions and examine the other kind of question you will see on both the Math Test—No Calculator and Math Test—Calculator sections: grid-ins. These are officially named "student-produced responses," because you have to do the calculations and find the answer on your own; there are no multiple-choice answers from which to choose.

Many students are intimidated by grid-ins. Don't be! Grid-in questions test the exact same mathematical concepts as the multiple-choice questions. The only difference is that there are no answer choices with which to work.

The grid-in questions are in a section of their own and arranged in order of difficulty from easy to hard.

TAKE A LOOK AT A GRID

The special answer grid has some very different sections. There are blank boxes at the top so you can actually write in your answer. Below the boxes are some circles that have fraction slashes and decimal points. You fill these in if your answer needs them. The largest section has circles with numbers in them. You have to fill in the circles to correspond to the answer you have written in the boxes. Yes, it's a lot to think about, but once you understand how to use the grid-ins, it's not a big deal.

Here is a sample grid:

NOTE: Remember that the student-produced responses will not be negative numbers and won't be greater than 9999.

HOW TO RECORD YOUR ANSWERS

On the SAT® exam, each set of grid-in questions starts with directions that look approximately like this:

DIRECTIONS: For these questions, solve the problem and enter your answer in the grid, as described below, on the answer sheet.

1. Although not required, it is suggested that you write your answer in the boxes at the top of the columns to help you fill in the circles accurately. You will receive credit only if the circles are filled in correctly.

2. Mark no more than one circle in any column.

3. No question has a negative answer.

4. Some problems may have more than one correct answer. In such cases, enter only one answer.

5. Mixed numbers such as $3\frac{1}{2}$ must be entered as 3.5 or $\frac{7}{2}$.

   If $3\frac{1}{2}$ is entered into the grid as , it will be interpreted as $\frac{31}{2}$, not $3\frac{1}{2}$.

304

Chapter 8

Grid-In
Strategies

6. **Decimal answers:** If you obtain a decimal answer with more digits than the grid can accommodate, it may be either rounded or truncated, but it must fill the entire grid.

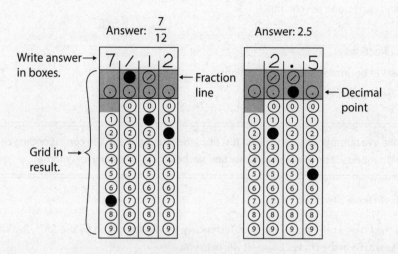

Answer: $\frac{7}{12}$ Answer: 2.5

Write answer → in boxes.

← Fraction line

← Decimal point

Grid in → result.

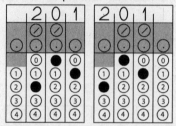

Answer: 201
Either position is correct.

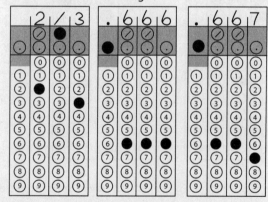

Acceptable ways to grid $\frac{2}{3}$ are:

Once you understand the following six rules, you can concentrate just on solving the math problems in this section.

1. Write your answer in the boxes at the top of the grid.

2. Mark the corresponding circles, one per column.

3. Start in any column.

4. Work with decimals or fractions.

5. Express mixed numbers as decimals or improper fractions.

6. If more than one answer is possible, enter any one.

NOTE: Don't use a comma in a number larger than 999. Just fill in the four digits and the corresponding circles. You only have circles for numbers, decimal points, and fraction slashes; there aren't any for commas.

Now let's look at these rules in more detail:

1. Write your answer in the boxes at the top of the grid. Technically, this isn't required by the SAT®. Realistically, it gives you something to follow as you fill in the circles. Do it—it will help you.

2. Make sure to mark the circles that correspond to the answer you entered in the boxes, one per column. The machine that scores the test can only read the circles, so if you don't fill them in, you won't get credit. Just entering your answer in the boxes is not enough!

3. You can start entering your answer in any column, if space permits. Unused columns should be left blank; don't put in zeroes. Look at this example:

Here are two ways to enter an answer of "150."

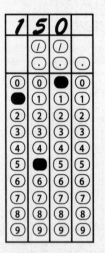 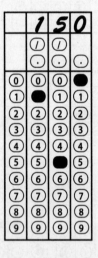

4. You can write your answer as a decimal or a fraction. For example, an answer can be expressed as $\frac{3}{4}$ or as .75. You don't have to put a zero in front of a decimal that is less than 1. Just remember that you have only four spaces to work with and that a decimal point or a fraction slash uses up one of the spaces.

 ALERT: Take the time to write your answer in the spaces. It will lessen your chances of filling in an incorrect circle.

For decimal answers, be as accurate as possible but keep it within four spaces. Say you get an answer of .1777, here are your options:

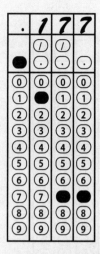 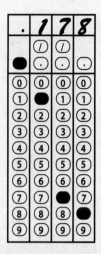

Answers .177 and .178 would both be marked correct.

Fractions do not have to be simplified unless they don't fit in the answer grid. For example, you can enter into the grid $\frac{4}{10}$, but you can't enter $\frac{12}{16}$ because you'd need five spaces. You would simplify it and enter $\frac{3}{4}$.

5. A mixed number has to be expressed as a decimal or as an improper fraction. If you tried to enter $1\frac{3}{4}$ into the grid, it would be scored as $\frac{13}{4}$, which would give you a wrong answer. Instead, you could enter the answer as 1.75 or as $\frac{7}{4}$.

The above answers are acceptable.

The above answer is unacceptable as representing the fraction $1\frac{3}{4}$.

ALERT: If the correct answer is a mixed number such as $5\frac{1}{4}$, you must enter it as 21/4 or as 5.25 in the answer grid. If you enter it as "51/4," it will read as "fifty-one fourths," and it will be marked incorrect.

6. Sometimes, the problems in this section will have more than one correct answer. Choose one and enter it.

For example, if a question asks for a prime number between 5 and 13, the answer could be 7 or 11. Enter 7 or enter 11, but don't put in both answers.

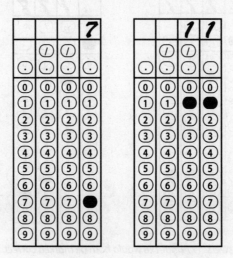

Either answer is acceptable but not both.

GUESSING ON GRID-INS CAN'T HURT YOU

Unfortunately, you cannot receive partial credit for grid-ins. Your answers are either completely correct or completely wrong. But no points are deducted for incorrect responses, so guessing is better than leaving a question blank.

EXERCISES: GRID-INS

EXERCISE 1

15 MINUTES—10 QUESTIONS

> **DIRECTIONS:** For these questions, solve the problem and enter your answer in the grid following each question, as described below.

1. Although not required, it is suggested that you write your answer in the boxes at the top of the columns to help you fill in the circles accurately. You will receive credit only if the circles are filled in correctly.

2. Mark no more than one circle in any column.

3. No question has a negative answer.

4. Some problems may have more than one correct answer. In such cases, enter only one answer.

5. Mixed numbers such as $3\frac{1}{2}$ must be entered as 3.5 or $\frac{7}{2}$.

   If $3\frac{1}{2}$ is entered into the grid as $\overline{3\mid\mid /\mid 2}$, it will be interpreted as $\frac{31}{2}$, not $3\frac{1}{2}$.

6. **Decimal answers:** If you obtain a decimal answer with more digits than the grid can accommodate, it may be either rounded or truncated, but it must fill the entire grid.

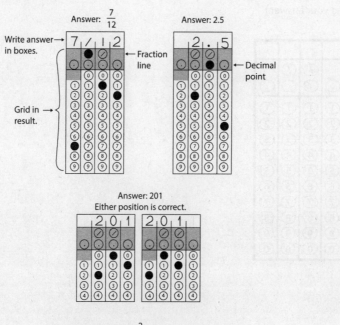

1. What is the slope of the line parallel to the line passing through the points (0, −4) and (−2, −8)?

SHOW YOUR WORK HERE

SHOW YOUR WORK HERE

2. Marion is paid $24 for 5 hours of work in the school office. Janet works 3 hours and makes $10.95. How much more per hour does Marion make than Janet? (Ignore the dollar sign when gridding your answer.)

310

Chapter 8

Grid-In
Strategies

www.petersons.com

3. The surface area of a cubical cage is 1,176 square feet. What is the length of a diagonal of one of its faces, accurate to the tenths place?

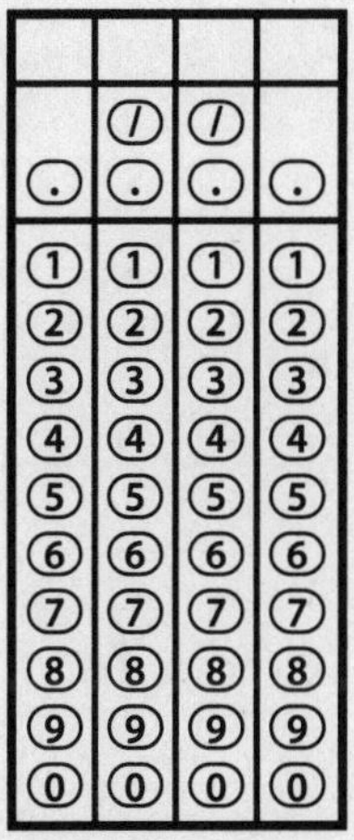

4. A car has an average mileage of 30 miles per gallon. If one gallon of gasoline costs $3.75, how many miles can the car travel on $20 worth of gasoline?

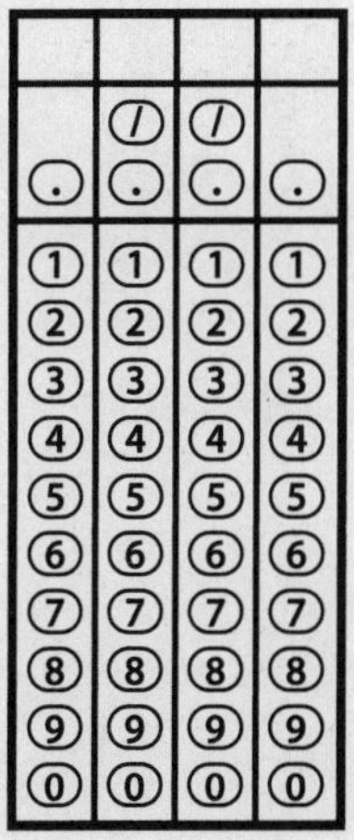

311

Chapter 8

Grid-In Strategies

5. If $a = \dfrac{3}{4}$, what is the value of $2a^2 - 1$?

6. Arc *AB* is on circle *O*. If the radius of circle *O* is 5 centimeters, and angle *AOB* measures 30°, what is the length of arc *AB* rounded to the nearest tenth of a centimeter?

7. If z is a solution of the equation $\sqrt{z} - 1 = 4$, what is the value of $2z^{-1}$?

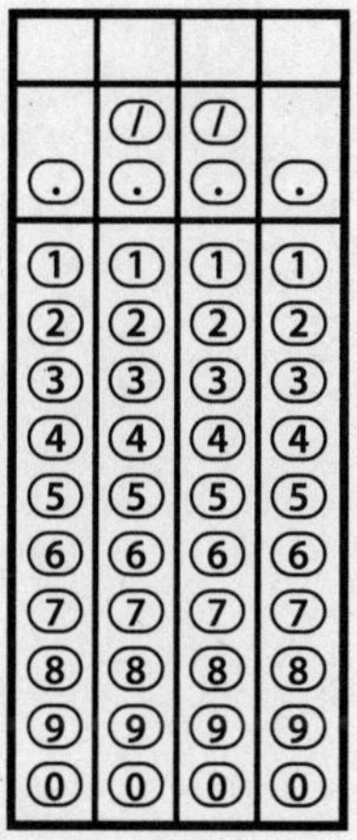

8. A cube with edges 3 centimeters long is made from solid aluminum. If the density of aluminum is approximately 2.7 grams per cubic centimeter, what is the weight of the cube to the nearest tenth of a gram?

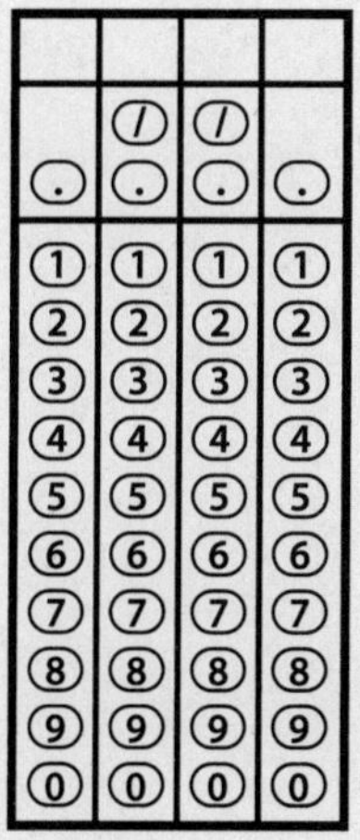

313

Chapter 8

Grid-In
Strategies

9. In May, Carter's Electronics sold 40 smartphones. In June, because of a special promotion, the store sold 80 smartphones. What is the percent of increase in the number of smartphones sold?

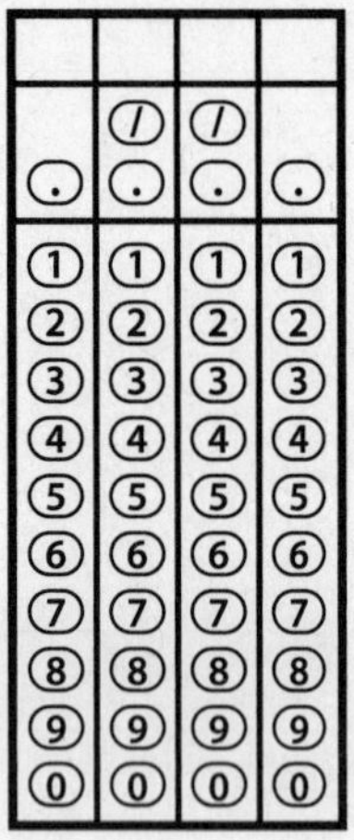

10. $\sqrt{21}\left(\dfrac{\sqrt{7}}{\sqrt{3}} - \dfrac{\sqrt{3}}{\sqrt{7}}\right)$

To what integer is the above expression equal?

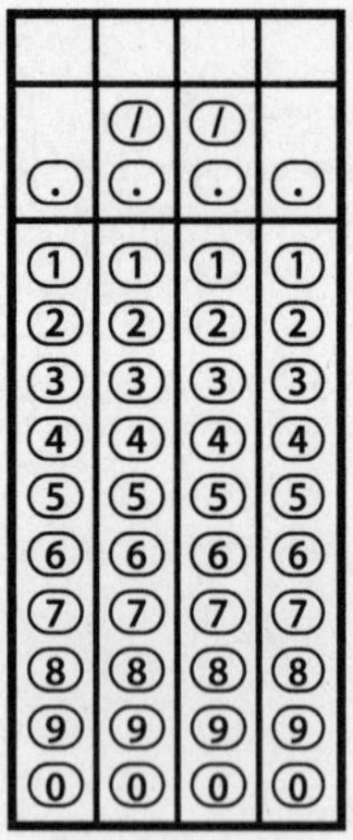

314

Chapter 8

Grid-In Strategies

15 MINUTES—10 QUESTIONS

DIRECTIONS: For these questions, solve the problem and enter your answer in the grid following each question, as described below.

1. Although not required, it is suggested that you write your answer in the boxes at the top of the columns to help you fill in the circles accurately. You will receive credit only if the circles are filled in correctly.

2. Mark no more than one circle in any column.

3. No question has a negative answer.

4. Some problems may have more than one correct answer. In such cases, grid only one answer.

5. Mixed numbers such as $3\frac{1}{2}$ must be entered as 3.5 or $\frac{7}{2}$.

   If $3\frac{1}{2}$ is entered into the grid as ⬚, it will be interpreted as $\frac{31}{2}$, not $3\frac{1}{2}$.

6. **Decimal answers:** If you obtain a decimal answer with more digits than the grid can accommodate, it may be either rounded or truncated, but it must fill the entire grid.

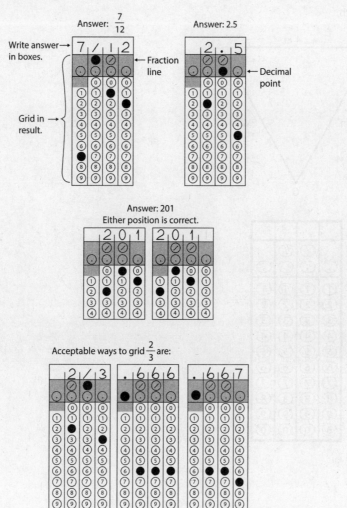

1. A craft shop sells handmade quilts and pillows in a ratio of 2 to 6 for one week. If 8 quilts are sold at the end of this week, how many pillows and quilts were sold all together?

2. What is the height of the triangle shown? Round to the nearest hundredth.

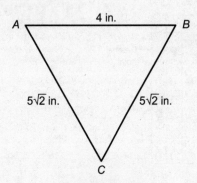

3. In a group of 40 students, 25 applied to Columbia and 30 applied to Cornell. If 3 students applied to neither Columbia nor Cornell, how many students applied to both schools?

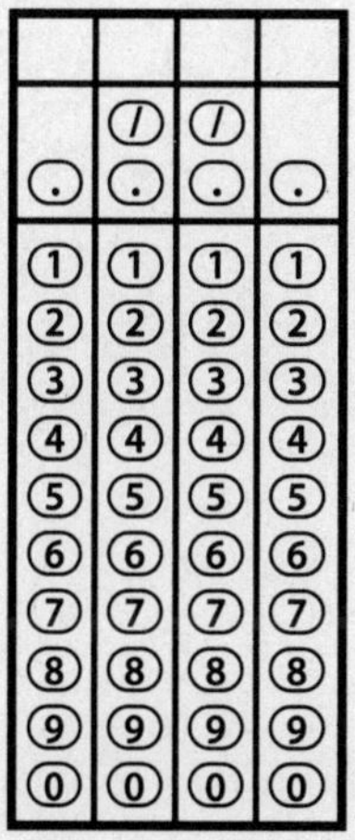

4. If $\dfrac{1}{6x^2 - 7x + 2} = \dfrac{2}{3}$ and $2 - 3x = \dfrac{1}{2}$,

what is the value of $2 - 2x$?

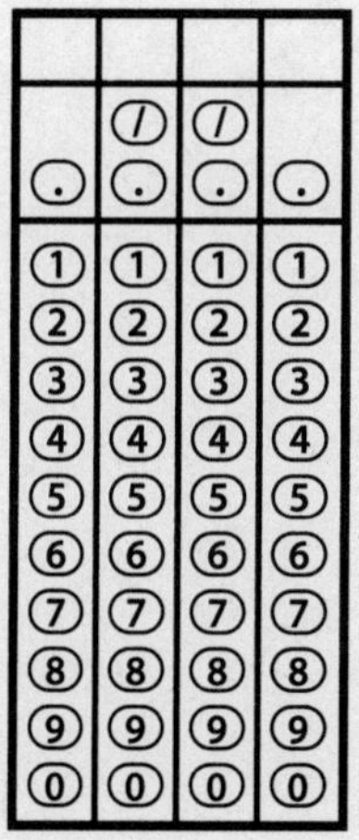

317

Chapter 8

Grid-In
Strategies

5. A gallon of water is added to 6 quarts of a solution that is 50% acid. What percent of the new solution is acid?

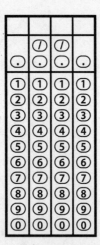

6. A gasoline tank is $\frac{1}{4}$ full. After 10 gallons of gasoline are added to the tank, its gauge indicates that the tank is $\frac{2}{3}$ full. Find the capacity of the tank in gallons.

7. A plane flies over Denver at 11:20 a.m. It passes over Coolidge, 120 miles from Denver, at 11:32 a.m. Find the rate of the plane in miles per hour.

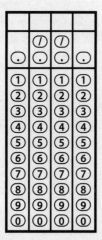

8. Solve for w: $\dfrac{4}{4-3w} = \dfrac{2}{w}$.

9. Find the mean of this set of numbers:
0, 0, 5, 6, 6, 10, 14, 23.

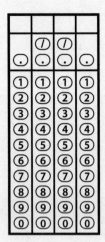

10. If (x, y) is a solution to the system of equations below, what is a possible value of $x + y$?

$$y = x^2 - 8x + 7$$
$$y = x - 1$$

320

Chapter 8

Grid-In
Strategies

EXERCISE 1: ANSWER KEY AND EXPLANATIONS

1. 2	**3.** 19.8	**5.** $\frac{1}{8}$	**7.** $\frac{2}{25}$	**9.** 100
2. 1.15	**4.** 160	**6.** 2.6	**8.** 72.9	**10.** 4

1. **The correct answer is 2.** The slope of the given line is $\frac{-8-(-4)}{-2-0}=2$. Since parallel lines have the same slope, the slope is 2.

2. **The correct answer is 1.15.**

   Marion's hourly wage is $\frac{\$24}{5}$, or $4.80.

   Janet's hourly wage is $\frac{\$10.95}{3}$, or $3.65.

   $4.80 − $3.65 = $1.15

   (You do not need to enter the dollar sign in the grid.)

3. **The correct answer is 19.8.** Let e be an edge of a face of this cube. The surface area is $6e^2$. Solve the following equation for e:

   $$6e^2 = 1{,}176$$
   $$e^2 = 196$$
   $$e = 14$$

   Let d be a diagonal of an edge. Use the Pythagorean theorem to find d:

   $$14^2 + 14^2 = d^2$$
   $$2 \cdot 14^2 = d^2$$
   $$14\sqrt{2} = d$$
   $$d \approx 19.8$$

4. **The correct answer is 160.**

   $$30\left(\frac{20}{3.75}\right) = 160$$

5. **The correct answer is $\frac{1}{8}$.**

   $$2\left(\frac{3}{4}\right)^2 - 1 = 2\left(\frac{9}{16}\right) - 1 = \frac{9}{8} - 1 = \frac{1}{8}$$

6. **The correct answer is 2.6.** The circumference of the circle is $2\pi(5) = 10\pi$.

   $$\frac{30}{360}(10\pi) \approx 2.6$$

7. **The correct answer is $\frac{2}{25}$.**
   First, solve for z:

   $$\sqrt{z} = 5$$
   $$z = 25$$

   Then solve the equation.

   $$2z^{-1} = \frac{2}{z} = \frac{2}{25}$$

8. **The correct answer is 72.9.** The formula for volume of a cube is s^3.

   Therefore, $3^3 = 27$.

   $27(2.7) = 72.9$

9. **The correct answer is 100.** When computing the percent of increase (or decrease), use $\frac{\text{difference}}{\text{original}} \times 100$. In this case, the difference is 80 − 40, which is 40. The original amount sold was 40, so $\frac{40}{40} \times 100 = 100\%$ increase.

10. **The correct answer is 4.**

    $$\sqrt{21}\left(\frac{\sqrt{7}}{\sqrt{3}} - \frac{\sqrt{3}}{\sqrt{7}}\right) = \sqrt{21}\left(\frac{\sqrt{7} \cdot \sqrt{7} - \sqrt{3} \cdot \sqrt{3}}{\sqrt{3} \cdot \sqrt{7}}\right)$$
    $$= \sqrt{21}\left(\frac{7-3}{\sqrt{21}}\right)$$
    $$= 4$$

321

Chapter 8

Grid-In Strategies

| **1.** 32 | **3.** 18 | **5.** 30 | **7.** 600 | **9.** 8 |
| **2.** 6.78 | **4.** 3 | **6.** 24 | **8.** $\frac{4}{5}$ | **10.** 15 or 1 |

1. **The correct answer is 32.** Let x be the number of pillows sold. Set up and solve the following proportion:

$$\frac{2}{6} = \frac{8}{x}$$
$$2x = 48$$
$$x = 24$$

The number of quilts and pillows sold is $24 + 8 = 32$.

2. **The correct answer is 6.78.** Draw a perpendicular bisector from C to the opposite base, as shown:

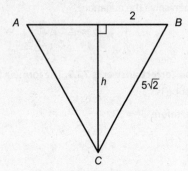

Using the Pythagorean theorem yields:

$$2^2 + h^2 = \left(5\sqrt{2}\right)^2$$
$$4 + h^2 = 50$$
$$h^2 = 46$$
$$h = \sqrt{46} \approx 6.78$$

3. **The correct answer is 18.**

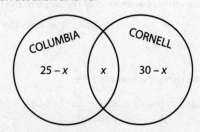

$$25 - x + x + 30 - x = 37$$
$$55 - x = 37$$
$$18 = x$$

4. **The correct answer is 3.** Solve as follows:

$$\frac{1}{6x^2 - 7x + 2} = \frac{2}{3}$$
$$\frac{1}{(2x-1)(3x-2)} = \frac{2}{3}$$
$$\frac{1}{(2x-1)\left(-\frac{1}{2}\right)} = \frac{2}{3}$$
$$\frac{-2}{(2x-1)} = \frac{2}{3}$$
$$-6 = 2(2x-1)$$
$$-3 = 2x - 2$$
$$3 = 2 - 2x$$

5. **The correct answer is 30.**

	No. of quarts	% acid	Amount of acid
Original	6	50	3
Added	4	0	0
New	10		3

$$\frac{3}{10} = 30\%$$

Note: Ignore the percent symbol when entering your answer in the grid.

6. **The correct answer is 24.**

10 gallons is $\frac{2}{3} - \frac{1}{4}$ of the tank.

$$\frac{2}{3} - \frac{1}{4} = \frac{8-3}{12} = \frac{5}{12}$$
$$\frac{5}{12}x = 10$$
$$5x = 120$$
$$x = 24$$

7. **The correct answer is 600.** The plane covers 120 miles in 12 minutes, or $\frac{1}{5}$ hour.

In $\frac{5}{5}$, or 1 hour, it covers 5(120), or 600 miles.

8. **The correct answer is $\frac{4}{5}$.** Cross-multiply and solve for w:

$$\frac{4}{4-3w} = \frac{2}{w}$$
$$4w = 2(4-3w)$$
$$4w = 8 - 6w$$
$$10w = 8$$
$$w = \frac{8}{10} = \frac{4}{5}$$

9. **The correct answer is 8.** Add the numbers and divide this sum by the number of values, namely 8:

$$\frac{0+0+5+6+6+10+14+23}{8} = \frac{64}{8} = 8$$

10. **The correct answer is 15 or 1 (both answers are acceptable.**

$$y = x^2 - 8x + 7$$
$$y = x - 1$$
$$x^2 - 8x + 7 = x - 1$$
$$x^2 - 9x + 8 = 0$$
$$(x-8)(x-1) = 0$$
$$x = 8 \text{ or } x = 1$$

If $x = 8$, then $y = 8 - 1 = 7$
If $x = 1$, then $y = 1 - 1 = 0$
$x + y = 15$ or $x + y = 1$

323

SUMMING IT UP

- When you use a grid to answer the student-produced response questions, follow these six rules:

    1. Write your answer in the boxes at the top of the grid.

    2. Mark the corresponding circles, one per column.

    3. Start in any column.

    4. Work with decimals or fractions.

    5. Express mixed numbers as decimals or improper fractions.

    6. If more than one answer is possible, enter any one.

- Remember that grid-ins test the same concepts as multiple-choice math.

- The most important advice for grid-ins? Don't be intimidated.

WANT TO KNOW MORE?

Access additional practice questions, helpful lessons, valuable tips, and top-notch strategies for the following grid-in review topics in *Peterson's Online Course for the SAT® Exam*:

- Grid-Ins

- Problem Solving

- Word Problems

To purchase and access the course, go to **www.petersons.com/testprep/sat**.

CHAPTER 9:
NUMBERS AND OPERATIONS

OVERVIEW

- Operations with Fractions
- Test for Divisibility
- Exercise: Operations with Fractions
- Word Problems Involving Fractions
- Exercise: Word Problems Involving Fractions
- Complex Numbers
- Exercise: Complex Numbers
- Direct and Inverse Variation
- Exercise: Direct and Inverse Variation
- Finding Percentages
- Exercise: Finding Percentages
- Percentage Word Problems
- Exercise: Percentage Word Problems
- Summing It Up

325

Chapter 9

Numbers and Operations

OPERATIONS WITH FRACTIONS

The four basic **arithmetic** operations are addition, subtraction, multiplication, and division.

ADDING AND SUBTRACTING

When adding or subtracting fractions, you must remember that the numbers must have the same (common) denominator.

Example:

Add $\frac{1}{3} + \frac{2}{5} + \frac{3}{4}$.

Solution:

The lowest number that is divisible by 3, 5, and 4 is 60. Therefore, use 60 as the common denominator. Convert each fraction to fractions with the common denominator, 60, by multiplying each numerator by the same factor as you must multiply the denominator by to result in the common denominator of 60.

$$\frac{20}{60} + \frac{24}{60} + \frac{45}{60} = \frac{89}{60}$$
$$= 1\frac{29}{60}$$

Fractions should be written in the simplest form. Often, in multiple-choice questions, you may find that the answer you have correctly computed is not among the choices but an equivalent fraction is. Be careful!

In simplifying fractions involving large numbers, it is helpful to be able to tell whether a factor is common to both numerator and denominator before a lengthy trial division. Certain tests for divisibility help with this.

TEST FOR DIVISIBILITY

To test if a number is divisible by:	Check to see:
2	if it is even
3	if the sum of the digits is divisible by 3
4	if the number formed by the last two digits is divisible by 4
5	if its last digit is a 5 or 0
6	if it is even and the sum of the digits is divisible by 3
8	if the number formed by the last three digits is divisible by 8
9	if the sum of the digits is divisible by 9
10	if its last digit is 0

Example:

Simplify: $\dfrac{3{,}525}{4{,}341}$

Solution:

This fraction can be simplified by dividing by 3, since the sum of the digits of the numerator is 15 and those of the denominator add up to 12, both are divisible by 3.

$$\frac{3{,}525}{4{,}341} = \frac{1{,}175}{1{,}447}$$

The resulting fraction meets no further divisibility tests and therefore has no common factor listed above. Larger divisors would be unlikely on the SAT® exam.

To add or subtract mixed numbers, it is again important to remember common denominators. In subtraction, you must borrow in terms of the common denominator.

Addition:
$$43\frac{2}{5} = 43\frac{6}{15}$$
$$+\;8\frac{1}{3} = +\;8\frac{5}{15}$$
$$\rule{3cm}{0.4pt}$$
$$51\frac{11}{15}$$

Subtraction:
$$43\frac{2}{5} = 43\frac{6}{15} = 42\frac{21}{15}$$
$$-6\frac{2}{3} = -6\frac{10}{15} = -6\frac{10}{15}$$
$$\rule{3cm}{0.4pt}$$
$$36\frac{11}{15}$$

MULTIPLYING

To multiply fractions, always try to divide common factors where possible before actually multiplying. In multiplying mixed numbers, always rename them as improper fractions first.

Multiply: $\dfrac{\cancel{2}}{\cancel{5}} \cdot \dfrac{\overset{2}{\cancel{10}}}{\cancel{11}} \cdot \dfrac{\overset{9}{\cancel{99}}}{\underset{55}{\cancel{110}}} = \dfrac{18}{55}$

Multiply: $4\dfrac{1}{2} \cdot 1\dfrac{2}{3} \cdot 5\dfrac{1}{5}$

$$\dfrac{\overset{3}{\cancel{9}}}{\cancel{2}} \cdot \dfrac{\cancel{5}}{\cancel{3}} \cdot \dfrac{\overset{13}{\cancel{26}}}{\cancel{5}} = 39$$

DIVIDING

To divide fractions or mixed numbers, remember to multiply by the reciprocal of the divisor (the number after the division sign).

$$\text{Divide: } 4\frac{1}{2} \div \frac{3}{4} = \frac{\overset{3}{\cancel{9}}}{\cancel{2}} \cdot \frac{\overset{2}{\cancel{4}}}{\cancel{3}} = 6$$

$$\text{Divide: } 62\frac{1}{2} \div 5 = \frac{\overset{25}{\cancel{125}}}{2} \cdot \frac{1}{\cancel{5}} = 12\frac{1}{2}$$

To simplify complex fractions (fractions within fractions), multiply every term by the least common multiple of all denominators in order to clear all fractions in the given numerator and denominator.

Example:

$$\frac{\dfrac{1}{2}+\dfrac{1}{3}}{\dfrac{1}{4}+\dfrac{1}{6}}$$

Solution:

The least number that can be used to clear all fractions is 12. Multiplying each term by 12 yields:

$$\frac{\dfrac{1}{2}+\dfrac{1}{3}}{\dfrac{1}{4}+\dfrac{1}{6}} = \frac{\dfrac{12}{2}+\dfrac{12}{3}}{\dfrac{12}{4}+\dfrac{12}{6}} = \frac{6+4}{3+2} = \frac{10}{5} = 2$$

Example:

$$\frac{\dfrac{3}{4}+\dfrac{2}{3}}{1-\dfrac{1}{2}}$$

Solution:

Again, multiply by 12.

$$\frac{\dfrac{3}{4}+\dfrac{2}{3}}{1-\dfrac{1}{2}} = \frac{\dfrac{36}{4}+\dfrac{24}{3}}{12-\dfrac{12}{2}} = \frac{9+8}{12-6} = \frac{17}{6} = 2\frac{5}{6}$$

EXERCISE: OPERATIONS WITH FRACTIONS

DIRECTIONS: Work out each problem in the space provided.

---

1. **Add:** $7\frac{1}{6} + 3\frac{11}{12}$

2. **Add:** $\frac{1}{2} + \frac{1}{4} + \frac{1}{8} + \frac{1}{16}$

3. **Subtract:** $5\frac{3}{4}$ from $10\frac{1}{2}$.

4. **Subtract:** $1\frac{7}{11}$ from $2\frac{1}{22}$.

329

Chapter 9

Numbers and Operations

5. **Multiply:** $\frac{15}{8} \cdot \frac{12}{25} \cdot \frac{2}{9}$

6. **Multiply:** $\frac{3}{4} \cdot \frac{3}{4} \cdot \frac{3}{4}$

7. **Divide:** $\frac{1}{5} \div 5$

---

8. **Divide:** $3\dfrac{2}{3} \div 1\dfrac{5}{6}$

9. **Simplify:** $\dfrac{\dfrac{5}{6} - \dfrac{1}{3}}{2 + \dfrac{1}{5}}$

10. **Simplify:** $4\left(\dfrac{1}{6} + \dfrac{1}{12}\right)$

11. **Simplify:** $\left(\dfrac{1}{2} - \dfrac{1}{3}\right)\left(\dfrac{1}{2} + \dfrac{1}{3}\right)$

12. **Simplify:** $\dfrac{4}{15} \div \left(\dfrac{1}{5} + \dfrac{1}{3}\right)$

330

Chapter 9

Numbers and Operations

1. $11\frac{1}{12}$	3. $4\frac{3}{4}$	5. $\frac{1}{5}$	7. $\frac{1}{25}$	9. $\frac{5}{22}$	11. $\frac{5}{36}$
2. $\frac{15}{16}$	4. $\frac{9}{22}$	6. $\frac{27}{64}$	8. 2	10. 1	12. $\frac{1}{2}$

1. **The correct answer is $11\frac{1}{12}$.**

$$7\frac{1}{6} + 3\frac{11}{12} = 7\frac{2}{12} + 3\frac{11}{12}$$
$$= 10\frac{13}{12}$$
$$= 11\frac{1}{12}$$

2. **The correct answer is $\frac{15}{16}$.**

$$\frac{1}{2} + \frac{1}{4} + \frac{1}{8} + \frac{1}{16} = \frac{8}{16} + \frac{4}{16} + \frac{2}{16} + \frac{1}{16}$$
$$= \frac{8+4+2+1}{16}$$
$$= \frac{15}{16}$$

3. **The correct answer is $4\frac{3}{4}$.**

$$10\frac{1}{2} = 9\frac{3}{2} = 9\frac{6}{4}$$

$$\begin{array}{r} 9\frac{6}{4} \\ -5\frac{3}{4} \\ \hline 4\frac{3}{4} \end{array}$$

4. **The correct answer is $\frac{9}{22}$.**

$$2\frac{1}{22} - 1\frac{7}{11} = 2\frac{1}{22} - 1\frac{14}{22}$$
$$= 1\frac{23}{22} - 1\frac{14}{22}$$
$$= \frac{9}{22}$$

5. **The correct answer is $\frac{1}{5}$.**

$$\frac{15}{8} \cdot \frac{12}{25} \cdot \frac{2}{9} = \frac{5 \cdot 3}{4 \cdot 2} \cdot \frac{4 \cdot 3}{5 \cdot 5} \cdot \frac{2}{3 \cdot 3} = \frac{1}{5}$$

6. **The correct answer is $\frac{27}{64}$.**

$$\frac{3}{4} \cdot \frac{3}{4} \cdot \frac{3}{4} = \frac{27}{64}$$

7. **The correct answer is $\frac{1}{25}$.**

$$\frac{1}{5} \cdot \frac{1}{5} = \frac{1}{25}$$

8. **The correct answer is 2.**

$$\frac{11}{3} \cdot \frac{6}{11} = 2$$

9. **The correct answer is $\frac{5}{22}$.**

$$\frac{25-10}{60+6} = \frac{15}{66} = \frac{5}{22}$$

Each term was multiplied by 30.

10. **The correct answer is 1.**

$$4\left(\frac{1}{6} + \frac{1}{12}\right) = 4\left(\frac{2}{12} + \frac{1}{12}\right)$$
$$= 4\left(\frac{3}{12}\right)$$
$$= \left(\frac{12}{12}\right)$$
$$= 1$$

331

Chapter 9

Numbers and Operations

11. The correct answer is $\dfrac{5}{36}$.

$$\left(\frac{1}{2}-\frac{1}{3}\right)\left(\frac{1}{2}+\frac{1}{3}\right)=\left(\frac{3}{6}-\frac{2}{6}\right)\left(\frac{3}{6}+\frac{2}{6}\right)$$
$$=\frac{1}{6}\cdot\frac{5}{6}$$
$$=\frac{5}{36}$$

12. The correct answer is $\dfrac{1}{2}$.

$$\frac{4}{15}\div\left(\frac{1}{5}+\frac{1}{3}\right)=\frac{4}{15}\div\left(\frac{3}{15}+\frac{5}{15}\right)$$
$$=\frac{4}{15}\div\frac{8}{15}$$
$$=\frac{4}{\cancel{15}}\cdot\frac{\cancel{15}}{8}$$
$$=\frac{4}{8}$$
$$=\frac{1}{2}$$

332

Chapter 9

Numbers and Operations

WORD PROBLEMS INVOLVING FRACTIONS

Fraction problems deal with parts of a whole.

Example:

If a class consists of 12 boys and 18 girls, what part of the class is boys?

Solution:

The class consists of 12 boys out of 30 total students, or $\dfrac{12}{30} = \dfrac{2}{5}$. So boys represent $\dfrac{2}{5}$ of the class.

Notice that, to find the solution, you must add the boys and girls to find the total number of students. Problems may require more than one calculation as you can see in this example.

Example:

One-quarter of this year's seniors have averages above 90. One-half of the remainder have averages between 80 and 90 inclusive. What part of the senior class have averages below 80?

Solution:

We know that $\dfrac{1}{4}$ have averages above 90.

$\dfrac{1}{2}$ of $\dfrac{3}{4}$, or $\dfrac{3}{8}$, have averages between 80 and 90 inclusive.

$\dfrac{1}{4} + \dfrac{3}{8} = \dfrac{2}{8} + \dfrac{3}{8} = \dfrac{5}{8}$ have averages 80 and above.

Therefore, $\dfrac{3}{8}$ of the class have averages below 80.

Example:

14 is $\dfrac{2}{3}$ of what number?

Solution:

$$14 = \dfrac{2}{3}x$$

Divide each side of the equation by $\dfrac{2}{3}$, which is the same as multiplying the reciprocal, or $\dfrac{3}{2}$.

$$21 = x$$

Example:

If John has *p* hours of homework and has worked for *r* hours, what part of his homework is yet to be done?

Solution:

If John had 5 hours of homework and had worked for 3 hours, you would first find he had 5 − 3 hours, or 2 hours, yet to do. This represents $\frac{2}{5}$ of his work. Using letters, his remaining work is represented by $\frac{p-r}{p}$.

 TIP If a problem is given with letters in place of numbers, the same reasoning must be applied as for numbers. If you are not sure how to proceed, replace the letters with numbers to determine the steps that must be taken.

EXERCISE: WORD PROBLEMS INVOLVING FRACTIONS

> **DIRECTIONS:** Work out each problem. Circle the letter of your choice.

1. A team played 30 games, of which it won 24. What part of the games played did the team lose?

   A. $\dfrac{4}{5}$

   B. $\dfrac{1}{4}$

   C. $\dfrac{1}{5}$

   D. $\dfrac{3}{4}$

2. If Germaine earns $X a week, and he saves $Y, what part of his weekly salary does he spend?

   A. $\dfrac{X}{Y}$

   B. $\dfrac{X-Y}{X}$

   C. $\dfrac{X-Y}{Y}$

   D. $\dfrac{Y-X}{X}$

3. What part of an hour elapses between 11:50 a.m. and 12:14 p.m.?

   A. $\dfrac{2}{5}$

   B. $\dfrac{7}{30}$

   C. $\dfrac{17}{30}$

   D. $\dfrac{1}{6}$

SHOW YOUR WORK HERE

Chapter 9

Numbers and
Operations

4. One half of the employees of Acme Co. earn salaries above $18,000 annually. One third of the remainder earn salaries between $15,000 and $18,000. What part of the staff earns below $15,000?

   A. $\dfrac{1}{6}$

   B. $\dfrac{2}{3}$

   C. $\dfrac{1}{2}$

   D. $\dfrac{1}{3}$

5. David received his allowance on Sunday. He spends $\dfrac{1}{4}$ of his allowance on Monday and $\dfrac{2}{3}$ of the remainder on Tuesday. What part of his allowance is left for the rest of the week?

   A. $\dfrac{1}{13}$

   B. $\dfrac{1}{9}$

   C. $\dfrac{1}{4}$

   D. $\dfrac{1}{3}$

6. A piece of fabric is cut into three sections so that the first is three times as long as the second, and the second section is three times as long as the third. What part of the entire piece is the smallest section?

   A. $\dfrac{1}{13}$

   B. $\dfrac{1}{9}$

   C. $\dfrac{1}{4}$

   D. $\dfrac{1}{3}$

336

Chapter 9

Numbers and Operations

7. A factory employs *M* men and *W* women. What part of its employees are women?

   A. $\dfrac{M}{W}$

   B. $\dfrac{M+W}{W}$

   C. $\dfrac{W}{M-W}$

   D. $\dfrac{W}{M+W}$

8. A motion was passed by a vote of 5:3. What part of the votes cast were in favor of the motion?

   A. $\dfrac{5}{8}$

   B. $\dfrac{5}{3}$

   C. $\dfrac{3}{5}$

   D. $\dfrac{3}{8}$

9. In a certain class, the ratio of men to women is 3:5. If the class has 24 people in it, how many are women?

   A. 9

   B. 12

   C. 15

   D. 18

10. If a baby otter can swim at an average rate of $1\frac{3}{8}$ miles per hour, how long would it take it to swim $4\frac{1}{2}$ miles downstream with a current moving at a rate of $\frac{3}{4}$ miles per hour?

   A. $7\frac{1}{2}$ hours

   B. 6 hours

   C. $3\frac{3}{11}$ hours

   D. $2\frac{2}{17}$ hours

11. Ben's Tae Kwon Do class lasts for $1\frac{3}{4}$ hours. So far, he has been in class for $\frac{5}{6}$ of an hour. How many minutes remain until the class is finished?

   A. 50

   B. 55

   C. 65

   D. 70

12. Zain's gas tank is $\frac{1}{8}$ full. After she adds 8 gallons of gas to the tank, it is then $\frac{5}{6}$ full. Approximately how many gallons of gas can her tank hold?

   A. 9

   B. 11

   C. 13

   D. 17

338

Chapter 9

Numbers and Operations

1. C	3. A	5. C	7. D	9. C	11. B
2. B	4. D	6. A	8. A	10. D	12. B

1. **The correct answer is C.** The team lost 6 games out of 30. $\dfrac{6}{30} = \dfrac{1}{5}$

2. **The correct answer is B.** Germaine spends $X - Y$ out of X. $\dfrac{X - Y}{X}$

3. **The correct answer is A.** 10 minutes elapse by noon, and another 14 after noon, making a total of 24 minutes. There are 60 minutes in an hour. $\dfrac{24}{60} = \dfrac{2}{5}$

4. **The correct answer is D.** One half earn over $18,000. One third of the other $\dfrac{1}{2}$, or $\dfrac{1}{6}$, earn between $15,000 and $18,000. This accounts for $\dfrac{1}{2} + \dfrac{1}{6}$, or $\dfrac{3}{6} + \dfrac{1}{6} = \dfrac{4}{6} = \dfrac{2}{3}$ of the staff, leaving $\dfrac{1}{3}$ to earn below $15,000.

5. **The correct answer is C.** David spends $\dfrac{1}{4}$ on Monday and $\dfrac{2}{3}$ of the other $\dfrac{3}{4}$, or $\dfrac{1}{2}$, on Tuesday, leaving only $\dfrac{1}{4}$ for the rest of the week.

6. **The correct answer is A.** Let the third or shortest section $= x$. Then the second section $= 3x$, and the first section $= 9x$. The entire piece of fabric is then $13x$, and the shortest piece represents $\dfrac{x}{13x}$, or $\dfrac{1}{13}$, of the entire piece.

7. **The correct answer is D.** The factory employs $M + W$ people, of which W are women.

8. **The correct answer is A.** For every 5 votes in favor, 3 were cast against. Therefore, 5 out of every 8 votes cast were in favor of the motion.

9. **The correct answer is C.** The ratio of women to the total number of people is 5:8. We can set up a proportion. If $\dfrac{5}{8} = \dfrac{x}{24}$, then $x = 15$.

10. **The correct answer is D.** The otter's speed going downstream with the current is:

$$\left(1\dfrac{3}{8} + \dfrac{3}{4}\right) = 1\dfrac{3}{8} + \dfrac{6}{8}$$
$$= 1\dfrac{9}{8}$$
$$= 2\dfrac{1}{8} \text{ miles per hour}$$

Compute this quotient:

$$4\dfrac{1}{2} \div 2\dfrac{1}{8} = \dfrac{9}{2} \div \dfrac{17}{8}$$
$$= \dfrac{9}{2} \cdot \dfrac{8}{17}$$
$$= \dfrac{36}{17}$$
$$= 2\dfrac{2}{17} \text{ hours}$$

339

Chapter 9

Numbers and Operations

11. **The correct answer is B.** The time remaining in the class is $1\frac{3}{4} - \frac{5}{6} = \frac{7}{4} - \frac{5}{6} = \frac{21}{12} - \frac{10}{12} = \frac{11}{12}$ of an hour. Since there are 60 minutes in one hour, the number of minutes to which this corresponds is $\frac{11}{12}(60) = 55$.

12. **The correct answer is B.** Let x be the number of gallons of gas the tank can hold. Then, $\frac{1}{8}x + 8 = \frac{5}{6}x$. Solve for x:

$$\frac{1}{8}x + 8 = \frac{5}{6}x$$
$$24 \cdot \left(\frac{1}{8}x + 8\right) = 24 \cdot \left(\frac{5}{6}x\right)$$
$$3x + 192 = 20x$$
$$192 = 17x$$
$$x = \frac{192}{17} = 11\frac{5}{17}$$

The tank holds approximately 11 gallons of gas.

Chapter 9

Numbers and Operations

COMPLEX NUMBERS

A **complex number** is a number made up of a real number and an imaginary number. It can be written in standard form $a + bi$, where a and b are real numbers and i is an imaginary unit.

$$i = \sqrt{-1}, \, i^2 = -1$$

For example, in the complex number $2 + 3i$ the real number is 2 and the imaginary number is $3i$.

Complex numbers can be added, subtracted, multiplied, and divided.

ADDING COMPLEX NUMBERS

To add complex numbers, add the real numbers and the imaginary numbers separately.

Sum: $(a + bi) + (c + di) = (a + c) + (b + d)i$

Example:

Add: $(2 + 3i) + (8 + 4i)$

Solution:

Add the real numbers and then the imaginary numbers.

$$(2 + 8) + (3i + 4i) = 10 + 7i$$

SUBTRACTING COMPLEX NUMBERS

To subtract complex numbers, subtract the real numbers and the imaginary numbers separately.

Difference: $(a + bi) - (c + di) = (a - c) + (b - d)i$

Example:

Subtract: $(2 + 3i) - (8 + 4i)$

Solution:

Subtract the real numbers and then the imaginary numbers.

$$(2 + 3i) - (8 + 4i) = (2 - 8) + (3i - 4i) = -6 - i$$

MULTIPLYING COMPLEX NUMBERS

Multiplying complex numbers is like multiplying polynomials by using the distributive property or the FOIL method.

Product: $(a + bi)(c + di) = (ac) + (adi) + (bci) + (bd)i^2$

Example:

Multiply: $3i(-2 + 9i)$

Solution:

Distribute $3i$ to all of the terms in the parentheses.

$$3i(-2+9i) = (3i)(-2)+(3i)(9i)$$
$$= (3i)(-2)+27i^2$$
$$i^2 = \left(\sqrt{-1}\right)\left(\sqrt{-1}\right) = -1$$
$$= -6i + 27(-1)$$
$$= -27 - 6i$$

Example:

Multiply: $(2 + 3i)(8 + 4i)$

Solution:

Find the sum of the products of the **F**irst terms, the **O**uter terms, the **I**nner terms, and the **L**ast terms of the binomials. The acronym FOIL stands for First Outer Inner Last and will help you to remember how to multiply two binomials.

When simplifying an expression that involves complex numbers, simplify i^2 to -1.

$$(2+3i)(8+4i) = (2 \cdot 8)+(2 \cdot 4i)+(8 \cdot 3i)+(3i \cdot 4i)$$
$$= 16 + 8i + 24i + 12i^2$$
$$= 16 + 32i + 12(-1)$$
$$= 4 + 32i$$

Simplify and write in standard form $a + bi$.

DIVIDING COMPLEX NUMBERS

Dividing complex numbers is more complicated because the denominator cannot contain a radical. This process is called **rationalizing the denominator**. In order to make the denominator rational, you must use its **complex conjugate**. The product of two complex conjugates is always a real number $a^2 + b^2$. The numbers $2 + 8i$ and $2 - 8i$ are examples of complex conjugates, and their product is the real number $2^2 + 8^2 = 4 + 64 = 68$.

Complex conjugates: $(a + bi)$ and $(a - bi)$

Product of complex conjugates: $(a + bi)(a - bi) = a^2 + b^2$

Example:

Simplify: $\dfrac{8}{7i}$

Solution:

Rationalize the denominator by multiplying the numerator and denominator by i.

$$\frac{8}{7i} = \frac{8}{7i} \cdot \frac{i}{i} = \frac{8i}{7i^2} = \frac{8i}{7(-1)} = \frac{8i}{-7}$$

Example:

Simplify: $\dfrac{4 + 2i}{-3 + 5i}$

Solution:

Rationalize the denominator by multiplying the numerator and denominator by the conjugate for the denominator. Then simplify by combining like terms.

$$\frac{4 + 2i}{-3 + 5i} = \frac{4 + 2i}{-3 + 5i} \cdot \frac{-3 - 5i}{-3 - 5i}$$

$$= \frac{-12 - 20i - 6i - 10}{9 + 15i - 15i - 25i^2}$$

$$= \frac{-12 - 20i - 6i - 10(-1)}{9 + 15i - 15i - 25(-1)}$$

$$= \frac{-2 - 26i}{9 + 25}$$

$$= \frac{-2 - 6i}{34}$$

$$= \frac{-2}{34} - \frac{26i}{34}$$

$$= \frac{-1}{17} - \frac{13i}{17}$$

Recall that $i^2 = -1$.

EXERCISE: COMPLEX NUMBERS

DIRECTIONS: Work out each problem. Circle the letter of your choice.

1. **Add:** $(8 + 2i) + (2 - 3i)$

   SHOW YOUR WORK HERE

   A. $15i$

   B. $5 + 4i$

   C. $6 + i$

   D. $10 - i$

2. **Add:** $\left(1 - \dfrac{1}{2}i\right) + (4 + 2i)$

   A. $5 - \dfrac{3}{2}i$

   B. $5 + \dfrac{3}{2}i$

   C. $\dfrac{7}{2}i$

   D. $\dfrac{13}{2}i$

3. **Subtract:** $(-9 + 4i) - (3 + 7i)$

   A. $-6 - 3i$

   B. $-2 + i$

   C. $-12 - 3i$

   D. $-i$

4. **Subtract:** $\left(\dfrac{3}{5} - \dfrac{1}{2}i\right) - \left(-\dfrac{3}{10} - 2i\right)$

   A. $\dfrac{9}{10} + \dfrac{3}{2}i$

   B. $\dfrac{9}{10} - \dfrac{3}{2}i$

   C. $\dfrac{3}{10} - \dfrac{3}{2}i$

   D. $\dfrac{3}{10} - \dfrac{5}{2}i$

5. **Multiply:** $(-5i)(-4i)i$

   A. $20i$

   B. $-\sqrt{20}\,i$

   C. $-20i$

   D. $\sqrt{20}\,i$

6. **Multiply:** $(-5i)(12 - 3i)$

SHOW YOUR WORK HERE

   A. $8 + 17i$

   B. $-15 - 60i$

   C. $15 + 60i$

   D. $-8 + 17i$

7. **Multiply:** $(4 - 6i)(1 - 2i)$

   A. $4 + 12i$

   B. $4 - 12i$

   C. $8 + 14i$

   D. $-8 - 14i$

8. **Compute:** $(2 - 3i)^2$

   A. $-5 + 12i$

   B. $-5 - 12i$

   C. 13

   D. -5

9. **Simplify:** $\dfrac{-5i}{4i + 11}$

   A. $-4 - 11i$

   B. $\dfrac{20 - 55i}{137}$

   C. $\dfrac{-20 - 55i}{137}$

   D. $4 + 11i$

10. **Simplify:** $\dfrac{17 - i}{3i}$

   A. $\dfrac{1}{3} - \dfrac{17}{3}i$

   B. $\dfrac{1}{3} + \dfrac{7}{3}i$

   C. $\dfrac{34}{5} + \dfrac{2}{5}i$

   D. $-\dfrac{1}{3} - \dfrac{17}{3}i$

345

Chapter 9

Numbers and Operations

11. Simplify: $\dfrac{3-5i}{3+5i}$

SHOW YOUR WORK HERE

    A. $\dfrac{8}{17}+\dfrac{15}{17}i$

    B. $\dfrac{8}{17}-\dfrac{15}{17}i$

    C. $-\dfrac{8}{17}+\dfrac{15}{17}i$

    D. $-\dfrac{8}{17}-\dfrac{15}{17}i$

12. Simplify: $\dfrac{-3+5i}{-3-4i}$

    A. $-\dfrac{29}{5}-\dfrac{27}{5}i$

    B. $\dfrac{-11}{25}-\dfrac{27}{25}i$

    C. $\dfrac{21}{25}-\dfrac{27}{25}i$

    D. $\dfrac{11}{7}+\dfrac{27}{7}i$

346

Chapter 9

Numbers and Operations

| 1. D | 3. C | 5. C | 7. D | 9. C | 11. D |
| 2. B | 4. A | 6. B | 8. B | 10. D | 12. B |

1. The correct answer is D.

$$(8 + 2i) + (2 - 3i) = (8 + 2) + (2i - 3i) = 10 - i$$

2. The correct answer is B.

$$\left(1 - \frac{1}{2}i\right) + (4 + 2i) = (1 + 4) + \left(-\frac{1}{2} + 2\right)i = 5 + \frac{3}{2}i$$

3. The correct answer is C.

$$(-9 + 4i) - (3 + 7i) = (-9 - 3) + (4i - 7i)$$
$$= -12 - 3i$$

4. The correct answer is A.

$$\left(\frac{3}{5} - \frac{1}{2}i\right) - \left(-\frac{3}{10} - 2i\right) = \left(\frac{3}{5} - \left(-\frac{3}{10}\right)\right) + \left(-\frac{1}{2} - (-2)\right)i$$
$$= \left(\frac{3}{5} + \frac{3}{10}\right) + \left(-\frac{1}{2} + 2\right)i$$
$$= \left(\frac{6}{10} + \frac{3}{10}\right) + \frac{3}{2}i$$
$$= \frac{9}{10} + \frac{3}{2}i$$

5. The correct answer is C.

$$(-5i)(-4i)i = (20)(i^2)(i) = -20i$$

6. The correct answer is B.

$$(-5i)(12 - 3i) = (-5i)(12) + (-5i)(-3i)$$
$$= -60i + 15i^2$$
$$= -60i + 15(-1)$$
$$= -15 - 60i$$

7. The correct answer is D.

$$(4 - 6i)(1 - 2i) = (4) + (-8i) + (-6i) + (12i^2)$$
$$= 4 + (-14i) + (-12)$$
$$= -8 - 14i$$

8. The correct answer is B.

$$(2 - 3i)^2 = (2 - 3i)(2 - 3i)$$
$$= 4 - 6i - 6i + 9i^2$$
$$= 4 - 12i - 9$$
$$= -5 - 12i$$

9. The correct answer is C.

$$\frac{-5i}{11 + 4i} = \frac{-5i}{11 + 4i} \cdot \frac{11 - 4i}{11 - 4i}$$
$$= \frac{-5i(11 - 4i)}{(11 + 4i)(11 - 4i)}$$
$$= \frac{-55i + 20i^2}{121 - 44i + 44i + 16i^2}$$
$$= \frac{-20 - 55i}{121 + 16}$$
$$= \frac{-20 - 55i}{137}$$

10. The correct answer is D.

$$\frac{17 - i}{3i} = \frac{17 - i}{3i} \cdot \frac{i}{i}$$
$$= \frac{(17 - i)(i)}{3i^2}$$
$$= \frac{17i - i^2}{3(-1)}$$
$$= \frac{1 + 17i}{-3}$$
$$= -\frac{1}{3} - \frac{17}{3}i$$

347

Chapter 9

Numbers and Operations

11. **The correct answer is D.** Multiply the numerator and denominator by the conjugate of the denominator. Then, simplify:

$$\frac{3-5i}{3+5i} = \frac{3-5i}{3+5i} \cdot \frac{3-5i}{3-5i}$$

$$= \frac{9-15i-15i+25i^2}{9-25i^2}$$

$$= \frac{9-30i-25}{9+25}$$

$$= \frac{-16-30i}{34}$$

$$= -\frac{8}{17} - \frac{15}{17}i$$

12. **The correct answer is B.**

$$\frac{-3+5i}{-3-4i} = \frac{-3+5i}{-3-4i} \cdot \frac{-3+4i}{-3+4i}$$

$$= \frac{(-3+5i)(-3+4i)}{(-3-4i)(-3+4i)}$$

$$= \frac{9-12i-15i+20i^2}{9-12i+12i-16i^2}$$

$$= \frac{9-12i-15i+20(-1)}{9-12i+12i-16(-1)}$$

$$= \frac{9-27i+(-20)}{9+(-16)(-1)}$$

$$= \frac{-11-27i}{25}$$

$$= \frac{-11}{25} - \frac{27}{25}i$$

348

Chapter 9

Numbers and Operations

DIRECT AND INVERSE VARIATION

DIRECT VARIATION

Two quantities are said to **vary directly** if as one increases, the other increases, and, as one decreases, the other decreases.

For example, the amount of sugar needed in a recipe varies directly with the amount of butter used. The number of inches between two cities on a map varies directly with the number of miles between the cities. The equation $y = ax$ represents direct variation between x and y, and y is said to vary directly with x. The variable a is called the constant of variation. By dividing each side by x, you can see that the ratio for the variable is the constant a.

Example:

Hooke's Law states that the distance d a spring stretches varies directly with the force F that is applied to it. Suppose a spring stretches 15 inches when a force of 9 lbs. is applied. Write an equation that relates d to F, and state the constant of variation.

Solution:

You are comparing the distance that a spring stretches with the force that is applied, so $\dfrac{d}{15} = \dfrac{F}{9}$. Solving for d in terms of F, you get $d = \dfrac{5}{3}F$. The constant of variation is $\dfrac{5}{3}$.

Example:

The weight of a person on the Moon varies directly with the weight of a person on Earth. A person who weighs 100 lbs. on Earth weighs 16.6 lbs. on the Moon. How much would a person who weighs 120 lbs. on Earth weigh on the Moon?

Solution:

Start with the equation $y = ax$, where y is the weight of a person on the Moon and x is the weight of a person on Earth.

$$y = ax$$
$$16.6 = a(100)$$
$$0.166 = a$$

The equation $y = 0.166x$ gives the weight y on the Moon of a person who weighs x pounds on Earth. To solve the example, substitute $x = 120$ in the equation to determine the weight of the person on the Moon.

$$y = 0.166x$$
$$y = 0.166(120)$$
$$y = 19.92$$

A person who weighs 120 lbs. on Earth would weigh 19.92 lbs. on the Moon.

349

Chapter 9

Numbers and Operations

INVERSE VARIATION

Two quantities are said to **vary inversely** if, as one increases, the other decreases.

For example, the number of workers hired to paint a house varies inversely with the number of days the job will take. A doctor's stock of flu vaccine varies inversely with the number of patients injected. The number of days a given supply of cat food lasts varies inversely with the number of cats being fed.

The equation $xy = a$, where $a \neq 0$, represents inverse variation between x and y, and y is said to vary inversely with x. The variable a is called the constant of variation.

 Whenever two quantities vary directly, you can find a missing term by setting up a proportion. However, be very careful to compare the same units, in the same order, on each side of the equal sign.

Example:

The number of songs that can be stored on a hard drive varies inversely with the size of the song. A certain hard drive can store 3,000 songs when the average size of the song is 3.75 MB. Write an equation that gives the number of songs y that will fit on the hard drive as a function of the average song size x.

Solution:

First, write an inverse variation equation that relates x and y. Then substitute 3,000 for y and 3.75 for x.

$$xy = a$$
$$y = \frac{a}{x}$$
$$3{,}000 = \frac{a}{3.75}$$
$$11{,}250 = a$$

The inverse variation equation for this situation is $y = \dfrac{11{,}250}{x}$.

EXERCISE: DIRECT AND INVERSE VARIATION

DIRECTIONS: Work out each problem. Circle the letter of your choice.

---

1. If 60 feet of uniform wire weighs 80 pounds, what is the weight of 2 yards of the same wire?

   A. $2\frac{2}{3}$ pounds

   B. 6 pounds

   C. 8 pounds

   D. 120 pounds

2. A gear 50 inches in diameter turns a smaller gear 30 inches in diameter. If the larger gear makes 15 revolutions, how many revolutions does the smaller gear make in that time?

   A. 9

   B. 12

   C. 20

   D. 25

3. The time it takes to construct a rock concert stage varies inversely with the number of workers. If 10 people work, it takes 4 days to finish the construction. How long does the job take if 14 people work?

   A. $2\frac{1}{2}$ days

   B. $2\frac{6}{7}$ days

   C. 3 days

   D. $3\frac{2}{7}$ days

4. If a furnace uses 40 gallons of oil in a week, how many gallons, to the nearest gallon, does it use in 10 days?

   A. 4

   B. 28

   C. 57

   D. 58

SHOW YOUR WORK HERE

5. A recipe requires 13 ounces of sugar and 18 ounces of flour. If only 10 ounces of sugar are used, how much flour, to the nearest ounce, should be used?

   A. 13

   B. 14

   C. 15

   D. 23

6. A bottle of 20 aspirin costs \$8.25. If the cost, y, varies directly with the number of aspirin, x, what is the approximate cost of a bottle of 325 aspirin?

   A. \$9.50

   B. \$11.25

   C. \$13.40

   D. \$15.30

7. A school has enough bread to feed 30 children for 4 days. If 10 more children are added, how many days will the bread last?

   A. $1\dfrac{1}{3}$

   B. $2\dfrac{2}{3}$

   C. 3

   D. $5\dfrac{1}{3}$

8. The intensity of a sound, I, varies inversely with the square of the distance, d, from the sound. If the distance is reduced by a factor of $\dfrac{1}{4}$, by what factor will the intensity of the sound increase?

   A. 4

   B. 8

   C. 12

   D. 16

352

Chapter 9

Numbers and Operations

9. The number of ceramic tiles, x, laid on a kitchen floor varies directly with the amount of time, y, spent laying the tile. If it takes 20 minutes to lay 12 tiles, how long does it take to lay 190 tiles?

   A. 1 hour, 36 minutes

   B. 1 hour, 54 minutes

   C. 2 hours, 10 minutes

   D. 2 hours, 25 minutes

10. The height, H, and base radius, R, of the water in a right circular cylinder vary inversely to keep the volume of water constant. When the height is 1.2 feet, the base radius is 0.35 feet. What is the base radius when the height is 1.4 feet?

    A. 0.25 feet

    B. 0.3 feet

    C. 0.4 feet

    D. 0.55 feet

11. The price per person, y, for a catered event varies inversely with the number of people attending the event, x. It costs $20 per person if 45 people attend. What is the approximate cost per person if 65 people attend?

    A. $9

    B. $13.85

    C. $15.50

    D. $22.25

12. The profit, P, earned from sales of handcrafted cheeseboards is directly proportional to the number of cheeseboards sold, x. What is the variation equation?

    A. $P = k + x$

    B. $P = \dfrac{1}{kx^2}$

    C. $P = kx$

    D. $P = \dfrac{k}{x}$

353

Chapter 9

Numbers and Operations

1. C	3. B	5. B	7. C	9. B	11. B
2. D	4. C	6. C	8. D	10. B	12. C

1. **The correct answer is C.** You are comparing feet with pounds. The more feet, the more pounds. This is DIRECT. Remember to rename yards as feet:

$$\frac{60}{80} = \frac{6}{x}$$
$$60x = 480$$
$$x = 8$$

2. **The correct answer is D.** The larger a gear, the fewer times it revolves in a given period of time. This is INVERSE.

$$50 \cdot 15 = 30 \cdot x$$
$$750 = 30x$$
$$25 = x$$

3. **The correct answer is B.** The variation equation is $P = \frac{k}{t}$. Using the given information, we can find k: $10 = \frac{k}{4}$, so that $k = 40$. So the model is $P = \frac{40}{t}$. The time is takes to complete the job if 14 people work is the solution of the equation $14 = \frac{40}{t}$. This solution is $t = \frac{40}{14} = \frac{20}{7} = 2\frac{6}{7}$ days.

4. **The correct answer is C.** The more days, the more oil. This is DIRECT. Remember to rename the week as 7 days.

$$\frac{40}{7} = \frac{x}{10}$$
$$7x = 400$$
$$x = 57\frac{1}{7}$$

5. **The correct answer is B.** The more sugar, the more flour. This is DIRECT.

$$\frac{13}{18} = \frac{10}{x}$$
$$13x = 180$$
$$x = 13\frac{11}{13}$$

6. **The correct answer is C.** The variation equation is $y = kx$. Using the given information, we can find k: $8.25 = 200k$, so that $k = \frac{8.25}{200} = 0.04125$. Hence, $y = 0.04125x$. The cost of 325 aspirin is $y = 0.04125(325) = 13.40$.

7. **The correct answer is C.** The more children, the fewer days. This is INVERSE.

$$30 \cdot 4 = 40 \cdot x$$
$$120 = 40x$$
$$3 = x$$

8. **The correct answer is D.**

$$I\left(d^2\right) = k$$
$$I\left(\frac{d}{4}\right)^2 = k$$
$$I\left(\frac{d^2}{16}\right) = k$$
$$I\left(d^2\right) = 16k$$

9. **The correct answer is B.** The variation equation is $y = kx$. Using the given information, we can find k: $12 = k(20)$ so that $k = \frac{3}{5}$. So $y = \frac{3}{5}x$. The time it takes is $\frac{3}{5}(190) = 114$ minutes, or 1 hour, 54 minutes, to lay 190 tiles.

10. **The correct answer is B.** The variation equation is $H = \frac{k}{R}$. Using the given information, we can find k: $1.2 = \frac{k}{0.35}$, so that $k = (1.2)(0.35) = 0.42$. So the model is $H = \frac{0.42}{R}$. The desired base radius R satisfies the equation $1.4 = \frac{0.42}{R}$. Solving for R yields $R = \frac{0.42}{1.4} = 0.3$.

354

Chapter 9

Numbers and Operations

11. **The correct answer is B.** The variation equation is

$y = \dfrac{k}{x}$. Using the given information, we can find k:

$20 = \dfrac{k}{45}$, so that $k = (20)(45) = 900$. So the model is

$y = \dfrac{900}{x}$. The cost per person if 65 people attend is

$y = \dfrac{900}{65} \approx \$13.85$.

12. **The correct answer is C.** The equation is $P = kx$, where k is the constant of proportionality.

355

Chapter 9

Numbers and Operations

FINDING PERCENTAGES

PERCENT EQUIVALENTS

Percent means "out of 100." If you understand this concept, it becomes very easy to rename a percentage as an equivalent decimal or fraction.

$$5\% = \frac{5}{100} = 0.05$$

$$2.6\% = \frac{2.6}{100} = 0.026$$

$$c\% = \frac{c}{100} = \frac{1}{100} \cdot c = 0.01c$$

$$\frac{1}{2}\% = \frac{\frac{1}{2}}{100} = \frac{1}{100} \cdot \frac{1}{2} = \frac{1}{100} \cdot 0.5 = 0.005$$

Certain fractional equivalents of common percentages occur frequently enough that they should be memorized. Learning the values in the following table will make your work with percentage problems much easier.

Percentage-Fraction Equivalents

$50\% = \frac{1}{2}$	$90\% = \frac{9}{10}$	$12\frac{1}{2}\% = \frac{1}{8}$
$25\% = \frac{1}{4}$	$33\frac{1}{3}\% = \frac{1}{3}$	$37\frac{1}{2}\% = \frac{3}{8}$
$75\% = \frac{3}{4}$	$20\% = \frac{1}{5}$	$62\frac{1}{2}\% = \frac{5}{8}$
$10\% = \frac{1}{10}$	$40\% = \frac{2}{5}$	$87\frac{1}{2}\% = \frac{7}{8}$
$30\% = \frac{3}{10}$	$60\% = \frac{3}{5}$	$16\frac{2}{3}\% = \frac{1}{6}$
$70\% = \frac{7}{10}$	$80\% = \frac{4}{5}$	$83\frac{1}{3}\% = \frac{5}{6}$

Most percentage problems can be solved by using the following proportion:

$$\frac{\%}{100} = \frac{\text{part}}{\text{whole}}$$

Although this method works, it often yields unnecessarily large numbers that are difficult to compute. Following are examples of the four basic types of percentage problems and different methods for solving them.

How to Solve Percentage Problems

- To change a % to a decimal, remove the % sign and divide by 100. This has the effect of moving the decimal point two places to the LEFT.

- To change a decimal to a %, add the % sign and multiply by 100. This has the effect of moving the decimal point two places to the RIGHT.

- To change a % to a fraction, remove the % sign and divide by 100. This has the effect of putting the % over 100 and simplifying the resulting fraction.

- To change a fraction to a %, add the % sign and multiply by 100.

To Find a Percentage of a Number

Example:

Find 27% of 92.

Solution:

Proportional Method	Shorter Method
	Rename the percentage as its decimal or fraction equivalent and multiply. Use fractions only when they are among the familiar ones given in the previous chart.
$$\frac{27}{100} = \frac{x}{92}$$ $$100x = 2,428$$ $$x = 24.84$$	$$\begin{array}{r} 92 \\ \times 0.27 \\ \hline 644 \\ 184 \\ \hline 24.84 \end{array}$$

Example:

Find $12\frac{1}{2}\%$ of 96.

Solution:

Proportional Method	Decimal Method	Fractional Method
$$\frac{12\frac{1}{2}}{100}=\frac{x}{96}$$ $$100x = 1,200$$ $$x = 12$$	$$\begin{array}{r} 0.125 \\ \times\ \ 96 \\ \hline 750 \\ 1125 \\ \hline 12.000 \end{array}$$	$$\frac{1}{8}\cdot 96 = 12$$

Which method is easiest? It really pays to memorize those fractional equivalents.

TO FIND A NUMBER WHEN A PERCENTAGE OF IT IS GIVEN

Example:

7 is 5% of what number?

Solution:

Proportional Method	Shorter Method
$$\frac{5}{100}=\frac{7}{x}$$ $$5x = 700$$ $$x = 140$$	Translate the problem into an algebraic equation. In doing this, the percentage must be written as a fraction or decimal. $$7 = 0.05x$$ $$700 = 5x$$ $$140 = x$$

Example:

20 is $33\frac{1}{2}$ of what number?

Solution:

Proportional Method	Shorter Method
$\dfrac{33\frac{1}{2}}{100} = \dfrac{20}{x}$ $33\frac{1}{3}x = 2{,}000$ $\dfrac{100}{3}x = 2{,}000$ $100x = 6{,}000$ $x = 60$	$20 = \dfrac{1}{3}x$ $60 = x$

Just think of the time you will save and the number of extra problems you will solve if you know that $33\frac{1}{3}\% = \frac{1}{3}$.

To Find What Percentage One Number Is of Another

Example:

90 is what percent of 1,500?

Solution:

Proportional Method	Shorter Method
$\dfrac{x}{100} = \dfrac{90}{1{,}500}$ $1{,}500x = 9{,}000$ $15x = 90$ $x = 6$	Put the part over the whole. Simplify the fraction and multiply by 100. $\dfrac{90}{1{,}500} = \dfrac{9}{150} = \dfrac{3}{50} \cdot 100 = 6$

Example:

7 is what percent of 35?

Solution:

Proportional Method	Shorter Method
$\dfrac{x}{100} = \dfrac{7}{35}$ $35x = 700$ $x = 20$	$\dfrac{7}{35} = \dfrac{1}{5} = 20\%$

Example:

18 is what percent of 108?

Solution:

Proportional Method	Shorter Method
$\dfrac{x}{100} = \dfrac{18}{108}$ $108x = 1{,}800$ Time-consuming long division is necessary to get: $x = 16\dfrac{2}{3}$	$\dfrac{18}{108} = \dfrac{9}{54} = \dfrac{1}{6} = 16\dfrac{2}{3}\%$ Once again, if you know the fraction equivalents of common percents, computation can be done in a few seconds.

TO FIND A PERCENTAGE OVER 100

Example:

Find 125% of 64.

Solution:

Proportional Method	Decimal Method	Fractional Method
$\dfrac{125}{100} = \dfrac{x}{64}$ $100x = 8{,}000$ $x = 80$	$\begin{array}{r} 64 \\ \times\ 1.25 \\ \hline 320 \\ 128 \\ \underline{64} \\ 80.00 \end{array}$	$1\dfrac{1}{4} \cdot 64$ $\dfrac{5}{4} \cdot 64 = 80$

Example:

36 is 150% of what number?

Solution:

Proportional Method	Decimal Method	Fractional Method
$\dfrac{150}{100} = \dfrac{36}{x}$ $150x = 3{,}600$ $15x = 360$ $x = 24$	$36 = 1.50x$ $360 = 15x$ $24 = x$	$36 = 1\dfrac{1}{2}x$ $36 = \dfrac{3}{2}x$ $72 = 3x$ $24 = x$

Example:

60 is what percent of 50?

Solution:

Proportional Method	Fractional Method
$\dfrac{x}{100} = \dfrac{60}{50}$ $50x = 6{,}000$ $5x = 600$ $x = 120$	$\dfrac{60}{50} = \dfrac{6}{5} = 1\dfrac{1}{5} = 120\%$

EXERCISE: FINDING PERCENTAGES

DIRECTIONS: Work out each problem. Circle the letter of your choice.

1. Write 1.001% as a decimal.

   A. 0.01001

   B. 0.1001

   C. 10.1

   D. 100.1

2. Write 3.4% as a fraction.

   A. $\dfrac{34}{1,000}$

   B. $\dfrac{34}{10}$

   C. $\dfrac{34}{100}$

   D. $\dfrac{340}{100}$

3. Write $\dfrac{17}{2}$% as a percentage.

   A. 8.5%

   B. 85%

   C. 0.085%

   D. 850%

4. Find 60% of 70.

   A. 4,200

   B. 420

   C. 42

   D. 4.2

5. What is 175% of 16?

   A. 28

   B. 24

   C. 22

   D. 12

SHOW YOUR WORK HERE

6. What percent of 40 is 16?

   A. 20%

   B. $2\frac{1}{2}$%

   C. $33\frac{1}{3}$%

   D. 40%

7. What percent of 0.02 is 0.005?

   A. 4.0

   B. 2.5

   C. 25

   D. 40

8. $4 is 20% of what?

   A. $5

   B. $20

   C. $200

   D. $500

9. $\frac{9}{5}$ is $20\frac{1}{4}$% of what number?

   A. $\frac{9}{80}$

   B. $\frac{80}{9}$

   C. $\frac{81}{400}$

   D. $\frac{45}{4}$

10. What percent of 2 is 0.004?

    A. 0.02

    B. 0.2

    C. 2

    D. 20

363

Chapter 9

Numbers and Operations

11. Write 0.02 as a percentage.

    A. 0.0002%

    B. 0.002%

    C. 20%

    D. 2%

12. Find $5\frac{2}{5}\%$ of $2\frac{1}{2}$.

    A. $\dfrac{27}{2}$

    B. $\dfrac{1}{50}$

    C. $\dfrac{27}{200}$

    D. $\dfrac{1}{20}$

364

Chapter 9

Numbers and Operations

| 1. A | 3. D | 5. A | 7. C | 9. B | 11. D |
| 2. A | 4. C | 6. D | 8. B | 10. B | 12. C |

1. **The correct answer is A.** Move the decimal point to the left two places to get the equivalent decimal 0.01001.

2. **The correct answer is A.**

$$3.4\% = \frac{3.4}{100} = \frac{34}{1,000}$$

3. **The correct answer is D.**

$$\frac{17}{2} = 8\frac{1}{2} = 8.5$$

This is equivalent to 850%.

4. **The correct answer is C.**

$$60\% = \frac{3}{5} \rightarrow \frac{3}{5} \cdot 70 = 42$$

5. **The correct answer is A.**

$$175\% = 1\frac{3}{4} \rightarrow \frac{7}{4} \cdot 16 = 28$$

6. **The correct answer is D.**

$$\frac{16}{40} = \frac{2}{5} = 40\%$$

7. **The correct answer is C.** Let x denote the desired percentage. Solve the following proportion:

$$\frac{x}{100} = \frac{0.005}{0.02}$$
$$\frac{x}{100} = 0.25$$
$$x = 25$$

8. **The correct answer is B.**

$$20\% = \frac{1}{5}, \text{ so } 4 = \frac{1}{5}x$$
$$20 = x$$

9. **The correct answer is B.** $20\frac{1}{4}\% = \frac{81}{4}\% = \frac{81}{400}$.

Let x be the unknown number. Then, $\frac{81}{400}x = \frac{9}{5}$.

Solving for x yields $\frac{9}{5} \cdot \frac{400}{81} = \frac{80}{9}$.

10. **The correct answer is B.** Let x denote the desired percent. Then, $\frac{x}{100}(2) = 0.004$. Solve for x, as follows:

$$\frac{x}{100}(2) = 0.004$$
$$x = \frac{100}{2}(0.004)$$
$$x = \frac{0.4}{2} = 0.2$$

11. **The correct answer is D.** $0.02 = \frac{2}{100} = 2\%$

12. **The correct answer is C.** $5\frac{2}{5}\% = \frac{27}{5}\% = \frac{27}{500}$.

Now, apply this to $2\frac{1}{2} = \frac{5}{2}$ to obtain $\frac{27}{500} \cdot \frac{5}{2} = \frac{27}{200}$.

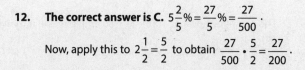

365

Chapter 9

Numbers and
Operations

PERCENTAGE WORD PROBLEMS

Certain types of business situations are excellent applications of percentages.

PERCENTAGE OF INCREASE OR DECREASE

The **percentage of increase or decrease** is found by putting the amount of increase or decrease over the original amount and renaming this fraction as a percentage.

Example:

Over a five-year period, the enrollment at South High dropped from 1,000 students to 800. Find the percentage of decrease.

Solution:

$$\frac{1,000-800}{1,000}=\frac{200}{1,000}=\frac{20}{100}=20\%$$

Example:

A company normally employs 100 people. During a slow spell, the company fired 20% of its employees. By what percentage must the company now increase its staff to return to full capacity?

Solution:

$$20\%=\frac{1}{5} \quad \rightarrow \quad \frac{1}{5}\cdot 100=20\%$$

The company now has 100 − 20 = 80 employees. If it then increases its staff by 20, the percentage of increase is $\frac{20}{80}=\frac{1}{4}$, or 25%.

 In word problems, *of* can usually be interpreted to mean *times* (in other words, *multiply*).

DISCOUNT

A **discount** is usually expressed as a percent of the marked price that will be deducted from the marked price to determine the sale price.

Example:

Bill's Hardware offers a 20% discount on all appliances during a sale week. If they take advantage of the sale, how much must the Russells pay for a washing machine marked at $280?

Solution:

Long Method	Shorter Method
$20\% = \dfrac{1}{5}$ $\dfrac{1}{5} \cdot 280 = \$56$ discount $\$280 - \$56 = \$224$ sale price The danger inherent in this method is that $56 is sure to be among the multiple-choice answers.	If there is a 20% discount, the Russells will pay 80% of the marked price. $80\% = \dfrac{4}{5}$ $\dfrac{4}{5} \cdot 280 = \$224$ sale price

Example:

A store offers a television set marked at $340 less discounts of 10% and 5%. Another store offers the same television set also marked at $340 with a single discount of 15%. How much does the buyer save by buying at the better price?

Solution:

In the first store, the initial discount means the buyer pays 90%, or $\dfrac{9}{10}$, of $340, which is $306. The additional 5% discount means the buyer pays 95% of $306, or $290.70. Note that the second discount must be figured on the first sale price. Taking 5% off $306 is a smaller amount than taking the additional 5% off $340. The second store will therefore have a lower sale price. In the second store, the buyer will pay 85% of $340, or $289, making the price $1.70 less than in the first store.

COMMISSION

Many salespeople earn money on a commission basis. In order to encourage sales, they are paid a percentage of the value of goods sold. This amount is called a **commission**.

Example:

A salesperson at Brown's Department Store is paid $80 per week in salary plus a 4% commission on all her sales. How much will that salesperson earn in a week in which she sells $4,032 worth of merchandise?

Solution:

Find 4% of $4,032 and add this amount to $80.

$$
\begin{array}{r}
4032 \\
\times\, 0.04 \\
\hline
\end{array}
$$
$$\$161.28 + \$80 = \$241.28$$

Example:

Bill Olson delivers frozen food for a delivery service and keeps 8% of all money collected. One month he was able to keep $16. How much did he forward to the delivery service?

Solution:

First, determine how much he collected by finding the number that 16 is 8% of.

$$16 = 0.08x$$
$$1,600 = 8x$$
$$200 = x$$

If Bill collected $200 and kept $16, he gave the delivery service $200 − $16, or $184.

TAXES

Taxes are a percentage of money spent or money earned.

Example:

Noname County collects a 7% sales tax on automobiles. If the price of a car is $8,532 before taxes, what will this car cost once sales tax is added in?

Solution:

Find 7% of $8,532 to determine tax and then add it to $8,532. This can be done in one step by finding 107% of $8,532.

$$
\begin{array}{r}
\$8,532 \\
\times 1.07 \\
\hline
59724 \\
85320 \\
\hline
\$9,129.24
\end{array}
$$

Example:

If the tax rate in Anytown is $3.10 per $100, what is the annual real estate tax on a house assessed at $47,200?

Solution:

$$\text{annual tax} = \text{tax rate} \cdot \text{assessed value}$$

$$
\begin{aligned}
&= \left(\frac{\$3.10}{\$100}\right)(47,200) \\
&= (0.031)(47,200) \\
&= \$1,463.20
\end{aligned}
$$

369

Chapter 9

Numbers and Operations

EXERCISE: PERCENTAGE WORD PROBLEMS

DIRECTIONS: Work out each problem. Circle the letter of your choice.

---

1. What was the original price of a phone that sold for $70 during a 20%-off sale?

   A. $56

   B. $84

   C. $87.50

   D. $90

2. How many dollars does a salesperson earn on a sale of $800 at a commission of 2.5%?

   A. 20

   B. 200

   C. 2,000

   D. 20,000

3. At a selling price of $273, a refrigerator yields a 30% profit on the cost. What selling price will yield a 10% profit on the cost?

   A. $210

   B. $221

   C. $231

   D. $235

4. A store is having a sale on jeans. The manager marks the price down by 30%. A customer has a coupon that gives an additional 10% off the sale price. If the original price was $65, what is the cost of the jeans after the discounts are applied?

   A. $35.75

   B. $40.95

   C. $45.50

   D. $58.50

SHOW YOUR WORK HERE

370

Chapter 9

Numbers and Operations

5. The net price of a certain article is $306 after successive discounts of 15% and 10% off the marked price. What is the marked price?

   A. $234.09

   B. $382.50

   C. $400

   D. $408

SHOW YOUR WORK HERE

6. In preparation for the holiday season, a store marks up the price of its most popular electronic toys by 15%. If such a toy was x dollars before the markup, which of these expressions represents the cost after the markup?

   A. $x + 1.15$ dollars

   B. $0.85x$ dollars

   C. $1.15x$ dollars

   D. $\dfrac{x}{0.85}$ dollars

7. A baseball team has won 40 games out of 60 played. It has 32 more games to play. How many of these must the team win to make its record 75% for the season?

   A. 26

   B. 28

   C. 29

   D. 30

8. If prices are reduced 25% and sales increase 20%, what is the net effect on gross receipts?

   A. They increase by 5%.

   B. They decrease by 5%.

   C. They increase by 10%.

   D. They decrease by 10%.

9. A salesperson earns 5% on all sales between $200 and $600, and 8% on the part of the sales over $600. What is her commission in a week in which her sales total $800?

   A. $20

   B. $36

   C. $46

   D. $78

371

Chapter 9

Numbers and Operations

10. If the enrollment at State U. was 3,000 in 1998 and 12,000 in 2008, what was the percent of increase in enrollment?

SHOW YOUR WORK HERE

   A. 400%

   B. 300%

   C. 25%

   D. 3%

11. Seventy percent of the members of a gym are male, and 40% of the males regularly compete in organized events. What percent of the members of the gym are males who regularly compete?

   A. 25%

   B. 28%

   C. 30%

   D. 42%

12. A salesperson receives a salary of $100 a week and a commission of 5% on all sales. What must be the amount of sales for a week in which the salesperson's total weekly income is $360?

   A. $6,200

   B. $5,200

   C. $2,600

   D. $720

372

Chapter 9

Numbers and Operations

1. C	**3.** C	**5.** C	**7.** C	**9.** C	**11.** B
2. A	**4.** B	**6.** C	**8.** D	**10.** B	**12.** B

1. **The correct answer is C.** $70 represents 80% of the original price.

$$70 = 0.80x$$
$$700 = 8x$$
$$\$87.50 = x$$

2. **The correct answer is A.**

$$2.5\% = \frac{2.5}{100}$$

The commission is $\frac{2.5}{100}(800) = \$20$.

3. **The correct answer is C.**

$$1.30x = 273$$
$$13x = 2{,}730$$
$$x = \$210 = \text{cost}$$

$273 represents 130% of the cost.

The new price will add 10% of cost, or $21, for profit.

New price = $231

4. **The correct answer is B.** The discounted price due to the markdown is $65 – 0.3($65) = $45.50. Applying the 10% coupon yields the final cost of $45.50 – $45.50(0.10) = $40.95.

5. **The correct answer is C.**

If marked price = m, first sale price = $0.85m$, and net price = $0.90(0.85m) = 0.765m$

$$0.765m = 306$$
$$m = 400$$

In this case, it would be easy to work from the answer choices.

15% of $400 is $60, making a first sale price of $340.

10% of this price is $34, making the net price $306.

Choices A, B, and D would not give a final answer in whole dollars.

6. **The correct answer is C.** Add 15% of x to x to get the cost after the mark-up. Doing so yields $x + 0.15x = 1.15x$.

7. **The correct answer is C.** The team must win 75%, or $\frac{3}{4}$, of the games played during the entire season. With 60 games played and 32 more to play, the team must win $\frac{3}{4}$ of 92 games, and $\frac{3}{4} \cdot 92 = 69$. Since 40 games have already been won, the team must win 29 additional games.

8. **The correct answer is D.** Let original price = p, and original sales = s. Therefore, original gross receipts = ps. Let new price = $0.75p$, and new sales = $1.20s$. Therefore, new gross receipts = $0.90ps$. Gross receipts are only 90% of what they were.

9. **The correct answer is C.** Five percent of sales between $200 and $600 is 0.05(600) = $30. Then, 8% of sales over $600 is 0.08(200) = $16. Total commission = $30 + $16 = $46.

10. **The correct answer is B.** There was an increase of 9,000 students. To determine the percent of this increase in enrollment:

$$\frac{9{,}000}{3{,}000} = 3 = 300\%$$

11. **The correct answer is B.** 40% of 70% of x, the total number of members, is $(0.40)(0.70)x = 0.28x$. So 28% of members are males who regularly compete.

12. **The correct answer is B.**

Let s = sales

$$\$100 + 0.05s = 360$$
$$0.05s = 260$$
$$5s = 26{,}000$$
$$s = \$5{,}200$$

373

Chapter 9

Numbers and Operations

SUMMING IT UP

- If the arithmetic looks complex, try to simplify it first.

- If a problem is given with letters in place of numbers, the same reasoning must be applied as for numbers. If you are not sure how to proceed, replace the letters with numbers to determine the steps that must be taken.

- Fractions should be written in the simplest form. Often, in multiple-choice questions, you may find that the answer you have correctly computed is not among the choices but an equivalent fraction is. Be careful!

- Whenever two quantities vary directly, you can find a missing term by setting up a proportion. However, be very careful to compare the same units, in the same order, on each side of the equal sign.

- When solving percentage problems, remember the following:

  - To change a % to a decimal, remove the % sign and divide by 100. This has the effect of moving the decimal point two places to the LEFT.

  - To change a decimal to a %, add the % sign and multiply by 100. This has the effect of moving the decimal point two places to the RIGHT.

  - To change a % to a fraction, remove the % sign and divide by 100. This has the effect of putting the % over 100 and simplifying the resulting fraction.

  - To change a fraction to a %, add the % sign and multiply by 100.

- In problems dealing with percentages, you may be presented with certain types of business situations, such as taxes or commissions. For problems asking about the percentage of increase or decrease, put the amount of increase or decrease over the original amount and rename that fraction as a percentage. A discount is usually expressed as a percentage of the marked price that will be deducted from the marked price to determine the sale price.

374

ONLINE
PREP

WANT TO KNOW MORE?

Access additional practice questions, helpful lessons, valuable tips, and top-notch strategies for the following numbers and operations review topics in *Peterson'sOnline Course for the SAT® Exam*:

- Arithmetic Strategy

- Hard Arithmetic

- Percent Word Problems

- Proportions and Rates

- Word Problems

- Working Backwards

To purchase and access the course, go to **www.petersons.com/testprep/sat**.

CHAPTER 10:
BASIC ALGEBRA

OVERVIEW

- Signed Numbers
- Exercise: Signed Numbers
- Linear Equations
- Exercise: Linear Equations
- Simultaneous Equations
- Exercise: Simultaneous Equations
- Exponents
- Exercise: Exponents
- Quadratic Equations
- Exercise: Quadratic Equations
- Literal Equations
- Exercise: Literal Equations
- Roots and Radicals
- Exercise: Roots and Radicals
- Monomials and Polynomials
- Exercise: Monomials and Polynomials
- Problem Solving in Algebra
- Exercise: Problem Solving in Algebra
- Inequalities
- Exercise: Inequalities
- Summing It Up

SIGNED NUMBERS

To solve algebra problems, you must be able to compute accurately with signed numbers.

Addition: To add signed numbers with the same sign, add the magnitudes of the numbers and keep the same sign. To add signed numbers with different signs, subtract the magnitudes of the numbers and use the sign of the number with the greater magnitude.

Subtraction: When subtracting a positive number from a negative number, add the magnitudes and make the difference (the answer) negative. When subtracting a negative number from a positive number, add the magnitude and make the difference positive. When asked to find the difference or a distance between a negative number and a positive number, the answer will always be positive.

Multiplication: If there is an odd number of negative signs, the product is negative. An even number of negative signs gives a positive product.

Division: If the signs are the same, the quotient is positive. If the signs are different, the quotient is negative.

Practicing these basic operations with signed numbers will help you on the more difficult problems on the SAT° Exam in which these and more complex skills are tested.

EXERCISE: SIGNED NUMBERS

DIRECTIONS: Work out each problem. Circle the letter next to your choice.

1. What is the sum of –6 and 8?

   A. –14

   B. 14

   C. –2

   D. 2

2. When –4 and –5 are added, what is the sum?

   A. –9

   B. 9

   C. –1

   D. 1

3. Subtract –8 from –3.

   A. –11

   B. –5

   C. 5

   D. 11

4. Subtract 8 from –2.

   A. –10

   B. –6

   C. 6

   D. 10

SHOW YOUR WORK HERE

5. Compute the product of –9 and 3.

  A. –6

  B. 6

  C. –27

  D. 27

6. What is the product of $(-6)\left(+\dfrac{1}{2}\right)(-10)$?

  A. $-15\dfrac{1}{2}$

  B. $15\dfrac{1}{2}$

  C. –30

  D. 30

7. Find the quotient: $\dfrac{(-6)(8)}{-12}$

  A. 36

  B. 4

  C. –36

  D. –4

8. Last winter the meteorology class recorded the daily temperatures. The coldest recorded temperature was –37 degrees Fahrenheit, and the warmest was 38 degrees Fahrenheit. How many degrees warmer was the warmest day than the coldest day?

  A. –75

  B. –1

  C. 1

  D. 75

Chapter 10

Basic Algebra

9. The highest point in California is Mt. Whitney with an elevation of 14,494 feet. The lowest point is Death Valley with an elevation of –294 feet. How much higher is the base of a tree at the top of Mt. Whitney than a person standing at the lowest point in Death Valley?

   A.   294 feet

   B.   14,200 feet

   C.   14,494 feet

   D.   14,788 feet

10. A submarine started at an elevation of –1,250 feet, or 1,250 feet below sea level, and it submerged another 25 feet per second. It continued to submerge for 10 seconds. What was its new elevation?

   A.   –1,500 feet

   B.   –1,000 feet

   C.   250 feet

   D.   1,500 feet

1. D	3. C	5. C	7. B	9. D
2. A	4. A	6. D	8. D	10. A

1. **The correct answer is D.** The larger of the two whole number parts determines the sign. So 8 + (–6) = 2.

2. **The correct answer is A.** In adding numbers with the same sign, add their magnitudes (4 + 5 = 9) and keep the same sign.

3. **The correct answer is C.** –3 – (–8) = –3 + 8 = 5

4. **The correct answer is A.** –2 – 8 = –2 + (–8) = –10

5. **The correct answer is C.** (–9)(3) = –27

6. **The correct answer is D.** The product of an even number of negative numbers is positive.

$$\frac{6}{1}\left(\frac{1}{2}\right)(10) = 30$$

7. **The correct answer is B.**

$$\frac{(-6)(8)}{-12} = \frac{-48}{-12} = 4$$

8. **The correct answer is D.** When subtracting a positive number from a negative number, you add the magnitude and make the difference positive. This is like a distance question. It's really asking what the distance is on the number line from –37 to +38. Try to picture the number line. Add the magnitudes and make the answer positive:

$$-37 - 38 = -75$$

The difference is 75 degrees.

9. **The correct answer is D.** This question is really asking about distance between two things, so the answer will be positive. You can figure it is 14,494 feet from the top of Mt. Whitney to sea level, and then another 294 feet to get to the lowest point of Death Valley. Add the two numbers: 14,494 + 294 = 14,788.

10. **The correct answer is A.** Find the additional distance submerged. Multiply –25 by 10. When multiplying a negative number by a positive, the product is negative.

$$-25 \times 10 = -250$$

Subtract 250 from –1,250. When subtracting a positive number from a negative number, add the magnitude and make the difference (the answer) negative:

$$1,250 + 250 = 1,500$$

The answer is –1,500.

379

Chapter 10

Basic Algebra

LINEAR EQUATIONS

The next step in solving algebra problems is mastering linear equations. Whether an equation involves numbers or only variables, the basic steps are the same.

FOUR-STEP STRATEGY

1. If there are fractions or decimals, remove them by multiplication.

2. Collect all terms containing the unknown for which you are solving on the same side of the equation. Remember that whenever a term crosses the equal sign from one side of the equation to the other, it must "pay a toll." That is, it must change its sign.

3. Determine the coefficient of the unknown by combining similar terms or factoring when terms cannot be combined.

4. Divide both sides of the equation by this coefficient.

 If you have a string of multiplications and divisions to do and the number of negative factors is even, the result will be positive; if the number of negative factors is odd, the result will be negative.

Example:

Solve for x: $5x - 3 = 3x + 5$

Solution:

$$2x = 8$$
$$x = 4$$

Example:

Solve for x: $\dfrac{3}{4}x + 2 = \dfrac{2}{3}x + 3$

Solution:

Multiply by 12:

$$9x + 24 = 8x + 36$$
$$x = 12$$

Example:

Solve for x: $0.7x + 0.04 = 2.49$

Solution:

Multiply by 100:

$$70x + 4 = 249$$
$$70x = 245$$
$$x = 3.5$$

An equation that is true for every value of the variable is called an **identity**. It has infinitely many solutions. An equation has **no solution** if no value for the variable will make the equation true.

Example:

Solve for x: $0.5(6x + 4) = 3x + 2$

Solution:

First, simplify each side of the equation. Then solve for x:

$$3x + 2 = 3x + 2$$
$$3x = 3x$$
$$x = x$$

Since $x = x$ is always true, the original equation has infinitely many solutions and is an *identity*.

Example:

Solve for x: $9x + 7 = x + 2(4x + 3)$

Solution:

First, simplify each side of the equation. Then solve for x:

$$9x + 7 = x + 8x + 6$$
$$9x + 7 = 9x + 6$$
$$7 = 6$$

Since $7 \neq 6$, the original equation has *no solution*.

If you eliminate the variable in the process of solving the equation, then you will have either infinitely many solutions or no solution.

Example:

In the equation $ax + 7 = 2x + 3$, for which values of a will the equation have no solutions?

Solution:

If $a = 2$, the original equation becomes $2x + 7 = 2x + 3$. Since $2x + 7 \neq 2x + 3$ there are *no solutions* that make the equation true.

Real-World Linear Equations

A **literal equation** is an equation that involves two or more variables. You can solve for one variable in terms of the others using the properties of equalities. A **formula** is a literal equation that defines a relationship among quantities. For example, the perimeter of a rectangle can be found using the formula $P = 2l + 2w$, where P = perimeter, l = length, and w = width.

Example:

What is the width of a rectangle with perimeter 42 and length 8?

Solution:

Using the formula $P = 2l + 2w$, where P = perimeter, l = length, and w = width, solve for the variable w.

Substitute the values that you know into the formula.

$$42 = 2(8) + 2w$$
$$42 = 16 + 2w$$
$$42 - 16 = 2w$$
$$26 = 2w$$
$$\frac{26}{2} = w$$
$$13 = w$$

The width of the rectangle is 13 units.

Example:

The drama club sold student and adult tickets to its spring play. The adult tickets cost $15 each, and the student tickets cost $10 each. Tickets sales were $4,050. If 120 adult tickets were sold, how many student tickets were sold?

Solution:

Using the formula $R = 15a + 10s$, where R = revenue from ticket sales, a = adult tickets, and s = student tickets, solve it for the variable s.

Substitute the values that you know into the formula.

$$4,050 = 15(120) + 10s$$
$$4,050 = 1,800 + 10s$$
$$4,050 - 1,800 = 10s$$
$$2,250 = 10s$$
$$\frac{2,250}{10} = s$$
$$225 = s$$

The drama club sold 225 student tickets.

EXERCISE: LINEAR EQUATIONS

> **DIRECTIONS:** Work out each problem. Circle the letter of your choice.

SHOW YOUR WORK HERE

1. If $5x + 6 = 10$, then x equals

    A. $\dfrac{16}{5}$

    B. $\dfrac{5}{16}$

    C. $-\dfrac{5}{4}$

    D. $\dfrac{4}{5}$

2. Solve for z: $3 - 2z = 9 + 4z$

    A. 3

    B. −1

    C. 0

    D. 6

3. Solve for y: $\frac{3}{4}y - 2 = \frac{1}{6}y$

    A. $\frac{7}{2}$

    B. $\frac{24}{7}$

    C. $\frac{2}{7}$

    D. $\frac{7}{24}$

4. If $7x = 3x + 12$, then $2x + 5 =$

    A. 10

    B. 11

    C. 12

    D. 13

5. Solve for w: $-8 + 4w = -2(3 - w)$

    A. -4

    B. 0

    C. 1

    D. 4

6. Solve for x: $\frac{2x + 9}{7} = \frac{3x + 8}{2}$

    A. No solution

    B. Infinitely many solutions

    C. $\frac{17}{38}$

    D. $-\frac{38}{17}$

7. Solve for N: $0.2(1 - 5N) = 0.5(1 - 2N)$

    A. 0

    B. 0.3

    C. No solution

    D. Infinitely many solutions

8. The formula for the area of a triangle is $A = \frac{1}{2}bh$. Find the base of the triangle if the area is 28 in.^{2} and its height is 7 in.

   A. 2 in.

   B. 8 in.

   C. 98 in.

   D. 196 in.

9. Membership to Iron Gym costs $40 per month plus a $30 registration fee. The monthly cost is deducted automatically from your account. If your starting balance is $350, how many months will you be able to go to the gym before you have to add money to your account?

   A. 6

   B. 7

   C. 8

   D. 9

10. Lauren started a small wreath-making business. She earns $50 per wreath that she sells. She purchased $1,500 worth of materials when she started the business. How many wreaths must she sell to break even?

    A. 15

    B. 30

    C. 45

    D. 60

385

Chapter 10

Basic Algebra

1. D	3. B	5. C	7. C	9. C
2. B	4. B	6. D	8. B	10. B

1. **The correct answer is D.**

$$5x = 4$$
$$x = \frac{4}{5}$$

2. **The correct answer is B.**

$$3 - 2z = 9 + 4z$$
$$3 = 9 + 6z$$
$$-6 = 6z$$
$$-1 = z$$

3. **The correct answer is B.** Start by clearing the fractions. Solve as follows:

$$\frac{3}{4}y - 2 = \frac{1}{6}y$$
$$12 \cdot \left(\frac{3}{4}y - 2\right) = 12 \cdot \left(\frac{1}{6}y\right)$$
$$9y - 24 = 2y$$
$$7y - 24 = 0$$
$$7y = 24$$
$$y = \frac{24}{7}$$

4. **The correct answer is B.** Solve for x:

$$4x = 12$$
$$x = 3$$
$$2x + 5 = 3(3) + 5 = 11$$

5. **The correct answer is C.**

$$-8 + 4w = -2(3 - w)$$
$$-8 + 4w = -6 + 2w$$
$$-2 + 4w = 2w$$
$$-2 = -2w$$
$$1 = w$$

6. **The correct answer is D.**

$$\frac{2x + 9}{7} = \frac{3x + 8}{2}$$
$$2(2x + 9) = 7(3x + 8)$$
$$4x + 18 = 21x + 56$$
$$-17x = 38$$
$$x = -\frac{38}{17}$$

7. **The correct answer is C.**

$$0.2(1 - 5N) = 0.5(1 - 2N)$$
$$0.2 - 0.2(5N) = 0.5 - 0.5(2N)$$
$$0.2 - N = 0.5 - N$$
$$0.2 = 0.5$$

Since the final equation is false, we conclude the equation has no solution.

8. **The correct answer is B.** Solve the formula for b. Then substitute in the values of the variables.

$$A = \frac{1}{2}bh$$
$$\frac{2A}{h} = b$$
$$\frac{2(28)}{7} = b$$
$$8 = b$$

9. **The correct answer is C.**

$$40x + 30 = 350$$
$$40x = 320$$
$$x = 8$$

10. **The correct answer is B.** Let x be the number of wreaths Lauren needs to sell to break even. Then $50x = 1,500$. Divide both sides by 50 to get $x = 30$.

SIMULTANEOUS EQUATIONS

In solving equations with two unknowns, you must work with two equations simultaneously. The object is to eliminate one of the two unknowns and solve for the resulting single unknown.

Example:

Solve for x: $2x - 4y = 2$
$3x + 5y = 14$

Solution:

Multiply the first equation by 5:

$$10x - 20y = 10$$

Multiply the second equation by 4:

$$12x + 20y = 56$$

Since the y-terms now have the same numerical coefficients, but with opposite signs, you can eliminate them by adding the two equations. If they had the same signs, you would eliminate them by subtracting the equations.

Add the equations:

$$10x - 20y = 10$$
$$12x + 20y = 56$$
$$\overline{22x = 66}$$
$$x = 3$$

Since you were only asked to solve for x, stop here. If you were asked to solve for both x and y, you would now substitute 3 for x in either equation and solve the resulting equation for y.

$$3(3) + 5y = 14$$
$$9 + 5y = 14$$
$$\overline{5y = 5}$$
$$y = 1$$

In the previous example, the system of equations has exactly one solution (3, 1). It is also possible for a system of equations to have no solution or infinitely many solutions.

Example:

Solve the system: $-12x + 8y = 2$
$\qquad\qquad\qquad 3x - 2y = 7$

Solution:

Multiply the second equation by 4, so that the *x*-terms and *y*-terms have the same numerical coefficients:

$$-12x + 8y = 2$$
$$12x - 8y = 28$$

Now add the equations:

$$-12x + 8y = 2$$
$$\underline{12x - 8y = 28}$$
$$0 = 30$$

Since $0 \neq 30$, there is no solution to the system.

Example:

Solve the system: $3x - 2y = -15$
$$x - \frac{2}{3}y = -5$$

Solution:

Multiply the second equation by 3, so that the *x*- and *y*-terms have the same numerical coefficients:

$$3x - 2y = -15$$
$$3x - 2y = -15$$

Now subtract the equations:

$$3x - 2y = -15$$
$$\underline{3x - 2y = -15}$$
$$0 = 0$$

Since $0 = 0$ is an identity, there are infinitely many solutions to the system.

Example:

For which value of a will the system $\begin{aligned} 3x - 4y &= 12 \\ ax - 3y &= 9 \end{aligned}$ have infinitely many solutions?

Solution:

Consider solving each equation for y:

$$y = \frac{3}{4}x - 3$$

$$y = \frac{a}{3x - 3}$$

To have infinitely many solutions, $\frac{3}{4} = \frac{a}{3}$.

So $a = \frac{9}{4}$.

Example:

Solve the system: $\begin{aligned} x^2 + y &= 9 \\ x - y &= -3 \end{aligned}$

Solution:

Add the equations to eliminate the y-variable:

$$\begin{aligned} x^2 + y &= 9 \\ x - y &= -3 \\ \hline x^2 + x &= 6 \end{aligned}$$

Set the equation equal to 0 and solve for x:

$$x^2 + x - 6 = 0$$

Factor to solve for x:

$$(x - 2)(x + 3) = 0$$

$$x = 2 \text{ or } x = -3$$

Find the corresponding y-values by substituting each value of x into the linear equation.

$$2 - y = -3; y = 5 \text{ and}$$
$$-3 - y = -3; y = 0$$

There are 2 possible solutions for the system: (2, 5) and (–3, 0). Check each in both equations.

$$1^{st} \text{ equation: } \left(x^2\right) + y = 9 \text{ and } \left(x\right)^2 + y = 9$$
$$\left(2\right)^2 + 5 = 9 \qquad \left(-3\right)^2 + 0 = 9$$
$$9 = 9 \qquad\qquad 9 = 9$$

$$2^{nd} \text{ equation: } \left(x\right) - y = -3 \text{ and } \left(x\right) - y = -3$$
$$\left(2\right) - 5 = -3 \qquad \left(-3\right) - 0 = -3$$
$$-3 = -3 \qquad\qquad -3 = -3$$

The solutions to the system are (2, 5) and (–3, 0).

APPLICATIONS OF SYSTEMS

Systems of equations can be used to solve many real-life problems.

Example:

Computer Connect, Inc. makes and sells computer parts. The material for each part costs $3.00 and sells for $12.75 each. The company spends $1,200 on additional expenses each month. How many computer parts must the company sell each month in order to break even?

Solution:

The break-even point is when the income equals the expenses. The first equation $12.75x = y$ represents the income. The second equation $3x + 1{,}200 = y$ represents expenses.

$$y = 12.75x$$
$$y = 3.00x + 1{,}200$$

Solve the system by subtracting the second equation from the first.

$$y = 12.75x$$
$$\underline{y = 3.00x + 1{,}200}$$
$$0 = 9.75x - 1{,}200$$
$$-9.75x = -1{,}200$$
$$x = \frac{-1{,}200}{-9.75}$$
$$x \approx 123.08$$

To break even, the company would have to sell at least 124 computer parts.

Example:

Jordan and Alex are planning a vacation. They plan to spend some of the time in Naples, Florida, and the rest of time in Key West. They estimate that it will cost $250 per day in Naples and $325 per day in Key West. If they plan to vacation a total of 8 days and have a budget of $2,375. How many days should they spend in each city?

Solution:

To write the equations, let x = the number of days in Naples and y = the number of days in Key West. The first equation $x + y = 8$ represents the total number of days on vacation. The second equation, $250x + 325y = 2,375$, represents total cost.

The system of equations is:
$$x + y = 8$$
$$250x + 325y = 2,375$$

Solve the system by multiplying the first equation by 325 and then subtract the second equation from the first.

$$
\begin{array}{r}
325x + 325y = 2,600 \\
\underline{250x + 325y = 2,375} \\
75x = 225 \\
x = 3
\end{array}
$$

Since $x + y = 8$, if $x = 3$ then $y = 5$. The couple can spend 3 days in Naples and 5 days in Key West.

Solving Systems of Inequalities by Graphing

Systems of inequalities are solved using the same methods as systems of equations. Recall that you must reverse the sign of the inequality if you multiply or divide by a negative value.

391

Chapter 10

Basic Algebra

You can graph a system of linear inequalities in the coordinate plane. The solution of the system is where the graphs of the inequalities overlap. Recall, that an inequality with a < or > sign, is graphed as a dashed line, while an inequality with a ≤ or ≥ is graphed with a solid line. A solid line shows that answers along the line are included in the solution set for that inequality.

Example:

What system of inequalities is represented by the graph shown?

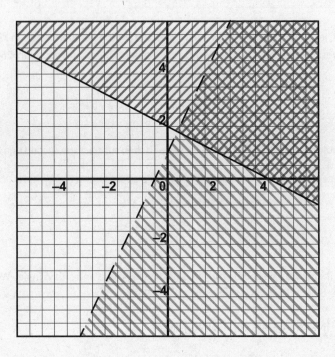

Solution:

First write the inequality that represents the region bounded by the solid line, using two points along the line and the slope-intercept formula $y = mx + b$, replacing the equal sign with a comparison symbol.

$$y \geq -0.5x + 2$$

Then write the inequality that represents the region bounded by the dashed line.

$$y < 2x + 1$$

The graph shows the intersection of the system $y \geq -0.5x + 2$
$$y < 2x + 1$$

Example:

Solve the system of inequalities by graphing: $x + 2y \leq 8$
$$3x - y \geq 3$$

Solution:

First solve each inequality for y to rewrite in slope-intercept form:

1st inequality: $x + 2y \leq 8$
$$2y \leq -x + 8$$
$$y \leq -\frac{1}{2}x + 4$$

2nd inequality: $3x - y \geq 3$
$$-y \geq -3x + 3$$
$$y \leq 3x - 3$$

Then graph each inequality.

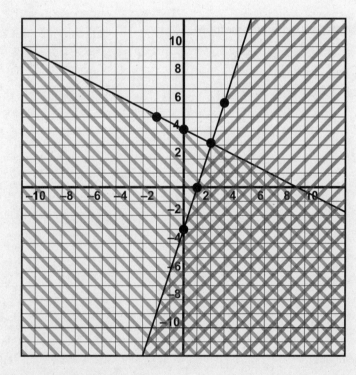

The solution is the region where the graphs overlap.

EXERCISE: SIMULTANEOUS EQUATIONS

DIRECTIONS: Work out each problem. Circle the letter of your choice.

1. What is the value of $x + y$ if the pair (x, y) satisfies the following system?

    $$\begin{cases} x = 2y - 14 \\ y = 5x + 1 \end{cases}$$

    SHOW YOUR WORK HERE

    A. 3

    B. 6

    C. 9

    D. 15

2. What is the value of y^2 if the pair (x, y) satisfies the following system?

    $$\begin{cases} 3y + 2x = -4 \\ 2y - x = 16 \end{cases}$$

    A. 8

    B. 16

    C. 28

    D. 49

Chapter 10

Basic Algebra

3. Solve the system:

    $$2y = x + 16$$
    $$-\frac{1}{2}x + y = -2$$

    A. No solution

    B. Infinitely many solutions

    C. 0

    D. All positive values

4. Solve the system for y:

    $$x - y^2 = 2$$
    $$2x + 5y = 7$$

    A. $y = 11, 2.25$

    B. $y = 0.5, -3$

    C. $y = 1.75, 17$

    D. Infinitely many solutions

5. Solve the system:

$$14y = -2x + 23$$
$$2(x + 7y) = 23$$

A. 0

B. All negative values

C. No solution

D. Infinitely many solutions

6. What system of inequalities is shown in the graph?

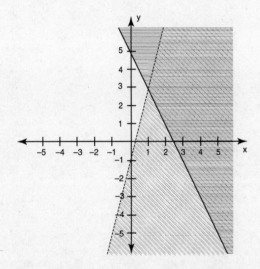

A.
$$y < 4x - 1$$
$$2x + y \geq 5$$

B.
$$y > 4x - 1$$
$$-2x + y \geq 5$$

C.
$$y > 4x + 1$$
$$2x - y \geq 5$$

D.
$$y \geq 4x - 1$$
$$2x + y \geq -5$$

7. Speedy Rent-A-Car charges $45 a day plus $0.60 per mile driven to rent a car. Zippy Rental charges $40 a day plus $0.70 per mile driven to rent a car. After how many miles would it cost the same amount to rent a car from either Speedy Rent-A-Car or Zippy Rental?

A. 25 miles

B. 50 miles

C. 75 miles

D. 100 miles

8. Andi can work a total of no more than 35 hours per week at her two jobs. She earns \$30 per hour giving music lessons and \$45 per hour working as a life coach. She must earn at least \$800 per week. Which system of inequalities can be used to determine the pairs of the number of hours spent at each job that would enable her to earn at least \$800?

A. $\begin{cases} 35(x+y) \geq 800 \\ \quad\quad x+y \leq 35 \end{cases}$

B. $\begin{cases} x \leq 35 \\ y \geq 800 \end{cases}$

C. $\begin{cases} \quad\quad x+y \geq 35 \\ 35x+45y \geq 800 \end{cases}$

D. $\begin{cases} \quad\quad x+y \leq 35 \\ 35x+45y \geq 800 \end{cases}$

9. Determine the value of $\dfrac{y}{x}$ if the pair (x, y) satisfies the following system?

$$\begin{cases} 3x+y=1 \\ -3x+4y=9 \end{cases}$$

A. -6

B. $-\dfrac{2}{3}$

C. 2

D. $\dfrac{8}{3}$

396

Chapter 10

Basic Algebra

10. Find the solution of the following system.

$$\begin{cases} y+\dfrac{3}{4}x=1 \\ y=-\dfrac{3}{4}x-1 \end{cases}$$

A. $x=0, y=-1$

B. $x=0, y=1$

C. Infinitely many solutions

D. No solution

1. C	3. A	5. D	7. B	9. A
2. B	4. B	6. A	8. D	10. D

1. **The correct answer is C.** Substitute the expression for y given by the second equation in for y in the first equation and solve the resulting for x:

$$x = 2(5x+1)-14$$
$$x = 10x+2-14$$
$$x = 10x-12$$
$$12 = 9x$$
$$\frac{4}{3} = x$$

Plug in this x-value into the second equation to determine the value of y: $y = 5\left(\frac{4}{3}\right)+1 = \frac{23}{3}$

Thus, $x+y = \frac{4}{3}+\frac{23}{3} = \frac{27}{3} = 9$

2. **The correct answer is B.** Multiply the second equation by 2 and add the result to the first equation to eliminate x: $7y = 28$, so that $y = 4$. Hence $4^2 = 16$.

3. **The correct answer is A.** Multiply the second equation by 2 and add to eliminate a variable.

$$2y = x+16$$
$$-\frac{1}{2}x+y = -2$$
$$\underline{-x+2y = 16}$$
$$\underline{x-2y = 4}$$
$$0 = 20$$

Since $0 \neq 20$, there is no solution.

4. **The correct answer is B.** Eliminate the x-variable and solve for y.

$$x-y^2 = 2$$
$$\underline{2x+5y = 7}$$
$$2x-2y^2 = 4$$
$$\underline{2x+5y = 7}$$
$$2y^2+5y = 3$$
$$2y^2+5y-3 = 0$$
$$(2y-1)(y+3) = 0$$
$$y = \frac{1}{2},\ -3$$

5. **The correct answer is D.**

$$14y = -2x+23$$
$$\underline{2(x+7y) = 23}$$
$$2x+14y = 23$$
$$\underline{2x+14y = 23}$$
$$0 = 0$$

Since $0 = 0$ is always true, there are infinitely many solutions.

6. **The correct answer is A.** First write the inequality that represents the region bounded by the dashed line using two points and the slope intercept formula.

$$y < 4x-1$$

Then write the inequality that represents the region bounded by the solid line.

$$y \geq -2x+5$$

The graph shows the intersection of the system:

$$y < 4x-1$$
$$2x+y \geq 5$$

397

Chapter 10

Basic Algebra

7. **The correct answer is B.** The system of equations that represents the cost of renting a car from the places is:

$$y = 45 + 0.6x$$
$$y = 40 + 0.7x$$

Solve this system by subtracting the second equation from the first. The solution is 50 miles.

Rewrite the equations so that you can eliminate the y variable. So:

$$40 = -0.7x + y$$
$$-45 = 0.6x - y$$

Add the second equation to the first to eliminate the y variable: $-5 = -0.1x$. When simplified, $x = 50$. Therefore, 50 is the number of miles it would take for the cost (y) of both rental companies to be equal.

8. **The correct answer is D.** Let x be the number of hours spent giving music lessons and y the number of hours spent working as a life coach. Since the total number of hours worked in one week cannot exceed 35, we have the inequality $x + y \leq 35$. Next, the amount earned working x hours giving music lessons is $35x$ dollars, and the amount earned working y hours as a life coach is $45y$ dollars. The sum of these two amounts must be at least \$800. This gives the inequality $35x + 45y \geq 800$. The desired system is given in choice D.

9. **The correct answer is A.** Add the two equations to eliminate x: $5y = 10$, so that $y = 2$. Plug this into the first equation for y and solve for x: $3x + 2 = 1$, so that $3x = -1$ and $x = -\dfrac{1}{3}$. Thus $\dfrac{y}{x} = \dfrac{2}{-\dfrac{1}{3}} = 2(-3) = -6$.

10. **The correct answer is D.** Substitute the expression for y given by the second equation into y in the first equation to obtain the equation $\left(-\dfrac{3}{4}x - 1\right) + \dfrac{3}{4}x = 1$. This is equivalent to the false statement $-1 = 1$. This system has no solution.

398

Chapter 10

Basic Algebra

EXPONENTS

An exponent is a mathematical notation indicating that a number, called the base, has been multiplied one or more times by itself. For example, in the term 2^3, the 2 is the base and the ^{3} is the exponent. This term means "two times two times two" and is read "two to the third power." The word *power* tells how many times the base number appears in the multiplication.

$$x^3 = x \text{ times } x \text{ times } x$$
$$x^2 = x \text{ times } x$$
$$x^1 = x$$
$$x^0 = 1$$

 Commit to memory small powers of small numbers that come up in many questions. For example, the powers of 2: 2, 4, 8, 16, 32, . . . the powers of 3: 3, 9, 27, 81, . . . and so on.

THE FIVE RULES OF EXPONENTS

1. To multiply powers of the same base, add the exponents.

$$x^2 \text{ times } x^3 = x^{2+3} = x^5$$
$$x^5 \text{ times } x^4 = x^{5+4} = x^9$$

2. To divide powers of the same base, subtract the exponent of the divisor from the exponent of the dividend.

$$\frac{x^6}{x^2} = x^{6-2} = x^4$$
$$\frac{x^{10}}{x^3} = x^{10-3} = x^7$$

3. Negative powers represent reciprocals.

$$x^{-1} = \frac{1}{x}$$
$$\left(\frac{x^3}{y^5}\right)^{-2} = \left(\frac{y^5}{x^3}\right)^2 = \frac{y^{10}}{x^6}$$

Chapter 10

Basic Algebra

4. To find the power of a power, multiply the exponents.

$$(x^2)^3 = x^{(2)(3)} = x^6$$

$$(x^3y^5)^2 = x^{(3)(2)}y^{(5)(2)} = x^6y^{10}$$

A variable base with an even exponent has two values, one positive and one negative.

$x^2 = 25$; x could be positive 5 or negative 5.

A variable base can be zero (unless otherwise stated in the problem). In that case, no matter what the exponent, the value of the term is zero.

Is x^4 always greater than x^2? No; if x is zero, then x^4 and x^2 are equal.

When the base is a fraction between 0 and 1, the larger the exponent, the smaller the value of the term.

Which is greater, $\left(\dfrac{37}{73}\right)$ or $\left(\dfrac{37}{73}\right)^2$? The correct answer is $\left(\dfrac{37}{73}\right)$ because $\left(\dfrac{37}{73}\right)$ is almost $\dfrac{1}{2}$, while $\left(\dfrac{37}{73}\right)^2$ is about $\dfrac{1}{4}$.

5. Fractional exponents represent roots.

$$x^{\frac{1}{2}} = \sqrt{x}$$

$$x^{\frac{1}{3}} = \sqrt[3]{x}$$

$$x^{\frac{2}{5}} = \left(\sqrt[5]{x}\right)^2$$

$$= \sqrt[5]{x^2}$$

400

Chapter 10

Basic Algebra

EXERCISE: EXPONENTS

DIRECTIONS: Work out each problem. Circle the letter of your choice.

1. $p^8 \times q^4 \times p^4 \times q^8 =$

   A. $p^{12}q^{12}$

   B. p^4q^4

   C. $p^{32}q^{32}$

   D. $p^{64}q^{64}$

2. $(x^2y^3)^4 =$

   A. x^6y^7

   B. x^8y^{12}

   C. $x^{12}y^8$

   D. x^2y

3. $\dfrac{x^{16}y^6}{x^4y^2} =$

   A. $x^{20}y^8$

   B. x^4y^3

   C. $x^{12}y^3$

   D. $x^{12}y^4$

4. Suppose $z^3 = -27$ and $y^2 = 16$. What is the minimum possible value for $y - z$?

   A. -7

   B. -1

   C. 1

   D. 7

401

Chapter 10

Basic Algebra

5. $a^{-4} \times a^{-3} =$

   A. $\dfrac{1}{a^{12}}$

   B. $\dfrac{1}{a^{7}}$

   C. a^{7}

   D. a^{12}

6. $x^{\frac{2}{3}} x^{\frac{1}{2}} =$

   A. $\sqrt[3]{x}$

   B. $\sqrt[5]{x^{3}}$

   C. $\left(\sqrt[6]{x}\right)^{7}$

   D. $\dfrac{1}{\sqrt[5]{x^{2}}}$

7. $\dfrac{w^{-5}}{w^{-10}} =$

   A. $\dfrac{1}{w^{2}}$

   B. w^{5}

   C. w^{15}

   D. w^{2}

8. $\left(x^{-3}y^{2}\right)^{-4} =$

   A. $\dfrac{1}{x^{7}y^{2}}$

   B. $\dfrac{y^{8}}{x^{12}}$

   C. xy^{6}

   D. $\dfrac{x^{12}}{y^{8}}$

402

Chapter 10

Basic Algebra

9. $\dfrac{x^{\frac{5}{6}}}{x^{\frac{2}{9}}} =$

A. $x^{\frac{5}{27}}$

B. $x^{\frac{11}{18}}$

C. $\dfrac{1}{x^{\frac{11}{18}}}$

D. $\dfrac{1}{x^{\frac{5}{27}}}$

10. $\left(\dfrac{w^2 y^{-3}}{w^{-4} y^{-5}}\right)^{-2} =$

A. $w^6 y^2$

B. $\dfrac{1}{w^6 y^2}$

C. $\dfrac{1}{w^{12} y^4}$

D. $w^{12} y^4$

403

Chapter 10

Basic Algebra

1. A	**3.** D	**5.** B	**7.** B	**9.** B
2. B	**4.** B	**6.** C	**8.** D	**10.** C

1. **The correct answer is A.** The multiplication signs do not change the fact that this is the multiplication of terms with a common base and different exponents. Solve this kind of problem by adding the exponents.

$$p^{8+4} \times q^{4+8} = p^{12}q^{12}$$

2. **The correct answer is B.** To raise a power to a power, multiply the exponents. $x^{(2)(4)}y^{(3)(4)} = x^8 y^{12}$

3. **The correct answer is D.** All fractions are implied division. When dividing terms with a common base and different exponents, subtract the exponents. Therefore, $16 - 4 = 12$ and $6 - 2 = 4$.

4. **The correct answer is B.** First, $z = -3$ and y can be either -4 or 4. The possible values of $y - z$ are as follows:

$$-4 - (-3) = -4 + 3 = -1$$
$$4 - (-3) = 4 + 3 = 7$$

The smallest value is -1.

5. **The correct answer is B.** To multiply, add the exponents. The resulting exponent will be negative, which means you need to take the reciprocal.

$$a^{-4} \times a^{-3} = a^{-4 + (-3)}$$
$$= a^{-7}$$
$$= \frac{1}{a^7}$$

6. **The correct answer is C.** To multiply, add the exponents. Then, use the rules for rational exponents to convert to root form.

$$x^{\frac{2}{3}}x^{\frac{1}{2}} = x^{\frac{2}{3}+\frac{1}{2}}$$
$$= x^{\frac{7}{6}}$$
$$= \left(\sqrt[6]{x}\right)^7$$

7. **The correct answer is B.**

$$\frac{w^{-5}}{w^{-10}} = \frac{w^{10}}{w^5}$$
$$= w^{10-5}$$
$$= w^5$$

8. **The correct answer is D.**

$$\left(x^{-3}y^2\right)^{-4} = x^{(-3)(-4)}y^{2(-4)}$$
$$= x^{12}y^{-8}$$
$$= \frac{x^{12}}{y^8}$$

9. **The correct answer is B.**

$$\frac{x^{\frac{5}{6}}}{x^{\frac{2}{9}}} = x^{\frac{5}{6}-\frac{2}{9}}$$
$$= x^{\frac{15}{18}-\frac{4}{18}}$$
$$= x^{\frac{11}{18}}$$

10. **The correct answer is C.**

$$\left(\frac{w^2 y^{-3}}{w^{-4}y^{-5}}\right)^{-2} = \left(\frac{w^2 w^4 y^5}{y^3}\right)^{-2}$$
$$= \left(w^6 y^2\right)^{-2}$$
$$= \frac{1}{\left(w^6 y^2\right)^2}$$
$$= \frac{1}{w^{6 \cdot 2}y^{2 \cdot 2}}$$
$$= \frac{1}{w^{12}y^4}$$

404

Chapter 10

Basic Algebra

QUADRATIC EQUATIONS

ROOTS AND FACTORING

In solving quadratic equations, remember that there will always be two roots, even though these roots may be equal. A complete quadratic equation is of the form $ax^2 + bx + c = 0$.

ALERT: Don't forget: In working with any equation, if you move a term from one side of the equal sign to the other, you must change its sign.

Example:

Factor: $x^2 + 7x + 12 = 0$

Solution:

$$(x + 3)(x + 4) = 0$$

The last term of the equation is positive; therefore, both factors must have the same sign, since the last two terms multiply to a positive product. The middle term is also positive; therefore, both factors must be positive, since they also add to a positive sum.

$$(x + 4)(x + 3) = 0$$

If the product of two factors is 0, each factor may be set equal to 0, yielding the values for x of -4 or -3.

Example:

Factor: $x^2 + 7x - 18 = 0$

Solution:

$$(x + 9)(x - 2) = 0$$

Now you are looking for two numbers with a product of -18; therefore, they must have opposite signs. To yield $+7$ as a middle coefficient, the numbers must be $+9$ and -2.

$$(x + 9)(x - 2) = 0$$

This equation gives the roots -9 and $+2$.

Incomplete quadratic equations are those in which b or c is equal to 0.

Example:

Solve for x: $x^2 - 16 = 0$

Solution:

$$x^2 = 16$$
$$x = \pm 4$$

Remember, there must be two roots.

Example:

Solve for x: $4x^2 - 9 = 0$

Solution:

$$4x^2 = 9$$
$$x^2 = \frac{9}{4}$$
$$x = \pm \frac{3}{2}$$

Example:

Solve for x: $x^2 + 4x = 0$

Solution:

Never divide through an equation by the unknown, as this would yield an equation of lower degree having fewer roots than the original equation. Always factor this type of equation.

$$x(x + 4) = 0$$

The roots are 0 and −4.

Example:

Solve for x: $4x^2 - 9x = 0$

Solution:

$$x(4x - 9) = 0$$

The roots are 0 and $\dfrac{9}{4}$.

The **quadratic formula** can also be used to find the solutions to quadratic equations $ax^2 + bx + c = 0$ where a, b, and c are real numbers and $a \neq 0$.

$$x = \frac{-b \pm \sqrt{b^2 - 4ac}}{2a}$$

Example:

Use the quadratic formula to solve for x: $2x^2 + 7x = 3$

Solution:

Write the equation in standard form: $2x^2 + 7x - 3 = 0$. Then, identify the values of a, b, and c and substitute them into the quadratic formula.

$$a = 2, b = 7, \text{ and } c = -3$$
$$x = \frac{-b \pm \sqrt{b^2 - 4ac}}{2a}$$
$$x = \frac{-7 \pm \sqrt{(7)^2 - 4(2)(-3)}}{2(2)}$$
$$x = \frac{-7 \pm \sqrt{73}}{4}$$

The solutions are $x = \dfrac{-7 + \sqrt{73}}{4} \approx 0.386$ or $x = \dfrac{-7 - \sqrt{73}}{4} \approx -3.886$

407

Chapter 10

Basic Algebra

EXERCISE: QUADRATIC EQUATIONS

> **DIRECTIONS:** Work out each problem. Circle the letter of your choice.

1. Solve for x: $x^2 - 2x - 15 = 0$

   SHOW YOUR WORK HERE

   A. $+5$ or -3

   B. -5 or $+3$

   C. -5 or -3

   D. $+5$ or $+3$

2. Solve for x: $x^2 + 12 = 8x$

   A. $+6$ or -2

   B. -6 or $+2$

   C. -6 or -2

   D. $+6$ or $+2$

3. Solve for x: $4x^2 = 12$

   A. $\sqrt{3}$

   B. 3 or -3

   C. $\sqrt{3}$ or $-\sqrt{3}$

   D. $\sqrt{3}$ or $\sqrt{-3}$

4. Solve for x: $3x^2 = 4x$

   A. $\dfrac{4}{3}$

   B. $\dfrac{4}{3}$ or 0

   C. $-\dfrac{4}{3}$ or 0

   D. $\dfrac{4}{3}$ or $-\dfrac{4}{3}$

5. Solve for x: $2x^2 + 3x = 7$

   A. $x = \dfrac{3+\sqrt{47}}{4}, x = \dfrac{3-\sqrt{47}}{4}$

   B. $x = \dfrac{3+\sqrt{65}}{4}, x = \dfrac{3-\sqrt{65}}{4}$

   C. $x = \dfrac{-3+\sqrt{47}}{4}, x = \dfrac{-3-\sqrt{47}}{4}$

   D. $x = \dfrac{-3+\sqrt{47}}{4}, x = \dfrac{-3-\sqrt{47}}{4}$

6. Solve for x: $3x^2 - 27 = 0$

   A. -3 or 3

   B. -27 or 27

   C. $-3\sqrt{3}$ or $3\sqrt{3}$

   D. $-\sqrt{3}$ or $\sqrt{3}$

7. Solve for x: $x(x-9) = -20$

   A. -20 or -11

   B. 11 or 20

   C. 4 or 5

   D. -5 or -4

8. Solve for x: $\dfrac{1}{3}x^2 - \dfrac{7}{6}x = -1$

   A. $-\dfrac{2}{3}$ or $-\dfrac{1}{2}$

   B. $\dfrac{2}{3}$ or $\dfrac{1}{2}$

   C. $-\dfrac{3}{2}$ or -2

   D. $\dfrac{3}{2}$ or 2

9. Solve for x: $2x^2 + 3x - 1 = 0$

SHOW YOUR WORK HERE

A. $\dfrac{1}{2}$ or -1

B. $\dfrac{-3+\sqrt{17}}{4}$ or $\dfrac{-3-\sqrt{17}}{4}$

C. -5 or $\dfrac{7}{2}$

D. $-\dfrac{3}{4}+\sqrt{17}$ or $-\dfrac{3}{4}-\sqrt{17}$

10. Solve for x: $4x^2 = 1$

A. 4 or -4

B. $\dfrac{1}{4}$ or $-\dfrac{1}{4}$

C. $\dfrac{1}{2}$ or $-\dfrac{1}{2}$

D. 2 or -2

410

Chapter 10

Basic Algebra

1. A	3. C	5. D	7. C	9. B
2. D	4. B	6. A	8. D	10. C

1. **The correct answer is A.**

$$(x-5)(x+3) =$$
$$x = 5 \text{ or } -3$$

2. **The correct answer is D.**

$$x^2 - 8x + 12 = 0$$
$$(x-6)(x-2) = 0$$
$$x = 6 \text{ or } 2$$

3. **The correct answer is C.**

$$x^2 = 3$$
$$x = \sqrt{3} \text{ or } -\sqrt{3}$$

4. **The correct answer is B.**

$$3x^2 - 4x = 0$$
$$x(3x-4) = 0$$
$$x = 0 \text{ or } \frac{4}{3}$$

5. **The correct answer is D.** Write the equation in standard form:

$$2x^2 + 3x - 7 = 0.$$

$a = 2$, $b = 3$, and $c = -7$.

$$x = \frac{-3 \pm \sqrt{(3)^2 - 4(2)(-7)}}{2(2)}$$
$$x = \frac{-3 \pm \sqrt{65}}{4}$$

The solutions are $x = \dfrac{-3+\sqrt{65}}{4}$ or $x = \dfrac{-3-\sqrt{65}}{4}$.

6. **The correct answer is A.** Isolate the squared term and take the square root of both sides:

$$3x^2 - 27 = 0$$
$$3x^2 = 27$$
$$x^2 = 9$$
$$x = \pm 3$$

7. **The correct answer is C.** Bring all terms to the left side and factor:

$$x(x-9) = -20$$
$$x^2 - 9x + 20 = 0$$
$$(x-4)(x-5) = 0$$
$$x = 4, 5$$

8. **The correct answer is D.** Clear the fractions, bring all terms to the left side, and factor:

$$\frac{1}{3}x^2 - \frac{7}{6}x = -1$$
$$6\left(\frac{1}{3}x^2 - \frac{7}{6}x\right) = 6(-1)$$
$$2x^2 - 7x = -6$$
$$2x^2 - 7x + 6 = 0$$
$$(2x-3)(x-2) = 0$$
$$x = \frac{3}{2}, 2$$

9. **The correct answer is B.** Use the quadratic formula:

$$x = \frac{-3 \pm \sqrt{3^2 - 4(2)(-1)}}{2(2)} = \frac{-3 \pm \sqrt{17}}{4}$$

10. **The correct answer is C.** Divide both sides by 4 and then take the square root:

$$4x^2 = 1$$
$$x^2 = \frac{1}{4}$$
$$x = \pm\sqrt{\frac{1}{4}}$$
$$x = \pm\frac{1}{2}$$

411

Chapter 10

Basic Algebra

LITERAL EQUATIONS

There are many equations that can be used to represent common problems, such as distance. The equation to find distance, given rate and time, is written as $d = rt$. An equation which is solved for one variable in particular, such as d in the distance formula, is called a **literal equation**. Here are some examples:

Example:

Solve for l in the equation $P = 2l + 2w$.

Solution:

Subtract $2w$ from both sides of the equation. This will eliminate it from the right side of the equation.

$$P - 2w = 2l$$

Divide both sides of the equation to solve for l.

$$\frac{P - 2w}{2}; \frac{P}{2} - w = l$$

Example:

Solve for c in the equation $E = mc^2$.

Solution:

Divide both sides by m. This will eliminate it from the right side of the equation.

$$\frac{E}{m} = c^2$$

Take the square root of both sides to solve for c.

$$\sqrt{\frac{E}{m}} = c$$

Example:

The volume of a cone can be found using the formula $V = \frac{1}{3}\pi r^2 h$. Solve for r.

Solution:

Divide both sides by h: $\frac{V}{h} = \frac{1}{3}\pi r^2$

Divide both sides by pi: $\frac{V}{\pi h} = \frac{1}{3}r^2$

Multiply both sides by 3: $3 \times \frac{V}{\pi h} = \frac{1}{3}r^2 \times 3$

Take the square root of both sides: $\sqrt{3 \times \frac{V}{\pi h}} = r$

EXERCISE: LITERAL EQUATIONS

DIRECTIONS: Work out each problem. Circle the letter of your choice.

---

1. Solve for x: $z = 5x - 25xy$

   SHOW YOUR WORK HERE

   A. $\dfrac{z}{-20y} = x$

   B. $\dfrac{z}{1-5y} = x$

   C. $\dfrac{z}{5-25y} = x$

   D. $\dfrac{z}{30y} = x$

2. A bakery orders vanilla beans at a cost of $12.45 for a package of 10. There is a shipping cost of $6 for all sizes of shipments. Which of the following shows the equation solved for p, the total number of packages purchased, where c is the total cost of the order?

   A. $p = 6c + 12.45$

   B. $p = 12.45c + 6$

   C. $p = \dfrac{c}{12.45} - 6$

   D. $p = \dfrac{c-6}{12.45}$

3. The distance between two points is determined by the equation below, where x_1 and x_2 are the x-coordinates of two points, and y_1 and y_2 are the y-coordinates of the two points.

   $$d = \sqrt{\left(x_2 - x_1\right)^2 + \left(y_2 - y_1\right)^2}$$

   Which shows the equation solved for y_2?

   A. $y_2 = \sqrt{d^2 - \left(x_2 - x_1\right)^2} + y_1$

   B. $y_2 = \sqrt{d - \left(x_2 - x_1\right)} + y_1$

   C. $y_2 = \sqrt{d - \left(x_2 - x_1\right)} + y_1$

   D. $y_2 = \sqrt{d^2 - \left(x_2 - x_1\right)^2} + y_1$

4. Solve for x_1: $y_2 - y_1 = m(x_1 - x_2)$

   A. $x_1 = \dfrac{y_2 - y_1}{m} - x_2$

   B. $x_1 = y_2 - y_1 + mx_2$

   C. $x_1 = \dfrac{y_2 - y_1 + mx_2}{m}$

   D. $x_1 = \dfrac{y_2 - y_1 + x_2}{m}$

5. The formula for converting degrees Fahrenheit to degrees Celsius is shown below.

$$C = \frac{5}{9}(F - 32)$$

Which equation shows the formula correctly solved for F?

   A. $\dfrac{9}{5}(C + 32) = F$

   B. $\dfrac{C}{\frac{9}{5}} - 32 = F$

   C. $\dfrac{9}{5}C - 32 = F$

   D. $\dfrac{9}{5}C + 32 = F$

6. Solve for f: $\dfrac{1}{f} = \dfrac{1}{a} + \dfrac{1}{b}$

   A. $f = a + b$

   B. $f = \dfrac{ab}{a + b}$

   C. $f = ab$

   D. $f = \dfrac{ba}{b - a}$

414

Chapter 10

Basic Algebra

7. Solve for A: $C = \dfrac{3B}{A}$

   A. $A = \dfrac{3B}{C}$

   B. $A = 3BC$

   C. $A = 3B - C$

   D. $A = \dfrac{C}{3B}$

8. Solve for A: $C = \dfrac{BA}{B-A}$

   A. $A = CB + (B+1)$

   B. $A = CB - (B+C)$

   C. $A = \dfrac{CB}{B+C}$

   D. $A = \dfrac{CB}{B+1}$

9. Solve for b_1: $A = \dfrac{1}{2}h(b_1 + b_2)$

   A. $b_1 = \dfrac{A}{2} \cdot h - b_2$

   B. $b_1 = \dfrac{2A - b_2}{h}$

   C. $b_1 = \dfrac{2A + b_2}{h}$

   D. $b_1 = \dfrac{2A - hb_2}{h}$

10. Solve for t_2: $B = \dfrac{A}{M(t_1 - t_2)}$

    A. $t_2 = \dfrac{BMt_1}{A} - B$

    B. $t_2 = A - BMt_1$

    C. $t_2 = \dfrac{BMt_1 - A}{BM}$

    D. $t_2 = \dfrac{BMt_1 + A}{B}$

415

Chapter 10

Basic Algebra

1. C	3. A	5. D	7. A	9. D
2. D	4. C	6. B	8. C	10. C

1. **The correct answer is C.** Factor out an x from both terms on the right side of the equation: $z = x(5 - 25y)$

   Divide both sides by $5 - 25y$:

   $$\frac{z}{5 - 25y} = x$$

2. **The correct answer is D.** The total cost, c, is determined by the equation $12.45p + 6 = c$. To solve for p, subtract 6 from both sides. Divide both sides by 12.45 to isolate p.

3. **The correct answer is A.** Solve for y_2 by squaring both sides to remove the square root from the right side.

   $$d^2 = (x_2 - x_1)^2 + (y_2 - y_1)^2$$

   Subtract the term $(x_2 - x_1)^2$ from both sides.

   $$d^2 - (x_2 - x_1)^2 = (y_2 - y_1)^2$$

   Take the square root of both sides to eliminate the exponent on the right side.

   $$\sqrt{d^2 - (x_2 - x_1)^2} = y_2 - y_1$$

   Add y_1 to both sides of the equation.

   $$\sqrt{d^2 - (x_2 - x_1)^2} + y_1 = y_2$$

4. **The correct answer is C.**

   $$y_2 - y_1 = m(x_1 - x_2)$$
   $$y_2 - y_1 = mx_1 - mx_2$$
   $$y_2 - y_1 + mx_2 = mx_1$$
   $$x_1 = \frac{y_2 - y_1 + mx_2}{m}$$

5. **The correct answer is D.** To solve for F, divide both sides by $\frac{5}{9}$ or multiply both sides by $\frac{9}{5}$.

   $$\frac{9}{5}C = F - 32$$

   Add 32 to both sides to isolate F.

   $$\frac{9}{5}C + 32 = F$$

6. **The correct answer is B.** To solve for f, first multiply both sides of the equation by f to move it into the numerator.

   $$1 = \frac{f}{a} + \frac{f}{b}$$

   Multiply by b and then by a to write the fractions with a common denominator, ab.

   $$1 = \frac{fb}{ab} + \frac{fa}{ab}$$

   Add the fractions.

   $$1 = \frac{fb + fa}{ab}$$

   Multiply both sides of the equation by ab.

   $$ab = fb + fa$$

   Factor f out of the terms on the right side of the equation.

   $$ab = f(b + a)$$

   Divide both sides of the equation by $(b + a)$.

   $$\frac{ab}{a + b} = f$$

416

Chapter 10

Basic Algebra

7.   The correct answer is A.

$$C = \frac{3B}{A}$$
$$AC = 3B$$
$$A = \frac{3B}{C}$$

8.   The correct answer is C.

$$C = \frac{BA}{B - A}$$
$$C(B - A) = BA$$
$$CB - CA = BA$$
$$CB = BA + CA$$
$$CB = A(B + C)$$
$$A = \frac{CB}{B + C}$$

9.   The correct answer is D.

$$A = \frac{1}{2}h(b_1 + b_2)$$
$$2A = h(b_1 + b_2)$$
$$2A = hb_1 + hb_2$$
$$2A - hb_2 = hb_1$$
$$b_1 = \frac{2A - hb_2}{h}$$

10.   The correct answer is C.

$$B = \frac{A}{M(t_1 - t_2)}$$
$$BM(t_1 - t_2) = A$$
$$BMt_1 - BMt_2 = A$$
$$BMt_1 - A = BMt_2$$
$$t_2 = \frac{BMt_1 - A}{BM}$$

417

Chapter 10

Basic Algebra

ROOTS AND RADICALS

ADDING AND SUBTRACTING

Rules for adding and subtracting radicals are much the same as for adding and subtracting variables. Radicals must be exactly the same if they are to be added or subtracted, and they merely serve as a label that does not change.

$$4\sqrt{2} + 3\sqrt{2} = 7\sqrt{2}$$
$$\sqrt{2} + 2\sqrt{2} = 3\sqrt{2}$$
$$\sqrt{2} + \sqrt{3} \text{ cannot be added}$$

Sometimes, when radicals are not the same, simplification of one or more radicals will make them the same. Remember that radicals are simplified by factoring out any perfect square factors.

$$\sqrt{27} + \sqrt{75}$$
$$\sqrt{9 \cdot 3} + \sqrt{25 \cdot 3}$$
$$3\sqrt{3} + 5\sqrt{3} = 8\sqrt{3}$$

MULTIPLYING AND DIVIDING

In multiplying and dividing, treat radicals in the same way as you treat variables. They are factors and must be handled as such.

$$\sqrt{2} \cdot \sqrt{3} = \sqrt{6}$$
$$2\sqrt{5} \cdot 3\sqrt{7} = 6\sqrt{35}$$
$$\left(2\sqrt{3}\right)^2 = 2\sqrt{3} \cdot 2\sqrt{3} = 4 \cdot 3 = 12$$
$$\frac{\sqrt{75}}{\sqrt{3}} = \sqrt{25} = 5$$
$$\frac{10\sqrt{3}}{5\sqrt{3}} = 2$$

SIMPLIFYING

To simplify radicals that contain a sum or difference under the radical sign, add or subtract first, then take the square root.

$$\sqrt{\frac{x^2}{9} + \frac{x^2}{16}} = \sqrt{\frac{16x^2 + 9x^2}{144}} = \sqrt{\frac{25x^2}{144}} = \frac{5|x|}{12}$$

If you take the square root of each term before combining, you would have $\frac{x}{3} + \frac{x}{4}$, or $\frac{7x}{12}$, which is clearly not the same answer. Remember that $\sqrt{25}$ is 5. However, if you write that $\sqrt{25}$ as $\sqrt{16 + 9}$, you cannot say it is $4 + 3$, or 7. *Always* combine the quantities within a radical sign into a single term before taking the square root.

418

Chapter 10

Basic Algebra

RADICALS

In solving equations containing radicals, always get the radical alone on one side of the equation; then square both sides to remove the radical and solve. Remember that all solutions to radical equations must be checked, as squaring both sides may sometimes result in extraneous roots.

Example:

Solve for x: $\sqrt{x+5} = 7$

Solution:

$$x + 5 = 49$$

$$x = 44$$

Checking, we have $\sqrt{49} = 7$, which is true.

Example:

Solve for x: $\sqrt{x} = -6$

Solution:

You may have written the answer: $x = 36$.

Checking, we have $\sqrt{36} = -6$, which is not true, as the radical sign means the positive, or principal, square root only.

This equation has no solution because $\sqrt{36} = 6$, not -6.

Example:

Solve for x: $\sqrt{x^2 + 6} - 3 = x$

Solution:

$$\sqrt{x^2+6} - 3 = x$$
$$\sqrt{x^2+6} = x + 3$$
$$x^2 + 6 = x^2 + 6x + 9$$
$$6 = 6x + 9$$
$$-3 = 6x$$
$$-\frac{1}{2} = x$$

Checking, we have

$$\sqrt{6\frac{1}{4}} - 3 = -\frac{1}{2}$$

$$\sqrt{\frac{25}{4}} - 3 = -\frac{1}{2}$$

$$\frac{5}{2} - 3 = -\frac{1}{2}$$

$$2\frac{1}{2} - 3 = -\frac{1}{2}$$

$$-\frac{1}{2} = -\frac{1}{2}$$

This is a true statement. Therefore, $\frac{1}{2}$ is a true root.

ROOTS AS FRACTIONAL POWERS

Roots can also be written as fractional exponents to make them easier for you to work with. The square root of 4 ("$\sqrt{4}$"), for example, can also be written as $4^{\frac{1}{2}}$. The value of a square root includes both the positive and negative root, so $\sqrt{4} = \pm 2$ and $4^{\frac{1}{2}} = \pm 2$.

To write an *n*th root as a fractional exponent, use the root as the denominator of the fraction under 1 or $\sqrt[n]{x} = x^{\frac{1}{n}}$.

Use the laws of exponents to solve radical expressions and equations.

Example:

Simplify: $\sqrt{3x} \cdot \sqrt{3x}$

   A. $9x^2$

   B. $6x$

   C. $3x^2$

   D. $3x$

Solution:

$$\sqrt{3x} \cdot \sqrt{3x} = (3x)^{\frac{1}{2}} \cdot (3x)^{\frac{1}{2}}$$

$$= (3x)^{\frac{1}{2} + \frac{1}{2}}$$

$$= 3x$$

EXERCISE: ROOTS AND RADICALS

DIRECTIONS: Work out each problem. Circle the letter of your choice.

1. What is the sum of $\sqrt{12} + \sqrt{27}$?

   SHOW YOUR WORK HERE

   A. $\sqrt{29}$

   B. $3\sqrt{5}$

   C. $13\sqrt{3}$

   D. $5\sqrt{3}$

2. Compute: $\sqrt{48} - \sqrt{27}$

   A. $\sqrt{3}$

   B. $5\sqrt{3}$

   C. $\sqrt{21}$

   D. $7\sqrt{3}$

3. What is the product of $\sqrt{18x}$ and $\sqrt{2x}$, where x is greater than 0?

   A. $6x^2$

   B. $6x$

   C. $36x^2$

   D. $6\sqrt{x}$

4. Solve for x: $\dfrac{\sqrt{2}}{x - \sqrt{2}} = \sqrt{6}$

   A. $\dfrac{2}{\sqrt{3}}$

   B. $\sqrt{2}$

   C. $\dfrac{1 - \sqrt{6}}{\sqrt{2}}$

   D. $\dfrac{1 + \sqrt{6}}{\sqrt{3}}$

5. Solve for x: $\sqrt{1 - 3x} = 4$

   A. 12

   B. 16

   C. −5

   D. $\dfrac{7}{3}$

421

Chapter 10

Basic Algebra

6. Solve for x: $8\sqrt{x}+7=3\sqrt{x}+17$

SHOW YOUR WORK HERE

A. -2

B. $\sqrt{2}$

C. 2

D. 4

7. To which of these expressions is $\sqrt[3]{81x^6y^5}$ equal?

A. $9x^3y^2\sqrt[3]{y}$

B. $3\sqrt[3]{3}\,x^3y^2$

C. $9x^2y\sqrt[3]{3y}$

D. $3x^2y\sqrt[3]{3y^2}$

8. Divide $6\sqrt{45}$ by $3\sqrt{5}$.

A. 6

B. 9

C. 15

D. 30

9. $\sqrt{\dfrac{y^2}{25}+\dfrac{y^2}{16}}=$

A. $\dfrac{2y}{9}$

B. $\dfrac{9y}{20}$

C. $\dfrac{y}{9}$

D. $\dfrac{|y|\sqrt{41}}{20}$

10. To which of these expressions is the following equal:

$\dfrac{\sqrt{16}-\sqrt[4]{16}}{\sqrt[3]{16}}?$

A. 0

B. $\dfrac{1}{\sqrt[3]{2}}$

C. 1

D. $\sqrt[3]{2}$

1. D	3. B	5. C	7. D	9. D
2. A	4. D	6. D	8. A	10. B

1. **The correct answer is D.**

$$\sqrt{12} = \sqrt{4}\sqrt{3} = 2\sqrt{3}$$
$$\sqrt{27} = \sqrt{9}\sqrt{3} = 3\sqrt{3}$$
$$2\sqrt{3} + 3\sqrt{3} = 5\sqrt{3}$$

2. **The correct answer is A.** Simplify each radical term and then combine:

$$\sqrt{48} - \sqrt{27} = \sqrt{16 \cdot 3} - \sqrt{9 \cdot 3}$$
$$= \sqrt{16}\sqrt{3} - \sqrt{9}\sqrt{3}$$
$$= 4\sqrt{3} - 3\sqrt{3}$$
$$= \sqrt{3}$$

3. **The correct answer is B.**

$$\sqrt{18x} \cdot \sqrt{2x} = \sqrt{36x^2} = 6x$$

4. **The correct answer is D.** Cross-multiply and then solve the resulting linear equation:

$$\frac{\sqrt{2}}{x - \sqrt{2}} = \sqrt{6}$$
$$\sqrt{2} = \sqrt{6}\left(x - \sqrt{2}\right)$$
$$\sqrt{2} = \sqrt{6}x - \sqrt{2} \cdot \sqrt{6}$$
$$\sqrt{2} + \sqrt{2} \cdot \sqrt{6} = \sqrt{6}x$$
$$\sqrt{2}\left(1 + \sqrt{6}\right) = \sqrt{6}x$$
$$x = \frac{\sqrt{2}\left(1 + \sqrt{6}\right)}{\sqrt{6}}$$
$$x = \frac{\cancel{\sqrt{2}}\left(1 + \sqrt{6}\right)}{\cancel{\sqrt{2}}\sqrt{3}} = \frac{1 + \sqrt{6}}{\sqrt{3}}$$

5. **The correct answer is C.** Square both sides and then solve the resulting linear equation:

$$\sqrt{1 - 3x} = 4$$
$$1 - 3x = 16$$
$$1 - 16 = 3x$$
$$-15 = 3x$$
$$x = -5$$

6. **The correct answer is D.** Subtract 7 from each side of the equation: $8\sqrt{x} = 3\sqrt{x} + 10$.

Subtract $3\sqrt{x}$ from each side: $5\sqrt{x} = 10$.

Divide each side by 5: $\sqrt{x} = 2, x = 4$.

7. **The correct answer is D.** Take out expressions that are cubes from the radicand:

$$\sqrt[3]{81x^6y^5} = \sqrt[3]{3^3 \cdot 3 \cdot \left(x^2\right)^3 \cdot y^3 \cdot y^2} = 3x^2y\sqrt[3]{3y^2}$$

8. **The correct answer is A.**

$$\frac{6\sqrt{45}}{3\sqrt{5}} = 2\sqrt{9} = 2 \cdot 3 = 6$$

9. **The correct answer is D.**

$$\sqrt{\frac{y^2}{25} + \frac{y^2}{16}} = \frac{\sqrt{16y^2 + 25y^2}}{400}$$
$$= \frac{\sqrt{41y^2}}{400} = \frac{|y|\sqrt{41}}{20}$$

10. **The correct answer is B.** Simplify each radical first. Then combine like terms:

$$\frac{\sqrt{16} - \sqrt[4]{16}}{\sqrt[3]{16}} = \frac{\sqrt{4^2} - \sqrt[4]{2^4}}{\sqrt[3]{2^3 \cdot 2}} = \frac{4 - 2}{2\sqrt[3]{2}} = \frac{\cancel{2}}{\cancel{2}\sqrt[3]{2}} = \frac{1}{\sqrt[3]{2}}$$

423

Chapter 10

Basic Algebra

MONOMIALS AND POLYNOMIALS

When we add a collection of expressions together, each expression is called a **term**. *Monomial* means one term. For example, we might say that $2x + 3y^2 + 7$ is the sum of three terms, or three monomials. When we talk about a monomial, we generally mean a term that is just the product of constants and variables, possibly raised to various powers. Examples might be 7, $2x$, $-3y^2$, and $4x^2z^5$. The constant factor is called the *coefficient* of the variable factor. Thus, in $-3y^2$, -3 is the coefficient of y^2.

If we restrict our attention to monomials of the form Ax^n, the sums of such terms are called **polynomials** (in one variable). Expressions like $3x + 5$, $2x^2 - 5x + 8$, and $x^4 - 7x^5 - 11$ are all examples of polynomials. The highest power of the variable that appears is called the **degree** of the polynomial. The three examples just given are of degree 1, 2, and 5, respectively.

In evaluating monomials and polynomials for negative values of the variable, the greatest pitfall is keeping track of the minus signs. Always remember that in an expression like $-x^2$, the power 2 is applied to the x, and the minus sign in front should be thought of as (-1) times the expression. If you want to have the power apply to $-x$, you must write $(-x)^2$.

Combining Monomials

Monomials with identical variable factors can be added together by adding their coefficients. So $3x^2 + 4x^2 = 7x^2$. Of course, subtraction is handled the same way, thus:

$$3x^4 - 9x^4 = -6x^4$$

Monomials are multiplied by taking the product of their coefficients and taking the product of the variable part by adding exponents of factors with like bases. So $(3xy^2)(2xy^3) = 6x^2y^5$.

Monomial fractions can be simplified to simplest form by dividing out common factors of the coefficients and then using the usual rules for subtraction of exponents in division. An example might be:

$$\frac{6x^3y^5}{2x^4y^3} = \frac{3y^2}{x}$$

Example:

Combine into a single monomial: $\dfrac{8x^3}{4x^2} - 6x$

Solution:

The fraction simplifies to $2x$, and $2x - 6x = -4x$.

COMBINING POLYNOMIALS AND MONOMIALS

Polynomials are added or subtracted by just combining like monomial terms in the appropriate manner. Thus,

$$(3x^2 - 3x - 4) + (2x^2 + 5x - 11)$$

is summed by removing the parentheses and combining like terms, to yield

$$5x^2 + 2x - 15.$$

In subtraction, when you remove the parentheses with a minus sign in front, be careful to change the signs of *all* the terms within the parentheses. So:

$$\left(3x^2 - 3x - 4\right) - \left(2x^2 + 5x - 11\right) = 3x^2 - 3x - 4 - 2x^2 - 5x + 11$$
$$= x^2 - 8x + 7$$

(Did you notice that $3x^2 - 2x^2 = 1x^2$, but the "1" is not shown?)

To multiply a polynomial by a monomial, use the distributive property to multiply each term in the polynomial by the monomial factor. For example, $2x(2x^2 + 5x - 11) = 4x^3 + 10x^2 - 22x$.

When multiplying a polynomial by a polynomial, you are actually repeatedly applying the distributive property to form all possible products of the terms in the first polynomial with the terms in the second polynomial. The most common use of this is in multiplying two **binomials** (polynomials with two terms), such as $(x + 3)(x - 5)$. In this case, there are four terms in the result, $x \cdot x = x^2$; $x(-5) = -5x$; $3 \cdot x = 3x$; and $3 \cdot (-5) = -15$; but the two middle terms are added together to give $-2x$. Thus, the product is $x^2 - 2x - 15$.

This process is usually remembered as the **FOIL method**. That is, form the products of First, Outer, Inner, Last, as shown in the figure below.

$$(x + 3)(x - 5) = x^2 + (-5x + 3x) - 15$$

Example:

If *d* is an integer, and $(x + 2)(x + d) = x^2 - kx - 10$, what is the value of $k + d$?

Solution:

The product of the two last terms, $2d$, must be -10. Therefore, $d = -5$. If $d = -5$, then the sum of the outer and inner products becomes $-5x + 2x = -3x$, which equals $-kx$. Hence, $k = 3$, and $k + d = 3 + (-5) = -2$.

FACTORING MONOMIALS

Factoring a monomial simply involves reversing the distributive property. For example, if you are looking at $4x^2 + 12xy$, you should see that $4x$ is a factor of both terms. Hence, you could just as well write this as $4x(x + 3y)$. Multiplication using the distributive property will restore the original formulation.

Example:

If $3x - 4y = -2$, what is the value of $9x - 12y$?

Solution:

Although you seem to have one equation in two unknowns, you can still solve the problem, because you do not need to know the values of the individual variables. Just rewrite:

$$9x - 12y = 3(3x - 4y).$$

Since $3x - 4y = -2$, $9x - 12y$ is 3 times -2, or -6.

426

Chapter 10

Basic Algebra

EXERCISE: MONOMIALS AND POLYNOMIALS

DIRECTIONS: Work out each problem. Circle the letter of your choice.

---

1. $6x^3(x^2)^3 =$

   SHOW YOUR WORK HERE

   A. $6x^7$

   B. $6x^8$

   C. $6x^9$

   D. $6x^{10}$

2. $(-4a^3bc^3)^3 =$

   A. $-12a^{27}bc^9$

   B. $64a^6b^4c^6$

   C. $-64a^9b^3c^9$

   D. $-12a^6b^4c^6$

3. $\left(-2z^3\right)^2 \cdot \left(-3z^2\right)^3 =$

   A. $108\,z^{17}$

   B. $-108\,z^{12}$

   C. $36\,z^{12}$

   D. $36\,z^{10}$

4. Simplify: $\dfrac{3x^3y - 9x^2}{xy^2}$

   A. $\dfrac{-6xy}{xy^2}$

   B. $\dfrac{3x(xy-3)}{y^2}$

   C. $\dfrac{3x^2 - 9x}{y}$

   D. $3x^2 - 9x$

5. $(a^3 + 4a^2 - 11a + 4) - (8a^2 + 2a + 4) =$

   A. $-3a^2 - 13a$

   B. $a^3 - 12a^2 - 13a - 8$

   C. $a^3 - 4a^2 - 9a + 8$

   D. $a^3 - 4a^2 - 13a$

6. $(4x^3 - 2x + 5) + (8x^2 - 2x - 10) =$

   A. $4x^3 + 8x^2 - 4x - 5$

   B. $12x^2 - 4x - 5$

   C. $12x^3 - 5$

   D. $4x^3 + 8x^2 + 15$

7. Multiply: $(2 - 3x^2)(4x - 1)$

   A. $-12x^3 + 3x^2 + 8x - 2$

   B. $-12x^3 + 2$

   C. $12x^3 + 3x^2 - 2$

   D. $2x + 3x^2$

8. Multiply: $(x^2 - 1)(2x^3 + 5)$

   A. $2x^5 + 5x^2$

   B. $-2x^3 - 5$

   C. $2x^5 - 2x^3 + 5x^2 - 5$

   D. $2x^6 - 5x^2 - 2x^3 - 5$

9. $\left(\dfrac{9xy^3z^2}{33x^2yz^5}\right)^2 =$

   A. $\dfrac{9y^4}{121x^2z^6}$

   B. $\dfrac{3xz^3}{y^2}$

   C. $\dfrac{3y^4}{11x^3z^5}$

   D. $\dfrac{9y^2}{121xz^3}$

10. $6x(2 - 3x) - x(2x + 1) =$

    A. $16x^2 + 12x$

    B. $-20x^2 + 11x$

    C. $-6x^2 - 3x$

    D. $-2x^2 + 9x + 1$

428

Chapter 10

Basic Algebra

1. C	**3.** B	**5.** D	**7.** A	**9.** A
2. C	**4.** B	**6.** A	**8.** C	**10.** B

1. **The correct answer is C.**

$$6x^3\left(x^2\right)^3 = \left(6 \cdot x^3\right) \cdot \left(x^2\right)^3$$
$$= 6 \cdot x^3 \cdot x^{(2 \cdot 3)}$$
$$= 6 \cdot x^3 \cdot x^6$$
$$= 6 \cdot x^9$$
$$= 6x^9$$

2. **The correct answer is C.** Apply the exponent rules, as follows:

$$\left(-4a^3bc^3\right)^3 = (-4)^3 a^9 b^3 c^9 = -64a^9 b^3 c^9$$

3. **The correct answer is B.** Apply the exponent rules, as follows:

$$\left(-2z^3\right)^2 \cdot \left(-3z^2\right)^3 = (-2)^2 z^6 \cdot (-3)^3 z^6$$
$$= 4z^6 \cdot (-27)z^6$$
$$= -108z^{12}$$

4. **The correct answer is B.** The variable x can be factored out of the all the terms in the numerator and denominator of the fraction:

$$\frac{3x^3 y - 9x^2}{xy^2} = \frac{3x^2 y - 9x^1}{(1)y^2}$$
$$= \frac{3x^2 y - 9x}{y^2}$$

Factor the term $3x$ out of the expression in the numerator: $3x(xy - 3)$.

Because y appears in only one of the terms in the numerator, it cannot be factored out of either the numerator or the denominator.

5. **The correct answer is D.** The term a^3 will remain because there are no other like terms to subtract. Subtract the squared terms: $4a^2 - 8a^2 = -4a^2$; the single variable terms $-11a - 2a = -13a$; and the integer terms $-4 - 4 = 0$. Combining these terms with a^3 gives us $a^3 - 4a^2 - 13a$.

6. **The correct answer is A.** The only like terms that may be combined are

$$(-2x) + (-2x) = -4x \text{ and } +5 + (-10) = 5 - 10 = -5.$$

Combine all the terms to get $4x^3 + 8x^2 - 4x - 5$.

7. **The correct answer is A.** FOIL the binomials, as follows:

$$\left(2 - 3x^2\right)\left(4x - 1\right) = 2(4x) - 2(1) - \left(3x^2\right)(4x) + \left(3x^2\right)(1)$$
$$= -12x^3 + 3x^2 + 8x - 2$$

8. **The correct answer is C.** Use the FOIL method to multiply:

First: $(x^2)(2x^3) = 2x^5$

Outer: $(x^2)(5) = 5x^2$

Inner: $(-1)(2x^3) = -2x^3$

Last: $(-1)(5) = -5$

Combine the terms to get $2x^5 - 2x^3 + 5x^2 - 5$.

9. **The correct answer is A.** Apply the exponent rules, as follows:

$$\left(\frac{9xy^3 z^2}{33x^2 yz^5}\right)^2 = \left(\frac{3y^2}{11xz^3}\right)^2 = \frac{9y^4}{121x^2 z^6}$$

10. **The correct answer is B.** Use the distributive property and combine like terms:

$$6x(2 - 3x) - x(2x + 1) = 12x - 18x^2 - 2x^2 - x$$
$$= -20x^2 + 11x$$

PROBLEM SOLVING IN ALGEBRA

When you are working with algebraic word problems, remember that before you begin solving the problem you should be absolutely certain that you understand precisely what you need to answer. Once this is done, show what you are looking for algebraically. Write an equation that translates the words of the problem to the symbols of mathematics. Then solve that equation by using the techniques you just learned.

This section reviews the types of algebra problems most frequently encountered on the SAT® exam. Thoroughly familiarizing yourself with the problems that follow will help you to translate and solve all kinds of word problems.

SOLVING TWO LINEAR EQUATIONS IN TWO UNKNOWNS

Many word problems lead to equations in two unknowns. Usually, one needs two equations to solve for both unknowns, although there are exceptions. There are two generally used methods to solve two equations in two unknowns. They are the method of **substitution** and the method of **elimination by addition and subtraction**.

We'll illustrate both methods via example. Here is one that uses the method of substitution.

Example:

Mr. Green took his four children to the local craft fair. The total cost of their admission tickets was $14. Mr. and Mrs. Molina and their six children had to pay $23. What was the cost of an adult ticket to the craft fair, and what was the cost of a child's ticket?

Solution:

Expressing all amounts in dollars, let x = cost of an adult ticket and let y = cost of a child's ticket.

$$\text{For the Greens: } x + 4y = 14$$

$$\text{For the Molinas: } 2x + 6y = 23$$

The idea of the method of substitution is to solve one equation for one variable in terms of the other and then substitute that solution into the second equation. So we solve the first equation for x, because that is the simplest one to isolate:

$$x = 14 - 4y$$

and substitute into the second equation:

$$2(14 - 4y) + 6y = 23$$

This gives us one equation in one unknown that we can solve:

$$28 - 8y + 6y = 23$$

$$-2y = -5; y = 2.5$$

Now that we know $y = 2.5$, we substitute this into $x = 14 - 4y$ to get:

$$x = 14 - 4(2.5) = 4$$

Thus, the adult tickets were $4 each, and the children's tickets were $2.50 each.

Here is an example using the method of elimination.

Example:

Paul and Denise both have after-school jobs. Two weeks ago, Paul worked 6 hours, Denise worked 3 hours, and they earned a total of $39. Last week, Paul worked 12 hours, Denise worked 5 hours, and they earned a total of $75. What is each one's hourly wage?

Solution:

Again, let us express all amounts in dollars. Let x = Paul's hourly wage, and let y = Denise's hourly wage.

$$\text{For the first week: } 6x + 3y = 39$$

$$\text{For the second week: } 12x + 5y = 75$$

The idea of the method of elimination is that adding equal quantities to equal quantities gives a true result. So we want to add some multiple of one equation to the other one so that if we add the two equations together, one variable will be eliminated. In this case, it is not hard to see that if we multiply the first equation by −2, the coefficient of x will become −12. Now when we add the two equations, x will be eliminated. Hence,

$$
\begin{array}{r}
-12x - 6y = -78 \\
12x + 5y = 75 \\
\hline
-y = -3
\end{array}
$$

Thus, $y = 3$. We now substitute this into either of the two equations. Let's use the first:

$$6x + (3)(3) = 39; x = 5.$$

Thus, Denise makes only $3 per hour, while Paul gets $5.

WORD PROBLEMS IN ONE OR TWO UNKNOWNS

Word problems can be broken down into a number of categories. To do **consecutive integer** problems, you need to remember that consecutive integers differ by 1, so a string of such numbers can be represented as $n, n + 1, n + 2 \ldots$

Rate-time-distance problems require you to know the formula $d = rt$. That is, distance equals rate times time.

Here are some examples of several types of word problems.

431

Chapter 10

Basic Algebra

Example:

Movie tickets are $13.50 for adults and $8 for senior citizens. On Saturday night, a total of 436 adults and senior citizens attended, and the movie theater collected $4,885 from these adults and senior citizens. How many senior citizens were at the movie theater?

Solution:

To solve the problem, you must write two different equations using the data in the question. Let a be the number of adults and s represent senior citizens.

$$a + s = 436$$

You also know that $a \times \$13.50$ can be used to find the total amount the movie theater collected for adult tickets and $s \times \$8$ to find the total amount collected for senior citizen tickets. Together these dollar amounts total $4,885.

$$13.5a + 8s = 4,885$$

Solve using elimination, by multiplying the first equation by –8 to eliminate one of the variables during addition of the equations:

$$(-8)(a + s) = (-8)(436)$$
$$-8a + -8s = -3,488$$

Add the equations:

$$-8a + -8s = -3,488$$
$$+13.5a + 8s = 4,885$$
$$5.5a = 1,397$$
$$a = 254$$

254 adults attended, so $436 - 254 = 182$ senior citizens were at the movie theater.

Example:

A supermarket places two orders for regular and extra-large packages of paper towels. The first order had 48 regular and 120 extra-large packages and cost $644.40. The second order had 60 regular and 40 extra-large and cost $338. What is the difference in cost between a regular and extra-large package of paper towels?

Solution:

Write two equations using the data given in the question. Use r to represent a regular package of paper towels and e to represent an extra-large package.

$$48r + 120e = 644.40$$
$$60r + 40e = 338$$

Multiply the bottom equation by –3 to eliminate e:

$$(-3)(60r + 40e) = (-3)(338)$$
$$-180r - 120e = -1,014$$

Add the two equations:

$$48r + 120e = 644.4$$
$$+ -180r - 120e = -1,014$$
$$-132r = -369.6$$
$$r = 2.8$$

The price of a regular package of paper towels is $2.80. To find the price of an extra-large package, substitute 2.8 into one of the equations:

$$(48)(2.8) + 120e = 644.4$$
$$120e = 510$$
$$e = 4.25$$

The difference in cost between an extra-large package and a regular package of paper towels is:

$$\$4.25 - \$2.80 = \$1.45$$

Example:

It took Andrew 15 minutes to drive downtown at 28 miles per hour to get a pizza. How fast did he have to drive back in order to be home in 10 minutes?

Solution:

15 minutes is $\frac{1}{4}$ of an hour. Hence, going 28 miles per hour, the distance to the pizza parlor can be computed using the formula $d = rt$; $d = (28)\left(\frac{1}{4}\right) = 7$ miles. Since 10 minutes is $\frac{1}{6}$ of an hour, we have the equation $7 = r\frac{1}{6}$.

Multiplying by 6, $r = 42$ mph.

FRACTION PROBLEMS

A fraction is a ratio between two numbers. If the value of a fraction is $\frac{2}{3}$, it does not mean the numerator must be 2 and the denominator 3. The numerator and denominator could be 4 and 6, respectively, or 1 and 1.5, or 30 and 45, or any of infinitely many combinations. All you know is that the ratio of numerator to denominator will be 2:3. Therefore, the numerator may be represented by $2x$, the denominator by $3x$, and the fraction by $\frac{2x}{3x}$.

Example:

The value of a fraction is $\frac{3}{4}$. If 3 is subtracted from the numerator and added to the denominator, the value of the fraction is $\frac{2}{5}$. Find the original fraction.

Solution:

Let the original fraction be represented by $\frac{3x}{4x}$. If 3 is subtracted from the numerator and added to the denominator, the new fraction becomes $\frac{3x-3}{4x+3}$.

We know that the value of the new fraction is $\frac{2}{5}$.

$$\frac{3x-3}{4x+3} = \frac{2}{5}$$

Cross-multiply to eliminate fractions.

$$15x - 15 = 8x + 6$$
$$7x = 21$$
$$x = 3$$

Therefore, the original fraction is $\frac{3x}{4x} = \frac{9}{12}$.

Chapter 10
Basic Algebra

EXERCISE: PROBLEM SOLVING IN ALGEBRA

> **DIRECTIONS:** Work out each problem. Circle the letter of your choice.

1. A train with a heavy load travels from Albany to Binghamton at 15 miles per hour. After unloading the load, it travels back from Binghamton to Albany at 20 miles per hour. The trip from Albany to Binghamton took 1.5 hours longer than the return trip. Which of the following equations can be used to calculate the time, t, it took for the train to go from Albany to Binghamton?

   A. $1.5t = 20t$

   B. $15t = 20t - 30$

   C. $t = 20t - 30$

   D. $15t = 20 + 30$

2. If a fleet of m buses uses g gallons of gasoline every two days, how many gallons of gasoline will be used by 4 buses every five days?

   A. $\dfrac{10g}{m}$

   B. $10gm$

   C. $\dfrac{10m}{g}$

   D. $\dfrac{20g}{m}$

3. A faucet is dripping at a constant rate. If, at noon on Sunday, 3 ounces of water have dripped from the faucet into a holding tank and, at 5 p.m. on Sunday, a total of 7 ounces have dripped into the tank, how many ounces will have dripped into the tank by 2:00 a.m. on Monday?

   A. 10

   B. $\dfrac{51}{5}$

   C. 12

   D. $\dfrac{71}{5}$

4. Prior to the 2016 Summer Olympics, the world record in 800-meter freestyle swimming was approximately 8 minutes and 15 seconds. Marta is recording her times in seconds, *s*, for the 800-meter freestyle competition at her school. Which expression below could be used to calculate Marta's time as a percentage of that world record?

A. $\dfrac{s}{8.25} \times 100$

B. $\left(\dfrac{s}{60} \div 8.15\right) \times 100$

C. $\left(\dfrac{s}{60} \div 495\right) \times 100$

D. $\dfrac{s}{495} \times 100$

5. Jill is four years older than Beth. Beth's age is three years less than twice Laura's age. How old is Jill if the sum of all three ages is 43 years?

A. 9

B. 15

C. 19

D. 22

6. Tania has nine more $5 bills than $10 bills, and three times as many $10 bills as $1 bills. If the total amount of money she has is $965, how many $10 bills does she have?

A. 20

B. 45

C. 60

D. 69

7. An experienced cashier can check out six customers in 10 minutes. A novice cashier can check out four customers in 10 minutes. How long would it take the two cashiers, working together, to check out 85 customers?

A. 1 hour

B. 1 hour, 10 minutes

C. 1 hour, 25 minutes

D. 1 hour, 45 minutes

8. The sum of four consecutive even numbers is 140. What is the second smallest of these numbers?

   A. 30

   B. 34

   C. 36

   D. 40

9. At a yoga studio, you can either pay $130 for a monthly membership and $5 per class you attend, or you can just pay $15 per class you attend. Which of the following systems of linear equations could be used to determine how many classes, x, you would need to attend for the monthly costs to be the same?

   A. $\begin{cases} C = 130(x+5) \\ C = 15 + x \end{cases}$

   B. $\begin{cases} C = 130 + 5x \\ C = 15x \end{cases}$

   C. $\begin{cases} C = 5x \\ C = 15x \end{cases}$

   D. $\begin{cases} C = 130 \\ C = 5x \end{cases}$

10. Nick burns 10 calories per minute rowing and 12 calories per minute lifting weights. He spends 45 minutes total rowing and lifting weights and burns 504 calories in so doing. Which of these systems of linear equations could be used to determine the number of minutes rowing, x, and the number of minutes spent lifting weights, y?

   A. $\begin{cases} 22(x+y) = 504 \\ x + y = 45 \end{cases}$

   B. $\begin{cases} 10 + 12 = 504x \\ y = 45 + x \end{cases}$

   C. $\begin{cases} 10x + 12y = 45 \\ x + y = 504 \end{cases}$

   D. $\begin{cases} 10x + 12y = 504 \\ x + y = 45 \end{cases}$

| 1. B | 3. D | 5. C | 7. C | 9. B |
| 2. A | 4. D | 6. C | 8. B | 10. D |

1. **The correct answer is B.** Use the distance formula $d = rt$. The train's rate from Albany to Binghamton is 15mph. Its time can be expressed as t. The train's rate from Binghamton to Albany is 20mph. Its time can be expressed as $t - 1.5$.

   For the trip from Albany to Binghamton: $d = 15t$

   For the trip from Binghamton to Albany:

   $$d = 20(t - 1.5) = 20t - 30$$

   Since the distance from Albany to Binghamton is equal to the distance from Binghamton to Albany, we can set these two expressions equal to each other:

   $$15t = 20t - 30$$

2. **The correct answer is A.** Running m buses for two days is the same as running one bus for $2m$ days. If we use g gallons of gasoline, each bus uses $\frac{g}{2m}$ gallons each day. So if you multiply the number of gallons per day used by each bus by the number of buses and the number of days, you should get total gasoline usage.

   That is, $\frac{g}{2m} \times (4)(5) = \frac{10g}{m}$.

3. **The correct answer is D.** In 5 hours, 4 ounces $(7 - 3)$ have dripped. Therefore, the drip rate is $\frac{4}{5}$ of an ounce per hour.

   From 5:00 p.m. on Sunday until 2:00 a.m. on Monday is 9 hours, which means the total will be:

   $$7 + \frac{4}{5} \times 9 = 7\frac{36}{5} = \frac{71}{5}$$

4. **The correct answer is D.** Convert the world record of 8 minutes and 15 seconds to seconds by multiplying 8 minutes $\times$ 60 sec/min = 480 seconds. Add 15:

   $$480 + 15 = 495 \text{ seconds.}$$

   Divide Marta's time, s, by the world record, 495: $\frac{s}{495}$ and multiply by 100 to express it as a percent. So the correct answer is $\frac{s}{495} \times 100$.

5. **The correct answer is C.** Let x be Laura's age (in years). Beth's age is $2x - 3$ years and Jill's age is $(2x - 3) + 4$ years. Summing these expressions and setting them equal to 43 yields the following equation to solve for x:

   $$x + (2x - 3) + (2x - 3) + 4 = 43$$
   $$5x - 2 = 43$$
   $$5x = 45$$
   $$x = 9$$

   Jill's age is $2(9) - 3 + 4 = 19$ years.

6. **The correct answer is C.** Let x be the number of $1 bills. There are $3x$ $10 bills and $3x + 9$ $5 bills. Multiply the number of each type of bill by the dollar value of that bill, add these expressions, and set the sum equal to 965 to obtain the following equation:

   $$1x + 10(3x) + 5(3x + 9) = 965$$
   $$x + 30x + 15x + 45 = 965$$
   $$46x = 920$$
   $$x = 20$$

   There are $3(20) = 60$ $10 bills.

438

Chapter 10

Basic Algebra

7. **The correct answer is C.** The number of customers checked out in 10 minutes by the pair of cashiers is $6 + 4 = 10$. The rate at which the pair checks out customers is 10 customers per 10 minutes, or 60 customers per hour (since 1 hour = 60 minutes). The time it takes the pair to check out 85 customers is

$\frac{85}{60}$ hour = 1 hour, 25 minutes.

8. **The correct answer is B.** Let x be the smallest of the four consecutive even integers. The other three are $x + 2, x + 4$, and $x + 6$. Since the sum is 140, we get the equation:

$$x + (x+2) + (x+4) + (x+6) = 140$$
$$4x + 12 = 140$$
$$4x = 128$$
$$x = 32$$

The four consecutive even integers are 32, 34, 36, and 38. The second smallest is 34.

9. **The correct answer is B.** The cost, C, of the version in which a customer pays a monthly membership is $C = 130 + 5x$, where x is the number of classes attended that month. The cost of the other option is $15x$. Since we are asked to find the number of classes for which the costs are the same, this is also equal to C. Hence the desired system is given in choice B as follows:

$$\begin{cases} C = 130 + 5x \\ C = 15x \end{cases}$$

10. **The correct answer is D.** First, the sum of the number of minutes spent rowing and the number of minutes spent lifting weights is 45 minutes; this gives the equation $x + y = 45$. To get the other equation, we account for the number of calories burned performing each exercise. The number of calories burnt for x minutes rowing is $10x$ and the number burned for y minutes of lifting weights is $12y$. The sum must be 504, which yields the equation $10x + 12y = 504$. The desired system is given in choice D as follows:

$$\begin{cases} 10x + 12y = 504 \\ x + y = 45 \end{cases}$$

439

Chapter 10

Basic Algebra

INEQUALITIES

Algebraic inequality statements are solved just as equations are solved—by isolating the variable on one side, factoring and canceling wherever possible. However, one important rule distinguishes inequalities from equations: whenever you multiply or divide by a negative number, the inequality symbol must be reversed.

Example:

Solve for x: $3 - 5x > 18$

Solution:

Add -3 to both sides:

$$-5x > 15$$

Divide by -5, remembering to reverse the inequality:

$$x < -3$$

Example:

Solve for x: $5x - 4 > 6x - 6$

Solution:

Collect all x terms on the left and numerical terms on the right. Remember that, as with equal signs in equations, if a term crosses the inequality symbol, the term changes its sign.

$$-x > -2$$

Divide (or multiply) by -1:

$$x < 2$$

INEQUALITY SYMBOLS

Inequalities usually have many solutions (after all, there are a lot of quantities that are not equal to each other!), and solving an inequality means finding all its solutions. The following symbols are used when solving inequalities:

> greater than	< less than	≥ greater than or equal to	≤ less than or equal to

PROPERTIES OF INEQUALITIES

In the properties below, assume that a, b, and c are real numbers.

Addition Property of Inequality	Subtraction Property of Inequality
If $a > b$, then $a + c > b + c$	If $a > b$, then $a - c > b - c$
If $a < b$, then $a + c < b + c$	If $a < b$, then $a - c < b - c$
Multiplication Property of Inequality	**Division Property of Inequality**

$c > 0$
 	
  If $a > b$, then $ac > bc$
 	
  If $a < b$, then $ac < bc$
 	
$c < 0$
 	
  If $a > b$, then $ac < bc$
 	
  If $a < b$, then $ac > bc$
	$c > 0$
	
	  If $a > b$, then $\dfrac{a}{c} > \dfrac{b}{c}$
	
	  If $a < b$, then $\dfrac{a}{c} < \dfrac{b}{c}$
	
	$c < 0$
	
	  If $a > b$, then $\dfrac{a}{c} < \dfrac{b}{c}$
	
	  If $a < b$, then $\dfrac{a}{c} > \dfrac{b}{c}$

These properties are also true for inequalities that include the $\leq$ and $\geq$ symbols.

Example:

The meeting room can hold at most 250 people. If 182 people have already been admitted, how many more people can be allowed into the meeting room?

Solution:

Let x = number of people that can be admitted.

$$182 + x \leq 250$$
$$182 - 182 + x \leq 250 - 182$$
$$x \leq 68$$

There can be at most 68 more people admitted to the meeting room.

441

Chapter 10

Basic Algebra

Example:

To stay healthy, an adult's goal should be to walk at least 10,000 steps each day. A fitness tracker showed that a person had walked 6,349 steps. What is the minimum number of steps this person can take to reach this goal?

Solution:

Let x = number of steps.

$$6,349 + x \geq 10,000$$
$$6,349 - 6,349 + x \geq 10,000 - 6,349$$
$$x \geq 3,651$$

The person must walk at least 3,651 more steps.

Example:

Alexander plans on mowing lawns this summer. He charges $20 per lawn. How many lawns will he have to mow in order to earn at least $575?

Solution:

Let x = number of lawns.

$$20x \geq 575$$
$$\frac{20x}{20} \geq \frac{575}{20}$$
$$x \geq 28.75$$

Alexander must mow at least 29 lawns to earn at least $575.

You can also use the properties of inequality to solve multi-step inequalities.

Example:

The marching band members are making a banner for the pep rally. The banner is in the shape of a rectangle that is 12 ft. long. They have no more than 32 ft. of fringe for the banner. What are the possible widths of the banner?

Solution:

Let w = width of the banner and l = length of the banner. Use the perimeter formula $(2l + 2w \leq P)$ to find the possible allowable widths.

$$2(12) + 2w \leq 32$$
$$24 + 2w \leq 32$$
$$2w \leq 8$$
$$\frac{2w}{2} \leq \frac{8}{2}$$
$$w \leq 4$$

The width of the banner can be 4 ft. or less.

Example:

A prepaid cell phone has a balance of $40. Calls are $0.04 per minute, and texts are $0.07 per text. If 342 texts were used, how many minutes can be used for calls?

Solution:

Let x = number of minutes used on calls and y = number of texts.

$$0.04x + 0.07y \leq 40$$
$$0.04x + 0.07(342) \leq 40$$
$$0.04x + 23.94 \leq 40$$
$$0.04x \leq 16.06$$
$$\frac{0.04x}{0.04} \leq \frac{16.06}{0.04}$$
$$x \leq 401.5$$

The number of minutes that can be used for calls is 401 or fewer.

EXERCISE: INEQUALITIES

DIRECTIONS: Work out each problem. Circle the letter of your choice.

1. If $3x - 8 \geq 4x$, then

   A. $-8 \leq x$

   B. $-8 \geq x$

   C. $-8 < x$

   D. $-8 > x$

2. If $-9x + 7 < 43$, then

   A. $x \geq -4$

   B. $x \leq -4$

   C. $x > -4$

   D. $x < -4$

3. The admission to the local carnival is $6. You want to play games that cost $1.50 per game. If you have $30, how many games can you play?

   A. At least 24

   B. No more than 20

   C. Less than or equal to 16

   D. Greater than or equal 20

4. You order a bouquet of flowers that contains roses and carnations. You have only $48 to spend. Roses cost $3 each, and carnations cost $1.25 each. How many roses can be in the bouquet if there are 18 carnations in the bouquet? Let *r* represent the number of roses.

   A. $r \geq 8$

   B. $r \leq 9$

   C. $r \geq 9$

   D. $r \leq 8$

SHOW YOUR WORK HERE

5. Bike rentals cost $15 for the first 2 hours and $6 for any additional hours. Ali wants to bike for more than 2 hours, but she has only $35. Which inequality represents the situation where h is the total number of hours Ali can bike?

   A. $6 + 15h \le 35$

   B. $6(h - 2) + 15 \le 35$

   C. $6h + 15 \le 35$

   D. $6(h + 2) + 15 \le 35$

6. Selena is adding trim to a rectangular tablecloth that measures 108 inches long. If she has 330 inches of trim, what is the greatest possible width of the tablecloth?

   A. At most 54 inches

   B. At most 57 inches

   C. At most 222 inches

   D. At most 114 inches

7. If $-36 \le -3x$, then

   A. $x \ge -33$.

   B. $x \le 12$.

   C. $x \ge 12$.

   D. $x \le -33$.

8. If $3x > -12$, then

   A. $x > -4$.

   B. $x < -4$.

   C. $x > -15$.

   D. $x < -15$.

445

Chapter 10

Basic Algebra

9. Adam spent less than $110 on a pair of gloves and four headbands. The pair of gloves cost $45. If x is the cost (in dollars) of one headband, which inequality can be used to determine the maximum cost of one headband?

   A. $4(x + 45) < 110$

   B. $4x < 110 + 45$

   C. $45 + 4x < 110$

   D. $45(4) + x < 100$

10. The sum of two consecutive odd integers is at most 85. Which inequality could be used to find the largest pair of such integers?

   A. $x + (x + 1) \geq 85$

   B. $x + (x + 2) \geq 85$

   C. $x + (x + 1) \leq 85$

   D. $x + (x + 2) \leq 85$

446

Chapter 10

Basic Algebra

1. B	3. C	5. B	7. B	9. C
2. C	4. D	6. B	8. A	10. D

1. **The correct answer is B.** Subtracting $3x$ from both sides leaves $-8 \geq x$.

2. **The correct answer is C.**

$$-9x + 7 < 43$$
$$-9x < 36$$
$$x > -4$$

By dividing by -9, you reverse the inequality sign.

3. **The correct answer is C.**

$$6 + 1.5x \leq 30$$
$$1.5x \leq 24$$
$$\frac{1.5x}{1.5} \leq \frac{24}{1.5}$$
$$x \leq 16$$

4. **The correct answer is D.**

$$3r + 1.25c \leq 48$$
$$3r + 1.25(18) \leq 48$$
$$3r + 22.5 \leq 48$$
$$3r \leq 25.5$$
$$\frac{3r}{3} \leq \frac{25.5}{3}$$
$$r \leq 8.5$$

There can only be at most 8 roses in the bouquet.

5. **The correct answer is B.** The cost for the first 2 hours is $15. Subtract the 2 hours from the total number of hours (h), and multiply by $6 an hour to compute the cost for the number of hours over 2. Be sure to add the initial $15 for the first 2 hours:

$$6(h - 2) + 15 \leq 35$$

6. **The correct answer is B.**

$$2l + 2w \leq 330$$
$$2(108) + 2w \leq 330$$
$$216 + 2w \leq 330$$
$$2w \leq 114$$
$$\frac{2w}{2} \leq \frac{114}{2}$$
$$w \leq 57$$

The tablecloth can be at most 57 in. wide.

7. **The correct answer is B.** Divide both sides by -3 and reverse the inequality sign:

$$-36 \leq -3x$$
$$12 \geq x$$
$$x \leq 12$$

8. **The correct answer is A.** Divide both sides by 3. The inequality sign stays the same.

$$3x > -12$$
$$x > -4$$

9. **The correct answer is C.** To solve, you need an expression for the total cost; in other words, the cost of the pair of gloves plus the cost of 4 headbands, or $45 + 4x$. This must be less than 110, so the desired inequality is $45 + 4x < 110$.

10. **The correct answer is D.** Let x be the smaller of the two odd integers. The next consecutive odd integer is $x + 2$. Since the sum of these two integers must not exceed 85, we get the inequality $x + (x + 2) \leq 85$.

447

Chapter 10

Basic Algebra

SUMMING IT UP

- In complex questions, don't look for easy solutions.

- Always keep in mind what is being asked.

- Keep the negatives and positives straight when you're doing polynomial math.

- Don't be distracted by strange symbols.

- An equation can have one solution, infinitely many solutions, or no solutions.

- Let a, b, and c be real numbers.

   - If $a > b$, then $a + c > b + c$

   - If $a < b$, then $a + c < b + c$

   - If $a > b$, then $a - c > b - c$

   - If $a < b$, then $a - c < b - c$

   - If $c > 0$, then if $a > b$, then $ac > bc$ and if $a < b$, then $ac < bc$

   - If $c < 0$, then if $a > b$, then $ac < bc$ and if $a < b$, then $ac > bc$

- You can graph a system of linear inequalities in the coordinate plane. The solution of the system is where the graphs of the inequalities overlap.

WANT TO KNOW MORE?

Access more practice questions, valuable lessons, helpful tips, and expert strategies for the following basic algebra review topics in *Peterson's Online Course for the SAT® Exam*:

- Algebra Strategy

- Inequalities

- Linear Equations

- Polynomials

- Quadratics

- Solving Equations

To purchase and access the course, go to **www.petersons.com/testprep/sat**.

CHAPTER 11:
GEOMETRY

OVERVIEW

- Geometric Notation
- Angle Measurement
- Intersecting Lines
- Area
- Circles
- Volume
- Triangles
- Parallel Lines
- Coordinate Geometry
- Exercise: Geometry
- Summing It Up

GEOMETRIC NOTATION

1. A **point** is represented by a dot and denoted by a capital letter.

Point *P*

2. A **line** can be denoted in two different ways. First, a small letter can be placed next to the line. For example, the diagram below depicts line *l*. The arrowheads on both ends of the line indicate that lines extend infinitely in both directions.

3. A line can also be denoted by placing a small double-headed arrow over two of its points. The diagram below depicts line $\overleftrightarrow{AB}$.

4. A **line segment** is the part of a line between two of its points, which are called the endpoints of the line segment. A line segment is denoted by placing a small line segment over the two endpoints. The diagram below depicts the line segment $\overline{AB}$.

5. The length of a line segment is denoted by placing its two endpoints next to each other. In the diagram below, $CD = 7$.

6. Two line segments that have the same length are said to be **congruent**. The symbol for congruence is $\cong$. Thus, if $AB = 12$ and $EF = 12$, then $\overline{AB}$ is congruent to $\overline{EF}$, or $\overline{AB} \cong \overline{EF}$.

7. A **ray** is the part of a line beginning at one point, called the **endpoint**, and extending infinitely in one direction. A ray is denoted by placing a small one-headed arrow over its endpoint and another point on the ray. The first diagram below depicts the ray $\overrightarrow{AB}$, and the second diagram depicts the ray $\overleftarrow{AC}$.

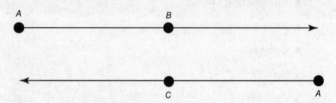

8. Two lines that cross each other are said to **intersect**. Two lines that do not intersect are said to be **parallel**. The symbol $\parallel$ is used to represent parallel lines. In the diagrams below, line k intersects line l at point P, while lines m and n are parallel, that is, $m \parallel n$.

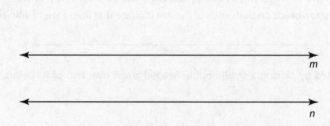

ANGLE MEASUREMENT

1. When two rays share a common endpoint, they form **angles**. The point at which the rays intersect is called the **vertex** of the angle, and the rays themselves are called the **sides** of the angle.

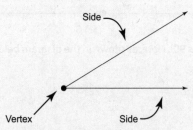

2. The symbol for angle is ∠. Angles can be denoted in several different ways. The most common way to denote an angle is to name a point on one side, then the vertex, and then a point on the other side as shown in the diagram below.

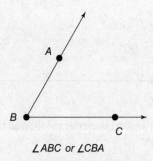

∠ABC or ∠CBA

Angles can also be denoted by writing a letter or a number within the angle, as shown below.

If there is no ambiguity, an angle can be named by simply naming the vertex.

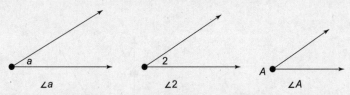

∠a   ∠2   ∠A

3. The size of an angle is measured in **degrees**. The symbol for degree is °. A full circle contains 360°, and all other angles can be measured as a fractional part of a full circle. Typically, the measure of an angle is written in the interior of the angle, near the vertex.

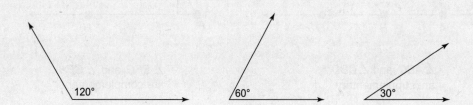

120°   60°   30°

4. A **straight angle** is an angle that measures 180°.

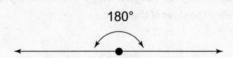

5. A **right angle** is an angle that measures 90°. Note, as shown in the diagram below, a "box" is used to represent a right angle.

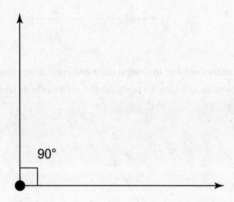

6. The measure of an angle is denoted by writing the letter m followed by the name of the angle. For example, m∠ABC = 45° tells that angle *ABC* has a measure of 45°.

7. Two angles that have the same number of degrees are said to be **congruent**. Thus, if m∠P = m∠Q, then ∠P ≅ ∠Q.

8. Two angles whose measures add up to 180° are said to be **supplementary**. Two angles whose measures add up to 90° are said to be **complementary**.

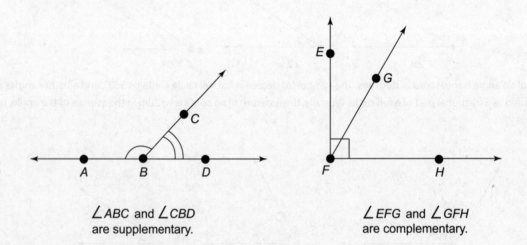

∠ABC and ∠CBD
are supplementary.

∠EFG and ∠GFH
are complementary.

9. To convert degrees to radians, multiply the degree measure by $\dfrac{\pi \text{ radians}}{180°}$.

Example:

Convert 85° to radians:

Solution:

$$85° = 85\left(\frac{\pi \text{ radians}}{180°}\right) = \frac{17\pi}{36}$$

To convert from radians to degrees, multiply the radian measure by $\frac{180°}{\pi \text{ radians}}$.

Example:

Convert $\frac{\pi}{6}$ radians to degrees:

Solution:

$$\frac{\pi}{6} = \left(\frac{\pi \text{ radians}}{6}\right)\left(\frac{180°}{\pi \text{ radians}}\right) = 30°$$

INTERSECTING LINES

1. When two lines intersect, four angles are formed. The angles opposite each other are congruent.

    $\angle 1 \cong \angle 3$ and $\angle 2 \cong \angle 4$

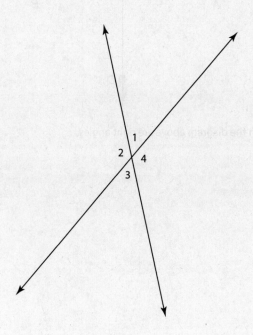

2. When two lines intersect, the angles adjacent to each other are supplementary.

m∠5 + m∠6 = 180°

m∠6 + m∠7 = 180°

m∠7 + m∠8 = 180°

m∠8 + m∠5 = 180°

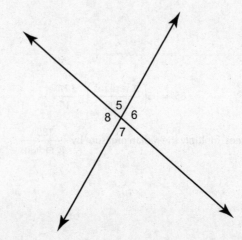

If you know the measure of any one of the four angles formed when two lines intersect, you can determine the measures of the other three. For example, if m∠1 = 45°, then m∠3 = 45°, and m∠2 = m∠4 = 180° − 45° = 135°.

3. Two lines that intersect at right angles are said to be *perpendicular*. In the figure below, $\overrightarrow{AB}$ is perpendicular to $\overrightarrow{CD}$. This can be denoted as $\overrightarrow{AB} \perp \overrightarrow{CD}$.

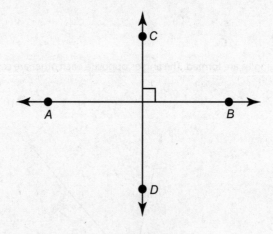

Note that all four of the angles in the diagram above are right angles.

AREA

Many of the geometry problems you will encounter on the SAT® exam will ask about the **perimeter** or **area** of a polygon. A **polygon** is a closed plane figure that consists of straight line segments called *sides*. The perimeter of a closed plane figure is the distance around the figure and is computed by adding all the lengths of the segments/sides that form its outer boundary. The area of a two-dimensional plane figure is the number of unit squares needed to cover it. The units of area measure are square inches, square feet, square yards, square centimeters, square meters, and so on. Following are useful area formulas for common plane figures:

1. Rectangle $= bh$

Area $= 6 \cdot 3 = 18$

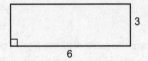

2. Parallelogram $= bh$

Area $= 8 \cdot 4 = 32$

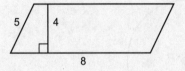

3. Square $= s^2$

Area $= 6^2 = 36$

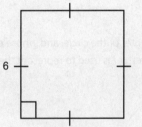

Square $= \dfrac{1}{2}d^2$ (d = diagonal)

Area $= \dfrac{1}{2}(10)(10) = 50$

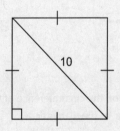

4. Triangle $= \dfrac{1}{2}bh$

Area $= \dfrac{1}{2}(12)(4) = 24$

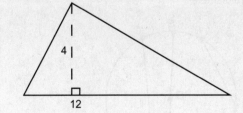

455

Chapter 11

Geometry

5. Trapezoid = $\frac{1}{2}h(b_1 + b_2)$

Area = $\frac{1}{2}(5)(16) = 40$

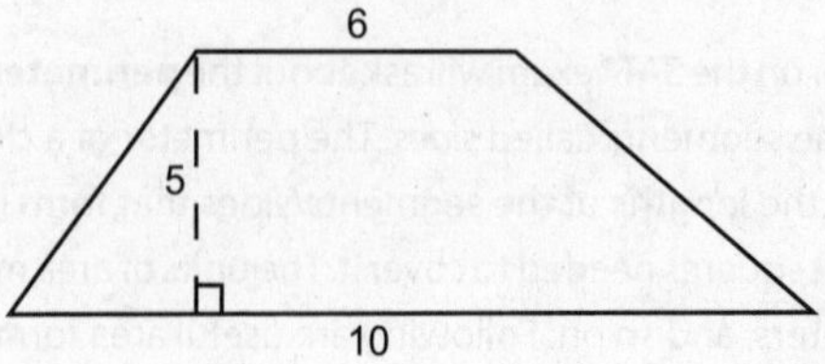

CIRCLES

1. A **circle** is a closed flat figure formed by a set of points all of which are the same distance from a point called the **center**. The boundary of the circle is called the **circumference**, and the distance from the center to any point on the circumference is called the **radius**. A circle is denoted by naming the point at its center, that is, the circle whose center is at point *P* is called circle *P*.

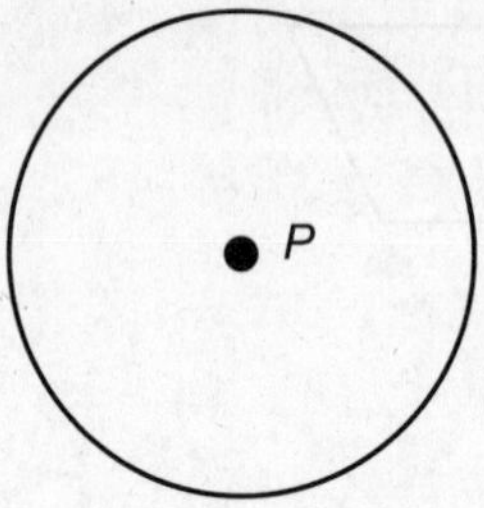

2. A **diameter** of a circle is a line segment that passes through the center of the circle, and whose endpoints lie on the circle. The diameter of a circle is twice as long as its radius. Typically, the letter *r* is used to represent the radius of a circle, and the letter *d* is used to represent the diameter.

$2r = d$

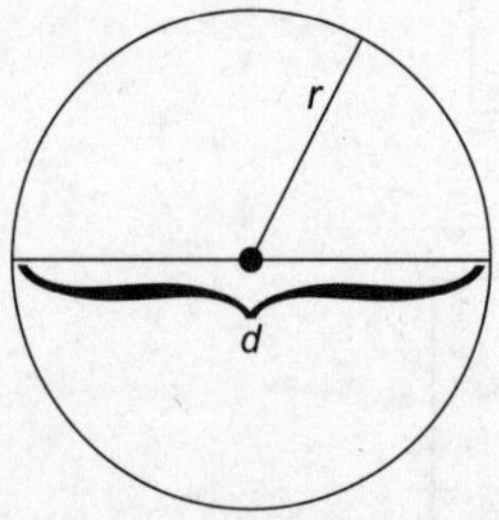

3. A **chord** of a circle is a line segment both of whose endpoints lie on the circumference of the circle. The chords of a circle have different lengths, and the length of the longest chord is equal to the diameter.

$\overline{AB}$, $\overline{CD}$, and $\overline{EF}$ are chords of circle *O*. $\overline{EF}$ is also a diameter.

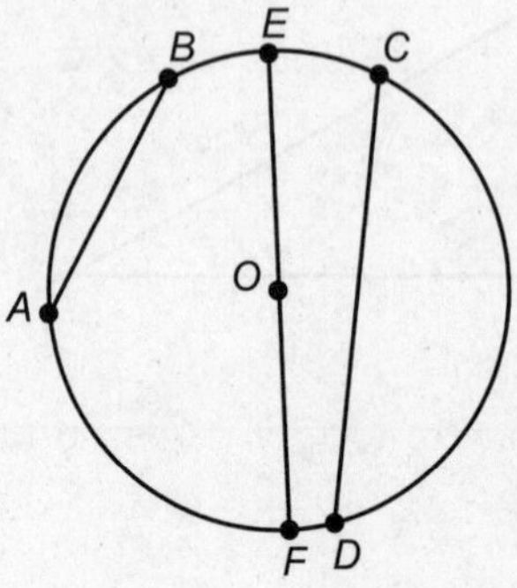

4. A **tangent** is a line that intersects the circle at exactly one point. A radius drawn to the point of intersection is perpendicular to the tangent line.

$\overline{OQ} \perp \overleftrightarrow{CD}$

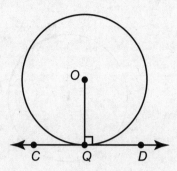

5. A **central angle** is an angle that is formed by two radii of a circle. As the diagram below shows, the vertex of a central angle is the center of the circle.

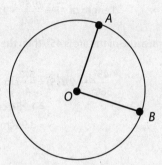

Central angle ∠ AOB

6. A central angle is equal in degrees to the measure of the arc that it intercepts. That is, a 40° central angle intercepts a 40° arc, and a 90° central angle intercepts a 90° arc.

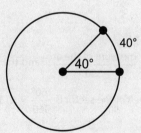

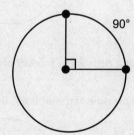

7. An **arc** is a piece of the circumference of a circle. The symbol ⌢ placed on top of the two endpoints is used to denote an arc. For example, $\widehat{MN}$ is indicated in the figure below.

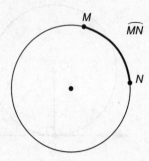

8. The **measure of an arc** is in degrees. The arc's length depends on the size of the circle because it represents a fraction of the circumference.

$$\text{Length of } \widehat{AB} = \frac{m\widehat{AB}}{360} \cdot 2\pi r$$

If the radius of a circle is 5 cm and the measure of the arc is 45°, then the length of the arc is

$$\frac{45°}{360°} \cdot 2\pi(5) = \frac{5\pi}{4} \text{ cm}$$
$$= 1.25\pi \text{ cm}$$
$$\approx 3.93 \text{ cm}$$

9. The **area of a circle** is measured using the formula πr^2. If the diameter of the circle is 12, its radius is 6:

Area of a circle $= \pi r^2$

Area $= \pi(6)^2 = 36\pi$

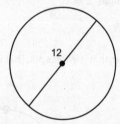

10. The **area of a sector** of a circle is the product of the ratio $\dfrac{\text{measure of the arc}}{360°}$ and the area of the circle. If the radius of

a circle is 3 cm and the measure of the arc is 60°, then the area of the sector is $\dfrac{60°}{360°} \cdot \pi(3)^2 = \dfrac{9\pi}{6} = \dfrac{3\pi}{2} \text{ cm}^2$.

Area of sector $AOB = \dfrac{m\widehat{AB}}{360} \cdot \pi r^2$

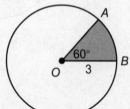

 When an SAT® exam problem asks you to find the area of a shaded region, you probably won't be able to calculate it directly. That's OK— instead, think of the shaded region as being whatever is left over when one region is subtracted or removed from a larger region. Use the formulas you know to find those two regions and perform the necessary subtraction.

11. The **length of a chord** of a circle is the product of $2r$ and $\sin\left(\dfrac{\text{measure of the central angle}}{2}\right)$. If the radius of a circle is

4 inches and the measure of the central angle is 60°, then the length of the chord is $2(4)\sin\left(\dfrac{60°}{2}\right) = 8\sin(30°) = 4$ inches.

(In a right-angled triangle, the **sine** of an angle is the length of the opposite side divided by the length of the hypotenuse. The abbreviation is **sin**.)

VOLUME

1. The volume of a right rectangular prism is equal to the product of its length, width, and height.

$V = lwh$

$V = (6)(2)(4) = 48$

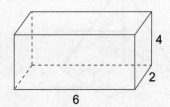

2. The volume of a cube is equal to the cube of an edge.

$V = e^3$

$V = (5)^3 = 125$

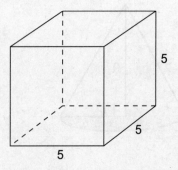

3. The volume of a right circular cylinder is equal to π times the square of the radius of the base times the height.

$V = \pi r^2 h$

$V = \pi(5)^2(3) = 75\pi$

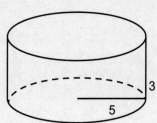

4. The volume of a sphere is equal to $\frac{4}{3}\pi$ times the cube of the radius.

$$V = \frac{4}{3}\pi r^3$$

$$v = \frac{4}{3}\pi(3)^3 = \frac{4}{3}\pi(27) = 36\pi$$

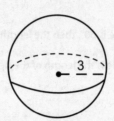

5. The volume of a right square pyramid is equal to $\frac{1}{3}$ times the product of the square of the side and the height.

$$V = \frac{1}{3}s^2h$$

$$V = \frac{1}{3}(2)^2(6)$$

$$V = 8$$

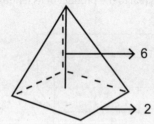

6. The volume of a right circular cone is equal to $\frac{1}{3}\pi$ times the product of the square of the radius and the height.

$$V = \frac{1}{3}\pi r^2h$$

$$V = \frac{1}{3}\pi(6)^2(9)$$

$$V = 108\pi$$

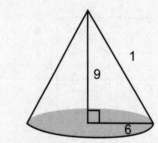

TRIANGLES

1. A **triangle** is a polygon with three sides. A **vertex** of a triangle is a point at which two of its sides meet. The symbol for a triangle is $\triangle$, and a triangle can be named by writing its three vertices in any order.

    $\triangle ABC$ contains sides $\overline{AB}$, $\overline{BC}$, and $\overline{AC}$, and angles $\angle A$, $\angle B$, and $\angle C$.

    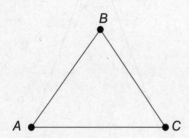

2. The sum of the measures of the angles in a triangle is 180°. Therefore, if the measures of any two of the angles in a triangle are known, the measure of the third angle can be determined.

3. In any triangle, the longest side is opposite the largest angle and the shortest side is opposite the smallest angle. In the triangle below, if $a° > b° > c°$, then $\overline{BC} > \overline{AC} > \overline{AB}$.

    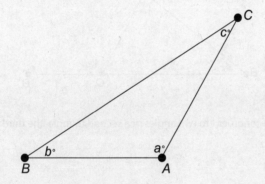

4. If two sides of a triangle are congruent, the angles opposite these sides are also congruent.

    If $\overline{AB} \cong \overline{AC}$, then $\angle B \cong \angle C$.

    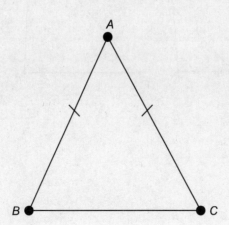

5. If two angles of a triangle are congruent, the sides opposite these angles are also congruent.

If $\angle B \cong \angle C$, then $\overline{AB} \cong \overline{AC}$.

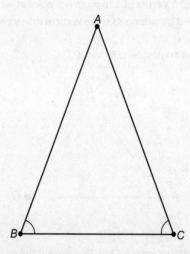

6. In the following diagram, $\angle 1$ is called an **exterior** angle. The measure of an exterior angle of a triangle is equal to the sum of the measures of the two **remote interior** angles, that is, the two interior angles that are the farthest away from the exterior angle.

$m \angle 1 = 115°$

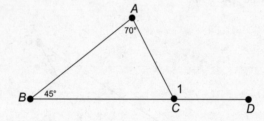

7. If two angles of one triangle are congruent to two angles of a second triangle, the third angles are also congruent.

$\angle D \cong \angle A$

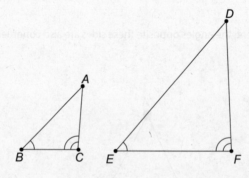

RIGHT TRIANGLES

1. **Pythagorean theorem**: The Pythagorean theorem states that the square of a hypotenuse (the leg opposite the right angle) of a right triangle is equal to the sum of the squares of the other two legs $a^2 + b^2 = c^2$.

$$(\text{leg})^2 + (\text{leg})^2 = (\text{hypotenuse})^2$$
$$4^2 + 5^2 = x^2$$
$$16 + 25 = x^2$$
$$41 = x^2$$
$$\sqrt{41} = x$$

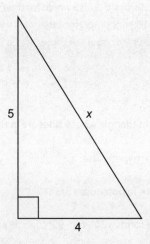

 Remember that in a right triangle, you can use the two legs (the two sides other than the hypotenuse) as base and altitude.

2. **Pythagorean triples**: These are sets of whole numbers that satisfy the Pythagorean theorem. When a given set of numbers, such as 3-4-5, forms a Pythagorean triple ($3^2 + 4^2 = 5^2$), any multiples of this set, such as 6-8-10 or 15-20-25, also form a Pythagorean triple. The most common Pythagorean triples that should be memorized are:

3-4-5
5-12-13
8-15-17
7-24-25

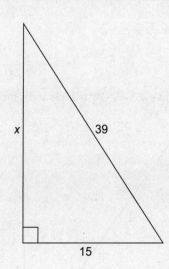

Squaring the numbers 15 and 39 in order to apply the Pythagorean theorem would take too much time. Instead, recognize the hypotenuse as 3(13). Suspect a 5-12-13 triangle. Since the given leg is 3(5), the missing leg must be 3(12), or 36, with no computation and a great saving of time.

3. The 30°-60°-90° triangle is a special right triangle whose sides are in the ratio of $x : \sqrt{3} : 2x$.

   a. The leg opposite the 30° angle is $\frac{1}{2}$ • hypotenuse.

   b. The leg opposite the 60° angle is $\frac{1}{2}$ • hypotenuse • $\sqrt{3}$.

   c. An altitude in an equilateral triangle forms a 30°–60°–90° triangle and is therefore equal to $\frac{1}{2}$ • hypotenuse • $\sqrt{3}$.

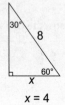

$x = 4$

$y = 5\sqrt{3}$

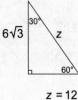

$z = 12$

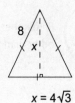

$x = 4\sqrt{3}$

4. The 45°–45°–90° triangle (isosceles right triangle) is a special right triangle whose sides are in the ratio of x: $x : \sqrt{2}$

   a. Each leg is $\frac{1}{2}$ • hypotenuse • $\sqrt{2}$.

   b. The hypotenuse is leg • $\sqrt{2}$.

   c. The diagonal in a square forms a 45°–45°–90° triangle and is therefore equal to the length of one side • $\sqrt{2}$.

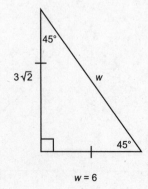

$w = 6$

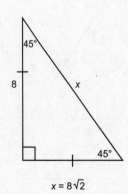

$x = 8\sqrt{2}$

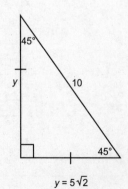

$y = 5\sqrt{2}$

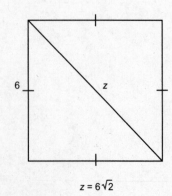

$z = 6\sqrt{2}$

5. One way to solve SAT® geometry questions that involve 30°–60°–90° triangles and 45°–45°–90° triangles is to use right triangle trigonometric relationships. In the triangle below, side $\overline{AB}$ is called the side **adjacent** to $\angle A$, side $\overline{BC}$ is called the side **opposite** $\angle A$, and side $\overline{AC}$ is the **hypotenuse**. Relative to $\angle A$, the trigonometric ratios **sine**, **cosine**, and **tangent** are defined as shown.

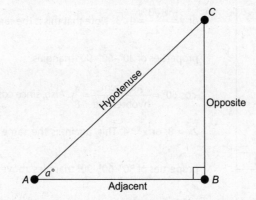

$$\text{sine } a° = \sin a° = \frac{\text{opposite}}{\text{hypotenuse}}$$

$$\text{cosine } a° = \cos a° = \frac{\text{adjacent}}{\text{hypotenuse}}$$

$$\text{tangent } a° = \tan a° = \frac{\text{opposite}}{\text{adjacent}}$$

The table below shows the values of the sine, cosine, and tangent for 30°, 45°, and 60°.

Angle a	sin $a°$	cos $a°$	tan $a°$
30°	$\dfrac{1}{2}$	$\dfrac{\sqrt{3}}{2}$	$\dfrac{\sqrt{3}}{3}$
45°	$\dfrac{\sqrt{2}}{2}$	$\dfrac{\sqrt{2}}{2}$	1
60°	$\dfrac{\sqrt{3}}{2}$	$\dfrac{1}{2}$	$\sqrt{3}$

By using the values of sine, cosine, and tangent above, problems involving 30°–60°–90° triangles and 45°–45°–90° triangles can also be solved. For example, consider the 30°-60°–90° triangle with hypotenuse of length 8. The computations that follow show how to determine the lengths of the other two sides.

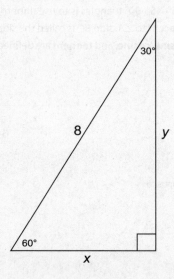

$\text{sine } 60° = \dfrac{\text{opposite}}{\text{hypotenuse}} = \dfrac{y}{8}$. Also, since , then $\dfrac{y}{8} = \dfrac{\sqrt{3}}{2}$. Cross-multiply to get $2y = 8\sqrt{3}$,

or $y = \dfrac{8\sqrt{3}}{2} = 4\sqrt{3}$. Note that this is the same answer that would be obtained using the

properties of 30°–60°–90° triangles.

$\cos 60° = \dfrac{\text{adjacent}}{\text{hypotenuse}} = \dfrac{x}{8}$. Also, since $\cos 60° = \dfrac{1}{2}$, then $\dfrac{x}{8} = \dfrac{1}{2}$. Cross-multiply to get

$2x = 8$, or $x = 4$. This, again, is the same answer that would be obtained using the

properties of 30°–60°–90° triangles above.

Here are two sample problems:

Example:

Suppose a building has a handicap ramp that rises 2.5 ft. and forms a 3° angle with the ground. How far from the base of the building is the start of the ramp? Round your answer to the nearest tenth.

Solution:

$$\tan 3° = \frac{2.5}{x}$$
$$x = \frac{2.5}{\tan 3°}$$
$$x = 47.7 \text{ feet}$$

466

Chapter 11

Geometry

Example:

Suppose a 26-ft. wire is attached to the top of a pole and staked in the ground at a 40-degree angle. Estimate the height of the pole.

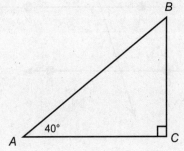

Solution:

$$\sin 40° = \frac{x}{26}$$
$$26 \sin 40° = x$$
$$16.7 \text{ ft.} \approx x$$

To find how far the stake is from the ground, you can use the Pythagorean theorem:

$$a^2 + b^2 = c^2$$
$$16.7^2 + b^2 = 26^2$$
$$19.9 \text{ ft.} \approx x$$

PARALLEL LINES

1. If two parallel lines are cut by a transversal, the alternate interior angles are congruent.

   If $\overleftrightarrow{AB} \perp \overleftrightarrow{CD}$, then

   $\angle 1 \cong \angle 3$, and

   $\angle 2 \cong \angle 4$.

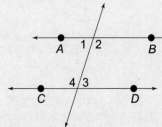

2. If two parallel lines are cut by a transversal, the corresponding angles are congruent.

   If $\overleftrightarrow{AB} \parallel \overleftrightarrow{CD}$, then

   $\angle 1 \cong \angle 5$,

   $\angle 2 \cong \angle 6$,

   $\angle 3 \cong \angle 7$, and

   $\angle 4 \cong \angle 8$.

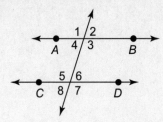

3. If two parallel lines are cut by a transversal, interior angles on the same side of the transversal are supplementary.

If $\overleftrightarrow{AB} \parallel \overleftrightarrow{CD}$, then

∠1 is supplementary to ∠4, and

∠2 is supplementary to ∠3.

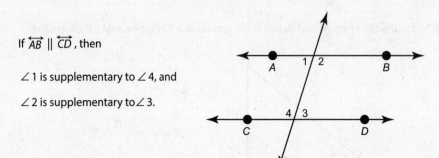

COORDINATE GEOMETRY

1. Lines and other geometric figures can be positioned on a plane by means of the **rectangular coordinate system**. The rectangular coordinate system consists of two number lines that are perpendicular and cross each other at their **origins** (0 on each of the number lines). The horizontal number line is called the *x*-axis, and the vertical number line is called the *y*-axis.

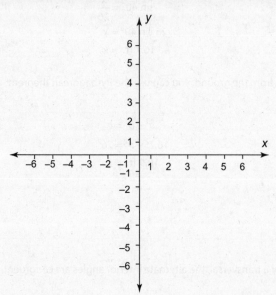

2. Any point on the plane can be designated by a pair of numbers. The first number is called the **x-coordinate** and indicates how far to move to the left (negative) or to the right (positive) on the **x-axis**, and the second number is called the **y-coordinate** and tells how far to move up (positive) or down (negative) on the **y-axis**. Generically, a point on the plane can be written as (x, y). When two points need to be expressed generically, they are typically written as (x_1, y_1) and (x_2, y_2).

The points (2, 3), (−4, 1), (−5, −2), and (2 −4) are graphed on a coordinate system as shown below.

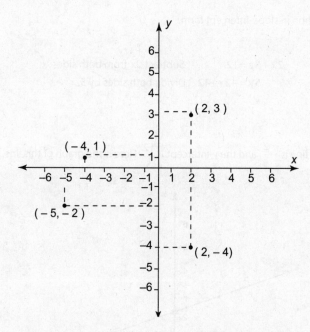

3. The **slope** of a straight line is a number that measures how steep the line is. Traditionally, the variable m is used to stand for the slope of a line. By convention, a line that increases from left to right has a positive slope, and a line that decreases from left to right has a negative slope. A horizontal line has a slope of 0 since it is "flat," and a vertical line has an undefined slope.

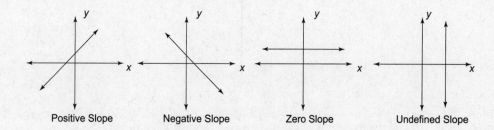

Positive Slope   Negative Slope   Zero Slope   Undefined Slope

4. If (x_1, y_1) and (x_2, y_2) are any two points on a line, the slope is given by the formula $m = \dfrac{(y_2 - y_1)}{(x_2 - x_1)}$.

Therefore, for example, if a line contains the points (5, 7) and (3, 4), the slope would be $m = \dfrac{7-4}{5-3} = \dfrac{3}{2}$. A slope of $\dfrac{3}{2}$ represents the fact that for every 2 units moved horizontally along the x-axis, the line rises vertically 3 units.

5. An equation of degree one that contains the variables x and/or y raised to the first power, but no higher, will always have a straight line as its graph. A very convenient way to write the equation of a line is in the **slope-intercept** form, $y = mx + b$. In this form, m represents the slope of the line, and b is the **y-intercept**, that is, the point where the graph crosses the y-axis.

Example:

Consider the line represented by the equation $2x + 5y = 12$.

Solution:

Begin by writing this equation in slope-intercept form.

$$2x + 5y = 12 \qquad \text{Subtract } 2x \text{ from both sides.}$$
$$5y = -2x + 12 \qquad \text{Divide both sides by 5.}$$
$$y = -\frac{2}{5}x + \frac{12}{5}$$

Therefore, the slope of the line is $-\frac{2}{5}$, and the y-intercept is $\frac{12}{5}$. Here is the graph of this line.

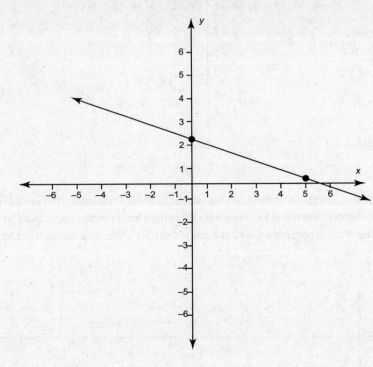

The following are sample problems:

Example:

Write the equation of the line containing the point (2, 1) and having slope 5.

Solution:

Begin by taking the slope-intercept form $y = mx + b$, and substituting $m = 5$, to obtain $y = 5x + b$. To determine the value of the y-intercept b, substitute the coordinates of the point (2, 1) into the equation.

$$y = 5x + b \quad \text{Substitute } (2, 1).$$
$$1 = 5(2) + b \quad \text{Solve for } b.$$
$$1 = 10 + b$$
$$-9 = b$$

Therefore, the equation of the line is $y = 5x - 9$.

Example:

Graph the function $f(x) = 2x + 5$.

Solution:

Begin by recognizing that the slope is 2 and the y-intercept is (0, 5). To graph this function, first graph the point (0, 5). Then move up 2 units and then to the right 1 unit. This location is (1, 7). Starting at (0, 5) again, go down 2 units and then to the left 1 unit. This location is (−1, 3). Connect these points to form the graph of the function $f(x) = 2x + 5$.

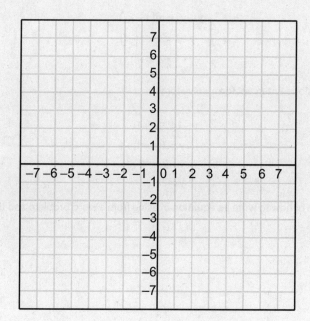

You can write an equation of a line from a graph given any two points on the line. First, use the two points to find the slope. Then use the point–slope form of an equation of a line: $y - y_1 = m(x - x_1)$. As an example, consider the graph shown below.

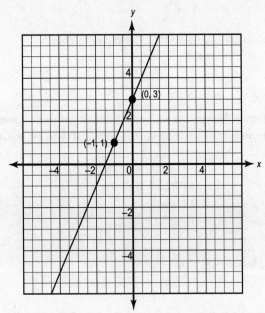

You need to first find the slope using two points on the line.

The slope formula is $m = \dfrac{y_2 - y_1}{x_2 - x_1}$. Use the points (0, 3) and (–1, 1) to find the slope.

$$m = \frac{y_2 - y_1}{x_2 - x_1} = \frac{1 - 3}{-1 - 0} = \frac{-2}{-1} = 2$$

Use the point–slope form and either given point.

$$y - y_1 = m(x - x_1)$$
$$y - 1 = 2(x - (-1))$$
$$y - 1 = 2(x + 1)$$

To write this equation in slope–intercept form, solve for y.

$$y - 1 = 2(x + 1)$$
$$y = 2(x + 1) + 1$$
$$y = 2x + 2 + 1$$
$$y = 2x + 3$$

Here is a sample question of how to write an equation of a line from a word problem and then graph the equation using the intercepts.

Example:

You decide to purchase holiday gift cards for your family. You have $300 to spend on the cards, and you purchase cards for either $20 or $30. What are three combinations of cards that you can purchase?

Solution:

To write an equation that represents this situation, first define your variables.

Let x = number of $20 gift cards purchased and y = number of $30 gift cards purchased.

Now write an equation to represent the situation.

$20x + 30y = 300$

Use the intercepts to draw the graph.

$$20x + 30y = 300$$
$$20(0) + 30y = 300$$
$$30y = 300$$
$$y = 10$$

$$20x + 30y = 300$$
$$20x + 30(0) = 300$$
$$20x = 300$$
$$x = 15$$

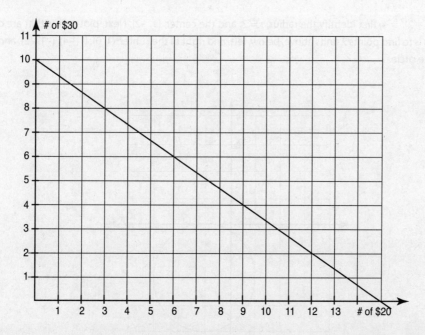

You cannot purchase a fraction of a card, so only the integer combinations can be solutions. You can purchase fifteen $20 cards and zero $30 cards, six $20 cards and six $30 cards, or zero $20 cards and ten $30 cards. (Although the question only asked for three answers, the other possible combinations are twelve $20 gift cards and two $30 gift cards, nine $20 gift cards and four $30 gift cards, and three $20 gift cards and eight $30 gift cards.)

6. The standard form of the equation of a circle with center at (h, k) and radius r is $(x - h)^2 + (y - k)^2 = r^2$. For example, to graph $y^2 = -x^2 + 64$, first rewrite the equation in standard form: $x^2 + y^2 = 64$. Then identify the radius, $r = 8$, and the center, $(0, 0)$. Now plot points that are on the circle: $(0, 8)$, $(0, -8)$, $(-8, 0)$, and $(8, 0)$. Connect the points to draw the circle.

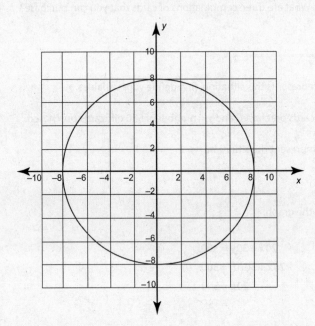

To graph $(x - 1)^2 + (y + 2)^2 = 4$, first identify the radius, $r = 2$, and the center, $(1, -2)$. Next, plot points that are on the circle. The easiest way to do this is to find points 2 units above, below, left, and right of the center: $(1, 0)$, $(1, -4)$, $(-1, -2)$, and $(3, -2)$. Connect the points to draw the circle.

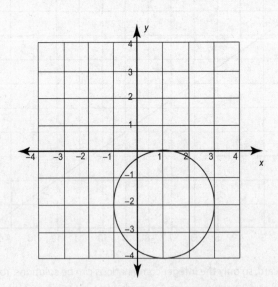

7. Parallel lines have the same slope. Therefore, one way to tell whether two lines are parallel or not is to write them in slope-intercept form and compare the slopes. To write the equation of the line that is parallel to the line $y = 3x + 7$ and contains the point (5, 2), begin by noting that the equation of the line we are looking for must have a slope of 3, just like the line $y = 3x + 7$. Thus, it must be of the form $y = 3x + b$.

$$y = 3x + b$$
$$y = 3x + b \qquad \text{Substitute (5, 2).}$$
$$2 = 3(5) + b \qquad \text{Solve for } b.$$
$$2 = 15 + b$$
$$-13 = b$$

Therefore, the equation of the line is $y = 3x - 13$.

8. The slopes of perpendicular lines are **negative reciprocals** of each other. That is, if a line has a slope of $\dfrac{a}{b}$, then the slope of the perpendicular line would be $-\dfrac{b}{a}$. Thus, the line perpendicular to the line with slope $\dfrac{2}{5}$ would have a slope of $-\dfrac{5}{2}$.

To write the equation of the line that is perpendicular to the line $y = \dfrac{1}{2}x - 7$ and contains the point (4, −3), begin by noting that the equation of the line to be determined has a slope of −2. Thus, the equation must be of the form $y = -2x + b$.

$$y = -2x + b \qquad \text{Substitute (4, −3).}$$
$$-3 = -2(4) + b \qquad \text{Solve for } b.$$
$$-3 = -8 + b$$
$$b = 5$$

Therefore, the equation of the line is $y = -2x + 5$.

475

Chapter 11

Geometry

EXERCISE: GEOMETRY

DIRECTIONS: Work out each problem. Circle the letter of your choice.

1. Determine the value of z:

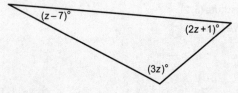

SHOW YOUR WORK HERE

A. 24

B. 31

C. 45

D. 61

2. Determine the volume of a right circular cone with base diameter 8 inches and height $\frac{5}{2}$ inches.

A. 20π cubic inches

B. $\frac{40}{3}\pi$ cubic inches

C. 40π cubic inches

D. $\frac{20}{3}\pi$ cubic inches

3. If the radius of a circle is decreased by 10%, by what percentage is its area decreased?

A. 10%

B. 19%

C. 21%

D. 81%

4. A spotlight is mounted on the ceiling 5 feet from one wall of a room and 10 feet from the adjacent wall. How many feet is it from the intersection of the two walls?

A. 15

B. $5\sqrt{2}$

C. $5\sqrt{5}$

D. $10\sqrt{2}$

5. A sphere has a diameter of 3 cm, and a cone has a height of 10 cm and a radius of 1.5 cm. How much bigger is the volume of the cone than the volume of the sphere?

A. $0.5\,\pi$

B. π

C. $3\,\pi$

D. $4.5\,\pi$

6. Find the value of y, assuming *ABCD* is a parallelogram:

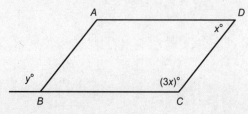

A. 45

B. 90

C. 135

D. 180

7. If $\overline{PQ} \cong \overline{QS}$, $\overline{QR} \cong \overline{RS}$ and the measure of angle *PRS* = 100°, what is the measure, in degrees, of angle *QPS*?

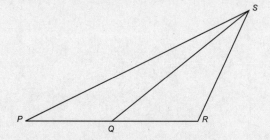

Note: Figure not drawn to scale

A. 10

B. 15

C. 20

D. 25

477

Chapter 11

Geometry

8. Find the area of the shaded region:

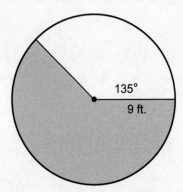

135°

9 ft.

A. 27π square feet

B. 81π square feet

C. $\frac{243}{8}$ square feet

D. $\frac{405\pi}{8}$ square feet

9. The edges of a rectangular box are in the ratio 2:3:7. If the volume of the box is 1,134 cubic meters, what is the length of the longest edge?

A. 3 meters

B. 6 meters

C. 9 meters

D. 21 meters

478

Chapter 11

Geometry

10. The surface area of a cube is 150 square feet. How many cubic feet are there in the volume of the cube?

A. 30

B. 50

C. 100

D. 125

11. What is the length of segment *PQ*?

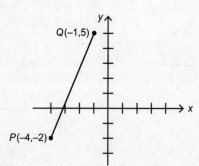

- **A.** $\sqrt{10}$
- **B.** $\sqrt{58}$
- **C.** $2\sqrt{10}$
- **D.** $2\sqrt{5}$

12. A square is inscribed in a circle of area 18π. Find a side of the square.

- **A.** 3
- **B.** 6
- **C.** $3\sqrt{2}$
- **D.** $6\sqrt{2}$

13. The cost of a 4-inch by 4-inch ceramic tile is *x* dollars. What is the cost of *y* square feet of such tiles?

- **A.** 9*xy* dollars
- **B.** 3*xy* dollars
- **C.** *xy* dollars
- **D.** $\dfrac{xy}{9}$

14. If a triangle of base 6 has the same area as a circle of radius 6, what is the altitude of the triangle?

- **A.** 6π
- **B.** 8π
- **C.** 10π
- **D.** 12π

479

Chapter 11

Geometry

15. What is the value of *x* in the figure?

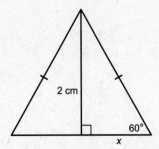

2 cm

60°

x

- **A.** 1 cm
- **B.** 2 cm
- **C.** $\dfrac{2}{\sqrt{3}}$
- **D.** $\dfrac{3}{\sqrt{2}}$

16. What is the circumference of a circle with an area of $\dfrac{49\pi}{4}$ square feet?

- **A.** $\dfrac{49\pi}{2}$
- **B.** 7π feet
- **C.** $\dfrac{7\pi}{2}$
- **D.** 14π feet

17. The ice compartment of a refrigerator is 8 inches long, 4 inches wide, and 5 inches high. How many ice cubes will it hold if each cube is 2 inches on an edge?

- **A.** 8
- **B.** 10
- **C.** 12
- **D.** 16

18. What is the equation of the line passing through the points (1, –4) and (–4, –1)?

- **A.** $5x - 3y = 17$
- **B.** $3x - 5y = 17$
- **C.** $5x + 3y = -17$
- **D.** $3x + 5y = -17$

19. What is the volume of a sphere with diameter $\frac{1}{3}$ inch?

   A. $\frac{4\pi}{81}$

   B. $\frac{\pi}{162}$

   C. $\frac{\pi}{54}$

   D. $\frac{2\pi}{27}$

20. In triangle PQR, $\overline{QS}$ and $\overline{SR}$ are angle bisectors (meaning $\angle PQS$ is congruent to $\angle SQR$, and $\angle PRS$ is congruent to $\angle SRQ$), and the measure of angle $P = 80°$. How many degrees are there in angle QSR?

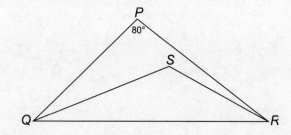

   A. 115°

   B. 120°

   C. 125°

   D. 130°

21. What is the equation of a circle with center (2, -4) and radius 9?

   A. $(x + 2)^2 + (y - 4)^2 = 9$

   B. $(x + 2)^2 + (y - 4)^2 = 81$

   C. $(x - 2)^2 + (y + 4)^2 = 81$

   D. $(x - 2)^2 + (y + 4)^2 = 3$

22. What is the value of *y* in the figure?

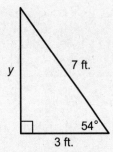

3 ft.

A. $3\sin 54°$

B. $7\sin 54°$

C. $\dfrac{\cos 54°}{7}$

D. $7\cos 54°$

23. What is the equation of the line containing the points (4, 6) and (3, 8)?

A. $y = -2x + 14$

B. $y = 2x + 14$

C. $y = -2x + 2$

D. $y = 2x - 2$

24. What is the equation of the line that runs perpendicular to the line $y - 2x = 0$ and passes through the point (−4, 0)?

A. $y = 2x + 8$

B. $y = \dfrac{1}{2}x - 4$

C. $y = 2x - 4$

D. $y = -\dfrac{1}{2}x - 2$

25. What is the area of the following region?

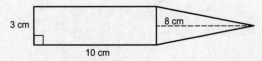

A. 24 square centimeters

B. 30 square centimeters

C. 42 square centimeters

D. 54 square centimeters

482

Chapter 11

Geometry

1. B	**6.** C	**11.** B	**16.** B	**21.** C
2. B	**7.** C	**12.** B	**17.** D	**22.** B
3. B	**8.** D	**13.** A	**18.** D	**23.** A
4. C	**9.** D	**14.** D	**19.** B	**24.** D
5. C	**10.** D	**15.** C	**20.** D	**25.** C

1. **The correct answer is B.** The sum of the three angles in a triangle is 180. This yields the equation:

$$(z-7)+(2z+1)+3z=180$$
$$6z-6=180$$
$$6z=186$$
$$z=31$$

2. **The correct answer is B.** The radius, r, is one-half the diameter or 4 inches. Using this with the height $h = \dfrac{5}{2}$ inches in the volume formula yields the following:

$$V=\frac{1}{3}\pi r^2 h=\frac{1}{3}\pi(4)^2\left(\frac{5}{2}\right)=\frac{40\pi}{3} \text{ cubic inches}$$

3. **The correct answer is B.** If the radii of the two circles have a ratio of 10:9, the areas have a ratio of 100:81. Therefore, the decrease is 19 out of 100, or 19%.

4. **The correct answer is C.**

$$5^2+10^2=x^2$$
$$25+100=x^2$$
$$x^2=125$$
$$x=\sqrt{125}=\sqrt{25}\sqrt{5}=5\sqrt{5}$$

5. **The correct answer is C.** The volume of the sphere is calculated using the formula $V = \dfrac{4}{3}\pi r^3$:

$$V=\frac{4}{3}\pi(1.5)^3=4.5\pi$$

The volume of the cone is calculated using the formula $V = \dfrac{1}{3}\pi r^2 h$:

$$V=\frac{1}{3}\pi(1.5)^2(10)=7.5\pi$$

Since $7.5\pi - 4.5\pi = 3\pi$, the volume of the cone is 3π bigger than the volume of the sphere.

6. **The correct answer is C.** Same side angles in a parallelogram sum to 180 degrees. So $x + 3x = 180$, so that $4x = 180$ and $x = 45$. Also, opposite angles are congruent, hence the measure of angle *CBA* is also 45 degrees. So $y + 45 = 180$; thus $y = 135$.

7. **The correct answer is C.**

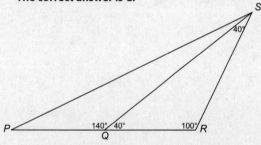

Since $\overline{QR} \cong \overline{RS}$, $\angle RQS \cong \angle RSQ$. There are 80° left in the triangle, so each of these angles is 40°.

$\angle SQP$ is supplementary to $\angle SQR$, making it 140°.

Since $\overline{QP} \cong \overline{QS}$, $\angle QPS \cong \angle QSP$. There are 40° left in the triangle, so each of these angles is 20°.

483

Chapter 11

Geometry

8. **The correct answer is D.** The central angle corresponding to the shaded region is $360 - 135 = 225$ degrees. So the area of the shaded region is $\frac{225}{360} \cdot \pi \cdot (9)^2 = \frac{405\pi}{8}$ square feet.

9. **The correct answer is D.** The width, length, and height of the rectangular box are $2x$, $3x$, and $7x$, for some real number x. Since the volume is the product of the width, length, and height, we get the equation:

$$(2x)(3x)(7x) = 1{,}134$$
$$42x^3 = 1{,}134$$
$$x^3 = 27$$
$$x = 3$$

The longest edge is $3(7) = 21$ meters.

10. **The correct answer is D.** The surface area of a cube is made up of 6 equal squares. If each edge of the cube is x, then

$$6x^2 = 150$$
$$x^2 = 25$$
$$x = 5$$

$$\text{Volume} = (\text{edge})^3 = 5^3 = 125$$

11. **The correct answer is B.** Use the distance formula:

$$\sqrt{\left(-4 - (-1)\right)^2 + \left(-2 - 5\right)^2} = \sqrt{(-3)^2 + (-7)^2}$$
$$= \sqrt{9 + 49}$$
$$= \sqrt{58}$$

12. **The correct answer is B.**

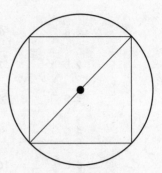

The diagonal of the square will be a diameter of the circle.

$$\pi r^2 = 18\pi$$
$$r^2 = 18$$
$$r = \sqrt{18} = \sqrt{9}\sqrt{2} = 3\sqrt{2}$$

The diameter is $6\sqrt{2}$ and, since the triangles are $45°$–$45°$–$90°$, a side of the square is 6.

13. **The correct answer is A.** There are nine 4-inch by 4-inch tiles in one square-foot tile. So the cost of one square-foot tile is $9x$ dollars. Thus, the cost of y square-foot tiles is $9xy$ dollars.

14. **The correct answer is D.** The area of the circle is $(6)^2\pi$, or 36π. In the triangle,

$$\frac{1}{2}(6)(h) = 36\pi$$
$$3h = 36\pi$$
$$h = 12\pi$$

484

Chapter 11

Geometry

15. **The correct answer is C.** The triangle is equilateral, so the height bisects the base. Thus, the length of the base is $2x$ cm; so all three sides have length $2x$ cm. The hypotenuse of the right triangle is $2x$. The base is x cm and height is 2 cm. Using the Pythagorean theorem yields the following:

$$2^2 + x^2 = (2x)^2$$
$$4 + x^2 = 4x^2$$
$$4 = 3x^2$$
$$x^2 = \frac{4}{3}$$
$$x = \sqrt{\frac{4}{3}}$$
$$x = \frac{2}{\sqrt{3}}$$

16. **The correct answer is B.** Let r be the radius of the circle. Then, $\pi r^2 = \frac{49}{4}\pi$. Solve for r:

$$\pi r^2 = \frac{49}{4}\pi$$
$$r^2 = \frac{49}{4}$$
$$r = \sqrt{\frac{49}{4}}$$
$$r = \frac{7}{2}$$

The circumference is $2\pi\left(\frac{7}{2}\right) = 7\pi$ feet.

17. **The correct answer is D.** The compartment will hold 2 layers, each of which contains 2 rows of 4 cubes each. This leaves a height of 1 inch on top empty. Therefore, the compartment can hold 16 cubes.

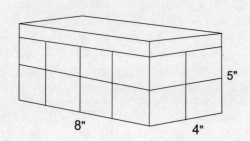

18. **The correct answer is D.** The slope of the line is $m = \frac{-1-(-4)}{-4-1} = -\frac{3}{5}$. Using the point-slope formula for the equation of a line, namely $y - y_1 = m(x - x_1)$, with the point $(1, -4)$, yields:

$$y - y_1 = m\left(x - x_1\right)$$
$$y - (-4) = -\frac{3}{5}(x - 1)$$
$$y + 4 = -\frac{3}{5}x + \frac{3}{5}$$
$$y = -\frac{3}{5}x - \frac{17}{5}$$
$$5y = -3x - 17$$
$$3x + 5y = -17$$

19. **The correct answer is B.** Let R be the radius of the sphere so that $R = \frac{1}{2}\left(\frac{1}{3}\right) = \frac{1}{6}$ inch. The volume is

$$V = \frac{4}{3}\pi R^3 = \frac{4}{3}\pi\left(\frac{1}{6}\right)^3 = \frac{4\pi}{3} \cdot \frac{1}{216} = \frac{\pi}{162} \text{ cubic inches.}$$

20. **The correct answer is D.** If m $\angle P = 80°$, there are 100° left between $\angle PQR$ and $\angle PRQ$. If they are both bisected, there will be 50° between $\angle SQR$ and $\angle SRQ$, leaving 130° for $\angle QSR$.

21. **The correct answer is C.** The standard form for a circle is $(x - h)^2 + (y - k)^2 = r^2$, where (h, k) is the center and r is the radius. Here, $h = 2$, $k = -4$, and $r = 9$. Substituting these in and simplifying yields the equation $(x - 2)^2 + (y + 4)^2 = 81$.

22. **The correct answer is B.** $\sin 54° = \frac{y}{7}$ so that $y = 7\sin 54°$.

485

Chapter 11

Geometry

23. **The correct answer is A.** The formula for the slope of a line is $m = \dfrac{(y_2 - y_1)}{(x_2 - x_1)}$, where (x_1, y_1) and (x_2, y_2) are any two points on the line. In this problem, the two points are $(4, 6)$ and $(3, 8)$, so $m = \dfrac{(y_2 - y_1)}{(x_2 - x_1)} = \dfrac{8 - 6}{3 - 4} = \dfrac{2}{-1} = -2$.

Use either point and the slope to complete the equation.

$$y = mx + b$$
$$6 = (-2)(4) + b$$
$$6 = -8 + b$$
$$14 = b$$

So the equation of the line is $y = -2x + 14$.

24. **The correct answer is D.** The given line's equation can be written as $y = 2x$. Its slope is 2, so the slope of the desired line, being perpendicular to this one, is $-\dfrac{1}{2}$. Using the point-slope formula for the equation of a line, namely $y - y_1 = m(x - x_1)$, with the point $(-4, 0)$, yields:

$$y - 0 = -\frac{1}{2}(x + 4)$$
$$y = -\frac{1}{2}x - 2$$

25. **The correct answer is C.** The area of the rectangular portion is $(3 \text{ cm})(10 \text{ cm}) = 30$ square centimeters. The area of the triangle portion is $\dfrac{1}{2}(3 \text{ cm})(8 \text{ cm}) = 12$ square centimeters. So the area of the entire region is $30 + 12 = 42$ square centimeters.

486

Chapter 11

Geometry

SUMMING IT UP

- Lines and line segments are the basic building blocks for most geometry problems.

- If a geometry problem provides a figure, mine it for clues. If a geometry problem doesn't provide a figure, sketch one.

- If a geometry problem deals with a quadrilateral or circle, look to form triangles by drawing lines through the figure.

- Geometry diagrams on the SAT® exam are not always drawn to scale. If the diagram is not drawn to scale, you may want to redraw it.

WANT TO KNOW MORE?

Access more practice questions, valuable lessons, helpful tips, and expert strategies for the following geometry review topics in *Peterson's Online Course for the SAT® Exam:*

- Angles

- Geometry Strategy

- Hard Geometry

- Quadrilaterals

- Radian Measures

- Right Triangles

- Triangle Properties

- Trigonometry

- Word Problems

To purchase and access the course, go to **www.petersons.com/testprep/sat.**

487

Chapter 11

Geometry

CHAPTER 12:
FUNCTIONS AND INTERMEDIATE ALGEBRA

OVERVIEW

- Functions
- Exercise: Functions
- Integer and Rational Exponents
- Exercise: Integer and Rational Exponents
- Solving Complex Equations
- Exercise: Solving Complex Equations
- Linear, Quadratic, and Exponential Functions
- Exercise: Linear, Quadratic, and Exponential Functions
- Summing It Up

FUNCTIONS

DEFINITIONS AND NOTATION

Let D and R be any two sets of numbers. A **function** is a rule that assigns to each element of D one and only one element of R. The set D is called the **domain** of the function, and the set R is called the **range**. A function can be specified by listing all of the elements in the first set next to the corresponding elements in the second set or by giving a rule or a formula by which elements from the first set can be associated with elements from the second set.

As an example, let the set $D = \{1, 2, 3, 4\}$ and set $R = \{5, 6, 7, 8\}$. The diagram below indicates a particular function, f, by showing how each element of D is associated with an element of R.

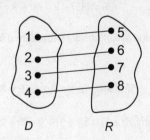

This diagram shows that the domain value of 1 is associated with the range value of 5. Similarly, 2 is associated with 6, 3 is associated with 7, and 4 is associated with 8. The function f can also be described in words by saying that f is the function that assigns to each domain value x the range value $x + 4$.

Typically, the letter x is used to represent the elements of the domain and the letter y is used to represent the elements of the range. This enables us to write the equation $y = x + 4$ to express the rule of association for the function above.

Note that as soon as a domain value x is selected, a range value y is determined by this rule. For this reason, x is referred to as the **independent variable**, and y is called the **dependent variable**.

Often, the rule of association for a function is written in **function notation**. In this notation, the symbol $f(x)$, which is read "f of x," is used instead of y to represent the range value. Therefore, the rule for our function can be written $f(x) = x + 4$. If you were asked to determine which range value was associated with the domain value of, say, 3, you would compute $f(x) = f(3) = 3 + 4 = 7$. Note that, in this notation, the letter f is typically used to stand for "function," although any other letter could also be used. Therefore, this rule could also be written as $g(x) = x + 4$.

Example:

Using function notation, write the rule for a function that associates, to each number in the domain, a range value that is 7 less than 5 times the domain value.

Solution:

$$f(x) = 5x - 7$$

Example:

Use the function from the problem above to determine the range value that is associated with a domain value of −12.

Solution:

$$f(-12) = 5(-12) - 7 = -60 - 7 = -67$$

Example:

If $f(x) = 8x + 9$, determine the value of $f(5)$, $f(q)$, $f(p^2)$, and $f(r + 3)$.

Solution:

$$f(5) = 8(5) + 9 = 40 + 9 = 49$$

In the same way, to determine the value of $f(q)$, simply substitute q for the value of x in the rule for $f(x)$. Therefore, $f(q) = 8q + 9$.

$$\text{Similarly, } f(p^2) = 8(p^2) + 9 = 8p^2 + 9.$$

$$\text{Similarly, } f(r + 3) = 8(r + 3) + 9 = 8r + 24 + 9 = 8r + 33.$$

490

Chapter 12

Functions
and
Intermediate
Algebra

FAMILIES OF FUNCTIONS

A **family** of functions is a group of functions with similar characteristics. The **parent function** is the most basic function in a family.

A **linear function** is a function whose graph is a straight line. $f(x) = x$ is the parent function for all linear functions. A **quadratic function** is a function whose graph is a parabola. The graph shown, $f(x) = x^2$, is the parent function for all quadratic functions.

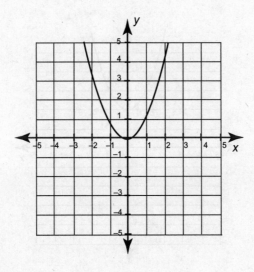

Example:

Compare $f(x) = 2x^2$ to $f(x) = x^2$.

Solution:

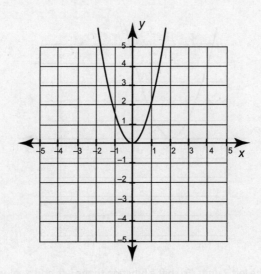

The graphs $f(x) = 2x^2$ and $f(x) = x^2$ both open up, have (0, 0) as their vertices, and have the same axis of symmetry $x = 0$. The graph $f(x) = 2x^2$ is narrower than the graph of $f(x) = x^2$.

Example:

How does the graph $f(x) = x^2 + 2$ compare to the parent function $f(x) = x^2$?

Solution:

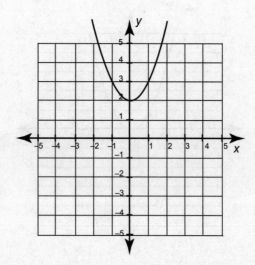

The graph $f(x) = x^2 + 2$ is two units higher than $f(x) = x^2$. The function $f(x) = x^2$ has been shifted up 2 units. The shifting, or **translating**, of a function is called a **transformation**. To move a function up, add a value b to the function: $f(x) = x^2 + b$. To move a function down, subtract a value b from the function: $f(x) = x^2 - b$.

The function $f(x) = (x + 2)^2$ looks like the following:

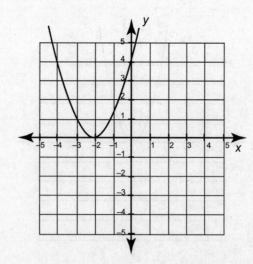

Its graph has been shifted to the left 2 units. To shift a function to the left, add a value b to inside the function: $f(x) = (x + b)^2$. To shift a function to the right, subtract a value b to inside the function:

$$f(x) = (x - b)^2.$$

The function $-f(x)$ is $f(x)$ flipped upside down (across the x-axis), while $f(-x)$ is the mirror of $f(x)$ (flipped across the y-axis):

$-f(x)$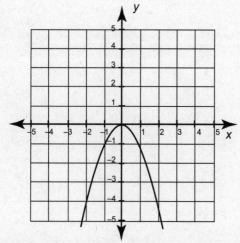

$f(-x)$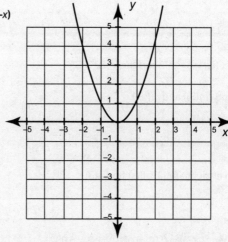

Example:

Describe how the function $f(x) = -2x^2 + 3$ compares with the graph $f(x) = x^2$.

Solution:

Both graphs have the same axis of symmetry but the graph $f(x) = -2x^2 + 3$ opens downward and is narrower than the graph of $f(x) = x^2$. The vertex of $f(x) = -2x^2 + 3$ is 3 units higher than the vertex of $f(x) = x^2$.

PERFORM OPERATIONS ON FUNCTIONS AND COMPOSITIONS

You can add, subtract, multiply, and divide any two functions.

Let $f(x) = 4x^2$ and $g(x) = x^2 + 9x + 6$

Addition: $f(x) + g(x) = 4x^2 + (x^2 + 9x + 6) = 5x^2 + 9x + 6$

Subtraction: $f(x) - g(x) = 4x^2 - (x^2 + 9x + 6) = 3x^2 - 9x - 6$

Multiplication: $f(x) \cdot g(x) = 4x^2(x^2 + 9x + 6) = 4x^4 + 36x^3 + 24x^2$

Division: $\dfrac{f(x)}{g(x)} = \dfrac{4x^2}{x^2 + 9x + 6}$

The composition of functions involves applying two functions in succession. The composition of a function $g(x)$ with a function $f(x)$ is written as $g(f(x))$, read as "g of f of x."

Example:

Let $f(x) = 6x^3 + 2$ and $g(x) = 2x^2 - 8$.

Find $f(g(3))$ and $g(f(3))$.

Solution:

To evaluate $f(g(3))$, first find $g(3)$.

$$g(3) = 2(3)^2 - 8 = 10$$

Then $f(g(3)) = f(10) = 6(10)^3 + 2 = 6,002.$

To evaluate $g(f(3))$, first find $f(3)$.

$$f(3) = 6(3)^3 + 2 = 164$$

Then $g(f(164)) = g(164) = 2(164)^2 - 8 = 53,784.$

Generally, $f(g(x)) \neq g(f(x))$.

494

Chapter 12

Functions
and
Intermediate
Algebra

EXERCISE: FUNCTIONS

DIRECTIONS: Work out each problem. Circle the letter of your choice.

1. What is the effect on the graph of the function $f(x) = 2x^2 + 5$ when it is changed to $f(x) = 2x^2 - 3$?

   A. The graph gets narrower.

   B. The graph opens down.

   C. The graph gets wider.

   D. The graph shifts down the y-axis.

2. What is the highest point on the graph of the parabola $g(x) = -(x+4)^2 - 5$?

   A. $(4, 5)$

   B. $(-4, 5)$

   C. $(-4, -5)$

   D. $(4, -5)$

3. If $m(x) = x(x+5)$ and $n(x) = 1 - \frac{1}{2}x^2$, compute $(m-n)(-2)$.

   A. -7

   B. -6

   C. -5

   D. -1

4. The profit from selling x number of sweatshirts can be described by the function $p(x) = 22x - 230$. What is the profit if 200 sweatshirts are sold?

   A. $4,170

   B. $4,280

   C. $4,400

   D. $4,630

495

Chapter 12

Functions
and
Intermediate
Algebra

5. If $d(x) = \dfrac{9 - x^2}{16 + x^2}$ and $e(x) = \sqrt{x}$, compute $(e \circ d)(x)$.

SHOW YOUR WORK HERE

A. $\dfrac{\sqrt{x}\left(9 - x^2\right)}{16 + x^2}$

B. $\dfrac{9 - x}{16 + x}$

C. $\dfrac{3 - x}{4 + x}$

D. $\sqrt{\dfrac{9 - x^2}{16 + x^2}}$

6. A company sells designer keychains. Its monthly revenue is modeled by $R(x) = 27x$, and its costs are modeled by $C(x) = 7x + 1{,}200$, where x is the number of keychains sold. Find $R(x) - C(x)$.

A. $-34x + 1{,}200$

B. $20x + 1{,}200$

C. $20x - 1{,}200$

D. $34x - 1{,}200$

7. Which of these functions is the result of shifting $f(x) = |x|$ down 5 units?

A. $g(x) = |x - 5|$

B. $g(x) = |x| - 5$

C. $g(x) = |x + 5|$

D. $g(x) = -5|x|$

8. You earn $17.50 per hour at your job. You are given a raise of 2% after 5 months. In addition, you receive $1 per hour for being a model employee. Find your new hourly wage if the $1 raise is applied before the 2% raise.

A. $18.13

B. $18.15

C. $18.85

D. $18.87

9. If $f(x) = x - \dfrac{1}{x}$ and $g(x) = x + \dfrac{1}{x}$, compute $(f \bullet g)\left(-\dfrac{1}{2}\right)$.

SHOW YOUR WORK HERE

   A. $-\dfrac{15}{4}$

   B. -2

   C. 0

   D. $\dfrac{3}{4}$

10. If $j(x) = 2\sqrt{x} - 1$ and $k(x) = |1 - x|$, compute $(j \circ k)(-3)$.

   A. 1

   B. 3

   C. 7

   D. Not defined

497

Chapter 12

**Functions
and
Intermediate
Algebra**

1. D	3. C	5. D	7. B	9. A
2. C	4. A	6. C	8. D	10. B

1. **The correct answer is D.** The vertex of the graph changes from (0, 5) to (0, –3). The original graph is translated down.

2. **The correct answer is C.** The standard form for a quadratic function is $f(x) = a(x - h)^2 + k$, where the vertex is (h, k); this is the highest point on the function if a is negative, as in the given function. Here, $h = -4$ and $k = -5$, so that the vertex is $(-4, -5)$.

3. **The correct answer is C.** $(m - n)(-2) = m(-2) - n(-2)$. Observe:

$$m(-2) = -2(3) = -6$$

$$n(-2) = 1 - \frac{1}{2}(-2)^2 = 1 - \frac{1}{2}(4) = 1 - 2 = -1$$

So $(m - n)(-2) = -6 - (-1) = -6 + 1 = -5$.

4. **The correct answer is A.**

$p(200) = 22(200) - 230 = 4,170$. The profit is $4,170.

5. **The correct answer is D.**

$$(e \circ d)(x) = e(d(x))$$
$$= e\left(\frac{9 - x^2}{16 + x^2}\right)$$
$$= \sqrt{\frac{9 - x^2}{16 + x^2}}$$

6. **The correct answer is C.**

$$R(x) - C(x) = 27x - (7x + 1,200)$$
$$= 27x - 7x - 1,200$$
$$= 20x - 1,200$$

7. **The correct answer is B.** Moving a function down 5 units is performed by subtracting 5 from the output, which here is $|x|$. The desired function is $g(x) = |x| - 5$.

8. **The correct answer is D.** Let x be your hourly wage. The function for the 2% raise is $f(x) = x + .02x = 1.02x$. The function for the $1 raise is $g(x) = x + 1$. The composition $f(g(x))$ represents the hourly wage when the $1 raise is applied before the 2% raise.

$$f(g(x)) = f(x + 1)$$
$$= 1.02(x + 1)$$
$$= 1.02(17.5 + 1)$$
$$= 1.02(18.50)$$
$$= 18.87$$

So, your new hourly wage is $18.87.

9. **The correct answer is A.**

First,
$$(f \cdot g)(x) = f(x) \cdot g(x)$$
$$= \left(x - \frac{1}{x}\right) \cdot \left(x + \frac{1}{x}\right)$$
$$= x^2 - \frac{1}{x^2}$$

Then,
$$(f \cdot g)\left(-\frac{1}{2}\right) = \left(-\frac{1}{2}\right)^2 - \frac{1}{\left(-\frac{1}{2}\right)^2}$$
$$= \frac{1}{4} - \frac{1}{\frac{1}{4}}$$
$$= \frac{1}{4} - 4$$
$$= -\frac{15}{4}$$

10. **The correct answer is B.** $(j \circ k)(-3) = f(k(-3))$. Since $k(-3) = |1 - (-3)| = |4| = 4$, we see that

$$f(k(-3)) = f(4)$$
$$= 2\sqrt{4} - 1$$
$$= 2(2) - 1$$
$$= 4 - 1$$
$$= 3$$

498

Chapter 12

Functions and Intermediate Algebra

INTEGER AND RATIONAL EXPONENTS

Chapter 10: "Basic Algebra" contains the definitions and the rules for positive integer exponents. The following section extends these definitions to integer and rational exponents.

INTEGER EXPONENTS

Negative exponents are defined in the following way:

For any positive integer n, $x^{-n} = \dfrac{1}{x^n}$. For example, $4^{-2} = \dfrac{1}{4^2} = \dfrac{1}{16}$.

Similarly, $\left(\dfrac{2}{3}\right)^{-4} = \left(\dfrac{3}{2}\right)^4 = \dfrac{3^4}{2^4} = \dfrac{81}{16}$.

All of the properties of exponents discussed in Chapter 11 apply to expressions with negative exponents as well. Thus, the

expression $x^{-7} \cdot x^4$ is equal to $x^{-3} = \dfrac{1}{x^3}$, and $\dfrac{y^{-5}}{y^{-11}} = y^{-5-(-11)} = y^{-5+11} = y^6$.

Examples:

Determine the value of the following expressions:

a. $8^{-2} \cdot 8^4$

b. $x^5 \cdot x^{-5}$

c. $\dfrac{y^4}{y^{-9}}$

d. $\dfrac{x^{-2} y^9}{x^7 y^3}$

Solutions:

a. $8^{-2} \cdot 8^4 = 8^2 = 64$

b. $x^5 \cdot x^{-5} = x^0 = x$

c. $\dfrac{y^4}{y^{-9}} = y^4 y^9 = y^{13}$

d. $\dfrac{x^{-2} y^9}{x^7 y^3} = \dfrac{y^{9-3}}{x^{7-(-2)}} = \dfrac{y^6}{x^9}$

499

Chapter 12

Functions
and
Intermediate
Algebra

Examples:

a. If $f(x) = 5^{-x}$, what is the value of $f(-2)$?

b. If $f(x) = 5^{-x}$, what is the value of $f(2)$?

Solutions:

a. $f(-2) = 5^{-(-2)} = 5^2 = 25$

b. $f(2) = 5^{-2} = \dfrac{1}{5^2} = \dfrac{1}{25}$

RATIONAL EXPONENTS

The definition of exponents can also be extended to include rational numbers:

For a rational number, x to the power of $\dfrac{1}{n}$ is defined as the nth root of x. In other words, $x^{\frac{1}{n}}$ is equal to $\sqrt[n]{x}$.

Therefore, $\sqrt{5}$ can be written as $5^{\frac{1}{2}}$.

Similarly, $8^{\frac{1}{3}}$ represents $\sqrt[3]{8}$ and is thus equal to 2.

Next, $x^{\frac{m}{n}}$ is defined to mean $(x^{\frac{1}{n}})^m$, for $x > 0$ and $n > 0$. Therefore, when you are given a number with a rational exponent, the numerator represents the power to which the number is to be raised, and the denominator represents the root to be taken. The expression $16^{\frac{5}{4}}$ tells you to take the fourth root of 16 and then raise the result to the fifth power. This expression can be evaluated in the following way: $16^{\frac{5}{4}} = \left(\sqrt[4]{16}\right)^5 = (2)^5 = 32$

In summary, all of the properties of exponents apply to expressions with rational exponents.

Examples:

Determine the value of the following expressions:

a. $27^{\frac{1}{3}}$

b. $64^{-\frac{2}{3}}$

c. $2x^{\frac{5}{6}} \cdot 3x^{-\frac{1}{3}}$

Solutions:

a. $27^{\frac{1}{3}} = \sqrt[3]{27} = 3$

b. $64^{-\frac{2}{3}} = \left(\dfrac{1}{64}\right)^{\frac{2}{3}} = \left(\sqrt[3]{\dfrac{1}{64}}\right)^2 = \left(\dfrac{1}{4}\right)^2 = \dfrac{1}{16}$

c. $2x^{\frac{5}{6}} \cdot 3x^{-\frac{1}{3}} = 6x^{\frac{5}{6}-\frac{1}{3}} = 6x^{\frac{1}{2}}$

Examples:

Simplify the following expressions:

a. $\left(25a^6\right)^{\frac{1}{2}}$

b. $\dfrac{b^{\frac{1}{3}}}{b^{-\frac{2}{3}}}$

c. $\left(c^{-\frac{1}{8}}d^{\frac{3}{4}}\right)^{16}$

d. $\sqrt{4x^3} \cdot \sqrt{8x^5}$

Solutions:

a. $\left(25a^6\right)^{\frac{1}{2}} = 25^{\frac{1}{2}}\left(a^6\right)^{\frac{1}{2}} = \sqrt{25}a^3 = 5a^3$

b. $\dfrac{b^{\frac{1}{3}}}{b^{-\frac{2}{3}}} = b^{\frac{1}{3}}b^{\frac{2}{3}} = b^{\frac{1}{3}+\frac{2}{3}} = b^1 = b$

c. $\left(c^{-\frac{1}{8}}d^{\frac{3}{4}}\right)^{16} = \left(c^{-\frac{1}{8}}\right)^{16}\left(d^{\frac{3}{4}}\right)^{16} = c^{-2}d^{12} = \dfrac{d^{12}}{c^2}$

d. $\sqrt{4x^3} \cdot \sqrt{8x^5} = 4^{\frac{1}{2}}x^{\frac{3}{2}} \cdot 8^{\frac{1}{2}}x^{\frac{5}{2}}$

$= 4^{\frac{1}{2}} \cdot 8^{\frac{1}{2}}x^{\frac{3}{2}}x^{\frac{5}{2}}$

$= 2\left(2\sqrt{2}\right)x^{\frac{3}{2}+\frac{5}{2}}$

$= 4\sqrt{2}x^4$

501

Chapter 12

Functions
and
Intermediate
Algebra

EXERCISE: INTEGER AND RATIONAL EXPONENTS

DIRECTIONS: Work out each problem. Circle the letter of your choice.

---

1. Simplify the expression: $\sqrt{8x} \cdot \sqrt{4x^3}$

   A. $32x^{\frac{3}{2}}$

   B. $16\sqrt{2x^4}$

   C. $4x^4$

   D. $4\sqrt{2}x^2$

2. Simplify the expression: $\sqrt{25x^4y^6} \cdot \sqrt{3x^3y^5}$

   A. $3x^{\frac{7}{2}}y^{\frac{11}{2}}$

   B. $5\sqrt{3}x^{\frac{7}{2}}y^{\frac{11}{2}}$

   C. $15x^{12}y^{11}$

   D. $75x^7y^{11}$

3. Which of these expressions is equivalent to $\left(\dfrac{4x^{-3}y^2}{3x^4y^{-1}}\right)^{-2}$?

   A. $\dfrac{4x^9y^3}{3}$

   B. $\dfrac{9x^{14}}{16y^6}$

   C. $\dfrac{16y^6}{9x^{14}}$

   D. $\dfrac{3}{4x^9y^3}$

4. Simplify the expression: $\dfrac{a^5b^{-2}c^{-3}}{a^{-2}b^4c^{-2}}$

   A. $\dfrac{a^7}{b^6c}$

   B. $\dfrac{a^7c}{b^2}$

   C. $\dfrac{a^3}{b^2c}$

   D. $\dfrac{a^3c^5}{b^2}$

SHOW YOUR WORK HERE

502

Chapter 12

Functions
and
Intermediate
Algebra

5. Which of these expressions is equivalent to $-\left(a^2 b^{-2}\right)^{-\frac{1}{2}}$?

SHOW YOUR WORK HERE

A. $\dfrac{a}{b}$

B. $-\dfrac{a}{b}$

C. $\dfrac{b}{a}$

D. $-\dfrac{b}{a}$

6. Simplify the expression: $\left(49x^4 y^8 z^{-6}\right)^{\frac{1}{2}}$

A. $49x^2 y^4 z^6$

B. $7x^3 y^4 z^3$

C. $\dfrac{y^4}{7x^2 z^3}$

D. $\dfrac{7x^2 y^4}{z^3}$

7. Which of these expressions is equivalent to $\dfrac{\sqrt[4]{81x^8 y^{16}}}{\sqrt[4]{x^{24} y^{20}}}$?

A. $\dfrac{3}{x^4 y}$

B. $\dfrac{3}{x^{15} y^4}$

C. $3x^4 y$

D. $3x^{15} y^4$

8. Which of these expressions is equivalent to $\dfrac{64x^{\frac{2}{3}}}{\left(64x^3\right)^{\frac{1}{2}}}$?

A. $\dfrac{2}{x^{\frac{5}{6}}}$

B. $\dfrac{2}{x}$

C. $\dfrac{8}{x^{\frac{5}{6}}}$

D. $2x$

503

Chapter 12

Functions
and
Intermediate
Algebra

9. Which of these expressions is equivalent to $\left(-\dfrac{1}{2}x^3 \right)^{-3}$?

A. $\dfrac{-8}{x^9}$

B. $\dfrac{x^9}{8}$

C. $-8x^9$

D. $-\dfrac{1}{8x^6}$

SHOW YOUR WORK HERE

10. Compute $64^{\frac{2}{3}} - 27^{\frac{1}{3}}$.

A. $\sqrt[3]{37}$

B. 5

C. 13

D. 19

504

Chapter 12

**Functions
and
Intermediate
Algebra**

1. D	3. B	5. D	7. A	9. A
2. B	4. A	6. D	8. C	10. C

1. The correct answer is D.

$$\sqrt{8x} \cdot \sqrt{4x^3} = (8x)^{\frac{1}{2}}(4x^3)^{\frac{1}{2}}$$
$$= \left(2\sqrt{2}x^{\frac{1}{2}}\right)\left(2x^{\frac{3}{2}}\right)$$
$$= 4\sqrt{2}x^2$$

2. The correct answer is B.

$$\left(25x^4y^6\right)^{\frac{1}{2}}\left(3x^3y^5\right)^{\frac{1}{2}} = 5x^2y^3 \cdot 3^{\frac{1}{2}}x^{\frac{3}{2}}y^{\frac{5}{2}}$$
$$= 5 \cdot 3^{\frac{1}{2}}x^{2+\frac{3}{2}}y^{3+\frac{5}{2}}$$
$$= 5\sqrt{3}x^{\frac{7}{2}}y^{\frac{11}{2}}$$

3. The correct answer is B. Apply the exponent rules.

$$\left(\frac{4x^{-3}y^2}{3x^4y^{-1}}\right)^{-2} = \left(\frac{4y^2y^1}{3x^4x^3}\right)^{-2}$$
$$= \left(\frac{4y^3}{3x^7}\right)^{-2}$$
$$= \left(\frac{3x^7}{4y^3}\right)^2$$
$$= \frac{3^2\left(x^7\right)^2}{4^2\left(y^3\right)^2}$$
$$= \frac{9x^{14}}{16y^6}$$

4. The correct answer is A.

$$\frac{a^5b^{-2}c^{-3}}{a^{-2}b^4c^{-2}} = a^{5-(-2)}b^{-2-4}c^{-3-(-2)}$$
$$= a^7b^{-6}c^{-1} = \frac{a^7}{b^6c}$$

5. The correct answer is D.

$$-\left(a^2b^{-2}\right)^{-\frac{1}{2}} = -\left(a^2\right)^{-\frac{1}{2}}\left(b^{-2}\right)^{\frac{1}{2}}$$
$$= -a^{-1}b^1$$
$$= -\frac{b}{a}$$

6. The correct answer is D.

$$\left(49x^4y^8z^{-6}\right)^{\frac{1}{2}} = 49^{\frac{1}{2}}x^{\frac{4}{2}}y^{\frac{8}{2}}z^{\frac{-6}{2}}$$
$$= 7x^2y^4z^{-3}$$
$$= \frac{7x^2y^4}{z^3}$$

7. The correct answer is A. Compute each radical and then simplify the resulting quotient using the exponent rules:

$$\frac{\sqrt[4]{81x^8y^{16}}}{\sqrt[4]{x^{24}y^{20}}} = \frac{\sqrt[4]{81} \cdot \sqrt[4]{x^8} \cdot \sqrt[4]{y^{16}}}{\sqrt[4]{x^{24}} \cdot \sqrt[4]{y^{20}}}$$
$$= \frac{3x^2y^4}{x^6y^5}$$
$$= \frac{3}{x^4y}$$

8. The correct answer is C.

$$\frac{64x^{\frac{2}{3}}}{\left(64x^3\right)^{\frac{1}{2}}} = \frac{64x^{\frac{2}{3}}}{(64)^{\frac{1}{2}}\left(x^3\right)^{\frac{1}{2}}}$$
$$= \frac{64x^{\frac{2}{3}}}{8x^{\frac{3}{2}}}$$
$$= \frac{8}{x^{\frac{3}{2}-\frac{2}{3}}}$$
$$= \frac{8}{x^{\frac{5}{6}}}$$

505

Chapter 12

Functions and Intermediate Algebra

9.   The correct answer is A.

$$\left(-\frac{1}{2}x^3\right)^{-3} = \left(-\frac{1}{2}\right)^{-3}\left(x^3\right)^{-3}$$
$$= (-2)^3\left(x^3\right)^{-3}$$
$$= -8x^{-9}$$
$$= -\frac{8}{x^9}$$

10.   The correct answer is C.

$$64^{\frac{2}{3}} - 27^{\frac{1}{3}} = \left(64^{\frac{1}{3}}\right)^2 - 27^{\frac{1}{3}}$$
$$= 4^2 - 3$$
$$= 16 - 3$$
$$= 13$$

506

Chapter 12

Functions
and
Intermediate
Algebra

www.petersons.com

SOLVING COMPLEX EQUATIONS

Chapter 10: "Basic Algebra" describes how to solve linear and quadratic equations. The following section discusses how to solve some of the more complex equations and inequalities that appear on the SAT® exam.

EQUATIONS INVOLVING RATIONAL EXPRESSIONS

A **rational expression** is a fraction that contains variables in the numerator and/or the denominator. The quickest way to solve equations containing rational expressions is to determine the least common denominator (LCD) of all of the fractions in the equation and then eliminate the fractions by multiplying each term in the equation by this LCD. There are four steps involved in solving such an equation:

1. Find the LCD of all of the rational expressions in the equation.
2. Multiply *every* term on both sides of the equation by this LCD.
3. Solve the resulting equation using the methods previously explained.
4. Check the solution to make certain that it actually solves the equation.

Note that step 4, checking the solution, is crucial because sometimes the process produces a solution that does not actually solve the equation. Such extraneous solutions need to be eliminated.

Example:

Solve for x: $\dfrac{7x}{5} + \dfrac{3}{8} = 10$

Solution:

The LCD of the two fractions in the equation is 40, so every term must be multiplied by 40.

$$40\left(\frac{7x}{5}\right) + 40\left(\frac{3}{8}\right) = 40(10) \qquad \text{Perform the multiplications.}$$
$$8(7x) + 5(3) = 400$$
$$56x + 15 = 400 \qquad \text{Subtract 15 from both sides.}$$
$$56x = 385 \qquad \text{Divide both sides by 56.}$$
$$x = \frac{385}{56} = \frac{55}{8} = 6\frac{7}{8}$$

Check that the answer is correct by substituting $\dfrac{55}{8}$ into the original equation.

507

Chapter 12

Functions
and
Intermediate
Algebra

Example:

Solve for x: $\dfrac{5}{x-4} - \dfrac{3}{x+4} = \dfrac{36}{x^2-16}$

Solution:

Begin by finding the LCD of the three fractions. Note that since $x^2 - 16 = (x - 4)(x + 4)$, the LCD is $(x - 4)(x + 4)$. Each term must be multiplied by this.

$$(x-4)(x+4)\left(\frac{5}{x-4}\right) - (x-4)(x+4)\left(\frac{3}{x+4}\right) = \left(\frac{36}{x^2-16}\right)(x-4)(x+4)$$

$$\begin{aligned}
(x+4)(5) - (x-4)(3) &= 36 && \text{Distribute.} \\
5x + 20 - 3x + 12 &= 36 && \text{Combine like terms.} \\
2x + 32 &= 36 && \text{Subtract 32 from both sides.} \\
2x &= 4 && \text{Divide by 2.} \\
x &= 2
\end{aligned}$$

To check the solution, substitute 2 into the equation:

$$\frac{5}{x-4} - \frac{3}{x+4} = \frac{36}{x^2-16}$$

$$\frac{5}{2-4} - \frac{3}{2+4} = \frac{36}{2^2-16}$$

$$-\frac{5}{2} - \frac{3}{6} = -\frac{36}{12}$$

$$-3 = -3$$

Therefore, the solution is $x = 2$.

508

Chapter 12

Functions
and
Intermediate
Algebra

Example:

Solve for x: $\dfrac{1}{5} - \dfrac{1}{6} = \dfrac{1}{x}$

Solution:

The LCD is $30x$. Multiply all terms by the LCD.

$$(30x)\left(\frac{1}{5}\right) - (30x)\left(\frac{1}{6}\right) = \frac{1}{x}(30x)$$

$$6x - 5x = 30$$

$$x = 30$$

If you check the value $x = 30$ in the original equation, you will find that it works.

RADICAL EQUATIONS

Equations that have variables in their radicands are called **radical equations**. For example, $\sqrt{x} = 16$ is a radical equation. To solve this radical equation, square both sides:

$$\sqrt{x} = 16$$
$$\left(\sqrt{x}\right)^2 = 16^2$$
$$x = 256$$

Check $x = 256$ in the original equation.

$$\sqrt{x} = 16$$
$$\sqrt{256} = 16?$$
$$16 = 16$$

The solution works.

Extraneous solutions may occur when you raise both sides of a radical equation to an even power. For example, if you square both sides of the equation $x = 5$ you get $x^2 = 25$. This new equation has two solutions, -5 and 5, but only 5 is the solution to the original equation.

Note the four steps involved in solving a radical equation:

1. Isolate the radical on one side of the equation.
2. Raise both sides of the equation to the same power to eliminate the radical.
3. Solve the resulting equation.
4. Check the solution.

Examples:

Solve each equation.

a. $\sqrt{2x+3} = 7$

b. $\sqrt[3]{4x-5} = 3$

c. $\sqrt[4]{2x+8} - 2 = 2$

d. $x + 2 = \sqrt{11x+12}$

509

Chapter 12

Functions and Intermediate Algebra

a.

$$\sqrt{2x+3}=7$$

$$\left(\sqrt{2x+3}\right)^2=7^2$$

$$2x+3=49$$

$$2x=46$$

$$x=23 \quad \text{Check the solution.}$$

$$\sqrt{2x+3}=7$$

$$\sqrt{2(23)+3}=7?$$

$$\sqrt{49}=7?$$

$$7=7 \qquad \text{The solution is 23}$$

b.

$$\sqrt[3]{4x-5}=3$$

$$\left(\sqrt[3]{4x-5}\right)^3=3^3$$

$$4x-5=27$$

$$4x=32$$

$$x=8 \quad \text{Check the solution.}$$

$$\sqrt[3]{4x-5}=3$$

$$\sqrt[3]{4(8)-5}=3?$$

$$\sqrt[3]{27}=3?$$

$$3=3 \qquad \text{The solution is 8.}$$

c.

$$\sqrt[4]{2x+8}-2=2$$

$$\sqrt[4]{2x+8}=4$$

$$\left(\sqrt[4]{2x+8}\right)^4=(4)^4$$

$$2x+8=256$$

$$2x=248$$

$$x=124 \quad \text{Check the solution.}$$

$$\sqrt[4]{2x+8}-2=2$$

$$\sqrt[4]{2(124)+8}-2=2?$$

$$\sqrt[4]{256}-2=2?$$

$$4-2=2?$$

$$2=2 \qquad \text{The solution is 124.}$$

d.

$$x+2=\sqrt{11x+12}$$

$$(x+2)^2=\left(\sqrt{11x+12}\right)^2$$

$$x^2+4x+4=11x+12$$

$$x^2-7x-8=0$$

$$(x-8)(x+1)=0$$

$$x=8, x=-1$$

Check the solution $x = 8$.

$$x+2=\sqrt{11x+12}$$

$$8+2=\sqrt{11(8)+12}?$$

$$10=\sqrt{100}?$$

$$10=10 \qquad \text{The solution is 8.}$$

Check the solution $x = -1$.

$$x+2=\sqrt{11x+12}$$

$$-1+2=\sqrt{11(-1)+12}?$$

$$1=\sqrt{1}?$$

$$1=1 \qquad \text{The solution is }-1.$$

The solutions are $x = 8$ and $x = -1$.

510

Chapter 12

Functions
and
Intermediate
Algebra

EXERCISE: SOLVING COMPLEX EQUATIONS

DIRECTIONS: Work out each problem. Circle the letter of your choice.

1. Solve for x: $\dfrac{2}{x-2} - \dfrac{5}{x+2} = \dfrac{2}{x^2-4}$

   A. $x = -4$

   B. $x = -2$

   C. $x = 2$

   D. $x = 4$

2. Solve for x: $\dfrac{3x}{3x-1} + \dfrac{3}{1-3x} = -1$

   A. -2

   B. $\dfrac{2}{3}$

   C. 2

   D. No solution

3. Solve for a: $\dfrac{3}{a-7} + \dfrac{5}{a^2-13a+42} = \dfrac{7}{a-6}$

   A. $a = -18$

   B. $a = -9$

   C. $a = 9$

   D. $a = 18$

4. Solve for x: $\dfrac{x}{x+1} = \dfrac{3}{x+3}$

   A. $-\sqrt{3}$ and $\sqrt{3}$

   B. 3

   C. -1 and 3

   D. 9

5. Solve for x: $\sqrt{5-4x} - x = 0$

   A. -5 and 1

   B. -1 and 5

   C. 1

   D. 5

511

Chapter 12

**Functions
and
Intermediate
Algebra**

6. Solve the equation: $\sqrt[4]{3x-2}+1=6$

    A. $x=1$

    B. $x=9$

    C. $x=17$

    D. $x=209$

7. Solve for x: $\sqrt[3]{4x^2-2x}=\sqrt[3]{5-10x}$

    A. 0

    B. $-\dfrac{5}{2}$ and $\dfrac{1}{2}$

    C. $-\dfrac{2}{5}$ and 2

    D. No solution

8. Solve the equation: $x=\sqrt{16x+225}$

    A. $x=45$

    B. $x=25$

    C. $x=-9$

    D. $x=-25$

9. Solve for t: $\dfrac{t}{4}+\dfrac{2t}{9}\geq\dfrac{3t-14}{6}$

    A. $t\leq 84$

    B. $t\leq 42$

    C. $t\geq 42$

    D. $t\geq 84$

10. Solve for x: $\sqrt[4]{\dfrac{5}{3x}}=1$

    A. $\dfrac{5}{3}$

    B. $\dfrac{3}{5}$

    C. -2

    D. $\dfrac{5}{12}$

512

Chapter 12

Functions and Intermediate Algebra

1. D	3. C	5. C	7. B	9. A
2. B	4. A	6. D	8. B	10. A

1. **The correct answer is D.** The LCD of the fractions in the equation $\dfrac{2}{x-2} - \dfrac{5}{x+2} = \dfrac{2}{x^2-4}$ is $(x-2)(x+2)$.

Multiply all terms by the LCD.

$$(x-2)(x+2)\frac{2}{x-2} - (x-2)(x+2)\frac{5}{x+2} = \frac{2}{x^2-4}(x-2)(x+2)$$
$$2(x+2) - 5(x-2) = 2$$
$$2x + 4 - 5x + 10 = 2$$
$$-3x + 14 = 2$$
$$-3x = -12$$
$$x = 4$$

Remember that you should check the answer to make certain that it solves the equation.

2. **The correct answer is B.** Rewrite the left side so that both fractions have the same denominator. Then, combine the fractions, cross-multiply, and solve for x:

$$\frac{3x}{3x-1} + \frac{3}{1-3x} = -1$$
$$\frac{3x}{3x-1} - \frac{3}{3x-1} = -1$$
$$\frac{3x-3}{3x-1} = -1$$
$$3x - 3 = -(3x - 1)$$
$$3x - 3 = -3x + 1$$
$$6x = 4$$
$$x = \frac{2}{3}$$

513

Chapter 12

**Functions
and
Intermediate
Algebra**

3. **The correct answer is C.** Note that $a^2 - 13a + 42 = (a-7)(a-6)$, so the LCD of the fractions in the equation is $(a-7)(a-6)$.

Now, multiply by the LCD.

$$(a-7)(a-6)\frac{3}{a-7} + (a-7)(a-6)\frac{5}{(a-7)(a-6)} = \frac{7}{a-6}(a-7)(a-6)$$
$$3a - 18 + 5 = 7(a-7)$$
$$3a - 13 = 7a - 49$$
$$4a = 36$$
$$a = 9$$

This solution checks.

4. The correct answer is A. Cross-multiply and then solve the resulting quadratic equation:

$$\frac{x}{x+1} = \frac{3}{x+3}$$
$$x(x+3) = 3(x+1)$$
$$x^2 + 3x = 3x + 3$$
$$x^2 = 3$$
$$x = \pm\sqrt{3}$$

5. The correct answer is C. Isolate the radical term on one side. Then, square both sides and solve the resulting quadratic equation:

$$\sqrt{5-4x} - x = 0$$
$$\sqrt{5-4x} = x$$
$$5 - 4x = x^2$$
$$x^2 + 4x - 5 = 0$$
$$(x+5)(x-1) = 0$$
$$x = -5, 1$$

Substituting these into the original equation shows that 1 is a solution, but –5 is not.

6. The correct answer is D.

$$\sqrt[4]{3x-2} + 1 = 6$$
$$\sqrt[4]{3x-2} = 5$$
$$3x - 2 = 625$$
$$3x = 627$$
$$x = 209$$

7. The correct answer is B. Cube both sides. Then solve the resulting quadratic equation:

$$\sqrt[3]{4x^2-2x} = \sqrt[3]{5-10x}$$
$$4x^2 - 2x = 5 - 10x$$
$$4x^2 + 8x - 5 = 0$$
$$(2x-1)(2x+5) = 0$$
$$x = \frac{1}{2}, -\frac{5}{2}$$

8. The correct answer is B.

$$x = \sqrt{16x + 225}$$
$$x^2 = 16x + 225$$
$$x^2 - 16x - 225 = 0$$
$$(x-25)(x+9) = 0$$
$$x = 25, -9$$

Note when you substitute $x = -9$ into the equation, you get $-9 = 9$. This means that –9 is an extraneous solution. The only solution is 25.

9. The correct answer is A. To solve $\frac{t}{4} + \frac{2t}{9} \geq \frac{3t-14}{6}$, multiply by the LCD of 36.

$$(36)\frac{t}{4} + (36)\frac{2t}{9} \geq (36)\frac{3t-14}{6}$$
$$9t + 8t \geq 6(3t-14)$$
$$17t \geq 18t - 84$$
$$-t \geq -84$$
$$t \leq 84$$

10. The correct answer is A. Raise both sides to the 4th power to eliminate the radical. Then solve the resulting linear equation:

$$\sqrt[4]{\frac{5}{3x}} = 1$$
$$\frac{5}{3x} = 1$$
$$5 = 3x$$
$$x = \frac{5}{3}$$

514

Chapter 12

Functions
and
Intermediate
Algebra

LINEAR, QUADRATIC, AND EXPONENTIAL FUNCTIONS

A **linear function** is a function of the form $f(x) = mx + b$, where m and b are real numbers. A **quadratic function** is a function of the form $g(x) = ax^2 + bx + c$, where $a \neq 0$ and a, b, and c are real numbers. An **exponential function** is a function of the form $f(x) = ab^x$ where base b is a positive integer greater than 1. These functions are important, because they can be used to model many real-world occurrences.

APPLICATIONS OF LINEAR FUNCTIONS

Let's look at an example of a real-world application of a linear function.

> In order to manufacture a new car model, a carmaker must initially spend $750,000 to purchase the equipment needed to start the production process. After this, it costs $7,500 to manufacture each car. In this case, the *cost function* that associates the cost of manufacturing cars to the number of cars manufactured is $C(x) = 7,500x + 750,000$, where x represents the number of cars manufactured, and $C(x)$ represents the cost of x cars. For example, the cost of making 7 cars is $C(7) = 7,500(7) + 750,000 = 52,500 + 750,000 = \$802,500$.

The above cost function is a linear function with $b = 750,000$ and $m = 7,500$. What is the domain of this function? Note that even though nothing has been said specifically about the domain, the only values that make sense as domain values are the non-negative integers, 0, 1, 2, 3, 4, 5, ... In such a situation, assume that the domain contains only the values that make sense.

Example:

Using the cost function for the carmaker discussed in the example above, how much would it cost to make 24 cars?

Solution:

To solve this, you need to determine the value of $C(24)$.

$$C(24) = 7,500(24) + 750,000 = 180,000 + 750,000 = \$930,000$$

Example:

Using the same cost function, determine how many cars could be made for $990,000.

Solution:

In this problem, you are told that the value of $C(x)$ is $990,000, and you need to find the value of x. To do this, solve the equation:

$$990,000 = 75,000(x) + 750,000 \quad \text{Subtract 750,000 from both sides.}$$
$$240,000 = 7,500x \quad \text{Divide by 7,500.}$$
$$32 = x$$

Therefore, for $990,000, 32 cars can be manufactured.

Example:

In the town of Kenmore, a taxi ride costs $2.50 plus an extra $0.50 per mile. Write a function that represents the cost of taking a taxi ride, using x to represent the number of miles traveled.

Solution:

$$C(x) = \$2.50 + 0.50x$$

If a ride costs $0.50 a mile, then the cost for x miles will be $0.50x$. Add to this the initial fee of $2.50 a ride.

Example:

You purchased shorts for $8 per pair, plus a shirt for $6. Write a function that represents the cost of your purchases, where x represents the number of pairs of shorts you purchase. How much did you spend if you purchased 5 pairs of shorts?

Solution:

$$f(x) = 8x + 6$$

Let $x = 5$, so $f(5) = 8(5) + 6 = 46$.

Example:

A bus pass has a starting value of $60. Each ride costs $2.50. Write a function that represents the remaining balance on the bus pass, where x represents the number of rides taken. How much money is left on the pass after 12 rides?

Solution:

$$f(x) = 60 - 2.5x$$

Let $x = 12$, so $f(12) = 60 - 2.5(12) = 30$.

There is $30 remaining on the pass after 12 rides.

The Graph of a Linear Function

Typically, when a function is graphed, the independent variable is graphed along the x-axis, and the dependent variable is graphed along the y-axis.

516

Chapter 12

Functions
and
Intermediate
Algebra

The taxi ride function from the previous problem is a linear function. In order to graph this function, you must first determine the domain. Note that the domain, once again, must consist of non-negative numbers. Next, determine a few values that satisfy the rule for the function. For example, when $x = 0$, $C(0) = \$2.50 + 0.50(0) = \$2.50$. A few additional simple computations will lead to the following table of values.

x	C(x)
0	$2.50
1	$3.00
2	$3.50
3	$4.00

If these points are plotted on a graph, you will see that they all lie on the same line. The entire graph of the taxi ride cost function is shown here.

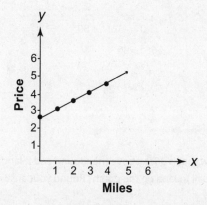

In general, the graph of any linear function is either a straight line or (depending on the domain) a portion of a straight line. The value of m represents the slope of the line, and the value of b is the y-intercept.

APPLICATIONS OF QUADRATIC FUNCTIONS

Quadratic functions can also be used to model certain real-world happenings. To understand these functions better, suppose a coffee manufacturer has a revenue function given by $R(x) = 40{,}000x - 2{,}000x^2$, where x represents the amount of coffee produced in tons per week. Let's consider some of the values for this function.

If $x = 0$, $R(x) = 40{,}000(0) - 2{,}000(0)^2 = 0$ represents the obvious fact that if no coffee is produced, there is no revenue.

That $R(1) = 40{,}000 - 2{,}000 = 38{,}000$ tells that the revenue from 1 ton of coffee is $38,000.

Similar computations show that $R(10) = \$200{,}000$ and $R(11) = \$198{,}000$.

Note that the revenue is smaller if 11 tons of coffee are produced than if 10 tons are produced. There are a number of possible reasons for this. Perhaps, for example, at the 11-ton level, more is produced than can be sold, and the coffee company must pay to store the overage.

517

Chapter 12

Functions
and
Intermediate
Algebra

The function $h(t) = -16t^2 + h_0$ models the height of an object dropped from an initial height h_0 (in feet) after t seconds. Use this function to work through the following examples.

Example:

An object is dropped from the roof of a building that is 80 ft. tall. How long will it take the object to hit the ground? Round your answer to the nearest hundredth of a second.

Solution:

$h(t) = -16t^2 + h_0$

Here $h_0 = 80$, so $h(t) = -16t^2 + 80$.

Substitute 0 in for $h(t)$ and solve the equation for t.

$$0 = -16t^2 + 80$$
$$16t^2 = 80$$
$$t^2 = 5$$
$$t \approx \pm 2.24$$

Example:

Suppose you drop a ball from a window that is 36 ft. above the ground and it lands on a porch that is 4 ft. above the ground. How long does it take for the ball to land on the porch? Round your answer to the nearest hundredth of a second.

Solution:

$h(t) = -16t^2 + h_0$

Here $h_0 = 36$, so $h(t) = -16t^2 + 36$.

Substitute 4 for $h(t)$, because the ball will hit the porch at 4 feet above 0, or ground level. Solve the equation for t.

$$4 = -16t^2 + 36$$
$$16t^2 = 32$$
$$t^2 = 2$$
$$t \approx \pm 1.41$$

It will take approximately 1.41 seconds for the object to land on the porch.

518

Chapter 12

Functions
and
Intermediate
Algebra

THE GRAPH OF A QUADRATIC FUNCTION

As you just saw, the graph of a linear function is always a straight line. To determine what the graph of a quadratic function looks like, consider the graph of the quadratic function $R(x) = 40{,}000x - 2{,}000x^2$. Negative numbers must be excluded from the domain. A few computations lead to the table here.

x	R(x)
0	0
3	102,000
5	150,000
9	198,000
10	200,000
11	198,000
15	150,000
17	102,000
20	0

The graph of $R(x)$ is shown here.

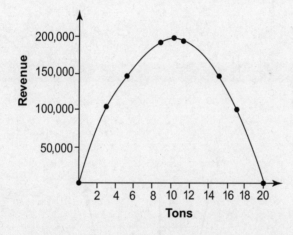

The graph shown above is called a **parabola**. This parabola is said to "open down." The highest point on the parabola, (10, 200,000), is called the **extreme point**.

Recall that the general form of a quadratic function is $g(x) = ax^2 + bx + c$. In general, the graph of any quadratic function will be a parabola. If $a > 0$, the parabola will "open up," and if $a < 0$, the parabola will "open down." If the parabola opens up, its extreme point (or vertex) is the minimum value of the function, and if the parabola opens down, its vertex is the maximum value of the function.

The coordinates of the vertex of a parabola are $\left[\dfrac{-b}{2a}, f\left(\dfrac{-b}{2a} \right) \right]$.

Example:

Sketch the graph of the function $f(x) = x^2 - x - 2$.

Solution:

Since the function is quadratic, the graph will be a parabola. Note that the value of a, the number in front of the x^2-term is 1, so the parabola opens up. The x-coordinate of the minimum point is $x = \dfrac{-b}{2a} = \dfrac{-(1)}{2(1)} = \dfrac{1}{2}$, and the y-coordinate of this point is

$$f\left(\frac{1}{2}\right) = \left(\frac{1}{2}\right)^2 - \frac{1}{2} - 2$$
$$= \frac{1}{4} - \frac{1}{2} - 2$$
$$= -2\frac{1}{4}$$

In order to sketch a parabola, it is helpful to determine a few points on either side of the vertex.

x	f(x)
−2	4
−1	0
0	−2
1	−2
2	0
3	4

The graph is shown here.

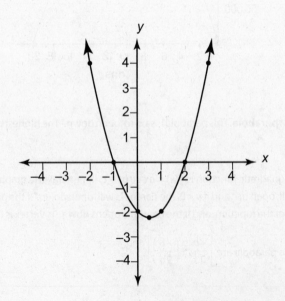

Example:

What is the relationship between the graph of the function $h(x) = ax^2 + bx$ and the graph of the function $j(x) = ax^2 + bx + 7$?

Solution:

If (x, y) is a point on the graph of $h(x)$, then $(x, y + 7)$ will be a point on the graph of $j(x)$. Therefore, the two graphs have exactly the same size and shape. The graph of $j(x)$ can be obtained by taking the graph of $h(x)$ and "lifting" each point 7 units, that is, increasing the y-coordinate of each point by 7.

APPLICATIONS OF EXPONENTIAL FUNCTIONS

If $a > 0$ and $b > 1$, then the function $f(x) = ab^x$ is an **exponential growth function** and b is called the **growth factor**. If $a > 0$ and $0 < b < 1$, then the function $f(x) = ab^x$ is an **exponential decay function** and b is called the **decay factor**.

An exponential growth function can model the number of students in a high school. Suppose the number of students in 2011 is given by $f(x) = 1{,}250(1.13)^x$, where x is the number of years since 2011. Let's consider some of the values for this function. If $x = 0$, then $f(x) = 1{,}250(1.13)^0 = 1{,}250$ represents the student population in 2011. If $x = 1$, then $f(x) = 1{,}250(1.13)^1 = 1{,}413$ represents the student population after 1 year. Similar computations show that $f(x) = 1{,}596$ when $x = 2$ and $f(x) = 2{,}303$ when $x = 5$.

An exponential decay function can model the value of an automobile. Suppose the value of the automobile is given by $f(x) = 35{,}000(0.85)x$, where x is the number of years since the automobile was purchased. Let's consider some of the values for this function. If $x = 0$, then $f(x) = 35{,}000(0.85)^0 = 35{,}000$ represents the value of the automobile at the time of purchase. If $x = 2$, then $f(x) = 35{,}000(0.85)^2 = 25{,}287.50$ represents the value of the automobile after 2 years. Similar computations show that $f(x) = 15{,}529.69$ when $x = 5$ and $f(x) = 3{,}057.40$ when $x = 15$.

THE GRAPH OF AN EXPONENTIAL FUNCTION

To determine what the graph of an exponential function looks like, consider the graph of the exponential function $f(x) = 52{,}50(0.9)^x$, where $f(x)$ is the value of a jet ski in dollars after x years.

The initial value of the jet ski is $5,250 and the percent of decrease per year is 10%. Some of the computations along with the graph of $f(x)$ is a curve that falls from left to right and gets less and less steep as x increases. The x-axis is a horizontal asymptote.

x	f(x)
0	5,250
1	4,725
5	3,100
8	2,260
12	1,482.8
15	1,080
25	339.21

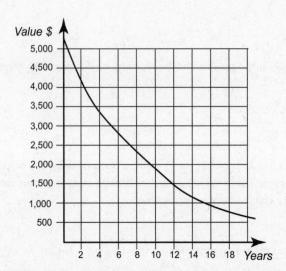

COMPARING LINEAR AND EXPONENTIAL GROWTH FUNCTIONS

Suppose you can choose how you will get your allowance. The first option is to get $5 a week every week. The second option is to get $0.50 for the first week, $1 for the second week, $2 for the third, and so on, by doubling the amount each week. Which option will pay you more?

Option 1: $y = 5x$, where x is the number of weeks you were paid your allowance and y is the total amount of money you have been paid so far.

Option 2: $y = (0.5)(2)^{x-1}$, where x is the number of weeks you were paid your allowance and y is the total amount of money you have been paid so far.

As you can see from the tables, Option 1 pays more until the 8th week. After that, Option 2 will always pay more since you are doubling a larger number.

Option 1: $y = 5x$

x (week)	1	2	3	4	5	6	7	8	9	10
y (total)	5	10	15	20	25	30	35	40	45	50

Option 2: $y = (0.5)(2)^{x-1}$

x (week)	1	2	3	4	5	6	7	8	9	10
y (total)	0.5	1	2	4	8	16	32	64	128	256

Option 1 is a linear function that is increasing at a constant rate, and Option 2 is an exponential function that is increasing rapidly as x gets bigger. You would chose Option 2 to be paid the most.

522

Chapter 12

**Functions
and
Intermediate
Algebra**

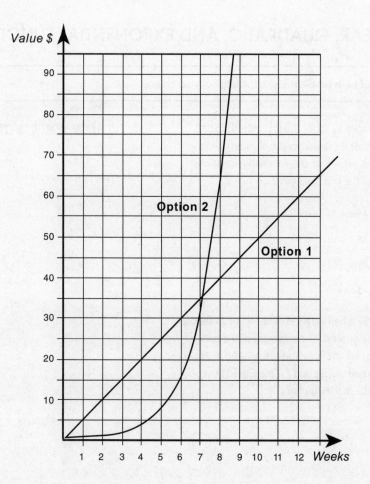

EXERCISE: LINEAR, QUADRATIC, AND EXPONENTIAL FUNCTIONS

DIRECTIONS: Work out each problem. Circle the letter of your choice.

1. A taxi company charges $2.25 for the first mile and $0.45 for each mile thereafter. If x stands for the number of miles a passenger travels, which of the following functions relates the length of the trip to its cost?

   A. $f(x) = 2.25 + 0.45(x + 1)$

   B. $f(x) = 2.25 + 0.45(1 - x)$

   C. $f(x) = 2.25 + 0.45(x - 1)$

   D. $f(x) = 2.25 + 0.45x$

2. A soccer player kicks a ball with initial speed of 24 feet per second from the ground. The trajectory of the ball is described by the quadratic function $h(t) = -16t^2 + 24t$, where $h(t)$ is measured in feet and t is measured in seconds. How long is the ball in the air?

   A. 1 second

   B. $\dfrac{3}{2}$ seconds

   C. 2 seconds

   D. $\dfrac{5}{2}$ seconds

3. At the Four Seasons bowling alley, it costs $1.50 to rent shoes and $2.50 for each game played. Which of the following functions relates the number of games played, x, to the cost in dollars?

   A. $f(x) = 4.00x$

   B. $f(x) = 2.50 + 1.50x$

   C. $f(x) = 1.50x - 2.50$

   D. $f(x) = 2.50x + 1.50$

SHOW YOUR WORK HERE

524

Chapter 12

Functions
and
Intermediate
Algebra

4. In order to raise money for a charity, Deb makes cakes to sell at a school bake sale. Her profit function is $P(x) = \$4.50x - \$15$. How many cakes must she sell in order to earn $66 for the charity?

A. 15

B. 16

C. 18

D. 20

5. For which domain value[s] of the function $f(x) = x^2 + 3x - 10$ does $f(x) = 0$?

A. 2

B. −2

C. −5

D. 2 and −5

6. The growth in population of a small town since 1983 is described by the function $P(t) = 1880(1.12)^t$, where t is the number of years since 1983 and $P(t)$ is the number of people. What is the population in the year 1983?

A. 226

B. 1,880

C. 2,106

D. 2,358

7. What is the x-coordinate of the extreme point of the function $f(x) = 7x^2 - 28x + 16$?

A. $x = \dfrac{1}{2}$

B. $x = -\dfrac{1}{2}$

C. $x = 2$

D. $x = -2$

8. Which of the following functions can be used to model exponential growth?

A. $f(x) = \dfrac{1}{5^x}$

B. $g(x) = 2 \cdot \left(\dfrac{4}{5}\right)^{-x}$

C. $h(x) = 4 \cdot (0.9)^x$

D. $j(x) = \left(\dfrac{1}{3}\right)^{x+6}$

9. A ball is dropped from a height of 20 ft. above the ground. Given $h(t) = -16t^2 + h_0$, how long will it be before the ball hits the ground?

A. About 2.0 seconds

B. About 1.56 seconds

C. About 1.12 seconds

D. About 0.89 seconds

10. The value of a car can be modeled by the equation $f(x) = 38{,}000(0.89)^x$, when x is the number of years since the car was purchased and $f(x)$ is the value of the car. What is the approximate value of the car after 6 years?

A. About $19,000

B. About $22,000

C. About $28,000

D. About $30,000

ANSWER KEY AND EXPLANATIONS

1. C	3. D	5. D	7. C	9. C
2. B	4. C	6. B	8. B	10. A

1. **The correct answer is C.** The cost for the first mile on a trip of x miles is $2.25. After this, there are still $x - 1$ miles to go, and the cost for each of these miles is $0.45. Therefore, the total cost of the trip, in dollars, is $2.25 + 0.45(x - 1)$.

2. **The correct answer is B.** Solve $h(t) = 0$. The larger of the two solutions is the amount of time the ball is in the air.

$$h(t) = -16t^2 + 24t = 0$$
$$-8t(2t - 3) = 0$$
$$t = 0, \frac{3}{2}$$

   The ball is in the air for $\frac{3}{2}$ seconds.

3. **The correct answer is D.** The cost of x games, at $2.50 a game, is $2.50x$. Adding the $1.50 cost of shoe rental to this leads to the function $f(x) = 2.50x + 1.50$.

4. **The correct answer is C.** You are asked to find the value of x for which $4.50x - 15 = 66$.

$$4.50x - 15 = 66$$
$$4.50x - 15 = 66 \quad \text{Add 15 to both sides.}$$
$$4.50x = 81 \quad \text{Divide by 4.50 (or 4.5).}$$
$$x = 18$$

   Therefore, Deb must sell 18 cakes to make $66.

5. **The correct answer is D.** In order to answer this question, you need to solve the quadratic equation $x^2 + 3x - 10 = 0$.

$$x^2 + 3x - 10 = 0 \quad \text{Factor the left-hand side.}$$
$$(x + 5)(x - 2) = 0 \quad \text{Set each factor equal to 0.}$$
$$x + 5 = 0 \quad x - 2 = 0$$
$$x = -5 \quad x = 2$$

   Thus, $f(x) = x^2 + 3x - 10 = 0$ at $x = -5$ and $x = 2$.

6. **The correct answer is B.** The year 1983 corresponds to $t = 0$. So the population in 1983 is $P(0) = 1,880$.

7. **The correct answer is C.** The vertex of a quadratic function is given by the formula $x = \frac{-b}{2a}$, where a is the coefficient of the x^2-term and b is the coefficient of the x-term. In this case, then, the vertex is

$$x = \frac{-b}{2a} = \frac{-(-28)}{2(7)} = \frac{28}{14} = 2.$$

8. **The correct answer is B.** A function that models exponential growth is of the form $y = A \cdot b^x$, where A is positive and $b > 1$. Note that

$$g(x) = 2 \cdot \left(\frac{4}{5}\right)^{-x} = 2 \cdot \left(\frac{5}{4}\right)^x \text{ is of this form.}$$

9. **The correct answer is C.** The model giving the height h of the ball (in feet) after t seconds is $h(t) = -16t^2 + 20$. Substitute 0 in for $h(t)$ and solve the equation. The ball will hit the ground about 1.12 seconds after it is dropped.

10. **The correct answer is A.** Substitute 6 for x in the equation $f(x) = 38,000(0.89)^x$, and solve the equation. The car will be worth approximately $19,000 after 6 years.

527

Chapter 12

Functions
and
Intermediate
Algebra

SUMMING IT UP

- A function is a rule that assigns exactly one output to each input. In other words, each member of the domain corresponds to exactly one member of the range.

- In function notation, the rule of association for a function is written as $f(x)$ to represent the range value.

- For any positive integer n, $x^{-n} = \dfrac{1}{x^n}$.

- For a rational number, x to the power of $\dfrac{1}{n}$ is defined as the nth root of x. In other words, $x^{\frac{1}{n}}$ is equal to $\sqrt[n]{x}$.

- A *linear function* is a function of the form $f(x) = mx + b$, where m and b are real numbers.
   - In general, the graph of any linear function is either a straight line or depending on the domain) a portion of a straight line.

- A *quadratic function* is a function of the form $g(x) = ax^2 + bx + c$, where $a \neq 0$ and a, b, and c are real numbers.
   - In general, the graph of any quadratic function will be a parabola.

- An *exponential function* is a function of the form $f(x) = abx$ where base b is a positive integer greater than 1.
   - In general, the graph of any exponential function will curve sharply as it rapidly increases or decreases.

- There are four steps involved in solving a rational equation:
   1. Find the LCD of all of the rational expressions in the equation.
   2. Multiply *every* term on both sides of the equation by this LCD.
   3. Solve the resulting equation using the methods previously explained.
   4. Check the solution to make certain that it actually solves the equation.

- There are four steps involved in solving a radical equation:
   1. Isolate the radical on one side of the equation.
   2. Raise both sides of the equation to the same power to eliminate the radical.
   3. Solve the resulting equation.
   4. Check the solution.

528

Chapter 12

Functions
and
Intermediate
Algebra

 ONLINE PREP

WANT TO KNOW MORE?

Access more practice questions, valuable lessons, helpful tips, and expert strategies for the following topics about functions and intermediate algebra in *Peterson's Online Course for the SAT® Exam*:

- 2 Equations—2 Unknowns
- Exponential Functions
- Functions
- Hard Algebra
- Inequalities
- Linear Equations
- Rational Expressions
- Quadratic Systems

To purchase and access the course, go to **www.petersons.com/testprep/sat**.

CHAPTER 13:
DATA ANALYSIS, STATISTICS, AND PROBABILITY

OVERVIEW

- Calculating Measures of Center and Spread
- Weighted Average
- Exercise: Calculating Measures of Center and Spread
- Probability
- Exercise: Probability
- Data Interpretation
- Exercise: Data Interpretation
- Statistics
- Exercise: Statistics
- Summing It Up

529

Chapter 13

Data Analysis, Statistics, and Probability

CALCULATING MEASURES OF CENTER AND SPREAD

ARITHMETIC MEAN, MEDIAN, MODE, AND RANGE

A set of data values may be summarized, using measures of center and/or measures of spread. Measures of center include mean, median, and mode and represent the center of the data. Measures of spread include range and standard deviation and represent how spread out the data values are within a data set. Standard deviation will be presented later in this chapter, when discussing ways to compare two data distributions. You will not be required to calculate standard deviation. Instead, you will need understand its meaning and how to use it to compare data sets.

Peterson's SAT® Prep Guide 2019

The Arithmetic Mean

An **average** or **arithmetic mean** is a value that is computed by dividing the sum of a set of terms by the number of terms in the collection. To find the average (arithmetic mean) of a group of n numbers, simply add the numbers and divide by n.

Example:

Find the average (arithmetic mean) of 32, 50, and 47.

Solution:

$$\begin{array}{r} 32 \\ 50 \\ +47 \\ \hline 129 \end{array} \qquad \begin{array}{r} 43 \\ 3\overline{)129} \end{array}$$

Another type of arithmetic mean problem gives you the arithmetic mean and asks for the missing term.

Example:

The average (arithmetic mean) of three numbers is 43. If two of the numbers are 32 and 50, find the third number.

Solution:

Using the definition of arithmetic mean, write the equation:

$$\frac{32+50+x}{3}=43$$
$$32+50+x=129$$
$$82+x=129$$
$$x=47$$

MEDIAN AND MODE

In order to find the **median** of a group of numbers, list the numbers in numerical order from smallest to largest. The median is the number in the middle. For example, the median of the numbers 3, 3, 5, 9, and 10 is 5. Note that, typically, the median and the arithmetic mean are not the same. In this problem, for example, the arithmetic mean is $30 \div 5 = 6$.

If there is an even number of numbers, the median is equal to the arithmetic mean of the two numbers in the middle. For example, to find the median of 3, 3, 5, 7, 9, and 10, note that the two middle numbers are 5 and 7. The median, then, is $\frac{5+7}{2}=6$.

The **mode** of a group of numbers is simply the number that occurs most frequently. Therefore, the mode of the group of numbers 3, 3, 5, 7, 9, and 10 is 3. If all of the numbers in a group only appear once, then there is no mode. A data set can have more than one mode.

Example:

What are the arithmetic mean, the median, and the mode of the following group of eight numbers?

2, 7, 8, 9, 9, 9, 10, and 10

Solution:

The sum of the eight numbers is 64, so the arithmetic mean is 64 ÷ 8 = 8.

Since this data set has an even number of data values, the median is the arithmetic mean of the two numbers in the middle. Since these numbers are both 9, the median is $\frac{9+9}{2} = 9$.

The mode is the number that occurs most often, which is also 9.

RANGE

The **range**, or the spread, of a data set is the difference between the greatest and least data values. To find the range of a set of data, first write the values in ascending order to make sure that you have found the least and greatest values. Then, subtract the least data value from the greatest data value.

Example:

Celia kept track of the average price of a gallon of gas over the last 10 years. Her data is shown in the table below. What is the range in the average price of gas?

Solution:

Year	Average price/gallon in U.S. dollars
2006	2.00
2007	2.08
2008	2.44
2009	3.40
2010	2.85
2011	2.90
2012	3.50
2013	4.20
2014	3.80
2015	3.25

Write the data in order from least to greatest:

2.00 2.08 2.44 2.85 2.90 3.25 3.40 3.50 3.80 4.20

Subtract the least value from the greatest value: 4.20 – 2.00 = 2.20.

$2.20 is the range or spread of the data.

WEIGHTED AVERAGE

If asked to find the arithmetic mean of a group of numbers in which some of the numbers appear more than once, simplify the computation by using the **weighted average** formula. For example, suppose the question asks for the average (arithmetic mean) age of a group of 10 friends. If four of the friends are 17, and six of the friends are 19, determine the average in the usual way:

$$\text{Average age} = \frac{17+17+17+17+19+19+19+19+19+19}{10} = \frac{182}{10} = 18.2$$

However, the computation can be done more quickly by taking the *weights* of the ages into account. The age 17 is weighted four times, and the age 19 is weighted six times. The average can then be computed as follows:

$$\text{Average age} = \frac{4(17)+6(19)}{10} = \frac{182}{10} = 18.2$$

Example:

Andrea has four grades of 90 and two grades of 80 during the spring semester of calculus. What is her average (arithmetic mean) in the course for this semester?

Solution:

Calculating Using Average Formula	Calculating Using Weighted Average Formula
$\frac{90+90+90+90+80+80}{6} = \frac{520}{6} = 86\frac{2}{3}$	$\frac{(90 \cdot 4)+(80 \cdot 2)}{6} = \frac{520}{6} = 86\frac{2}{3}$

Be sure not to average 90 and 80, since there are four grades of 90 and only two grades of 80.

AVERAGE RATE

The **average rate** for a trip is the total distance covered, divided by the total time spent. Recall that distance can be determined by multiplying the rate by the time, that is, $d = rt$.

Example:

In driving from New York to Boston, Mr. Portney drove for 3 hours at 40 miles per hour and 1 hour at 48 miles per hour. What was his average rate for this portion of the trip?

Solution:

$$\text{Average rate} = \frac{\text{Total distance}}{\text{Total time}}$$

$$\text{Average rate} = \frac{3(40)+1(48)}{3+1}$$

$$\text{Average rate} = \frac{168}{4} \quad 42 \text{ miles per hour}$$

Since more of the trip was driven at 40 mph than at 48 mph, the average should be closer to 40 than to 48, which it is. This will help you to check your answer or to pick out the correct choice in a multiple-choice question.

EXERCISE: CALCULATING MEASURES OF CENTER AND SPREAD

> **DIRECTIONS:** Work out each problem. Circle the letter of your choice.

1. The following are the amounts spent by nine families on purchasing gifts during the holiday season:

   $150 $325 $150 $250 $400 $175 $150 $325 $250

   What is the mode amount spent?

   A. $150

   B. $250

   C. $325

   D. $400

SHOW YOUR WORK HERE

2. The costs of five different airlines' tickets from Dallas to Boston are shown in the table below.

Airline	Ticket Cost
A	$356
B	$298
C	$312
D	$304
E	$283

   A sixth airline also offers flights from Dallas to Boston. The median price of the tickets from the six airlines, including those shown in the table, is $308. The range of the ticket prices is $77. What is the cost of the sixth airline's ticket?

   A. $385

   B. $360

   C. $279

   D. $231

3. The temperatures (in degrees Fahrenheit) recorded daily in a greenhouse during the month of April are as follows:

70 72 66 70 72 71 70 70 66 68
70 68 71 72 70 78 70 66 69 78
68 66 68 70 72 68 68 70 70 72

What is the range?

A. 12

B. 20

C. 70

D. 78

4. Mike was comparison shopping for used copies of a textbook. He decided that he will purchase the book which costs the median price of the following list of prices:

$35 $52 $42 $48 $37 $48 $38

What price does he pay?

A. $37

B. $38

C. $42

D. $48

5. Seven students were asked to report the number of nights per week they work at a part-time job. Here are their responses:

0 6 3 3 5 4 0

What is the mean number of nights worked by these students?

A. 3

B. 4

C. 5

D. 6

6. Max is selling his car. He looks at the selling prices of the same type of car at five local car dealerships to determine a fair price for his car. The selling prices are listed below.

   $7,505 $7,630 $7,995 $7,029 $7,135 $7,995

   What is the approximate average (arithmetic mean) selling price for the type of car Max is trying to sell?

   A. $7,995

   B. $7,548

   C. $7,512

   D. $7,505

7. Susan has an average (arithmetic mean) of 86 on three examinations. What grade must she receive on her next test to raise her average (arithmetic mean) to 88?

   A. 90

   B. 94

   C. 96

   D. 100

8. The photography club sold calendars that were created using the best photos from their collection the previous year. Each of the 12 members sold calendars on Saturday; the number each sold is reported below:

   20 5 18 18 15 12 18 14 8 10 15 3

   What is the range?

   A. 13

   B. 15

   C. 17

   D. 18

9. The ages of 14 US presidents at inauguration are listed here in order of their presidencies. Which of the following correctly compares the average (arithmetic mean), median, and mode of their ages?

   54 51 60 62 43 55 56 61 52 69 64 46 54 47

   A. mode < mean < median

   B. mode < median < mean

   C. median < mode < mean

   D. median < mean < mode

535

Chapter 13

Data Analysis, Statistics, and Probability

10. Amaya drives on two types of roads for her trip. She averages 53 miles per hour on city roads and 59 miles per hour on the highway. Amaya drives her car on a trip that has twice as many highway miles as city road miles. She drives a total of 552 miles. What is her average speed for the whole trip? Round your answer to the nearest whole.

    A. 55 miles per hour

    B. 56 miles per hour

    C. 57 miles per hour

    D. 58 miles per hour

11. Last year, a software company paid each of its four administrative assistants $33,000, each of its two programmers $75,000, and a senior manager $140,000. How many of these employees earned less than the mean salary?

    A. 0

    B. 4

    C. 6

    D. 7

12. A statistician computes the average (arithmetic mean), median, and range of a data set consisting of 65 numbers. Because one of the numbers in the set is much greater than all the others, the statistician suspects the number is an error and recalculates the statistics after removing this largest value (called an "outlier"). Which of the following statements is true?

    A. After the greatest value is removed, the average, median, and range must decrease.

    B. After the greatest value is removed, the range must decrease, but the average and median may not be affected.

    C. After the greatest value is removed, the average and the range must decrease, but the median may not be affected.

    D. After the greatest value is removed, the median and the range will change, but the average may not be affected.

536

Chapter 13

Data Analysis,
Statistics, and
Probability

1. A	3. A	5. A	7. B	9. B	11. B
2. B	4. C	6. B	8. C	10. C	12. C

1. **The correct answer is A.** The value that occurs most often in the data set is the mode; here, it is $150.

2. **The correct answer is B.** List the given ticket costs from least to greatest:

   $283, $298, $304, $312, $356

   Add $77 to the least cost to determine if the unknown cost is also the greatest cost:

   $$283 + 77 = 360$$

   Use the value to find the median of the tickets:

   $283, $298, $304, $312, $356, $360

   Find the average (mean) of $304 and $312, which is $308.

   The unknown ticket cost is $360.

3. **The correct answer is A.** The range is the difference between the largest value and smallest value in a data set. Here, that difference is $78 - 66 = 12$.

4. **The correct answer is C.** First, arrange the dollar amounts in increasing order:

   $35 $37 $38 $42 $48 $48 $52

   The median is the dollar amount in the fourth place from the left, which is $42.

5. **The correct answer is A.** Add the seven values and then divide the sum by 7:

   $$\frac{0+6+3+3+5+4+0}{7} = \frac{21}{7} = 3$$

6. **The correct answer is B.**

   $$\frac{7,505 + 7,630 + 7,995 + 7,029 + 7,135 + 7,995}{6}$$

   $$= \frac{45,289}{6}$$

   $$= 7,548.167$$

   The approximate average of the cars' selling prices is $7,548.

7. **The correct answer is B.**

   $$\frac{3(86) + x}{4} = 88$$

   $$258 + x = 352$$

   $$x = 94$$

8. **The correct answer is C.** The range is the difference between the largest value and smallest value in a data set. Here, that difference is $20 - 3 = 17$.

9. **The correct answer is B.** First, put the ages of the presidents in order.

   43, 46, 47, 51, 52, 54, 54, 55, 56, 60, 61, 62, 64, 69

   The mode of their ages is 54, which is the only repeated age.

   The median of their ages is the middle number, which is the average of 54 and 55, or 54.5.

   The average or arithmetic mean is found by adding their ages and dividing by 14.

   $$\frac{43 + 46 + 47 + 51 + 52 + 54 + 54 + 55 + 56 + 60 + 61 + 62 + 64 + 69}{14}$$

   $$= \frac{774}{14}$$

   $$= 55.3$$

   Now order the three values: 54 < 54.5 < 55.3, which means that mode < median < mean.

537

Chapter 13

Data Analysis, Statistics, and Probability

10.   **The correct answer is C.** Amaya drove for a time on city roads at 53 miles/hour and twice as much time on the highway at 59 miles/hour, so her average speed was as follows:

$$\frac{53x + 59(2x)}{3x} = \frac{171x}{3x} = 57$$

The average speed for the entire trip was 57 miles per hour.

11.   **The correct answer is B.** Add the values and divide the sum by 7 to determine the mean salary:

$$\frac{4(\$33,000) + 2(\$75,000) + \$140,000}{7} = \frac{\$422,000}{7} \approx \$60,286$$

Four of the employees earn a salary below the mean.

12.   **The correct answer is C.** Removing the greatest value from a data set will always result in reducing the arithmetic mean (unless all values in the data set are equal). The range will also decrease: after removing the outlier, the greatest value in the new data set will be a lower number, so the difference between that number and the least value will decrease.

To see that the median may or may not change, consider these two possible cases:

1.   When the original data set is listed from least to greatest, the 33rd value—the median—is *not* equal to the 32nd value. After removing the outlier, the data set has 64 values. The median is now the average of the 32nd and 33rd values, which will be different from the 33rd value. In this case, the median would change when the greatest value is removed.

2.   After listing the values from least to greatest, the 33rd and 32nd values in the original data set are equal. In that case, the median will be the same before and after the outlier is removed.

Because we do not know which of the two situations above describes the data set, we do not know whether the median will change when the largest value is removed.

538

Chapter 13

Data Analysis,
Statistics, and
Probability

PROBABILITY

Probability is a numerical way of measuring the likelihood that a specific outcome will happen. The probability of a specific outcome is always a number between 0 and 1. An outcome with a probability of 0 cannot possibly happen, and an event with a probability of 1 will definitely happen. Therefore, the nearer the probability of an event is to 0, the less likely the event is to happen, and the nearer the probability of an event is to 1, the more likely the event is to happen.

There are two types of probability: **theoretical probability** and **experimental probability**. Theoretical probability is defined by theory, whereas experimental probability is defined by outcomes of actual trials.

Theoretical probability is calculated as the ratio of the number of favorable outcomes to the number of possible outcomes (i.e., sample space). This type of probability is independent of the outcomes of any trials. The theoretical probability of event A is represented as follows:

$$P(A) = \frac{\text{number of favorable outcomes}}{\text{number of possible outcomes}}$$

Experimental probability is calculated as the ratio of the number of times event A actually occurs to the number of trials. Outcomes in an experiment may or may not be equally likely. The experimental probability of event A is represented as follows:

$$P(A) = \frac{\text{number of times event A occurs}}{\text{number of trials}}$$

If an experiment has n possible, equally likely outcomes, the probability of each specific outcome is defined to be $\frac{1}{n}$. When tossing a coin, the theoretical probability of getting heads, written $P(H)$, is $\frac{1}{2}$, since heads is one of two equally likely outcomes, namely heads or tails. When a die is thrown, there are six possible outcomes, namely 1, 2, 3, 4, 5, or 6, so the probability of tossing an odd number is $\frac{3}{6}$ since there are 3 odd numbers (or 3 favorable outcomes), and 6 possible outcomes. This probability reduces to $\frac{1}{2}$.

CONDITIONAL PROBABILITY

The probability of an event occurring after another event has already occurred is called **conditional probability**.

The notation for conditional probability is $P(B|A)$, which is read as "the probability of B given A."

If both events A and B are **independent**, where the result of B is not affected by the result of A, then the conditional probability of B given A is equal to the probability of B.

$$P(B|A) = P(B)$$

Likewise, if both events A and B are independent, where the result of A is not affected by the result of B, then the conditional probability of A given B is equal to the probability of A.

$$P(A|B) = P(A)$$

If both events A and B are **dependent**, where the result of B is affected by the result of A (or the result of A is affected by the result of B), then the conditional probability of B given A or A given B may be calculated using a few different methods. In probability situations involving dependent events, the way in which the question is asked will determine which equation to use.

The Multiplication Rule for dependent events states the following:

$$P(A \text{ and } B) = P(A) \cdot P(B \mid A)$$

or

$$P(A \text{ and } B) = P(B) \cdot P(A \mid B)$$

Using algebra, the following equations can be derived:

$$P(B \mid A) = \frac{P(A \text{ and } B)}{P(A)}$$

$$P(A \mid B) = \frac{P(A \text{ and } B)}{P(B)}$$

Example:

Of 100 people who work out at a gym, there are 45 people who take yoga classes, 55 people who take weightlifting classes, and 15 people who take both yoga and weightlifting. What is the probability that a randomly selected person takes weightlifting, given that the person also takes yoga?

Solution:

This question is asking you to find the probability that a person is taking weightlifting, given that he or she is also taking yoga (or $P(A \mid B)$). This probability is found by writing the following equation:

$$P(A \mid B) = \frac{P(A \text{ and } B)}{P(A)} = \frac{0.15}{0.45} = \frac{1}{3}$$

Note: It may be helpful to use letters that more closely represent the pieces of the problem. For example, you may wish to use $P(Y)$ to represent the probability of taking yoga classes and $P(W)$ to represent the probability of taking weightlifting classes. The probability of taking both would be written as $P(Y \text{ and } W)$.

The conditional probability that a person who takes weightlifting also takes yoga is $\frac{1}{3}$.

INDEPENDENT EVENTS

If events A and B are independent, then the probability of event B is not affected by the result of event A.

Example:

Adam tosses a coin and then tosses another coin. What is the probability that he gets heads or tails on the second toss, given that he gets heads on the first toss?

Solution:

We are going to use H to denote heads and T to denote tails.

Since the events are independent, we can write the following:

$$P(H \text{ or } T|H) = P(H)$$

Since $P(H) = \dfrac{1}{2}$, we know that the probability of getting heads or tails on the second toss, given that the first toss gives heads, is also equal to $\dfrac{1}{2}$.

Example:

Again suppose that Adam tosses a coin and then tosses another coin. What is the probability that he gets heads on the first toss and tails on the second toss?

Solution:

Since the events are independent and the tosses can be distinguished, the probability can be represented as

$$P(H \text{ and } T) = P(H) \cdot P(T) = \dfrac{1}{2} \cdot \dfrac{1}{2} = \dfrac{1}{4}.$$

If Adam tosses two coins at the same time (and the toss that gives either result doesn't matter), the probability of getting heads and tails is $\dfrac{1}{2}$ because making a list would show that there are two favorite outcomes out of a sample space of four; i.e., the list HT, HH, TH, and TT shows that HT and TH have heads and tails, in some order. The ratio, $\dfrac{2}{4}$, reduces to $\dfrac{1}{2}$.

DEPENDENT EVENTS

If events A and B are dependent, then the probability of event B is affected by the result of event A.

Example:

What is the probability of choosing a black 5, not replacing the card, and then choosing a red 5 from the same standard deck of cards?

Solution:

There are two red 5s and two black 5s in a standard deck of 52 cards. Removing a black 5 from the deck will leave only 51 cards in the deck, so the probability can be found like so:

$$P(A \text{ and } B) = \dfrac{2}{52} \times \dfrac{2}{51} = \dfrac{1}{663}$$

TWO-WAY TABLES AND PROBABILITY

Data on the exam is often represented in two-way tables like the one in the example below. Be careful to read the correct row or column that represents the information in the problem. These tables are often used for two or three problems in a row.

Example:

Hattie is a member of the honor society. All members of the society are polled to determine how many hours they spend studying per week and whether they prefer math or science classes. The results are shown in the table below.

	Science	Math	Total
0–3 hours per week	4	2	6
4–6 hours per week	6	7	13
Total	10	9	19

What is the probability that an honor society member selected at random prefers math, given that the member studies 4–6 hours per week?

Solution:

There are a total of 13 students who study 4–6 hours per week, and 7 of them prefer math. So the probability is $\frac{7}{13}$.

542

Chapter 13

Data Analysis, Statistics, and Probability

EXERCISE: PROBABILITY

DIRECTIONS: Work out each problem. Circle the letter of your choice.

1. Which of these pairs of events is dependent?

   A. Running a race and sweating

   B. Tossing a coin and then tossing a second coin

   C. Rolling a die and then tossing a coin

   D. Choosing a student from a math class and then choosing a student from a different math class

2. A poll asked 100 visitors at a national park the distance they hiked during their visit. The table shows the data collected based on the visitors' ages and hiking distances.

	18–25 years old	26–35 years old	Total
0–2 miles	16	22	38
2–4 miles	20	17	37
4+ miles	11	14	25
Total	47	53	100

   What is the probability that a visitor hiked more than 4 miles, given that the visitor was 18–25 years old?

   A. $\dfrac{11}{14}$

   B. $\dfrac{11}{25}$

   C. $\dfrac{11}{36}$

   D. $\dfrac{11}{47}$

3. What is the probability of selecting three black cards from a deck of 52 cards if each card is replaced before the next one is selected?

   A. $\dfrac{1}{256}$

   B. $\dfrac{1}{16}$

   C. $\dfrac{1}{52}$

   D. $\dfrac{1}{13}$

SHOW YOUR WORK HERE

543

Chapter 13

Data Analysis, Statistics, and Probability

4. Slips of paper numbered 1 through 15 are placed in a bag. A student selects a slip from the bag without looking. What is the probability that the number selected is 9, given that it is known to be an odd number?

   A. $\dfrac{1}{10}$

   B. $\dfrac{1}{8}$

   C. $\dfrac{1}{7}$

   D. $\dfrac{1}{15}$

5. The two-way frequency table below shows the results of a poll regarding video game play. The poll asked 150 randomly selected people the amount of time they spend playing video games each week and the type of game they most like to play. The table shows frequencies of each category.

	1–3 hours	3–5 hours	5+ hours	Total
Role-playing	12	15	16	43
Platform	24	19	18	61
Action	33	35	28	96
Total	69	69	62	200

   What is the probability that a person plays 3–5 hours of games per week, given that they prefer platform games?

   A. $\dfrac{19}{35}$

   B. $\dfrac{19}{42}$

   C. $\dfrac{19}{61}$

   D. $\dfrac{19}{69}$

544

Chapter 13

Data Analysis, Statistics, and Probability

6. Which question below describes the probability of two dependent events?

    A. Two coins are flipped. What is the probability of the second coin landing heads up, if the first coin landed tails up?

    B. Two number cubes are rolled. What is the probability of rolling two even numbers?

    C. A card is selected from a deck of 52 cards. What is the probability of selecting 3 hearts in a row, if each card is replaced after being selected?

    D. A bag contains 5 red marbles and 6 blue marbles. What is the probability of selecting two marbles of different colors, without replacement of the marbles?

SHOW YOUR WORK HERE

7. A summer camp held a fishing tournament. The participants selected the type of bait they would use. The table below shows the first type of fish caught by each participant and the bait they used.

	Perch	Bass	Trout	Catfish	Total
Live Bait	10	4	4	6	24
Artificial Bait	5	5	2	0	12
Total	15	9	6	6	36

What is the probability that a participant's first catch was a bass, given that artificial bait was used?

SHOW YOUR WORK HERE

    A. $\dfrac{1}{4}$

    B. $\dfrac{5}{9}$

    C. $\dfrac{5}{12}$

    D. $\dfrac{5}{36}$

545

Chapter 13

Data Analysis, Statistics, and Probability

8. Salena buys seven tickets in a raffle in which 50 tickets are sold. There are three prizes given: first, second, and third. What is the probability that she wins both first and second prizes?

   A. $\dfrac{7}{50}$

   B. $\dfrac{3}{175}$

   C. $\dfrac{36}{2,401}$

   D. $\dfrac{49}{2,500}$

9. During a science experiment, two studies of chemical reactions are conducted. Each experiment requires a hypothesis. Hypothesis A is correct $\dfrac{5}{7}$ of the times the experiment is conducted. Hypothesis B is correct $\dfrac{3}{4}$ of the times the experiment is conducted. If the two hypotheses do not affect each other, what is the probability that both hypotheses A and B are correct?

   A. $\dfrac{15}{28}$

   B. $\dfrac{5}{7}$

   C. $\dfrac{3}{4}$

   D. $\dfrac{8}{11}$

546

Chapter 13

Data Analysis, Statistics, and Probability

10. Gustav finds that during daily marching band practice he correctly completes all steps $\frac{7}{8}$ of the time. During daily symphonic band practice he correctly plays each piece of music $\frac{11}{12}$ of the time. The probability that he completes all steps in marching band and plays each piece of music correctly in symphonic band during the same day is $\frac{3}{5}$.

What is the probability that he correctly completes all steps during marching band, given that he plays each piece correctly in symphonic band?

A. $\frac{24}{35}$

B. $\frac{36}{55}$

C. $\frac{11}{20}$

D. $\frac{21}{40}$

11. A hockey team roster has 20 players on it. There are 12 forwards, 6 defensemen, and 2 goaltenders. If three players are selected at random without replacement, find the probability that all three are defensemen.

A. $\frac{1}{57}$

B. $\frac{2}{57}$

C. $\frac{27}{1,000}$

D. $\frac{3}{20}$

12. Kendra keeps loose change in a purse. If there are 8 dimes, 3 quarters, and 4 pennies in the purse and she chooses one coin without looking in the purse, what is the probability that the coin she selects is either a dime or a quarter?

A. $\frac{1}{5}$

B. $\frac{8}{15}$

C. $\frac{1}{2}$

D. $\frac{11}{15}$

| 1. A | 3. B | 5. C | 7. C | 9. A | 11. A |
| 2. D | 4. B | 6. D | 8. B | 10. B | 12. D |

1. **The correct answer is A.** Events are dependent if the occurrence of one event can affect the probability of the other. Of the pairs listed, running a race and sweating are dependent.

2. **The correct answer is D.** There are a total of 47 visitors who are 18–25 years old. In that age group, 11 of those visitors walked more than 4 miles, so the probability is $\frac{11}{47}$.

3. **The correct answer is B.** Since the card is placed back into the deck after each selection is made, you are always drawing a card from the full 52-card deck. So the selections are independent of each other. There are 26 black cards in the deck, so the probability of selecting a black card is $\frac{26}{52}=\frac{1}{2}$. The probability of selecting four black cards, one after the other, under these conditions, is $\frac{1}{2}\cdot\frac{1}{2}\cdot\frac{1}{2}\cdot\frac{1}{2}=\frac{1}{16}$.

4. **The correct answer is B.** This is a conditional probability. Since we are given that the number is odd, we reduce the sample space from 15 numbers to one including only the numbers 1, 3, 5, 7, 9, 11, 13, 15. There are 8 numbers here, each of which is equally likely to be selected. The probability of selecting the 9, given that the number is known to be odd, is $\frac{1}{8}$.

5. **The correct answer is C.** There are 61 total people who play platform games. Of those 61 people, 19 play for 3–5 hours, so the probability is $\frac{19}{61}$.

6. **The correct answer is D.** Situations that state there is no replacement have an event that is dependent on the other. In this case, the second chosen marble is dependent on the marble that was chosen first because there will be one less marble in the bag and it must be a different color.

7. **The correct answer is C.** There are 12 total fish caught using artificial bait. The number of bass caught out of those 12 is 5, so the probability is $\frac{5}{12}$.

8. **The correct answer is B.** The probability of Salena winning first prize is $\frac{7}{50}$. Once that prize is awarded, that winning ticket is discarded from the original lot of 50 tickets, and the next one is selected for second prize. The probability of Salena winning second prize is $\frac{6}{49}$. The probability that she wins both first and second prizes is the product of these two numbers: $\frac{7}{50}\cdot\frac{6}{49}=\frac{3}{175}$.

9. **The correct answer is A.** The probability of each hypothesis is independent of the other. The probability of both events occurring can be found by

$$P(A \text{ and } B) = P(A) \times P(B) = \frac{5}{7} \times \frac{3}{4} = \frac{15}{28}.$$

10. **The correct answer is B.** The probability of correctly completing the marching steps, given he plays each piece correctly in symphonic band, can be found by

$$\frac{P(A \text{ and } B)}{P(B)} = \frac{\frac{3}{5}}{\frac{11}{12}} = \frac{3}{5} \times \frac{12}{11} = \frac{36}{55}.$$

11. **The correct answer is A.** The probability that the first selection is a defenseman is $\frac{6}{20}$. The second selection is made from a lot of 19 players, 5 of whom are defensemen; the probability that the second selection is a defenseman is $\frac{5}{19}$. Finally, the third selection is made from a lot of 18 players, 4 of whom are defensemen; the probability that the third selection is a defenseman is $\frac{4}{18}$. The probability that three defensemen are selected is the product of these probabilities: $\frac{6}{20} \cdot \frac{5}{19} \cdot \frac{4}{18} = \frac{1}{57}$.

12. **The correct answer is D.** The probability is $\frac{8+3}{15} = \frac{11}{15}$.

549

Chapter 13

Data Analysis, Statistics, and Probability

DATA INTERPRETATION

WORKING WITH DATA IN TABLES

Some SAT® exam questions ask you to solve mathematical problems based on data contained in tables. All such problems are based on problem-solving techniques that have already been reviewed. The trick when working with tables is to make certain that you select the correct data needed to solve the problem. Take your time reading each table so that you understand exactly what information the table contains. Carefully select data from the correct row and column. As you will see, things are even trickier when a problem involves more than one table.

In order to illustrate problem solving with tables, consider the two tables below. The three questions that follow are based on the data within these tables.

Paul, Mark, and Bob are computer salespeople. In addition to their regular salaries, they each receive a commission for each computer they sell. The number of computers that each salesperson sold during a particular week, as well as their commission amounts, is shown in the tables below.

Number of Computers Sold

	Monday	Tuesday	Wednesday	Thursday	Friday
Paul	9	3	12	6	4
Mark	6	3	9	1	5
Bob	8	4	5	7	8

Commission per Sale

Paul	$15
Mark	$20
Bob	$25

Example:

What is the total amount of the commissions that Bob earned over the entire week?

Solution:

This problem concerns only Bob, so ignore the information for Mark and Paul. Over the course of the week, Bob sold $8 + 4 + 5 + 7 + 8 = 32$ computers. The second table tells us that Bob earns $25 per sale, so the total amount of his commission would be $25 \times 32 = \$800$.

Example:

What is the total amount of commission money earned by Paul, Mark, and Bob on Thursday?

Solution:

To solve this problem, focus only on what happened on Thursday. Ignore the data for the other four days. Be careful not to add the number of computers sold by the three people, since they each earn a different commission per sale.

- On Thursday, Paul sold 6 computers and earned a $15 commission for each computer sold, so Paul earned $15 × 6 = $90.

- Mark sold 1 computer, so based on his $20 commission, he earned $20.

- Bob sold 7 computers and earned a $25 commission per machine, so he made $25 × 7 = $175.

- Overall, the amount of commission on Thursday is $90 + $20 + $175 = $285.

Example:

On what day did Paul and Mark earn the same amount in commission?

Solution:

You can save yourself a lot of time if you look at the tables before you start to compute. Note that Mark's commission is larger than Paul's, and so the only way they could have earned the same amount is if Paul sold more computers than Mark. The only days that Paul sold more computers than Mark were Monday, Wednesday, and Thursday, so those are the only days that need to be considered. By observation, you can see the following:

- On Thursday, Paul made much more in commission than Mark, so eliminate Thursday.

- On Monday, Paul earned $15 × 9 = $135 and Mark earned $20 × 6 = $120. This means that the answer must be Wednesday.

- To be certain, note that on Wednesday Paul earned $15 × 12 = $180, and Mark earned $20 × 9 = $180 also.

CORRELATION AND SCATTERPLOTS

If two variables have a relationship such that when one variable changes, the other changes in a predictable way, the two variables are **correlated**. For example, there is a correlation between the number of hours an employee works each week and the amount of money the employee earns—the more hours the employee works, the more money the employee earns. Note that in this case, as the first variable increases, the second variable increases as well. These two variables are **positively correlated**.

Sometimes, when one variable increases, a second variable decreases. For example, the more that a store charges for a particular item, the fewer of that item will be sold. In this case, these two variables are **negatively correlated**.

Sometimes, two variables are not correlated; that is, a change in one variable does not affect the other variable in any way. For example, the number of cans of soda that a person drinks each day is not correlated with the amount of money the person earns.

One way to determine whether two variables are correlated is to sketch a **scatterplot**. A scatterplot is a graph in which the *x*-axis represents the values of one variable and the *y*-axis represents the values of the other variable. Several values of one variable and the corresponding values of the other variable are measured and plotted on the graph:

- If the points appear to form a straight line, or are close to forming a straight line, then it is likely that the variables are correlated.

- If the line has a positive slope (rises up left to right), the variables are positively correlated.

- If the line has a negative slope (goes down left to right), the variables are negatively correlated.

- If the points on the scatterplot seem to be located more or less at random, then it is likely that the variables are not correlated.

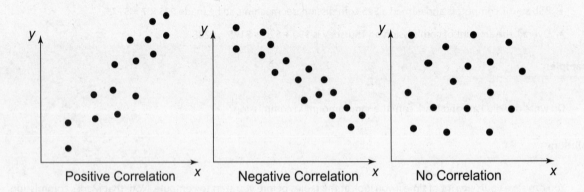

It is rare that the points on a scatterplot will all lie exactly on the same line. However, if there is a strong correlation, it is likely that there will be a line that could be drawn on the scatterplot that comes close to all of the points. Statisticians call the line that comes the closest to all of the points on a scatterplot the **line of best fit**. Without performing any computations, it is possible to visualize the location of the line of best fit, as the diagrams below show:

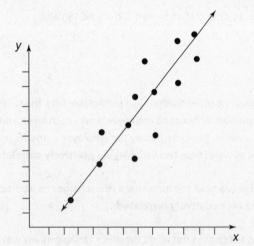

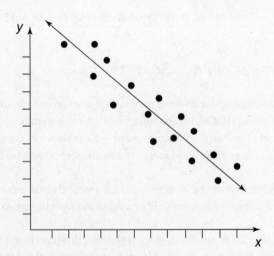

Example:

Which of the following slopes is the closest to the slope of the line of best fit for the scatterplot shown here?

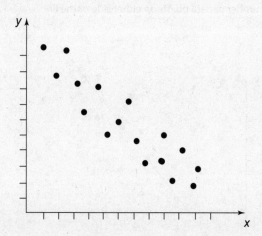

A. 3

B. 1

C. 0

D. −1

Solution:

Begin by sketching in the line of best fit in its approximate location.

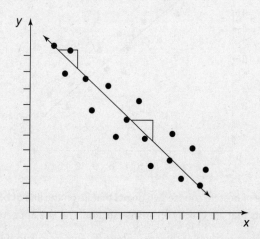

This line has a negative slope, since it decreases from left to right. In addition, the slope appears to be about −1, because if you move one unit horizontally from a point on the line, you need to move one unit vertically downward to return to the line. Since you can see that the points represent a negative correlation, the slope of the line of best fit will have to be negative, and choice D represents the only negative slope. **The correct answer is D.**

EQUATION OF LINE OF BEST FIT

You may see questions that ask you to create a line of best fit and give the equation for this line. Again, there is some approximation involved in determining a line of best fit. Look at the following scatterplot. Imagine a line that would come closest to all the data points and include an equal number of data points on either side of the line.

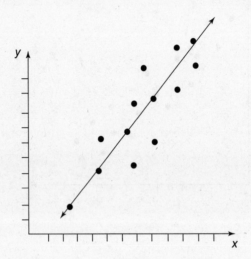

Notice the line of best fit below has 8 points above and 8 points below the line.

Note that the line of best fit does not have to cross any of the data points. In this case, the line of best fit goes through the middle of the data and does not include any of the actual data points.

554

Chapter 13

Data Analysis,
Statistics, and
Probability

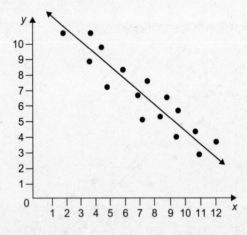

To determine the equation of the line of best fit, choose two points that lie on the line of best fit. You may have to approximate points if the line does not have points that are exactly on an intersection. The line appears to have points at (6, 8) and (12, 3).

Use these two points to determine the equation of the line of best fit. First, calculate the slope, m, using the slope formula $\frac{y_2 - y_1}{x_2 - x_1}$. Plug x- and y-values into the equation: $\frac{3-8}{12-6} = -\frac{5}{6}$. The slope-intercept formula is $y = mx + b$.

So far, we have $y = -\frac{5}{6}x + b$

Substitute the x- and y-values from one of the points into the equation. Using the point (6, 8), we can write:

$$8 = \frac{-5}{6}(6) + b$$

$$8 = -5 + b$$

$$b = 13$$

The equation of the line of best fit is $y = \frac{-5}{6}x + 13$.

MAKING PREDICTIONS

The following scatterplot shows the average number of books borrowed on a weekly basis for years 2000–2009 at a local library.

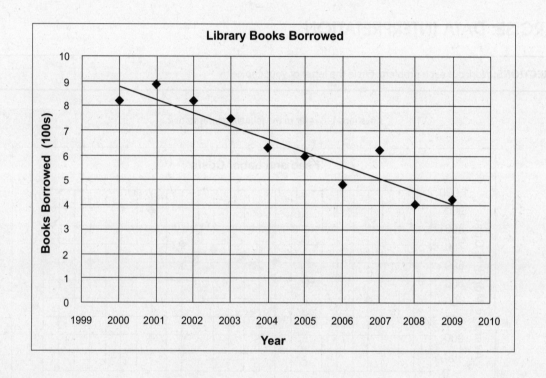

Example:

If the trend continued, about how many books were borrowed in 2010?

Solution:

Use the slope of the line to make predictions about data points that are not shown. According to the slope, the average number of books borrowed weekly goes down approximately 0.6 × 100 = 60 books every year. Multiply by 100 because, according to the title of the vertical axis, the numbers are in the 100s. The expected value for the number of books borrowed in 2009 was 400. The slope says we should expect that number to decrease by 60 every year, so you can predict that there were 340 books borrowed in 2010.

You have seen data that show a linear correlation, which may be represented by a line of best fit. In other cases, data may be better modeled by quadratic or exponential functions. When given a data set or plotted data, look to see if the data looks linear, parabolic, or representative of exponential growth or decay. Quadratic and exponential function models may easily be determined by entering the data into a spreadsheet or graphing calculator and selecting the appropriate function type (quadratic or exponential). The technology will provide output for the equation of the function. (The same procedure can be done with lines of best fit, as well.) Quadratic and exponential function models can also be estimated using the same sort of procedure described with the linear correlations above. Just note that not all data sets will be most appropriately modeled by a linear function.

Note that linear growth represents growth by a common difference, whereas exponential growth represents growth by a common factor. A real-world example of linear growth is simple interest, whereas a real-world example of exponential growth is compound interest.

EXERCISE: DATA INTERPRETATION

DIRECTIONS: Work out each problem. Circle the letter of your choice.

Questions 1–3 refer to the following information.

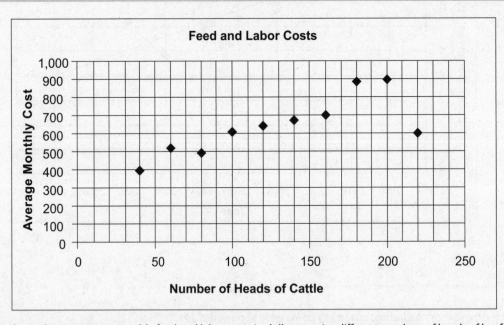

The scatterplot above shows average monthly feed and labor costs in dollars to raise different numbers of heads of beef cattle.

1. Which of the following best represents the slope of the line of best fit for this data?

   SHOW YOUR WORK HERE

   A. 200

   B. $\frac{1}{2}$

   C. $\frac{10}{9}$

   D. 2

2. Based on the scatterplot, what is the equation of the line of best fit?

A. $y = 200x + 400$

B. $y = 2x + 320$

C. $y = 2x + 380$

D. $y = \dfrac{1}{2}x + 380$

3. If the trend continued, what would be the average monthly feed and labor costs to raise 500 heads of beef cattle?

A. $1,380

B. $1,000

C. $880

D. $600

SHOW YOUR WORK HERE

| Questions 4–6 refer to the following information. |

Geographic Area	Attended College	Did Not Attend College	No Response	Total
Northeast	72,404	68,350	29,542	170,296
Northwest	88,960	125,487	48,960	263,407
Southeast	115,488	96,541	65,880	277,909
Southwest	79,880	65,874	13,840	159,594
Total	356,732	356,252	158,222	871,206

A survey was conducted in different geographic areas of a large state, covering the entire state population, pertaining to college attendance for people over the age of 30. The table above displays a summary of the survey results.

4. According to the table, for which group did the highest percentage of people report that they had attended college?

A. Northeast

B. Northwest

C. Southeast

D. Southwest

SHOW YOUR WORK HERE

557

Chapter 13

Data Analysis, Statistics, and Probability

5. Of the people living in the northeast who reported that they did not attend college, 1,000 people were selected at random to do a follow-up survey in which they were asked if they were interested in attending adult education classes. There were 665 people who said they were interested in attending adult education classes. Using the data from both the initial survey and the follow-up survey, which of the following is most likely to be an accurate statement?

   A. About 48,149 people living in the northeast who did not attend college would be interested in adult education classes.

   B. About 45,453 people living in the northeast who did not attend college would be interested in adult education classes.

   C. About 19,645 people living in the northeast who did not attend college would be interested in adult education classes.

   D. Most people in the state are not interested in taking adult education classes.

6. What is the relative frequency of the number of people who attended college statewide, according to the survey?

   A. 0.18

   B. 0.41

   C. 0.43

   D. 0.5

558

Chapter 13

Data Analysis, Statistics, and Probability

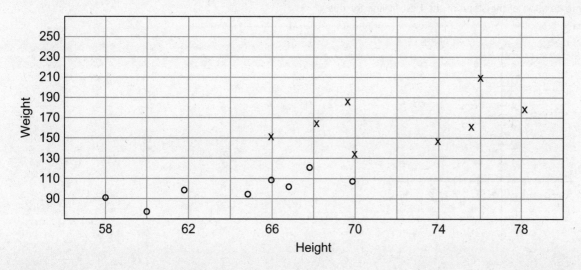

The scatterplot above shows the heights, in inches, and weights, in pounds, of 16 women and men at a health club. The women are represented by O's. The men are X's.

7. Which is a true statement about the data?

   A. The heights and weights are more strongly correlated for women than for men, and the slope of the line of best fit for women is greater than the slope for men.

   B. The heights and weights are more strongly correlated for women than for men, and the slope of the line of best fit for men is greater than the slope for women.

   C. The heights and weights are more strongly correlated for men than for women, and the slope of the line of best fit for women is greater than the slope for men.

   D. The heights and weights are more strongly correlated for men than for women, and the slope of the line of best fit for men is greater than the slope for women.

8. Assume the 16 people whose data is plotted in the scatterplot are a random sample representing the entire health club membership. For what height would we expect a male and female club member to have roughly the same weight?

   A. 60 inches

   B. 66 inches

   C. 72 inches

   D. Based on the data, we would expect any male club member to weigh more than a female club member of the same height.

559

Chapter 13

Data Analysis, Statistics, and Probability

9. The following scatterplot shows a relationship between two variables *x* and *y*. Which of the following is the best approximation of the slope of the best fit line for this data?

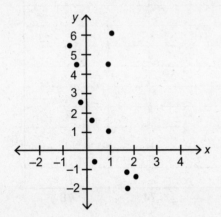

SHOW YOUR WORK HERE

A. −3

B. −1

C. 1

D. 3

10. The following scatterplot shows a relationship between two variables *x* and *y*. What is true about the correlation between *x* and *y*?

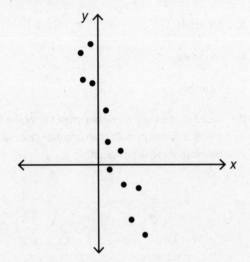

A. No correlation

B. Strongly negatively correlated

C. Strongly positively correlated

D. Weakly positively correlated

A product rating site gathers data on the price, *p*, and quality of a product, *x*, (on a scale of 0 to 100, where 100 is a perfect rating). The scatterplot below shows recent data for slow cookers.

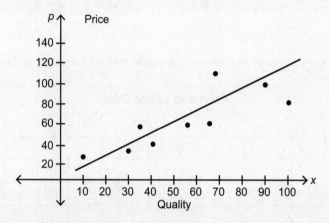

The best fit line for this data has equation $p = 0.9x + 15$.

11. What is the predicted price of a slow cooker if the quality rating is 95?

    A. $80.00

    B. $88.90

    C. $100.50

    D. $120.00

12. According to the best fit line, if you pay $51 for the slow cooker, what is its approximate expected quality rating?

    A. 36

    B. 40

    C. 45

    D. 50

SHOW YOUR WORK HERE

1. D	**3.** A	**5.** B	**7.** B	**9.** A	**11.** C
2. C	**4.** D	**6.** B	**8.** A	**10.** B	**12.** B

1. **The correct answer is D.** First, draw an estimated line of best fit, through the points, as shown below:

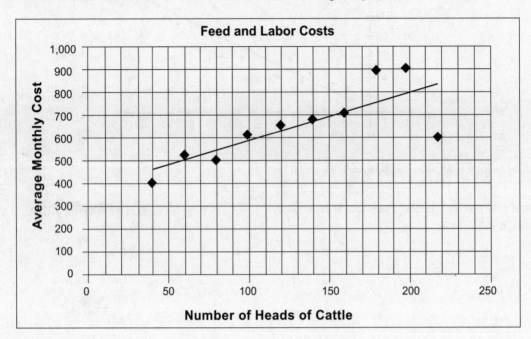

Feed and Labor Costs

Next, choose two points that lie on, or close to, this estimated line of best fit. We can use the points, (60, 500) and (160, 700), since it looks like they lie on, or close to, the drawn line.

Use these coordinates in the slope formula: $\dfrac{y_2 - y_1}{x_2 - x_1} = \dfrac{700 - 500}{160 - 60} = \dfrac{200}{100} = 2$

2. **The correct answer is C.** Using $m = 2$ as the slope (from Question 1), insert a set of xy-coordinates into the slope-intercept form, or $y = mx + b$. Substituting the x- and y-values from the point, (60, 500), into the equation gives $500 = 2(60) + b$, which simplifies as $500 = 120 + b$ and finally as $b = 380$. Rewriting the slope-intercept form with the slope of 2 and y-intercept of 380 gives $y = 2x + 380$.

3. **The correct answer is A.** Use the equation of the line of best fit to make predictions. Plug in 500 for the x-value: $y = 2(500) + 380 = 1,000 + 380 = 1,380$.

4. **The correct answer is D.** The percentage of people who attended college in the southwest region is

$\dfrac{79,880}{159,594} \approx 0.5 = 50\% \cdot$

The percentages for the other areas are:

Northeast: $\dfrac{72,404}{170,296} \approx 0.425 \approx 43\%$

Northwest: $\dfrac{88,960}{263,407} \approx 0.337 \approx 34\%$

Southeast: $\dfrac{115,488}{277,909} \approx 0.415 \approx 42\%$

5.   The correct answer is B. Extrapolating from the second survey, we can predict that $\frac{665}{1,000} = 66.5\%$ of the total population of the northeast will likely be interested in taking adult education classes. Applying this to the total northeast population who reported that they did not attend college: $68,350 \times 0.665 = 45,453$ people in this population are likely to be interested in adult education classes.

6.   The correct answer is B. The relative frequency of college graduates in the survey is calculated by taking the total number of people who reported having attended college and dividing by the total number of people in the survey:

$$\frac{356,732}{871,206} \approx 0.41$$

7.   The correct answer is B. See the estimated lines of best fit for women (W) and men (M):

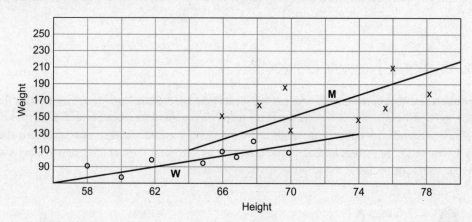

The O's generally are closer to line W than the X's are to line M, so the correlation is stronger for women. The slope of line W is about $\frac{1}{3}$; for M it is roughly $\frac{2}{3}$.

8.   The correct answer is A. Extending line M downward, it would intersect W at roughly (60, 83). At this point of intersection, the expected height (60 inches) and weight of a man or woman would be the same.

9.   The correct answer is A. The slope is negative since the points fall from left to right. To decide between choices A and B, notice that the points (0, 6) and (2, 0) are very close to the cluster of points in the scatterplot. Using these two points generates a line with slope –3. This steepness characterizes the pattern shown more than does a line with slope –1.

10.   The correct answer is B. The points are closely packed together and they fall from left to right. So the data is strongly negatively correlated.

11.   The correct answer is C. Evaluate the best line of fit when $x = 95$ to get the cost: $p = 0.9(95) + 15 = \$100.50$.

12.   The correct answer is B. Solve the equation $51 = 0.9x + 15$ to get the expected quality rating. Doing so yields $0.9x = 36$, so that $x = \frac{36}{0.9} = 40$.

Chapter 13

Data Analysis, Statistics, and Probability

STATISTICS

COMPARING DATA SETS USING SHAPE, CENTER, AND SPREAD

Statistics questions on the SAT® exam require using measures of central tendency, meaning the mean (average), median, and mode of a data set. You will need to be familiar with the shape, center, and spread of data. The shape of the data refers to the normal distribution curve, which we examine below. The center could be the average (arithmetic mean) or the median of the data values in the set. The spread is the range of the data, or the standard deviation of the data that describes the distance between values in a data set.

Data may be presented in tables, bar graphs, and via other methods, so it is important to be familiar with different types of data presentation.

STANDARD DEVIATION—NORMAL DISTRIBUTION

A **standard deviation** describes how far the data values in a set are from the mean or how much they "deviate" from the mean. The graphs below are both normal distribution curves. In the graph on the left, since much of the data clusters closely around the mean, there is a small standard deviation. In the graph on the right, since the data is more spread out, there is a larger standard deviation. If these were sets of test scores for Class A and Class B on a math exam, most of the scores in Class A would be very close to the average score, but, in Class B, the scores would be more varied.

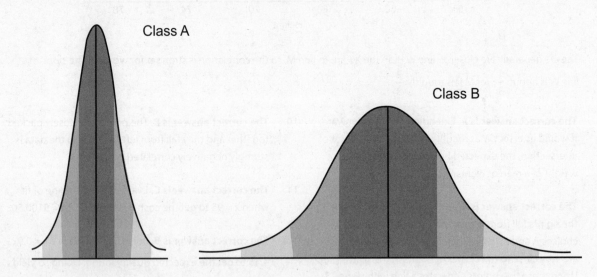

What You Really Need to Know About Standard Deviation

You won't have to calculate the standard deviation, but it is important to understand how to use it. If data has a normal distribution, the empirical rule states the following:

- Approximately 68% of the data falls within 1 standard deviation of the mean.
- Approximately 95% of the data falls within 2 standard deviations of the mean.
- Approximately 99.7% of the data falls within 3 standard deviations of the mean.

Let's see how this works with a table of data. The table below lists the number of students enrolled in six different sections of algebra, A, B, C, D, E, and F, offered by a college. First calculate the mean.

	A	B	C	D	E	F
Number of Students	18	23	15	19	28	11

$$\text{mean} = \frac{18+23+15+19+28+11}{6} = \frac{114}{6} = 19$$

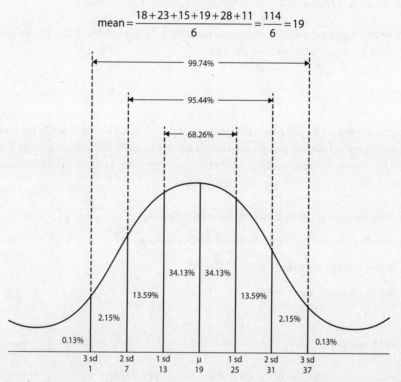

The mean is always in the middle. Here, it is 19, and the standard deviation is approximately 6.

The standard deviation of this data set is given as 6. In this example, the standard deviation of 6 means that approximately 68% of the algebra sections have between 19 − 6, or 13 students and 19 + 6, or 25 students, plus or minus 1 standard deviation.

Approximately 95% of the algebra sections lie within 2 standard deviations, meaning the sections have between 7 and 31 students.

Confidence Intervals and Measurement Errors

Measurement or sampling errors will usually occur when data cannot be collected about an entire population. If, for example, we are trying to determine the mean salary of people living in a city with 3.5 million people, we would probably use a smaller random sample of several hundred to several thousand people that was representative of the population. The difference between the mean salary of the actual population and that of the sample population is called a *measurement* or *sampling error*. The sampling error decreases as the sample size increases, since there is more data that should more accurately reflect the true population. Here's an example:

A packaging company is gathering data about how many oranges it can fit into a crate. It takes a sample of 36 crates out of a total shipment of 5,540 crates. The sample mean is 102 oranges with a sampling error of 6 oranges at a 95% confidence interval.

What Does the Confidence Interval Mean?

In this case, it means that based on the sample, you can be 95% confident that the true population mean for the entire shipment is between 102 – 6 and 102 + 6, or 96 and 108 oranges per crate.

A confidence interval tells you how close the sample mean is to the actual mean of the entire population.

COMPARING DATA SETS USING MEAN AND STANDARD DEVIATION

You may have two sets of data with similar means and ranges but different standard deviations. For the data set with the greater standard deviation, more of the data are farther from the mean.

Example:

A coach is deciding between 2 baseball players to recruit to his team. He is looking at player performance over the past 10 seasons. Both players have the same mean batting average of 0.270 and the same range of batting averages (0.080) over the past 10 seasons. However, Player A's batting averages have a higher standard deviation than Player B's batting averages. What does this indicate about each player?

A. Player A is more likely to hit better than his mean batting average.

B. Player B is more likely to hit better than his mean batting average.

C. Player A's batting average is more erratic.

D. Player B's batting average is more erratic.

566

Chapter 13

Data Analysis,
Statistics, and
Probability

Solution:

A greater standard deviation in a data set means that the data values are more spread out, or erratic, meaning performance varied more. Essentially, Player B's batting average is more dependable; he more frequently batted close to his batting average than did Player A. So, if the manager is looking for reliability, he may want to choose Player B for his team. **The correct answer is C.**

MAKING INFERENCES USING SAMPLE DATA

Frequently, a population is too large for every data value to be measured. Instead, a random sample of the population is used to make inferences about the true population.

Example:

An online retailer wants to determine the average dollar value of an order that it receives on a daily basis. Based on a random sample of 200 orders, the mean dollar value is $72 and the standard deviation is $5.

The normal distribution curve would look like this:

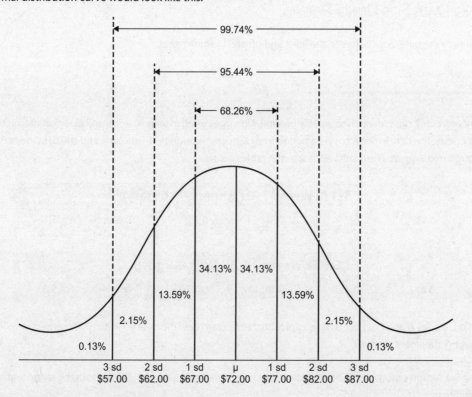

If the sample used is representative of the true population, what can be concluded about the true population of shoppers?

A. The mean of the true population is $72.

B. Most shoppers spend between $62 and $82.

C. All shoppers spend between $57 and $87.

D. The mode of the size of an order is $72.

Solution:

Shoppers who spent between $62 and $82 fall within 2 standard deviations of the mean of the sample population. Approximately 95% of the shoppers fall within 2 standard deviations of the mean. Thus, it can be concluded that most shoppers spend between $62 and $82. Though the sample is representative, it does not indicate that the mean of the true population is equal to the mean of the sample population, so choice A is incorrect. Approximately 99.7% of the population lies within 3 standard deviations of the mean, which, in this case, is between $57 and $87—but this is not all shoppers, so choice C is not fully supported. We don't know the mode of the data, so choice D is not correct. **The correct answer is B.**

COMPARING DATA SETS USING SPREAD

The spread is simply the difference between the least and greatest value in a set.

Example:

Todd's meteorology class researched weekly precipitation (measured in inches) in a tropical region during two 6-week periods. The data in Set A covers a period from January through mid-February, and the data in Set B is from July through mid-August. The results appear in the tables below.

Set A: Weeks 1–6 (January–February)					
0.43	1.73	1.93	0.28	0.08	1.18

Set B: Weeks 27–32 (July–August)					
0.20	0.01	0.00	0.08	0.04	0.00

Given that Data Set A and Data Set B have approximate standard deviations of 0.79 and 0.08, respectively, which of the following statements is true?

A. Data Set A shows more variability in data values than Data Set B, as evidenced by both the range and standard deviation.

B. Data Set A shows more variability in data values than Data Set B, as evidenced only by the range.

C. Data Set A shows less variability in data values than Data Set B, as evidenced by both the range and standard deviation.

D. Data Set A shows less variability in data values than Data Set B, as evidenced only by the standard deviation.

568

Chapter 13

Data Analysis, Statistics, and Probability

Solution:

To calculate range, write the data values in order from least to greatest for each set:

Set A: 0.08; 0.28; 0.43; 1.18; 1.73; 1.93

Set B: 0.00; 0.00; 0.01; 0.04; 0.08; 0.20

Find the difference between the least and greatest value for each set:

Set A: Range = 1.93 – 0.08 = 1.85

Set B: Range = 0.20 – 0.00 = 0.20

The range in Set A is greater. Since a higher standard deviation indicates more variability in data values about the mean, Data Set A has a higher level of variability than Data Set B. So, both measures of spread indicate that Data Set A shows more variability in data values. **The correct answer is A.**

COMPARING DATA SETS USING MEDIAN AND MODE

Using the same data sets about tropical precipitation, let's look at problems involving median and mode.

Example:

Set A: Weeks 3–8 (January–February)					
0.43	1.73	1.93	0.28	0.08	1.18

Set B: Weeks 29–34 (July–August)					
0.20	0.01	0.00	0.08	0.04	0.00

Which is true about the two sets of data above?

A.   The mode of Set A is greater than the mode of Set B.

B.   The mode of Set B is greater than the mode of Set A.

C.   The median of Set A is greater than the median of Set B.

D.   The median of Set B is greater than the median of Set A.

Solution:

In this case, Set A does not have a mode, because there is no data value that appears more than once. So we cannot make any statements involving the mode of Set A.

Calculate the median of both sets of data. The median is the number in the middle of a data set when all the values are written in increasing order:

$$\text{Set A: } 0.08, 0.28, 0.43, 1.18, 1.73, 1.93$$

Here, the two middle numbers are 0.43 and 1.18, so we take their average:

$$\text{Median of Set A: } \frac{0.43 + 1.18}{2} = \frac{1.61}{2} = 0.805$$

We perform the same set of calculations for set B:

$$\text{Set B: } 0.00, 0.00, 0.01, 0.04, 0.08, 0.20$$

$$\text{Median of Set B: } \frac{0.01 + 0.04}{2} = \frac{0.05}{2} = 0.025$$

From this we can see that the median of Set A is greater than the median of Set B. **The correct answer is C.**

EVALUATING REPORTS AND SURVEYS

To evaluate a report about a set of data, it is important to consider the appropriateness of the data collection method. Random sampling ensures that every member of the population has an equally likely chance of being chosen. This data collection method type reduces bias and measurement error. There are different types of random sampling techniques that a researcher may use.

Example:

A local politician wants to gauge how her constituents feel about the installation of a gas pipeline that will border her district. Which of the following would allow the politician to make a valid conclusion about the opinions of her constituents?

A. Survey a random sample of local Democrats

B. Survey a sample of citizens who volunteer to provide responses

C. Survey an intact group of senior citizens at a local event

D. Survey a random sample of citizens at a local library

Solution:

Let's analyze each of these options. First is the random sample of local Democrats in Choice A. This may seem like a good choice. However, it excludes members of other parties and their opinions. Choice B may seem okay at first, but such a sample will likely promote bias of the data, since the individuals responding will likely have strong viewpoints that may not be shared by others in the district. Choice C also seems like an acceptable choice at first, but this sampling method excludes other age groups. Data obtained from this sampling technique cannot be generalized to the population, as a whole. Choice D would allow for a valid conclusion (or generalization to the population), since a random sample is used and a library will likely have patrons who have varying beliefs, backgrounds, ages, and so on. Choice D does not exclude any age or party and will result in the smallest sampling error. **The correct answer is D.**

When considering whether the data in a report is representative of a population, it is important to consider the demographics of the population being studied. Their habits, behaviors, and perhaps incomes will influence their decisions and even their ability to be included in the report. The type of survey that will include the widest range of habits, behaviors, and incomes of the people being studied is likely the most representative. As discussed above, the use of random sampling reduces the sampling error and bias and results in sample data that may be used to represent the population from which the sample came.

571

Chapter 13

Data Analysis, Statistics, and Probability

EXERCISE: STATISTICS

DIRECTIONS: Work out each problem. Circle the letter of your choice.

---

1. The tables below show the number of employees in two different groups of an organization in different age ranges.

Production

Age Range	Number of Employees
20–24	4
25–29	8
30–34	25
35–39	19
40–44	17

Design

Age Range	Number of Employees
20–24	2
25–29	4
30–34	6
35–39	33
40–44	38

Which of the following conclusions can be made about the data above?

A. The range of ages is greater in production than in design.

B. The range of ages is greater in design than in production.

C. The median age is greater in production than in design.

D. The median age is greater in design than in production.

2. A nursery wants to know if a certain fertilizer is helping its rose bushes grow more roses per bush. The nursery uses the fertilizer on one plot, Plot A, of rose bushes but does not use fertilizer on another plot, Plot B. All the rose bushes in both plots were planted at the same time. The charts below show the number of flowers on each bush for the two plots.

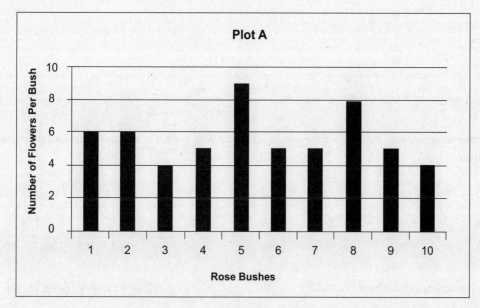

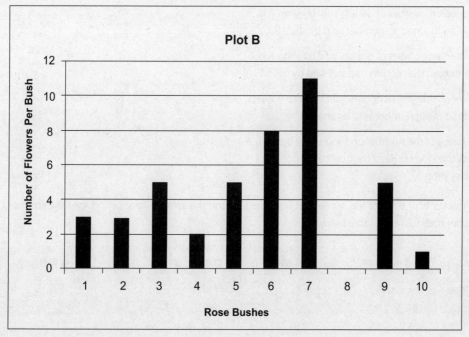

Which of the following conclusions could be logically drawn based on the data?

A. The mean number of roses in Plot A is greater, so plot A likely benefited from the fertilizer.

B. The mean number of roses in Plot B is greater, so plot B likely benefited from NOT having the fertilizer.

C. The fertilizer had no effect on the rose bushes.

D. There is not enough information to make any conclusion.

3. If the mean and standard deviation of a bell-shaped distribution are 2.0 and 0.75, respectively, what interval contains about 95% of the data?

SHOW YOUR WORK HERE

A. (0.5, 3.5)

B. (1.25, 2.75)

C. (1.5, 2.5)

D. (1.0, 3.0)

4. The number of donuts sold during the time-period between 6 a.m. and 8 a.m. by two local donut shops for one week is shown below:

Shop	M	T	W	Th	F	Sat	Sun
A	780	700	890	600	1,200	1,200	930
B	650	750	900	700	860	940	1,200

Which of the following statements is true?

SHOW YOUR WORK HERE

A. The median number of donuts sold by shop A is less than the median number sold by shop B.

B. The median number of donuts sold by shop A is greater than the median number sold by shop B.

C. The mean number of donuts sold by shop A is less than the mean number sold by shop B.

D. The range of the number of donuts sold by shop A is less than the range of the number of donuts sold by shop B.

5. A coffee retailer kept track of the number of customers during the same 6-hour period over the course of two days and recorded her findings in the table below.

	1–2 p.m.	2–3 p.m.	3–4 p.m.	4–5 p.m.	5–6 p.m.	6–7 p.m.
Sunday	24	22	28	35	38	35
Monday	11	18	18	22	44	30

Which of the following is a valid conclusion to be drawn from the data in the tables?

SHOW YOUR WORK HERE

A. The coffee shop is busier later in the day.

B. There are probably never more than 50 customers in the coffee shop.

C. The average number of customers is higher on the weekends than during the week.

D. The range of data on the two days is equal.

6. A sample of athletes was chosen, and the times it took them to complete an obstacle course was recorded. The mean time was 35 minutes and standard deviation was 4.25 minutes. If the sample is representative of the population of all athletes attempting the obstacle course, what conclusion can be drawn about the population of all athletes attempting the course?

   A. All athletes complete the course in no more than 47.75 minutes.

   B. The median completion time is 35 minutes.

   C. Most athletes finish the course in between 26.5 minutes and 43.5 minutes.

   D. No athlete completes the course in less than 25 minutes.

7. The data set below represents the number of hits a baseball player gets per game for 10 games.

$$0 \quad 3 \quad 1 \quad 1 \quad 0 \quad 2 \quad 0 \quad 1 \quad 3 \quad 2$$

Which of the following statements is true?

   A. The median number hits per game for this player is 2.

   B. The data set is bimodal.

   C. The mean number hits per game for this player is 1.

   D. The range of the number of hits this player gets per game is 2.

8. The margin of error is +/− 20 points for a 95% confidence interval for a given set of data. The researcher in charge of the data wants to obtain a lower margin of error. Which of the following is the best approach for the researcher, if he wishes to decrease the margin of error?

   A. Increase the confidence level to 98%.

   B. Decrease the confidence level to 90%.

   C. Obtain another sample of the same size.

   D. Decrease the sample size.

575

Chapter 13

Data Analysis, Statistics, and Probability

9. A poll was taken by the local university to determine which candidate is most likely to win the upcoming congressional race. The poll was conducted by selecting every fifth person who walked into a coffee shop in the largest city of the congressional district. Which of the following best describes the poll?

   A. The poll is a representative sample because it was done in the largest city in the district.

   B. The poll is a representative sample because it was done randomly.

   C. The poll is not a representative sample because it was done only in the largest city in the district.

   D. The poll is not a representative sample because it was done randomly.

10. The double occupancy room rates at 40 five-star hotels in Los Angeles is normally distributed with a mean of $280 and a standard deviation of $48.25. Which is the range of values, in dollars, around the mean that includes 95% of the room rates?

   A. $280.00–$328.25

   B. $231.75–$280.00

   C. $231.75–$328.25

   D. $183.50–$376.50

576

Chapter 13

**Data Analysis,
Statistics, and
Probability**

11. A researcher wants to measure the opinions of university students regarding global climate change. Which of the following poll results would most likely provide reliable data about the opinions of the entire population of university students?

   A. The researcher interviewed 60 students selected at random at a political rally attended by about 16% of university students.

   B. The researcher interviewed 55 students in a physics laboratory on campus.

   C. The researcher randomly selected 100 students from the complete roster of registered students, and emailed an interview invitation. Twelve percent participated.

   D. The researcher randomly selected 100 students from the complete roster of registered students, and emailed an offer of $5 to participate in an interview. Fifty percent participated.

12. A public health group investigates a claim that "Brand Y" cigarettes have less than 18 milligrams of tar per cigarette, and that this is less tar than "Brand X" cigarettes have. The group tests 16 randomly selected cigarettes for each brand. The findings are shown in the charts below.

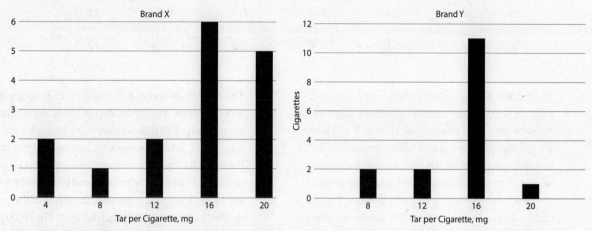

Which conclusion is supported by the data?

A. The average (arithmetic mean) tar per cigarette is higher for Brand Y than for Brand X, although the average is less than 18 milligrams for Brand Y.

B. The average (arithmetic mean) tar per cigarette is higher for Brand X than for brand Y, although the average is less than 18 milligrams for both brands.

C. The average (arithmetic mean) tar per cigarette is higher for Brand X, and it is greater than 18 milligrams.

D. The average (arithmetic mean) tar per cigarette is the same for the two brands. Brand X has greater variability, so it is more likely that a Brand X cigarette will have more than 18 grams of tar than it is that a Brand Y cigarette will exceed that amount of tar.

1. D	3. A	5. A	7. B	9. C	11. D
2. A	4. B	6. C	8. B	10. D	12. D

1. **The correct answer is D.** We don't have exact ages, which is why we can't conclude anything about the range of ages and can eliminate choices A and B. There are 73 employees in the production group, so the median age is the 37th data value when the ages are written in ascending order, which would be in the 30–34 age range. There are 83 employees in the design group. The median age is the 42nd data value, which falls in the 35–39 age range. Thus the median age for the design group is higher.

2. **The correct answer is A.** First focus on the mean number of roses on the bushes in Plot A:

$$\frac{6+6+4+5+9+5+5+8+5+4}{10} = \frac{57}{10} = 5.7$$

Then, look at those in Plot B:

$$\frac{3+3+5+2+5+8+11+0+5+1}{10} = \frac{43}{10} = 4.3$$

On average, the bushes in Plot A grew more roses and so likely benefited from the fertilizer.

3. **The correct answer is A.** For a bell-shaped curve, 95% of the data occurs within two standard deviations of the mean. Here, this is 2.0: 2(0.75) = 0.5 to 2.0 + 2(0.75) = 3.5. So the interval (0.5, 3.5) is the desired answer.

4. **The correct answer is B.** The median number of donuts sold by shop A is 890, and the median number sold by shop B is 860. Statement B is true.

5. **The correct answer is A.** It is difficult to conclude that there are never more than 50 customers in the shop, as choice B says, because we don't have enough data. As for choice C, while the mean for Sunday is higher than the mean for Monday, the sample size of 2 days is not enough to make a conclusion about the weekends versus the weekdays in general. The range of the two data sets are not equal to each other, so choice D is incorrect. Sunday's range: 38 – 22 = 16 and Monday's range: 44 – 11 = 33.

6. **The correct answer is C.** The interval containing 95% of the data is 35 – 2(4.25) = 26.5 to 35 + 2(4.25) = 43.5. This is the majority of the time, so statement C is true.

7. **The correct answer is B.** There are two values that occur the same number of times, and this number exceeds the frequency of all other data values. These two data values are 0 and 1. The data set has two modes, or is bimodal.

8. **The correct answer is B.** The data has already been collected, so decreasing the sample size is not possible without redoing the study. Decreasing the sample size would increase the margin of error. Also, obtaining a new sample would not necessarily reduce the margin of error. Increasing the confidence level would increase the margin of error, while decreasing the confidence interval would decrease the margin of error. This is true because increased confidence levels have higher critical values that, when multiplied by the ratio of the population standard deviation to the square root of n, result in higher margins of error. For example, for a population standard deviation of 3 and sample size of 30, a 95% confidence level would give a margin of error equal to the product of $1.96 \cdot \frac{3}{\sqrt{n}}$, or approximately 1.07. A 90% confidence level would give a margin of error equal to the product of $1.645 \cdot \frac{3}{\sqrt{n}}$, or approximately 0.90. Notice the margin of error decreased with the decreased level of confidence. Decreasing the confidence level would decrease the margin of error.

9. **The correct answer is C.** A representative sample should allow for random selection within the entire population, not just random selection from one part of the population.

10. **The correct answer is D.** Ninety-five percent of the rates fall within 2 standard deviations of the mean, meaning within $48.25 \times 2 = \$96.50$ of the mean price of $280.00 and $280.00 + 96.50 = 376.50$ and $280.00 - 96.50 = 183.50$.

11. **The correct answer is D.** Although the interview at the rally would yield the greatest number of respondents, the population of political-event attendees—only 15 percent of all students—probably differs from the general population of students in their opinions about public policy issues, including climate change. Similarly, in a chemistry lab, the students interviewed are more likely to be science students; their opinions, though possibly more authoritative, could be expected to differ from the larger population of university students. Random selection from the entire student body is most likely to provide a sample that represents the general population, and the larger sample in choice D makes it more reliable than choice C. There is no reason to think that the offer of a small incentive would bias the sample.

12. **The correct answer is D.** To calculate the mean tar per cigarette for Brand X, divide the total amount of tar in all Brand X cigarettes by the number of cigarettes, 16. Based on the bar chart we have the following (Inside the parentheses is the amount of tar multiplied by the number of cigarettes with that much tar.):

$$\frac{(4 \times 2) + (8 \times 1) + (12 \times 2) + (16 \times 6) + (20 \times 5)}{16} = \frac{236}{16} = 14.75$$

For Brand Y the corresponding calculation is:

$$\frac{(8 \times 2) + (12 \times 2) + (16 \times 11) + (20 \times 1)}{16} = \frac{236}{16} = 14.75$$

The average tar per cigarette is 14.75 milligrams for both brands. Only choice D correctly states that this average is the same for both. The statement that tar in Brand X is more variable than in Brand Y is also correct. Note as well that 5 of 16 tested Brand X cigarettes had more than 18 mg of tar, but only 1 of 16 Brand Y cigarettes exceeded that amount.

579

Chapter 13

Data Analysis, Statistics, and Probability

SUMMING IT UP

- Not all problems that deal with averages will ask you to solve for the average of a set of quantities.

- The trick when working with tables is to make sure you select the correct data needed to solve the problem.

- Take your time reading each table.

- Observe trends with scatterplots, and use lines or curves to predict unknown values.

- Read data representations carefully when comparing data sets.

- Pay attention to sampling methods when you evaluate survey data.

WANT TO KNOW MORE?

Access more practice questions, helpful lessons, valuable tips, and expert strategies for the following data analysis, statistics, and probability topics in *Peterson's Online Course for the SAT® Exam:*

- Data Interpretation

- Mean, Median, and Mode

- Percent Word Problems

- Ratios

- Word Problems

To purchase and access the course, go to **www.petersons.com/testprep/sat**.

580

Chapter 13

**Data Analysis,
Statistics, and
Probability**

PART VII:
PRACTICE TESTS
FOR THE SAT® EXAM

Chapter 14: SAT® Exam Practice Tests

CHAPTER 14:
SAT® EXAM PRACTICE TESTS

OVERVIEW

- Introduction to the Practice Tests
- Practice Test 1
- Practice Test 2
- Practice Test 3
- Practice Test 4
- Practice Test 5

INTRODUCTION TO THE PRACTICE TESTS

On test day, you will see these important reminders on the first page of your exam booklet:

- You must use a No. 2 pencil when taking the test; you may not use a pen or mechanical pencil.

- You may not share any questions with anyone. This is considered a violation of College Board's "Test Security and Fairness" policies, and it could cause your scores to be canceled.

- You are not permitted to take the test booklet out of the testing room.

In addition to filling in your name and Test Center information on your answer sheet, you'll be asked to fill in two different codes that will be on your test booklet. Each test booklet has a unique code, and there will be a grid-in form to fill in with your "TEST ID" and "FORM CODE" letters and numbers.

The general directions for the test will look something like this:

- You may only work on one section at a time.

- If you complete a section before time is called, check your work on that section only. You are not permitted to work on any other section.

The directions for marking your answers will likely include the following recommendations:

- Mark your answer sheet properly—be sure to completely fill in the answer circle.

- Be careful to mark only one answer for each question.

- Don't make any stray marks on the answer sheet.

- If you need to erase your answer, make sure you do so completely.

- Be sure to use the answer spaces that correspond to the question numbers.

You will be able to use your test booklet for scratch work, but you won't get credit for any work done in your test booklet. When time is called at the end of each section, you will not be permitted to transfer answers from your test booklet to your answer sheet.

Any information, ideas, or opinions presented in any of the passages you will see on the exam that have been taken from other sources or published material do not represent the opinions of the College Board.

Scoring on the exam is as follows:

- You will receive one point for each correct answer.
- You will not lose points for wrong answers, so you should attempt to answer every question even if you aren't completely sure of the correct answer.

Your testing supervisor will announce when to open the test booklet, so be sure to wait until you're told to do so. For the purposes of this practice test, be sure you have a timer to set for 65 minutes for the Section 1: Reading Test.

The answer sheets for each test section, including lined paper for the essay, appear on the next pages.

Following the Answer Keys and Explanations for these Practice Tests, you will find details on how to score your work.

GOOD LUCK!

584

Chapter 14

SAT® Exam
Practice
Tests

www.petersons.com

Section 1: Reading Test

1. Ⓐ Ⓑ Ⓒ Ⓓ   12. Ⓐ Ⓑ Ⓒ Ⓓ   23. Ⓐ Ⓑ Ⓒ Ⓓ   33. Ⓐ Ⓑ Ⓒ Ⓓ   43. Ⓐ Ⓑ Ⓒ Ⓓ
2. Ⓐ Ⓑ Ⓒ Ⓓ   13. Ⓐ Ⓑ Ⓒ Ⓓ   24. Ⓐ Ⓑ Ⓒ Ⓓ   34. Ⓐ Ⓑ Ⓒ Ⓓ   44. Ⓐ Ⓑ Ⓒ Ⓓ
3. Ⓐ Ⓑ Ⓒ Ⓓ   14. Ⓐ Ⓑ Ⓒ Ⓓ   25. Ⓐ Ⓑ Ⓒ Ⓓ   35. Ⓐ Ⓑ Ⓒ Ⓓ   45. Ⓐ Ⓑ Ⓒ Ⓓ
4. Ⓐ Ⓑ Ⓒ Ⓓ   15. Ⓐ Ⓑ Ⓒ Ⓓ   26. Ⓐ Ⓑ Ⓒ Ⓓ   36. Ⓐ Ⓑ Ⓒ Ⓓ   46. Ⓐ Ⓑ Ⓒ Ⓓ
5. Ⓐ Ⓑ Ⓒ Ⓓ   16. Ⓐ Ⓑ Ⓒ Ⓓ   27. Ⓐ Ⓑ Ⓒ Ⓓ   37. Ⓐ Ⓑ Ⓒ Ⓓ   47. Ⓐ Ⓑ Ⓒ Ⓓ
6. Ⓐ Ⓑ Ⓒ Ⓓ   17. Ⓐ Ⓑ Ⓒ Ⓓ   28. Ⓐ Ⓑ Ⓒ Ⓓ   38. Ⓐ Ⓑ Ⓒ Ⓓ   48. Ⓐ Ⓑ Ⓒ Ⓓ
7. Ⓐ Ⓑ Ⓒ Ⓓ   18. Ⓐ Ⓑ Ⓒ Ⓓ   29. Ⓐ Ⓑ Ⓒ Ⓓ   39. Ⓐ Ⓑ Ⓒ Ⓓ   49. Ⓐ Ⓑ Ⓒ Ⓓ
8. Ⓐ Ⓑ Ⓒ Ⓓ   19. Ⓐ Ⓑ Ⓒ Ⓓ   30. Ⓐ Ⓑ Ⓒ Ⓓ   40. Ⓐ Ⓑ Ⓒ Ⓓ   50. Ⓐ Ⓑ Ⓒ Ⓓ
9. Ⓐ Ⓑ Ⓒ Ⓓ   20. Ⓐ Ⓑ Ⓒ Ⓓ   31. Ⓐ Ⓑ Ⓒ Ⓓ   41. Ⓐ Ⓑ Ⓒ Ⓓ   51. Ⓐ Ⓑ Ⓒ Ⓓ
10. Ⓐ Ⓑ Ⓒ Ⓓ   21. Ⓐ Ⓑ Ⓒ Ⓓ   32. Ⓐ Ⓑ Ⓒ Ⓓ   42. Ⓐ Ⓑ Ⓒ Ⓓ   52. Ⓐ Ⓑ Ⓒ Ⓓ
11. Ⓐ Ⓑ Ⓒ Ⓓ   22. Ⓐ Ⓑ Ⓒ Ⓓ

Section 2: Writing and Language Test

1. Ⓐ Ⓑ Ⓒ Ⓓ   10. Ⓐ Ⓑ Ⓒ Ⓓ   19. Ⓐ Ⓑ Ⓒ Ⓓ   28. Ⓐ Ⓑ Ⓒ Ⓓ   37. Ⓐ Ⓑ Ⓒ Ⓓ
2. Ⓐ Ⓑ Ⓒ Ⓓ   11. Ⓐ Ⓑ Ⓒ Ⓓ   20. Ⓐ Ⓑ Ⓒ Ⓓ   29. Ⓐ Ⓑ Ⓒ Ⓓ   38. Ⓐ Ⓑ Ⓒ Ⓓ
3. Ⓐ Ⓑ Ⓒ Ⓓ   12. Ⓐ Ⓑ Ⓒ Ⓓ   21. Ⓐ Ⓑ Ⓒ Ⓓ   30. Ⓐ Ⓑ Ⓒ Ⓓ   39. Ⓐ Ⓑ Ⓒ Ⓓ
4. Ⓐ Ⓑ Ⓒ Ⓓ   13. Ⓐ Ⓑ Ⓒ Ⓓ   22. Ⓐ Ⓑ Ⓒ Ⓓ   31. Ⓐ Ⓑ Ⓒ Ⓓ   40. Ⓐ Ⓑ Ⓒ Ⓓ
5. Ⓐ Ⓑ Ⓒ Ⓓ   14. Ⓐ Ⓑ Ⓒ Ⓓ   23. Ⓐ Ⓑ Ⓒ Ⓓ   32. Ⓐ Ⓑ Ⓒ Ⓓ   41. Ⓐ Ⓑ Ⓒ Ⓓ
6. Ⓐ Ⓑ Ⓒ Ⓓ   15. Ⓐ Ⓑ Ⓒ Ⓓ   24. Ⓐ Ⓑ Ⓒ Ⓓ   33. Ⓐ Ⓑ Ⓒ Ⓓ   42. Ⓐ Ⓑ Ⓒ Ⓓ
7. Ⓐ Ⓑ Ⓒ Ⓓ   16. Ⓐ Ⓑ Ⓒ Ⓓ   25. Ⓐ Ⓑ Ⓒ Ⓓ   34. Ⓐ Ⓑ Ⓒ Ⓓ   43. Ⓐ Ⓑ Ⓒ Ⓓ
8. Ⓐ Ⓑ Ⓒ Ⓓ   17. Ⓐ Ⓑ Ⓒ Ⓓ   26. Ⓐ Ⓑ Ⓒ Ⓓ   35. Ⓐ Ⓑ Ⓒ Ⓓ   44. Ⓐ Ⓑ Ⓒ Ⓓ
9. Ⓐ Ⓑ Ⓒ Ⓓ   18. Ⓐ Ⓑ Ⓒ Ⓓ   27. Ⓐ Ⓑ Ⓒ Ⓓ   36. Ⓐ Ⓑ Ⓒ Ⓓ

Section 3: Math Test—No Calculator

1. Ⓐ Ⓑ Ⓒ Ⓓ   4. Ⓐ Ⓑ Ⓒ Ⓓ   7. Ⓐ Ⓑ Ⓒ Ⓓ   10. Ⓐ Ⓑ Ⓒ Ⓓ   13. Ⓐ Ⓑ Ⓒ Ⓓ
2. Ⓐ Ⓑ Ⓒ Ⓓ   5. Ⓐ Ⓑ Ⓒ Ⓓ   8. Ⓐ Ⓑ Ⓒ Ⓓ   11. Ⓐ Ⓑ Ⓒ Ⓓ   14. Ⓐ Ⓑ Ⓒ Ⓓ
3. Ⓐ Ⓑ Ⓒ Ⓓ   6. Ⓐ Ⓑ Ⓒ Ⓓ   9. Ⓐ Ⓑ Ⓒ Ⓓ   12. Ⓐ Ⓑ Ⓒ Ⓓ   15. Ⓐ Ⓑ Ⓒ Ⓓ

Section 3: Math Test—No Calculator

16. ☐☐☐☐   17. ☐☐☐☐   18. ☐☐☐☐   19. ☐☐☐☐   20. ☐☐☐☐

Section 4: Math Test—Calculator

1. Ⓐ Ⓑ Ⓒ Ⓓ	7. Ⓐ Ⓑ Ⓒ Ⓓ	13. Ⓐ Ⓑ Ⓒ Ⓓ	19. Ⓐ Ⓑ Ⓒ Ⓓ	25. Ⓐ Ⓑ Ⓒ Ⓓ
2. Ⓐ Ⓑ Ⓒ Ⓓ	8. Ⓐ Ⓑ Ⓒ Ⓓ	14. Ⓐ Ⓑ Ⓒ Ⓓ	20. Ⓐ Ⓑ Ⓒ Ⓓ	26. Ⓐ Ⓑ Ⓒ Ⓓ
3. Ⓐ Ⓑ Ⓒ Ⓓ	9. Ⓐ Ⓑ Ⓒ Ⓓ	15. Ⓐ Ⓑ Ⓒ Ⓓ	21. Ⓐ Ⓑ Ⓒ Ⓓ	27. Ⓐ Ⓑ Ⓒ Ⓓ
4. Ⓐ Ⓑ Ⓒ Ⓓ	10. Ⓐ Ⓑ Ⓒ Ⓓ	16. Ⓐ Ⓑ Ⓒ Ⓓ	22. Ⓐ Ⓑ Ⓒ Ⓓ	28. Ⓐ Ⓑ Ⓒ Ⓓ
5. Ⓐ Ⓑ Ⓒ Ⓓ	11. Ⓐ Ⓑ Ⓒ Ⓓ	17. Ⓐ Ⓑ Ⓒ Ⓓ	23. Ⓐ Ⓑ Ⓒ Ⓓ	29. Ⓐ Ⓑ Ⓒ Ⓓ
6. Ⓐ Ⓑ Ⓒ Ⓓ	12. Ⓐ Ⓑ Ⓒ Ⓓ	18. Ⓐ Ⓑ Ⓒ Ⓓ	24. Ⓐ Ⓑ Ⓒ Ⓓ	30. Ⓐ Ⓑ Ⓒ Ⓓ

31. ☐☐☐☐   32. ☐☐☐☐   33. ☐☐☐☐   34. ☐☐☐☐   35. ☐☐☐☐

36. ☐☐☐☐   37. ☐☐☐☐   38. ☐☐☐☐

Section 5: Essay

www.petersons.com

SECTION 1: READING TEST

65 Minutes—52 Questions

TURN TO SECTION 1 OF YOUR ANSWER SHEET TO ANSWER THE QUESTIONS IN THIS SECTION.

DIRECTIONS: Each passage (or pair of passages) in this section is followed by a number of multiple-choice questions. After reading each passage, select the best answer to each question based on what is stated or implied in the passage or passages and in any supplementary material, such as a table, graph, chart, or photograph.

Questions 1–10 are based on the following passage.

PASSAGE I

The following passage has been taken from the "The Bride Comes to Yellow Sky," by Stephen Crane. It is a western short story that was first published in 1898. The protagonist is Jack Potter, who returns to the town of Yellow Sky with his bride.

The great Pullman was whirling onward with such dignity of motion that a glance from the window seemed simply to prove that the plains of Texas were pouring
Line eastward. Vast flats of green grass, dull-hued spaces
5 of mesquite and cactus, little groups of frame houses, woods of light and tender trees, all were sweeping into the east, sweeping over the horizon, a precipice.

A newly married pair had boarded this coach at San Antonio. The man's face was reddened from many days
10 in the wind and sun, and a direct result of his new black clothes was that his brick-colored hands were constantly performing in a most conscious fashion. From time to time he looked down respectfully at his attire. He sat with a hand on each knee, like a man waiting in a bar-
15 ber's shop. The glances he devoted to other passengers were furtive and shy.

The bride was not pretty, nor was she very young. She wore a dress of blue cashmere, with small reservations of velvet here and there, and with steel buttons
20 abounding. She continually twisted her head to regard her puff sleeves, very stiff, straight, and high. They embarrassed her. It was quite apparent that she had cooked, and that she expected to cook, dutifully. The blushes caused by the careless scrutiny of some pas-
25 sengers as she had entered the car were strange to see upon this plain, under-class countenance, which was drawn in placid, almost emotionless lines.

They were evidently very happy. "Ever been in a parlor-car before?" he asked, smiling with delight.

30 "No," she answered; "I never was. It's fine, ain't it?"

"Great! And then after a while we'll go forward to the diner, and get a big layout. Finest meal in the world. Charge a dollar."

"Oh, do they?" cried the bride. "Charge a dollar?
35 Why, that's too much—for us—ain't it Jack?"

"Not this trip, anyhow," he answered bravely. "We're going to go the whole thing."

Later he explained to her about the trains. "You see, it's a thousand miles from one end of Texas to
40 the other; and this train runs right across it, and never stops but for four times." He had the pride of an owner. He pointed out to her the dazzling fittings of the coach, and in truth her eyes opened wider as she contemplated the sea-green figured velvet, the
45 shining brass, silver, and glass, the wood that gleamed as darkly brilliant as the surface of a pool of oil. At one end a bronze figure sturdily held a support for a separated chamber, and at convenient places on the ceiling were frescoes in olive and silver.

50 To the minds of the pair, their surroundings reflected the glory of their marriage that morning in San Antonio. This was the environment of their new estate; and the man's face in particular beamed with an elation that made him appear ridiculous to the
55 negro porter. This individual at times surveyed them from afar with an amused and superior grin. On other occasions he bullied them with skill in ways that did not make it exactly plain to them that they were being bullied. He subtly used all the manners of the most
60 unconquerable kind of snobbery. He oppressed them, but of this oppression they had small knowledge, and they speedily forgot that infrequently a number of travelers covered them with stares of derisive enjoyment. Historically, there was supposed to be
65 something infinitely humorous in their situation.

CONTINUE

1 The passage might best be described as

- **A.** an analysis of a man's acceptance of his social status.
- **B.** an account of a couple's anticipation of married life.
- **C.** a description of train travel in nineteenth-century Texas.
- **D.** a criticism of class consciousness in the nineteenth century.

2 It can be inferred from the passage that Jack

- **A.** wants to impress his new bride.
- **B.** is likely a farmhand or rancher.
- **C.** is used to being treated as an inferior.
- **D.** wants to change his station in life.

3 Which choice provides the best evidence for the answer to the previous question?

- **A.** Lines 12–15 ("From time . . . barber's shop.")
- **B.** Lines 17–22 ("The bride . . . embarrassed her.")
- **C.** Lines 31–37 ("'Great! . . . whole thing.")
- **D.** Lines 50–55 ("To the . . . negro porter.")

4 As used in line 2, "dignity" most nearly means

- **A.** splendor.
- **B.** respectability.
- **C.** superiority.
- **D.** gracefulness.

5 Jack and his bride might best be described as

- **A.** firm and resolute in their decisions.
- **B.** nervous and fearful about their trip.
- **C.** awkward and self-conscious in the setting.
- **D.** amazed and bewildered by the landscape.

6 Which choice provides the best evidence for the answer to the previous question?

- **A.** Lines 4–7 ("Vast flats . . . precipice.")
- **B.** Lines 12–16 ("From time . . . furtive and shy.)
- **C.** Lines 30–33 ("'No,' she . . . a dollar.")
- **D.** Lines 50–55 ("To the . . . negro porter.")

7 In lines 23–27 ("The blushes . . . emotionless lines."), why does the narrator note that the bride's blushing seemed so out of place on her face?

- **A.** To emphasize the degree to which other passengers are staring
- **B.** To express the bride's extreme happiness with her marriage
- **C.** To communicate that the bride is lacking in self-confidence
- **D.** To underscore that the bride is strikingly unattractive

8 As used in line 53, "estate" most nearly means

- **A.** project.
- **B.** interests.
- **C.** property.
- **D.** standing.

9 In lines 55–64 ("This individual . . . derisive enjoyment."), the narrator maintains that the

- **A.** porter mocks the couple, making Jack and his bride believe they are being catered to.
- **B.** couple barely notices the contemptuous way they are treated by the porter.
- **C.** porter is openly hostile to the couple, making the trip painful for them.
- **D.** couple has become used to the rude behavior of the porter.

10 What is the main rhetorical effect of lines 10–13 ("and a … his attire")?

A. To illustrate how nervous and awkward the groom is

B. To show how much the groom is used to using his hands

C. To convey how unaccustomed the groom is to wearing dress clothes

D. To show how happy the groom is about being married

Questions 11–21 are based on the following passage.

The following passage has been taken from American Ornithology *by Alexander Wilson, a Scottish-American naturalist. Dubbed "the Father of American Ornithology," Wilson is regarded as the greatest American ornithologist after Audubon. His nine-volume* American Ornithology *was published between 1808 and 1814.*

About the twenty-fifth of April the Hummingbird usually arrives in Pennsylvania; and about the tenth of May begins to build its nest. This is generally fixed on
Line the upper side of a horizontal branch, not among the
5 twigs, but on the body of the branch itself. Yet I have known instances where it was attached by the side to an old moss-grown trunk; and others where it was fastened on a strong rank stalk, or weed, in the garden; but these cases are rare. In the woods it very often chooses
10 a white oak sapling to build on; and in the orchard, or garden, selects a pear tree for that purpose. The branch is seldom more than ten feet from the ground. The nest is about an inch in diameter, and as much in depth. A very complete one is now lying before me, and the materials
15 of which it is composed are as follows: —The outward coat is formed of small pieces of bluish grey lichen that vegetates on old trees and fences, thickly glued on with the saliva of the bird, giving firmness and consistency to the whole, as well as keeping out moisture. Within
20 this are thick matted layers of the fine wings of certain flying seeds, closely laid together; and lastly, the downy substance from the great mullein, and from the stalks of the common fern, lines the whole. The base of the nest is continued round the stem of the branch, to which it
25 closely adheres; and, when viewed from below, appears a mere mossy knot or accidental protuberance. The eggs are two, pure white, and of equal thickness at both ends. . . . On a person's approaching their nest, the little proprietors dart around with a humming sound, passing
30 frequently within a few inches of one's head; and should the young be newly hatched, the female will resume her

place on the nest even while you stand within a yard or two of the spot. The precise period of incubation I am unable to give; but the young are in the habit, a short
35 time before they leave the nest, of thrusting their bills into the mouths of their parents, and sucking what they have brought them. I never could perceive that they carried them any animal food; tho, from circumstances that will presently be mentioned, I think it highly
40 probable they do. As I have found their nest with eggs so late as the twelfth of July, I do not doubt but that they frequently, and perhaps usually, raise two broods in the same season.

The hummingbird is extremely fond of tubular
45 flowers, and I have often stopt, with pleasure, to observe his maneuvers among the blossoms of the trumpet flower. When arrived before a thicket of these that are full blown, he poises, or suspends himself on wing, for the space of two or three seconds, so steadily, that his wings
50 become invisible, or only like a mist; and you can plainly distinguish the pupil of his eye looking round with great quickness and circumspection; the glossy golden green of his back, and the fire of his throat, dazzling in the sun, form altogether a most interesting appearance. The
55 position into which his body is usually thrown while in the act of thrusting his slender tubular tongue into the flower, to extract its sweets, is exhibited in the figure on the plate. When he alights, which is frequently, he always prefers the small dead twigs of a tree, or bush,
60 where he dresses and arranges his plumage with great dexterity. His only note is a single chirp, not louder than that of a small cricket or grasshopper, generally uttered while passing from flower to flower, or when engaged in fight with his fellows; for when two males meet at
65 the same bush, or flower, a battle instantly takes place; and the combatants ascend in the air, chirping, darting and circling around each other, till the eye is no longer able to follow them. The conqueror, however, generally returns to the place, to reap the fruits of his victory. I
70 have seen him attack, and for a few moments tease the King-bird; and have also seen him, in his turn, assaulted by a humble-bee, which he soon put to flight. He is one of those few birds that are universally beloved; and amidst the sweet dewy serenity of a summer's morning,
75 his appearance among the arbours of honeysuckles, and beds of flowers, is truly interesting.

CONTINUE

11 The author is mostly concerned with

    A. describing the characteristics of the hummingbird.

    B. explaining how hummingbirds build their nests.

    C. convincing the reader that hummingbirds are interesting.

    D. interpreting the meaning of certain hummingbird behaviors.

12 Based on lines 1–3 ("About the twenty-fifth of April . . . to build its nest."), it can generally be assumed that hummingbirds

    A. take two weeks to build their nests.

    B. migrate elsewhere for the winter.

    C. cannot be found in places farther north.

    D. are mostly solitary animals.

13 As used in line 3, "fixed" most nearly means

    A. adjusted.

    B. intended.

    C. aligned.

    D. secured.

14 In lines 13–26 ("A very complete one . . . accidental protuberance."), the author is mainly concerned with how the hummingbird

    A. uses nearby plants in the nest.

    B. builds compact, complicated nests.

    C. builds the nest over a period of time.

    D. constructs a nest that is waterproof.

15 It can be inferred from the passage that hummingbirds

    A. stay in the nest for years at a time.

    B. are fiercely protective of their eggs and young.

    C. have a sweet, though notably quiet, song.

    D. feed only on the sweet nectar of flowers.

16 Which choice provides the best evidence for the answer to the previous question?

    A. Lines 28–33 ("On a person's . . . the spot.")

    B. Lines 33–37 ("The precise . . . brought them.")

    C. Lines 37–40 ("I never . . . they do.")

    D. Lines 61–64 ("His only . . . with his fellows;")

17 As it is used in line 60, "dresses" most nearly means

    A. oils.

    B. dons.

    C. shuffles.

    D. neatens.

18 In lines 49–50, the author notes that the hummingbird's "wings become invisible, or only like a mist" to

    A. show how transparent the wings are.

    B. emphasize how fast the wings are moving.

    C. point out that the sun reflects off the wings.

    D. reiterate that the hummingbird is beautiful.

19 In lines 68–69 ("The conqueror . . . fruits of his victory."), "fruits of his victory" refers to

    A. the dead twigs of a tree.

    B. a female hummingbird.

    C. the nectar of a flower.

    D. the other combatant.

20 Which choice provides the best evidence for the answer to the previous question?

    A. Lines 1–3 ("About the twenty-fifth . . . its nest.")

    B. Lines 58–61 ("When he alights, . . . dexterity.")

    C. Lines 63–65 ("passing from . . . or flower,)

    D. Lines 66–68 ("and the combatants . . . follow them.")

21 The author most likely references the kingbird in lines 69–71 ("I have seen . . . King-bird.") to

    A. highlight the many dangers that confront hummingbirds.

    B. describe how the hummingbird stays close to its nest.

    C. emphasize that the hummingbird is an aggressive bird.

    D. introduce the idea that the hummingbird does not only fight for self-defense.

Questions 22–31 are based on the following passage and supplementary material.

The passage is excerpted from information provided by the National Oceanic and Atmospheric Administration (NOAA) at http://www.noaa.gov.

Over half a mile taller . . . than Mt. Everest, Mauna Kea in Hawai'i is more than 6 miles tall, from its base on the ocean floor to its summit two miles above the
Line surface of the Pacific Ocean. This island mountain is only
5 one of many features found on the ocean floor. Besides being the base for islands, the ocean floor also includes continental shelves and slopes, canyons, oceanic ridges, trenches, fracture zones, abyssal hills, abyssal plains, volcanoes, and seamounts. Not just rock and mud, these
10 locations are the sites of exotic ecosystems that have rarely been seen or even explored.

Plate Tectonics and the Ocean Floor

The shape of the ocean floor, its bathymetry, is largely a result of a process called plate tectonics. The outer rocky layer of the Earth includes about a dozen
15 large sections called tectonic plates that are arranged like a spherical jigsaw puzzle floating on top of the Earth's hot flowing mantle. Convection currents in the molten mantle layer cause the plates to slowly move about the Earth a few centimeters each year. Many ocean
20 floor features are a result of the interactions that occur at the edges of these plates.

The shifting plates may collide (converge), move away (diverge), or slide past (transform) each other. As plates converge, one plate may dive under the other,
25 causing earthquakes, forming volcanoes, or creating deep ocean trenches such as the Mariana Trench. Where plates are pulled away (diverge) from each other, molten magma flows upward between the plates, forming mid-ocean ridges, underwater volcanoes, hydrothermal

30 vents, and new ocean floor crust. The Mid-Atlantic Ridge is an example of this type of plate boundary. . . .

Marine Life and Exploration on the Ocean Floor

Over the last decade, more than 1500 new species have been discovered in the ocean by marine biologists and other ocean scientists. Many of these newly
35 discovered species live deep on the ocean floor in unique habitats dependent on processes resulting from plate movement, underwater volcanoes, and cold water seeps. The discovery of deep ocean hydrothermal vent ecosystems in 1977 forced scientists to redefine living
40 systems on our planet. Considered one of the most important scientific discoveries of the last century, organisms in this deep, dark ecosystem rely on chemicals and a process called chemosynthesis as the base of their food web and not on sunlight and photosynthesis as in
45 other previously described ecosystems. . . .

Hydrothermal vents form along mid-ocean ridges, in places where the sea floor moves apart very slowly (6 to 18 cm per year) as magma wells up from below. (This is the engine that drives Earth's tectonic plates apart,
50 moving continents and causing volcanic eruptions and earthquakes.) When cold ocean water seeps through cracks in the sea floor to hot spots below, hydrothermal vents belch a mineral-rich broth of scalding water. Sometimes, in very hot vents, the emerging fluid turns
55 black, creating a "black smoker," because dissolved sulfides of metals (iron, copper, and several heavy metals) instantaneously precipitate out of solution when they mix with the cold surrounding seawater.

Unlike plants that rely on sunlight, bacteria living
60 in and around the dark vents extract their energy from hydrogen sulfide (HS) and other molecules that billow out of the seafloor. Just like plants, the bacteria use their energy to build sugars out of carbon dioxide and water. Sugars then provide fuel and raw material for the rest of
65 the microbes' activities.

Why Is Chemosynthesis Important?

Chemosynthetic deep-sea bacteria form the base of a varied food web that includes shrimp, tubeworms, clams, fish, crabs, and octopi. All of these animals must be adapted to endure the extreme environment of the
70 vents—complete darkness; water temperatures ranging from 2°C (in ambient seawater) to about 400°C (at the vent openings); pressures hundreds of times that at sea level; and high concentrations of sulfides and other noxious chemicals.

CONTINUE

Practice Test 1

Why is photosynthesis important?

75 Aquatic and terrestrial plants form the base of varied food webs that may include small fish and crabs, larger fish, and eventually, humans.

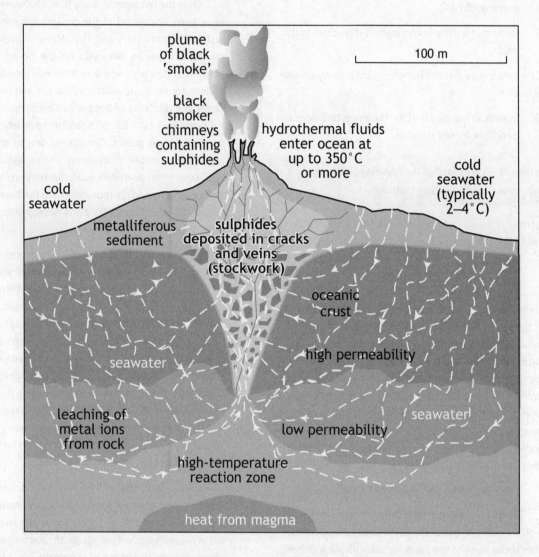

22 Which best describes the function of the opening sentence ("Over half a mile taller . . . the Pacific Ocean.")?

  A. It shows how unusual and extraordinary some ocean features are.

  B. It emphasizes that Mt. Everest is not the world's tallest mountain.

  C. It describes the geography of island mountains in the Pacific Ocean.

  D. It compares the geography of Mt. Everest to that of Mauna Kea.

23 The author uses the simile "like a spherical jigsaw puzzle" (line 16) to illustrate that

  A. each plate plays a critical role.

  B. the earth is sphere-shaped.

  C. each plate is symmetrical.

  D. the plates fit together.

24 The movement of the earth's tectonic plates is a function of

    A. earthquakes and volcanoes.

    B. the movement of ocean tides.

    C. new ocean floor crust.

    D. the moving molten mantle layer.

25 Which inference can you make about scientists' pre-1977 understanding of deep ocean hydrothermal vent ecosystems?

    A. Scientists did not know how organisms in deep ocean hydrothermal vent ecosystems survived.

    B. Scientists believed that colliding plates caused the formation of deep ocean hydrothermal vents.

    C. Scientists determined that some sea life can move easily between shallow waters and deep ocean hydrothermal vent ecosystems.

    D. Scientists believed minerals could be mined from deep ocean hydrothermal vent ecosystems.

26 Which choice provides the best evidence for the answer to the previous question?

    A. Lines 32–34 ("Over the . . . ocean scientists.")

    B. Lines 40–44 ("Considered one . . . web.")

    C. Lines 46–48 ("Hydrothermal vents . . . from below.")

    D. Lines 54–58 ("Sometimes, in . . . surrounding seawater.")

27 As it is used in line 61, "billow" most nearly means

    A. flow.

    B. crest.

    C. wave.

    D. inflate.

28 The author devotes the first half of the passage to an explanation of plate tectonics in order to

    A. describe the geography of the ocean floor.

    B. explain the conditions that create hydrothermal vents.

    C. compare hydrothermal vents to underwater volcanoes.

    D. argue that hydrothermal vents are a unique ecosystem.

29 Which choice provides the best evidence for the answer to the previous question?

    A. Lines 5–9 ("Besides being . . . and seamounts.")

    B. Lines 34–38 ("Many of . . . water seeps.")

    C. Lines 46–48 ("Hydrothermal vents . . . from below.")

    D. Lines 48–51 ("This is the engine . . . and earthquakes.")

30 As used in line 74, "noxious" most nearly means

    A. annoying.

    B. harmful.

    C. offensive.

    D. unusual.

31 Why does the passage mention photosynthesis in line 44?

    A. To aid in explaining the concept of chemosynthesis, the author briefly compares it to photosynthesis.

    B. Photosynthesis is one of the most important scientific discoveries of the last century.

    C. Photosynthesis is an integral part of varied food webs.

    D. The main goal of the passage is to help the reader more fully understand the importance of photosynthesis.

CONTINUE

*The passage is an excerpt from "How the Other Half Lives," by Jacob
Riis. It was published in 1890 and documented the squalid living
conditions in the tenements of New York City.*

The old question, what to do with the boy, assumes
a new and serious phase in the tenements. Under the
best conditions found there, it is not easily answered.
Line In nine cases out of ten he would make an excellent
5 mechanic, if trained early to work at a trade, for he is
neither dull nor slow, but the short-sighted despotism
of the trades unions has practically closed that avenue
to him. Trade-schools, however excellent, cannot supply
the opportunity thus denied him, and at the outset the
10 boy stands condemned by his own to low and ill-paid
drudgery, held down by the hand that of all should labor
to raise him.

Home, the greatest factor of all in the training of
the young, means nothing to him but a pigeon-hole
15 in a coop along with so many other human animals. Its
influence is scarcely of the elevating kind, if it have any.
The very games at which he takes a hand in the street
become polluting in its atmosphere. With no steady
hand to guide him, the boy takes naturally to idle ways.
20 Caught in the street by the truant officer, or by the
agents of the Children's Societies, peddling, perhaps, or
begging, to help out the family resources, he runs the
risk of being sent to a reformatory, where contact with
vicious boys older than himself soon develop the latent
25 possibilities for evil that lie hidden in him. The city has
no Truant Home in which to keep him, and all efforts
of the children's friends to enforce school attendance
are paralyzed by this want. The risk of the reformatory
is too great. What is done in the end is to let him take
30 chances—with the chances all against him. The result is
the rough young savage, familiar from the street. Rough

as he is, if any one doubt that this child of common clay
have in him the instinct of beauty, of love for the ideal of
which his life has no embodiment, let him put the matter
35 to the test. Let him take into a tenement block a handful
of flowers from the fields and watch the brightened
faces, the sudden abandonment of play and fight that
go ever hand in hand where there is no elbow-room,
the wild entreaty for "posies," the eager love with which
40 the little messengers of peace are shielded, once possessed; then let him change his mind. I have seen an
armful of daisies keep the peace of a block better than
a policeman and his club, seen instincts awaken under
their gentle appeal, whose very existence the soil in
45 which they grew made seem a mockery. . . .

Yet, as I knew, that dismal alley with its bare brick
walls, between which no sun ever rose or set, was
the world of those children. It filled their young lives.
Probably not one of them had ever been out of the sight
50 of it. They were too dirty, too ragged, and too generally
disreputable, too well hidden in their slum besides, to
come into line with the Fresh Air summer boarders.

With such human instincts and cravings, forever
unsatisfied, turned into a haunting curse; with appetite
55 ground to keenest edge by a hunger that is never fed,
the children of the poor grow up in joyless homes to
lives of wearisome toil that claims them at an age when
the play of their happier fellows has but just begun. Has
a yard of turf been laid and a vine been coaxed to grow
60 within their reach, they are banished and barred out
from it as from a heaven that is not for such as they. I
came upon a couple of youngsters in a Mulberry Street
yard a while ago that were chalking on the fence their
first lesson in "writin'."

65 And this is what they wrote: "Keeb of te Grass." They
had it by heart, for there was not, I verily believe, a green
sod within a quarter of a mile. Home to them is an empty
name.

32 The passage is mainly concerned with establishing that

A. there are very few job opportunities available for poor people.

B. the condition of the tenements condemns children to lives of misery.

C. more education is needed to help elevate the children of the poor.

D. children who live in poverty naturally turn to crime to support themselves.

33 As it is used in line 18, "polluting" most nearly means

A. dirty.

B. dangerous.

C. corrupting.

D. rowdy.

34 In line 10, "condemned by his own" means that the boy is

A. denounced because of his character.

B. criticized by his family members.

C. held back by his own community.

D. ridiculed by teachers in his school.

35 Which choice provides the best evidence for the answer to the previous question?

A. Lines 17–18 ("The very . . . atmosphere.")

B. Lines 20–21 ("Caught . . . Societies")

C. Lines 25–26 ("The city . . . keep him")

D. Lines 29–30 ("What is done . . . against him.")

36 In lines 14–15, the author uses the metaphor of the pigeon coop to establish that the tenement is

A. as filthy as a cage in which animals are kept.

B. completely devoid of privacy for its tenants.

C. the only housing available for any person.

D. merely a place to live and lacks any positive influences.

37 As it is used in line 19, "idle" most nearly means

A. unproductive.

B. vain.

C. immature.

D. simple.

38 The author suggests taking flowers to the tenement child to show that

A. he has the capacity to appreciate exquisite things.

B. he is always bored and will play with anything.

C. there are few flowers growing in the tenements.

D. the policemen patrolling the tenements are brutal.

39 Which choice provides the best evidence for the answer to the previous question?

A. Lines 30–31 ("The result . . . the street.")

B. Lines 31–35 ("Rough as . . . the test.")

C. Lines 41–45 ("I have . . . a mockery.")

D. Lines 46–48 ("Yet, as . . . those children.")

40 What seems to be the author's main perspective on children who live in tenements?

A. They are more inherently evil than other children.

B. They are less intelligent than other children.

C. Their parents are to blame for not forcing them to attend school.

D. The conditions of the tenements are to blame for the children's misery.

41 The author provides the story of the "writin'" in the last paragraph to show that tenement children

A. do not know how to spell.

B. are in need of good schools.

C. have no access to green spaces.

D. are prone to vandalism.

CONTINUE

42 The author suggests in lines 25–28 that a truant home

    A. is no different from a reformatory.

    B. does not enforce school attendance.

    C. is full of vicious young boys.

    D. is necessary but unavailable.

Questions 43–52 are based on the following two passages.

Passage 1 is a letter written by Robert Schumann to Clara Wieck in 1838.

Passage 2 is a letter from Napoleon Bonaparte to his wife Josephine, written in 1796.

PASSAGE 1

Robert Schumann to Clara Wieck (1838)

I have a hundred things to write to you, great and small, if only I could do it neatly, but my writing grows more and more indistinct, a sign, I fear, of heart
Line
weakness. There are terrible hours when your image
5 forsakes me, when I wonder anxiously whether I have ordered my life as wisely as I might, whether I had any right to bind you to me, my angel, or can really make you as happy as I should wish. These doubts all arise, I am inclined to think, from your father's attitude towards me.
10 It is so easy to accept other people's estimate of oneself. Your father's behaviour makes me ask myself if I am really so bad—of such humble standing—as to invite such treatment from anyone. Accustomed to easy victory over difficulties, to the smiles of fortune, and to affection, I
15 have been spoiled by having things made too easy for me, and now I have to face refusal, insult, and calumny. I have read of many such things in novels, but I thought too highly of myself to imagine I could ever be the hero of a family tragedy of the Kotzebue sort myself. If I had
20 ever done your father an injury, he might well hate me; but I cannot see why he should despise me and, as you say, hate me without any reason. But my turn will come, and I will then show him how I love you and himself; for I will tell you, as a secret, that I really love and respect
25 your father for his many great and fine qualities, as no one but yourself can do. I have a natural inborn devotion and reverence for him, as for all strong characters, and it makes his antipathy for me doubly painful. Well, he may some time declare peace, and say to us, "Take each
30 other, then."

You cannot think how your letter has raised and strengthened me. . . . You are splendid, and I have much more reason to be proud of you than of me. I have made up my mind, though, to read all your wishes in your face.
35 Then you will think, even though you don't say it, that your Robert is a really good sort, that he is entirely yours, and loves you more than words can say. You shall indeed have cause to think so in the happy future. I still see you as you looked in your little cap that last evening. I still
40 hear you call me *du*. Clara, I heard nothing of what you said but that *du*. Don't you remember?

PASSAGE 2

Napoleon Bonaparte to Josephine Bonaparte (1796)

I have not spent a day without loving you; I have not spent a night without embracing you; I have not so much as drunk a single cup of tea without cursing the pride
45 and ambition which force me to remain separated from the moving spirit of my life. In the midst of my duties, whether I am at the head of my army or inspecting the camps, my beloved Josephine stands alone in my heart, occupies my mind, fills my thoughts. If I am moving away
50 from you with the speed of the Rhône torrent, it is only that I may see you again more quickly. If I rise to work in the middle of the night, it is because this may hasten by a matter of days the arrival of my sweet love. Yet in your letter of the 23rd and 26th Ventôse, you call me *vous*.
55 Vous yourself! Ah! wretch, how could you have written this letter? How cold it is! And then there are those four days between the 23rd and the 26th; what were you doing that you failed to write to your husband? . . . Ah, my love, that *vous,* those four days make me long for
60 my former indifference. Woe to the person responsible! May he, as punishment and penalty, experience what my convictions and the evidence (which is in your friend's favour) would make me experience! Hell has no torments great enough! *Vous! Vous!* Ah! How will things stand in
65 two weeks? . . . My spirit is heavy; my heart is fettered and I am terrified by my fantasies. . . . You love me less; but you will get over the loss. One day you will love me no longer; at least tell me; then I shall know how I have come to deserve this misfortune. . . .

---

43 Both passages are primarily concerned with the subject of

    A. jealousy.

    B. commitment.

    C. work.

    D. being apart.

44 As it is used in line 28, "antipathy" most nearly means

   A. indifference.

   B. mistrust.

   C. rudeness.

   D. dislike.

45 We can infer from Passage 1 that Clara's father's feelings about Robert have caused Robert to

   A. dislike Clara's father.

   B. question his and Clara's future.

   C. doubt Clara's love for him.

   D. question Clara's character.

46 Which choice provides the best evidence for the answer to the previous question?

   A. Lines 4–9 ("There are . . . towards me.")

   B. Lines 11–13 ("Your father's . . . from anyone.")

   C. Lines 22–26 ("But my . . . can do.")

   D. Lines 35–37 ("Then you . . . can say.")

47 Napoleon's letter to Josephine suggests that she

   A. wishes she could fight alongside her husband.

   B. has little to occupy her time.

   C. is distracting him from his responsibilities.

   D. has never regretted her marriage to him.

48 Which choice provides the best evidence for the answer to the previous question?

   A. Lines 42–43 ("I have . . . you")

   B. Lines 43–46 ("I have . . . my life.")

   C. Lines 46–48 ("In the . . . heart")

   D. Lines 49–51 ("If I . . . quickly.")

49 As it is used in line 52, "hasten" most nearly means

   A. stretch out.

   B. speed up.

   C. force.

   D. cause.

50 We can infer that Clara's letter to Robert was different from Josephine's letter to Napoleon in that Clara's letter

   A. made Robert doubt himself.

   B. made Robert question her loyalty.

   C. left Robert feeling encouraged.

   D. left Robert feeling confused.

51 In each passage, the author recollects something his beloved said. But the effect of Josephine's words (lines 53–56) differ from the effect of Clara's words (lines 39–41) in that

   A. Josephine's words have hurt Napoleon.

   B. Clara's words have offended Robert.

   C. Josephine's words have calmed Napoleon.

   D. Clara's words have humbled Robert.

52 We can infer that both Robert and Napoleon

   A. are modest people.

   B. anger quickly.

   C. tend to be indecisive.

   D. suffer from self-doubt.

STOP

If you finish before time is called, you may check your work on this section only.
Do not turn to any other section.

SECTION 2: WRITING AND LANGUAGE TEST

35 Minutes—44 Questions

TURN TO SECTION 2 OF YOUR ANSWER SHEET TO ANSWER THE QUESTIONS IN THIS SECTION.

DIRECTIONS: Each passage below is accompanied by a number of multiple-choice questions. For some questions, you will need to consider how the passage might be revised to improve the expression of ideas. Other questions will ask you to consider how the passage might be edited to correct errors in sentence structure, usage, or punctuation. A passage may be accompanied by one or more graphics—such as a chart, table, or graph—that you will need to refer to in order to best answer the question(s).

Some questions will direct you to an underlined portion of a passage—it could be one word, a portion of a sentence, or the full sentence itself. Other questions will direct you to a particular paragraph or to certain sentences within a paragraph, or you'll be asked to think about the passage as a whole. Each question number refers to the corresponding number in the passage.

After reading each passage, select the answer to each question that most effectively improves the quality of writing in the passage or that makes the passage follow the conventions of Standard Written English. Many questions include a "NO CHANGE" option. Select that option if you think the best choice is to leave that specific portion of the passage as it is.

Questions 1–11 are based on the following passage.

Burma: has it truly changed?

A rigid red-and-white sign **1** erected on a rural road in Burma reads, "[The Military] AND THE PEOPLE IN ETERNAL UNITY. ANYONE ATTEMPTING TO DIVIDE THEM IS OUR ENEMY."

It's no wonder that Burma, also known as Myanmar, inspired two of the most well-known books about totalitarianism: **2** *Animal Farm* and *Nineteen Eighty-Four?* The books sprang from the mind of a man who, as a teenager, sought adventure with the British Imperial Police Force in the 1920s. Five years after Eric Arthur Blair began his tour of duty in the far-flung, **3** obscure Asian colony, he returned to his homeland, shed his uniform, changed his name to George Orwell, and started a new career as a novelist.

1

A. NO CHANGE

B. born

C. floated

D. dripped

2

A. NO CHANGE

B. *Animal Farm* and *Nineteen Eighty-Four.*

C. *Animal Farm* and *Nineteen Eighty-Four,*

D. *Animal Farm* and *Nineteen Eighty-Four!*

3

A. NO CHANGE

B. darkened

C. obvious

D. uncertain

CONTINUE

The contrasts Orwell saw still exist. This land of haunting beauty, with its history of human rights violations, **4** had also sparked filmmaker Ron Fricke's imagination. He and his crew traveled to 25 countries to shoot images for his non-verbal film *Samsara* (2013). *Samsara* means "the ever-turning wheel of life" in Sanskrit. The sequences shot in Bagan, Burma, are almost dreamlike in quality, especially because, as in the rest of the film, there is no dialogue or narration. **5** Only music accompanies scenes of hundreds of Buddhist temples as they seemingly float upon seas of green foliage. Watching these scenes, it is hard to believe that Burma has seen violent years of civil war, ethnic cleansing, and forced labor. But such problems, as well as those of economic stagnation and corruption, can usually be traced back to the military regime, which took power in 1962 through a coup. The military manages **6** the country's major industries and has also been accused of controlling Burma's substantial heroin exports.

The Irish rock band U2 dedicated their song "Walk On" to Burmese academic Aung San Suu Kyi, who was under house arrest from 1989 until 2010 because of her pro-democracy stance. **7** The members of U2 have a history of incorporating their political views into their music. Her National League for Democracy (NLD) won the 1990 elections with an overwhelming majority, but she was not allowed to serve.

4

A. NO CHANGE

B. have also sparked

C. also sparked

D. will also spark

5

A. NO CHANGE

B. As they seemingly float above seas of green foliage, only music accompanies scenes of hundreds of Buddhist temples.

C. Only music accompanies scenes, as they seemingly float above seas of green foliage, of hundreds of Buddhist temples.

D. Only music accompanies scenes, of hundreds of Buddhist temples, as they seemingly float above a sea of green foliage.

6

A. NO CHANGE

B. the countries major industries

C. the countrys major industries

D. the countries' major industries

7 The writer is considering deleting the underlined sentence. Should the writer do this?

A. Yes, because the sentence does not support the main idea of the paragraph.

B. Yes, because the sentence should be moved to the beginning of the paragraph.

C. No, because the sentence expands upon the main idea of the paragraph.

D. No, because the sentence introduces an important detail about Burma.

8 <u>An honor given out, in 1991 given out to people, by the Nobel Committee since 1901, and organizations, she received the Nobel Peace Prize.</u>

The lyrics of U2's song are about doing what's right, even if it requires personal sacrifice. **9** <u>Not surprisingly, the album was banned and not allowed to be distributed in Burma. Anyone caught attempting to smuggle it into the country would have been imprisoned for three to twenty years for smuggling.</u>

[1] Military rule supposedly ended in 2011. **10** [2] However, it's too soon to be sure that the people of this land are finally free of the ever-watching gaze of Big Brother. [3] Then-Secretary of State Hillary Clinton visited in 2011 and President Obama in 2012. [4] Soon after, the European Union lifted sanctions against Burma and offered it financial aid. [5] There are signs that the country is emerging from **11** <u>their isolation.</u> However, it's too soon to be sure that the people of this land are finally free of the ever-watching gaze of Big Brother.

8 Which of the following most effectively presents the ideas in this sentence?

A. NO CHANGE

B. In 1991 she received the Nobel Peace Prize, an honor given out to people and organizations by the Nobel Committee since 1901.

C. The Nobel Peace Prize, since 1901 by the Nobel Committee, she received in 1991, an honor given out to people and organizations.

D. Given out to people, an honor in 1991, since 1901 and organizations, the Nobel Peace Prize she received, and organizations.

9

A. NO CHANGE

B. Not surprisingly, the album was banned. Anyone caught attempting to smuggle it into the country would have been imprisoned for three to twenty years.

C. Not surprisingly, the album was banned and not allowed to be distributed in Burma. Anyone caught attempting to smuggle it into the country would have been imprisoned for three to twenty years.

D. Not surprisingly, the album was banned from things that could be smuggled into Burma. Anyone caught attempting to obtain it in the country would have been imprisoned for three to twenty years.

10 To make this paragraph most logical, sentence 2 should be

A. kept where it is now.

B. placed before sentence 4.

C. placed after sentence 5.

D. removed.

11

A. NO CHANGE

B. its isolation

C. our isolation

D. your isolation

CONTINUE

John Dewey and Education

John Dewey, an American educator and philosopher of education, was a prolific writer on the subject. He was particularly interested in the place of education in a democratic republic.

The place of public education within a democratic society has been widely discussed and debated through the years. Perhaps no one has written more widely on the subject in the United States than John Dewey, **12** a philosopher and teacher, whose theories on education have a large social component, that is, an emphasis on education **13** as a social act, and the classroom or learning environment as a replica of society.

Dewey defined various aspects or characteristics of education. First, **14** they were a necessity of life inasmuch as living beings needed to maintain themselves through a process of renewal. Therefore, just as humans needed **15** sleep; food; water; and shelter for physiological renewal, they also needed education to renew their minds, assuring that their socialization kept pace with physiological growth.

12 Which choice provides the most relevant detail?

A. NO CHANGE

B. sometimes called "the father of public education,"

C. the son of a grocer in Burlington, Vermont,

D. a university professor who taught ethics and logic,

13

A. NO CHANGE

B. as a social act, and the classroom, or learning environment, as a replica of society

C. as a social act and the classroom or learning environment as a replica of society

D. as a social act and the classroom, or learning environment, as a replica of society

14

A. NO CHANGE

B. it was

C. we were

D. he was

15

A. NO CHANGE

B. sleep: food: water: and shelter

C. sleep, food, water; and shelter

D. sleep, food, water, and shelter

16 The main aspect of education was its social component, which was to be accomplished by providing the young with an environment that would provide a nurturing atmosphere to encourage the growth of their as yet undeveloped social customs.

17 The final aspect of public education was the provision of direction to youngsters, who might otherwise be left in uncontrolled situations, without the steadying and organizing influences of school. Direction was not to be of an **18** autonomous nature, but rather indirect through the selection of the school situations in which the youngster participated.

19 On the other hand, Dewey saw public education as a catalyst for growth. Since the young came to school capable of growth, it was the role of education to provide opportunities for that growth to occur. The successful school environment is one in which a desire for continued growth is created—a desire that extends throughout one's life beyond the end of formal education. . . .

---

16 The writer is considering revising the underlined portion of the sentence to read as follows:

A second aspect of education was its social component,

Should the writer make this revision here?

A. Yes, because the change improves the organization.

B. Yes, because the change clarifies the aspects of education.

C. No, because the change eliminates information that supports the main idea of the paragraph.

D. No, because the change makes the organization of this part of the passage unclear.

17

A. NO CHANGE

B. Leaving youngsters in uncontrolled situations, without the steadying and organizing influences of school, would not provide them with direction.

C. Without school, youngsters would have no direction.

D. A third aspect of public education was the provision of direction to youngsters, who might otherwise be left in uncontrolled situations, without the steadying and organizing influences of school.

18

A. NO CHANGE

B. uncertain

C. overt

D. abstract

19

A. NO CHANGE

B. Finally,

C. In retrospect,

D. Therefore,

CONTINUE

Neither did Dewey's model see education as a means by which the past was recapitulated. Instead, **20** education was a continuous reconstructions of experiences, grounded very much in the present environment.

21 The nature of the larger society that supports the educational system, since Dewey's model places a heavy emphasis on the social component, is of paramount importance. The ideal larger society, according to Dewey, is one in which the interests of a group are all shared by all of its members and in which interactions with other groups are free and full. According to Dewey, education in such a society should provide members of the group a stake or interest in social relationships and the ability to **22** subjugate change without compromising the order and stability of the society.

20

A. NO CHANGE

B. educations were continuous reconstructions of experiences

C. education was a continuous reconstruction of experience

D. education was experiences being continuously reconstructed

21

A. NO CHANGE

B. The nature of the larger society that supports the educational system is of paramount important since Dewey's model places a heavy emphasis on the social component.

C. Of paramount importance, since Dewey's model places a heavy emphasis on the social component, is the nature of the larger society that supports the educational system.

D. Since Dewey's model places a heavy emphasis on the social component, the nature of the larger society that supports the educational system is of paramount importance.

22

A. NO CHANGE

B. negotiate

C. complicate

D. obfuscate

The study of plant life is very different from the study of animal life because of unique plant characteristics. The following passage provides an overview of those characteristics, along with some plant classifications that are of interest to scientists.

 Compared to animals, plants present unique problems in demographic studies. The idea of counting living individuals becomes difficult given perennials that reproduce vegetatively <u>by sending out runners or rhizomes, splitting at the stem base, or by producing arching canes that take root where they touch the ground.</u> In these ways some individuals, given sufficient time, can extend out over a vast area.

Each plant life span has a basic associated life form. *Annual plants* live for 1 year or less. Their average life span is 1–8 months, depending on the species and on the environment where they are located (the same desert plant may complete **25** its life cycle in 8 months one year and in 1 month the next, depending on the amount of rain it receives). Annuals with extremely short life cycles are classified as *ephemeral* plants. An example of an ephemeral is *Boerrhavia repens* of the Sahara Desert, which can go from seed to seed in just 10 days. Annuals are herbaceous, which means that they lack a secondary meristem that produces lateral, woody tissue. They complete their life cycle after seed production for several reasons: nutrient depletion, hormone changes, or inability of non-woody tissue to withstand unfavorable environmental conditions following the growing season. A few species can persist for more than a year in uncommonly favorable conditions.

Biennial plants are also herbaceous, but usually live for 2 years. <u>Their first year is spent in vegetative growth, which generally takes place more below ground than above.</u> Reproduction occurs in the second year, and this is followed by the completion of the life cycle. Under poor growing conditions, or by experimental manipulation, the vegetative stage can be drawn out for more than 1 year.

23 Which of the following would make the most effective introductory sentence to this passage?

A. When it comes to the study of plants and animals, there are distinct differences between each.

B. When it comes to the study of plants and animals, there are no obvious and discernible differences.

C. Let's learn more about some unique animals and plants!

D. Have you ever studied various life forms in science class?

24

A. NO CHANGE

B. by sending out runners or rhizomes, a split at the stem base, or the production of arching canes that take root where they touch the ground.

C. by sending out runners or rhizomes, splitting at the stem base, or in the production of arching canes that take root where they touch the ground.

D. by sending out runners or rhizomes, splitting at the stem base, or producing arching canes that take root where they touch the ground.

25

A. NO CHANGE

B. it's

C. its'

D. it is

26 The writer is considering deleting the underlined sentence. Should the writer do this?

A. Yes, because it doesn't support the main idea of the paragraph.

B. Yes, because it is out of place in the paragraph.

C. No, because it describes vegetative growth.

D. No, because it describes what happens in the first year.

CONTINUE

Herbaceous perennials typically live for 20–30 years, although some species have been known to live for 400–800 years. These plants die back to the root system and root crown at the end of each growing season. The root system becomes woody, but the above-ground system is herbaceous. **27** An initial vegetative state first, popular landscaping plants, they then bloom and reproduce yearly after making them popular landscaping plants. Sometimes they bloom only once at the conclusion of their life cycle. Because herbaceous perennials have no growth rings, it is difficult to age them. Methods that have been used to age them include counting leaf scars and **28** reducing the rate of spread in *tussock* (clumped) forms.

29 *Suffrutescent* shrubs (hemixyles) falls somewhere between herbaceous perennials and true shrubs. They develop perennial, woody tissue only near the base of their **30** stems. The rest of the shoot system is herbaceous and dies back each year. They are small and short-lived compared to true shrubs.

31 *Woody perennials* (trees and shrubs) have the longest life spans. Shrubs live on average 30–50 years. Broadleaf trees (angiosperm) average 200–300 years, and conifer (needles) trees average 500–1,000 years. Woody perennials spend approximately the first 10 percent of their life span in a juvenile, totally vegetative state before they enter a combined reproductive and vegetative state, achieving a peak of reproduction several years before the conclusion of their life cycle.

27 Which choice most effectively maintains the paragraph's focus on relevant information and ideas?

A. NO CHANGE

B. Their initial vegetative state lasts 2–8 years, which is an adaptation that is not seen in animals.

C. Blooming and reproducing early, herbaceous perennials include such plants as hollyhocks, aster, and yarrow.

D. They have a juvenile, vegetative stage for the first 2–8 years, then bloom and reproduce yearly.

28

A. NO CHANGE

B. hedging

C. estimating

D. valuing

29

A. NO CHANGE

B. *Suffrutescent* shrubs (hemixyles) fall

C. *Suffrutescent* shrub (hemixyles) fall

D. *Suffrutescent* shrubs (hemixyles) has fallen

30 Which choice most effectively combines the two sentences at the underlined portion?

A. stems, the rest of the shoot system

B. stems because the rest of the shoot system

C. stems: the rest of the shoot system

D. stems; the rest of the shoot system

31

A. NO CHANGE

B. *Woody perennials*—trees and shrubs—have the longest life spans.

C. *Woody perennials,* trees and shrubs, have the longest life spans.

D. *Woody perennials* "trees and shrubs" have the longest life spans.

32 <u>Irregardless</u> of the life span, annual or perennial, one can identify about eight important age states in an individual plant or population. They are: (1) viable seed, (2) seedling, (3) juvenile, (4) immature, (5) mature, (6) initial reproductive, (7) maximum vigor (reproductive and vegetative), and (8) senescent. If a population shows all eight states, it is **33** <u>stable</u> and is most likely a part of a *climax* community. If it shows only the last four states, it may not maintain itself and may be part of a *seral* community.

32

A. NO CHANGE

B. Regardless

C. Irregardless

D. Regarding less

33 Which choice is most consistent with the style and tone of the passage?

A. NO CHANGE

B. diminishing

C. ephemeral

D. uniform

Questions 34–44 are based on the following passage and supplementary chart.

Variations in wage

34 [1] Within certain fields, workers are especially likely to receive different salaries. [2] According to the Bureau of Labor Statistics (BLS), large differences in wages can be explained by a variety of factors. [3] Commercial pilots, for example, had a median annual wage **35** of $75,620: more than double the median for all occupations in May 2014. [4] But that median figure **36** diminishes the fact that the gap between the 90th percentile wage and the 10th percentile wage was more than $100,000. [5] In other words, just because someone chooses to be a commercial pilot does not necessarily mean he or she will earn as much as the top earners in the field.

34 For the sake of the cohesion of this paragraph, sentence 1 should be placed

- A. where it is now.
- B. after sentence 2.
- C. after sentence 3.
- D. after sentence 4.

35

- A. NO CHANGE
- B. of $75,620 more than double
- C. of $75,620; more than double
- D. of $75,620—more than double

36

- A. NO CHANGE
- B. contradicts
- C. conceals
- D. equivocates

Table 1. Arts, Entertainment, and Sports Occupations with More than $100,000 Wage Difference, May 2014

Occupation	Employment	Median wage	10th percentile wage	90th percentile wage[1]	Wage difference[2]
Actors[3]	59,210	$41,230	$18,720	>$187,200	>$168,480
Athletes and sports competitors	11,520	43,350	20,190	>187,200	>167,010
Producers and directors	97,300	69,100	31,380	>187,200	>155,820
Broadcast news analysts	4,310	61,450	28,210	182,470	154,260
Art directors	33,140	85,610	45,060	168,040	122,980
Film and video editors	24,460	57,210	25,520	145,620	120,100
Musicians and singers[3]	38,900	50,250	18,680	137,510	118,830

Footnotes:

(1) BLS does not publish specific estimates for percentile wages above $187,200 per year. Where the percentile wage is greater than $187,200, the wage is shown with a greater-than sign (>).

(2) Wage differences with a greater-than sign (>) were calculated using $187,200, the highest percentile wage that BLS publishes.

(3) In occupations in which workers typically are paid by the hour and work less than the standard 2,080 hours per year, BLS reports only hourly wages. For comparison purposes in calculating wage differences, the hourly wage was multiplied by 2,080 to get an annual wage.

Source: Occupational Employment Statistics survey, Bureau of Labor Statistics

Why wages vary

Everyone is **37** <u>unique</u>. Each person comes to a position with her own set of skills, a capacity for adapting to the demands of the job, and **38** <u>their</u> own personal strengths and weaknesses. In addition, job titles can be **39** <u>deceiving</u>. No two jobs are identical. In some fields, this allows for opportunity to advance dramatically in terms of rank and earnings. There are the fields in which these differences are very obvious, such as professional sports or the entertainment field.

In occupations with less variability among workers, wage differences are usually **40** <u>vast</u>. Fast food cooks, for example, earn similar wages. Workers in this occupation have fewer opportunities for advancement and higher pay than other occupations. Nevertheless, there are a variety of factors that **41** <u>effect</u> how much a person earns.

Credentials. In some jobs, having advanced education is necessary for advancement. In other careers, holding a professional license or training credentials will increase a worker's wage.

Experience. Experienced workers usually earn more than those newer to the field. Employers will pay more for a skilled employee, especially in fields in which they are in high demand.

37

A. NO CHANGE
B. common
C. normal
D. typical

38

A. NO CHANGE
B. our
C. its
D. her

39

A. NO CHANGE
B. tenuous
C. impractical
D. incidental

40

A. NO CHANGE
B. noticeable
C. small
D. productive

41

A. NO CHANGE
B. affect
C. infect
D. reflect

CONTINUE

Job tasks. Jobs that are more complex or that demand more responsibility often pay more. **42**

Location. In the US, a worker doing the same job as another in a different state may earn a very different salary. **43** <u>Some of the factors—cost of living and the local demand for the skill these are—behind this, variation.</u> For example, in New York City, the cost of living is high and workers will be paid more than their counterparts in Billings, Montana.

Performance. In highly competitive fields, such as sports, only a small percentage of athletes will experience great success. There will be many athletes who experience only little or moderate success, **44** <u>and consequently their median wage will rank below everyone except broadcast news analysts.</u>

42 Which of the following, if added to the passage, would best support the author's point of view regarding job tasks in the previous sentence?

A. Even within the same company, two workers with the same job title will sometimes be given the exact same tasks and receive different wages as a result.

B. Even within the same company, two workers with the same job title will sometimes be given different tasks and receive different wages as a result.

C. Even within the same company, two workers with the same job title will sometimes be given different tasks and receive the same wages as a result.

D. Even within the same company, two workers with the same job title will sometimes be given the same tasks and receive the same wages as a result.

43

A. NO CHANGE

B. Cost of living and the local demand for the skill: some of the factors behind this variation.

C. Some of the factors behind this variation, cost of living and the local demand for the skill.

D. Some of the factors behind this variation include cost of living and the local demand for the skill.

44 Which choice completes the sentence with accurate data based on the supplementary table?

A. NO CHANGE.

B. and consequently their median wage will rank below everyone except actors.

C. and consequently their median wage will rank above only singers and musicians.

D. and consequently their median wage will rank above only film and video editors.

STOP

If you finish before time is called, you may check your work on this section only.
Do not turn to any other section.

SECTION 3: MATH TEST—NO CALCULATOR

25 Minutes—20 Questions

TURN TO SECTION 3 OF YOUR ANSWER SHEET TO ANSWER THE QUESTIONS IN THIS SECTION.

DIRECTIONS: For **Questions 1–15,** solve each problem, select the best answer from the choices provided, and fill in the corresponding circle on your answer sheet. For **Questions 16–20,** solve the problem and enter your answer in the grid on the answer sheet. The directions **before Question 16** will provide information on how to enter your answers in the grid.

ADDITIONAL INFORMATION:

1. The use of a calculator in this section is **not permitted**.
2. All variables and expressions used represent real numbers unless otherwise indicated.
3. Figures provided in this test are drawn to scale unless otherwise indicated.
4. All figures lie in a plane unless otherwise indicated.
5. Unless otherwise specified, the domain of a given function f is the set of all real numbers x for which $f(x)$ is a real number.

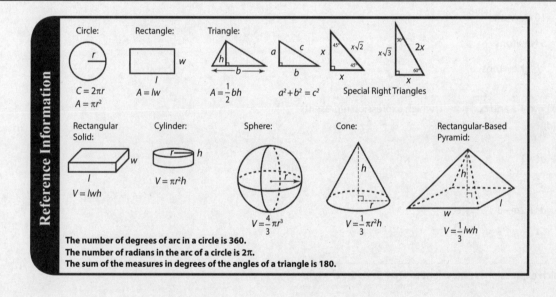

Reference Information

Circle:
$C = 2\pi r$
$A = \pi r^2$

Rectangle:
$A = lw$

Triangle:
$A = \frac{1}{2}bh$

$a^2 + b^2 = c^2$

Special Right Triangles

Rectangular Solid:
$V = lwh$

Cylinder:
$V = \pi r^2 h$

Sphere:
$V = \frac{4}{3}\pi r^3$

Cone:
$V = \frac{1}{3}\pi r^2 h$

Rectangular-Based Pyramid:
$V = \frac{1}{3}lwh$

The number of degrees of arc in a circle is 360.
The number of radians in the arc of a circle is 2π.
The sum of the measures in degrees of the angles of a triangle is 180.

CONTINUE

1 One angle of a triangle measures 82°. The other two angles have a ratio of 2:5. Find the number of degrees in the smallest angle of the triangle.

A. 14

B. 28

C. 38

D. 82

SHOW YOUR WORK HERE

2 The total force required to move an object through the air is given by $T = \sqrt{F_x^2 + F_y^2 + F_z^2}$, where F_x is the x-component of the force, F_y is the y-component of the force, and F_z is the z-component of the force. If the total force is 15 Newtons and the x- and z-components are both equal to twice the y-component of the force, what is the value of F_z?

A. 15 Newtons

B. 10 Newtons

C. 5 Newtons

D. $\sqrt{5}$ Newtons

3 If $f(x) = x^2 + 2$ and $g(x) = x - 1$, which expression represents $f(g(a))$?

A. $a^2 + 1$

B. $a^2 - 2$

C. $a^2 + 2a - 3$

D. $a^2 - 2a + 3$

4 Which expression is equivalent to $-(y + 3x)^2 - 2(2x^2 - 3y^2)$?

A. $-4y^2 - 13x^2$

B. $-4y^2 - 6xy - 13x^2$

C. $5y^2 + 6xy + 13x^2$

D. $5y^2 - 6xy - 13x^2$

SHOW YOUR WORK HERE

5 Simplify:

$$\frac{x^2 - y^2}{x - y}$$

A. $\dfrac{xy}{x + y}$

B. $\dfrac{x + y}{xy}$

C. $x + y$

D. xy

6 Which of the following complex numbers is equivalent to $(3 - i)(8 + 4i)$?

A. $20 - (-4i)$

B. $20 + 4i$

C. $24 - 4i$

D. $28 + 4i$

7 Which of these expressions is equivalent to $(x + y)^2 - (x - y)^2$?

A. 0

B. $2y^2$

C. $4xy$

D. $4xy + 2y^2$

8 An economist studied the labor forces in several randomly selected states. He found the average minimum wage of these states was $7.50, with a 95% confidence interval of ±0.25. How should the economist interpret the data?

A. States that have a minimum wage below $7.75 represent 95% of the states.

B. States that have a minimum wage above $7.25 represent 95% of the states.

C. There is a 95% probability that a randomly selected state will have a minimum wage between $7.25 and $7.75.

D. There is a 95% probability that the actual average minimum wage of all states is between $7.25 and $7.75.

CONTINUE

9

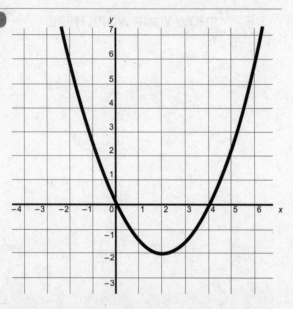

The curve shown on the *xy*-plane represents the function *f(x)*. Which of these equations represents the same function?

A. $y = \frac{1}{2}x^2 - 2x$

B. $y = x^2 - 4x$

C. $y = x^2 + 4x$

D. $y = \frac{1}{2}x^2 + 2x$

10 A 10% saline solution is to be mixed with a 40% saline solution to obtain 5 liters of a 20% saline solution. Which system of equations can be used to find the number of liters of the 10% solution, *x*, that will be needed to be combined with the number of liters of the 40% solution, *y*?

A. $0.1x + 0.4y = 1$
   $x + y = 5$

B. $0.1x + 0.4y = 5$
   $x + y = 5$

C. $0.1x + 0.4y = 1$
   $x + y = 1$

D. $0.1x + 0.4y = 5$
   $x + y = 1$

11. Over time, the radioactive substance plutonium-241 (Pu-241) breaks down, changing into other chemicals. Through this process of "radioactive decay," the mass of a sample of Pu-241 decreases. This change in mass could be modeled by what exponential function? I is the initial mass of the Pu-241, and t is the elapsed time in years.

A. $M(t) = I + e^{-0.048}t$

B. $M(t) = I - te^{-0.048}$

C. $M(t) = Ie^{0.048}t$

D. $M(t) = Ie^{-0.048}t$

12.
$$2x + 3y = 3$$
$$x = 2 - 9y$$

If (x, y) is the solution of the system of equations above, what is the value of y?

A. $-\dfrac{7}{15}$

B. $\dfrac{1}{15}$

C. $\dfrac{2}{9}$

D. $\dfrac{3}{2}$

13. What is the equation of the line that is parallel to $y = 5x + 7$ and contains the point $(1, 3)$?

A. $y = -5x + 8$

B. $y = 5x - 2$

C. $y = 5x + 3$

D. $y = 5x + 2$

14. When Rafael parked his car in the city garage for 3 hours, the charge was $5. When he parked his car for 5 hours, the charge was $6.50. If the cost of parking a car in the city garage is a linear function of time in hours, which function represents the charge, y, to park for x hours?

A. $y = \dfrac{5}{3}x$

B. $y = 1.3x$

C. $y = 3x + 5$

D. $y = 0.75x + 2.75$

CONTINUE

15 What is the solution of the equation
$3(x - 9) = 4x + 3(1 - 2x)$?

A. −4

B. 6

C. 12

D. 30

SHOW YOUR WORK HERE

CONTINUE

DIRECTIONS: For **Questions 16–20,** solve the problem and enter your answer in the grid, as described below, on the answer sheet.

1. Although not required, it is suggested that you write your answer in the boxes at the top of the columns to help you fill in the circles accurately. You will receive credit only if the circles are filled in correctly.

2. Mark no more than one circle in any column.

3. No question has a negative answer.

4. Some problems may have more than one correct answer. In such cases, enter only one answer.

5. **Mixed numbers** such as $3\frac{1}{2}$ must be entered as 3.5 or $\frac{7}{2}$.

   If $3\frac{1}{2}$ is entered into the grid as $\overline{3\,|\,1\,|\,/\,|\,2}$, it will be interpreted as $\frac{31}{2}$, not $3\frac{1}{2}$.

6. **Decimal answers:** If you obtain a decimal answer with more digits than the grid can accommodate, it may be either rounded or truncated, but it must fill the entire grid.

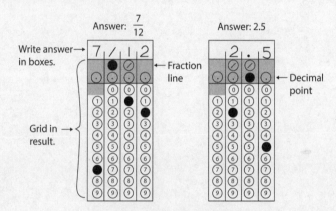

Answer: $\frac{7}{12}$ Answer: 2.5

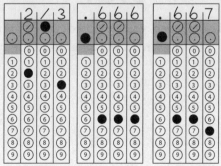

Answer: 201
Either position is correct.

Acceptable ways to grid $\frac{2}{3}$ are:

CONTINUE

16 What is the length of the arc of a circle with diameter 5 inches corresponding to a central angle of 144°? Round your answer to the nearest hundredth of an inch.

SHOW YOUR WORK HERE

17 If x is the solution of the equation $\frac{1}{4}\left(2 - \frac{1}{3}x\right) = x - \frac{1}{3}(x - 3)$, what is the value of x^2?

18 What is a solution of $x^2 + 4 = 9x - x^2$?

19 What is the x-intercept of the graph of $y - 3 = 5(x - 2)$?

20 Find a solution of $\sqrt{x + 3} = x - 3$.

STOP

If you finish before time is called, you may check your work on this section only.
Do not turn to any other section.

SECTION 4: MATH TEST—CALCULATOR

55 Minutes—38 Questions

TURN TO SECTION 4 OF YOUR ANSWER SHEET TO ANSWER THE QUESTIONS IN THIS SECTION.

DIRECTIONS: For **Questions 1–30,** solve each problem, select the best answer from the choices provided, and fill in the corresponding circle on your answer sheet. For **Questions 31–38,** solve the problem and enter your answer in the grid on the answer sheet. The directions **before Question 31** will provide information on how to enter your answers in the grid.

ADDITIONAL INFORMATION:

1. The use of a calculator in this section is **permitted**.
2. All variables and expressions used represent real numbers unless otherwise indicated.
3. Figures provided in this test are drawn to scale unless otherwise indicated.
4. All figures lie in a plane unless otherwise indicated.
5. Unless otherwise specified, the domain of a given function f is the set of all real numbers x for which $f(x)$ is a real number.

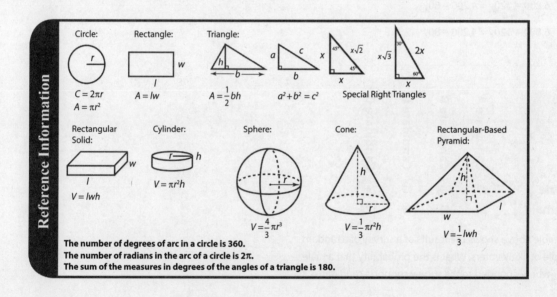

Reference Information

Circle:
$C = 2\pi r$
$A = \pi r^2$

Rectangle:
$A = lw$

Triangle:
$A = \frac{1}{2}bh$

$a^2 + b^2 = c^2$

Special Right Triangles

Rectangular Solid:
$V = lwh$

Cylinder:
$V = \pi r^2 h$

Sphere:
$V = \frac{4}{3}\pi r^3$

Cone:
$V = \frac{1}{3}\pi r^2 h$

Rectangular-Based Pyramid:
$V = \frac{1}{3}lwh$

The number of degrees of arc in a circle is 360.
The number of radians in the arc of a circle is 2π.
The sum of the measures in degrees of the angles of a triangle is 180.

CONTINUE

1 A salesperson earns twice as much in December as in each of the other months of a year. What part of this salesperson's entire year's earnings is earned in December?

A. $\dfrac{1}{7}$

B. $\dfrac{2}{13}$

C. $\dfrac{1}{6}$

D. $\dfrac{2}{11}$

2 Village A has a population of 6,800 that is decreasing at a rate of 120 per year. Village B has a population of 4,200 that is increasing at a rate of 80 per year. Which equation can be used to find the number of years, y, until the population of the two villages will be equal?

A. $6,800 - 120y = 4,200 + 80y$

B. $6,800 + 120y = 4,200 - 80y$

C. $6,800 - 120y = 4,200 - 80y$

D. $6,800 + 120y = 4,200 + 80y$

3

	Candidate A	Candidate B	Candidate C	Candidate D
Male	27	29	35	24
Female	24	49	45	17

The table above shows the results of a survey of a random sample of likely voters. What is the probability that a male voter who responded to the survey supports candidate C?

A. $\dfrac{7}{50}$

B. $\dfrac{7}{23}$

C. $\dfrac{7}{16}$

D. $\dfrac{7}{9}$

4 The formula for converting temperatures from degrees Fahrenheit to degrees Celsius is $C = \frac{5}{9}(F - 32)$. Solve the formula for F.

   A. $F = \frac{5}{9}(C + 32)$

   B. $F = \frac{5}{9}(C - 32)$

   C. $F = \frac{9}{5}C - 32$

   D. $F = \frac{9}{5}C + 32$

5 A recent study showed that 15% of the salmon that pass through turbines in hydroelectric dams are killed. If an initial population of 50,000 salmon must pass through n turbines, which function models the number of salmon that will survive?

   A. $A(n) = 50,000 - 0.15n$

   B. $A(n) = 50,000 - 0.85n$

   C. $A(n) = 50,000 \times 0.15^n$

   D. $A(n) = 50,000 \times 0.85^n$

6 The equation $f(x) = 1.5x + 15$ models the growth of a bamboo shoot, where x represents the number of days and $f(x)$ represents the height of the shoot in feet. Determine how many days it will take the bamboo shoot to reach a height of 19.5 feet.

   A. 1

   B. 2

   C. 3

   D. 4

CONTINUE

7 A random sample of women and men were surveyed to determine car style preference. The results of the survey are represented by the two-way frequency table below.

	Women	Men	Total
SUV	47	36	83
Pickup Truck	20	38	58
Van	28	36	64
Sedan	59	54	113
Total	154	164	318

The difference in the percentage of male respondents who selected pickup trucks and the percentage of female respondents who selected pickup trucks is how many percentage points? (Round to the nearest whole point.)

A. 6

B. 31

C. 10

D. 18

8 A high school principal wanted to estimate the mean of the grade point averages of students in her school. She randomly selected a group of students and found the mean grade point average to be 2.8 on a four-point scale, with a 95% confidence interval of ±0.2. How should the principal interpret the data?

A. Students with a grade point average below 3.0 make up 95% of the students in the school.

B. Students with a grade point average above 2.6 make up 95% of the students in the school.

C. There is a 95% probability that a randomly selected student will have a grade point average between 2.6 and 3.0.

D. There is a 95% probability that the actual mean grade point average of all students in the school is between 2.6 and 3.0.

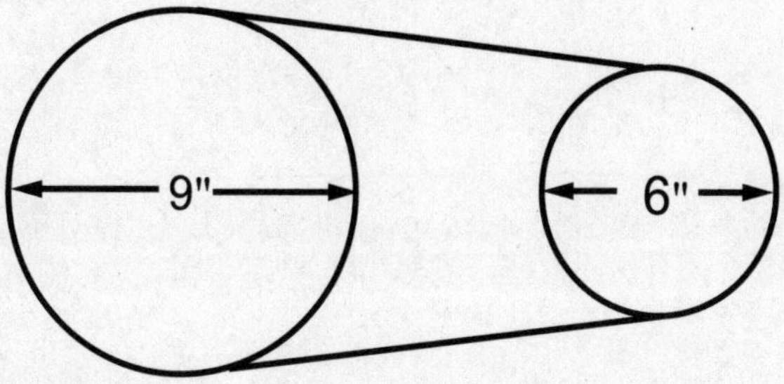

A pulley having a 9-inch diameter is belted to a pulley having a 6-inch diameter, as shown in the figure. The ratio of the number of revolutions per minute of these pulleys is 9:6. The small pulley is turned by a motor. When the small pulley turns, the larger pulley also turns. If the large pulley runs at 120 rpm, how fast does the small pulley run, in revolutions per minute?

A. 80

B. 100

C. 160

D. 180

10

$$y = x^2 - 7x + 10$$
$$x - y = 4$$

If (x, y) is a solution of the system of equations above, what is the value of y^2?

A. 2

B. $\dfrac{9}{2}$

C. $18 - 8\sqrt{2}$

D. 14

11 The water level of a swimming pool measuring 75 feet by 42 feet is to be raised 4 inches. How many gallons of water must be added to accomplish this? (7.48 gal. = 1 cubic ft.)

A. 1,684

B. 7,854

C. 12,600

D. 94,248

CONTINUE

SHOW YOUR WORK HERE

12 A cargo ship carries mid-sized and large luxury automobiles. The average (arithmetic mean) weight of the mid-sized cars carried on board is 1,590 kg. Large luxury cars on the ship average 1,980 kg. If the ship carries more than twice as many mid-sized cars as large luxury cars, which could be the average weight of all cars on board?

A. 1,580 kg

B. 1,699 kg

C. 1,725 kg

D. 1,785 kg

13 The distance from the center of a circle to a chord is 5. If the length of the chord is 24, what is the length of the radius of the circle?

A. 5

B. 10

C. 13

D. 26

14 A 40-pound bag of garden soil contains 0.8 cubic feet of soil. What is the weight, in pounds, of the garden soil needed to cover a 12-foot by 12-foot square garden to a depth of 3 inches?

A. 1,152

B. 1,800

C. 4,608

D. 5,760

15 The demand for a certain product can be defined by the function $y = 500 - 12x$, where y is the number of units of the product that can be sold at a price of x dollars. Which statement must be true?

A. If the price of the product decreases by $1, the number of units that can be sold decreases by 12.

B. If the price of the product increases by $12, the number of units that can be sold decreases by 1.

C. The y-intercept of the graph of the function represents the units of the product that can be sold at a cost of $1.

D. The x-intercept of the graph of the function represents the price at which no units of the product will be sold.

16

$$y = (x - 5)(x + 1)$$

The equation above represents a parabola. Which of the following equivalent forms of the equation shows the coordinates of the vertex of the parabola as constants or coefficients?

A. $y = x^2 - 4x - 5$

B. $y = (x - 2)^2 - 9$

C. $y = x(x - 4) - 5$

D. $y + 5 = x^2 - 4x$

Questions 17–19 refer to the following graph.

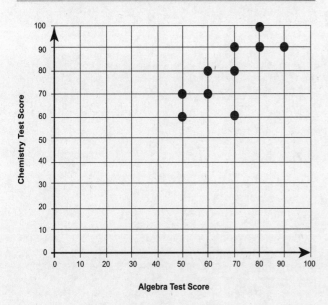

The scatterplot above shows the scores for 10 students on their most recent algebra and chemistry tests.

17 What is the arithmetic mean of the students' algebra test scores?

A. 68

B. 70

C. 79

D. 80

SHOW YOUR WORK HERE

CONTINUE

Peterson's SAT® Prep Guide 2019

629

18 A line of best fit of the data is given by $y = 0.76x + 27.6$, where x is a student's algebra test score and y is a student's chemistry test score. Which interpretation is valid?

SHOW YOUR WORK HERE

A. The average chemistry test score is 27.6 points higher than the average algebra test score.

B. The average algebra test score is 0.76 times the average chemistry test score.

C. Students with higher algebra test scores tended to have higher chemistry test scores.

D. There is not enough information to determine a relationship between the students' chemistry test scores and their algebra test scores.

19 Using the line of best fit, $y = 0.76x + 27.6$, what is the predicted algebra test score of a student with a chemistry test score of 70, rounded to the nearest whole number?

A. 50

B. 56

C. 77

D. 81

20 The velocity of an object dropped from a tower is given by the function $v(t) = -9.8t$, where t is the number of seconds after the object was dropped and $v(t)$ is given in meters per second. If the object hits the ground at 4 seconds, which inequality shows the possible values of $v(t)$?

A. $-39.2 \leq v(t) \leq 0$

B. $-2.45 \leq v(t) \leq 0$

C. $0 \leq v(t) \leq 2.45$

D. $0 \leq v(t) \leq 39.2$

21 To predict the results of an election for city council, a polling company surveyed 200 randomly selected likely voters within the city. Of those surveyed, 80 planned to vote for candidate A. The polling company reported a margin of error of 3.5%. What is a reasonable estimate of the percentage of likely voters who support candidate A?

A. Between 36.5% and 43.5%

B. Between 46.5% and 53.5%

C. Between 56.5% and 63.5%

D. Between 76.5% and 83.5%

22 Corporate Average Fuel Economy, a set of US fuel economy standards, sets targets for fuel economy for cars and light trucks. The target for the year 2020 is 42 miles per gallon, and for 2025, it is 54.5 miles per gallon. Which function can be used to estimate progress toward the goal y years after 2020 until 2025?

A. $g(y) = 54.5 - 2.5y$

B. $g(y) = 42 - 2.5y$

C. $g(y) = 54.5 + 2.5y$

D. $g(y) = 42 + 2.5y$

23 A municipal light plant buys energy from windmill farms that have two sizes of windmills. Small windmills produce 1.45 megawatts of power, and large windmills produce 2.75 megawatts of power. Which inequality represents the number of small windmills, x, and large windmills, y, needed to supply the light plant with a total power supply of at least 200 megawatts?

A. $2.75x + 1.45y \leq 200$

B. $1.45x + 2.75y \geq 200$

C. $2.75x + 1.45y \geq 200$

D. $1.45x + 2.75y \leq 200$

24 If x_1 and x_2 are the solutions of $x^2 - 4x = 3$, what is $|x_2 - x_1|$?

A. 0

B. 2

C. 4

D. $2\sqrt{7}$

CONTINUE

25 A group of 18 coins has a total value of $3.10. If the coins consist only of quarters and nickels, how many more quarters are there than nickels?

A. 3

B. 4

C. 7

D. 11

26 Which graph would be drawn to represent an economy that is growing at a fixed percentage rate?

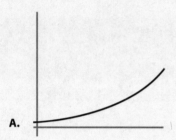

A.

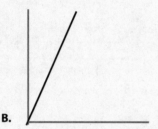

B.

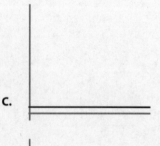

C.

D.

27 You are at the top of a 150-foot cliff and wish to rappel down to the ground. You can safely descend at a rate of 4 feet per second. Which of the following functions expresses your elevation above the ground, d, as a function of time, t?

   A. $d(t) = 4t + 150$

   B. $d(t) = 150t - 4$

   C. $d(t) = -4t + 150$

   D. $d(t) = 4t - 150$

28 Which quadrant does the solution set for the system of inequalities below NOT intersect?

$$\begin{cases} -2y > 3(x-6) \\ 2y > 6 - 3x \end{cases}$$

   A. Quadrant I

   B. Quadrant II

   C. Quadrant III

   D. Quadrant IV

29

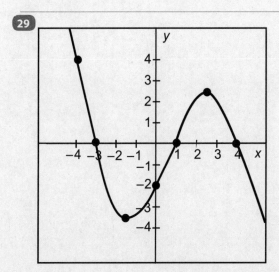

A polynomial function $p(x)$ is shown on the xy-coordinate plane. If $q(x)$ is a quadratic function, which of these equations can represent $p(x)$?

   A. $p(x) = (x - 1)q(x)$

   B. $p(x) = (x + 2)q(x)$

   C. $p(x) = (x - 3)q(x)$

   D. $p(x) = (x + 4)q(x)$

⊙ **CONTINUE**

30 The points $(-3, 2)$ and $(3, 2)$ are the endpoints of a diameter of a circle. Which equation represents the circle?

A. $(x - 2)^2 + y^2 = 3$

B. $(x - 2)^2 + y^2 = 6$

C. $x^2 + (y - 2)^2 = 9$

D. $x^2 + (y - 2)^2 = 16$

SHOW YOUR WORK HERE

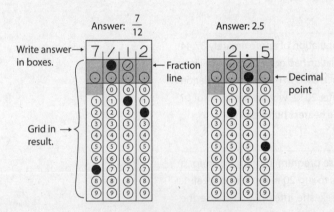
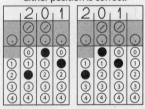
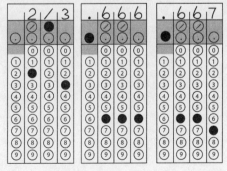

31 A local politician requested donations to pay for the cost of a radio ad. Twelve donors offered to split the cost equally, so they each paid $75. If the politician had been able to find 20 donors to equally split the same cost, how much would each have paid?

32 When $(3+i)^3$ is rewritten as $a + bi$, what is the value of b? (Note: $i = \sqrt{-1}$)

33 You must insure a shipment of diamonds and rubies. The diamonds are valued at $12,000 per carat, and the rubies are $9,000 per carat. Diamonds range in size from 1 to 6 carats. Rubies range from 2 to 4 carats. If there are at most one-third as many diamonds as rubies, what is the greatest possible value of the shipment in dollars, per gemstone? Enter a whole number with no comma.

34 In 2012, Algeria had a population of approximately 37.44 million. In 2013, the population had grown to 38.19 million. If the function $p(t) = a \cdot b^t$ is used to model the population in millions, $p(t)$, t years after 2012, what is the value of b? Round your answer to the nearest hundredth.

35 Juliette begins an exercise program in preparation for a half-marathon. She plans to run 20 miles during Week 1. For each subsequent week, she intends to increase the miles run for that week by 10% of the number she ran the previous week. How many miles will Juliette then run during Week 3?

SHOW YOUR WORK HERE

36 You have 160 yards of fencing material. If you want to construct a rectangular pen with a width between 10 and 20 yards, inclusive, what is the longest that such a pen can be, in yards?

37
$$3.6x + 2.4y = 12$$
$$x - y = 2$$

If (x, y) is a solution of the system of equations above, what is the value of y?

38 The function $f(x) = x^2 - 4$ is translated 3 units to the right to create function $g(x)$. What is the value of $g(9)$?

STOP

**If you finish before time is called, you may check your work on this section only.
Do not turn to any other section.**

SECTION 5: ESSAY

50 Minutes—1 Essay

> **DIRECTIONS:** The essay gives you an opportunity to show how effectively you can read and comprehend a passage and write an essay analyzing the passage. In your essay, you should demonstrate that you have read the passage carefully, present a clear and logical analysis, and use language precisely.
>
> Your essay will need to be written on the lines provided in your answer booklet. You will have enough space if you write on every line and keep your handwriting to an average size. Try to print or write clearly so that your writing will be legible to the readers scoring your essay.

> As you read the passage below, consider how Elizabeth Roberts-Pedersen uses the following:
>
> - Evidence, such as facts, statistics, or examples, to support claims.
> - Reasoning to develop ideas and to connect claims and evidence.
> - Stylistic or persuasive elements, such as word choice or appeals to emotion, to add power to the ideas expressed.

Adapted from "From Shell Shock to PTSD: Proof of War's Traumatic History" by Elizabeth Roberts-Pedersen, originally published by The Conversation *on April 14, 2015. Elizabeth Roberts-Pedersen is a lecturer in history at the University of Western Sydney in Australia. (This passage was edited for length. To read the complete article, see http://theconversation.com.)*

1 2015 marks several important First World War anniversaries: the centenary of the first use of poison gas in January; the centenary of the Gallipoli landings and the Armenian genocide in April. It is also 100 years since *The Lancet* published Charles S. Myers' article, "A Contribution to the Study of Shell Shock."

The study of shell shock

2 Myers' article is generally regarded as the first use of the term "shell shock" in medical literature. It was used as a descriptor for "three cases of loss of memory, vision, smell and taste" in British soldiers admitted to a military hospital in France.

3 While Myers presented these cases as evidence of the spectacular concussive effects of artillery on the Western Front, British medical opinion soon came to regard these symptoms as psychological in origin. The men presenting to medical officers with tics, tremors, and palpitations, as well as more serious symptoms of "functional" blindness, paralysis, and loss of speech, were not concussed—but nor were they necessarily cowards or malingerers.

4 Instead, these were men simply worn down by the unprecedented stresses of trench warfare—in particular, the effort required to push out of one's mind the prospect of joining the ranks of the maimed or the corpses lying in no man's land. . . .

5 For contemporaries and later for historians, shell shock came to encapsulate all the horror of this new form of industrialized warfare. As historian Jay Winter suggests, it moved "from a diagnosis into a metaphor." . . .

Developing a diagnosis

6 It is tempting to view shell shock as the unambiguous turning point in psychiatry's history, popularizing the idea that unconscious processes might produce symptoms that operate separately from moral qualities such as endurance and courage. However, scholarship over the last 15 years suggests that this position was far from widely accepted.

7 . . . The notion that many patients had some "predisposing" weakness—independent of their combat experiences—persisted throughout the interwar period and into the Second World War.

CONTINUE

8   It wasn't until the Vietnam War that this formulation was reversed, which in turn bridged the gap between combatant syndromes and the civilian sphere.

9   This development is only comprehensible as part of a broader political context. The notion that the Vietnam War exacted a form of psychic damage on American soldiers was championed by the anti-war activists of Vietnam Veterans Against the War (VVAW) and psychiatrists Chaim Shatan and Robert Jay Lifton. "Post-Vietnam syndrome," Shatan wrote, was caused by the "unconsummated grief" of a brutal and brutalizing war.

10 The VVAW's advocacy was instrumental in securing official recognition for this condition. It was included in 1980 in the third edition of the *Diagnostic and Statistical Manual of Mental Disorders* (*DSM-III*) as "post-traumatic stress disorder."

11 PTSD's inclusion in *DSM-III* legitimated the suffering of Vietnam veterans and held out the possibility of subsidized medical care and compensation. But the *DSM-III* definition of PTSD was significant in two additional ways.

12 First, it identified the disorder as a condition that could afflict soldiers and civilians alike—not a diagnosis exclusive to combat, like shell shock.

13 Second, it focused attention on the continuing effects of a traumatic experience, rather than on the personality and constitution of the patient.

14 The ramifications of these changes have been immense. PTSD and a broader field of "traumatology" are now entrenched in psychiatric and popular discourse. In Australia, we now assume that warfare is objectively traumatizing, and that governments ought to provide medical and financial support for affected service personnel, even if a recent Four Corners program confirmed that this is not always the case.

How is PTSD viewed today?

15 Though PTSD has its origins in opposition to the Vietnam War, the politics of the condition are now largely ambivalent, with its significance shifting according to circumstance.

16 This point is well illustrated by the film *American Sniper*, which demonstrates the possibility of two contrary positions. After his return to civilian life, SEAL sniper Chris Kyle (Bradley Cooper) is shown to be suffering from some characteristic after-effects of combat. …

    …

17 The real Chris Kyle was shot dead by Eddie Ray Routh [another veteran] in 2013. At trial, the accused's lawyers pursued a defense of insanity, compounded by the inadequate care provided by veterans' mental health services. Routh was found guilty of Kyle's murder in March of 2015.

18 In the 100 years since Myers' article on shell shock, the psychological consequences of war remain as relevant as ever.

Write an essay in which you explain how the writer builds an argument to persuade her audience that she is offering proof of war's traumatic history. In your essay, analyze how Elizabeth Roberts-Pedersen uses one or more of the features listed above (or features of your own choice) to strengthen the logic and persuasiveness of her argument. Be sure that your analysis focuses on the most relevant aspects of the passage.

Your essay should not explain whether you agree with Elizabeth Roberts-Pedersen's claims, but rather explain how she builds an argument to persuade her audience.

STOP

If you finish before time is called, you may check your work on this section only.
Do not turn to any other section.

1. B	**12.** B	**23.** D	**34.** C	**45.** B
2. A	**13.** D	**24.** D	**35.** B	**46.** A
3. C	**14.** B	**25.** A	**36.** D	**47.** C
4. D	**15.** B	**26.** B	**37.** A	**48.** C
5. C	**16.** A	**27.** A	**38.** A	**49.** B
6. B	**17.** D	**28.** B	**39.** B	**50.** C
7. A	**18.** B	**29.** C	**40.** D	**51.** A
8. D	**19.** C	**30.** B	**41.** C	**52.** D
9. B	**20.** C	**31.** A	**42.** D	
10. C	**21.** C	**32.** B	**43.** B	
11. A	**22.** A	**33.** C	**44.** D	

READING TEST RAW SCORE [   ]
(Number of correct answers)

1. **The correct answer is B.** The narrator's description of Jack and his bride, of their wonder at their surroundings and happiness at their marriage, makes choice B the correct answer. Choice A is incorrect because though Jack seems awkward in his surroundings, he does not seem aware of his lower social standing compared to other passengers. Though the passage provides a great deal of insight about the people who traveled on trains and the luxury in which they traveled, choice C is incorrect because the primary focus is on the newly married couple and their interactions. While Jack and his bride do seem self-conscious on the train (lines 15–16), and while other passengers seem to regard them with derision (lines 62–64), the passage does not delve deeply into issue of class and class consciousness, so choice D is also incorrect.

2. **The correct answer is A.** The couple's trip on the opulent train, as well as specific luxuries that Jack points out to his bride (such as in lines 31–33), makes choice A the correct answer. Choice B is misleading, as Jack's face is "reddened from many days in the wind and sun" (lines 9 and 10), suggesting that he works outside but not necessarily as a farmhand or rancher. Choice C is incorrect because, while the couple seem to shrug off the stares of other passengers (lines 62–64), readers get the distinct impression that they are not used to being around people of a higher social standing. Choice D is not correct because Jack does not suggest through deeds or words that he wants more than he has.

3. **The correct answer is C.** In lines 31–37, Jack's enthusiastic tone in responding to his bride's delight ("Great!") and his "brave" assurance that they are "going to go the whole thing" when she questions if they can afford the dining car make choice C the correct answer. While choice A (lines 12–15) suggests that Jack is aware of his formal clothes and may want to make a good impression, it is not clear that he wants to impress his bride with his appearance. Therefore, choice A is incorrect. Because it involves the bride and the other passengers' perceptions of her, choice B (lines 17–22) is also incorrect. Though choice D (lines 50–55) suggests that the couple views their marriage favorably, there is no indication in these lines that Jack wants to impress his bride.

4. **The correct answer is D.** In the first sentence, the phrase "whirling onward with such dignity of motion that a glance from the window seemed simply to prove that the plains of Texas were

Practice Test 1 — ANSWERS

pouring eastward" (lines 1–4) suggests that the train was moving very smoothly, so choice D is the correct answer as *gracefulness* suggests a lack of turbulence. Choices A and C are incorrect because, while they may suggest that the ride is better than expected, they do not describe the smooth movement that the sentence emphasizes. Choice B is a synonym of *dignity*, but it does not suit the context of the sentence.

5. **The correct answer is C.** The expressions of both Jack and his bride, as well as the intimation that they are not wholly comfortable in their attire (lines 12–15 and 20–22), make choice C correct. The pair seems happy about their marriage, but there is no suggestion that they are resolute about their decision to marry or about any other decision, so choice A is incorrect. Choice B is a distortion because, while they seem slightly nervous, there is no evidence to suggest that they are nervous about the trip itself. Choice D is incorrect because, although they are amazed at the train's interior, they do not seem to notice the landscape.

6. **The correct answer is B.** The couple's awkwardness and self-consciousness is best supported by Jack's nervous and shy countenance, choice B. The description of the landscape is a distraction and does not support the inference that the couple feels self-conscious, so choice A is incorrect. Choice C is off-base because it suggests the bride is concerned about the cost, rather than how the couple might appear to others. Choice D is incorrect because the narrator's likening the state of their marriage to their surroundings does not suggest that they were either comfortable or uncomfortable in their surroundings.

7. **The correct answer is A.** The narrator notes the other passengers' "careless scrutiny" (line 24) and emphasizes that the bride's countenance is "emotionless" (line 27). The inference is that the other passengers were staring to such a degree that the bride's usually "placid" face flushed red with embarrassment, making choice A correct. While the narrator notes in the following sentence that the pair are "very happy" (line 28), there is no evidence to suggest that she is blushing from happiness, so choice B is not correct. While the "careless scrutiny" (line 24) likely led to self-consciousness, there is no evidence to support the idea that the bride is generally lacking in self-confidence. Therefore, choice C is incorrect. Choice D is misleading, because the narrator notes only that the bride is plain, not unattractive.

8. **The correct answer is D.** In the preceding sentence the narrator notes that "their surroundings reflected the glory of their marriage that morning in San Antonio" (lines 50–52). The glory of their new estate, then, refers to their new standing as a married couple, so choice D is correct. While *estate* can refer to social standing, in this case, the couple's newly married status helps to give context to the word, so choice A is incorrect. Choice B is off-base, as *interests* do not fit the context. While *estate* does refer to property, the context of the sentence does not support this definition of the word. Therefore, choice C is incorrect.

9. **The correct answer is B.** The narrator notes that the couple "had small knowledge" (line 61) of the porter's bullying, so choice B is correct. There is no indication they are being openly mocked, nor that the couple feels catered to, so choice A is incorrect. The narrator describes the couple's enjoyment and does not suggest that anyone was openly hostile to them, thus choice C is not correct. The couple "had small knowledge" of the porter's bullying, so choice D cannot be correct because they could not have become used to behavior they had small knowledge of.

10. **The correct answer is C.** Because the author describes the new black suit as the cause when he says the groom's "brick-colored hands were constantly performing in a most conscious fashion" (lines 11–12), choice C is the correct answer. Although the groom is nervous in general, here the focus is on how his clothes have led to certain hand gestures, so choice A is insufficient because it does not take that important detail into consideration; it only focuses on the groom's awkwardness and not what is causing that awkwardness. Choice B is incorrect, because although the author brings up the weathered condition of the groom's hands, he uses it as a contrast to the new clothes; the fact that the groom's hands are "brick-colored," which may indicate that he works with his hands, is not the most important message conveyed by these lines. Choice D is also incorrect because the groom's happiness is not described in this part of the story, and when he expresses happiness, it is with a natural openness. For example, he smiles with delight (line 20) or beams with elation (lines 53–54).

11. **The correct answer is A.** The passage covers nest building, feeding, and other behaviors, so choice A is correct. Choice B is incorrect, because how hummingbirds build their nests is just one detail in the passage, and it fails to capture the idea of the passage as a whole. Choice C is also incorrect because while the author

notes that the hummingbird is interesting, the author is more concerned with detailing the hummingbird's behavior neutrally than convincing the reader of anything. Choice D is incorrect because the author does not, for example, explain why the hummingbird builds nests where it does but rather describes its behavior. Interpretation is not as important as description in this particular passage.

12. **The correct answer is B.** By noting in line 1 that the birds arrive "about the twenty-fifth of April," the author is implying that hummingbirds are elsewhere before that, and since winter ends only one month before the twenty-fifth of April, it is reasonable to conclude that birds migrate elsewhere during the wintertime. The time span the author gives is between the time the birds arrive and the time they begin building their nest (lines 1–3), so there is not enough information in these lines to support choice A. There is no indication that some birds do not migrate farther north of Pennsylvania, so choice C is not a correct assumption. By referring to "the hummingbird," the author is not referring to a singular one, but rather to those species that migrate to Pennsylvania. Therefore, choice D is not the best answer choice.

13. **The correct answer is D.** The author is describing how the nest is stuck to the branch and provides a context clue in the form of a synonym (*attached*) in line 6, so *secured* (choice D) is correct. Because neither choice A nor choice B make sense in the context of the sentence, they are incorrect. While choice C makes sense in the context, it does not make sense when the synonym (*attached*) in line 6 is taken into account, and so it is incorrect.

14. **The correct answer is B.** The author notes the materials in each layer and uses phrases like "firmness and consistency" and "closely laid together," making choice B the correct answer since it covers the entirety of lines 13–26. While the author does cite a number of different plants that go into the nest, this is just a single detail in lines 13–26 and not the main focus of the section as a whole, so choice A is incorrect. Though it might be assumed that such an intricate nest takes time to build, the author does not note time as a factor, so choice C is not the best answer. While the author notes that the bird's saliva helps keep out moisture, this is not the main focus of lines 13–26 as a whole, so choice D is also incorrect.

15. **The correct answer is B.** The author notes the female's bold reaction to people approaching her nest, which makes choice B correct. There is no specific mention of

how long hummingbirds stay in their nest, but based on the suggestion that they migrate and that their young only stay in their nests a "short time" (lines 34–35), it is reasonable to conclude that choice A is incorrect. Though the author mentions that hummingbird chirps are "not louder than that of a small cricket or grasshopper," it is also noted that a hummingbird's "only note is a single chirp," making choice C incorrect. The author notes that the females most likely carry "animal food" to their young, so choice D is also incorrect.

16. **The correct answer is A.** Lines 28–33 reveal that the hummingbird will dart around a person's head to protect its eggs and young, which is a bold reaction from such a tiny creature. Choice B (lines 33–37) refers to the duration that chicks are in the nest, and thus does not support the inference. Choice C (lines 37–40) refers to what hummingbirds eat, and it also does not support the inference. Choice D (lines 61–64) is incorrect because it includes details about a hummingbird's voice and does not support the idea that the female guards her young.

17. **The correct answer is D.** Choice D is correct because the bird is putting its feathers in order, or neatening them, which the author's use of the word *arrange* supports. Choice A is incorrect because there is no suggestion that the hummingbird oils itself at all in this passage. Choice B is a synonym for *wears*, but in this context, it suggests that the hummingbird is not always wearing its feathers, which does not make sense. It is not clear what it would mean for a bird to "shuffle" its feathers, so choice C does not make much sense either.

18. **The correct answer is B.** When something moves extremely fast, it can be nearly impossible to see, making it seem almost invisible, which makes choice B the most plausible answer. Birds do not have transparent wings, and if the hummingbird did, this would probably be an amazing enough detail for the author to note. Since there is no specific mention of the hummingbird having transparent wings, choice A is not a strong answer. The sun reflecting off the wings might make them seem shiny, but it would not make them "become invisible," so choice C is also incorrect. Something needs to be visible in order to be beautiful, so choice D does not make sense.

19. **The correct answer is C.** In lines 64–65, the author notes that, "for when two males meet at the same bush, or flower, a battle instantly takes place." When the author says the victor "returns to the same place," the reference must be the bush or flower, a conclusion

reinforced by line 57 in which the author describes how the hummingbird "extracts its sweets" from the flower. Thus, choice C is correct. Though the author notes in line 59 that the hummingbird tends to alight on the "dead twigs of a tree," there is no indication that this is the place the bird returns to after battle, so choice A is incorrect. Similarly, although the two combatants are male, the author has not indicated that the males are battling over females. Rather, the battle seems to be over access to food, so choice B is also incorrect. Choice D is off-base, as the author only mentions the conqueror returning "to the same place."

20. **The correct answer is C.** In lines, 63–65, the author explains how the hummingbird moves from flower to flower and how the two male combatants meet over a flower, which implies that they are fighting over that flower and the nectar it contains. So choice C is correct. While the author begins the passage with a description of the nesting habits of females, nesting and mating are not discussed in the second paragraph, so choice A (lines 1–3) is incorrect. The mention of dead twigs does not refer to any specific territory, making choice B (lines 58–61) incorrect. The reference to another male hummingbird provides no support for the idea that "fruits of his victory" refers to the nectar of flowers, so choice D (lines 66–68) is incorrect.

21. **The correct answer is C.** Lines 69–71 describe the hummingbird as attacking another bird, which emphasizes its aggressive nature. These lines portray the hummingbird as a danger, rather than a bird vulnerable to dangers, so choice A does not make sense. Choice B is also incorrect, as the author describes the female hummingbird as staying on its nest (lines 31–32), and these lines, which refer to the male, have nothing to do with the bird's proximity to its nest. Choice D is incorrect because the description of how male hummingbirds attack each other that appeared earlier in the paragraph (lines 63–67) already introduced the idea that they do not only fight for self-defense.

22. **The correct answer is A.** By invoking Mt. Everest in line 1, the world's tallest mountain, the author is intent on showing that there are equally extraordinary and exotic geographical features on the ocean floor, making choice A the correct answer. While the author does emphasize that Mauna Kea is actually taller, that isn't the point of the opening sentence. Instead, the author continues describing the many geographical features found on the ocean floor. Therefore, choice B is incorrect. The author does not describe the geography of Mauna Kea or any other island mountain, so choice C is incorrect.

Because there is no other mention of Mt. Everest in the passage, choice D is also incorrect.

23. **The correct answer is D.** The pieces of a jigsaw puzzle fit together as the tectonic plates do, so choice D is correct. As the author does not note individual plates and the role each plays, choice A is incorrect. Although the author refers to the spherical shape of the Earth in line 16, it is not the earth's shape that is most important here, so choice B is incorrect. Because the author does not describe the shape of each plate, choice C is not a conclusion that can be reached based on the information in line 16.

24. **The correct answer is D.** In lines 16–18, the author describes the tectonic plates as "floating on top of the Earth's hot flowing mantle" and notes that "convection currents in the molten mantle layer cause the plates to slowly move," so choice D is correct. Earthquakes and volcanoes are a result of the movement of the plates (lines 22–26), so choice A is incorrect. There is no mention of ocean tides in this passage, so choice B is also incorrect. The upward flow of magma in diverging plates causes new ocean floor crust (lines 27–30), which does not cause the tectonic plates to move, so choice C is not correct.

25. **The correct answer is A.** The passage indicates that the major discovery of 1977 was that organisms in deep ocean hydrothermal vent ecosystems eat chemicals (lines 40–45). Since eating is key to survival, this supports choice A. The passage does not specify when scientists came to believe that colliding plates caused the formation of deep ocean hydrothermal vents, so choice B is not the best answer. In lines 66–76, the author describes the food web found in this ecosystem and notes that these animals must be adapted to survive in the extreme environment. There is no indication that the animals move between environments, so choice C is incorrect. While there are many metals that spew from the vents, there is no indication that scientists had any interest in whether or not these minerals could be mined, so choice D is also incorrect.

26. **The correct answer is B.** In lines 39–44, the author notes that the discovery forced scientists to "redefine living systems on our planet" and then goes on to note "other previously described ecosystems" that rely on sunlight and photosynthesis as the basis of their food web. This makes choice B the correct answer. Lines 32–34 do not provide evidence because the author has not yet tied the new species to the existence of an ecosystem that relies on chemosynthesis, so choice A is

incorrect. The way hydrothermal vents are formed does not support the inference about organisms in deep ocean hydrothermal vent ecosystems, so choice C is incorrect. Similarly, the kinds of metals that spew from the vents support bacteria that form the base of the chemosynthetic food web, but the existence of these metals does not support the inference about what scientists knew about organisms in deep ocean hydrothermal vent ecosystems before 1977. Thus, choice D is also incorrect.

27. **The correct answer is A.** In line 61, the author describes "molecules that billow out of the seafloor." Because of the context, we know that the molecules are somehow emerging from the seafloor, but there is no indication that it is forceful, so choice A seems the most reasonable answer. *Crest* indicates a very specific movement, and since there is no indication of a cresting pattern in the passage, choice B is not the best answer. *Wave* indicates a movement and can be used as a synonym for *billow*, but it does not indicate the continuous forward movement indicated in line 61, so choice C is not the best answer. Choice D implies that the molecules change size, which is not implied in the passage.

28. **The correct answer is B.** In lines 12–13, the author notes, "The shape of the ocean floor, its bathymetry, is largely a result of a process called plate tectonics." The author goes on to describe how the movement of plates causes hydrothermal vents (lines 26–30), so choice B is the correct answer. While the author does describe the geography of the ocean floor, this description is general, and the geography of the ocean's floor is not the passage's main idea, so choice A is incorrect. The suggestion that the same forces that create volcanoes also create hydrothermal vents is tangential and has little impact on the passage's main idea, thus choice C is also incorrect. While the author describes the ecosystems around hydrothermal vents as different from those that rely on photosynthesis, the discussion of plate tectonics does not support the inference that they are unusual. Therefore, choice D is not correct.

29. **The correct answer is C.** The passage describes the features of hydrothermal vents, so the discussion of plate tectonics serves to explain how hydrothermal vents are formed. In lines 46–48, the author explains how the movement of the plates causes the formation of hydrothermal vents, so choice C is correct. In lines 5–9, the author introduces the geography of the ocean floor but has not yet mentioned hydrothermal vents, so choice A is incorrect. In lines 34–38, the author notes

that many species have been discovered in this unique environment, but there is no general discussion of the formation of hydrothermal vents. Thus, choice B is not correct. Lines 48–51 note that the main causes of hydrothermal vents are also responsible for volcanoes and earthquakes, but the information is parenthetical and not as extensive as in the previous lines, so choice D is also incorrect.

30. **The correct answer is B.** Lines 69–74 provide a description of an "extreme environment," including darkness and extreme temperatures that would kill most other forms of life, signaling that *harmful* (choice B) is the answer. Though they could be used as synonyms for *noxious* in another context, choices A and C are not strong enough to support the idea of the extremely inhospitable environment that the author is describing in the paragraph. Likewise, choice D is incorrect because while the environment described is unusual, the focus is more on the idea that it is inhospitable, i.e., harmful to most forms of life that we know even though animals in this region are adapted to survive exposure to these chemicals.

31. **The correct answer is A.** By briefly comparing a familiar concept (photosynthesis) with a new concept (chemosynthesis), the author hopes the reader will catch on to the new topic more easily. Choice B is incorrect because lines 40–43 mention chemosynthesis as one of the most important scientific discoveries of the last century, not photosynthesis. Photosynthesis is indeed an integral part of varied food webs (lines 75–77). However, choice C is incorrect because that is not why it is mentioned in line 44. Although the importance of photosynthesis is mentioned, it is clearly not the main goal of the passage, making choice D incorrect.

32. **The correct answer is B.** The passage begins with a sentence that focuses on boys who live in the tenements. The passage ends with the idea that "Home to them is an empty name," referring again to the tenements, so choice B is correct. Though much of the first paragraph is a discussion of the lack of job opportunities, the main focus of the passage is on the lack of opportunities for children living in the tenements, so choice A is not correct. The author does allude to education in lines 8, 27, and 64, but again, it is not the main focus of the passage, thus choice C is also incorrect. The second paragraph deals with delinquency but only within the context of the tenements. Since the main focus of the passage as a whole is not how impoverished children often turn to crime, choice D is incorrect.

33. **The correct answer is C.** Both the preceding and following sentences discuss the idea that the tenements are not "elevating" (line 16) and contribute to "idle" (line 19) ways, so the context makes choice C the correct answer. While polluting can mean "dirty," the author here is concerned more with the child's character development, so choice A is incorrect. There is no evidence to suggest that the games are dangerous, thus choice B is also incorrect. Similarly, the context does not suggest that the author is referring to the games as having a noisy character, so choice D is not correct.

34. **The correct answer is C.** The context of the tenements helps make clear that the author is referring to the people who make up the child's community when he writes that "the boy stands condemned by his own …" (line 10), so choice C is the correct answer. Because the author's reference to "the boy" is a reference to all boys in the tenement, choice A cannot be correct. Choice B is incorrect because the author's discussion is more about the corrosive effects of the entire community, not of the smaller family unit. There is no indication that the children go to school, so choice D is also incorrect.

35. **The correct answer is B.** Lines 20–21 provide examples of the boy's "own," the people who should be helping him but are letting him down: the truant officer and the agents of the Children's Societies. Choice A (lines 17–18) deals with the games the boy plays, not the people who are failing to protect him. Choice C (lines 25–26) is about environments—the city and the Truant Home—not the people who run them and fail the boy. Choice D (lines 29–30) refers to factors affecting the boy in a vague way that does not place any blame on specific people who should be helping him.

36. **The correct answer is D.** Again, the author's focus is on the tenements as spirit-crushing, which is supported in lines 15–16: "Its influence is scarcely of the elevating kind, if it have any." Thus, choice D is the correct answer. While the author speaks of "so many other human animals" (line 15), creating an image of packed cages, there is no suggestion that the tenements are filthy, only that they don't provide an environment that helps grow a boy's character, so choice A is not the best answer. Choice B assumes that the biggest problem with tenement life is the lack of privacy, and since the author never suggests that this is true, this is not a very logical interpretation of the pigeon coop metaphor. Choice C makes an incorrect generalization, suggesting that every person lives in a tenement, which is simply untrue.

37. **The correct answer is A.** The author demonstrates the meaning of *idle* in the sentence that follows the word (line 20–25), in which the author describes the boy doing things that will not help him and may lead him into trouble. Thus, choice A is the correct answer. The implication that *idle* ways will lead to trouble does not support *vain* (choice B) as an answer. Similarly, there is no indication that the boy acts younger than he is, so choice C is incorrect. Actions can be simple without being unproductive, so choice D is not the best interpretation of how the author uses *idle* in this context.

38. **The correct answer is A.** The author notes in lines 31–35: "Rough as he is, if any one doubt that this child of common clay have in him the instinct of beauty, of love for the ideal of which his life has no embodiment, let him put the matter to the test." Thus, choice A is the correct answer. Because the context suggests the author is speaking of the child's "instinct for beauty," choice B is incorrect. While there is a suggestion that no flowers grow in the tenements, choice C is incorrect because the author's focus here is on the child and his (or her) potential, as evidenced by the sentence cited above. Similarly, the reference to the police and their tactics suggests brutality in dealing with the children. The focus, again, is on the child's potential, so choice D is incorrect.

39. **The correct answer is B.** Lines 32–34 ("if anyone doubt that this child of common clay have in him the instinct of beauty, of love for the ideal of which his life has no embodiment") support the idea that the tenement child has a capacity to appreciate beauty, so choice B is the correct answer. Neither choice A nor choice D suggests the child has the capacity to appreciate beauty, given his (or her) surroundings. While choice C suggests the calming effect of flowers and juxtaposes this with the image of a policeman's brutal tactics (lines 41–44), it does not suggest the capacity to appreciate the "ideal."

40. **The correct answer is D.** The author suggests that growing up in a "joyless" (line 56) tenement condemned children to "low and ill-paid drudgery" (lines 10–11). Although the author describes the children negatively, even using the word *evil* in line 25, he does not suggest that the children are inherently different from other children, making choices A and B incorrect. In lines 18–19, he mentions the lack of a "steady hand to guide" the children as a factor in these children taking to "idle ways." However, he does not directly mention the children's parents, making choice C incorrect.

41. **The correct answer is C.** In lines 58–61, the author notes that tenement children "banished and barred" from "a yard of turf" as from "a heaven that is not for such as they," and notes later that there was not "a green sod within a quarter of a mile," making choice C is the correct answer. While the author notes that this is "their first lesson in 'writin,'" the point is more about what they wrote, so choice A is not correct. Similarly, choice B is incorrect, as the author does not mention lack of schooling in this paragraph. There is no support for choice D, as the focus in this paragraph is on children's play.

42. **The correct answer is D.** The author notes that "The city has no Truant Home" and that efforts to get the child to go to school "are paralyzed by this want," or this need for a truant home, so choice D is the correct answer. The author notes in the lines that precede lines 25–28 that a reformatory is full of "vicious boys," but the author sees a "want" or need for a truant home, so choices A and C are incorrect. The suggestion that the city needs a truant home because the boy won't go to school suggests the opposite of choice B.

43. **The correct answer is B.** In line 36, Robert expresses his devotion to Clara by saying that he is "entirely yours," and likewise, Napoleon begins his letter by noting that "I have not spent a day without loving you; I have not spent a night without embracing you." Both letters express a devotion and commitment to the relationship, so choice B is the correct answer. While Napoleon's letter betrays his jealousy, Robert's letter contains no note of jealousy, so choice A is incorrect. Napoleon's letter notes his "pride and ambition" that force him away from Josephine, a reference to his work, but Robert's letter mentions no such reference, so choice C is incorrect. Likewise, choice D is incorrect, as Robert's letter does not lament that the two are apart.

44. **The correct answer is D.** The author notes in lines 21–22, "but I cannot see why he should despise me and, as you say, hate me without any reason." Thus, choice D is correct. The synonyms *despise* and *hate* suggest that choice A is incorrect, as indifference implies little feeling. Similarly, choices B and C are incorrect, as *hate* and *despise* suggest dislike, not mistrust or rudeness.

45. **The correct answer is B.** In lines 5–7, the author notes, "I wonder anxiously whether . . . I had any right to bind you to me, my angel" and then goes on to write in lines 8–9, "These doubts all arise, I am inclined to think, from your father's attitude towards me." Thus, choice B is correct. Choice A is incorrect, as Robert notes in lines 24–25, "I really love and respect your father." There is no

indication that he doubts Clara's love for him. In fact, lines 31–32 suggest otherwise: "You cannot think how your letter has raised and strengthened me." Therefore, choice C is incorrect. In lines 32–33, Robert writes, "You are splendid, and I have much more reason to be proud of you than of me," so choice D is also incorrect.

46. **The correct answer is A.** In lines 5–7, the author notes, "I wonder anxiously whether … I had any right to bind you to me, my angel" and then goes on to write in lines 8–9, "These doubts all arise, I am inclined to think, from your father's attitude towards me." Thus, choice A is correct. Choice B is incorrect, as Robert doubts himself in these lines, not his relationship with Clara. In lines 22–26, Robert expresses his admiration for Clara's father, sentiments that do not support the inference, so choice C is incorrect. Likewise, choice D suggests a new commitment by Robert to their relationship, which is also incorrect.

47. **The correct answer is C.** Napoleon makes it clear that he spends so much time thinking about how much he misses Josephine that it is distracting him from his responsibilities as a military leader (line 46–49), so choice C is the best answer. There is no indication in the letter that Josephine wishes she could fight alongside her husband, so choice A is incorrect. Choice B is also incorrect, as Napoleon questions whether she is too busy to write to her husband (lines 56–58), which implies that she might have quite a few things to occupy her time. Napoleon imagines that Josephine may no longer love him one day (lines 67–68), or has even found someone else to love already, which indicates that she could regret marrying him, so choice D is not the best answer.

48. **The correct answer is C.** Napoleon writes in lines 46–48: "In the midst of my duties, whether I am at the head of my army or inspecting the camps, my beloved Josephine stands alone in my heart," suggesting that he is thinking about Josephine when he should be thinking about his responsibilities as a military leader. In choice A (lines 42–43), he is merely stating that he thinks about Josephine constantly without implying that those thoughts distract him from anything. Choice B (lines 43–46) may support the idea that thoughts of Josephine distracted Napoleon from enjoying a cup of tea, but they do not support the idea that those thoughts distracted him from his responsibilities. Choice D (lines 49–51) indicates the efforts he is taking to return to Josephine as quickly as possible without suggesting that these efforts distract him from his responsibilities as a military leader.

49. **The correct answer is B.** The context—Napoleon's desire to see Josephine—and the phrase "by a matter of days" (line 53) suggest that choice B is the correct answer. Choice A is incorrect, as stretching out the time would delay his ability to see Josephine. *Force* (choice C) does not make sense when added to the phrase "by a matter of days." Likewise, choice D is incorrect because *cause* does not suggest the idea that Napoleon wants to make the days go by more quickly.

50. **The correct answer is C.** In lines 31–32, Robert writes to Clara: "You cannot think how your letter has raised and strengthened me. …" whereas Napoleon writes to Josephine in lines 55–56: "Ah! wretch, how could you have written this letter? How cold it is!" Thus, choice C is the correct answer. While Robert does indeed express doubts, those doubts seem to stem from the attitude of Clara's father, not Clara's letter, so choice A is incorrect. Robert does not question Clara's loyalty, though Napoleon does question Josephine's, thus choice B is also incorrect. Clara's letter to Robert only seems to have strengthened his love for her, rather than made him feel confused, so choice D is not correct.

51. **The correct answer is A.** Napoleon is incensed and crushed that Josephine used *vous* (a formal way of addressing someone) in her letter (line 59), whereas Robert is delighted by the memory of Clara calling him *du* (line 40). Therefore, choice A is the correct answer, and choice B is incorrect. Likewise, choice C is incorrect because rather than calming Napoleon, the use of *vous* has made him angry. Choice D is incorrect, as there is no evidence that Robert feels humbled by her words.

52. **The correct answer is D.** In line 10, Robert notes, "It is so easy to accept other people's estimate of oneself." Similarly, Napoleon writes in lines 66–69, "You love me less; but you will get over the loss. One day you will love me no longer; at least tell me; then I shall know how I have come to deserve this misfortune. …" Choice D then is the correct answer. Neither Robert nor Napoleon show any evidence of being modest, thus choice A is incorrect. There is no evidence to support the idea that Robert angers quickly, whereas Napoleon seems quick to anger. Thus, choice B is not correct. While Robert seems indecisive, Napoleon does not. In fact, he seems to make up his mind about Josephine quickly, so choice C is also incorrect.

1. A	**10.** C	**19.** B	**28.** C	**37.** A
2. B	**11.** B	**20.** C	**29.** B	**38.** D
3. A	**12.** B	**21.** D	**30.** D	**39.** A
4. C	**13.** C	**22.** B	**31.** A	**40.** C
5. A	**14.** B	**23.** A	**32.** B	**41.** B
6. A	**15.** D	**24.** D	**33.** A	**42.** B
7. A	**16.** A	**25.** A	**34.** B	**43.** D
8. B	**17.** D	**26.** D	**35.** D	**44.** B
9. B	**18.** C	**27.** D	**36.** C	

WRITING AND LANGUAGE TEST RAW SCORE ☐
(Number of correct answers)

1. **The correct answer is A.** This choice makes the most sense given the context of the sentence. A standing structure added to an area, like a sign on a road, is typically *erected*. It is not *born*, so choice B is incorrect. It is also unlikely that the sign *floated* or *dripped*, so choices C and D are incorrect.

2. **The correct answer is B.** Choice B is correct because the sentence is declarative and therefore requires a period. Choice A is incorrect because the sentence is not a question. Choice C is incorrect because it creates a run-on. Choice D is incorrect because the sentence is not an exclamation.

3. **The correct answer is A.** Choice A is correct because *obscure* supports the characterization of the colony as "far-flung" and out-of-the-way. Choice B is incorrect because there is no indication that the colony is not well-lit. Choice C is incorrect because the colony is the opposite of obvious. Choice D is incorrect because *uncertain* implies vagueness, which isn't intended here.

4. **The correct answer is C.** Choice C is correct because the sentence requires the simple past tense. Choice A is incorrect because this is past perfect tense. Choice B is incorrect because it is in the plural past tense, and it should be singular. Choice D is incorrect because it is in the future tense.

5. **The correct answer is A.** Choice A is correct because the phrase "as they seemingly float above seas of green foliage" modifies, and thus must follow, "Buddhist temples." Choices B and C are incorrect because they make it unclear what the modifying clause refers to. Choice C is incorrect because the use of commas is wrong.

6. **The correct answer is A.** Choice A is correct because *country's* is a singular possessive noun referring to Burma. Choice B is incorrect because it is plural, not possessive. Choice C is incorrect because it requires an apostrophe before the *s*. Choice D is incorrect because it is plural possessive.

7. **The correct answer is A.** The sentence should be deleted because it is irrelevant to the passage. Choice B is incorrect because it does not belong in the passage at all. Choice C is incorrect because it does not expand upon the main idea but introduces an unrelated detail. Choice D is incorrect, because it is a detail about the rock band, not the country.

8. **The correct answer is B.** This version most effectively and clearly presents the ideas in this sentence. The disorganization of ideas and information in choices A, C, and D creates confusion.

Answer Keys and Explanations

9. **The correct answer is B.** Only choice B eliminates redundancies while still communicating that the album was banned and that smugglers were punished. Choice A is incorrect because "not allowed to be distributed in Burma" and "for smuggling" are redundant. Choice C is incorrect because "not allowed to be distributed in Burma" is redundant. Choice D is incorrect; as written, it implies that some things can be legally smuggled into Burma. It also inaccurately suggests that merely trying to obtain the album in Burma, not smuggle it in, carried a possible sentence of imprisonment for three to twenty years.

10. **The correct answer is C.** Sentence 2 should not be placed after sentence 1 (choice A) because it doesn't fit logically into the order of events in the paragraph. Similarly, it would not make sense for this sentence to be placed before sentence 4 (choice B), since sentences 3 and 4 talk about improvements in Burma since the ending of the military rule, and this sentence would interrupt the flow of ideas. Placed after sentence 5 (choice C), sentence 2 provides a conclusion that highlights Burma's uncertain future in spite of the end of its military rule. Therefore, it is a logical component of the paragraph and should not be removed (choice D).

11. **The correct answer is B.** Choice B is correct because the pronoun *its* refers to *the country*, which is a singular noun. Choices A, C, and D are incorrect because they do not correctly refer to the antecedent, "the country."

12. **The correct answer is B.** Noting that Dewey is known as "the father of public education" sets up the rest of the passage and provides information that supports the main idea of the passage. Although accurate, choices A, C, and D do not support the main idea of the paragraph and introduce ideas that are not developed in the passage.

13. **The correct answer is C.** Choice C is correct because this part of an extended prepositional phrase introduced by the phrase "emphasis on." Because of this, no commas are necessary as they would separate the preposition from its other subjects ("the classroom" or "learning environment"). Choice A is incorrect because the comma causes confusion about the subject of the preposition "on." Choice B is incorrect for the same reason and also because "or learning environment" is a restrictive phrase and does not require commas. Choice D is incorrect because "or learning environment" is a restrictive phrase and does not require commas.

14. **The correct answer is B.** Choice B is correct because the antecedent is *education*, which means the pronoun should be *it*. Choice A is incorrect because it implies that the antecedent is "aspects or characteristics." Choice C is incorrect because the passage is not written in the first person and there is no antecedent it could logically refer to. Choice D is incorrect because it implies that the antecedent is Dewey, which is incorrect.

15. **The correct answer is D.** Choice D is correct because semicolons are only necessary when the list items themselves contain commas. Since they don't, this series only requires commas. Choices A and C are incorrect because they misuse semicolons. Choice B is incorrect because it misuses colons.

16. **The correct answer is A.** Changing *another* to *a second* improves the organization because it includes an ordinal number as the previous and following paragraphs do. Choice B is incorrect because it does not clarify the aspects of education. Choice C is incorrect because the change does not eliminate supporting information. Choice D is incorrect because the change does not negatively affect the organization.

17. **The correct answer is D.** The following paragraph of the passage discusses a fourth aspect of Dewey's philosophy of education, and the paragraph after that discusses a fifth aspect, making the use of the word *final* in choice A incorrect. Choice D is correct because the use of the word *third* helps keep the passage organized. Choices B and C are less desirable choices than choice D because they do not help readers to orient themselves.

18. **The correct answer is C.** Choice C is correct because the context clue "but rather" suggests a word that is the opposite of *indirect*, and *overt* comes closest to this meaning. Choices A, B, and D are incorrect because they do not make sense in the context of the sentence.

19. **The correct answer is B.** Choice B is correct because it effectively sets up the fourth and final item in a list of examples. Choice A is incorrect because it implies a contrast which is unsupported by the context. Choice C is incorrect because it suggests the author is looking back, which is unsupported by the context. Choice D is incorrect because it suggests a conclusion, which the paragraph is not.

20. **The correct answer is C.** Choice C is correct because the noun *education* must agree in number with *reconstruction*. Choices A, B, and D are incorrect because *education* must be singular in order to be in agreement with *reconstruction*.

21. **The correct answer is D.** In choice D, the subordinate clause that begins with *since* should precede the second part of the sentence that it qualifies. Choice A is incorrect because the subordinate clause is illogical in the middle of the sentence. Choice B is incorrect because the subordinate clause helps set up the rest of the sentence and belongs at the beginning. Choice C is incorrect because the arrangement of the clauses is awkward and difficult to follow.

22. **The correct answer is B.** Choice B supports the implication that members of the group could find a way to enact and undergo change without causing social instability. Choice A is incorrect because it suggests that change is a negative thing that must be overcome. Choices C and D are incorrect because they both imply meanings that are not supported by the context of the sentence.

23. **The correct answer is A.** An effective opening sentence for this paragraph and passage would introduce the notion of differences between the study of plants and the study of animals, a notion further elaborated upon in the following sentence, so choice A is correct. Choice B is incorrect because it provides information that refutes this notion. Choice C is incorrect because the exploration of unique animals and plants is not the focus or intent of the passage. Choice D is incorrect because a school-level study of various life forms does not effectively introduce the main ideas in the passage.

24. **The correct answer is D.** Choice D accurately employs parallel structure. Choice A is incorrect because the word *by* before "producing arching canes" is unnecessary and prevents the clause from being parallel. Choice B is incorrect because each part of the clause is constructed in a different way ("by sending," "a split," "the production"). Choice C is incorrect because the last part of the clause ("in the production . . .") is not constructed like the rest of the clause.

25. **The correct answer is A.** Choice A is correct because *its* is a possessive determiner that refers to "desert plant." Choice B is incorrect because *it is* a contraction of "it is." Choice C is incorrect because it is not a word. Choice D is incorrect because it does not make sense in the sentence.

26. **The correct answer is D.** This sentence should not be deleted because it provides useful and relevant information regarding the lifecycles of biennial plants Choice A is incorrect because this information does support the main idea of the paragraph. Choice B is incorrect because the current placement of the sentence is correct in the organization of the paragraph. Choice C is incorrect because the information in this sentence does not provide a helpful illustrative contrast of presented ideas for readers.

27. **The correct answer is D.** This version most effectively and clearly presents the ideas in this sentence. The disorganization of ideas and information in choices A, B, and C create confusion.

28. **The correct answer is C.** Choice C is correct because the context of the sentence suggests a word that refers to an attempt to determine a number. Choices A and B are incorrect because *reducing* and *hedging* suggest actions that are not supported by the context of the sentence. Choice D is incorrect because it suggests a valuation of quality and worth rather than an attempt at counting.

29. **The correct answer is B.** Choice B is correct because the subject "*suffrutescent* shrubs (hemixyles)" is plural and must be followed by the plural verb, *fall*. Choice A is incorrect because the subject is plural and the verb is singular. Choice C is incorrect because the subject is singular and the verb is plural. Choice D is incorrect because the subject is plural and the verb is singular and not in the present tense.

30. **The correct answer is D.** Choice D is correct because both sentences are closely related, independent clauses. Choice A is incorrect because a comma is not sufficient to join two independent clauses. Choice B is incorrect because there is no cause/effect relationship present, which the word "because" implies. Choice C is incorrect because a colon is only used to separate independent clauses when the second clause explains or amplifies the first, which is not the case here.

31. **The correct answer is A.** The parentheses in choice A correctly indicate that the phrase "trees and shrubs" is supplemental information and not necessary for understanding the rest of the sentence. Choice B is incorrect because dashes are used to call attention to the text that they surround, which is not intended here. Choice C is incorrect because it makes it unclear whether woody perennials are trees and shrubs, or if the author is talking about them in addition to trees and shrubs. Choice D is not correct because quotation marks are not used to set off extraneous information, but rather to highlight specific words or to cast doubt on a word or phrase.

Answer Keys and Explanations

32. The correct answer is B. Choice B is correct because *regardless* is the correct form of this conventional expression. Choices A, C, and D are incorrect variations of this phrase.

33. The correct answer is A. Choice A is correct because the context suggests that if the eight age states exist, the population is healthy, viable, and not going anywhere. Choice B is incorrect because it suggests the population is shrinking, which is not implied by the context. Choice C is incorrect because it suggests impermanence, which is not implied by the text. Choice D is incorrect because it suggests that the population is homogenous, which is not implied by the context.

34. The correct answer is B. Choice B is correct because sentence 2 makes a broad statement about differences in wages and makes the most sense as an introductory statement. Choice A is incorrect because sentence 1 is not the best introductory statement. Choices C and D are incorrect because sentences 3 and 4 expand on an idea presented in sentence 2.

35. The correct answer is D. Choice D is correct because the dash helps draw attention to the supplemental information that follows it. Choice A is incorrect because a colon is not used to introduce a dependent clause that expands on an independent clause. Choice B is incorrect because there should be punctuation to separate the number from the rest of the sentence. Choice C is incorrect because a semicolon is used to join two independent clauses.

36. The correct answer is C. Choice C is correct because the context implies that the author wants to suggest that the median figure hides the fact that the gap was more than $100,000. Choice A is incorrect because it does not make sense in the sentence—the median figure doesn't reduce the fact. Choice B is incorrect because the author is not presenting a disagreement. Choice D is incorrect because the context does not suggest vagueness and it is grammatically incorrect.

37. The correct answer is A. The point being made in this paragraph is that everyone is different and comes with an individualized set of skills for different jobs. Therefore, describing them as *unique* is most appropriate. The adjectives in the other answer choices don't support this notion and are incorrect.

38. The correct answer is D. Choice D is correct because the antecedent in this sentence is "each person," and the pronoun *she* was used previously to refer to the antecedent. Choices A, B, and C are incorrect because they do not align with "her" in number and gender.

39. The correct answer is A. Choice A is correct because the author's point is that "no two jobs are identical" and that because of this, job titles can be misleading. Choice B is incorrect as it suggests a weak or unconvincing connection, which doesn't make sense in the context of the sentence. Choice C is incorrect because the sentence is not talking about the practicality of job titles. Choice D is incorrect because the sentence is not suggesting job titles are unplanned or unimportant.

40. The correct answer is C. This sentence is highlighting the reduced variability in certain occupations, which would indicate that wage differences, if any, would be small. Referring to these wage differences as vast, noticeable, or productive wouldn't support the notion of reduced variability, so answer choices A, B, and D are incorrect.

41. The correct answer is B. Choice B is correct because the author is listing the factors that influence, lead to, or affect, how much a person earns. Choice A is incorrect because the verb *effect* is used to suggest someone has succeeded in making something happen, which is not intended here. Choices C and D are incorrect because they do not make sense in the context of the sentence.

42. The correct answer is B. The author's point of view regarding job tasks, as evidenced in the previous sentence, is that jobs with different responsibilities will result in different wages. Choice B is the only option that supports this notion. Choices A, C, and D either don't support this or directly negate this notion.

43. The correct answer is D. Choice D corrects the fact that this sentence lacks a verb and is incomplete by adding *include*. Choices A, B, and C are incorrect because they are not complete sentences.

44. The correct answer is B. Choice B is correct because the only job with a lower median wage than athletes is actor. Choice A is incorrect because broadcast news analysts do not have a lower median wage than actors. Choices C and D are incorrect because only actors have a median wage lower than athletes' median wage.

1. B	5. C	9. A	13. B	17. 4/9 or 0.44
2. B	6. D	10. A	14. D	18. 4 or 1/2
3. D	7. C	11. D	15. B	19. 1.4 or 7/5
4. D	8. D	12. B	16. 6.28	20. 6

MATH TEST—NO CALCULATOR RAW SCORE
(Number of correct answers)

1. **The correct answer is B.** Let the other two angles be $2x$ and $5x$. Thus,

$$2x + 5x + 82 = 180$$
$$7x = 98$$
$$x = 14$$
$$2x = 28$$
$$5x = 70$$

The smallest angle of the triangle is $= 28°$.

2. **The correct answer is B.** Solve the following equation for F_y:

$$T = \sqrt{F_x^2 + F_y^2 + F_z^2}$$
$$15 = \sqrt{\left(2F_y\right)^2 + F_y^2 + \left(2F_y\right)^2}$$
$$15 = \sqrt{9F_y^2}$$
$$15 = 3F_y$$
$$5 = F_y$$

Therefore, $F_z = 2 \times F_y = 10$ Newtons.

3. **The correct answer is D.**

$$g(a) = a - 1$$
$$f(a-1) = (a-1)^2 + 2 = a^2 - 2a + 1 + 2$$
$$f(g(a)) = a^2 - 2a + 3$$

4. **The correct answer is D.**

$$-(y+3x)^2 - 2(2x^2 - 3y^2) = -(y^2 + 6xy + 9x^2) - 4x^2 + 6y^2$$
$$= -y^2 - 6xy - 9x^2 - 4x^2 + 6y^2$$
$$= 5y^2 - 6xy - 13x^2$$

5. **The correct answer is C.** The numerator is the difference between perfect squares; $x^2 - y^2$ is equal to the product of $(x + y)$ and $(x - y)$. Therefore,

$$\frac{x^2 - y^2}{x - y} = \frac{(x+y)(x-y)}{x-y} = x + y$$

6. **The correct answer is D.**

$$(3-i)(8+4i) = 24 + 12i - 8i - 4i^2$$
$$= 24 + 4i - (-4)$$
$$= 28 + 4i$$

7. **The correct answer is C.**

$$(x+y)^2 - (x-y)^2 = x^2 + 2xy + y^2 - \left(x^2 - 2xy + y^2\right)$$
$$= x^2 + 2xy + y^2 - x^2 + 2xy - y^2$$
$$= 4xy$$

8. **The correct answer is D.** The confidence interval indicates the interval within which the estimated population parameter is likely to fall. A 95% confidence interval of ±0.25 means that it can be said, with 95% confidence, that the average minimum wage of all states will fall between $0.25 above the average of the randomly selected states and $0.25 below the average of the randomly selected states. The economist found the average of the randomly selected states to be $7.50, so $7.50 + $0.25 = $7.75, and $7.50 − $0.25 = $7.25. Therefore, the average minimum wage of all states will be found within the range of $7.25 and $7.75, with 95% confidence.

9. **The correct answer is A.** The graph shows that $y = 0$ when $x = 0$ or $x = 4$, so the equation must take the form $y = ax(x − 4)$. We can use the vertex, $(2, −2)$, to find the value of a:

$$-2 = a(2)(2-4) = -4a \rightarrow a = \frac{1}{2}$$

Substituting this value into the equation, we get:

$$y = \frac{1}{2}x\left(x-4\right)$$
$$= \frac{1}{2}x^2 - 2x$$

10. **The correct answer is A.** The amount of the solutions x and y combined must equal 5 liters, so $x + y = 5$. The amount of salt in the two solutions, $0.1x$ and $0.4y$, must combine to equal the amount of salt in the total: $(0.2)(5) = 1$

11. **The correct answer is D.** Choices A and C would both result in values greater than l for all values of $t > 0$. Choice B is not an exponential function.

12. **The correct answer is B.** Substitute the expression equivalent to x from the second equation into the first equation and solve:

$$2(2 - 9y) + 3y = 3$$
$$4 - 18y + 3y = 3$$
$$4 - 15y = 3$$
$$-15y = -1$$
$$y = \frac{1}{15}$$

13. **The correct answer is B.** The slope of the line $y = 5x + 7$ is 5, and a line parallel to this line would have the same slope. Therefore, the desired line is of the form $y = 5x + b$. Substitute $(1, 3)$ into this equation to compute the value of b:

$$3 = 5 \times 1 + b$$
$$-2 = b$$

Thus, the equation of the line is $y = 5x − 2$.

14. **The correct answer is D.** The function that models the cost of parking is linear, so it must be of the form $y = mx + b$, where y is the cost after x hours. Solve for m and b using the information provided.

$$5 = m(3) + b$$
$$6.5 = m(5) + b$$

Multiply the first equation by −1 and add the two equations to obtain:

$$1.5 = 2m$$
$$0.75 = m$$

So $y = 0.75x + b$. You could solve for b, but that is not necessary because only one of the answer choices has a coefficient of 0.75 on x.

15. **The correct answer is B.**

$$3(x - 9) = 4x + 3(1 - 2x)$$
$$3x - 27 = 4x + 3 - 6x$$
$$3x - 27 = -2x + 3$$
$$5x = 30$$
$$x = 6$$

16. **The correct answer is 6.28.** First, convert the central angle to radians by multiplying $144°$ by $\frac{\pi}{180°}$; this gives $\frac{4\pi}{5}$ radians. Next, the diameter of the circle is 5 inches, so its radius is 2.5 inches. Therefore, the length of the desired arc is

$$S = r\theta = (2.5 \text{ inches}) \cdot \left(\frac{4\pi}{5}\right) \approx \frac{(10)(3.14)}{5} \text{ inches}$$
$$= 6.28 \text{ inches}$$

17. The correct answer is $\frac{4}{9}$ (4/9) or .444.

$$\frac{1}{4}\left(2-\frac{1}{3}x\right)=x-\frac{1}{3}(x-3)$$

Multiply both sides by 12 (which is the least common multiple of 3 and 4) to clear the fractions.

$$3\left(2-\frac{1}{3}x\right)=12x-4(x-3)$$
$$6-x=12x-4x+12$$
$$6-x=8x+12$$
$$-6=9x$$
$$-\frac{6}{9}=x$$
$$-\frac{2}{3}=x$$

So $x^2=\left(-\frac{2}{3}\right)^2=\frac{4}{9}$.

18. The correct answer is 4 or $\frac{1}{2}$ (1/2) or .5.

$$x^2+4=9x-x^2$$
$$2x^2-9x+4=0$$
$$(2x-1)(x-4)=0$$
$$x=\frac{1}{2}\text{ or }x=4$$

19. The correct answer is 1.4 or $\frac{7}{5}$ (7/5).

To find the x-intercept, set y equal to 0 and solve for x:

$$0-3=5(x-2)$$
$$-3=5x-10$$
$$7=5x$$
$$\frac{7}{5}=x$$

20. The correct answer is 6.

$$\sqrt{x+3}=x-3$$
$$\left(\sqrt{x+3}\right)^2=(x-3)^2$$
$$x+3=x^2-6x+9$$
$$0=x^2-7x+6$$
$$0=(x-6)(x-1)$$
$$x=6\text{ or }x=1$$

Because $\sqrt{1+3}=2\neq 1-3=-2$, only $x=6$ is an actual solution.

Section 4: Math Test—Calculator

1. B	**9.** D	**17.** A	**25.** B	**33.** 48000
2. A	**10.** A	**18.** C	**26.** A	**34.** 1.02
3. B	**11.** B	**19.** B	**27.** C	**35.** 24.2
4. D	**12.** B	**20.** A	**28.** C	**36.** 70
5. D	**13.** C	**21.** A	**29.** A	**37.** 0.8
6. C	**14.** B	**22.** D	**30.** C	**38.** 32
7. C	**15.** D	**23.** B	**31.** 45	
8. D	**16.** B	**24.** D	**32.** 26	

MATH TEST—CALCULATOR RAW SCORE
(Number of correct answers)

1. **The correct answer is B.** Let x = amount earned each month other than December. Since the salesperson earned twice as much in December as in every other month, $2x$ = amount earned in December. Then, the entire earnings are $11x + 2x = 13x$. The proportion of earnings earned in December can be expressed as
$$\frac{2x}{13x} = \frac{2}{13}.$$

2. **The correct answer is A.** Because the population of village A is decreasing by 120 per year, the population in year y will be $6,800 - 120y$. Because the population of village B is increasing by 80 per year, the population in year y will be $4,200 + 80y$. Set the two expressions equal to find when the populations will be the same: $6,800 - 120y = 4,200 + 80y$.

3. **The correct answer is B.** There are a total of $27 + 29 + 35 + 24 = 115$ males who responded to the survey. Of the 115 males, 35 support candidate C:
$$\frac{35}{115} = \frac{7}{23}$$

4. **The correct answer is D.**
$$C = \frac{5}{9}(F - 32)$$
$$\frac{9}{5}C = F - 32$$
$$\frac{9}{5}C + 32 = F$$
$$F = \frac{9}{5}C + 32$$

5. **The correct answer is D.** Because this is a percent decrease, an exponential model is appropriate. A model for exponential decay is $f(t) = a(1 - r)t$, where a is the initial amount, and r is the decay rate. The initial amount is 50,000 and the decay rate is 0.15, so the appropriate model in this case is
$A(n) = 50,000(1 - 0.15)^n = 50,000 \times 0.85^n$.

6. **The correct answer is C.** Substitute 19.5 for $f(x)$ and solve the resulting equation for x:
$$19.5 = 1.5x + 15$$
$$4.5 = 1.5x$$
$$3 = x$$

7. **The correct answer is C.** Thirty-eight men selected pickup trucks out of a total of 164 men who responded (right-most column). So the ratio of male respondents who selected pickup trucks to the total number of male respondents can be represented $\frac{38}{164}$, which is approximately 23.2%. Twenty women selected pickup trucks out of a total of 154 women who responded. The ratio of female respondents who selected pickup trucks to the total number of female respondents can be represented as $\frac{20}{154}$, which is approximately 13%. The difference in percentage points may be represented as 23.2 – 13%, which is approximately 10%, indicating a difference in percentage points of approximately 10.

8. **The correct answer is D.** The confidence interval indicates the interval within which the estimated population parameter is likely to fall. A 95% confidnece interval of ±0.2 means that it can be said, with 95% confidence, that the mean grade point average of all students will fall between 0.2 points above the mean of the randomly selceted students' GPAs and 0.2 points below that mean.

9. **The correct answer is D.** The 6-inch pulley will revolve 9 times for every 6 revolutions of the 9-inch pulley, so set up the proportion this way:

$$\frac{9}{6} = \frac{x}{120}$$
$$6x = 1,080$$
$$x = 180$$

10. **The correct answer is A.** Since $x - y = 4$, $y = x - 4$. Substitute $x - 4$ for y in the first equation and solve for x. Then use $y = x - 4$ to find y and square that value.

$$x - 4 = x^2 - 7x + 10$$
$$0 = x^2 - 8x + 14$$
$$x = \frac{-(-8) \pm \sqrt{(-8)^2 - 4(1)(14)}}{2(1)} = 4 \pm \sqrt{2}$$
$$y = x - 4 = (4 \pm \sqrt{2}) - 4 = \pm\sqrt{2}$$
$$y^2 = 2$$

11. **The correct answer is B.** Four inches is $\frac{1}{3}$ ft. The volume of the added level is:

$75 \times 42 \times \frac{1}{3} = 1,050$ cubic ft. There are 7.48 gallons in 1 cubic ft., so 1,050 cubic ft. × 7.48 gal./cubic ft. = 7,854 gallons.

12. **The correct answer is B.** If there were exactly twice as many mid-sized cars as large luxury cars, then the average weight of all cars would be the average weight of two mid-sized and one large car. That average would be:

$$\frac{2 \cdot 1,590 + 1,980}{3} = \frac{5,160}{3}$$
$$= 1,720 \text{ kg}$$

Because there are *more* than twice as many mid-sized cars as large luxury cars on board, the average weight of all cars must be less than it would be for exactly twice as many. So the average weight of all cars must be less than 1,720 kg. A lower bound on the average weight of all cars is 1,590 kg, because the average weight of all cars cannot be less than the average weight of the lighter cars. The average weight

must be greater than 1,590 kg, because the problem implies that there is at least one large luxury car. Thus, the average weight of all cars must be between 1,590 kg and 1,720 kg; an average weight of 1,699 kg falls within this interval.

13. **The correct answer is C.**

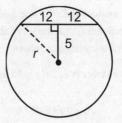

A radius drawn perpendicular to a chord bisects the chord. Construct the radius as shown above.

$$5^2 + 12^2 = r^2$$
$$25 + 144 = r^2$$
$$169 = r^2$$
$$13 = r$$

14. **The correct answer is B.** Three inches equal 0.25 feet. To cover the garden, we'll need 12 feet × 12 feet × 0.25 feet = 36 cubic feet of garden soil.

$$\frac{x \text{ pounds}}{36 \text{ cubic feet}} = \frac{40 \text{ pounds}}{0.8 \text{ cubic feet}}$$
$$x = \frac{(40)(36)}{0.8}$$
$$x = 1,800$$

15. **The correct answer is D.** The x-intercept occurs at the point where $y = 0$, or where no products will be sold.

16. **The correct answer is B.** To find the equation that shows the vertex of the parabola, change from factored form to standard form, and then complete the square:

$$y = (x - 5)(x + 1)$$
$$y = x^2 - 4x - 5$$
$$y = x^2 - 4x + 4 - 5 - 4$$
$$y = (x - 2)^2 - 9$$

Remember, the vertex of the parabola is found when the equation is written in the form $y = a(x - h)^2$. You won't need to perform any calculations if you recognize that only choice B is written in this form.

17. **The correct answer is A.** The arithmetic mean of the algebra test scores is:

$$\frac{50+50+60+60+70+70+70+80+80+90}{10}$$
$$=\frac{680}{10}$$
$$=68$$

18. **The correct answer is C.** The slope of the line of best fit is positive, indicating that the y-variable tends to increase as the x-variable increases.

19. **The correct answer is B.** Set $y = 70$ and solve for x:

$$70 = 0.76x + 27.6$$
$$42.4 = 0.76x$$
$$x = \frac{42.4}{0.76} \approx 56$$

20. **The correct answer is A.** At $t = 0$, the object is moving at $-9.8(0) = 0$ meters per second. At $t = 4$ seconds, the object is moving at $-9.8(4) = -39.2$ meters per second. The velocity must be equal to or between these two extremes.

21. **The correct answer is A.**

$$\frac{80}{200} = 40\%$$
$$40\% - 3.5\% = 36.5\%$$
$$40\% + 3.5\% = 43.5\%$$

22. **The correct answer is D.** Use a linear model as the basis for the estimate. The rate of change is $\frac{54.5-42}{2025-2020} = 2.5$

In 2020, the target is 42, and the target increases by 2.5 each year.

23. **The correct answer is B.** Multiply 1.45 by x and 2.75 by y. The total power supply must be at least 200, so the inequality is $1.45x + 2.75y \geq 200$.

24. **The correct answer is D.** First, find the solutions:

$$x^2 - 4x = 3$$
$$x^2 - 4x + 4 = 7$$
$$(x-2)^2 = 7$$
$$x - 2 = \pm\sqrt{7}$$
$$x = 2 \pm \sqrt{7}$$

Then, find the absolute value of the difference of the solutions:

$$\left|\left(2+\sqrt{7}\right)-\left(2-\sqrt{7}\right)\right| = 2\sqrt{7}$$

25. **The correct answer is B.** Let n be the number of nickels and q be the number of quarters. Then, solve the resulting system of equations:

$$0.05n + 0.25q = 3.10$$
$$n + q = 18 \rightarrow q = 18 - n$$
$$0.05n + 0.25(18 - n) = 3.10$$
$$0.05n + 4.5 - 0.25n = 3.10$$
$$-0.2n = -1.4$$
$$n = 7$$

Since there are 7 nickels, there must be 11 quarters: $11 - 7 = 4$.

26. **The correct answer is A.** Because the rate of growth is a fixed percentage, an exponential graph is appropriate.

27. **The correct answer is C.** Because you are descending, the rate of change in elevation is negative and equal to to -4 feet per second. The initial height is 150 feet at $t = 0$. So, the linear function is $d(t) = -4t + 150$.

28. **The correct answer is C.** The following is the solution set:

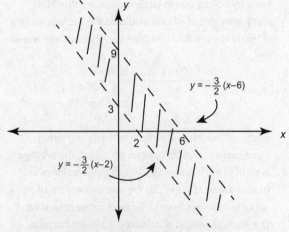

Notice that the solution set does not intersect Quadrant III.

29. **The correct answer is A.** Since 1 is a zero of the graph, $(x - 1)$ is a factor of the polynomial.

30. **The correct answer is C.** Since $(-3, 2)$ and $(3, 2)$ are the endpoints of a diameter of a circle, the center of the circle is at $(0, 2)$ and the radius of the circle is 3. The general form of the equation of a circle with center (a, b) and radius r is $(x - a)^2 + (y - b)^2 = r^2$. Substituting the values for a, b, and r, we obtain $x^2 + (y - 2)^2 = 9$.

31. **The correct answer is 45.** Let x equal the total cost.

$$\frac{x}{12} = 75$$
$$x = 900$$
$$\frac{900}{20} = 45$$

32. **The correct answer is 26.**

$$
\begin{aligned}
(3+i)^3 &= (3+i)(3+i)^2 \\
&= (3+i)(9+6i+i^2) \\
&= (3+i)(9+6i+(-1)) \\
&= (3+i)(8+6i) \\
&= 24+18i+8i+6i^2 \\
&= 24+26i-6 \\
&= 18+26i
\end{aligned}
$$

The imaginary part of $a + bi$ is bi. Therefore, in this case, $b = 26$.

33. **The correct answer is 48000.** The shipment's greatest possible value occurs if all gemstones are at their maximum weight in carats. Furthermore, because the largest diamonds have greater value (6 carats × \$12,000 per carat = \$72,000) than the largest rubies (4 carats × \$9,000 per carat = \$36,000), the maximum possible total value occurs if there are exactly one-third as many diamonds as rubies—the greatest possible number of diamonds. If T is the total number of gemstones, then the number of diamonds is $\frac{1}{3} \times T$ and the number of rubies is $\frac{2}{3} \times T$. The maximum total value of the shipment is:

$$
\begin{aligned}
&\frac{1}{3} \cdot T \cdot \$72,000 + \frac{2}{3} \cdot T \cdot \$36,000 \\
&= \$24,000(T) + \$24,000(T) \\
&= \$48,000(T)
\end{aligned}
$$

If the value of T gemstones is \$48,000(T), then the value per gemstone is \$48,000.

34. **The correct answer is 1.02.** Because this is an exponential growth model, divide the population in 2013 by the population in 2012 to find the value of b:
(38.19 million) ÷ (37.44 million) ≈ 1.02.

35. **The correct answer is 24.2.** As shown below, Juliette will run 22 miles in Week 2 and 24.2 miles in Week 3.

$$20 \times 1.1 = 22$$
$$22 \times 1.1 = 24.2$$

36. **The correct answer is 70 yards.** The perimeter, P, of a rectangle is $2l + 2w = P$. We are given that $P = 160$. The largest value of l occurs when the smallest value of w is used. So, using $w = 10$ yards and $P = 160$ yards in this formula yields:

$$
\begin{aligned}
2l + 2(10) &= 160 \\
2l + 20 &= 160 \\
2l &= 140 \\
l &= 70
\end{aligned}
$$

So the longest that such a pen can be is 70 yards.

37. **The correct answer is 0.8.**

$$3.6x + 2.4y = 12$$
$$x - y = 2$$

Multiply the second equation by 3.6 and subtract it from the first equation. Then, solve for y:

$$
\begin{aligned}
3.6x + 2.4y &= 12 \\
-3.6x - 3.6y &= 7.2 \\
\hline
6y &= 4.8 \\
y &= 0.8
\end{aligned}
$$

38. **The correct answer is 32.** Since $g(x)$ is a translation of $f(x)$ 3 units to the right, $g(x) = f(x - 3)$:

$$
\begin{aligned}
g(9) &= f(9 - 3) \\
&= f(6) \\
&= 6^2 - 4 \\
&= 32
\end{aligned}
$$

SECTION 5: ESSAY

Analysis of Passage

In the right-hand column, you will find an analysis of the passage by Elizabeth Roberts-Pedersen, noting how the writer used evidence, reasoning, and stylistic or persuasive elements to support her claims, connect the claims and evidence, and add power to the ideas she expressed. Check to see if you evaluated the passage in a similar way.

1   2015 marks several important First World War anniversaries: the centenary of the first use of poison gas in January; the centenary of the Gallipoli landings and the Armenian genocide in April. It is also 100 years since *The Lancet* published Charles S. Myers' article, "A Contribution to the Study of Shell Shock."

1   *The writer provides a historical context to support her central idea: people have long known that war is psychologically traumatic.*

The study of shell shock

2   Myers' article is generally regarded as the first use of the term "shell shock" in medical literature. It was used as a descriptor for "three cases of loss of memory, vision, smell and taste" in British soldiers admitted to a military hospital in France.

2   *The writer lays the groundwork for her argument by providing facts about and describing the symptoms of this trauma, which was initially called "shell shock."*

3   While Myers presented these cases as evidence of the spectacular concussive effects of artillery on the Western Front, British medical opinion soon came to regard these symptoms as psychological in origin.

3   *The writer supports her argument with facts that show that "shell shock," which was at first used to describe symptoms caused by "concussive effects of artillery," came to be seen as "psychological in origin."*

4   The men presenting to medical officers with tics, tremors, and palpitations, as well as more serious symptoms of "functional" blindness, paralysis, and loss of speech, were not concussed—but nor were they necessarily cowards or malingerers.

4   *The writer strengthens her argument with facts that demonstrate those suffering from shell shock were suffering genuine psychological trauma, and were not, as often believed, cowards or people trying to avoid combat. The author's examples of "functional" problems shows that even without physical damage, people can become deaf, mute, or paralyzed because of psychological damage.*

5   Instead, these were men simply worn down by the unprecedented stresses of trench warfare—in particular, the effort required to push out of one's mind the prospect of joining the ranks of the maimed or the corpses lying in no man's land. . . .

5   *The writer offers evidence that shows the psychological effects of combat.*

6 For contemporaries and later for historians, shell shock came to encapsulate all the horror of this new form of industrialized warfare. As historian Jay Winter suggests, it moved "from a diagnosis into a metaphor."

   ...

6 *The writer quotes a historian who views shell shock not only as devastating in itself, but as absolute confirmation of the horrors of war.*

Developing a diagnosis

7 It is tempting to view shell shock as the unambiguous turning point in psychiatry's history, popularizing the idea that unconscious processes might produce symptoms that operate separately from moral qualities such as endurance and courage. However, scholarship over the last 15 years suggests that this position was far from widely accepted.

7 *The writer makes the point that even though shell shock was being generally accepted as a legitimate condition, there was still resistance to the idea.*

8 ... The notion that many patients had some "predisposing" weakness—independent of their combat experiences—persisted throughout the interwar period and into the Second World War.

8 *Continuing to trace resistance to the validity of shell shock, the writer cites one opposing argument. She also provides additional historical perspective, saying that resistance continued even into WWII.*

9 It wasn't until the Vietnam War that this formulation was reversed, which in turn bridged the gap between combatant syndromes and the civilian sphere.

9 *The writer completes this part of her argument, providing a specific time frame (the Vietnam War) for when shell shock was fully legitimized as a combat-related condition. She also identifies this period as a time when the concept of trauma-caused damage began to be extended to civilian experiences outside of military participation.*

10 This development is only comprehensible as part of a broader political context. The notion that the Vietnam War exacted a form of psychic damage on American soldiers was championed by the anti-war activists of Vietnam Veterans Against the War (VVAW) and psychiatrists Chaim Shatan and Robert Jay Lifton.

10 *The writer provides historical, political, and social contexts for this acceptance.*

11 "Post-Vietnam syndrome," Shatan wrote, was caused by the "unconsummated grief" of a brutal and brutalizing war.

11 *The writer uses the evocative words brutal and brutalizing to communicate the particular horrors of the Vietnam War.*

12 The VVAW's advocacy was instrumental in securing official recognition for this condition. It was included in 1980 in the third edition of the *Diagnostic and Statistical Manual of Mental Disorders (DSM-III)* as "post-traumatic stress disorder."

12 *The writer provides facts and dates to show when "shell shock" was officially recognized as a legitimate condition and when it was renamed post-traumatic stress disorder (PTSD).*

13 PTSD's inclusion in *DSM-III* legitimated the suffering of Vietnam veterans and held out the possibility of subsidized medical care and compensation. But the *DSM-III* definition of PTSD was significant in two additional ways.

First, it identified the disorder as a condition that could afflict soldiers and civilians alike—not a diagnosis exclusive to combat, like shell shock.

Second, it focused attention on the continuing effects of a traumatic experience, rather than on the personality and constitution of the patient.

14 The ramifications of these changes have been immense. PTSD and a broader field of "traumatology" are now entrenched in psychiatric and popular discourse. In Australia, we now assume that warfare is objectively traumatizing, and that governments ought to provide medical and financial support for affected service personnel, even if a recent Four Corners program confirmed that this is not always the case.

How is PTSD viewed today?

15 Though PTSD has its origins in opposition to the Vietnam War, the politics of the condition are now largely ambivalent, with its significance shifting according to circumstance.

This point is well illustrated by the film *American Sniper*, which demonstrates the possibility of two contrary positions. After his return to civilian life, SEAL sniper Chris Kyle (Bradley Cooper) is shown to be suffering from some characteristic after-effects of combat. . . .

…

The real Chris Kyle was shot dead by Eddie Ray Routh [another veteran], in 2013. At trial, the accused's lawyers pursued a defense of insanity, compounded by the inadequate care provided by veterans' mental health services. Routh was found guilty of Kyle's murder in March of 2015.

16 In the 100 years since Myers' article on shell shock, the psychological consequences of war remain as relevant as ever.

13 *The writer explains why official recognition of PTSD was so important. She details how the shift in emphasis from the patient to the experience removed the stigma from those suffering from PTSD.*

14 *The writer cites benefits that sufferers of PTSD can now receive as a consequence of the improved attitude toward PTSD.*

15 *The writer addresses the perception of PTSD today, citing two recent examples of former soldiers linked to PTSD.*

16 *The writer concludes her argument by juxtaposing these modern instances of PTSD with the article that introduced the term "shell shock" and restating her central idea: The psychological consequences of war are as relevant and deserving of attention today as they were 100 years ago. By referring to the 100 years since Myers' article on shell shock, the writer reinforces her central idea that she is offering "proof of war's traumatic history."*

The following are examples of a high-scoring and low-scoring essay, based on the passage by Elizabeth Roberts-Pedersen.

High-Scoring Essay

Elizabeth Roberts-Pedersen claims that the psychological consequences of war have always been with us; it just took time for us to realize it. To convince us, she uses evidence and reasoning that carefully develop and reinforce her premise. With a few persuasive elements, her article brings us to the same conclusion: war has severe consequences that don't disappear when peace is declared.

Roberts-Pedersen begins the discussion of PTSD by citing an article published 100 years ago that contained the first mention of a condition known at the time as shell shock. Soldiers suffering from shell shock were described as having physical symptoms, such as blindness and paralysis. At first attributed to the effects of artillery, the medical community soon accepted the cause as the stress and exhaustion of combat rather than physical injury. Unfortunately, the men were considered to be weak individuals by popular medical opinion of the time.

In the section titled "Developing a diagnosis," Roberts-Pedersen uses reason to explain how popular opinion toward this condition changed and uses evidence to prove that the change occurred. She credits the Vietnam War and the public's response to the war for the change. Anti-war activists and psychiatrists promoted a description of Vietnam veterans' condition as grief caused by a "brutal and brutalizing war." The phrasing shows us that the soldiers with this condition are victims of the war, just as soldiers who are physically wounded in combat are. The image of veterans with shell shock morphed from "weak individuals" to "noble heroes who suffer from brutal acts of war." The evidence she cites for this claim is the addition of post-traumatic stress disorder (PTSD) to the official medical manual, *Diagnostic and Statistical Manual of Mental Disorders* (*DSM-III*). She explains the consequences by showing the cause (including the condition in the manual) with its effects (people with PTSD are now treated well by the military).

In the final section, Roberts-Pedersen reminds us of the *American Sniper* movie. Both the hero and the villain in the movie have combat experience. Regardless of the men's conditions, the audience easily distinguishes the hero from the villain. Understanding of the medical condition first described 100 years ago is needed to understand the movie. This final piece of evidence persuades us that PTSD is a condition that continues to affect lives today, and we need to see it with clear eyes.

Low-Scoring Essay

Elizabeth Roberts-Pedersen is a writer familiar with shell shock, which is called PTSD today. She first discovered shell shock 100 years ago and wrote about it in a medical book. Shell shock was a head injury that happens when men close to the bomb are shocked when the bomb explodes. The light is bright enough to blind them and the sound can make them deaf and dumb or paralyze them. They studied this in three British soldiers who were in a French hospital.

Doctors studied this a long time and changed the name to PTSD. They changed the name because the same thing can happen when people who aren't in the military get shocked by something bad. Now, it's a stress disorder that doctors can treat with medicine. Civilians can get it now after a bad thing happens like a riot or a bombing but they don't get as stressed about it anymore. Now they can cure it or at least treat it.

The writer uses a movie I saw called American Sniper. The sniper does some stuff during the war and gets PTSD. A bad guy who was also in a military unit killed the sniper. He tries to tell people that he had PTSD and that's why he killed the sniper.

The writer says that the story in the movie, which is true, is proof that PTSD still happens today. You hear about it in the news pretty often. That makes it important for people to know about, which is why she wrote about it and why we should know about it.

COMPUTING YOUR SCORES

Now that you've completed this practice test , it's time to compute your scores. Simply follow the instructions on the following pages, and use the conversion tables provided to calculate your scores. The formulas provided will give you as close an approximation as possible of how you might score on the actual SAT® exam.

To Determine Your Practice Test Scores

1. After you go through each of the test sections (Reading, Writing and Language, Math—No Calculator, and Math—Calculator) and determine which answers you got right, be sure to enter the number of correct answers in the box below the answer key for each of the sections.

2. Your total score on the practice test is the sum of your Evidence-Based Reading and Writing Section score and your Math Section score. To get your total score, convert the raw score—the number of questions you got right in a particular section—into the "scaled score" for that section, and then you'll calculate the total score. It sounds a little confusing, but we'll take you through the steps.

To Calculate Your Evidence-Based Reading and Writing Section Score

Your Evidence-Based Reading and Writing Section score is on a scale of 200–800. First determine your Reading Test score, and then determine your score on the Writing and Language Test.

1. Count the number of correct answers you got on the **Section 1: Reading Test.** Remember that there is no penalty for wrong answers. **The number of correct answers is your raw score.**

2. Go to **Raw Score Conversion Table 1: Section and Test Scores** on page 667. Look in the "Raw Score" column for your raw score, and match it to the number in the "Reading Test Score" column.

3. Do the same with **Section 2: Writing and Language Test** to determine that score.

4. Add your Reading Test score to your Writing and Language Test score.

5. Multiply that number by 10. This is your Evidence-Based Reading and Writing Section score.

To Calculate Your Math Section Score

Your Math score is also on a scale of 200–800.

1. Count the number of correct answers you got on the **Section 3: Math Test—No Calculator** and the **Section 4: Math Test—No Calculator**. Again, there is no penalty for wrong answers. **The number of correct answers is your raw score.**

2. Add the number of correct answers on the Section 3: Math Test—No Calculator and the Section 4: Math Test—No Calculator.

3. Use the **Raw Score Conversion Table 1: Section and Test Scores** on page 667 and convert your raw score into your Math Section score.

To Obtain Your Total Score

Add your score on the Evidence-Based Reading and Writing Section to the Math Section score. This is your total score on this Practice Test, on a scale of 400–1600.

Subscores Provide Additional Information

Subscores offer you greater details about your strengths in certain areas within literacy and math. The subscores are reported on a scale of 1–15 and include Heart of Algebra, Problem Solving and Data Analysis, Passport to Advanced Math, Expression of Ideas, Standard English Conventions, Words in Context, and Command of Evidence.

Heart of Algebra

The **Heart of Algebra subscore** is based on questions from the **Math Test** that focus on linear equations and inequalities.

- Add up your total correct answers from these sections:
    - ○ Math Test—No Calculator: Questions 12, 13–15, 17–19
    - ○ Math Test—Calculator: Questions 2, 6, 13, 15, 20, 22, 23, 25, 27, 28, 31, 37
- Your Raw Score = the total number of correct answers from all of these questions.
- Use the **Raw Score Conversion Table 2: Subscores** on page 668 to determine your **Heart of Algebra** subscore.

Problem Solving and Data Analysis

The **Problem Solving and Data Analysis subscore** is based on questions from the **Math Test** that focus on quantitative reasoning, the interpretation and synthesis of data, and solving problems in rich and varied contexts.

- Add up your total correct answers from these questions:
    - ○ Math Test—No Calculator: Questions 8, 10
    - ○ Math Test—Calculator: Questions 1, 3, 5, 7–9, 12, 14, 17–19, 21, 26, 33, 35
- Your Raw Score = the total number of correct answers from all of these questions.
- Use the **Raw Score Conversion Table 2: Subscores** on page 668 to determine your **Problem Solving and Data Analysis** subscore.

Passport to Advanced Math

The **Passport to Advanced Math subscore** is based on questions from the **Math Test** that focus on topics central to your ability to progress to more advanced math, such as understanding the structure of expressions, reasoning with more complex equations, and interpreting and building functions.

- Add up your total correct answers from these questions:
    - ○ Math Test—No Calculator: Questions 2–4, 6, 9, 11, 16
    - ○ Math Test—Calculator: Questions 4, 10, 16, 24, 29, 34, 36, 38
- Your Raw Score = the total number of correct answers from all of these questions.
- Use the **Raw Score Conversion Table 2: Subscores** on page 668 to determine your **Passport to Advanced Math** subscore.

Expression of Ideas

The **Expression of Ideas subscore** is based on questions from the **Writing and Language Test** that focus on topic development, organization, and rhetorically effective use of language.

- Add up your total correct answers from these questions in Section 2: Writing and Language Test:
    - ○ Questions 1, 3, 7–10, 12, 16–19, 22, 23, 26–28, 30, 33, 34, 36, 37, 39, 42, 44
- Your Raw Score = the total number of correct answers from all of these questions.
- Use the **Raw Score Conversion Table 2: Subscores** on page 668 to determine your Expression of Ideas subscore.

Standard English Conventions

The **Standard English Conventions subscore** is based on questions from the **Writing and Language Test** that focus on sentence structure, usage, and punctuation.

- Add up your total correct answers from these questions in Section 2: Writing and Language Test:
    - ○ Questions 2, 4–6, 11, 13–15, 20, 21, 24, 25, 29, 31, 32, 35, 38, 40, 41, 43
- Your Raw Score = the total number of correct answers from all of these questions.
- Use the **Raw Score Conversion Table 2: Subscores** on page 668 to determine your **Standard English Conventions** subscore.

Words in Context

The **Words in Context subscore** is based on questions from the **Reading Test** and the **Writing and Language Test** that address word/phrase meaning in context and rhetorical word choice.

- Add up your total correct answers from these questions in Sections 1 and 2:
  - Reading Test: Questions 4, 8, 13, 17, 27, 30, 33, 36, 44, 49
  - Writing and Language Test: Questions 1, 3, 18, 22, 28, 33, 36, 39
- Your Raw Score = the total number of correct answers from all of these questions.
- Use the **Raw Score Conversion Table 2: Subscores** on page 668 to determine your **Words in Context** subscore.

Command of Evidence

The **Command of Evidence subscore** is based on questions from the **Reading Test** and the **Writing and Language Test** that ask you to interpret and use evidence found in a wide range of passages and informational graphics, such as graphs, tables, and charts.

- Add up your total correct answers from Sections 1 and 2:
  - Reading Test: Questions 3, 6, 16, 20, 26, 29, 39, 42, 46, 48
  - Writing and Language Test: Questions 7, 8, 12, 16, 23, 26, 42, 44
- Your Raw Score = the total number of correct answers from all of these questions.
- Use the **Raw Score Conversion Table 2: Subscores** on page 668 to determine your **Command of Evidence** subscore.

CROSS-TEST SCORES

The SAT® exam also reports two cross-test scores: Analysis in History/Social Studies and Analysis in Science. These scores are based on questions in the Reading Test, Writing and Language Test, and both Math Tests that ask you to think analytically about texts and questions in these subject areas. Cross-test scores are reported on a scale of 10–40.

Analysis in History/Social Studies

- Add up your total correct answers from these questions:
  - Reading Test: Questions 32–52
  - Writing and Language Test: Questions 1, 3, 7–10
  - Math Test—No Calculator: Question 8
  - Math Test—Calculator: Questions 2, 3, 21, 22, 26, 31, 34
  - Your Raw Score = the total number of correct answers from all of these questions.
  - Use the **Raw Score Conversion Table 3: Cross-Test Scores** on page 669 to determine your Analysis in History/Social Studies cross-test score.

Analysis in Science

- Add up your total correct answers from these questions:
  - Reading Test: Questions 11–31
  - Writing and Language Test: Questions 23, 26, 27, 28, 30, 33
  - Math Test—No Calculator: Questions 10, 11
  - Math Test—Calculator: Questions 4–6, 9, 20, 23
- Your Raw Score = the total number of correct answers from all of these questions.
- Use the **Raw Score Conversion Table 3: Cross-Test Scores** on page 669 to determine your Analysis in Science cross-test score.

Raw Score Conversion Table 1: Section and Test Scores

Raw Score	Math Section Score	Reading Test Score	Writing and Language Test Score	Raw Score	Math Section Score	Reading Test Score	Writing and Language Test Score	Raw Score	Math Section Score	Reading Test Score	Writing and Language Test Score
0	200	10	10	20	450	22	23	40	610	33	36
1	200	10	10	21	460	23	23	41	620	33	37
2	210	10	10	22	470	23	24	42	630	34	38
3	230	11	10	23	480	24	25	43	640	35	39
4	240	12	11	24	480	24	25	44	650	35	40
5	260	13	12	25	490	25	26	45	660	36	
6	280	14	13	26	500	25	26	46	670	37	
7	290	15	13	27	510	26	27	47	670	37	
8	310	15	14	28	520	26	28	48	680	38	
9	320	16	15	29	520	27	28	49	690	38	
10	330	17	16	30	530	28	29	50	700	39	
11	340	17	16	31	540	28	30	51	710	40	
12	360	18	17	32	550	29	30	52	730	40	
13	370	19	18	33	560	29	31	53	740		
14	380	19	19	34	560	30	32	54	750		
15	390	20	19	35	570	30	32	55	760		
16	410	20	20	36	580	31	33	56	780		
17	420	21	21	37	590	31	34	57	790		
18	430	21	21	38	600	32	34	58	800		
19	440	22	22	39	600	32	35				

Conversion Equation 1 Section and Test Scores

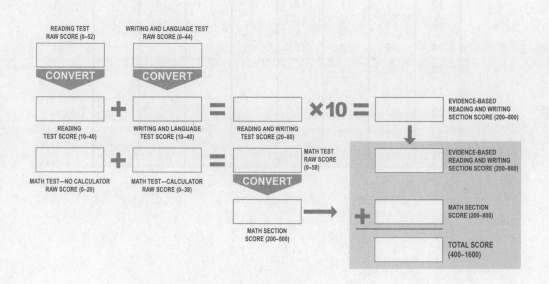

RAW SCORE CONVERSION TABLE 2: SUBSCORES

Raw Score (# of correct answers)	Expression of Ideas	Standard English Conventions	Heart of Algebra	Problem Solving and Data Analysis	Passport to Advanced Math	Words in Context	Command of Evidence
0	1	1	1	1	1	1	1
1	1	1	1	1	3	1	1
2	1	1	2	2	5	2	2
3	2	2	3	3	6	3	3
4	3	2	4	4	7	4	4
5	4	3	5	5	8	5	5
6	5	4	6	6	9	6	6
7	6	5	6	7	10	6	7
8	6	6	7	8	11	7	8
9	7	6	8	8	11	8	8
10	7	7	8	9	12	8	9
11	8	7	9	10	12	9	10
12	8	8	9	10	13	9	10
13	9	8	9	11	13	10	11
14	9	9	10	12	14	11	12
15	10	10	10	13	14	12	13
16	10	10	11	14	15	13	14
17	11	11	12	15		14	15
18	11	12	13			15	15
19	12	13	15				
20	12	15					
21	13						
22	14						
23	14						
24	15						

Conversion Equation 2 Subscores

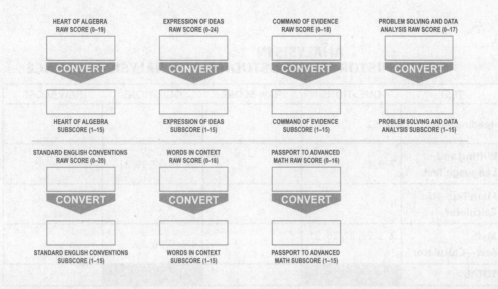

HEART OF ALGEBRA RAW SCORE (0–19)	EXPRESSION OF IDEAS RAW SCORE (0–24)	COMMAND OF EVIDENCE RAW SCORE (0–18)	PROBLEM SOLVING AND DATA ANALYSIS RAW SCORE (0–17)
CONVERT	CONVERT	CONVERT	CONVERT
HEART OF ALGEBRA SUBSCORE (1–15)	EXPRESSION OF IDEAS SUBSCORE (1–15)	COMMAND OF EVIDENCE SUBSCORE (1–15)	PROBLEM SOLVING AND DATA ANALYSIS SUBSCORE (1–15)

STANDARD ENGLISH CONVENTIONS RAW SCORE (0–20)	WORDS IN CONTEXT RAW SCORE (0–18)	PASSPORT TO ADVANCED MATH RAW SCORE (0–16)
CONVERT	CONVERT	CONVERT
STANDARD ENGLISH CONVENTIONS SUBSCORE (1–15)	WORDS IN CONTEXT SUBSCORE (1–15)	PASSPORT TO ADVANCED MATH SUBSCORE (1–15)

Raw Score Conversion Table 3: Cross-Test Scores

Raw Score (# of correct answers)	Analysis in History/Social Studies Cross-Test Score	Analysis in Science Cross-Test Score	Raw Score (# of correct answers)	Analysis in History/Social Studies Cross-Test Score	Analysis in Science Cross-Test Score
0	10	10	18	28	26
1	10	11	19	29	27
2	11	12	20	30	27
3	12	13	21	30	28
4	14	14	22	31	29
5	15	15	23	32	30
6	16	16	24	32	30
7	17	17	25	33	31
8	18	18	26	34	32
9	20	19	27	35	33
10	21	20	28	35	33
11	22	20	29	36	34
12	23	21	30	37	35
13	24	22	31	38	36
14	25	23	32	38	37
15	26	24	33	39	38
16	27	24	34	40	39
17	28	25	35	40	40

CONVERSION EQUATION 3: CROSS-TEST SCORES

	ANALYSIS IN HISTORY/SOCIAL STUDIES		**ANALYSIS IN SCIENCE**	
TEST	**QUESTIONS**	**RAW SCORE**	**QUESTIONS**	**RAW SCORE**
Reading Test	32–52		11–31	
Writing and Language Test	7–9, 43		23, 26, 27, 29, 31	
Math Test—No Calculator	8		10, 11	
Math Test—Calculator	2. 3. 21, 22, 26, 31, 34		4–6, 9, 20, 23	
TOTAL				

ANALYSIS IN HISTORY/
SOCIAL STUDIES
RAW SCORE (0–35)

CONVERT

ANALYSIS IN HISTORY/
SOCIAL STUDIES
CROSS-TEST SCORE (10–40)

ANALYSIS IN SCIENCE
RAW SCORE (0–35)

CONVERT

ANALYSIS IN SCIENCE
CROSS-TEST SCORE (10–40)

Section 1: Reading Test

1. Ⓐ Ⓑ Ⓒ Ⓓ   12. Ⓐ Ⓑ Ⓒ Ⓓ   23. Ⓐ Ⓑ Ⓒ Ⓓ   33. Ⓐ Ⓑ Ⓒ Ⓓ   43. Ⓐ Ⓑ Ⓒ Ⓓ
2. Ⓐ Ⓑ Ⓒ Ⓓ   13. Ⓐ Ⓑ Ⓒ Ⓓ   24. Ⓐ Ⓑ Ⓒ Ⓓ   34. Ⓐ Ⓑ Ⓒ Ⓓ   44. Ⓐ Ⓑ Ⓒ Ⓓ
3. Ⓐ Ⓑ Ⓒ Ⓓ   14. Ⓐ Ⓑ Ⓒ Ⓓ   25. Ⓐ Ⓑ Ⓒ Ⓓ   35. Ⓐ Ⓑ Ⓒ Ⓓ   45. Ⓐ Ⓑ Ⓒ Ⓓ
4. Ⓐ Ⓑ Ⓒ Ⓓ   15. Ⓐ Ⓑ Ⓒ Ⓓ   26. Ⓐ Ⓑ Ⓒ Ⓓ   36. Ⓐ Ⓑ Ⓒ Ⓓ   46. Ⓐ Ⓑ Ⓒ Ⓓ
5. Ⓐ Ⓑ Ⓒ Ⓓ   16. Ⓐ Ⓑ Ⓒ Ⓓ   27. Ⓐ Ⓑ Ⓒ Ⓓ   37. Ⓐ Ⓑ Ⓒ Ⓓ   47. Ⓐ Ⓑ Ⓒ Ⓓ
6. Ⓐ Ⓑ Ⓒ Ⓓ   17. Ⓐ Ⓑ Ⓒ Ⓓ   28. Ⓐ Ⓑ Ⓒ Ⓓ   38. Ⓐ Ⓑ Ⓒ Ⓓ   48. Ⓐ Ⓑ Ⓒ Ⓓ
7. Ⓐ Ⓑ Ⓒ Ⓓ   18. Ⓐ Ⓑ Ⓒ Ⓓ   29. Ⓐ Ⓑ Ⓒ Ⓓ   39. Ⓐ Ⓑ Ⓒ Ⓓ   49. Ⓐ Ⓑ Ⓒ Ⓓ
8. Ⓐ Ⓑ Ⓒ Ⓓ   19. Ⓐ Ⓑ Ⓒ Ⓓ   30. Ⓐ Ⓑ Ⓒ Ⓓ   40. Ⓐ Ⓑ Ⓒ Ⓓ   50. Ⓐ Ⓑ Ⓒ Ⓓ
9. Ⓐ Ⓑ Ⓒ Ⓓ   20. Ⓐ Ⓑ Ⓒ Ⓓ   31. Ⓐ Ⓑ Ⓒ Ⓓ   41. Ⓐ Ⓑ Ⓒ Ⓓ   51. Ⓐ Ⓑ Ⓒ Ⓓ
10. Ⓐ Ⓑ Ⓒ Ⓓ   21. Ⓐ Ⓑ Ⓒ Ⓓ   32. Ⓐ Ⓑ Ⓒ Ⓓ   42. Ⓐ Ⓑ Ⓒ Ⓓ   52. Ⓐ Ⓑ Ⓒ Ⓓ
11. Ⓐ Ⓑ Ⓒ Ⓓ   22. Ⓐ Ⓑ Ⓒ Ⓓ

Section 2: Writing and Language Test

1. Ⓐ Ⓑ Ⓒ Ⓓ   10. Ⓐ Ⓑ Ⓒ Ⓓ   19. Ⓐ Ⓑ Ⓒ Ⓓ   28. Ⓐ Ⓑ Ⓒ Ⓓ   37. Ⓐ Ⓑ Ⓒ Ⓓ
2. Ⓐ Ⓑ Ⓒ Ⓓ   11. Ⓐ Ⓑ Ⓒ Ⓓ   20. Ⓐ Ⓑ Ⓒ Ⓓ   29. Ⓐ Ⓑ Ⓒ Ⓓ   38. Ⓐ Ⓑ Ⓒ Ⓓ
3. Ⓐ Ⓑ Ⓒ Ⓓ   12. Ⓐ Ⓑ Ⓒ Ⓓ   21. Ⓐ Ⓑ Ⓒ Ⓓ   30. Ⓐ Ⓑ Ⓒ Ⓓ   39. Ⓐ Ⓑ Ⓒ Ⓓ
4. Ⓐ Ⓑ Ⓒ Ⓓ   13. Ⓐ Ⓑ Ⓒ Ⓓ   22. Ⓐ Ⓑ Ⓒ Ⓓ   31. Ⓐ Ⓑ Ⓒ Ⓓ   40. Ⓐ Ⓑ Ⓒ Ⓓ
5. Ⓐ Ⓑ Ⓒ Ⓓ   14. Ⓐ Ⓑ Ⓒ Ⓓ   23. Ⓐ Ⓑ Ⓒ Ⓓ   32. Ⓐ Ⓑ Ⓒ Ⓓ   41. Ⓐ Ⓑ Ⓒ Ⓓ
6. Ⓐ Ⓑ Ⓒ Ⓓ   15. Ⓐ Ⓑ Ⓒ Ⓓ   24. Ⓐ Ⓑ Ⓒ Ⓓ   33. Ⓐ Ⓑ Ⓒ Ⓓ   42. Ⓐ Ⓑ Ⓒ Ⓓ
7. Ⓐ Ⓑ Ⓒ Ⓓ   16. Ⓐ Ⓑ Ⓒ Ⓓ   25. Ⓐ Ⓑ Ⓒ Ⓓ   34. Ⓐ Ⓑ Ⓒ Ⓓ   43. Ⓐ Ⓑ Ⓒ Ⓓ
8. Ⓐ Ⓑ Ⓒ Ⓓ   17. Ⓐ Ⓑ Ⓒ Ⓓ   26. Ⓐ Ⓑ Ⓒ Ⓓ   35. Ⓐ Ⓑ Ⓒ Ⓓ   44. Ⓐ Ⓑ Ⓒ Ⓓ
9. Ⓐ Ⓑ Ⓒ Ⓓ   18. Ⓐ Ⓑ Ⓒ Ⓓ   27. Ⓐ Ⓑ Ⓒ Ⓓ   36. Ⓐ Ⓑ Ⓒ Ⓓ

Section 3: Math Test—No Calculator

1. Ⓐ Ⓑ Ⓒ Ⓓ   4. Ⓐ Ⓑ Ⓒ Ⓓ   7. Ⓐ Ⓑ Ⓒ Ⓓ   10. Ⓐ Ⓑ Ⓒ Ⓓ   13. Ⓐ Ⓑ Ⓒ Ⓓ
2. Ⓐ Ⓑ Ⓒ Ⓓ   5. Ⓐ Ⓑ Ⓒ Ⓓ   8. Ⓐ Ⓑ Ⓒ Ⓓ   11. Ⓐ Ⓑ Ⓒ Ⓓ   14. Ⓐ Ⓑ Ⓒ Ⓓ
3. Ⓐ Ⓑ Ⓒ Ⓓ   6. Ⓐ Ⓑ Ⓒ Ⓓ   9. Ⓐ Ⓑ Ⓒ Ⓓ   12. Ⓐ Ⓑ Ⓒ Ⓓ   15. Ⓐ Ⓑ Ⓒ Ⓓ

Practice Test 2 — ANSWERS

Section 3: Math Test—No Calculator

16. **17.** **18.** **19.** **20.**

Section 4: Math Test—Calculator

1. Ⓐ Ⓑ Ⓒ Ⓓ   7. Ⓐ Ⓑ Ⓒ Ⓓ   13. Ⓐ Ⓑ Ⓒ Ⓓ   19. Ⓐ Ⓑ Ⓒ Ⓓ   25. Ⓐ Ⓑ Ⓒ Ⓓ

2. Ⓐ Ⓑ Ⓒ Ⓓ   8. Ⓐ Ⓑ Ⓒ Ⓓ   14. Ⓐ Ⓑ Ⓒ Ⓓ   20. Ⓐ Ⓑ Ⓒ Ⓓ   26. Ⓐ Ⓑ Ⓒ Ⓓ

3. Ⓐ Ⓑ Ⓒ Ⓓ   9. Ⓐ Ⓑ Ⓒ Ⓓ   15. Ⓐ Ⓑ Ⓒ Ⓓ   21. Ⓐ Ⓑ Ⓒ Ⓓ   27. Ⓐ Ⓑ Ⓒ Ⓓ

4. Ⓐ Ⓑ Ⓒ Ⓓ   10. Ⓐ Ⓑ Ⓒ Ⓓ   16. Ⓐ Ⓑ Ⓒ Ⓓ   22. Ⓐ Ⓑ Ⓒ Ⓓ   28. Ⓐ Ⓑ Ⓒ Ⓓ

5. Ⓐ Ⓑ Ⓒ Ⓓ   11. Ⓐ Ⓑ Ⓒ Ⓓ   17. Ⓐ Ⓑ Ⓒ Ⓓ   23. Ⓐ Ⓑ Ⓒ Ⓓ   29. Ⓐ Ⓑ Ⓒ Ⓓ

6. Ⓐ Ⓑ Ⓒ Ⓓ   12. Ⓐ Ⓑ Ⓒ Ⓓ   18. Ⓐ Ⓑ Ⓒ Ⓓ   24. Ⓐ Ⓑ Ⓒ Ⓓ   30. Ⓐ Ⓑ Ⓒ Ⓓ

31. **32.** **33.** **34.** **35.**

36. **37.** **38.**

Section 5: Essay

_____

_____

_____

_____

_____

_____

_____

_____

_____

_____

_____

_____

_____

_____

_____

_____

_____

_____

_____

_____

_____

_____

_____

_____

_____

_____

_____

_____

www.petersons.com

SECTION 1: READING TEST

65 Minutes—52 Questions

TURN TO SECTION 1 OF YOUR ANSWER SHEET TO ANSWER THE QUESTIONS IN THIS SECTION.

DIRECTIONS: Each passage (or pair of passages) in this section is followed by a number of multiple-choice questions. After reading each passage, select the best answer to each question based on what is stated or implied in the passage or passages and in any supplementary material, such as a table, graph, chart, or photograph.

Questions 1–11 are based on the following passage and supplementary material.

"Sedentary Death Syndrome: Public Health Menace" was authored by Rob Wilkins, a member of the National Federation of Professional Trainers (NFPT). The NFPT certifies personal fitness trainers to understand the fundamental exercise science principles in order to provide safe and effective fitness programs to individuals or small groups. The article appears on NFPT's website, http://www.nfpt.com.

"In the United States, even the Grim Reaper is flabby."
– Dr. Frank W. Booth, University of Missouri-Columbia

Line
Being fat and physically inactive now has a name—Sedentary Death Syndrome or "SeDS." Approximately 2.5
5   million Americans will die prematurely in the next ten years due to SeDS, a number greater than all alcohol, guns, motor vehicles, illicit drug use, and sexual behavior related deaths combined.

Research has identified SeDS as the second
10   largest threat to public health (heart disease remains the number one cause of death for Americans) and is expected to add as much as $3 trillion to healthcare costs over ten years, more than twice the tax cut recently passed by the US Senate. Frank W. Booth, a professor
15   at the University of Missouri-Columbia, stated that he invented the term SeDS to emphasis his point that, in the United States, even the Grim Reaper is flabby.

Professor Booth's goal is to make the public and the federal government pay more attention and spend
20   more money on getting the average American to become more physically active. "We knew that there were approximately 250,000 people in the United States each year dying of inactivity-related diseases, but the phrase inactivity-related disease lacks pizzazz,"
25   Booth said. Without a catchy name, the condition wasn't getting enough attention, he said. "One day while I was out jogging, it hit me: Why not call it SeDS?"

Approximately two-thirds of American adults are currently overweight or obese according to the Center

30   for Science in the Public Interest (CSPI). Due to the fact that more than one-fourth of Americans are not physically active in their leisure time, obesity has doubled, and Type 2 diabetes (also known as adult-onset diabetes) has increased tenfold. Type 2 diabetes
35   is a devastating disease that may lead to complications such as blindness, kidney failure, heart disease, circulatory problems that can result in amputation, and premature death.

Between 1982–1994, one third of all new cases of
40   Type 2 diabetes were among people ages 10–19. The then-Surgeon General of the United States recently observed that, "We are raising the most overweight youngsters in American history." In 2011–2012, 8.4% of 2- to 5-year-olds had obesity compared with 17.7%
45   of 6- to 11-year-olds, and 20.5% of 12- to 19-year-olds.

Studies indicate that currently about 17% of the nation's children are obese. This is not surprising, considering that the average American child spends 900 hours per year in school but 1,200 hours watching
50   television, according to the TV-Turnoff Network.

The problem is made worse by the fact that fewer than 3 in 10 high school students get at least 60 minutes of physical activity every day. Less than half (48%) of all adults meet the 2008 Physical Activity
55   Guidelines.

"Our bodies were designed to be physically active," said Scott Gordon of East Carolina University. The trouble is that hard work, from farming to simply doing household chores without appliances, is no
60   longer part of ordinary life for most people, he said. Gordon called for activity to be put back in. "In adults, this may mean planning exercise into your daily routine," he said. "However, it may be as simple as taking the stairs instead of the elevator a couple of
65   times a day." Booth and his supporters said a special effort must be made to reach children, so they won't turn fat and weak like their parents and, also like their

CONTINUE

parents, get sick and die early. "Perhaps the greatest tragedy is that ailments previously associated with
70 the middle-aged and older population will now affect our children and will serve to drastically decrease their quality of life," said researcher Ron Gomes of the University of Delaware.

All Americans may incur a severe decline in their
75 health due to consistent physical inactivity. Thirty-five known conditions are exacerbated by physical inactivity; they include arthritis pain, arrhythmias, breast cancer, colon cancer, congestive heart failure, depression, gallstone disease, heart attack, hypertension, obesity,
80 osteoporosis, peripheral vascular disease, respiratory problems, Type 2 diabetes, sleep apnea, and stroke.

Providing enjoyable experiences is a potent strategy for increasing activity levels in youth, their attitude about the value of exercise, and ultimately
85 long-term health outcome. Introducing and making exercise fun for young children may help them develop commitment and a positive attitude toward physical activity as they go through adolescence and adulthood.

1 The author most likely selected the particular causes of death in lines 6–7 ("alcohol . . . behavior") to

A. shock the reader with the various ways one could die.

B. prove that SeDS has become the most common cause of death.

C. show that some of the most common causes of death are not as common as SeDS.

D. prevent the reader from engaging in destructive and self-destructive behavior.

2 The structure of the article is designed to

A. present opinions backed up by factual detail.

B. frighten readers who are ignoring their weight issues.

C. offer testimonials from those who are most affected.

D. focus on statistical data and how it is being interpreted.

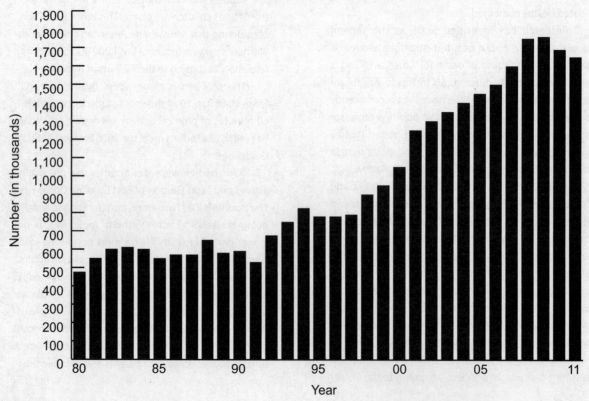

Number in Thousands of New Cases of Diagnosed Diabetes Among Adults Aged 18–79 Years, U.S. 1980–2011

3 The author includes a quote featuring the Grim Reaper in line 1 to

  A. indicate the gravity of a problem.

  B. lighten the tone of an otherwise serious article.

  C. to make the concept of death more understandable.

  D. frighten the reader with a scary image.

4 Based on the passage, which choice best describes the relationship between the design of our bodies and the fact that obesity has doubled?

  A. Humans are naturally prone to obesity.

  B. Weight gain is passed from parents to children.

  C. People eat more in order to perform modern activities.

  D. Physical work is no longer part of most people's lives.

5 As used in line 4, "sedentary" most nearly means

  A. inactive.

  B. robust.

  C. sudden.

  D. obese.

6 The author indicates that SeDS

  A. may soon surpass heart disease as the number one cause of death.

  B. has made Dr. Frank W. Booth a respected and well-known professor.

  C. does not affect young people significantly.

  D. has financial negative impacts as well as physical ones.

7 Which choice provides the best evidence for the answer to the previous question?

  A. Lines 11–13 ("and is . . . ten years")

  B. Lines 14–15 ("Frank . . . Columbia")

  C. Lines 18–20 ("Professor . . . money")

  D. Lines 21–23 ("We knew . . . diseases")

8 It can reasonably be inferred from the passage and the chart that drastic increases in new cases of Type 2 diabetes began around

  A. 1980.

  B. 1988.

  C. 1998.

  D. 2009.

9 As used in line 24, "pizzazz" most nearly means

  A. research.

  B. oomph.

  C. seriousness.

  D. clarity.

10 The passage most strongly suggests which of the following?

  A. A catchy name will motivate people to lose weight.

  B. Moving the body is essential to health.

  C. Type 2 diabetes is another form of obesity.

  D. Children can have good habits despite poor role models.

11 Which choice provides the best evidence for the answer to the previous question?

  A. Lines 18–21 ("Professor . . . active")

  B. Lines 30–34 ("Due to . . . tenfold")

  C. Lines 34–38 ("Type 2 . . . death")

  D. Lines 68–73 ("Perhaps . . . Delaware")

CONTINUE

Questions 12–22 are based on the following passage.

This passage is excerpted from Helen Hunt Jackson's A Century of Dishonor, *published in 1881. In 1879, Jackson became a Native American rights activist after witnessing a speech by Ponca chief Standing Bear.*

There are within the limits of the United States between two hundred and fifty and three hundred thousand Indians, exclusive of those in Alaska. The
Line names of the different tribes and bands as entered in
5 the statistical table, so the Indian Office Reports, number nearly three hundred.

There is not among these three hundred bands of Indians one which has not suffered cruelly at the hands either of the Government or of white settlers. The poorer,
10 the more insignificant, the more helpless the band, the more certain the cruelty and outrage to which they have been subjected. This is especially true of the bands on the Pacific slope. These Indians found themselves all of a sudden surrounded by and caught up in the great
15 influx of gold-seeking settlers, as helpless creatures on a shore are caught up in a tidal wave. There was not time for the Government to make treaties; not even time for communities to make laws. The tale of the wrongs, the oppressions, the murders of the Pacific-slope Indians in
20 the last thirty years would be a volume by itself, and is too monstrous to be believed.

It makes little difference, however, where one opens the record of the history of the Indians; every page and every year has its dark stain. The story of one tribe is the
25 story of all, varied only by differences of time and place; but neither time nor place makes any difference in the main facts. Colorado is as greedy and unjust in 1880 as was Georgia in 1830, and Ohio in 1795; and the United States Government breaks promises now as deftly as
30 then, and with an added ingenuity from long practice.

One of its strongest supports in so doing is the wide-spread sentiment among the people of dislike to the Indian, of impatience with his presence as a "barrier to civilization" and distrust of it as a possible danger.
35 The old tales of the frontier life, with its horrors of Indian warfare, have gradually, by two or three generations' telling, produced in the average mind something like an hereditary instinct of questioning and unreasoning aversion which it is almost impossible to dislodge or
40 soften.

President after president has appointed commission after commission to inquire into and report upon Indian affairs, and to make suggestions as to the best methods of managing them. The reports are
45 filled with eloquent statements of wrongs done to the Indians, of perfidies on the part of the Government; they counsel, as earnestly as words can, a trial of the simple and unperplexing expedients of telling truth, keeping promises, making fair bargains, dealing justly in all ways
50 and all things. These reports are bound up with the Government's Annual Reports, and that is the end of them.

The history of the Government connections with the Indians is a shameful record of broken treaties and unfulfilled promises. The history of the border white
55 man's connection with the Indians is a sickening record of murder, outrage, robbery, and wrongs committed by the former, as the rule, and occasional savage outbreaks and unspeakably barbarous deeds of retaliation by the latter, as the exception.
60 Taught by the Government that they had rights entitled to respect, when those rights have been assailed by the rapacity of the white man, the arm which should have been raised to protect them has ever been ready to sustain the aggressor.
65 The testimony of some of the highest military officers of the United States is on record to the effect that, in our Indian wars, almost without exception, the first aggressions have been made by the white man. . . . Every crime committed by a white man against an Indian
70 is concealed and palliated. Every offense committed by an Indian against a white man is borne on the wings of the post or the telegraph to the remotest corner of the land, clothed with all the horrors which the reality or imagination can throw around it. Against such influ-
75 ences as these are the people of the United States need to be warned.

---

12 The author's description of government inquiries into the handling of Native American affairs in lines 41–51 suggests that the author

A. claims no responsibility for the unjust treatment Native Americans have suffered historically.

B. believes that the government reports were more concerned with voicing insincere support for Native Americans than making substantive changes.

C. supposes that presidents have not been critical of how Native Americans have been treated historically.

D. acknowledges that the government understands the problem and is well equipped to determine a viable solution.

13 The author refers to different states and different times (lines 22–30) as a way of

A. showing that abuses against Native Americans are widespread across geography and history.

B. pointing out which states had the worst records of abuse against Native Americans.

C. showing that these abuses against Native Americans no longer occur in America.

D. defining where abuses against Native Americans in the southern United States occurred.

14 Which choice provides the best evidence for the answer to the previous question?

A. Lines 22–23 ("It makes . . . the Indians")

B. Lines 24–25 ("The story . . . place")

C. Lines 28–30 ("the United . . . as then")

D. Line 30 ("with . . . practice")

15 What explanation does the author give for why abuses against Native Americans were allowed to go unchecked and unpunished in lines 16–18?

A. Old tales of Native Americans attacks on the frontier were persistent.

B. The government tended to break treaties and abuse its own laws.

C. The government sympathized with gold-seeking settlers instead of Native Americans.

D. The Pacific slope was lawless and chaotic during the gold rush.

16 The author states that the abuses Native Americans suffered were not

A. completely unjustified.

B. limited to a particular tribe.

C. well documented enough.

D. recorded before 1795.

17 The author is primarily concerned with

A. explaining how the government can atone for the abuses it has committed against Native Americans.

B. arguing that Native Americans have been systematically abused throughout US history.

C. explaining the causes and effects of the government's abuses against Native Americans.

D. presenting opposing viewpoints as to why the United States has had conflicts with Native Americans.

18 As used in line 70, "palliated" most nearly means

A. intensified.

B. misunderstood.

C. eased.

D. excused.

19 Which of the following summaries of the last paragraph is the most accurate?

A. The generals of the US Army suggest that they had to be aggressive to keep Native Americans from defeating them and that sometimes there were crimes committed against Native Americans. Both sides spread their interpretation of events across the nation.

B. In court hearings, soldiers discussed how the white man often took the fight to Native Americans in order to move them off the land and that there were occasions when this resulted in savage behavior by both parties.

C. Proof that the white man was the aggressor in almost every conflict comes from the US Army itself and the offenses of white men are disguised while the few offenses of Native Americans are widely exaggerated.

D. The history of the conflicts between Native Americans and white men is one of gross injustice and extreme crimes against the tribes most of the time, while horrible crimes against white people are generally few and far between.

CONTINUE

20 The author suggests that the government has

    A. tried to convince Native Americans that they have the same rights as all other Americans.

    B. only just begun to make efforts to ensure that Native Americans are treated fairly.

    C. made a conscious effort to force Native Americans out of the United States.

    D. tried to conceal the crimes that Native Americans have committed against white men.

21 Which choice provides the best evidence for the answer to the previous question?

    A. Lines 60–61 ("Taught by . . . respect")

    B. Lines 62–64 ("the arm . . . aggressor")

    C. Lines 65–68 ("The testimony . . . white man…")

    D. Lines 70–73 ("Every offense . . . land")

22 As used in line 58, "barbarous" most nearly means

    A. silent.

    B. steadfast.

    C. calculated.

    D. brutal.

Questions 23–32 are based on the following passage and supplementary material.

Robert E. Lee and his family lived on a plantation estate in Arlington, Virginia, up until 1861. When the Civil War broke out, he and his family departed for safer quarters. Lee became the commander of the Rebel field forces in 1862. His former home is now a National Park site. The full-length text of the following passage, provided by the National Park Service, can be found at http://www.nps.gov/arho/learn/historyculture/slavery.htm.

Slavery at Arlington

From its earliest days, Arlington House was home not only to the Custis and Lee families who occupied the mansion, but to dozens of slaves who lived and labored on the estate.

Line
5   For nearly sixty years, Arlington functioned as a complex society made up of owners and slaves, whites and blacks. To some observers, on the surface, Arlington appeared as a harmonious community in which owner and slave often lived and worked side by side. Yet an

10 invisible gulf separated the two, as slaves were the legal property of their owners. The enslaved possessed no rights, could not enter into legally binding contracts, and could be permanently separated from their families at a moment's notice.

15   In 1802, the first slaves to inhabit Arlington arrived with their owner, George Washington Parke Custis. The grandson of Martha Washington and adopted grandson of George Washington, Custis had grown up at Mount Vernon, as had many of his slaves. Upon Martha Wash-

20 ington's death, Custis inherited her slaves and purchased others who belonged to his mother. In all, Custis owned nearly 200 slaves and as many as 63 lived and worked at Arlington. The others worked on his other two plantations near Richmond, Virginia.

25   Once at Arlington, the slaves constructed log cabins for their homes and began work on the main house. Using the red clay soil from the property and shells from the Potomac river, they made the bricks and stucco for the walls and exterior of the house. The slaves also

30 harvested timber from the Arlington forest, which was used for the interior flooring and supports. The slaves were responsible for keeping up the house and laboring on the plantation, working to harvest corn and wheat, which was sold at market in Washington.

35   Custis saw his daughter marry Lt. Robert E. Lee at Arlington in 1831. Robert and Mary Anna came to call Arlington home and Custis was a prominent figure in the lives of the seven Lee children. In his later years, Custis did not stray far from Arlington. He made his

40 will in 1855, and he increasingly relied on his son-in-law, Col. Lee, to handle his tangled business affairs. Until his death, Custis retained his old bedchamber in the north wing of the mansion, where he died after a short illness on October 10, 1857.

45 Some slaves had very close relationships with the family members, though these relationships were governed by the racial hierarchy that existed between slaves and slaveholders. Mr. Custis relied heavily on his carriage driver, Daniel Dotson, and Mrs. Lee had a personal rela-
50 tionship with the head housekeeper, Selina Gray. As Mary's arthritis increasingly restricted her activities through the years, she depended on Selina for assistance. As evidence of their close bond, Mrs. Lee entrusted Selina with the keys to the plantation at the time of the Lees' evacuation
55 in May 1861.

There is evidence that some slaves at Arlington had opportunities not widely afforded to slaves elsewhere. Mrs. Custis, a devout Episcopalian, tutored slaves in basic reading and writing so that they could read the Bible.
60 Mrs. Lee and her daughters continued this practice even though Virginia law had prohibited the education of slaves by the 1840s. Mrs. Custis also persuaded her husband to free several women and children.

Some of these emancipated slaves settled on the
65 Arlington estate, including Maria Carter Syphax who lived with her husband on a seventeen-acre plot given to her by the Custises at the time of her emancipation around 1826.

While such allowances may have improved the quality of life for the Arlington slaves, most black men
70 and women on the estate remained legally in bondage until the Civil War. In his will, Custis stipulated that all the Arlington slaves should be freed upon his death if the estate was found to be in good financial standing or within five years otherwise. When Custis died in 1857,
75 Robert E. Lee—the executor of the estate—determined that the slave labor was necessary to improve Arlington's financial status. The Arlington slaves found Lee to be a more stringent taskmaster than his predecessor. Eleven slaves were "hired out" while others were sent to the other
80 estates. In accordance with Custis's instructions, Lee officially freed the slaves on December 29, 1862.

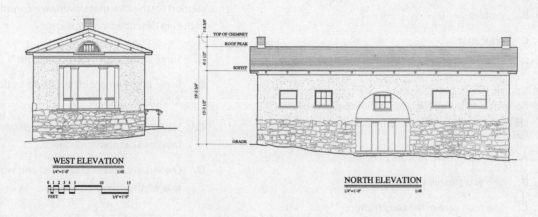

WEST ELEVATION
1/4" = 1'-0"   1:48

NORTH ELEVATION
1/4" = 1'-0"   1:48

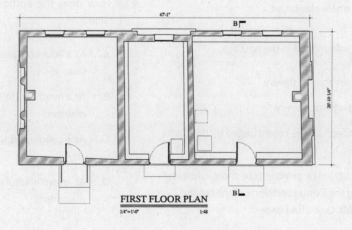

FIRST FLOOR PLAN
1/4" = 1'-0"   1:48

The room at the east end on the lower level housed the summer kitchen, with cooks' quarters above. The center room at the lower level was a washroom, with the washerwoman's quarters above. The rooms at the west end housed various domestic slaves, including the coachmen, gardener, and housekeeper.

CONTINUE

23 What is the most likely purpose of the passage?

   A. To inform people about the evils of slavery

   B. To persuade people that slavery was not so terrible

   C. To describe the history of Arlington House

   D. To illustrate how slaves lived before the Civil War

24 Why did Mrs. Custis teach her slaves to read?

   A. So they could teach other slaves and become self-sufficient

   B. So they could read their contracts with their owners

   C. So they could teach her children to read

   D. So they could read the Bible

25 As used in line 60, "practice" most nearly means

   A. repetition.

   B. custom.

   C. education.

   D. profession.

26 According to the information in the passage, how was the life of Selina Gray different from that of other slaves?

   A. She didn't have to work as hard.

   B. She was trusted by Mrs. Lee.

   C. She took care of the Lee children.

   D. She ran the whole plantation.

27 According to the information in the passage,

   A. Mrs. Custis was against slavery.

   B. Mrs. Lee was against slavery.

   C. Maria Carter Syphax was emancipated by the Curtis family.

   D. Mr. Custis's son-in-law proved to be more interested in improving the living conditions of the family's slaves than Mr. Custis had been.

28 How was Robert E. Lee related to George Washington?

   A. Lee married the daughter of Washington's grandson.

   B. Lee married George Washington's granddaughter.

   C. Lee's son married Martha Washington's granddaughter.

   D. Lee's father was Martha Washington's nephew.

29 Which choice provides the best evidence for the answer to the previous question?

   A. Lines 15–16 ("the first slaves . . . Parker Custis.")

   B. Lines 19–21 ("Upon Martha . . . his mother.")

   C. Lines 35–36 ("Custis saw . . . in 1831.")

   D. Lines 36–38 ("Robert . . . Lee children.")

30 Which of the following is NOT stated in the passage as support for the idea that slaves were considered property in the era described in the passage?

   A. Some of the slaves were "hired out."

   B. Some of the emancipated slaves settled on the Arlington estate.

   C. Slaves could be permanently separated from their families at a moment's notice.

   D. Owners and slaves often lived and worked side by side on the Arlington estate.

31 How does the author use the phrase "invisible gulf" (line 10)?

   A. As a figure of speech—related to differences in stature.

   B. As a maritime definition—related to a hidden body of water.

   C. As a geographical reference—related to a ravine or abyss.

   D. As an architectural description—related to building placement.

32 In the context of the passage, what is the best definition of the word "afforded" (line 57)?

A. Spared or given up without risk

B. Had sufficient money to pay for

C. Provided or supplied

D. Purchased in exchange for

Questions 33–42 are based on the following passages.

Passage 1 is excerpted from the U.S. Environmental Protection Agency website. Passage 2 is excerpted from the article "Science Has Spoken: Global Warming Is a Myth" by Oregon Institute of Science and Medicine chemists, Arthur B. Robinson and Zachary W. Robinson. This article was published in the Wall Street Journal *in 1997.*

PASSAGE 1

Climate change is happening

Our Earth is warming. Earth's average temperature has risen by 1.4°F over the past century and is projected to rise another 2 to 11.5°F over the next hundred years.
Line Small changes in the average temperature of the planet
5 can translate to large and potentially dangerous shifts in climate and weather.

The evidence is clear. Rising global temperatures have been accompanied by changes in weather and climate. Many places have seen changes in rainfall, resulting in more
10 floods, droughts, or intense rain, as well as more frequent and severe heat waves. The planet's oceans and glaciers have also experienced some big changes—oceans are warming and becoming more acidic, ice caps are melting, and sea levels are rising. As these and other changes become more
15 pronounced in the coming decades, they will likely present challenges to our society and our environment.

Humans are largely responsible for recent climate change. Over the past century, human activities have released large amounts of carbon dioxide and other
20 greenhouse gases into the atmosphere. The majority of greenhouse gases come from burning fossil fuels to produce energy, although deforestation, industrial processes, and some agricultural practices also emit gases into the atmosphere.
25 Greenhouse gases act like a blanket around Earth, trapping energy in the atmosphere and causing it to warm. This phenomenon is called the greenhouse effect and is natural and necessary to support life on Earth. However, the buildup of greenhouse gases can change Earth's
30 climate and result in dangerous effects to human health and welfare and to ecosystems.

Our lives are connected to the climate. Human societies have adapted to the relatively stable climate we have enjoyed since the last ice age, which ended several
35 thousand years ago. A warming climate will bring changes that can affect our water supplies, agriculture, power and transportation systems, the natural environment, and even our own health and safety.

Some changes to the climate are unavoidable.
40 Carbon dioxide can stay in the atmosphere for nearly a century, so Earth will continue to warm in the coming decades. The warmer it gets, the greater the risk for more severe changes to the climate and Earth's system. Although it's difficult to predict the exact impacts of
45 climate change, what's clear is that the climate we are accustomed to is no longer a reliable guide for what to expect in the future.

We can reduce the risks we will face from climate change. By making choices that reduce greenhouse gas
50 pollution and preparing for the changes that are already underway, we can reduce risks from climate change. Our decisions today will shape the world our children and grandchildren will live in.

PASSAGE 2

[The global warming] hypothesis predicts that
55 global temperatures will rise significantly, indeed catastrophically, if atmospheric carbon dioxide rises. Most of the increase in atmospheric carbon dioxide has occurred during the past 50 years, and the increase has continued during the past 20 years. Yet there has been no significant
60 increase in atmospheric temperature during those 50 years, and during the 20 years with the highest carbon dioxide levels, temperatures have decreased.

In science, the ultimate test is the process of experiment. If a hypothesis fails the experimental test, it must be
65 discarded. Therefore, the scientific method requires that the global warming hypothesis be rejected.

Why, then, is there continuing scientific interest in "global warming"? There is a field of inquiry in which scientists are using computers to try to predict the
70 weather—even global weather over very long periods. But global weather is so complicated that current data and computer methods are insufficient to make such predictions. Although it is reasonable to hope that these methods will eventually become useful, for now computer
75 climate models are very unreliable.

CONTINUE

So we needn't worry about human use of hydrocarbons warming the Earth. We also needn't worry about environmental calamities, even if the current, natural warming trend continues: After all the Earth has been much
80 warmer during the past 3,000 years without ill effects.

But we should worry about the effects of the hydrocarbon rationing being proposed at Kyoto. Hydrocarbon use has major environmental benefits. A great deal of research has shown that increases in atmospheric
85 carbon dioxide accelerate the growth rates of plants and also permit plants to grow in drier regions. Animal life, which depends upon plants, also increases.

33 Upon which concepts do both passages fully agree?

A. That global warming has been proven by evidence

B. That an increase in overall temperature is manageable

C. That levels of atmospheric carbon dioxide have increased

D. That usual weather patterns have been affected

34 Which choice provides the best evidence for the answer to the previous question?

A. Lines 4–6 ("Small changes . . . and weather.")

B. Lines 28–31 ("However, the . . . to ecosystems.")

C. Lines 56–61 ("Most of the . . . 20 years.")

D. Lines 81–82 ("But we should . . . at Kyoto.")

35 Which point of view characterizes both passages?

A. One of scientists taking neutral positions

B. One of fanatics defending a cause

C. One of humans concerned for global well-being

D. One of debaters directly addressing readers as "you"

36 Both the author of Passage 1 and the author of Passage 2 agree that humans

A. can have positive impacts on the environment.

B. are accountable for the rise of global warming.

C. have proven to be able to adapt to climate changes throughout history.

D. shouldn't worry about hydrocarbons warming the Earth.

37 The terms such as "potentially dangerous, severe, dangerous effects" in Passage 1 and terms such as "no significant, insufficient, unreliable" in Passage 2 create tones that are

A. the same because they both create a sense of danger.

B. different because one is based on scientific evidence and the other is speculative.

C. the same because they are both very technical.

D. different because one is alarming and the other is assuring.

38 As used in line 15, "pronounced" most nearly means

A. articulated.

B. announced.

C. inconspicuous.

D. noticeable.

39 In both passages, the authors present information by

A. listing a sequence of events that begins in the past and continues into the future.

B. discussing the causes of a situation and the resulting lack of effects.

C. comparing two different approaches to a problem and determining which will be most effective.

D. defining the problems the world faces and then offering solutions to them.

40 The essential difference between the arguments the two sets of authors present is whether or not

A. hydrocarbons should be controlled.

B. climate and weather can be modified by humans.

C. atmospheric elements pose a threat to human life.

D. the production of hydrocarbons is a natural result of human activity.

41 Which choice provides the best evidence for the answer to the previous question?

A. Lines 20–24 ("The majority . . . into the atmosphere.")

B. Lines 40–42 ("Carbon dioxide . . . coming decades.")

C. Lines 54–56 ("The global . . . dioxide rises.")

D. Lines 83–86 ("A great . . . drier regions.")

42 As used in line 5, "translate" most nearly means

A. language translation.

B. expand.

C. transform.

D. explain.

Questions 43–52 are based on the following passage.

The following is an excerpt from a short story, "Miss Tempy's Watchers," by Sarah Orne Jewett, a novelist and short-story writer who lived from 1849–1909. In the story, two women watch over their deceased friend on the evening before her funeral and share their memories of her.

The time of year was April; the place was a small farming town in New Hampshire, remote from any railroad. One by one the lights had been blown out in
Line the scattered houses near Miss Tempy Dent's, but as her
5 neighbors took a last look out of doors, their eyes turned with instinctive curiosity toward the old house where a lamp burned steadily. They gave a little sigh. "Poor Miss Tempy!" said more than one bereft acquaintance; for the good woman lay dead in her north chamber, and
10 the lamp was a watcher's light. The funeral was set for the next day at one o'clock.

The watchers were two of her oldest friends. Mrs. Crowe and Sarah Ann Binson. They were sitting in the kitchen because it seemed less awesome than the
15 unused best room, and they beguiled the long hours by steady conversation. One would think that neither topics nor opinions would hold out, at that rate, all through the long spring night, but there was a certain degree of excitement just then, and the two women had risen to
20 an unusual level of expressiveness and confidence. Each had already told the other more than one fact that she had determined to keep secret; they were again and again tempted into statements that either would have found impossible by daylight. Mrs. Crowe was knitting a
25 blue yarn stocking for her husband; the foot was already

so long that it seemed as if she must have forgotten to narrow it at the proper time. Mrs. Crowe knew exactly what she was about, however; she was of a much cooler disposition than Sister Binson, who made futile attempts
30 at some sewing, only to drop her work into her lap whenever the talk was most engaging.

Their faces were interesting—of the dry, shrewd, quick-witted New England type, and thin hair twisted neatly back out of the way. Mrs. Crowe could look
35 vague and benignant, and Miss Binson was, to quote her neighbors, a little too sharp-set, but the world knew that she had need to be, with the load she must carry supporting an inefficient widowed sister and six unpromising and unwilling nieces and nephews. The
40 eldest boy was at last placed with a good man to learn the mason's trade. Sarah Ann Binson, for all her sharp, anxious aspect never defended herself, when her sister whined and fretted.

She was told every week of her life that the poor
45 children would never have had to lift a finger if their father had lived, and yet she had kept her steadfast way with the little farm, and patiently taught the young people many useful things for which, as everybody said, they would live to thank her. However pleasureless her
50 life appeared to outward view, it was brimful of pleasure to herself.

Mrs. Crowe, on the contrary, was well-to-do, her husband being a rich farmer and an easy-going man. She was a stingy woman, but for all of that she looked
55 kindly; and when she gave away anything, or lifted a finger to help anybody, it was thought a great piece of beneficence, and a compliment, indeed, which the recipient accepted with twice as much gratitude as double the gift that came from a poorer and more
60 generous acquaintance. Everybody liked to be on good terms with Mrs. Crowe. Socially, she stood much higher than Sarah Ann Binson.

---

43 The two women are in Miss Tempy Dent's house because they are

A. waiting to tell other friends and family that she has died.

B. staying with the body so it isn't alone until it is buried.

C. conducting a funeral service following Miss Tempy's requests.

D. visiting Miss Tempy Dent, but she has died.

CONTINUE

44 The theme of this excerpt can best be described as

A. old friends often grow closer when they lose a friend.

B. the bonds of friendship remain strong even in death.

C. trying to stay awake all night isn't hard for dear friends.

D. the living carry on the traditions of the dead.

45 In lines 24–27, the author describes the stocking Mrs. Crowe was knitting to show that she

A. was too distracted to do a good job.

B. had never knitted anything before.

C. had forgotten her husband's measurements.

D. did not really want to be where she was.

46 Even though these two women are very different, the author shows that they are getting closer by

A. having them sit in the kitchen instead of the best room.

B. having Mrs. Crowe give Sarah Ann something nice.

C. explaining that Sarah Ann was actually very happy.

D. describing the intimacy of their conversation.

47 Which choice provides the best evidence for the answer to the previous question?

A. Lines 16–20 ("One would . . . and confidence.")

B. Lines 20–24 ("Each had . . . daylight.")

C. Lines 27–29 ("Mrs. Crowe . . . Binson")

D. Lines 29–31 ("who made . . . engaging.")

48 Which choice provides the best summary of what happened between Mrs. Crowe and Sarah Ann Binson in Miss Tempy's kitchen?

A. Both women found it hard to fill up the long hours.

B. Both women had become excited by the intimacy they shared.

C. Mrs. Crowe did not reveal as much as Sarah Ann Binson.

D. Sarah Ann Binson revealed her love of pleasure and freedom.

49 Mrs. Crowe and Sarah Ann Binson are

A. not very trusting.

B. the same age.

C. focused on their work.

D. from different social standings.

50 Which choice provides the best evidence for the answer to the previous question?

A. Lines 1–3 ("The time of . . . any railroad.")

B. Lines 13–16 ("They were . . . conversation.")

C. Lines 49–53 ("However . . . easy-going man.")

D. Lines 60–61 ("Everybody . . . Mrs. Crowe.")

51 As used in line 36, "sharp-set" most nearly means

A. eager.

B. bored.

C. absentminded.

D. cheap.

52 As used in line 42, "aspect" most nearly means

A. face.

B. angle.

C. attitude.

D. component.

STOP

If you finish before time is called, you may check your work on this section only.

Do not turn to any other section.

SECTION 2: WRITING AND LANGUAGE TEST

35 MINUTES—44 QUESTIONS

TURN TO SECTION 2 OF YOUR ANSWER SHEET TO ANSWER THE QUESTIONS IN THIS SECTION.

DIRECTIONS: Each passage below is accompanied by a number of multiple-choice questions. For some questions, you will need to consider how the passage might be revised to improve the expression of ideas. Other questions will ask you to consider how the passage might be edited to correct errors in sentence structure, usage, or punctuation. A passage may be accompanied by one or more graphics—such as a chart, table, or graph—that you will need to refer to in order to best answer the question(s).

Some questions will direct you to an underlined portion of a passage—it could be one word, a portion of a sentence, or the full sentence itself. Other questions will direct you to a particular paragraph or to certain sentences within a paragraph, or you'll be asked to think about the passage as a whole. Each question number refers to the corresponding number in the passage.

After reading each passage, select the answer to each question that most effectively improves the quality of writing in the passage or that makes the passage follow the conventions of Standard Written English. Many questions include a "NO CHANGE" option. Select that option if you think the best choice is to leave that specific portion of the passage as it is.

Questions 1–11 are based on the following passage.

Code Talking

In September of 1992, a group of American heroes who had gone unrecognized for many years was honored by the United States Pentagon. Consisted of thirty-five Navajo code talkers.

1

A. NO CHANGE

B. Having consisted of

C. A group which were made of

D. It consisted of

CONTINUE

During World War II, the United States Marines needed to develop a [2] code, for communicating top-secret information. [3] It being the case that they would then have access to information about United States Marines tactics and troop movements, it was crucial that enemy forces not be able to decipher the code.

[2]

A. NO CHANGE

B. code for communicating

C. code, for communicating,

D. code for communicating,

[3]

A. NO CHANGE

B. It was crucial to the United States, that enemy forces not be able to decipher the code, having access to information about Marines tactics and troop movements.

C. It was crucial that enemy forces be unable to decipher the code because, if they did, they would have access to information about the Marines' tactics and troop movements.

D. Crucially, the enemy forces were unable to decipher the code, which would have access to the Marines' tactics and troop movements.

The military recruited a small group of Navajos to create a code based on their language. **4** The Navajo language was chosen because many of the top military officials at the time were Navajo. First, it was extremely difficult to learn and virtually unknown outside the Navajo community in the American Southwest. **5** However, the Navajo language does not have a written form; it uses no alphabet. Its complexity and **6** obscurity made it the perfect basis for a code.

The first group of Navajo recruits attended boot camp in 1942. Afterward, they set to work developing a vast dictionary of code words for military terms based on the Navajo language. Each code talker had to memorize the dictionary before being sent to a Marine unit. Once they were stationed with a unit, the code talkers used telephones and radios to transmit encoded orders and information.

While the Navajo language was complicated, the code was even more complex. A code talker receiving a message heard a stream of Navajo words. **7** The receiver had to translate the words into English. Then the receiver had to use the first letter of each English equivalent to spell out a word. Adding to the difficulty of breaking the code was the fact that most letters could be indicated by the code talkers with more than one Navajo word.

4 Which choice most effectively sets up the information that follows?

A. NO CHANGE

B. The Navajo language was chosen because the Navajo people were famous for their military history.

C. The Navajo people had often been called on to help the American government in the past.

D. The Navajo language made an excellent code for a few essential reasons.

5

A. NO CHANGE

B. Furthermore

C. Likewise

D. As a result

6

A. NO CHANGE

B. uncertainty

C. beauty

D. clarity

7 Which choice most effectively joins the two sentences?

A. The receiver had to translate the words into English, and then the receiver had to use the first letter of each English equivalent to spell out a word.

B. The receiver had to translate the words into English, and then use the first letter of each English equivalent to spell out a word.

C. The receiver had to translate the words into English even though the receiver had to then use the first letter of each English equivalent to spell out a word.

D. The receiver had to translate the words into English because the receiver had to use the first letter of each English equivalent to spell out a word.

CONTINUE

Though able to crack the codes of other military branches, enemy forces never managed to **8** perceive what the Marines' Navajo code talkers said. The code talkers were renowned for the **9** speed, and accuracy, with which they **10** worked.

11 Because the Navajo language was common only in the American Southwest, the work of the code talkers remained unacknowledged until quite recently. Half a century later, in 1992, thirty-five former code talkers and their families attended the dedication of the Navajo Code Talker Exhibit at the United States Pentagon, and officially took their place in military history.

8

A. NO CHANGE

B. fathom

C. elucidate

D. decipher

9

A. NO CHANGE

B. speed, and accuracy

C. speed and accuracy

D. speed and accuracy,

10

A. NO CHANGE

B. will work

C. are working

D. have been working

11 Which choice provides information that best supports the claim made by the sentence?

A. NO CHANGE

B. had to be translated into English words and letters

C. took a long time to decode by people who didn't speak English

D. remained part of a classified code for many years

Dian Fossey

Who was **12** <u>Dian Fossey.</u> Dian Fossey was a researcher, a visionary, and a pioneer in the field of animal conservation. More specifically, Fossey dedicated her life to preserving Africa's endangered mountain gorilla.

Fossey **13** <u>was born in San Francisco and</u> made her first trip to Africa in 1963. At the time, she was 31 years old. In the course of her trip, she met Dr. Louis Leakey, a **14** prominent archaeologist and anthropologist. Dr. Leakey believed in the importance of research on large apes and encouraged Fossey to undertake such a study. **15** <u>After accepting the research challenge from Dr. Leakey, mountain gorillas became a research topic.</u>

12

A. NO CHANGE

B. Dian Fossey?

C. Dian Fossey,

D. Dian Fossey!

13 The writer is considering deleting the underlined portion of the sentence. Should the writer make this deletion?

A. Yes, because this information should be provided earlier in the passage.

B. Yes, because this information doesn't support the main idea of the paragraph.

C. No, because this information supports the main idea of the paragraph.

D. No, because this information is important to the organization of the passage.

14

A. NO CHANGE

B. imminent

C. infamous

D. egregious

15

A. NO CHANGE

B. After accepting the research challenge from Dr. Leakey, Fossey chose mountain gorillas as the topic of her research.

C. Mountain gorillas, after accepting the research challenge from Dr. Leakey, became the topic of Fossey's research.

D. Fossey chose mountain gorillas after accepting the research challenge from Dr. Leakey, as her research topic.

CONTINUE

Fossey began her work in the African country of Zaire, but was forced to leave because of political unrest. She moved to another African country, Rwanda, where she established a research camp in a national park. **16** They're, she spent thousands of hours observing the behavior of gorillas. Her steadfast patience won the trust of the animals, and they began to **17** except her presence among them. As a result, she was able to observe behaviors that had never been seen by humans before.

Spending so much time observing the gorillas, Fossey naturally distinguished among them and had particular favorites. One of these favorites was a young male gorilla named Digit. Digit was later killed by a poacher, an illegal hunter of protected animals. **18** Fossey was really, really sad. She began a public campaign to raise awareness about the problem of gorilla poaching, a practice that threatened their continued existence. In 1989, **19** it will be predicted that there were only 620 mountain gorillas left. Fossey's campaign earned worldwide attention and support, and she continued to live and work in Africa for many years thereafter.

16

A. NO CHANGE

B. Their

C. There

D. Where

17

A. NO CHANGE

B. undertake

C. assume

D. accept

18

A. NO CHANGE

B. Fossey was crushed.

C. Fossey was super-duper sad.

D. Fossey was stunned and saddened.

19

A. NO CHANGE

B. it was predicted

C. it is predicted

D. he is predicting

20 In 1980, Fossey took a teaching position at Cornell University and wrote a book, *Gorillas in the Mist*, that brought further attention to the **21** deteriorating numbers of mountain gorillas. Afterward, Fossey returned to Rwanda, and spent the rest of her life working to protect the mountain gorilla. Even after her mysterious death, Fossey's work continued make an impact.

Today, **22** the population of mountain gorillas in Rwanda is rising thanks to the legacy of Dian Fossey.

20 At this point, the writer is considering adding the following sentence:

She had always been interested in dancing and learning new and interesting dance moves.

Should the writer make this addition here?

A. Yes, because this information provides information necessary to understand the paragraph.

B. Yes, because this information makes a good transition from the previous paragraph.

C. No, because this information is not necessary and doesn't support the main idea of the paragraph.

D. No, because this information should be placed at the end of the passage.

21

A. NO CHANGE

B. declining

C. demeaning

D. degrading

22 The writer is considering deleting the underlined sentence. Should the writer do this?

A. No, because it serves as a fitting conclusion to the passage

B. No, because it fully explains why the mountain gorilla population is rising.

C. Yes, because it contradicts the information presented in the passage.

D. Yes, because this information is not necessary.

CONTINUE

Questions 23–33 are based on the following passage and supplementary material.

Tamarin Families

Deep in the rainforests of Brazil, tiny creatures known as "kings of the jungle" inhabit the trees. These creatures, similar in size to squirrels, have bright, reddish-orange coats and hairless faces; their fur **23** obscures their faces like the mane of a lion. Accordingly, these highly endangered monkeys are called golden lion tamarins.

Tamarins live in small family units of up to nine individuals. **24** Offspring are generally born in pairs, and all members of the group will pitch in to help care for them. Tamarins that participate in caring for their newborn siblings tend to become **25** better parents.

23

A. NO CHANGE

B. surrounds

C. covers

D. marks

24 The writer is considering deleting the underlined sentence. Should the writer do this?

A. No, because this is useful and relevant contextual information.

B. No, because it explains why family units are relatively small.

C. Yes, because it should be placed earlier in the paragraph.

D. Yes, because this information interrupts the flow of the paragraph.

25

A. NO CHANGE

B. better parents than tamarins that do not.

C. better parents than other tamarins.

D. better parents than older tamarins.

[1] Tamarins are diurnal, meaning **26** they are active during the daytime. [2] At night, they seek shelter in tree hollows. [3] They are omnivorous, eating fruits, insects, and occasionally small lizards and snakes, which are **27** one in the same to them. [4] Tamarins spend their time in trees, using their fingers to grip the branches. **28** [5] However, they dislike direct sunlight, and so are well-suited to the dense foliage of the forest.

26

A. NO CHANGE

B. it is

C. he is

D. it will be

27

A. NO CHANGE

B. one with the same

C. one and the same

D. one the same

28 To make this paragraph the most logical, sentence 5 should be placed

A. where it is now.

B. before sentence 1.

C. before sentence 2.

D. before sentence 4.

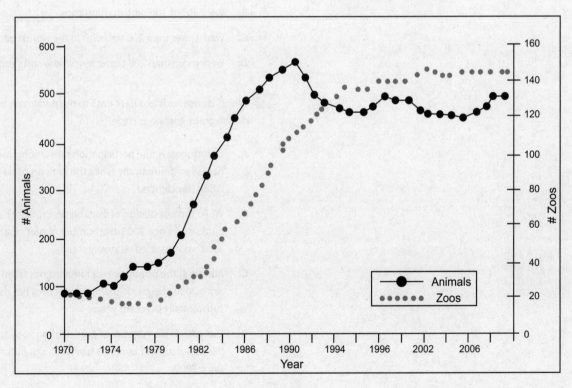

Used with permission. Ballou, J. D., J. Mickelberg, D. Field, and N. Lindsey. 2009. Population Management Recommendations for the International Ex-situ Population of Golden Lion Tamarins (Leontopithecus rosalia). National Zoological Park, Washington, D.C.

CONTINUE

Golden lion tamarins inhabit a distinct ecological **29** niche, they are found only in the eastern rainforests of Brazil. As farmers clear the rainforest to grow cash crops, the habitat of the tamarins has decreased drastically; as a result, the survival of the species is in extreme danger. Ecologists estimate that there are only one thousand tamarins remaining in the wild.

[1] In the 1970s, a conservation campaign was initiated to save the tamarins. **30** [2] It has grown to address the problem from several angles, including managing and restoring the disappearing habitat of the tamarins, breeding tamarins in captivity and in the wild, and reintroducing tamarins into their natural environment. [3] At this time, there **31** were about 140 participating zoos. [4] The movement began as a collaborative effort by the National Zoological Park in Washington, the Smithsonian Institute, and the Rio de Janeiro Primate Center. [5] As part of this effort, a number of zoos around the world have participated in helping to breed tamarins in captivity. **32**

29

A. NO CHANGE

B. niche they,

C. niche they

D. niche; they

30 To make this paragraph most logical, sentence 2 should be

A. kept where it is now.

B. placed before sentence 1.

C. placed after sentence 4.

D. removed.

31 At this point, the writer wants to add specific information that supports the main idea of the paragraph. Which choice most effectively completes the sentence with relevant and accurate information based on the graph (previous page)?

A. NO CHANGE

B. were about 300 participating zoos.

C. were fewer than 200 tamarins in the world's zoos.

D. were more than 200 tamarins in the world's zoos.

32 Which choice adds accurate data to the paragraph based on the graph (previous page)?

A. Unfortunately, the participation rate among zoos has fallen dramatically while the tamarin population has climbed.

B. While the population of tamarins in captivity has fluctuated since 2000, the number of participating zoos has remained relatively steady.

C. Although the population of tamarins has fallen since 2000, the participation rate of zoos has risen substantially in recent years.

D. Sadly, both the number of participating zoos and the population of tamarins has fallen significantly since 2000.

So far, efforts to return these animals back into their natural habitat have been **33** <u>fruitful</u>, making the golden lion tamarin one of very few species to be successfully reintroduced into the wild.

33

A. NO CHANGE

B. problematic

C. lucrative

D. delayed

Questions 34–44 are based on the following passage.

Classical architecture, the origins of which can be traced to ancient Rome, is characterized by a strict and **34** terminable adherence to the principles of coherence, exactness, and detail.

35 The basis of the classical style was the manner in which a building's space was divided so as to create a coherent whole. An example of a plan for the division of a building's space was **36** the tripartite plan. This plan would divide the space in a particular building into three equal parts. Such a plan would be followed no matter what the purpose of the building—churches, homes, or public government buildings could all be designed with such a plan. Even gardens, designed in the classical style, might have a three-part plan.

34

A. NO CHANGE

B. inclement

C. rigorous

D. contentious

35 At this point, the writer is considering adding the following sentence:

Over time, the classical tripartite plan spilled over from architecture to other arts—music, poetry, and dance—and it is not uncommon to have a three-part hierarchy within those artistic areas as well.

Should the writer make this addition here?

A. Yes, because it adds interesting detail to the paragraph.

B. Yes, because it provides an accurate introduction to the paragraph.

C. No, because this information should be added at the end of the paragraph.

D. No, because this information does not support the main idea of the paragraph.

36 Which choice most effectively combines the sentences at the underlined portion?

A. the tripartite plan, and this plan would

B. the tripartite plan would

C. the tripartite plan, it would

D. the tripartite plan, which would

Once the framework of a building designed in the classical style was established, architectural elements were added. While **37** columns are fairly typical architectural element, there are five types in particular that are the most **38** common: the *Doric, Ionic, Corinthian, Tuscan,* and *Composite*. Each column was distinctive and of a certain specified proportion, base to top. Just as the building follows a tripartite plan, so the columns themselves have a three-part organization. Above the column is a horizontal piece, called the *entablature*; then comes the column itself, which is tall and cylindrical; and finally comes the platform, or *crepidoma*, upon which the column rests.

Each of these elements also maintains a three-part organization. The *entablature* is divided into three parts— **39** cornice, the frieze, and the architrave. The column includes the capital, the shaft, and the base. **40**

37

A. NO CHANGE

B. columns are fairly typical architectural elements

C. column is a fairly typical architectural elements

D. columns is fairly typical architectural elements

38

A. NO CHANGE

B. common: the *Doric* and *Ionic*, *Corinthian*, and *Tuscan*, and *Composite*.

C. common; the *Doric Ionic*; and *Corinthian*; *Tuscan* and *Composite*.

D. common: the *Doric* and *Ionic*; *Corinthian*, *Tuscan*, and *Composite*.

39

A. NO CHANGE

B. cornice, frieze, and the architrave.

C. the cornice, the frieze, and the architrave.

D. the cornice, the frieze, and architrave.

40 Which of the following sentences, if added here, support the author's ideas in the first sentence of the paragraph?

A. The crepidoma was a single solid mass of steps that supported the rest of the column.

B. The crepidoma sometimes included a sloping ramp, particularly in large temples.

C. The crepidoma maintains the three-part division with its three steps.

D. The crepidoma, though, was not often used in Doric columns.

CONTINUE

Classical architecture is filled with conventions that while not obvious to most viewers, become apparent upon closer analysis. For example, **41** classical buildings must stand free; it cannot touch the sides of other buildings because, in the view of the classicist, each building is a world within a world of **42** his own. Consequently, organizing groups of buildings became problematic for rule-following, classical architects because of **43** differentiated violations of spatial conventions. The classical mode required adherence to formal rules that were sometimes impossible to impose on groups of buildings. **44**

41

A. NO CHANGE

B. a classical building must stand free; we cannot touch

C. classical buildings must stand free; you cannot touch

D. classical buildings must stand free; they cannot touch

42

A. NO CHANGE

B. their

C. its

D. the buildings

43

A. NO CHANGE

B. perceived

C. comprehended

D. extricated

44 Which choice most effectively establishes the main topic of the final paragraph?

A. The rules of classical architecture include dividing a building and its features into tripartite groups of three.

B. Classical architects were all quite interested in building on a mass scale during the time in which they lived.

C. A classical building must stand free and be a world unto itself, which is why no classical buildings connect to each other.

D. The numerous and strict conventions of classical architecture, such as the idea that a building must stand on its own, were not always easy for classical builders to abide by.

STOP

If you finish before time is called, you may check your work on this section only.
Do not turn to any other section.

SECTION 3: MATH TEST—NO CALCULATOR

25 MINUTES—20 QUESTIONS

TURN TO SECTION 3 OF YOUR ANSWER SHEET TO ANSWER THE QUESTIONS IN THIS SECTION.

DIRECTIONS: For **Questions 1–15,** solve each problem, select the best answer from the choices provided, and fill in the corresponding circle on your answer sheet. For **Questions 16–20,** solve the problem and enter your answer in the grid on the answer sheet. The directions **before Question 16** will provide information on how to enter your answers in the grid.

ADDITIONAL INFORMATION:

1. The use of a calculator in this section is **not permitted**.
2. All variables and expressions used represent real numbers unless otherwise indicated.
3. Figures provided in this test are drawn to scale unless otherwise indicated.
4. All figures lie in a plane unless otherwise indicated.
5. Unless otherwise specified, the domain of a given function *f* is the set of all real numbers *x* for which *f(x)* is a real number.

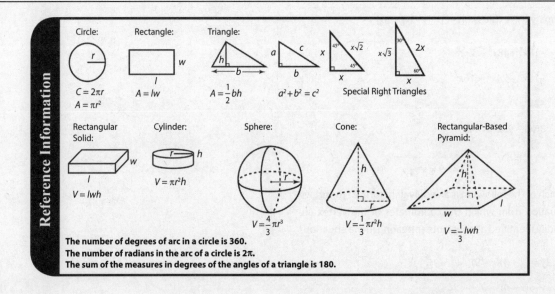

The number of degrees of arc in a circle is 360.
The number of radians in the arc of a circle is 2π.
The sum of the measures in degrees of the angles of a triangle is 180.

Practice Test 2 — MATH — NO CALCULATOR

1 Simplify the expression $(4x^2 - 5x + 8) - (3x^2 - 5 - 2x)$.

  A. $x^2 - 3x + 13$

  B. $x^2 - 3x + 3$

  C. $x^2 - 7x + 13$

  D. $x^2 - 7x + 3$

2 Which expression is equivalent to $x^{\frac{2}{3}} \cdot x^{-\frac{4}{3}}$?

  A. $-\sqrt[3]{x^8}$

  B. $-\sqrt[3]{x^2}$

  C. $\sqrt[3]{x^2}$

  D. $\dfrac{1}{\sqrt[3]{x^2}}$

3 Simplify the expression $-2[x(1 - 3x) + 3x]^2$.

  A. $-18x^4 + 48x^3 - 32x^2$

  B. $-18x^4 - 24x^3 + 16x^2$

  C. $-2x^2$

  D. $36x^4 - 96x^3 + 64x^2$

4
$$8x - 9 = x^2 - y$$

Which of the following is an equivalent form of the above equation from which the coordinates of the vertex are readily identified as constants appearing in the equation?

  A. $y = (x + 1)(x - 9)$

  B. $y = (x - 4)^2 - 7$

  C. $y = x^2 - 8x + 9$

  D. $x = \sqrt{y + 7} + 4$

5 If $a + 4b = 16$, what is the value of $-5[-3a + 2(4b + a) - 12b]$?

  A. 80

  B. 16

  C. -16

  D. -80

6

$$S = 2\pi r^2 + 2\pi rh$$

The formula above relates the surface area S of a cylinder to an expression involving the radius r and the height h. Which of the following gives h in terms of S and r?

A. $h = \dfrac{S}{2\pi r} - r$

B. $h = \dfrac{S}{2\pi r} + r$

C. $h = \dfrac{2\pi r^2 - S}{2\pi r}$

D. $h = \dfrac{S + 2\pi r^2}{2\pi r}$

7 A group of economists performed a study on the decreasing population in a small town for a time period of 10 years. They determined that as a result of factors such as loss of jobs and a poor economy, the population of the town decreased by about 3.5% each year. Which of the following equations accurately describes the population of the town, P, in terms of its initial population, P_0, and n, the number of years of the study?

A. $P = P_0(0.965)^n$

B. $P = P_0(0.965)n$

C. $P = P_0(1.035)^n$

D. $P = P_0(1.035)n$

8 If f is a linear function and $f(4) = 2$ and $f(6) = 10$, which of the following could be the function f?

A. $f(x) = x - 2$

B. $f(x) = 2x - 2$

C. $f(x) = 2x - 6$

D. $f(x) = 4x - 14$

SHOW YOUR WORK HERE

CONTINUE

9

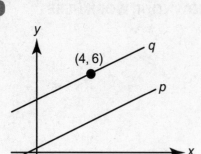

Note: Figure not drawn to scale.

In the figure above, lines p and q are parallel. If $y = x + 1$ represents the equation of line p, what is the y-intercept of line q?

A. 2

B. 3

C. 4

D. 5

10 A certain brand of yogurt is sold in either large or small cups. If 3 small cups and 2 large cups hold 30 ounces of yogurt, and 4 small cups and 1 large cup hold 25 ounces of yogurt, how much yogurt, in ounces, does a large cup of yogurt hold?

A. 2 ounces

B. 4 ounces

C. 7 ounces

D. 9 ounces

11

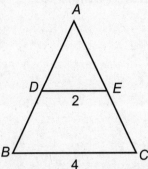

Note: Figure not drawn to scale.

In the figure above, $\overline{DE}$ is parallel to $\overline{BC}$ and $AD = 3$. What is the length of segment BD?

A. 2

B. 3

C. 4

D. 6

12 The sales for gasoline at a local station during a given year are described by the function $p(x) = -3(x-5)^2 + 173$, where $x = 1, 2, \ldots 12$; $x = 1$ corresponds to the month of January; and $p(x)$ is measured in hundred thousands of dollars. What does the number 173 in the formula represent?

A. The number of thousands of gallons sold, on average.

B. The total profit (in hundred thousands of dollars) for the year.

C. The maximum monthly sales (in hundred thousands of dollars) for the months of the year being described.

D. The month during which the sales were the highest.

13 If $(x + 2)^2 - (x - 3)^2 = 0$, which of the following are possible values of x?

A. $\frac{1}{2}$ only

B. -2 and 3

C. -3 and 2

D. no solution

CONTINUE

14 What is the equation of the circle for which the points $(-2, 3)$ and $(4, 9)$ are the endpoints of one of its diameters?

SHOW YOUR WORK HERE

A. $(x-1)^2 + (y-6)^2 = 2\sqrt{3}$

B. $(x+1)^2 + (y+6)^2 = 18$

C. $(x-1)^2 + (y-6)^2 = 18$

D. $(x+1)^2 - (y+6)^2 = 2\sqrt{3}$

15 A line in the xy-plane with the slope $-\dfrac{4}{5}$ passes through the point $(3, 4)$. Which of the following points lies on the line?

A. $(-5, 12)$

B. $(-2, 0)$

C. $(7, -1)$

D. $(13, -4)$

DIRECTIONS: For **Questions 16–20,** solve the problem and enter your answer in the grid, as described below, on the answer sheet.

1. Although not required, it is suggested that you write your answer in the boxes at the top of the columns to help you fill in the circles accurately. You will receive credit only if the circles are filled in correctly.

2. Mark no more than one circle in any column.

3. No question has a negative answer.

4. Some problems may have more than one correct answer. In such cases, enter only one answer.

5. **Mixed numbers** such as $3\frac{1}{2}$ must be entered as 3.5 or $\frac{7}{2}$.

   If $3\frac{1}{2}$ is entered into the grid as $\overline{3\,|\,1\,/\,2}$, it will be interpreted as $\frac{31}{2}$, not $3\frac{1}{2}$.

6. **Decimal answers:** If you obtain a decimal answer with more digits than the grid can accommodate, it may be either rounded or truncated, but it must fill the entire grid.

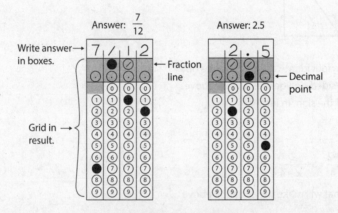

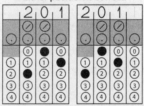

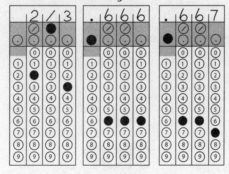

CONTINUE

16 Miguel is making a new garden. He is buying a new wheelbarrow and bags of peat moss. Each bag weighs 30 pounds and the wheelbarrow weighs 50 pounds. If his truck can carry a maximum of 1,500 pounds in the bed, what is the greatest number of whole bags of peat moss he can carry in the bed of his truck, along with the wheelbarrow?

SHOW YOUR WORK HERE

17

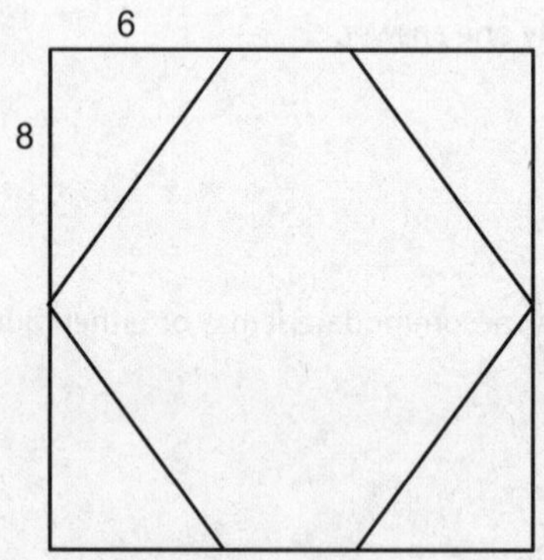

A sign is made by cutting four identical right triangles out of a square, leaving a 6-sided polygon, as shown above. What is the perimeter of the sign, in inches?

18

$$\frac{5x+2}{x-4} = 5 + \frac{b}{x-4}$$

What is the value for b that will make the equation above true?

19

$$y = 3x - 4$$
$$y = 2x - 5$$

According to the system of equations above, what is the value of xy?

20

$$6x - 5y = 9$$
$$-18x + by = -27$$

What value of b will make the system of equations above have infinitely many solutions?

STOP

If you finish before time is called, you may check your work on this section only.
Do not turn to any other section.

SECTION 4: MATH TEST—CALCULATOR

55 Minutes—38 Questions

TURN TO SECTION 4 OF YOUR ANSWER SHEET TO ANSWER THE QUESTIONS IN THIS SECTION.

> **DIRECTIONS:** For **Questions 1–30**, solve each problem, select the best answer from the choices provided, and fill in the corresponding circle on your answer sheet. For **Questions 31–38,** solve the problem and enter your answer in the grid on the answer sheet. The directions **before Question 31** will provide information on how to enter your answers in the grid.

ADDITIONAL INFORMATION:

1. The use of a calculator in this section is **permitted**.
2. All variables and expressions used represent real numbers unless otherwise indicated.
3. Figures provided in this test are drawn to scale unless otherwise indicated.
4. All figures lie in a plane unless otherwise indicated.
5. Unless otherwise specified, the domain of a given function f is the set of all real numbers x for which $f(x)$ is a real number.

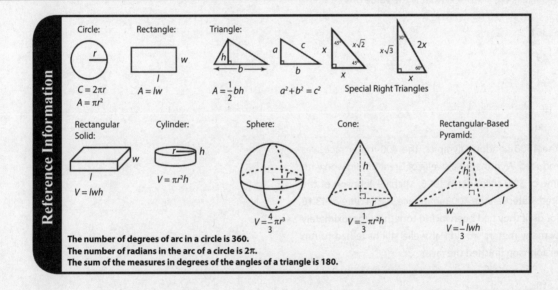

The number of degrees of arc in a circle is 360.
The number of radians in the arc of a circle is 2π.
The sum of the measures in degrees of the angles of a triangle is 180.

CONTINUE

1

Price	Number of houses sold
Under $60,000	10
$60,000–$299,999	5
$300,000–$499,999	3
$500,000–$999,999	5
Over $1 million	2

The table above shows the prices of houses sold in one month in Homeville. What could the median price of these houses be?

A. $58,000

B. $281,000

C. $320,000

D. $480,000

2 If $2[-3 - (2 - 4x)] = -3^2 + x$, what is the value of x^{-2}?

A. 361

B. 49

C. 14

D. 9

3 In the 1908 London Olympics, the 400-meter race was introduced. Wyndham Halswelle of Great Britain won with a time of 50.0 seconds. In 1996, Michael Johnson of the United States ran the 400-meter race with a time of 43.18 seconds. If they had been racing together, approximately how many meters would Halswelle still have had to run after Johnson finished the race?

A. 10

B. 25

C. 55

D. 100

4 If 18 − 6x is 4 less than −8, what is the value of −3x?

A. −15

B. −5

C. 5

D. 15

SHOW YOUR WORK HERE

5

1,000 milligrams = 1 gram

1,000 grams = 1 kilogram

Ibuprofen is an over-the-counter drug used to treat arthritis and relieve pain, fever, and swelling. The dose contained in a standard tablet is 200 mg. If ibuprofen is sold in cartons of 24 bottles, with 250 standard tablets per bottle, how much pain medication is in the carton in all?

A. 0.12 kilograms

B. 1.2 kilograms

C. 12 kilograms

D. 120 kilograms

6 A local newspaper reported a poll of 100 adults that found 80% of respondents were in favor of building a new school. The poll was taken by asking random parents picking up their students after school. Which of the following statements about the sampling method for this poll is NOT true?

A. The sampling method was not representative of the town as a whole because some students take the bus home.

B. The sampling method was not representative of the town as a whole because not everyone has children who go to school.

C. The sampling method was not representative of the town as a whole because the population of the town is much greater than 100.

D. The sampling method was not representative of the town as a whole because people who do not have students in school are less likely to support a new school.

CONTINUE

The graph below shows the population of a small town, from the years 2007 through 2015.

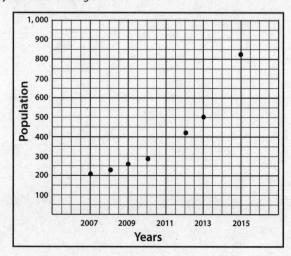

SHOW YOUR WORK HERE

---

7 Assuming that the population growth trend continues, what is the best prediction for the difference in the town's population from 2011 to 2014?

A. 663

B. 515

C. 358

D. 305

---

8 Assuming the data is described by the function $P(x) = Ae^{bx}$, which of the following values of b is the best choice if the points (2009, 250) and (2013, 500) lie on its graph?

A. $\ln 16$

B. $\ln 2$

C. $\frac{1}{4}\ln 2$

D. $\sqrt[4]{\ln 2}$

9 The median salary at a large biotech company is $45,000. The mean salary is $60,000. Which of the following statements best explains the difference between the mean and the median?

A. There are a few people at the biotech company with very low salaries.

B. There are a few people at the biotech company with very high salaries.

C. Most of the salaries at the biotech company are between $45,000 and $60,000.

D. All of the salaries at the biotech company are within a small range.

10 Mount Asgard in Auyuittuq (pronounced: *ow-you-eet-took*) National Park, Baffin Island, Nunavut, was used in the opening scene for the James Bond movie *The Spy Who Loved Me*. A stuntman skis off the edge of the mountain, free-falls for several seconds, and then opens a parachute. The height, h, in meters, of the stuntman above the ground t seconds after he opens the parachute is represented by the equation $h(t) = -10.5t + 980$. What does the 980 in the equation represent?

A. The speed of the stuntman

B. The height of the mountain

C. The height of the stuntman when he opens the parachute

D. The total length of time the stuntman is in the air

11 According to Einstein's theory of relativity, an object cannot travel faster than the speed of light, which is approximately 180,000 miles per second. If x represents the speed of an object measured in miles per hour, which inequality represents the range of possible speeds for the object?

A. $x \leq 648,000,000$

B. $x \geq 648,000,000$

C. $x \leq 180,000$

D. $x \geq 180,000$

SHOW YOUR WORK HERE

CONTINUE

12 Consider the following diagram:

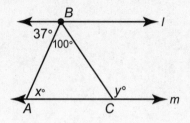

Assuming that lines *l* and *m* are parallel, determine the value of *x*.

A. 37

B. 43

C. 137

D. 143

13 The price of a 1 GB memory card is *x* dollars. A coupon for 15% is applied to the cost of a purchase of *T* memory cards, and a 6% tax is then applied to the discounted amount. Finally, a special state employee discount of 10% is applied to the final amount. Which of the following expressions represents the savings compared to the cost without any discounts?

A. $0.910(x + T)$ dollars

B. $0.8109xT$ dollars

C. $0.2491xT$ dollars

D. $0.1581(x + T)$ dollars

14 What real values of *z*, if any, satisfy the equation
$$\frac{1}{1+z} = \frac{4}{z+z^2} + 1 ?$$

A. No solution

B. 0

C. −2 only

D. −2 and 2

SHOW YOUR WORK HERE

A food truck sells sandwiches for $5.95 each and beverages in cans or bottles. A beverage in a bottle costs the same as a beverage in a can. Which of the following statements is true about the equation that represents the food truck revenue, $5.95x + 1.75y = z$?

A. x is the number of customers served.

B. z is the number of customers served.

C. y is the number of beverages sold.

D. y is the number of sandwiches sold.

16

$$2x + y \geq a$$
$$x + 2y \geq b$$

In the xy-plane, if $(-1, -1)$ is a solution to the system of inequalities above, which of the following relationships must be true about a and b?

A. $a > b > 0$

B. $a < b < 0$

C. $b < a < 0$

D. $a < 0$ and $b < 0$

---

17 Alex is baking cupcakes and cookies. The cupcake pan holds 15 cupcakes, and the cookie pan holds 18 cookies. Alex wants to make at least twice as many pans of cookies as pans of cupcakes, but no more than 165 total cookies and cupcakes. Which of the following system of inequalities fits the situation?

A. $18x + 15y \leq 165$
$\quad\quad x \leq 2y$

B. $18x + 15y \leq 165$
$\quad\quad x \geq 2y$

C. $18x + 15y < 165$
$\quad\quad x < 2y$

D. $18x + 15y < 165$
$\quad\quad x > 2y$

18 Which of the following equals x, if $3\sqrt{x}+8=20$?

A. 4

B. 8

C. 12

D. 16

19 According to historians, Archimedes proved that a crown made for his king was not pure gold. Suppose the crown had a mass of 800 grams and a volume of 50cc. The density of gold is about 19 grams per cc, and the density of silver is about 10.5 grams per cc. The system below models this relationship (G = volume of gold, S = volume of silver).

$$G+S=50$$
$$19G+10.5S=800$$

If the crown contained both silver and gold, about what percent of the crown's volume is silver?

A. 19 percent

B. 36 percent

C. 62 percent

D. 81 percent

SHOW YOUR WORK HERE

SHOW YOUR WORK HERE

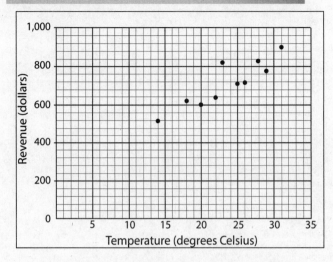

The graph above displays the total revenue R in dollars for an ice cream shop when the temperature is T degrees Celsius.

20 Which of the following best describes the association between R and T?

A. Strong positive correlation

B. Strong negative correlation

C. Weak positive correlation

D. Weak negative correlation

21 Which of the following is the line of best fit for the data in the graph?

A. $y = 500 + 1.2x$

B. $y = 1.33x$

C. $y = 20x + 250$

D. $y = 725$

22 For which of the following values of a does the equation $ax^2 - x + 2$ have two complex conjugate solutions?

A. -5

B. $-\dfrac{1}{2}$

C. $\dfrac{1}{8}$

D. $\dfrac{2}{3}$

CONTINUE

23 If $(x + 1)$ and $(x + 5)$ are the only linear factors of $f(x)$, which of the following graphs shows a possible graph of the function f?

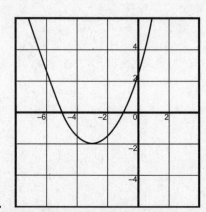

A.

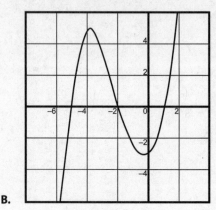

B.

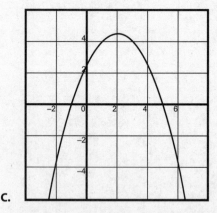

C.

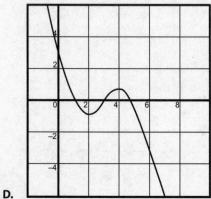

D.

24 The graph of a parabola has *x*-intercepts at 4 and –2 and a *y*-intercept at 8. Which of the following could be the equation of the graph?

A. $y = -(x - 1)^2 + 9$

B. $y = x^2 - 2x + 8$

C. $y = (x - 1)^2 - 9$

D. $y = x^2 + 2x - 8$

25 The table below displays the results of a study on the health status of people in four age groups. Using this data, a demographer calculates that the probability that a person in the age group she studies will be in excellent health is 0.512. What group is she studying?

Age	Health Status				
	Excellent	Very Good	Good	Fair/ Poor	TOTAL
> 12 years	10,715	6,996	2,542	231	20,484
12–17 years	12,146	7,744	3,738	536	24,164
18–44 years	32,307	27,208	18,909	5,293	83,717
45–64 years	7,932	10,548	9,683	5,336	33,499
TOTAL	63,100	52,496	34,872	11,396	

A. Adults aged 18–44

B. Adults aged 18–44 in excellent or very good health

C. Children under 12 years old

D. Children and teenagers aged 17 or under

SHOW YOUR WORK HERE

CONTINUE

26 If *k* is a negative constant less than −1, which of the following could be the graph of $y = kx^2 + bx + c$?

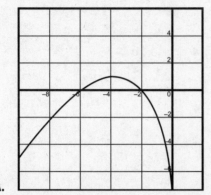

A.

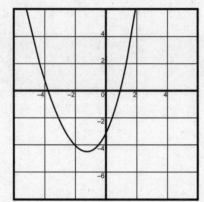

B.

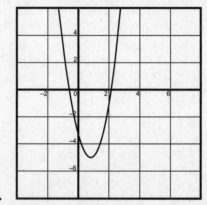

C.

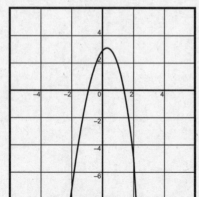

D.

An educational researcher chose 200 randomly selected students at a local college and asked them how they would best categorize their political inclinations. The results are shown in the table below.

	Liberal	Moderate	Conservative
Seniors	6	18	34
Juniors	20	42	30
Sophomores	8	6	4
Freshmen	22	8	2

27 What is the probability that a junior of this group is a conservative?

A. $\dfrac{17}{29}$

B. $\dfrac{9}{15}$

C. $\dfrac{2}{9}$

D. $\dfrac{15}{46}$

28 Given a total of 4,000 students at the college, about how many of those students would categorize themselves as moderates?

A. About 74

B. About 1,120

C. About 1,400

D. About 1,480

SHOW YOUR WORK HERE

29 A recent poll found that 11% of the respondents approve of the job that the US Congress is doing. The margin of error for the poll was ± 3% with 95% confidence interval. Which of the following statements is a conclusion that can accurately be drawn from this poll?

A. 95% of the time that such a poll is conducted, the true approval rate is between 8% and 14%.

B. The true percentage of people who approve of the job that the US Congress is doing is between 8% and 14%.

C. The pollsters are 95% confident that the true percentage of people who approve of the job that the US Congress is doing is between 86% and 92%.

D. The pollsters are 95% confident that the true percentage of people who approve of the job that the US Congress is doing is between 8% and 14%.

30 Line m intersects the x-axis at $(3, 0)$ and the y-axis at $(0, -2)$. Line n passes through the origin and is perpendicular to line m. Which of the following is an equation of line n?

A. $y = \dfrac{3}{2}x$

B. $y = \dfrac{2}{3}x$

C. $y = -\dfrac{3}{2}x$

D. $y = -\dfrac{2}{3}x$

SHOW YOUR WORK HERE

1. Although not required, it is suggested that you write your answer in the boxes at the top of the columns to help you fill in the circles accurately. You will receive credit only if the circles are filled in correctly.

2. Mark no more than one circle in any column.

3. No question has a negative answer.

4. Some problems may have more than one correct answer. In such cases, enter only one answer.

5. **Mixed numbers** such as $3\frac{1}{2}$ must be entered as 3.5 or $\frac{7}{2}$.

   If $3\frac{1}{2}$ is entered into the grid as $\overline{3\,|\,1\,/\,2}$, it will be interpreted as $\frac{31}{2}$, not $3\frac{1}{2}$.

6. **Decimal answers:** If you obtain a decimal answer with more digits than the grid can accommodate, it may be either rounded or truncated, but it must fill the entire grid.

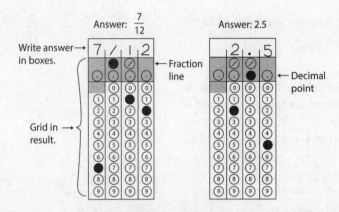

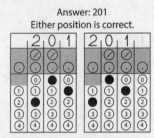

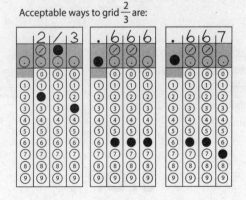

31 A baboon troop has 60 members, 35% of which are male. What is the ratio of males to females in the baboon troop? (Grid your answer as a fraction.)

SHOW YOUR WORK HERE

32 During a recent baseball season, 2 hitters on a team had a total of 66 home runs. Batter *B* had 14 fewer home runs than batter *A*. How many home runs did batter *A* hit?

33 If the average (arithmetic mean) of the set of numbers shown below is 15, then what is the value of the number N?

$$\{14, 19, 12, 16, N, 17\}$$

34
$$3(5 - 2x) = -4(cx + 4)$$

What value for *c* in the equation above will make the equation have no solutions?

35 The base of a circular cylinder has a radius that is equal to twice its height. The diameter of a sphere is the same as the height of the cylinder. How many times larger is the volume of the cylinder as compared to the volume of the sphere?

36
$$f(x) = 3x^2 - 4x + 8$$
$$g(x) = 2x - 5$$

Use the functions above to find the value of $g(f(-2))$.

37
$$y = 2x - 3$$
$$y = -3(x - 1)^2 + 4$$

According to the system of equations above, what is one value of *x*?

38 The total rainfall in Plainville increased by 25% from 2012 to 2013. The rainfall decreased by 30% from 2013 to 2014. Then, it increased again by 40% from 2014 to 2015. What was the percent of increase in rainfall from 2012 to 2015? Express your final answer as a decimal.

STOP

**If you finish before time is called, you may check your work on this section only.
Do not turn to any other section.**

SECTION 5: ESSAY

50 MINUTES—1 ESSAY

DIRECTIONS: The essay gives you an opportunity to show how effectively you can read and comprehend a passage and write an essay analyzing the passage. In your essay, you should demonstrate that you have read the passage carefully, present a clear and logical analysis, and use language precisely.

Your essay will need to be written on the lines provided in your answer booklet. You will have enough space if you write on every line and keep your handwriting to an average size. Try to print or write clearly so that your writing will be legible to the readers scoring your essay.

As you read the passage below, consider how Jessica Smartt Gullion uses the following:
- Evidence, such as facts, statistics, or examples, to support claims.
- Reasoning to develop ideas and to connect claims and evidence.
- Stylistic or persuasive elements, such as word choice or appeals to emotion, to add power to the ideas expressed.

Will guns on campus lead to grade inflation?

Adapted from "Will Guns on Campus Lead to Grade Inflation?" by Jessica Smartt Gullion, originally published in The Conversation *on April 27, 2015. Jessica Smartt Gullion is an assistant professor of sociology at Texas Woman's University.*

1   Texas college professors may soon face a dilemma between upholding professional ethics and protecting their lives.

2   The Texas legislature appears poised to approve a bill that would allow college students to carry firearms to class. Called "campus carry," public universities in Texas will not be allowed to ban guns on their campuses, once the law is passed, although private schools could enact their own prohibitions.

3   Its backers argue that students have the right to protect themselves on campuses with handguns. The lobbying extends to sponsoring crash courses such as the NRA University, a two-hour seminar course for college students.

4   With this proposed law, a question coming up for many academics is whether they would be forced to give As to undeserving students, just so they can avoid being shot.

5   This is not as farfetched as it sounds. In my five years as a college professor, I have had experience with a number of emotionally distressed students who resort to intimidation when they receive a lesser grade than what they feel they deserve.

Threats on campus

6   Here is an example of one such threatening experience: One evening in a graduate course, after I handed back students' papers, a young woman stood up and pointed at me. "This is unacceptable!" she screamed as her body shook in rage.

7   She moved toward the front of the class waving her paper in my face and screamed again, "unacceptable!" After a heated exchange, she left the room and stood outside the door sobbing.

8   All this was over receiving a B on a completely low-stakes assignment.

CONTINUE

9   What followed was even more startling. The following week, the student brought along a muscle-bound man to class. He watched me through the doorway window for the entire three hours of the class, with his arms folded across his chest.

10 And if this wasn't enough, the young woman's classmates avoided me on campus because, they said, they were afraid of getting caught in the crossfire should she decide to shoot me.

11 After that, every time she turned in a paper I cringed and prayed that it was good so that I wouldn't have to give her anything less than an A.

12 Learning from this experience, now I give papers back only at the end of the class or just "forget" to bring them with me.

13 I was lucky that the student didn't have a gun in my classroom. Other professors have not been so lucky.

14 Last year, a student at Purdue shot his instructor in front of a classroom of students. In another incident in 2009, a student at Northern Virginia Community College tried to shoot his math professor on campus. And, in 2000, a graduate student at the University of Arkansas shot his English professor.

15 In each of these states, carrying handguns on campus was illegal at the time of the shooting, although a bill was introduced in Arkansas earlier this year to allow students to carry guns.

Grade inflation

16 Despite these and other shootings, a new trend has emerged across the United States that supports guns on college campuses.

17 Eight states allow firearms onto college campuses, and 11 states are now considering similar legislation.

18 We know that some students will carry guns whether it is legal or not. One study found that close to 5 percent of undergraduates had a gun on campus and that almost two percent had been threatened with a firearm while at school.

...

19 Who would want to give a student a low grade and then get shot for it?

20 Many majors are highly competitive and require certain GPAs for admission. Students on scholarships and other forms of financial aid must maintain high grades to keep their funding. It's no surprise that some students might resort to any means necessary to keep up their GPAs.

21 An international student once cried in my office and begged me to change his F to an A, as without it, his country would no longer pay for him to be in the United States. I didn't. He harassed me by posting threatening messages on Facebook.

22 So, the question is, will we soon see a new sort of grade inflation, with students earning a 4.0 GPA with their firepower rather than brain power? And if so, what sort of future citizenry will we be building on our campuses?

Write an essay in which you explain how Jessica Smartt Gullion builds an argument to persuade her audience that firearms should not be allowed on college campuses. In your essay, analyze how she uses one or more of the features listed previously (or features of your own choice) to strengthen the logic and persuasiveness of her argument. Be sure that your analysis focuses on the most relevant aspects of the passage.

Your essay should not explain whether you agree with Jessica Smartt Gullion's claims, but rather explain how she builds an argument to persuade her audience.

STOP

If you finish before time is called, you may check your work on this section only.
Do not turn to any other section.

1. C	12. B	23. C	34. C	45. A
2. A	13. A	24. D	35. C	46. D
3. B	14. B	25. B	36. A	47. B
4. D	15. D	26. B	37. D	48. B
5. A	16. B	27. C	38. D	49. D
6. D	17. B	28. A	39. D	50. C
7. A	18. D	29. C	40. C	51. A
8. C	19. C	30. D	41. C	52. C
9. B	20. A	31. A	42. C	
10. B	21. A	32. C	43. B	
11. B	22. D	33. C	44. A	

READING TEST RAW SCORE
(Number of correct answers) [ ]

1. **The correct answer is C.** The causes of death the author lists are thought to be very common causes, but by stating that SeDS is a more common cause than all of those other causes combined shows that SeDS is more severe than they are. Some of the causes of death may be shocking to some readers, but the author has a much more important reason for listing them than their shock value, so choice A is not the best answer. The author only shows that SeDS is more common than the causes of death he lists in lines 6–7, but in lines 10–11, he states that there is one cause of death more common than SeDS, so choice B is incorrect. The causes of death listed in lines 6–7 are all destructive or self-destructive, but choice D implies that the author's main concern is stopping readers from engaging in these forms of behavior when the overall purpose of the passage is to explain the dangers of SeDS.

2. **The correct answer is A.** In lines 1–2 and 14–27, the article presents the opinions of Frank Booth first, accompanied by factual details. These are followed by quotes from Scott Gordon (lines 56–65) and Ron Gomes (lines 68–73), along with other facts and charts illustrating statistics about diabetes. Choice B is incorrect because the information is not presented in a sensational manner; it is concerned with facts and opinions from experts. Those affected are not quoted,

so choice C is also incorrect. Choice D focuses only on statistics, and the article does not discuss how the statistics are interpreted, so it is incorrect as well.

3. **The correct answer is B.** The Grim Reaper is a traditional image of a cloaked skeleton that represents the inevitability of death, but the image of a flabby skeleton is so absurd that it is comical. Since the rest of the article is extremely serious, it is reasonable to conclude that the author included the humorous quote in line 1 to lighten the tone of an otherwise serious article, so choice B is the best answer. Choice A is incorrect because the silliness of the image of a flabby Grim Reaper actually undercuts the gravity of the problem of SeDS. Choice C is incorrect because the idea of a flabby Grim Reaper is intended to be silly and ironic, which is almost the opposite effect of being relatable. Choice D is incorrect because although images of the Grim Reaper can be frightening, the silliness of a flabby Grim Reaper undercuts that image's scariness.

4. **The correct answer is D.** The article says that the human body has evolved over time to do physical work like farming and household chores, but machines now do much of that work, which leads

Practice Test 2—ANSWERS

to obesity (lines 56–60). Choice A introduces an idea that information in the article never supports. Children do inherit different body types, but this article is not about the dangers of a particular body type acquired naturally; it is about how inactivity can cause people to become unnaturally obese, so choice B is not the best answer. The author argues that people are now more sedentary than in previous generations, but choice C implies that people need to eat more because modern life requires a great deal of physical activity. This conclusion contradicts a main point in the passage.

5. **The correct answer is A.** Frank Booth wanted to emphasize that a lack of exercise or activity leads to obesity and even death, so he chose *sedentary* as a synonym for *inactive* to add pizzazz to a condition that needs greater attention (lines 21–27). Choice B is actually the opposite meaning, referring to health and energy. Choice C echoes another health issue: Sudden Infant Death Syndrome, which refers to children who die mysteriously as infants. The process the article discusses is not sudden or restricted to children. Choice D describes the result of inactivity, but does not define it.

6. **The correct answer is D.** The author refers to the heavy cost of treating SeDS in the article (lines 12–13), which supports choice D. Although Dr. Frank W. Booth comes off as an authority on SeDS in this article, there is no indication that the syndrome is responsible for making him respected or well known. The author's discussion of how many people between the ages of 10 and 19 suffer from Type 2 diabetes caused by SeDS in lines 39–40 contradicts the conclusion in choice C.

7. **The correct answer is A.** Choice A discusses the heavy healthcare costs ($3 trillion) of treating SeDS (lines 11–13). Choice B is incorrect because it merely introduces an authority on SeDS; it makes no comment on the financial burden the syndrome creates. While choice C refers to money by stating that Dr. Booth believes the government should spend more on preventing SeDS, he does not present this proposal in a negative light, so choice C is not as strong of an answer as choice A is. Choice D only discusses the negative physical impacts of SeDS; it does not refer to the financial ones.

8. **The correct answer is C.** In 1998, new cases of Type 2 diabetes began to drastically increase and grow continuously every year, until the number peaked in 2009. Choice A is the start of the chart, and although it shows an increasing trend overall, there are many decreases as well. Choice D is the highest number of new cases reported, but it is not the beginning of

continuing increases because the number of cases falls off the following year.

9. **The correct answer is B.** Booth states that he wanted to come up with "a catchy name" (line 25), something that would get people's attention. Based on this statement, it is logical to conclude that *pizzazz* means "oomph," or bold and attention getting. Choice A makes sense within the context of the sentence, but it changes the meaning of the sentence and doesn't convey the idea of a catchy name, which is what the sentence discusses. Choice C suggests that "inactivity-related disease" (line 23) is too frivolous, with the author saying that it is not "catchy" (line 25) enough to grab the public's attention, implying that "inactivity-related disease" is too dry and serious. This contradicts the conclusion in choice C. Choice D is incorrect because "inactivity-related disease" is a much clearer and more descriptive term than SeDS.

10. **The correct answer is B.** The author includes quotes stating that "Our bodies were designed to be physically active" (lines 56–57) and that "this may mean planning exercise into your daily routine" (lines 62–63), which supports the conclusion in choice B since physical inactivity causes SeDS. Choice A is incorrect because the author sees a catchy name as simply a way to make people aware of the problem. Choice C is incorrect because although the article connects the rise in Type 2 diabetes with obesity, it is only one health issue the article discusses. Choice D is also incorrect because of the narrowness of its focus. The article brings up the importance of children developing better habits than their parents, but is not the overarching theme of the passage.

11. **The correct answer is B.** Choice B (lines 30–34) establishes a clear link between the number of Americans who are not physically active and the doubling of the obesity rate. Choice A (lines 18–21) mentions the fact that one person wants more money to be allocated to helping Americans be more active, but doesn't link obesity to fitness. Choice C (lines 34–38) describes the complications of Type 2 diabetes but doesn't refer to obesity. Choice D (lines 68–73) explains the connection between children and ailments associated with obesity but doesn't indicate how essential it is for all human beings to be physically active.

12. **The correct answer is B.** Although the government professes that wrongs done to the Native Americans should be corrected, the author's use of the phrase "simple and unperplexing expedients" (lines 47–48)

suggests that the author believes the government's intentions are not sincere, so choice B is correct. The lines state that the government acknowledges that Native Americans have suffered "wrongs" (line 45) and that the government is responsible for committing such "perfidies" (line 46), or untrustworthy actions, which contradicts choice A. The author states that "President after president" (line 41) initiated these reports describing government injustices committed against Native Americans, which contradicts choice C. While the author may think the government has some under-standing of the plight of Native Americans, she shows that she does not believe that it is "well equipped to determine a viable solution" by implying that the government only voices insincere support for Native Americans while failing to make substantive changes to improve their situation.

13. **The correct answer is A.** By citing abuses against Native Americans in a variety of US states across a period of 85 years, the author shows how government abuses against Native Americans are widespread across geography and history. Choice B is not the best answer because, although specific states are mentioned, they are simply used as examples and there is no indication that these states have the worst records of abuse against Native Americans. Choice C implies that because the dates cited are not recent, the problems have stopped, yet the second half of the sentence explains that the government "breaks promises now as deftly as then." Choice D is incorrect because it implies that the lines are specifically focused on a particular region, which is not true since the states mentioned are not all southern states and the author suggests that abuses against Native Americans have been committed in different places.

14. **The correct answer is B.** Lines 24–25 state that "The story of one tribe is the story of all, varied only by differences of time and place," and since this story is that of the abuses Native Americans have suffered at the hands of the government, the lines show that the abuses have been committed across geography ("place") and history ("time"). So choice B is the best answer. Choice A (lines 22–23) is less effective because it only refers to history ("the record of the history of the Indians"), not geography. Choice C (lines 28–30) refers only to geography ("the United States"), not history. Choice D (line 30) is incorrect because it merely refers to how the abuses are being committed ("with added ingenuity"), not how they have been committed across history and geography.

15. **The correct answer is D.** In lines 16–18 ("There . . . laws"), the author talks about an area that was settled so quickly that there wasn't a chance to create laws to protect Native Americans amidst the chaos of the gold rush. Consequently, settlers could do whatever they wanted to the tribes, unregulated by any treaty. While the author mentions that the tales described in choice A existed, she does not use them to explain why abuses against Native Americans during the gold rush were allowed to go unchecked and unpunished. Choice B is incorrect because there were no treaties or laws to break during the chaotic and lawless period described in lines 16–18. Choice C is incorrect because although white settlers and the government were both responsible for abuses against Native Americans, the author does not suggest that there was any particular sympathy between those two particular parties.

16. **The correct answer is B.** In lines 24–25, the author states that "The story of one tribe is the story of all," which is his way of saying that the abuses Native Americans suffered were not limited to a particular tribe. The author expresses nothing but outrage in sympathy with Native Americans throughout the passage, contradicting choice A completely. Choice C is incorrect because the author regularly cites documen-tation of the abuses Native Americans suffered at the hands of the government ("The reports are filled with eloquent statements of wrongs done to the Indians . . . The history of the Government connections with the Indians is a shameful record of broken treaties and unfulfilled promises."). Choice D makes an unsubstan-tiated assumption based on the fact that 1795 is the earliest year mentioned in this particular article.

17. **The correct answer is B.** Throughout the article, the author passionately argues that Native Americans have been systematically abused by both the government and white settlers, citing examples of such abuses as "murder, outrage, [and] robbery." However, the author never explains how the government could atone for those abuses, so choice A is incorrect. The author is mainly concerned with detailing the government's abuse of Native Americans; she does not really get into the causes and effects of those abuses, so choice C is not the best answer. The author never presents opposing viewpoints of why the United States has had conflicts with Native Americans; she only argues her own position that the government has been abusive, so choice D is not the best answer either.

18. **The correct answer is D.** The author repeatedly refers to concealing or explaining away the offenses of white settlers against Native Americans, so *excused* is the best

Answer Keys and Explanations

synonym for *palliated* as it is used in line 70. Choice A has the opposite meaning of "*palliated.*" Choice B would imply that there might be some justification for white men's crimes against Native Americans; that those crimes are merely misunderstood. This contradicts the pro-Native American stance the author expresses throughout the entire passage. *Eased* can be used as a synonym for *palliated,* but it is not appropriate for this particular context since one it does not really make sense to ease a crime.

19. **The correct answer is C.** Choice C is the best summary because it accurately states that the army admits they were the aggressor. The few times Native Americans did something horrible (lines 67–68), the events were played up as worse than they were (lines 70–74), while the army's crimes were played down (lines 69–70). Choice A gets some of the facts wrong and makes assumptions that aren't in the original paragraph. Choice B does the same and interprets "testimony" as literally referring to a courtroom. Choice D is too simplistic and leaves out much of the pertinent information of the paragraph.

20. **The correct answer is A.** While the author is clear that she feels the government has denied Native Americans their human rights, she also suggests that the government has tried to convince them that they have the same rights as all other Americans. The author states that the government's abuse of Native Americans is ongoing ("the United States Government breaks promises now as deftly as then"), which contradicts choice B. While she argues that the government's treatment of Native Americans has been extremely unjust, she never accuses the government of having an agenda to actually drive Native Americans out of the country. The author acknowledges that Native Americans have committed crimes against white men, but states that these crimes are widely reported (lines 70–74: "Every offense committed by an Indian . . . around it."), which contradicts choice D.

21. **The correct answer is A.** Lines 60–61 show that the government has taught Native Americans that they have rights even if the government has not honored its own teachings. Choice B (lines 62–64) only comments on the government's failure to honor its teachings; it does not explain what has been taught, which is necessary to serve as evidence to support the previous question's answer. Choice C (lines 65–68) moves on to a new topic (white man's aggression toward Native Americans) that has nothing to do with the previous question. Lines 70–73 deal with Native American crimes against white people, and the only answer choice

related to that topic in the previous question incorrectly suggests that the government has tried to conceal these crimes, so choice D is incorrect under any circumstances.

22. **The correct answer is D.** The author uses the word *barbarous* to describe the retaliations of Native Americans against white people that are "unspeakable." It is logical to conclude that the attacks are unspeakable because they are so brutal and violent, so choice D is the best answer. An attack can be silent, but this would not make it unspeakable, so choice A does not make much sense. *Steadfast* generally has positive connotations, meaning admirably consistent or loyal, yet an attack would most likely be unspeakable because it is horrible. Therefore, the correct answer should have negative connotations, and that eliminates choice B. Similarly, an attack can be calculated, but it is more logical for an attack to be unspeakable because of its brutality than its level of calculation, so choice C is not the most sensible answer.

23. **The correct answer is C.** The main theme in the passage describes the people who lived at Arlington House—slaves and owners—and includes information about how the house was constructed and by whom as well as the history of the plantation's ownership. There is no language that suggests the author wished to persuade readers (choice B). Although the author makes it clear how disadvantaged slaves were, the passage does not focus on the evils of slavery (choice A). Although the passage includes some information about the lives of slaves (choice D) its overall focus is the history of the plantation.

24. **The correct answer is D.** The text explains that Mrs. Custis "tutored slaves in basic reading and writing so that they could read the Bible" (lines 58–59) because she was a very religious woman. There is no indication that she wanted them to be able to teach the skills to anyone else, so choices A and C can be eliminated. The passage never mentions any other reading material, so choice B is incorrect.

25. **The correct answer is B.** Although the most common use of the word *practice* is to repeat an activity regularly in order to gain proficiency, that is not how the word is used in this sentence, making choice A incorrect. Instead, the author uses this word to mean a regular activity that became customary. Mrs. Custis initiated the tutoring of the slaves (lines 58–59). Her daughter-in-law, Mrs. Lee, "continued this practice" (line 60). Although the activity happened to involve education, that is not the meaning of the word in this sentence, making choice C

incorrect. Also, tutoring was not the official profession of either of the women, making choice D incorrect.

26. **The correct answer is B.** The text tells us that Selina was given the keys to the plantation (lines 53–54), which implies great trust in the days of slavery. As head housekeeper, she may also have cared for the Lee children (choice C) but that information is not in the passage. Being head of housekeeping is not the same as running the whole plantation (choice D); while housekeeping of a large mansion is hard work, the text doesn't compare it to the fieldwork of other slaves, (choice A).

27. **The correct answer is C.** In lines 64–67, Maria Carter Syphax is named as one of the emancipated slaves who settled on the Arlington estate. Choice D is incorrect because the opposite of this statement is stated in lines 77–78. Regarding choices A and B, it is stated in the passage that Mrs. Custis and Mrs. Lee tutored slaves despite it being against the law (lines 60–61). It is stated that Mrs. Custis persuaded her husband to free several of their female and child slaves (lines 62–63). It is stated that Mrs. Lee had a close relationship with the head housekeeper (lines 49–54). However, Mrs. Custis's and Mrs. Lee's general view of slavery is not discussed in the passage, making choices A and B incorrect.

28. **The correct answer is A.** According to the passage, Robert E. Lee was related to George Washington through marriage (lines 17–18 and line 35). The fact that Lee married Washington's great granddaughter eliminates choice B. The passage never mentions whether any of Lee's seven children were even sons, so choice B is incorrect. There is no discussion of Lee's father at all, which means there is no evidence supporting choice D either.

29. **The correct answer is C.** Lines 35–36 state that Robert E. Lee married Custis's daughter after the author had already explained that Custis was George Washington's grandson. Lines 15–16 only introduce Custis and do not explain his relationship to George Washington at all, so choice A is not a strong answer. Lines 19–21 only show that Custis had some sort of relationship with Martha Washington, since he inherited slaves from her, but it does not explain the exact nature of that relationship, so choice B is not the best evidence for the previous answer. Similarly, lines 36–38 show that Lee and Custis had a relationship but fail to explain what that relationship is, so choice D is incorrect.

30. **The correct answer is D.** Choice D is stated in lines 8–9 as a reason for Arlington seeming like a "harmonious community." It is mentioned to set up the contrast between how it looked to "observers" and the reality of slaves being considered property, without any rights. If slaves were not considered property, they could not be "hired out" (line 79) by their owners, making choice A incorrect. Although it's true that the passage states that choice B is true (lines 64–65), the owners wouldn't have had the right to emancipate their slaves if they had not been considered to be the property of the owners, making choice B incorrect. The most straight-forward reasons directly supporting the idea that slaves were the property of their owners are listed in lines 12–14. One of these is choice C, rendering it incorrect.

31. **The correct answer is A.** The "invisible gulf" the author mentions is one of separation between slaves and owners in terms of privilege and human rights. While *gulf* can describe a body of water, as in choice B; a chasm, as in choice C; or a physical gap, as in choice D, here the author's use is metaphorical.

32. **The correct answer is C.** In this context, *afford* does not refer to money as in choice B, but to things provided to others. Since slaves were property, and treated as such, few owners thought about teaching them to read or write. There is no risk implied in this use of the word, choice A, or any suggestion of the tutoring being given in exchange for something else as in choice D.

33. **The correct answer is C.** Both passages agree that the amount of carbon dioxide in our atmosphere has increased (lines 18–20 and lines 56–59). However, choice A is disputed by the second passage, and choice B is disputed by the first passage. Choice D is refuted by the second passage as being too complicated to prove or predict.

34. **The correct answer is C.** Only choice C specifically mentions carbon dioxide levels, which the first passage implies the same by stating that "Carbon dioxide can stay in the atmosphere for nearly a century, so Earth will continue to warm in the coming decades" in lines 40–42. Choice A (lines 4–6) discusses some of the effects of carbon dioxide levels but does not confirm their increase. Choice B (lines 28–31) discusses the changes to the atmosphere without specifically mentioning increased carbon dioxide levels. Choice D (lines 81–82) directly counters any attempts to limit carbon dioxide but doesn't support the fact there are increases.

35. **The correct answer is C.** Both passages address the reader as *we* or *our*, indicating a shared interest among humans. Each passage is trying to persuade the reader to one viewpoint, thus making choice A incorrect.

Choice B is too strong a description since both passages try to convince with logic rather than pure emotionalism. Choice D is incorrect because there are no second-person or "you" statements in the passages.

36. **The correct answer is A.** The author of Passage 1 believes that human actions could reduce the impact of global warming on the environment and shows this by stating "By making choices that reduce greenhouse gas pollution and preparing for the changes that are already underway, we can reduce risks from climate change" (lines 49–51). The authors of Passage 2 do not believe in global warming, but still believe in humans' capacity to improve the environment by advocating human rationing of hydrocarbon and stating that "Hydrocarbon use has major environmental benefits" in lines 82–83. Choice B is incorrect because the authors of Passage 2 do not even believe in global warming. Only the author of Passage 1 discusses how humans have adapted to climate changes throughout history, so choice C is incorrect. Only the author of Passage 2 voices the suggestion in choice D by stating that "we needn't worry about human use of hydrocarbons warming the Earth" in lines 76–77.

37. **The correct answer is D.** The purpose of Passage 1 is to convince readers that global warming is a danger, and the alarming tone of language such as "potentially dangerous, severe, dangerous effects" reinforces that purpose. The second passage attempts to refute any cause for concern by describing the evidence supporting global warming with terms such as "no significant, insufficient, unreliable," which attempts to assure the reader that there is nothing to worry about. Therefore, choice D is the best answer. Based on these evaluations, only Passage 1 creates a sense of danger, so choice A is incorrect. While one could certainly argue that the first passage is based on scientific evidence and the second is speculative, the terms in this answer choice do not differ because one set is scientific and the other is speculative, so choice B is not the best answer. The passages are not overly technical, and the terms repeated in this answer choice certainly do not refute that fact, so choice C is not the best answer.

38. **The correct answer is D.** The sentence refers to symptoms of climate change becoming more recognizable. *Pronounced* can refer to the way something is said or *articulated* (choice A); however , that meaning doesn't fit the context. Choice C has the opposite meaning from the meaning of *pronounced* as used in the passage. *Pronounced* can refer to a declaration or announcement (choice B) but that meaning also does not fit the context.

39. **The correct answer is D.** Both passages define a problem—the first discusses a lack of sufficient concern about global warming and the second discusses misplaced concern about global warming—and offer solutions to those problems when the author Passage 1 implores the reader to reduce the risks of global warning and the authors of Passage 2 recommend greater use of hydrocarbons. Therefore, choice D is the best answer. Choice A suggests a timeline of events. Although both authors reference past and future events, information is not presented sequentially. Only the author of Passage 2 argues that there is a lack of effects regarding global warming, so choice B fails to describe how information is presented in both passages. Neither passage compares two approaches to the global warming problem, so choice C is incorrect.

40. **The correct answer is C.** The first passage focuses only on the negative effects of atmospheric carbon dioxide, and the second passage states that hydrocarbons do not have a negative effect. Choices A and D are incorrect because there is no mention of hydrocarbons in Passage 1. The author of Passage 1 believes that human intervention could have a positive impact on global warming, which indicates a belief that climate and weather can be somewhat modified by humans, but the authors of Passage 2 make no such suggestions, so choice B is incorrect.

41. **The correct answer is C.** The author of the second passage is quoting those he or she disagrees with, such as the author of the first passage. Choice A (lines 20–24) highlights only the sources of greenhouse gases and does not encapsulate the major differences between these arguments. Choice B (lines 40–42) focuses on the long-term effects of carbon dioxide but doesn't summarize the two competing arguments. Choice D (lines 83–86) focuses only on beneficial effects of increased atmospheric carbon dioxide.

42. **The correct answer is C.** The word *transform* (choice C) correctly fits with the idea of changes becoming shifts and suggests that the effects of climate change may be unpredictable. Language translation (choice A) is the process of converting words and meaning from one language into another; however, that is not the way in which *translate* is used here. The effects the authors mention could include expansion, but that is too narrow a definition for the context, which makes choice B incorrect. Choice D refers to helping someone understand something, which does not fit the context of the sentence.

43. The correct answer is B. The two women are fulfilling a tradition common to many cultures, in which the living stay with the body of a friend or family member so it doesn't have to be alone. The tradition partly grew out of the possibility that the deceased might revive, as sometimes happened in the days before doctors were readily available. Choice A is incorrect; it is clear that word has already spread that Miss Tempy died (lines 7–8). Choice C has no supporting evidence in the story. Choice D is a presumption that is also unsupported by details in the story.

44. The correct answer is A. While performing a duty to a friend, two of her oldest, dearest friends draw closer to each other (lines 20–22). Choice B is incorrect because the focus of the story is the relationship between the two remaining friends. Choice C may be true but is incidental. Choice D may also be true but is not central to the story.

45. The correct answer is A. The author explains in lines 19–24 how stimulating the conversation between the women was ("the two women had risen to an unusual level of expressiveness . . . they were again and again tempted into statements that either would have found impossible by daylight"), so it is reasonable to assume that Mrs. Crowe was so distracted by this conversation that she failed to notice that the stocking she was knitting was becoming too long (lines 24–27). Choices B and C reach very specific conclusions that evidence in the passage does not support, and as already stated, the author's description of Mrs. Crowe's conversation with Sarah Ann Binson indicates a likelier answer to this question. That stimulating conversation also indicates that Mrs. Crowe did want to be where she was; otherwise, she would not be very interested in the conversation, so choice D is not the best conclusion either.

46. The correct answer is D. Choice D shows that under this special circumstance, the women are bonding. Choice A is a minor detail that doesn't reflect their friendship. Choice B does not happen in the story, although it is mentioned as a trait of Mrs. Crowe's. Choice C is part of the author's description of Sarah Ann, but it doesn't indicate closeness to Mrs. Crowe.

47. The correct answer is B. In lines 20–24, the author states that the two women were telling each other secrets and saying things that they never would have said under other circumstances ("statements that either would have found impossible by daylight"), indicating the intimacy of their conversation. Therefore, choice B is the best answer. Choice A (lines 16–20) indicates the liveliness of the conversation ("there was a certain degree of excitement just then, and the two women had risen to an unusual level of expressiveness and confidence") but not the intimacy of it. Choice C (lines 27–29) only describes a difference between the two women. Choice D (lines 29–31) shows that the conversation was "engaging," but not that it was especially intimate.

48. The correct answer is B. During the long night together talking, both women reveal secrets and say things they would never have said under normal circumstances. Choice A is a supposition the author makes, presuming they wouldn't have enough to talk about all night long, but that doesn't prove to be the case. Choice C reflects the characterization of Mrs. Crowe as "knowing exactly what she was about" (lines 27–28) and "a cooler disposition" (lines 28–29) yet she is so involved in her conversation that she doesn't notice she is knitting a sock that is too long. Choice D reflects the author's comment that her life is filled with pleasure, but she also says that, to outward appearances, Sarah Ann Binson was burdened by caring for her family (lines 37–39).

49. The correct answer is D. Choice D is correct because despite Mrs. Crowe's higher social standing (lines 61–62) the women easily fill a long night with intimate talk. Their intimate conversation indicates that they are very trusting, at least when talking to each other, so choice A is not the best answer. Choice B assumes they are the same age, but this detail isn't mentioned in the passage. Neither seems overly concerned with her work (Mrs. Crowe is not paying attention to her knitting and Sarah Ann Binson keeps setting her sewing down to talk instead), so choice C is not the best conclusion.

50. The correct answer is C. Lines 49–53 indicate that Sara Ann Binson seemed to live a "pleasureless" life because she had to work so hard on her small farm, while Mrs. Crowe was "well-to-do" with a "rich" husband. Therefore, choice C is the best answer. Choice A (lines 1–3) merely establishes the passage's setting and implies nothing about its two main characters. Choice B (lines 13–16) establishes what the two women are doing and suggests nothing about their social standing. Choice D (lines 60–61) only indicates public perception of Mrs. Crowe, and its failure to mention Sarah Ann Binson makes it weak evidence for the previous answer.

51. **The correct answer is A.** Sarah Ann would have to be eager to carry the load of her family as discussed in the rest of the sentence, and since the author seems to be establishing a contrast between public perception of Sarah Ann and the "vague" (line 34) Mrs. Crowe, choice A is the best contrast to Mrs. Crowe's vagueness. That contrast also eliminates choice C since *absentminded* is too close in meaning to *vague*. Sarah Ann's hard work indicates that people would not view her as *bored*, so choice B does not make much sense. While she may be restless, the focus of the sentence is on how much responsibility she shoulders for her relatives. The fact that Sarah Ann Binson does not have much money does not mean that she was cheap, since one who does not have much to spend does not have the luxury of cheapness, so choice D is not the best answer.

52. **The correct answer is C.** Although several of the answer choices are synonyms of *aspect*, the only one that would truly make sense in place of the word in this particular line is "attitude," since it is Sarah Ann Binson's attitude that appears to be *sharp* and *anxious*. It would not make sense to write "for all her sharp, anxious face," even though *face* can be used to mean *aspect* in another context, so choice A is not the best answer. Choice B is another synonym of *aspect* that would not make sense in this context. Choice D is incorrect, because although *aspect* is sometimes misused to mean *component*, this is not exactly what it means, and *component* would not make sense in this context anyway.

1. D	**10.** A	**19.** B	**28.** C	**37.** B
2. B	**11.** D	**20.** C	**29.** D	**38.** A
3. C	**12.** B	**21.** B	**30.** C	**39.** C
4. D	**13.** B	**22.** A	**31.** B	**40.** C
5. B	**14.** A	**23.** B	**32.** B	**41.** D
6. A	**15.** B	**24.** A	**33.** A	**42.** C
7. B	**16.** C	**25.** B	**34.** C	**43.** B
8. D	**17.** D	**26.** A	**35.** C	**44.** D
9. C	**18.** D	**27.** C	**36.** D	

WRITING AND LANGUAGE TEST RAW SCORE [　　　　]
(Number of correct answers)

1. **The correct answer is D.** This sentence is a fragment requiring a subject, which the pronoun *it* provides. Choices B and C do not work because the specific subject doesn't have a verb—*having* and *were* are part of the descriptive phrase, not the direct action of the subject.

2. **The correct answer is B.** The phrase "for communicating" is set off by a comma in the passage, but because the description "for communicating" modifies *code* by defining the purpose of that code, "for communicating" is a restrictive phrase and should not be separated from the word or phrase it modifies. This makes choices A and C incorrect because the comma after *code* separates the restrictive phrase and the word it modifies. Choice D is incorrect because the comma after *communicating* is incorrect.

3. **The correct answer is C.** Choice C is the only choice that makes clear who has the access and the only choice that states the intended purpose concisely. Choice A is incorrect because the construction "it being the case that they would" is wordy. Choice D places "enemy forces" near the beginning of the sentence, but it creates confusion in the second clause that implies that the code, not the enemy forces, would have access to the tactics and troop movements. Choice B is incorrect because "having access" is ambiguous.

4. **The correct answer is D.** This sentence accurately supports the information in the paragraph and passage, that the US military selected the Navajo language as the foundation for a secret code for a few specific reasons—namely, its "complexity and obscurity." There's no evidence to suggest that many of the top military officials at the time were Navajo, so choice A is incorrect. There's also no evidence to support the notion that the Navajo language was chosen because the Navajo people were famous for their military history, so choice B is incorrect. Furthermore, there's no evidence to support the notion that the Navajo people had often been called on to help the American government in the past, so choice C is also incorrect.

5. **The correct answer is B.** This sentence provides an additional reason why the Navajo language made an excellent code, which makes *furthermore* the best choice. Choice A is incorrect because *However* indicates a contrast, which is not implied by the context. Choice C is incorrect because *Likewise* would make sense only if the sentence were making a comparison. Choice D is incorrect because *As a result* suggests that the sentence is drawing a conclusion, but this is not supported by the context.

6. **The correct answer is A.** Choice A maintains the paragraph's implication that the Navajo language is largely unknown or obscure, a quality that would make the language ideal for the Marines' purpose. Choice B is incorrect because *uncertainty* implies that the language is nonsensical and incomprehensible, which is not the

point. Choice C is incorrect because *beauty* would not make a language perfect for a code. Choice D is incorrect because *clarity* is not a desirable quality for a code that is intended to be unbreakable.

7. **The correct answer is B.** Choice B correctly joins two independent clauses with a comma and a coordinating conjunction. Choice A does not effectively combine the two sentences because it repeats the subject, forming an awkward sentence. Choices C and D are incorrect because they imply that the second clause is dependent on the first clause, which changes the meaning of the sentence.

8. **The correct answer is D.** Choice D accurately suggests that the enemy forces attempted, but did not succeed, in interpreting (or deciphering) the code. Choices A and B are incorrect because they do not fit the intended meaning of the sentence and therefore do not make sense in the context. Choice C is incorrect because *elucidate* means to "explain something," which is the opposite of what the Marines tried to achieve by using Navajo code talkers.

9. **The correct answer is C.** No commas are needed to separate "speed and accuracy" from the rest of the sentence, as this adverbial phrase does not need to be set off from the verb (the work of the code talkers). For this reason, choices A and D are incorrect. Choice B is incorrect because "speed and accuracy" contains a conjunction and does not require a comma.

10. **The correct answer is A.** Choice A maintains the simple past tense, which is established earlier in the sentence. Choices B, C, and D are incorrect because they contain inappropriate shifts in verb tense.

11. **The correct answer is D.** This choice best supports the claims made by the rest of this sentence. The work of the code talkers had to remain largely a secret and unacknowledged for many years because the code was still being used actively. Choices A, B, and C don't explain why the work of the code talkers had to remain unacknowledged, so they are incorrect.

12. **The correct answer is B.** "Who was Dian Fossey" is a question and thus requires a question mark. Choices A, C, and D are incorrect because they do not include a question mark.

13. **The correct answer is B.** Knowing where Fossey was born is irrelevant to the rest of the passage; it doesn't support the main idea of the paragraph or the passage, which is Fossey's work with gorillas. Therefore, choices C and D are incorrect. Choice A is incorrect because this

information does not need to be included anywhere in the passage.

14. **The correct answer is A.** Choice A correctly portrays Dr. Louis Leakey as a well-known and well-respected scholar in the field. Choice B is incorrect because *imminent* refers to something that is about to happen and therefore does not make sense. Choices C and D both imply that Dr. Leakey is bad or disreputable, which is not supported by the context.

15. **The correct answer is B.** Choice B corrects the dangling modifier by making it clear that Fossey decided to focus her research on mountain gorillas. Choice A is incorrect because it contains a dangling modifier. Choice C and D are incorrect because they contain misplaced modifiers.

16. **The correct answer is C.** The sentence is attempting to show where Fossey observed gorillas, so *There* is the correct word to start the sentence. Choice A is incorrect because *they're*, a contraction that means "they are," does not fit within the context of the sentence. Choice B is incorrect because *Their* is a possessive determiner and does not fit in this context. Choice D is incorrect because *Where* makes the sentence a fragment.

17. **The correct answer is D.** Choice D is correct because the sentence is talking about how the animals welcomed Fossey. Choice A is incorrect because it confuses *except*, which refers to something that is apart from other things, with the word *accept*. Choices B and C are incorrect because they are used incorrectly in this context.

18. **The correct answer is D.** Only choice D maintains the tone and style of the rest of the passage. Choices A, B, and C are incorrect because they are much more informal than the rest of the passage.

19. **The correct answer is B.** The opening of the sentence (*In 1989*) indicates that the action in this sentence has already happened, so the past tense is required. Therefore, choice B is correct. Choices A, C, and D employ incorrect verb tense forms.

20. **The correct answer is C.** The writer should not add the sentence because, while the information might or might not be true, the writer doesn't expand on it, and it doesn't support the main idea of the paragraph—that Fossey continued to work to save gorillas for the rest of her life. Choice A is incorrect because the information does not support the main idea of the paragraph. Choice B is incorrect because the information is not necessary to the transition between paragraphs. Choice

D is incorrect because the information is not necessary anywhere in the passage.

21. **The correct answer is B.** Choice B is correct because *declining* accurately communicates that the number of gorillas as falling. Choice A is incorrect because it suggests a diminishment of quality, not number. Choices C and D both imply humiliation, which is not supported by the context.

22. **The correct answer is A.** This sentence serves as an accurate and useful conclusion that connects the work Fossey did while she was alive to its impact on the population of mountain gorillas in Rwanda today. While the gorilla population growth can be attributed to Fossey's dedication to their conservation, the sentence does not fully explain why the population is rising (choice B). This sentence does not contradict the rest of the passage (choice C); it ties together the main idea of the passage and concludes the passage, so it is not unnecessary (choice D).

23. **The correct answer is B.** Choice B is correct because *surrounds* maintains the comparison the author makes between a tamarin's fur and a lion's mane. Choices A and C are incorrect because the first part of the sentence describes their "hairless faces," so the notion of fur obscuring or covering the face is inappropriate. Choice D is incorrect because it is vague and ambiguous.

24. **The correct answer is A.** The writer should not delete the underlined sentence. This information supports the main idea of the paragraph, and the sentence appears in the correct place in the logical organization of the paragraph. Choice B is incorrect because this sentence does not explain the previous sentence; rather, it adds a detail that is further explained in the next sentence. Choice C is incorrect because moving the sentence would interrupt the organizational flow of the paragraph. Choice D is incorrect because this information does not interrupt the flow of ideas in the paragraph.

25. **The correct answer is B.** Choice B clarifies the comparison between tamarins that assist in the care of newborns with those that do not. Choice A is incorrect because the failure to note what is being compared leads to confusion. Choices C and D are incorrect because the comparisons are vague or incorrect.

26. **The correct answer is A.** The pronoun *they* correctly refers to the plural antecedent "tamarins" and the verb *are* is in the present tense like the rest of the paragraph. Choices B and D are incorrect because the pronoun *it* is

singular. Choice C is incorrect because "tamarins" are gender-neutral.

27. **The correct answer is C.** Choice C corrects the conventional expression to "one and the same." Choices A, B, and D are incorrect because they do not reflect the proper use of this conventional expression.

28. **The correct answer is C.** Sentence 5 provides more information about tamarins' diurnal activities and thus should naturally follow sentence 1. The word *however* also implies that the sentence provides information that somehow contrasts with the previous sentence and the idea that tamarins dislike sunlight contrasts with the notion that they are active during the day. Choices A, B, and D are incorrect because sentence 5 does not make sense in those positions.

29. **The correct answer is D.** The semicolon in choice D correctly connects two independent clauses. Choice A is incorrect because a comma may not be used to separate independent clauses without the use of a coordinating conjunction. Choice B is incorrect because it doesn't fix the comma splice; it just moves it. Choice C is incorrect because the sentence requires punctuation to fix the grammatical error.

30. **The correct answer is C.** Sentence 2 is a direct follow-up to sentence 4 because sentence 4 explains the movement's beginning, and sentence 2 explains the movement's expansion and growth since its beginning. Placing sentence 2 before sentence 1 (choice B) is not logical, because it would be unclear what *it* is referencing. Sentence 3 talks about how many participating zoos there were at the beginning of the campaign introduced in sentence 1, and is therefore a logical follow up to it. Leaving sentence 2 between them (choice A) interrupts this natural flow by talking about the expansion of the movement. Sentence 2 provides supporting details about the accomplishments of the conservation campaign started by the National Zoological Park in Washington, the Smithsonian Institute, and the Rio de Janeiro Primate Center. Therefore, it should not be removed (choice D).

31. **The correct answer is B.** Choice B clarifies the ambiguous pronoun *it* by inserting the reference to "the campaign." Choice C is incorrect because *it* does not refer to "the problem." Choice D is incorrect because it simply replaces one pronoun with another, which does nothing to clarify what the pronoun refers to.

32. **The correct answer is B.** Choice B accurately states that tamarin populations have fluctuated in recent years while the number of zoos participating in the program

has not. Choice A is incorrect because the graph does not show any decline in the participation of zoos. Choice C is incorrect because the participation rate of zoos has not risen substantially in recent years. Choice D is incorrect because neither the number of participating zoos nor the population of tamarins has fallen significantly since 2000.

33. **The correct answer is A.** Choice A accurately suggests the efforts have been successful. Choice B is incorrect because the sentence suggests success rather than a problem. Choice C is incorrect because the sentence does not mention making money. Choice D is incorrect because it suggests their plan is off schedule, but this is not supported by the sentence.

34. **The correct answer is C.** Choice C supports the idea of "strict" adherence to principles. Choice A is incorrect because it suggests the adherence is temporary, which is not supported by the context. Choices B and D are incorrect because they do not make sense in the context of the sentence.

35. **The correct answer is C.** This information supports the main idea of the paragraph and provides a logical conclusion to the paragraph, so it should be placed at the end. Choice A is incorrect because, although the information might be interesting, it is out of place and disrupts the flow of ideas in the paragraph. Choice B is incorrect because it is a conclusion, not an introduction. Choice D is incorrect because, although the information supports the main idea of the paragraph, it is out of place.

36. **The correct answer is D.** Choice D uses a transition word and comma to combine the sentences in a grammatically correct and concise way. Choice A is incorrect; and suggests additional but equal information, but the second clause modifies the first and is not equal. Choice B is incorrect because it is syntactically incorrect. Choice C incorrectly separates two independent clauses with a comma.

37. **The correct answer is B.** In choice B, the plural noun *columns* is in agreement with the second plural noun *elements*, and the statement contains the plural verb *are*. Choice A is incorrect because the plural noun *columns* is not in agreement with the singular noun *element*. Choice C is incorrect because the singular noun *column* is not in agreement with the plural noun *elements*. Choice D is incorrect because the noun *columns* is plural and the verb *is* is singular.

38. **The correct answer is A.** The items in the list need only be separated by commas. Choice B is incorrect because the conjunction *and* is incorrectly used in several places. Choices C and D are incorrect because they incorrectly and unnecessarily use a semicolon.

39. **The correct answer is C.** Only choice C maintains parallel structure by including *the* before each of item in the series. Choices A, B, and D are incorrect because they do not provide parallel structure because the article *the* is not used consistently.

40. **The correct answer is C.** Choice C correctly continues and supports the paragraph's purpose of providing examples of how each element is divided into three parts. The paragraph currently discusses how the *entablature* and column are divided into three parts, and choice C continues that purpose by describing the three parts of the *crepidoma,* the third element. Choices A, B, and D are incorrect because they do not support the purpose or topic of the paragraph.

41. **The correct answer is D.** The antecedent "classical buildings" is plural, which means the pronoun must also be plural. Choices A, B, and C are incorrect because they contain antecedents and pronouns that are not in agreement.

42. **The correct answer is C.** *Its* is a possessive determiner that refers to the singular noun *building*. Choices A and B are incorrect because the antecedent is *building,* so the pronoun should be gender neutral and singular. Choice D is incorrect because *buildings* should be singular possessive.

43. **The correct answer is B.** *Perceived* means "recognized," which fits with the meaning of the sentence. Choice A is incorrect because it describes the violations as being different, which is not what the author intends. Choices C and D are incorrect because neither makes sense in the context of the sentence.

44. **The correct answer is D.** Choice D follows the paragraph's focus on the difficulty of following the strict conventions of classical architecture. Choice A is incorrect because it focuses on information from a previous paragraph. Choice B is incorrect because it is a general statement that is unsupported by the information in the passage. Choice C is incorrect because it makes a hyperbolic generalization that is not supported by the paragraph.

1. A	**5.** A	**9.** A	**13.** A	**17.** 48
2. D	**6.** A	**10.** D	**14.** C	**18.** 22
3. A	**7.** A	**11.** B	**15.** D	**19.** 7
4. B	**8.** D	**12.** C	**16.** 48	**20.** 15

MATH TEST—NO CALCULATOR RAW SCORE
(Number of correct answers)

1. **The correct answer is A.** Subtract like terms when simplifying the expression: $4x^2 - 3x^2 = x^2$, $-5x - (-2x) = -3x$, and $8 - (-5) = 13$. Put together, the expression is $x^2 - 3x + 13$.

2. **The correct answer is D.** To simplify the expression, first add the exponents, and then use the rule that a negative exponent is equal to the reciprocal of the positive exponent of the same number. Finally, rewrite the rational exponent in radical form:

$$x^{\frac{2}{3}} \cdot x^{-\frac{4}{3}} = x^{-\frac{2}{3}}$$
$$= \frac{1}{x^{\frac{2}{3}}}$$
$$= \frac{1}{\sqrt[3]{x^2}}$$

3. **The correct answer is A.**

$$-2\left[x(1-3x)+3x\right]^2 = -2\left[x-3x^2+3x\right]^2$$
$$= -2\left[+3x^2+4x\right]^2$$
$$= -2\left[9x^4-24x^3+16x^2\right]$$
$$= -18x^4+48x^3-32x^2$$

4. **The correct answer is B.** The vertex of a parabola is found when the equation is written in the form $y = a(x - h)^2 + k$. You don't need to perform any calculations, because only choice B is written in this form.

5. **The correct answer is A.** Rewrite the expression as a multiple of $a + 4b$:

$$-5\left[-3a+2(4b+a)-12b\right] = -5\left[-3(a+4b)+2(a+4b)\right]$$
$$= -5\left[-(a+4b)\right]$$
$$= 5(a+4b)$$
$$= 5(16)$$
$$= 80$$

6. **The correct answer is A.** Divide both sides by $2\pi r$ to simplify, then solve for h:

$$S = 2\pi r^2 + 2\pi rh$$
$$\frac{S}{2\pi} = \frac{2\pi r^2 + 2\pi h}{2\pi r}$$
$$\frac{S}{2\pi r} = r + h$$
$$\frac{S}{2\pi r} - r = h$$

7. **The correct answer is A.** The population will be reduced by 3.5% each year, so each year the population is multiplied by $(1 - 0.035)$, or (0.965). The only answer choice that shows repeated multiplication of (0.965) through the use of the exponent n is choice A: $P = P_0(0.965)^n$.

8. **The correct answer is D.** Substitute the values 4 and 6 for x and check which equation has the correct function values for both, or calculate the slope between the points and substitute one point to find the y-intercept:

$$\frac{10-2}{6-4}=4$$
$$y=4x+b$$
$$2=4(4)+b$$
$$-14=b$$
$$y=4x-14$$

9. **The correct answer is A.** The standard slope-intercept form of the equation of a line is $y = mx + b$, where m is the slope of the line and b is the y-intercept. Therefore, the slope of line p equals 1. Since lines p and q are parallel, their slopes are equal. Therefore, the slope of line q equals 1. Let line q be represented by the standard equation of a line, $y = mx + b$. Since the slope of line q equals 1, substitute $m = 1$ in the equation: $y = x + b$.

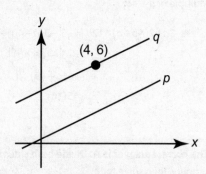

Note: Figure not drawn to scale.

From the above figure, we know that point (4, 6) lies on line q. Therefore, $x = 4$ and $y = 6$ must satisfy the equation of the line. Substitute these values in the above equation and solve for b, which is the y-intercept:

$$6=4+b$$
$$2=b$$

Therefore, the y-intercept of line q equals 2.

10. **The correct answer is D.** Write equations based on the information given; let s = a small cup and L = a large cup. Multiply the first equation by 4 and the second one by 3, so that s gets eliminated during the subtraction. Then solve for L:

$$4(3s+2L=30)$$
$$-3(4s+L=25)$$
$$\overline{}5L=45$$
$$L=9$$

11. **The correct answer is B.** If the angles of a triangle are equal to the corresponding angles of another triangle, the two triangles are similar. Also remember that when two triangles are similar, their corresponding sides are proportional.

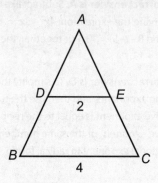

Note: Figure not drawn to scale.

$\overline{DE}$ is parallel to $\overline{BC}$, so $\angle ABC$ and $\angle ADE$ are corresponding angles; therefore, $\angle ABC = \angle ADE$. Similarly, $\angle ACB = \angle AED$. Also, the angle at point A is common to both triangles. Thus, all three angles of triangle ABC are congruent with the corresponding angles of triangle ADE.

Therefore, triangle ABC and triangle ADE are similar and their corresponding sides are proportional.

Now set up a proportion of their corresponding sides and solve for the length of segment AB:

$$\frac{AB}{AD}=\frac{BC}{DE}$$
$$\frac{AB}{3}=\frac{4}{2}$$
$$\frac{AB}{3}=2$$
$$AB=6$$

Therefore, the length of segment BD is $AB - AD = 6 - 3 = 3$.

12. **The correct answer is C.** Because $-3(x-5)^2$ will always be negative, $p(x)$, the sales in month x, will always be less than or equal to 173. $p(x) = 173$ when $x = 5$. So 173 is the maximum monthly sales.

13. **The correct answer is A.** You can work backward with the answer choices to determine the value of x. None of the values works except $x = \dfrac{1}{2}$:

$$(x+2)^2 - (x-3)^2 = \left(\frac{5}{2}\right)^2 - \left(-\frac{5}{2}\right)^2$$
$$= \frac{25}{4} - \frac{25}{4}$$
$$= 0$$

14. **The correct answer is C.**

The center of the circle is the midpoint of the segment with endpoints $(-2, 3)$ and $(4,9)$: $\left(\dfrac{-2+4}{2}, \dfrac{3+9}{2}\right) = (1, 6)$. The diameter is the length of the segment with endpoints $(-2, 3)$ and $(4, 9)$:

$\sqrt{\left(4-(-2)\right)^2 + \left(9-3\right)^2} = \sqrt{72} = 6\sqrt{2}$. So the radius is half of the diameter, or $3\sqrt{2}$. Finally, using the standard form for the equation of the circle, we conclude that its equation is $(x-1)^2 + (y-6)^2 = 18$.

15. **The correct answer is D.** Check each answer choice to see if the slope between the point $(3, 4)$ and the given coordinates is $-\dfrac{4}{5}$. Only choice D gives us this answer:

$$\frac{y-4}{x-3} = -\frac{4}{5}$$
$$\frac{-4-4}{13-3} = \frac{-8}{10} = -\frac{4}{5}$$

16. **The correct answer is 48.** Let x be the number of 30-pound bags that Miguel can safely carry. Because his truck can safely carry only a maximum of 1,500 pounds, the weight of the bags plus the weight of the wheelbarrow has to be equal to or less than that, which gives us the inequality $30x + 50 \leq 1,500$. Solve for x to get the number of bags:

$$30x + 50 \leq 1,500$$
$$30x \leq 1,450$$
$$x \leq 48.33$$

Because Miguel can't take partial bags, he can safely take 48 bags.

17. **The correct answer is 48.**

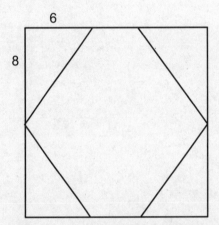

We know that each side of the square has length 16 since two triangle sides of length 8 form one side of the square. From this, we know that the shortest sides of the hexagonal sign must equal 4: the square side – 2 triangle edges = $16 - 2(6) = 4$. Now all we have to do is find the hypotenuse of one triangle and multiply it by 4.

Use the Pythagorean theorem: $a^2 + b^2 = c^2$, where c is the length of the hypotenuse. In this case: $8^2 + 6^2 = c^2$, $64 + 36 = c^2$, $100 = c^2$, and $10 = c$.

So the perimeter of the sign is $10(4) + 4(2) = 40 + 8 = 48$ inches.

18. **The correct answer is 22.** To solve for b, first multiply both sides by $x - 4$ to get $5x + 2 = 5x - 20 + b$. Then, subtract $5x - 20$ from both sides to get $22 = b$.

$$\frac{5x+2}{x-4} = 5 + \frac{b}{x-4}$$
$$5x + 2 = 5(x-4) + b$$
$$5x + 2 = 5x - 20 + b$$
$$5x - 5x + 2 + 20 = b$$
$$b = 22$$

19. The correct answer is 7.

$$3x - 4 = 2x - 5$$
$$x = -1$$
$$y = 3(-1) - 4 = -7$$
$$xy = (-1)(-7) = 7$$

20. The correct answer is 15.

$$-3(6x - 5y) = -3(9)$$
$$-18x + 15y = -27$$

For a system of equations to have infinitely many solutions, the equations must be equivalent. To make $6x - 5y = 9$ equivalent to $-18x + by = -27$, you can multiply $6x - 5y = 9$ by some factor so that the coefficient of x will be -18 and the constant on the right side will be -27. That factor is -3. When we multiply the first equation by -3, it becomes $-18x + 15y = -27$. That will be equivalent to the second equation when $b = 15$.

1. B	**9.** B	**17.** B	**25.** D	**33.** 12
2. B	**10.** C	**18.** D	**26.** D	**34.** 1.5 or 3/2
3. C	**11.** A	**19.** B	**27.** D	**35.** 24
4. A	**12.** A	**20.** A	**28.** D	**36.** 51
5. B	**13.** C	**21.** C	**29.** D	**37.** 2
6. C	**14.** A	**22.** D	**30.** C	**38.** .225
7. D	**15.** C	**23.** A	**31.** 7/13	
8. C	**16.** D	**24.** A	**32.** 40	

MATH TEST—CALCULATOR RAW SCORE
(Number of correct answers)

1. **The correct answer is B.** The table shows the prices of 25 houses. The median price is the price in the middle, or the price that is greater than exactly 12 other prices and less than exactly 12 other prices. This price must be greater than $60,000 because the table shows that only 10 houses sold for $60,000 or less. The median price must be less than $300,000 because only 10 houses sold for $300,000 or more (bottom three rows of the table).

2. **The correct answer is B.**

$$2\left[-3-(2-4x)\right]=-3^{2}+x$$
$$2\left[-5+4x\right]=-9+x$$
$$-10+8x=-9+x$$
$$-1=-7x$$
$$\frac{1}{7}=x$$

So $x^{-2}=\left(\frac{1}{7}\right)^{-2}=49.$

3. **The correct answer is C.** Johnson ran the 400-meter race in 43.18 seconds. In that time, Halswelle ran at a rate of 8 meters per second (400 meters/50 seconds = 8 meters/second). So he would have run 43.18 seconds × 8 meters/second = 345.44 meters. Halswelle would have had about 55 more meters to run before reaching the end of the 400-meter race.

4. **The correct answer is A.** The description can be written as $18-6x=-8-4$, which is equivalent to $18-6x=-12$. Subtracting 18 from both sides gives $-6x=-30$. Since $-3x$ is half of $-6x$, dividing both sides by 2 gives $-3x=-15$.

5. **The correct answer is B.** The total amount of pain medication is 24(250)(200) = 1,200,000 milligrams. The answers are all in kilograms, so convert the measure in milligrams to kilograms one step at a time: 1,200,000 milligrams = 1,200 grams, and 1,200 grams = 1.2 kilograms.

6. **The correct answer is C.** A sample is not equivalent to the population, and just because a sample is smaller than the population does not mean that it is not representative.

7. **The correct answer is D.** The slope of the curve is increasing as the number of years increases. The population increases from 290 to 425 in the span between 2010 and 2012. So the estimated population for 2011 is 357.50. Similarly, the population increases from 500 to 825 in the span between 2013 and 2015. So the estimated population for 2014 is 662.50. Thus, the predicted difference in the population between the years 2014 and 2011 is 305.

8. **The correct answer is C.** Substitute the points (2009, 250) and (2013, 500) into the equation to obtain two equations involving A and b:

$$250 = Ae^{b(2009)}$$
$$500 = Ae^{b(2013)}$$

Observe that $500 = Ae = Aeb(2009)$.

$$250e^{-b(2009)} = A$$
$$500e^{-b(2013)} = A$$
$$250e^{-b(2009)} = 500e^{-b(2013)}$$
$$250e^{-b(2009)}e^{b(2013)} = 500$$
$$e^{4b} = 2$$
$$4b = \ln 2$$
$$b = \frac{1}{4}\ln 2$$

9. **The correct answer is B.** If the mean is significantly greater than the median, there must be some values that are much greater than the rest in order to increase the mean.

10. **The correct answer is C.** In the equation $h(t) = -0.5t + 980$, 980 represents the height above the ground of the stuntman when he opens the parachute. At the moment the parachute opens, $t = 0$, and $h(0) = 280$.

11. **The correct answer is A.** Convert 180,000 miles per second to miles per hour by using the fact that there are 3,600 seconds in one hour:

$$180,000 \text{ miles per second} = 180,000(3,600) \text{ miles per hour}$$
$$= 648,000,000 \text{ miles per hour}$$

Since an object's speed cannot exceed this value, the inequality is $x \leq 648,000,000$.

12. **The correct answer is A.** Angle BAC and the angle labeled 37° are corresponding angles formed by the segment AB transversing parallel lines l and m.

Corresponding angles are congruent, so the measure of angle $BAC = 37°$.

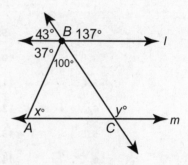

13. **The correct answer is C.** The cost of T memory cards is xT dollars. The cost after the 15% discount is applied is $0.85xT$ dollars. The cost after the 6% tax is applied is $0.85xT + 0.06(0.85xT) = 0.901xT$ dollars. Finally, applying the 10% discount to that amount yields a total cost for the purchase of $0.901xT - 0.10(0.901xT) = 0.8109xT$ dollars. Without any discount, the cost of T memory cards is $xT + 0.06xT = 1.06xT$ dollars. So the savings is $1.06xT - 0.8109xT = 0.2491xT$ dollars.

14. **The correct answer is A.** Multiply both sides of the equation by $z + z^2$ to clear the fractions:

$$(z + z^2) \cdot \frac{1}{1+z} = (z + z^2) \cdot \left[\frac{4}{z + z^2} + 1 \right]$$
$$z = 4 + (z + z^2)$$
$$0 = 4 + z^2$$

Since the right side is always positive (in fact, it is never less than 4), this equation has no solution. You could also arrive at this answer by substituting 0 and −2 for z in the equation. Since neither value makes the equation true, choices B, C, and D are eliminated.

15. **The correct answer is C.** If $5.95 is the cost per sandwich, then $5.95x$ is the revenue from sandwiches, and y must be the number of beverages sold, since the number of beverages sold is an unknown value, and z must be the total revenue.

16. **The correct answer is D.** Substituting −1 for x and −1 for y in both inequalities shows that both a and b are less than −3. Choices B and C *might* be true, but choice D must be true.

17. **The correct answer is B.** Let x = number of pans of cookies and y = number of pans of cupcakes. Then the number of cookies and cupcakes that Alex bakes are $18x$ and $15y$, respectively. Alex wants at least twice as many pans of cookies as pans of cupcakes, $x \geq 2y$. The total number of cookies and cupcakes, $18x + 15y$, must be less than or equal to ("no more than") 165. Choice B includes both of those inequalities.

18. **The correct answer is D.** Isolate $\sqrt{x}$ on one side of the equation and then square both sides to solve.

$$3\sqrt{x} + 8 = 20$$
$$3\sqrt{x} = 12$$
$$\sqrt{x} = 4$$
$$x = 16$$

19. **The correct answer is B.** First, solve the system of equations for S:

$$G + S = 50$$
$$\underline{19G + 10.5S = 800}$$
$$19G + 19S = 950$$
$$\underline{-19G + 10.5S = 800}$$
$$8.5S = 150$$
$$S = 17.65$$
$$S \approx 18$$

S is the volume of silver in the crown. Divide that by the total volume of the crown to determine the percentage (by volume) of the crown that is silver:

$$\frac{18}{50} = 0.36$$
$$= 36\%$$

20. **The correct answer is A.** The trend of the graph is positive, and most of the data points are close to a line, so the association is a strong positive correlation.

21. **The correct answer is C.** The trend of the graph is positive, most of the data points are close to a line, and the line for $y = 20x + 250$ goes through the center of the data. The other graphs don't go through the center or don't follow the trend of data.

22. **The correct answer is D.** A quadratic equation $ax^2 + bx + c = 0$ has two complex conjugate solutions when the radicand in the quadratic formula $\frac{-b \pm \sqrt{b^2 - 4ac}}{2a}$ is negative. To figure out the radicand for the given equation, keep a as the variable a, then define $b = -1$, and $c = 2$. So the radicand $b^2 - 4ac$ is $(-1)^2 - 4(a) \cdot (2) = 1 - 8a$. This expression is negative whenever $a > \frac{1}{8}$. The only answer option for which this is true is choice D.

23. **The correct answer is A.** Because the function has factors $(x - 1)$ and $(x + 5)$, and there are no other linear factors, the graph of $f(x)$ must have zeros when $x - 1 = 0$ and $x + 5 = 0$, and nowhere else. Thus, the only x-intercepts for $f(x)$ are 1 and −5. Answer B is incorrect because it includes an additonal x-intercept as (−2, 0).

24. **The correct answer is A.** The y-intercept indicates that when $x = 0$, $y = 8$. Substituting $x = 0$ into all the answer choices, you can see that only choices A and B are true. Then use the x-intercept $x = 4$, $y = 0$ to see that only choice A is correct for those values.

25. **The correct answer is D.** Observe that 10,715 + 12,146 = 22,861 study subjects in the under 12 and 12–17 age groups are in excellent health. The total number of subjects in the two age groups is 20,484 + 24,164 = 44,648. The probability that one of these subjects is in excellent health is the number of such subjects in excellent health divided by the total number of subjects in the group:

$$\frac{22,861}{44,648} \approx 0.512$$

26. **The correct answer is D.** If $k < -1$, then the graph must open downward and be relatively steep. The graph of a quadratic equation is always a parabola, which eliminates choice A.

27. **The correct answer is D.** There were 92 juniors, and, of those, 30 students categorized themselves politically as conservative: $\dfrac{30}{92} = \dfrac{15}{46}$

28. **The correct answer is D.** Of the 200 students surveyed, there were 74 students total who categorized themselves as moderates.

$$\frac{74}{200} \times 4,000 = 1,480$$

29. **The correct answer is D.** The 95% confidence that the margin of error is ± 3% is important, and choices A and B ignore the confidence interval. Choice C is not correct because there are likely people who don't know or have no opinion of the job that the US Congress is doing. Only choice D accurately uses the confidence interval and the data given in the problem.

30. **The correct answer is C.** First, find the slope of line m using the points on the line:

$$\frac{-2-0}{0-3} = \frac{2}{3}$$

A line that is perpendicular to line m will have a slope that is the negative reciprocal of that slope, so the slope of line n is $-\dfrac{3}{2}$, which means that choice C is correct.

31. **The correct answer is $\dfrac{7}{13}$ (7/13).** First, determine how many male baboons there are in the troop; 35% of 60 equals 21. So, there are 21 males and 39 females. Since the fraction $\dfrac{21}{39}$ won't fit into the grid, you must reduce. Divide both the numerator and the denominator by 3 to get $\dfrac{7}{13}$.

32. **The correct answer is 40.** Write and solve an equation that represents the home runs hit by batters A and B, and solve for the desired number.

n = number of home runs by batter A

$n - 14$ = number of home runs by batter B

$$n + n - 14 = 66$$
$$2n - 14 = 66$$
$$2n = 80$$
$$n = 40$$

33. **The correct answer is 12.** There are six numbers in the set. If their mean is 15, then we know $S/6 = 15$, where S is the sum of the numbers in the set. From that, see that

the sum of the numbers is 90. If $14 + 19 + 12 + 16 + N + 17 = 90$, then $N = 12$.

34. **The correct answer is 1.5 or 3/2.** First simplify the equation, and then determine which value of c will make the equation have no solutions, which is when the coefficient for $x = 0$.

$$3(5-2x) = -4(cx+4) \qquad 4c - 6 = 0$$
$$15 - 6x = -4cx - 16 \qquad 4c = 6$$
$$4cx - 6x = -31 \qquad c = 1.5$$

35. **The correct answer is 24.** Let h be the height of the cylinder. Its radius is $2h$, so the volume of the cylinder is $\pi(2h)^2 h = 4\pi h^3$. Since h is the diameter of the sphere, its radius is $\dfrac{h}{2}$.

Volume of the sphere =

$$\frac{4}{3}\pi\left(\frac{h}{2}\right)^3 = \frac{1}{6}\pi h^3$$

Observe: Volume of the cylinder =

$$4\pi h^3 = 24\left(\frac{1}{6}\pi h^3\right) = 24 \times \text{volume of the sphere}$$

36. **The correct answer is 51.**

$$f(-2) = 3(-2)^2 - 4(-2) + 8 = 28$$
$$g(28) = 2(28) - 5 = 51$$
$$g(f(-2)) = 51$$

37. **The correct answer is 2.** First, combine the equations by substituting $2x - 3$ for y in the second equation. Then solve for x:

$$2x - 3 = -3(x-1)^2 + 4$$
$$2x - 3 = -3x^2 + 6x - 3 + 4$$
$$0 = -3x^2 + 4x + 4$$
$$0 = (3x + 2)(-x + 2)$$
$$x = -\frac{2}{3}, 2$$

Negative answers cannot be gridded, so the only correct answer is 2.

38. **The correct answer is .225.** To find the percent of change, multiply $1.25(1 - 0.3)(1.4)$ to show the three years of change as (1.225). This is equivalent to a 22.5% increase. The equivalent decimal is 0.225. Since there are only 4 spaces in the grid-in box, ignore the zero (0), and just grid in the decimal point and 225 so it appears as .225.

Section 5: Essay

Analysis of Passage

The following is an analysis of the passage by Jessica Smartt Gullion, noting how the writer used evidence, reasoning, and stylistic or persuasive elements to support her claims, connect the claims and evidence, and add power to the ideas she expressed. Check to see if you evaluated the passage in a similar way.

Will guns on campus lead to grade inflation?

By Jessica Smartt Gullion, Assistant Professor of Sociology at Texas Woman's University

1   Texas college professors may soon face a dilemma between upholding professional ethics and protecting their lives.

2   The Texas legislature appears poised to approve a bill that would allow college students to carry firearms to class. Called "campus carry," public universities in Texas will not be allowed to ban guns on their campuses, once the law is passed, although private schools could enact their own prohibitions.

3   Its backers argue that students have the right to protect themselves on campuses with handguns. The lobbying extends to sponsoring crash courses such as the NRA University, a two-hour seminar course for college students.

4   With this proposed law, a question coming up for many academics is whether they would be forced to give As to undeserving students, just so they can avoid being shot.

5   This is not as farfetched as it sounds. In my five years as a college professor, I have had experience with a number of emotionally distressed students who resort to intimidation when they receive a lesser grade than what they feel they deserve.

Threats on campus

6   Here is an example of one such threatening experience: One evening in a graduate course, after I handed back students' papers, a young woman stood up and pointed at me. "This is unacceptable!" she screamed as her body shook in rage.

7   She moved toward the front of the class waving her paper in my face and screamed again, "unacceptable!" After a heated exchange, she left the room and stood outside the door sobbing.

1   The writer starts her argument by articulating her central concern: Texas college professors may soon be forced to put fear for their safety above professional ethics.

2   The writer states her reason for this concern: a pending Texas law that permits college students to carry guns on campuses.

3   The writer establishes her credibility and fairness by stating the reason why some legislators support this bill.

4   The writer returns to her central concern, expressing it in more detail: some instructors might give undeserved high grades to avoid being shot.

5   The writer provides facts about herself: she has been a college professor for five years and has had experience with students who intimidate instructors. By citing her background, the writer establishes her credentials as someone qualified to write about this topic and make this argument.

6   The writer provides a specific example drawn from her own experience. This makes her argument more personal and further strengthens her credibility—she truly knows what she is talking about. In addition, the writer makes this story extremely vivid using powerful words (screamed; shook in rage).

7   The writer continues to use evocative words (waving her paper in my face; heated exchange; sobbing).

Answer Keys and Explanations

8   All this was over receiving a B on a completely low-stakes assignment.

9   What followed was even more startling. The following week, the student brought along a muscle-bound man to class. He watched me through the doorway window for the entire three hours of the class, with his arms folded across his chest.

10 And if this wasn't enough, the young woman's classmates avoided me on campus because, they said, they were afraid of getting caught in the crossfire should she decide to shoot me.

11 After that, every time she turned in a paper I cringed and prayed that it was good so that I wouldn't have to give her anything less than an A.

12 Learning from this experience, now I give papers back only at the end of the class or just "forget" to bring them with me.

13 I was lucky that the student didn't have a gun in my classroom. Other professors have not been so lucky.

14 Last year, a student at Purdue shot his instructor in front of a classroom of students. In another incident in 2009, a student at Northern Virginia Community College tried to shoot his math professor on campus. And, in 2000, a graduate student at the University of Arkansas shot his English professor.

15 In each of these states, carrying handguns on campus was illegal at the time of the shooting, although a bill was introduced in Arkansas earlier this year to allow students to carry guns.

Grade Inflation

16 Despite these and other shootings, a new trend has emerged across the US that supports guns on college campuses.

17 Eight states allow firearms onto college campuses and 11 states are now considering similar legislation.

18 We know that some students will carry guns whether it is legal or not. One study found that close to five percent of undergraduates had a gun on campus and that almost two percent had been threatened with a firearm while at school.

. . .

8   *The writer underscores the volatility of this student by using the phrase "all this" and pointing out that she received a respectable grade (a B) on an assignment that wasn't particularly important. The writer is implying that this woman's response to the grade was not rational, and she might have been angrier (and potentially more dangerous) if this were a major assignment.*

9   *The writer adds more details to the story, again carefully choosing words to paint a vivid picture (a muscle-bound man; the entire three hours; arms folded across his chest). Here, the writer evokes sympathy for herself and, by extension, all college teachers who have experienced (or who might experience) something similar.*

10 *The writer points out that the consequence of this experience went beyond her and one student, extending to her interactions with her other students.*

11 *The writer concludes the story by relating the effects this experience had on her, driving home the point that she is speaking from personal experience and eliciting more sympathy from the reader. She chooses her words carefully (cringed; prayed) for maximum impact.*

12 *The writer makes the reader aware that this experience has had a lasting effect on her.*

13 *The writer returns to her central point: students having guns on campuses.*

14 *The writer cites three other incidents in which college students shot or tried to shoot instructors on a college campus.*

15 *The writer points out that in these incidents carrying handguns on campus was illegal. Thus she implies that things could get much worse on campuses where carrying handguns is allowed.*

16 *The writer points that even with the issue of students shooting instructors, there is support for guns on college campuses.*

17 *The writer uses statistics to support this claim.*

18 *The writer underscores her point that guns on campus are a big problem and cites a study to support this claim.*

19　Who would want to give a student a low grade and then get shot for it?

19　*The writer asks a rhetorical question to support her argument that guns on campus could motivate instructors to give undeserved high grades.*

20　Many majors are highly competitive and require certain GPAs for admission. Students on scholarships and other forms of financial aid must maintain high grades to keep their funding. It's no surprise that some students might resort to any means necessary to keep up their GPAs.

20　*The writer provides reasons why some students are desperate to maintain good grades, bolstering her claim that students can become violent if they receive disappointing grades.*

21　An international student once cried in my office and begged me to change his F to an A, as without it, his country would no longer pay for him to be in the U.S. I didn't. He harassed me by posting threatening messages on Facebook.

21　*Citing another example from her past, the writer describes what a student who was dependent on good grades did to her. She is again showing that her concern is well-founded and arousing the reader's sympathy by relating a personal experience.*

22　So, the question is, will we soon see a new sort of grade inflation, with students earning a 4.0 GPA with their firepower rather than brain power? And if so, what sort of future citizenry will we be building on our campuses?

22　*The writer concludes her argument with two rhetorical questions. She also chooses words that create strong images ("students earning a 4.0 GPA with their firepower rather than brain power" and "what sort of future citizenry will we be building on our campuses").*

Sample Essays

The following are examples of a high-scoring and low-scoring essay, based on the passage by Jessica Smartt Gullion.

High-Scoring Essay

The right to bear arms is highly contested in the United States. Rather than entering the national fray, Jessica Smartt Gullion focuses on only the right of college students to carry guns on campus. To persuade readers that college students should not be allowed to carry guns, she uses examples from her experience as a college professor to demonstrate the connection between grades and violence directed at the professors who assign those grades. Examples of violent incidents at other universities show that her experience is not unique. She brings the examples to life with words that evoke emotion, revealing the stress and fear that classroom violence creates. Gullion concludes by posing rhetorical questions that ask readers to consider the effect of guns in the college classroom.

Gullion presents the issue in a single clear sentence. At first, the claim seems extreme—professors might be killed for giving students poor grades for poor performance. She provides some background information, explaining the "campus carry" bill that would permit students at public universities in Texas to carry guns on campus. To balance the article's viewpoint, the writer briefly explains the opposing view that students should be armed to protect themselves. The article then circles back, bringing the information together by reminding readers that her concern is that professors who give poor grades for poor performance put themselves in danger.

To ward off readers' first impression that her concern is unrealistic, she admits that it may seem farfetched. However, she states that students have tried to intimidate her into giving better grades a number of times in the five years that she has been a college professor. In the next section, she uses emotional words that bring a threatening situation to life.

By simply placing the words "threats" and "campus" together, the "Threats on campus" heading brings an immediate sense of danger to a location where readers expect to feel safe. Gullion recounts a story of a violent event in her classroom. Emotional words such as "screamed" and "body shook with rage" help readers feel the shock and fear the exchange generated. The writer points out that the student's reaction was caused by getting a decent grade on an unimportant assignment. Without actually saying it, Gullion has made readers wonder what could have happened if the grade had been lower, if the assignment were more important, or if the student had been armed. The confrontation in the classroom didn't end there. The tale of the muscle-bound man watching her silently for three hours increased the "creepiness" rating of the incident and demonstrated some long-term effects. Even without a "campus carry" law, other students worried about the possibility of a shooting. Gullion describes how she cringed when the student turned in assignments after that.

Reinforcing the danger by supporting her personal experience with facts, Gullion identifies three separate incidents in which students shot their teachers. She makes the possibility of being shot for giving bad grades to students seem like it is not farfetched at all.

Sometimes, Gullion reasons, more is at stake for a student than grades. Poor grades can cause a student to be rejected for admission to a particular field of study, lose a scholarship, or lose the opportunity to study in the United States. Any of these results could change a student's life forever.

The rhetorical questions in the conclusion ask readers what they think about "campus carry" laws after the information she presented. Using the words "firepower" and "brain power" lays out the two options side by side. Firepower is the physical, violent option. Brain power is the smart, nonviolent option. She clearly wants readers to choose brain power by voting against any law that would allow students to carry guns on campus. If readers don't choose brain power, Gullion fears for the result.

Low-Scoring Essay

The Texas legislature thinks it would be safer if people carried guns everywhere they go, including college classes. Jessica Smartt Gullion disagrees. She has been a college professor for five years. In five years, she has been threatened by students a number of times. She's afraid that if students can carry guns, she might be shot.

Jessica Gullion thinks students might shoot her if she gives them bad grades. She tells stories about two times that she was threatened. One of the students brought a stalker to class with her just to threaten the teacher after getting a bad grade. The stalker might have shot the teacher if guns were allowed. Later, she talks about another stalker who threatened her on Facebook before he was forced to leave the country because his grades were bad.

The writer gives some statistics that show that five percent of college students already carry guns on college campuses. Making it legal, would mean that even more students would carry guns. Although the writer worries about being shot by a student on purpose, she could also worry about being shot accidentally if students try to shoot each other in the classroom.

At the end of the article, the writer asks if teachers will give better grades to students who are armed. She thinks students who get good grades by threatening teachers will make worse citizens than students who are smart and study to get good grades.

COMPUTING YOUR SCORES

Now that you've completed this practice test, it's time to compute your scores. Simply follow the instructions on the following pages, and use the conversion tables provided to calculate your scores. The formulas provided will give you as close an approximation as possible of how you might score on the actual SAT® exam.

To Determine Your Practice Test Scores

1. After you go through each of the test sections (Reading, Writing and Language, Math—No Calculator, and Math—Calculator) and determine which answers you got right, be sure to enter the number of correct answers in the box below the answer key for each of the sections.

2. Your total score on the practice test is the sum of your Evidence-Based Reading and Writing Section score and your Math Section score. To get your total score, convert the raw score—the number of questions you got right in a particular section—into the "scaled score" for that section, and then you'll calculate the total score. It sounds a little confusing, but we'll take you through the steps.

To Calculate Your Evidence-Based Reading and Writing Section Score

Your Evidence-Based Reading and Writing Section score is on a scale of 200–800. First determine your Reading Test score, and then determine your score on the Writing and Language Test.

1. Count the number of correct answers you got on the **Section 1: Reading Test.** Remember that there is no penalty for wrong answers. **The number of correct answers is your raw score.**

2. Go to **Raw Score Conversion Table 1: Section and Test Scores** on page 757. Look in the "Raw Score" column for your raw score, and match it to the number in the "Reading Test Score" column.

3. Do the same with **Section 2: Writing and Language Test** to determine that score.

4. Add your Reading Test score to your Writing and Language Test score.

5. Multiply that number by 10. This is your Evidence-Based Reading and Writing Section score.

To Calculate Your Math Section Score

Your Math score is also on a scale of 200–800.

1. Count the number of correct answers you got on the **Section 3: Math Test—No Calculator** and the **Section 4: Math Test—No Calculator**. Again, there is no penalty for wrong answers. **The number of correct answers is your raw score.**

2. Add the number of correct answers on the Section 3: Math Test—No Calculator and the Section 4: Math Test—No Calculator.

3. Use the **Raw Score Conversion Table 1: Section and Test Scores** on page 757 and convert your raw score into your Math Section score.

To Obtain Your Total Score

Add your score on the Evidence-Based Reading and Writing Section to the Math Section score. This is your total score on this Practice Test, on a scale of 400–1600.

Subscores Provide Additional Information

Subscores offer you greater details about your strengths in certain areas within literacy and math. The subscores are reported on a scale of 1–15 and include Heart of Algebra, Problem Solving and Data Analysis, Passport to Advanced Math, Expression of Ideas, Standard English Conventions, Words in Context, and Command of Evidence.

Heart of Algebra

The **Heart of Algebra subscore** is based on questions from the **Math Test** that focus on linear equations and inequalities.

- Add up your total correct answers from these sections:
  - Math Test—No Calculator: Questions 3, 8–10, 15, 16, 19, 20
  - Math Test—Calculator: Questions 2, 4, 10, 11, 15–17, 19, 30, 32, 34
- Your Raw Score = the total number of correct answers from all of these questions.
- Use the **Raw Score Conversion Table 2: Subscores** on page 758 to determine your **Heart of Algebra** subscore.

Problem Solving and Data Analysis

The **Problem Solving and Data Analysis subscore** is based on questions from the **Math Test** that focus on quantitative reasoning, the interpretation and synthesis of data, and solving problems in rich and varied contexts.

- Add up your total correct answers from these questions:
  - Math Test—No Calculator: none
  - Math Test—Calculator: Questions 1, 5–9, 13, 20, 21, 25, 27–29, 31, 33, 35, 38
- Your Raw Score = the total number of correct answers from all of these questions.
- Use the **Raw Score Conversion Table 2: Subscores** on page 758 to determine your **Problem Solving and Data Analysis** subscore.

Passport to Advanced Math

The **Passport to Advanced Math subscore** is based on questions from the **Math Test** that focus on topics central to your ability to progress to more advanced math, such as understanding the structure of expressions, reasoning with more complex equations, and interpreting and building functions.

- Add up your total correct answers from these questions:
  - Math Test—No Calculator: Questions 1, 2, 4–7, 12, 13, 18
  - Math Test—Calculator: Questions 14, 18, 23, 24, 26, 36, 37
- Your Raw Score = the total number of correct answers from all of these questions.
- Use the **Raw Score Conversion Table 2: Subscores** on page 758 to determine your **Passport to Advanced Math** subscore.

Expression of Ideas

The **Expression of Ideas subscore** is based on questions from the **Writing and Language Test** that focus on topic development, organization, and rhetorically effective use of language.

- Add up your total correct answers from these questions in Section 2: Writing and Language Test:
  - Questions 3, 4, 5, 7, 8, 11, 13, 15, 17, 18, 20, 21, 23, 24, 28, 30, 32–35, 43, 44
- Your Raw Score = the total number of correct answers from all of these questions.
- Use the **Raw Score Conversion Table 2: Subscores** on page 758 to determine your **Expression of Ideas** subscore.

Standard English Conventions

The **Standard English Conventions subscore** is based on questions from the **Writing and Language** Test that focus on sentence structure, usage, and punctuation.

- Add up your total correct answers from these questions in Section 2: Writing and Language Test:
  - Questions 1, 2, 6, 9, 10, 12, 14, 16, 19, 25–27, 29, 36–42
  - Your Raw Score = the total number of correct answers from all of these questions.
- Use the **Raw Score Conversion Table 2: Subscores** on page 758 to determine your **Standard English Conventions** subscore.

Words in Context

The **Words in Context subscore** is based on questions from the **Reading Test** and the **Writing and Language Test** that address word/phrase meaning in context and rhetorical word choice.

- Add up your total correct answers from these questions in Sections 1 and 2:
  - Reading Test: Questions 5, 9, 18, 22, 38, 42, 51, 52
  - Writing and Language Test: Questions 6, 8, 14, 17, 23, 33, 34, 43
- Your Raw Score = the total number of correct answers from all of these questions.
- Use the **Raw Score Conversion Table 2: Subscores** on page 758 to determine your **Words in Context** subscore.

Command of Evidence

The **Command of Evidence subscore** is based on questions from the **Reading Test** and the **Writing and Language Test** that ask you to interpret and use evidence found in a wide range of passages and informational graphics, such as graphs, tables, and charts

- Add up your total correct answers from Sections 1 and 2:
  - Reading Test: Questions 7, 11, 14, 21, 29, 30, 34, 41, 47, 50
  - Writing and Language Test: Questions 4, 11, 15, 31, 32, 40
- Your Raw Score = the total number of correct answers from all of these questions.
- Use the **Raw Score Conversion Table 2: Subscores** on page 758 to determine your **Command of Evidence** subscore.

CROSS-TEST SCORES

The SAT® exam also reports two cross-test scores: Analysis in History/Social Studies and Analysis in Science. These scores are based on questions in the Reading Test, Writing and Language Test, and both Math Tests that ask you to think analytically about texts and questions in these subject areas. Cross-test scores are reported on a scale of 10–40.

Analysis in History/Social Studies

- Add up your total correct answers from these questions:
  - Reading Test: Questions 12–32
  - Writing and Language Test: Questions 3, 4, 11, 15, 22, 35
  - Math Test—No Calculator: None
  - Math Test—Calculator: Questions 3, 6–8, 19, 27–29
- Your Raw Score = the total number of correct answers from all of these questions.
- Use the **Raw Score Conversion Table 3: Cross-Test Scores** on page 759 to determine your Analysis in History/Social Studies cross-test score.

Analysis in Science

- Add up your total correct answers from these questions:
  - Reading Test: Questions 1–11, 33–42
  - Writing and Language Test: Questions 23, 24, 28, 30, 32, 33
  - Math Test—No Calculator: Questions 7, 12
  - Math Test—Calculator: Questions 5, 10, 11, 25, 31, 38
- Your Raw Score = the total number of correct answers from all of these questions.
- Use the **Raw Score Conversion Table 3: Cross-Test Scores** on page 759 to determine your Analysis in Science cross-test score.

Raw Score Conversion Table 1: Section and Test Scores

Raw Score	Math Section Score	Reading Test Score	Writing and Language Test Score	Raw Score	Math Section Score	Reading Test Score	Writing and Language Test Score	Raw Score	Math Section Score	Reading Test Score	Writing and Language Test Score
0	200	10	10	20	450	22	23	40	610	33	36
1	200	10	10	21	460	23	23	41	620	33	37
2	210	10	10	22	470	23	24	42	630	34	38
3	230	11	10	23	480	24	25	43	640	35	39
4	240	12	11	24	480	24	25	44	650	35	40
5	260	13	12	25	490	25	26	45	660	36	
6	280	14	13	26	500	25	26	46	670	37	
7	290	15	13	27	510	26	27	47	670	37	
8	310	15	14	28	520	26	28	48	680	38	
9	320	16	15	29	520	27	28	49	690	38	
10	330	17	16	30	530	28	29	50	700	39	
11	340	17	16	31	540	28	30	51	710	40	
12	360	18	17	32	550	29	30	52	730	40	
13	370	19	18	33	560	29	31	53	740		
14	380	19	19	34	560	30	32	54	750		
15	390	20	19	35	570	30	32	55	760		
16	410	20	20	36	580	31	33	56	780		
17	420	21	21	37	590	31	34	57	790		
18	430	21	21	38	600	32	34	58	800		
19	440	22	22	39	600	32	35				

Conversion Equation 1 Section and Test Scores

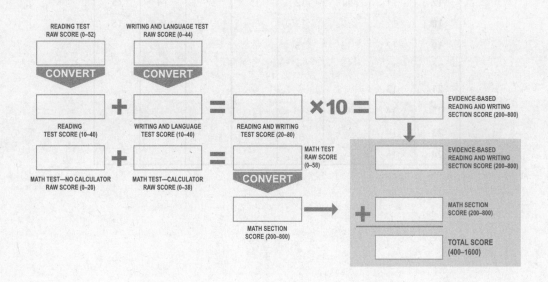

Computing Your Scores

RAW SCORE CONVERSION TABLE 2: SUBSCORES

Raw Score (# of correct answers)	Expression of Ideas	Standard English Conventions	Heart of Algebra	Problem Solving and Data Analysis	Passport to Advanced Math	Words in Context	Command of Evidence
0	1	1	1	1	1	1	1
1	1	1	1	1	3	1	1
2	1	1	2	2	5	2	2
3	2	2	3	3	6	3	3
4	3	2	4	4	7	4	4
5	4	3	5	5	8	5	5
6	5	4	6	6	9	6	6
7	6	5	6	7	10	6	7
8	6	6	7	8	11	7	8
9	7	6	8	8	11	8	8
10	7	7	8	9	12	8	9
11	8	7	9	10	12	9	10
12	8	8	9	10	13	9	10
13	9	8	9	11	13	10	11
14	9	9	10	12	14	11	12
15	10	10	10	13	14	12	13
16	10	10	11	14	15	13	14
17	11	11	12	15		14	15
18	11	12	13			15	15
19	12	13	15				
20	12	15					
21	13						
22	14						
23	14						
24	15						

CONVERSION EQUATION 2 SUBSCORES

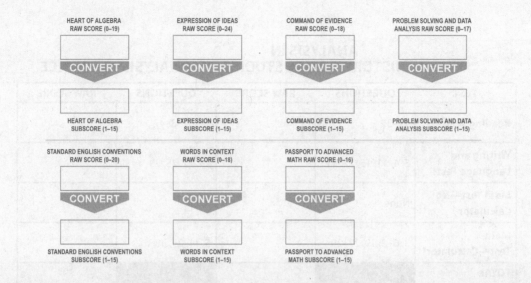

HEART OF ALGEBRA RAW SCORE (0–19)	EXPRESSION OF IDEAS RAW SCORE (0–24)	COMMAND OF EVIDENCE RAW SCORE (0–18)	PROBLEM SOLVING AND DATA ANALYSIS RAW SCORE (0–17)
CONVERT	CONVERT	CONVERT	CONVERT
HEART OF ALGEBRA SUBSCORE (1–15)	EXPRESSION OF IDEAS SUBSCORE (1–15)	COMMAND OF EVIDENCE SUBSCORE (1–15)	PROBLEM SOLVING AND DATA ANALYSIS SUBSCORE (1–15)

STANDARD ENGLISH CONVENTIONS RAW SCORE (0–20)	WORDS IN CONTEXT RAW SCORE (0–18)	PASSPORT TO ADVANCED MATH RAW SCORE (0–16)
CONVERT	CONVERT	CONVERT
STANDARD ENGLISH CONVENTIONS SUBSCORE (1–15)	WORDS IN CONTEXT SUBSCORE (1–15)	PASSPORT TO ADVANCED MATH SUBSCORE (1–15)

RAW SCORE CONVERSION TABLE 3: CROSS-TEST SCORES

Raw Score (# of correct answers)	Analysis in History/Social Studies Cross-Test Score	Analysis in Science Cross-Test Score	Raw Score (# of correct answers)	Analysis in History/Social Studies Cross-Test Score	Analysis in Science Cross-Test Score
0	10	10	18	28	26
1	10	11	19	29	27
2	11	12	20	30	27
3	12	13	21	30	28
4	14	14	22	31	29
5	15	15	23	32	30
6	16	16	24	32	30
7	17	17	25	33	31
8	18	18	26	34	32
9	20	19	27	35	33
10	21	20	28	35	33
11	22	20	29	36	34
12	23	21	30	37	35
13	24	22	31	38	36
14	25	23	32	38	37
15	26	24	33	39	38
16	27	24	34	40	39
17	28	25	35	40	40

CONVERSION EQUATION 3: CROSS-TEST SCORES

TEST	ANALYSIS IN HISTORY/SOCIAL STUDIES		ANALYSIS IN SCIENCE	
	QUESTIONS	RAW SCORE	QUESTIONS	RAW SCORE
Reading Test	12–32		1–11, 33–42	
Writing and Language Test	3, 4, 11, 15, 22, 35		19, 22, 25, 29	
Math Test—No Calculator	None		7, 12	
Math Test—Calculator	3, 6–8, 19, 27–29		5, 11, 25, 38	
TOTAL				

ANALYSIS IN HISTORY/
SOCIAL STUDIES
RAW SCORE (0–35)

CONVERT

ANALYSIS IN HISTORY/
SOCIAL STUDIES
CROSS-TEST SCORE (10–40)

ANALYSIS IN SCIENCE
RAW SCORE (0–35)

CONVERT

ANALYSIS IN SCIENCE
CROSS-TEST SCORE (10–40)

Section 1: Reading Test

1. Ⓐ Ⓑ Ⓒ Ⓓ	12. Ⓐ Ⓑ Ⓒ Ⓓ	23. Ⓐ Ⓑ Ⓒ Ⓓ	33. Ⓐ Ⓑ Ⓒ Ⓓ	43. Ⓐ Ⓑ Ⓒ Ⓓ
2. Ⓐ Ⓑ Ⓒ Ⓓ	13. Ⓐ Ⓑ Ⓒ Ⓓ	24. Ⓐ Ⓑ Ⓒ Ⓓ	34. Ⓐ Ⓑ Ⓒ Ⓓ	44. Ⓐ Ⓑ Ⓒ Ⓓ
3. Ⓐ Ⓑ Ⓒ Ⓓ	14. Ⓐ Ⓑ Ⓒ Ⓓ	25. Ⓐ Ⓑ Ⓒ Ⓓ	35. Ⓐ Ⓑ Ⓒ Ⓓ	45. Ⓐ Ⓑ Ⓒ Ⓓ
4. Ⓐ Ⓑ Ⓒ Ⓓ	15. Ⓐ Ⓑ Ⓒ Ⓓ	26. Ⓐ Ⓑ Ⓒ Ⓓ	36. Ⓐ Ⓑ Ⓒ Ⓓ	46. Ⓐ Ⓑ Ⓒ Ⓓ
5. Ⓐ Ⓑ Ⓒ Ⓓ	16. Ⓐ Ⓑ Ⓒ Ⓓ	27. Ⓐ Ⓑ Ⓒ Ⓓ	37. Ⓐ Ⓑ Ⓒ Ⓓ	47. Ⓐ Ⓑ Ⓒ Ⓓ
6. Ⓐ Ⓑ Ⓒ Ⓓ	17. Ⓐ Ⓑ Ⓒ Ⓓ	28. Ⓐ Ⓑ Ⓒ Ⓓ	38. Ⓐ Ⓑ Ⓒ Ⓓ	48. Ⓐ Ⓑ Ⓒ Ⓓ
7. Ⓐ Ⓑ Ⓒ Ⓓ	18. Ⓐ Ⓑ Ⓒ Ⓓ	29. Ⓐ Ⓑ Ⓒ Ⓓ	39. Ⓐ Ⓑ Ⓒ Ⓓ	49. Ⓐ Ⓑ Ⓒ Ⓓ
8. Ⓐ Ⓑ Ⓒ Ⓓ	19. Ⓐ Ⓑ Ⓒ Ⓓ	30. Ⓐ Ⓑ Ⓒ Ⓓ	40. Ⓐ Ⓑ Ⓒ Ⓓ	50. Ⓐ Ⓑ Ⓒ Ⓓ
9. Ⓐ Ⓑ Ⓒ Ⓓ	20. Ⓐ Ⓑ Ⓒ Ⓓ	31. Ⓐ Ⓑ Ⓒ Ⓓ	41. Ⓐ Ⓑ Ⓒ Ⓓ	51. Ⓐ Ⓑ Ⓒ Ⓓ
10. Ⓐ Ⓑ Ⓒ Ⓓ	21. Ⓐ Ⓑ Ⓒ Ⓓ	32. Ⓐ Ⓑ Ⓒ Ⓓ	42. Ⓐ Ⓑ Ⓒ Ⓓ	52. Ⓐ Ⓑ Ⓒ Ⓓ
11. Ⓐ Ⓑ Ⓒ Ⓓ	22. Ⓐ Ⓑ Ⓒ Ⓓ			

Section 2: Writing and Language Test

1. Ⓐ Ⓑ Ⓒ Ⓓ	10. Ⓐ Ⓑ Ⓒ Ⓓ	19. Ⓐ Ⓑ Ⓒ Ⓓ	28. Ⓐ Ⓑ Ⓒ Ⓓ	37. Ⓐ Ⓑ Ⓒ Ⓓ
2. Ⓐ Ⓑ Ⓒ Ⓓ	11. Ⓐ Ⓑ Ⓒ Ⓓ	20. Ⓐ Ⓑ Ⓒ Ⓓ	29. Ⓐ Ⓑ Ⓒ Ⓓ	38. Ⓐ Ⓑ Ⓒ Ⓓ
3. Ⓐ Ⓑ Ⓒ Ⓓ	12. Ⓐ Ⓑ Ⓒ Ⓓ	21. Ⓐ Ⓑ Ⓒ Ⓓ	30. Ⓐ Ⓑ Ⓒ Ⓓ	39. Ⓐ Ⓑ Ⓒ Ⓓ
4. Ⓐ Ⓑ Ⓒ Ⓓ	13. Ⓐ Ⓑ Ⓒ Ⓓ	22. Ⓐ Ⓑ Ⓒ Ⓓ	31. Ⓐ Ⓑ Ⓒ Ⓓ	40. Ⓐ Ⓑ Ⓒ Ⓓ
5. Ⓐ Ⓑ Ⓒ Ⓓ	14. Ⓐ Ⓑ Ⓒ Ⓓ	23. Ⓐ Ⓑ Ⓒ Ⓓ	32. Ⓐ Ⓑ Ⓒ Ⓓ	41. Ⓐ Ⓑ Ⓒ Ⓓ
6. Ⓐ Ⓑ Ⓒ Ⓓ	15. Ⓐ Ⓑ Ⓒ Ⓓ	24. Ⓐ Ⓑ Ⓒ Ⓓ	33. Ⓐ Ⓑ Ⓒ Ⓓ	42. Ⓐ Ⓑ Ⓒ Ⓓ
7. Ⓐ Ⓑ Ⓒ Ⓓ	16. Ⓐ Ⓑ Ⓒ Ⓓ	25. Ⓐ Ⓑ Ⓒ Ⓓ	34. Ⓐ Ⓑ Ⓒ Ⓓ	43. Ⓐ Ⓑ Ⓒ Ⓓ
8. Ⓐ Ⓑ Ⓒ Ⓓ	17. Ⓐ Ⓑ Ⓒ Ⓓ	26. Ⓐ Ⓑ Ⓒ Ⓓ	35. Ⓐ Ⓑ Ⓒ Ⓓ	44. Ⓐ Ⓑ Ⓒ Ⓓ
9. Ⓐ Ⓑ Ⓒ Ⓓ	18. Ⓐ Ⓑ Ⓒ Ⓓ	27. Ⓐ Ⓑ Ⓒ Ⓓ	36. Ⓐ Ⓑ Ⓒ Ⓓ	

Section 3: Math Test—No Calculator

1. Ⓐ Ⓑ Ⓒ Ⓓ	4. Ⓐ Ⓑ Ⓒ Ⓓ	7. Ⓐ Ⓑ Ⓒ Ⓓ	10. Ⓐ Ⓑ Ⓒ Ⓓ	13. Ⓐ Ⓑ Ⓒ Ⓓ
2. Ⓐ Ⓑ Ⓒ Ⓓ	5. Ⓐ Ⓑ Ⓒ Ⓓ	8. Ⓐ Ⓑ Ⓒ Ⓓ	11. Ⓐ Ⓑ Ⓒ Ⓓ	14. Ⓐ Ⓑ Ⓒ Ⓓ
3. Ⓐ Ⓑ Ⓒ Ⓓ	6. Ⓐ Ⓑ Ⓒ Ⓓ	9. Ⓐ Ⓑ Ⓒ Ⓓ	12. Ⓐ Ⓑ Ⓒ Ⓓ	15. Ⓐ Ⓑ Ⓒ Ⓓ

Practice Test 3 — ANSWERS

Section 3: Math Test—No Calculator

16. [grid-in answer box] 17. [grid-in answer box] 18. [grid-in answer box] 19. [grid-in answer box] 20. [grid-in answer box]

Section 4: Math Test—Calculator

1. A B C D   7. A B C D   13. A B C D   19. A B C D   25. A B C D
2. A B C D   8. A B C D   14. A B C D   20. A B C D   26. A B C D
3. A B C D   9. A B C D   15. A B C D   21. A B C D   27. A B C D
4. A B C D   10. A B C D   16. A B C D   22. A B C D   28. A B C D
5. A B C D   11. A B C D   17. A B C D   23. A B C D   29. A B C D
6. A B C D   12. A B C D   18. A B C D   24. A B C D   30. A B C D

31. [grid-in answer box] 32. [grid-in answer box] 33. [grid-in answer box] 34. [grid-in answer box] 35. [grid-in answer box]

36. [grid-in answer box] 37. [grid-in answer box] 38. [grid-in answer box]

Section 5: Essay

SECTION 1: READING TEST

65 Minutes—52 Questions

TURN TO SECTION 1 OF YOUR ANSWER SHEET TO ANSWER THE QUESTIONS IN THIS SECTION.

> **DIRECTIONS:** Each passage (or pair of passages) in this section is followed by a number of multiple-choice questions. After reading each passage, select the best answer to each question based on what is stated or implied in the passage or passages and in any supplementary material, such as a table, graph, chart, or photograph.

Questions 1–11 are based on the following passage.

The U.S. Geological Survey (USGS) is a government agency whose goal is to provide reliable scientific information about the Earth, including minimizing loss from natural disasters. This excerpt is from the organization's website. For the full passage, please visit http://earthquake.usgs.gov/learn.

Earthquakes, Megaquakes, and the Movies

Throughout the history of Hollywood, disaster films have been sure-fire winners for moviemakers. ... With amazing special effects, it's easy to get caught up in the
Line fantasy disaster epic. What makes a great science fantasy
5 film often bears no relation to real facts or the hazards people truly face.

The U.S. Geological Survey is the lead federal agency responsible for researching, monitoring and forecasting geologic hazards such as earthquakes,
10 volcanoes and landslides. ... Let's start with some **science-based information** on earthquakes.

Earthquakes are naturally occurring events outside the powers of humans to create or stop. An earthquake is caused by a sudden slip on a fault, much
15 like what happens when you snap your fingers. Before the snap, you push your fingers together and sideways. Because you are pushing them together, friction keeps them from slipping. When you apply enough stress to overcome this friction, your fingers move suddenly,
20 releasing energy. The same "stick-slip" process goes on in the earth. Stresses in the Earth's outer layer push the sides of the fault together. The friction across the surface of the fault holds the rocks together so they do not slip immediately when pushed sideways. Eventually enough
25 stress builds up and the rocks slip suddenly, releasing energy in waves that travel through the rock to cause the shaking that we feel during an earthquake.

Earthquakes typically originate several to tens of miles below the surface of the Earth. It takes
30 decades to centuries to build up enough stress to make a large earthquake, and the fault may be tens to hundreds of miles long. People cannot prevent earthquakes from happening or stop them once they've started— giant nuclear explosions at shallow depths, like those
35 in some movies, won't actually stop an earthquake.

It's well known that California, the Pacific Northwest, and Alaska all have frequent earthquakes, some of which are quite damaging. Some areas of the country are more at risk than others, but, in fact, **42 of
40 the 50 states could experience damaging ground shaking** from an earthquake in 50 years (which is the typical lifetime of a building), and 16 states have a relatively high likelihood of experiencing damaging ground shaking.

45 **The two most important variables affecting earthquake damage are the intensity of ground shaking and the quality of the engineering of structures in the region.** The level of shaking is controlled by the proximity of the earthquake source
50 to the affected region and the types of rocks that seismic waves pass through en route (particularly those at or near the ground surface). Generally, the bigger and closer the earthquake, the stronger the shaking. But there have been large earthquakes with
55 very little damage because they caused little shaking or because the buildings were built to withstand that shaking. In other cases, moderate earthquakes have caused significant damage because the shaking was locally amplified, or because the structures were
60 poorly engineered.

The idea of a "Mega-Quake"—an earthquake of magnitude 10 or larger—is very unlikely. Earthquake magnitude is based in part on the length of faults— the longer the fault, the larger the earthquake. **The
65 simple truth is that there are no known faults capable of generating a magnitude 10 or larger "mega-quake."** ...

Then there's this business of California falling off into the ocean. NOT TRUE! The ocean is not a

CONTINUE

70 great hole into which California can fall, but is itself land at a somewhat lower elevation with water above it. It's impossible that California will be swept out to sea. Instead, southwestern California is moving slowly (2 inches per year) towards Alaska. 15 million years (and many earth-
75 quakes) from now, Los Angeles and San Francisco will be next-door neighbors.

Another popular cinematic and literary device is a fault that opens during an earthquake to swallow up an inconvenient character. But the ground moves parallel to
80 a fault during an earthquake, not away from it. If the fault could open, there would be no friction. Without friction, there would be no earthquake. Shallow crevasses can form during earthquake-induced landslides, lateral spreads, or other types of ground failures. **Faults, however, do not**
85 **gape open during an earthquake.**

So when you see the next big disaster film, rest assured that movies are just entertainment. Enjoy them! And then go learn about the real-world science behind disasters, and if you live in an area where hazards exist,
90 take the suggested steps to protect you and your family.

1 Which of the following best describes the author's purpose in writing this article?

A. To counter the myths about earthquakes driven by fictional films

B. To explain to people the causes and effects of earthquakes

C. To show how Hollywood distorts science

D. To give people advice about what to do if an earthquake strikes

2 According to the passage, earthquakes are caused mainly by

A. the existence of faults in the earth's crust.

B. stresses in the earth's crust that cause a fault to slip.

C. two faults in the earth's crust pressing against each other.

D. the quality of the engineering of structures in the region.

3 Who is the target audience of the article?

A. The general public

B. Scientists

C. Filmmakers

D. Science teachers

4 How does the article counter the claim that in the future part of California may fall off into the ocean?

A. It states that it would be a disaster.

B. It states that sea level rise will prevent it.

C. It explains the similarity between California and Alaska.

D. It explains how the ocean is just land covered by water.

5 Which choice provides the best evidence for the answer to the previous question?

A. Lines 69–71 ("The ocean . . . above it.")

B. Lines 71–72 ("It's impossible . . . out to sea.")

C. Lines 72–74 ("Instead, southwestern . . . towards Alaska.")

D. Lines 74–76 ("15 million years . . . neighbors.")

6 As used in line 25, "stress" most nearly means

A. anxiety.

B. weight.

C. pressure.

D. emphasis

7 In 1989, an earthquake caused extensive damage to San Francisco, California. Based only on information in the article, this most likely occurred because

  A. The earthquake source was very near the affected region and the buildings were poorly constructed.

  B. San Francisco has had earthquakes many times before, and they were all destructive.

  C. City officials never thought the city would experience an earthquake, so they were unprepared.

  D. The faults were deep and numerous across the country.

8 Which choice provides the best evidence for the answer to the previous question?

  A. Lines 13–22 ("An earthquake is . . . the fault together.")

  B. Lines 28–32 ("Earthquakes typically . . . miles long.")

  C. Lines 45–48 ("The two most important . . . in the region.")

  D. Lines 79–81 ("But the ground . . . be no friction.")

9 In line 59, "amplified" most nearly means

  A. lifted.

  B. supplemented.

  C. intensified.

  D. made louder.

10 How does the use of the phrase "inconvenient character" (line 79) affect the tone of the passage?

  A. It reveals a negative attitude about unscientific data.

  B. It illustrates a mocking tone toward how the storylines are written.

  C. It reveals a scholarly attitude about science.

  D. It communicates a warning about inaccurate scientific information.

11 How does the author refute the idea that an earthquake could cause the earth to open up and swallow people and things?

  A. By pointing out that the idea of the earth opening up is portrayed in movies

  B. By noting that there are no known faults capable of producing a "mega-quake"

  C. By explaining that the ground moves parallel to a fault during an earthquake

  D. By suggesting that subsequent landslides can cause crevasses to open up

CONTINUE

Questions 12–22 are based on the following passages and supplementary material.

After the Constitution was drafted, it had to be ratified by at least nine of the thirteen states. The following two passages illustrate the debate over ratification.

Passage 1 is from Patrick Henry's speech, made as governor of Virginia on June 5, 1778, at the state's convention to ratify the constitution. Passage 2 is from an essay written by James Madison, which first appeared in a New York newspaper on June 6, 1788, and later became part of what is now known as the Federalist Papers.

PASSAGE 1

If you make the citizens of this country agree to become the subjects of one great consolidated empire of America, your government will not have sufficient

Line
5   energy to keep them together. Such a government is incompatible with the genius of republicanism. There will be no checks, no real balances, in this government. What can avail your specious, imaginary balances, your rope-dancing, chain-rattling ridiculous ideal checks and contrivances? But, sir, "we are not feared by foreigners;

10   we do not make nations tremble." Would this constitute happiness or secure liberty? I trust, sir, our political hemisphere will ever direct their operations to the security of those objects.

This Constitution is said to have beautiful features;

15   but when I come to examine these features, sir, they appear to me horribly frightful. Among other deformities, it has an awful squinting; it squints toward monarchy, and does not this raise indignation in the breast of every true American? Your president may easily become king.

20   Your Senate is so imperfectly constructed that your dearest rights may be sacrificed to what may be a small minority; and a very small minority may continue for ever unchangeably this government, altho horridly defective. Where are your checks in this government? Your strong-

25   holds will be in the hands of your enemies. It is on a supposition that your American governors shall be honest that all the good qualities of this government are founded; but its defective and imperfect construction puts it in their power to perpetrate the worst of mischiefs should they

30   be bad men; and, sir, would not all the world, blame our distracted folly in resting our rights upon the contingency of our rulers being good or bad? Show me that age and country where the rights and liberties of the people were placed on the sole chance of their rulers being good men

35   without a consequent loss of liberty! I say that the loss of that dearest privilege has ever followed, with absolute certainty, every such mad attempt.

PASSAGE 2

In order to lay a due foundation for that separate and distinct exercise of the different powers of government,

40   which to a certain extent is admitted on all hands to be essential to the preservation of liberty; it is evident that each department should have a will of its own; and consequently should be so constituted that the members of each should have as little agency as possible in the

45   appointment of the members of the others …. It is equally evident that the members of each department should be as little dependent as possible on those of the others for the emoluments annexed to their offices. Were the executive magistrate, or the judges, not independent of the

50   legislature in this particular, their independence in every other would be merely nominal. But the great security against a gradual concentration of the several powers in the same department, consists in giving to those who administer each department the necessary constitutional

55   means and personal motives to resist encroachments of the others. The provision for defense must in this, as in all other cases, be made commensurate to the danger of attack. Ambition must be made to counteract ambition. The interest of the man must be connected with the

60   constitutional rights of the place. It may be a reflection on human nature, that such devices should be necessary to control the abuses of government. But what is government itself, but the greatest of all reflections on human nature? If men were angels, no government would be

65   necessary. If angels were to govern men, neither external nor internal controls on government would be necessary. In framing a government which is to be administered by men over men, the great difficulty lies in this: you must first enable the government to control the governed; and

70   in the next place oblige it to control itself. A dependence on the people is, no doubt, the primary control on the government; but experience has taught mankind the necessity of auxiliary precautions.

12 Which of the following best represents the differences in point of view of the authors of the two passages?

- **A.** Henry was concerned about the balance of power, and Madison was concerned about concentration of wealth.

- **B.** Henry worried about too much power in the hands of the government, and Madison worried about too much power in any one branch of government.

- **C.** Henry was focused on states' rights, and Madison was focused on adding the Bill of Rights to the Constitution.

- **D.** Henry was afraid of a return to monarchy, and Madison was afraid of government corruption.

13 Which represents the best summary of Patrick Henry's objection to the drafted Constitution?

- **A.** It overemphasizes the need for checks and balances.

- **B.** It leaves too much power in the hands of the people.

- **C.** It does not centralize power enough.

- **D.** It makes government dependent on people who are flawed.

14 Which of the following rhetorical choices is made by Henry and not by Madison?

- **A.** Second-person voice

- **B.** Passive voice

- **C.** Questions

- **D.** Alliteration

15 What was Madison's strongest counterargument to those who were concerned about a strong central government?

- **A.** Government must reflect human nature.

- **B.** People are drastically flawed and can never be trusted.

- **C.** People would have no influence over their government.

- **D.** As long as the powers are separated, power will not be concentrated.

"GIVE ME LIBERTY, OR GIVE ME DEATH !"
PATRICK HENRY delivering his great speech on the Rights of the Colonies, before the Virginia Assembly.

CONTINUE

16 Which choice provides the best evidence for the answer to the previous question?

A. Lines 51–56 ("But the great . . . of the others.")

B. Lines 62–64 ("But what is . . . nature?")

C. Lines 64–65 ("If men were . . . would be necessary.")

D. Lines 70–73 ("A dependence on . . . auxiliary precautions.")

17 What do these two statements show about how their authors viewed human nature?

Henry, lines 32–35: "Show me that age and country where the rights and liberties of the people were placed on the sole chance of their rulers being good men without a consequent loss of liberty!

Madison, lines 65–66: "If angels were to govern men, neither external nor internal controls on government would be necessary."

A. Henry and Madison both believed that people are too flawed to be trusted with complete control.

B. Henry and Madison both believed rulers do not care about the rights and liberties of the people they govern.

C. Henry didn't trust ordinary people to be rulers, and Madison believed all people could be trusted to wield complete control.

D. Henry believed that government is unnecessary for a free people, and Madison believed that government needs to be regulated.

18 In lines 9–10, Henry suggests that he believes the framers of the Constitution felt a need to

A. display their power to Americans.

B. intimidate other countries.

C. secure happiness and liberty.

D. build strong international relationships.

19 Based on the information in this passage, what kind of government does Henry think is best?

A. Monarch

B. Republic

C. Autocracy

D. Plutocracy

20 Which choice provides the best evidence for the answer to the previous question?

A. Lines 2–3 ("one great . . . of America.")

B. Line 5 ("the genius . . . republicanism.")

C. Line 17 ("it squints . . . monarchy")

D. Line 19 ("Your president . . . become king.")

21 As it is used in line 42, "department" most nearly means

A. executive.

B. territory.

C. level.

D. branch.

22 As used in line 57, "commensurate" most nearly means

A. proportional.

B. provisional.

C. dependent.

D. relevant.

This article is excerpted from the National Oceanic and Atmospheric Administration Fisheries website (NOAA). The public agency provides science news and scientific findings related to the Earth and the Earth's atmosphere. This article describes the finding of a tiny, rare shark. For the full passage, please visit www.nmfs.noaa.gov/stories.

NOAA and Tulane researchers identify second possible specimen ever found.

A very small and rare species of shark is swimming its way through scientific literature. But don't worry, the chances of this inches-long vertebrate biting through your
Line swimsuit is extremely slim, because if you ever spotted
5 one, you'd be the third person to ever do so.

This species common name is the "pocket shark," though those in the field of classifying animals refer to it by its scientific name *Mollisquama* sp., according to a new study published in the international journal of taxonomy
10 *Zootaxa*. While it is small enough to, yes, fit in your pocket, it's dubbed "pocket" because of the distinctive orifice above the pectoral fin—one of many physiological features scientists hope to better understand.

"The pocket shark we found was only 5 and a half
15 inches long, and was a recently born male," said Mark Grace of NOAA Fisheries' Pascagoula, Miss., Laboratory, lead author of the new study, who noted the shark displayed an unhealed umbilical scar. "Discovering him has us thinking about where mom and dad may be, and how they got to
20 the Gulf. The only other known specimen was found very far away, off Peru, 36 years ago."

Interestingly, the specimen Grace discovered wasn't found in the ocean, per se, but rather in the holdings of NOAA's lab in Pascagoula. It was collected in the deep sea
25 about 190 miles offshore Louisiana during a 2010 mission by the NOAA Ship *Pisces* to study sperm whale feeding. Grace, who was part of that mission after the rare shark was collected, and upon uncovering the sample at the lab years later, recruited Tulane University researchers Michael
30 Doosey and Henry Bart, and NOAA Ocean Service genetics expert Gavin Naylor, to give the specimen an up-close examination.

A tissue sample was collected, and by tapping into the robust specimen collection of Tulane University's
35 Biodiversity Research Institute, scientists were able to place the specimen into the genus *Mollisquama*. Further genetic analysis from Naylor indicates that pocket sharks are closely related to the kitefin and cookie cutter species, fellow members of the shark family *Dalatiidae*. Like other

40 *Dalatiidae* shark species it is possible that pocket sharks when hungry may remove an oval plug of flesh from their prey (various marine mammals, large fishes, and squid).

The specimen is part of the Royal D. Suttkus Fish Collection at Tulane University's Biodiversity Research
45 Institute in Belle Chasse, La., and it is hoped that further study of the specimen will lead to many new discoveries. Already, the specimen—when compared to the 1979 specimen taxonomic description—is found to have a series of glands along the abdomen not previously noted.
50 Partners at the Smithsonian National Museum of Natural History in Washington, D.C., and American Natural History Museum in New York City have also contributed to the study of this shark.

"This record of such an unusual and extremely rare
55 fish is exciting, but it's also an important reminder that we still have much to learn about the species that inhabit our oceans," Grace added.

---

23 What does the article illustrate about how scientific information is gathered?

A. Multiple scientific institutions are needed to form any strong scientific conclusion.

B. Luck plays an essential role whenever scientists work to gather information.

C. All scientific research is recorded in journals.

D. Scientists in different locations often share their findings.

---

24 According to the passage, the pocket shark got its name because of

A. its small size.

B. the orifice near its fin.

C. the way it can be carried in a pocket.

D. its markings that resemble pockets.

---

25 The author indicates that the most likely key to determining how the pocket shark ended up in the Gulf would be

A. a study of the area around the Gulf.

B. a comparison between the Gulf and Peru.

C. a study of sharks native to the Gulf.

D. the discovery of its parents.

CONTINUE

26 Which choice provides the best evidence for the answer to the previous question?

- A. Lines 14–15 ("The pocket . . . born male")
- B. Lines 15–18 ("Mark Grace . . . scar.")
- C. Lines 18–21 ("Discovering . . . ago.")
- D. Lines 22–24 ("Interestingly . . . Pascagoula.")

27 According to the passage, what information was most important in determining the species of the shark?

- A. The length of the shark
- B. The "pocket" feature that made it unique
- C. Tissue samples to provide genetic information
- D. Its position in the food chain

28 How did scientists determine the age of the pocket fish they found?

- A. The number of lines on the fins
- B. Its size in comparison to other pocket fish
- C. Its size in comparison to other fish found in the same area
- D. A scar

29 According to the passage, scientists were so excited about finding a pocket shark because the sharks are

- A. evidence of a new family of sharks.
- B. the only known species that has pockets.
- C. proof that a single breed can live in vastly different waters.
- D. so unique and so few of them have been found.

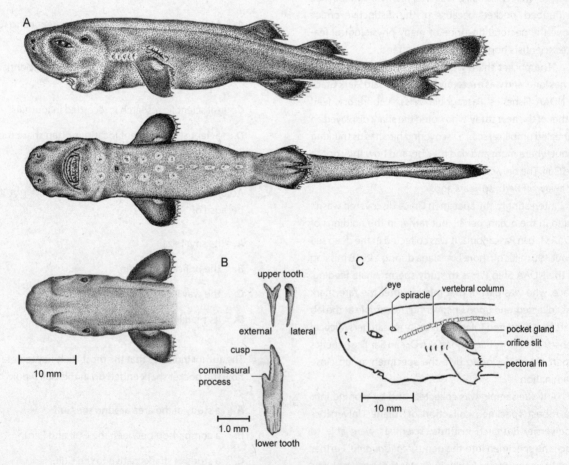

Credit: Dr. Mark Grace, Zootaxa 3948 (3): 587–600

30 Which choice provides the best evidence for the answer to the previous question?

A. Lines 20–21 ("The only . . . years ago.")

B. Lines 27–28 ("Grace . . . collected")

C. Lines 36–39 ("Further genetic . . . *Dalatiidae*")

D. Lines 54–57 ("This record . . . added.")

31 Based on its use in line 34, "robust" most nearly means

A. typical.

B. healthy.

C. varied.

D. distinguished.

32 According to the passage, kitefin sharks

A. eat oval-shape pieces of flesh.

B. do not feed on squid.

C. are identical to pocket sharks.

D. were discovered after pocket sharks.

Questions 33–42 are based on the following passage.

The following passage is excerpted from Mark Twain's essay, *"Fenimore Cooper's Literary Offenses"* (1895). James Fenimore Cooper (1789–1851) was a popular writer whose works were published in the first half of the 19th century.

[James Fenimore] Cooper's art has some defects. In one place in *Deerslayer*, and in the restricted space of two-thirds of a page, Cooper has scored 114 offences against

Line literary art out of a possible 115.

5 . . . In his little box of stage properties he kept six or eight cunning devices. A favorite one was to make a moccasined person tread in the tracks of the moccasined enemy, and thus hide his own trail. Cooper wore out barrels and barrels of moccasins in working that trick.

10 Another stage-property that he pulled out of his box pretty frequently was his broken twig. Every time a Cooper person is in peril, and absolute silence is worth four dollars a minute, he is sure to step on a dry twig. There may be a hundred handier things to step on, but . . . Cooper requires

15 him to turn out and find a dry twig; and if he can't do it, go and borrow one. In fact, the Leather Stocking Series ought to have been called the Broken Twig Series.

If Cooper had any real knowledge of Nature's ways of doing things, he had a most delicate art in concealing the

20 fact. For instance: one of his acute Indian experts, Chingachgook (pronounced Chicago, I think), has lost the trail of a person he is tracking through the forest. Neither you nor I could ever have guessed out the way to find it. It was very different with Chicago. He turned a running stream out

25 of its course, and there, in the slush in its old bed, were that person's moccasin-tracks. The current did not wash them away, as it would have done in all other like cases—no, even the eternal laws of Nature have to vacate when Cooper wants to put up a delicate job of woodcraft on the reader.

30 . . . In the *Deerslayer* tale, Cooper has a stream which is fifty feet wide where it flows out of a lake; it narrows to twenty as it meanders along for no given reason; and yet when a stream acts like that it ought to be required to explain itself. Cooper narrowed it to less than twenty to

35 accommodate some Indians. He bends a "sapling" to the form of an arch over this narrow passage, and conceals six Indians in its foliage. They are "laying" for a settler's scow or ark, which is coming up the stream on its way to the lake. Its rate of progress cannot be more than a mile an hour.

40 The ark is one hundred and forty feet long; the dwelling is ninety feet long. The idea of the Indians is to drop softly and secretly from the arched sapling as the

CONTINUE

ark creeps along under it. It will take the ark a minute and a half to pass under. It will take the ninety-foot
45 dwelling a minute to pass under. Now, then, what did the six Indians do? It would take you thirty years to guess. Their chief warily watched the canal-boat as it squeezed along under him, and when he had got his calculations fined down to exactly the right shade,
50 as he judged, he let go and dropped. And missed the house! He missed the house and landed in the stern of the scow. It was not much of a fall, yet it knocked him silly. He lay there unconscious. If the house had been ninety-seven feet long he would have made the trip.
55 The fault was Cooper's, not his. There still remained in the roost five Indians.

The boat has passed under and is now out of their reach. Let me explain what the five did—you would not be able to reason it out for yourself. No. 1 jumped for the
60 boat, but fell in the water astern of it. Then No. 2 jumped for the boat, but fell in the water still farther astern of it. Then No. 3 jumped for the boat and fell a good way astern of it. Then No. 4 jumped for the boat and fell in the water away astern. Then even No. 5 made a jump for
65 the boat—for he was a Cooper Indian. . . .

I may be mistaken, but it does seem to me that *Deerslayer* is not a work of art in any sense; it does seem to me that it is destitute of every detail that goes to the making of a work of art; in truth, it seems to me that
70 *Deerslayer* is just simply a literary delirium tremens.

33 The main purpose of the third paragraph is to

   A. point out flaws in Cooper's arguments.

   B. mock Cooper's inability to write about nature.

   C. criticize Cooper's treatment of Native Americans.

   D. explain how Cooper described a stream bed in one of his stories.

34 Which of the following words best describes the tone of Twain's critique?

   A. Exhausted

   B. Scholarly

   C. Cheery

   D. Humorous

35 Which choice provides the best evidence for the answer to the previous question?

   A. Lines 3–4 ("Cooper has . . . possible 115.")

   B. Lines 8–9 ("Cooper wore . . . that trick.")

   C. Line 65 ("for he . . . Cooper Indian.")

   D. Lines 66–67 ("it does seem . . . work of art")

36 As used in line 5, "stage properties" most nearly means

   A. literary tricks.

   B. dramatic license.

   C. stage rules.

   D. scripts for a drama.

37 Why did Twain include a pronunciation guide to the Native American Indian name Chingachgook (lines 20–21)?

   A. To make it easier for people to read his essay

   B. To mock Cooper's book

   C. To show respect for the Native American tribe

   D. To illustrate that Cooper's work was about actual Native American peoples

38 What is Twain's basic overall criticism of Cooper's work?

   A. Cooper's books are too complicated.

   B. Cooper's work is too self-serious.

   C. Cooper's plots did not make sense.

   D. Cooper's stories are boring.

39 Which choice provides the best evidence for the answer to the previous question?

   A. Lines 3–4 ("Cooper has . . . possible 115.")

   B. Lines 34–35 ("Cooper narrowed . . . some Indians.")

   C. Lines 58–59 ("Let me . . . for yourself.")

   D. Lines 64–65 ("Then even . . . Cooper Indian.")

40 According to Twain's criticism in the passage, how did Cooper characterize Native Americans?

A. They were athletic and smart.

B. They were cunning and dangerous.

C. They were sneaky and inept.

D. They were gentle and respectful.

41 How does Twain use the term "delirium tremens" in line 70?

A. As an analogy

B. As a simile

C. As a historical reference to Cooper's drinking problems

D. As a historical reference to Cooper's mental health

42 As used in line 68, "destitute" most nearly means

A. impoverished.

B. full.

C. void.

D. capable.

Questions 43–52 are based on the following passage.

Pulitzer prize-winning writer Willa Cather worked as a reporter and also wrote several novels and short stories. This excerpt is from one of her more popular short stories, written in 1905.

Paul's Case: A Study in Temperament

It was Paul's afternoon to appear before the faculty of the Pittsburgh High School to account for his various misdemeanors. He had been suspended a week ago, *Line* and his father had called at the Principal's office and
5 confessed his perplexity about his son. Paul entered the faculty room suave and smiling. His clothes were a trifle outgrown, and the tan velvet on the collar of his open overcoat was frayed and worn; but for all that there was something of the dandy in him, and he wore
10 an opal pin in his neatly knotted black four-in-hand, and a red carnation in his buttonhole. This latter adornment the faculty somehow felt was not properly significant of the contrite spirit befitting a boy under the ban of suspension.
15 Paul was tall for his age and very thin, with high, cramped shoulders and a narrow chest. His eyes were remarkable for a certain hysterical brilliancy, and he continually used them in a conscious, theatrical sort of way, peculiarly offensive in a boy. The pupils were abnormally
20 large, as though he was addicted to belladonna, but there was a glassy glitter about them which that drug does not produce.

When questioned by the Principal as to why he was there Paul stated, politely enough, that he wanted to
25 come back to school. This was a lie, but Paul was quite accustomed to lying; found it, indeed, indispensable for overcoming friction. His teachers were asked to state their respective charges against him, which they did with such a rancor and aggrievedness as evinced that this
30 was not a usual case. Disorder and impertinence were among the offenses named, yet each of his instructors felt that it was scarcely possible to put into words the cause of the trouble, which lay in a sort of hysterically defiant manner of the boy's; in the contempt which they
35 all knew he felt for them, and which he seemingly made not the least effort to conceal. Once, when he had been making a synopsis of a paragraph at the blackboard, his English teacher had stepped to his side and attempted to guide his hand. Paul had started back with a shudder
40 and thrust his hands violently behind him. The astonished woman could scarcely have been more hurt and embarrassed had he struck at her. The insult was so

CONTINUE

involuntary and definitely personal as to be unforgettable. In one way and another he had made all of his teachers, men and women alike, conscious of the same feeling of physical aversion. In one class he habitually sat with his hand shading his eyes; in another he always looked out the window during the recitation; in another he made a running commentary on the lecture, with humorous intention.

His teachers felt this afternoon that his whole attitude was symbolized by his shrug and his flippantly red carnation flower, and they fell upon him without mercy, his English teacher leading the pack. He stood through it smiling, his pale lips parted over his white teeth. (His lips were constantly twitching, and he had a habit of raising his eyebrows that was contemptuous and irritating to the last degree.) Older boys than Paul had broken down and shed tears under that baptism of fire, but his set smile did not once desert him, and his only sign of discomfort was the nervous trembling of the fingers that toyed with the buttons of his overcoat, and an occasional jerking of the other hand that held his hat. Paul was always smiling, always glancing about him, seeming to feel that people might be watching him and trying to detect something. This conscious expression, since it was as far as possible from boyish mirthfulness, was usually attributed to insolence or "smartness."

43 Based on the passage, what is the best way to describe the story?

A. It's a character study.

B. It's an account of a real-life character.

C. It's a psychological story with a complicated plot.

D. It's a story that emphasizes the setting.

44 What was the reason that Paul was asked to go to the principal's office?

A. To explain to the teachers why he wanted to return to school

B. To explain to the faculty why he had been misbehaving

C. To explain to the principal why he was late for class

D. To explain to his parents why he had been suspended

45 Why did Paul wear a red carnation?

A. To show respect for the faculty

B. To show remorse

C. To make himself appear wealthy

D. To defy the faculty

46 The reader can infer from the passage that the feelings of Paul's teachers toward him may be described mostly as

A. frustration and anger.

B. sadness and confusion.

C. indifference and coldness.

D. hope and tenderness.

47 Which choice provides the best evidence for the answer to the previous question?

A. Lines 3–5 ("He had been . . . about his son.")

B. Lines 11–14 ("This latter . . . ban of suspension.")

C. Lines 27–30 ("His teachers . . . not a usual case.")

D. Lines 44–46 ("In one way . . . physical aversion.")

48 According to the author, Paul's English teacher

A. had experience dealing with emotional students.

B. took Paul's dislike of being touched personally.

C. was too impatient to allow Paul to write on his own.

D. had to endure hearing Paul make comments on her lecture.

49 How does Cather show a connection between Paul's feeling and his actions?

A. She describes how subtle signals reflect Paul's mood or disposition.

B. She describes his reactions compared to how others would react in similar circumstances.

C. She gives details about his physical appearance and that of the teachers.

D. She provides details about his behavior and the way it is interpreted by others.

50 Which choice provides the best evidence for the answer to the previous question?

   A.   Lines 54–55 ("He stood . . . white teeth.")

   B.   Lines 55–58 ("His lips were . . . last degree.")

   C.   Lines 58–63 ("Older boys . . . his hat.")

   D.   Lines 66–68 ("This conscious . . . or smartness.")

51 Based on the passage, which meaning of the word "temperament" is used in the title "A Study in Temperament"?

   A.   Complexion

   B.   Adjustment

   C.   Mood

   D.   Personality

52 As in line 9, "dandy" most nearly means someone who

   A.   is first-rate in his class.

   B.   dresses with elegance and care.

   C.   is carefree.

   D.   is brilliant.

STOP

If you finish before time is called, you may check your work on this section only.
Do not turn to any other section.

SECTION 2: WRITING AND LANGUAGE TEST

35 Minutes—44 Questions

TURN TO SECTION 2 OF YOUR ANSWER SHEET TO ANSWER THE QUESTIONS IN THIS SECTION.

DIRECTIONS: Each passage below is accompanied by a number of multiple-choice questions. For some questions, you will need to consider how the passage might be revised to improve the expression of ideas. Other questions will ask you to consider how the passage might be edited to correct errors in sentence structure, usage, or punctuation. A passage may be accompanied by one or more graphics—such as a chart, table, or graph—that you will need to refer to in order to best answer the question(s).

Some questions will direct you to an underlined portion of a passage—it could be one word, a portion of a sentence, or the full sentence itself. Other questions will direct you to a particular paragraph or to certain sentences within a paragraph, or you'll be asked to think about the passage as a whole. Each question number refers to the corresponding number in the passage.

After reading each passage, select the answer to each question that most effectively improves the quality of writing in the passage or that makes the passage follow the conventions of Standard Written English. Many questions include a "NO CHANGE" option. Select that option if you think the best choice is to leave that specific portion of the passage as it is.

Questions 1–11 are based on the following passage.

Elizabeth Blackwell, the Doctor

On January 23, 1849, in the town of Geneva, New York, Elizabeth Blackwell stepped onto the altar of the Presbyterian church and received her medical degree from the president of Geneva Medical College. This took <u>her place in history.</u> Blackwell had <u>denounced</u> the expectations of most of her teachers and classmates to become the country's first female doctor.

1

A. NO CHANGE

B. Receiving her medical degree led to giving her a place in history.

C. She took her place in history.

D. In doing so, she took her place in history.

2

A. NO CHANGE

B. defied

C. incited

D. met

As a young woman, Blackwell had worked as a school teacher, but she found herself unsatisfied. Once she realized that her dream was to be a doctor, she faced tremendous obstacles. There had never before been a female physician in America. At the time, educating a boy was considered **3** far more important than a girl. Blackwell's education did not prepare her for the challenges of medical school, and she had to work hard just to catch up. **4** To make up for the gaps in her education, the household of a physician became her home for the next several years. There, she had access to educational resources and received some medical training.

5 As she prepared to apply to medical school, Blackwell sought advice from physicians in New York and Philadelphia. She found that they **6** doubted she would be admitted to medical school; at least one advisor went so far as to suggest that she might disguise herself as a man in order to gain admittance. **7** Their advisors were not far from wrong in their prediction. Blackwell applied to well over a dozen medical colleges, but she received admission to only one—Geneva Medical College.

3

- **A.** NO CHANGE
- **B.** far more important than it was to a girl.
- **C.** far more important than educating a girl.
- **D.** far more important than opportunities for girls.

4

- **A.** NO CHANGE
- **B.** A physician's household, to make up for the gaps in her education, became her home for the next several years.
- **C.** Her home for the next several years, to make up for the gaps in her education, became a physician's household.
- **D.** To make up for the gaps in her education, she arranged to live in the household of a physician for the next several years.

5 Which choice provides the most logical introduction to the sentence?

- **A.** NO CHANGE
- **B.** After finishing medical school,
- **C.** While attending university,
- **D.** Before she applied to be a psychologist.

6

- **A.** NO CHANGE
- **B.** debated
- **C.** insisted
- **D.** supposed

7

- **A.** NO CHANGE
- **B.** Her
- **C.** His
- **D.** Your

Gaining admission to the college **8** has become the first in a long line of obstacles for Blackwell. She discovered that her fellow **9** students all of whom were men had elected as a joke to admit her to the medical program and were astonished when she actually showed up at the college to enroll for classes. The students were embarrassed by her presence in lectures on topics—such as human anatomy—that they considered unsuitable for mixed company.

Steadily, and with perseverance, Blackwell gained acceptance among the students and faculty. After she completed her degree, she continued **10** to face prejudice and biases, which were real obstacles and challenges against her because she was a woman, and outright barriers to her career. She was unable to establish the private practice she had hoped for. Nevertheless, Blackwell was successful, **11** but when she went to study at a hospital in Paris, she was assigned the same duties as young girls with no education at all.

8

A. NO CHANGE

B. becomes

C. became

D. will become

9

A. NO CHANGE

B. students all, of whom, were men had

C. students all of whom, were men had

D. students, all of whom were men, had

10

A. NO CHANGE

B. to face outright barriers to her career due to prejudice and biases.

C. to face a variety of significant barriers to her and her career.

D. to face barriers that obstructed her career and included bias because she was a woman.

11 Which choice most effectively maintains support for claims or points in the text?

A. NO CHANGE

B. but she is remembered for having been the first woman in America to receive a medical degree

C. and she had a distinguished career as a promoter of preventative medicine and as a champion of medical opportunities for women

D. but she lived an interesting life and had many opportunities to travel widely and meet new people

CONTINUE

Questions 12–22 are based on the following passage and supplementary material.

Rachel Carson, Protector of the Environment

Today, we can hardly imagine a world without websites, blogs, and articles that express concern for the environment. **12** Carson, a former marine biologist for the Fish and Game Service, **13** ruffled the feathers of a ton of people who had a vested interest in maintaining the status quo where the environment was concerned. Her credibility as a scientist and her personal courage enabled Carson to withstand the criticism heaped on her during her lifetime.

12 At this point, the writer is considering adding the following sentence:

But in 1962, when Rachel Carson's *Silent Spring* was published, this was not the case.

Should the writer do this?

A. Yes, because it provides the reader with a date and historical context.

B. Yes, because it informs the reader of how old Carson was when she got published.

C. No, because it inserts irrelevant information about an unimportant book.

D. No, because it divides the paragraph's focus between the book and Carson.

13

A. NO CHANGE

B. aggravated a lot of folks

C. inflamed the outsized egos of those

D. disturbed many

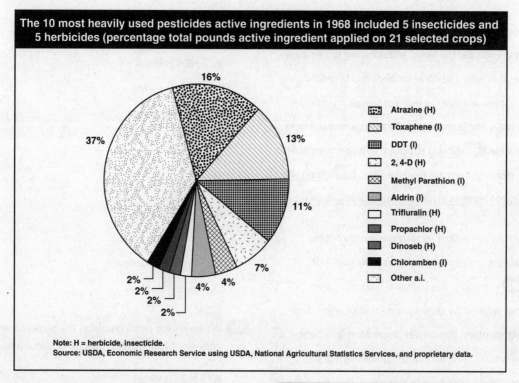

The 10 most heavily used pesticides active ingredients in 1968 included 5 insecticides and 5 herbicides (percentage total pounds active ingredient applied on 21 selected crops)

- Atrazine (H)
- Toxaphene (I)
- DDT (I)
- 2, 4-D (H)
- Methyl Parathion (I)
- Aldrin (I)
- Trifluralin (H)
- Propachlor (H)
- Dinoseb (H)
- Chloramben (I)
- Other a.i.

Note: H = herbicide, insecticide.
Source: USDA, Economic Research Service using USDA, National Agricultural Statistics Services, and proprietary data.

And what exactly was it that Rachel Carson did that was so **14** disturbing. She pointed out the dangers of **15** pesticides—DDT in particular—to the environment. DDT was designed to contain insect pests in gardens and on farmland after World War II. Most people considered it a "wonder chemical," **16** and by 1968, they used DDT to cover approximately 11% of all farmland.

14

A. NO CHANGE

B. disturbing?

C. disturbing!

D. disturbing:

15

A. NO CHANGE

B. pesticides—DDT in particular to

C. pesticides DDT in particular, to

D. pesticides (DDT) in particular to

16 Which choice completes the sentence with accurate data based on the chart?

A. NO CHANGE

B. and in fact, by 1968, DDT accounted for 11% of all pesticides used.

C. as it was believed to contain approximately 11% of all garden pests.

D. though only about 11% of all farmers and gardeners actually used it.

CONTINUE

Rachel Carson believed, however, that the pesticides were **17** dehydrating the soil and the rivers, and adhering to tree leaves and branches that were the home for birds and beneficial insects. She contended that the levels of chemical pesticides in plants, animals, and humans had already reached alarming levels. In her view, **18** he was so potent that they were able to penetrate systems and remain there for years, **19** giving way to possible improvements in general health and well-being.

The furor caused by Carson's writing was mostly felt by the chemical companies that produced pesticides. Not willing to **20** contradict the potential hazards of their products, they resisted by seeking to discredit Carson. And despite her credentials, Carson was discredited for a period of time. However, in 1970, with the establishment of the Environmental Protection Agency, the nation became more concerned with issues that Carson had raised.

Since 2001, DDT has been banned for agricultural use worldwide except in small quantities and only as part of a plan to transition to safer alternatives. The only places in which DDT is still allowed are those countries in which it is being used to combat malaria. **21** Since malaria kills more than 800,000 people every year, most of them children in Sub-Saharan Africa, Carson has been blamed for "millions of deaths," despite the studies that show that the pesticide can contribute to cancers, male infertility, miscarriages, developmental delay in children, and damage to the liver and nervous system.

17

A. NO CHANGE

B. appropriating

C. transcending

D. permeating

18

A. NO CHANGE

B. it was

C. the pesticides were

D. everything was

19 Which choice best completes the sentence and remains consistent with Carson's argument about pesticides?

A. NO CHANGE

B. providing a definitive link between cancer and pesticides.

C. leading to an alarming decrease in local bird populations.

D. potentially leading to a breakdown in tissue and immune systems.

20

A. NO CHANGE

B. acknowledge

C. propagate

D. solicit

21

A. NO CHANGE

B. Even though malaria kills 800,000 people every year, most of them children in Sub-Saharan Africa, Carson

C. Coincidentally, malaria kills 800,000 people every year, most of them children in Sub-Saharan Africa, Carson

D. Does malaria kill 800,000 people every year, most of them children in Sub-Saharan Africa, Carson

Were it not for those like Rachel Carson, **22** DDT would probably still be seen as "wonder chemicals," and the only way to combat malaria. Though still controversial, she was a scientist of vision and determination who changed the course of history and brought environmental issues to the world's attention.

Questions 23–33 are based on the following passage.

A Mayan Worldview

The ancient Mayans inhabited the area that now consists of **23** Mexico; Guatemala, Belize, Honduras; and El Salvador. Their rich civilization flourished from the third through the ninth centuries. **24** Among the many notable achievements of this society were the Mayan understanding of astronomy, which was manifest not only in Mayan science but in every aspect of the culture.

22

A. NO CHANGE

B. pesticides with DDT would probably still be seen as a "wonder chemical,"

C. DDT would probably still be seen as a "wonder chemical,"

D. DDT would probably still be seen as chemicals that are wondrous.

23

A. NO CHANGE

B. Mexico, Guatemala, Belize, Honduras, and El Salvador.

C. Mexico, Guatemala, Belize, Honduras; El Salvador.

D. Mexico Guatemala Belize Honduras El Salvador.

24

A. NO CHANGE

B. Among the many notable achievements of this society are the Mayan understanding of astronomy,

C. Among the many notable achievements of this society will be the Mayan understanding of astronomy,

D. Among the many notable achievements of this society was the Mayan understanding of astronomy,

CONTINUE

Ancient Mayans kept meticulous records of **25** the setting Sun, the moving Moon, and the rotation of the planets that were visible to the naked eye. Based on the solar year, they created a calendar which they used to keep track of time. So **26** astute were the Mayans' observations that they could predict such events as solar and lunar eclipses, and **27** the movement of the planets.

For the ancient Mayans, astronomy was not just a science; it was a combination of science, religion, and philosophy that found **28** it's way into many aspects of their lives, including architecture. Mayan ceremonial buildings, for example, were exactly aligned with compass points, so that at the fall and spring equinoxes, light would flood the interior of the building. These buildings were designed and built as acts of worship to the **29** Mayan gods. Science, architecture, and religion, then, were all intricately and beautifully blended.

25

A. NO CHANGE

B. the setting Sun, the moving Moon, and the rotating planets

C. the set sun, the moving moon, and the rotated planets

D. the setting Sun, the way the Moon moved, and the rotation of the planets

26

A. NO CHANGE

B. inept

C. expected

D. complicated

27 Which choice gives a supporting example that is most similar to the example already in the sentence?

A. NO CHANGE

B. the migration of birds.

C. the direction of the winds.

D. the flow of the tides.

28

A. NO CHANGE

B. its'

C. its

D. its's

29 Which choice most effectively combines the two sentences at the underlined portion?

A. Mayan gods: science

B. Mayan gods; science

C. Mayan gods, science

D. Mayan gods, but science

Government, too, was **30** <u>inextricably</u> linked with astronomy. The beginning and ending of the reigns of Mayan leaders appear to have been timed to coincide with astronomical events. Ancient Mayan artwork, carvings and murals show royalty wearing **31** <u>symbols: relating to the Sun, Moon, and sky.</u> The Mayans believed that the Sun and Moon were guided across the sky by benevolent gods, and that these gods needed human help to thwart the evil gods who wanted to stop them. Human intervention took the form of different rituals, including sacrifice. It was considered an honor to die for this cause, and those who were sacrificed were believed to have gained eternal life.

The planet Venus, which can often be seen by the unaided eye, played a large role in Mayan life. The Mayans used the appearance of Venus in the sky as a means of timing when they attacked enemies. The night sky, among its other duties, could then serve as a **32** <u>harvest calendar.</u>

33 <u>In short, the</u> ancient Mayans, in looking to the night sky for guidance, discovered a natural order around which they were able to base a rich and textured civilization.

30

A. NO CHANGE

B. bafflingly

C. greedily

D. embarrassingly

31

A. NO CHANGE

B. symbols, relating to the Sun, Moon, and sky.

C. symbols relating to the Sun, Moon, and sky.

D. symbols; relating to the Sun, Moon, and sky.

32 Which choice provides information that best supports the focus of this paragraph?

A. NO CHANGE

B. reminder of the season

C. reference point for direction

D. call to war

33

A. NO CHANGE

B. However,

C. Moreover,

D. Incidentally,

Questions 34–44 are based on the following passage.

The Real World

Our college employment counseling center recommended that students have mock interviews before setting out into the world for the real thing. For reasons that I still don't understand, I **34** <u>believed</u> that this applied to other people but not to me. Midway **35** <u>thorough</u> my senior year of college, I sent out resumes to several law firms in the area. I didn't consult with anybody about how to begin seeking a job. My plan was to work at a law firm for a couple of years before attending law school. I received a couple of responses and was thrilled to set up **36** <u>our</u> first interview at a prestigious law firm that had offices all over the world. **37** <u>It was exactly the type of environment in which I envisioned myself.</u>

34

A. NO CHANGE
B. know
C. denied
D. believe

35

A. NO CHANGE
B. threw
C. though
D. through

36

A. NO CHANGE
B. his
C. my
D. their

37 Which of the following sentences, if added, would most effectively conclude this paragraph?

A. NO CHANGE
B. I couldn't imagine enjoying working in this environment.
C. I really wish college never ended!
D. I needed more time to weigh my career options.

The position for which I was interviewing was a clerical job that, the interviewer made clear from the outset, would require long hours, late nights, and a great deal of filing and photocopying. I confidently announced to the interviewer that I didn't mind long hours and thankless assignments. **38** And then happily informed him that I wanted to work my way up and someday be his boss. I figured the surprised look on his face was because he wasn't used to seeing young men as ambitious and **39** enigmatic as I was. I would have kept going, had he not suggested moving on to another topic.

[1] I'm sorry to say that here I left nothing to the imagination. [2] I believed that my interviewer would value my stark honesty when I told him that my greatest **40** weakness's included not getting along with other people very well and a tendency to make more enemies than friends. **41** [3] In the next phase of the interview, I was asked to list my strengths and weaknesses. [4] The interviewer raised his eyebrows but said nothing, and I was certain that he knew he'd found his candidate. [5] After all, **42** I could've cared less about getting along with other people and I figured I wouldn't need to get along with people to photocopy and file, so I'd hit upon the perfect answer to a tricky question.

38

A. NO CHANGE

B. After happily informing him that I wanted to work my way up and someday be his boss.

C. Which is why I happily informed him that I wanted to work my way up and someday be his boss.

D. Then I happily informed him that I wanted to work my way up and someday be his boss.

39

A. NO CHANGE

B. articulate

C. conspicuous

D. incoherent

40

A. NO CHANGE

B. weaknesses'

C. weaknesses

D. weakness'

41 For the sake of cohesion, sentence 3 of this paragraph should be placed

A. where it is now.

B. before sentence 1.

C. before sentence 5.

D. at the beginning of the next paragraph.

42

A. NO CHANGE

B. I could have cared less

C. I could of cared less

D. I couldn't have cared less

CONTINUE

43 I did not get offered that job, nor the next several for which I interviewed at other firms. Eventually I paid a **44** <u>deferred</u> trip to the college job counseling office and got a few pointers on my technique. I am happy to say that while I never did end up going to law school, I have become a high school guidance counselor who specializes in helping students find internships in community businesses.

43 Which of the following would make the most effective opening sentence for this paragraph?

A. After the interview, I waited anxiously to hear back from the employer.

B. I never heard back from the employer about the job.

C. I met my friends for brunch over the following weekend.

D. I got married four years later, after dating for several years.

44

A. NO CHANGE

B. belated

C. hastened

D. disparaged

STOP

If you finish before time is called, you may check your work on this section only.
Do not turn to any other section.

SECTION 3: MATH TEST—NO CALCULATOR

25 Minutes—20 Questions

TURN TO SECTION 3 OF YOUR ANSWER SHEET TO ANSWER THE QUESTIONS IN THIS SECTION.

DIRECTIONS: For **Questions 1–15,** solve each problem, select the best answer from the choices provided, and fill in the corresponding circle on your answer sheet. For **Questions 16–20,** solve the problem and enter your answer in the grid on the answer sheet. The directions **before Question 16** will provide information on how to enter your answers in the grid.

ADDITIONAL INFORMATION:

1. The use of a calculator in this section is **not permitted**.
2. All variables and expressions used represent real numbers unless otherwise indicated.
3. Figures provided in this test are drawn to scale unless otherwise indicated.
4. All figures lie in a plane unless otherwise indicated.
5. Unless otherwise specified, the domain of a given function *f* is the set of all real numbers *x* for which *f(x)* is a real number.

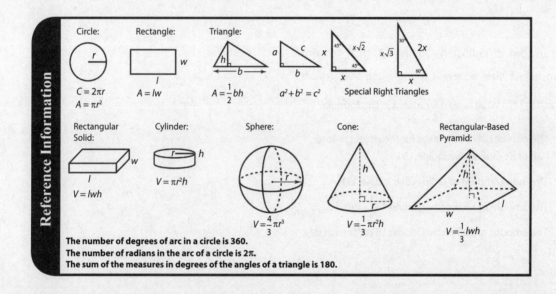

The number of degrees of arc in a circle is 360.
The number of radians in the arc of a circle is 2π.
The sum of the measures in degrees of the angles of a triangle is 180.

CONTINUE

1. Jared is beginning to track the number of steps he walks each day. Yesterday he walked 950 steps. He set a goal of increasing his steps per day by 125, with an eventual goal of walking at least 3,000 steps per day. Which of the following functions can be used to determine the number of steps Jared plans to take d days from yesterday?

    A. $f(d) = 3{,}000 - (950 + 125d)$

    B. $f(d) = 3{,}000 - 125d$

    C. $f(d) = 950 + 125d$

    D. $f(d) = 950 - 125d$

2. If $f(1) = 3$, $f(3) = -1$, $g(3) = 1$, and $g(-1) = 3$, what is the value of $f(g(3))$?

    A. -3

    B. -1

    C. 1

    D. 3

3. The amount of radioactive iodine 131 that remains in an object after d days is found using the formula $y = a(0.5)^{\frac{d}{8.02}}$. What does a represent in the formula?

    A. The number of days it takes for the object to lose half of its radioactive iodine 131

    B. The initial amount of radioactive iodine 131

    C. The amount of radioactive iodine 131 after d days

    D. The amount of radioactive iodine 131 lost each day

SHOW YOUR WORK HERE

4 An architect is designing the roof of a house that is to be symmetric, with two equal sides meeting exactly in the middle. The house is 30 feet wide. The peak of the roof is 8 feet above the house. If the outside of the roof is separated into two parts, how long is each part from the peak of the roof to its edge?

A.   15 ft.

B.   17 ft.

C.   23 ft.

D.   31 ft.

SHOW YOUR WORK HERE

5
$$y = 2(x - 5)^2 - 2$$

Which equation, where the *x*-intercepts appear as constants, is equivalent to the equation above?

A. $y = 2x^2 - 20x + 48$

B. $y = 2(x^2 - 10x + 24)$

C. $y = 2(x - 4)(x - 6)$

D. $y = (2x - 8)(x - 6)$

6 Which of the following graphs represents the equation $3x + y = 4$?

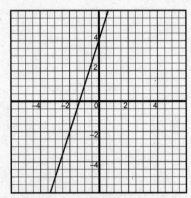

A.

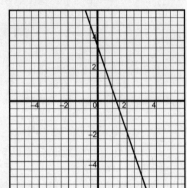

B.

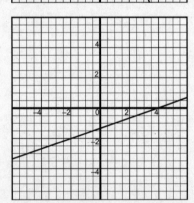

C.

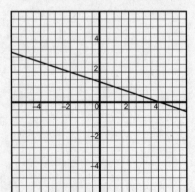

D.

7 Which of the following is an equation for the line through the point (2, 3) with a slope of –1?

A. $2x + 3y = -1$

B. $3x + 3y = 15$

C. $3x + 2y = 10$

D. $x + y = -5$

8
$$3x = 6y$$
$$2x^2 - y^2 = 14$$

If (x, y) is a solution to the system of equations above, then y^2 equals which value?

A. $\dfrac{x^2}{2}$

B. $\dfrac{14}{3}$

C. 2

D. $\sqrt{2}$

9 Which of the following is equivalent to $\dfrac{\sqrt[3]{\sqrt{z}}}{\sqrt[3]{z} \cdot \sqrt{z}}$?

A. z

B. z^{-1}

C. $z^{-\frac{2}{3}}$

D. $z^{\frac{1}{5}}$

10 Which of the following is the equation for the graph of a parabola that has a vertex at (3, –5) and a y-intercept at 13?

A. $y - 28 = (x - 3)(x + 5)$

B. $y = 2(x - 3)^2 - 5$

C. $y = (x - 3)^2 - 13$

D. $y = x^2 - 6x + 13$

CONTINUE

SHOW YOUR WORK HERE

11 The admission cost for a play is $12 for adults and $7 for children. Which system of equations can be used to determine the number of adults and number of children that attended if 117 people attended the play and the total amount collected for admission was $1,079?

A. $12x + 7y = 117$
$x + y = 1,079$

B. $12x + y = 117$
$x + 7y = 1,079$

C. $12x + 7y = 1,079$
$x + y = 117$

D. $x + 7y = 117$
$12x + y = 1,079$

12 Which of the following is equivalent to $\dfrac{4-i}{3+i}$ that can be found by multiplying by the complex conjugate of the denominator?

A. $\dfrac{1}{3}$

B. $\dfrac{17}{11+7i}$

C. $\dfrac{11-7i}{10}$

D. $\dfrac{13+i}{8}$

13 What is the solution to the equation $-6(t+1) = 2(1-3t) - 8$?

A. -8

B. -6

C. No solution

D. Infinitely many solutions

14 A small city in Spain grows at an average rate of 1.7% a year. The population of the city in 1980 was 2,845. The equation that models the city's population in 1990 is $P = 2,845e^{(0.017)(10)}$. What does 10 represent in the equation?

    A. The city's population in 1980

    B. The number of years

    C. The city's average growth rate

    D. The factor of increase of the city's population each year

15 If the expression $\dfrac{9x^2}{3x-2}$ is rewritten as an equivalent expression of the form $\dfrac{4}{3x-2} + A$, then A equals:

    A. $3x^2$

    B. $\dfrac{5x^2}{3x-2}$

    C. $(3x-2)^2$

    D. $(3x + 2)$

DIRECTIONS: For **Questions 16–20,** solve the problem and enter your answer in the grid, as described below, on the answer sheet.

1. Although not required, it is suggested that you write your answer in the boxes at the top of the columns to help you fill in the circles accurately. You will receive credit only if the circles are filled in correctly.

2. Mark no more than one circle in any column.

3. No question has a negative answer.

4. Some problems may have more than one correct answer. In such cases, enter only one answer.

5. **Mixed numbers** such as $3\frac{1}{2}$ must be entered as 3.5 or $\frac{7}{2}$.

   If $3\frac{1}{2}$ is entered into the grid as $\boxed{3\,|\,1\,/\,2}$, it will be interpreted as $\frac{31}{2}$, not $3\frac{1}{2}$.

6. **Decimal answers:** If you obtain a decimal answer with more digits than the grid can accommodate, it may be either rounded or truncated, but it must fill the entire grid.

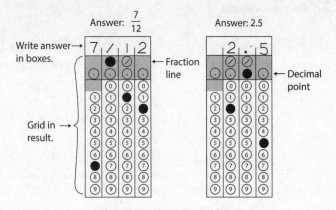

Answer: $\frac{7}{12}$ — Write answer in boxes. — Fraction line

Answer: 2.5 — Decimal point

Grid in result.

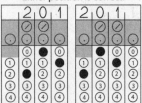

Answer: 201
Either position is correct.

Acceptable ways to grid $\frac{2}{3}$ are:

16 If $\sqrt{x+1} - 2 = 3$, what is the value of x?

17 Let b be a real number. For what value of b does the function $f(x) = x^2 - 2bx + (b^2 + 2b - 1)$ have one and only one x-intercept?

18

$$\frac{3x^2 - 4x - 18}{x+3} = 3x - c + \frac{21}{x+3}$$

What is the value for c that will make the equation above true?

19

$$y = 3x + 7$$
$$4x - ty = 5$$

According to the system of equations above, what is the value of t that makes the system of equations have no solutions?

20 A spherical scoop of ice cream is placed on top of a hollow ice cream cone. The scoop and cone have the same radius. The ice cream melts completely and it fills the cone to the top. How many times greater is the height of the cone than the radius of the cone?

STOP

If you finish before time is called, you may check your work on this section only.
Do not turn to any other section.

SECTION 4: MATH TEST—CALCULATOR

55 Minutes—38 Questions

TURN TO SECTION 4 OF YOUR ANSWER SHEET TO ANSWER THE QUESTIONS IN THIS SECTION.

DIRECTIONS: For **Questions 1–30,** solve each problem, select the best answer from the choices provided, and fill in the corresponding circle on your answer sheet. For **Questions 31–38,** solve the problem and enter your answer in the grid on the answer sheet. The directions **before Question 31** will provide information on how to enter your answers in the grid.

ADDITIONAL INFORMATION:

1. The use of a calculator in this section is **permitted**.
2. All variables and expressions used represent real numbers unless otherwise indicated.
3. Figures provided in this test are drawn to scale unless otherwise indicated.
4. All figures lie in a plane unless otherwise indicated.
5. Unless otherwise specified, the domain of a given function f is the set of all real numbers x for which $f(x)$ is a real number.

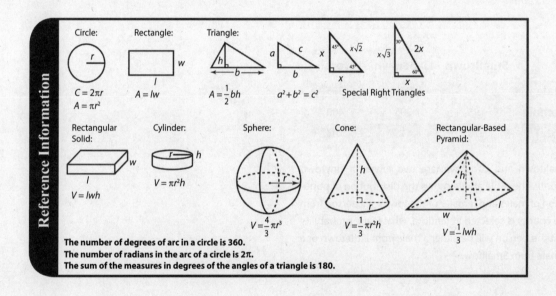

Reference Information

Circle:
$C = 2\pi r$
$A = \pi r^2$

Rectangle:
$A = lw$

Triangle:
$A = \frac{1}{2}bh$

$a^2 + b^2 = c^2$

Special Right Triangles

Rectangular Solid:
$V = lwh$

Cylinder:
$V = \pi r^2 h$

Sphere:
$V = \frac{4}{3}\pi r^3$

Cone:
$V = \frac{1}{3}\pi r^2 h$

Rectangular-Based Pyramid:
$V = \frac{1}{3}lwh$

The number of degrees of arc in a circle is 360.
The number of radians in the arc of a circle is 2π.
The sum of the measures in degrees of the angles of a triangle is 180.

CONTINUE

SHOW YOUR WORK HERE

1 A certain insect is estimated to travel 1,680 feet per year. At this rate, about how many months would it take for the insect to travel 560 feet?

A. 0.75

B. 3

C. 4

D. 5.5

2 A librarian is tracking the circulation of books at the library. Out of the books that had been loaned one day, 18 were renewed, 46 were returned on time, and 11 were returned late. At this rate, about how many books will be renewed if the library loans 25,000 books each year?

A. 4,000

B. 6,000

C. 9,000

D. 15,000

3

	Smalltown	Littletown	Total
Male	175	210	385
Female	195	205	400
Total	370	415	785

Smalltown and Littletown are two towns in Tinytown County. The table above shows the distribution of population of males and females of the towns. If a person from the county is selected at random, what is the probability that the person will be either a male from Littletown or a female from Smalltown?

A. $\dfrac{39}{74}$

B. $\dfrac{42}{83}$

C. $\dfrac{56}{157}$

D. $\dfrac{81}{157}$

4 Sixty incoming freshmen at a university are asked how many continents each has visited. The results are summarized in the frequency table below.

Continents Visited	Number of Students
1	12
2	18
3	14
4	8
5	6
6	2
Total Students Responding:	**60**

Given the data, which is a true statement about the median and mode of the data set?

A. The median is less than the mode.

B. The median is equal to the mode.

C. The median is greater than the mode.

D. The median and mode cannot be determined from the table.

5 Glen earns $10.25 per hour and pays $12.50 per day to commute to and from work on the bus. He wants to make sure that he works long enough to earn at least three times as much as he spends commuting. Which of the following inequalities best represents this situation?

A. $10.25h \geq 3(12.50)$

B. $3(10.25) \geq 12.50h$

C. $3(10.25h) \geq 12.50$

D. $h \geq 3(12.50)(10.25)$

6 Nadia spent 7 more hours on math homework last month than Peter. If they spent a total of 35 hours doing math homework last month, how many hours did Peter spend on math homework?

A. 7

B. 14

C. 21

D. 28

CONTINUE

7 If *c* is 22 percent of *e* and *d* is 68 percent of *e*, what is *d* – *c* in terms of *e*?

- **A.** 90*e*
- **B.** 46*e*
- **C.** 0.9*e*
- **D.** 0.46*e*

8
$$2x-9y<12$$
$$-3x+4y>5$$

Which of the following is a solution to the system of inequalities shown above?

- **A.** $(-4, -4)$
- **B.** $(-4, 4)$
- **C.** $(4, -4)$
- **D.** $(4, 4)$

9 If *n* = 7, what is 2*m*(16 – 6*n*) in terms of *m*?

- **A.** −52*m*
- **B.** −15*m*
- **C.** −14*m*
- **D.** 32*m*

10 Tessa wants to raise a total of at least $250 for her favorite charity. She has already raised $145. Tessa asks for $15 contributions from each person she contacts. Which inequality best represents this situation?

- **A.** $15x \geq 250$
- **B.** $145(15x) \geq 250$
- **C.** $145 + 15x \geq 250$
- **D.** $145 - 15x \geq 250$

Questions 11 and 12 refer to the following information.

A class raised money selling t-shirts, and then they began selling hats. The graph represents the total amount of money in the class account as the number of hats sold increases.

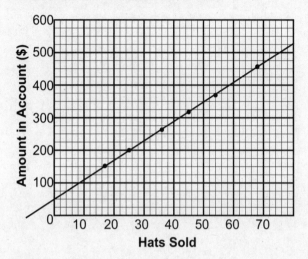

11 According to the graph, which of the following best approximates the number of hats that must be sold for the class to have raised a total of $400?

A. 54

B. 58

C. 64

D. 68

12 What does the slope of the line signify?

A. The amount of money already raised

B. The amount of money received per hat

C. The number of hats that are sold

D. The number of hats that must be sold to meet the fundraising goal

CONTINUE

13 A survey was conducted to determine whether the voters in a city of 38,000 would support funding a new park. A sample of 18 voters randomly selected from the voting list revealed that 11 voters favored funding the park, 4 voters did not want to fund the park, and 3 voters had no preference. Which of the following makes it least likely that a reliable conclusion can be drawn from the data?

A. The size of the sample population

B. The size of the city's population

C. The number of people with no preference

D. How the sample population was selected

14 In 2010, a census showed a city had a population of 22,500. The results of the census also showed that the mean income of the population was $72,350, and the median income was $65,580. Which of the following could describe the difference between the mean income and the median income of the population?

A. Most of the income values are between the mean and median income values.

B. There are a few income values that are much less than the other income values.

C. There are a few income values that are much greater than the other income values.

D. The range in income values is greater than the income value.

15 A group of *h* neighbors has 1,230 CDs they are selling at a yard sale. If each neighbor sells on average *x* CDs per day for *j* days of the yard sale, which of the following represents the total number of CDs that will be left when the yard sale is over?

A. $1,230 - jhx$

B. $1,230 - hx - j$

C. $1,230 - \dfrac{jx}{h}$

D. $1,230 + \dfrac{jx}{h}$

16

$$y = -16x^2 + 50x + 2$$

The equation above represents the height y of a ball, in feet, x seconds after it has been thrown upward. Which of the following best describes the meaning of the coefficient 50?

A. The height of the ball when it is thrown

B. The height of the ball after x seconds

C. The initial velocity of the ball when it is thrown

D. The acceleration of the ball's upward velocity

Questions 17 and 18 refer to the following information.

Quinn is moving across the state and needs to rent a moving truck that will fit her belongings. The table below shows the mileage rate and daily rental cost for trucks from three different companies.

	Mileage rate, b, in cents per mile	Rental rate, a, in dollars per day
Company J	15	19
Company K	10	30
Company L	12	25

The total cost, y, for renting the truck for one day and driving x miles is found by using the formula $y = a + 0.01bx$.

17 For which numbers of miles x is the cost of renting from Company J less than renting from Company K?

A. $x < 44$

B. $x < 55$

C. $x < 220$

D. $x < 980$

CONTINUE

18 If the relationship between the total cost, y, of renting the truck from Company L and driving it x miles for one day is graphed in the xy-plane, what does the slope of the line represent?

A. The daily rental cost for the truck

B. The cost to drive the truck each mile

C. The total cost for the miles driven

D. The total cost for renting and driving the truck

SHOW YOUR WORK HERE

Questions 19 and 20 refer to the following information.

A sample of the population in two neighborhood towns, Town A and Town B, was surveyed in order to determine the most popular types of house styles. The results of the survey are shown in the table.

| House Style | | |
House Style	Town A	Town B
Ranch	75	62
Colonial	25	65
Cape Cod	53	43
Victorian	20	32

19 According to the table above, what is the probability that a randomly selected house in Town B is a colonial house?

A. $\dfrac{65}{202}$

B. $\dfrac{17}{18}$

C. $\dfrac{31}{45}$

D. $\dfrac{25}{62}$

20 What is the probability that a randomly selected house is from Town B, given that its style is either a Cape Cod or a Ranch?

A. $\dfrac{105}{202}$

B. $\dfrac{233}{375}$

C. $\dfrac{105}{233}$

D. $\dfrac{7}{25}$

21 Let a and b be positive real numbers. What is the distance between the x-coordinates of the points of intersection of the graphs of $f(x) = b^2 - (x + a)^2$ and $g(x) = (x + a)^2 - b^2$?

A. $2b$

B. $2a$

C. $a + b$

D. $2(a + b)$

22

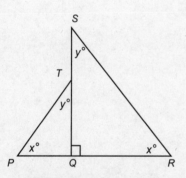

Note: Figure not drawn to scale.

In the figure above, if $QP = 11.5$, $TQ = 15$, and $QR = 46$, what is the value of SQ?

A. 65

B. 60

C. 49.5

D. 42.5

CONTINUE

23

$$1 = \frac{3}{x-4} + \frac{4}{x-3}$$

Which of the following are the values of x in the equation above?

A. $7 \pm 2\sqrt{3}$

B. $7 \pm \sqrt{62}$

C. $7 \pm \sqrt{86}$

D. $1, 13$

SHOW YOUR WORK HERE

---

24 A certain type of weather radar, known as a Base Reflectivity Radar, has a circumference of 572π miles. The central angle of a sector of the circle that the radar makes is $\frac{3\pi}{4}$. What is the area, in square miles, of the sector of the circle?

A. 858π square miles

B. $\frac{429\pi}{4}$ square miles

C. $\frac{61{,}347\pi}{2}$ square miles

D. $81{,}796\pi$ square miles

If w is a negative constant less than -1 and v is a positive constant greater than 1, which of the following could be the graph of $y = a(x + w)(x + v)$?

A.

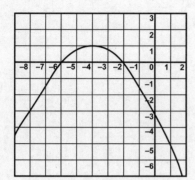

B.

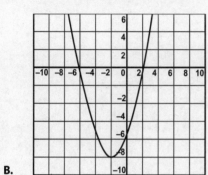

C.

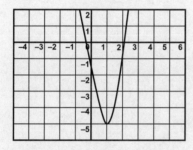

D.

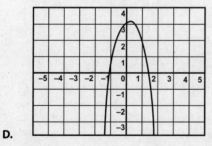

26

$$2x - 5y < 6$$
$$x + ay < -3$$

Which of the following must be true if the system of inequalities has solutions only in quadrants II and III?

A. $a < 0$

B. $a = 0$

C. $0 \le a \le 2.5$

D. $a > 2.5$

Questions 27 and 28 refer to the following information.

An astronomer records the luminosities (brightness) and temperatures of 19 "main sequence" stars, the most common type of star in the universe. The results are shown below with luminosity measured by comparison to the sun, and temperature in kelvins.

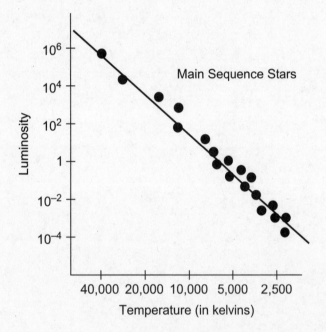

SHOW YOUR WORK HERE

27 How many of the stars observed by the scientist were hotter than 10,000K?

- **A.** 3
- **B.** 5
- **C.** 6
- **D.** 7

28 The sun's luminosity on the scale used here is 1. Based on the line of best fit, which of the following temperatures is closest to that of the sun's?

- **A.** 2,500
- **B.** 5,000
- **C.** 10,000
- **D.** 20,000

29 A recent national poll of adults in the United States found that 64% favor stricter emissions on power plants. The margin of error for the poll was ±4% with 95% confidence. Which of the following statements is a conclusion that can accurately be drawn from this poll?

- **A.** The true percentage of people who oppose stricter emissions of power plants is definitely between 32% and 40%.
- **B.** The true percentage of people who support stricter emissions of power plants is definitely between 60% and 68%.
- **C.** The pollsters are 95% confident that the true percentage of people who oppose stricter emissions of power plants is between 32% and 40%.
- **D.** The pollsters are 95% confident that the true percentage of people who support stricter emissions of power plants is between 60% and 68%.

30 The equation for the graph of a circle in the xy-plane is $x^2 + y^2 - 10x + 4y = -20$. What are the coordinates of the center of the circle?

- **A.** $(5, -2)$
- **B.** $(-5, 2)$
- **C.** $(10, -4)$
- **D.** $(-10, 4)$

CONTINUE

DIRECTIONS: For **Questions 31–38,** solve the problem and enter your answer in the grid, as described below, on the answer sheet.

---

1. Although not required, it is suggested that you write your answer in the boxes at the top of the columns to help you fill in the circles accurately. You will receive credit only if the circles are filled in correctly.

2. Mark no more than one circle in any column.

3. Mark no more than one circle in any column.

4. No question has a negative answer.

5. Some problems may have more than one correct answer. In such cases, enter only one answer.

6. **Mixed numbers** such as $3\frac{1}{2}$ must be entered as 3.5 or $\frac{7}{2}$.

   If $3\frac{1}{2}$ is entered into the grid as $3|1|/|2$, it will be interpreted as $\frac{31}{2}$, not $3\frac{1}{2}$.

7. **Decimal answers:** If you obtain a decimal answer with more digits than the grid can accommodate, it may be either rounded or truncated, but it must fill the entire grid.

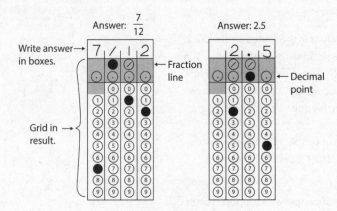

31 A bowling alley charges $4.50 per hour to use a lane. They also charge $2.50 to rent a pair of bowling shoes. Miguel and his friend rent a pair of bowling shoes each. The total cost before taxes is $16.25. How many hours did they bowl?

32 If $4s - 3 < 2$ and s is an integer, what is the greatest possible value of $4s + 5$?

33 If $2a - b = 7$ and $2a + 2b = 16$, what is the value of $3a + 7b$?

34 The current population of a certain type of organism is about 100 million. The population is currently increasing at an annual rate that will make the population double in 18 years. If this pattern continues, what will the population be, in millions, 54 years from now?

35 Sally sold pieces of her pottery for x dollars each at an art show. Paul sold pieces of his pottery for y dollars each at the same show. Paul sold four pieces of pottery for a total of $85, and Sally sold five pieces for a total of $40 more than Paul. How much more, in dollars, did Sally charge for each piece of her pottery than Paul charged for his? (Ignore the dollar sign when entering your answer in the grid.)

36 Carl knitted 4 more scarves this year than last year. If he knitted 16% more scarves this year than last year, how many did he knit this year?

37
$$y = 2x + 5$$
$$y = -2(x + 1)^2 + 3$$

If (x, y) is a solution to the system of equations above, what is one possible value of y?

38 The average GPA for the girl's lacrosse team for each year starting in 2012 and ending in 2016 has been 3.5. What is the lowest the GPA could be in 2017 so that the average GPA for all six years is at least 3.47? Round to the nearest hundredth.

STOP

If you finish before time is called, you may check your work on this section only.
Do not turn to any other section.

SECTION 5: ESSAY

50 Minutes—1 Essay

DIRECTIONS: The essay gives you an opportunity to show how effectively you can read and comprehend a passage and write an essay analyzing the passage. In your essay, you should demonstrate that you have read the passage carefully, present a clear and logical analysis, and use language precisely.

Your essay will need to be written on the lines provided in your answer booklet. You will have enough space if you write on every line and keep your handwriting to an average size. Try to print or write clearly so that your writing will be legible to the readers scoring your essay.

As you read the passage below, consider how Catherine Anderson uses the following:

- Evidence, such as facts, statistics, or examples, to support claims.
- Reasoning to develop ideas and to connect claims and evidence.
- Stylistic or persuasive elements, such as word choice or appeals to emotion, to add power to the ideas expressed.

Adapted from "Michael Graves sought to create joy through superior design" by Catherine Anderson, originally published in The Conversation on March 25, 2015. Catherine Anderson is Assistant Professor of Interior Architecture and Design at George Washington University. (This passage was edited for length.)

1   Visit the website of designer Michael Graves, and you'll be greeted with the words "Humanistic Design = Transformative Results." The mantra can double as Graves' philosophy. For Graves—who passed away at 80 earlier this month—paid no heed to architectural trends, social movements or the words of his critics. Instead, it was the everyday human being—the individual—who inspired and informed his work.

2   During a career that spanned over 50 years, Graves held firm to the belief that design could effect tremendous change in people's day-to-day lives. From small-scale kitchen products to immense buildings, a thread runs throughout his products: accessible, aesthetic forms that possess a sense of warmth and appeal.

3   Early in his career, Graves was identified as one of the New York Five, a group of influential architects who whole-heartedly embraced Modernism, the architectural movement that subscribed to the use of simple, clean lines, forms devoid of embellishments and modern materials such as steel and glass.

4   However, Graves is best described as a Post-Modernist. He eschewed the austerity of Modernism and its belief that "less is more," instead embracing history and references to the past. He rejected the notion that decoration, or ornament, was a "crime" (as Austrian architect Adolf Loos wrote in 1908); rather, he viewed it as a way for his architecture to convey meaning.

5   As the noted architectural historian Spiro Kostof explains in his book *A History of Architecture: Settings and Rituals*, "Post Modernists turn to historical memory . . . to ornament, as a way of enriching the language of architecture."

6   … Along these lines, Graves loathed the idea of intellectualizing his structures. Instead, he sought to make them accessible, understandable, and poignant to all passersby. . . .

7   In addition to designing buildings, Graves embarked upon a long and highly successful partnership with the Italian kitchenware company Alessi. . . . Graves' most famous Alessi design is his iconic teakettle . . . which had a cheerful red whistling bird and sky-blue handle. On sale since 1985, the best-selling product is still in production today.

8   In 1999, Minneapolis-based discount retail giant Target approached Graves with an offer to design a line of kitchen products, ranging from toasters to spatulas.

CONTINUE

9   While some might have shied away from having their work associated with a mega-corporation like Target, Graves wholly embraced the project. . . .

10 In all, Graves' collaboration with Target would last 13 years; during this time, the designer would become a household name, with millions of units of his products appearing in American homes.

11 Many of Graves' designs for Target—his spatula, can opener, and ice cream scoop—had chunky, sky-blue handles. Other appliances that were white . . . were sprinkled with touches of color. . . . Black and beige had no place in Graves' palette.

12 The option to select a better-looking product with a slightly higher price versus the same article but with a less expensive, nondescript appearance is now the norm for most consumers: good design (and function) are part and parcel of the customer experience (nowhere is this more evident than in Apple's rise to dizzying heights as arguably one of the world's most valuable brands).

13 It's an idea that's democratic in nature, and thinking about design through this lens led Graves to create thoughtful, appealing, and affordable products for the masses. . . .

14 As Graves' popularity rose, his critics leveled blistering commentaries about what they deemed a precipitous fall from grace—from a "trend beyond compare" to a "stale trend," as architecture critic Herbert Muschamp noted in a 1999 *New York Times* article. The notion that he had commodified design—and had somehow "cheapened" it—drew the disdain of those who once lauded his works.

15 Yet Graves remained true to his beliefs even into the last phase of his life. In 2003, after an illness left him paralyzed below the waist, he realized that the design of hospitals and equipment . . . could be redesigned and made more functional, comfortable, and visually appealing. He then went on to improve ubiquitous devices such as wheelchairs and walking canes. . . .

16 Consumers may not have ever known his architecture or what the critics thought of his work (or even realized they were buying one of his products). Graves didn't seem to mind. His goal was to provide well-designed items for everyday use rather than impress his detractors.

17 As he told NPR in 2002, "It's the kind of thing where you pick something up or use it with a little bit of joy . . . it puts a smile on your face."

Write an essay in which you explain how Catherine Anderson builds an argument to persuade her audience that Michael Graves' central concern was creating designs that helped "the everyday human being." In your essay, analyze how the writer uses one or more of the features listed previously (or features of your own choice) to strengthen the logic and persuasiveness of her argument. Be sure that your analysis focuses on the most relevant aspects of the passage.

Your essay should not explain whether you agree with Catherine Anderson's claims, but rather explain how she builds an argument to persuade her audience.

STOP

If you finish before time is called, you may check your work on this section only.
Do not turn to any other section.

1. A	**12.** B	**23.** D	**34.** D	**45.** D
2. B	**13.** D	**24.** B	**35.** B	**46.** A
3. A	**14.** A	**25.** D	**36.** A	**47.** C
4. D	**15.** D	**26.** C	**37.** B	**48.** B
5. A	**16.** A	**27.** C	**38.** C	**49.** A
6. C	**17.** A	**28.** D	**39.** C	**50.** C
7. A	**18.** B	**29.** D	**40.** C	**51.** D
8. C	**19.** B	**30.** D	**41.** A	**52.** B
9. C	**20.** B	**31.** C	**42.** C	
10. B	**21.** D	**32.** A	**43.** A	
11. C	**22.** A	**33.** B	**44.** B	

READING TEST RAW SCORE ☐
(Number of correct answers)

1. **The correct answer is A.** The overall main points of the article are all meant to dispel the myths surrounding earthquakes: how and why they occur. The article provides supporting details about the science of earthquakes, which also counter the Hollywood myths. Thus, choice A is the correct answer. While the author does explain the causes and effects of earthquakes, it is to dispel the myths created by Hollywood, thus choice B is incorrect. Choice C is incorrect, as the passage applies to earthquakes only and not to science in general. Choice D is incorrect as this topic is not covered in the passage.

2. **The correct answer is B.** The main causes of earthquakes are described in paragraph 3, which explains that "An earthquake is caused by a sudden slip on a fault" (lines 13–14) before stating that "Stresses in the Earth's outer layer push the sides of the fault together" (lines 21–22). The mere existence of faults is not what causes earthquakes; it is the actions to which those faults are subjected that are true causes, so choice A is not the best answer. An earthquake is caused by the actions on a single fault, so choice C is incorrect. The author only mentions the quality of the engineering of structures in the region in lines 47–48 in relation to the damage earthquakes cause, not the cause of earthquakes themselves, so choice D is incorrect.

3. **The correct answer is A.** The article is intended to separate fact from fiction for those who might be misinformed. Although there are a lot of scientific facts in the passage, the tone is casual and almost scolding in its refutation of the myths surrounding earthquakes, which the author makes clear in lines 86–90 ("So when you see . . . and your family."). Choice C is incorrect because filmmakers would not be particularly interested in being reminded that the films they make are often not based in reality. Choices B and D are incorrect as both scientists and science teachers would already know these facts.

4. **The correct answer is D.** The article counters the myths by pointing out in lines 69–72 that the ocean isn't a hole into which a land mass can fall, as the ocean is itself just land at a lower elevation. Thus, choice D is the correct answer. Choice A is incorrect because it accepts the myth as fact rather than countering it. Choice B is incorrect because while the author talks about the land mass under the ocean as being at a lower sea level than California, it is only to explain the geology of the region. Choice C is

incorrect because the author does not explain that California and Alaska are similar but rather that southern California is moving slowly toward Alaska.

5. **The correct answer is A.** The author notes in lines 69–71 that California cannot break off, as it is part of the land that makes up the ocean floor, only at a higher elevation. Thus, choice A is the correct answer. Choice B (lines 71–72) is incorrect, as it is not an explanation as much as a refutation. Choices C (lines 72–74) and D (lines 74–76) are incorrect, as they merely point out another feature of the geology of California; they do not clarify why California will not be swept out into the ocean.

6. **The correct answer is C.** In the context of this passage, *stress* is pressure that builds up in rocks. Only in human interactions does *stress* describe the pressure that builds up in people, causing worry and/or anxiety, so choice A is incorrect. Stress does not imply the idea of weight in the context of this passage, making choice B incorrect. It also does not mean "emphasis," so choice D is incorrect.

7. **The correct answer is A.** The passage makes it clear that the closer a region is to the earthquake source (lines 48–50); the more that region will be affected. The most likely reason that San Francisco, or any place, would experience so much damage is that it lacked buildings that could withstand the shaking from an earthquake, and the earthquake was probably very strong. Information in the passage makes it impossible to know whether or not choice B is true. The passage implies that earthquakes are a major concern in California (lines 36–38), so it is unlikely that its city officials never thought an earthquake, would occur in San Francisco. So even though the city was apparently unprepared for such a strong and damaging earth-quake, choice C is not entirely correct. Faults across the country are irrelevant to a situation in one particular city, so choice D is not correct.

8. **The correct answer is C.** Lines 45–48 clearly explain that the effects of an earthquake are dependent on the proximity of the earthquake source to the affected region, as well as the quality of the engineering of the structures that are shaken by the earthquake. Choice B (lines 28–32) is incorrect because these lines discuss the creation of an earthquake but do not mention the affected region of an earthquake. Similarly, choices A (lines 13–22) and D (lines 79–81) both contain lines that regard the attributes and causes of an earthquake but fail to address why a region is affected. Therefore, choices A and D are incorrect.

9. **The correct answer is C.** The word *amplified* is used to describe the shaking of a "moderate" earthquake that nevertheless causes "significant damage" in certain areas. It describes how in certain areas, a moderate condition is intensified, so choice C is the best answer. *Lifted* implies an upward movement, and it would not make sense to suggest that the earthquake's shaking was lifted above the surface of the earth, so choice A cannot be correct in this particular context. *Supplemented* means "added to," and it would not make sense for anything to be added to the shaking, so choice B is incorrect. While *amplified* can be used to mean "made louder," the volume of the earthquake's noise is not significant in this context; the intensity of its shaking and how that shaking started moderately but caused significant damage is, so choice D is incorrect.

10. **The correct answer is B.** The phrase reveals that disaster movies are made more dramatic for effect at the expense of scientific accuracy. Using the word *inconvenient* mocks the story; it implies that the earthquake is used as an easy way to write a character out of the story. Choices A, C, and D are incorrect because the use of the referenced phrase does not directly relate to scientific information within the passages, as stated in these choices.

11. **The correct answer is C.** The passage explains that friction is required for an earthquake (lines 81–82), making the idea of a gaping fault impossible, as a fault line could only open up without friction. Choice A is incorrect because although the concept is portrayed in movies, as described in lines 77–79, that fact does not refute the myth. Choice B is incorrect because this question is about earthquakes causing the ground to open up and not "mega-quakes." While the author does state that earthquakes can cause landslides (lines 82–84), he or she immediately follows this up by stating "Faults, however, do not gape open during an earth-quake." (lines 84-85), so choice D is incorrect.

12. **The correct answer is B.** Patrick Henry lashes out against concentrated power (Passage 1, lines 1–5). Madison, on the other hand, explains that power is essential, but separating the power of the government into different departments (branches) will act as a check on that power, ensuring that it cannot get out of control (Passage 2, sentence 1). Choices A, C, and D are incorrect because the statements made in them do not reflect the content of the passages.

13. **The correct answer is D.** Henry addresses the issue of concentrating power and says that it rests "on a

supposition that your American governors shall be honest" (lines 25–26), which, in his view, is a dangerous and unnecessarily risky assumption to make. Choice A is incorrect because Henry actually suggests the opposite of this conclusion, voicing concern about a lack of check and balances in lines 5–6 before speculating that a president who basically operates as a king could be the result of a lack of checks and balances in line 19. Choices B and C are both incorrect because neither correlate with the views of Henry and would therefore not be an objection of his.

14. **The correct answer is A.** Henry addresses the listener frequently as "sir" and as "you" throughout passage 1. Both Henry and Madison make use of the passive voice, making choice B incorrect. For example, in line 41, Madison states "…it is evident that …". Although Henry's speech might be described as livelier overall, he also uses the passive voice. For example, in line 14, he states that the "Constitution is said to have beautiful features." Both Henry and Madison make use of questions to engage the reader, making choice C incorrect. Neither Henry nor Madison use alliteration (the repetition of initial consonant sounds), making choice D incorrect.

15. **The correct answer is D.** Madison argues that a government whose powers are separated by design will act as controls, each branch on the other, and avoid concentration of power. Although Madison describes government as a reflection of human nature, this is not a counterargument to those who were concerned about a strong central government, so choice A does not make much sense. Choice B is incorrect because it exaggerates Madison's simple suggestion that people are not "angels" and require some monitoring from their fellow people to ensure that they always act in the people's best interests. Choice C is incorrect because Madison does state that the people should monitor the government to a certain degree.

16. **The correct answer is A.** Lines 51–56 describe how Madison believes the government should be divided into branches that would check and balance each other. This would serve to counteract the idea that the government is too centralized because the branches would allow for the power to be divided and would make it so that one branch would not have too much power. Choice B (lines 62–64) makes the mistake of concluding that choice A was the correct answer. Choice C (lines 64–65) makes the mistake that choice B was the correct answer to the previous question, and it was not. Choice D (lines 70–73) relates to people influencing the

government, which relates to choice C in the previous question, but since that answer choice was incorrect, choice D has no bearing on the correct answer to this question.

17. **The correct answer is A.** Henry and Madison's statements are both very similar, indicating that both men believed that even the most seemingly honest person was too flawed, too human, to be trusted with complete control of the people she or he ruled. Henry says that being "good men" is not enough to earn that trust, while Madison suggests that anyone short of being a complete "angel" could not be trusted with complete control. Choice B is too extreme; one does not have to be completely disinterested in the rights and liberties of the people they rule to be undeserving of complete control. Choice C is incorrect because both men are skeptical of allowing anyone to be trusted with complete control. Even though its statement about Madison is true, choice D is incorrect because Henry does not show that he did not believe government was necessary.

18. **The correct answer is B.** In lines 9–10, Henry voices his image of the framers of the Constitution with the words "we are not feared by foreigners; we do not make nations tremble," which suggest a desire to intimidate other countries, so choice B is correct. Since other countries ("foreigners . . . nations"), and not the American people, are the targets of these words, choice A is incorrect. In lines 10–11, Henry questions the idea that these intimidations would "constitute happiness or secure liberties" for Americans, so choice C is incorrect. These words of intimidation would have the opposite effect of building strong relationships with other countries, so choice D is incorrect.

19. **The correct answer is B.** In line 5 ("the genius of republicanism"), Henry praises a republican form of government (i.e., one that has elected representatives and is not run by a monarchy). Henry indicates that such a centralized government, as outlined in the Constitution, cannot work with the goals of forming a republican government. Choices A, C, and D are incorrect because Henry is adamant about his opposition to anything similar to a monarchial government, autocracy and plutocracy included.

20. **The correct answer is B.** Line 5 ("the genius of republicanism") clearly states that Henry believes that the ideal form of government is republicanism where all the people are represented. Choices C (line 17) and D (line 19) are similar because they both have to do with

the United States becoming a monarchy. Therefore, these choices are both incorrect. Choice A (lines 2–3) is incorrect because it does not have to do with Henry's preference in forms of government.

21. **The correct answer is D.** Madison's reference to "department" refers to the branches of the government that are outlined in the Constitution (executive, legislative, judicial), which is apparent from the context. An executive may be in charge of a department, but a single person would not constitute an entire government department, so choice A does not make sense. Choice B is not the best answer since a "territory" would more likely describe an area of land rather than a segment of government. Choice C is incorrect because *level* implies a hierarchy, which does not apply to this particular context.

22. **The correct answer is A.** In the context of the sentence, Madison is referring to how the checks on one department (or branch) would be in turn proportional to the checks on another department. One department would hold another in check to maintain a balance of power so that power would not get concentrated in one branch. Choices B, C, and D do not make sense in the context and are therefore incorrect.

23. **The correct answer is D.** The article mentions multiple scientists and institutions that all worked on identifying the shark and sharing their information so that it could be correctly cataloged and understood (lines 15–16, 29–31, and 50–53). The overall conclusion about methodology, therefore, shows that science can be a collaborative endeavor. Although the passage describes multiple institutions working together, this answer choice assumes that this is necessary for all examples of scientific information gathering. This conclusion is too general and baseless for choice A to be correct. Choice B is too extreme, since it assumes that the luck that led to the discovery of the pocket shark in this passage applies to all instances of scientific information gathering. Choice C also assumes that the circumstances in this passage will be true for all other instances of scientific information gathering.

24. **The correct answer is B.** Lines 10–12 state that while the shark is small enough to "fit in your pocket," it actually gets its name because of the pocket-like "orifice above the pectoral fin," which confirms that choice B is correct and eliminates choices A and C. The author never suggests that the pocket shark has markings that resemble pockets, so choice D is incorrect.

25. **The correct answer is D.** According to line 15, the pocket shark was a newborn, so it could not have transported itself to a place so far from where the only other pocket shark was discovered near Peru. Locating the parents, or "mom and dad" (line 19), could provide clues to how the newborn ended up in the Gulf, so choice D is the best answer. The author's mention of the shark's parents provides the best clue to this answer, while the absence of speculation about the area around the Gulf or whether or not the differences between the Gulf and Peru had any effect on the pocket shark's location make choices A and B less logical conclusions. The author provides no indication that studying sharks native to the Gulf would yield any information about how the pocket shark ended up there.

26. **The correct answer is C.** Choice C (lines 18–21) ties all the ideas that led to the answer to the previous question together. It mentions the desire to find the shark's parents, or "mom and dad," and learn how those parents got to the Gulf when the only other discovered pocket shark was located off Peru. Choice A (lines 14–15) only establishes that the pocket shark was a newborn and does not do as strong a job of establishing the importance of finding its parents as choice C does. Lines 15–18 only establish how scientists knew the shark was a newborn ("the shark displayed an unhealed umbilical scar"), so choice B is incorrect. Choice D (lines 22–24) only explains where Mark Grace found the pocket shark; it provides no insight about the importance of finding its parents.

27. **The correct answer is C.** Paragraph 5 explains that tissue samples were analyzed to get genetic information that could be compared to other specimens. Using this data, scientists could then determine how to classify the pocket shark. Choice A is not the best answer since other sharks could be the same length as the pocket shark, and lines 33–36 (A tissue . . . *Mollisquama*) explicitly explain how scientists used tissue samples to determine the shark's species. The author discusses the pocket-like orifice to explain how the shark got its name but never implies that this characteristic helped scientists determine its species. In lines 39–42, the author states that learning its species may provide clues to the shark's position in the food chain, not the other way around, so choice D is incorrect.

28. **The correct answer is D.** It is mentioned in the passage that scientists found an umbilical scar that had not healed, suggesting that the fish had been "recently born" (line 15). In lines 20–21, it is mentioned that only one other pocket fish had ever been found before, giving insufficient basis for comparison to determine age, making choice B incorrect. Choices A and C are not explicitly stated in the passage, and in any case, do not make sense in relation to fish.

29. **The correct answer is D.** The passage explicitly states that scientists were excited to discover the pocket shark because it is so unique and so few of them have been found (lines 4–5 and 20–21). Choice A is incorrect because the author actually places the pocket shark into the *Dalatiidae* shark family (lines 37–39) that existed before the pocket shark was discovered. While the pocket is "distinctive" (line 11), there is no evidence that the pocket shark is the only shark with such an orifice. Even if this is true, an explicit statement about why scientists are excited about its discovery renders choice B incorrect. The author mentions that pocket sharks were found in the Gulf and far away off Peru but does not offer this detail as the reason why scientists are so excited about its discovery, so choice C is incorrect.

30. **The correct answer is D.** Lines 54–57 explicitly state that it is "exciting" to find a shark that is so "unusual" and "rare," so choice D is correct. Choice A (lines 20–21) seems to make the mistake that the correct answer to the previous question was choice C (lines 36–39) when this is not the case. While lines 27–28 do indicate that the pocket shark is rare, they do not indicate that scientists are excited about that fact, so choice B is not the best answer. Choice C seems to make the mistake of assuming that choice A was the correct answer to the previous question when it was not.

31. **The correct answer is C.** *Robust* in this context describes a collection that has variety. A specimen is a sample used for testing, so it makes sense for the lab to have a large, substantial collection of marine animal samples for testing. Choices A, B, and D are incorrect because it cannot be inferred, based on the passage, that the "robust specimen collection" is how these choices describe it.

32. **The correct answer is A.** The kitefin is part of the *Dalatiidae* family, which is partially defined by how they remove oval plugs of flesh from their prey (lines 39–42). The passage also states that sharks in the *Dalatiidae* family eat squid (line 42), so choice B is incorrect. While

the pocket and kitefin sharks are from the same family, they cannot be identical; otherwise, there would be no reason to give them distinct names, so choice C does not make much sense. Whether the pocket shark was discovered before or after the kitefin shark cannot be conclusively determined from evidence in the passage, so choice D is not the best answer.

33. **The correct answer is B.** In lines 18–20, Twain announces his intention with a mocking turn of phrase ("If Cooper had any real knowledge of Nature's ways of doing things, he had a most delicate art in concealing the fact.") and goes on to describe an implausible description of nature in one of Cooper's stories, so choice B is the best answer. Cooper just seems to be telling a story in the tale of Chingachgook, not making an argument, so choice A is not the best answer. Although there is a Native American in the story Twain describes, he is more focused on criticizing Cooper's treatment of nature than his treatment of Native Americans, so choice C is not the best answer. Twain is making a point about Cooper's wider treatment of nature than how the writer specifically described a stream bed, so choice D is not the best answer choice.

34. **The correct answer is D.** For the entirety of the passage, Twain mocks Cooper's story, but he does so in a humorous way. For example, in the first paragraph Twain makes the humorously absurd suggestion that there is some way to score committing offenses against literary art (lines 3–4) and in lines 58–59, he describes the action of the novel, saying: "Let me explain what the five did—you would not be able to reason it out for yourself." This is sarcasm making mockery of the action of the characters in the book. It is light-hearted and expresses incredulity, thus setting a humorous tone. While Twain might be exhausted with reading Cooper's work, Twain's own writing is so sharp and witty that he never seems exhausted, himself, in this passage, so choice A is not the best answer. The voice of the passage is informal as evidenced by its abundant jokes, and as a result, not scholarly. This makes choice B incorrect. The tone of the passage is humorous; however, it is too biting to accurately be described as cheery and does not suggest optimism, making choice C incorrect.

35. **The correct answer is B.** Lines 8–9 illustrate the hyperbole that Twain uses to humorously describe how Cooper took liberty with his description of the techniques Native Americans used to track footprints to find and/or attack enemy tribes. In these lines, Twain's description of wearing out the moccasins in the process of following a trail pokes fun at the erroneous nature of Cooper's characterization. Choices A, C, and D are all critiques, but they do not express humor.

36. **The correct answer is A.** Twain refers to Cooper's use of various literary devices as "stage properties" (line 5) as a way to mock Cooper. The "barrels and barrels of moccasins" (line 9) is one example. Another is his description (in lines 10–17) of "the broken twig." The "stage properties" Twain refers to do not have anything to do with drama or theater, making choices B, C, and D incorrect.

37. **The correct answer is B.** The pronunciation guide (lines 20–21) is another way of mocking Cooper's book. Here, Twain describes the book and throws in, as an aside, the pronunciation key to indicate how far Cooper veers from reality, so much so that the Native Americans he describes might as well be called Chicago. Choices A and C are incorrect because Twain is writing satirically and does not actually intend for the reader to pronounce the Native American's name correctly. As the work is satire, Twain only intends to criticize Cooper, and illustrating that Cooper's work was about actual Native Americans would not achieve this goal. Therefore, choice D is incorrect.

38. **The correct answer is C.** The biggest and most frequent criticism Twain makes in the passage is to show how unrealistic and senseless the plot and characters are. For example, in describing the ark (paragraph 5), he explains how the timing is off for the entire scene, making its occurrence totally unreasonable. And here he jokes and ridicules the outcome: "He missed the house and landed in the stern of the scow. It was not much of a fall, yet it knocked him silly" (lines 51–53), showing how absurd the storyline is. If anything, Twain suggests that Cooper had a simplistic approach to creating stories since his books suffer from so many lazy plot holes (for example, the incompletely described passage of the ark in the fifth paragraph), so choice A is incorrect. While Twain's tone implies he may appreciate writing that does not take itself too seriously, an absence of humor is not one of the criticisms he lodges against Cooper's work, so choice B is not the best answer. Twain describes quite a bit of action in Cooper's stories, so "boring" may not be something of which they are guilty, and Twain certainly never suggests as much in this particular passage, so choice D can also be eliminated.

39. **The correct answer is C.** In lines 58–59, Twain addresses the reader to suggest that there is no way for the reader to figure out what is happening in a particular sequence in Cooper's story, which supports the idea that his stories do not make sense. Choice A (lines 3–4) is merely a hyperbolic description of Cooper's list of defects and illustrates Twain's style of satire. Choices B (lines 34–35) and D (lines 64–65) describe instances in which Cooper bent reality to suit his poor plotting, but neither sends a general message about the senselessness of Cooper's writing as well as choice C does.

40. **The correct answer is C.** Twain criticizes Cooper's characterization of the Native Americans as sneaky and inept. From line 30 to line 65, he describes a group of Native Americans attempting to sneak attack an ark but completely botching the job. They bumble through every attempt they make to attack the settlers (for example, they can't jump onto a very slow-moving boat, because they miscalculate the timing). The fact that they cannot make successful leaps onto the ark contradicts the notion that Cooper portrays Native Americans as athletic, and their ineptness indicates that he does not depict them as very smart either, so choice A is incorrect. The ineptness of these characters hardly makes them effectively cunning or dangerous, so choice B is wrong too. Cooper's Native American characters may be unable to plot an attack well, but they still plot an attack, so it would be wrong to conclude that Cooper characterizes Native Americans as gentle and respectful, choice D.

41. **The correct answer is A.** Twain's thesis is that Cooper's work is an extremely defective work of art. After strongly criticizing *Deerslayer* throughout the passage, Twain ends by comparing it to "a literary delirium tremens" (line 70). Because Twain doesn't use *like* or *as*, his comparison is an analogy, not a simile, making choice B incorrect. There are no references to any personal weaknesses in Cooper's character or mental state in the passage, making choices C and D incorrect. In addition, Twain's analogy is meant to be humorous, not personal.

42. **The correct answer is C.** In the context of the sentence, *destitute* means that the work is void of the variables that make a story artful. Although the word can mean impoverished, that meaning does not fit this context, making choice A incorrect. Choices B and D are both incorrect because they do not make sense in this context.

43. The correct answer is A. The overall descriptions are of the character Paul. The passage describes how he looks, his actions and reactions, and his emotions. Through the use of a narrator telling the story, it also describes how others react to him, giving the reader an outside perspective of the character. Thus, choice A is the correct answer. Choice B is incorrect because the passage description notes that it is from a short story and therefore fiction. Choice C is incorrect because there is no plot in the passage. Choice D is incorrect because it is the character of Paul—not any one setting—that is emphasized.

44. The correct answer is B. The author notes in lines 1–3 that it "was Paul's afternoon to appear before the faculty of the Pittsburgh High School to account for his various misdemeanors." Thus, choice B is the correct answer. Choice A is incorrect because, while the author notes that Paul does tell the principal that he wants to return to school, this was not the reason why he was asked to appear before the faculty. Choice C is incorrect because tardiness is not mentioned as one of Paul's infractions. Choice D is incorrect because, while his father calls the principal after Paul's suspension confessing that he is perplexed by his son's behavior, there is no mention that Paul's parents are in the principal's office at this time.

45. The correct answer is D. The carnation is obvious on his coat lapel, and it is a contrast to the way he is dressed in shabby clothes, as if he didn't care. And yet the carnation adds a note of frivolity and mockery to the seriousness of the event. It is a way of subtly communicating that he will do as he pleases, in defiance of the wishes of the faculty, thus choice D is the correct answer. Choice A is incorrect, as Paul does not wish to show respect to the faculty. Choice B is incorrect because Paul does not intend to show remorse. In fact, he intends to show defiance. Choice C is incorrect because if Paul wanted to appear wealthy, he would not wear shabby clothes.

46. The correct answer is A. The author notes in lines 29–30 that his teachers stated their charges against him with "such a rancor and aggrievedness as evinced that this was not a usual case," which indicates extreme feelings of frustration and anger, so choice A is the correct answer. While sadness and confusion can often be felt in conjunction with frustration and anger, the author's failure to mention such emotions makes choice B incorrect. Lines 51–54 indicate extreme emotions that contradict the conclusion in choice C, and the fact that these are negative emotions eliminates choice D.

47. The correct answer is C. In lines 27–30, the author notes that Paul's teachers stated their charges with "rancor and aggrievedness," words that suggest anger and frustration. Thus, choice C is the correct answer. Choice A (lines 3–5) is incorrect because these lines refer to Paul's father's feelings. Choice B (lines 11–14) is incorrect because, while it suggests that the teachers did not feel that Paul was contrite, it does not support the idea that they were angry and frustrated. Choice D (lines 44–46) is incorrect because these lines explain how the teachers interpreted Paul's feelings toward them.

48. The correct answer is B. When the English teacher took Paul's hand to guide him, he reacted by shuddering and thrusting "his hands violently behind him" (line 40). His teacher reacts to this with astonishment (lines 41–42) and "could scarcely have been more hurt and embarrassed had he struck at her," which supports choice B. Her astonishment and the fact that she took his reaction so personally suggest that she may not have much experience dealing with emotional students, so choice A is not the best answer. The author merely writes that she "attempted to guide his hand" (line 39); she does not suggest that the teacher took his hand because she was impatient with how slowly Paul was writing, so choice C is not the best answer. While Paul did make "a running commentary on the lecture" (line 49) in one of his classes, the author implies that this class took place in a different class from the English one, so choice D is not the best answer.

49. The correct answer is A. Paul's appearance is described in great detail, and his outer appearance is often betrayed by behavior that gives away his true feelings. For example, he smiles but his fingers tremble and play with the buttons on his coat (lines 61–62). Choices B, C, and D are incorrect because they do not describe Paul's actions and feelings; rather, they describe contrasts with others and their appearance and reactions.

50. The correct answer is C. Cather notes in her description of Paul playing with the buttons on his coat that it was the only outward sign of his discomfort, thus in lines 58–63, she connects his outer actions to his inner feelings, allowing the reader inside Paul's emotional state. Choice C then is the correct answer. Choices A (lines 54–55) and B (lines 55–58) are incorrect, as the lines do not interpret the meaning of Paul's facial expression. Choice D (lines 66–68) is incorrect, as the interpretation noted here is made by others and not necessarily reflective of Paul's feelings.

51. The correct answer is D. The word as used in the title suggests that the story is focused on the personality makeup of the protagonist. Thus, choice D is the correct answer. Choice A is incorrect because the narrator does not describe Paul's complexion. Choice B is incorrect, as the word does not make sense in the context. Choice C is incorrect, because the story is a description of a boy's behavior over a period of time, and mood suggests one particular moment or feeling.

52. The correct answer is B. A dandy is a person who is meticulous in the way he dresses and takes extreme care in his appearance. The paragraph in which the word is used is in the context of Paul's clothing, and *dandy* suits the characterization of Paul, so choice B is the correct answer. Choices A, C, and D are incorrect because the context is a description of Paul's dress.

1. D	**10.** B	**19.** D	**28.** C	**37.** A
2. B	**11.** C	**20.** B	**29.** B	**38.** D
3. C	**12.** A	**21.** A	**30.** A	**39.** B
4. D	**13.** D	**22.** C	**31.** C	**40.** C
5. A	**14.** B	**23.** B	**32.** D	**41.** B
6. A	**15.** A	**24.** D	**33.** A	**42.** D
7. B	**16.** B	**25.** B	**34.** A	**43.** A
8. C	**17.** D	**26.** A	**35.** D	**44.** B
9. D	**18.** C	**27.** A	**36.** C	

WRITING AND LANGUAGE TEST RAW SCORE [   ]
(Number of correct answers)

1. **The correct answer is D.** Choice D provides a transition between sentences and establishes the historical importance of Blackwell's accomplishment. Choice C does the latter but not the former. Choice A is awkward. Choice B unnecessarily repeats information already provided in the previous sentence.

2. **The correct answer is B.** The context of the paragraph makes clear that the expectations of those around her were that she would fail in becoming a doctor and that Blackwell had ignored or disregarded those expectations. Choice A is incorrect because her achievement was not a condemnation or criticism of the expectation that she would fail; it simply flouted it. Choice C is incorrect because *incite* means to encourage or inspire, and the context does not support the idea that she inspired the expectation that she would fail. Choice D is incorrect because the context makes clear that in earning her degree, Blackwell did not meet the expectations of her peers. Rather, she disregarded and far surpassed them.

3. **The correct answer is C.** The comparison here is between educating a boy and educating a girl, thus choice C is the correct answer. Choice A is incorrect because it illogically compares educating a boy to a girl, rather than to educating a girl. Choice B is incorrect because it illogically compares educating a boy to a girl's preference for education. Choice D is incorrect because it illogically compares educating a boy to opportunities for girls.

4. **The correct answer is D.** The phrase, "To make up for the gaps in her education," modifies *she* or Blackwell and should directly precede a reference to Blackwell to avoid confusion. Choice A is incorrect because the phrase appears to modify household. Choices B and C are incorrect because the phrase appears awkwardly in the middle of the sentence and it is unclear what it modifies.

5. **The correct answer is A.** The first part of the sentence, "As she prepared to apply to medical school," correctly tells the reader when the events of the sentence took place. Choices B and C incorrectly state when these events take place. Choice D incorrectly suggests that Blackwell wanted to be a psychologist.

6. **The correct answer is A.** This sentence provides significant context clues to help you determine the right word to include. The latter half of the sentence is building on a specific contention, saying "at least one advisor went so far as to suggest that she might disguise herself as a man in order to gain admittance." Such a notion suggests that her advisors felt great *doubt* that she would gain direct admittance to medical school, so choice A is correct. There is no evidence that there was any debate, insistence, or supposing going on, so the other answer choices are incorrect.

7. The correct answer is B. The antecedent of the pronoun is Blackwell, so the pronoun should be *her*, making choice B the correct answer. Choices A, C, and D do not agree with the antecedent *Blackwell*.

8. The correct answer is C. The sentence should be written in the simple past tense: *became* agrees with the verb tense used in the sentences that follow, thus choice C is the correct answer. Choice A is incorrect because it is in the present perfect tense while the sentence that follows is in the simple past tense. Choice B is incorrect because it is in the present tense, and all of the events take place in the distant past. Choice D is incorrect because it is in the future tense.

9. The correct answer is D. The phrase, "all of whom were men," is nonrestrictive, which means it must be set off by commas. Only choice D has the commas in the appropriate place to set off the entire phrase. Choice A is incorrect, as there are no commas to set off the nonrestrictive phrase. Choices B and C are incorrect because the commas are in the wrong place.

10. The correct answer is B. This choice reduces wordiness and redundancy, as experiencing prejudice and biases implies that obstacles and challenges were faced. Choice A is incorrect because, as stated, experiencing prejudice and biases implies that real obstacles and challenges were faced, so there's no need to restate it. Choice C is incorrect because it fails to specify that the challenges faced included prejudice and biases, which is significant information that should be included. Choice D is incorrect because the wording is awkward and would introduce confusion to the sentence.

11. The correct answer is C. Only choice C supports the idea that, although she faced barriers, she was successful by distinguishing herself as a promoter of preventative medicine and medical opportunities for women. Choice A is incorrect because it does not support the idea that she was successful, and it does not refer to her career after she graduated from medical school. Choice B is incorrect because it does not describe anything that Blackwell went on to do after she got her degree. Choice D is incorrect because it does not describe anything that Blackwell did in her career.

12. The correct answer is A. This choice provides useful historical context for when Carson's book was published, informing readers that few people in 1962 expressed concern about the environment. This helps advance the idea that Carson was brave for speaking out. Choice B is not correct, as Carson's age is not a

significant factor here. Choice C is incorrect because this information is not irrelevant, and the book is indeed an important publication. Choice D is incorrect because adding this sentence does not create a division in the focus of the paragraph.

13. The correct answer is D. The style of the passage is formal and objective, and only choice D corresponds with this style. Choices A and B are incorrect because they employ an informal style. Choice C is incorrect because it is not objective in referring to "outsized egos."

14. The correct answer is B. The sentence is a question and requires a question mark at the end. Choices A, C, and D are incorrect because the sentence is interrogative and requires a question mark.

15. The correct answer is A. In this sentence, the phrase "DDT in particular" represents a sharp break in thought and should be set off by dashes. The sentence as it is written is correct. Choice B is incorrect because a dash must be used at the beginning and end of the phrase to set it off from the rest of the sentence. Choice C is incorrect because while commas could be used to separate the phrase, they must be used before and after the phrase to be correct. While parenthesis could be used to set off the phrase, in choice D, they are only used to set off part of it, making it incorrect.

16. The correct answer is B. The information above the pie chart indicates that the chart refers to the most heavily used pesticides by percentage in 1968. Only choice B accurately notes this by referencing that DDT accounted for 11% of all pesticides used in that year. Choice A is incorrect because the chart does not show the amount of farmland that was sprayed with DDT. Choice C is incorrect because the chart does not indicate the percentage of pests contained by DDT. Choice D is incorrect because the chart does not show the percentage of farmers and gardeners who used DDT.

17. The correct answer is D. The context of the paragraph, as well as the point later in the paragraph that pesticides "were able to penetrate systems and remain there for years," indicates that the pesticides were seeping into, or permeating, the soil and rivers. Choice A is incorrect because there is no support for the idea that the pesticides sapped the water from soil and rivers. Choice B is incorrect because the pesticides could not seize the soil and rivers. Choice C is not correct because *transcend* does not make sense in the context.

18. The correct answer is C. In the original text, the incorrect pronoun *he* is used, creating confusion as to what noun it's replacing. For clarity, the sentence must restate the antecedent; thus, choice C is the correct answer. Choice B is incorrect because *it* does not agree with any antecedent in the preceding sentence. Choice D is incorrect because *everything* is illogical in the context.

19. **The correct answer is D.** Choice D maintains Carson's argument that pesticides are dangerous. Choice A is incorrect because it suggests that pesticides are beneficial to health. Choice B is incorrect because Carson is not making an argument about cancer specifically, nor does she definitively link the two. Choice C is incorrect because Carson is not talking about only bird populations.

20. **The correct answer is B.** The context of the paragraph suggests that the chemical companies were not willing to accept or admit the potential hazards of their product; thus, choice B is the correct answer. Choice A is incorrect because *contradict* suggests that they agreed with Carson, an idea not supported by the context. Choice C is incorrect because while it is likely true that chemical companies were not willing to "propagate" or communicate the potential hazards of their product, the fact that they discredited Carson suggests that they were even stronger in their reaction to her claims. Choice D is incorrect because *solicit*, or try to obtain, doesn't make sense in the context.

21. **The correct answer is A.** The first part of the sentence is a subordinating clause, and the subordinating conjunction *since* helps establish the clause's connection to the rest of the sentence. It explains why Carson is blamed for the deaths. Therefore, choice A is the correct answer. The other answer choices are incorrect because they deploy incorrect subordinating conjunctions and introduce confusion and awkwardness into the sentences.

22. **The correct answer is C.** The noun DDT must agree in number with "wonder chemical"; thus, choice C is the correct answer. Choice A is incorrect because DDT does not agree in number with "wonder chemicals." Likewise, choice B is incorrect because "pesticides" does not agree in number with "wonder chemical." Choice D is also incorrect because DDT does not agree in number with *chemicals*.

23. **The correct answer is B.** Because this is a simple list of countries, the items in the series should be set off by commas, choice B. Choices A and C are incorrect because the items are set off by both commas and semicolons. Choice D is incorrect because the lack of internal punctuation creates a grammatically incorrect sentence.

24. **The correct answer is D.** The subject and verb in a sentence must agree in number. In this case, only choice D reflects agreement of the subject and verb as well as appropriate verb tense. Choice A is incorrect because the subject of the sentence, "the Mayan understanding of astronomy," is singular and requires a singular verb, and *were* is plural. Choice B is incorrect because *are* is plural and is in the present tense rather than the past tense. Choice C is incorrect because the verb form *will be* is in the future tense, while the notable achievements of the Mayans occurred in the past.

25. **The correct answer is B.** All of the items in the list should be in the same form, or parallel. Only choice B reflects a parallel structure for all of the verbs: *setting*, *moving*, and *rotating*. The verbs in the other answer choices do not have parallel structure and are incorrect.

26. **The correct answer is A.** The context of the sentence suggests that the Mayans' observations were accurate, as they could predict eclipses and the movement of the planets. Only *astute* reflects this level of accuracy, so choice A is correct. Choice B is incorrect, as *inept* suggests the Mayans weren't skilled at making observations. Choice C is incorrect, as the observations were not "expected," given the time period in which they were made. Choice D is incorrect, as there's no evidence or support within the sentence that refers to the complexity of the Mayan's observations.

27. **The correct answer is A.** This answer ("the movement of the planets") provides an example that is related to astronomy, which is the main focus of the paragraph and sentence. Choices B, C, and D are incorrect because they provide examples that are inconsistent with the topic of astronomy.

28. **The correct answer is C.** *Its* is a possessive determiner and does not require an apostrophe, thus choice C is the correct answer. Choice A is incorrect because *it's* is a contraction of *it is*. Choices B and D are incorrect because they are not words.

29. **The correct answer is B.** A semicolon is used to join two related sentences that can stand on their own. Choice A is incorrect because a colon is not used to join two independent clauses. Choice C is incorrect because a comma may only be used to join two independent clauses if it is followed by a conjunction. Choice D is incorrect because, while it is followed by a conjunction, *but* indicates that the second clause is somehow at odds with the first.

30. **The correct answer is A.** The paragraph suggests that the link between government and astronomy was so complete that the two were inseparable, so choice A is the correct answer, as the word *inextricably* means in a manner that is impossible to separate. There's nothing in the passage to suggest that the link was baffling or embarrassing or that an element of greed was involved, so the other answer choices are incorrect.

31. **The correct answer is C.** No punctuation is required after *symbols* because the phrase that follows it is restrictive, or necessary for identifying which symbols. Only choice C contains no punctuation after *symbols*, so it is the correct answer. Choice A is incorrect because the colon is not correct. Choice B is incorrect because the comma sets the restrictive phrase off from *symbols*. Choice D is incorrect because a semicolon is used only to separate two independent clauses, and "relating to the Sun, Moon, and sky" is not an independent clause.

32. **The correct answer is D.** "Call to war" is correct because it supports the paragraph's focus on when the Mayans would attack their enemies. Choices A, B, and C are incorrect because they provide information that is inconsistent with the paragraph's focus.

33. **The correct answer is A.** The last paragraph is a short summary of the rest of the passage, as the phrase "in short," suggests. Thus, choice A is the correct answer. Choice B is incorrect because *however* indicates a contrast with information that preceded it. Choice C is incorrect because *moreover* suggests that the paragraph will include new information, which it does not. Choice D is also incorrect because *incidentally* suggests that a digression or side topic will follow.

34. **The correct answer is A.** In college, the narrator believed that the employment counselor's advice did not apply to him. Throughout the story, it was made apparent that the narrator was mistaken and should have taken the advice and done a mock interview. Choices B and D are incorrect because *know* and *believe* are is present tense, while the rest of the paragraph is past tense. Choice C is incorrect because it goes against the premise of the story. If the narrator denied that it applied to other people but not to him, he would have known it applied to him and would have done the mock interview. This does not make sense as an introduction to the rest of the story, which shows the narrator did not know how to properly behave and answer questions in a job interview.

35. **The correct answer is D.** The narrator has intended to use the preposition *through* here, and only choice D reflects the correct spelling. Choice A is incorrect because *thorough* is an adjective that means complete or exhaustive. Choice B is also incorrect because *threw* is the past tense of *throw*. Choice C is not correct because *though* functions as either an adverb meaning "however" or a conjunction meaning "while."

36. **The correct answer is C.** Because it is clear that the narrator is seeking a job, the correct possessive modifier before a noun must be *my*, as the passage is written in the first person and the narrator is referring to himself and no one else. Thus, choice C is the correct answer. Choice A is incorrect because *our* is plural in number and refers to the narrator and others, an incorrect reference. Choice B is not correct because there is no antecedent for *his* and the interview clearly belongs to the narrator. Choice D is also incorrect because there is no antecedent for *their*.

37. **The correct answer is A.** The sentence that currently concludes the paragraph provides an effective summation of the ideas in the paragraph, that the law firm that will be the location of the narrator's first interview is the ideal working environment. It also provides context for the paragraph that follows, letting readers know that this job is one that the narrator really wants to get. Choice B is the opposite of the narrator's actual thoughts about the law firm, and there's no evidence to suggest that choices C and D represent the narrator's actual beliefs.

38. **The correct answer is D.** A complete sentence contains both a subject and a predicate. The sentence as it stands is a fragment, as it does not contain a subject. Only choice D contains both a subject (*I*) and a predicate (*informed*). Choice A is incorrect because, as previously noted, it does not contain a subject. Choice B is incorrect, as it is a dependent clause, containing neither a subject nor a predicate. Choice C is incorrect because it, too, is a dependent clause.

39. **The correct answer is B.** The context of the paragraph suggests that the narrator thinks that he is ambitious and well-spoken, as he has articulated his goals to the interviewer. Only choice B fits with the context. Choice A is incorrect because *enigmatic* means mysterious, and there is nothing mysterious about the narrator. Further, the narrator wouldn't assume that the interviewer thought he was mysterious. Choice C is incorrect because means "noticeable." While this could potentially work, it is not usually considered an admirable trait in a job interview. In this case, *articulate* is a better fit. Choice D is incorrect because *incoherent* means unable to be understood, and the narrator clearly thinks he has made a good impression on the interviewer.

40. **The correct answer is C.** The context requires the plural form of *weakness*, which is *weaknesses*. Thus, choice C is the correct answer. Choice A is incorrect because it is a possessive form of *weakness*. Choice B is incorrect because it is the possessive form of the plural *weaknesses*, rather than just the plural. Choice D is not correct because it neither accurately reflects the plural of *weakness*, nor the possessive of the word.

41. **The correct answer is B.** Sentence 3 introduces the topic of the paragraph, which is the narrator's listing of his strengths and weaknesses. Because the sentence clearly introduces the main point of the paragraph, it belongs at the beginning of the paragraph. Choice B, then, is the correct answer, which makes choice A incorrect. Choice C is incorrect because it makes no sense to place the sentence after the sentences that tell the narrator's response to the interviewer's question. Choice D is incorrect, as the existing paragraph is where information regarding the phases of the interview fits best.

42. **The correct answer is D.** The conventional phrase, "I couldn't have cared less," expresses apathy, as the speaker cannot care any less. Only choice D reflects the correct usage. Choice A is incorrect because the narrator is suggesting that he actually *could* have cared less than he already does—the degree of care can be reduced. Choices B and C are incorrect for the same reason, though choice C also incorrectly uses "of" instead of "have."

43. **The correct answer is A.** The previous paragraph ends following the job interview, and this paragraph begins with the narrator not getting the job. An effective transition sentence would chronicle the waiting period between the interview and the hiring decision, so choice A is correct. Choice B is incorrect because the narrator did hear back about the job. Choices C and D are incorrect because they are outside the scope and context of the paragraph.

44. **The correct answer is B.** The word *eventually*, along with the narrator's admission in the first paragraph that he did not go to the college job counseling office when first advised to, suggests that the correct term here is *belated*, or overdue. Thus, choice B is the correct answer. Choice A is incorrect because *deferred* implies that he put off the trip with the intention of going at a later time, and there is no indication that the narrator did this. Choice C is incorrect because *hastened* suggests that the narrator made a speedy trip. Choice D is also incorrect, as *disparaged* means "belittled or criticized," an adjective that doesn't make sense in the context of describing his trip to the college job counseling office.

Section 3: Math Test—No Calculator

1. C	**5.** C	**9.** C	**13.** D	**17.** $\frac{1}{2}$ (1/2)
2. D	**6.** B	**10.** B	**14.** B	**18.** 13
3. B	**7.** B	**11.** C	**15.** D	**19.** $\frac{4}{3}$ (4/3)
4. B	**8.** C	**12.** C	**16.** 24	**20.** 4

MATH TEST—NO CALCULATOR RAW SCORE
(Number of correct answers)

1. **The correct answer is C.** The question asks for Jared's goal in steps per day after d days. He increases his goal by 125 steps each day, so after 1 day it will go up 125(1), after 2 days it will go up by 125(2), and after d days it will go up by $125d$ from his original amount of 950.

2. **The correct answer is D.** Use the correct order of evaluating functions. First evaluate $g(3) = 1$, then substitute in $f(g(3))$ as $f(1)$ to find that $f(g(3)) = 3$.

3. **The correct answer is B.** The formula for exponential decay is $y = a(1 - r)n$, where r is the rate of change, n is the number of times the rate is applied, a is the initial amount, and y is the amount remaining.

4. **The correct answer is B.** First, find half the length of the horizontal distance, which is 15 ft. Then, use the Pythagorean theorem to find the length of each of the slanted sides.

$$a^2 + b^2 = c^2$$
$$8^2 + 15^2 = c^2$$
$$64 + 225 = c^2$$
$$289 = c^2$$
$$17 = c$$

5. **The correct answer is C.** Distribute, combine like terms, and factor to identify the x-intercepts (4 and 6) as:

$$y = 2(x-5)^2 - 2$$
$$= 2(x^2 - 10x + 25) - 2$$
$$= 2x^2 - 20x + 48$$
$$= 2(x^2 - 10x - 24)$$
$$= 2(x-4)(x-6)$$

Answer choices A, B, and D are equivalent to the given equation, but they do not directly reveal that 4 and 6 are the x-intercepts.

6. **The correct answer is B.** Find the x- and y-intercepts of the given equation.

$$3x + y = 4$$
$$3(0) + y = 4$$
$$y = 4$$
$$3x + 0 = 4$$
$$x = \frac{4}{3}$$

Check the intercepts on the graph of each line to see if they match the intercepts of the equation in the problem. Only choice B has intercepts at (0, 4) and $\left(\frac{4}{3}, 0\right)$.

7. **The correct answer is B.** Use the point slope form of a linear equation to write the slope-intercept form of the equation:

$$y - y_1 = m(x - x_1)$$
$$y - 3 = -1(x - 2)$$
$$y - 3 = -x + 2$$
$$y = -x + 5$$

Then find the equation that is equivalent to the slope-intercept form:

$$3x + 3y = 15$$
$$3y = -3x + 15$$
$$y = -x + 5$$

8. **The correct answer is C.** The first equation simplifies to $x = 2y$. Substituting $2y$ for x into the second equation gives:

$$2(2y)^2 - y^2 = 14$$
$$2 \cdot 4y^2 - y^2 = 14$$
$$7y^2 = 14$$
$$y^2 = 2$$

9. **The correct answer is C.** Simplify the expression using the exponent rules:

$$\sqrt[3]{\sqrt{z}} = \left(z^{\frac{1}{2}}\right)^{\frac{1}{3}} = z^{\frac{1}{6}}$$

$$\sqrt[3]{z} \cdot \sqrt{z} = z^{\frac{1}{3}} \cdot z^{\frac{1}{2}} = z^{\frac{5}{6}}$$

$$\frac{\sqrt[3]{\sqrt{z}}}{\sqrt[3]{z} \cdot \sqrt{z}} = \frac{z^{\frac{1}{6}}}{z^{\frac{5}{6}}} = z^{\frac{1}{6} - \frac{5}{6}} = z^{-\frac{2}{3}}$$

10. **The correct answer is B.** The equation for a parabola with a vertex at (h, k) is $y = a(x - h)^2 + k$, and if the y-intercept is 13, then $(0, 13)$ is a point on the parabola, and $13 = a(0 - h)^2 - k$. Since $13 = 2(0 - 3)^2 - 5$, choice B is correct.

11. **The correct answer is C.** The amount per each type of admission is $12 and $17, so the total admission of $1,079 based upon number of adults and children is $12x + 7y$. The total number of people, 117, is represented by $x + y$.

12. **The correct answer is C.**

$$\frac{4-i}{3+i} \times \frac{3-i}{3-i} = \frac{11-7i}{10}$$

13. **The correct answer is D.** Solve the equation:

$$-6(t+1) = 2(1-3t) - 8$$
$$-6t - 6 = 2 - 6t - 8$$
$$-6 = -6$$

The equation has infinitely many solutions.

14. **The correct answer is B.** The formula for population growth is $P = P_o e^{rt}$, where P represents the total population, P_o represents the initial population, e represents the constant value, r represents the rate of growth, and t represents the time. The "10" in the problem represents the time, in years, between the two years of interest—the initial year 1980 and the city's population in 1990. There are 10 years between 1980 and 1990.

15. **The correct answer is D.** Long division reveals that 4 is the remainder when we divide $9x^2$ by $3x - 2$.

$$
\begin{array}{r}
3x + 2 \\
3x - 2 \overline{)\, 9x^2 } \\
\underline{9x^2 - 6x} \\
6x - 4 \\
\underline{ 4}
\end{array}
$$

In general, when we divide F by G and obtain quotient Q and remainder R, then $\frac{F}{G} = Q + \frac{R}{G}$. In this case:

$$\frac{9x^2}{3x-2} = (3x+2) + \frac{4}{3x-2}$$

16. **The correct answer is 24.** To solve this problem, first isolate $\sqrt{x+1}$ on one side of the equation. Then, square both sides:

$$\sqrt{x+1} - 2 = 3$$
$$\sqrt{x+1} = 5$$
$$x + 1 = 25$$
$$x = 24$$

Answer Keys and Explanations

17. **The correct answer is $\frac{1}{2}$ (1/2).** Complete the square on the function so that the vertex is readily identifiable:

$$f(x) = x^2 - 2bx + \left(b^2 + 2b - 1\right)$$
$$= \left(x^2 - 2bx + b^2\right) + \left(b^2 + 2b - 1\right) - b^2$$
$$= (x - b)^2 + (2b - 1)$$

The vertex is $(b, 2b - 1)$, and the parabola opens upward. The graph will have one x-intercept, which coincides with the vertex, if and only if $2b - 1 = 0$. That is, when $b = \frac{1}{2}$.

18. **The correct answer is 13.** To find the value of c, divide the numerator by the denominator using either long division or synthetic division. Remember that the remainder can be written as a fraction, with the remainder as the numerator and the divisor as the denominator.

$$\begin{array}{r} 3x - 13 \\ x + 3 \overline{\smash{\big)}\ 3x^2 - 4x - 18} \\ \underline{3x^2 + 9x} \\ -13x \\ \underline{-13x - 39} \\ 21 \end{array}$$

Here, the remainder is 21, so the fraction is equal to $3x - 13 + \frac{21}{x + 3}$. Set this equal to the expression in the equation to find that $c = 13$.

$$\frac{3x^2 - 4x - 18}{x + 3} = 3x - 13 + \frac{21}{x + 3}$$
$$c = 13$$

19. **The correct answer is $\frac{4}{3}$ (4/3).** The equations need to have the same slope but different y-intercepts. The first equation is already written in slope-intercept form. First, rewrite the second equation so that it is in slope-intercept form, then find the value for t that makes the slope 3. This should make the y-intercept different than 7.

$$4x - ty = 5$$
$$-ty = -4x + 5$$
$$y = \frac{-4x + 5}{-t}$$
$$y = \frac{-4x}{-t} + \frac{5}{-t}$$

So,

$$\frac{-4}{-t} = 3$$
$$4 = 3t$$
$$t = \frac{4}{3}$$

To check that the y-intercept is not 7:

$$\frac{5}{-t} = \frac{5}{-\frac{4}{3}}$$
$$= 5\left(-\frac{3}{4}\right)$$
$$= -\frac{15}{4}$$

20. **The correct answer is 4.** Use the formulas for the volume of a sphere and volume of a cone. Set the formulas equal to each other since their volumes are equal. In the formulas, r represents the radius of the cone or the radius of the circle, which are equal. The height of the cone is h. Solve for the value of $\frac{h}{r}$.

$$V_{cone} = V_{scoop}$$
$$\frac{1}{3}\pi r^2 h = \frac{4}{3}\pi r^3$$
$$h = \frac{\cancel{3}\left(\frac{4}{\cancel{3}}\cancel{\pi} r^{\cancel{3}}\right)}{\cancel{\pi}\, \cancel{r^2}}$$
$$h = 4r$$
$$\frac{h}{r} = 4$$

1. C	**9.** A	**17.** C	**25.** B	**33.** 36
2. B	**10.** C	**18.** B	**26.** C	**34.** 800
3. D	**11.** B	**19.** A	**27.** B	**35.** 3.75
4. C	**12.** B	**20.** C	**28.** B	**36.** 29
5. A	**13.** A	**21.** A	**29.** D	**37.** 1 or 3
6. B	**14.** C	**22.** B	**30.** A	**38.** 3.32
7. D	**15.** A	**23.** A	**31.** 2.5	
8. B	**16.** C	**24.** C	**32.** 9	

MATH TEST—CALCULATOR RAW SCORE
(Number of correct answers)

1. **The correct answer is C.** We must first determine how many feet the insect travels in an average month. Then we can determine how many months it will take for the insect to travel 560 feet. To determine the number of feet the insect travels per month, we divide the yearly total by 12:

$$\frac{1,680}{12} = 140$$

The insect travels 140 feet each month. To determine how many months it would take the insect to travel 560 feet, we divide the total number of feet (560) by the number of feet that the insect travels in a month (140):

$$\frac{560}{140} = 4$$

Traveling at a rate of 140 feet per month, it would take the insect 4 months to travel 560 feet.

2. **The correct answer is B.** The question asks for the number of books that will be renewed if the library loans 25,000 books. Use a proportion to solve. Note that 18 of 75 (=18 + 46 +11) books were renewed in one day.

$$\frac{18}{75} = \frac{x}{25,000}$$
$$75x = 18(25,000)$$
$$x = \frac{18(25,000)}{75}$$
$$x = 6,000$$

3. **The correct answer is D.** The number of males in Littletown is 210, and the number of females in Smalltown is 195. The probability of choosing a male who lives in Littletown is $\frac{210}{785}$, and the probability of choosing a woman who lives in Smalltown is $\frac{195}{785}$. The probability of choosing one or the other is the sum of the individual probabilities:

$$\frac{210}{785} + \frac{195}{785} = \frac{405}{785} = \frac{81}{157}$$

4. **The correct answer is C.** The median is 2.5. When, as in this case, there is an even number of values in a data set, we average the two middle values after listing all of the values from smallest to largest. In the case of the sixty students, the thirtieth number in the list will be 2, because there are 12 1's and 18 2's. The next value on the list, the thirty-first, is 3. So, the median is $\frac{2+3}{2} = 2.5$. The mode is 2, the most frequent value. We know this because 18 is the largest number in the column on the right. Hence, the median, 2.5, is greater than the mode, 2.

5. **The correct answer is A.** The total amount that Glen earns in one day is 10.25h where h is the number of hours Glen works, and 3(12.50) is three times what he spends commuting. If he wants to earn at least three times what he spends commuting, then choice A is the only answer that represents the situation.

6. **The correct answer is B.** If Peter spent x hours, then Nadia spent $x + 7$ hours on math homework, and together they spent $x + (x + 7) = 35$ hours. Solve for x:

$$x+(x+7)=35$$
$$2x+7=35$$
$$2x=28$$
$$x=14$$

7. **The correct answer is D.** Since c is 22 percent of e, c equals $(e \times 0.22)$, or $= 0.22e$. Likewise, because d is 68 percent of e, d equals $(e \times 0.68)$, or $= 0.68e$. To find the value of $d - c$ in terms of e, we can set up an equation:

$$d-c=(0.68e-0.22e)$$
$$d-c=0.46e$$

8. **The correct answer is B.** Graph the inequalities and look for where they overlap, or substitute each point into both inequalities to determine which point satisfies both inequalities.

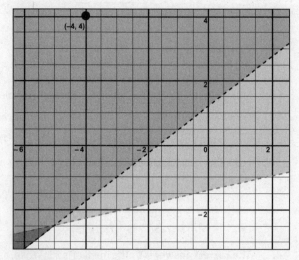

Only choice B is correct:

$$2x-9y<12 \qquad\qquad -3x+4y>5$$
$$2(-4)-9(4)<12 \qquad -3(-4)+4(4)>5$$
$$-8-36<12 \qquad\qquad 12+16>5$$

9. **The correct answer is A.** The question is just asking us to substitute the value that we are given for n and then to simplify the expression. We're asked to provide an answer in terms of m or, in other words, an answer that contains the variable m. Let's see what we get when we substitute 7 for n:

$$2m(16-6n)=2m\big[16-6(7)\big]$$
$$=2m(16-42)$$
$$=2m(-26)$$
$$=-52m$$

10. **The correct answer is C.** The total amount that she has raised is $145. If she gets $15 from each additional donor, then the total contributions will be equal to $145 + 15x$, where x is the number of contributions she gets from this point forward.

11. **The correct answer is B.** Read the graph and look for where the line has a vertical coordinate of $400. The closest approximation is 58 hats.

12. **The correct answer is B.** The x-axis of the graph shows the number of hats sold, and the y-axis shows the amount of money raised. Consequently, the slope of the line shows the amount of money received per hat.

13. **The correct answer is A.** A sample size of 18 people is not large enough to make a conclusion for a city of 38,000. The sample population was randomly selected, the size of the city population alone doesn't affect the reliability, and the number of people with no preference does not affect the reliability.

14. **The correct answer is C.** When the mean and median of a set of data are not the same, outliers tend to affect the mean more than the median. If some income values are much greater than the others, the mean will be greater than the median.

15. **The correct answer is A.** The amount of CDs sold would be equal to the number of days in the sale (j) times the number of neighbors (h) times the average number of CDs sold by each neighbor each day (x), or jhx. To determine the number of CDs that will be left after the total number of CDs, (jhx), are sold, we subtract jhx from 1,230. This value can be expressed as $1,230 - jhx$.

16. **The correct answer is C.** The formula that is useful for this problem is the formula for projectile motion: $y = 0.5at^2 + vt + h$, where a is the acceleration, v is the upward velocity, h is the initial height, t is the time in seconds, and y is the height after t seconds. Here, the coefficient, v, equals 50, so the correct answer must be choice C.

17. **The correct answer is C.** First, write equations that represent the price for each company. Then let the price from Company J be less than the price for Company K and solve the inequality.

$$\text{Company J}=0.15x+19$$
$$\text{Company K}=0.10x+30$$
$$0.15x+19<0.1x+30$$
$$0.05x<11$$
$$x<220$$

18. **The correct answer is B.** The daily rental cost for the truck is the y-intercept. The slope of the graph of this relationship is the per-mile cost. The total cost for the miles driven is $0.12x$. The total cost for driving the truck the entire distance is $0.12x + 25$.

19. **The correct answer is A.** To find the conditional probability that a randomly chosen house in Town B is a colonial house, first find the total number of houses that are in Town B: $62 + 65 + 43 + 32 = 202$. Then write and simplify a ratio of colonial houses in Town B to the total number of houses in Town B in the survey: $\dfrac{65}{202}$.

20. **The correct answer is C.** Reduce the set of outcomes under consideration to only those houses that are either Cape Cod or Ranch; this gives a total of $53 + 43 + 75 + 62 = 233$ outcomes. Of these, $62 + 43 = 105$ are from Town B. So the probability is $\dfrac{105}{233}$.

21. **The correct answer is A.** Set $f(x)$ equal to $g(x)$ and solve the equation that results to get the x-coordinates of the points of intersection:

$$b^2 - (x+a)^2 = (x+a)^2 - b^2$$
$$2b^2 = 2(x+a)^2$$
$$b^2 = (x+a)^2$$
$$\pm b = x + a$$
$$x = -a \pm b$$

So, the x-coordinates are $-a - b$ and $-a + b$. The difference between these two numbers is:

$$(-a + b) - (-a - b) = -a + b + a + b = 2b.$$

22. **The correct answer is B.** The key to solving this geometry problem is to recognize that the figure contains two similar triangles. We know that the triangles are similar because their corresponding angles are equal ($x = x$, $y = y$) and the two right angles at point Q are equal. Since the triangles have equal corresponding angles, we know that the sides are in proportion to one another.

We want to determine the ratio between the corresponding sides in the larger triangle, SQR, and the smaller triangle, TQP. We can do this by comparing the two corresponding sides for which we have measures. We're given the length of QP in the smaller triangle as 11.5. We're also given the length of its corresponding leg from the larger triangle, QR, as 46. How many times larger is QR than QP? If we divide 46 by 11.5, we see that QR is 4 times larger than QP.

The question asks us to determine the length of SQ, which is a side of the larger triangle, SQR. We know that the measure of its corresponding side in the smaller triangle, TQP, is TQ, which measures 15. We also know that all corresponding sides in the larger triangle, SQR, are 4 times longer than the ones in the smaller triangle, TQP, so SQ measures 4 times longer than TQ, or $4 \times 15 = 60$.

23. **The correct answer is A.** First, rewrite the equation as a quadratic one:

$$1 = \frac{3}{x-4} + \frac{4}{x-3}$$
$$(x-3)(x-4) = (x-3)(x-4)\left[\frac{3}{x-4} + \frac{4}{x-3}\right]$$
$$x^2 - 7x + 12 = 3x - 9 + 4x - 16$$
$$x^2 - 14x + 37 = 0$$

Now use the quadratic formula with $a = 1$, $b = -14$, and $c = 37$ to simplify:

$$x = \frac{14 \pm \sqrt{(-14)^2 - 4(37)}}{2}$$
$$x = \frac{14 \pm \sqrt{196 - 148}}{2}$$
$$x = 7 \pm 2\sqrt{3}$$

24. **The correct answer is C.** Use the circumference of the circle to find the radius.

$$C = 2\pi r$$
$$572\pi = 2\pi r$$
$$286 = r$$

Then use the measure of the central angle and the radius to find the area of the sector. The area of a sector is the product of the ratio

$$\frac{\text{measure of the central angle in radians}}{2\pi}$$

and the area of the circle:

$$A = \frac{\frac{3\pi}{4}}{2\pi}\pi(r)^2$$
$$A = \frac{3}{8}\pi(286)^2$$
$$A = \frac{61{,}347\pi}{2}$$

25. **The correct answer is B.** If $w < -1$ and $v > 1$, then the x-intercepts of the graph must be greater than 1 and less than -1. Choice D is incorrect because the graph shows an x-intercept exactly at $(-1, 0)$.

26. **The correct answer is C.** If you try values of a that are (1) less than zero, (2) greater than zero but less than 2.5, and (3) greater than 2.5, then you will be able to select the correct answer from among the choices provided. To graph more easily, note that the line corresponding to the first inequality is $y = \left(\dfrac{2}{5}\right)x - \dfrac{6}{5}$, and the line corresponding to the second inequality is $y = \left(-\dfrac{1}{a}\right)x - \dfrac{3}{a}$. The cases where $a = -1$, $a = 1$, and $a = 6$ are shown below. Only in the second graph, where $a = 1$, is the dark-gray solution completely within quadrants II and III (left of the y-axis). So among the choices, $0 \le a \le 2.5$ must be correct.

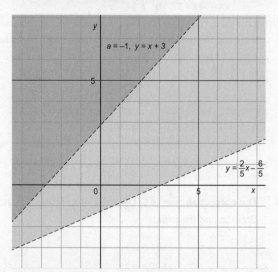

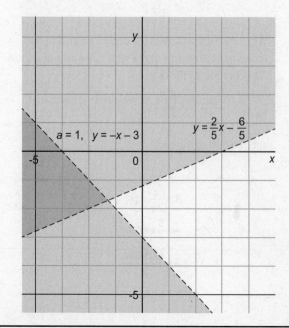

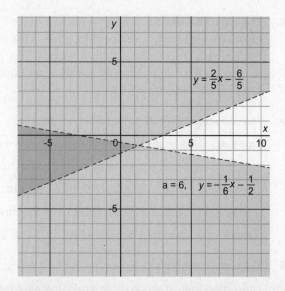

27. **The correct answer is B.** There are five dots to the left of a vertical line drawn upward from the 10,000K mark on the horizontal axis. Notice that the scale increases from right to left.

28. **The correct answer is B.** A horizontal line drawn through the mark at 1 on the vertical scale meets the line of best fit at a point closest to 5,000 on the horizontal axis. (The actual surface temperature of the sun is about 5,800K.)

29. **The correct answer is D.** The 95% confidence that the margin of error is $\pm\, 4\%$ is important, and choices A and B ignore the confidence interval. Choice C is not correct because there are likely people who don't know or have no opinion on whether there should be stricter emissions standards for power plants. Only choice D accurately uses the confidence interval and the data given in the problem.

30. **The correct answer is A.** Use completing the square to find the coordinates of the center of the circle. Separate the equation x- and y-terms:

$$x^2 + y^2 - 10x + 4y = -20$$
$$x^2 - 10x + y^2 + 4y = -20$$
$$\left(x^2 - 10x + 25\right) + \left(y^2 + 4y + 4\right) = -20 + 25 + 4$$
$$\left(x - 5\right)^2 + \left(y + 2\right)^2 = 9$$

The center is $(5, -2)$, because the standard form of the circle is $(x - h)^2 + (y - k)^2 = r^2$.

31. **The correct answer is 2.5.** Write an equation to represent the situation, and then solve:

$$16.25 = 2.5(2) + 4.5x$$
$$11.25 = 4.5x$$
$$2.5 = x$$

32. **The correct answer is 9.** Solve for the expression requested in the inequality, then interpret the answer in the context of the question asked:

$$4s - 3 < 2$$
$$4s < 5$$
$$s < \frac{5}{4}$$

We want an integer value for s that will maximize the value of $4s + 5$. The greatest integer less than $\frac{5}{4}$ is 1. Substitute 1 for s: $4s + 5 = 4(1) + 5 = 9$.

33. **The correct answer is 36.** Use the method of combination to determine the values of a and b. Start by subtracting the first equation from the second equation:

$$2a + 2b = 16$$
$$\underline{-(2a - b) = -(7)}$$
$$3b = 9$$
$$b = 3$$

Insert $b = 3$ into the first equation:

$$2a - (3) = 7$$
$$2a = 10$$
$$a = 5$$

Now you are ready to plug both values into the expression in question:

$$3a + 7b = 3(5) + 7(3)$$
$$= 15 + 21$$
$$= 36$$

34. **The correct answer is 800.** The formula for population growth is given in terms of n, the number of years. In order to solve this problem, plug the value of n, in this case 54, into the formula and calculate the value of the expression $100(2)^{\frac{n}{18}}$:

$$\text{Population (in millions) after } n \text{ years} = 100(2)^{\frac{n}{18}}$$
$$= 100(2)^{\frac{54}{18}}$$
$$= 100(2)^3$$
$$= 800$$

35. **The correct answer is 3.75.** Read the question carefully; it asks for the difference in the prices of one object, not the difference between the amounts of money they made, or any other quantity.

Since Paul sold four pieces of pottery for $85, he made $y = \frac{85}{4} = \$21.25$ per piece. Sally made $40 more than Paul did for all of her pieces, so she made $85 + $40 = $125 in total. Since she sold five pieces, she made $x = \frac{125}{5} = \$25.00$ per piece. Per piece, Sally made $x - y = $25 – $21.25 = $3.75 more than Paul did. The correct answer is 3.75.

36. **The correct answer is 29.** First, find the number of scarves knitted last year using a percent proportion. Then add 4 to find this year's new total.

$$\frac{16}{100} = \frac{4}{x}$$
$$16x = 400$$
$$x = \frac{400}{16}$$
$$x = 25$$
$$25 + 4 = 29$$

37. **The correct answer is 1 or 3.** First, combine the equations by substituting $2x + 5$ for y in the second equation. Then solve for x. Next, substitute the x-values back in and solve for y:

$$2x + 5 = -2(x + 1)^2 + 3$$
$$2x + 5 = -2x^2 - 4x - 2 + 3$$
$$0 = -2x^2 - 6x - 4$$
$$0 = -2(x + 2)(x + 1)$$
$$x = -1, -2$$
$$y = 2(-1) + 5 = 3$$
$$\text{or}$$
$$y = 2(-2) + 5 = 1$$

38. **The correct answer is 3.32.** Let x be the GPA for the year 2017. Compute the average of 3.5, 3.5, 3.5, 3.5, 3.5, and x:

$$\frac{3.5(5) + x}{6} = 3.47$$
$$17.5 + x = 20.82$$
$$x = 3.32$$

SECTION 5: ESSAY

ANALYSIS OF PASSAGE

The following is an analysis of the passage by Catherine Anderson, noting how the writer used evidence, reasoning, and stylistic or persuasive elements to support her claims, connect the claims and evidence, and add power to the ideas she expressed. Check to see if you evaluated the passage in a similar way.

1   Visit the website of designer Michael Graves, and you'll be greeted with the words "Humanistic Design = Transformative Results."

2   The mantra can double as Graves' philosophy. For Graves—who passed away at 80 earlier this month—paid no heed to architectural trends, social movements or the words of his critics.

3   Instead, it was the everyday human being—the individual—who inspired and informed his work.

4   During a career that spanned over 50 years, Graves held firm to the belief that design could effect tremendous change in people's day-to-day lives. From small-scale kitchen products to immense buildings, a thread runs throughout his products: accessible, aesthetic forms that possess a sense of warmth and appeal.

5   Early in his career, Graves was identified as one of the New York Five, a group of influential architects who whole-heartedly embraced Modernism, the architectural movement that subscribed to the use of simple, clean lines, forms devoid of embellishments and modern materials such as steel and glass.

6   However, Graves is best described as a Post-Modernist.

7   He eschewed the austerity of Modernism and its belief that "less is more," instead embracing history and references to the past.

8   He rejected the notion that decoration, or ornament, was a "crime" (as Austrian architect Adolf Loos wrote in 1908); rather, he viewed it as a way for his architecture to convey meaning.

9   As the noted architectural historian Spiro Kostof explains in his book *A History of Architecture: Settings and Rituals*, "Post Modernists turn to historical memory … to ornament, as a way of enriching the language of architecture."

10   …Along these lines, Graves

1   *Anderson lays the groundwork for the validity of her argument by referring the reader to an authoritative source on this subject—the website of Michael Graves.*

2   *The writer uses evocative words and phrases such as "mantra," double as, "philosophy," "paid no heed," and "trends."*

3   *The writer clearly states her central argument.*

4   *Anderson continues using evocative phrases: "held firm," "effect tremendous change," "immense buildings," "a thread runs throughout," a "sense of warmth and appeal."*

5   *She provides historical context by discussing Graves' early career and establishing his status as a Modernist architect. She also defines Modernism for the reader.*

6   *The writer expands her historical context by claiming that Graves was really a Post-Modernist. She then explains exactly what this means.*

7   *The writer uses evocative phrases to paint pictures for the reader: "eschewed the austerity," "embracing history," "rejected the notion."*

8   *Anderson enlivens her writing with a vivid word (crime) used by an authority and cites her source.*

9   *Anderson quotes an authoritative source to support her claim that Graves was a Post-Modernist.*

10   *The writer builds on this quotation to advance her argument that Graves was a Post-Modernist.*

11   loathed the idea of intellectualizing his structures. Instead, he sought to make them accessible, understandable and poignant to all passersby. …

12   In addition to designing buildings, Graves embarked upon a long and highly successful partnership with the Italian kitchenware company Alessi …

13   Graves' most famous Alessi design is his iconic teakettle … which had a cheerful red whistling bird and sky-blue handle. On sale since 1985, the best-selling product is still in production today.

14   In 1999, Minneapolis-based discount retail giant Target approached Graves with an offer to design a line of kitchen products, ranging from toasters to spatulas.

15   While some might have shied away from having their work associated with a mega-corporation like Target, Graves wholly embraced the project. …

16   In all, Graves' collaboration with Target would last 13 years; during this time, the designer would become a household name, with millions of units of his products appearing in American homes.

17   Many of Graves' designs for Target—his spatula, can opener and ice cream scoop—had chunky, sky-blue handles. Other appliances that were white … were sprinkled with touches of color. … Black and beige had no place in Graves' palette.

18   The option to select a better-looking product with a slightly higher price versus the same article but with a less expensive, nondescript appearance is now the norm for most consumers: good design (and function) are part and parcel of the customer experience

19   (nowhere is this more evident than in Apple's rise to dizzying heights as arguably one of the world's most valuable brands).

20   It's an idea that's democratic in nature, and thinking about design through this lens led Graves to create thoughtful, appealing and affordable products for the masses. …

21   As Graves' popularity rose, his critics leveled

22   blistering commentaries about what they deemed a precipitous fall from grace—from a "trend beyond compare" to a "stale trend," as

---

11   *The writer uses evocative phrases to make her argument vivid: "loathed the idea," "intellectualizing his structures," "poignant to all passersby."*

12   *Anderson points out that Graves did more than design buildings, mentioning his partnership with the Italian kitchenware company Alessi.*

13   *She also mentions one of Graves' famous creations for Alessi and points out that it sold extremely well.*

14   *Continuing her discussion of Graves' non-architectural creations, the writer refers to his work designing kitchen products for Target.*

15   *The writer anticipates a possible negative reaction to this work, pointing out that Graves "embraced" it.*

16   *Anderson legitimizes Graves' work with Target, saying his creations sold millions of units and that he became "a household name."*

17   *She gives the reader a strong sense of Graves' practical, everyday Target creations, naming specific products and describing what they looked like.*

18   *Anderson cites the significance of Graves' work with Target, pointing out that better design in everyday products has become the norm.*

19   *She supports this claim by citing Apple as an example of a company that routinely offers customers good design in its products.*

20   *The writer reasserts the importance of Graves' place in the movement to create "affordable products for the masses."*

21   *The writer provides historical context to trace the negative reaction to Graves' work with Target.*

22   *She brings this reaction to life using evocative phrases: "blistering commentaries, precipitous fall from grace, commodified design, drew the disdain of those who once lauded his works."*

23 architecture critic Herbert Muschamp noted in a 1999 *New York Times* article. The notion that he had commodified design—and had somehow "cheapened" it—drew the disdain of those who once lauded his works.

24 Yet Graves remained true to his beliefs even into the last phase of his life. In 2003, after an illness left him paralyzed below the waist, he realized that the design of hospitals and equipment . . . could be redesigned and made more functional, comfortable and visually appealing. He then went on to improve ubiquitous devices such as wheelchairs and walking canes. . . .

25 Consumers may not have ever known his architecture or what the critics thought of his work (or even realized they were buying one of his products). Graves didn't seem to mind. His goal was to provide well-designed items for everyday use rather than impress his detractors.

26 As he told NPR in 2002, "It's the kind of thing where you pick something up or use it with a little bit of joy … it puts a smile on your face."

23 *The writer cites a source to support her claim that there was a negative reaction to Graves' Target products.*

24 *Anderson provides additional historical context for Graves' later designs for common things and gives specific examples.*

25 *The writer provides psychological insight into Graves' personality and reasserts his primary goal: "to provide well-designed items for everyday use."*

26 *The writer concludes her argument with a quotation from Graves that supports her claim that his primary concern was quality design for the everyday human being.*

SAMPLE ESSAYS

The following are examples of a high-scoring and low-scoring essay, based on the passage by Catherine Anderson.

HIGH-SCORING ESSAY

Catherine Anderson is clearly a fan of Michael Graves's architecture and product design. Anderson identifies the everyday human being as Graves's inspiration. She gives a history of Graves' work, explaining how his focus on people inspired him. Anderson's word choices and descriptions bring Graves's products to life. Anderson's words are as warm and appealing as the products she describes. Supporting her descriptions with a history of Graves's designs and biographical details convinces readers to admire the products he designed and, perhaps, to buy one that fits in their own kitchens.

Anderson tells readers that Graves's career started as an architect in New York 50 years ago. She provides historical context by identifying Graves as one of an elite group of Modernist architects who designed simple, plain buildings constructed of the modern materials steel and glass. Because her description of Modernist architecture sounds cold and empty, Anderson hastens to say that Graves was actually a Post-Modernist architect whose creations were less plain and more inviting. He used embellishments in his architectural designs to convey meaning, which sounds more warm and comforting than the Modernist architectural style she described with the words *plain*, *steel and glass*, and *austerity*.

To support her statements, Anderson cites a well-known architectural expert who describes Post-Modernist architecture as enriched by ornamentation. She then uses appealing words to attract readers to Graves's work—*accessible*, *understandable*, and *poignant*.

Graves didn't design architecture only. He also designed common items, such as teakettles and spatulas, for common people. His most famous design is a quirky teakettle that has a sky-blue handle and a bright red bird that whistles when the water is hot enough to make tea. Just the image Anderson created of the whistling bird on the teakettle makes Graves's work sound fun and appealing. The kitchen products Graves designed are sold by Target, a store where the people who inspired Graves could afford to shop. They must be buying his products because millions of them have been purchased at Target and are still selling today.

While Graves's popularity rose among Target shoppers, it dropped among architecture critics. Anderson informs readers of the critics' changing attitudes by quoting their comments such as "stale trend" and "cheapened." Graves, however, heroically "remained true to his beliefs" by continuing to design attractive products that could be bought by average people.

In 2003 an illness made Graves a paraplegic. Instead of becoming bitter, like many people would have in the same situation, Graves looked around at the poorly designed medical products and decided that he could make improvements. Even a hospital environment benefited from his design abilities. He created products, such as wheelchairs and canes, that Anderson said were "more functional, comfortable and visually attractive."

Anderson closed the article by quoting Graves's comment that he hoped his products would make people smile. Anderson showed that throughout his life, Graves's main concern was creating designs for the average person. Just as he had hoped, his products have inspired, and continue to inspire, joy in the people who inspired him—especially when making tea.

LOW-SCORING ESSAY

Catherine Anderson started the article by focusing on Michael Graves's mantra of "Humanistic Design = Transformative Results." This means that focusing on people can make things better.

Michael Graves focused on people to design buildings and things they could use like teakettles and wheelchairs. Because Michael Graves likes people, he designed things that they would like, things that would make them happy.

Catherine Anderson says his products are warm and appealing. She describes a teakettle that's fun to use because it whistles. The buildings he designed have historical meaning because he added a lot of decorations. He said it's not a crime to build decorated buildings.

Michael Graves worked with Alessi to design attractive kitchen products that people liked a lot, like the whistling teakettle. He used warm colors like red to make it more appealing. Catherine Anderson describes his kitchen products as "chunky" and colorful. This makes them sound like things everyone would want to have. Because millions were sold at Target, he probably made a lot of money on them. That's a good reason to ignore the critics who didn't like his designs. The critics said his kitchen products were "stale," which is a clever food-related way to say they were old and boring. Regardless of the critics, his stuff is popular.

Michael Graves was pretty old when he got sick and couldn't walk. Because he couldn't walk, he designed wheelchairs and canes that he and other people could use. Catherine Anderson says they're "functional, comfortable and visually appealing." If Target sold them, they would probably be as popular as his teakettle.

Michael Graves died in 2015 when he was 80 years old. His buildings and products followed his mantra of "Humanistic Design = Transformative Results." He made things better by focusing on people. He improved a lot of things that he designed and made a lot of people happy. Catherine Anderson proved that the things he made were attractive and made people happy.

COMPUTING YOUR SCORES

Now that you've completed this practice test, it's time to compute your scores. Simply follow the instructions on the following pages, and use the conversion tables provided to calculate your scores. The formulas provided will give you as close an approximation as possible of how you might score on the actual SAT® exam.

TO DETERMINE YOUR PRACTICE TEST SCORES

1. After you go through each of the test sections (Reading, Writing and Language, Math—No Calculator, and Math—Calculator) and determine which answers you got right, be sure to enter the number of correct answers in the box below the answer key for each of the sections.

2. Your total score on the practice test is the sum of your Evidence-Based Reading and Writing Section score and your Math Section score. To get your total score, convert the raw score—the number of questions you got right in a particular section—into the "scaled score" for that section, and then you'll calculate the total score. It sounds a little confusing, but we'll take you through the steps.

TO CALCULATE YOUR EVIDENCE-BASED READING AND WRITING SECTION SCORE

Your Evidence-Based Reading and Writing Section score is on a scale of 200–800. First determine your Reading Test score, and then determine your score on the Writing and Language Test.

1. Count the number of correct answers you got on the **Section 1: Reading Test.** Remember that there is no penalty for wrong answers. **The number of correct answers is your raw score.**

2. Go to **Raw Score Conversion Table 1: Section and Test Scores** on page 850. Look in the "Raw Score" column for your raw score, and match it to the number in the "Reading Test Score" column.

3. Do the same with **Section 2: Writing and Language Test** to determine that score.

4. Add your Reading Test score to your Writing and Language Test score.

5. Multiply that number by 10. This is your Evidence-Based Reading and Writing Section score.

TO CALCULATE YOUR MATH SECTION SCORE

Your Math score is also on a scale of 200–800.

1. Count the number of correct answers you got on the questions in **Section 3: Math Test—No Calculator** and **Section 4: Math Test—No Calculator.** Again, there is no penalty for wrong answers. **The number of correct answers is your raw score.**

2. Add the number of correct answers on the Section 3: Math Test—No Calculator and the Section 4: Math Test—No Calculator.

3. Use the **Raw Score Conversion Table 1: Section and Test Scores** on page 850 and convert your raw score into your Math Section score.

TO OBTAIN YOUR TOTAL SCORE

Add your score on the Evidence-Based Reading and Writing Section to the Math Section score. This is your total score on this Practice Test, on a scale of 400–1600.

SUBSCORES PROVIDE ADDITIONAL INFORMATION

Subscores offer you greater details about your strengths in certain areas within literacy and math. The subscores are reported on a scale of 1–15 and include Heart of Algebra, Problem Solving and Data Analysis, Passport to Advanced Math, Expression of Ideas, Standard English Conventions, Words in Context, and Command of Evidence.

Heart of Algebra

The **Heart of Algebra subscore** is based on questions from the **Math Test** sections that focus on linear equations and inequalities.

- Add up your total correct answers from these sections:
  - Math Test—No Calculator: Questions 1, 6, 7, 11, 13, 14, 17, 19
  - Math Test—Calculator: Questions 6–8, 10, 15, 17, 18, 26, 31–33
- Your Raw Score = the total number of correct answers from all of these questions.
- Use the **Raw Score Conversion Table 2: Subscores** on page 851 to determine your **Heart of Algebra** subscore.

Problem Solving and Data Analysis

The **Problem Solving and Data Analysis subscore** is based on questions from the **Math Test** that focus on quantitative reasoning, interpretation and synthesis of data, and solving problems in rich and varied contexts.

- Add up your total correct answers from these questions:
  - Math Test—No Calculator: None
  - Math Test—Calculator: Questions 1–5, 11–14, 19, 20, 27–29, 35, 36, 38
- Your Raw Score = the total number of correct answers from all of these questions.
- Use the **Raw Score Conversion Table 2: Subscores** on page 851 to determine your **Problem Solving and Data Analysis** subscore.

Passport to Advanced Math

The **Passport to Advanced Math subscore** is based on questions from the **Math Test** that focus on topics central to your ability to progress to more advanced math, such as understanding the structure of expressions, reasoning with more complex equations, and interpreting and building functions.

- Add up your total correct answers from these questions:
  - Math Test—No Calculator: 2, 3, 5, 8–10, 15, 16, 18
  - Math Test—Calculator: Questions 9, 16, 21, 23, 25, 34, 37
- Your Raw Score = the total number of correct answers from all of these questions.
- Use the **Raw Score Conversion Table 2: Subscores** on page 851 to determine your **Passport to Advanced Math** subscore.

Expression of Ideas

The **Expression of Ideas subscore** is based on questions from the **Writing and Language Test** that focus on topic development, organization, and rhetorically effective use of language.

- Add up your total correct answers from these questions in Section 2: Writing and Language Test:
  - Questions 1, 2, 5, 6, 10–13, 16, 17, 19, 20, 26, 27, 29, 30, 32, 33, 37, 39, 41, 43, 44
- Your Raw Score = the total number of correct answers from all of these questions.
- Use the **Raw Score Conversion Table 2: Subscores** on page 851 to determine your Expression of Ideas subscore.

Standard English Conventions

The **Standard English Conventions subscore** is based on questions from the **Writing and Language Test** that focus on sentence structure, usage, and punctuation.

- Add up your total correct answers from these questions in Section 2: Writing and Language Test:
  - Questions 3, 4, 7–9, 14, 15, 18, 21–25, 28, 31, 35, 36, 38, 40, 42
- Your Raw Score = the total number of correct answers from all of these questions.
- Use the **Raw Score Conversion Table 2: Subscores** on page 851 to determine your **Standard English Conventions** subscore.

Words in Context

The **Words in Context subscore** is based on questions from the **Reading Test** and the **Writing and Language Test** that address word/phrase meaning in context and rhetorical word choice.

- Add up your total correct answers from these questions in Sections 1 and 2:
    - Reading Test: Questions 6, 9, 21, 22, 28, 31, 36, 42, 51, 52
    - Writing and Language Test: Questions 2, 6, 17, 20, 26, 30, 39, 44
- Your Raw Score = the total number of correct answers from all of these questions.
- Use the **Raw Score Conversion Table 2: Subscores** on page 851 to determine your **Words in Context** subscore.

Command of Evidence

The **Command of Evidence subscore** is based on questions from the **Reading Test** and the **Writing and Language Test** that ask you to interpret and use evidence found in a wide range of passages and informational graphics, such as graphs, tables, and charts.

- Add up your total correct answers from Sections 1 and 2:
    - Reading Test: Questions 5, 8, 16, 20, 26, 30, 35, 39, 47, 50
    - Writing and Language Test: Questions 5, 11, 12, 19, 27, 32, 37, 43
    - Your Raw Score = the total number of correct answers from all of these questions.
- Use the **Raw Score Conversion Table 2: Subscores** on page 851 to determine your **Command of Evidence** subscore.

CROSS-TEST SCORES

The SAT® exam also reports two cross-test scores: Analysis in History/Social Studies and Analysis in Science. These scores are based on questions in the Reading Test, Writing and Language Test, and both Math Tests that ask you to think analytically about texts and questions in these subject areas. Cross-test scores are reported on a scale of 10–40.

Analysis in History/Social Studies

- Add up your total correct answers from these questions:
    - Reading Test: Questions 12–22, 33–42
    - Writing and Language Test: Questions 26, 27, 29, 30, 32, 33
    - Math Test—No Calculator: Question 14
    - Math Test—Calculator: Questions 4, 13, 14, 19, 20, 29, 38
- Your Raw Score = the total number of correct answers from all of these questions.
- Use the **Raw Score Conversion Table 3: Cross-Test Scores** on page 852 to determine your Analysis in History/Social Studies cross-test score.

Analysis in Science

- Add up your total correct answers from these questions:
    - Reading Test: Questions 1–11, 23–32
    - Writing and Language Test: Questions 12, 13, 16, 17, 19, 20
    - Math Test—No Calculator: Question 3
    - Math Test—Calculator: Questions 1, 3, 16, 24, 27, 28, 34
- Your Raw Score = the total number of correct answers from all of these questions.
- Use the **Raw Score Conversion Table 3: Cross-Test Scores** on page 852 to determine your Analysis in Science cross-test score.

Raw Score Conversion Table 1: Section and Test Scores

Raw Score	Math Section Score	Reading Test Score	Writing and Language Test Score	Raw Score	Math Section Score	Reading Test Score	Writing and Language Test Score	Raw Score	Math Section Score	Reading Test Score	Writing and Language Test Score
0	200	10	10	20	450	22	23	40	610	33	36
1	200	10	10	21	460	23	23	41	620	33	37
2	210	10	10	22	470	23	24	42	630	34	38
3	230	11	10	23	480	24	25	43	640	35	39
4	240	12	11	24	480	24	25	44	650	35	40
5	260	13	12	25	490	25	26	45	660	36	
6	280	14	13	26	500	25	26	46	670	37	
7	290	15	13	27	510	26	27	47	670	37	
8	310	15	14	28	520	26	28	48	680	38	
9	320	16	15	29	520	27	28	49	690	38	
10	330	17	16	30	530	28	29	50	700	39	
11	340	17	16	31	540	28	30	51	710	40	
12	360	18	17	32	550	29	30	52	730	40	
13	370	19	18	33	560	29	31	53	740		
14	380	19	19	34	560	30	32	54	750		
15	390	20	19	35	570	30	32	55	760		
16	410	20	20	36	580	31	33	56	780		
17	420	21	21	37	590	31	34	57	790		
18	430	21	21	38	600	32	34	58	800		
19	440	22	22	39	600	32	35				

Conversion Equation 1 Section and Test Scores

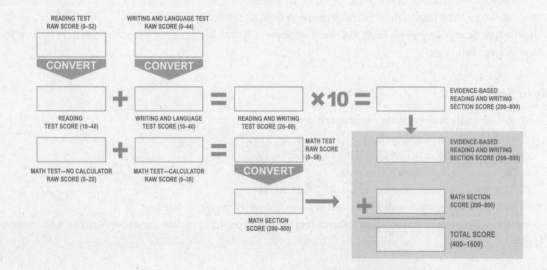

Raw Score (# of correct answers)	Expression of Ideas	Standard English Conventions	Heart of Algebra	Problem Solving and Data Analysis	Passport to Advanced Math	Words in Context	Command of Evidence
0	1	1	1	1	1	1	1
1	1	1	1	1	3	1	1
2	1	1	2	2	5	2	2
3	2	2	3	3	6	3	3
4	3	2	4	4	7	4	4
5	4	3	5	5	8	5	5
6	5	4	6	6	9	6	6
7	6	5	6	7	10	6	7
8	6	6	7	8	11	7	8
9	7	6	8	8	11	8	8
10	7	7	8	9	12	8	9
11	8	7	9	10	12	9	10
12	8	8	9	10	13	9	10
13	9	8	9	11	13	10	11
14	9	9	10	12	14	11	12
15	10	10	10	13	14	12	13
16	10	10	11	14	15	13	14
17	11	11	12	15		14	15
18	11	12	13			15	15
19	12	13	15				
20	12	15					
21	13						
22	14						
23	14						
24	15						

Computing Your Scores

CONVERSION EQUATION 2 SUBSCORES

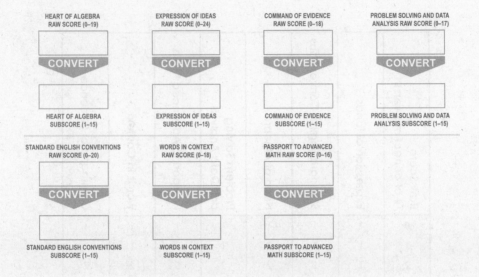

| | HEART OF ALGEBRA RAW SCORE (0–19) | EXPRESSION OF IDEAS RAW SCORE (0–24) | COMMAND OF EVIDENCE RAW SCORE (0–18) | PROBLEM SOLVING AND DATA ANALYSIS RAW SCORE (0–17) |
| CONVERT → | HEART OF ALGEBRA SUBSCORE (1–15) | EXPRESSION OF IDEAS SUBSCORE (1–15) | COMMAND OF EVIDENCE SUBSCORE (1–15) | PROBLEM SOLVING AND DATA ANALYSIS SUBSCORE (1–15) |

| | STANDARD ENGLISH CONVENTIONS RAW SCORE (0–20) | WORDS IN CONTEXT RAW SCORE (0–18) | PASSPORT TO ADVANCED MATH RAW SCORE (0–16) |
| CONVERT → | STANDARD ENGLISH CONVENTIONS SUBSCORE (1–15) | WORDS IN CONTEXT SUBSCORE (1–15) | PASSPORT TO ADVANCED MATH SUBSCORE (1–15) |

RAW SCORE CONVERSION TABLE 3: CROSS-TEST SCORES

Raw Score (# of correct answers)	Analysis in History/Social Studies Cross-Test Score	Analysis in Science Cross-Test Score	Raw Score (# of correct answers)	Analysis in History/Social Studies Cross-Test Score	Analysis in Science Cross-Test Score
0	10	10	18	28	26
1	10	11	19	29	27
2	11	12	20	30	27
3	12	13	21	30	28
4	14	14	22	31	29
5	15	15	23	32	30
6	16	16	24	32	30
7	17	17	25	33	31
8	18	18	26	34	32
9	20	19	27	35	33
10	21	20	28	35	33
11	22	20	29	36	34
12	23	21	30	37	35
13	24	22	31	38	36
14	25	23	32	38	37
15	26	24	33	39	38
16	27	24	34	40	39
17	28	25	35	40	40

CONVERSION EQUATION 3: CROSS-TEST SCORES

ANALYSIS IN HISTORY/SOCIAL STUDIES   ANALYSIS IN SCIENCE

TEST	QUESTIONS	RAW SCORE	QUESTIONS	RAW SCORE
Reading Test	12–22, 33–42		1–11, 23–32	
Writing and Language Test	26, 27–30, 32, 33		12, 13, 16, 17, 19, 20	
Math Test—No Calculator	14		3	
Math Test—Calculator	3, 13, 14, 19, 20, 29, 38		1, 4, 16, 24, 27, 28, 34	
TOTAL				

ANALYSIS IN HISTORY/
SOCIAL STUDIES
RAW SCORE (0–35)

CONVERT

ANALYSIS IN HISTORY/
SOCIAL STUDIES
CROSS-TEST SCORE (10–40)

ANALYSIS IN SCIENCE
RAW SCORE (0–35)

CONVERT

ANALYSIS IN SCIENCE
CROSS-TEST SCORE (10–40)

Section 1: Reading Test

1. Ⓐ Ⓑ Ⓒ Ⓓ   12. Ⓐ Ⓑ Ⓒ Ⓓ   23. Ⓐ Ⓑ Ⓒ Ⓓ   33. Ⓐ Ⓑ Ⓒ Ⓓ   43. Ⓐ Ⓑ Ⓒ Ⓓ
2. Ⓐ Ⓑ Ⓒ Ⓓ   13. Ⓐ Ⓑ Ⓒ Ⓓ   24. Ⓐ Ⓑ Ⓒ Ⓓ   34. Ⓐ Ⓑ Ⓒ Ⓓ   44. Ⓐ Ⓑ Ⓒ Ⓓ
3. Ⓐ Ⓑ Ⓒ Ⓓ   14. Ⓐ Ⓑ Ⓒ Ⓓ   25. Ⓐ Ⓑ Ⓒ Ⓓ   35. Ⓐ Ⓑ Ⓒ Ⓓ   45. Ⓐ Ⓑ Ⓒ Ⓓ
4. Ⓐ Ⓑ Ⓒ Ⓓ   15. Ⓐ Ⓑ Ⓒ Ⓓ   26. Ⓐ Ⓑ Ⓒ Ⓓ   36. Ⓐ Ⓑ Ⓒ Ⓓ   46. Ⓐ Ⓑ Ⓒ Ⓓ
5. Ⓐ Ⓑ Ⓒ Ⓓ   16. Ⓐ Ⓑ Ⓒ Ⓓ   27. Ⓐ Ⓑ Ⓒ Ⓓ   37. Ⓐ Ⓑ Ⓒ Ⓓ   47. Ⓐ Ⓑ Ⓒ Ⓓ
6. Ⓐ Ⓑ Ⓒ Ⓓ   17. Ⓐ Ⓑ Ⓒ Ⓓ   28. Ⓐ Ⓑ Ⓒ Ⓓ   38. Ⓐ Ⓑ Ⓒ Ⓓ   48. Ⓐ Ⓑ Ⓒ Ⓓ
7. Ⓐ Ⓑ Ⓒ Ⓓ   18. Ⓐ Ⓑ Ⓒ Ⓓ   29. Ⓐ Ⓑ Ⓒ Ⓓ   39. Ⓐ Ⓑ Ⓒ Ⓓ   49. Ⓐ Ⓑ Ⓒ Ⓓ
8. Ⓐ Ⓑ Ⓒ Ⓓ   19. Ⓐ Ⓑ Ⓒ Ⓓ   30. Ⓐ Ⓑ Ⓒ Ⓓ   40. Ⓐ Ⓑ Ⓒ Ⓓ   50. Ⓐ Ⓑ Ⓒ Ⓓ
9. Ⓐ Ⓑ Ⓒ Ⓓ   20. Ⓐ Ⓑ Ⓒ Ⓓ   31. Ⓐ Ⓑ Ⓒ Ⓓ   41. Ⓐ Ⓑ Ⓒ Ⓓ   51. Ⓐ Ⓑ Ⓒ Ⓓ
10. Ⓐ Ⓑ Ⓒ Ⓓ   21. Ⓐ Ⓑ Ⓒ Ⓓ   32. Ⓐ Ⓑ Ⓒ Ⓓ   42. Ⓐ Ⓑ Ⓒ Ⓓ   52. Ⓐ Ⓑ Ⓒ Ⓓ
11. Ⓐ Ⓑ Ⓒ Ⓓ   22. Ⓐ Ⓑ Ⓒ Ⓓ

Section 2: Writing and Language Test

1. Ⓐ Ⓑ Ⓒ Ⓓ   10. Ⓐ Ⓑ Ⓒ Ⓓ   19. Ⓐ Ⓑ Ⓒ Ⓓ   28. Ⓐ Ⓑ Ⓒ Ⓓ   37. Ⓐ Ⓑ Ⓒ Ⓓ
2. Ⓐ Ⓑ Ⓒ Ⓓ   11. Ⓐ Ⓑ Ⓒ Ⓓ   20. Ⓐ Ⓑ Ⓒ Ⓓ   29. Ⓐ Ⓑ Ⓒ Ⓓ   38. Ⓐ Ⓑ Ⓒ Ⓓ
3. Ⓐ Ⓑ Ⓒ Ⓓ   12. Ⓐ Ⓑ Ⓒ Ⓓ   21. Ⓐ Ⓑ Ⓒ Ⓓ   30. Ⓐ Ⓑ Ⓒ Ⓓ   39. Ⓐ Ⓑ Ⓒ Ⓓ
4. Ⓐ Ⓑ Ⓒ Ⓓ   13. Ⓐ Ⓑ Ⓒ Ⓓ   22. Ⓐ Ⓑ Ⓒ Ⓓ   31. Ⓐ Ⓑ Ⓒ Ⓓ   40. Ⓐ Ⓑ Ⓒ Ⓓ
5. Ⓐ Ⓑ Ⓒ Ⓓ   14. Ⓐ Ⓑ Ⓒ Ⓓ   23. Ⓐ Ⓑ Ⓒ Ⓓ   32. Ⓐ Ⓑ Ⓒ Ⓓ   41. Ⓐ Ⓑ Ⓒ Ⓓ
6. Ⓐ Ⓑ Ⓒ Ⓓ   15. Ⓐ Ⓑ Ⓒ Ⓓ   24. Ⓐ Ⓑ Ⓒ Ⓓ   33. Ⓐ Ⓑ Ⓒ Ⓓ   42. Ⓐ Ⓑ Ⓒ Ⓓ
7. Ⓐ Ⓑ Ⓒ Ⓓ   16. Ⓐ Ⓑ Ⓒ Ⓓ   25. Ⓐ Ⓑ Ⓒ Ⓓ   34. Ⓐ Ⓑ Ⓒ Ⓓ   43. Ⓐ Ⓑ Ⓒ Ⓓ
8. Ⓐ Ⓑ Ⓒ Ⓓ   17. Ⓐ Ⓑ Ⓒ Ⓓ   26. Ⓐ Ⓑ Ⓒ Ⓓ   35. Ⓐ Ⓑ Ⓒ Ⓓ   44. Ⓐ Ⓑ Ⓒ Ⓓ
9. Ⓐ Ⓑ Ⓒ Ⓓ   18. Ⓐ Ⓑ Ⓒ Ⓓ   27. Ⓐ Ⓑ Ⓒ Ⓓ   36. Ⓐ Ⓑ Ⓒ Ⓓ

Section 3: Math Test—No Calculator

1. Ⓐ Ⓑ Ⓒ Ⓓ   4. Ⓐ Ⓑ Ⓒ Ⓓ   7. Ⓐ Ⓑ Ⓒ Ⓓ   10. Ⓐ Ⓑ Ⓒ Ⓓ   13. Ⓐ Ⓑ Ⓒ Ⓓ
2. Ⓐ Ⓑ Ⓒ Ⓓ   5. Ⓐ Ⓑ Ⓒ Ⓓ   8. Ⓐ Ⓑ Ⓒ Ⓓ   11. Ⓐ Ⓑ Ⓒ Ⓓ   14. Ⓐ Ⓑ Ⓒ Ⓓ
3. Ⓐ Ⓑ Ⓒ Ⓓ   6. Ⓐ Ⓑ Ⓒ Ⓓ   9. Ⓐ Ⓑ Ⓒ Ⓓ   12. Ⓐ Ⓑ Ⓒ Ⓓ   15. Ⓐ Ⓑ Ⓒ Ⓓ

Practice Test 4 — ANSWERS

Section 3: Math Test—No Calculator

16.   17.   18.   19.   20.

Section 4: Math Test—Calculator

1. Ⓐ Ⓑ Ⓒ Ⓓ   7. Ⓐ Ⓑ Ⓒ Ⓓ   13. Ⓐ Ⓑ Ⓒ Ⓓ   19. Ⓐ Ⓑ Ⓒ Ⓓ   25. Ⓐ Ⓑ Ⓒ Ⓓ

2. Ⓐ Ⓑ Ⓒ Ⓓ   8. Ⓐ Ⓑ Ⓒ Ⓓ   14. Ⓐ Ⓑ Ⓒ Ⓓ   20. Ⓐ Ⓑ Ⓒ Ⓓ   26. Ⓐ Ⓑ Ⓒ Ⓓ

3. Ⓐ Ⓑ Ⓒ Ⓓ   9. Ⓐ Ⓑ Ⓒ Ⓓ   15. Ⓐ Ⓑ Ⓒ Ⓓ   21. Ⓐ Ⓑ Ⓒ Ⓓ   27. Ⓐ Ⓑ Ⓒ Ⓓ

4. Ⓐ Ⓑ Ⓒ Ⓓ   10. Ⓐ Ⓑ Ⓒ Ⓓ   16. Ⓐ Ⓑ Ⓒ Ⓓ   22. Ⓐ Ⓑ Ⓒ Ⓓ   28. Ⓐ Ⓑ Ⓒ Ⓓ

5. Ⓐ Ⓑ Ⓒ Ⓓ   11. Ⓐ Ⓑ Ⓒ Ⓓ   17. Ⓐ Ⓑ Ⓒ Ⓓ   23. Ⓐ Ⓑ Ⓒ Ⓓ   29. Ⓐ Ⓑ Ⓒ Ⓓ

6. Ⓐ Ⓑ Ⓒ Ⓓ   12. Ⓐ Ⓑ Ⓒ Ⓓ   18. Ⓐ Ⓑ Ⓒ Ⓓ   24. Ⓐ Ⓑ Ⓒ Ⓓ   30. Ⓐ Ⓑ Ⓒ Ⓓ

31.   32.   33.   34.   35.

36.   37.   38.

Section 5: Essay

SECTION 1: READING TEST

65 Minutes—52 Questions

TURN TO SECTION 1 OF YOUR ANSWER SHEET TO ANSWER THE QUESTIONS IN THIS SECTION.

DIRECTIONS: Each passage (or pair of passages) in this section is followed by a number of multiple-choice questions. After reading each passage, select the best answer to each question based on what is stated or implied in the passage or passages and in any supplementary material, such as a table, graph, chart, or photograph.

Questions 1–10 are based on the following passage and supplementary material.

From his humble beginnings, Herbert Hoover made his fortune in the mining industry. He earned his reputation as a humanitarian and skilled administrator during and after World War I and later served as Secretary of Commerce under both Presidents Harding and Coolidge. In 1928, he was nominated for president by the Republican Party. The following is an excerpt from a speech he gave at the end of his campaign against the Democratic nominee, New York Governor Alfred E. Smith.

During one hundred and fifty years we have builded up a form of self government and a social system which is peculiarly our own. It differs essentially from all others
Line in the world. It is the American system. . . . It is founded
5 upon the conception that only through ordered liberty, freedom and equal opportunity to the individual will his initiative and enterprise spur on the march of progress. And in our insistence upon equality of opportunity has our system advanced beyond all the world.
10 During [World War I] we necessarily turned to the government to solve every difficult economic problem. The government having absorbed every energy of our people for war, there was no other solution. For the preservation of the state the Federal Government became a
15 centralized despotism which undertook unprecedented responsibilities, assumed autocratic powers, and took over the business of citizens. To a large degree, we regimented our whole people temporally into a socialistic state. However justified in war time, if continued
20 in peace-time it would destroy not only our American system but with it our progress and freedom as well.
When the war closed, the most vital of issues both in our own country and around the world was whether government should continue their wartime ownership
25 and operation of many [instruments] of production and distribution. We were challenged with a . . . choice between the American system of rugged individualism and a European philosophy of diametrically opposed

doctrines, doctrines of paternalism and state socialism.
30 The acceptance of these ideas would have meant the destruction of self-government through centralization . . . [and] the undermining of the individual initiative and enterprise through which our people have grown to unparalleled greatness. . . .
35 I would like to state to you the effect that . . . [an interference] of government in business would have upon our system of self-government and our economic system. That effect would reach to the daily life of every man and woman. It would impair the very
40 basis of liberty and freedom. . . .
Let us first see the effect on self-government. When the Federal Government undertakes to go into commercial business it must at once set up the organization and administration of that business, and
45 it immediately finds itself in a labyrinth. . . . Commercial business requires a concentration of responsibility. Our government to succeed in business would need to become in effect a despotism. There at once begins the destruction of self-government. . . .
50 Liberalism is a force truly of the spirit, a force proceeding from the deep realization that economic freedom cannot be sacrificed if political freedom is to be preserved. [An expansion of the government's role in the business world] would cramp and cripple the
55 mental and spiritual energies of our people. It would extinguish equality and opportunity. It would dry up the spirit of liberty and progress. . . . For a hundred and fifty years liberalism has found its true spirit in the American system, not in the European systems.
60 I do not wish to be misunderstood. . . . I am defining general policy. . . . I have already stated that where the government is engaged in public works for purposes of flood control, of navigation, of irrigation, of scientific research or national defense . . . it will at
65 times necessarily produce power or commodities as a by-product.

CONTINUE

Nor do I wish to be misinterpreted as believing that the United States is a free-for-all and devil-take-the-hindmost. The very essence of equality of oppor-
70 tunity and of American individualism is that there shall be no domination by any group or [monopoly] in this republic. . . . It is no system of *laissez faire*. . . .

I have witnessed not only at home but abroad the many failures of government in business. I have
75 seen its tyrannies, its injustices, its destructions of self-government, its undermining of the very instincts which carry our people forward to progress. I have witnessed the lack of advance, the lowered standards of living, the depressed spirits of people working under
80 such a system. . . .

And what has been the result of the American system? Our country has become the land of oppor-tunity to those born without inheritance, not merely because of the wealth of its resources and industry but
85 because of this freedom of initiative and enterprise. Russia has natural resources equal to ours. . . . But she has not had the blessings of one hundred and fifty years of our form of government and our social system.

1 Based on the excerpt, which statement is true of Hoover's ideas about the government's role in business?

A. Government involvement in private businesses is justified during wartime, but not at other times.

B. Government cannot solve economic problems and should never be involved in private business.

C. Government stifles personal liberties and prevents businesses from making any profit.

D. Government is responsible for ensuring that private businesses make a profit.

2 Why did Hoover believe it was necessary to strengthen the federal government during wartime?

A. The United States was fighting despotism and therefore had to become despotic.

B. Only a socialistic government can function during wartime.

C. Most resources went toward the war effort, draining them for other uses in the economy.

D. Businesses acting by themselves could interfere with the war effort.

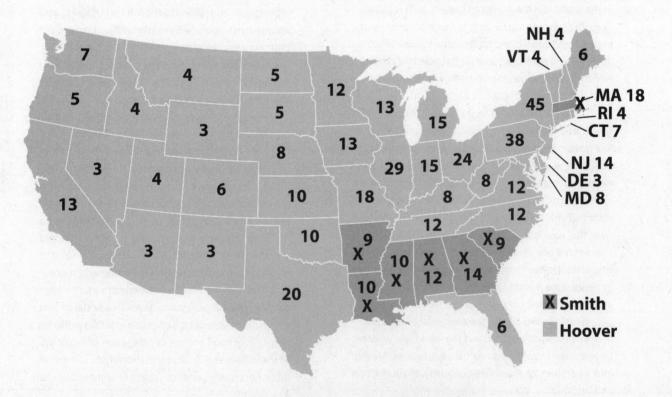

This map shows the electoral votes for each state in the presidential election of 1928, which Herbert Hoover won in a landslide.

3 Which choice provides the best evidence for the answer to the previous question?

A. Lines 10–11 ("During . . . problem.")

B. Lines 12–13 ("The government . . . other solution.")

C. Lines 13–15 ("For the . . . despotism")

D. Lines 15–17 ("which undertook . . . citizens.")

4 How does Hoover's speech change in lines 60–80 ("I do not wish . . . under such a system.")?

A. He changes his position by stating the opposite of all of the ideas he had stated in the passage previously.

B. He shows he wants to be understood by repeating the main points of everything he had discussed in the passage previously.

C. He shows that his beliefs are the beliefs of all Americans, and are therefore, moderate and widely acceptable.

D. He emphasizes that he wants to clarify his position and does so by providing details about his philosophy.

5 What is the most likely reason that Hoover includes lines 67–69 in his speech?

A. To appeal to more voters

B. To ensure his words are not twisted

C. To soften his position

D. To provide context for his views

6 According to the passage, Hoover believed liberalism to be

A. completely exclusive to the American system.

B. more prevalent in Europe than it is in America.

C. a defining characteristic of the American system.

D. a much better philosophy than conservatism.

7 Which choice provides the best evidence for the answer to the previous question?

A. Line 50 ("Liberalism . . . spirit")

B. Lines 53–54 ("An expansion . . . world")

C. Lines 55–56 ("It would . . . opportunity.")

D. Lines 58–59 ("liberalism . . . system")

8 Based on the passage, which of the following is the main doctrine Hoover advocates the United States should adopt now that war has ended?

A. Socialism

B. Despotism

C. Liberalism

D. Capitalism

9 As used in line 45, "labyrinth" most nearly means

A. maze.

B. cave.

C. bind.

D. landmine.

10 As used in line 18, "regimented" most nearly means

A. organized.

B. militarized.

C. bullied.

D. established.

CONTINUE

Passage 1 is an excerpt from a letter written by Harriet Beecher Stowe, the abolitionist and author of the best-selling novel Uncle Tom's Cabin *(1852). The book describes the horrors of slavery and is said to have helped promote the abolitionists' cause. The recipient of the letter, Mrs. Follen, a fellow abolitionist, was also a poet, editor, and novelist.*

Passage 2 is an excerpt from the memoir of Frederick Douglass, an active abolitionist who had escaped from slavery in 1838. After gaining his freedom, Douglass published Narrative of the Life of Frederick Douglass, An American Slave, Written by Himself *(1845). The passage describes how he planned his escape.*

PASSAGE 1

Harriet Beecher Stowe, from a letter to Mrs. Follen (1853)

I had two little curly-headed twin daughters to begin with, and my stock in this line was gradually increased, till I have been the mother of seven children,
Line the most beautiful and the most loved of whom lies
5 buried near my Cincinnati residence. It was at his dying bed and at his grave that I learned what a poor slave mother may feel when her child is torn away from her. In those depths of sorrow which seemed to me immeasurable, it was my only prayer to God that such anguish
10 might not be suffered in vain. There were circumstances about his death of such peculiar bitterness, of what seemed almost cruel suffering, that I felt that I could never be consoled for it unless this crushing of my own heart might enable me to work out some great good
15 to others . . .

I allude to this here because I have often felt that much that is in that book ("Uncle Tom") had its root in the awful scenes and bitter sorrows of that summer. It has left now, I trust, no trace on my mind except a deep
20 compassion for the sorrowful, especially for mothers who are separated from their children. . . .

I am now writing a work which will contain, perhaps, an equal amount of matter with *Uncle Tom's Cabin*. It will contain all the facts and documents upon
25 which that story was founded, and an immense body of facts, reports of trial, legal documents, and testimony of people now living South, which will more than confirm every statement in *Uncle Tom's Cabin*. I must confess that till I began the examination of facts in order to write this
30 book, much as I thought I knew before, I had not begun to measure the depth of the abyss. The law records of courts and judicial proceedings are so incredible as to fill me with amazement whenever I think of them. It seems

to me that the book cannot but be felt, and, coming
35 upon the sensibility awaked by the other, do something. I suffer exquisitely in writing these things. It may be truly said that I suffer with my heart's blood. Many times in writing *Uncle Tom's Cabin* I thought my heart would fail utterly, but I prayed earnestly that God would help me
40 till I got through, and still I am pressed beyond measure and above strength. . . .

PASSAGE 2

Recollection of Frederick Douglass

. . . It is impossible for me to describe my feelings as the time of my contemplated start grew near. I had a number of warm-hearted friends in Baltimore,—friends
45 that I loved almost as I did my life,—and the thought of being separated from them forever was painful beyond expression. It is my opinion that thousands would escape from slavery, who now remain, but for the strong cords of affection that bind them to their friends. The
50 thought of leaving my friends was decidedly the most painful thought with which I had to contend. The love of them was my tender point, and shook my decision more than all things else. Besides the pain of separation, the dread and apprehension of a failure exceeded what
55 I had experienced at my first attempt. The appalling defeat I then sustained returned to torment me. I felt assured that, if I failed in this attempt, my case would be a hopeless one—it would seal my fate as a slave forever. I could not hope to get off with anything less than the
60 severest punishment, and being placed beyond the means of escape. It required no very vivid imagination to depict the most frightful scenes through which I would have to pass, in case I failed. The wretchedness of slavery, and the blessedness of freedom, were perpetually before
65 me. It was life and death with me. But I remained firm and according to my resolution, on the third day of September, 1838, I left my chains, and succeeded in reaching New York without the slightest interruption of any kind.

---

11 The common thread of the experiences that stimulated the writing of Stowe and Douglass was that both of them

A. lost close friends to slavery.

B. experienced deaths in their families.

C. loved their children very deeply.

D. lost loved ones in terrible ways.

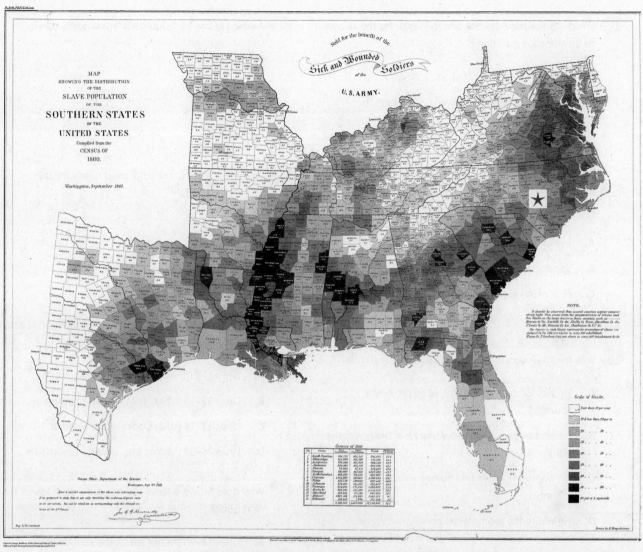

This map shows population and density of slaves in 1860.

(Credit: Historical Map & Chart Collection, Office of Coast Survey, NOAA)

12 Which choice provides the best partial evidence for the answer to the previous question?

A. Lines 1–3 ("I had two . . . children")

B. Lines 4–5 ("the most loved . . . residence.")

C. Lines 8–9 ("In those depths . . . immeasurable")

D. Lines 10–12 ("There were . . . suffering")

13 According to the passage, the process of writing *Uncle Tom's Cabin* was

A. artistically satisfying.

B. slow and difficult.

C. extremely painful.

D. a positive emotional release.

CONTINUE

14 Which choice provides the best evidence for the answer to the previous question?

    A. Lines 28–31 ("I must confess . . . abyss.")

    B. Lines 31–33 ("The law records . . . of them.")

    C. Lines 37–39 ("Many times . . . utterly")

    D. Lines 39–40 ("I prayed . . . got through")

15 Based on the passsage, what does Douglass think is the largest deterrent in reaching freedom?

    A. Leaving his hometown

    B. Separation from his friends

    C. Fear of the embarrassment that comes with failure

    D. Fear of the physical torture that comes with failure

16 Why might Douglass have given his narrative its title?

    A. He was almost illiterate and liked the way it sounded.

    B. He wanted people to know that he actually was the author.

    C. He wanted to make sure no one else could take his identity.

    D. He wanted to promote the abolitionist cause.

17 What do the passages suggest about the abolitionist movement in the mid-nineteenth century?

    A. Everyone was too afraid of negative repercussions to speak up against the evils of slavery.

    B. Some people wrote in order to expose the evils of slavery in an effort to abolish it.

    C. People in the North were the only ones who were angry about the evils of slavery.

    D. The conflict over slavery was only just beginning to heat up when these passages were written.

18 As used in line 36, "exquisitely" most nearly means

    A. beautifully.

    B. exhaustively.

    C. delightfully.

    D. intensely.

19 As used in line 51, "contend" most nearly means

    A. struggle.

    B. assert.

    C. debate.

    D. challenge.

20 What evidence suggests that Stowe's abolitionist activism was a way to memorialize her lost child?

    A. Lines 5–7 ("It was at . . . mother may feel")

    B. Lines 12–15 ("that I felt . . . good to others")

    C. Lines 17–18 ("that book . . . that summer.")

    D. Lines 36–37 ("It may be . . . heart's blood.")

21 Why does Stowe believe she needs to do research for her next book?

    A. Lines 18–20 ("It has left . . . the sorrowful")

    B. Lines 30–31 ("much as I . . . the abyss.")

    C. Lines 31–32 ("The law records . . . so incredible")

    D. Lines 37–39 ("Many times . . . fail utterly")

The following is a news item (May 4, 2015) from the Jet Propulsion Laboratory at the California Institute of Technology. The lab is part of NASA and is dedicated to the robotic exploration of space.

Traffic Around Mars Gets Busy

NASA has beefed up a process of traffic monitoring, communication, and maneuver planning to ensure that Mars orbiters do not approach each other too closely.

Line
5   Last year's addition of two new spacecraft orbiting Mars brought the census of active Mars orbiters to five, the most ever. NASA's Mars Atmosphere and Volatile Evolution (MAVEN) and India's Mars Orbiter Mission joined the 2003 Mars Express from ESA (the European Space Agency) and two from NASA: the 2001 Mars Odyssey and the 2006
10   Mars Reconnaissance Orbiter (MRO). The newly enhanced collision-avoidance process also tracks the approximate location of NASA's Mars Global Surveyor, a 1997 orbiter that is no longer working.

It's not just the total number that matters, but also
15   the types of orbits missions use for achieving their science goals. MAVEN, which reached Mars on Sept. 21, 2014, studies the upper atmosphere. It flies an elongated orbit, sometimes farther from Mars than NASA's other orbiters and sometimes closer to Mars, so it crosses altitudes
20   occupied by those orbiters. For safety, NASA also monitors positions of ESA's and India's orbiters, which both fly elongated orbits.

. . .

Traffic management at Mars is much less complex
25   than in Earth orbit, where more than 1,000 active orbiters plus additional pieces of inactive hardware add to hazards. As Mars exploration intensifies, though, and will continue to do so with future missions, precautions are increasing. The new process was established to manage this growth
30   as new members are added to the Mars orbital community in years to come.

All five active Mars orbiters use the communication and tracking services of NASA's Deep Space Network, which is managed at JPL [Jet Propulsion Laboratory]. This
35   brings trajectory information together, and engineers can run computer projections of future trajectories out to a few weeks ahead for comparisons.

"It's a monitoring function to anticipate when traffic will get heavy," said Joseph Guinn, manager of JPL's Mission
40   Design and Navigation Section. "When two spacecraft are predicted to come too close to one another, we give people a heads-up in advance so the project teams can start coordinating about whether any maneuvers are needed."

The amount of uncertainty in the predicted location
45   of a Mars orbiter a few days ahead is more than a mile (more than two kilometers). Calculating projections for weeks ahead multiplies the uncertainty to dozens of miles, or kilometers. In most cases when a collision cannot be ruled out from projections two weeks ahead, improved
50   precision in the forecasting as the date gets closer will rule out a collision with no need for avoidance action. Mission teams for the relevant orbiters are notified in advance when projections indicate a collision is possible, even if the possibility will likely disappear in subsequent projections.
55   This situation occurred on New Year's weekend, 2015.

On Jan. 3, automated monitoring determined that two weeks later, MAVEN and MRO could come within about two miles (three kilometers) of each other, with large uncertainties remaining in the exact passing dis-
60   tance. Although that was a Saturday, automatic messages went out to the teams operating the orbiters.

"In this case, before the timeline got short enough to need to plan an avoidance maneuver, the uncertainties shrank, and that ruled out the chance of the two spacecraft
65   coming too near each other," Guinn said. This is expected to be the usual pattern, with the advance warning kicking off higher-level monitoring and initial discussions about options.

If preparations for an avoidance maneuver were
70   called for, spacecraft commands would be written, tested, and approved for readiness, but such commands would not be sent to a spacecraft unless projections a day or two ahead showed probability of a hazardous conjunction. The amount of uncertainty about each spacecraft's exact
75   location varies, so the proximity considered unsafe also varies. For some situations, a day-ahead projection of two craft coming within about 100 yards (100 meters) of each other could trigger a maneuver.

The new formal collision-avoidance process for Mars
80   is part of NASA's Multi-Mission Automated Deep-Space Conjunction Assessment Process. A side benefit of it is that information about when two orbiters will be near each other—though safely apart—could be used for planning coordinated science observations. The pair could look at
85   some part of Mars or its atmosphere from essentially the same point of view simultaneously with complementary instruments.

CONTINUE

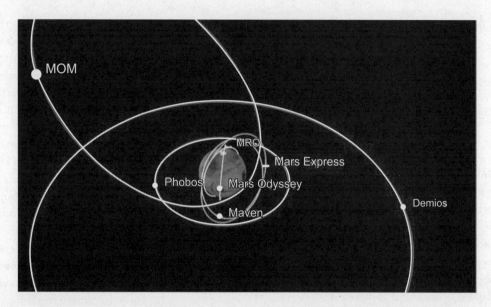

This graphic depicts the relative shapes and distances from Mars for five active orbiter missions plus the planet's two natural satellites. It illustrates the potential for intersections of the spacecraft orbits.

22 Which of the following is the best summary of the passage?

A. Gathering information from space requires careful and complex monitoring of spacecraft satellites.

B. The satellites orbiting Mars could collide, so monitoring and collision avoidance measures are necessary.

C. Planning for space satellites around other planets takes skilled teamwork.

D. Monitoring traffic around the Earth is more complex than monitoring the traffic around Mars.

23 Which areas are involved in monitoring Mars' satellites?

A. The United States, Russia, and India

B. Europe and the United States

C. India, Europe, and the United States

D. The United States, China, and Russia

24 According to information in the passage, what happened on New Year's weekend 2015?

A. Data indicated that there could be a collision.

B. Data gave scientists new information about the orbit of the satellites.

C. Scientists failed to react to a collision alert.

D. Two satellites experienced a devastating collision.

25 Which choice provides the best evidence for the answer to the previous question?

A. Lines 16–17 ("MAVEN . . . atmosphere.")

B. Lines 57–58 ("MAVEN . . . each other")

C. Lines 60–61 ("Although that . . . orbiters.")

D. Lines 63–65 ("the uncertainties . . . other")

26 Based on information given in the passage, the distances between satellites are

A. related to the degree of danger they pose.

B. impossible to calculate before it is too late.

C. minor details in satellite collision warning reports.

D. extremely constant without even a minimum of variation.

27 Which choice provides the best evidence for the answer to the previous question?

A. Lines 51–53 ("Mission teams . . . is possible")

B. Lines 57–58 ("MAVEN and . . . each other")

C. Lines 74–75 ("The amount . . . also varies")

D. Lines 79–81 ("The new formal . . . Assessment Process.")

28 Based on the passage, what is a potential benefit of two orbiters being close together for a period of time?

- **A.** They could look at Mars simultaneously and compare findings.
- **B.** They could test the collision alert systems more accurately.
- **C.** MAVEN and MRO could monitor each other's progress.
- **D.** Different countries could use it as a means of competition, testing which orbiter provides the most accurate data.

29 As the impending date of possible collision nears, predictions of distances

- **A.** become less accurate.
- **B.** become more accurate.
- **C.** maintain the same accuracy.
- **D.** becomes more difficult.

30 As used in line 73, "conjunction" most nearly means

- **A.** rejection.
- **B.** combination.
- **C.** contention.
- **D.** connection.

31 As used in line 36, "projections" most nearly means

- **A.** use of trajectory information.
- **B.** reference to future trajectories.
- **C.** comparisons to other trajectories.
- **D.** engineers can make comparisons.

Questions 32–42 are based on the following passage.

Potatoes were first cultivated in Peru by the Incas between 8000 and 5000 BCE. Today, potatoes make up the fourth-largest food crop in the world. In a ground-breaking agreement between the International Potato Center (known by its Spanish acronym CIP), the nonprofit organization ANDES, and the Association of the Potato Park communities, scientists are helping Peruvian farmers test and monitor many varieties of potatoes. One of their goals is to ensure continued diversity in potatoes—an action that could prevent disasters such as the Irish Potato Famine.

As world leaders gather in Lima to negotiate a new global climate deal at the UN Climate conference, this innovative, inclusive work shows the importance of new *Line* kinds of partnerships between scientists and farmers for
5 adaptation to climate change.

In the Peruvian highlands near Cusco, climate change has already impacted farmers in a fundamental way. Rising temperatures are correlated with increased pests and diseases, making it difficult to grow potatoes, their
10 staple food.

The effects of these temperature changes are very pronounced in the Potato Park, a valley outside of Cusco, where just 30 years ago, cultivation of native potato was routinely done at 3,800 meters.
15 Now, native potato cultivation starts at around 4,000 meters. In just 30 years, challenges associated with a warming climate have pushed potato cultivation up by 200 meters. The speed of this change in planting zones due to a warming climate is unprecedented as it is pushing
20 the farmers to the top of the mountain, beyond which there is no more soil or land.

In addition to moving to higher elevation for potato cultivation, Quechua farmers in the Potato Park are also responding to this challenge by stewarding over 1,440
25 cultivars of native potato. These include their own varieties plus cultivars that different entities have provided to the Park, 410 of which have come from CIP.

The five communities that make up the Potato Park are also working with CIP scientists in the characterization
30 of potato diversity, monitoring changes in potato varieties used over time and testing of varieties in different parts of the landscape, a combined territory of over 9,000 hectares.

Planting a diversity of potatoes provides a vital safeguard against crop failure—if disaster strikes, the farmers
35 will always have food. This strategy to reduce risk comes from their ancestors.

CONTINUE

The agreement with CIP has brought back varieties which had been collected from the communities in the 1960s but had since been lost. The resulting land-
40 scape-based gene bank is actively managed by the five Potato Park communities.

It provides a critical source of climate-resilient crops for adaptation, both locally and globally. Although gene banks conserve many food crops, they cannot safeguard
45 them all, and their collections are no longer evolving in response to climatic changes or accessible to farmers.

Alejandro Argumedo, Director of Programs of the Peruvian NGO ANDES explained: "The landmark agreement between CIP and the Potato Park for repa-
50 triation and monitoring of native potatoes represents a fundamental shift in approach. Rather than only collecting crops from farmers, scientists have also given farmers crops from their gene bank in return. The disease-free seeds and scientific knowledge gained
55 have boosted food security, and the new varieties have enhanced income, enabling the communities to develop novel food products."

Head of the CIP Genetic Resources-Genebank David Ellis said: "Through the agreement, first signed in
60 2004, CIP is increasing its understanding of how climate change is affecting potato diversity and agro-eco-systems, and through collaborative and mutually beneficial research with the farmers, it has continued to enhance knowledge, adaptation to climate change and
65 capacity development for sustaining potato production and traditional knowledge.

In Asia and Africa, hardy local landraces and live-stock breeds are also proving a vital resource in the struggle to cope with more extreme weather such as
70 droughts.

Krystyna Swiderska, Principal Researcher at IIED [International Institute for Environment and Devel-opment] said: "From China to Kenya, farmers have improved both resilience and productivity by crossing
75 resilient landraces with high-yielding modern varieties."

32 What is the relationship between plant diversity and climate change?

A. Plant diversity can provide some protection from crop failure due to climate change.

B. Increasing plant diversity with ancient varieties of potatoes may be more resilient to the higher temperatures associated with climate change.

C. In general, no variety of potato is adaptable to changes in climate.

D. The potato gene bank tries to ensure plant diversity but cannot save them from extinction.

33 According to the passage, how are potato farmers trying to combat climate change?

A. They will be attending the UN summit on climate change.

B. They are inventing new ways to exterminate pests.

C. They are planting more diverse seeds and plants.

D. They are experimenting with a different kind of staple food.

34 What kind of climate is best suited for potatoes?

A. Tropical

B. Cool

C. Hot

D. Moist

35 Which choice provides the best evidence for the answer to the previous question?

A. Lines 8–10 ("Rising temperatures . . . staple food.")

B. Lines 33–34 ("Planting a . . . crop failure")

C. Lines 43–46 ("Although gene . . . climatic changes")

D. Lines 60–63 ("CIP is . . . the farmers")

36 Which of the following is the best summary of the passage?

A. New farming techniques are helping Peruvian farmers adapt to a changing climate.

B. Peruvian farmers are part of an international group trying to fight the effects of climate change.

C. Ancestral growing techniques combined with new scientific methods are proving to be useful in combating the effects of climate change on Peruvian farmers.

D. Extreme weather conditions are proving difficult challenges for farmers all over the world.

37 What are the implications of climate change on world hunger?

A. It won't be affected.

B. It may enable the development of new crops to feed the world.

C. With the right scientific intervention, it could alleviate hunger.

D. It may get worse.

38 According to the passage, some farmers are dealing with the effects of climate change by

A. studying how to stop droughts.

B. planting a diversity of potatoes.

C. only growing modern potato varieties.

D. abandoning farming.

39 Which choice provides the best evidence for the answer to the previous question?

A. Lines 18–21 ("The speed . . . no more soil or land.")

B. Lines 33–35 ("Planting a diversity . . . will always have food.")

C. Lines 53–57 ("The disease-free seeds . . . novel food products.")

D. Lines 67–70 ("In Asia and Africa . . . such as droughts.")

40 As used in line 12, "pronounced" most nearly means

A. articulated.

B. official.

C. well-known.

D. noticeable.

41 What evidence does the text provide to show that potatoes were eaten by Peruvian people for a very long time?

A. Lines 25–27 ("These include . . . the Park")

B. Lines 28–31 ("Potato Park . . . over time")

C. Lines 35–36 ("This strategy . . . their ancestors.")

D. Lines 37–39 ("The agreement . . . been lost.")

42 As used in line 24, "stewarding" most nearly means

A. managing.

B. controlling.

C. regulating.

D. developing.

CONTINUE

Questions 43–52 are based on the following passage.

In his leisure time, Thomas Bulfinch (1796–1867) enjoyed writing condensed summaries of classical literature. Written for the general reader, "to popularize mythology and extend the enjoyment of elegant literature," his three volumes of classics were published under the title Bulfinch's Mythology. *This passage is an excerpt from chapter XXVII, The Trojan War.*

Minerva was the goddess of wisdom, but on one occasion she did a very foolish thing; she entered into competition with Juno and Venus for the prize of beauty.
Line It happened thus: At the nuptials of Peleus and Thetis
5 all the gods were invited with the exception of Eris, or Discord. Enraged at her exclusion, the goddess threw a golden apple among the guests, with the inscription, "For the fairest." Thereupon Juno, Venus, and Minerva each claimed the apple. Jupiter, not willing to decide
10 in so delicate a matter, sent the goddesses to Mount Ida, where the beautiful shepherd Paris was tending his flocks, and to him was committed the decision. The goddesses accordingly appeared before him. Juno promised him power and riches, Minerva glory and
15 renown in war, and Venus the fairest of women for his wife, each attempting to bias his decision in her own favor. Paris decided in favour of Venus and gave her the golden apple, thus making the two other goddesses his enemies. Under the protection of Venus, Paris sailed to
20 Greece, and was hospitably received by Menelaus, king of Sparta. Now Helen, the wife of Menelaus, was the very woman whom Venus had destined for Paris, the fairest of her sex. She had been sought as a bride by numerous suitors, and before her decision was made known, they
25 all, at the suggestion of Ulysses, one of their number, took an oath that they would defend her from all injury and avenge her cause if necessary. She chose Menelaus, and was living with him happily when Paris became their guest. Paris, aided by Venus, persuaded her to elope with
30 him, and carried her to Troy, whence arose the famous Trojan war, the theme of the greatest poems of antiquity, those of Homer and Virgil.

Menelaus called upon his brother chieftains of Greece to fulfill their pledge, and join him in his efforts
35 to recover his wife. They generally came forward, but Ulysses, who had married Penelope, and was very happy in his wife and child, had no disposition to embark in such a troublesome affair. He therefore hung back and Palamedes was sent to urge him. When Palamedes
40 arrived at Ithaca, Ulysses pretended to be mad. He yoked an ass and an ox together to the plough and began to sow salt. Palamedes, to try him, placed the infant Telemachus before the plough, whereupon the father

turned the plough aside, showing plainly that he was no
45 madman, and after that could no longer refuse to fulfill his promise. Being now himself gained for the undertaking, he lent his aid to bring in other reluctant chiefs, especially Achilles. This hero was the son of that Thetis at whose marriage the apple of Discord had been thrown
50 among the goddesses. Thetis was herself one of the immortals, a sea-nymph, and knowing that her son was fated to perish before Troy if he went on the expedition, she endeavoured to prevent his going. She sent him away to the court of King Lycomedes, and induced him
55 to conceal himself in the disguise of a maiden among the daughters of the king. Ulysses, hearing he was there, went disguised as a merchant to the palace and offered for sale female ornaments, among which he had placed some arms. While the king's daughters were engrossed
60 with the other contents of the merchant's pack, Achilles handled the weapons and thereby betrayed himself to the keen eye of Ulysses, who found no great difficulty in persuading him to disregard his mother's prudent counsels and join his countrymen in the war.

---

43 Which of the following is a theme used in this myth?

  A. Humans use deception to achieve goals.

  B. The gods have special powers of to control events.

  C. The bonds of marriage tie people's loyalties to one another.

  D. War is a dangerous undertaking that threaten human life.

---

44 According to the passage, Ulysses' reasons for not participating in the war were

  A. courageous.

  B. loyal.

  C. hypocritical.

  D. cowardly.

---

45 It can reasonably be inferred that Discord tossed the apple at the nuptials to

  A. find out who the fairest goddess truly was.

  B. reduce the ceremony to chaos and disharmony.

  C. get the three goddesses ejected from the nuptials.

  D. present a ceremonial gift to the three goddesses.

46 Why did Thetis try to prevent Achilles from going to Troy?

   A. She thought his presence might start a war.

   B. She didn't want him to marry Helen.

   C. She wanted him to ask King Lycomedes for his help.

   D. She didn't want her son to be killed in battle.

47 Based on the myth, what started the Trojan War?

   A. A fight over an apple

   B. A fight for the hand of Helen

   C. A test of Ulysses' loyalty

   D. The marriage of Peleus and Thetis

48 Which choice provides the best evidence for the answer to the previous question?

   A. Lines 19–21 ("Under . . . Sparta.")

   B. Lines 27–31 ("She chose . . . war")

   C. Lines 31–32 ("the theme . . . Virgil.")

   D. Lines 33–34 ("Menelaus . . . pledge")

49 What is the relationship between Telemachus and Ulysses?

   A. Telemachus was Ulysses' son.

   B. Telemachus was a god and Ulysses human.

   C. Telemachus was a prince and Ulysses was king of Sparta.

   D. Telemachus was an old man and Ulysses was his son.

50 Which choice provides the best evidence for the answer to the previous question?

   A. Lines 40–44 ("Ulysses . . . aside")

   B. Lines 46–48 ("Being . . . Achilles.")

   C. Lines 50–52 ("Thetis . . . Troy.")

   D. Lines 53–55 ("She sent . . . maiden")

51 As used in line 35, "recover" most nearly means

   A. retrieve.

   B. balance.

   C. salvage.

   D. repair.

52 As used in line 63, "prudent" most nearly means

   A. fierce.

   B. cautious.

   C. legal.

   D. indifferent.

STOP

If you finish before time is called, you may check your work on this section only.
Do not turn to any other section.

SECTION 2: WRITING AND LANGUAGE TEST

35 MINUTES—44 QUESTIONS

TURN TO SECTION 2 OF YOUR ANSWER SHEET TO ANSWER THE QUESTIONS IN THIS SECTION.

DIRECTIONS: Each passage below is accompanied by a number of multiple-choice questions. For some questions, you will need to consider how the passage might be revised to improve the expression of ideas. Other questions will ask you to consider how the passage might be edited to correct errors in sentence structure, usage, or punctuation. A passage may be accompanied by one or more graphics—such as a chart, table, or graph—that you will need to refer to in order to best answer the question(s).

Some questions will direct you to an underlined portion of a passage—it could be one word, a portion of a sentence, or the full sentence itself. Other questions will direct you to a particular paragraph or to certain sentences within a paragraph, or you'll be asked to think about the passage as a whole. Each question number refers to the corresponding number in the passage.

After reading each passage, select the answer to each question that most effectively improves the quality of writing in the passage or that makes the passage follow the conventions of Standard Written English. Many questions include a "NO CHANGE" option. Select that option if you think the best choice is to leave that specific portion of the passage as it is.

Questions 1–11 are based on the following passages and supplementary material.

The struggle of African Americans to make economic and political progress within the socioeconomic structure of the United States has been long and filled with setbacks. The following passages document some of the events in that long struggle and seek to explain why it has been so difficult.

PASSAGE 1

The Fight for African American Progress: The Economic Picture

Slavery—which lasted until 1865—and **1** comprehensive education guaranteed that African Americans remained socioeconomically disadvantaged until well into the twentieth century. Segregated schools were rarely on par with schools for whites; consequently, African Americans often found they could not compete with whites for jobs.

1 Which choice provides the most relevant detail?

A. NO CHANGE

B. inadequate

C. spacious

D. superior

CONTINUE

Increased opportunities for African Americans followed in the wake of the civil rights movement, African Americans were finally able to gain higher levels of education and achieve better positions in a variety of professions. In the 1980s, large numbers of African Americans moved into the upper middle class.

3 However, by the 1990s, there was a noticeable gap between low-income African Americans and those who were able to improve their socioeconomic status. By 2010, the economic status of many African American households had declined, **4** with the median net worth in 2009 less than half of what it had been in 2005. Today, many low-income African Americans do not have a place in the class structure because of poverty and underlying racial prejudice, particularly in urban areas. **5** Too often, urban neighborhoods become a place of high crime, poor schools, and substandard housing.

Median Net Worth of Households, 2005 and 2009
in 2009 dollars

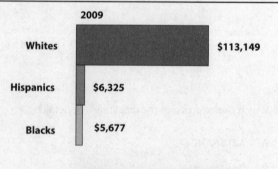

Source: Pew Research Center tabulation of Survey of Income and Program Particpation data

2

A. NO CHANGE

B. the civil rights movement and African Americans

C. the civil rights movement African Americans

D. the civil rights movement. African Americans

3

A. NO CHANGE

B. By the 1990s, there was a noticeable gap between low-income African Americans and those who were able to improve their socioeconomic status.

C. There was a noticeable gap between low-income African Americans and those who were able to improve their socioeconomic status by the 1990s.

D. However, there was a noticeable gap between low-income African Americans in the 1990s and those who were able to improve their socioeconomic status.

4 Which choice most effectively reflects information in the chart?

A. NO CHANGE

B. though the median net worth in 2009 was several times more than what it had been in 2005.

C. whereas the median net worth of white households grew by 50% from 2005 to 2009.

D. while the median net worth of white and Hispanic households grew modestly.

5

A. NO CHANGE

B. Too often, urban neighborhoods become places of high crime, poor schools, and substandard housing.

C. Too often, urban neighborhoods become a high-crime place with poor schools and substandard housing.

D. Too often, an urban neighborhood becomes places of high crime, poor schools, and substandard housing.

The Fight for African American Progress:
The Political Picture

 6 Only, with the enforcement of the Reconstruction Act of 1867 and the ratification of the Fifteenth Amendment did African Americans first win seats in Congress. On February 25, 1870, Hiram Revels of Mississippi became the first African American Senator. Later that same year, Joseph Rainey of South Carolina became the first African American member of the House of Representatives.

African Americans throughout the South became politically active soon after the close of the Civil War. A generation of African American leaders emerged, almost all of whom supported the Republican Party because **7** they had **8** discerned their rights.

6

A. NO CHANGE

B. Only with the enforcement of the Reconstruction Act of 1867, and the ratification of the Fifteenth Amendment,

C. Only with the enforcement of the Reconstruction Act of 1867 and the ratification of the Fifteenth Amendment

D. Only with the enforcement of the Reconstruction Act of 1867, and the ratification of the Fifteenth Amendment

7

A. NO CHANGE

B. he

C. we

D. it

8

A. NO CHANGE

B. evinced

C. championed

D. disputed

CONTINUE

During the 1890s and early 1900s, however, no African American won election to Congress, in part because of restrictive state election codes in some southern states. During World War I and in the following decade, African Americans who migrated to northern cities created the foundations for political organization in urban centers. Over the next three decades, African Americans won congressional seats in New York City, Detroit, and Philadelphia. In the wake of the civil rights movement, African Americans regained seats in the South. **10** The South is a beautiful part of the country, and you should seriously consider visiting it for your next vacation.

These members of Congress have traditionally served as advocates for all African Americans, not just their constituencies. During Reconstruction and the late nineteenth century, they worked to protect the voting rights of African Americans. They also called for expanded educational opportunities and land grants for freed slaves. In the mid-twentieth century, they focused on urban communities and urged federal programs for improved housing and job training. **11** The Congressional Black Caucus demonstrated a special concern for the protection of civil rights, the guarantee of equal opportunity in education, employment, and housing, and a broad array of foreign and domestic policy issues.

9

A. NO CHANGE

B. favorable

C. irrelevant

D. progressive

10 The writer is considering deleting the underlined sentence. Should the writer do this?

A. No, because it provides relevant details about the main topic of the paragraph.

B. No, because it provides context for the following paragraph.

C. Yes, because it introduces a detail that is not directly related to the topic of the paragraph.

D. Yes, because it creates a transition to the next paragraph.

11

A. NO CHANGE

B. The Congressional Black Caucus demonstrated a special concern for the protection of civil rights; the guarantee of equal opportunity in education, employment, and housing; and a broad array of foreign and domestic policy issues.

C. The Congressional Black Caucus demonstrated a special concern for the protection of civil rights the guarantee of equal opportunity in education employment and housing and a broad array of foreign and domestic policy issues.

D. The Congressional Black Caucus demonstrated a special concern for the protection of civil rights. The guarantee of equal opportunity in education. Employment and housing. And a broad array of foreign and domestic policy issues.

Morocco's Musical Traditions

Morocco has many rich musical traditions stemming from [12] their unique geographical conditions and a long history of intermingled cultures. For the past century, Morocco has attracted musicians and other artists from the west who wanted to learn from the country's creative and hospitable people. For instance, Jimi Hendrix's style of guitar playing was influenced by his travels to Marrakesh and Essaouira, where he discovered the rhythmic music of the Ganawa tribe. The Rolling Stones were fascinated with Morocco's music and made several trips there to hear it. During one of the Stones' stays, Brian Jones recorded an album of village folk music. [13] The Rolling Stones have also been influenced by such legendary African American musicians as Muddy Waters, Chuck Berry, and James Brown.

Morocco is located on the northeastern corner of Africa, only a few miles from the southern tip of Spain across the Strait of Gibraltar. Mountain ranges form the "backbone" of the country, running from the northeast to the southwest. Fertile plains stretch from the northern side of these mountains to the Mediterranean Sea and Atlantic Ocean. [14] This area covered with farmland and several large cities and towns is the most prosperous part of the country. Although the mountains themselves are quite rugged and rocky, there is plenty of water to support fruit orchards and isolated villages of goatherds. The southern side of the mountains is more arid, with rocky plateaus and several fertile river valleys descending gradually into the Sahara Desert. The river valleys are dotted with towns and villages that get smaller as the rivers dry up along the desert's edge. Several nomadic tribes travel among the villages and desert oases.

12

A. NO CHANGE

B. our

C. its

D. your

13 Which choice most effectively maintains the paragraph's focus on relevant information and ideas?

A. NO CHANGE

B. Jazz musicians such as Pharaoh Sanders and Ornette Coleman have also made pilgrimages, in search of Morocco's earthy, trance-inducing rhythms, and complex melodies.

C. The band once made a trip to Morocco in the late 1960s while waiting for the verdict on drug charges made against them in Great Britain.

D. Today, raj, a type of music from Algeria, is popular among young Moroccans for the way it mixes western rock with Jamaican reggae and Moroccan pop.

14

A. NO CHANGE

B. This area covered with farmland and several large cities and towns, is the most prosperous part of the country.

C. This area, covered with farmland and several large cities and towns, is the most prosperous part of the country.

D. This area, covered with farmland and several large cities and towns is the most prosperous part of the country.

CONTINUE

15 Berbers could be found in dense population clusters throughout the country. **16** <u>There</u> ancestors lived all along the North African coast until frequent invasions brought foreign rulers to many of the countries, including Morocco. However, invading Greeks, Romans, Vandals, and Turks found it all but impossible to control the Berbers who lived in the rugged and isolated mountain ranges. Despite ruling the country, foreigners could not conquer the stubborn Berber spirit. The Romans gave them their name, which eventually evolved into the term *barbarian*, although this is a **17** <u>misnomer</u> for such gracious and hospitable people.

Beginning in the seventh century, Arab legions invaded Morocco on several occasions. These invasions began to affect the region not only politically, but religiously as well. Eventually the Berbers and most of the other **18** <u>notorious</u> tribes became Islamic and adopted some elements of Arabic culture, including classical Arabic music. The strongest Arabic musical influence is found in their lyrics, which often praise Allah or refer to the Qur'an.

15 Which of the following would make the most effective opening sentence for this paragraph?

A. Foreign invaders found it impossible to conquer the Berbers.

B. The Berbers have long been the largest ethnic group in Morocco.

C. Ancestors of the Berbers lived in rugged, isolated mountain ranges.

D. Berbers are hospitable people, despite the origins of their name.

16

A. NO CHANGE

B. They're

C. Theyre

D. Their

17

A. NO CHANGE

B. euphemism

C. locution

D. reflection

18

A. NO CHANGE

B. autonomous

C. indigenous

D. illustrious

Despite these additional influences, the Berbers were still able to maintain most of their own beliefs and traditions. Traditional Berber music was performed solo or in larger ensembles, sometimes accompanied by dancers. Musicians could be found performing in the medina marketplaces in the older parts of towns. The musicians often got a performance started with improvisational banter, referring to one another and to people in the gathering crowd. Then they began to warm up their instruments as they continued jesting: **19** drum skins that had been heated over lanterns were thumped someone played a few chords on a flute or a lute some castanets clacked or a few dance steps were stomped out. This buildup set the dramatic tone for the frenzied music about to be played; it also encouraged the audience to toss out a few more coins.

Tribes of Saharan nomads, such as the Ganawa and the Tuareg, brought the music and musical traditions of West Africa to Morocco. **20** It traveled with the gold and salt caravans through Timbuktu and up to Marrakesh just across the Atlas Mountains. The most notable instruments were large, metal, double-castanets clapped between the fingers to make a galloping rhythm. Hand clapping, fast drumming, and harmonized chanting were also common elements of these southern Moroccan tribes.

19

A. NO CHANGE

B. drum skins, that had been, heated over lanterns were thumped a few chords, on a flute or a lute, were played some castanets were clacked or a few, dance steps were stomped out.

C. drum skins. That had been heated over lanterns. Were thumped, a few chords on a flute or a lute were played. Some castanets were clacked, or a few dance steps were stomped out.

D. drum skins that had been heated over lanterns were thumped, a few chords on a flute or a lute were played, some castanets were clacked, or a few dance steps were stomped out.

20

A. NO CHANGE

B. Our family

C. This music

D. Everything

Morocco's musical traditions were additionally influenced by the country's northern neighbor, Spain. Arabs had lived in southern Spain for several centuries before they were driven out during the Spanish Inquisition. Arab musicians from the Spanish region of Andalusia brought a sophisticated and intricate style of music back to North Africa. Much of this Andalusian music was played on the oud, an Arabian lute with a pear-shaped body, three rounded sound holes, a short, fretless neck, and five pairs of strings. **21** <u>Some researchers believe that Andalusian music found its way into the poetry of the troubadours.</u> Andalusian music, with its distinctly western classic sound, had in fact influenced the troubadours who played in the medieval courts of Europe. A good deal of southern European folk music, such as Flamenco, was influenced by Andalusian music.

Today many Moroccan musicians adeptly blend these various musical styles, perhaps playing an Andalusian melody over a Ganawa rhythm while chanting in praise of Allah. Their lively mixes are as naturally eclectic as the rest of Moroccan culture. A few musicians, such as Nouamane Lahlou, have taken practically the reverse path of Jimi Hendrix and Ornette Coleman, blending their Moroccan musical traditions with modern styles. **22** Yet the result is <u>similar. They</u> have created popular songs that have a more international appeal.

21 Which choice gives a second supporting example that is most similar to the example that precedes it in the paragraph?

A. NO CHANGE

B. The rebec, a predecessor of the violin, was also an instrument in Andalusian musical traditions.

C. Today, there are two basic types of ouds: Arabic and Turkish.

D. Folk traditions of Andalusia were embedded in the music of the region.

22 Which choice most effectively combines the two sentences at the underlined portion?

A. similar they

B. similar they,

C. similar: they

D. similar they—

Mildred Dresselhaus

Heralded as "The Queen of Carbon," Mildred Dresselhaus is a pioneer for women in science, especially physics and electrical engineering. **23** Born into a poor household in the Bronx, New York, Dresselhaus had **24** a stroke in luck when her brother won a scholarship to attend a music school in New York City. Dresselhaus soon joined him, and through music she became **25** cognizant of the fact that there were schools within the city that could offer her a better education. She secured a place at Hunter College High School—a school open only to girls.

23 At this point, the writer is considering adding the following sentence:

With all the honors Dresselhaus has received, she has never forgotten those who helped her, and she continues to help others pursue the field she loves.

Should the writer make this addition here?

A. Yes, because it provides a detail to reinforce the passage's main idea.

B. Yes, because it serves as an introduction to her childhood.

C. No, because it detracts from the main idea.

D. No, because it should be included later in the passage.

24

A. NO CHANGE

B. stroke and luck

C. stroke of luck

D. stroke of lucky

25

A. NO CHANGE

B. apprehensive

C. dismayed

D. astute

CONTINUE

After high school, she attended Hunter College with the goal of becoming a teacher. **This was a common career path for women in this era.** Fortunately, during her second year at Hunter, **27** **Dresselhaus met the celebrated Rosalyn Yalow—a woman who would eventually gain recognition for winning the Nobel Prize in Medicine.** With **28** Yalows encouragement, Dresselhaus began to explore science and became passionate about physics. After seeing a notice on a bulletin board, Dresselhaus applied for a Fulbright Scholarship in physics, despite having already been accepted into a graduate program for math. To her delight, she won a scholarship.

26 Which choice best supports the statement made in the previous sentence?

A. NO CHANGE

B. Hunter College was established in 1870 and is located in New York City.

C. Dresselhaus later received her master's degree from Radcliffe College.

D. By this point, she was not as interested in music.

27

A. NO CHANGE

B. Dresselhaus met Rosalyn Yalow—a woman who would eventually win the Nobel Prize in Medicine.

C. Dresselhaus met Rosalyn Yalow—a woman who would, a little later in her career, win one of the most prestigious awards in her field—the Nobel Prize in Medicine.

D. Dresselhaus met Rosalyn Yalow—a woman who would eventually, but later, win the Nobel Prize in Medicine.

28

A. NO CHANGE

B. Yalows'

C. Yalow

D. Yalow's

[1] The Fulbright Scholarship sent her to the Cavendish Laboratory in Cambridge, England. [2] In 1958, Dresselhaus received her Ph.D. in physics from the University of Chicago. 29 [3] There, only she had often been the woman in her classes. [4] Dresselhaus continued her research on the microwave properties of superconductors at Cornell University—after winning a two-year NSF post-doctoral fellowship. 30 [5] After Dresselhaus returned to the United States, her mentor Yalow persuaded her to continue her research.

After her two years at Cornell, Dresselhaus accepted a position at MIT. She first worked as a researcher for Lincoln Laboratories and later as a visiting professor of electrical engineering and computer science. While at MIT, Dresselhaus shifted her research from semiconductors to the structure of semimetals, especially graphite.

In 1968, she became a full professor, teaching condensed matter physics to engineering students, while continuing her research. Shortly thereafter, Dresselhaus began to achieve recognition for her work, recognition that has continued up to the present. She is celebrated as an 31 eminent scientist. In 2014, when President Obama awarded her the Medal of Freedom, he said, "Her influence is all around us, in the cars we drive, the energy we generate, the electronic devices that power our lives."

Although Dresselhaus is pleased to be recognized for her work in physics, perhaps her greatest enjoyment comes from her mentoring of numerous Ph.D. 32 students—about 20 percent of them women. Despite her age, Dresselhaus's 33 complacency with physics has not diminished. She says, "I am excited by my present research and am not yet anxious to stop working."

29

A. NO CHANGE

B. There, she had often been the only woman in her classes.

C. There, she had often only been the woman in her classes.

D. Only there, she had often been the woman in her classes.

30 For the sake of cohesion, sentence 5 of this paragraph should be placed

A. where it is now.

B. before sentence 1.

C. before sentence 2.

D. before sentence 3.

31

A. NO CHANGE

B. immanent

C. imminent

D. emigrant

32

A. NO CHANGE

B. students: about 20 percent of them women.

C. students; about 20 percent of them women.

D. students—about 20 percent of them: women.

33

A. NO CHANGE

B. indifference

C. ignorance

D. fascination

CONTINUE

Questions 34–44 are based on the following passage.

Sense of Smell

Smell is considered to be the most delicate of our five senses. It has many practical functions—allowing us, for example, to determine whether food has gone bad or to detect smoke when something is burning. **34** Some things smell good to us, and some things don't; our noses are powerful tools for recognizing familiar people and places or recalling old memories. Smells can remind us of our aunt's cooking or our second-grade classroom, just as an infant identifies the individual scents of its mother and father. Smell also factors into romance, which is why the perfume industry labors to extract and mix pleasure-provoking aromas. **35** The nose will even play a complementary role in tasting: if you plug your nose while eating, you will find that your food seems to lose some of its taste. It is certainly true that we can perceive much more subtle olfactory variations than visual or auditory ones.

34 Which choice most effectively sets up the examples given in this sentence?

A.   NO CHANGE

B.   Dogs have a stronger sense of smell;

C.   Our sense of smell offers a variety of helpful functions;

D.   Other senses are more acute than smell.

35

A.   NO CHANGE

B.   The nose even plays a complementary role in tasting:

C.   The nose even played a complementary role in tasting:

D.   The nose has played a complementary role in tasting:

Despite all of these known applications, our knowledge of just *how* the nose knows **36** is less than the knowledge of our other senses. First of all, it's often difficult to describe how something smells. It's relatively easy to identify a D major chord or paint a verbal picture of something that is silvery-blue, but the fragrance of a rose is more **37** concordant. The scent of one rose might be "flowery and sweet, with a touch of citrus," while that of another might be more "like honey and freshly-cut grass." **38** Therefore, scents have been classified by scientists into 10 groups, each of which is characterized by its volatile compounds.

36

A. NO CHANGE

B. is less than our other senses.

C. is less than that of how our other senses operate.

D. is less than how our other senses operate.

37

A. NO CHANGE

B. distinct

C. expansive

D. elusive

38 Which choice most effectively maintains support for claims or points in the text?

A. NO CHANGE

B. Even those employed in the perfume and food industries often have trouble agreeing on how to describe and categorize particular scents.

C. Yet many studies of scents attempt to classify new and interesting fragrance mediums.

D. Even wine aromas have been assigned to twelve different categories, each represented by a section of a wine aroma wheel.

CONTINUE

Sights and sounds are measured in terms of their wavelengths, **39** allowing us to make better art and music, which can be assessed with scientific instruments. Scent molecules are not as easy to quantify. **40** We know that molecules up to a certain mass have scents, but there are conflicting theories as to what determines their smell and how the nose records and transmits this information to the brain. Until recently, most experts believed us able to recognize a certain smell based on a molecule's shape. Such a theory asserts that when a scent molecule of a certain shape enters the nose and touches a receptor, like a key, it unlocks and triggers a particular smell, which is then sent to the brain. Likewise, a variety of different scent molecules can open a combination of locks, sending a mixture of scent signals to the brain ("smells like this spaghetti sauce has basil and garlic in it"). This "lock-and-key" theory does hold true for the shape and smell of many molecules. For instance, most molecules that contain an amine group will have a fishy smell. There are, however, many instances of similarly shaped molecules with different smells, and vice versa. For example, two **41** different shaped compounds will still smell like rotten eggs if they both contain sulfur.

39 The writer is considering deleting the underlined part of the sentence. Should the writer do this?

A. No, because it provides scientific details about the measurement of two of the senses.

B. No, because it provides comparative data about perception.

C. Yes, because it should be placed later in the passage.

D. Yes, because it adds irrelevant details.

40

A. NO CHANGE

B. We know that molecules up to a certain mass have scents because there are

C. Since we know that molecules up to a certain mass have scents, there are

D. We know that molecules up to a certain mass have scents, and there are

41

A. NO CHANGE

B. differently

C. differing

D. differ

Luca Turin, a biophysicist and perfume enthusiast, questioned these discrepancies and resolved to form a new theory of his own. Turin has performed many experiments that 42 invade the lock-and-key theory. He believes that out of literally millions of different smells, there are too many cases in which the shape does *not* determine the smell. He once demonstrated this assertion by comparing a hydrocarbon called camphane (the main component of camphor, sometimes used in cold medicines) with decaborane. Decaborane resembles camphane structurally, except that it has boron atoms where camphane has carbon atoms. According to the lock-and-key theory, both compounds should smell like camphor. However, the decaborane instead smells like rotten eggs (which is surprising, as it contains no sulfur). This example proves that molecular shape is not always the determining factor of smell.

Then what exactly *is* the determining 43 factor—Turin theorizes that the *vibration* of a molecule's atoms provides its signature smell. 44 The number of atoms and electrons connected within a molecule determine that molecule's particular vibration. The result of these minute shakes and quivers can be recorded as a particular frequency. The receptors in the nose, therefore, actually record the vibration of the molecules and transmit that information to the brain as a scent. This theory puts smell in the same category as sight and sound. Colors can be measured along a spectrum of light according to their wavelengths; tones can be measured along a spectrum of octaves according to their wavelengths. Turin claims that the same types of measurements can be taken with smells. Although the frequencies of scents are much more complicated to measure, measuring them is exactly what Turin has set out to do.

42

A. NO CHANGE
B. sanction
C. instigate
D. refute

43

A. NO CHANGE
B. factor?
C. factor.
D. factor!

44

A. NO CHANGE
B. The number of atoms and electrons within a molecule determines
C. The number of atoms and electrons within a molecule have determined
D. The number of atoms and electrons within a molecule will have determined

STOP

**If you finish before time is called, you may check your work on this section only.
Do not turn to any other section.**

SECTION 3: MATH TEST—NO CALCULATOR

25 Minutes—20 Questions

TURN TO SECTION 3 OF YOUR ANSWER SHEET TO ANSWER THE QUESTIONS IN THIS SECTION.

DIRECTIONS: For **Questions 1–15,** solve each problem, select the best answer from the choices provided, and fill in the corresponding circle on your answer sheet. For **Questions 16–20,** solve the problem and enter your answer in the grid on the answer sheet. The directions **before Question 16** will provide information on how to enter your answers in the grid.

ADDITIONAL INFORMATION:

1. The use of a calculator in this section is **not permitted**.
2. All variables and expressions used represent real numbers unless otherwise indicated.
3. Figures provided in this test are drawn to scale unless otherwise indicated.
4. All figures lie in a plane unless otherwise indicated.
5. Unless otherwise specified, the domain of a given function *f* is the set of all real numbers *x* for which *f*(*x*) is a real number.

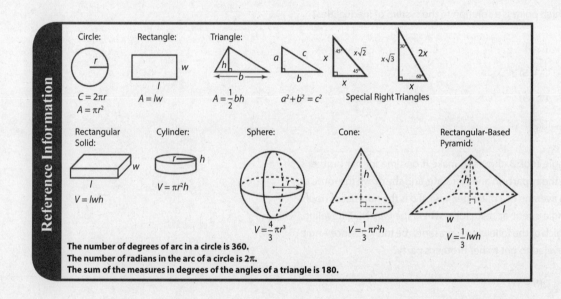

The number of degrees of arc in a circle is 360.
The number of radians in the arc of a circle is 2π.
The sum of the measures in degrees of the angles of a triangle is 180.

CONTINUE

1 If $3x - 2[1 - 2(x + 4)] = 5x$, what is the value of x?

A. -14

B. -7

C. 7

D. 12

2 Which expression shows the simplified form of

$(3x^2 - 7x + 5) - (-6x^2 + 5x - 4)$?

A. $-3x^2 - 2x + 1$

B. $-3x^2 - 12x + 9$

C. $9x^2 - 2x + 1$

D. $9x^2 - 12x + 9$

3
$$y \leq 3x - 4$$
$$5x + 4y \geq 6$$

Which point is a solution to the system of inequalities?

A. $(0, 0)$

B. $(-1, 5)$

C. $(2, -3)$

D. $(3, 4)$

4 Angie took $3x$ hours to make it on time for her brother's birthday party in another state, and she drove the route at an average of z miles per hour. If b is the number of hours Angie spent at rest stops, when she was NOT traveling, which of the following represents the total distance Angie traveled to get to her brother's party?

A. $z(b - 3x)$

B. $b - 3x$

C. $z(3x - b)$

D. $3xz - b$

5 If $3s - r = 9$ and $6s = 36$, what is the value of r?

A. 3

B. 6

C. 9

D. 12

SHOW YOUR WORK HERE

6 The distance, D, in miles from the city of Springfield of an approaching express train is modeled by $D = 209.6 - 55.9t$, where t is the elapsed time in hours since the train departed from Arlington. In this equation, what does the number 209.6 represent?

SHOW YOUR WORK HERE

A. The total amount of time it will take for the train to travel between the two cities

B. The negative velocity of the train

C. The distance between Arlington and Springfield

D. The decrease in the distance between the train and Springfield

7 If $f(x) = cx - \dfrac{d}{x}$, which of the following represents $f\left(\dfrac{1}{c}\right)$?

A. $1 - cd$

B. $1 + cd$

C. $c^2 - \dfrac{d}{c}$

D. $\dfrac{d}{c} - c^2$

8 Let a and b be positive real numbers. Consider the function $g(x) = (x^2 - a^2)(x^2 + b^2)$. Which of the following statements concerning $g(x)$ is true?

A. The graph of $g(x)$ crosses the x-axis twice.

B. $g(-b) = 0$

C. The graph of $g(x)$ never extends below the x-axis.

D. The graph of $g(x)$ does not have a y-intercept.

9 The x-intercepts of the function $g(x)$ are -2, 3, and 5. Which of the following is a factor of $g(x)$?

A. $x + 2$

B. $x + 3$

C. $x - 15$

D. $x - 30$

CONTINUE

10 An esteemed data scientist reports having discovered an extremely strong correlation between the total number of runs scored in Major League Baseball each week and the Friday closing price of stock for a medical device manufacturer, over a period of 22 weeks in 2014. Which explanation is most likely?

A. Either the run scoring affects the stock price, or the stock influences run scoring.

B. The run scoring and stock are both influenced by a single unknown factor.

C. The correlation is not possible; the data must be faked or erroneous.

D. The correlation is spurious, a coincidence. The data scientist may have searched for unrelated but matching patterns using data-mining tools.

SHOW YOUR WORK HERE

11 What is the value of a, if $x^{\frac{1}{5}} \bullet x^{\frac{4}{5}} = x^{-a}$?

A. −5

B. −1

C. 1

D. 5

12

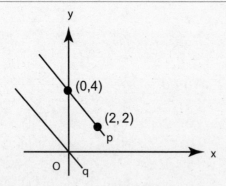

In the figure above, lines p and q are parallel. If point (x, y) lies on line q, which of the following represents the relationship between x and y?

A. $x + y = 0$

B. $x - y = 0$

C. $x + y = 1$

D. $x - y = -1$

13

In a right triangle DEF, $\sin F = \dfrac{2}{3}$ and m$\angle E = 90°$. Which of the following statements is true?

A. $\cos F = \dfrac{1}{3}$

B. $\tan F = 2$

C. $\cos D = \dfrac{2}{3}$

D. $\sin D = \dfrac{1}{3}$

14 A circle is drawn on an xy-plane. The diameter of the circle has endpoints at $(-9, 7)$ and $(15, -3)$. Which of the following is an equation for the graph of the circle?

A. $(x - 3)^2 + (y - 2)^2 = 169$

B. $(x - 3)^2 + (y - 2)^2 = 676$

C. $(x - 6)^2 + (y - 4)^2 = 169$

D. $(x - 6)^2 + (y - 4)^2 = 676$

15

$$\frac{3x^2 - 5x + 9}{x - 3}$$

Which expression is equivalent to the expression above?

A. $3x + 4 + \dfrac{21}{x - 3}$

B. $3x - 5 - \dfrac{6}{x - 3}$

C. $3x + 9 + \dfrac{36}{x - 3}$

D. $3x - 14 + \dfrac{51}{x - 3}$

CONTINUE

DIRECTIONS: For **Questions 16–20,** solve the problem and enter your answer in the grid, as described below, on the answer sheet.

1. Although not required, it is suggested that you write your answer in the boxes at the top of the columns to help you fill in the circles accurately. You will receive credit only if the circles are filled in correctly.

2. Mark no more than one circle in any column.

3. No question has a negative answer.

4. Some problems may have more than one correct answer. In such cases, enter only one answer.

5. **Mixed numbers** such as $3\frac{1}{2}$ must be entered as 3.5 or $\frac{7}{2}$.

   If $3\frac{1}{2}$ is entered into the grid as $\underline{3\,|\,1\,/\,2}$, it will be interpreted as $\frac{31}{2}$, not $3\frac{1}{2}$.

6. **Decimal answers:** If you obtain a decimal answer with more digits than the grid can accommodate, it may be either rounded or truncated, but it must fill the entire grid.

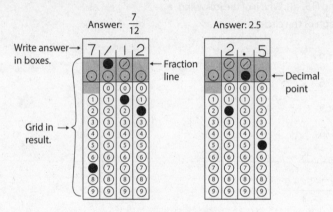

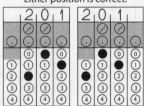

16 A ball is tossed into the air from 6 meters off of the ground, with a velocity of 13 meters per second. The equation that represents the height of the ball (h, in meters) at time (t, in seconds) is $h = 6 + 13t - 5t^2$. How many seconds will it take for the ball to hit the ground?

17 If $b = 6$ is a solution to the equation $6b + m = 270$, where m is a constant, what is the value of m?

18

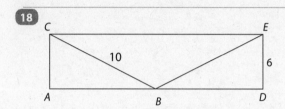

In the figure above, $ACED$ is a rectangle and B is the midpoint of $\overline{AD}$. What is the value of $\overline{AD}$?

19 What is the value of x, if $\sqrt{x+10} - \sqrt{2x-5} = 0$?

20

$$6x - \frac{3}{5}y = 2$$
$$kx - 6y = 20$$

In this system of equations, the coefficient k represents a constant. For what value of k does the system have infinitely many solutions?

STOP

If you finish before time is called, you may check your work on this section only.
Do not turn to any other section.

SECTION 4: MATH TEST—CALCULATOR

55 Minutes—38 Questions

TURN TO SECTION 4 OF YOUR ANSWER SHEET TO ANSWER THE QUESTIONS IN THIS SECTION.

DIRECTIONS: For **Questions 1–30**, solve each problem, select the best answer from the choices provided, and fill in the corresponding circle on your answer sheet. For **Questions 31–38**, solve the problem and enter your answer in the grid on the answer sheet. The directions **before Question 31** will provide information on how to enter your answers in the grid.

ADDITIONAL INFORMATION:

1. The use of a calculator in this section is **permitted**.
2. All variables and expressions used represent real numbers unless otherwise indicated.
3. Figures provided in this test are drawn to scale unless otherwise indicated.
4. All figures lie in a plane unless otherwise indicated.
5. Unless otherwise specified, the domain of a given function f is the set of all real numbers x for which $f(x)$ is a real number.

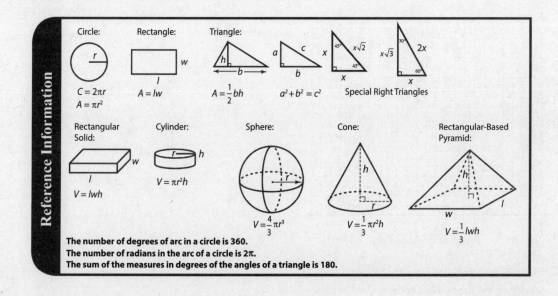

Reference Information

Circle:
$C = 2\pi r$
$A = \pi r^2$

Rectangle:
$A = lw$

Triangle:
$A = \frac{1}{2}bh$

$a^2 + b^2 = c^2$

Special Right Triangles

Rectangular Solid:
$V = lwh$

Cylinder:
$V = \pi r^2 h$

Sphere:
$V = \frac{4}{3}\pi r^3$

Cone:
$V = \frac{1}{3}\pi r^2 h$

Rectangular-Based Pyramid:
$V = \frac{1}{3}lwh$

The number of degrees of arc in a circle is 360.
The number of radians in the arc of a circle is 2π.
The sum of the measures in degrees of the angles of a triangle is 180.

CONTINUE

SHOW YOUR WORK HERE

1 A terabyte (TB) of information equals 1,024 gigabytes (GB). A server has a total capacity of 2 terabytes but can use only 90% of that capacity for storage. A company needs to store 920 100-GB files. What is the smallest number of servers the company must purchase to meet its need? It is OK to distribute individual files across servers; the total storage available must be equal to or greater than the total amount of information to be stored.

A. 49 servers

B. 50 servers

C. 499 servers

D. 500 servers

2 A major city performed a recent study to see the effect that snowfall totals have on the number of drivers on the road. The results of the study are represented in the scatterplot, where the x-axis represents the amount of snowfall and the y-axis represents the number of drivers. Which statement best describes the results of the study?

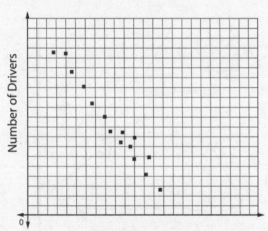

Amount of Snowfall

A. There is no correlation between the amount of snowfall and the number of drivers on the road.

B. There is a positive correlation between the amount of snowfall and the number of drivers on the road.

C. There is a negative correlation between the amount of snowfall and the number of drivers on the road.

D. The scatterplot does not display enough data to interpret a correlation between the amount of snowfall and the number of drivers on the road.

3 A candy store owner offers pre-mixed bags of jellybeans, taffies, and gummies. She wants to keep the cost of the candy in each bag at or under $3.10. Unit costs of the candies are as follows:

Jelly Beans	$0.046
Taffy	$0.069
Gummies	$0.038

Which of the following inequalities would best help the proprietor to know how many of each candy could go into a bag, given her budget?

A. $0.046J + 0.069T + 0.038G < 3.10$

B. $0.046J + 0.069T + 0.038G \leq 3.10$

C. $\dfrac{0.046}{J} + \dfrac{0.069}{T} + \dfrac{0.038}{G} < 3.10$

D. $\dfrac{0.046}{J} + \dfrac{0.069}{T} + \dfrac{0.038}{G} \leq 3.10$

4 Martina earns $480 per week plus 15% commission on all of her sales. Which shows the amount she earns each week as a function of her total sales, x?

A. $f(x) = 480(0.15x)$

B. $f(x) = 480 + 0.15x$

C. $f(x) = 480(15x)$

D. $f(x) = 480 + 15x$

5 The city of Smallville had an increase of 8% in its tax revenues from last year to this year. For next year, the mayor projects the city's tax revenues to increase by 10% from this year. What will be the total percent increase from last year to next year's projection?

A. 18%

B. 18.8%

C. 19%

D. 19.8%

CONTINUE

6 A random sample of people in a county were asked whether or not they drive more when gas prices decrease. Of the 682 people who responded, 471 of them said they do not drive more when gas prices decrease. If there are about 898,000 people living in the county, about how many people would be expected to not drive more when gas prices decrease?

A. 280,000

B. 320,000

C. 580,000

D. 620,000

7 A team of biologists randomly selected and weighed 322 lobsters caught in the Gulf of Maine. The mean measurement in the sample was 2.16 pounds, and the margin of error for this estimate was 0.18 pounds. The team plans to repeat the experiment with the goal of reducing the margin of error. Which of the following strategies would most likely result in a smaller margin of error for the estimated mean weight of captured Maine lobsters?

A. Randomly select and weigh 250 captured Maine lobsters.

B. Randomly select and weigh 322 lobsters caught off Maine and in surrounding waters outside the Gulf of Maine.

C. Randomly select and weigh 500 captured Maine lobsters.

D. Repeat the experiment using a different scale to weigh the lobsters.

8 There are 380 seats in a movie theater. The theater must collect at least $600 in admission per movie screening in order to make a profit. The prices for admission are $6.50 for children and $8.25 for adults. Solving which of the following systems of inequalities yields the number of child tickets, x, and the number of adult tickets, y, sold?

A. $x+y \geq 380$
$6.5x+8.25y \leq 600$

B. $x+y < 380$
$6.5x+8.25y > 600$

C. $x+y \leq 380$
$6.5x+8.25y \leq 600$

D. $x+y \leq 380$
$6.5x+8.25y \geq 600$

SHOW YOUR WORK HERE

9 A couch is on sale for 15% off the retail price r. A 6% sales tax is added to the sale price. Which expression represents the total cost of the couch, including the sales tax?

A. $0.15r + 1.06$

B. $0.85r + 1.06r$

C. $0.85r \times 1.06$

D. $0.15r \times 1.06r$

10 Which of the following equations could be used to determine the number of ounces of a 26% fertilizer solution that should be mixed with 80 ounces of a 12% fertilizer solution to make a 20% fertilizer solution?

A. $0.26x + 0.12(80) = 0.20(80 + x)$

B. $0.38(80 + x) = 0.20$

C. $0.26(80 - x) + 0.12x = 0.20(80)$

D. $0.26(80) + 0.12x = 0.20(x + 80)$

11 If $b \neq 1$ and $a = \dfrac{3}{b}$, which of the following expressions is equivalent to $\dfrac{a-3}{3b-3}$?

A. $-b$

B. $-\dfrac{1}{b}$

C. $-a$

D. $\dfrac{1}{a}$

12 Which of the following is equivalent to $3\sqrt[4]{x^3}$?

A. $3x^{\frac{4}{3}}$

B. $3x^{\frac{3}{4}}$

C. $3\left(x^3\right)^4$

D. $3\left(x^4\right)^{\frac{1}{3}}$

CONTINUE

13 Aaron earns $9 per hour working part-time at the pool and $11 per hour working part-time at the bakery. He needs to make at least $215 each week, but he cannot work more than a total of 25 hours each week. Which system of inequalities represents this situation, where x is the number of hours at the pool and y is the number of hours at the bakery?

SHOW YOUR WORK HERE

A. $9x + 11y \geq 215$
$x + y \leq 25$

B. $9x + 11y < 215$
$x + y < 25$

C. $9x + 11y < 215$
$x + y > 25$

D. $9x + 11y > 215$
$x + y \leq 25$

14 A car and an antique truck depart from the rest area at the base of a mountain at noon, both heading up the mountain. The average speed of the car is 15 miles per hour slower than twice the speed of the truck. In 3 hours, the car is 21 miles ahead of the truck. How fast is the car traveling?

A. 11 miles per hour

B. 22 miles per hour

C. 25 miles per hour

D. 29 miles per hour

15 What is the y-intercept of the line whose equation is $3x + 4y = 16$?

A. $\left(\dfrac{3}{4}, 0\right)$

B. $(4, 0)$

C. $\left(0, \dfrac{3}{4}\right)$

D. $(0, 4)$

Questions 16 and 17 refer to the following information.

The graph below shows the amount of radioactive material in y grams that remains after x days in a container. Each point shows a measured amount that remains, and the best fit relation between those points is drawn to connect those points.

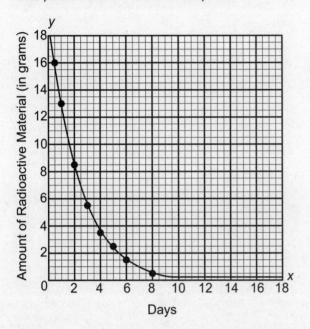

16 Which of the following equations would describe the relationship between the amount of radioactive material and the number of days that have passed?

A. $f(x) = 3x + 18$

B. $g(x) = 18 - 2.5x$

C. $h(x) = 18e^{0.5x}$

D. $j(x) = 18e^{-0.4x}$

17 If 2 grams were left, how many days had radioactive material been in the container?

A. 4

B. 5.5

C. 6.5

D. 8.5

18

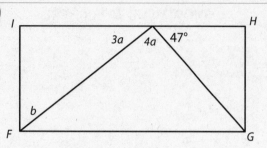

Note: Figure not drawn to scale.

In the rectangle *FGHI* above, what is the value of ∠*b*?

A.   17°

B.   20°

C.   33°

D.   45°

19   The population of a country has been growing at an annual rate of about 2.5%. The population in the year 2014 was estimated at 339,800. Which of the following equations shows the projected population of the country *x* years after 2010?

A. $y = 339,800(1.025)^x$

B. $y = 339,800(1.025)^{x-4}$

C. $y = 339,800(2.5)^x$

D. $y = 339,800(2.5)^{x-4}$

20   A city newspaper randomly surveyed 250 subscribers about their support for the mayor. Of the respondents, 27% said they supported the mayor, and the results had a margin of error of 3%. The newspaper ran a headline that less than 30% of city residents support the mayor. Which of the following statements best explains why the results do not support the conclusion stated in the headline?

A.   The sample size is too small.

B.   The percent of supporters could be more than 30.

C.   The margin of error is too large to make any conclusions.

D.   The sample is likely biased and not representative of the city.

21 Identify the value of a, if $a > 0$ and $\left(3^{-a}\right)^{\frac{2}{3}} = \left(9^{\frac{1}{a}}\right)^{-6}$.

A. $3\sqrt{3}$

B. $3\sqrt{2}$

C. $2\sqrt{3}$

D. $2\sqrt{2}$

Questions 22 and 23 refer to the following information.

The tables below give the number of days of rain per month for one year in Town A and Town B.

Town A		Town B	
Days of Rain Per Month	Frequency	Days of Rain Per Month	Frequency
5	1	1	1
6	3	3	3
7	2	5	2
8	1	9	1
9	2	12	2
10	1	15	1
11	2	19	2

22 Which of the following is true about the data shown in the tables?

A. The median number of days of rain is greater in Town A.

B. The median number of days of rain is greater in Town B.

C. The median number of days of rain is the same in both towns.

D. There is not enough information to compare the mean, median, or mode.

CONTINUE

SHOW YOUR WORK HERE

23 Which of the following is true about the standard deviation of the data shown in the tables?

A. The standard deviation of days of rain per month in Town A is greater.

B. The standard deviation of days of rain per month in Town B is greater.

C. The standard deviation of days of rain per month is the same in both towns.

D. There isn't enough information to calculate the standard deviations.

24 The graph of a linear function has intercepts at $(a, 0)$ and $(0, a)$. Which of the following is true about the slope of the graph of the function?

A. It is positive.

B. It is negative.

C. It is zero.

D. It is undefined.

25 What is the value of x in the diagram below?

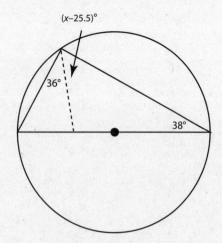

$(x-25.5)°$

$36°$

$38°$

Note: Figure not drawn to scale.

A. 16

B. 41.5

C. 54

D. 79.5

Questions 26 and 27 refer to the following information.

A poll surveyed 300 randomly selected voters for an upcoming city election. Of the respondents, 31% said that they will vote for Candidate A. The margin of error for the results was ±4% with 95% confidence.

26 Which of the following statements is best supported by the data?

   A. The sample size is too small to make an inference about the election.

   B. The margin of error is too large to make an inference about the election.

   C. The sample is likely biased, so an inference about the election cannot be made.

   D. The sample is likely unbiased and large enough to make an inference about the election.

27 Which of the following statements can be best drawn from this data?

   A. The actual percentage of voters who will vote for Candidate A is 27%.

   B. The actual percentage of voters who will vote for Candidate A is 35%.

   C. The actual percentage of voters who will vote for Candidate A is most likely between 27% and 35%.

   D. The actual percentage of voters who will vote for Candidate A is most likely between 91% and 99%.

CONTINUE

28 The diameter of Pluto's largest moon Charon is about 750 miles. The diameter of Pluto is about 2 times greater than the diameter of Charon. Which of the following best describes the volume of Pluto?

A. The volume of Pluto is about two times as great as the volume of Charon.

B. The volume of Pluto is about four times as great as the volume of Charon.

C. The volume of Pluto is about six times as great as the volume of Charon.

D. The volume of Pluto is about eight times as great as the volume of Charon.

29

$$y = -2$$
$$y = ax^2 - b$$

Which of the following values for a and b will make the system of equations above have one solution?

A. $a = 3, b = -3$

B. $a = -2, b = -2$

C. $a = -2, b = 2$

D. $a = 3, b = 3$

30

$$h(x) = -(x - 8)(x + 2)$$

Which of the following is an equivalent form of the function h above in which the maximum value of h appears as a constant or coefficient?

A. $h(x) = -x^2 + 16$

B. $h(x) = -x^2 + 6x + 16$

C. $h(x) = -(x + 3)^2 - 7$

D. $h(x) = -(x - 3)^2 + 25$

SHOW YOUR WORK HERE

DIRECTIONS: For **Questions 31–38**, solve the problem and enter your answer in the grid, as described below, on the answer sheet.

1. Although not required, it is suggested that you write your answer in the boxes at the top of the columns to help you fill in the circles accurately. You will receive credit only if the circles are filled in correctly.

2. Mark no more than one circle in any column.

3. No question has a negative answer.

4. Some problems may have more than one correct answer. In such cases, enter only one answer.

5. **Mixed numbers** such as $3\frac{1}{2}$ must be entered as 3.5 or $\frac{7}{2}$.

   If $3\frac{1}{2}$ is entered into the grid $\boxed{3\,|\,1\,/\,2}$, it will be interpreted as $\frac{31}{2}$, not $3\frac{1}{2}$.

6. **Decimal answers:** If you obtain a decimal answer with more digits than the grid can accommodate, it may be either rounded or truncated, but it must fill the entire grid.

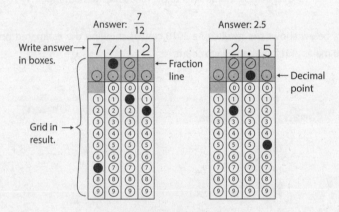

Answer: $\frac{7}{12}$ Answer: 2.5

Answer: 201
Either position is correct.

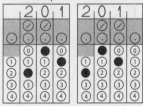

Acceptable ways to grid $\frac{2}{3}$ are:

31 Given $-5 > 4x-2 > -12$, what is a possible value of $-2x + 1$?

32 Amber has $25 to spend. She wants to buy a book that costs $12 and pens that cost $2.75 each. What is the greatest number of pens she can buy?

33 A team scored 74 points in a basketball game, not including foul shots. They scored on a total of 33 attempted shots, which are broken down into 2-point shots and 3-point shots, depending on where the shooter is standing on the court. How many 2-point shots did the team score in the game?

Questions 34 and 35 refer to the following information:

The data provided in the table below shows the results of a 2010 census showing the estimated population of four countries, in millions of people, divided into males and females in each country.

	Canada	China	Mexico	United States	Total
Males	16.9	696.3	55.9	153.1	922.2
Females	17.1	645.0	57.5	157.2	876.8
Total	34	1,341.3	113.4	310.3	1,799.0

34 If a person is chosen at random, what is the probability that the person is a female from China? Express your answer as a decimal rounded to the nearest hundredth.

SHOW YOUR WORK HERE

35 If a person is chosen at random, what is the probability that the person is from Mexico or the United States, given that the person is male? Express your answer as a decimal rounded to the nearest hundredth.

36
$$g(x) = \frac{1}{(x-6)^2 + 2(x-6) + 1}$$

For what value of x is the function g above undefined?

SHOW YOUR WORK HERE

A famous painting last sold for $300,000 ten years ago. Similar paintings have increased by about 14% annually in that time. The current owner of the painting is using the equation $V = 300(r)^t$ to model the value, V, in thousands of dollars t years after it was last sold.

37 What value should the current owner use for r?

38 What is the estimated value, to the nearest whole thousands of dollars, of the painting today? (Disregard the dollar sign and any commas when entering your answer. For instance, if your answer is $2,359,000, enter 2359 in the grid.)

STOP

If you finish before time is called, you may check your work on this section only.
Do not turn to any other section.

SECTION 5: ESSAY

50 Minutes—1 Essay

Directions: The essay gives you an opportunity to show how effectively you can read and comprehend a passage and write an essay analyzing the passage. In your essay, you should demonstrate that you have read the passage carefully, present a clear and logical analysis, and use language precisely.

Your essay will need to be written on the lines provided in your answer booklet. You will have enough space if you write on every line and keep your handwriting to an average size. Try to print or write clearly so that your writing will be legible to the readers scoring your essay.

As you read the passage below, consider how the writer, Marc de Rosnay, uses the following:

- Evidence, such as facts, statistics, or examples, to support claims.
- Reasoning to develop ideas and to connect claims and evidence.
- Stylistic or persuasive elements, such as word choice or appeals to emotion, to add power to the ideas expressed.

Adapted from "Milestones: what is the 'right' age for kids to travel alone, surf the web, learn about war?" by Marc de Rosnay, originally published by The Conversation *on January 4, 2015. Marc de Rosnay is a Professor and Head of Early Start at the School of Education at University of Wollongong, Australia. (This passage was edited for length.)*

1   Being a parent presents some problems. Irrespective of what you want, your children are going to take actions or be exposed to things that you may not relish. There is the ever-present possibility that they will experience things that you want to actively protect them from. The web provides some salient examples, like pornography. I really don't want my eight-year-old seeing pornography.

2   However, when my eight-year-old asks me an important Dungeons & Dragons question like, "Dad, can a paladin do magic and wear armour?" or he wants to know how solar panels operate, I always encourage him to look on the web. I've taught him to search on Google, to follow his curiosity, and I sometimes do it with him.

3   Ultimately, I want him to be able to seek answers to the questions that are interesting to him independently. He is guaranteed to run into something dodgy on the web, and my wife and I can take ordinary precautions.

4   To our way of thinking, however, more extreme precautions—prohibiting unsupervised internet use and high-level parental control—start to present their own risks.

5   One might ask, at what age should I allow my child to use the web unsupervised?

6   From the perspective of developmental and educational psychology, this is a slightly odd question. Let me explain. Most parents are familiar with the idea that certain developmental achievements happen at specific ages. Thus, infants become more wary of strangers at about nine months of age (stranger wariness), and they start to point communicatively by about 12 months of age (declarative pointing). These kinds of developments in the child's capacity are to be expected in all children given a typical environment; we call them developmental milestones.

…

CONTINUE

7   I spoke recently to a friend who wanted her ten-year-old daughter to be able to get to school, in the city, on public transport from the inner-west by herself. This particular young girl is very intelligent and responsible, I'm sure that she could have gotten herself to school at seven years of age. But there is no way her parents would have felt comfortable about that.

8   Why? For her parents to give her the independence to travel to school alone, they need to be satisfied not just that she can present her ticket, change trains, and get on the right bus, they need to be confident that she understands the importance of staying on the path, like Little Red Riding Hood.

9   This understanding is largely derived from countless conversations in which the parents have been able to convey important information about the world and the risks it presents to their daughter.

10 We know that children seek information from the people they trust, and from people who have a good record at providing useful information; actually, these two things are not unconnected. Between early childhood and mid-adolescence children have to understand all sort of things for which they need information from people they trust.

11 The information we convey to our children, and the manner in which we do it, helps prepare them for life. For most things, like knowledge about their bodies and sexuality, there is no particular moment at which children are ready for specific knowledge or experience, and much of this we can't control anyway.

12 But what we can do is answer their questions honestly in a manner that is appropriate for their age and conveys our values. The risks of overprotection are simple: children will grow up anyway but they won't have access to good information from people that they trust.

So what age is a good age?

13 It is very difficult to put an age on when a child should or shouldn't be able to grasp a new domain of independence. Your decisions will depend on specific circumstances . . . Managing risk is critical.

14 The web provides a salient example. By year five or six, today's children should have some freedom to search for the information they need independently. They can do this in a family space rather than in their bedroom. Talk to them honestly about the unsavoury content on the web; this will give them a framework for managing troubling or embarrassing content with you.

15 Independent action is also very important for children. Think back to your own childhood, there is a good chance that some of your fondest memories don't involve adults. Sometimes, children can walk to the shops before they are 12 years old, and around this time, they should be able to stay in the house for a little while as well.

…

16 Independence is linked to responsibility and much can be done to build responsibility in children before they undertake fully independent actions. But when you give your children independence you provide them with evidence that you trust them, and that trust fortifies responsibility in a way that supervised activity cannot.

> Write an essay in which you explain how Marc de Rosnay builds an argument to persuade his audience that being overly protective of children can be as risky as not protecting them enough. In your essay, analyze how the writer uses one or more of the features previously listed (or features of your own choice) to strengthen the logic and persuasiveness of his argument. Be sure that your analysis focuses on the most relevant aspects of the passage.
>
> Your essay should not explain whether you agree with Marc de Rosnay 's claims, but rather explain how he builds an argument to persuade his audience.

STOP

If you finish before time is called, you may check your work on this section only.
Do not turn to any other section.

1. A	12. D	23. C	34. B	45. B
2. C	13. C	24. A	35. A	46. D
3. B	14. C	25. B	36. C	47. B
4. D	15. B	26. A	37. D	48. B
5. B	16. B	27. C	38. B	49. A
6. C	17. B	28. A	39. B	50. A
7. D	18. D	29. B	40. D	51. A
8. C	19. A	30. D	41. C	52. B
9. A	20. B	31. B	42. A	
10. A	21. B	32. A	43. A	
11. D	22. B	33. C	44. C	

READING TEST RAW SCORE ☐
(Number of correct answers)

1. **The correct answer is A.** Hoover spends paragraph 2 explaining how the government's involvement in businesses was necessary to solve economic problems during World War I before concluding that although government involvement in businesses is "justified in war time, if continued in peace-time it would destroy not only our American system but with it our progress and freedom as well" (lines 19–21). Therefore, the best answer is choice A. The fact that Hoover defends government involvement in private businesses during wartime eliminates choice B, which argues that the government should *never* be involved in private businesses. Choice C is incorrect because it draws an extreme conclusion ("prevents businesses from making any profit") that Hoover never draws in the passage. Choice D is too simplistic, failing to take into account the role that government should play in business during wartime and not play during peacetime.

2. **The correct answer is C.** In lines 10–19, Hoover supports the idea that the government needed to take over businesses during World War I because the entire country was mainly focused on the war effort, so choice C is correct. Although Hoover does describe the government as having been despotic (line 15) during World War I, he does not draw the more philosophical conclusion that despotism is required to fight despotism in general, so choice A is not the best answer. Although Hoover says the government became more socialistic (lines 18–19) during the war, and this is generally acceptable only during wartime, he does not make the extreme conclusion that *only* a socialistic government can function during wartime, so choice B is not the best answer. He only discusses government takeover of businesses in terms of how it helps the economy and the war effort; he does not imply the more negative concept that businesses would actually hurt the war effort by continuing to run privately during wartime, so choice D is not the best answer choice.

3. **The correct answer is B.** In lines 12–13, Hoover explains that "The government having absorbed every energy of our people for war, there was no other solution," which supports the idea that the government needed to take over businesses during World War I because the entire country was mainly focused on the war effort. Choice A (lines 10–11) merely introduces the idea of the government becoming more involved in the economy; it does not get into why this was necessary, so it is inadequate evidence to support the previous correct answer. Choice C (lines 13–15) seems to make the mistake that choice A was the correct

answer to the previous question since both that choice and these lines refer to despotism. Choice D (lines 15–17) just goes on to define how the government became despotic, and that does not support the previous correct answer.

4. **The correct answer is D.** In these two paragraphs, Hoover explains that his general statements are not to be interpreted as extreme positions, and in doing so, he provides some details to clarify his position, beginning his clarification with the explicit introductory phrase "I do not wish to be misunderstood" (line 60). Hoover is merely clarifying his position in these paragraphs; he is not changing his position at all, so choice A is incorrect. Although Hoover does summarize a few of his previously made points in these paragraphs ("I have already stated . . . by-product"; lines 61–66), he does not repeat *every* point he had made in the passage up until this point, so choice B is incorrect. While Hoover does feel strongly about his position, he does not assume that his position is that of all Americans, which would be too extreme and too unrealistic since different individuals often have different ideas, so choice C is incorrect.

5. **The correct answer is B.** In line 67, Hoover states "Nor do I wish to be misinterpreted," because a misinterpretation of his words could lead someone to twist them into believing that he is saying something he does not intend to say, such as the belief that the United States should be a "free-for-all" (line 68), which would be an extreme interpretation of his position. Hoover is making a general statement about the government's role in private business in this passage; there is no evidence that he is trying to drum up votes for himself or anyone else, so choice A is incorrect. Hoover is only clarifying his position in these lines; he is not changing or softening his position, so choice C is incorrect. There is establishment of context in these lines, so choice D is also incorrect.

6. **The correct answer is C.** In lines 57–59, Hoover suggests that liberalism is a defining characteristic of the American system, so choice C is the best answer. Although Hoover believes that liberalism is a defining characteristic of the American system, he does not make the extreme judgment that America is the only liberal country, so choice A is incorrect. However, Hoover does say that liberalism is more important to the American system than the European system (lines 58–60), which is the opposite of the conclusion in choice B. Hoover never makes any comparison between liberalism and conservatism, which he does not mention at all in this passage, so choice D cannot be correct.

7. **The correct answer is D.** By defining liberalism as "the true spirit in the American system" (lines 58–59), Hoover is distinguishing it as the defining characteristic of that system, so choice D is correct. Choices A (line 50) and B (lines 53–54) simply make general statements about liberalism, neither of which connect it to the American system specifically, so these are not the best answer choices. Choice C (lines 55–56) only mentions an effect of expanding the government's role in business; it does not define the role of liberalism in the American system, so it is incorrect.

8. **The correct answer is C.** Hoover acknowledges despotism's importance during the war in lines 13–17. However, now that it has ended, he vouches for a return to liberalism, making choice B incorrect. He contrasts European and American doctrines, demonstrating that "rugged individualism" is favorable to "paternalism and state socialism" (lines 27–29), making choice A incorrect. Although it is implied that Hoover favors capitalism, this is not directly stated in the passage, making choice D incorrect.

9. **The correct answer is A.** A labyrinth is a maze or a puzzle, which in the context of the sentence shows that Hoover is referring to the problems that will ensue if government gets into business. The result, he says, will be a tangled mess of bureaucracy rather than a smooth operation.

10. **The correct answer is A.** In the context of this sentence, *regimented* refers to the organization of people or government. Although the context is military, the regiment here refers to the civilian population.

11. **The correct answer is D.** Stowe recalls how she was deeply affected by the loss of her young child (lines 5–15), while Douglass describes escaping from slavery. However, the fact that he left behind friends who remained slaves is certainly terrible too, so choice D is the best answer. Only Douglass discusses the loss of friends to slavery, so choice A is incorrect. Only Stowe discusses the death of a family member and the fact that she had children whom she loved deeply, so choices B and C can be eliminated.

12. **The correct answer is D.** In lines 10–12, Stowe explains how her son's death involved "cruel suffering," which partially supports the previous answer about how she and Douglass lost loved ones in terrible ways. Choice A (lines 1–3) merely introduces the idea that she had children. By dealing with how much Stowe loved her children, choice B (lines 4–5) seems to make the mistake that choice C (lines 8–9) was the correct answer to the

previous question. Choice C establishes that she felt terrible about her son's death, but it does not indicate that the circumstances of his death were especially terrible.

13. **The correct answer is C.** Stowe describes the process of writing *Uncle Tom's Cabin* in terms that emphasize how extremely painful it was to recount the terrible experiences of the slavery era (lines 36–39), so choice C is the best answer. She does not indicate that it was artistically satisfying, so choice A is incorrect, nor does she get into the actual work involved in writing it, so choice B is incorrect as well. While writing the book was extremely emotional, she describes it in negative terms, so choice D is not the most logical answer.

14. **The correct answer is C.** In lines 37–39, Stowe uses the phrase "I thought my heart would fail utterly" to illustrate how extremely painful it was to write *Uncle Tom's Cabin*, so choice C is the best answer. Choice A (lines 28–31) alludes to how terrible the circumstances of slavery were, which she illustrates by referring to "the depth of the abyss," but she doesn't explain how that affected her emotions, so it is not the best answer. Similarly, choice B (lines 31–33) deals with the law records and not Stowe's emotions, so it is also incorrect. Choice D (lines 39–40) explains how Stowe got through the extremely painful experience of writing *Uncle Tom's Cabin*; it does not establish the idea that writing the book was extremely painful.

15. **The correct answer is B.** In line 52–53, Douglass states leaving the friends he loved "shook [his] decision more than anything else." He mentions his hometown, Baltimore, briefly at the beginning of the passage. However, he never states that it was hard for him to leave the town specifically, rendering choice A incorrect. In lines 55–65, he discusses fear of failure at length, showing it does hinder him from reaching his freedom. However, this is not stated as the *largest* deterrent, making choices C and D incorrect.

16. **The correct answer is B.** The addition of "An American Slave, Written by Himself" reinforces the idea that it was unusual for a slave to write anything, no less a complete book. We can infer from the inclusion of this information in the title that Douglass wanted to make sure no one thought someone else had written the work.

17. **The correct answer is B.** Both passages are written documents of the evils of slavery created in the effort to abolish the vile practice, which supports choice B and eliminates choice A. There is no comparison between attitudes about slavery in the north and south in either

passage, and since there were many people in the south, such as slaves, who were terribly angry about the evils of slavery, choice C does not makes sense. Neither passage indicates when the conflict over slavery started heating up in relation to when these passages were written, so choice D is incorrect.

18. **The correct answer is D.** The only meaning of the word that makes sense in the sentence is choice D. Here Stowe is talking about the intense pain she felt when discovering that the slave experience was even worse than she had thought. Although *exquisite* can mean beautiful or delightful, in this context its meaning is "intensely."

19. **The correct answer is A.** In this part of the narrative, Douglass describes his feelings about leaving his friends when he escapes. These feelings are part of his struggle to make the final decision to attempt the escape, so in this context, he is contending with his feelings of pain about the decision.

20. **The correct answer is B.** In lines 12–15, Stowe expresses her deep sorrow and says what would make her feel better would be knowing that she could use her loss for some greater purpose. Her belief in the evil of slavery and acting on that belief through the abolitionist movement was one way she used to come to terms with her child's death.

21. **The correct answer is B.** The fact that Stowe felt she had to document what she wrote in the book indicates that some people questioned the validity of the premise of *Uncle Tom's Cabin*. Her research led her to discover, not that the book got it wrong, but that the treatment of slaves was even worse than she had imagined when writing *Uncle Tom's Cabin*. Choice B (lines 30–31) suggests that whatever ideas Stowe recorded in the book were incomplete, and she needed more work to further the truth.

22. **The correct answer is B.** The main idea of the passage is how NASA and its partners monitor the satellites orbiting around Mars to make sure they don't collide. A summary must include the main idea along with some other information that provides an overview of the entire text. Choice B includes both the main idea and the detail that explains the reason the satellites need monitoring. The passage doesn't discuss gathering information, choice A, and choice D is a detail.

23. **The correct answer is C.** The passage details the various spacecraft currently in orbit around Mars and their sponsoring areas, including several belonging to the United States, one to India, and one to the European Union (lines 4–14).

24. **The correct answer is A.** The passage describes a close call in which a collision alert was sounded because two satellites came within a close distance of each other (lines 55–60), triggering the plans put in place for such an event. The alarms are set so that the orbits can be closely monitored and steps taken to prevent a collision should they be needed. Over that weekend, the alarms went off, but no action was needed because it was determined that the satellites were not that close to each other after all (lines 62–65), a fact the scientists could not predict earlier. While the passage does not go into great detail about how the scientists reacted to the alert, it certainly does not indicate that they failed to respond to the alert completely, so choice C is incorrect. There was only a danger of collision during this period; the collision never actually occurred, so choice D is incorrect.

25. **The correct answer is B.** Lines 57–58 explain how the satellites MAVEN and MRO came within collision distance of each other, which provides evidence to support the correct answer to the previous question. Choice A (lines 16–17) merely introduces one of those satellites; it does not describe the circumstances in which it was involved on New Year's weekend 2015. Choice C (lines 60–61) explains how the message went out, not the more important details of what was in the message, so it is not the best answer. Choice D (lines 63–65) explains the resolution of the incident, not what that incident was, so it is not the best answer either.

26. **The correct answer is A.** According to the passage, the closer satellites come toward each other, the greater danger to human life and each other they pose, so choice A is the best answer. This fact also eliminates choice C. If it were impossible to calculate the distance between satellites until it was too late, there would be no preventative point in calculating at all, so choice B does not make sense. Also, if the distance never varied, there would be no point in reporting on satellites' distance from each other, so choice D is incorrect.

27. **The correct answer is C.** A satellite could collide if its orbital path crosses the orbital path of another satellite at the same time. Choice C (lines 74–75) explains this relationship. None of the other choices describes this relationship.

28. **The correct answer is A.** This answer is supported in lines 84–87, which imply that the two orbiters could compare findings, while viewing Mars from essentially the same perspective. Although the accuracy of the collision alert systems is discussed in the passage, testing their accuracy is never explicitly stated as a benefit of two orbiters being close together, rendering choice B incorrect. MAVEN and MRO are mentioned together in line 57, but their monitoring of each other's progress is never mentioned as a benefit, making choice C incorrect. Although the passage mentions that different countries operate different orbiters, there is no mention of competitiveness in accuracy, therefore, choice D is incorrect.

29. **The correct answer is B.** Lines 49–50 state that there is "improved prediction in the forecasting as the date gets closer." Lines 46–48 state that uncertainty "multiplies" the *further* you go away from the date, therefore choice A is incorrect. Choice C is incorrect because of both of these previously mentioned statements (lines 49–51 and lines 46–48), which show definitively that the accuracy shifts. The difficulty of the predictions is never discussed, therefore choice D is incorrect.

30. **The correct answer is D.** *Conjunction* is used in line 73 to describe the "connection" of satellites, causing a collision, so choice D is the best answer. Choice A can be eliminated because *rejection* has the opposite meaning of *connection*. While *combination* can be used as a synonym for *conjunction* in other contexts, it does not make sense in this particular context, so choice B can be eliminated. Choice C means *argument*, and while there would certainly be conflict between two satellites involved in a dangerous conjunction, they cannot actually argue as humans do.

31. **The correct answer is B.** In line 36, the word *future*, in "projections of future trajectories" explains when the data will be used, from which it can be inferred that *projection* is something forecast for later or at a future time. In this case the data consists of forecasts about the paths of the satellites in the future as they travel in their orbits.

32. **The correct answer is A.** Because climate change is already affecting the potato crops in Peru (lines 6–10), especially those at high altitudes, diversity of crops can help determine which varieties are better suited for the higher altitudes and warmer temperatures. Some ancient varieties could be resilient to warmer temperatures, but the statement does not explain how diversity of crops can be resilient to the effects of climate change

(choice B). According to the passage, it is possible to help potatoes adapt to changes in the climate (lines 63–66), so choice C is incorrect. Choice D is incorrect because lines 58–66 indicate that the gene bank could help save varieties of potatoes from extinction.

33. **The correct answer is C.** Diversity of crops can help alleviate disease and enhance adaptation to different environments, and the farmers are using more diverse plants and seedlings. This tactic will help fight crop failure and also help the crops to adapt to changing conditions as the farmers experiment with breeds of plants and seeds. Lines 1–2 only mention that world leaders attend the UN summit on climate change, not farmers, so choice A is incorrect. According to the passage, climate change is causing a rise in pests that devastate crops (lines 6–10), but it never suggests that scientists are working to invent new kinds of pesticides, so choice B is not the best answer. The passage does not suggest that the farmers are trying out a different kind of staple food (choice D).

34. **The correct answer is B.** The author explains that rising temperatures are making it difficult to grow potatoes (lines 8–9), so it is logical to conclude that relatively cool temperatures are best for growing potatoes. This confirms choice B as the best answer and eliminates choices A and C. A climate can be cool and moist, but since moisture level is not discussed in this passage, there is no evidence to support choice D.

35. **The correct answer is A.** Lines 8–10 explain how rising temperatures are bad for potato farming, confirming that relatively cool temperatures are ideal. Choice B (lines 33–34) is about the benefits of planting diverse potato species, not the effect of temperature on potatoes. Choice C (lines 43–46) is about the limitations of gene banks, so it is irrelevant to the correct answer to the previous question. Choice D (lines 60–63) is about how genetic researchers are working with farmers to solve the potato-farming problem.

36. **The correct answer is C.** Choice C is best because it includes the main idea of the passage—Peruvian farmers are working to combat the effects of climate change—and the idea that the strategies include both the old and the new. Choice A includes only one facet of this concept, and choices B and D are details that are not needed in a summary.

37. **The correct answer is D.** The passage describes the effects of farming the potato, a staple crop for thousands of people, and how climate change is reducing output of the crop. Although farmers and scientists are working together in Peru and other places, it will be challenging to stay ahead of the changes already occurring. These changes, as described in the passage, for example, having to move crops to higher altitudes, may have limited use; as the article states, the land at higher altitudes is scarce and rockier. The passage also states that efforts to maintain a gene bank to increase crop diversity are limited, and sometimes the crops don't respond well and/or not all farmers have access to the gene banks. These factors suggest that the problem could grow worse.

38. **The correct answer is B.** According to the passage, planting a diversity of potatoes ensures that farmers will always have food, making it a safe way of dealing with the effects of climate change. According to lines 69–70, droughts are a problem for farmers, but it is never suggested that these farmers are dealing with that issue by studying how to stop droughts themselves, so choice A is incorrect. Lines 73–75 mention that some farmers are working with modern varieties in reaction to climate change. However, they are crossing them with other varieties, so choice C is incorrect since it indicates that farmers are *only* growing modern varieties. While choice D is possible, it is not mentioned in the passage, so it cannot be deduced from the information provided.

39. **The correct answer is B.** Lines 33–35 directly state "planting a diversity of potatoes provides a safeguard against crop failure." Lines 18–21 could be mistakenly viewed as evidence for choice D in problem 38, but since choice D is incorrect in question 38, choice A is incorrect in question 39. Similarly, lines 67–70 mention droughts, so it could be viewed as a justification for choice A in question 38. However, because choice A is incorrect in 38, choice D is incorrect in 39. Lines 53–57 talk about disease-free seeds and scientific knowledge, neither of which are options for question 38. Therefore, they could not be evidence in question 39 and answer C is incorrect.

40. **The correct answer is D.** In some contexts, the word *pronounced* can mean "to articulate" (choice A), but in line 12, it is used to refer to how "noticeable" the temperature changes are in the Potato Valley; in fact, the entire passage describes the effects of climate change on crops in the Potato Valley, so those effects must be noticeable enough there to warrant such a discussion. Therefore, choice D is the best answer. Choices B and C do not make sense in this particular context.

Answer Keys and Explanations

41. The correct answer is C. The word *ancestors* suggests someone who existed hundreds of generations ago, so choice C (lines 35–36) indicates that the potato is a food that was grown for food a very long time ago. Choice D (lines 37–39) refers to the past, but one would not refer to relatives past as "ancestors" if they lived as recently as the 1960s. Choices A (lines 25–27) and B (lines 28–31) do not refer to past events at all.

42. The correct answer is A. Lines 23–25 refer to how the farmers care for their native plants; they are "managing" them as they try to find breeds that are hardier at higher altitudes and withstand some of the effects of higher temperatures. None of the other words conveys this exact meaning—the farmers can't control the seedlings (choice B), nor can they regulate them (choice C). The farmers are not developing the crops (choice D); scientists are working on that aspect.

43. The correct answer is A. The myth includes two examples of deception to achieve goals: one when Thetis sends Achilles to the court of King Lycomedes disguised as a young girl (lines 53–56) and the other when Ulysses disguises himself as a merchant to gain access to the royal palace (lines 56–57). Both acts show people trying to deceive others to get what they want. The gods aren't shown to control events so much as cleverly intervene in human endeavors, so choice B is incorrect. Marriage loyalties are shown as bonds that can be broken (Helen willingly went off with Paris though she was married to Menelaus (lines 27–30)), making choice C incorrect. There are several references to the dangers of war (choice D), but the men are encouraged to join the war efforts.

44. The correct answer is C. Ulysses had urged others to swear to defend Helen, but when he was called upon to do the same, he opted out because he didn't want to upset his happy life (lines 35–38). This decision was hypocritical (choice C). While refusing to participate in a war can be very courageous under certain circumstances, Ulysses's reasons were personal, selfish, and a violation of his own oath to protect Helen, so choice A can be eliminated. Choice B can be eliminated too since breaking an oath is a betrayal of loyalty. While it is possible that Ulysses was afraid, the passage never makes that clear, and the correct answer must be "according to the passage," so choice D is not the best answer.

45. The correct answer is B. The author states that Discord was "Enraged at her exclusion" (line 6) from the nuptials, and tossing the apple among the guests caused a disagreement among the goddesses Juno, Venus, and Minerva at the nuptials. Therefore, it is reasonable to conclude that she was trying to ruin the ceremony by reducing it to chaos and disharmony, so choice B is the best answer. There is no reason to believe Discord was actually interested in finding out who the fairest woman was; she just knew that introducing such a question would cause trouble, so choice A is not the best answer. There is no evidence that the three goddesses were in danger of being ejected from the nuptials, so choice C is not as strong an answer as choice B is. Since Discord was angry and her goal was to cause trouble, a motivation as sincere as the desire to present a gift is unlikely, so choice D is incorrect.

46. The correct answer is D. Lines 52–53 state that Thetis was afraid that Achilles might perish if he went to war. The battle was already beginning, so choice A is incorrect. Her objections were based on her fear for his safety, not any ideas about his future marriage plans, making choice B incorrect. Her plan for Achilles to go to King Lycomedes was not to ask for help (choice D), but rather so he could avoid being drafted to fight by concealing his true identity.

47. The correct answer is B. According to lines 21–31, the main cause of the Trojan War was the fight between Paris and Menelaus for Helen. It was the goddesses Juno, Venus, and Minerva who fought over the apple (lines 8–9), so choice A is incorrect. The war did prove that Ulysses was disloyal, since he refused to fight in it even though he had sworn an oath to fight, but these circumstances did not start the war, so choice C is incorrect. The marriage of Paris and Helen, not the marriage of Peleus and Thetis, started the war, so choice D is incorrect.

48. The correct answer is B. Lines 27–31 explain how Paris wanted the much-prized Helen for his wife even though she was married to Menelaus, and after he persuaded her to go with him, the Trojan War broke out. The men set out to bring Helen back to her rightful husband. Choice A (lines 19–21) only discusses the first meeting of Paris and Menelaus and says nothing about the conflict between the two men that led to the Trojan War. Choice C (lines 31–32) only mentions the legacy of the war; it does not explain the war's cause. Choice D (lines 33–34) explains how Menelaus began gathering soldiers to fight the war; it fails to mention how the war started, so it is incorrect.

49. **The correct answer is A.** Lines 39–46 reveal that Telemachus is Ulysses' son when the young child is put in danger, and Ulysses had to drop his guise as a madman to save him. The fact that Telemachus was Ulysses' son, and not the other way around, eliminates choice D. Both Telemachus and Ulysses were humans, but neither was royalty, making choices B and C incorrect.

50. **The correct answer is A.** In lines 40–44, Palamades intended to find out if Ulysses was actually mad or just pretending, and he tests Ulysses by putting the infant Telemachus in danger. Referring to how the "father" (line 43) failed the test by saving the infant reveals the relationship in choice A. Choice B (lines 46–48) just discusses the aftermath of the test and reveals nothing about the relationship between Ulysses and Telemachus. Choices C (lines 50–52) and D (lines 53–55) are about Thetis and her son, not Ulysses and his.

51. **The correct answer is A.** In line 35, the word *recover* refers to what Menelaus wants to do to his wife, whom Paris has taken. Therefore, the most sensible definition of the word in this context is "retrieve," which means "get back." Choices B, C, and D are all synonyms of *recover*, but none make sense in this particular context. Paris needed to retrieve his wife, not "balance" her, which probably would not make sense in any context, so choice B is incorrect. One salvages wrecked objects, not healthy human beings, so choice C is incorrect. Helen is not damaged, she is just missing, so choice D does not make sense either.

52. **The correct answer is B.** The context of lines 59–64 indicates that "prudent counsels" is associated with something told to Achilles by his mother. His mother had advised Achilles to adopt the disguise to avoid participating in the war, which reveals the cautiousness of her advice, so choice B is the best answer. Had his mother's advice been "fierce," she likely would have impelled Achilles to fight rather than hide, so choice A does not make sense. There is no evidence that there was some legal component to Achilles's mother's advice, so choice C does not make sense either. The cautiousness of her advice shows that Achilles's mother cared about her son very much, yet choice D is the opposite of caring.

SECTION 2: WRITING AND LANGUAGE TEST

1. B	**10.** C	**19.** D	**28.** D	**37.** D
2. D	**11.** B	**20.** C	**29.** B	**38.** B
3. A	**12.** C	**21.** B	**30.** C	**39.** D
4. A	**13.** B	**22.** C	**31.** A	**40.** A
5. B	**14.** C	**23.** D	**32.** A	**41.** B
6. C	**15.** B	**24.** C	**33.** D	**42.** D
7. D	**16.** D	**25.** A	**34.** C	**43.** B
8. C	**17.** A	**26.** A	**35.** B	**44.** B
9. A	**18.** C	**27.** B	**36.** C	

WRITING AND LANGUAGE TEST RAW SCORE

(Number of correct answers)

1. **The correct answer is B.** This sentence provides key context clues to help you determine if the underlined word is correct. The sentence requires an adjective to describe the type of education that would guarantee "that African Americans remained socioeconomically disadvantaged until well into the twentieth century." Clearly, this describes an inferior education. What word among the answer choices best fits this description? *Inadequate* (choice B) is correct. Choices A and D describe an opposite type of education. Choice C doesn't make sense; *spacious* isn't an appropriate adjective to describe an education.

2. **The correct answer is D.** This sentence contains two independent clauses that are neither separated by appropriate punctuation nor connected with a coordinating conjunction, making it a run-on sentence. Only choice D provides the appropriate punctuation in the form of a period, and thus it is correct. Choice A is incorrect, as a comma alone is inadequate to separate two independent clauses. Choice B is incorrect, as a coordinating conjunction like *and* must be preceded by a comma. Choice C is incorrect because it includes no punctuation at all.

3. **The correct answer is A.** The third paragraph contains information that contrasts with information that is presented in the previous paragraph, so using the transition *however* (choice A) makes a more effective sentence than those (choices B and C) which omit it.

Moving the phrase "by the 1990s" to the end of the sentence (choice C) also makes it less effective. Moving the decade to the middle of the sentence (choice D) makes the sentence harder to follow.

4. **The correct answer is A.** The chart shows the median net worth of households dropped from 2005 to 2009, with Black households showing a drop from $12,124 to $5,677. Thus, choice A is the correct answer, as the median net worth of Black households did drop to less than half of what it had been in 2005. Choice B is incorrect, as the median net worth *dropped*, not *rose*. Choices C and D are not correct because the median net worth of *all* households fell in the same time period.

5. **The correct answer is B.** In this sentence "urban neighborhoods" must agree in number with *places*, so choice B is the correct answer as both are plural. Choices A and C are incorrect because *place* is singular. Choice D is also incorrect because while *places* is plural, *neighborhood* is singular.

6. **The correct answer is C.** The first part of this sentence requires no punctuation, so choice C is correct. Choice A is incorrect because *only* should not be set off by a comma. Choice B is incorrect because "and the ratification of the Fifteenth Amendment" should not be separated by a comma from the preposition *with* as it is part of the prepositional phrase. Choice D is incorrect, as the entire phrase is an adverbial phrase that modifies "did win" and should not be separated by a comma.

7. **The correct answer is D.** The pronoun antecedent is "Republican Party," so the pronoun that refers to it should be singular and gender neutral. Thus, choice D is correct. Choice A is incorrect because *they* does not agree with the antecedent in number. Choice B is incorrect, as *he* is an incorrect shift in pronoun person. Choice C is also incorrect, as *we* is an incorrect shift in both person and number.

8. **The correct answer is C.** The context in this paragraph suggests that African Americans supported the Republican Party because the party somehow aided them in gaining rights. The best choice, then, is *championed* (choice C), as it implies that the Republican Party fought for the rights of African Americans. Choice A is incorrect because *discern* means "to perceive," which doesn't suggest a good enough reason for African Americans to support the party. Choice B is incorrect, as *evinced* means "reveal" and that, too, is not a strong enough reason for African Americans to support the party. Choice D is incorrect because African Americans would not support the Republican Party if the party disputed or argued against their rights.

9. **The correct answer is A.** The context suggests that the state election codes were somehow limiting for African American candidates, as they were not elected because of the codes. Thus, choice A, *restrictive*, is the correct answer. Choices B and D are incorrect, because *favorable* and *progressive* would be used to describe an opposite type of state election codes. Choice C is incorrect, because if the codes were "irrelevant," they could not be a contributing factor to African American losses.

10. **The correct answer is C.** The writer should delete the sentence because it introduces a detail that is not directly related to the topic of the paragraph. Choice A is incorrect because its details are irrelevant. Choice B is incorrect because the scenic aspect of the South is not necessary context for the following paragraph. Choice D is incorrect because the sentence does not provide a transition for the paragraph that follows.

11. **The correct answer is B.** A semicolon is used to link lists of items in which commas are used. Thus, choice B is the correct answer, as the semicolons help to avoid confusion by linking lists of items that already contain commas. Choice A is incorrect, as there is no way to discern the lists. Choice C is incorrect because the lack of internal punctuation creates a run-on sentence. Choice D is incorrect, as using periods in this way creates a bunch of grammatically incorrect sentence fragments.

12. **The correct answer is C.** The antecedent in this sentence is Morocco, so the pronoun *its* must be used for agreement. Thus, choice C is the correct answer. Choice A is incorrect because *they* does not correctly refer to Morocco but rather to Moroccans, a noun that is not used in this sentence. Choices B and D are incorrect, as there are no logical antecedents to which *our* and *your* might refer.

13. **The correct answer is B.** The paragraph is about the influence that Moroccan music has had on non-Moroccan musicians, and only choice B maintains this focus by pointing out how some jazz musicians were influenced by Moroccan music. Choices A and C are incorrect because the sentences take the focus off Moroccan music and on the people who influenced the Rolling Stones. Choice D is incorrect because it talks about how other types of music have influenced Moroccan music.

14. **The correct answer is C.** The clause "covered with farmland and several large cities and towns" is a nonrestrictive phrase, which means that it is not necessary for understanding the sentence; thus it should be set off with commas (choice C). Choice A is incorrect, as commas are necessary to indicate that the information contained within them is additional and nonessential. Choices B and D are incorrect because other commas are necessary in the sentences.

15. **The correct answer is B.** The existing initial sentence of the paragraph describes the "dense population clusters" of Berbers throughout Morocco. Which of the sentences among the answer choices would serve to introduce and support this fact? Choice B would make the most effective lead-in sentence. The other answer choices don't serve to introduce the initial contention of this paragraph. Choice A is incorrect because, although the author mentions foreign invaders, the main topic is to explain who the Berbers are. Choice C is incorrect because the author's focus is on who the Berbers are, not where their ancestors lived. Choice D is incorrect because this is a minor point in the paragraph.

16. **The correct answer is D.** Here, the possessive determiner *their* (choice D), is correct as the word describes ancestors belonging to the Berbers. Choice A is incorrect because *there* is an adverb telling where. Choice B is incorrect because *they're* is a contraction of "they are." Similarly, choice C is incorrect because *theyre* is the contraction of "they are" spelled incorrectly.

17. **The correct answer is A.** The context suggests that the word "barbarian" does not fit the Berber people, and *misnomer* means "inaccurate name." Thus, choice A is the correct answer. Choice B is incorrect, as *euphemism* means "a milder word for one considered too harsh," which is not what the context suggests. Choice C is incorrect, as *locution* refers to the way a word is pronounced. Choice D is incorrect because the context, that the Berbers are gracious and hospitable people, is not a reflection of the term *barbarian*, which suggests the opposite of gracious and hospitable.

18. **The correct answer is C.** The author explains that the Berbers and most of the other tribes became Islamic. The context, then, suggests that the other tribes were like the Berbers, which means they were indigenous, or native to the area. Choice C is the correct answer. Choice A is incorrect because *notorious* means "famous," usually for something bad, and there is no indication that this was so. Choice B is incorrect because *autonomous* means "independent," and the idea of autonomy, for the Berbers or any tribe, is not noted anywhere else. Choice D is incorrect because *illustrious* means "distinguished" and this, too, is not supported by the context.

19. **The correct answer is D.** This sentence requires proper internal punctuation to ensure clarity and appropriate grammatical construction. Choice D deploys appropriate internal punctuation to produce a clear, grammatically correct sentence. Choice A is incorrect; the sentence is a run-on as written. Choice B is also incorrect; the commas are placed inappropriately and create confusion. Choice C uses end punctuation (periods) inappropriately and creates sentence fragments.

20. **The correct answer is C.** It is unclear what the pronoun here refers to. For clarity, the sentence must restate the antecedent, thus choice C is correct. Choice A is incorrect because it is unclear whether *it* refers to the music, the traditions, or Morocco. Choice B is incorrect, as it doesn't make sense in this context. Choice D is incorrect because the rest of the paragraph focuses on the music and musical traditions, not everything that the caravans carried.

21. **The correct answer is B.** This answer provides another example of the instruments used in Andalusian music. Choice A is not an example; it describes another aspect of Andalusian traditions. Choice C gives a detail about the example given rather than a second example. Choice D provides further information about Andalusian culture and is not a further example of the types of instruments used.

22. **The correct answer is C.** As the second sentence is an explanation of the first, a colon would be an effective way to combine these two independent clauses. Choice A is incorrect because it creates a run-on sentence. Choices B and D use incorrect internal punctuation for this sentence.

23. **The correct answer is D.** The sentence would work better later in the passage, after Dresselhaus's honors have been described and before her mentoring is discussed. Choice A is incorrect because the sentence is not a detail that supports the main idea. Choice B is incorrect because the sentence is about her work later in life, not her childhood. Choice C is incorrect because the sentence does not detract from the main idea.

24. **The correct answer is C.** The conventional expression used here is "stroke of luck," which means a fortunate occurrence. Only choice C is an accurate representation of this expression. Choices A, B, and D are incorrect because they are inaccurate expressions.

25. **The correct answer is A.** The context suggests that Dresselhaus became aware that there were better schools in the area, as she later got into a school for girls. Choice A means the same as *aware*; thus, it is correct. Choice B is incorrect, as *apprehensive* means "worried," and there is no indication that Dresselhaus was worried. Choice C is incorrect, as *dismayed* means "alarmed," and there is no sense that she was alarmed. Choice D is incorrect, as *astute* doesn't fit the context.

26. **The correct answer is A.** The statement in the passage provides more information about why Dresselhaus's original goal was to become a teacher, so choice A is correct. Choice B is incorrect because it offers more information about Hunter College, rather than Dresselhaus's goals. Choice C is incorrect because it would fit better later in the passage. Choice D is incorrect because it does not relate to why Dresselhaus wanted to be a teacher.

27. **The correct answer is B.** Only choice B avoids wordiness and redundancy, making it the correct answer. Choice A is incorrect because *celebrated* and *gain recognition* make the sentence unnecessarily wordy. Choice C is incorrect because it is also wordy: "a little later in her career" could easily be substituted for *eventually*, and "one of the most prestigious awards in her field" is unnecessary. Choice D is incorrect because "but later" is redundant.

28. **The correct answer is D.** In this sentence, *Yalow* is possessive, and thus must be followed by *'s*. Only choice D reflects the correct spelling of this possessive noun. Choice A is incorrect because there is no apostrophe before the *s*. Choice B incorrectly places the apostrophe after the *s* instead of before it. Choice C is incorrect because it contains no apostrophe or *s*.

29. **The correct answer is B.** The context of the paragraph makes clear that often, there were no other women in the classes Dresselhau attended. The modifier *only* must appear directly before the word it modifies, in this case *woman*. Thus, choice B is the correct answer. Choice A is incorrect because placing the modifier before *she* makes the sentence unclear. Choice C is incorrect because *only* modifies the verb "had been," again making the sentence unclear. Choice D is incorrect because *only* modifies "there," suggesting that *there* was the only place she had been a woman.

30. **The correct answer is C.** The first sentence of the paragraph notes that Dresselhaus studied in Cambridge, England. And the second sentence notes that she received her Ph.D. from the University of Chicago. Since sentence 5 is about Dresselhaus returning to the United States to continue her research, it most logically fits between sentences 1 and 2. Thus, choice C is the correct answer. Choices A, B, and D are incorrect because they do not reflect a logical sequence of events.

31. **The correct answer is A.** The author's intention is to point out that Dresselhaus is a distinguished scientist, and only choice A reflects the correct spelling of the word *eminent*. Choices B and C are incorrect, as *immanent* means "inherent or within," and *imminent* means "impending or close at hand." Choice D is incorrect, as an emigrant is someone who leaves his or her own country to settle in another.

32. **The correct answer is A.** In this sentence, the phrase "about 20 percent of them women" represents a sharp break in thought, and it should be set off by a dash. The sentence as it is written is correct, so choice A is the correct answer. Choice B is incorrect because a colon is used before a list or explanation, and the phrase "about 20 percent of them women" is neither a list nor an explanation. Instead, it is additional information. A dash is more appropriate in this case. Choice C is incorrect because a semicolon is used to separate items in a series or two independent clauses. Although it employs a dash correctly, choice D includes a colon before *women*, an addition that is unnecessary and incorrect.

33. **The correct answer is D.** The context makes clear that Dresselhaus enjoys her work and is interested in it. Only *fascination* (choice D) conveys this idea. Choice A is incorrect, as *complacency* means "self-satisfied," but the word is usually used in the context of being stuck in a position and unwilling to move forward. Choice B is incorrect, as *indifference* would suggest that Dresselhaus had absolutely no interest in physics, which is incorrect. Choice C is incorrect, as *ignorance* suggests that Dresselhaus did not have a solid understanding of physics, which is incorrect.

34. **The correct answer is C.** Choice C correctly introduces the variety of useful functions that our sense of smell provides us. Choice A is incorrect because it does not effectively set up the information in the rest of the sentence—namely, the variety of functions our sense of smell provides. Choice B is incorrect because the focus is on humans rather than dogs. Choice D is incorrect because it focuses on other senses rather than on smell.

35. **The correct answer is B.** The paragraph is written in the present tense, as is the conditional clause that follows the colon. Thus, this clause must be written in the present tense, making choice B the correct answer. Choice A is incorrect, as the clause makes an inappropriate shift to the future tense. Choice C is incorrect because the clause makes an inappropriate shift to the past tense. Choice D is incorrect because the clause makes an inappropriate shift to the present perfect tense.

36. **The correct answer is C.** The comparison here is between our knowledge of how the nose works and our knowledge of how other senses work, thus choice C is the correct answer. Choice A is incorrect because it illogically compares our knowledge of how the nose works to our general knowledge about the other senses. Choice B is incorrect because it illogically compares our knowledge of how the nose works to our other senses, without specifying any particular thing about the other senses. Choice D is incorrect because it illogically compares our knowledge of how the nose works to how our other senses work, without mentioning the word *knowledge*.

37. **The correct answer is D.** The context of the paragraph suggests that the fragrance of a rose is difficult to pin down, as the author contrasts it with identifying a D major chord or describing something that is silvery-blue. The word *elusive* best captures this sense, as it means "difficult to capture or pin down." Thus, choice D is the correct answer. Choice A is incorrect because

concordant means "consistent," which is not what the author is trying to convey. Choice B is incorrect because *distinct* means "recognizably different or distinguishable," and the author's point is that a rose's scent, while recognizable, is difficult to describe. Choice C is also incorrect, as *expansive* means "covering a large space or area" and does not fit within the context of this sentence.

38. **The correct answer is B.** The paragraph makes the point that our knowledge of how the nose differentiates odors and our ability to categorize those odors is limited. Only choice B supports this point by noting that people who make scent their job have a hard time agreeing on how to classify or categorize scents. Choice A is incorrect because the fact that scientists have classified scents into 10 groups directly contradicts the point the author is making in the paragraph that our ability to categorize scents is limited. Choice C is incorrect because while it doesn't contradict the author's main point, it also doesn't support it. Choice D is incorrect because it also contradicts the author's main point that scents are hard to categorize, as wine aromas have been assigned to twelve different categories.

39. **The correct answer is D.** The writer should delete the underlined part of the sentence because it adds irrelevant details that are not related to the rest of the passage. Choices A and B are incorrect because they suggest adding irrelevant or erroneous information. Choice C is incorrect because it is irrelevant and shouldn't be included at all.

40. **The correct answer is A.** The context of the paragraph makes clear two points: We know that molecules up to a certain mass have scents and that there are conflicting theories as to what determines their smell and how the nose records and transmits this information to the brain. The second independent clause contrasts with the first, as it presents uncertainty while the first points out what we know. Thus, the coordinating conjunction *but* is the best way to join these two clauses. Choice A is the correct answer. Choices B and C are incorrect as they set up a causal relationship that is inaccurate. Choice D is incorrect as it doesn't accurately establish the contrast information presented in the two clauses.

41. **The correct answer is B.** The adverb *differently* is the correct modifier for *shaped*. Together these two words create a compound modifier for the word *compounds*. *Different* (choice A) and *differing* (choice C) are adjectives, which describe nouns, so neither are correct in this sentence. *Differ* is a verb and does not correctly modify the subject.

42. **The correct answer is D.** Turin's questioning of the lock-and-key theory along with the results of his experiments suggest that he has disproved the theory, which makes choice D the correct answer. Choice A is incorrect, as *invade* means to "enter and take control by force" and does not fit within the context of this sentence. Choice B is incorrect, as *sanction* means "to support," and Turin's experiments did not support the theory. Choice C is incorrect, as *instigate* means "to bring about or induce," which doesn't make sense in the context.

43. **The correct answer is B.** The sentence is clearly interrogative and thus requires a question mark at the end. Choice B, then, is the correct answer. Choice A is incorrect, as a dash is not used as end-of-sentence punctuation. Choice C is incorrect, as a period is used for a declarative sentence, and this sentence is interrogative. Choice D is incorrect because an exclamation point is used for an exclamatory statement, and this one is not.

44. **The correct answer is B.** The subject of the sentence is *number*, which is singular, so the verb should agree in number. Only *determines* agrees in number with the subject, so choice B is the correct answer. Choice A is incorrect, as *determine* is a plural verb. Choices C and D are incorrect because both contain plural verbs as well as shifts in tense.

1. B	**5.** C	**9.** A	**13.** C	**17.** 234
2. D	**6.** C	**10.** D	**14.** A	**18.** 16
3. D	**7.** A	**11.** B	**15.** A	**19.** 15
4. C	**8.** A	**12.** A	**16.** 3	**20.** 60

MATH TEST—NO CALCULATOR RAW SCORE
(Number of correct answers)

1. **The correct answer is B.**

$$3x - 2[1 - 2(x+4)] = 5x$$
$$3x - 2[-2x - 7] = 5x$$
$$3x + 4x + 14 = 5x$$
$$7x + 14 = 5x$$
$$2x = -14$$
$$x = -7$$

2. **The correct answer is D.** Subtract the two polynomials by combining like terms:

$$\left(3x^2 - 7x + 5\right) - \left(-6x^2 + 5x - 4\right)$$
$$= \left(3x^2 - (-6x^2)\right) + \left(-7x - 5x\right) + \left(5 - (-4)\right)$$
$$= 9x^2 - 12x + 9$$

3. **The correct answer is D.** To determine which point is correct, substitute each value into each inequality:

A. $0 \le 3(0) - 4$ **Wrong**
$5(0) + 4(0) \ge 6$

B. $5 \le 3(-1) - 4$ **Wrong**
$5(-1) + 4(5) \ge 6$

C. $-3 \le 3(2) - 4$ **Wrong**
$5(2) + 4(-3) \ge 6$

D. $4 \le 3(3) - 4$ **Correct**
$5(3) + 4(4) \ge 6$

4. **The correct answer is C.** Pick values for the numbers. Suppose $x = 1$. That means Angie took 3×1, or 3, hours to get to the party. If it took her 3 hours to get to the party, she could have stopped for 1 hour ($b = 1$) and driven 30 miles per hour ($z = 30$). If she took 3 hours to get to the party and she stopped for 1 hour, then she was only driving for 2 hours. That means that she must have driven 30×2, or 60, miles total. Now try the answer choices. Plug in $x = 1$, $b = 1$, and $z = 30$. The answer choice that is correct will also total 60. Choice C results in:

$$30(3 \times 1 - 1) = 30(3 - 1) = 30(2) = 60$$

It is the correct answer.

You can also solve this problem by thinking it through. You are looking for a distance, and distance = rate × time. The rate is z miles per hour. The time is the amount of time it took Angie to arrive at the party ($3x$) minus any time she stopped during the trip (b). So the time is $3x - b$. If you multiply the rate by the time to find the distance, you get $z(3x - b)$, which is choice C.

5. **The correct answer is C.** First, solve for s: $6s = 36$; $s = 6$. Now plug in 6 for s to solve for r: $3s - r = 9$; $3(6) - r = 9$; $18 - r = 9$; $-r = -9$; $r = 9$.

Another way you could solve this is to work backwards. After finding the value of s to be 6, plug in each answer choice as a value for r. For example, if you started with choice A: $3(6) - 3 = 18 - 3 = 15$, which is not 9, so eliminate choice A. You could try out each answer choice until you reached choice C and found that: $3(6) - 9 = 18 - 9 = 9$, so C is correct.

6. **The correct answer is C.** One way to see this is to consider the time before the train begins to move. No time has elapsed, so $t = 0$. The equation at this instant shows $D = 209.6 - 55.9(0)$; the train is 209.6 miles from Springfield. Because the train is still in Arlington at that time, 209.6 also equals the distance between the two cities.

7. **The correct answer is A.** In order to find the value of $f\left(\dfrac{1}{c}\right)$ plug $x = \dfrac{1}{c}$ into the given function and simplify:

$$f\left(\frac{1}{c}\right) = c\left(\frac{1}{c}\right) - \frac{d}{\frac{1}{c}} = 1 - cd$$

8. **The correct answer is A.** $g(x) = 0$ when either $(x^2 - a^2) = 0$ or $(x^2 + b^2) = 0$. The first of these has solutions $x = a$ and $x = -a$. The second one has only imaginary solutions, which do not yield x-intercepts. Therefore, the graph of $g(x)$ crosses the x-axis twice.

9. **The correct answer is A.** The factors of a function can be found from its x-intercepts through a process like below:

$$x = -2, x = 3, x = 5$$

$$x + 2 = 0, x - 3 = 0, x - 5 = 0$$

$$g(x) = f(x)(x + 2)(x - 3)(x - 5)$$

10. **The correct answer is D.** Correlation does not imply causation. Such coincidences do occur, and can be found on the data-rich internet. A statistician might want to point out such a correlation for educational purposes.

11. **The correct answer is B.** When multiplying exponential terms with the same base, exponents are added:

$$x^{\frac{1}{5}} \cdot x^{\frac{4}{5}} = x^{-a}$$

$$x^{\frac{1}{5} + \frac{4}{5}} = x^{-a}$$

$$x^{\frac{5}{5}} = x^{-a}$$

$$x^{1} = x^{-a}$$

$$-a = 1$$

$$a = -1$$

12. **The correct answer is A.** When two lines are parallel, their slopes are equal. Since you know that line p passes through points $(0, 4)$ and $(2, 2)$, you can use this information to find the slope of p:

$$\begin{aligned}\text{Slope of } p &= \frac{y_2 - y_1}{x_2 - x_1} \\ &= \frac{2 - 4}{2 - 0} \\ &= \frac{-2}{2} \\ &= -1\end{aligned}$$

Since lines p and q are parallel, their slopes must be equal. This means that the slope of q is also equal to -1.

Since you know that line q passes through points $(0, 0)$ and (x, y) and the slope is -1, you can write an equation representing the relationship between x and y:

$$\begin{aligned}\text{slope of } q = -1 &= \frac{y - y_1}{x - x_1} \\ &= \frac{y - 0}{x - 0} \\ &= \frac{y}{x}\end{aligned}$$

If $\dfrac{y}{x} = -1$, then $y = -x$ and $x + y = 0$.

13. **The correct answer is C.** In any right triangle the sine of one acute angle is equal to the cosine of the other acute angle.

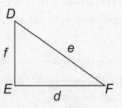

$$\begin{aligned}\sin F &= \frac{\text{opposite}}{\text{hypotenuse}} \\ &= \frac{f}{e} = \frac{2}{3}\end{aligned}$$

$$\begin{aligned}\cos D &= \frac{\text{adjacent}}{\text{hypotenuse}} \\ &= \frac{f}{e} = \frac{2}{3}\end{aligned}$$

14. **The correct answer is A.** First, find the center of the circle by finding the midpoint of its diameter.

$$\left(\frac{-9+15}{2}, \frac{7+(-3)}{2}\right) \rightarrow \left(\frac{6}{2}, \frac{4}{2}\right) \rightarrow (3,2)$$

Next, find the radius of the circle by finding half the length of the diameter:

$$\frac{\sqrt{(-9-15)^2+(7-(-3))^2}}{2}=13$$

Then, plug the center and the radius into the standard form for the equation of a circle and simplify:

$$(x-h)^2+(y-k)^2=r^2$$
$$(x-3)^2+(y-2)^2=13^2$$
$$(x-3)^2+(y-2)^2=169$$

15. **The correct answer is A.** Divide the two expressions using either long division or synthetic division:

$$\begin{array}{r} 3x+4 \\ x-3\overline{)3x^2-5x+9} \\ \underline{3x^2-9x} \\ 4x \\ \underline{4x-12} \\ 21 \end{array}$$

In general, when we divide F by G and obtain quotient Q and remainder R, then $\frac{F}{G}=Q+\frac{R}{G}$. In this case:

$$\frac{3x^2-5x+9}{x-3}=3x+4+\frac{21}{x-3}$$

Alternatively, you can use the remainder theorem to solve. Substitute 3 for x in numerator and the value should be the remainder.

$$3(3)^2-5(3)+9=27-15+9=21$$

16. **The correct answer is 3.** To find a solution, first set the equation equal to 0, since the height of the ball when it hits the ground is 0. Then, solve the equation for t using factoring.

$$0=6+13t-5t^2$$
$$0=5t^2-13t-6$$
$$0=(5t+2)(t-3)$$

$$5t+2=0; t=3$$

$$t=-\frac{2}{5}; t=3$$

Since the time cannot be negative, the solution is $t=3$. The ball will hit the ground in 3 seconds.

17. **The correct answer is 234.** Since m is a constant, that means that m must always have the same value. So use $b=6$ to solve for m.

$$6b+m=270$$
$$6(6)+m=270$$
$$36+m=270$$

After subtracting 36 from both sides of the equation, you will get $m=234$.

18. **The correct answer is 16.** You know that opposite sides of a rectangle are equal, so since $\overline{ED}=6$, $\overline{CA}$ must also equal 6. You know from the diagram that $\overline{CB}=10$. Since $\triangle ABC$ is a right triangle, you can use the Pythagorean theorem or what you know about 3-4-5 triangles to find the length of $\overline{AB}$.

Using the Pythagorean theorem: $a^2+b^2=c^2$; $6^2+b^2=10^2$; $36+b^2=100$; $b^2=64$; $b=8$. So now you know that $\overline{AB}=8$. You know that B is the midpoint of $\overline{AD}$ and that the midpoint divides a segment in half. That means that $\overline{AB}=\overline{BD}$. Since $\overline{AB}=8$, $\overline{BD}$ also equals 8. That means that the length of $\overline{AD}=8+8=16$.

19. **The correct answer is 15.** Transfer the radical expressions on the opposite sides of the equation and then square both sides:

$$\sqrt{x+10}-\sqrt{2x-5}=0$$
$$\sqrt{x+10}=\sqrt{2x-5}$$
$$\left(\sqrt{x+10}\right)^2=\left(\sqrt{2x-5}\right)^2$$
$$x+10=2x-5$$
$$10+5=2x-x$$
$$x=15$$

There is also a negative solution, but you can enter only postitive numbers in the grid.

20. **The correct answer is 60.** For the system to have infinite solutions, $kx-6y=20$ must be equivalent to $6x-\frac{3}{5}y=2$. For the two equations to be equivalent, there must be some number, say m, such that when we multiply both sides of $6x-\frac{3}{5}y=2$ by m, the result is $kx-6y=20$. Using only the right sides of the equations, we see that $2m=20$, so $m=10$. Then $10(6x)=kx$, so $k=60$.

SECTION 4: MATH TEST—CALCULATOR

1. B	**9.** C	**17.** B	**25.** D	**32.** 4
2. C	**10.** A	**18.** C	**26.** D	**33.** 25
3. B	**11.** B	**19.** B	**27.** C	**34.** .358 or .359
4. B	**12.** B	**20.** D	**28.** D	
5. B	**13.** A	**21.** B	**29.** C	**35.** .226 or .227
6. D	**14.** D	**22.** A	**30.** D	
7. C	**15.** D	**23.** B	**31.** Any number greater than 5/2 and less than 6.	**36.** 5
8. D	**16.** D	**24.** B		**37.** 1.14
				38. 1112

MATH TEST—CALCULATOR RAW SCORE
(Number of correct answers) ☐

1. **The correct answer is B.** The total storage available per server in gigabytes is 2 TB × 90% × 1,024 GB/TB. 2 × 0.9 × 1,024 = 1,843.2. The total storage needed is 920 × 100 GB = 92,000 GB. Dividing the total amount of storage needed by the amount available per server, we obtain $\frac{92,000}{1843.2} \approx 49.91$. Because 49 < 49.91 < 50, the smallest number of servers needed is 50.

2. **The correct answer is C.** A negative correlation is a relationship between two variables such that when one variable increases, the other variable decreases. The points on the scatterplot show that as the amount of snowfall increases, the number of drivers on the road decreases. Therefore, the scatterplot shows a negative correlation.

3. **The correct answer is B.** The cost of any set of candies is the cost of each piece multiplied by the number of pieces. Because the store owner wants to keep the cost "at or under" $3.10, it is OK for the cost to equal $3.10. The formula represents that fact by using the less-than-or-equal-to operator.

4. **The correct answer is B.** The amount of $480 is constant, and the amount she makes in commission depends on her total sales. The term that represents her commission should include the variable, and since she makes 15% of her total sales x, the term $0.15x$ represents the amount of commission. Adding both of these amounts together results in $f(x) = 480 + 0.15x$.

5. **The correct answer is B.** Choose an initial amount for the tax revenue for the town of $100,000. An increase of 8% would be an increase of $8,000 to $108,000. An additional 10% increase the next year would be another $10,800, for total revenue of $118,800. This is 18.8% more than the original $100,000.

6. **The correct answer is D.** 471 of the 682 respondents is about $\frac{471}{682} \approx 0.69 = 69\%$. To estimate the number of people in the county who will not drive more if gas prices drop, multiply the entire population by the percent in the random sample.

$$898,000(0.69) = 619,620$$

The answer that comes closest to this calculation is choice D.

7. **The correct answer is C.** Increasing the sample size tends to reduce the margin of error; reducing sample size tends to increase the error. There is no reason to believe that including lobsters from outside Maine would reduce the margin of error, and sampling from a population other than the population of interest reduces confidence in any conclusions about the population of interest. Margin of error is a measure of the difference between sample statistics and population statistics caused by random variation among samples. An alternate measurement device (choice D) would not necessarily be more accurate, and the measurement procedure does not affect random variation.

8. **The correct answer is D.** There are 380 seats in the theater, so the total number of tickets that can be sold is at most 380. The theater will sell x child tickets and y adult tickets for a maximum of 380 tickets, or $x + y \leq 380$. The income from the tickets will be \$6.50 per child, or $6.5x$, and \$8.25 per adult, or $8.25y$. The total amount the theater collects, $6.5x + 8.25y$, has to be at least \$600, or $6.5x + 8.25y \geq 600$. Only choice D shows both of these inequalities.

9. **The correct answer is C.** The discount is 15%, or $1 - 0.15 = 0.85$ of the retail price, which is $0.85r$. The 6% sales tax is added to this discounted cost, which is the same as multiplying by 1.06. The expression combining those two is $0.85r \times 1.06$.

10. **The correct answer is A.** If x is the number of ounces of 26% fertilizer solution, then the total amount in ounces of pure fertilizer in the mixture will be $0.26x + 0.12(80)$. The second term is the ounces of pure fertilizer in 80 ounces of 12% solution. The total amount of pure fertilizer in the resulting 20% solution can also be expressed as follows:

20% × the total ounces of mixed solution = $0.20(80 + x)$. The table below summarizes the information.

	% fertilizer	Number of ounces	Number of ounces of pure fertilizer
26% solution	0.26	x	$0.26x$
12% solution	0.12	80	$0.12(80)$
End result 20% solution	0.20	$80 + x$	$0.20(80 + x)$

Therefore, the equation is $0.26x + 0.12(80) = 0.20(80 + x)$.

11. **The correct answer is B.** You know that b cannot equal 1. Pick values for a and b. For example, suppose $b = 6$. That would mean that $a = 0.5$, because $ab = 3$. Plug in these values for the expression given:

$$\frac{a-3}{3b-3} = \frac{0.5-3}{3(6)-3}$$
$$= \frac{-2.5}{15}$$
$$= -\frac{5}{2} \times \frac{1}{15}$$
$$= -\frac{1}{6}$$

Since $b = 6$, $-\frac{1}{6} = -\frac{1}{b}$, which matches choice B.

12. **The correct answer is B.** Simplify the expression:

$$3\sqrt[4]{x^3} = 3\left(x^3\right)^{\frac{1}{4}} = 3x^{\frac{3}{4}}$$

13. **The correct answer is A.** The amount earned per hour is $9x$ for the pool and $11y$ for the bakery, and needs to be at least \$215, so $9x + 11y \geq 215$ represents this. The total number of hours needs to be at most 25, so $x + y \leq 25$ represents this. Only choice A shows both of these inequalities.

14. **The correct answer is D.**

	Distance (in miles)	Rate (in mph)	Time (in hours)
Car	$d + 21$	$2r - 15$	3
Truck	d	r	3

Using distance equals rate times time, we get the following system of equations:

$$\begin{cases} d + 21 = 3(2r - 15) \\ d = 3r \end{cases}$$

To solve this system, substitute the expression for d given by the second equation for d in the first equation to get an equation involving only r. Solve the equation as follows:

$$3r + 21 = 3(2r - 15)$$
$$3r + 21 = 6r - 45$$
$$3r = 66$$
$$r = 22$$

So the car is traveling at the rate of $2(22) - 15 = 29$ miles per hour.

15. **The correct answer is D.** The slope-intercept form of the equation of a line is $y = mx + b$, where m is the slope of the line and b is the y-intercept. The coordinates of the y-intercept are $(0, b)$.

In order to solve this problem, transform the given equation into the slope-intercept form:

$$3x + 4y = 16$$
$$4y = -3x + 16$$
$$y = -\frac{3}{4}x + 4$$

Comparing the above equation with the slope-intercept equation, $y = mx + b$, you can see that $b = 4$.

Therefore, the coordinates of the y-intercept are $(0, 4)$.

16. **The correct answer is D.** The graph is that of a decreasing exponential function. These are of the form $E(x) = A \cdot b^{-cx}$, where A, b, and c are positive constants. The function in choice D is the only one of this form.

17. **The correct answer is B.** Use the curve to draw a horizontal line at $y = 2$. Connect that intersection point vertically to the x-axis. This corresponds to 5.5 days, since the x-axis scale is 0.5 days.

18. **The correct answer is C.** You know that the angles labeled $3a$, $4a$, and $47°$ all lie on the same line. You know that a straight line measures $180°$, so you can find the value of a by adding:

$$3a + 4a + 47° = 180°$$
$$7a + 47° = 180°$$
$$7a = 133°$$
$$a = 19°$$

If $a = 19°$, then $3a = 3(19°) = 57°$. Angle l and the angles labeled b and $3a$ form a triangle. The sum of the angles of a triangle is $180°$. Since $FGHI$ is a rectangle, you know that angle $l = 90°$. So:

$$180° = 57° + 90° + b$$
$$180° = 147 + b$$
$$33° = b$$

19. **The correct answer is B.** Note that in the question it asks for the projected population x years after 2010, but it gives the population in 2014. The equation must take into account this difference.

The formula for exponential growth is $y = a(1 + r)n$, where a is the initial amount, r is the rate at which the amount is increasing, and n is the number of times that the amount increases at that rate. In this question $a = 339,800$, $r = 0.025$, and $n = x - 4$. Plugging these values into the formula, we get $y = 339,800(1 + 0.025)^{x-4}$, which is choice B.

20. **The correct answer is D.** The sample is likely biased since they only asked subscribers of their newspaper. Also, subscribers of the newspaper may not live in the city.

21. **The correct answer is B.** To solve this problem, first convert 9 into an exponential term with base 3, so that both sides have the same base. Then equate powers on both sides. Also remember that when raising an exponential term with another power, exponents are multiplied, thus $(xm)n = x^{m \times n}$.

$$\left(3^{-a}\right)^{\frac{2}{3}} = \left(9^{\frac{1}{a}}\right)^{-6}$$

$$\left(3^{-a}\right)^{\frac{2}{3}} = \left[\left(3^2\right)^{\frac{1}{a}}\right]^{-6}$$

$$3^{\frac{-2a}{3}} = 3^{\frac{-12}{a}}$$

$$-2a^2 = -36$$

$$a^2 = 18$$

$$a = \sqrt{18}$$

$$a = \sqrt{9 \times 2}$$

$$a = \sqrt{9} \times \sqrt{2}$$

$$a = 3\sqrt{2}$$

22. **The correct answer is A.** For Town A, the median is 7.5, because the number of days of rain per month was 7 or fewer for one half of the 12 recorded values, and was 8 or greater for the other half. For Town B, the median falls between 5 and 9, so it is 7. The median is greater for Town A. This is the only statement among the answer choices that is true.

23. **The correct answer is B.** The numbers of days of rain have a much greater variation in Town B than in Town A. You can see this by comparing the range of values for Town A, $11 - 5 = 6$, to the range for Town B, $19 - 1 = 18$. Since standard deviation is a measure of variation, choice B is correct.

24. **The correct answer is B.** Consider an example that would make the statement in the question true. If the intercepts of a function are at $(a, 0)$ and $(0, a)$, then they could be at $(3, 0)$ and $(0, 3)$. The slope of the line through those points is:

$$\frac{3-0}{0-3} = \frac{3}{-3} = -1$$

OR

$$\frac{a-0}{0-a} = \frac{a}{-a} = -1$$

25. **The correct answer is D.** An inscribed triangle that passes through the center forms a right triangle. So the missing angle measure is $90 - 36 = 54$. Using the given expression $x - 25.5 = 54$, $x = 79.5$.

26. **The correct answer is D.** There is nothing to indicate that the sample is biased or too small, or that the margin of error is too large, so choice D is best supported by the data.

27. **The correct answer is C.** The 95% confidence that the margin of error is ±4% means that there is a high probability that the actual percent of the voters that will vote for Candidate A is 31%, ±4%, or between 27% and 35% (assuming poll respondents are truthful).

28. **The correct answer is D.** We can calculate and compare their actual volumes or the ratio of their volumes.

$$V_{Pluto} = \frac{4}{3}\pi r^3 \qquad V_{Charon} = \frac{4}{3}\pi r^3$$

$$= \frac{4}{3}\pi(750)^3 \qquad = \frac{4}{3}\pi\left(\frac{750}{2}\right)^3$$

$$\approx 1{,}766{,}250{,}00 \qquad \approx 220{,}781{,}250$$

$$\frac{1{,}766{,}250{,}000}{220{,}781{,}250} = 8$$

OR

$$\frac{V_{Pluto}}{V_{Charon}} = \frac{\frac{4}{3}\pi(2r)^3}{\frac{4}{3}\pi r^3}$$

$$= \frac{8r^3}{r^3}$$

$$= 8$$

The ratio of the volumes of any two spheres where the diameter of one sphere is twice the diameter of the other sphere is always 8 to 1.

29. **The correct answer is C.** For the system to have exactly one real solution, the graph of the system will be a line and a parabola that is tangent to the line. For the parabola to be tangent to the line, it must have its vertex along that line. Since the graph of $y = ax^2$ has its vertex along the line $y = 0$, then $y = ax^2 - 2$ has its vertex along the line $y = -2$. Another way to solve this is to substitute -2 for y in to $y = ax^2 - b$, giving $ax^2 - b + 2 = 0$. Then substitute the a and b values given in each answer choice into this equation to see how many solutions each pair yields. Only choice C gives exactly one solution for x ($x = 0$).

30. **The correct answer is D.** Remember that the vertex form of a quadratic equation is $h(x) = a(x - h)^2 + k$, where k is the minimum or maximum value of the function. Since in this question h is the equation for a parabola that opens down, it will have a maximum at k when written in vertex form. Choices C and D are both in vertex form, but only choice D is equivalent to the original function. Check by writing both in standard form:

$$-(x-8)(x+2) = -(x-3)^2 + 25$$
$$-(x^2 - 6x - 16) = -(x^2 - 6x + 9) + 25$$
$$-x^2 + 6x + 16 = -x^2 + 6x + 16$$

31. **The correct answer is any number greater than $\frac{5}{2}$ and less than 6.** Notice that the expression in the middle of the inequality, $4x - 2$, is equivalent to the expression we need to evaluate, $-2x + 1$, multiplied by -2. We can rewrite the given inequality by dividing all parts by -2. Multiplying or dividing an inequality by a negative number reverses the inequality signs, as shown in the second step below.

$$-5 > 4x - 2 > -12$$
$$\frac{-5}{-2} < \frac{4x - 2}{-2} < \frac{-12}{-2}$$
$$\frac{5}{2} < -2x + 1 < 6$$

32. **The correct answer is 4.** Write and solve an inequality to find the number of pens she can buy, and then interpret the answer, including the remainder.

$$2.75x + 12 \leq 25$$
$$2.75x \leq 13$$
$$x \leq 4.\overline{72}$$

Since she can't buy fractions of a pen, the greatest number of pens that Amber can buy is 4.

33. **The correct answer is 25.** Write and solve a system of equations. Let $x =$ the number of 2-point shots made and $y =$ the number of 3-point shots made.

$$x + y = 33$$
$$2x + 3y = 74$$

Multiply the first equation by 2:

$$2(x + y) = 2 \times 33$$
$$2x + 2y = 66$$

Now subtract the second equation from this new one:

$$2x + 2y = 66$$
$$\underline{-(2x + 3y) = 74}$$
$$-y = -8$$
$$y = 8$$

Substitute $y = 8$ into the initial equation:

$$x + y = 33$$
$$x + 8 = 33$$
$$x = 25$$

34. **The correct answer is .358 or .359.** The number of females in China is 645 million. The total number of people represented in the table is 1,799 million. The probability that a random person chosen in this census is a female in China is $\frac{645}{1,799} \approx 0.358$.

You can enter this in the grid as .358 or as .359.

35. **The correct answer is.226 or .227.** Reduce the set of outcomes that you use to the first row because you are told that the person is male. Thus, we use 922.2 outcomes instead of 1,799.0. Now, the probability that the person from this group is Mexican or from the United States is $\frac{55.9 + 153.1}{922.2} \approx 0.23$.

You can enter this in the grid as .226 or as .227.

36. **The correct answer is 5.** A function like g is undefined when the denominator is equal to 0, so set the denominator equal to 0 and solve for x:

$$(x - 6)^2 + 2(x - 6) + 1 = 0$$
$$x^2 - 12x + 36 + 2x - 12 + 1 = 0$$
$$x^2 - 10x + 25 = 0$$
$$(x - 5)^2 = 0$$
$$x - 5 = 0$$
$$x = 5$$

37. **The correct answer is 1.14.** Substitute 1.14 for r because there is an increase of 14%, so r should be 1 + 0.14, or 1.14, in order to match the standard form for exponential growth.

38. **The correct answer is 1112.** Substitute 1.14 for r to represent a 14% increase and 10 for t to represent 10 years after it was last sold:

$$V = 300(1.14)^{10}$$
$$= 1,112.166$$

This is rounded to 1,112, which is 1,112 thousands of dollars.

Section 5: Essay

Analysis of Passage

The following is an analysis of the passage by Marc de Rosnay, noting how the writer used evidence, reasoning, and stylistic or persuasive elements to support his claims, connect the claims and evidence, and add power to the ideas he expressed. Check to see if you evaluated the passage in a similar way.

1 Being a parent presents some problems. Irrespective of what you want, your children are going to take actions or be exposed to things that you may not relish. There is the ever-present possibility that they will experience things that you want to actively protect them from.

1 *The writer begins his argument by pointing out that there are problems inherent in raising a child and names the issue that is central to his essay: children are going to do things or be exposed to things a parent will not like.*

2 The web provides some salient examples, like pornography. I really don't want my eight-year-old seeing pornography.

2 *The writer then cites a specific example: the web.*

3 However, when my eight-year-old asks me an important Dungeons & Dragons question like, "Dad, can a paladin do magic and wear armour?" or he wants to know how solar panels operate, I always encourage him to look on the web.

3 *The writer establishes his legitimacy to write about this topic by mentioning that he is the parent of an eight-year-old boy.*

4 I've taught him to search on Google, to follow his curiosity, and I sometimes do it with him.

4 *Using his relationship with his son as an example, the writer describes a situation in which a parent gives a child free access to the web.*

5 Ultimately, I want him to be able to seek answers to the questions that are interesting to him independently.

5 *The writer states why he believes he is right to give his child free access to the web.*

6 He is guaranteed to run into something dodgy on the web, and my wife and I can take ordinary precautions.

6 *De Rosnay returns to the issue of children being exposed to things a parent will not like, admitting that his son "is guaranteed" to encounter something objectionable on the web. He then raises the possibility of taking precautions against this situation. However, these precautions are "ordinary," or reasonable.*

7 To our way of thinking, however, more extreme precautions—prohibiting unsupervised internet use and high-level parental control—start to present their own risks.

7 *The writer states his central argument: extreme precautions can present their own risks.*

8 One might ask, at what age should I allow my child to use the web unsupervised?

8 *Proceeding with his argument, the writer asks a rhetorical question.*

9 From the perspective of developmental and educational psychology, this is a slightly odd question. Let me explain. Most parents are familiar with the idea that certain developmental achievements happen at specific ages. Thus, infants become more wary of strangers at about nine months of age (stranger wariness), and they start to point communicatively by about 12 months of age (declarative pointing). These kinds of developments in

9 *The writer answers his question by explaining that some developmental achievements (developmental milestones) occur at specific ages.*

the child's capacity are to be expected in all children given a typical environment; we call them developmental milestones.

10 I spoke recently to a friend who wanted her ten-year-old daughter to be able to get to school, in the city, on public transport from the inner-west by herself. This particular young girl is very intelligent and responsible, I'm sure that she could have gotten herself to school at seven years of age. But there is no way her parents would have felt comfortable about that.

11 Why? For her parents to give her the independence to travel to school alone, they need to be satisfied not just that she can present her ticket, change trains, and get on the right bus, they need to be confident that she understands the importance of staying on the path, like Little Red Riding Hood.

This understanding is largely derived from countless conversations in which the parents have been able to convey important information about the world and the risks it presents to their daughter.

12 We know that children seek information from the people they trust, and from people who have a good record at providing useful information; actually, these two things are not unconnected. Between early childhood and mid-adolescence children have to understand all sort of things for which they need information from people they trust.

13 The information we convey to our children, and the manner in which we do it, helps prepare them for life.

14 For most things, like knowledge about their bodies and sexuality, there is no particular moment at which children are ready for specific knowledge or experience, and much of this we can't control anyway.

15 But what we can do is answer their questions honestly in a manner that is appropriate for their age and conveys our values.

16 The risks of overprotection are simple: children will grow up anyway but they won't have access to good information from people that they trust.

10 Again referring to his personal experience, the writer cites a specific example of a parent wrestling with the question of how much freedom to give her child.

11 The writer explores the problems this question raises, citing some of the specific issues a parent must address.

12 The writer changes perspective from the personal to the objective to discuss how children seek and acquire information.

13 The writer lays the foundation for his argument by talking about the importance of parents allowing children to acquire information: it helps prepare them for life.

14 De Rosnay strengthens his argument by pointing out that often there is no ideal moment to communicate "specific knowledge or experience." He also points out that parents have little or no control over when their children acquire specific knowledge or experience.

15 The writer supports his central argument by stating what parents do have control over: answering children's questions honestly and appropriately.

16 The writer strengthens his central argument by citing the risks of overprotection: children will not gain good information from people they trust.

So what age is a good age?

17 It is very difficult to put an age on when a child should or shouldn't be able to grasp a new domain of independence. Your decisions will depend on specific circumstances . . . Managing risk is critical.	*17 De Rosnay returns to the essay's central question (the ideal age to let a child acquire new independence), stressing the crucial role played by the different factors in each situation.*
18 The web provides a salient example.	*18 The writer returns to his first specific example: the web.*
19 By year five or six, today's children should have some freedom to search for the information they need independently.	*19 The writer suggests an age at which a child should have "some freedom" to use the web independently.*
20 They can do this in a family space rather than in their bedroom. Talk to them honestly about the unsavoury content on the web; this will give them a framework for managing troubling or embarrassing content with you.	*20 The writer suggests some precautions parents can take as they give children this freedom.*
Independent action is also very important for children. Think back to your own childhood, there is a good chance that some of your fondest memories don't involve adults. Sometimes, children can walk to the shops before they are 12 years old, and around this time, they should be able to stay in the house for a little while as well.	
. . .	
21 Independence is linked to responsibility and much can be done to build responsibility in children before they undertake fully independent actions. But when you give your children independence you provide them with evidence that you trust them, and that trust fortifies responsibility in a way that supervised activity cannot.	*21 The writer concludes his argument by summing up his reasoning: giving children independence shows that you trust them, which in turn teaches children to be responsible; denying children independence by overprotecting them does not give them the same trust-fosters-responsibility experience.*

SAMPLE ESSAYS

The following are examples of a high-scoring and low-scoring essay, based on the passage by Marc de Rosnay.

HIGH-SCORING ESSAY

The central argument in this article is that parents have to give their children a certain amount of freedom to help them grow up to be responsible, independent adults. Marc de Rosnay says that children will be exposed to things that parents won't like, but a good parent gives a child freedom and support. If a parent teaches the child how to handle things that are unpleasant or dangerous, the child learns to be independent and stay safe. Overprotecting children can pose risks because these children may not learn to protect themselves. To convince us of his viewpoint, de Rosnay uses knowledge about childhood development, examples from his experience as a parent, and logic.

As they grow up, children will be exposed to things that parents won't like, such as Internet pornography. De Rosnay establishes his qualification to write about this topic by revealing that he has an eight-year-old son and he's encouraged him to search for information on the Internet. This gives us an example of a danger—pornography on the Internet—and de Rosnay's response—allowing his son to use the Internet. He explains that he taught his son to use Google and he sometimes uses the Internet with him.

De Rosnay uses logic to explain this decision. (1) He wants his son to be able to use the Internet without his help. (2) He takes precautions (which he calls "ordinary") to protect his son from objectionable material. (3) Forms of overprotection, like forbidding his son to use the Internet without supervision or setting up a high level of parental control, can also cause problems.

The author poses a rhetorical question to ask how old a child should be to use the Internet without supervision. This question is really about how a parent determines when a child is old enough to do anything, and de Rosnay uses logic to answer it. He uses the term "developmental milestone" to discuss the age at which most children acquire a skill, such as declarative pointing at the age of 12 months. More complex skills aren't acquired at a particular age because the skill is more complicated and factors like the environment and the child's maturity are different.

De Rosnay provides an example of a complex skill. His friend wanted her ten-year-old daughter to be able to use public transportation to go to school. However, the girl would have to change trains and take a bus to get from home to school. More importantly, she had to understand the dangers she could face and how to avoid them, which meant her parents had to prepare her.

Using this example, the author connects to how parents can prepare their children for life—where children will face all kinds of new experiences, including some that are dangerous. He argues that the best a parent can do is answer questions in a way that is honest and appropriate for the child's age, and conveys good values. Children taught this way will trust their parents and go to their parents for information and help when they need it. He contrasts this with overprotected children who have not learned that they can get good information from their parents, and so won't turn to their parents for help.

The author acknowledges that it is difficult to say how much independence a child should have at a specific age. He cites differences in parents, children, and the amount of risk in a situation (like a bad neighborhood). He does say that children should have some independence on the Internet by the age of five or six, but also suggests that parents take the precaution of making access available in a family space (as opposed to the child's bedroom). He also gives milestones for other independent activities like staying home alone.

To wrap up his argument, de Rosnay uses logic to link responsibility, independence, and trust. He believes that trusting children makes them more responsible. Responsibility leads to giving a child more independence. Giving more independence shows more trust. The cycle starts with trusting the child. As the cycle continues, the child eventually grows up and becomes an independent, responsible adult. De Rosnay's examples and logic create a solid argument for giving a child as much independence as the child can handle while providing a framework to help the child mature.

In his article called "Milestones: what is the 'right' age for kids to travel alone, surf the web, learn about war?" Marc de Rosnay looks at what ages kids should be allowed to do certain things like surfing the Internet, walking to school, and watching the news.

Marc de Rosnay is the head of a school in Australia, which is why he knows about child development. In his own life, Marc determined that his eight-year-old son was old enough to use the Internet alone. He thinks his son would probably use the Internet alone anyway, so trying to keep him from using it would cause problems.

Marc de Rosnay asks when children should be allowed to do other things like riding a bike. He says that Dutch people start riding bikes at 2 because riding bikes is really popular there. They learn how to ride by watching other people do it and then imitating them.

Marc de Rosnay gives ages when children should be able to do certain things. They should go to the store alone at 10-14 years, surf the Internet at 5-6 years old, stay home alone at 11 years old, visit a war memorial at 6-8 years old, and watch the news or read the newspaper at 7-9 years old.

In conclusion, Marc de Rosnay says it's hard to know when children can do some things alone. Parents just have to trust their children.

COMPUTING YOUR SCORES

Now that you've completed this practice test, it's time to compute your scores. Simply follow the instructions on the following pages, and use the conversion tables provided to calculate your scores. The formulas provided will give you as close an approximation as possible of how you might score on the actual SAT® exam.

To Determine Your Practice Test Scores

1. After you go through each of the test sections (Reading, Writing and Language, Math—No Calculator, and Math—Calculator) and determine which answers you got right, be sure to enter the number of correct answers in the box below the answer key for each of the sections.

2. Your total score on the practice test is the sum of your Evidence-Based Reading and Writing Section score and your Math Section score. To get your total score, convert the raw score—the number of questions you got right in a particular section—into the "scaled score" for that section, and then you'll calculate the total score. It sounds a little confusing, but we'll take you through the steps.

To Calculate Your Evidence-Based Reading and Writing Section Score

Your Evidence-Based Reading and Writing Section score is on a scale of 200–800. First determine your Reading Test score, and then determine your score on the Writing and Language Test.

1. Count the number of correct answers you got on the **Section 1: Reading Test.** Remember that there is no penalty for wrong answers. **The number of correct answers is your raw score.**

2. Go to **Raw Score Conversion Table 1: Section and Test Scores** on page 945. Look in the "Raw Score" column for your raw score, and match it to the number in the "Reading Test Score" column.

3. Do the same with **Section 2: Writing and Language Test** to determine that score.

4. Add your Reading Test score to your Writing and Language Test score.

5. Multiply that number by 10. This is your Evidence-Based Reading and Writing Section score.

To Calculate Your Math Section Score

Your Math score is also on a scale of 200–800.

1. Count the number of correct answers you got on the **Section 3: Math Test—No Calculator** and the **Section 4: Math Test—No Calculator.** Again, there is no penalty for wrong answers. **The number of correct answers is your raw score.**

2. Add the number of correct answers on the **Section 3: Math Test—No Calculator** and the **Section 4: Math Test—No Calculator.**

3. Use the **Raw Score Conversion Table 1: Section and Test Scores** on page 945 and convert your raw score into your Math Section score.

To Obtain Your Total Score

Add your score on the Evidence-Based Reading and Writing Section to the Math Section score. This is your total score on this Practice Test, on a scale of 400–1600.

Subscores Provide Additional Information

Subscores offer you greater details about your strengths in certain areas within literacy and math. The subscores are reported on a scale of 1–15 and include Heart of Algebra, Problem Solving and Data Analysis, Passport to Advanced Math, Expression of Ideas, Standard English Conventions, Words in Context, and Command of Evidence.

Heart of Algebra

The **Heart of Algebra subscore** is based on questions from the **Math Test** that focus on linear equations and inequalities.

- Add up your total correct answers from these questions:
  - Math Test—No Calculator: Questions 1, 3–6, 12, 17, 20
  - Math Test—Calculator: Questions 3, 4, 8–10, 13, 15, 24, 31–33
- Your Raw Score = the total number of correct answers from all of these questions.
- Use the **Raw Score Conversion Table 2: Subscores** on page 946 to determine your **Heart of Algebra** subscore.

Problem Solving and Data Analysis

The **Problem Solving and Data Analysis subscore** is based on questions from the **Math Test** that focus on quantitative reasoning, interpretation and synthesis of data, and solving problems in rich and varied contexts.

- Add up your total correct answers from these questions:
  - Math Test—No Calculator: 10
  - Math Test—Calculator: Questions 1, 2, 5–7, 14, 16, 17, 20, 22, 23, 26, 27, 34, 35, 38
- Your Raw Score = the total number of correct answers from all of these questions.
- Use the **Raw Score Conversion Table 2: Subscores** on page 946 to determine your **Problem Solving and Data Analysis** subscore.

Passport to Advanced Math

The **Passport to Advanced Math subscore** is based on questions from the **Math Test** that focus on topics central to your ability to progress to more advanced math, such as understanding the structure of expressions, reasoning with more complex equations, and interpreting and building functions.

- Add up your total correct answers from these questions:
  - Math Test—No Calculator: Questions 2, 7–9, 11, 15, 16, 19
  - Math Test—Calculator: Questions 11, 12, 19, 21, 29, 30, 36, 37
- Your Raw score = the total number of correct answers from all of these questions.
- Use the **Raw Score Conversion Table 2: Subscores** on page 946 to determine your **Passport to Advanced Math** subscore.

Expression of Ideas

The **Expression of Ideas subscore** is based on questions from the **Writing and Language Test** that focus on topic development, organization, and rhetorically effective use of language.

- Add up your total correct answers from these questions in Section 2: Writing and Language Test.
  - Questions 1, 3, 4, 8–10, 13, 15, 17, 18, 21–23, 25–27, 30, 33, 34, 37–39, 41, 42
- Your Raw Score = the total number of correct answers from all of these questions.
- Use the **Raw Score Conversion Table 2: Subscores** on page 946 to determine your **Expression of Ideas** subscore.

Standard English Conventions

The **Standard English Conventions** subscore is based on questions from the **Writing and Language Test** that focus on sentence structure, usage, and punctuation.

- Add up your total correct answers from these questions in Section 2: Writing and Language Test.
  - Questions 2, 5–7, 11, 12, 14, 16, 19, 20, 24, 28, 29, 31, 32, 35, 36, 40, 43, 44
- Your Raw Score = the total number of correct answers from all of these questions.
- Use the **Raw Score Conversion Table 2: Subscores** on page 946 to determine your **Standard English Conventions** subscore.

Words in Context

The **Words in Context** subscore is based on questions from the **Reading Test** and the **Writing and Language Test** that address word/phrase meaning in context and rhetorical word choice.

- Add up your total correct answers from these questions in Sections 1 and 2:
  - Reading Test: Questions 9, 10, 18, 19, 30, 31, 40, 42, 51, 52
  - Writing and Language Test: Questions 8, 9, 17, 18, 25, 33, 37, 42
- Your Raw Score = the total number of correct answers from all of these questions.
- Use the **Raw Score Conversion Table 2: Subscores** on page 946 to determine your **Words in Context** subscore.

Command of Evidence

The **Command of Evidence** subscore is based on questions from the **Reading Test** and the **Writing and Language Test** that ask you to interpret and use evidence found in a wide range of passages and informational graphics, such as graphs, tables, and charts.

- Add up your total correct answers from these questions in Sections 1 and 2:
  - Reading Test: Questions 3, 8, 12, 14, 25, 27, 35, 39, 48, 50
  - Writing and Language Test: Questions 4, 10, 13, 21, 23, 26, 34, 38
- Your Raw Score = the total number of correct answers from all of these questions.
- Use the **Raw Score Conversion Table 2: Subscores** on page 946 to determine your **Command of Evidence** subscore.

CROSS-TEST SCORES

The SAT® exam also reports two cross-test scores: Analysis in History/Social Studies and Analysis in Science. These scores are based on questions in the Reading Test, Writing and Language Test, and both Math Tests that ask you to think analytically about texts and questions in these subject areas. Cross-test scores are reported on a scale of 10–40.

Analysis in History/Social Studies

- Add up your total correct answers from these sections:
  - Reading Test: Questions 1–10, 11–21
  - Writing and Language Test: Questions 13, 15, 17, 18, 21, 23
  - Math Test—No Calculator: None
  - Math Test—Calculator: Questions 5, 6, 19, 20, 26, 27, 34, 35
- Your Raw Score = the total number of correct answers from all of these questions.
- Use the **Raw Score Conversion Table 3: Cross-Test Scores** on page 947 to determine your **Analysis in History/Social Studies** cross-test score.

Analysis in Science

- Add up your total correct answers from these sections:
  - Reading Test: Questions 22–31, 32–42
  - Writing and Language Test: Questions 34, 37–39, 41, 42
  - Math Test—No Calculator: Question 16
  - Math Test—Calculator: Questions 2, 7, 16, 17, 22, 23, 28
- Your Raw Score = the total number of correct answers from all of these questions.
- Use the **Raw Score Conversion Table 3: Cross-Test Scores** on page 947 to determine your **Analysis in Science** cross-test score.

Raw Score Conversion Table 1: Section and Test Scores

Raw Score	Math Section Score	Reading Test Score	Writing and Language Test Score	Raw Score	Math Section Score	Reading Test Score	Writing and Language Test Score	Raw Score	Math Section Score	Reading Test Score	Writing and Language Test Score
0	200	10	10	20	450	22	23	40	610	33	36
1	200	10	10	21	460	23	23	41	620	33	37
2	210	10	10	22	470	23	24	42	630	34	38
3	230	11	10	23	480	24	25	43	640	35	39
4	240	12	11	24	480	24	25	44	650	35	40
5	260	13	12	25	490	25	26	45	660	36	
6	280	14	13	26	500	25	26	46	670	37	
7	290	15	13	27	510	26	27	47	670	37	
8	310	15	14	28	520	26	28	48	680	38	
9	320	16	15	29	520	27	28	49	690	38	
10	330	17	16	30	530	28	29	50	700	39	
11	340	17	16	31	540	28	30	51	710	40	
12	360	18	17	32	550	29	30	52	730	40	
13	370	19	18	33	560	29	31	53	740		
14	380	19	19	34	560	30	32	54	750		
15	390	20	19	35	570	30	32	55	760		
16	410	20	20	36	580	31	33	56	780		
17	420	21	21	37	590	31	34	57	790		
18	430	21	21	38	600	32	34	58	800		
19	440	22	22	39	600	32	35				

Conversion Equation 1 Section and Test Scores

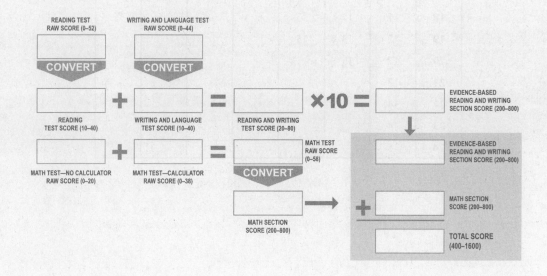

Raw Score Conversion Table 2: Subscores

Raw Score (# of correct answers)	Expression of Ideas	Standard English Conventions	Heart of Algebra	Problem Solving and Data Analysis	Passport to Advanced Math	Words in Context	Command of Evidence
0	1	1	1	1	1	1	1
1	1	1	1	1	3	1	1
2	1	1	2	2	5	2	2
3	2	2	3	3	6	3	3
4	3	2	4	4	7	4	4
5	4	3	5	5	8	5	5
6	5	4	6	6	9	6	6
7	6	5	6	7	10	6	7
8	6	6	7	8	11	7	8
9	7	6	8	8	11	8	8
10	7	7	8	9	12	8	9
11	8	7	9	10	12	9	10
12	8	8	9	10	13	9	10
13	9	8	9	11	13	10	11
14	9	9	10	12	14	11	12
15	10	10	10	13	14	12	13
16	10	10	11	14	15	13	14
17	11	11	12	15		14	15
18	11	12	13			15	15
19	12	13	15				
20	12	15					
21	13						
22	14						
23	14						
24	15						

Conversion Equation 2 Subscores

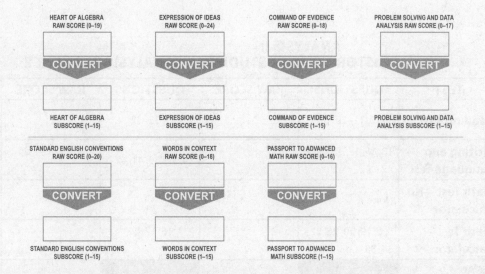

HEART OF ALGEBRA RAW SCORE (0–19)	EXPRESSION OF IDEAS RAW SCORE (0–24)	COMMAND OF EVIDENCE RAW SCORE (0–18)	PROBLEM SOLVING AND DATA ANALYSIS RAW SCORE (0–17)
CONVERT	CONVERT	CONVERT	CONVERT
HEART OF ALGEBRA SUBSCORE (1–15)	EXPRESSION OF IDEAS SUBSCORE (1–15)	COMMAND OF EVIDENCE SUBSCORE (1–15)	PROBLEM SOLVING AND DATA ANALYSIS SUBSCORE (1–15)

STANDARD ENGLISH CONVENTIONS RAW SCORE (0–20)	WORDS IN CONTEXT RAW SCORE (0–18)	PASSPORT TO ADVANCED MATH RAW SCORE (0–16)
CONVERT	CONVERT	CONVERT
STANDARD ENGLISH CONVENTIONS SUBSCORE (1–15)	WORDS IN CONTEXT SUBSCORE (1–15)	PASSPORT TO ADVANCED MATH SUBSCORE (1–15)

Raw Score Conversion Table 3: Cross-Test Scores

Raw Score (# of correct answers)	Analysis in History/Social Studies Cross-Test Score	Analysis in Science Cross-Test Score	Raw Score (# of correct answers)	Analysis in History/Social Studies Cross-Test Score	Analysis in Science Cross-Test Score
0	10	10	18	28	26
1	10	11	19	29	27
2	11	12	20	30	27
3	12	13	21	30	28
4	14	14	22	31	29
5	15	15	23	32	30
6	16	16	24	32	30
7	17	17	25	33	31
8	18	18	26	34	32
9	20	19	27	35	33
10	21	20	28	35	33
11	22	20	29	36	34
12	23	21	30	37	35
13	24	22	31	38	36
14	25	23	32	38	37
15	26	24	33	39	38
16	27	24	34	40	39
17	28	25	35	40	40

CONVERSION EQUATION 3: CROSS-TEST SCORES

TEST	ANALYSIS IN HISTORY/SOCIAL STUDIES		ANALYSIS IN SCIENCE	
	QUESTIONS	RAW SCORE	QUESTIONS	RAW SCORE
Reading Test	1–10, 11–20		22–31, 32–42	
Writing and Language Test	13, 15, 17, 18, 21, 22		34, 37–39, 41, 42	
Math Test—No Calculator	None		16	
Math Test—Calculator	5, 6, 19, 20, 26, 27, 34, 35		2, 7, 16, 17, 22, 23, 28	
TOTAL				

ANALYSIS IN HISTORY/
SOCIAL STUDIES
RAW SCORE (0–35)

CONVERT

ANALYSIS IN HISTORY/
SOCIAL STUDIES
CROSS-TEST SCORE (10–40)

ANALYSIS IN SCIENCE
RAW SCORE (0–35)

CONVERT

ANALYSIS IN SCIENCE
CROSS-TEST SCORE (1–40)

Section 1: Reading Test

1. Ⓐ Ⓑ Ⓒ Ⓓ 12. Ⓐ Ⓑ Ⓒ Ⓓ 23. Ⓐ Ⓑ Ⓒ Ⓓ 33. Ⓐ Ⓑ Ⓒ Ⓓ 43. Ⓐ Ⓑ Ⓒ Ⓓ
2. Ⓐ Ⓑ Ⓒ Ⓓ 13. Ⓐ Ⓑ Ⓒ Ⓓ 24. Ⓐ Ⓑ Ⓒ Ⓓ 34. Ⓐ Ⓑ Ⓒ Ⓓ 44. Ⓐ Ⓑ Ⓒ Ⓓ
3. Ⓐ Ⓑ Ⓒ Ⓓ 14. Ⓐ Ⓑ Ⓒ Ⓓ 25. Ⓐ Ⓑ Ⓒ Ⓓ 35. Ⓐ Ⓑ Ⓒ Ⓓ 45. Ⓐ Ⓑ Ⓒ Ⓓ
4. Ⓐ Ⓑ Ⓒ Ⓓ 15. Ⓐ Ⓑ Ⓒ Ⓓ 26. Ⓐ Ⓑ Ⓒ Ⓓ 36. Ⓐ Ⓑ Ⓒ Ⓓ 46. Ⓐ Ⓑ Ⓒ Ⓓ
5. Ⓐ Ⓑ Ⓒ Ⓓ 16. Ⓐ Ⓑ Ⓒ Ⓓ 27. Ⓐ Ⓑ Ⓒ Ⓓ 37. Ⓐ Ⓑ Ⓒ Ⓓ 47. Ⓐ Ⓑ Ⓒ Ⓓ
6. Ⓐ Ⓑ Ⓒ Ⓓ 17. Ⓐ Ⓑ Ⓒ Ⓓ 28. Ⓐ Ⓑ Ⓒ Ⓓ 38. Ⓐ Ⓑ Ⓒ Ⓓ 48. Ⓐ Ⓑ Ⓒ Ⓓ
7. Ⓐ Ⓑ Ⓒ Ⓓ 18. Ⓐ Ⓑ Ⓒ Ⓓ 29. Ⓐ Ⓑ Ⓒ Ⓓ 39. Ⓐ Ⓑ Ⓒ Ⓓ 49. Ⓐ Ⓑ Ⓒ Ⓓ
8. Ⓐ Ⓑ Ⓒ Ⓓ 19. Ⓐ Ⓑ Ⓒ Ⓓ 30. Ⓐ Ⓑ Ⓒ Ⓓ 40. Ⓐ Ⓑ Ⓒ Ⓓ 50. Ⓐ Ⓑ Ⓒ Ⓓ
9. Ⓐ Ⓑ Ⓒ Ⓓ 20. Ⓐ Ⓑ Ⓒ Ⓓ 31. Ⓐ Ⓑ Ⓒ Ⓓ 41. Ⓐ Ⓑ Ⓒ Ⓓ 51. Ⓐ Ⓑ Ⓒ Ⓓ
10. Ⓐ Ⓑ Ⓒ Ⓓ 21. Ⓐ Ⓑ Ⓒ Ⓓ 32. Ⓐ Ⓑ Ⓒ Ⓓ 42. Ⓐ Ⓑ Ⓒ Ⓓ 52. Ⓐ Ⓑ Ⓒ Ⓓ
11. Ⓐ Ⓑ Ⓒ Ⓓ 22. Ⓐ Ⓑ Ⓒ Ⓓ

Section 2: Writing and Language Test

1. Ⓐ Ⓑ Ⓒ Ⓓ 10. Ⓐ Ⓑ Ⓒ Ⓓ 19. Ⓐ Ⓑ Ⓒ Ⓓ 28. Ⓐ Ⓑ Ⓒ Ⓓ 37. Ⓐ Ⓑ Ⓒ Ⓓ
2. Ⓐ Ⓑ Ⓒ Ⓓ 11. Ⓐ Ⓑ Ⓒ Ⓓ 20. Ⓐ Ⓑ Ⓒ Ⓓ 29. Ⓐ Ⓑ Ⓒ Ⓓ 38. Ⓐ Ⓑ Ⓒ Ⓓ
3. Ⓐ Ⓑ Ⓒ Ⓓ 12. Ⓐ Ⓑ Ⓒ Ⓓ 21. Ⓐ Ⓑ Ⓒ Ⓓ 30. Ⓐ Ⓑ Ⓒ Ⓓ 39. Ⓐ Ⓑ Ⓒ Ⓓ
4. Ⓐ Ⓑ Ⓒ Ⓓ 13. Ⓐ Ⓑ Ⓒ Ⓓ 22. Ⓐ Ⓑ Ⓒ Ⓓ 31. Ⓐ Ⓑ Ⓒ Ⓓ 40. Ⓐ Ⓑ Ⓒ Ⓓ
5. Ⓐ Ⓑ Ⓒ Ⓓ 14. Ⓐ Ⓑ Ⓒ Ⓓ 23. Ⓐ Ⓑ Ⓒ Ⓓ 32. Ⓐ Ⓑ Ⓒ Ⓓ 41. Ⓐ Ⓑ Ⓒ Ⓓ
6. Ⓐ Ⓑ Ⓒ Ⓓ 15. Ⓐ Ⓑ Ⓒ Ⓓ 24. Ⓐ Ⓑ Ⓒ Ⓓ 33. Ⓐ Ⓑ Ⓒ Ⓓ 42. Ⓐ Ⓑ Ⓒ Ⓓ
7. Ⓐ Ⓑ Ⓒ Ⓓ 16. Ⓐ Ⓑ Ⓒ Ⓓ 25. Ⓐ Ⓑ Ⓒ Ⓓ 34. Ⓐ Ⓑ Ⓒ Ⓓ 43. Ⓐ Ⓑ Ⓒ Ⓓ
8. Ⓐ Ⓑ Ⓒ Ⓓ 17. Ⓐ Ⓑ Ⓒ Ⓓ 26. Ⓐ Ⓑ Ⓒ Ⓓ 35. Ⓐ Ⓑ Ⓒ Ⓓ 44. Ⓐ Ⓑ Ⓒ Ⓓ
9. Ⓐ Ⓑ Ⓒ Ⓓ 18. Ⓐ Ⓑ Ⓒ Ⓓ 27. Ⓐ Ⓑ Ⓒ Ⓓ 36. Ⓐ Ⓑ Ⓒ Ⓓ

Section 3: Math Test—No Calculator

1. Ⓐ Ⓑ Ⓒ Ⓓ 4. Ⓐ Ⓑ Ⓒ Ⓓ 7. Ⓐ Ⓑ Ⓒ Ⓓ 10. Ⓐ Ⓑ Ⓒ Ⓓ 13. Ⓐ Ⓑ Ⓒ Ⓓ
2. Ⓐ Ⓑ Ⓒ Ⓓ 5. Ⓐ Ⓑ Ⓒ Ⓓ 8. Ⓐ Ⓑ Ⓒ Ⓓ 11. Ⓐ Ⓑ Ⓒ Ⓓ 14. Ⓐ Ⓑ Ⓒ Ⓓ
3. Ⓐ Ⓑ Ⓒ Ⓓ 6. Ⓐ Ⓑ Ⓒ Ⓓ 9. Ⓐ Ⓑ Ⓒ Ⓓ 12. Ⓐ Ⓑ Ⓒ Ⓓ 15. Ⓐ Ⓑ Ⓒ Ⓓ

Section 3: Math Test—No Calculator

16. [grid-in bubble grid]
17. [grid-in bubble grid]
18. [grid-in bubble grid]
19. [grid-in bubble grid]
20. [grid-in bubble grid]

Section 4: Math Test—Calculator

1. Ⓐ Ⓑ Ⓒ Ⓓ
2. Ⓐ Ⓑ Ⓒ Ⓓ
3. Ⓐ Ⓑ Ⓒ Ⓓ
4. Ⓐ Ⓑ Ⓒ Ⓓ
5. Ⓐ Ⓑ Ⓒ Ⓓ
6. Ⓐ Ⓑ Ⓒ Ⓓ
7. Ⓐ Ⓑ Ⓒ Ⓓ
8. Ⓐ Ⓑ Ⓒ Ⓓ
9. Ⓐ Ⓑ Ⓒ Ⓓ
10. Ⓐ Ⓑ Ⓒ Ⓓ
11. Ⓐ Ⓑ Ⓒ Ⓓ
12. Ⓐ Ⓑ Ⓒ Ⓓ
13. Ⓐ Ⓑ Ⓒ Ⓓ
14. Ⓐ Ⓑ Ⓒ Ⓓ
15. Ⓐ Ⓑ Ⓒ Ⓓ
16. Ⓐ Ⓑ Ⓒ Ⓓ
17. Ⓐ Ⓑ Ⓒ Ⓓ
18. Ⓐ Ⓑ Ⓒ Ⓓ
19. Ⓐ Ⓑ Ⓒ Ⓓ
20. Ⓐ Ⓑ Ⓒ Ⓓ
21. Ⓐ Ⓑ Ⓒ Ⓓ
22. Ⓐ Ⓑ Ⓒ Ⓓ
23. Ⓐ Ⓑ Ⓒ Ⓓ
24. Ⓐ Ⓑ Ⓒ Ⓓ
25. Ⓐ Ⓑ Ⓒ Ⓓ
26. Ⓐ Ⓑ Ⓒ Ⓓ
27. Ⓐ Ⓑ Ⓒ Ⓓ
28. Ⓐ Ⓑ Ⓒ Ⓓ
29. Ⓐ Ⓑ Ⓒ Ⓓ
30. Ⓐ Ⓑ Ⓒ Ⓓ

31. [grid-in bubble grid]
32. [grid-in bubble grid]
33. [grid-in bubble grid]
34. [grid-in bubble grid]
35. [grid-in bubble grid]

36. [grid-in bubble grid]
37. [grid-in bubble grid]
38. [grid-in bubble grid]

Section 5: Essay

SECTION 1: READING TEST

65 Minutes—52 Questions

TURN TO SECTION 1 OF YOUR ANSWER SHEET TO ANSWER THE QUESTIONS IN THIS SECTION.

> **DIRECTIONS:** Each passage (or pair of passages) in this section is followed by a number of multiple-choice questions. After reading each passage, select the best answer to each question based on what is stated or implied in the passage or passages and in any supplementary material, such as a table, graph, chart, or photograph.

Questions 1–11 are based on the following passage.

Snail-Sniffing Dogs in the Galapagos

The Galapagos Islands, which belong to Ecuador, are located approximately 906 km (563 mi.) west of the mainland. Because of their isolation, these volcanic islands are home to a variety of unique species, such as gigantic land tortoises and marine iguanas. As more people have visited and settled on the islands, however, it has become increasingly difficult to protect the native plants and animals.

The following text has been adapted from Ecosystem Restoration: Invasive Snail Detection Dogs, *which was originally published by Galapagos Conservancy (www.galapagos.org). Galapagos Conservancy is a conservation group that collaborates with scientists worldwide to ensure protection of the Galapagos Islands. (For the complete article, see http://galapagos.org/conservation.)*

In Galapagos, native species are threatened by introduced, invasive species such as goats, rats, pigs, and cats, among many others. While much has
Line been accomplished in the management of existing
5 invasive species, the islands are constantly at risk of new unwanted species arriving each day. The Giant African Land Snail (GALS)—the largest species of snail found on land, growing to nearly 8 inches in length—is one such new invasive that has taken up residence in
10 Galapagos. Known to consume at least 500 different types of plants, scientists consider the GALS to be one of the most destructive snail species in the world. It now poses a serious threat to the native snails and plants of Galapagos.
15 Invasive Giant African Land Snails were first detected on Santa Cruz Island in 2010, and currently less than 20 hectares (50 acres) are infested—but the snails are expanding their range every wet season. Experience has shown that once an invasive species becomes estab-
20 lished, it is almost impossible to remove. At this point in time, it is still possible to eradicate the GALS from Galapagos if additional management techniques are integrated into current activities.

Previously, staff from the Galapagos Agency
25 for the Regulation and Control of Biosecurity and Quarantine (ABG) had to search for and collect GALS on rainy nights using headlamps—an extremely challenging and unsustainable solution to the permanent eradication of the snails. Dogs, on the other
30 hand, have an incredible sense of smell and can be trained to detect scents imperceptible to the human nose, making them ideal for the detection of the GALS. Detection dogs have been used for finding contraband drugs and shark fins in Galapagos, but not
35 for other purposes. This project entails utilizing two scent detection dogs to detect GALS in order to help clear currently affected areas and search for previously undetected populations in the islands.

During the first phase of the project, which
40 took place in the fall of 2014, two detection dogs were trained by Dogs for Conservation (DFC) in the United States to specifically detect GALS. Darwin, a golden Labrador retriever, was rescued after he was unable to successfully complete a service dog training
45 program, and Neville, a black Labrador retriever, was saved from a shelter. Darwin and Neville were selected for this project based on their detection abilities and temperament for working with multiple handlers, in preparation for work with new handlers in Galapagos.
50 In December of 2014, the dogs were brought to Galapagos where six ABG staff were trained as handlers for this and future detection projects. Many had never worked with dogs before and had to learn the basics of canine behavior, learning theory, scent theory, training
55 methods, and handling skills. New kennels were built by ABG personnel with materials funded through this project in order to house the dogs.

Both dogs required a period of acclimation to Galapagos and to their new roles. The dogs could only
60 be trained on dead snails in the US due to biosecurity risks for this highly invasive species, so additional

CONTINUE

training was needed upon their arrival in Galapagos to transition them to live snails and snail eggs. Darwin and Neville have now been fully trained to detect the
65 invasive snails, and the dogs will be regularly assisting with GALS eradication and monitoring on Santa Cruz.

DFC continues to provide guidance and support to the GALS K9 team, with whom they are in weekly communication. Future updates to the project will be
70 posted … as they occur. This project is also serving as a pilot to establish a permanent canine detection program in the Galapagos. Expertly trained dogs and experienced handlers will be a highly cost-effective detection tool for ongoing biosecurity programs aimed at eliminating
75 targeted invasive species that threaten the unique and fragile ecosystems of Galapagos.

1 What is the purpose of this article?

A. To bring tourists to the Galapagos

B. To raise money for the organization

C. To inform the public about the problems of invasive species

D. To persuade people that it is important to keep species of animals and plants from becoming extinct

2 Which statement best represents the main idea of the passage?

A. Dogs can help reduce invasive species in the Galapagos.

B. Scientists have found no way to reduce invasive species in the Galapagos.

C. Galapagos ecosystems include unique species.

D. Organizations are working together to rid the Galapagos of invasive species.

3 Why do the Galapagos have a unique ecosystem?

A. Islands can only support certain kinds of species.

B. There were no mammals there until humans brought them.

C. Only certain types of animals and plants can live there because of the climate.

D. It was isolated for a long time, so humans did not interfere with the natural ecosystems.

4 Which best describes the threat of GALS to the Galapagos Islands?

A. Their growth patterns

B. Their eating habits

C. Their ability to hide from detection

D. Their ability to survive in hot climates

5 According to the passage, the GALS problem on the Galapagos Islands

A. has been solved by hunting dogs.

B. has been exaggerated by the media.

C. is steadily growing worse every year.

D. is the biggest problem affecting the islands.

6 Which choice provides the best evidence for the answer to the previous question?

A. Lines 10–12 ("Known to . . . the world.")

B. Lines 17–18 ("the snails . . . season.")

C. Lines 24–29 ("Previously, staff . . . the snails.")

D. Lines 59–61 ("The dogs . . . biosecurity risks")

7 Why did the scientists decide to try using dogs to find the GALS?

A. Dogs are friendly animals that are easy to work with.

B. Dogs can also be trained to find illicit drugs.

C. Dogs are trainable and able to find GALS by smell.

D. Dogs can go into the small spaces in which GALS hide.

8 Which choice provides the best evidence for the answer to the previous question?

A. Lines 29–32 ("Dogs, on . . . human nose")

B. Lines 33–34 ("Detection . . . drugs")

C. Lines 35–37 ("This project . . . areas")

D. Lines 39–40 ("During the . . . 2014")

9 As used in line 60, "biosecurity" most nearly means

A. safe handling of animals.

B. safety from dangerous animals and plants.

C. protection to keep wildlife from extinction.

D. protection of an ecosystem from invasive species.

10 As used in line 58, "acclimation" is best defined as

A. adjusting to changes in the environment.

B. conforming to one's surroundings.

C. adaptation of a species.

D. modification of behavior.

11 Why are dogs considered an invasive species to the Galapagos?

A. The dogs' sense of smell helps them find native species and use them for food.

B. The dogs required time to get acclimated to the environment.

C. The dogs did not inhabit the Galapagos until brought by humans.

D. The dogs once thrived on the Galapagos, but they had depleted their limited food sources.

Questions 12–22 are based on the following passage.

The following is an excerpt from a speech given by President Jimmy Carter, spoken and broadcast from the White House library two weeks after he took office. Prior to Carter's election, the country had faced a severe oil shortage and rising prices for oil and related products.

Report to the American People (February 2, 1977)

The extremely cold weather this winter has dangerously depleted our supplies of natural gas and fuel oil and forced hundreds of thousands of workers off the job.
Line
5 I congratulate the Congress for its quick action on the Emergency Natural Gas Act, which was passed today and signed just a few minutes ago. But the real problem—our failure to plan for the future or to take energy conservation seriously—started long before this winter, and it will take much longer to solve.

10 I realize that many of you have not believed that we really have an energy problem. But this winter has made all of us realize that we have to act.

Our program will emphasize conservation. The amount of energy being wasted which could be saved is
15 greater than the total energy that we are importing from foreign countries. We will also stress development of our rich coal reserves in an environmentally sound way; we will emphasize research on solar energy and other renewable energy sources; and we will maintain strict safeguards on
20 necessary atomic energy production.

The responsibility for setting energy policy is now split among more than 50 different agencies, departments, and bureaus in the Federal Government. Later this month, I will ask the Congress for its help in combining many of
25 these agencies in a new energy department to bring order out of chaos. Congressional leaders have already been working on this for quite a while.

We must face the fact that the energy shortage is permanent. There is no way we can solve it quickly. But
30 if we all cooperate and make modest sacrifices, if we learn to live thriftily and remember the importance of helping our neighbors, then we can find ways to adjust and to make our society more efficient and our own lives more enjoyable and productive. Utility companies
35 must promote conservation and not consumption. Oil and natural gas companies must be honest with all of us about their reserves and profits. We will find out the difference between real shortages and artificial ones. We will ask private companies to sacrifice, just as private
40 citizens must do.

CONTINUE

All of us must learn to waste less energy. Simply by keeping our thermostats, for instance, at 65 degrees in the daytime and 55 degrees at night we could save half the current shortage of natural gas.

45 There is no way that I, or anyone else in the Government, can solve our energy problems if you are not willing to help. I know that we can meet this energy challenge if the burden is borne fairly among all our people—and if we realize that in order to solve our
50 energy problems we need not sacrifice the quality of our lives.

The Congress has made great progress toward responsible strip-mining legislation, so that we can produce more energy without unnecessary destruction
55 of our beautiful lands. My administration will support these efforts this year. We will also ask Congress for its help with legislation which will reduce the risk of future oil tanker spills and help deal with those that do occur.

I would like to tell you now about one of the things
60 that I have already learned in my brief time in office. I have learned that there are many things that a president cannot do. There is no energy policy that we can develop that would do more good than voluntary conservation. There is no economic policy that will do as much as
65 shared faith in hard work, efficiency, and in the future of our system.

12 What is the most likely reason that Carter gave this speech?

   A. He wanted to reassure people that he was going to make the United States energy independent.

   B. As a new president, he wanted to start a dialogue with the people.

   C. He wanted to explain the severity of the energy crisis and what needed to be done to address it.

   D. He wanted people to understand the limitations of the president.

13 What is the theme of the speech?

   A. The United States has a long-term energy problem.

   B. There are many ways to conserve energy.

   C. People need to use less energy in their homes.

   D. The government cannot solve environmental problems.

14 Which of the following actions does Carter propose that the government take to help solve the problem?

   A. Lowering the thermostats

   B. Forming a new energy department

   C. Developing coal reserves

   D. Protecting the environment from oil spills

15 Which of the following best represents the belief system illustrated in Carter's speech?

   A. The idea that the United States should be energy independent

   B. The concept of shared sacrifice

   C. The idea that the environment needs to be protected by volunteers

   D. The concept of equal powers among the three branches of government

16 What does Carter think should be the foundation for conserving energy?

   A. The responsible use of strip mining to produce more energy

   B. The reduction of indoor temperatures to conserve fuel

   C. The use of solar and other renewable energy sources

   D. A voluntary policy in which people share in creating efficiency

17 How does Carter try to convince the public that everyone needs to participate to solve the problem?

   A. He describes how utility companies are also promoting conservation, not consumption.

   B. He explains that all people waste a lot of energy.

   C. He tells the public to lower the thermostats in their homes, which can save natural gas.

   D. He explains that the energy crisis requires some major sacrifices.

18 Which choice provides the best evidence for the answer to the previous question?

    A. Lines 34–35 ("Utility companies . . . consumption.")

    B. Lines 37–38 ("We will . . . ones.")

    C. Line 41 ("All of . . . energy.")

    D. Lines 41–43 ("Simply . . . at night")

19 Which of the following best explains the tone of the speech?

    A. Carter speaks bluntly about the problem but also tries to be persuasive and optimistic in order to encourage everyone to work together.

    B. Carter is speaking on national television and wants his audience to keep listening to him, so his tone is light and informal, even though the topic is a serious one.

    C. Carter is deeply concerned over the energy problem, so the tone of the speech is stern and authoritative because he wants people to follow his requests.

    D. Carter wants to be taken seriously, so he avoids persuasive language; instead, he speaks with informative, matter-of-fact neutrality.

20 Which choice provides the best evidence for the answer to the previous question?

    A. Lines 45–48 ("There is no . . . challenge")

    B. Lines 52–53 ("The Congress . . . legislation")

    C. Lines 55–56 ("My administration . . . year.")

    D. Lines 59–60 ("I would . . . office.")

21 As used in line 2, "depleted" most nearly means

    A. consumed.

    B. replaced.

    C. weakened.

    D. wasted.

22 Explain how the word "reserves" is used in line 17 and line 37.

    A. In the first use, "reserves" refers to something protected in order to prevent easy access to it; in the second use, it refers to something that is difficult to obtain.

    B. In the first use, "reserves" refers to something discarded; in the second use; it refers to something set aside in case of emergencies.

    C. In the first use, "reserves" refers to something saved in case of future needs; in the second use, it refers to being set aside in order to raise prices.

    D. In the first use, "reserves" refers to something not used because there is an excess; in the second use, it refers to something that belongs to someone else.

CONTINUE

Rudyard Kipling (1865–1936) was one of the most popular English writers of his era, authoring stories, novels, and poems, many of which take place in colonial India, where he was born and lived as a young child and returned to as a young adult. "The Arrest of Lieutenant Golightly," one of his earliest stories, was first published in an English-language newspaper in India where Kipling worked as a journalist. The following is an excerpt from that story.

If there was one thing on which Golightly prided himself more than another, it was looking like "an Officer and a gentleman." He said it was for the honor of the

Line Service that he attired himself so elaborately; but those
5 who knew him best said that it was just personal vanity. There was no harm about Golightly. … He recognized a horse when he saw one, … he played a very fair game at billiards, and was a sound man at the whist-table. Everyone liked him; and nobody ever dreamed of seeing
10 him handcuffed on a station platform as a deserter. But this sad thing happened.

He was going down from Dalhousie, at the end of his leave—riding down. He had cut his leave as fine as he dared, and wanted to come down in a hurry.
15 It was fairly warm at Dalhousie [a town in India in the hills, used as a summer retreat for British personnel] and knowing what to expect below, he descended in a new khaki suit—tight fitting—of a delicate olive-green; a peacock-blue tie, white collar, and a snowy white solah
20 [a plant made into fabric used in hat-making] helmet. He prided himself on looking neat even when he was riding post. He did look neat, and he was so deeply concerned about his appearance before he started that he quite forgot to take anything but some small change with
25 him. He left all his notes at the hotel. His servants had gone down the road before him, to be ready in waiting at Pathankote with a change of gear.

Twenty-two miles out of Dalhousie it began to rain—not a mere hill-shower, but a good, tepid mon-
30 soonish downpour. Golightly bustled on, wishing that he had brought an umbrella. The dust on the roads turned into mud, and the pony mired a good deal. So did Golightly's khaki gaiters. But he kept on steadily and tried to think how pleasant the coolth was.
35 His next pony was rather a brute at starting, and Golightly's hands being slippery with the rain, con-trived to get rid of Golightly at a corner. He chased the animal, caught it, and went ahead briskly. The spill had not improved his clothes or his temper, and he had
40 lost one spur. He kept the other one employed. By the time that stage was ended, the pony had had as much exercise as he wanted, and, in spite of the rain, Golightly

was sweating freely. At the end of another miserable half-hour, Golightly found the world disappear before
45 his eyes in clammy pulp. The rain had turned the pith of his huge and snowy solah-topee into an evil-smelling dough, and it had closed on his head like a half-opened mushroom. Also the green lining was beginning to run.

Golightly did not say anything worth recording
50 here. He tore off and squeezed up as much of the brim as was in his eyes and ploughed on. The back of the helmet was flapping on his neck and the sides stuck to his ears, but the leather band and green lining kept things roughly together, so that the hat did not actually
55 melt away where it flapped.

Presently, the pulp and the green stuff made a sort of slimy mildew which ran over Golightly in several directions—down his back and bosom for choice. The khaki color ran too … and sections of Golightly were
60 brown, and patches were violet, and contours were ochre, and streaks were ruddy red, and blotches were nearly white, according to the nature and peculiarities of the dye. When he took out his handkerchief to wipe his face and the green of the hat-lining and the purple
65 stuff that had soaked through on to his neck from the tie became thoroughly mixed, the effect was amazing.

He went to the Station-Master to negotiate for a first-class ticket to Khasa, where he was stationed. The booking-clerk said something to the Station-Master, the
70 Station-Master said something to the Telegraph Clerk, and the three looked at him with curiosity. They asked him to wait for half-an-hour, while they telegraphed to Umritsar for authority. So he waited, and four constables came and grouped themselves picturesquely round him.
75 Just as he was preparing to ask them to go away, the Station-Master said that he would give the Sahib [term of respect; like calling someone "sir" in English] a ticket to Umritsar, if the Sahib would kindly come inside the booking-office. Golightly stepped inside, and the next
80 thing he knew was that a constable was attached to each of his legs and arms, while the Station-Master was trying to cram a mailbag over his head.

---

23 Which of the following best describes the tone of the story?

A. Disgust

B. Mocking

C. Ironic

D. Proud

24 Which choice provides the best evidence for the answer to the previous question?

A. Lines 1–3 ("If there . . . gentleman.")

B. Lines 6–7 ("There was . . . saw one")

C. Lines 7–8 ("he played . . . whist-table.")

D. Line 9 ("Everyone . . . him")

25 Even though the author says "this sad thing happened," which detail from the passage shows that Kipling considers Golightly to be responsible for what happened to him?

A. He did look neat, and he was so deeply concerned about his appearance before he started that he quite forgot to take anything but some small change with him.

B. He prided himself on looking neat even when he was riding post.

C. Golightly bustled on, wishing that he had brought an umbrella.

D. His next pony was rather a brute at starting, and Golightly's hands being slippery with the rain, contrived to get rid of Golightly at a corner.

26 Which of the following best explains the identity and actions of the main character, Golightly?

A. He's a proper military man leaving his post.

B. He's a British soldier trying to escape capture by the Indian government.

C. He's an outlaw trying to escape capture.

D. He's a British businessman on a trip overseas.

27 Which choice provides the best evidence for the answer to the previous question?

A. Lines 9–11 ("nobody ever . . . happened.")

B. Lines 12–13 ("He was going . . . his leave")

C. Lines 15–16 ("It was fairly . . . personnel")

D. Lines 17–20 ("he descended . . . helmet.")

28 How does Kipling make fun of his character Golightly?

A. His explanation of Golightly's vanity is satiric.

B. His description of Golightly's experience shows how he has trouble coping with the severe rainstorms in India.

C. He gives a detailed description of how silly Golightly looks.

D. He shows that Golightly had difficulty riding the horse.

29 Why did Kipling provide such detail about Golightly's looks?

A. To make fun of his vanity and usual appearance

B. To show how intense the climate is in India

C. To help the reader understand the setting

D. To describe the problems of the British military in India

30 How are lines 50–51 ("He tore off . . . ploughed on.") distinguished from the rest of the text in the passage?

A. Kipling describes the character's verbal response to the situation.

B. The narrator interjects his own viewpoint.

C. It adds internal dialogue to the story.

D. The narrator describes Golightly's thoughts rather than his appearance.

31 What is the meaning of the sentence: "He had cut his leave as fine as he dared." (lines 13–14)?

A. He dared to take leave without telling the authorities.

B. He arranged to take as much time as he could without getting in trouble.

C. He was daring in leaving the military post because it was dangerous.

D. He wanted to leave, but was afraid he'd get caught.

32 As used in line 32, "mired" most nearly means

A. sped.

B. slowed.

C. pooled.

D. ate.

CONTINUE

Questions 33–42 are based on the following passages and supplementary material.

Passage 1 is an excerpt from a speech modeled on the Declaration of Independence, written and read by Elizabeth Cady Stanton at the Woman's Rights Convention, held in Seneca Falls, New York, July 19, 1848. About 300 people attended the event and about a third (68 women and 32 men) signed the declaration.

Passage 2 is excerpted from The Narrative of Sojourner Truth, *the memoir of a slave in pre-Civil War New York. Born into slavery as Isabella, after being freed in 1827, she took the name Sojourner Truth to express her strong faith. Because Truth was illiterate, she dictated her story to the writer Olive Gilbert, whom she had met in Massachusetts. The book was published in 1850 and was widely distributed by Abolitionists to help further their cause.*

PASSAGE 1

Declaration of Sentiments

The history of mankind is a history of repeated injuries and usurpations on the part of man toward woman, having in direct object the establishment of
Line an absolute tyranny over her. To prove this, let facts be
5 submitted to a candid world.

He has never permitted her to exercise her inalienable right to the elective franchise.

He has compelled her to submit to laws, in the formation of which she had no voice.

10 He has withheld from her rights which are given to the most ignorant and degraded men—both natives and foreigners.

Having deprived her of this first right of a citizen, the elective franchise, thereby leaving her without rep-
15 resentation in the halls of legislation, he has oppressed her on all sides.

He has made her, if married, in the eye of the law, civilly dead.

He has taken from her all right in property, even to
20 the wages she earns.

He has made her, morally, an irresponsible being, as she can commit many crimes with impunity, provided they be done in the presence of her husband. In the covenant of marriage, she is compelled to
25 promise obedience to her husband, he becoming, to all intents and purposes, her master—the law giving him power to deprive her of her liberty, and to administer chastisement.

He has so framed the laws of divorce, as to what
30 shall be the proper causes, and in the case of separation, to whom the guardianship of the children shall be given,

as to be wholly regardless of the happiness of women—the law, in all cases, going upon a false supposition of the supremacy of man, and giving all power into his hands.

35 After depriving her of all rights as a married woman, if single, and the owner of property, he has taxed her to support a government which recognizes her only when her property can be made profitable to it. …

He has endeavored, in every way that he could, to
40 destroy her confidence in her own powers, to lessen her self-respect, and to make her willing to lead a dependent and abject life. . . .

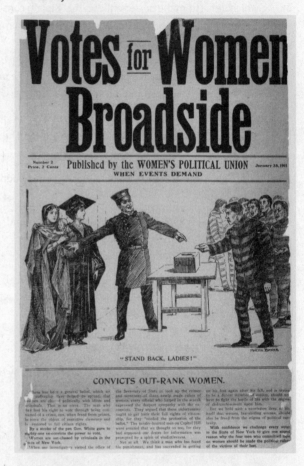

(Credit: Women's Political Union, 1911. Library of Congress)

PASSAGE 2

From: The Narrative of Sojourner Truth

After emancipation had been decreed by the State, some years before the time fixed for its consummation,
45 Isabella's master told her if she would do well, and be faithful, he would give her "free papers," one year before she was legally free by statute. In the year 1826, she had a badly diseased hand, which greatly diminished her usefulness; but on the arrival of July 4, 1827, the time
50 specified for her receiving her "free papers," she claimed the fulfillment of her master's promise; but he refused

granting it, on account (as he alleged) of the loss he had sustained by her hand. She plead that she had worked all the time, and done many things she was not wholly able to do, although she knew she had been less useful than formerly; but her master remained inflexible. Her very faithfulness probably operated against her now, and he found it less easy than he thought to give up the profits of his faithful Bell, who had so long done him efficient service.

But Isabella inwardly determined that she would remain quietly with him only until she had spun his wool—about one hundred pounds—and then she would leave him, taking the rest of the time to herself. "Ah!" she says, with emphasis that cannot be written, "the slaveholders are TERRIBLE for promising to give you this or that, or such and such a privilege, if you will do thus and so; and when the time of fulfillment comes, and one claims the promise, they, forsooth, recollect nothing of the kind; and you are, like as not, taunted with being a LIAR; or, at best, the slave is accused of not having performed *his* part or condition of the contract." "Oh!" said she, "I have felt as if I could not live through the *operation sometimes*. Just think of us! *so* eager for our pleasures, and just foolish enough to keep feeding and feeding ourselves up with the idea that we should get what had been thus fairly promised; and when we think it is almost in our hands, find ourselves flatly denied! Just think! how *could* we bear it?"

33 What was Stanton's purpose in writing and speaking the Declaration of Sentiments?

   A. She wanted to show that women could write important documents.

   B. She wanted to shock the audience in upstate New York.

   C. She wanted to show why women needed rights.

   D. She wanted to gain support for equal protection of minorities.

34 What is the effect of repeating the phrase "He has"?

   A. It shows how strongly she feels about how women were treated.

   B. It emphasizes the transgressions of men against women.

   C. It makes the speech dull because it repeats the same words.

   D. It makes the speech more like the Declaration of Independence.

35 Which rhetorical device is used by Elizabeth Cady Stanton but not by Soujourner Truth?

   A. Anaphora

   B. Third-person voice

   C. Italics for emphasis

   D. Metaphor

36 How does Stanton support her argument that women have been forced into obedience?

   A. She explains that women can't work outside the home.

   B. She expresses anger at the idea that women are not allowed to vote.

   C. She expresses dismay at how children can be taken from mothers in cases of divorce or separation.

   D. She explains how marriage legally compels women to obey their husbands.

37 What does Stanton mean by "elective franchise" as used in line 14?

   A. The sport of elections

   B. The business of elections

   C. The team needed for elections

   D. The right to vote

38 What do the two passages suggest about what women and slaves had in common?

   A. Neither women nor slaves could get paid for their work.

   B. Both women and slaves had to take care of the children in a family.

   C. Women had to obey their husbands; slaves had to obey their masters.

   D. Men made and broke promises to both women and slaves.

CONTINUE

39 Which of the following statements is true about the two passages?

- **A.** They both display a tone of anger at their lack of freedom.
- **B.** Stanton's tone is angry and Truth's tone is sad.
- **C.** Truth's tone is bitter; Stanton's tone is outrage.
- **D.** They both show a tone of frustration.

40 What set Isabella's master apart from other slaveholders?

- **A.** He didn't mistreat her as much.
- **B.** He allowed her to learn to read and write.
- **C.** He finally did set her free before he had to.
- **D.** He made promises he didn't keep.

41 Which choice provides the best evidence for the answer to the previous question?

- **A.** Lines 45–47 ("Isabella's . . . by statute.")
- **B.** Lines 47–49 ("In the year . . . usefulness")
- **C.** Lines 50–51 ("she claimed . . . promise")
- **D.** Lines 53–55 ("She plead . . . able to do")

42 In line 57, Truth says that her "faithfulness probably operated against her." What does she mean by this phrase?

- **A.** Her faith in God would help her through the difficulties operating against her.
- **B.** Her loyalty made her more important and valuable to her master.
- **C.** She needed to be faithful to her God so that her master would not break his promises.
- **D.** She needed to be faithful in the face of her master's inflexibility.

Questions 43–52 are based on the following passage and supplementary material.

The following passage has been adapted from "New Dinosaur's Keen Nose Made It a Formidable Predator, Penn Study Finds" by Katherine Unger Baillie, originally published by the University of Pennsylvania, May 11, 2015. (This passage was edited for length.)

New Dinosaur's Keen Nose Made It a Formidable Predator

A researcher from the University of Pennsylvania has identified a species of dinosaur closely related to *Velociraptor*, the group of creatures made infamous by
Line the movie *Jurassic Park*. The newly named species likely
5 possessed a keen sense of smell that would have made it a formidable predator.

Steven Jasinski, a doctoral student in the School of Arts & Science's Department of Earth and Environmental Science at Penn, and acting curator of paleontology
10 and geology at the State Museum of Pennsylvania, discovered the new species while investigating a specimen originally assigned to a previously known species. His analysis suggests the fossil—part of the dinosaur's skull—actually represents a brand new species, which
15 Jasinski has named *Saurornitholestes sullivani*. The creature's genus name Saurornitholestes, which means "lizard bird thief," gives a sense of what the prehistoric predator would have looked like. These animals were lightly built with long legs and jaws lined with teeth,
20 and they are believed to be very distant relatives of today's birds.

. . .

The specimen, roughly 75 million years old, was discovered by paleontologist Robert Sullivan in the
25 Bisti/De-Na-Zin Wilderness Area of New Mexico in 1999. When first described, scientists believed it was a member of *Saurornitholestes langstoni*, a species of theropod dinosaurs in the Dromaeosauridae family that had been found in present-day Alberta, Canada.
30 But when Jasinski . . . began a comparative analysis of the specimen to other *S. langstoni* specimens, he found subtle differences. Notably, he observed that the surface of the skull corresponding with the brain's olfactory bulb was unusually large. This finding implies
35 a powerful sense of smell.

"This feature means that *Saurornitholestes sullivani* had a relatively better sense of smell than other dromaeosaurid dinosaurs, including *Velociraptor*, *Dromaeosaurus*, and *Bambiraptor*," Jasinski said. "This keen
40 olfaction may have made *S. sullivani* an intimidating predator as well."

S. sullivani comes from the end of the time of dinosaurs, or the Late Cretaceous, and represents the only named dromaeosaur from this period in North America south of Montana.

At the time *S. sullivani* lived, North America was split into two continents separated by an inland sea. This dinosaur lived on the western shores in an area called Laramidia. Numerous dromaeosaurs, which are commonly called raptors, are known from more northern areas in Laramidia, including Alberta, Canada, and Montana. However, *S. sullivani* represents the only named dromaeosaur from the Late Cretaceous of southern Laramidia.

S. sullivani shared its world with numerous other dinosaurs. . . . Though a distinct species, *S. sullivani* appears to be closely related to *S. langstoni*. Finding the two as distinct species further shows that differences existed between dinosaurs between the northern and southern parts of North America.

At less than 3 feet at its hip and roughly 6 feet in length, *S. sullivani* was not a large dinosaur. However, previous findings of related species suggest the animal would have been agile and fast, perhaps hunting in packs and using its acute sense of smell to track down prey.

"Although it was not large, this was not a dinosaur you would want to mess with," Jasinski said.

43 Which of the following is the best statement of the main idea of the article?

A. The *S. sullivani* was a predator aided by its keen sense of smell.

B. The new species resembled today's birds.

C. Scientific discoveries make important contributions to our knowledge of prehistoric animals.

D. Recent fossil evidence identified a new species of dinosaur.

44 What conclusion can you draw from the way the *S. sullivani* species was discovered?

A. Students can sometimes make amazing discoveries.

B. Scientific investigations can yield surprising results.

C. Students do important work with academics in their field of studies.

D. Some discoveries are attributable to chance.

A pair of S. sullivani attack a young hadrosaur. (Illustration by Mary P. Williams)

CONTINUE

45 According to the passage, a strong sense of smell helps a predator because it

A. would help a predator find food.

B. could help a predator sense danger.

C. would make up for poor eyesight.

D. could help a predator find a mate.

46 What does the name of the new species tell us about this dinosaur?

A. Dinosaurs are named after real people.

B. The name tells us where the dinosaur fossils were found.

C. Dinosaurs are given names based on where they lived.

D. The name suggests what it might have looked like.

47 Which choice provides the best evidence for the answer to the previous question?

A. Lines 14–15 ("brand new . . . *sullivani*.")

B. Lines 18–21 ("These animals . . . birds.")

C. Lines 23–24 ("The specimen . . . Robert Sullivan")

D. Lines 26–27 ("When first . . . *langstoni*")

48 Based on the passage, which of the following was NOT a predatory advantage for the *S. sullivani*?

A. Sense of smell

B. Speed

C. Jaws lined with teeth

D. Size

49 How did scientists recognize that the fossil they found was a new species?

A. The fossil was larger than others that they had found previously.

B. By comparing it to other fossils, they noticed differences in the skull.

C. By looking at its closest relatives, they realized this was a different species.

D. The fossil had different markings than other species.

50 Which choice provides the best evidence for the answer to the previous question?

A. Lines 7–9 ("Steven Jasiniski . . . at Penn")

B. Lines 30–32 ("But when . . . differences.")

C. Lines 34–35 ("This finding . . . smell.")

D. Lines 42–43 ("*S. sullivani* . . . Cretaceous")

51 As used in line 6, "formidable" most nearly means

A. frightened.

B. inspiring.

C. impressive.

D. difficult.

52 As used in line 34, "olfactory" most nearly means

A. bulb.

B. sense of smell.

C. surface of the skull.

D. unusually large.

STOP

**If you finish before time is called, you may check your work on this section only.
Do not turn to any other section.**

SECTION 2: WRITING AND LANGUAGE TEST

35 MINUTES—44 QUESTIONS

TURN TO SECTION 2 OF YOUR ANSWER SHEET TO ANSWER THE QUESTIONS IN THIS SECTION.

DIRECTIONS: Each passage below is accompanied by a number of multiple-choice questions. For some questions, you will need to consider how the passage might be revised to improve the expression of ideas. Other questions will ask you to consider how the passage might be edited to correct errors in sentence structure, usage, or punctuation. A passage may be accompanied by one or more graphics—such as a chart, table, or graph—that you will need to refer to in order to best answer the question(s).

Some questions will direct you to an underlined portion of a passage—it could be one word, a portion of a sentence, or the full sentence itself. Other questions will direct you to a particular paragraph or to certain sentences within a paragraph, or you'll be asked to think about the passage as a whole. Each question number refers to the corresponding number in the passage.

After reading each passage, select the answer to each question that most effectively improves the quality of writing in the passage or that makes the passage follow the conventions of Standard Written English. Many questions include a "NO CHANGE" option. Select that option if you think the best choice is to leave that specific portion of the passage as it is.

Questions 1–11 are based on the following passage.

The Glass Ceiling

"The Glass Ceiling" is a metaphor that refers to the imperceptible and subversive forms of discrimination women in the workforce encounter when pursuing upper-level management positions. A popular phrase in the 1980s, it has become less widely used over the ensuing years. **1** Other phrases from past decades are still in frequent use. However, as recent data make clear, "The Glass Ceiling" remains a solid barrier to women working in **2** America!

1 The writer is considering deleting the underlined sentence. Should the writer do this?

- **A.** No, because it provides a detail that supports the main topic of the paragraph.
- **B.** No, because it acts as a transition to the next paragraph.
- **C.** Yes, because it repeats information that has been provided.
- **D.** Yes, because it is a detail that is irrelevant to the main topic of the paragraph.

2

- **A.** NO CHANGE
- **B.** America.
- **C.** America?
- **D.** America...

CONTINUE

According to data from the U.S. Bureau of Labor Statistics and the Pew Research Center, women make up 57.2% of the nation's workforce ❸ but hold 5% of CEO only positions in Fortune 500 companies. Women also account for only 17% of board membership at Fortune 500 companies. While these percentages note a minimal increase in female leadership over the ❹ passed thirty years, barriers still seem to exist.

❺ In 1995, a bipartisan Federal Glass Ceiling Commission was formed; to determine the root of gender discrimination within corporate America. The committee, headed by Secretary of Labor Robert Reich, noted that "At the highest levels of corporations the promise of reward for preparation and pursuit of excellence is not equally available to members of all groups." Two barriers that contributed most to "The Glass Ceiling" ❻ effect were "supply barriers" and "internal business barriers."

❸

A. NO CHANGE

B. but hold only 5% of CEO positions in Fortune 500 companies.

C. but hold 5% of only CEO positions in Fortune 500 companies.

D. but hold 5% of CEO positions only in Fortune 500 companies.

❹

A. NO CHANGE

B. passing

C. passive

D. past

❺

A. NO CHANGE

B. In 1995, a bipartisan Federal Glass Ceiling Commission, was formed to determine the root of gender discrimination within corporate America.

C. In 1995, a bipartisan Federal Glass Ceiling Commission was formed to determine the root of gender discrimination within corporate America.

D. In 1995 a bipartisan Federal Glass Ceiling Commission was formed to determine the root of gender discrimination; within corporate America.

❻

A. NO CHANGE

B. affect

C. effective

D. affection

"Supply barriers" represent the lack of leadership, education, and experience women are given access to during high school and college. Corporations have viewed this lack of access as an educational reform issue, not a business issue, and they do not think it's **7** her responsibility to fix it. However, corporations are **8** equipped with both financial and educational resources to overcome this "supply barrier." If corporations are serious about ending discrimination in the workplace, they need to invest in educational programs that train women to be future leaders. This includes creating more mentoring programs and school-to-work initiatives and providing more educational scholarships.

9 The difference between what corporate executives say they want to do. In regard to discrimination, and efforts being made (or not made) to end discriminatory practices is another issue. Talking the talk and not walking the walk is what the "internal business barrier" is all about. The reason for this discrepancy is that many white males working in the highly competitive corporate America believe they are "losing the corporate game, losing control, and losing opportunity." In essence, white men in corporate leadership feel threatened by including women in their ranks.

7

A. NO CHANGE

B. their

C. his

D. your

8

A. NO CHANGE

B. implemented

C. furnished

D. supplied

9

A. NO CHANGE

B. The difference between what corporate executives say they want to do; in regard to discrimination, and

C. The difference between what corporate executives say they want to do and in regard to discrimination and

D. The difference between what corporate executives say they want to do in regard to discrimination and

CONTINUE

10 While many efforts have been made to prevent overt discriminatory practices, 65% of women still see gender bias as a barrier they have to overcome. **11** <u>Until women can be as equals accepted in the corporate sphere, "The Glass Ceiling" will remain firmly intact.</u>

10 Which of the following sentences would make an effective opening sentence to this paragraph?

A. Ending discrimination against women in the workforce is a relatively easy problem to fix.

B. Ending discrimination against women in the workforce is an involved, complicated process.

C. There are plenty of opportunities for women to find fulfillment and success.

D. Technology is helping modern societies overcome issues involving gender bias.

11

A. NO CHANGE

B. Until women can be accepted as equals in the corporate sphere, "The Glass Ceiling" will remain firmly intact.

C. Until women can be accepted as equally in the corporate sphere, "The Glass Ceiling" will remain firmly intact.

D. Until women can be accepted in the corporate sphere as equally, "The Glass Ceiling" will remain firmly intact.

The Library of Congress

The Library of Congress is the world's largest and most open library. **12** With collections numbering more than 158 million items on 838 miles of shelving, it includes materials in 470 languages; the basic manuscript collections of 23 presidents of the United States; maps and atlases that have aided explorers and navigators in charting both the world and outer space; and the earliest motion pictures and examples of recorded sound, as well as the latest databases and software packages. **13** The Library's services extend, not only to members and committees of Congress, but also to the executive, and judicial branches of government, to libraries throughout the nation and the world, and to scholars, researchers, artists, and scientists who use its resources.

14 This was not always the case. When President John Adams signed the bill that provided for the removal of the seat of government to the new capital city of Washington in 1800, he created a reference library for Congress only. The bill provided, among other items, $5,000 "for the purchase of such books as may be necessary for the use of Congress—and for putting up a suitable apartment for containing them therein. . . ."

After this small congressional library was destroyed by fire along with the Capitol building in 1814, former President Thomas Jefferson offered as a **15** substitute his personal library, accumulated over a span of fifty years. It was considered to be one of the finest in the United States. Congress accepted Jefferson's offer. Thus the foundation was laid for a great national library.

12

A. NO CHANGE

B. It is difficult to maintain such a vast collection—

C. Among the collections of

D. Already collections number

13

A. NO CHANGE

B. The Library's services extend not only to members and committees of Congress, but also to the executive and judicial branches of government; to libraries throughout the nation and the world; and to scholars researchers, artists, and scientists

C. The Library's services extend not only to members and committees of Congress, but also to the executive and judicial branches, of government, to libraries throughout the nation, and the world and to scholars, researchers, artists, and scientists

D. The Library's services, extend not only to members and committees of Congress, but also to the executive and judicial branches of government to libraries, throughout the nation and the world, and to scholars, researchers, artists, and scientists

14

A. NO CHANGE

B. A little history is in order here.

C. Nevertheless, John Adams signed a bill to create the library.

D. We're lucky we have this institution.

15

A. NO CHANGE

B. replacement

C. stand-in

D. copy

CONTINUE

By the close of the Civil War, the collections of the Library of Congress had grown to 82,000 volumes and were still principally used by members of Congress and committees. In 1864, President Lincoln appointed as Librarian of Congress a man who was to transform the Library: Ainsworth Rand Spofford, who opened the Library to the public and greatly expanded **16** it's collections. Spofford successfully advocated a change in the copyright law so that the **17** Library would receive two, free copies of every book, map, chart, dramatic, or musical composition, engraving, cut, print, or photograph submitted for copyright. Predictably, Spofford soon filled all the Capitol's library rooms, attics, and hallways. In 1873, he then won another lobbying effort, for a new building to permanently house the nation's growing collection and reading rooms to serve scholars and the reading public. The result was the Thomas Jefferson Building, completed in 1897. Since then, two more buildings have been constructed to house the Library's **18** ever-expanding collection.

The first librarian in the new building was a newspaperman with no previous library experience, John Russell Young. He quickly realized that the Library had to get control of the collections that had been overflowing the rooms in the Capitol. Young set up organizational units and devised programs that changed the Library. **19** Instead of being essentially an acquisitions operation, it became an efficient processing factory that organized the materials and made them useful.

16

A. NO CHANGE

B. it collections

C. its collections

D. its' collections

17

A. NO CHANGE

B. Library would receive two free copies of every book, map, chart, dramatic or musical composition engraving, cut, print, or photograph, submitted for copyright.

C. Library would receive two, free copies of every book, map, chart, dramatic or musical composition; engraving, cut, print, or photograph submitted for copyright

D. Library would receive two free copies of every book, map, chart, dramatic or musical composition, engraving, cut, print, or photograph submitted for copyright.

18

A. NO CHANGE

B. ever-existing

C. ever-expending

D. ever-expounding

19 Which choice most effectively sets up the information that follows?

A. NO CHANGE

B. In spite of being essentially an acquisitions operation,

C. Once it was essentially an acquisitions operation,

D. In addition to it being essentially an acquisitions operation,

20 Formerly head of the Boston Public Library, Herbert Putnam succeeded Young. Putnam served as Librarian of Congress for 40 years. While Librarian, Spofford had collected the materials, Young had organized them, and Putnam set out to ensure that they would be used. **21** They took the Library of Congress directly into the national library scene and made its holdings known and available to the smallest community library in the most distant part of the country.

20

A. NO CHANGE

B. Young was succeeded. Herbert Putnam had formerly been head of the Boston Public Library.

C. Young was succeeded by someone else—Herbert Putnam, former head of the Boston Public Library.

D. Young was succeeded after only two years by Herbert Putnam, formerly the head of the Boston Public Library.

21

A. NO CHANGE

B. Them

C. He

D. We

CONTINUE

In about 1912, both Librarian Putnam and members of Congress became concerned about the distance that was widening between the Library and its employer, the Congress. Various states had begun to set up "legislative reference bureaus," which brought together skilled teams of librarians, economists, and political scientists whose purpose was to respond quickly to questions that arose in the legislative process. Congress wanted the same kind of service for itself, so Putnam designed such a unit for the Library of Congress. Called the Legislative Reference Service, it went into operation in 1914 to prepare indexes, digests, and compilations of law that the Congress might need, but it quickly became a specialized reference unit for information transfer and research. This service was the forerunner of the Library's current Congressional Research Service. **22**

22 Which choice best describes a conclusion that can be drawn from the chart?

A. There are more public university than private university libraries that are similar in scope and scale to the Library of Congress.

B. University libraries of the same scope and scale as the Library of Congress are more common than one would expect.

C. When it comes to university libraries of the same scope and scale as the Library of Congress, the private sector is doing more to create them than the public sector.

D. As the years go on, university libraries of the same scope and scale as the Library of Congress are rapidly increasing.

Number of Libraries in Volume Category

Institutional characteristic	Less than 5,000	5,000–9,999	10,000–19,999	20,000–29,999	30,000–49,999	50,000–99,999	100,000–249,999	250,000–499,999	500,000–999,999	1,000,000 or more
All higher education institutions	320	158	241	450	450	691	747	275	153	160
Control										
Public	43	57	77	145	297	362	231	146	106	109
Private	277	101	136	96	153	329	516	129	47	51
Level										
Total 4-year and above	115	48	90	89	155	361	673	273	151	160
Doctor's	12	6	8	5	14	35	131	83	93	151
Master's	35	19	24	22	39	177	378	151	51	9
Bachelor's	68	23	58	61	102	148	164	39	7	0
Less than 4-year	205	110	123	152	295	330	74	2	2	0
Size (FTE enrollment)										
Less than 1,500	309	138	186	193	257	352	363	36	4	1
1,500 to 4,999	9	20	26	47	185	249	297	135	36	7
5,000 or more	2	0	1	1	8	90	87	104	113	152
Carnegie classification (1994)										
Research I and II	0	0	0	0	0	0	1	1	10	113
Doctoral I and II	1	0	0	0	0	0	10	20	44	35
Master's I and II	1	0	3	4	3	47	211	164	76	9
Baccalaureate I and II	1	5	5	6	26	178	292	66	17	3
Associate of Arts	150	75	85	150	317	328	74	2	1	0
Specialized	50	33	67	60	82	116	126	21	3	0
Not classified	117	45	53	21	2	22	33	1	2	0

Source: U.S. Department of Education, National Center for Education Statistics, 1996 Integrated Postsecondary Education Data System, "Academic Libraries Survey" (IPEDS-L: 1996).

Lavinia & Emily

The Homestead was quiet and still, a preternatural quiet Lavinia Dickinson had become all too accustomed to. Looking around her sister [23] Emily's now forever empty bedroom that contained nothing, Lavinia recalled some verses penned by Emily many years ago:

> The bustle in a house
> The morning after death
> Is solemnest of industries
> Enacted upon earth, —
>
> The sweeping up the heart,
> And putting love away
> We shall not want to use again
> Until eternity.

Some people wondered at Emily's seeming [24] preoccupation with death. But Lavinia found it natural for her [25] sisters inquisitive mind to be drawn to exploring this final journey in the cycle of life, especially since Emily had seen so many loved ones pass into eternal slumber. Emily had always had a curious mind, and a voracious appetite for learning. She also greatly enjoyed being in nature. Faith was something she refused to accept blindly, without thought, much to the chagrin of the Calvinist community around her. For Emily, faith was more than rote belief.

> Faith is a fine invention
> For gentlemen who see;
> But microscopes are prudent
> In an emergency!

23

A. NO CHANGE

B. Emily's now forever empty bedroom, Lavinia recalled some verses

C. Emily's bedroom, Lavinia recalled some verses

D. Emily's now forever empty bedroom, Lavinia recalled some verses and poetry

24

A. NO CHANGE

B. predisposition

C. predilection

D. predetermination

25

A. NO CHANGE

B. sister's

C. sisters'

D. sister

26 Emily had felt very fully her isolation as one "standing alone in rebellion" of faith. Reading **27** <u>through</u> her letters and the poems Emily had hidden away, Lavinia realized just how isolated her beloved sister had felt. Perhaps that was why the self-professed "belle of Amherst" had withdrawn so much from the public sphere.

Emily felt, quite keenly, the limitations of womanhood. Lavinia still remembered the indignation Emily had expressed during the Whig Convention of 1852 when women were not allowed to be delegates. "Why can't *I* be a Delegate? ...don't I know all about Daniel Webster, and the Tariff and the Law?" **28**

26 Which of the following sentences would make an effective addition to this paragraph?

A. One reason for Emily's sense of isolation was her resistance to common ideas of her time.

B. One reason for Emily's sense of isolation was her refusal to take part in social events.

C. One reason for Emily's sense of isolation was her need to be alone to write poetry.

D. One reason for Emily's sense of isolation was her house's remote location.

27

A. NO CHANGE

B. tough

C. though

D. thought

28 At this point, the writer is considering adding the following sentence:

But Lavinia also knew that her sister was not cut out for politics and all the socializing and public display it would entail.

Should the writer make this addition here?

A. Yes, because it adds more information about Emily's personality.

B. Yes, because it explains the contrast between Emily's words and actions.

C. No, because it detracts from the point about women's issues.

D. No, because it is not relevant to Emily's life.

Yes, it seemed to Lavinia that her sister had most decidedly felt the trappings of being a woman. And, as much as **29** they tried to eschew them **30** by not becoming a wife or mother, she still felt trapped by society's strict bonds.

I Never Hear the Word "Escape"

I never hear the word "escape"
Without a quicker blood,
A sudden expectation,
A flying attitude.

I never hear of prisons broad
By soldiers battered down,
But I tug childish at my bars, —
Only to fail again!

Emily never understood the power of the gift she had been **31** given?

The Duel

I took my power in my hand.
And went against the world;
'T was not so much as David had,
But I was twice as bold.

I aimed my pebble, but myself
Was all the one that fell.
Was it Goliath was too large,
Or only I too small?

Sitting in the stillness of Emily's room, surrounded by her internal monologue expressed through thousands of poems, **32** it was deciding by Lavinia that it was time the world knew the full treasure her sister was. **33**

29

A. NO CHANGE

B. we

C. she

D. her

30 Which choice best fits with the style and tone of the passage?

A. NO CHANGE

B. by never being a wife or mother

C. by postponing choosing to be a wife or mother

D. by refusing the role of wife or mother

31

A. NO CHANGE

B. given!

C. given.

D. given;

32

A. NO CHANGE

B. decide

C. decided

D. decide

33 Which of the following would make an effective concluding sentence for this paragraph and passage?

A. The world will never know this unique treasure.

B. The world was about to receive a gift it would long cherish.

C. The world already had enough special voices.

D. The world is approximately 4.5 billion years old.

What Is Sleep?

Scientists have known for some years that sleep is important to human health. In fact, cases of long-term sleep deprivation have even led to death. **34** Yet, scientists are still studying this unique state in which humans spend a third of their lives.

35 [1] It isn't only current scientists who are intrigued with sleep. [2] Throughout history, people have attempted to understand this remarkable experience. [3] Many centuries ago, for example, sleep was regarded as a type of anemia of the brain. [4] Alcmaeon, a Greek scientist, believed that blood retreated into the blood vessels, and the partially starved brain went to sleep. [5] Plato supported the idea that the soul left the body during sleep, wandered through the world, and woke up the body when it returned. [6] During the twentieth century, great strides were made in the study of sleep.

Recently, more scientific explanations of sleep have been proposed. Looking at them, we see a variety of ideas about the nature of sleep. **36** Research may be able to help people who have sleep disorders. According to one theory, the brain is put to sleep by a chemical agent that accumulates in the body when it is awake. Another theory is that weary branches of certain nerve cells break connections with neighboring cells. The flow of impulses required for staying awake is then disrupted. These more recent theories have to be subjected to laboratory research.

34

A. NO CHANGE

B. Scientists are yet studying

C. Scientists are studying yet

D. Yet, scientists study still

35 Which sentence in this paragraph is the BEST choice to move to the fourth paragraph to create a more logical sequence?

A. Sentence 1

B. Sentence 2

C. Sentence 4

D. Sentence 6

36 Which choice most effectively sets up the information that follows?

A. NO CHANGE

B. Some of the newer ideas may yield important data about the science of sleep.

C. Although science has not yet solved the mysteries of sleep, breakthroughs are imminent.

D. However, some of the old ideas may prove to be correct.

Why do we sleep? Why do we dream? Modern sleep research is said to have begun in the 1920s with the **37** discovery of a machine that could measure brain waves, the electroencephalograph (EEG). The study of sleep was further enhanced in the 1950s, **38** and Eugene Aserinsky, a graduate student at the University of Chicago, and Nathaniel Kleitman, his professor, observed periods of rapid eye movements (REMs) in sleeping subjects. When awakened during these REM periods, subjects almost always remembered dreaming. **39** Nevertheless, when awakened during non-REM phases of sleep, the subjects rarely could recall their dreams. Aserinsky and Kleitman used EEGs and other machines in an attempt to learn more about REMs and sleep patterns.

40 Guided by REMs, it became possible for investigators to "spot" dreaming from outside and then **41** awaken the sleeper to collect dream stories. They could also **42** altar the dreamers' experiences with noises, drugs, or other stimuli before or during sleep. Thankfully, it appears the body takes care of itself by temporarily paralyzing muscles during REM sleep, preventing the dreamer from "acting out" dream activities.

37

A. NO CHANGE
B. invention
C. idea
D. suggestion

38

A. NO CHANGE
B. when
C. or
D. so

39

A. NO CHANGE
B. Even so,
C. As predicted,
D. On the other hand,

40 Which choice sets up the most logical introduction to the sentence?

A. NO CHANGE
B. Regardless of REMs,
C. No longer hampered by REMs,
D. Nevertheless, with REMs,

41

A. NO CHANGE
B. wake up
C. view
D. study

42

A. NO CHANGE
B. alter
C. alternate
D. alternative

CONTINUE

Since the mid-1950s researchers **43** has been drawn into sleep laboratories. There, bedrooms adjoin other rooms that contain EEGs and other equipment. The EEG amplifies signals from sensors on the face, head, and other parts of the body, which together yield tracings of respiration, pulse, muscle tension, and changes of electrical potential in the brain that are sometimes called brain waves. These recordings supply clues to the changes of the sleeping person's activities. These sleep studies have changed long-held beliefs that sleep was an inactive, or passive, state only used for rest and recuperation. As scientists have learned more about the purpose of sleep and dreams during REM **44** sleep. They are now turning to the study of sleep disorders to learn more about problems during sleep.

43

A. NO CHANGE

B. were been drawn

C. have been drawn

D. was drawn

44

A. NO CHANGE

B. sleep—they

C. sleep; they

D. sleep, they

STOP

If you finish before time is called, you may check your work on this section only.
Do not turn to any other section.

SECTION 3: MATH TEST—NO CALCULATOR

25 Minutes—20 Questions

TURN TO SECTION 3 OF YOUR ANSWER SHEET TO ANSWER THE QUESTIONS IN THIS SECTION.

DIRECTIONS: For **Questions 1–15,** solve each problem, select the best answer from the choices provided, and fill in the corresponding circle on your answer sheet. For **Questions 16–20,** solve the problem and enter your answer in the grid on the answer sheet. The directions **before Question 16** will provide information on how to enter your answers in the grid.

ADDITIONAL INFORMATION:

1. The use of a calculator in this section is **not permitted**.
2. All variables and expressions used represent real numbers unless otherwise indicated.
3. Figures provided in this test are drawn to scale unless otherwise indicated.
4. All figures lie in a plane unless otherwise indicated.
5. Unless otherwise specified, the domain of a given function f is the set of all real numbers x for which $f(x)$ is a real number.

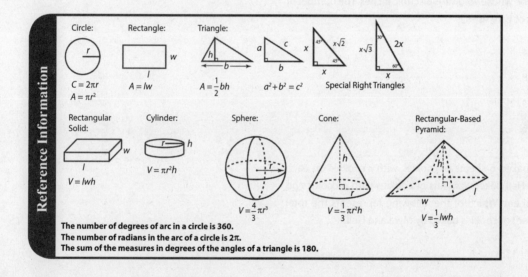

Reference Information

Circle:
$C = 2\pi r$
$A = \pi r^2$

Rectangle:
$A = lw$

Triangle:
$A = \frac{1}{2}bh$

$a^2 + b^2 = c^2$

Special Right Triangles

Rectangular Solid:
$V = lwh$

Cylinder:
$V = \pi r^2 h$

Sphere:
$V = \frac{4}{3}\pi r^3$

Cone:
$V = \frac{1}{3}\pi r^2 h$

Rectangular-Based Pyramid:
$V = \frac{1}{3}lwh$

The number of degrees of arc in a circle is 360.
The number of radians in the arc of a circle is 2π.
The sum of the measures in degrees of the angles of a triangle is 180.

CONTINUE

SHOW YOUR WORK HERE

1 If $\dfrac{x+2}{5} = m$ and $m = -3$, what is the value of x?

A. -17

B. -15

C. -5

D. -1

2 If $d = m - \dfrac{50}{m}$, and m is a positive number, then as m increases in value, d

A. increases in value.

B. decreases in value.

C. increases, then decreases.

D. decreases, then increases.

3 Pieces of wire are soldered together so as to form the edges of a cube whose volume is 64 cubic inches. The number of inches of wire used is

A. 24.

B. 48.

C. 64.

D. 96.

4 Myra baked 6 sheets of cookies with r cookies on each sheet. Neil baked 7 sheets of cookies with p cookies on each sheet. Which of the following represents the total number t of cookies baked by Myra and Neil?

A. $t = 13pr$

B. $t = 42pr$

C. $t = 6r + 7p$

D. $t = 7r + 6p$

5 If $b = a + 3$ and $c = -a^2 + 3a + 10$, then what is $b^2 - 2c$ in terms of a?

A. $2(a + 3)^2(-a + 5)(a + 2)$

B. $3a^2 - 6a - 2$

C. $-a^2 + 6a + 29$

D. $3a^2 - 11$

6

$$y = \frac{(x-3)^3}{4}$$

Which expression is equivalent to x?

A. $\sqrt{4y} + 3$

B. $\sqrt{4y+3}$

C. $\sqrt[3]{4y} + 3$

D. $\sqrt[3]{4y+3}$

7 Hannah recently purchased a plant that grows 4.5 centimeters each week. The height of Hannah's plant can be found using the equation $h = 4.5w + 6$, where h is the height of the plant in centimeters, and w is the number of weeks. What is the meaning of the 6 in the equation?

A. Hannah's plant will be 6 centimeters tall after 4.5 weeks.

B. Hannah's plant grows 6 centimeters each week.

C. Hannah's plant will grow for 6 weeks.

D. Hannah's plant was initially 6 centimeters tall.

8 $(x)^6 + (2x^2)^3 + (3x^3)^2 =$

A. $5x^5 + x^6$

B. $17x^5 + x^6$

C. $6x^6$

D. $18x^6$

Question 9 refers to the following graph.

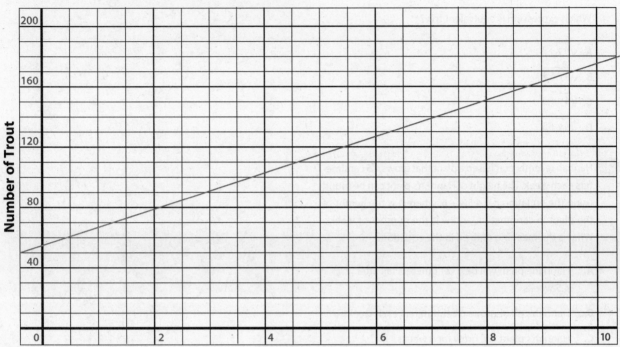

Number of Days

9 Stephen was studying the population of a certain trout pond. When he started his study, there were 55 trout in the pond. He observed the pond each day for 10 days and observed that there were 12 new trout each day. The graph above represents the relationship between the number of trout in the pond and the number of days. Which of the following is an equation for the graph?

SHOW YOUR WORK HERE

A. $y = 12x + 55$

B. $y = 10x + 12$

C. $y = 55x + 12$

D. $y = 12x + 10$

10 Which of the following is equal to $\left(-\dfrac{27}{8}\right)^{-\frac{1}{3}}$?

A. $-\dfrac{3}{2}$

B. $-\dfrac{2}{3}$

C. $\dfrac{2}{3}$

D. $\dfrac{3}{2}$

11 The area of a square is $49x^2$. What is the length of a diagonal of the square?

A. $7x$

B. $7x\sqrt{2}$

C. $14x$

D. $\dfrac{7x}{\sqrt{2}}$

SHOW YOUR WORK HERE

12 The distance, s, in feet that an object falls in t seconds when dropped from a height is obtained by use of the formula $s = 16t^2$. When graphed, what is the meaning of the slope between any two points in the graph?

A. The height in feet from where the object falls

B. The average speed, in feet per second, of the object as it falls

C. The time in seconds it takes for the object to fall to the ground

D. The acceleration, in feet per second squared, of the object as it falls

13
$$D + B = 24$$
$$4D + 2B = 84$$

In this system of equations, the first equation represents the total number of dogs, D, and birds, B, in a pet store. The second equation represents the number of legs a dog has, $4D$, and the number of legs a bird has, $2B$. How many dogs and birds are in the pet store?

A. $D = 6; B = 18$

B. $D = 18; B = 6$

C. $D = 24; B = 84$

D. $D = 60; B = 24$

14
$$f(x) = x^2 - 4x - 21$$

Which of the following is an equivalent equation that shows the zeros of the function as coefficients or constants?

A. $f(x) = (x - (-7))(x - 3)$

B. $f(x) = (x - 7)(x - (-3))$

C. $f(x) = (x - 2)^2 - 21$

D. $f(x) = (x - 2)^2 - 25$

CONTINUE

15 Which equation represents the equation of a line perpendicular to $y = 3x - 2$ that goes through the point $(1, 3)$?

SHOW YOUR WORK HERE

A. $y = -3x + 6$

B. $y = -\dfrac{1}{3}x + \dfrac{10}{3}$

C. $y = -\dfrac{1}{3}x + \dfrac{9}{3}$

D. $y = 3x$

DIRECTIONS: For **Questions 16–20,** solve the problem and enter your answer in the grid, as described below, on the answer sheet.

1. Although not required, it is suggested that you write your answer in the boxes at the top of the columns to help you fill in the circles accurately. You will receive credit only if the circles are filled in correctly.

2. Mark no more than one circle in any column.

3. No question has a negative answer.

4. Some problems may have more than one correct answer. In such cases, enter only one answer.

5. **Mixed numbers** such as $3\frac{1}{2}$ must be entered as 3.5 or $\frac{7}{2}$.

    If $3\frac{1}{2}$ is entered into the grid as $\boxed{3\,|\,1\,/\,2}$, it will be interpreted as $\frac{31}{2}$, not $3\frac{1}{2}$.

6. **Decimal answers:** If you obtain a decimal answer with more digits than the grid can accommodate, it may be either rounded or truncated, but it must fill the entire grid.

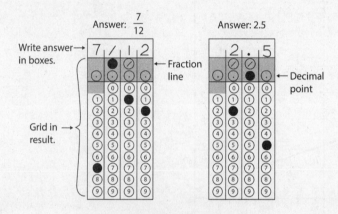

Answer: $\frac{7}{12}$ Answer: 2.5

Write answer → in boxes.   ← Fraction line   ← Decimal point

Grid in → result.

Answer: 201
Either position is correct.

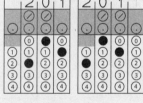

Acceptable ways to grid $\frac{2}{3}$ are:

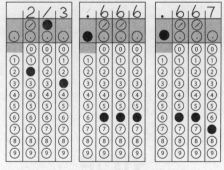

CONTINUE

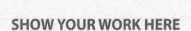

16

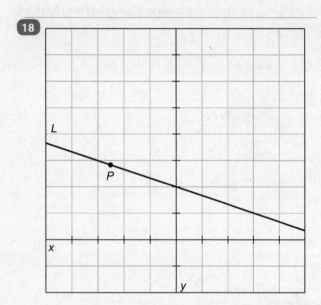

In the figure above, $x =$

17 The only factors of the function f are $(x + 3)^2$ and $(3x - 2)$. What is the product of its three zeroes?

18

A line drawn through point p perpendicular to line L will have what slope?

19

$$\sqrt{4 - x^2} = \sqrt{3x}$$

What is one solution to the equation?

20

$$2x + 3y = 7$$
$$ax - 12y = b$$

According to the system of equations above, what is the value of ab that will make the system of equations have an infinite number of solutions?

STOP

If you finish before time is called, you may check your work on this section only.

Do not turn to any other section.

SECTION 4: MATH TEST—CALCULATOR 🖩

55 Minutes—38 Questions

TURN TO SECTION 4 OF YOUR ANSWER SHEET TO ANSWER THE QUESTIONS IN THIS SECTION.

DIRECTIONS: For **Questions 1–30**, solve each problem, select the best answer from the choices provided, and fill in the corresponding circle on your answer sheet. For **Questions 31–38,** solve the problem and enter your answer in the grid on the answer sheet. The directions **before Question 31** will provide information on how to enter your answers in the grid.

ADDITIONAL INFORMATION:

1. The use of a calculator in this section is **permitted.**
2. All variables and expressions used represent real numbers unless otherwise indicated.
3. Figures provided in this test are drawn to scale unless otherwise indicated.
4. All figures lie in a plane unless otherwise indicated.
5. Unless otherwise specified, the domain of a given function f is the set of all real numbers x for which $f(x)$ is a real number.

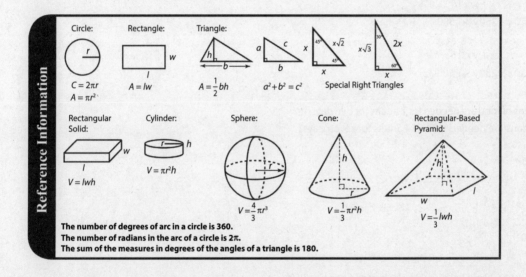

Reference Information

Circle:
$C = 2\pi r$
$A = \pi r^2$

Rectangle:
$A = lw$

Triangle:
$A = \frac{1}{2}bh$

$a^2 + b^2 = c^2$

Special Right Triangles

Rectangular Solid:
$V = lwh$

Cylinder:
$V = \pi r^2 h$

Sphere:
$V = \frac{4}{3}\pi r^3$

Cone:
$V = \frac{1}{3}\pi r^2 h$

Rectangular-Based Pyramid:
$V = \frac{1}{3}lwh$

The number of degrees of arc in a circle is 360.
The number of radians in the arc of a circle is 2π.
The sum of the measures in degrees of the angles of a triangle is 180.

CONTINUE

1 If $9x + 5 = 23$, what is the numerical value of $18x + 5$?

   A. 46

   B. 41

   C. 36

   D. 32

SHOW YOUR WORK HERE

2 A pickup truck has maximum load capacity of 1,500 pounds. Bruce is going to load small radiators, each weighing 150 pounds, and large radiators, each weighing 250 pounds, into the truck. There are 15 radiators to choose from. Which system of linear inequalities represents this situation?

   A. $x + y < 15$
      $150x + 250y < 1,500$

   B. $x + y \geq 15$
      $150x + 250y \geq 1,500$

   C. $x + y > 15$
      $150x + 250y > 1,500$

   D. $x + y \leq 15$
      $150x + 250y \leq 1,500$

3 If 15 cans of food are needed for 7 adults for two days, how many cans are needed to feed 4 adults for seven days?

   A. 15

   B. 20

   C. 25

   D. 30

4 Fiona earns $28 per hour working for herself. She saves 25% of her income to pay taxes. Which function can be used to determine the after-tax amount Fiona earns for working x hours?

   A. $f(x) = 28(0.25x)$

   B. $f(x) = 28 + 0.25x$

   C. $f(x) = 28(0.75x)$

   D. $f(x) = 28 + 0.75x$

Total Annual Sales

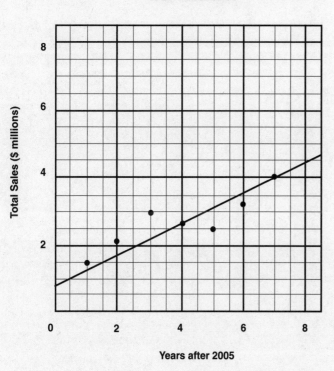

Years after 2005

The graph above represents the sales for a company after 2005.

5 Which phrase best describes the correlation between the years after 2005 and the total sales?

A. Weak negative

B. Strong negative

C. Weak positive

D. Strong positive

6 Which equation best models the data shown in the graph?

A. $y = 0.4x + 1$

B. $y = x + 0.5$

C. $y = 1.5^x$

D. $y = 0.5^x$

CONTINUE

7 If a box of notepaper costs $4.20 after a 40% discount, what was its original price?

   A. $2.52

   B. $5.88

   C. $7.00

   D. $10.50

8 The average attendance at basketball games at a local university over the last 10 years can be modeled by the equation $y = 329x + 6,489$, where y represents the average attendance at basketball games x years after 2004. Which of the following describes the meaning of 329 in the equation?

   A. The average attendance at basketball games in 2004.

   B. The total attendance at basketball games in 2004.

   C. The annual increase in average attendance at basketball games.

   D. The total increase in average attendance at basketball games for the last 10 years.

9 One supercomputer can process a job 1.5 times faster than another supercomputer. When both supercomputers are used simultaneously to complete a job, the job is completed in 3 hours. How long would it take the slower supercomputer to complete the job alone?

   A. $\frac{2}{3}$ hour

   B. 4.5 hours

   C. 6 hours

   D. 7.5 hours

SHOW YOUR WORK HERE

10 A local library had 25,825 books at the beginning of 2010. Since then, it has added 375 books each year. The library can fit a maximum of 35,000 books. If x represents the number of years after the start of 2010, which inequality shows the number of years that the library can continue adding books at this pace without adding space?

A. $35,000 - 375 \leq x$

B. $35,000 \leq 375x$

C. $35,000 \geq 375x - 25,825$

D. $35,000 \geq 375x + 25,825$

11

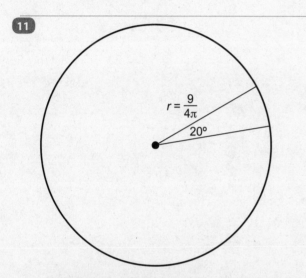

Note: Figure not drawn to scale.

Given the circle shown above, what is the length of the arc formed by the 20° angle?

A. $\dfrac{45}{\pi}$

B. $\dfrac{\pi}{4}$

C. $\dfrac{1}{2}$

D. $\dfrac{1}{4}$

12 A study was performed to determine if a new medication, Z, helps people who suffer from a certain affliction. A group of 500 randomly selected people who have the affliction were included in the study. Of the group, 200 people were given Z, 200 people were given an old medication, Y, and another 100 people received no treatment. The data showed that people who received Z had significantly decreased effects of the affliction, more than people who received no treatment or who were given medicine Y. Based on the design and results of the study, which of the following is an appropriate conclusion?

A. Z is likely to lessen the effects of the affliction in people who suffer from the affliction.

B. Z is likely to lessen the effects of the affliction better than any other medication.

C. Z is likely to lessen the effects of the affliction for anyone who takes the medication.

D. Z is likely to lessen the effects of the affliction for those who received no treatment.

13 One model for the growth of atmospheric carbon dioxide based on data from Mauna Loa observatory in Hawaii uses the quadratic equation, $C = 0.013t^2 + 0.518t + 310.44$, where C is the concentration in parts per million (PPM) and t is the number of years since 1950. Suppose we want to compare the concentrations predicted by that quadratic model to a model predicting linear—constant year-to-year—growth. Base the linear growth model on the data from 2000 and 2010 shown below. Which statement best describes the difference predicted by the two models for the year 2100?

Year	CO_2 concentration (PPM)
2000	370
2010	390

A. The quadratic model predicts a concentration in the year 2100 that is about 90 PPM less than the linear model predicts.

B. The quadratic model predicts a concentration in the year 2100 that is about 10 PPM greater than the linear model predicts.

C. The quadratic model predicts a concentration in the year 2100 that is about 90 PPM greater than the linear model predicts.

D. The quadratic model predicts a concentration in the year 2100 that is about 110 PPM greater than the linear model predicts.

SHOW YOUR WORK HERE

14 After installing a circular pond with diameter 12 feet, Kosi decided to install an 18-inch walkway around the entire pond. The stone costs $7.25 per square foot. What is the total cost of the stone for the walkway?

A. $130.50

B. $461.23

C. $819.96

D. $1,281.18

15 If $a^2 + 12a = 45$ and $a < 0$, what is the value of $a + 6$?

A.   −15

B.   −9

C.   −3

D.   3

CONTINUE

The graph provided shows the population of California, in millions, from the years 1860 to 1980. Each point represents the population at a particular year. The best fit relation between the points is drawn to connect them.

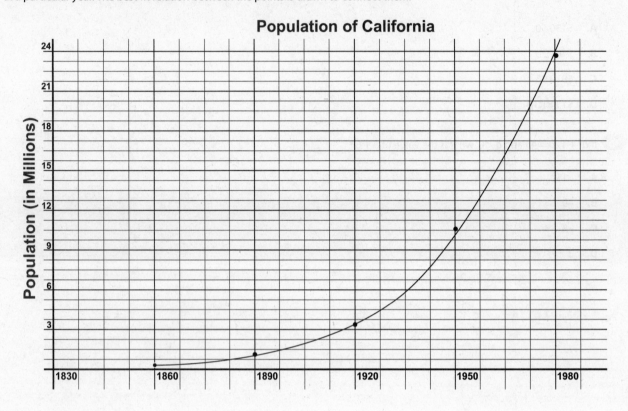

Population of California

16 Which phrase describes the relationship between the population and the number of years?

   A. Linear increasing

   B. Linear decreasing

   C. Exponential growth

   D. Exponential decay

17 Based on the graph, which of the following would be the best prediction of the population of California in 1990?

   A. 20 million

   B. 23 million

   C. 25 million

   D. 30 million

SHOW YOUR WORK HERE

18 A rectangular sign is cut down by 10% of its height and 30% of its width. What percent of the original area remains?

A. 37%

B. 57%

C. 63%

D. 70%

19 A recent report states that if you were to eat each meal in a different restaurant in New York City, it would take you more than 19 years to cover all of New York City's eating places, assuming that you eat three meals a day. On the basis of this information, the number of restaurants in New York City

A. exceeds 20,500.

B. is fewer than 20,000.

C. exceeds 21,000 but does not exceed 21,500.

D. exceeds 21,500.

20

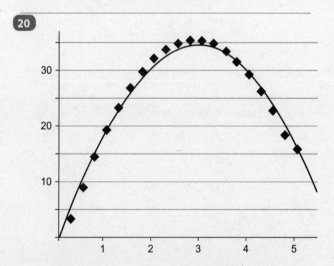

What is the best interpretation of the graph above, which shows the line of best fit drawn through a set of data points recorded in an experiment?

A. The distance from the thrower of a ball thrown horizontally, versus time, fitting a quadratic model

B. The distance from the thrower of a ball thrown horizontally, versus time, fitting a nonlinear model

C. The distance from the thrower of a ball thrown vertically, versus time, fitting a quadratic model

D. The distance from the thrower of a ball thrown vertically, versus time, fitting an exponential model

CONTINUE

21

$$\frac{3x-1}{2x+3}-\frac{2x+3}{3x-1}$$

Which of the following is equivalent to the expression above?

A. $\dfrac{5x^2-18x-8}{6x^2+7x-3}$

B. $\dfrac{x-4}{6x^2+7x-3}$

C. $\dfrac{5x^2+10}{6x^2+7x-3}$

D. $\dfrac{5x^2-12x-8}{6x^2+7x-3}$

SHOW YOUR WORK HERE

Questions 22 and 23 refer to the following graph.

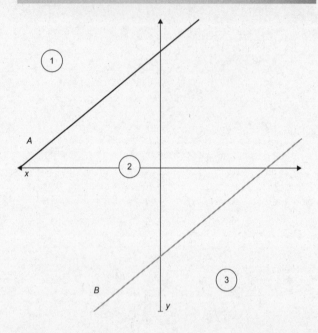

22 Lines *A* and *B* shown in the graph have equal slope. If lines *A* and *B* represent a system of two equations with two variables, then how many solutions does the system have?

A. 1 solution

B. Infinitely many solutions

C. No solution

D. Not enough information is provided to determine the number of solutions.

---

23 We convert the equation for line A, $y = mx + a$, to an inequality by replacing "=" with "<". We convert the equation for B, $y = mx + b$, by changing "=" to ">". Which statement is true?

A. A point, (x, y), satisfying both inequalities, would lie in Region 1 of the graph.

B. A point, (x, y), satisfying both inequalities, would lie in Region 2 of the graph.

C. A point, (x, y), satisfying both inequalities, would lie in Region 3 of the graph.

D. There is no point, (x, y) that would satisfy both inequalities.

24 The number of people living in a certain city has been growing at a constant rate of about 3.8% each year since 1980. The population in 2000 was 38,500. If y is the population of the city x years after 1980, which equation best represents this situation?

A. $y = 18,260(1.038)^x$

B. $y = 38,500(1.38)^x$

C. $y = 38,500(1.038)^x$

D. $y = 81,172(1.38)^x$

25 If $f(x) = |x|$ and $g(x) = -\dfrac{1}{x}$, then for $x < 0$, $g(f(x)) =$

A. $-\dfrac{1}{x}$

B. 0

C. $\left|\dfrac{1}{x}\right|$

D. $\dfrac{1}{x}$

CONTINUE

Questions 26 and 27 refer to the following information.

A recent poll surveyed a random selection of 850 likely voters in a state election. Of the sample, 31% say that they favor candidate A, and 18% say that they favor candidate B. The margin of error reported for this was ±3.4% with 95% confidence.

26 Which of the following statements can accurately be drawn from this data?

    A.   The margin of error is too large to make any conclusions.

    B.   The sample of likely voters doesn't represent all voters.

    C.   The sample size is too small to represent the voters across the entire state.

    D.   The sample was randomly selected and is large enough to make conclusions.

27 Which of the following statements can accurately be drawn from this data?

    A.   The true percentage of likely voters who will vote for candidate A is 31%.

    B.   The true percentage of likely voters who will vote for candidate A is most likely between 27.6% and 34.4%.

    C.   The true percentage of likely voters who will vote for candidate B is 18%.

    D.   The true percentage of likely voters who will vote for someone other than candidate A or candidate B is most likely between 45.6% and 52.4%.

28 In a certain course, a student takes eight tests, all of which count equally. When figuring out the final grade, the instructor drops the best and the worst grades and averages the other six. The student calculates that his average for all eight tests is 84%. After dropping the best and the worst grades, the student averages 86%. What was the average of the best and the worst grades?

A. 68

B. 73

C. 78

D. 88

29

$$x^2 + y^2 - 8x + 12y = 144$$

What is the length of the radius of the circle with the equation above?

A. 6

B. 12

C. 14

D. 24

30 If a represents a real number, what condition must a satisfy so that the graph of $f(x) = 2(3a - x) - (5 + ax)$ does not intersect Quadrant III?

A. $a < \dfrac{5}{6}$

B. $-2 \leq a < \dfrac{5}{6}$

C. $a > \dfrac{5}{6}$

D. $a \leq -2$

CONTINUE

DIRECTIONS: For **Questions 31–38,** solve the problem and enter your answer in the grid, as described below, on the answer sheet.

1. Although not required, it is suggested that you write your answer in the boxes at the top of the columns to help you fill in the circles accurately. You will receive credit only if the circles are filled in correctly.

2. Mark no more than one circle in any column.

3. No question has a negative answer.

4. Some problems may have more than one correct answer. In such cases, enter only one answer.

5. **Mixed numbers** such as $3\frac{1}{2}$ must be entered as 3.5 or $\frac{7}{2}$.

    If $3\frac{1}{2}$ is entered into the grid as $\overline{3\,|\,1\,/\,2}$, it will be interpreted as $\frac{31}{2}$, not $3\frac{1}{2}$.

6. **Decimal answers:** If you obtain a decimal answer with more digits than the grid can accommodate, it may be either rounded or truncated, but it must fill the entire grid.

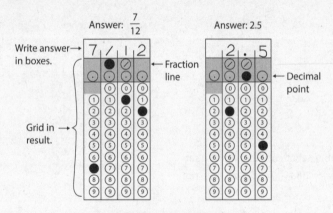

Answer: $\frac{7}{12}$ Answer: 2.5

Write answer in boxes.
Fraction line
Decimal point
Grid in result.

Answer: 201
Either position is correct.

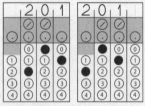

Acceptable ways to grid $\frac{2}{3}$ are:

31 The 50 members of a governing body of an organization have held office for the following number of complete terms. (Note that a zero means that the member is currently in the process of serving his or her first term.)

Number of Complete Terms Served	Number of Members
0	6
1	13
2	21
3	4
4	5
5	1

What is the mean number of terms served by the members of this governing body?

32 If $\dfrac{x}{12}+\dfrac{x}{18}=1$, what is the value of x?

33 An African elephant can lift a total of approximately 660 pounds with its trunk. A small bundle of twigs weighs 12 pounds. If an African elephant lifts a small log that weighs 50 pounds, what is the greatest number of small twig bundles that it could theoretically lift in addition to the log?

CONTINUE

Questions 34 and 35 refer to the following information.

The table below shows the party affiliations of the 45 US presidents, whose terms began in the eighteenth, nineteenth, twentieth, or twenty-first centuries.

Party	Century				Total
	18th	19th	20th	21st	
Federalist	2	0	0	0	2
Democratic-Republican	0	4	0	0	4
Democrat	0	8	7	1	16
Whig	0	4	0	0	4
Republican	0	7	10	2	19
Total	2	23	17	3	45

34 In what century did the highest percentage of Democrats serve as president? Enter your answer as a two-digit number (for example, enter "18" for the eighteenth century).

35 To the nearest percentage point, what percentage of US presidents have *not* been Democrats or Republicans? Members of the "Democratic-Republican" party were neither Democrats nor Republicans. Enter your answer as a two-digit number.

36

$$5x + 4y = 11$$
$$6x - 8y = 10$$

In the system of equations above, what is the value of y?

37 A car travels from town A to town B, a distance of 360 miles, in 9 hours. How many hours would the same trip have taken had the car traveled 5 mph faster?

38

$$\frac{2}{x+2} + \frac{3}{x-5} = \frac{4x+7}{x^2 - 3x - 10}$$

What is the solution to the equation shown above?

STOP

If you finish before time is called, you may check your work on this section only.
Do not turn to any other section.

SECTION 5: ESSAY

50 Minutes—1 Essay

DIRECTIONS: The essay gives you an opportunity to show how effectively you can read and comprehend a passage and write an essay analyzing the passage. In your essay, you should demonstrate that you have read the passage carefully, present a clear and logical analysis, and use language precisely.

Your essay will need to be written on the lines provided in your answer booklet. You will have enough space if you write on every line and keep your handwriting to an average size. Try to print or write clearly so that your writing will be legible to the readers scoring your essay.

As you read the passage below, consider how the writers, Alex Jensen and Susan M. McHale, use the following:

- Evidence, such as facts, statistics, or examples, to support claims.
- Reasoning to develop ideas and to connect claims and evidence.
- Stylistic or persuasive elements, such as word choice or appeals to emotion, to add power to the ideas expressed.

Adapted from *"What makes siblings from the same family so different? Parents"* by Alex Jensen and Susan M. McHale, originally published in *The Conversation*, July 6, 2015. Alex Jensen is an Assistant Professor of Human Development at Brigham Young University. Susan M. McHale is a Professor of Human Development and Family Studies at Pennsylvania State University.

What makes siblings from the same family so different? Parents

1   A colleague related the following story: while running errands with her 11- and 7-year-old daughters, a back seat battle began to rage. My colleague's attempts to defuse the situation only led to a shouting match about who was to blame for the skirmish. Finally the 11-year-old proclaimed to her sister, "You started it the day you were born and took away Mom's love!"

2   This pair of sisters fight frequently, and from their mother's perspective, part of the reason is that the two have little in common. As it turns out, their situation is not unique.

3   Despite the fact that siblings are, on average, 50% genetically similar, are often raised in the same home by the same parents, attend the same schools and have many other shared experiences, siblings are often only as similar to each other as they are to children who are growing up across town or even across the country.

4   So, what is it that makes two siblings from the same family so different?

What makes the difference?

5   As researchers of sibling and family relationships, we knew that at least one answer to this question comes from theory and data showing that, at least in some families, siblings try to be different from one another and seek to establish a unique identity and position in their family.

6   From a child's perspective, if an older brother excels at school, it may be easier to attract her parents' attention and praise by becoming a star athlete than by competing with her brother to get the best grades. In this way, even small differences between siblings can become substantial differences over time.

7   But parents may also play a role. For instance, when parents notice differences between their children, children may pick up on parents' perceptions and beliefs about those differences. This, in turn, can increase sibling differences.

CONTINUE

8   We wanted to test these ideas to see what makes siblings different. So, we used data from first- and second-born teenage siblings from 388 two-parent families to examine sibling differences in school performance.

9   We asked mothers and fathers to report on whether they thought the two siblings differed in their academic abilities, and if so, which sibling was more capable. We also collected school grades from both siblings' report cards.

Preference for the firstborn

10   Our analyses showed some interesting results: parents tended to believe that the older sibling was better in school. This was even when older siblings did not actually receive better grades, on average.

11   This may be a product of parents having greater expectations for firstborns or that, at any given time, the older sibling is undertaking more advanced school work.

12   There was, however, an exception to this pattern: in families with older brothers and younger sisters, parents rated the younger sibling as being more capable. In fact, in those families, younger sisters received better grades than their older brothers.

13   Our findings also showed that it was not sibling differences in school grades that predicted parents' ratings of their children's abilities. Rather, parents' beliefs about differences in their children's abilities predicted later sibling differences in school grades.

14   In other words, when parents believed one child was more capable than the other, that child's school grades improved more over time than their sibling's.

Sustaining beliefs

15   Although we expected that children's school grades and parents' beliefs about their children's relative abilities would be mutually influential, it turned out that parents' beliefs did not change much over their children's teenage years.

16   Instead, sibling differences in school grades did change and were predicted by parents' beliefs. In this way, parents' beliefs about differences between their children may encourage the development of actual sibling difference.

17   The above comment by an 11-year-old highlights that children are sensitive to their place and value in the family—relative to those of their siblings. Parents may strive to show their love for their children, but they also should be aware that small differences in how they treat their children can have large effects—including on their children's development and adjustment and also on the sibling relationship.

18   Indeed, some research suggests that sibling conflict arises when children try to be different from their siblings.

19   My colleague may be correct that her daughters fight frequently because they have nothing in common. But their conflicts may also be motivated by her daughter's perception that their differences started on the day her sister was born "and took away Mom's love."

> Write an essay in which you explain how the writers build an argument to persuade their audience that parents are the reason why siblings from the same family behave differently. In your essay, analyze how Alex Jensen and Susan M. McHale use one or more of the features previously listed (or features of your own choice) to strengthen the logic and persuasiveness of their argument. Be sure that your analysis focuses on the most relevant aspects of the passage.
>
> Your essay should not explain whether you agree with the writers' claims but rather explain how they build an argument to persuade their audience.

STOP

If you finish before time is called, you may check your work on this section only.
Do not turn to any other section.

1. C	**12.** C	**23.** B	**34.** B	**45.** A
2. A	**13.** A	**24.** B	**35.** A	**46.** D
3. D	**14.** C	**25.** A	**36.** D	**47.** B
4. B	**15.** B	**26.** A	**37.** D	**48.** D
5. C	**16.** D	**27.** A	**38.** C	**49.** B
6. B	**17.** B	**28.** C	**39.** D	**50.** B
7. C	**18.** C	**29.** A	**40.** C	**51.** C
8. A	**19.** A	**30.** B	**41.** A	**52.** B
9. D	**20.** A	**31.** B	**42.** B	
10. A	**21.** A	**32.** B	**43.** D	
11. C	**22.** C	**33.** C	**44.** C	

READING TEST RAW SCORE [   ]
(Number of correct answers)

1. **The correct answer is C.** The overall idea of the article emphasizes the problem of GALS, an invasive species that threatens the ecosystems of the islands. The article is informational and does not attempt to persuade readers (choice D), encourage them to visit (choice A), or raise money (choice B).

2. **The correct answer is A.** The main discussion of the article is about how scientists are trying to contain and eliminate GALS by using trained dogs to detect them. Choice B is incorrect because it states the opposite of the correct answer. Choice C is a true statement, but it is not the main idea of the article. Choice D is also true, but the article does not focus on how organizations are collaborating; rather its emphasis is on training dogs to help solve the specific problem of one invasive species.

3. **The correct answer is D.** The first four lines of the introductory paragarph before the article mentions the location of the islands, which are quite a distance from any mainland. This fact of geography likely kept people from settling there for a long time. This meant that the natural ecosystems were in balance.

4. **The correct answer is B.** The article explains that the GALS is very destructive because it eats so many different types of plants (lines 10–12). Once this snail enters a population, it takes over by reproducing quickly and eating plant species that keep the ecosystems in balance. While their ability to hide (choice C) makes them difficult to find, the threat comes from their eating habits.

5. **The correct answer is C.** According to the passage, GALS only affected 50 acres of land as of its writing (lines 15–18), but they are covering more ground every year, and since they will destroy much needed plant life on that ground, choice C is the best answer. Although dogs are being used in an effort to solve the GALS problem, that problem has not been solved yet, so choice A is not the best answer. There is no discussion of media treatment of the problem in this passage, so choice B is incorrect, nor is the GALS problem compared to other invasive species problems on the island, so choice D cannot be determined.

6. **The correct answer is B.** Choice B (lines 17–18) explains how GALS are covering more ground "every wet season," and since they will destroy the plant life on that ground, this proves that the problem is getting worse with each passing season or year. Choice A (lines 10–12) introduces the problem; it does not explain how it is getting worse, which is what the correct answer to the previous question states. Choices C (lines 24–29) and D (lines 59–61) only explain efforts to solve the problem; they are not evidence that shows how the problem is steadily growing worse every year.

7. **The correct answer is C.** Dogs have a very highly developed sense of smell and can be trained to follow a scent that humans cannot detect (lines 29–33), so choice C is the best answer. Dogs were not chosen based on their ease of interaction with people or for their ability to find drugs, so choice A and choice B are incorrect. The passage never indicates that GALS hide in small spaces or that dogs track them in such spaces, so choice D is incorrect.

8. **The correct answer is A.** Lines 29–32 reveal that dogs "have an incredible sense of smell and can be trained to detect scents," which is basically a rewording of the correct answer to the previous question, so choice A is best. Choice B (lines 33–34) seems to have mistaken choice B for the correct answer to the previous question, since it references how dogs can detect drugs. Choice C (lines 35–37) describes how dogs are used in the project, not why they are ideal for the project. Choice D (lines 39–40) just explains when the first phase of the project began.

9. **The correct answer is D.** *Biosecurity* is a combined form of the prefix *bio-* (meaning life) and *security*. As used in the passage, the word refers to security from harmful biological species. The word is not related to handling of plants or animals, choices A and B. The article does not mention extinction (choice C). Here, *biosecurity* is protection of the ecosystems (choice D).

10. **The correct answer is A.** *Acclimation*, as used in the context provided, describes how the dogs had to adjust to the Galapagos, which was not their native environment. *Conforming* (choice B) suggests blending in rather than adjusting. *Adaptation* (choice C) is a process that takes many years, not a few days or weeks. Training is a type of behavior *modification* (choice D), but it is unrelated to acclimation.

11. **The correct answer is C.** Dogs are not native to the Galapagos, which are islands far from any mainland, inhabited mostly by species unique to the islands, such as giant tortoises and iguanas. Dogs were brought to the islands (lines 50–52) by people to help them find the invasive species that are upsetting the balance found on the islands. The dogs' sense of smell makes them good hunters for the invasive species on the islands, but that does not explain why they are invasive, so choice A is incorrect. The text explains that the dogs had to be acclimated both to the islands and their trainers, but their adjustment was so that they could be trained properly for their role as hunters. This acclimation does not explain why they would be considered invasive, so choice B is incorrect. Choice D is incorrect because the text does not say that dogs ever thrived on the islands or were predators of any native species; it only stated that the dogs brought by the project helped in finding a particular invasive species so that it could be eradicated.

12. **The correct answer is C.** In lines 6–12, Carter explains how important it is for people to grasp the severity of the energy problem. In lines 13–28, he explains how he plans to address the problem. Although energy independence was cited as a goal, it was not a reason for his speech, so choice A is incorrect. This passage has a very specific and important purpose: addressing the energy crisis; choice B incorrectly concludes that merely engaging with the public was its main purpose. Carter does mention at the end of his speech how he understands the limitations of the office, but that idea is not the reason for addressing the public, so choice D is incorrect.

13. **The correct answer is A.** The overriding idea that Carter emphasizes is that the energy problem is not new; it is complex; it will take a long time to fix it (lines 6–9); and many people, the public included, will have to work together to change it (lines 45–47). There are many ways to conserve energy (choice B), but this is not the specific focus of the passage. Carter's urging people to use less energy in their homes (choice C) is a detail. Carter never claims that government cannot solve environmental problems (choice D).

14. **The correct answer is C.** Developing coal reserves is an example of how the United States could decrease its dependence on foreign sources of energy (lines 16–17). Carter proposes that people lower their thermostats in lines 41–44 (choice A) but that is not a government action. He also proposes consolidating different agencies to form a new cabinet-level department (lines 24–26), but that is not an action that would solve the energy problem, so choice B is incorrect. Protection from oil spills (choice D) would help mitigate pollution and stop the waste of energy, but it is not mentioned as a way to solve the problem.

15. **The correct answer is B.** Throughout his speech, Carter references the public and its role in addressing the problem. He emphasizes that the problem affects everyone and that everyone needs to participate to help solve it. He says that the sacrifices needed to be made by the public should be "borne fairly among all our people" (lines 48–49). Choice A is true, but it is not a belief system. Choice D is referenced when he explains the limitations of presidential power, but that is not a belief system; it is a part of the Constitution.

16. **The correct answer is D.** Carter explains how he believes that if everyone cooperates and contributes to conservation, the problem will get solved more easily and quickly (lines 47–49). Although he mentions all of the other choices as actions that can be taken, his main thrust is to appeal to people acting together as a nation to be more energy efficient.

17. **The correct answer is B.** By detailing the amount of waste (lines 13–16), Carter shows people that it won't be all that difficult to conserve energy; simple, small changes can make a difference if enough people participate. Choices A and C are ideas that he mentions, but they are not statements that support his argument that people can make a difference by conserving the energy they now waste. People generally are not willing to make sacrifices for the sake of making sacrifices; they need a reason to convince them to make such sacrifices, so choice D is not the best answer.

18. **The correct answer is C.** In line 41, President Carter makes a very simple and direct statement about how everyone must participate in energy conservation to solve the crisis, so choice C is the best answer. Choice A (lines 34–35) seems to have mistaken choice A for the correct answer to the previous question since it mentions utility companies. Carter is not yet talking about what the citizens he is addressing need to do in lines 37–38, so choice B is not the best answer. Choice D (lines 41–43) describes one thing people can do to conserve energy; it is not a plea for them to conserve.

19. **The correct answer is A.** Because Carter is addressing the public, he makes suggestions that people can easily do and tries to encourage conservation. He speaks directly and plainly to the people in an effort to get them on board. The fact that he is on television (choice B) is irrelevant. The speech is not authoritarian (choice C)—it is the opposite: an effort to enlist the citizenry in solving a national problem. Because he recognizes the depth of the problem and needs to persuade the citizenry about participating, his tone is not merely informational, so choice D is incorrect.

20. **The correct answer is A.** In lines 45–48, Carter speaks bluntly about the energy crisis in a way that shows how the public needs to be involved in solving it ("There is no way that I, or anyone else in the Government, can solve our energy problems if you are not willing to help."). However, he also shows his optimism by stating, "I know that we can meet this energy challenge . . ." Therefore, choice A is the best answer. Choice B (lines 52–53) is optimistic, but it fails to capture the blunt and persuasive tone of the rest of the passage. Choice C (lines 55–56) is matter of fact about the Carter administration's plans; it is not blunt, persuasive, or optimistic. Choice D (lines 59–60) merely introduces a new topic, and does not serve as evidence of the passage's overall tone.

21. **The correct answer is A.** In the context of lines 1–3, *depleted* means "consumed" or used up. Carter is speaking about the overall supplies, not individual waste. The supplies were used during the cold winter months. The energy sources were not "weakened," (choice C) or "wasted" (choice D) or "replaced" (choice B).

22. The correct answer is C. In both of these sentences, the word *reserves* refers to something that is saved for future use. In the first use ("We will also stress development of our rich coal reserves in an environmentally sound way…"), the reserves are lands that contain coal that has not yet been mined; they are reserved for future use. In the second use ("Oil and natural gas companies must be honest with all of us about their reserves and profits."), the reserves are oil and gas supplies that are set aside in order to raise prices.

23. The correct answer is B. The attention to detail is designed to show how ridiculous Golightly looked (lines 18–20). The descriptions show the character to be helpless in the face of a normal event—a rainstorm (lines 28–30). Contrasted with his vanity, the picture Kipling paints is mocking (choice B). Disgust, irony, and pride are not shown, so choices A, C, and D are incorrect.

24. The correct answer is B. Lines 6–7 offer Golightly's ability to recognize a horse as one of his virtues; since this is something almost anyone can do, it is hardly a virtue of any significance and can be interpreted as an instance of the author mocking Golightly. Choice A (lines 1–3) makes a statement about Golightly's desires, but those desires are not ridiculous enough to reveal the passage's overall mocking tone. Choice C (lines 7–8) reveals that Golightly had some abilities when it came to playing games, and does not mock him for those abilities. Choice D (line 9) seems to express genuine sympathy for Golightly, so it is hardly mocking.

25. The correct answer is A. In the passage, Kipling states that Golightly's focus on his appearance led him to not take enough money with him (lines 22–25). This results in him negotiating with the Station Master for a first-class ticket and his subsequent arrest. His pride, lack of an umbrella, and fall from his horse may have been contributing factors to his arrest, but none is the best answer: It was not pride alone that led to the arrest; even with an umbrella, Golightly would still have had no money for a ticket; and Golightly was not responsible for the fall, as it was an accident.

26. The correct answer is A. Golightly is described as an officer (lines 1–3). We are told he was taking a leave of his post, which would indicate a military post (lines 12–13). There is no indication that he was trying to escape capture by the Indian government, so choice B is incorrect. Golightly was not an outlaw, so choice C is incorrect, nor was he a businessman on an overseas trip (choice D).

27. The correct answer is A. The previous correct answer classifies Golightly as a proper military man leaving his post. In lines 9–10, "nobody ever dreamed of seeing him handcuffed" because he was so proper, and the description of him as a "deserter" shows that he left his post, because that is the crime of which deserters are guilty. Choice B merely shows the direction in which Golightly was heading when things went wrong for him. Choice C helps to establish setting; it says nothing about Golightly, himself. Choice D describes what Golightly was wearing; it does not say what he does.

28. The correct answer is C. Kipling piles on the missteps Golightly makes, each one adding to the other, making Golightly look silly and inept throughout the passage. For a person whose title is "officer," Golightly does not show professionalism or skill at handling a relatively minor problem. The rainstorm (choice B) is a backdrop for the setting in which he falters and is not in itself a way to make fun of the character. There is no satire shown, so choice A is incorrect. Golightly's trouble with the horse (choice D) went beyond "difficulty."

29. The correct answer is A. It is the detail of the descriptions that give the story its mocking tone and attitude. Kipling sets up the character by describing his intense vanity, which contrasts with the way he looks when caught in the rainstorm (lines 44–66). The details are not relevant to any of the other choices.

30. The correct answer is B. Throughout the excerpt, Kipling uses an omniscient narrator to tell the story. But in this line, the narrator editorializes and injects his own opinion. Instead of describing the character's response, the narrator judges it and then continues to describe Golightly's behavior. The narrator does not report the character's verbal response or add dialogue.

31. The correct answer is B. Lines 13–14 present an idiomatic way of saying that Golightly was pushing the envelope to the greatest extent possible without ruffling feathers in the line of command. His capture by the authorities was a result of misidentification because he was so unrecognizable from being out in the rainstorm and falling off the horse. He was doing what was expected, so there was nothing to get caught doing (choice D), except that he looked suspicious to others in his disheveled state. Choice A is contrary to the meaning of the text; he had told his superiors. The sentence is about how much leave he could take, not about leaving without permission.

32. **The correct answer is B.** Lines 31–32 explain that the pony was walking through mud, which would logically slow down its pace, so choice B is the best answer and choice A can be eliminated. A mire is a muddy pool, but it makes no sense to say that a pony "pooled," so choice C can be eliminated. Indicating that the pony started eating at this point in line 32 would not flow naturally from the previous statement about how the path had turned into mud, so choice D is not the best answer.

33. **The correct answer is C.** The content of the speech shows Stanton's concern about how women were treated unfairly, with few rights. Although some people at the time may have been shocked by her speech, her purpose was not shock value (choice B), but to inform and persuade. Although she was sympathetic to the plight of minorities/African Americans, this speech was focused on women's issues, so choice D is incorrect.

34. **The correct answer is B.** Stanton repeats the phrase "He has" to list each of the transgressions of men against women's rights. The repetition emphasizes and magnifies these transgressions and makes the point that they can't be ignored. Stanton did feel strongly (choice A), but the use of repetition does not indicate strength of feeling, it shows strength of her argument. Although Stanton did use the Declaration of Independence as a model (choice D), the repetition is not part of that model.

35. **The correct answer is A.** Stanton uses anaphora through repetition of the phrase "He has" throughout the passage (lines 6, 8, 10, etc.). Truth does not employ this technique. Both authors use third-person voice, so choice B is incorrect. Only Truth uses italics for emphasis, such as "how *could* we bear it?" (line 77), so choice C is incorrect. Neither author uses metaphor, so choice D is incorrect.

36. **The correct answer is D.** In lines 24–28, Stanton shows how women have been enslaved by the legal system and by men, who are considered superior. Some women did have jobs outside the home, as is implied by lines 19–20 (choice A), but Stanton explains that they were not allowed to keep their wages. Women were not allowed to vote, and Stanton includes this in her list of grievances, but voting rights is not directly related to obedience. Choice C is implied by lines 29–32, but this issue is not directly related to obedience.

37. **The correct answer is D.** *Franchise* is another word for the right to vote. By pairing the word with *elective* in line 14, the focus is on the right to vote in elections. Stanton emphasizes how women are deprived of this basic right. A more modern meaning of franchise is in sports, indicating a team that is a member of a larger group or league. At the time of the speech, there were no such sports leagues, and the word was commonly used to refer to the right to vote.

38. **The correct answer is C.** The commonality is in the necessity for obedience. For women, obedience to their husbands was the rule of law (lines 24–66); for slaves, it was a given that they had to obey their masters. In some cases, women did get paid for their work (choice A), and women, whether or not they were slaves, were generally in charge of children, whether their own or others' (choice B). While some men may break promises, only the Sojourner text discusses how her master continually broke his promises to her, so choice D is incorrect.

39. **The correct answer is D.** Stanton's list of grievances shows her frustration and resulting anger at the system that has denied women basic rights. Truth's narrative expresses her feelings of frustration at being promised her freedom only to have it denied. Truth doesn't show anger (choice A), sadness (choice B), or bitterness (choice C). She shows resolve and determination to get her freedom.

40. **The correct answer is C.** He was willing to give her freedom before he had to, and the introduction tells us that she was granted her freedom in 1827, before it was legally mandated. Forcing her to work longer than he had originally said was a form of mistreatment, making choice A incorrect. He did not allow her to learn to read and write, which was why her narrative is told through someone else's voice (choice B). Although he did make promises that he didn't keep (choice D), Truth suggests that all slaveholders used this tactic to get more work out of their slaves.

41. **The correct answer is A.** Lines 45–47 convey the relative good treatment of Isabella's master as he set her free before she was legally required to go free. Choice B (lines 47–49) makes a statement about Isabella's physical condition; it does not reveal anything about her master, so it cannot serve as evidence to support the previous correct answer. Choice C (lines 50–51) simply says that Isabella's master honored a promise he made to her, but one can make a promise to mistreat someone else, so this is not the best piece of evidence to support the previous correct answer. Choice D (lines 53–55) makes a statement about the work Isabella did, and if anything, it shows that her master was inconsiderate by making her do work "she was not wholly able to do."

42. **The correct answer is B.** Although Truth had great religious faith, the faithfulness referred to here is not about religion (choices A and C); it is about loyalty (choice B). Truth reminisces here about her service to her master. He had asked that she be a faithful servant (lines 45–46), which she was, but then she recognizes that, ironically, this is exactly why she has become so valuable to her master (lines 56–59).

43. **The correct answer is D.** The overall main idea encompasses the discovery and its meaning (a new species). Choices A and B are details that support the main idea. Choice C is a general statement that could be a conclusion, but it is not the main idea.

44. **The correct answer is C.** The article describes how the discovery was made by a student and other researchers (lines 7–12). The discovery was important because it identified a new species (lines 12–14) and will help scientists and researchers continue to add to our body of knowledge about prehistoric mammals. The discovery wasn't totally by chance because Jasinski was conducting related research (choice D). Choices A and B are general statements that could have general application, but they are not conclusions based on facts in the article.

45. **The correct answer is A.** Lines 65–66 explicitly state how its sense of smell made the *S. sullivani* an effective predator as it used "its acute sense of smell to track down prey." Choices B, C, and D could all be correct in another context, but this question specifies that the answer must be determined "according to the passage," which does not provide evidence for any answer except for choice A.

46. **The correct answer is D.** The meaning of the genus name *Saurornitholestes* provides clues about the dinosaur's appearance (lines 15–21). None of the Latin names indicates where the fossils were found (choice B) or where the dinosaurs lived (choice C). The discovered species was named after a human, as are others on occasion, but the name does not reveal anything about the dinosaur.

47. **The correct answer is B.** The first part of the dinosaur's name, *Saurornitholestes*, means "lizard bird thief" (line 17), and lines 19–21 reveal that it had physical characteristics similar to those of birds (it was "lightly built with long legs") and lizards (it had "jaws lined with teeth"). Choice A merely states the Latin name without explaining what it means, so unless the reader speaks Latin, there is little way to use this information to learn anything about how the dinosaur looked. The fact that Robert Sullivan discovered the dinosaur explains why the second part of its name is *sullivani*, but it says nothing about how the dinosaur looked. Choice D merely mentions a mistake in classifying the dinosaur; it provides no clue to what its name says about its appearance.

48. **The correct answer is D.** Lines 61–62 and lines 67–68 state the *S. sullivani* was not a large dinosaur. Therefore, it did not have size on its side. It did have a superior sense of smell, though, as stated in lines 65–66, so choice A is incorrect. Lines 18–21 indicates that its jaws were lined with teeth, which would be an advantage, making choice C incorrect. Lines 63–66 state that the dinosaur was "agile and fast" which would help it "track down prey," making choice B incorrect.

49. **The correct answer is B.** The passage explains the process by which Jasinski noticed that the species he was examining differed from the description of what was expected (lines 30–34). He didn't recognize this because of either the size of the fossil (choice A) or its markings (choice D). Scientists did not know what its closest relatives were because they had not yet realized that it was a different species, so choice C is incorrect.

50. **The correct answer is B.** The author states that Jasinski realized that the fossil actually had "subtle differences" (line 32) from the one to which he compared it and was, therefore, a different species. Choice A merely introduces Jasinski; it says nothing about how he figured out he had found a new species. Choice C explains one of the things Jasinski discovered about the dinosaur; it does not suggest that the dinosaur's sense of smell is how he knew he was dealing with a new species. Choice D only explains when the dinosaur lived.

51. The correct answer is C. *Formidable* can mean "impressive" in the sense of its size or power, and in this context, the predator—the newly discovered species—would have been threatening to other species. The predator might have even been frightened at times, but this is not a defining characteristic of predators, which are generally thought to inspire fear more than feel it, so choice A is not the best answer. Choice B would be an odd description of the effectiveness of a predator, so it is not a very good answer either. While "difficult" can be used as a synonym for *formidable*, it would be better used to describe an opponent in a contest, not a predator that presents more of a danger than a challenge, so choice D is not the best answer choice.

52. The correct answer is B. Lines 34–35 provide context clues that the olfactory bulb is related to the sense of smell. The organs that are used for smell are contained in that part of the skull, which was unusually large, but the clue is in the next sentence that defines "olfactory." These clues eliminate choices A, C, and D, which are not supported by the passage. Choice A would create a redundancy, translating "olfactory bulb" as "bulb bulb."

Section 2: Writing and Language Test

1. D	**10.** B	**19.** A	**28.** C	**37.** B
2. B	**11.** B	**20.** D	**29.** C	**38.** B
3. B	**12.** A	**21.** C	**30.** D	**39.** D
4. D	**13.** B	**22.** A	**31.** C	**40.** A
5. C	**14.** A	**23.** B	**32.** C	**41.** A
6. A	**15.** B	**24.** A	**33.** B	**42.** B
7. B	**16.** C	**25.** B	**34.** A	**43.** C
8. A	**17.** D	**26.** A	**35.** D	**44.** D
9. D	**18.** A	**27.** A	**36.** B	

WRITING AND LANGUAGE TEST RAW SCORE
(Number of correct answers)

1. **The correct answer is D.** The underlined sentence should be deleted because other phrases from the 1980s are not related to the Glass Ceiling. Choices A and B are incorrect because the sentence should not be kept. It does not support the main topic nor does it act as a transition. Choice C is incorrect because it is not information that has already been provided.

2. **The correct answer is B.** The proper end punctuation for this sentence is a period. Any other punctuation will be grammatically incorrect or inappropriately change the tone or intent of the sentence. Thus, choice B is the correct answer. Choice A is incorrect because ending the sentence with an exclamation point injects emotion that is missing from the rest of the passage. It is like shouting at the reader. Choice C is incorrect because this sentence is not a question. Choice D is incorrect because ending the sentence with an ellipsis suggests the thought isn't finished, which is not the case.

3. **The correct answer is B.** As written, the text has a syntax error. The intention of the writer is to say that the number of women in CEO positions in Fortune 500 companies is just 5% of the total. To convey this, the modifier *only* has to be placed correctly in the sentence—before 5%. Choice B does this, so that's the correct answer. Choices A and C are incorrect because they say women hold 5% of CEO positions (but may or may not hold that percentage of any other positions), and they take the emphasis off the low figure of 5% and place it on CEO positions; this is not what the writer means to say. Choice D is incorrect

because it says women hold 5% of CEO positions in Fortune 500 companies (but may or may not hold that percentage in other kinds of companies), and it takes the emphasis off the low figure of 5% and places it on Fortune 500 companies; this is not what the writer means to say.

4. **The correct answer is D.** This sentence requires a word that means "having existed or taken place in a period before the present," which is what *past* means. Therefore, choice D is the correct answer. Choice A is incorrect because *passed* is the past tense of *pass*. (*Past* and *passed* are commonly confused words.) Choice B is incorrect because *passing* doesn't have the right meaning for this sentence. While it refers to time going by, it changes the sense of the sentence by referring to passing years rather than events that have taken place. Choice C is incorrect because the word *passive* doesn't make sense in this sentence.

5. **The correct answer is C.** The only internal punctuation this sentence requires is a comma after the introductory phrase "In 1995," making choice C the correct answer. Choice A is incorrect because it includes a semicolon after *formed*, which makes the rest of the sentence a fragment. Choice B is incorrect because, while it removes the incorrect semicolon, it introduces a new error by including a second comma after *Commission*. Choice D is not correct because, while it removes the incorrect semicolon, it introduces two new errors by removing the comma after 1995 and by placing a semicolon after *discrimination*, which creates a sentence fragment.

6. **The correct answer is A.** This sentence requires a word that means "result," or "something caused by something else," which is the meaning of *effect*—a noun that means "the result of something." Therefore, choice A is the correct answer. Choice B is incorrect because *affect* is the wrong word for this sentence. It is a verb that means "to bring about a result." (*Effect* and *affect* are commonly confused words. One way to know the difference between them is to remember that after you *affect* something, there is an *effect*.) Choice C is incorrect because the word *effective* doesn't make sense in this sentence. Choice D is incorrect because the word *affection* doesn't make sense in this sentence.

7. **The correct answer is B.** The sentence uses the plural pronoun form *they* earlier in the sentence, which provides a clue that another plural pronoun is needed here to replace the plural noun *corporations*. Therefore, choice B is correct. The pronouns among the other answer choices are singular, and are incorrect.

8. **The correct answer is A.** The corporations have the financial and educational resources to overcome this "supply barrier"; therefore, they are "equipped" with them. *Implemented* (choice B) is incorrect because the corporations are not implementing the resources; this word choice is therefore contradictory to the point of the passage. Both *furnished* (choice C) and *supplied* (choice D) imply someone or something had given the corporations these resources, which is not supported in the passage. The source of the resources is never mentioned. The point of the sentence is simply that the corporations are equipped with the necessary resources to solve this issue, they just are not using them. Therefore, choice A is best.

9. **The correct answer is D.** The original punctuation creates a sentence fragment. Combining the text eliminates the fragment, so choice D is the correct answer. Choice A is incorrect because the period after *do* creates a sentence fragment. Choice B is incorrect because, while it eliminates the incorrect period, it introduces a new error by replacing the period with a semicolon to separate the two dependent clauses. Choice C is not correct because, although it removes the incorrect period, it introduces a new error by including the conjunction *and*. With this addition, the sentence no longer makes sense.

10. **The correct answer is B.** This paragraph discusses some of the obstacles and challenges that persist regarding gender discrimination and bias that have proven difficult to overcome. A good opening sentence would support this notion, which choice B does. Choices A and C provide direct opposition to this point of view, and are incorrect. Choice D is out of context and unsupported by this paragraph and passage. Therefore, it is incorrect.

11. **The correct answer is B.** The writer is saying that women must be accepted "as equals" in the corporate sphere. Only choice B places this modifier after *accepted*, the correct position in the sentence. Therefore, choice B is the correct answer. Choice A is incorrect because the modifying phrase "as equals" is not placed in the right part of the sentence, creating a syntax error. Choice C is incorrect because, while it repositions the modifying phrase, it introduces a new error by using the adverb form of *equally*. Choice D is incorrect because, while it repositions the modifying phrase (which could be correct in this part of the sentence), it, too, uses the adverb form of *equally*.

12. **The correct answer is A.** The sentence as is introduces details that describe the entire collection. Choice B adds information not supported by the passage. Choice C implies the examples are not inclusive. Choice D is incorrect because *Already* has no meaning in the context of the sentence.

13. **The correct answer is B.** Semicolons are needed when items in a series already contain commas. Choice B correctly shows the proper separation of items in a series with semicolons and commas. Choice A incorrectly places commas after *extend* and *executive*. Choice C incorrectly places a comma after *branches* and incorrectly eliminates the comma after *world*. Choice D incorrectly places a comma after *services* and incorrectly eliminates the comma after *government*.

14. **The correct answer is A.** The author is introducing a new topic (going from an overview of the modern Library of Congress to its beginnings), and pointing out that the Library did not start out as large as it is today. The sentence in the original text is the best transition phrase for cohesion, so choice A is the correct answer. Choice B might sound correct, but it changes the tone of the passage from formal to informal, so it is not the best answer. Choice C is incorrect because it changes the sense and meaning of the text and creates a sentence that does not support the main idea of the paragraph. Choice D might appear to be correct, but like choice B, it changes the tone of the passage from formal to informal, so it is not the best answer.

15. **The correct answer is B.** After the original Library of Congress was destroyed, the nation needed a new, similar institution. In other words, the library had to be replaced. Therefore, choice B is the correct answer. Choice A is incorrect because while it suggests a new library, it also suggests the continued presence of the original library, which was not the case. Choice B is the better answer because it is a more precise word in this context. Choice C also indicates a new library, but like choice A, it suggests the continued presence of the original library. Choice D is not correct because the new library was a replacement as opposed to a copy of the old library.

16. **The correct answer is C.** *Its* is a possessive determiner and does not require an apostrophe. Thus, choice C is the correct answer. Choice A is incorrect because *it's* is a contraction of "it is." Choice B is incorrect because it makes no sense. Choice D is incorrect because *its'* is not a word.

17. **The correct answer is D.** This text requires seven commas, and only choice D has all the necessary commas in the right places. Choice A incorrectly places commas after *two* and *dramatic*. Choice B incorrectly leaves out a comma after *composition* and incorrectly places a comma after *photograph*. Choice C incorrectly places a comma after *two* and a semicolon after *composition*.

18. **The correct answer is A.** The library's collection keeps growing—it is ever-expanding. Thus, choice A is the correct answer. Choice B is incorrect because it changes the meaning of the sentence to say that the library's collection always exists. This is not what the author means. Choice C is incorrect because it makes no sense. Choice D is incorrect because it also makes no sense.

19. **The correct answer is A.** Choice A best expresses the idea that Young instigated the change. Choice B is incorrect because it implies that there was opposition to the change. Choice C implies that it had to be an acquisitions library first before making the change. Choice D is incorrect because the introductory phrase implies that there was an addition to the operation rather than a replacement of one system for another.

20. **The correct answer is D.** In this paragraph the author is shifting from John Russell Young to Herbert Putnam. Choice D adds the phrase "after only two years," a detail with additional information that gives the reader a fuller sense of this story and creates a smoother transition. Therefore, choice D is the correct answer. Choices A, B, and C make the shift from Young to Putnam, but none of them has the additional information or makes as smooth a transition as choice D, so none of them is the best answer.

21. **The correct answer is C.** This paragraph is mainly about Herbert Putnam, and Putnam (in the previous sentence) is the antecedent of the pronoun that starts this sentence. Putnam is one person, so the singular pronoun *he* is required. Therefore, choice C is the correct answer. Choice A is incorrect because if *they* is used, the meaning of the sentence changes—it means Spofford, Young, and Putnam "took the Library of Congress directly into the national library scene." Choice B is incorrect because *them* is the objective case, and this sentence requires a pronoun in the subjective case. Choice D is incorrect because the antecedent of the pronoun that starts this sentence is *Putnam*, so a singular pronoun is required.

22. **The correct answer is A.** The last column of the chart shows information for the largest libraries (the category of the Library of Congress). According to the chart, there are 109 of these in the private sector and 51 in the private sector. So there are more public than private libraries similar in scope and scale to the Library of Congress, making choice A correct. Choices B, C, and D are incorrect because the chart does not support these conclusions.

23. **The correct answer is B.** As written, this sentence contains a redundancy—empty and contained nothing mean the same thing. Choice B eliminates this redundancy. Choice C is not the best answer because, while it eliminates the redundancy, it changes the sense and intent of the sentence, taking away the weight and urgency of the bedroom being "forever empty." Choice D is incorrect because, although it eliminates the original redundancy, it adds a new one: verses and poetry are the same thing.

24. **The correct answer is A.** Emily Dickinson had a seeming obsession with death, which was a common theme in many of her poems. *Predisposition* (choice B) is a tendency to act or think in a particular way, *predilection* (choice C) is a preference for something, and *predetermination* (choice D) is the doctrine (usually associated with Calvinism) that God has foreordained every event throughout eternity. None of these words express Dickinson's attitude toward death.

25. **The correct answer is B.** Emily is the sister in question, so this sentence calls for a singular possessive pronoun. Choice B is the possessive pronoun for *sister*, so it is the correct answer. Choice A is incorrect because it is the plural of *sister*, not the possessive pronoun for the word. Choice C is incorrect because it is a plural possessive pronoun (for *sisters*), not a singular possessive pronoun (for *sister*). Choice D is incorrect because it is not a possessive pronoun.

26. **The correct answer is A.** The paragraph is mainly about Emily's isolation and the reason for it. In Emily's own words, she was "one 'standing alone in rebellion' of faith" as she resisted ideas common to her time. Only choice A refers to this, which makes it the correct answer. Choice B might seem like a good answer, but Emily's refusal to take part in social events stemmed from her sense of isolation rather than acting as the cause of it. The passage does not say she became isolated after refusing to participate in social events; it implies her refusal to be social was a decision she made because she felt so isolated. Choices C and D are incorrect because they are not supported by the passage. The author does not say either of these reasons caused Emily's sense of isolation.

27. **The correct answer is A.** Choice A is the only choice that supplies the correct word *through* for this sentence. Choices B, C, and D are all incorrect because none of these words makes sense in the sentence.

28. **The correct answer is C.** The writer should not add the sentence because it detracts from the point about women's issues. The added sentence focuses on the idea of Emily being involved in politics, which is not the point Lavinia is making. Choices A and B are incorrect because the information is not directly related to the point being made by Lavinia. Choice D is incorrect because, although the statement is about Emily's life, it is misplaced in the midst of Lavinia's thoughts about how Emily viewed the limitations society imposed on women.

29. **The correct answer is C.** Because it is clear that it was Emily who felt "the trappings of being a woman," the required word is the singular subjective pronoun *she*. Thus, choice C is the correct answer. Choice A is incorrect because *they* is plural. If *they* is used, the sentence appears to be saying that both Emily and Lavinia "tried to eschew" the trappings of being a woman, which is not supported by the passage; in addition, the rest of the sentence will make no sense because *her* is used toward the end of the sentence. Choice B is incorrect because there is no antecedent for *we*. Choice D is incorrect because the sentence calls for a subjective pronoun; *her* is a possessive or an objective pronoun.

30. **The correct answer is D.** The passage is written in a formal style and has a literary tone. Instead of saying Emily did not accept the role of women, the author writes she "eschewed" "the trappings of being a woman." Only choice D matches this style and tone, so it is the correct answer. Choices A, B, and C are incorrect because while each conveys this same thought, the uninspired word choice in each answer does not match the style or tone of the passage. Choice C is also unnecessarily wordy.

31. **The correct answer is C.** The proper end punctuation for this sentence is a period. Most other punctuation will be grammatically incorrect or inappropriately change the tone or intent of the sentence. Thus, choice C is the correct answer. Choice A is incorrect because this sentence is not a question. Choice B is incorrect because ending the sentence with an exclamation point injects emotion that is missing from the rest of the passage and is inappropriate here. Choice D is not correct because it is incorrect to end a sentence with a semicolon.

Answer Keys and Explanations

32. The correct answer is C. The correct form of the verb "to decide" is the past tense *decided*—the preceding word *was* provides a helpful context clue to make this determination. Choices A and D feature incorrect verb tenses for this sentence. Choice B is a noun, and is not appropriate given the context of this sentence.

33. The correct answer is B. This passage chronicles the early years of the famous writer Emily Dickinson, whom the world would eventually get to know and cherish, and the preceding sentence provides an important context clue to answer this question: "…it was time the world knew the full treasure her sister was." Choice B makes the best sense to follow and build upon this notion and is the correct answer. Choices A, C, and D are incorrect and don't make sense given the context of the passage.

34. The correct answer is A. The point of this opening paragraph is to establish the fact that even though scientists have long known that sleep is important to human health, they continue to study sleep. The "even though" part of this idea is conveyed by the word *yet*, which must be placed in the right part of the sentence if the sentence is to make sense. Only choice A does this, making it the correct answer. Choices B and C are incorrect because they change the meaning of the sentence by eliminating the "even though" element that the writer wants to convey, and they demonstrate clumsy syntax. Choice D is incorrect because while it places *yet* correctly in the sentence, the rest of this answer demonstrates clumsy syntax.

35. The correct answer is D. This passage is mainly concerned with past theories about sleep. The fourth paragraph addresses sleep study in the twentieth century. Sentence 6 (choice D) refers to advances in the study of sleep that were made during the twentieth century, so the passage would have a more logical sequence if this sentence were moved to the fourth paragraph. Thus, choice D is the correct answer. Choices A and B are incorrect because the first two sentences serve as transitions to the topic of past theories about sleep and should remain in this paragraph. Sentence 4 (choice C) is incorrect because it describes one of these past theories about sleep. Therefore, it, too, should remain in this paragraph.

36. The correct answer is B. The sentence in choice B leads to the introduction of the theories that follow. Choice A is incorrect because it is irrelevant to this part of the passage. Choices C and D are incorrect because the text does not imply either statement.

37. The correct answer is B. This sentence tells the reader that modern sleep research began with a machine. Machines are created, or invented, and only choice B conveys this idea. Choices A, C, and D are incorrect because each conveys a different idea. A machine isn't discovered (choice A), though a new use for a machine may be discovered. The passage makes it clear that sleep study went beyond the idea (choice C) or suggestion (choice D) of a machine.

38. The correct answer is B. The second part of the sentence is a subordinate clause, and a subordinating conjunction is necessary to establish the clause's connection to the beginning of the sentence: The study of sleep was enhanced *as a result of* Aserinsky and Kleitman's work. Choice B is the only answer with a subordinating conjunction. Choices A, C, and D are not correct because they are all coordinating conjunctions that, if used, change the meaning of the sentence. Choice A makes the enhancement of sleep study and Aserinsky and Kleitman's work separate and equal things rather than one being the result of the other. Choice C creates a sentence that does not make sense. Choice D changes the cause and effect: it means that Aserinsky and Kleitman did their work *because* the study of sleep was enhanced.

39. The correct answer is D. The link between the ideas in this sentence and the previous sentence is contradiction. Subjects awakened during REM sleep almost always remembered dreaming; *but* subjects awakened during non-REM sleep could rarely recall dreams. To convey this idea, a contradictory transition word or phrase is required. Only choice D provides the right phrase. Choices A and B are incorrect because, while these phrases can indicate contradiction, in this case each creates a sentence that does not make sense. Choice C is incorrect because the passage does not say any predictions were made about what would happen during this study.

40. The correct answer is A. The underlined phrase leads directly to the idea presented in the second part of the sentence. Choice B is incorrect because this part of the passage links to REMs; it is not regardless of them. Choice C is incorrect because it contains an erroneous implication. Choice D is incorrect because the adverb used implies that there is contradictory text preceding it, which there is not.

41. **The correct answer is A.** *Awaken* is more concise and active than the phrase "wake up"; therefore, B is not the best choice. In order to "collect dream stories" (the purpose stated in the second half of the sentence), it is necessary for the dreamer to wake up and share his or her stories verbally. Stories cannot be told simply by viewing or studying a sleeping person, so C and D are incorrect.

42. **The correct answer is B.** The intent of this sentence is to talk about changing dreamers' experiences. Only choice B is the correct word to communicate this (*alter* means "to change"). Choice A is incorrect because the definition of *altar* is "a usually raised structure or place on which sacrifices are offered or incense is burned in worship." (*Alter* and *altar* are frequently confused words.) Choice C is incorrect because it creates a sentence that means scientists could switch dreamers' various experiences for one another. Choice D is incorrect because it creates a sentence that does not make sense. (*Alternate* and *alternative* are frequently confused words.)

43. **The correct answer is C.** The subject and verb in a sentence must agree in number. The subject of this sentence (*researchers*) is plural, so a plural verb in the right tense is required. Only choice C reflects agreement between the subject and verb, as well as appropriate verb tense. Choice A is incorrect because the subject of the sentence (*researchers*) is plural, and "has been drawn" is singular. Choice B is plural but there is no such verb as "were been drawn." Choice D is incorrect because "was drawn" is singular.

44. **The correct answer is D.** The original punctuation creates a sentence fragment. Combining the text in a grammatically correct way eliminates the fragment, and only choice D does this. Choice A is incorrect because the period after *sleep* creates the sentence fragment. Choice B is incorrect because, while it eliminates the incorrect period after *sleep*, replacing the period with a dash creates a sentence that does not make sense. Choice C is not correct because, although it removes the incorrect period, it introduces a different error by replacing it with a semicolon. Semicolons are used with complete thoughts. The first part of this sentence is not a complete thought, so choice C does not correct the original fragment.

Section 3: Math Test—No Calculator

1. A	**5.** D	**9.** A	**13.** B	**17.** 6
2. A	**6.** C	**10.** B	**14.** B	**18.** 3
3. B	**7.** D	**11.** B	**15.** B	**19.** 1
4. C	**8.** D	**12.** B	**16.** 50	**20.** 224

MATH TEST—NO CALCULATOR RAW SCORE
(Number of correct answers)

1. **The correct answer is A.** Substitute the value for m and solve for x:

$$\frac{x+2}{5} = m$$
$$\frac{x+2}{5} = -3$$
$$x+2 = -15$$
$$x = -17$$

2. **The correct answer is A.** If h is any positive quantity, then letting $d_h = (m+h) - \frac{50}{m+h}$, we can see that dh is greater than d, since h is greater than zero, and $\frac{50}{m}$ is greater than $\frac{50}{m+h}$. Therefore, d increases as m does.

3. **The correct answer is B.** The volume of a cube is $V = s^3$. A side of this cube is $\sqrt[3]{64}$ in. Since there are 12 edges to a cube, the amount of wire needed is 12×4 in., or 48 inches.

4. **The correct answer is C.** The total number of cookies is equal to the sum of the cookies that Myra baked plus the cookies Neil baked. Myra baked 6 sheets of r cookies, or $6r$ cookies, and Neil baked 7 sheets of p cookies, or $7p$ cookies. The total number of cookies must be $6r + 7p$.

5. **The correct answer is D.** Substitute $a + 3$ for b, and $-a^2 + 3a + 10$ for c, into the expression $b^2 - 2c$ and combine terms.

$$(a+3)^3 - 2(-a^2 + 3a + 10)$$
$$= a^2 + 6a + 9 + 2a^2 - 6a - 20$$
$$= a^2 + 2a^2 + 6a - 6a + 9 - 20$$
$$= 3a^2 - 11$$

6. **The correct answer is C.**

$$y = \frac{(x-3)^3}{4}$$
$$4y = (x-3)^3$$
$$\sqrt[3]{4y} = x - 3$$
$$\sqrt[3]{4y} + 3 = x$$

7. **The correct answer is D.** The plant grows 4.5 centimeters a week, and that is represented by the $4.5w$ in the equation. Since the 6 is a constant in the equation, this represents the initial height of the plant. Therefore, the plant must have been 6 centimeters tall when Hannah bought it.

8. **The correct answer is D.**

$$x^6 + (2x^2)^3 + (3x^3)^2 = x^6 + 8x^6 + 9x^6 = 18x^6$$

9. **The correct answer is A.** The graph shows that the y-intercept is approximately at the point (0, 55). The equation that shows a y-intercept of 55 is in choice A. To further verify, substitute points in for the number of days to find the corresponding number of trout. For example, substitute 10 in for x: $y = 12(10) + 55 = 120 + 55 = 175$. The point (10,175) is on the graph.

10. **The correct answer is B.**

$$\left(-\frac{27}{8}\right)^{-\frac{1}{3}} = \left(-\frac{8}{27}\right)^{\frac{1}{3}} = -\frac{2}{3}$$

1. B	**9.** D	**17.** D	**25.** D	**33.** 50
2. D	**10.** D	**18.** C	**26.** D	**34.** 20
3. D	**11.** D	**19.** A	**27.** B	**35.** 22
4. C	**12.** A	**20.** C	**28.** C	**36.** 1/4 or .025
5. D	**13.** D	**21.** A	**29.** C	
6. A	**14.** B	**22.** C	**30.** C	**37.** 8
7. C	**15.** B	**23.** B	**31.** 1.84	**38.** 11
8. C	**16.** C	**24.** A	**32.** 36/5 or 7.2	

MATH TEST—CALCULATOR RAW SCORE
(Number of correct answers)

1. **The correct answer is B.** If $9x + 5 = 23$, $9x = 18$, and $x = 2$. Thus, $18x + 5 = 36 + 5 = 41$.

2. **The correct answer is D.** There can be at most 15 radiators, so $x + y \leq 15$. Each small radiator weighs 150 pounds, so the combined weight of all the small radiators is represented by $150x$. Each large radiator weighs 250 pounds, represented by $250y$. The maximum load can be equal to but not exceed 1,500 pounds: $150x + 250y \leq 1,500$.

3. **The correct answer is D.** Each adult needs 15 cans/7 adults $= \dfrac{15}{7}$ cans in two days, or $\left(\dfrac{1}{2}\right)\left(\dfrac{15}{7}\right) = \dfrac{15}{14}$ cans per adult per day. Multiply this by the number of adults and by the number of days:

$$\frac{15}{14}(4 \text{ adults})(7 \text{ days}) = 30 \text{ cans of food}$$

4. **The correct answer is C.** Fiona's non-taxed amount is 75% of what she earns each hour, or $0.75x$. This is multiplied by the hourly rate, which in this case is $28, leading to the expression $28(0.75x)$.

5. **The correct answer is D.** The data are increasing and stay relatively close to a line of best fit that would pass through the center of the points. This means that there is a strong positive correlation between the years after 2005 and the total sales.

6. **The correct answer is A.** Using a line that passes through (2, 1.9) and (6, 3.5), the slope is

$$\frac{3.5 - 1.9}{6 - 2} = \frac{1.6}{4} = 0.4$$

The line passes through (0, 1), making the equation $y = 0.4x + 1$.

7. **The correct answer is C.** Let $x =$ original price. Then:

$$0.60x = \$4.20$$
$$\text{or} \quad 6x = \$42.00$$
$$x = \$7.00$$

8. **The correct answer is C.** The number 329 represents the slope of the graph of the equation, which is the rate of increase in attendance.

Answer Keys and Explanations

9. **The correct answer is D.** When they work together, the faster supercomputer will complete 1.5, or $\frac{3}{2}$, times the work of the slower supercomputer. That means the slower supercomputer does $\frac{2}{5}$ of the work, and the faster computer does $\frac{3}{5}\left(\frac{2}{5}\times\frac{3}{2}=\frac{3}{5}\right)$. If the slower supercomputer completes $\frac{2}{5}$ of the job in 3 hours, then it woud take 7.5 hours to complete the entire job alone:

$$\frac{2}{5}t = 3 \text{ hours}$$
$$2t = 15 \text{ hours}$$
$$t = 7.5 \text{ hours}$$

10. **The correct answer is D.** The number of books that the library adds is 375x, or 375 times the number of years. The total number of books must be the sum of 375x and 25,825 (the number they already have), not to exceed 35,000.

11. **The correct answer is D.** First, we convert 20° to radians: $\frac{\pi \text{ radians}}{180°}$ x 20° $= \frac{\pi}{9}$ radians. Then, we use the formula for the length of an arc, s, formed by an angle of θ radians on a circle of radius, r: $s = r\theta$. Evaluating this formula for the given radius and central angle measure, in radians, gives $\frac{9}{4\pi} \cdot \frac{\pi}{9} = \frac{1}{4}$. So the length of the arc that intercepts the given central angle is $\frac{1}{4}$.

12. **The correct answer is A.** Choice C is incorrect because we cannot say with certainty that a medication will help all people who need it. Choice D doesn't make sense; the medication cannot help people who don't take it. Choice B is incorrect because we only compared Z against one other medication, Y. The inference can be applied only to the given medications and populations.

13. **The correct answer is D.** To use the quadratic model, substitute $t = 150$ into the given equation:

$$C = 0.013(150)^2 + 0.518 \times 150 + 310.44 = 680.64$$

For the linear model, note that the constant rate of change of carbon dioxide concentration based on the data in the table is $\frac{390-370}{2010-2000} = \frac{20}{10} = 2$ PPM increase per year. So the increase from 2000 to 2100 would be 200 PPM, meaning that the concentration in 2100 would be 370 + 200 = 570 PPM. The quadratic model predicts a higher concentration in 2100, by about 110 PPM.

14. **The correct answer is B.** Draw the following diagram:

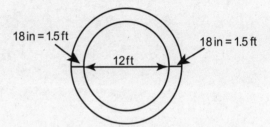

The area of the pond plus the walkway:

The diameter is 15 feet, so the area is $\pi\left(\frac{15}{2}\right)^2 = \frac{225\pi}{4}$ square feet.

The area of the pond only:

The diameter is 12 feet, so the area is $\pi\left(\frac{12}{2}\right)^2 = 36\pi$ square feet.

So the area of the walkway is the difference of these two areas: $\frac{225\pi}{4} - 36\pi = \frac{81}{4}\pi$ square feet. Therefore, the cost is $(\$7.25)\left(\frac{81}{4}\pi\right) \approx \$461.23$.

15. **The correct answer is B.** We can rewrite the equation as a quadratic set equal to zero, and factor or apply the quadratic formula. Here we factor:

$$a^2 + 12a - 45 = 0$$
$$(a+15)(a-3) = 0$$
$$a = -15 \text{ or } a = 3$$

We are given a < 0, so it must be that $a = -15$, and $a + 6 = -9$.

16. **The correct answer is C.** The graph shows points connected by a curve with an increasing positive slope that approximates an exponential graph, so this is exponential growth.

17. **The correct answer is D.** The graph shows an exponential growth curve, and the population of California in 1980 is approximately 24 million. Therefore, choices A and B can be eliminated, because based on the exponential growth, the population in 1990 would be more than the population in 1980. It appears on the graph that 25 million was reached before 1980. So 30 million (choice D) would be the best prediction.

18. **The correct answer is C.** Let the original sign be 10 by 10.

Then, the new sign is 7 by 9.

$$\frac{63}{100} = 63\%$$

19. **The correct answer is A.** Three meals a day times 365 days per year means there are $3 \times 365 = 1{,}095$ meals in one year. Over 19 years, there are $1{,}095 \times 19 = 20{,}805$ meals. Therefore, the number of restaurants in New York City exceeds 20,500.

20. **The correct answer is C.** The graph shows the distance decreasing after about three units of time, which is what a ball thrown vertically upward does, but not a ball thrown horizontally. The shape of the graph is roughly a parabola, which is the graph of a quadratic equation.

21. **The correct answer is A.** Subtract by using a common denominator, and then simplify:

$$\frac{3x-1}{2x+3} - \frac{2x+3}{3x-1} = \frac{(3x-1)(3x-1)}{(2x+3)(3x-1)} - \frac{(2x+3)(2x+3)}{(3x-1)(2x+3)}$$

$$= \frac{(3x-1)^2 - (2x+3)^2}{(2x+3)(3x-1)}$$

$$= \frac{5x^2 - 18x - 8}{6x^2 + 7x - 3}$$

22. **The correct answer is C.** A solution to the system would be a pair of values, (x, y), satisfying both equations. Such a solution would be represented on the graph as a point (or a set of points) that lies on both lines. Because lines A and B are parallel, they do not intersect, so no point lies on both lines. There is no solution to the system of equations represented by lines A and B.

23. **The correct answer is B.** The coordinates of any point (x, y) lying below line A satisfy the inequality $y < mx + a$. On the graph, Regions 2 and 3 lie below line A. Any point lying above line B satisfies $y > mx + b$; these points are in regions 1 and 2. To satisfy both point inequalities, (x, y) must lie in region 2.

24. **The correct answer is A.** To write an exponential equation for this situation, you need to find P, the population in 1980. Use the formula for exponential growth and the known population 20 years after 1980.

$$38{,}500 = P(1 + 0.038)^{20}$$

$$\frac{38{,}500}{(1.038)^{20}} = P$$

$$18{,}260 \approx P$$

25. **The correct answer is D.** If $x < 0$, then $f(x) = |x| = -x$. Then $g(f(x)) = g(-x)$. Finally, $g(-x) = \left(\frac{1}{-x}\right) = \frac{1}{x}$. For instance, assume $x = -3$: then, $f(-3) = 3$ and $g(f(-3)) = g(3) = -\frac{1}{3}$.

26. **The correct answer is D.** The sample size leads to the margin of error that is given with the data. As long as the margin of error is considered when making conclusions, those conclusions are reasonable.

27. **The correct answer is B.** The 95% confidence that the margin of error is ±3.4% is important, and choices A and C ignore the confidence interval. Choice D is not correct, because this interval is centered on 49%, instead of 51%, which is the number of people who support a different candidate or no candidate at this time. Only choice B accurately uses the confidence interval and the data given in the problem.

28. **The correct answer is C.** If the average for the eight tests is 84%, then the sum of the eight tests must be 8 times 84, or 672. For the six tests, the sum must be 6 times 86, or 516. The two dropped tests must have accounted for 156 points. 156 divided by 2 is 78.

Answer Keys and Explanations

29. **The correct answer is C.** Complete the square to write the equation in standard form for a circle:

$$x^2 + y^2 - 8x + 12y = 144$$
$$x^2 - 8x + y^2 + 12y = 144$$
$$\left(x^2 - 8x + 16\right) + \left(y^2 + 12y + 36\right) = 144 + 16 + 36$$
$$(x - 4)^2 + (y + 6)^2 = 196$$

Since 196 is 14^2, the radius is 14.

30. **The correct answer is C.** First, put the function into slope-intercept form:

$$f(x) = 2(3a - x) - (5 + ax)$$
$$= 6a - 2x - 5 - ax$$
$$= -(2 + a)x + (6a - 5)$$

In order for the graph to not intersect Quadrant III, $(2 + a)$ must be nonnegative so that the slope of the line is negative or zero AND the y-intercept $(6a - 5)$ must be positive. This gives two conditions: $-(2 + a) \leq 0$ AND $6a - 5 > 0$. Solving these inequalities yields $a \geq -2$ AND $a > \frac{5}{6}$. Both conditions must hold. So it must be the case that $a > \frac{5}{6}$.

31. **The correct answer is 1.84.** Compute the mean as follows:

$$\frac{0(6) + 1(13) + 2(21) + 3(4) + 4(5) + 5(1)}{50} = 1.84$$

32. **The correct answer is 36/5 or 7.2.** Begin by multiplying all terms of the equation by the LCD of 36:

$$36\left(\frac{x}{12}\right) + 36\left(\frac{x}{18}\right) = 1(36)$$
$$3x + 2x = 36$$
$$5x = 36$$
$$x = \frac{36}{5} = 7\frac{1}{5} = 7\frac{2}{10} = 7.2$$

33. **The correct answer is 50.** Write and solve an inequality that represents the situation. Then interpret the solution:

$$50 + 12x \leq 660$$
$$12x \leq 610$$
$$x \leq 50.8$$

Since the elephant cannot lift part of a bundle, the greatest number of bundles it can lift is 50.

34. **The correct answer is 20.** In the twentieth century, 7 of the 17 presidents were Democrats. $\frac{7}{17} = 41\%$, rounded to the nearest percentage point. The percentages for the nineteenth and twenty-first centuries are 35% and 33%, respectively.

35. **The correct answer is 22.** Presidents from the Federalist, Democratic-Republican, and Whig parties total $2 + 4 + 4 = 10$. The total number of presidents is 45. $\frac{10}{45} \approx 0.222$. Rounding to the nearest whole percent gives 22%.

36. **The correct answer is 1/4 or 0.25.** Solve using elimination so that the x-terms are eliminated:

$$-6(5x + 4y) = -6(11)$$
$$5(6x - 8y) = 5(10)$$

$$\begin{array}{r} -30x - 24y = -66 \\ + \quad 30x - 40y = 50 \\ \hline -64y = -16 \end{array}$$

$$y = \frac{16}{64}$$
$$= \frac{1}{4}$$

37. **The correct answer is 8.** Distance = rate × time:

$$360 = r(9)$$
$$40 = r$$

If r were $40 + 5 = 45$

$$d = rt$$
$$360 = 45t$$
$$t = 8$$

38. **The correct answer is 11.** Solve using a common denominator, and check your answer:

$$\frac{2}{x+2}+\frac{3}{x-5}=\frac{4x+7}{x^2-3x-10}$$

$$\frac{2(x-5)}{(x+2)(x-5)}+\frac{3(x+2)}{(x-5)(x+2)}=\frac{4x+7}{x^2-3x-10}$$

$$\frac{2x-10+3x+6}{x^2-3x-10}=\frac{4x+7}{x^2-3x-10}$$

$$5x-4=4x+7$$

$$x=11$$

$$\frac{2}{11+2}+\frac{3}{11-5}=\frac{4(11)+7}{(11)^2-3(11)-10}$$

$$\frac{2}{13}+\frac{3}{6}=\frac{51}{78}$$

$$\frac{2(6)}{13(6)}+\frac{3(13)}{6(13)}=\frac{51}{78}$$

$$\frac{51}{78}=\frac{51}{78}$$

Section 5: Essay

Analysis of Passage

The following is an analysis of the passage by Alex Jensen and Susan M. McHale, noting how the writers used evidence, reasoning, and stylistic or persuasive elements to support their claims, connect the claims and evidence, and add power to the ideas the writers expressed. Check to see if you evaluated the passage in a similar way.

What makes siblings from the same family so different? Parents

1. A colleague related the following story: while running errands with her 11- and 7-year-old daughters, a back seat battle began to rage. My colleague's attempts to defuse the situation only led to a shouting match about who was to blame for the skirmish. Finally the 11-year-old proclaimed to her sister, "You started it the day you were born and took away Mom's love!"

2. This pair of sisters fight frequently, and from their mother's perspective, part of the reason is that the two have little in common. As it turns out, their situation is not unique.

3. Despite the fact that siblings are, on average, 50% genetically similar, are often raised in the same home by the same parents, attend the same schools and have many other shared experiences,

4. siblings are often only as similar to each other as they are to children who are growing up across town or even across the country.

5. So, what is it that makes two siblings from the same family so different?

What makes the difference?

6. As researchers of sibling and family relationships, we knew that at least one answer to this question comes from

7. theory and data showing that, at least in some families, siblings try to be different from one another and seek to establish a unique identity and position in their family.

8. From a child's perspective, if an older brother excels at school, it may be easier to attract her parents' attention and praise by becoming a star athlete than by competing with her brother to get the best grades. In this way, even small differences between siblings can become substantial differences over time.

1. The writers begin the essay with an anecdote drawn from personal experience. This story (which includes the evocative statement "You... took away Mom's love!") immediately makes the essay more personal and prepares the reader to engage with the writers' argument.

2. The writers broaden their point of view from the personal to the objective and give the reader more perspective on the topic.

3. The writers use statistics and factual information to provide context for and lay the foundation of their argument.

4. Jensen and McHale clearly state a key premise of their argument — siblings are rarely similar. Having said this, they now have to support the rest of their argument: parents are the reason for these differences.

5. The writers pose a rhetorical question to introduce support for their argument.

6. The writers provide their backgrounds, which show why they're qualified to be making this argument: they are researchers of sibling and family relationships.

7. The writers refer to theory and data that support their argument: "some siblings try to be different from one another, and seek to establish a unique identity and position in their family."

8. The writers go into more detail about this information, presenting a concrete example that is easily understood by the reader.

9   But parents may also play a role. For instance, when parents notice differences between their children, children may pick up on parents' perceptions and beliefs about those differences. This, in turn, can increase sibling differences.

9   The writers now discuss the role of parents in sibling differences, paving the way to support the central point in their argument: parents are a major force in sibling differences.

10 We wanted to test these ideas to see what makes siblings different. So, we used data from first- and second-born teenage siblings from 388 two-parent families to examine sibling differences in school performance.

10 The writers explain how they tested the validity of their argument.

11 We asked mothers and fathers to report on whether they thought the two siblings differed in their academic abilities, and if so, which sibling was more capable. We also collected school grades from both siblings' report cards.

11 The writers provide more detailed information about the study they conducted to test the validity of their argument.

Preference for the firstborn

12 Our analyses showed some interesting results: parents tended to believe that the older sibling was better in school. This was even when older siblings did not actually receive better grades, on average.

12 The writers provide results of their study that revealed parents' perceptions of and ideas about older siblings. Specifically, parents tended to believe that the older sibling was better in school (whether this was true or not).

13 This may be a product of parents having greater expectations for firstborns or that, at any given time, the older sibling is undertaking more advanced school work.

13 The writers go into more detail about parents' perceptions of and ideas about older siblings.

14 There was, however, an exception to this pattern: in families with older brothers and younger sisters, parents rated the younger sibling as being more capable. In fact, in those families, younger sisters received better grades than their older brothers.

14 The writers go into further detail about results of their study. This detail shows a difference in how parents regarded their children, apparently favoring girls over boys in the area of academic capability.

15 Our findings also showed that it was not sibling differences in school grades that predicted parents' ratings of their children's abilities. Rather, parents' beliefs about differences in their children's abilities predicted later sibling differences in school grades.

15 The writers provide additional details from their study, showing parental beliefs and attitudes toward their children's abilities greatly affected sibling differences regarding academic performance.

16 In other words, when parents believed one child was more capable than the other, that child's school grades improved more over time than their sibling's.

16 Jensen and McHale explain these details and show how they support their argument: When parents believed one child was more academically capable than the other, that child's school grades improved more over time than their sibling's.

Sustaining beliefs

17 Although we expected that children's school grades and parents' beliefs about their children's relative abilities would be mutually influential, it turned out that parents' beliefs did not change much over their children's teenage years.

17 The writers provide information showing that once parents form perceptions and beliefs about their children's academic abilities, these attitudes and ideas do not greatly change.

18   Instead, sibling differences in school grades did change and were predicted by parents' beliefs. In this way, parents' beliefs about differences between their children may encourage the development of actual sibling difference.

18   *Jensen and McHale use the information revealed by their study to prove their argument: While parents' beliefs about their children's academic abilities did not change, sibling differences in school grades did. Thus, "parents' beliefs about differences between their children may encourage the development of actual sibling difference."*

19   The above comment by an 11-year-old highlights that children are sensitive to their place and value in the family—relative to those of their siblings. Parents may strive to show their love for their children, but they also should be aware that small differences in how they treat their children can have large effects—including on their children's development and adjustment and also on the sibling relationship.

19   *The writers strengthen their argument by returning to their introductory anecdote and summing up what their study revealed: "Children are sensitive to their place and value in the family," and differences in how parents treat their children can have "large effects" on them.*

20   Indeed, some research suggests that sibling conflict arises when children try to be different from their siblings.

20   *The writers conclude the essay by referring to research that supports the mother's statement in the introductory anecdote: sibling conflict can be created "when children try to be different from their siblings."*

21   My colleague may be correct that her daughters fight frequently because they have nothing in common.

21   *While this may seem like the writers are giving up on their argument, acknowledging their colleague might be right about the cause of her daughters' conflicts demonstrates the writers' honesty and objectivity.*

22   But their conflicts may also be motivated by her daughter's perception that their differences started on the day her sister was born "and took away Mom's love."

22   *Jensen and McHale then end the essay by offering additional insight about their colleague's daughters. Here, they provide an alternative explanation for the girls' differences, restating their argument and repeating the 11-year-old girl's evocative remark: the conflict between these two siblings may also be motivated by the girl's belief that the birth of her younger sister changed their mother's behavior toward the older girl because the younger sister "took away Mom's love."*

SAMPLE ESSAYS

The following are examples of a high-scoring and low-scoring essay, based on the passage by Alex Jenson and Susan M. McHale.

HIGH-SCORING ESSAY

No two siblings are alike. Alex Jensen and Susan M. McHale are two university professors who investigated the reasons for the differences between siblings. They concluded that parents cause the differences. To explain their conclusion, they use professional authority, personal experience, statistics, results of a study they conducted, and references to other research.

Professional authority is established immediately—both authors are identified as university professors in the area of human development. In the second section, they reinforce their authority by stating that they are researchers of sibling and family relationships. This demonstrates their knowledge specifically in the area of siblings. Readers can trust their conclusions.

The article begins with a personal story of two young siblings who constantly fight. During a particular fight, the 11-year-old girl accuses her 7-year-old sister of starting the fight when she was born and "took away mom's love." This harsh accusation hooks readers into wondering about the real cause of sibling differences.

A quick look at statistics provided by the authors reveals many reasons for siblings to be similar rather that different. Siblings are 50% genetically similar and share the same parents, schools, and other experiences. Again, this makes the reader wonder about the cause of sibling differences.

The answer comes from theory and data, reinforcing their role as authorities in the subject. One cause, the authors state, is that siblings try to be different from each other to be unique in the family. They support this with an example of how one sibling can choose to excel at athletic pursuits because an older sibling already excels in academics. Over time, one small choice made to be different, such as joining a soccer team, causes other, bigger differences. One sibling becomes an athlete while the other becomes a scholar.

Finally, the authors address the role of parents in sibling differences. They theorize that parents notice small differences between children and children react to their parents' perceptions by becoming even more different. To confirm their theory, the authors conducted a study of the first and second siblings in 388 two-parent homes. Readers can easily see the study as a reasonable approach to determining the cause of the differences. The authors asked parents about their perceptions of their children's academic abilities and compared the perceptions to the children's report cards. In effect, they compared parents' perceptions to actual performance.

The authors present the analysis of the study results. Parents seem to expect the oldest sibling to perform better than the younger child, even though it wasn't always true. They describe an exception: If the older sibling is male and the younger sibling is female, the parents expect the girl to perform better academically, and the girl does get better grades than her brother.

The authors present their findings. Overall, the authors determined that parents' perception caused siblings' academic performance. If the parents believed that Suzy would perform better that Sally, Suzy's grades would improve until they were better than Sally's. Over time, parents' perceptions caused behaviors to change; behaviors did not cause parents' perceptions to change.

Parents have a large role in shaping their children and the relationship between their children. The authors briefly cite other research that points to differences between siblings as the cause of conflict between siblings.

At the end of the article, the authors return to the personal story told at the beginning of the article. The authors' colleague says that the conflict between her daughters is caused by the differences between the daughters. After reading the authors' findings though, readers can conclude that the differences are caused by the parents. Hence, the conflict between the siblings is actually caused by the parents. The authors have successfully presented their theory and their results to convince readers that parents should be more aware of the effect they have on their children.

Low-Scoring Essay

Alex Jensen and Susan M. McHale are two professors who researched the cause of sibling rivalry. They start the article with a story about two sisters having a fight in the backseat of a car. One of the girls accuses the other of stealing Mom's love. It refers to the age-old argument that "Mom loves you best."

The researchers look at some of the reasons that siblings fight even though they share so many of the same things, including genes, parents, schools, and probably clothes. They conclude that siblings try to be different on purpose so they can have a unique place in the family. The differences might start as things their parents notice like, "You're better at math than Mike," or "You run faster than Jake." Eventually, the small differences that parents notice become big things. Jake becomes an accountant because he's better at math. Mike becomes a gym teacher and coaches at the local high school because he's a better athlete.

The authors talk about a study they did about sibling rivalry. The differences between the siblings are caused by the way that parents expect the children to act. Children act the way they do to get attention.

The authors tell us that parents should be careful about the characteristics they encourage in their children and the perceptions they talk about. The "Mom loves you best" argument can shape children's lives. Parents should be careful to say good things about their children and interact evenly with both children. Then, no one will win the "Mom loves you best" argument and siblings will fight less.

COMPUTING YOUR SCORES

Now that you've completed this practice test , it's time to compute your scores. Simply follow the instructions on the following pages, and use the conversion tables provided to calculate your scores. The formulas provided will give you as close an approximation as possible of how you might score on the actual SAT® exam.

TO DETERMINE YOUR PRACTICE TEST SCORES

1. After you go through each of the test sections (Reading, Writing and Language, Math—No Calculator, and Math—Calculator) and determine which answers you got right, be sure to enter the number of correct answers in the box below the answer key for each of the sections.

2. Your total score on the practice test is the sum of your Evidence-Based Reading and Writing Section score and your Math Section score. To get your total score, convert the raw score—the number of questions you got right in a particular section— into the "scaled score" for that section, and then you'll calculate the total score. It sounds a little confusing, but we'll take you through the steps.

TO CALCULATE YOUR EVIDENCE-BASED READING AND WRITING SECTION SCORE

Your Evidence-Based Reading and Writing Section score is on a scale of 200–800. First determine your Reading Test score, and then determine your score on the Writing and Language Test.

1. Count the number of correct answers you got on the **Section 1: Reading Test.** Remember that there is no penalty for wrong answers. **The number of correct answers is your raw score.**

2. Go to **Raw Score Conversion Table 1: Section and Test Scores** on page 1036. Look in the "Raw Score" column for your raw score, and match it to the number in the "Reading Test Score" column.

3. Do the same with **Section 2: Writing and Language Test** to determine that score.

4. Add your Reading Test score to your Writing and Language Test score.

5. Multiply that number by 10. This is your Evidence-Based Reading and Writing Section score.

TO CALCULATE YOUR MATH SECTION SCORE

Your Math score is also on a scale of 200–800.

1. Count the number of correct answers you got on the **Section 3: Math Test—No Calculator** and the **Section 4: Math Test— No Calculator**. Again, there is no penalty for wrong answers. **The number of correct answers is your raw score.**

2. Add the number of correct answers on the Section 3: Math Test—No Calculator and the Section 4: Math Test—Calculator.

3. Use the **Raw Score Conversion Table 1: Section and Test Scores** on page 1036 and convert your raw score into your Math Section score.

TO OBTAIN YOUR TOTAL SCORE

Add your score on the Evidence-Based Reading and Writing Section to the Math Section score. This is your total score on this Practice Test, on a scale of 400–1600.

SUBSCORES PROVIDE ADDITIONAL INFORMATION

Subscores offer you greater details about your strengths in certain areas within literacy and math. The subscores are reported on a scale of 1–15 and include Heart of Algebra, Problem Solving and Data Analysis, Passport to Advanced Math, Expression of Ideas, Standard English Conventions, Words in Context, and Command of Evidence.

Heart of Algebra

The **Heart of Algebra subscore** is based on questions from the **Math Test** that focus on linear equations and inequalities.

- Add up your total correct answers from these sections:
    - Math Test—No Calculator: Questions 1, 4, 7, 9, 13, 15, 18, 20
    - Math Test—Calculator: Questions 1, 2, 4, 8–10, 13, 21, 32, 33, 36
- Your Raw Score = the total number of correct answers from all of these questions.
- Use the **Raw Score Conversion Table 2: Subscores** on page 1037 to determine your **Heart of Algebra** subscore.

Problem Solving and Data Analysis

The **Problem Solving and Data Analysis subscore** is based on questions from the **Math Test** that focus on quantitative reasoning, interpretation and synthesis of data, and solving problems in rich and varied contexts.

- Add up your total correct answers from these questions:
    - Math Test—No Calculator: None
    - Math Test—Calculator: Questions 3, 5–7, 12, 16–20, 26–28, 31, 34, 35, 37
- Your Raw Score = the total number of correct answers from all of these questions.
- Use the **Raw Score Conversion Table 2: Subscores** on page 1037 to determine your **Problem Solving and Data Analysis** subscore.

Passport to Advanced Math

The **Passport to Advanced Math subscore** is based on questions from the **Math Test** that focus on topics central to your ability to progress to more advanced math, such as understanding the structure of expressions, reasoning with more complex equations, and interpreting and building functions.

- Add up your total correct answers from these questions:
    - Math Test—No Calculator: Questions 2, 5, 6, 8, 10, 12, 14, 17, 19
    - Math Test—Calculator: Questions 15, 22–25, 30, 38
- Your Raw Score = the total number of correct answers from all of these questions.
- Use the **Raw Score Conversion Table 2: Subscores** on page 1037 to determine your **Passport to Advanced Math** subscore.

Expression of Ideas

The **Expression of Ideas subscore** is based on questions from the **Writing and Language Test** that focus on topic development, organization, and rhetorically effective use of language.

- Add up your total correct answers from these questions in Section 2: Writing and Language Test:
    - Questions 1, 3, 6, 8, 10, 12, 14, 15, 18–20, 22, 24, 26–28, 30, 33, 35–37, 39–41
- Your Raw Score = the total number of correct answers from all of these questions.
- Use the **Raw Score Conversion Table 2: Subscores** on page 1037 to determine your Expression of Ideas subscore.

Standard English Conventions

The **Standard English Conventions subscore** is based on questions from the **Writing and Language Test** that focus on sentence structure, usage, and punctuation.

- Add up your total correct answers from these questions in Section 2: Writing and Language Test:
    - Questions 2, 4, 5, 7, 9, 11, 13, 16, 17, 21, 23, 25, 29, 31, 32, 34, 38, 42–44
- Your Raw Score = the total number of correct answers from all of these questions.
- Use the **Raw Score Conversion Table 2: Subscores** on page 1037 to determine your **Standard English Conventions** subscore.

Words in Context

The **Words in Context subscore** is based on questions from the **Reading Test** and the **Writing and Language Test** that address word/phrase meaning in context and rhetorical word choice.

- Add up your total correct answers from these questions in Sections 1 and 2:
  - ° Reading Test: Questions 9, 10, 21, 22, 23, 31, 32, 37, 42, 51, 52
  - ° Writing and Language Test: Questions 6, 8, 15, 18, 24, 27, 37, 41
- Your Raw Score = the total number of correct answers from all of these questions.
- Use the **Raw Score Conversion Table 2: Subscores** on page 1037 to determine your **Words in Context** subscore.

Command of Evidence

The **Command of Evidence subscore** is based on questions from the **Reading Test** and the **Writing and Language Test** that ask you to interpret and use evidence found in a wide range of passages and informational graphics, such as graphs, tables, and charts.

- Add up your total correct answers from Sections 1 and 2:
  - ° Reading Test: Questions 6, 8, 18, 20, 24, 27, 35, 41, 47, 50
  - ° Writing and Language Test: Questions 1, 10, 12, 19, 26, 28, 36, 40
- Your Raw Score = the total number of correct answers from all of these questions.
- Use the **Raw Score Conversion Table 2: Subscores** on page 1037 to determine your **Command of Evidence** subscore.

CROSS-TEST SCORES

The SAT® exam also reports two cross-test scores: Analysis in History/Social Studies and Analysis in Science. These scores are based on questions in the Reading Test, Writing and Language Test, and both Math Tests that ask you to think analytically about texts and questions in these subject areas. Cross-test scores are reported on a scale of 10–40.

Analysis in History/Social Studies

- Add up your total correct answers from these questions:
  - ° Reading Test: Questions 12–20, 22, 33–42
  - ° Writing and Language Test: Questions 12, 14, 15, 18–20
  - ° Math Test—No Calculator: None
  - ° Math Test—Calculator: Questions16, 17, 24, 26, 27, 31, 34, 35
- Your Raw Score = the total number of correct answers from all of these questions.
- Use the **Raw Score Conversion Table 3: Cross-Test Scores** on page 1038 to determine your Analysis in History/Social Studies cross-test score.

Analysis in Science

- Add up your total correct answers from these questions:
  - ° Reading Test: Questions 1–11, 43–52
  - ° Writing and Language Test: Questions 35–37, 39, 40
  - ° Math Test—No Calculator: Questions 7, 9, 12, 13
  - ° Math Test—Calculator: Questions 12, 20, 33
- Your Raw Score = the total number of correct answers from all of these questions.
- Use the **Raw Score Conversion Table 3: Cross-Test Scores** on page 1038 to determine your Analysis in Science cross-test score.

RAW SCORE CONVERSION TABLE 1: SECTION AND TEST SCORES

Raw Score	Math Section Score	Reading Test Score	Writing and Language Test Score	Raw Score	Math Section Score	Reading Test Score	Writing and Language Test Score	Raw Score	Math Section Score	Reading Test Score	Writing and Language Test Score
0	200	10	10	20	450	22	23	40	610	33	36
1	200	10	10	21	460	23	23	41	620	33	37
2	210	10	10	22	470	23	24	42	630	34	38
3	230	11	10	23	480	24	25	43	640	35	39
4	240	12	11	24	480	24	25	44	650	35	40
5	260	13	12	25	490	25	26	45	660	36	
6	280	14	13	26	500	25	26	46	670	37	
7	290	15	13	27	510	26	27	47	670	37	
8	310	15	14	28	520	26	28	48	680	38	
9	320	16	15	29	520	27	28	49	690	38	
10	330	17	16	30	530	28	29	50	700	39	
11	340	17	16	31	540	28	30	51	710	40	
12	360	18	17	32	550	29	30	52	730	40	
13	370	19	18	33	560	29	31	53	740		
14	380	19	19	34	560	30	32	54	750		
15	390	20	19	35	570	30	32	55	760		
16	410	20	20	36	580	31	33	56	780		
17	420	21	21	37	590	31	34	57	790		
18	430	21	21	38	600	32	34	58	800		
19	440	22	22	39	600	32	35				

CONVERSION EQUATION 1 SECTION AND TEST SCORES

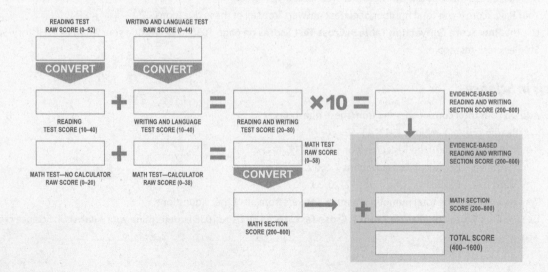

Raw Score (# of correct answers)	Expression of Ideas	Standard English Conventions	Heart of Algebra	Problem Solving and Data Analysis	Passport to Advanced Math	Words in Context	Command of Evidence
0	1	1	1	1	1	1	1
1	1	1	1	1	3	1	1
2	1	1	2	2	5	2	2
3	2	2	3	3	6	3	3
4	3	2	4	4	7	4	4
5	4	3	5	5	8	5	5
6	5	4	6	6	9	6	6
7	6	5	6	7	10	6	7
8	6	6	7	8	11	7	8
9	7	6	8	8	11	8	8
10	7	7	8	9	12	8	9
11	8	7	9	10	12	9	10
12	8	8	9	10	13	9	10
13	9	8	9	11	13	10	11
14	9	9	10	12	14	11	12
15	10	10	10	13	14	12	13
16	10	10	11	14	15	13	14
17	11	11	12	15		14	15
18	11	12	13			15	15
19	12	13	15				
20	12	15					
21	13						
22	14						
23	14						
24	15						

CONVERSION EQUATION 2 SUBSCORES

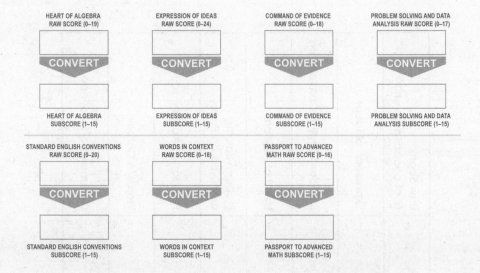

RAW SCORE CONVERSION TABLE 3: CROSS-TEST SCORES

Raw Score (# of correct answers)	Analysis in History/Social Studies Cross-Test Score	Analysis in Science Cross-Test Score		Raw Score (# of correct answers)	Analysis in History/Social Studies Cross-Test Score	Analysis in Science Cross-Test Score
0	10	10		18	28	26
1	10	11		19	29	27
2	11	12		20	30	27
3	12	13		21	30	28
4	14	14		22	31	29
5	15	15		23	32	30
6	16	16		24	32	30
7	17	17		25	33	31
8	18	18		26	34	32
9	20	19		27	35	33
10	21	20		28	35	33
11	22	20		29	36	34
12	23	21		30	37	35
13	24	22		31	38	36
14	25	23		32	38	37
15	26	24		33	39	38
16	27	24		34	40	39
17	28	25		35	40	40

ANALYSIS IN HISTORY/SOCIAL STUDIES   ANALYSIS IN SCIENCE

TEST	QUESTIONS	RAW SCORE	QUESTIONS	RAW SCORE
Reading Test	12–22, 33–42		1–11, 43–52	
Writing and Language Test	12–22		34–44	
Math Test—No Calculator	None		7, 9, 12, 13	
Math Test—Calculator	16, 17, 24, 26, 27, 31, 34, 35		12, 20, 33	
TOTAL				

ANALYSIS IN HISTORY/
SOCIAL STUDIES
RAW SCORE (0–35)

ANALYSIS IN SCIENCE
RAW SCORE (0–35)

CONVERT   CONVERT

ANALYSIS IN HISTORY/
SOCIAL STUDIES
CROSS-TEST SCORE (10–40)

ANALYSIS IN SCIENCE
CROSS-TEST SCORE (10–40)

PART VIII: APPENDICES

A: Parents' Guide to College Admission Testing

B: Math Formulas for Memorization

Appendix A: Parents' Guide to College Admission Testing

GETTING INVOLVED

The first step in creating a plan to help your teen prepare for college admissions tests is to define your role. As a parent, you already play a variety of roles in raising your children, wearing different hats at different times. You may find yourself acting as mentor, chauffeur, cook, coach, mediator, or even prison warden. All of these roles require different time commitments and often even require you to acquire new skills.

When it comes to helping your teen tackle the SAT® exam, you might feel confused about which role to take. Many parents find becoming involved with their teen's education a bit challenging. Teenagers can have a hard time accepting their parents as teachers. Sometimes, when parents try to teach their teen, their efforts lead to the three "F's": *failure, friction,* and *frustration.* When these experiences arise, parents may conclude that they have no role to play in their child's education.

Of course, nothing could be further from the truth. In fact, there are many roles parents should choose to play in helping their teens prepare for college admissions tests.

ROLES FOR PARENTS

You can play a variety of roles in helping your teen prepare for college admissions tests. In guiding your teen, you may choose to be one, or any combination, of the following:

- Buyer
- Advocate
- Supporter
- Helper
- Organizer
- Manager
- Tutor

1043

Appendix A

Parents'
Guide to
College
Admission
Testing

THE BUYER

"Here's the money for the SAT® test-prep books you want to buy."

This parent feels that it is the teenager's job to prepare for college admissions tests, and the parent's job is to offer financial support. The teenager is the main decision maker and is responsible for obtaining the necessary materials and services. This parental role is supportive and not too time-consuming, although it may present problems for parents who are on a tight budget.

THE ADVOCATE

"How does your school help juniors prepare for the SAT® exam?"

This parent believes that it is the school's job to prepare students for the test. The parent starts the ball rolling and requests information from school personnel about what services are available. The teenager may or may not be involved in this information-gathering process. Most parents feel comfortable in this role, as it requires little time and is accepted by both school personnel and teachers.

THE SUPPORTER

"I know it's a tough test. I see you're working hard and spending a lot of time studying for it."

This parent believes that the teenager has the major responsibility in preparing for the test. The teenager is the decision maker, and the parent offers suggestions and support. The parent is understanding, empathetic, and non-critical. This can be a comfortable parental role since it is non-threatening to the teenager, is positive, and requires a minimal amount of time.

THE HELPER

"I picked up this SAT® practice book and made a list of some tutoring courses for you."

This parent believes that it is the parent's job to help the teenager with his plans, but that it is up to the teenager to make the final decisions. This parent helps only when asked and follows the teen's timetable when possible. This is a comfortable role since it is supportive, non-threatening, and not time-consuming. However, this role might pose problems for working parents who do not have flexible schedules.

THE ORGANIZER

"I've signed you up to take a test-prep course."

This parent feels that the teenager should not be responsible for the arrangements involved in test preparation. The parent assumes a major role in establishing a timetable, finding out about resources, arranging for services, and purchasing materials. The teenager's responsibility is to follow the parent's game plan. In short, the parent provides the framework so that the teenager can spend her time preparing effectively. This role is time-consuming and parent-directed.

THE MANAGER

"After you study your vocabulary words for 30 minutes, you can use the car."

This parent believes that good intentions are not enough to make her child perform well on the SAT® exam. She believes in the rule "work first, play later." Firm guidelines and consequences are established to keep the ball rolling. The degree to which the teenager is involved in planning and implementing this approach depends on a number of factors, such as the teenager's maturity and motivation.

NOTE: Educators and legislators recognize the importance of having parents involved in their children's education. Research shows that, when they have been taught how to do it, parents can successfully teach their teens.

Your comfort with this role is related to the extent to which you believe in the "work first, play later" philosophy. If you already ascribe to this rule in raising your children, extending it to SAT® exam preparation will be an easy task. Patience and willingness to check on study behavior are also important factors to consider when thinking about the role of manager.

1044

Appendix A

Parents'
Guide to
College
Admission
Testing

www.petersons.com

THE TUTOR

"I'll explain the algebra problem to you."

Parents who take on the role of tutor believe that they can work effectively with their teenager on academic subjects. These parents offer direct instruction in one or more of the test areas, such as vocabulary, reading comprehension, geometry, or algebra.

 Remember, no single role is superior to the other. Find roles that are best suited to you and your teenager's needs.

WHICH ROLE IS FOR YOU?

Defining your role requires two steps:

1. Collecting information about yourself
2. Using this information systematically, as you decide which role you want to take on and when

To collect information about yourself, take the following "Parent Survey."

PARENT SURVEY

	LOW	MEDIUM	HIGH
1. How much money is available for test preparation, tutoring books, etc.?	Up to $25 for books	$25–$150 for books and tutoring	More than $150 for courses, books, etc.
2. Do you question school personnel?	Never. I feel uncomfortable.	Sometimes, if it is important.	Usually. It's my right.
3. Do you make supportive statements about academic achievements?	Not usually. I don't want to spoil my child.	Sometimes, if grades are good.	Frequently, especially about trying hard.
4. What resources are available in your school or community?	I don't have the faintest idea!	I thought I saw an advertisement for an SAT® course.	I know a tutor and saw an SAT® book in the store.
5. How involved do you feel?	I don't know if I should be involved.	I'll do what I can if I'm asked.	This is important! I'll help whenever I can.
6. How much time are you willing to devote to SAT® exam preparation?	1–3 hours total	1–2 hours per week	3 or more hours per week
7. How efficient is your decision making?	It's either too slow or too hasty.	Sometimes good, but it's a tiresome process.	Usually good. I consider options and select one.
8. Who should be the primary decision maker?	Not me. It's not my job!	I'll make decisions sometimes.	Me. I have more experience.

	LOW	MEDIUM	HIGH
9. How organized are you?	I lose papers, forget dates, and am often late.	I write schedules but forget to follow them.	A place for everything and everything in its place!
10. How comfortable are you with your teenager?	It's tough being around my child.	Some days are good, others aren't.	Minor problems, but we get along.
11. How firm or consistent are your limits?	No one listens to me. I nag and yell.	My children know the rules, but I forget to enforce them.	My children follow the rules.
12. Do you have reading and math skills?	Minimal skills; low confidence.	Some skills; average confidence.	Strong skills; high confidence.
13. How effective are you as your teenager's teacher?	We always end up fighting.	Sometimes it works, sometimes it doesn't.	It's not easy, but we work together.

Choosing Your Role by Interpreting Your Survey Responses

While there are no hard and fast rules to use in choosing a role, your answers to the survey questions will help you select your role in a systematic way. Using your survey responses, you can use the following guidelines to identify which roles to try first. Remember that any combination of roles is good. To help clarify:

- **The roles of buyer, advocate, and supporter** are appropriate if a majority of your answers fall in the LOW or MEDIUM columns. These roles demand the least amount of direct parent-as-teacher involvement, yet they are an important part of test preparation. Most parents can assume these roles.

- **The roles of helper, organizer, and manager** require that the majority of your answers fall in the MEDIUM or HIGH columns. These roles involve more constant and direct interaction with your teen. Some parents can assume these roles.

- **The role of tutor** is the most demanding role and requires that at least 11 out of 13 responses fall in the MEDIUM or HIGH columns. There are few parents who can comfortably and successfully assume this role.

Depending on your time and resources, you may, for example, want to begin in the advocate and supporter roles, followed by that of a buyer. If necessary, you could find someone else to act as a manager and tutor. Or, alternatively, you might find yourself best suited to being an organizer, manager, helper, and supporter right away.

BECOMING ACTIVE

Parents entrust their most valuable assets—their children—to the schools. As an investor in your child's education, you have the same concerns as any other person investing in the future. Unfortunately, sometimes parents are made to feel that the school is the "expert." In some schools, parents are viewed as meddlers if they ask for, or insist upon, information about their children's progress. As a parent, you can, and should, be involved in your teen's education, even at the secondary level. Don't be afraid to pursue information on your teen's behalf—you need to be informed, ask questions, offer suggestions, and reject suggestions if they aren't the right solutions to the problems!

HOW TO APPROACH YOUR TEENAGER

For the first time, your teen may be striving for independence and questioning himself or herself and the future. These changes may make your role as a parent additionally tough, and you may find it hard to help your teen prepare for college admissions tests. The key to reaching your teen is to focus on where he or she is academically and personally.

GETTING INFORMATION FROM DIFFERENT SOURCES

To design your SAT® exam preparation plan, you'll need to get up-to-date information about your teenager from several sources, including yourself, your teenager, and the school. Your child's guidance counselor is a primary source of information, since he or she can provide information from classroom teachers and across various subject areas.

YOU AND YOUR TEEN

The first source of information is you. Parents must neither overestimate nor underestimate the importance of their own information about their teenager. You can be most effective if you know which questions to ask and whom to ask. You need to know about your teenager's concerns, goals, attitudes, academics, work habits, general behavior, and special strengths and weaknesses.

To initiate this step, ask your teen to meet with you for an hour to discuss college plans and how he or she feels about preparing for the SAT® exam. You can begin by asking your teen for his or her opinions on matters concerning his or her education and future goals. In this first conversation, you can ask about colleges he or she is considering. Because many colleges suggest that its applicants' test scores fall within a certain range, information about the college's requirements is important. The required scores may affect the amount of time and the kind of commitment required for the test preparation.

You may also want to ask your teen to evaluate his or her study skills and the kind of study skills needed to prepare for the SAT® exam. Some teenagers work effectively in groups. Others are uncomfortable or distracted when studying in a group. Students' work habits and interactions with other people also influence their attitudes toward college admissions tests and their scores. Your teenager's reaction to tests in general is an important factor to take into consideration.

Don't feel rejected if your teen says, "I don't want to meet. I know what to do." Don't push it; just try again later. The timing may be right on the second go-around.

> **NOTE:** Taking the SAT® exam can create a lot of stress. Excessive anxiety interferes with test performance. Collecting information from your teenager will help identify his or her problems and concerns, so you can help reduce test-prep stress.

THE SCHOOL

Another important source of information is the school. Guidance counselors, teachers, and others, such as coaches or band directors, can tell you about your teenager's attitudes and interactions with peers and adults outside the home. These attitudes may influence your teen's college selection and in turn lead you to the most appropriate type of preparation for the college admissions tests.

Your teen's guidance counselor can review previous standardized test scores with you and discuss differences in performance between tests and grades. Reviewing standardized test scores and grades can help you establish realistic guidelines for SAT® exam preparation.

Teachers and counselors can also describe specific weaknesses that might block an otherwise solid test performance. In addition, they can offer information about your child's work habits, such as whether homework is submitted on time or how well-organized his or her papers are.

1047

Appendix A

Parents'
Guide to
College
Admission
Testing

Additional Options

Independent school counselors, or educational consultants, are another alternative to consider. These types of counselors are not affiliated with a school and work as private consultants. If you lack confidence in your teen's counselor or feel that the counselor is too busy to provide the extensive work necessary for appropriate college planning, you may want to work with an educational consultant.

A private consultant may work with students from all over the United States and foreign countries. This broader perspective can provide more diverse options for your child. Many independent counselors also have firsthand experience as college admissions officers and therefore are aware of the kind of information that should be collected and ways of presenting such information to colleges.

WHAT TO ASK

The following is a list of questions you'll want to ask yourself, your teen, and school personnel or educational consultants.

Goals

- What career choices is your teen considering?

- Are there specific colleges your teen wants to attend?

- What range of SAT® exam scores do those colleges require? (Or are these scores optional?)

Attitudes

- How confident is your teen about his or her ability to succeed?

- What attitude does your teen have toward school and school personnel?

- Are your teen's friends a good influence in terms of future plans?

- How helpful is the family in terms of school success?

- What is your teen's attitude toward college admissions tests?

Academics

- How has your teen done on other standardized tests?

- Do standardized test scores accurately reflect your teen's skills or abilities?

- Do your teen's grades accurately reflect his or her skills or abilities?

- What are your teen's areas of strength?

- What are your teen's areas of weakness?

1048

Appendix A

Parents'
Guide to
College
Admission
Testing

Work Habits

- How effective are your teen's organizational and study skills?

- Does your teen do better with certain study procedures (e.g., in a group or listening to recorded lectures)?

- How effective are your teen's test-taking skills?

- Are there obstacles that might interfere with effective test preparation (e.g., a job or extracurricular activities)?

- Are there barriers to effective test-taking (e.g., struggles with long reading passages or not liking multiple-choice tests)?

Behavior

- To what degree does your teen need or accept help?

- To what degree is your teen a good decision maker?

- How good is your teen at self-managing or being a self-starter?

- To what degree does your teen test limits or rules?

- How well does your teen cope with stress or adversity?

- How well does your teen relate to school personnel and teachers?

- How well does your teen relate to peers and classmates?

- How well does your teen relate to family members?

- With whom will your teen talk about problems (e.g., a sibling or a neighbor)?

Special Issues

- Does your teen have special talents or abilities?

- Does your teen have special challenges or obstacles?

- Have special challenges or obstacles been addressed previously?

- In what way will any of these issues affect preparation for the college admissions tests?

SAT® Exam

- How do students in your teen's school perform on the test?

- How did your teen perform on other college admissions tests?

- How do your teen's test scores compare with others in the class?

- What services do school personnel provide for SAT® exam preparation?

By asking these questions, you can really focus on your teenager. By answering these questions now, you'll reveal information gaps, identify consistencies or inconsistencies in opinions or behaviors, highlight strengths and weaknesses, and begin your systematic plan for helping your teen.

1049

Appendix A

Parents'
Guide to
College
Admission
Testing

HOW TO USE THE INFORMATION

To get the most out of the information you have collected, pay particular attention to the following issues:

- **Consistency of answers provided by each of the sources**—for example, whether the counselor's answers conflict with your teenager's answers

- **Trends that emerge**—such as better work this year or more anxiety than last year

- **Gaps in information**—such as no previous standardized test scores available

- **Strengths and weaknesses**—such as being well organized or having poor reading comprehension

YOUR TEEN'S STRENGTHS

All teenagers have strengths. However, some teenagers' strengths are more obvious than others. As a parent, your job includes the following:

- Identifying, highlighting, maintaining, and increasing existing strengths

- Providing opportunities for new strengths to develop

Strengths may be grouped into several broad categories—knowledge, work habits, attitude, behavior, and special. To help clarify:

- **Strengths in the knowledge area** include mastering basic skills, achieving good grades, and having a potential for learning.

- **Strengths in the area of work habits** include applying skills and knowledge in an organized and effective way and achieving desired goals.

- **Strengths in the area of attitude** include having clear goals, optimism, motivation, and self-confidence.

- **Strengths in the behavior category** refer to the teenager's ability to cope, follow rules, and get along with peers and adults.

- **Special strengths** may include talents in areas such as music, art, writing, or science.

Too frequently, both parents and teachers forget to focus on the positive. They zero in on the weaknesses rather than on the strengths. To avoid this common mistake, review the information you have collected and list your teen's strengths and special talents in the following chart. We'll come back to filling in the problem areas later.

1050

Appendix A

Parents'
Guide to
College
Admission
Testing

SOURCE		KNOWLEDGE	WORK HABITS	ATTITUDE	BEHAVIOR	SPECIAL
Parent	Strength					
	Problem					
Teenager	Strength					
	Problem					
School	Strength					
	Problem					

Remember to discuss these strengths with your teenager, especially if he or she does not recognize his or her own strengths or talents. Building your teen's confidence is important and will pay off enormously.

IDENTIFYING SPECIFIC PROBLEM AREAS

Several kinds of problems may become obvious as you collect information about your teenager. These problem areas may be grouped into the same five categories we used to identify strengths.

KNOWLEDGE PROBLEMS

Students with knowledge problems may make statements such as "I'm not even sure about getting all the ratio and proportion problems right," or "I hate reading," or "I never do those grammar parts—I skip most of them."

Knowledge problems include the following:

- Lack of mastery of basic skills, such as arithmetic

- Lack of understanding of rules and concepts in more advanced areas, such as geometry

- Lack of experience, which leaves gaps in some areas covered on the SAT® exam

- Difficulties in one or more of the following: remembering previously learned material, analyzing material, or putting information together (e.g., as in a report)

Your teenager may have a knowledge problem in only one area, which may or may not have an effect on any other area. For example, Marcus, a 10th-grader, had a reading problem, and testing showed that he read two years below his present grade level. His computation skills were good, and he did well in algebra. However, word problems were his downfall. In this case, a knowledge problem in one area had an effect on another area.

1051

Appendix A

Parents'
Guide to
College
Admission
Testing

WORK-HABITS PROBLEMS

Statements such as "I can't find my notes," "I think I left my books at school," or "I'll study later, after my favorite TV show" signal work-habits problems.

Here are a few examples of work-habits problems:

- Poor study habits
- Test anxiety
- Ineffective test-taking skills
- Lack of organization
- Difficulty estimating how long a task will take

Teenagers with work-habit problems lack the skills necessary to study effectively or to apply the knowledge they have during a testing situation. These teenagers may work too slowly and be unable to complete portions of the test, or they may work too quickly and inadvertently skip questions and make careless errors.

ATTITUDE PROBLEMS

Students with attitude problems may make statements such as "It doesn't matter how much I study, I'll never be able to do it," or "I don't care—the SAT® doesn't matter anyway."

Attitude problems involve the following:

- Unrealistic self-image and academic goals
- Over- or underestimation of the importance of the SAT® exam

On the one hand, teenagers may be overly optimistic in thinking that they are smart, do not need to prepare for the SAT® exam, and can get into any college on the basis of grades alone. On the other hand, teenagers may have an overly negative view of their ability and therefore avoid school, worry about grades, panic on tests, and can be difficult or quarrelsome.

Attitude problems can influence the degree to which teenagers are willing to spend time and energy preparing for the SAT® exam.

BEHAVIOR PROBLEMS

Teenagers with behavior problems are likely to make statements such as "I don't have to study just because you say so," or "I know I should study, but I just can't make myself do it," or "I keep getting headaches when I think about the SAT®."

The following are a few behavior problems you may encounter with your teen:

- Poor self-control
- Lack of responsible behavior
- Inability to get along with peers, adults, or family
- Drug and/or alcohol abuse
- Inability or unwillingness to follow rules and maintain commitments in school and in the community

Teenagers with behavior problems usually use ineffective ways of coping with stress, are overly dependent or rebellious, are unable to control anger, and are unwilling to face or discuss problems with adults.

1052

Appendix A

Parents'
Guide to
College
Admission
Testing

SPECIAL PROBLEMS

Teenagers with special problems may make statements such as "I've always had trouble with spelling and reading," or "I know I have physical problems, but I want to try to go to college," or "I can do those questions; I just need more time."

Special problems include these conditions:

- Specific learning disabilities

- Severe physical, sensory, or emotional limitations

- Language barriers

- Disadvantaged backgrounds that may result in a lack of culturally enriching experiences

Special problems may prevent or affect your teen's ability to take the test. If your teenager is eligible, he or she may be able to take the SAT® exam with certain accommodations, such as extended time. Be sure to review the options and eligibility requirements and submit an accommodations request well in advance, as it can take several weeks to be approved.

To begin designing an SAT® plan, you need to review your teenager's problems. List these problems on the same chart where you have already listed the teenager's strengths. When discussing these problems with your teenager, remember to talk about his or her strengths as well.

HOW TO USE THE INFORMATION ABOUT YOUR TEEN

After collecting information about your teenager, you should summarize the information by reviewing the chart you completed. Remember that strengths, along with weaknesses, may exist in each area. Keep the following in mind as you evaluate and summarize the information you have gathered:

- The number of sources that agree or disagree

- The number of objective measures that agree or disagree, such as tests, grades, or reports

- The number of times you are aware of the strength or problem—for example, if your teenager always seems to be studying or is always complaining

1053

Appendix A

Parents'
Guide to
College
Admission
Testing

WORKING WITH YOUR TEEN'S GUIDANCE COUNSELOR

Relative to college admissions tests, the counselor's role is to help students understand the nature of these tests, the benefits of study and coaching, what test to take and when, and whether to retake a test in order to achieve a higher score.

The counselor can help you and your teen summarize information about how prepared your teen is for the SAT® exam and can discuss strengths and weaknesses in light of current and past test results and grades. Making an appointment with your teen's guidance counselor now will enable you to make reasonable decisions about a course of action.

DEVELOPING EFFECTIVE WORK HABITS

In addition to assessing knowledge of English, math, and other content areas, the SAT® exam tests how well your teen takes standardized tests. Part of becoming a successful test-taker involves developing effective work habits. Developing these habits now will save your teen lots of frustration, time, and energy and will inevitably improve his or her test scores.

MANAGING TIME

Consider the following example. John is a fairly good student and earns *B*'s and *C*'s in his high school courses. He is concerned about the SAT® exam and wants to do well. During a practice test, he plods through each section and spends extra time on some of the more difficult questions. He doesn't finish parts of the test. His practice SAT® test scores are unnecessarily low because he didn't have time to answer all of the questions he could have easily handled. John's test behavior indicates that he needs help in work habits, especially in learning to manage his time and pace himself during the test.

When people work in factories or offices, they are usually told how much time should be spent on different tasks. This process ensures productivity, allowing workers to know what is expected of them and helping them pace themselves so that they get the most done in the least amount of time. Similarly, your teen will also benefit from learning how to manage the time he has to take the SAT® exam. Before taking the tests, he or she should know the following:

- How many questions are on each section of the test

- How much time is provided for each section

- Approximately how much time can be given to each question if he or she is to complete the test and if all of the questions are of equal difficulty

- The kinds of questions that he or she can't do and should skip until completing those questions he or she can definitely answer correctly

With test-taking, managing time means that your teen can predict what he or she has to do, how long it should take, how to pace himself or herself to get the job done, and how to leave time to check his or her work. Although most testing centers have clocks, your teen should wear an approved watch during the test (and practice tests) to keep track of time and check his or her pacing.

GETTING ORGANIZED AND STICKING TO TASKS

Now consider the case of another test-taker, Emma. The following takes place in her parents' kitchen after dinner:

7:05 p.m. "Mom, did you see my SAT® practice book?"

7:10 p.m. "Mom, I found some paper. Where are some pencils?"

7:15 p.m. "Oh, I'd better text Liam to see if I have a ride tomorrow!"

7:20 p.m. "What time is it?"

7:22 p.m. "I need to get on the computer."

7:25 p.m. "That's enough math! I think I'll do some vocabulary."

7:40 p.m. "I hate vocabulary! I'll go back to math."

Emma displays several work-habits problems. One problem is that she hasn't recognized what she can't do during study time—for example, disrupting herself by sending a text message. Another problem is that Emma jumps from task to task, breaking her own concentration.

Good work habits entail being organized. Teenagers need to learn how to organize materials, list what has to be done, and specify how much time might be needed to complete each job. Study styles may differ, but teenagers must find the most effective ways to use their time and follow their own plans.

1054

Appendix A

Parents'
Guide to
College
Admission
Testing

Students like Emma benefit from guidelines to follow during study time, such as the following:

- Spend at least 20–30 minutes on each activity, maintaining concentration, and building up skills.

- Stick to some basic study rules, including not avoiding work because it is too difficult or boring.

- Invoke the rule: "Work first, play later." For example, text, go online, or make phone calls only after work is completed.

Sticking to a task is an essential work habit. Unless she changes her habits, Emma will not reach the critical test-related goal: accurately completing the greatest number of problems she can within specific time limits. Emma is also operating under some misconceptions. She really believes that she is working hard and that her fatigue is a result of studying. She may also begin to think that she is not as bright as her friends because they are getting better results on practice tests. All of these potential problems can be resolved by changing her work habits.

IF IT WORKS, DON'T CHANGE IT

Another 10th-grader, Caleb, likes his comforts. He loads up on soda and chips before he settles down to work. The radio is an essential part of his lifestyle. When his mother and sisters pass by his room, they see him sprawled on his bed with a small light turned on and papers and books all over the floor. Sometimes he's sound asleep. Because he seems so casual, everybody stops by and talks to him.

Some parents might assume that the manner in which Caleb goes about studying is totally ineffective. It doesn't appear that any teenager could concentrate and maintain attention curled up in bed with music blaring, people walking in and out, poor lighting, and a nap now and then. Most parents would be right. Caleb's parents had been concerned and were annoyed by his work habits. However, Caleb earns high grades in school, and on the first SAT® exam he took, he scored more than 600 on the reading and writing sections. He has also shown his parents how his speed is increasing on certain practice SAT® exercises. In this case, the parents have specific information and assurance that their son's work habits work for him, despite appearing inefficient.

Your objective here is to check the effectiveness of your teenager's work habits. Consider what effect these habits have on classroom or college admissions test performance. Remember to have your teen take a practice test under actual SAT® exam conditions to see how his or her work habits hold up.

TAMING THE PROCRASTINATOR

Procrastination is a common problem for teens. Leslie is an 11th-grader having a conversation with her father, Mr. Rand.

> **Mr. Rand:** "Did you start to study for the SAT®?"
>
> **Leslie:** "No, it's in two months."
>
> **Mr. Rand:** "Shouldn't you start now?"
>
> **Leslie:** "I wish you would stop nagging me. I can take care of myself."

Here's another scenario, between Mrs. Sanchez and her 11th-grader, Ricky:

> **Mrs. Sanchez:** "I haven't seen that SAT® book around. Are you studying in school?"
>
> **Ricky:** "I started looking at it, but it's so long I'll never get through it."

Putting off work occurs when people feel overwhelmed, don't know where to begin, feel pressured to get other things done, or are distracted by other things they would rather do. Parents who recognize this work-habit problem in their teenagers may have similar habits themselves.

1055

Appendix A

Parents'
Guide to
College
Admission
Testing

Procrastination becomes a particular problem for the following reasons:

- Time is limited; when time is limited, people feel pressure.

- There can be a penalty for delay—for example, you might miss the SAT® because your payment was not received on time.

- Avoiding work increases the load, rather than decreases it.

By taking into account the time available before the SAT® exam and the preparation that has to be done, you can help your teenager create a sensible plan that divides one seemingly overwhelming task into smaller and more manageable ones. Predicting what has to be done, and doing those tasks one by one, gives teenagers control over feelings of being swamped and unable to cope.

A WORK-HABITS CHECKLIST

To help your teenager develop effective work habits, ask him or her questions regarding time management, materials, atmosphere, and space. You may want to use the following checklist.

Time Management

☐ Are there signals to others that this is a study time (e.g., a "Do Not Disturb" sign)?
☐ Are there rules set up for the study time (e.g., no phone calls or no visitors)?
☐ Is a time schedule agreed upon and posted?
☐ Are study breaks scheduled?

Materials

☐ Is a clock or kitchen timer available?
☐ Are supplies handy (e.g., pencils, eraser, computer)?
☐ Does the seating encourage attention and alert behavior (e.g., a chair and a desk rather than a bed)?

Atmosphere

☐ Is the lighting adequate?
☐ Is the noise level low?
☐ Is the area visually nondistracting?
☐ Is the area well-ventilated and does it have a moderate temperature?

Space

☐ Is there a special place designated (e.g., desk, room, or area) for studying?
☐ Is this space away from the main traffic of the home?
☐ Is the space large enough to allow for writing?
☐ Is there space available for storing or filing materials?

1056

Appendix A

Parents'
Guide to
College
Admission
Testing

HOW TO HELP YOUR TEEN WITH WORK HABITS

Teenagers have difficulty finding time to do homework or household chores, but they usually seem to have a lot of time to text or talk on the phone, go online, or hang out with friends. Managing time comes down to establishing priorities. Here are some guidelines that you can use to help your teenager use his or her time more effectively:

- Set a realistic study schedule that doesn't interfere too much with normal activities.

- Divide the task into small and manageable parts—for example, instead of trying to memorize 2,000 vocabulary words in two weeks, have your teen learn and use five new words a day, three times a week.

- Use what has just been learned whenever possible—for example, talk about, joke about, and use new vocabulary words.

- Find times that are best for concentration and, if possible, have your teen avoid studying at times when he or she is tired, hungry, or irritable.

- Plan a variety of study breaks, such as music or jogging, to revive concentration.

- Encourage your teenager to get a group of friends together to practice taking the exam, review test items, compare answers, and/or discuss the ways they used to solve the problems. Such a group can range in size from two to six students.

WHY CREATE A PLAN?

It takes more than good intentions to do well on a college admissions test. It takes time, organization, and hard work. A test-prep plan provides the means for converting good intentions into meaningful test preparation. Take note of the specifics needed for an effective plan:

- Goals

- Responsibilities of parent and teenager

- Available resources

- Schedules

- Budgets

- Instruction

- Possible problems or concerns

By clearly establishing who is responsible for what, a test-prep plan removes many sources of conflict between parent and teenager and allows each person to channel all of his or her efforts toward the goal of improving test scores.

CREATING TEST-PREP PLANS

Let's look at some step-by-step ways of creating test-prep plans and what to expect as you create a plan for your teen.

1057

Appendix A

Parents'
Guide to
College
Admission
Testing

Make Time to Plan

Family life is hectic. Finding time to sit down and talk together is frequently a problem. Like a well-managed business, families with educational concerns and goals also need to have planning meetings. They need to find the time and place that will allow for discussion and working together.

Setting up a time to talk about a plan with your teen will work best if you approach him or her when he or she is most apt to be receptive. How you proceed is as important as what you do. A first step in developing a plan is to set goals.

 Some teenagers need to review a specific skill or subject; others have problems that require intensive instruction and practice. Since each teenager is unique, each test-prep plan must be individually tailored to fit specific needs.

List Goals

Goals help identify in a concrete way what you want to happen, such as your teen raising his or her verbal score by 40 to 60 points. Sometimes teenagers choose goals that are too general, such as doing geometry problems more accurately or completing the reading section more rapidly. Goals should be specific to the SAT® even when they include study skills. For example, just having a goal of studying for 30 minutes a night does not guarantee improvement. The following list contains some sample goals.

For accuracy:	Increase the number of correct math and vocabulary test answers.
For speed:	Decrease the time needed to read comprehension exercises while maintaining an understanding of what is read.
For speed and accuracy:	Decrease the time needed to read comprehension exercises and increase understanding of what is read.
For quantity:	Increase the number of problems tried or completed.
For frequency:	Study vocabulary words and do essay writing practice exercises for about 30 minutes at least three times per week.
For duration:	Increase study sessions to 1 hour, adding additional practice math problems.

After outlining the goals, the next step in planning is to prepare a schedule.

 Remember to take action in a way that is sensitive to your teen's needs and schedules.

1058

Appendix A

Parents'
Guide to
College
Admission
Testing

www.petersons.com

Make a Schedule

A test-preparation schedule should include a timetable and weekly or daily activity lists. First make the timetable. You can use a regular calendar that covers the time between the current date and the date of the SAT® exam. To make your timetable, write down all activities related to preparing for the test and the test date on the calendar.

You should also keep weekly and/or daily lists to identify specific tasks, such as the type or number of practice exercises to be completed. Such scheduling spells out the tasks ahead of time, reduces unnecessary worrying, and allows for more realistic planning. Often, teenagers become overwhelmed by the thought of all that has to be done and end up doing nothing. Writing a list and assigning times to each task tends to make these jobs more doable and more realistic.

Talk About Costs

Although you want to do everything possible for your teen's college admissions test preparation, cost is an important consideration. Most families' budgets are already strained without adding the expenses of materials, tutors, or commercial courses—especially since test preparation comes at a time when parents are trying to save money for college tuition.

Regardless of who pays the bill—the parent, the teenager, or both—budgets should be discussed. The estimated costs of various alternatives should also be outlined. Any budget limits and expected responsibilities should be proposed. By discussing these issues up front, you clarify problems and provide a realistic basis for decision making.

Find Out About Resources

Your community may have a variety of resources to help teenagers prepare for college admissions tests. However, it may take a little detective work to find them. For example, many religious groups and local organizations, such as your department of recreation, senior center, or the town library, sponsor young-adult activities. These groups usually know skilled people within the community who would be willing to help teenagers study for the SAT® exam. In addition, parent or community groups may also be willing to sponsor special activities if they are aware of teenagers' needs.

Match Materials to Your Teen's Goals

You and your teen should now select which books, equipment, and/or specialized materials will be used. You should match these materials to your teenager's goals. Consider drawing on information from teachers or counselors, previous standardized tests, and test-prep books that analyze the SAT® exam. Material can be purchased, borrowed, or shared by several teenagers.

Locate a Tutor

In finding a tutor, you should consider someone who has experience with the college admissions tests. You may actually hire more than one tutor, since instruction may be provided by volunteers, peers, schoolteachers, or professional tutors. Discuss various tutoring options with your teen.

1059

Appendix A

Parents'
Guide to
College
Admission
Testing

FIND A PLACE TO PRACTICE AND STUDY

Regardless of your plan's specifics, your teen needs a suitable place in which to study. Teenagers who register for courses or who receive tutoring have to practice test-taking at home, too. It is important to select a quiet study place at home or at school for SAT® homework assignments or for sessions with the tutor. It is also smart to turn off phones, the TV, computers, and mobile devices to reduce interruptions and distractions while your teen is preparing for the test. Some students do well working in a library or another area set aside for quiet study.

ANTICIPATE POSSIBLE HURDLES

Some common problems that arise during the test-prep process include:

- The teenager doesn't work well with the tutor.

- The instructor gets sick.

- The study group falls apart.

- One of the parents loses a job, so money is no longer available for a commercial course.

More subtle problems can occur when:

- Teenagers set unrealistic goals and then feel tired, frustrated, and angry.

- Parents become worried that their teenager isn't making enough progress.

- Parents feel angry and disappointed when things don't work out exactly as planned.

When managing a plan, you must assume that problems will arise and that plans have to be changed to deal with these problems. Helping your teenager shift gears and learn how to make adjustments is vital preparation for the real world and a valuable skill for him or her to learn now.

WAYS TO TRACK PROGRESS

Here are some ways you can check on your teen's performance progress:

- Keep records for each study session.

- Keep track of the number of problems completed correctly.

- Keep track of how much time it takes to complete the work.

- Review the records to see if changes to the plan need to be made.

- Make sure your teen is focused on the specific test sections or questions that need special attention.

Teenagers can check on their progress in several ways. These methods include calendars, checklists, charts, and graphs. The best method is the one that your teen will regularly use.

1060

Appendix A

Parents'
Guide to
College
Admission
Testing

You should comment on performance when the progress has occurred, not a week or two later. Teenagers usually do not want anyone to know that they are studying for the tests, so it's best to comment when no one else is around. You should also be especially sensitive to how your teenager will receive any comments about his or her work. Teenagers often view these helpful hints as criticism, even when they are offered in a positive way. You may find it easier to use notes or humor as a way of making a point that can be accepted by your teen. For example, Anne's father wrote her the following note:

> *Dear Anne:*
>
> *I see that you're keeping track of the number of problems you complete for the SAT. Looks as if you're doing at least 2–3 more problems each time—HOORAY!*

Research suggests that tracking progress can positively influence a student's performance. Remember the days when you hung your children's drawings on the refrigerator? Recognition still goes a long way. Post progress charts where they can be seen and acknowledged.

FIXING PROBLEMS

When teenagers are not progressing as anticipated, parents frequently jump to conclusions and think that the teenager has done something wrong. It may appear that the teenager is lazy. In fact, he or she may just be feeling overwhelmed, confused, and exhausted. When you become aware of problems, you may need to take a second look at the situation, looking for specific performance obstacles.

Rather than blaming your teenager, or labeling his or her behavior as right or wrong, you might consider behavior in terms of its being efficient or inefficient. To help you pinpoint what's going on, you may want to ask your teenager two questions:

- How is your study schedule working?

- Are you learning what you thought you would?

Your teen can give you the information to zero in on the specific problem. Some common problems teenagers face stem from unrealistic goals, unsuitable materials, and inefficient organization.

APPLYING SOLUTIONS

Usually there is more than one solution for every identified problem. Here are some common SAT® test-prep problems and a variety of possible solutions.

1061

Appendix A

Parents'
Guide to
College
Admission
Testing

Problem:

The teen seems to give up because it appears to him or her that the material is too complicated.

Solution:

Remind the teen that habits are like muscles. The first time someone goes for a run, it may seem very difficult, but it gets easier each time the person does it. Incorporating regular study time for the SAT® into the day will become easier the more the teen does it. If necessary, have the teen start small so she or he will be energized by successes.

Problem:

Progress is slower than anticipated and there isn't enough time left to reach the original goal.

Solutions:

Lower the expectations about the scores.

Rearrange the study schedule.

Provide more intensive instruction.

Schedule the test at a later date.

Shoot for a later college admissions date.

Problem:

The teenager is studying, but he or she does not remember anything the next day.

Solutions:

Change from group to individual tutoring.

Change from reading the information to listening to some of the information.

Practice aloud before doing the test exercises.

Study in a different place.

Check that the teaching materials match the required skills. Also try to determine how the teen learns best and use the information to leverage those strengths. For example, some students remember better if they write things down by hand rather than if they type them. Other students benefit from talking out loud as they work through the steps of a difficult concept.

1062

Appendix A

Parents'
Guide to
College
Admission
Testing

Problem:

The teenager is studying, but he or she seems to lose things and waste time.

Solution:

Give him or her information and techniques that will help him or her to become better organized.

Problem:

The teenager seems frantic and appears to be spending too much time studying.

Solution:

Provide some written material that will help him or her rank what has to be done in order of importance.

Review the goals, costs, and benefits, but keep in mind that the test is part of a larger picture.

NOTE: Keep in mind that the idea is to study more effectively, not necessarily longer.

MOTIVATING YOUR TEENAGER

Studying for the test usually isn't fun. It is hard work and teenagers need encouragement to keep going.

Sometimes teenagers are motivated because they immediately taste success. For example, Rico studied for a chemistry test and received an A. It is highly likely that he will study for the next test because he saw that his work paid off.

Checking on progress on the SAT® practice tests is important. Doing so gives your teenager the opportunity to realize that his or her work does pay off and progress is being made.

Sometimes parents need to boost motivation when they see signs of fatigue or signals that their teenager is being turned off to studying. If you are trying to find ways to encourage your teenager, consider the following:

- Make positive statements, such as "I know you're working hard."

- Provide extra treats, such as a special dinner or extra use of the car.

- Leave a small, humorous gift in their room, such as a giant pencil or a silly figurine.

- Organize some special event, such as going to the movies, a concert, or out to eat with another family whose teenager is also taking the test.

- Do some chore for your teenager so that your teen has more time to study.

Regardless of the system of rewards, remember to be positive, low-key, and avoid negative or punishing situations. The goal is to encourage and support effective studying, not to control your teenager. By establishing realistic goals and rewards, you help your teenager do his or her best and show him or her that you really care.

1063

Appendix A

Parents'
Guide to
College
Admission
Testing

SETTING UP REWARDS

Like everyone else, not all teenagers are motivated the same way. This is why it's helpful to know as much as possible about your teen's personality. Some teens feel very comfortable with a lot of structure and being held accountable by a tutor, parent, or teacher. Others are fine with a lot of structure as long as the purpose behind it makes sense to them. Highly independent teens may perceive it as "being told what to do," however. Challenge teens for whom choice is essential to come up with their own plan for test preparation. These teens can be very good at "thinking outside the box" and may be more motivated by proving they can succeed doing things their way than by any other reward.

Sometimes, you need to put into practice methodical and consistent ways to make sure that plans are followed. In other words, you may need to make sure that certain events occur after, and only after, a task is completed. The following examples show how you can build in rewards for work accomplished.

- Ron tends to be forgetful. For a month, he had not done the vocabulary exercises he agreed to do. He and his parents worked out a plan so that if a certain number of exercises were completed on Tuesday and Thursday nights, he could have the car on Fridays.

- Diana, on the other hand, did not want the car—she loved talking on the phone. Her family devised a plan that required her to work on her writing exercises for 30 minutes, three nights a week, before she could talk on the phone.

- You can also set up a tracking system using counters such as paper clips, to record short blocks of study time—a half hour, for example. Each counter can represent something the student can use as he or she wishes. For example, each paper clip might represent a half hour that can be spent with friends or playing sports.

Research also shows that linking habits—also called anchoring or stacking habits—makes a person more likely to accomplish them. Have the student choose an activity he or she performs every day, then link a desired new habit to an existing one. For example, if Rose takes 5 minutes every night before she brushes her teeth to be sure that she's written out her study plan for the next day and gathered all the materials she will need, she's more likely to do so. The new habit, writing the study plan, is linked to an established habit, brushing her teeth.

This final list of questions is provided to help you check on your teen's progress and iron out problems. When plans are well-managed, trouble spots are easily identified and changes can usually be made without anyone feeling that he or she has failed, especially the teenager.

MANAGING YOUR PLAN: A CHECKLIST

❑   Is progress being checked using charts, checklists, graphs, or other means?

❑   Do charts or graphs show any problems?

❑   What adjustments are necessary?

❑   Have alternative solutions been considered?

❑   Are any additional resources or checklists necessary?

❑   Has progress been made toward the goals?

Originally published in a slightly different form in *Parent's Guide to the SAT® & ACT®* (Lawrenceville, NJ: Peterson's, 2005), 27–133. Reprinted by permission of the authors.

Appendix B: Math Formulas for Memorization

NUMBERS AND OPERATIONS

Imaginary Unit, i	$i = \sqrt{-1};\ i^2 = -1$
Adding Complex Numbers	$(a + bi)(c + di) = (a + c)(b + d)i$
Subtracting Complex Numbers	$(a + bi) - (c + di) = (a - c) + (b - d)i$
Multiplying Complex Numbers	$(a + bi)(c + di) = (ac) + (adi) + (bci) + (bd)i^2$
Complex Conjugates	$(a + bi)$ and $(a - bi)$
Product of Complex Conjugates	$(a + bi)(a - bi) = a^2 + b^2$
Direct Variation	$y = ax$, where is the constant of variation
Inverse Variation	$y = \dfrac{a}{x}$, where is the constant of variation and $a \neq 0$.
Percent Increase	$\text{Percent Increase} = \dfrac{\text{Amount of Increase}}{\text{Original Amount}} \times 100$
Percent Decrease	$\text{Percent Decrease} = \dfrac{\text{Amount of Decrease}}{\text{Original Amount}} \times 100$

BASIC ALGEBRA

Rules of Exponents	$x^m \cdot x^n = x^{m+n}$ $\dfrac{x^m}{x^n} = x^{m-n}$ $x^{-n} = \dfrac{1}{x^n}$ $\left(x^m\right)^n = x^{m \cdot n}$ $x^{\frac{m}{n}} = \sqrt[n]{x^m}$
Standard Form of a Quadratic Equation	$ax^2 + bx + c = 0$
Quadratic Formula	$x = \dfrac{-b \pm \sqrt{b^2 - 4ac}}{2a}$

1065

Appendix B

Math
Formulas for
Memorization

Peterson's SAT® Prep Guide 2019

Convert Degrees to Radians	Multiply degree measure by $\dfrac{\pi \text{ radians}}{180°}$
Convert Radians to Degrees	Multiply radian measure by $\dfrac{180°}{\pi \text{ radians}}$
Area of a Rectangle	$A = bh$
Area of a Parallelogram	$A = bh$
Area of a Square	$A = s^2$
Area of a Triangle	$A = \dfrac{1}{2}bh$
Area of a Trapezoid	$A = \dfrac{1}{2}h(b_1 + b_2)$
Length of an Arc on a Circle	Length of $\overset{\frown}{AB} = \dfrac{m\overset{\frown}{AB}}{360°} \cdot 2\pi r$
Area of a Circle	$A = \pi r^2$
Circumference of a Circle	$C = 2\pi r$
Area of a Sector of a Circle	Area of sector $AOB = \dfrac{m\overset{\frown}{AB}}{360°} \cdot \pi r^2$
Length of a Chord of a Circle	Length of chord $= 2r \cdot \sin\left(\dfrac{\text{measure of central angle}}{2}\right)$, where r represents the radius
Volume of a Right Rectangular Prism	$V = lwh$
Volume of a Cube	$V = s^3$
Volume of a Right Circular Cylinder	$V = \pi r^2 h$
Volume of a Sphere	$V = \dfrac{4}{3}\pi r^3$
Volume of a Right Circular Cone	$V = \dfrac{1}{3}\pi r^2 h$
Pythagorean Theorem	$a^2 + b^2 = c^2$, where a and b are legs of a right triangle and c is its hypotenuse
30-60-90 Right Triangle	Side length opposite the 30° angle: x Side length opposite the 60° angle: $x\sqrt{3}$ Side length opposite the right angle: $2x$
45-45-90 Right Triangle	Side lengths opposite both 45° angles: x Side length opposite the right angle: $x\sqrt{2}$

1066

Appendix B

Math
Formulas for
Memorization

www.petersons.com